WALTER A. MUSCIANO
WARBIRDS OF THE *SEA*
A History of Aircraft Carriers
& Carrier-Based Aircraft

Schiffer Military/Aviation History
Atglen, PA

Acknowledgements

The author extends his sincere thanks to the following who provided information and photographs: Lois Lovisolo and Grumman Corporation; Gordon S. Williams, Marilyn A. Phipps and the Boeing Company; Brendan Morrissey and British Aerospace; Virginia C. Schultz, Mary Beth Straight, Dottie Sappington and United States Naval Institute; Rita Forenbach; Kaman Aircraft; Alice S. Creighton and United States Naval Academy; Dave Ekstrand; P.D. Batten and Westland Helicopters Limited; U.S. Marine Corps; Timothy J. Beecher, Harry Gann, Thomas J. Downey and McDonnell Douglas; Nicholas Sampsidis; Richard Scherer; Russell D. Egnor, Pat Toombs, Jeanne J. Thomas USN, and News Photo Division, Office of Information, U.S. Navy; Vickers Armstrong Ltd.; Charles R. Haberlein Jr., H.A. Vadnais, Jr., E.C. Finney Jr., and U.S. Naval Historical Center; Barbara L. Burger, Elizabeth Hill, Fred Pernell and U.S. National Archives; British Air Ministry (Navy); Bazan of Ferrol; Argentine Navy; Musee de la Marine; Royal Navy; George Page and Curtiss Aeroplane and Motor Co.; Aerospatiale; Regia Aeronautica; L. Steffo and Fincantieri Cantieri Navali Italiani S.p.A.; A.E. Ferko; Ryan Aeronautical Corporation; Fairey Aviation Co. Ltd.; Meredith McRoberts and Marine Log; Lockheed Aircraft Corporation; Mac Taggart, Scott & Co. Ltd.; D.C. Bateman and British Ministry of Defence (Navy); Newport News Shipbuilding; Hans Justus Meier; Edna Carrozza and Rolls-Royce Inc.; Lockheed-California Company; U.S. Department of Defense; Italian Navy; Swedish Air Force; James Ruggieri; Brewster Aeronautical Corporation; James Lynch, Fred Hartman and United Technologies/Sikorsky; Bell Helicopter Textron Inc.; Henry Tremont; H. J. "Jerry" Dalton, Jr., Paul Bower and Vought Aircraft Company; British Information Service; N.H. Hauprich; Service Historique de la Marine; Sal Marrone; Dan Hagedorn and National Air & Space Museum; Albert L. Lewis; Royal Canadian Armed Forces; U.S. Information Agency; George G. Sharp, Inc. Marine Design; Arthur L. Schoeni and Ling-Temco-Vought; U.S. Air Force; Lt. Col. O. Keith Williams, USMC (Ret); Dale Glasgow; U.S.Army Air Corps; Jonna D. Manes and Raytheon Company; E.C.P. Armees, Paris; Curtiss-Wright Corporation; L.F. Lovell, D. Richardson and the Fleet Air Arm Museum; John Regan; Avions Marcel Dassault-Brequet Aviation; Shirley Manfredi; Blackburn Aeroplane and Motor Co. Ltd.; Brian Andresen; William Lodge; Capt. James F. Grabb, USCG (Ret) and the American Society of Naval Engineers; Richard Rodi; U.S. Army Signal Corps; Ines White; J. M. Syverson and North American Rockwell; Breda Meccanica Bresciana; General Dynamics; Boeing Helicopters; Marconi Space & Defence Systems; Marine National/ECP Armees; Peter Doyle; Daniel J. Lenihan, Chief, Submerged Cultural Resources Unit, U.S. National Park Service; Bundesarchiv; British Information Service; United Aircraft Corporation; North American Rockwell; Convair; French Marine Nationale; Royal Australian Navy; General Electric Company; Col. George F. Britt, USMC (Ret.); Rex B. Beisel Jr.; Mike Walker and Operational Archives, U.S. Naval Historical Center; David Dodds and British Aerospace Dynamics; Thomas G. Dickinson, M.D.; Royal Netherlands Navy; Capt. Donald Edge, USN (Ret.); and Capt. E. Earle Rogers II, USN (Ret.).

Special thanks to Margaret Musciano, whose review of the manuscript made this volume possible.

Dedicated to
My Beloved Grandchildren
Kirsten and Derek
With Love and Pride

"It is well that war is so terrible or we should become too fond of it."

Robert E. Lee
(1807-1870) Confederate Commander In Chief
American Civil War

Dust jacket artwork by Steve Ferguson, Colorado Springs,. CO

RED SKY FOR YANKEE STATION

The dust jacket illustration shows a broad panorama of Carrier Wing 21 over "Yankee Station" in the Tonkin Gulf during the summer of 1967. A pair of MiG killer Vought F-8 Crusaders have just "busted the deck" of the *USS Bon Homme Richard* beneath "a red sky at night, sailor's delight."

The U.S. Navy entered the missile-age of aerial combat over Southeast Asia on June 17, 1965 when F-4 Phantom pilot CDR Lou Page and back-seater Lt. John Smith scored the first confirmed aerial victory of the Vietnam War. Two more Navy kills occurred over a span of five months, followed by a six month lull. The air war then broadened in June of 1966 when Carrier Air Wing CVW-21 aboard the the *USS Hancock* accounted for the first kill by an F-8 Crusader of the Vietnam War made by the "Checkmates" of VF-211. Only a week later, two more Checkmates from the "Hanna" had victories confirmed. The aerial contest continued sporadically for the next nine months and yielded another seven Navy victories.

In January of 1967, CVW-21 returned for its third tour, this time aboard the *USS Bon Homme Richard* where the Checkmates of VF-211 and the "Checkertails" of sister outfit VF-24 engaged in a series of intense aerial duels beginning in May. By the end of July, the "Sadies of Bonny Dick" had accounted for nine more MiG kills; five by VF-24 and four by VF-211 (plus a single victory scored by an A-4 Skyhawk pilot of VA-76). Although no other carrier wing ever surpassed the "baker's dozen" of confirmed victories compiled by the men of the Hanna and Bonny Dick.

Only six more aerial victories would be accrued by the Crusaders in 1968 as the majority of MiG encounters would come to the carrier squadrons flying the superior F-4 Phantom II. On January 12, 1973, VF-161 Phantom driver Lt. Vic Kavoleski and back-seater Lt. Jim Wise scored the last aerial kill of the Southeast Asian war. It was the sixty-seventh kill for the U.S. Navy where all but three of their victims had ultimately fallen to missiles.

Book Design by Robert Biondi.

Printed in the United States of America.
ISBN: 0-88740-583-5

We are interested in hearing from authors with book ideas on related topics.

Published by Schiffer Publishing Ltd.
77 Lower Valley Road
Atglen, PA 19310
Please write for a free catalog.
This book may be purchased from the publisher.
Please include $2.95 postage.
Try your bookstore first.

Preface

Writing and illustrating this book is the logical consequence of a lifetime of interest, hobby and vocation dedicated to the history, design and performance of aircraft-capable ships and shipboard aircraft.

Ever since childhood I have been fascinated by aircraft carriers and their airplanes. As early as five years old I fell in love with the beautiful *Lexington/Saratoga* carriers and when the *Ranger* appeared my child's eye thought it was ugly because it was not like my "*Lady Lex*."

Then came the breathtaking Boeing F4B, Curtiss Goshawk and Helldiver biplanes and, by that time, I had become an avid model builder of ships and planes which I pursued with a passion.

My appetite for any scrap of information, clippings, photos, etc. about my beloved shipboard planes and carriers became insatiable. In fact, I have referred to some of these old clippings for bits of historic information in this volume.

Soon I was designing my own model planes and carriers but, somehow, all the carriers resembled *Lady Lex*. I dreamed of designing full size carriers and shipboard aircraft, as do many youngsters, but my dream was realized because I spent a very happy and satisfying half-century working on designs of shipboard aircraft and aircraft capable ships.

When the George G. Sharp marine design organization was selected to design the *Casablanca* class mini-carriers Mr. Sharp, knowing my avid interest in carriers and shipboard aircraft, asked me to prepare the basic conceptual design. Yes, my design did resemble *Lady Lex*, only smaller! At the age of 20, the beauty of *USS Lexington* was still ingrained in my soul. I was told that the bow flare into the flight deck was great; however, something far more simple and basic was needed. Then a blueprint of the converted cargo ship escort carrier *USS Charger* was unfolded as an example of what was desired, "only better." Aesthetics were crushed and practicality took charge.

When I was approached to write a book about aircraft carriers, I knew that shipboard aircraft, the Warbirds of the Sea, had to be included because the carrier and its planes are inseparable. One cannot write, discuss or even think about one without the other.

This book is the first to combine the history of shipborne aircraft with that of aircraft carriers in a narrative that covers every facet of shipboard naval aviation.

One objective for writing this book is to share my research and interests with the reader who has an avid interest in aircraft carriers, shipboard aircraft and carrier warfare history, as well as the conception and development of the aircraft carrier and shipboard aircraft. The other objective is to introduce the story of aircraft carriers and shipboard aircraft to the neophyte and to readers with casual interest in the subject. The book has been written to entertain as well as inform the reader and I hope you enjoy reading this fascinating story as much as I enjoyed writing it.

Walter A. Musciano
Lodi, New Jersey

Contents

List of Illustrations *(Drawings by the Author)*

Foreword

As a career naval officer I was privileged to serve on aircraft carriers and destroyers for many years and witnessed the astounding changes that made naval airpower the force it is today. However, I am indebted to Walter A. Musciano and *Warbirds of the Sea* for understanding the continuum of progress that produced the entire picture of the how and why things happened to give the United States Navy the premier naval air force.

Historians, naval personnel, designers and constructors of aircraft carriers and carrier aircraft, as well as the general public, now have a clear and intelligible record of how naval airpower came into being. Walter A. Musciano used his experience as a ship and naval aircraft designer and student of naval and aviation history, strategy and tactics to become a syllogist who sets about understanding in depth the syllogistic argument that made naval air power possible.

The two major premises followed in *Warbirds of the Sea* are that ships are major weapon system platforms, and that aircraft are also major weapon system platforms. To my knowledge this book is the first to clearly define the symbiosis that flows from these major premises. The mutually beneficial relationship that developed between the warship and warplane is now recognized as naval airpower.

Walter Musciano's interest in both ships and naval aircraft enabled him to use his superb skills with words and drawings to tell both stories. His extensive and thorough scientific understanding of the key technical decisions that were made to produce the aircraft carrier and carrier aircraft are clearly presented in Warbirds of the Sea.

The human element in technical progress was not neglected in this book. Even the loss of life is shown to be a positive element in the process that considers all options. I am pleased that Musciano included the human element.

The Author has a deep interest and understanding of the application of weapon systems in combat. His natural curiosity about the real nature of things has led him to insights about naval airpower that can be of value at the highest level of the United States Government.

Musciano's life-long passion with ship and aircraft design has solved the mysteries of how naval airpower happened. Ultimately, his analysis of naval airpower in *Warbirds of the Sea* will be used as a guide to measure the value of similar studies.

Allen Jones, Jr., Capt. USN (Ret.)

Capt. Jones enlisted in the U.S. Navy in 1943 and was commissioned in 1946 at Tulane University. He served on the *Essex* class aircraft carrier *USS Randolph* CV-15; and the destroyers *USS Epperson* and *USS Robert L. Wilson.*

After attending the United States Naval War College he became commanding officer of *USS Cook*, *USS Tingey*, and *USS Paricutin*. He retired from the U.S. Navy in 1973 and became involved in the design of revolutionary high speed naval combat ships and innovative steering systems for which he has been awarded patents.

Prologue

There is no single weapon so formidable, so flexible, and so capable of projecting enormous power as the aircraft carrier and its air wing. The modern aircraft carrier is truly a most amazing, all-inclusive weapon which can attack any military target on land, on or beneath the sea, and in the air, while simultaneously defending itself. It is highly mobile and flexible in action free to select the preferred battlefield in which to launch its brood of fighters and bombers. So important has the carrier and its air wing become that, in recent history, U.S. presidents have selected carriers to be sent to world trouble spots as a show of force to avoid an escalating conflict.

Aircraft Carriers

As with many weapons that played a significant role in World War II, the aircraft carrier was used, in embryonic form, during World War I. Having evolved through three-quarters of a century of development and refinement, the carrier and its aircraft have emerged as one of the most sophisticated weapons known to man.

Carrier History

The history of the aircraft carrier is the story of a time of revolution in naval warfare. The carrier was born in the era of battleships and battle cruisers which were the main striking force of the world's fleets; responsible for bombardment, sea warfare, and blockade. Their guns had a range of about 20 miles; insignificant when compared to the range of airplanes. Yet, the early carriers were subordinate to these ships of the line and were used to gather intelligence

Literally floating cities, air bases, and forts the Supercarrier must be designed, not only to remain afloat under many adverse conditions, but must travel at 30 plus knots and be capable of safely negotiating violent maneuvers. This dramatic photograph has caught USS Enterprise (CVAN-65) in a sharp turn to starboard or right turn. Observe the angle of heel to port which appears dangerously severe to the casual observer; however, careful design by the architects and engineers of the U.S. Navy and Newport News Shipbuilding & Drydock Co. has enabled this ninety-thousand ton giant to conduct the maneuvers safely. (Official U.S. Navy Photograph, News Photo Division)

Below: The enormous size of a supercarrier under construction is hard to conceive and unbelievable even when confronted in reality. This is USS Enterprise (CVAN-65) under construction in the graving dock at Newport News, Virginia. Iron workers, electricians, pipefitters, insulation specialists, joiner workers, HVAC technicians, welders, steamfitters, painters, and many other trades are represented by the thousands of workers who swarm over the giant ship like so many ants over a giant lizard. Unseen in this photograph are the many workers inside the hull and superstructure. Observe the scaffolding around the island which at one time encompassed the hull. (Newport News S.B. & D.D. Co.)

This overall view of a typical World War II geared steam turbine powerplant shows the high pressure turbine (10); low pressure turbine (11); and high speed gears (12). The high speed gears drive the low speed gear, below them, which turns the propeller shaft. One or more heavy lift trolley hoists (13) are necessary to lift heavy machinery components for repair or maintenance. Four engine rooms are installed in the typical aircraft carrier along with four boiler or fire rooms which are not shown. (WAM Foto)

about the strength and disposition of the enemy fleet by sending the aircraft to scout ahead of the main fleet. Aircraft from the early carriers were also used as "spotters" to direct the big guns of the battle fleet. World War II changed the carrier's role from that of a subordinate to that of the principal ship of the fleet; displacing the battleship and battle cruiser into virtual oblivion. The character of war at sea was truly revolutionized by the advent of the aircraft carrier.

Carrier Statistics

From an engineering standpoint the modern Supercarrier is unbelievably complex and massive. Displacing almost 100,000 tons, these 300,000 horsepower Goliaths sport 1,000 feet long flight decks with an area of over four and one-half acres! Carriers are far more complex than any other naval design. In addition to the propulsion power plant, operating crew, missile defense systems, fuel, and stores common to the average surface combatant the modern Supercarrier must include: 300,000 gallons of aviation fuel; accommodation for 3,000 air wing crew in addition to the 3,000 operating crew; cavernous hangar space for 90 or more fighters, attack planes, helicopters, and multiengine ASW (Anti Submarine Warfare) planes and that's not all. Up to four powerful steam catapults capable of accelerating a 30 ton airplane to 150 miles per hour in a 300 feet run, plus arresting gear capable of stopping this plane as it touches down at that same speed are necessary for this mobile air base. Also needed are engine and aircraft shops and spare parts stowage plus 2,000

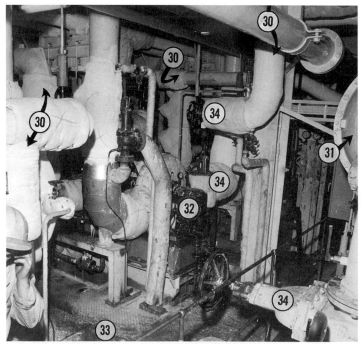

Beneath the Operating Level of the Engine Room is the Engine Room Floor level which is full of pumps (32); piping (30); heaters and coolers (heat exchangers) (31); and valves (34). Beneath the Engine Room Floor Plates (33) is an eerie world of darkness filled with piping of every description carrying ballast water; bilge stops; fuel; cooling water for machinery; and firemain water. (WAM Foto)

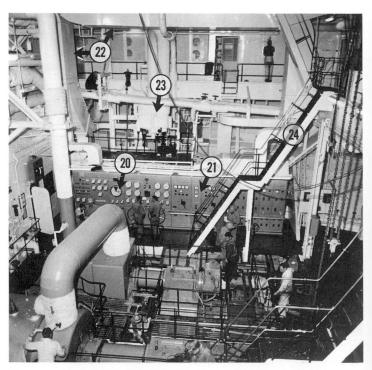

The operating level of a World War II steam powerplant engine room included the Main Engine Room Guage Board (20); the Main Switchboard (21); Ventilation Ducts (22); and Access Inclined Ladder (24). The large handwheels at the Main Engine Room Guage Board are to control the steam valves to the turbines. These huge valves are encased in insulation(23). Below the operating level is the Engine Room Floor grating which contains a myriad of pumps, heaters, coolers and piping that serve the powerplant and the basic safety of the ship. (WAM Foto)

An ordnance technician is adjusting the nose plug/fuse of a 1,000 pound bomb in the bomb magazine. Bombs and shells are carefully stowed in racks so they can't shift as the carrier rolls and pitches in heavy seas. Magazines are fitted with automatic sprinkler flooding systems. (Official U.S. Navy Photograph)

The carrier pilots are officers and eat in relative style in the wardroom. This is a corner of the Essex Class carrier USS Yorktown (CV-10) wardroom showing a table setting before the remaining officers arrive. The appointments on an aircraft carrier are more comfortable than those of smaller ships such as frigates, destroyers and submarines. (Official U.S. Navy Photograph)

tons of aircraft missiles, bombs and other munitions. The modern aircraft carrier makes its own oxygen and nitrogen in a manufacturing plant below the flight deck; oxygen being necessary for the plane crews and the inert nitrogen needed to inflate the airplane tires as well as to isolate highly flammable stores. High speed (30-35 knots) is essential to assist in the launching and retrieval of the planes. Up to four massive elevators are needed to move the planes between the flight and hangar decks.

Carrier Provisions

Fresh water is important and, on a large carrier, 40,000 gallons of potable (drinking) water are distilled from sea water every day. Dry and refrigerated spaces to store enough food for a 90 day voyage are needed. A partial list of food includes 10,000 pounds of roast beef; 17,000 pounds of chicken; 10,000 dozen eggs; 33,000 pounds of potatoes; 3,000 pounds of broccoli; and 26,000 pounds of hamburger meat. Bread and cake are baked on board from thousands of pounds of flour. On an American Supercarrier 18,000 hot meals are served every day and fresh fruit is available at every meal. Most activities have a fast-food area open 24 hours every day.

Carrier Aircraft

The planes are also a breed apart from the conventional shore-based combat planes. Catapult fittings and arresting hook are mandatory as is a reinforced fuselage capable of absorbing the shock and stresses of catapult launches and arrested landings. Carrier planes strike the flight deck with incredible force; therefore, they must have exceptionally strong landing gears. Flotation gear and/or life rafts, and life vests are often necessary.

Wing Folding

Probably the most spectacular and challenging carrier plane requirement is the folding wing and, on some aircraft, folding parts of the fuselage. This is necessary in order to fit as many aircraft as can be stowed into the smallest possible hangar and to keep the size of the aircraft elevators to a minimum. A myriad of wing folding techniques have been tried for three-quarters of a century. At the onset wing folding was accomplished manually by the plane handlers and this system continued into World War II on some designs. Wings were folded back laterally; twisted 90 degrees and folded back; and folded upward over the fuselage which is the system preferred by most designers today. Photographs in the following chapters will illustrate many wing folding designs. Hydraulically operated wing folding mechanisms actuated by the pilot from the cockpit are universally used in modern jets. Considering the hydraulic tubing, electrical cable, electronic wiring, etc. traversing the fold joint and the tremendous force imposed on the wings of a maneuvering jet fighter it is impossible not to admire the wing folding mechanism which can withstand loads of 10G and more, plus articulate the traversing hardware at the joint.

Corrosion

Aviation writers often neglect one of the major problems associated with carrier-based aircraft; corrosion. The marine environment readily provides a saltwater electrolyte between dissimilar metals in the plane's structure; thereby, starting galvanic activity much like that found in a wet cell battery. In this activity one of the metals can be eaten away to the point of fatigue. The most common forms of corrosion caused by the saltwater environment are: pitting, exfoliation (the metal sloughing off in layers), crevice, and filiform (threadlike pieces separating from the structure). Aluminum alloy, magnesium, titanium, and high strength steels are all susceptible to the ravages of saltwater. The saltwater problem is as old as carrier aircraft having caused rotted wood and mildewed doped fabric on the early shipboard planes. Countless millions are

Vought Corsair IIs, Grumman Intruders, and McDonnell Douglas Phantom II fighters, arranged high above the sea on the USS Franklin D. Roosevelt Flight Deck, are covered with salt sea spray. The corrosive salt water penetrates the smallest scratch in the paint to attack the aluminum and magnesium components. Salt water will also enter the hangar when the roll-up doors are open. The corrosive salt is inescapable. (Official U.S. Navy Photograph, News Photo Division)

spent on coating research and the results will be covered chronologically in subsequent chapters.

Aircraft Carrier Pilots

Actually, the modern aircraft carrier can be compared to the medieval castle because it is a self-sufficient society which embodies hierarchical relationships, rituals, physical conditions, and psychological roles which have not changed in a thousand years. The carrier pilot is a modern knight, supported by the feudal society of the ship, and flying a supersonic jet instead of riding a charging horse. The carrier pilots' confraternity is cemented by the conviction that they are the best in the world and the ship exists only for them. Conversely, the pilots exist for the purpose of defending their ship and destroying the enemy.

Highly Skilled Pilots

Carrier operations demand highly skilled pilots because the carrier pilot's training places emphasis on catapult shots and arrested land-

ings. Even when at sea the entire air wing conducts practice carrier operations including the very difficult and dangerous night landings. Some squadrons have mounted a bulletin board in the ready room on which every pilot's landing grades are prominently posted. This encourages those pilots whose landings are not perfect to improve their skill.

Many Extra Duties

Unlike his shore-based counterpart the carrier pilot has many nonflying duties. A carrier squadron is complete in itself with operations, administration, and maintenance records all handled by the pilots who are the unit's officers. In the event of reassignment the pilots must complete the many tasks required to transfer about 230 enlisted men, 30 officers, about 25 airplanes, and all the spare parts, supplies and support equipment. Despite the large size of the carrier, space is at a premium; therefore, carrier squadrons do not enjoy the luxury of having support officers assigned to the many necessary tasks as do land-based squadrons.

Aircraft operating from ships are constantly exposed to corrosive salt water or salt-laden atmosphere. This Westland Lynx helicopter is receiving a salt water bath on the helo pad of HMS Birmingham during rough seas. (Royal Navy Photo, Courtesy Westland Helicopters Limited)

Aircraft Carriers, Carrier Aircraft And Pilots Are Unique

The carrier, the planes, and the pilots are all unique in their own category; a well-matched team that has no equal and one that forges the most flexible and formidable weapon of war.

War Philosophy And The Aircraft Carrier

War? Yes, the carrier and its air wing are instruments of war; an activity that has been with mankind throughout recorded history.

The Sun Tzu Doctrines

The oldest known philosophy about war was written 25 centuries ago by an ancient Chinese military leader, Sun Tzu. His revealing book "The Art of War" has been available in Russian for several centuries and was required reading by all members of the Soviet

Aircraft carriers have many operations and spaces that are not found on the average naval ship. One of these is the Air Plot Room in which air wing commanders keep tabs on all aircraft in the air. This is the Air Plot Room on USS Yorktown (CV-10). (Official U.S. Navy Photograph)

The pilots' Ready Room is one of the few spaces on a World War II aircraft carrier that was air conditioned. The Ready Room doubles as a lecture hall and a general meeting place for the pilots to discuss tactics and other operational problems. As the name suggests, the Ready Room is where the pilots are briefed and debriefed and where they await word of their next assignment. Note the parachutes on the chairs, steel helmets hanging overhead and recognition models of friendly and enemy aircraft (arrows). (Official U.S. Navy Photograph)

political/military establishment. The ideas of Sun Tzu were adopted by Mao Tse-tung for his famous Little Red Book of strategic and tactical doctrines. "The Art of War" first appeared in the West in 1782 as a French translation and it has been said that Napoleon followed its theories. Sun Tzu's war philosophy was translated into English in 1905. His doctrines are very simple, yet most profound:

"Break the enemy's resistance without fighting" is a very desirable goal which can be accomplished by the aircraft carrier. The very appearance of a carrier force near a trouble spot can bring diplomats running to the conference table.

"Take the initiative; don't fight defensive wars." Again, the carrier is the ideal weapon as was proven in the Mediterranean Sea, North Sea, and the Pacific Ocean when the Allied Nations pressed forward with their carriers at a time when conditions appeared hopeless.

"Employ indirect tactics and maintain tactical flexibility." The very fact that aircraft carriers are mobile weapons that can strike where and when least expected and then shift into another attack affords them the ability to fulfill this Sun Tzu doctrine.

"Employ deception whenever possible." As will be seen in later chapters, the Japanese Navy used deceptive tactics during World War II and succeeded in luring a U.S. naval force away from its duty by using harmless decoy carriers as bait. The Japanese Navy admired Sun Tzu.

Clausewitz on War

In the arena of international politics, war is the last resort. As the famous German military theorist, Karl von Clausewitz (1780-1831), wrote in his eight monumental volumes "On War": "War is a Continuation of diplomacy by other means." "On War" is the most sig-

Karl von Clausewitz wrote on understanding war and his work "On War" is required reading in military academies. He was the first military theorist to advocate limited war. (U.S. Naval Academy)

nificant attempt in Western history to understand war and it is required reading in the world's military academies. Clausewitz was the first to advocate limited war. He rejected wars of blind passion and the utter destruction of the enemy. Instead, Clausewitz viewed war as a rational act and wrote: "War can never be divorced from political life, and whenever this occurs – we are left with something pointless and devoid of sense." He reasoned that war must have a specific objective and this objective should be revealed to the enemy prior to the start of hostilities with the hope that the objective will be gained peacefully. Clausewitz also felt that the force used in war should be scaled to the importance of the objective. He rejected all-out war and "unconditional surrender" because this only prolongs the fighting which creates needless casualties, drains the nation's wealth, and loses sight of the initial objective. Clausewitz would never have approved the use of nuclear weapons.

The Clausewitz doctrines had a profound influence on Soviet strategy: ". . . avoid large confrontations and achieve your objectives one at a time." Lenin, especially, appreciated this Clausewitz statement: "A conqueror is always a lover of peace; he would like to make his entry into our country unopposed."

The aircraft carrier with its air wing has demonstrated that it can direct all of its might against the enemy as in World War II; yet it can also exercise restraint as demonstrated in the 1986 attack on Libya. This ability to strike anywhere in the world with measured response to a crisis makes the carrier's air wing the ideal weapon to fulfill the General von Clausewitz theories.

Sea Power and Admiral Mahan

Another famous military theoretician who has strongly influenced naval strategy was Rear Admiral Alfred Thayer Mahan (1840-1914). As a U.S. naval officer he wrote 20 books and 23 essays on naval strategy and is considered one of the world's leading naval theorists. His most read and studied book "The Influence of Sea Power upon History" stresses the relationship between seapower and national greatness. Mahan's doctrine specifies a healthy seaborne foreign commerce, reliable foreign ports of trade as sources of materials and markets for exports, and most important is the means to protect these sea lines of communication and trade by force; force limited to the prevailing conditions.

Admiral Mahan's observations of naval influence on land wars are profound; especially those concerning sea lines of communication (SLOC). His observation of the British Navy's influence on the Napoleonic Wars was summarized as: "Those far-distant storm-beaten ships, on which Napoleon's soldiers never looked, stood between them and the domination of the world."

Alfred Thayer Mahan stressed the relationship between seapower and national greatness. He felt a navy should be able to protect its country's Sea Lines of Communication and that fleets should be built up in peacetime. (U.S. Naval Historical Center)

Admiral Mahan is much revered by the U.S. Navy and in May 1950 the Naval War College, in cooperation with the Naval Historical Center, celebrated the centenary of "The Influence of Sea Power Upon History" with a conference and exhibit. Caught in a sardonic mood, Secretary of War Henry L. Stimson once noted that the U.S. Navy Department, ". . . seems to retire from the realm of logic into a dim religious world in which Neptune was God, Mahan his prophet, and the United States Navy the only true church."

Again, we find the aircraft carrier and its air wing to be ideally suited to fulfill Mahan's theories. The air wing can clear the lines of communication beneath the waves, on the sea surface and in the skies above; a real triple threat to would-be blockaders.

Mahan also argued that nations should build their fleets during peacetime and, in this philosophy, he was not alone. In the Fourth Century B.C. Flavius Vegetius Renatus made this profound observation in the prologue of his "De Rei Militari": "Let him who desires peace, prepare for war." America's first president, George Washington, is quoted as saying: "In times of peace, prepare for war." They knew that wars are won with weapons forged in peacetime.

Air Power and Colonel Douhet

Guilio Douhet was one of the early apostles of air power who wrote, as early as 1910, that future wars would be decided in the air and that aviation would be the critical element in any future conflict. Colonel Douhet criticized the Italian High Command with such vigor because of its indifference to air power that he was imprisoned but, when it became obvious that he was correct, Colonel Douhet was promoted to the Directorate of Aviation. In 1920 he wrote his prophetic "Command of the Air."

Once more it is evident that carrier aircraft meet the requirements of a famous military theorist; the ability to strike from the air was precisely Colonel Douhet's argument. His profound statement: "To prepare for war demands exercise of the imagination" is more relevant today than it was in 1910.

Landmass And Maritime Nations

It is to be expected that nations with extensive coastlines as the United States and island nations as Britain and Japan will have naval forces of considerable size. Conversely, nations with enormous landmass and little navigable coastline are not expected to develop large navies. The former Admiral of the Fleet of the Soviet Union, S.G. Gorshkov, has studied Clausewitz, Mahan, and Douhet with great intensity, resulting in the Soviet Union's concentration in the development of a powerful navy, even including aircraft carriers; most unusual for a landmass nation.

Admiral Anderson And The Importance Of Aircraft Carriers

To conclude; it is worthy to quote from a speech presented on November 17, 1961 by the U.S. Navy Chief of Naval Operations (CNO) Admiral George W. Anderson, Jr., whose prophetic words stated: "Far from being obsolete in our missile age, the importance of our carrier forces in the pattern of world events has become even more pronounced, and with new weapons the aircraft carrier will demon-

Admiral George W. Anderson, Jr. forecast a greater role for the aircraft carrier in the missile age despite the efforts of politicians and misled theoreticians to minimize the carrier's importance because they thought missiles could replace them. (Official U.S. Navy Photograph)

strate even greater effectiveness as one of the most flexible weapons systems ever conceived by man." Admiral Anderson had the vision to realize the importance of the aircraft carrier at a time when the future of the carrier in the U.S. Navy was questioned by politicians and misled naval theoreticians, alike. It is because of the foresight of men like Admiral Anderson that the aircraft carrier program moved forward.

Unique And A Breed Apart

It is obvious that aircraft carriers, carrier aircraft, and carrier-based pilots are unique and an incomparable breed apart from all others. Also learned is that these men and weapons meet the strategic and tactical requirements of the most respected military theorists. The sophisticated, awesome Supercarriers and space-age carrier borne jets did not develop overnight. It took men with vision, willing to risk everything, including their lives to realize their dreams and theories. This is the story about to unfold; the carriers and their air groups in peace and war throughout their years of development and into the future.

CHAPTER I
CONCEPTION:
BEGINNING -1918

Early Interest in Shipboard Aircraft and Carriers • Early American Interest in Military Aircraft • First Shipboard Flights • Royal Navy Interest In Aviation • Seaplane Development • The First Catapults • Royal Navy Shipboard Experiments • Arming The Airplane • Early Carrier Conversions • Short 184 Seaplane • World War I Begins • Landplanes Replace Seaplanes • A Carrier Milestone: HMS Campania • Turret Top Takeoff Platforms • More Royal Navy Carrier Conversions • Large Fast Carrier Conversion • Lansing - Ishii Agreement • Through-Deck Carriers • Unified Royal Air Force = Death of RNAS • Last Shipboard Zeppelin Victory • Sopwith Sea Camel 2F.1 • U.S. Naval Aviation in World War I • Peace

O ne of the many results of naval aviation has been to make sea-based power more significant and influential than ever in the shaping of nations.

chanics responsible for refitting the airplanes and for keeping them always ready for flight." It was not until 16 years later that the first airplane operated from a ship.

EARLY INTEREST IN SHIPBOARD AIRCRAFT AND CARRIERS

As with many of the revolutionary ideas affecting our times, U.S. Naval aviation can trace its origins to the American Civil War. Although captive balloons had been in use on land since the war's beginning, it was not until August 3, 1861 that John La Mountain ascended in a balloon that was moored to the deck of the Union steam transport "Fanny" to observe Confederate gun batteries at Sewell's Point, Virginia, near Hampton Roads. These waterborne reconnaissance operations proved so successful that a specially designed balloon boat was constructed. This was topped with an unobstructed flight deck; elliptical in plan form and much wider than the hull. Named the "George Washington Parke Custis", this revolutionary craft served as a base for many successful observation flights by balloonist Thaddeus Lowe and is often called the first aircraft carrier.

The Aircraft Carrier Prophet

Clement Ader was a French aviation pioneer who, many historians claim, made two successful manned flights in 1890 and 1891 in steam engine powered airplanes. More important is the fact that Ader visualized the prospect of naval aviation in a book titled "L'Aviation Militaire", published in 1895. The outstanding passage in his book describes the aircraft carrier as we know it today. Ader wrote: ". . . an aircraft carrier will become indispensable. Such ships will be very differently constructed from anything in existence today. To start with, the deck will have been cleared of any obstacles; it will be a flat area, as wide as possible, not conforming to the lines of the hull and will resemble a landing strip. The speed of this ship will have to be at least as great as that of cruisers or even greater . . . Servicing the airplanes will have to be done below this deck in the hull . . . Access to this lower deck will be by means of a large elevator long enough and wide enough to take an aircraft with its wings folded . . . Along the sides will be the workshops of the me-

Often called the first aircraft carrier, George Washington Parke Custis was an American Civil War specially-designed balloon boat used by Union Forces to observe Confederate gun batteries and troop movements. Note the spacious, virtually unobstructed Flight Deck that foreshadowed the modern aircraft carrier. (Official U.S. Navy Photograph)

PREVIOUS: Eugene Ely lifts his Curtiss off USS Pennsylvania on the return leg of his landing-takeoff round trip between the ship and San Francisco's Presidio. Note the U.S. Navy launches on the ready to rescue Ely in case of a ditching. (Eugene B. Ely Scrapbooks, Vol.I, page 49, U.S. Naval Historical Center)

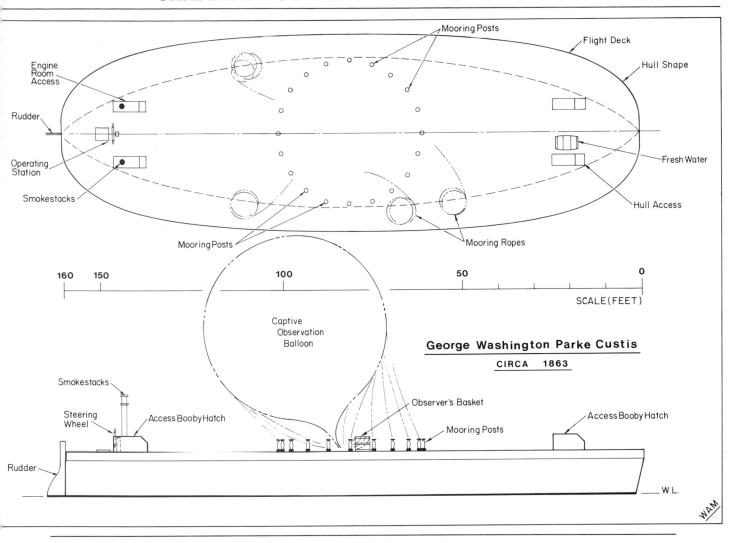

George Washington Parke Custis

CIRCA 1863

EARLY AMERICAN INTEREST IN MILITARY AIRCRAFT

The United States took early interest in the military uses of airplanes even before the Wright Brothers' historic flight and continued after this epic event.

Teddy Roosevelt Interested in Aviation

In 1898 the Assistant Secretary of the Navy, Theodore Roosevelt, became intensely interested in Professor Samuel P. Langley's unmanned flying machine and realized the possibilities of applying aviation to sea power. Roosevelt had recommended that the Secretary of the Navy establish an interservice board to determine the military value of the airplane. This joint board reported favorably for the use of airplanes as weapons of war; however, it took five more years of experimentation before the Wright Brothers made their first flight at Kitty Hawk in 1903.

U.S. Army Buys First Airplane

On February 10, 1908 the U.S. Army signed a contract with the Wright Brothers for, ". . . one (1) heavier-than-air flying machine, in accordance with Signal Corps Specification No. 486, dated December 23, 1907." This was the first airplane to be purchased and owned by any government; cost was 25,000 dollars.

Captain Chambers and the Battleship Admirals

Admiral William S. Cowles, Chief of the U.S. Navy Bureau of Equipment, had written several memoranda to the Secretary of the Navy in 1908 requesting authority to purchase airplanes. All were ignored. The U.S. Navy soon found itself in a most embarrassing situation when persistent newsmen and enthusiastic citizens questioned the Navy's reluctance to buy airplanes. Finally, in September, 1910 the Navy Department detached Captain Washington Irving Chambers from his command of the battleship *USS Louisiana* and assigned him the task of keeping informed of aviation developments and to answer all correspondence on aviation subjects for the Bureau of Equipment. Chambers was an aggressive, able and farseeing officer and soon became an avid supporter of naval aviation. It was an uphill fight because the U.S. Navy, as with most navies of that time, was run by the battleship admirals who saw no useful purpose for the airplane.

FIRST SHIPBOARD FLIGHTS

During a strategy meeting with his two assistants Chambers agreed that flying a plane from a battleship would get the admirals' attention. The cruiser *USS Birmingham* was anchored in Hampton Roads,

NAVY DEPARTMENT,

WASHINGTON,

March 25, 1898.

Sir:

Mr. Walcott, Director of the Geological Survey, has just been in to see me, having seen the President. He has shown me some interesting photographs of Professor Langley's flying machine. The machine has worked. It seems to me worth while for this government to try whether it will not work on a large enough scale to be of use in the event of war. For this purpose I recommend that you appoint two officers of scientific attainments and practical ability, who in conjunction with two officers appointed by the Secretary of War, shall meet and examine into this flying machine, to inform us whether or not they think it could be duplicated on a large scale, to make recommendation as to its practicability and prepare estimates as to the cost.

I think this is well worth doing.

This board should have the power to call in outside experts like R. H. Thurston, President Sibley College, Cornell University, and Octave Schanute, President of American Society of Civil Engineers, at Chicago.

Very respectfully,

T. Roosevelt
Assistant Secretary.

The Honorable,

The Secretary

Assistant Secretary of the Navy Theodore Roosevelt wrote this letter to the Secretary of the Navy John D. Long. With the Spanish-American War imminent, Roosevelt foresaw the use of airplanes by the military. (Official U.S. Navy Photo, U.S. Naval Historical Center)

Virginia, so Chambers obtained permission to use this ship for his test. An 83 foot wooden flight deck was constructed over the bow of the ship. Captain Chambers invited the Wright Brothers to conduct the test but they refused. He then approached Glenn H. Curtiss, another early American aviation pioneer, who reacted with great enthusiasm. Curtiss recommended Eugene B. Ely for the flight because Ely was his best exhibition pilot.

Eugene B. Ely

Eugene B. Ely was born in 1886 and grew up in Davenport, Iowa. Being very mechanically inclined, upon graduating from Iowa State University he was attracted to automobiles and soon became an expert driver. Road racing and work as a chauffeur led him to San Francisco where he married a pretty local girl, Mabel Hall. The pair moved to Oregon where Ely took a job as an auto salesman. In early 1910 his boss became the Northwest Agent for Curtiss planes but was afraid to fly so Ely offered to fly the demonstration Curtiss but smashed the plane. Eugene bought the wreck, repaired it, and within a month had taught himself to fly! On October 5 he received Federal Pilot's License No. 17.

Ely Meets Curtiss

Eugene and Mable toured the U.S. and Canada where Ely flew in air meets and on exhibition flights. He met Glenn Curtiss at a Minneapolis flying meet and Curtiss was so impressed with Ely that he signed him on as part of the Curtiss team.

The First Shipboard Takeoff

Ely readily agreed to make the takeoff from *USS Birmingham*. On the afternoon of November 14, 1910, a gloomy Monday with fog and rain showers, Eugene Ely climbed into the 100 horsepower Curtiss biplane, gunned the eight-cylinder Vee engine and rolled down the wooden runway but did not lift off. Instead, the Curtiss went off the edge of the deck and plunged towards the water! Ely managed to level off and zoom upwards as the wheels and propeller dipped into the water. The intrepid pilot was unable to tell where he was heading because his goggles had been covered with spray. As soon as he cleared his vision he sighted a strip of land in Norfolk called Willoughby Spit and landed there instead of circling the harbor and touching down in the Norfolk Navy Yard as originally planned.

This was a memorable feat for it proved that airplanes could operate from ships. Captain Chambers was overjoyed at Ely's success and when he discovered that the U.S. Navy had no reward for Ely he contacted John Barry Ryan, head of the U.S. Aeronautical Reserve. Ryan had offered a 500 dollar prize for the first reservist who made a ship-to-shore flight. Eugene Ely was not a reservist but Chambers convinced Ryan to make Ely a lieutenant in the U.S. Aeronautical Reserve and award him the 500 dollars. In return Ely presented his splintered propeller to John Barry Ryan.

The First Shipboard Landing

Yet to be proven was whether an airplane could land on a battleship as well. The dynamic Chambers made arrangements to use the battle-

Eugene Ely and his wife, Mabel, with their Curtiss pusher in Birmingham, Alabama in 1910. The pair toured the U.S. and Canada, where Eugene flew in air meets and on exhibition flights. Ely received U.S. Federal Pilot's License No. 17. (Eugene B. Ely Scrapbooks, Vol.I, page 3, U.S. Naval Historical Center)

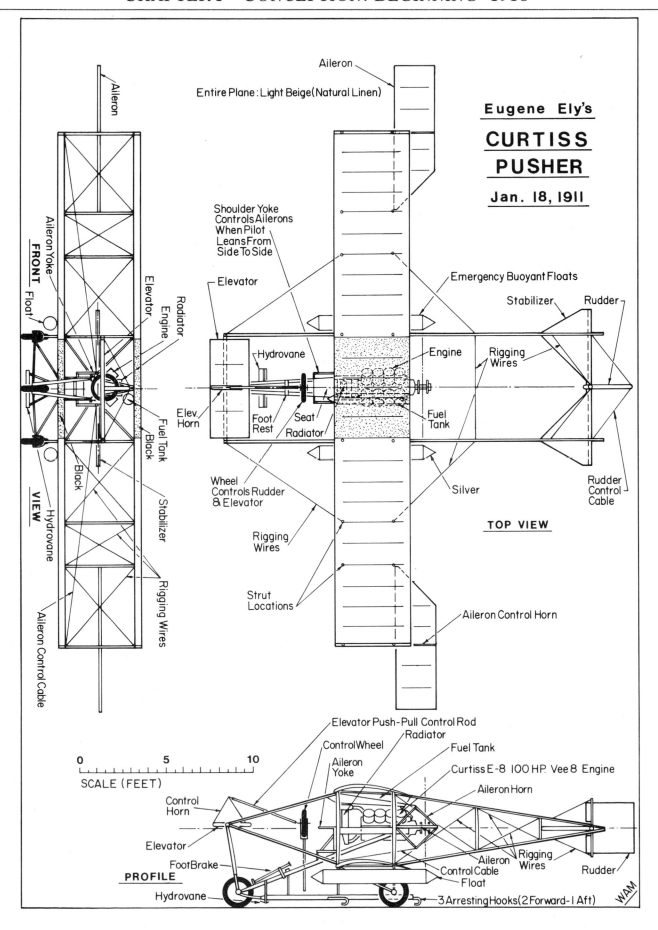

Aileron

Entire Plane : Light Beige (Natural Linen)

Eugene Ely's

CURTISS
PUSHER

Jan. 18, 1911

Aileron

Aileron Yoke

FRONT

Float

Radiator

Engine

Elevator

Shoulder Yoke Controls Ailerons When Pilot Leans From Side To Side

Elevator

Emergency Buoyant Floats

Stabilizer   Rudder

Hydrovane

Engine

Rigging Wires

Elev. Horn

Fuel Tank Black

Foot Rest

Seat

Radiator

Fuel Tank

VIEW

Black

Hydrovane

Stabilizer

Rigging Wires

Aileron Control Cable

Wheel Controls Rudder & Elevator

Rigging Wires

Strut Locations

Silver

Rudder Control Cable

TOP VIEW

Aileron Control Horn

Elevator Push-Pull Control Rod

Radiator

Control Wheel

Fuel Tank

Aileron Yoke

Curtiss E-8 100 H.P. Vee 8 Engine

Aileron Horn

| 0 | 5 | 10 |

SCALE (FEET)

Control Horn

Elevator

Foot Brake

Aileron Control Cable

Float

Aileron

Rigging Wires

Rudder

PROFILE

Hydrovane

3 Arresting Hooks (2 Forward - 1 Aft)

WAM

Eugene Ely in his 100 horsepower Curtiss pusher has just run off the USS Birmingham Flight Deck and is heading toward the waters of Hampton Roads. The plane's wheels and propeller touched the water before the intrepid pilot was able to climb to safety. This historic flight on November 14, 1910 was the world's first takeoff from a ship. (Official U.S. Navy Photograph, U.S. Naval Historic Center)

At 10 o'clock in the morning of January 18, 1911 Eugene Ely was checking his Curtiss on San Francisco's Presidio Army Air Field preparatory to his flight to USS Pennsylvania. Notice the cylindrical floats under the lower wing for bouyancy in the event of a ditching. (Eugene B. Ely Scrapbooks, Vol.III, page 55, U.S. Naval Historical Center)

ship *USS Pennsylvania*, which was moored in San Francisco Bay, for the experiment and Ely agreed to make the flight. A 127 x 32 foot wooden runway was erected over the *Pennsylvania*'s quarterdeck, but the problem of the moment was how to stop the plane after touchdown. Someone remembered that Hugh A. Robinson, an innovative circus performer, had been using a proven system in one of his acts to stop a car in which he performed the loop-de-loop. The stopping mechanism consisted of a series of ropes laying across the car's path with a 50 pound sandbag tied to the end of each rope. The car was fitted with a retractable hook. As the car left the loop-de-loop it sped directly towards the terrified spectators; however, the hook was then lowered in time to grapple the sand-

bagged ropes which, by dragging the sandbags, brought the car to a stop in front of the grandstand! The Curtiss was fitted with three nonretractable hooks. Forty-four 100-pound sandbags and 22 lengths of rope were added to the runway or flight deck. A canvas crash barrier was also erected at the forward end of the runway in the event the sandbags did not stop the Curtiss.

At 10:53 in the morning of January 18, 1911 Ely took off from the Presidio in San Francisco (which in 1911 was an Army airfield) and flew 13 miles to *USS Pennsylvania*. A 10 miles per hour tailwind forced the Curtiss to approach the deck at 40 miles per hour instead of the normal 30 miles per hour.

Caught at the moment he shut down the engine, Eugene Ely is about to alight on the USS Pennsylvania Flight Deck in San Francisco Bay. This first landing on a ship was witnessed by hundreds of sailors perched on the highest spot they could find on the ship. (Official U.S. Navy Photograph News Photo Division)

With his Curtiss at rest after the historic landing on January 18, 1911 Ely is escorted from the plane as crew members disconnect the sandbags that stopped the Curtiss. Note the canvas barriers in the foreground to stop the plane if the sandbags did not work. (Eugene Ely Scrapbooks, Vol.I, page 50, U.S. Naval Historical Center)

Eugene Ely waits by his plane until all is in readiness for his takeoff from USS Pennsylvania. Note the bicycle inner tubes around Ely's shoulders, back and chest which were intended to protect the pilot in the event of a crash as well as to provide some buoyancy in case of a ditching. Observe the hydrovane behind the nose wheel. (Eugene B. Ely Scrapbooks, Vol.IV, page 18, U.S. Naval Historical Center)

The pilot caught the 12th transverse rope with his hooks and came to a safe stop. Whistles blew and crowds cheered as Ely was mobbed by scores of well-wishers. Captain C.F. Pond, *Pennsylvania*'s Commanding Officer, proclaimed this feat as: "the most important landing of a bird since the dove flew back to the Ark."

Ely had the ropes removed from the deck 45 minutes later. His plane was turned around and he then took off and flew back to the Presidio.

Naval experts who witnessed this important event were very impressed and the *San Francisco Examiner* exclaimed: "Eugene Ely Revises World's Naval Tactics." Ely is quoted as saying: "For the first time in my life, the feeling that I had actually done a great thing came over me."

Ely's Fatal Crash

When asked about retiring Ely replied, a bit philosophically: "I guess I will be like the rest of them, keep at it until I'm killed." On October 19, 1911 at the Georgia State Fair Grounds in Macon, Ely was demonstrating his plane before 8,000 delighted spectators. During one of his maneuvers he put his plane into a shallow dive from

which it did not recover. Ely managed to jump clear but he died of a broken neck.

Eugene Ely was not a reckless daredevil. He was a very intelligent and educated individual who could have contributed even more to the science of aeronautics. The fact that in 1911 there was neither private or government money for investment in flying machines forced men like Ely into exhibition flying, living out of a suitcase, cheap hotels, plus the danger of a job which was beneath his talent.

The October 28, 1911 issue of *Aero* magazine printed the following account about Ely's death: "The crowd was uncontrolled and fought about his machine for several minutes after the fall. During the struggle Ely's tie, cap, and other articles of clothing disappeared." The man who pioneered carrier aviation certainly deserved better than that.

It was not until 1933 that Eugene Ely was honored, posthumously, with the Distinguished Flying Cross.

The U.S. Navy did not pursue Ely's valuable demonstration of mating the airplane to ships; and the aircraft carrier, as such, was left for the British to develop.

ROYAL NAVY INTEREST IN AVIATION

The British Admiralty's first interest in aviation was stimulated by the fact that the German Fleet was equipped with Zeppelin airships for scouting purposes. In 1909 the Admiralty ordered a 500 foot airship of their own from Vickers; officially known as the R-1, but unofficially called the *Mayfly*. As the R-1 was being brought out of its hangar in September 1911 *Mayfly* was caught by a gust of wind that destroyed it before the craft had ever flown. The two officers appointed to administer the *Mayfly*, Captain Murray Sueter and Commander Oliver Schwann, were not at all discouraged and pressed on to develop British naval aviation.

Civilians Assist the Admiralty

During this period the vast majority of airplanes in Britain were sold to private individuals who flew them for enjoyment. This resulted in the formation of flying clubs in which several airplanes could use the same flying field. The British Aero Club was one of the most active. Two civic minded members of the Aero Club made the Admiralty an offer it could could not refuse: Mr. Frank McClean offered to lend two airplanes to the Royal Navy while Mr. G.B. Cockburn offered free flying lessons to four naval officers at the Aero Club's flying field on the island of Sheppy. Lieutenants Charles R. Samson, Arthur Longmore and Reginald Gregory of the Royal Navy, and Captain Eugene Gerrard of the Royal Marines were chosen for the lessons and they reported for their new duties in March 1911.

SEAPLANE DEVELOPMENT

Attention in naval aircraft had turned to seaplanes as more suitable for naval applications. The first recorded use of aircraft operation from water was in March 1910 when French aviator Henri Fabre took off from the waters near Marseille; however, Fabre was unable to land on the water.

U.S. Navy's First Plane and Naval Aviators

In an attempt to secure a U.S. Navy contract Glenn Curtiss installed a single float on one of his flying machines which became the first successful seaplane. Curtiss demonstrated this craft on February 17, 1911 by landing alongside the *USS Pennsylvania* in San Diego Harbor, having the craft hoisted aboard, and then lowered onto the water again from which Curtiss promptly took off. This operation caught the U.S.Navy's attention and the Secretary of the Navy, George von Meyer, approved the purchase of naval aircraft. On May 8, 1911 the Navy Department ordered two Curtiss Triad tricycle landplanes which were converted to seaplanes or hydroplanes. The Curtiss Triad flew its acceptance trials at Hammondsport, N.Y. on July 1, 1911. In preparing the specifications for the U.S. Navy purchase Captain Chambers included the requirement that Curtiss was to be responsible to instruct two U.S. Navy officers to fly the planes. Lieutenants Theodore Gordon Ellyson and John H. Towers were chosen for this training and became U.S. Naval Aviators No. 1 and 3 respectively. Naval Aviator No. 2 was Lieutenant John Rodgers who was to be trained by the Wright Brothers. At last, the

The U.S. Navy's first plane was the Curtiss Triad ordered on May 8, 1911. Originally a tricycle landplane, the craft was converted into a single float seaplane because the Navy thought a seaplane was more suitable for naval operations. Appearing in the photo are: (10) Glen Curtiss; (20) Theodore Ellyson; (30) Capt. Washington Irving Chambers; (40) John Towers. (U.S. National Archives)

Glenn Curtiss sits at the wheel of the four-cylinder "Lizzie" he had designed and built as a basic trainer for his military students. From left the students are U.S. Marine Lieutenant John McClaskey, U.S. Army Captain Paul Beek, Lieutenant John H. Towers and Lieutenant Theodore Ellyson. (U.S. Naval Historical Center)

Standing near the tail of the Curtiss Triad are the pioneers of American naval aviation. From left are Glenn Curtiss, Captain Chambers, John Towers, Theodore Ellyson and a Curtiss employee. (U.S. Naval Historical Center)

birth of U.S. Naval Aviation had become a reality. Despite this modest but farsighted beginning, America gradually lost its naval leadership. By the end of the year five countries had more certified pilots than the U.S. France led with 353 pilots, compared with only 26 pilots in America, of whom only eight were military airmen.

The First Flying Boat
Glenn Curtiss made the first flying boat in 1910 and tested the plane during that summer. Ellyson and Towers flew the Curtiss design in mid-1911 amid great enthusiasm. The U.S. Navy showed some in-

U.S. Naval Aviator No. 1, Lieutenant Theodore Ellyson, checks the controls preparatory to takeoff in a Curtiss pusher. He was the test pilot for many Curtiss innovations. (U.S. National Archives)

U.S. Naval Aviator No. 3, Lieutenant John H. Towers, was in the U.S. Naval Academy Class of 1906 and learned to fly in 10 weeks with Ellyson as his instructor. He remained in the Navy completing important assignments through two world wars. (U.S. National Archives)

Glenn Curtiss rides the world's first amphibian out of the water and onto shore during the first water-to-land-to-water flight. At Captain Chamber's instigation, Curtiss added three wheels to the Triad's single float. (U.S. Naval Historical Center)

The Wright Brothers used a catapult or accelerator to assist their biplanes to gain speed quickly for takeoff. A weight, suspended in the framework tower, was connected to the plane by a rope via a series of pulleys. When the weight was dropped it pulled the plane forward. (U.S. Naval Historical Center)

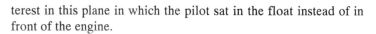

terest in this plane in which the pilot sat in the float instead of in front of the engine.

The First Amphibian

The indefatigable Captain Chambers mused to himself; could a plane be made to fly from land as well as water? He approached Curtiss with this question. Glenn Curtiss added three wheels to the single float of this biplane; a small wheel at the bow and two larger wheels on either side of the stern of the float. After test flights proved successful from both land and water, Curtiss made the first water-to-land-to-water flight at North Island, California. In this historic flight Curtiss took off from water and landed on shore. After a short roll he took off again and returned to the water. The amphibian had been born.

THE FIRST CATAPULTS

On March 13, 1912 Captain Chambers was assigned to the U.S. Navy Bureau of Navigation in order that he could devote all of his

time to aeronautics. Chambers had hardly gotten accustomed to his new desk when he began working on ideas to improve the operation of aircraft from ships. He knew that landplanes could land and take off from ships; however, the flight deck occupied too much valuable space. Chambers also appreciated the fact that seaplanes could be lowered into the water from ships, take off to perform their mission, land beside the ship and be hoisted aboard; however too much time was lost lowering and raising the plane from the sea. He then hit upon the idea of using a compressed air catapult to launch planes away from ships in the quickest manner over the shortest run.

Wright Brothers' Catapult

The Wright Brothers had been using a catapult or accelerator type of launching device that consisted of a heavy weight suspended in a framework tower. Through a system of pulleys a rope led from the weight to the aircraft and, when the weight was released, it pulled the plane forward. Captain Chamber's idea was high-tech for 1912.

Theodore "Spuds" Ellyson prepares to test the new compressed air catapult which is mounted on a long float in the water. Note that this 1912 Curtiss design has no forward elevator control surface. (U.S. National Archives)

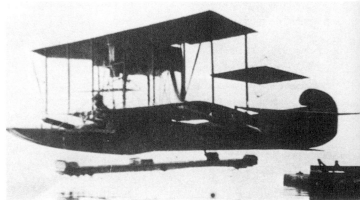

The Curtiss flying boat in a catapult launch with Ellyson at the controls. The plane has just left the float and the wheeled trolley has fallen clear of the hull. Here again the forward elevator has been omitted. (U.S. National Archives)

First Catapult Trial

The first catapult trial was held at Annapolis and Theodore Ellyson was the test pilot. A track was installed on a wharf and a wheeled wooden trolley was fitted to the tracks. The aircraft was carried by the trolley which was connected to the compressed air piston connecting rod via a series of pulleys to multiply the effect of the 40 inch piston travel. The trial was conducted in a slight cross-wing and the full 290 pounds per square inch pressure was turned on at once. Halfway through the run the trolley arose from the tracks, throwing the plane in the air. The cross-wind lifted the starboard or right wing which threw the plane into the water. Both plane and pilot survived the accident unharmed.

Second Catapult Trial

The next trial was at the Washington Navy Yard on November 12, 1912 with Ellyson, again, as the test pilot. This time the trolley was held to the tracks with reverse flanges and more wheels were added. The catapult was mounted on a long float so it could be directed into the wind. The air valve was opened slowly and when the trolley left the rails at the end of the run, the Curtiss climbed gradually in a steady flight.

The operation was repeated later in the month with the new Curtiss flying boat that the U.S. Navy had just purchased. Although Curtiss, Chambers and Ellyson were elated at the catapult success, it remained dormant for several years due to official apathy.

ROYAL NAVY SHIPBOARD EXPERIMENTS

Samson, Gregory, Longsmore, and Gerrard, having learned to fly the primitive box-like planes built by the Short Brothers, began to study how they might be adapted to naval purposes. The planes were too flimsy to take floats; therefore, cylindrical air bags were lashed to the landing gear and tailskid area.

First Water Takeoff and Landing

By the time the Short biplanes had been fitted with the air bags Commander Oliver Schwann, who had access to a sturdier float equipped Avro biplane, made Britain's first takeoff from water on November 18, 1911. During the following month Lieutenant Longmore landed an air bag-fitted Short S.27 on the River Medway but was unable to take off due to the bulk and resistance of the air bags.

First Takeoff From Moving Ship

In an effort to overcome the takeoff problem Lieutenant Samson supervised the construction of a wooden platform over the bow of the battleship *HMS Africa* and, flying a Short S.27, he took off this

Commander Schwann's Avro seaplane is towed to the ready dock prior to the first British seaplane takeoff. (Air Ministry [Navy])

Commander Oliver Schwann made the first takeoff from water in Britain on November 18, 1911. The commander is shown in the cockpit of the 35 horsepower, four-cylinder Green engine-powered Avro seaplane as the crew ready the plane for the flight. The plane crashed upon landing. (Air Ministry [Navy])

The Short S.27 rests on the wooden launching platform of HMS Hibernia from which Lieutenant Charles R. Samson flew the plane on May 4, 1912. This was the world's first takeoff from a moving ship. (Ministry of Defence [Navy])

Lieutenant Samson leaves the platform of HMS Hibernia in his Short S.27 on May 4, 1912. The landing gear was fitted with streamlined cylindrical floats, wheels, and skids. (Ministry of Defence [Navy])

deck on January 10, 1912 and landed alongside the ship. On May 4 Lieutenant Samson made the world's first takeoff from a moving ship when he took off from a platform on *HMS Hibernia* while the ship was steaming at 10 knots. He landed ashore with his wheel and air bag-equipped Short S.27. Lieutenant Gregory duplicated this feat on May 9 from the same ship. As more sturdy aircraft were developed the air bag idea was abandoned in favor of rigid floats.

Murray Sueter; Air Department Director

The Admiralty was so inspired by the activities of these officers that, by the end of 1912, the Royal Flying Corps was divided into two distinct sections; a separate naval wing and a separate military wing. Murray Sueter was installed in the Admiralty as the first Director of the Air Department. The Naval Wing soon boasted 16 assorted aircraft and 22 pilots.

ARMING THE AIRPLANE

"Time spent on reconnaissance is seldom wasted." This British strategy governed the basic objective in the application of the airplane for naval purposes. Despite this intent, considerable experimentation was conducted in arming military aircraft. On June 30, 1910 Glenn Curtiss pioneered the technique of bombing by dropping a number of dummy bombs on a land target in the shape of a ship. During January 1911, U.S. Navy Lieutenant M.S. Crissy dropped a live bomb from a Wright biplane piloted by Philip Parmelee. These bombs were hand-held and it was a rather hit or miss technique. This encouraged Lieutenant Riley Scott to invent the first bomb sight with which he won 75,000 francs in a French bombing contest in 1912. Lieutenant Samson had experimented with dummy bombs during that same year. Seaplanes of greater power and strength were coming from the Short Brothers factory and these had been fitted with guns ranging in size from 1 1/2 pounders to 6 pounders. On July 28, 1914 Squadron Commander Arthur Longmore (later to become Air Field Marshal Sir) launched the first torpedo from a Short seaplane. This weapon was 14 inches in diameter and weighed 810 pounds.

Aircraft Radio

Communications also progressed. In the summer of 1913 radio signals were transmitted from a Short seaplane and four shore stations were established at Calshot, Cromarty, Great Yarmouth, and Felixstowe.

The Airplane Goes To War

Aerial reconnaissance and bombing were used for the first time by Italian aircraft during the Italo-Turkish War of 1911-1912. The Italians dropped improvised bombs, hand grenades, and propaganda leaflets from their Bleriot XI monoplanes. The airplane was now also a weapon and not only a mobile crow's nest.

Despite the success of Ely's and Samson's demonstrations the U.S. Navy and the Royal Navy proceeded slowly and cautiously.

EARLY CARRIER CONVERSIONS

The early experiments conducted by Charles Samson in launching aircraft from ramps installed on battleships convinced the Admi-

ralty that aircraft should take part in fleet maneuvers. The annual naval exercises scheduled for the summer of 1913 afforded the ideal opportunity to apply the use of aircraft with the fleet.

HMS Hermes Seaplane Carrier Conversion

The protected cruiser *HMS Hermes* was selected for conversion to a seaplane carrier. This ship was of the *Highflyer* class, launched in 1898. The twin screws were driven by triple expansion reciprocating steam engines developing 10,000 horsepower from steam generated in 18 coal fired boilers. Displacement of this 350 foot ship was 5,650 tons. Speed was 20 knots. Main armament was (11) 6 inch guns and armor consisted of a 3 inch thick deck and gun shields. The conversion included the addition of cranes fore and aft to hoist the seaplanes aboard plus a sloping takeoff deck running from the wheelhouse to the bow. Canvas shelters were erected on the forecastle and quarterdeck.

Seaplane Operation

Three seaplanes were to be carried and the method of launching is most interesting. The forward crane placed the Short Folder seaplane on a wheeled dolly on the takeoff deck.

During takeoff the plane rode on the dolly until the seaplane became airborne, leaving the dolly on the deck. Landing was made on the water and either crane hoisted the plane onto the ship.

Short Folder

The Short Folder seaplane was the first British plane to have folding wings to facilitate stowage on airplane carriers. Since this biplane had the rather large wingspan of 67 feet, folding wings were necessary. The wings folded laterally 90 degrees aft until they became parallel to the fuselage.

HMS Ark Royal Conversion

Inclement weather prevented *Hermes* and her aircraft from participating in fleet exercises; however, the Folders were launched and retrieved repeatedly with such success that the Admiralty decided to provide the Royal Navy with a ship constructed specifically for the purpose of operating airplanes at sea. Winston Churchill, as First Sea Lord, was very enthusiastic about this project and ordered it to proceed without delay.

A collier-grain bulk carrier had been under construction at the Blyth Shipyard with only the framework completed.

This was purchased by the Admiralty in May 1914 and completely redesigned except for the hull lines. The powerplant was retained but relocated aft with the superstructure, as in modern tankers, in order to have an uninterrupted 130 foot flying off deck. An adjacent hatch opened into a 150 foot cargo hold for the stowage of seven airplanes plus workshops, ammunition and aviation fuel. Two large steam powered cranes were installed, flanking the flying off deck. A 3,000 horsepower triple expansion steam engine drove the ship to a speed of 11 knots. This 352 foot ship displaced 7,450 tons. No inclined takeoff ramp was fitted as was on *Hermes*; all landplanes or dollied seaplanes being launched directly from the flying off deck which was parallel to the waterline. As with *Hermes*, the seaplanes landed in the water and were hoisted aboard by the cranes which placed them on the flying off deck or into the hatchway to

HMS Ark Royal was the first ship constructed specifically for the purpose of operating airplanes at sea. Engine room was located aft in order to have a long uninterrupted flying off deck. The speed of 11 knots produce insufficient WOD for troublefree takeoffs. HMS Ark Royal served as a Catapult Aircraft Merchant ship (CAM) during World War II; renamed HMS Pegasus. (Ministry of Defence [Navy])

the hold. Landplanes had to land on shoreside fields or ditch alongside the carrier and be rescued. It is to the designers' credit that this ship met the basic requirements of the aircraft carrier with nothing more than their imagination and designing talent to work with. This

A Short 184 torpedo plane is lifted from the water onto HMS Ark Royal by one of the two powerful cranes. (U.S. Naval Historical Center)

revolutionary ship was renamed *HMS Ark Royal*, commemorating another *Ark Royal* of the 17th Century which served with honor under the command of Sir Francis Drake in fighting the Spanish Armada.

Russian Seaplane Carriers

Imperial Russia demonstrated considerable interest in seaplane carriers during the 1914-1918 War, having converted eight noncombatants for that purpose. They are: 3,285 ton *Almaz*; 9,250 ton *Alexander I* and *Nicolai I* (renamed *Respublikanek* and *Aviator*, respectively, after the Revolution); 3,800 ton *Orlica*; 3,152 ton *Romania*; 2,369 ton *Regele Carol*; 3,418 ton *Dacia* and 3;418 ton *Imperator Trayan*. All saw service in the Black Sea except *Orlica* which was used in the Baltic Sea. These ships carried from four to eight aircraft which were operated from the water because no flying off deck was fitted. Speeds were 18-19 knots.

Japanese Seaplane Carrier

Japan also showed early interest in air capable ships. In the summer of 1914 the cargo vessel *Lethington* was converted into the seaplane carrier *Wakamiya*. *Lethington* was a British built ship which Japan had captured from Russia in 1905 during the Russo-Japanese War. This 7,720 ton vessel was powered by a 1,600 horsepower triple expansion steam engine which propelled the craft to nine knots. Japan had joined the Allies during World War I and the seaplane carrier *Wakayima* took part in a raid on the German enclave at Tsingtao, China in September 1914 with her seaplanes sinking a German minelayer and damaging shore installations. The Japanese Naval Air Service had trained six officers to fly in 1912. One of the officers was Chikuhei Nakajima who was soon to become a famous airplane designer and founder of the renowned aircraft company of that name. Despite the fact that Nakajima was producing his first aircraft, a two-place seaplane, the Japanese Navy continued to fly British Sopwith and Short seaplanes as well as some French Farman seaplanes throughout the war.

French Seaplane Carrier

The French were not far behind in trying the aircraft carrier. In 1914 the old cruiser *Foudre* was selected to have a flying off deck erected over the bow and a hangar installed on the quarter deck. Rene Caudron, later to become a famous airplane designer, made the first takeoff from the ship in the harbor of St. Raphael on May 8; however, in actual service only seaplanes were carried and these were hoisted in and out of the water as with *Empress*, *Engadine* and *Riviera*. *Foudre* was France's first and last attempt at aircraft carriers in World War I and all interest remained dormant for the next eight years.

SHORT 184 SEAPLANE

The two-seater Short 184 was the result of constant refinement of the Folder and also featured folding wings. This craft was made by Short Brothers, the oldest established designers and builders of airplanes in Britain. Oswald and Eustace had founded the company in 1898, making balloons, and when their older brother, Horace, joined them in 1908 they began to manufacture airplanes on the Isle of Sheppy. The 184 was powered by a variety of engines ranging from 225 to 275 horsepower which gave the 5,500 pound plane a speed of 80 to 85 miles per hour. The craft was designed for reconnaissance work and bombing, in addition to torpedo attack tasks. It could carry bombs ranging in size from 65 pounders to 520 pounders. The 184 established the Short Brothers' reputation as quality aircraft constructors and 650 of these fabric covered wooden frame seaplanes were built.

A Short 184, with a torpedo slung between the main floats, is lowered to the water. Short 184 torpedo planes scored the world's first and second aircraft-launched torpedo sinkings. Both planes operated from HMS Ben-My-Chree. (Ministry of Defence [Navy])

The triple-bay folding wings of the Short 184 duplicate those of earlier Short Folder; hinging on the rear spar. Observe the large radiator atop the engine cowl which must have hindered the pilot's forward view. Also note the cylindrical floats under the wingtips to support the wing in the event the plane tips during takeoff or landing. (U.S. National Archives)

France converted the aging cruiser Foudre with a flying off deck, hangar, and lifting booms. In actual service only seaplanes were carried and these were hoisted in and out of the water. (Marine National/ECP Armees)

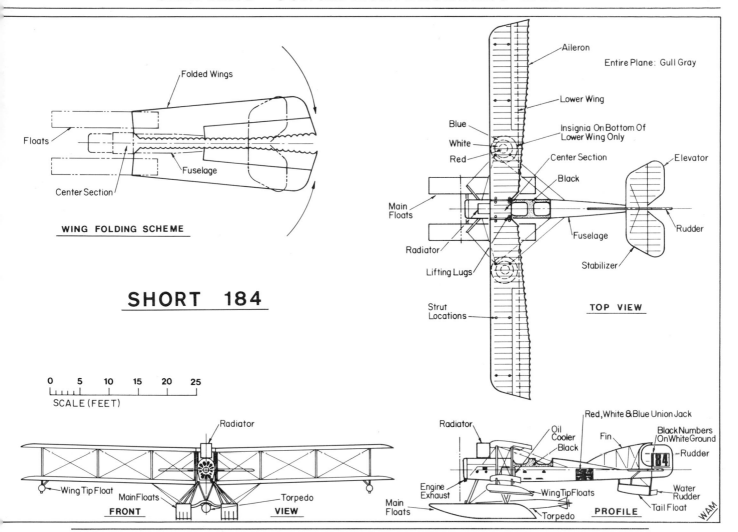

WING FOLDING SCHEME

SHORT 184

SCALE (FEET)

FRONT VIEW

TOP VIEW

PROFILE

WORLD WAR I BEGINS

World War I began in August 1914 while *Ark Royal* was still under construction and was not scheduled for completion until the end of the year.

Empress, Engadine and Riviera Conversions

In view of the war emergency the Admiralty requisitioned three cross-channel steamers; *Empress, Engadine* and *Riviera*. These ships were converted to carry four seaplanes each, but they were not fitted with flying off decks. The seaplanes were lowered into the water for takeoff and were retrieved in the same way after flight. The ships were not aircraft carriers in the true sense of the word; more like what were to be known as seaplane tenders in later years. This operating scenario limited the aircraft's usefulness because, due to the frail construction, the floats tended to break up if the sea was the least bit rough. Records indicate that several planes were lost in choppy seas. The ships were commissioned in late 1914.

Although *Ark Royal* was a more useful design, its slow speed proved a detriment to its ability to keep up with the fleet. Conversely, *Empress, Engadine* and *Riviera* boasted twice the speed of *Ark Royal* but did not have the aircraft launching ability. In addition, they did not satisfy the need for endurance to keep up with the far ranging fleet.

Vindex, Ben-My-Chree and *Manxman* Conversions

The Admiralty now turned to three Isle of Man steam packets which were larger and even faster than the converted cross-channel steamers. The selection to be converted was *Ben-My-Chree*, *Vindex* (former *Viking*) and *Manxman*. These steam turbine powered (11,000 to 14,000 horsepower) craft attained speeds of 21 to 25 knots and displaced 2,500 to 3,800 tons. Conversion proceeded through the winter and two craft were commissioned in Spring 1915. Conversion included a rigid hangar on the main deck aft of the superstructure and an inclined forward flying off ramp. Accommodations for four to eight aircraft were provided. The ships were also fitted with 12 pounder and 3 pounder guns for defense. *Manxman* was commissioned in spring 1916.

Early Royal Navy Air Raids

While the development of sea-going combat aircraft was making progress, the Royal Naval Air Service, or RNAS, was demonstrating the real potential of air power for the first time over the European mainland. Early in the war Charles R. Samson was in charge of a small force of 10 aircraft based in Belgium whose principal objective was to carry out reconnaissance flights over land and sea, and to engage any enemy planes or Zeppelins; however, Samson decided to do more.

HMS Ben-My-Chree had been an Isle of Man steam packet converted into a seaplane carrier. Four to eight aircraft could be carried in the hangar aft of the smokestacks. The ship had a speed of about 23 knots. Note the mast and boom for lifting seaplanes. (The Fleet Air Arm Museum)

Another Isle of Man conversion was HMS Manxman which differed from Ben-My-Chree with a large structural crane on the fantail for lifting the increasingly heavy seaplanes onto the deck. (William Lodge Photo, Courtesy Brian Andresen)

After an unsuccessful raid on September 22 in which the British failed to find their objective Samson sent four pilots flying Sopwith Tabloids on another raid over Germany on October 8. This flight was more successful. Commander Spencer Grey dropped 20 pound bombs on the Cologne railroad station while Flight Lieutenant R.L.G. Marix bombed Zeppelin sheds at Dusseldorf. Not only did one of the sheds burst into flame but it destroyed the new Zeppelin *LZ 9* which was moored inside. Zeppelins were regarded as the primary menace to the Royal Navy which is why they were chosen as the target on this very first strategic bombing raid.

First Shipboard Aircraft Raid
As *Ark Royal* was nearing completion, *Empress, Engadine* and *Riviera* were launching their planes for the first offensive operation by shipboard aircraft. It was on Christmas Day 1914 that these seaplanes took off to attack airship sheds in Cuxhaven and Wilhelmshaven. Flight Commander F.J. Rutland made history when he flew reconnaissance from *Engadine* during early stages of the Battle of Jutland.

HMS Hermes Sinks
In the meantime, *HMS Hermes* was in action in the Atlantic operating Short Folders. On October 31, 1914 she was torpedoed by a German submarine off Calais, France and sunk.

First Aerial Torpedo Victory
HMS Ark Royal and seven seaplanes went to the Eastern Mediterranean to provide photographic reconnaissance, gunnery control and infantry support during the early stages of the Dardanelles campaign.

Her slow speed made *Ark Royal* very vulnerable to German submarines which were appearing with greater frequency in the Eastern Mediterranean; whereupon she was replaced by *Ben-My-Chree* during May 1915.

HMS Ben-My-Chree was equipped with the new Short Type 184 seaplane which was the first practical torpedo-carrying aircraft. On August 12, 1915 Flight Commander C.H.K. Edmonds took off from *Ben-My-Chree* and made the first ever airborne torpedo attack on a 5,000 ton Turkish supply ship. Flying at an altitude of only 15 feet, Edmonds released the torpedo at a range of 300 yards and sank the ship. A few weeks later a Turkish tugboat was sunk by a torpedo launched from another Short 184.

Zeppelin Menace
The thorn in the Royal Navy's side was the relative impunity of the German airships as they surveyed the British Fleet from their safe altitude. Seaplanes could not reach the airships; therefore, two Bristol Scout biplane landplanes were loaded in the Hangar aboard *HMS Vindex*. The first takeoff was made on November 3, 1915 to prove the feasibility of launching landplanes from the 64 foot forward deck. This flight was made by Flight Sublieutenant H.F. Towler and is considered a milestone in the development of the aircraft carrier.

LANDPLANES REPLACE SEAPLANES
German Zeppelins continued to harass the Royal Navy unmolested until August, 1916 when Flight Lieutenant C.T. Freeman took off the deck of *Vindex* in his Bristol Scout to intercept a high-flying Zeppelin by dropping Rankin darts. The airship got away but the practicability of operations from airplane carriers had been demonstrated.

Also in 1916, Rear Admiral Vaughn-Lee, Director of Air Services, proposed seaplane equipped carriers forming a sort of early warning interception screen in the North Sea and English Channel however, it very quickly became apparent that once the Zeppelin was sighted seaplanes would consume so much time getting ready for the launch that they could never catch up with the airship. Further, the seaplanes did not have the performance to reach the intruders. A successful interception demanded aircraft of higher performance that could become airborne in short order; namely landplane fighters.

Landplane Torpedo-Bomber Specified
On October 9, 1916 Commodore Murray Sueter, Director of the Air Department of the Admiralty, issued what was called a "Most Secret Memorandum". It asked Sopwith to investigate the design and construction of a torpedo-carrying landplane capable of carrying one or two 1,000 pound torpedoes plus enough fuel for missions up to four hours' endurance. The craft must be capable of operation from an aircraft carrier. The memo went on to suggest the possibility of using catapults to assist the plane to become airborne. The interesting part of Commodore Sueter's memorandum is that he specified a landplane to operate from an aircraft carrier.

The Sopwith Tabloid created a sensation in 1913 because it was diminutive, hence the name, and exhibited remarkable performance. Observe the skis extending forward of the landing gear to prevent nose-overs or propeller breakage. A seaplane version won the coveted Schneider Trophy Race at Monaco flown by C. Howard Pixton. (British Aerospace, Courtesy Brendan Morrissey)

Developed from the Schneider Trophy winner, the 100 horsepower Sopwith Schneider closely resembled its progenitor except for the tail float and the diagonal member between the float struts. Note the cockard insignia on the bottom of the upper wing. (British Aerospace, Courtesy Brendan Morrissey)

This beautifully maintained Sopwith Baby is suspended in the entrance foyer of The Fleet Air Arm Museum, RNAS Yeovilton, Somerset, England. The Baby is very similar to the Schneider except for the rudder shape, open engine cowling, and 130 horsepower engine. These craft saw naval action in the early days of World War I. (WAM Foto)

A few months later in February 1917 the British Grand Fleet Aircraft Committee made the surprise recommendation to replace the Sopwith Baby and Tabloid seaplanes operating from Campania with Sopwith Pup landplanes.

Sopwith Tabloid

The Sopwith Tabloid was a very small unarmed single-seater biplane which created a sensation when it made its appearance in 1913. It was named Tabloid because, like the Tabloid newspaper, it was smaller than the usual aircraft of that period. Designed specifically for demonstration flying and racing, the 80 horsepower Gnome rotary engine propelled the aircraft to a speed of 92 miles per hour with a rate of climb of 1,200 feet per minute; a performance that had never before been achieved with a biplane. The craft had a wingspan of 25 feet and weight was only 1,500 pounds. The Sopwith Tabloid was equally at home as a landplane or seaplane. In fact, a seaplane version won the coveted Schneider Trophy for 1914 and spun off equally famous designs; the 100 horsepower Sopwith Schneider and the 110 to 130 horsepower Sopwith Baby. These planes served early in the war as both shore-based and shipboard aircraft. The success of the biplane reversed the growing tendency toward a preference for monoplane designs, which was not to return for two decades!

Bristol Scout

The prototype Bristol 206 Scout was designed by Frank Barnwell and made its maiden flight during February 1914. The production Scout was the "C" model powered by an 80 horsepower rotary engine manufactured by either Gnome, Clerget, or Le Rhone. The Admiralty ordered 24 for the RNAS. The 24 foot wingspan craft weighed 1,415 pounds and attained a maximum speed of 109 miles per hour at 3,000 feet. Service ceiling was 14,000 feet. In view of the fact that the plane was built for scouting it was unarmed. Most of the RNAS Bristol Scouts were used for anti-Zeppelin patrols armed with canisters of incendiary Rankin darts. By late 1915 the Model "D" had been developed, powered with a 100 horsepower Monosoupape engine, of which the Admiralty ordered fifty.

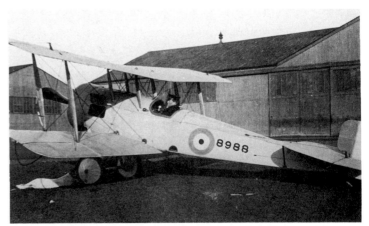

The Bristol Scout D served in the RNAS for anti-Zeppelin patrol duty. Instead of machine guns, the Bristol was armed with incendiary darts to drop on the huge airships. (Air Ministry [Navy])

Murray Sueter, shown here as Rear Admiral Sir Murray Sueter, is the British counterpart of the American Captain Chambers as the Father of British Carrier Aviation. He was a co-administrator of the dirigible, Mayfly; conceived the idea for the Campania conversion; Sopwith Cuckoo and many others that led to Britain's leadership in carrier aviation. He was the Director of the Air Department in The Admiralty. (The Fleet Air Arm Museum)

Captain Oliver Schwann was a co-administrator of the dirigible Mayfly; made the first British takeoff from water; and became commanding officer of Campania. He was one of the leading pioneers in the development of British Naval Aviation. (The Fleet Air Arm Museum)

Sopwith Pup

The Sopwith Pup, which had been recommended by the Grand Fleet Aircraft Committee, was universally acclaimed to have had the finest flying qualities of any airplane of World War I. Although a bit underpowered, virtually all who flew the Pup considered it to be the most perfect flying machine ever made. The nickname Pup is most unusual for a warplane. The Sopwith design immediately preceding the Pup was the larger two-seater 1 1/2 Strutter; therefore, the new smaller plane was looked upon as the offspring of the 1 1/2 Strutter, i.e. the Pup. It was not the official name at all but the men who flew and serviced her persisted in calling her Pup. In fact, the authorities tried to prevent the use of the name Pup, but were unsuccessful.

The Sopwith Pup went into service with the Royal Flying Corps and the Royal Naval Air Service in 1916. Powered by an 80 horsepower Le Rhone rotary engine the craft had a top speed of 111 miles per hour. The service ceiling was 17,500 feet. Standard armament was a single Vickers machine gun mounted atop the fuselage in front of the pilot; however, some Pups were armed with the lighter Lewis machine gun firing upward through a cutout in the upper wing center section. The Pup will appear again when the RNAS endeavors to learn the secret of landing safely on aircraft carriers.

Sopwith Cuckoo

Sopwith accepted Commodore Sueter's request to develop a tor-

pedo-carrying landplane and by June 1917 the prototype made its initial appearance. This Sopwith design was a single-seater biplane designated T.1; however, because, like the cuckoo, it lays its eggs in other birds' nests the T.1 was soon called the Cuckoo. The landing gear was a very sturdy divided type without the standard cross axle in order to be able to launch the 18 inch, 1,000 pound torpedo from under the fuselage.

The Cuckoo basic structure was wood with fabric covering and the wings folded back laterally as on the 184 and Folder. The prototype was powered by a 200 horsepower Hispano-Suiza engine; however, the demand for this engine to power the famous SE 5 fighters forced the Cuckoo production aircraft to be fitted with either the 200 horsepower Sunbeam Arab, 200 horsepower Rolls-Royce Falcon III, or the 200 horsepower Wolseley W.4A Viper en-

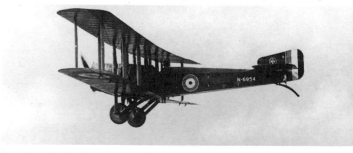

The Sopwith Cuckoo was the first torpedo-carrying landplane. In order to launch the 18 inch, 1,000 pound torpedo the landing gear was designed to leave off the conventional cross axle. Wings folded for stowage on carriers. (Imperial War Museum)

gines. Maximum speed of this 3,883 pound plane with the Arab engine was 103 miles per hour.

The official trials were held in July 1917 and a total of 350 aircraft were ordered. It proved a very pleasant plane to fly, even with the torpedo. The Armistice was signed as Cuckoo number 90 was delivered and; therefore, the contract was cancelled. Although the Sopwith Cuckoo made its appearance too late to make a name for itself, it did pave the way for the future torpedo planes which achieved so much during World War II. Of interest is the fact that a British Air Mission sold six of these aircraft to Japan in 1922 giving the Japanese Navy its first experience with a combat technique that it learned to use so well.

The final conversion of Campania reveals the new dual forward smokestacks, removal of tall crane masts and forward superstructure, and extension of the takeoff ramp. Note the relocated bridge between the new smokestacks. (Peter Doyle Collection)

A CARRIER MILESTONE: *HMS CAMPANIA*

Captain Murray Sueter began to realize that the ideal airplane carrier had to combine high speed with endurance and capaciousness, and to this end he selected the Cunard Line *Campania* for conversion to an aircraft carrier. Built in 1892, *Campania* had been a Blue Ribbon record breaking passenger liner during the turn of the century and was now scheduled for scrapping. The Admiralty purchased the liner in late 1914 and conversion began at once with the addi-

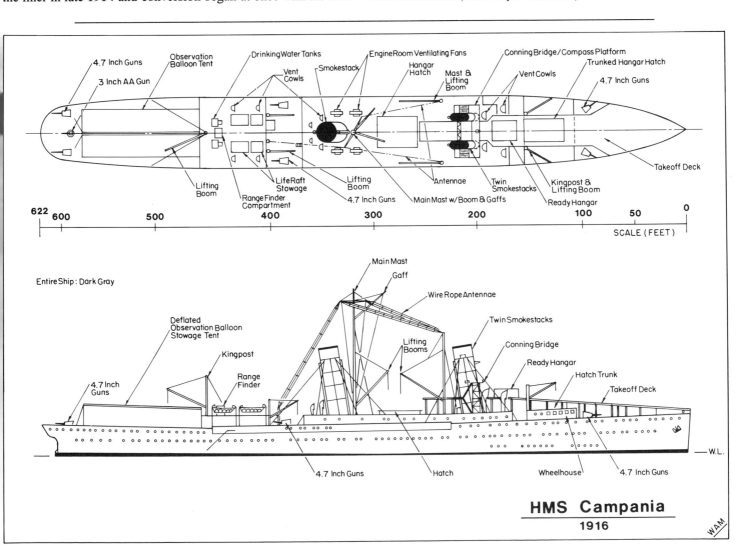

HMS Campania
1916

tion of cranes and a short inclined flying off deck. Six single-mounted 4.7 inch guns were installed on the main deck, one on each side; forward, amidships, and aft.

Second *Campania* Conversion

The initial conversion proved unsatisfactory because, despite its 18,000 ton displacement and 600 foot length, *Campania* could operate no more aircraft than the much smaller Isle of Man packets. Further modifications were accomplished by Cammell, Laird's shipyard which included replacing the forward smokestack with two side by side thinner stacks set far enough apart so the take off ramp could be extended between them. The extended ramp was lengthened to 165 feet and inclined downward towards the bow. The ramp displaced the navigating bridge so it was moved to a new location between the new smokestacks and supported by them, 15 feet above the ramp. The 30,000 horsepower ship could now handle six to eight aircraft. The holds could accommodate 12 planes plus aviation fuel and spare parts. Speed was 23 knots. In addition to the airplanes *Campania* was designed to stow and operate an observation kite balloon from its quarterdeck to be used for immediate observation duties rather than long range reconnaissance.

Campania Joins the Fleet

With Captain Oliver Swann in command the *Campania* home base was an anchorage in Scapa Flow. This is the same Oliver Schwann mentioned earlier but since then had changed his name to an Anglicized version of his very German sounding name. On May 30, 1916 Swann received a preparatory signal radioed to all ships of the Grand Fleet at 5:35 PM. A further order was received one and one half hours later to raise steam for full speed and by 9:00 PM *Campania* was ready to proceed to sea. A SNAFU occurred when Captain Swann failed to receive the executive order sent out at 10:54 PM and it was not for several hours that he was aware that the Fleet had sailed. He quickly weighed anchor and sped after the Fleet which was on its way to engage the German Fleet in what became known as the Battle of Jutland.

Campania's absence from the battle was not known until midnight nor was it known until 2:00 AM that she had left Scapa Flow. In view of the many German submarines in the area plus the fact that no destroyer escort was available, Admiral John Jellico ordered

Campania to return to Scapa Flow, which she reached at 9:15 AM, May 31.

Just how much help the *Campania* planes would have given to Jellico is conjecture; however, the German Fleet was helped by the high-flying reconnaissance of no less than 10 Zeppelins.

Campania was, indeed, a luckless ship because on August 19, 1916 the German Fleet made a sortie showing some eagerness to do battle; however, *Campania* could not sail to meet the Germans due to engine trouble. By contrast, a Zeppelin sighted the larger British Fleet in time to warn Admiral Reinhard Scheer, who quickly retired back to Kiel rather than engage in a suicidal battle.

Fairey Campania Shipboard Aircraft

HMS Campania was the first aircraft carrier in history to have had an airplane specifically designed for her use and the only carrier to have an airplane named after her. The Fairey Campania was the first British plane specifically designed for carrier operation. This two-seater, reconnaissance, float equipped biplane made its appearance in 1916 and proved a medicre design which had an undistinguished career. Structure was wire-braced wood with fabric covering. The wings could be folded, as on the Short designs, for stowage in the hold. The 5,706 pound, 275 horsepower version of the Campania had a maximum speed of 82 miles per hour and a service ceiling of 6,900 feet.

TURRET TOP TAKEOFF PLATFORMS

The Royal Navy also began taking an interest in turret top takeoff platforms in 1917. Experience with the Sopwith Pup showed that, with a wing loading of only five pounds per square foot and a power loading of 16.4 pounds per horsepower, the plane required a takeoff run of only 20 feet into a 20 knot wind. In view of the very small platform required for takeoff it was decided to erect one atop the forward turret of light cruisers, starting with the *HMS Yarmouth*. The first flight from this platform was made in June 1917 by Flight Commander F.J. Rutland who also made the first reconnaissance flight from the *HMS Engadine*.

Turret Top Platform Airship Victory

After only two months had elapsed the idea of operating fighters

A Fairey Campania seaplane flies off the HMS Furious Takeoff Deck leaving its four-wheel trolley on the deck. This system had been used since the first seaplane carrier conversion in 1913. The decision to use landplanes and the introduction of the catapult ended the trolley takeoff. (Ministry of Defence [Navy])

This close-up of the seaplane takeoff trolley reveals the guidance shoe that rides in the centerline slot in the deck. This keeps the seaplane on a straight run during takeoff. (Ministry of Defence [Navy])

from cruisers paid off. On August 21, 1917 *HMS Yarmouth* was escorting a squadron of minelayers in Heligoland Bight when a German airship came into view. Flight Sublieutenant B.S. Smart ran to his Pup and took off from the platform. The Sopwith climbed laboriously to 7,000 feet and slipped above the dirigible unseen. He swooped towards the intruder broadsides and fired incendiary bullets from his single machine gun. First a flicker and then sudden, spectacular, flaming destruction engulfed the *L 22* as it fell into the sea! The victor ditched his plane and was picked up by *HMS Prince*. Smart was awarded the Distinguished Service Order for this feat.

Takeoff Platform Variations

Sublieutenant Smart's encouraging victory stimulated further development of the basic platform idea. Soon rotating takeoff platforms were mounted amidships on some vessels. These had the advantage of heading the plane into the wind without requiring the ship to change its direction; however, the takeoff platform was always installed atop a gun turret on battle cruisers. The first battle cruiser test flight was made from a turret platform on *HMS Repulse* that was positioned 42 degrees off the starboard bow. This flight was made on October 1, 1917 into a 31 miles per hour wind. Once again the test pilot was Flight Commander F.J. Rutland.

By the early months of 1918 all Royal Navy battle cruisers had been fitted with turret platforms. Eventually, portable wooden planked extensions were added to the platforms to lengthen them for the longer takeoff run required by the larger and heavier two-seater reconnaissance Sopwith 1 1/2 Strutters. Also added was a quick-release device which held the planes back until the engine developed full power, then it released the Sopwith for takeoff.

MORE ROYAL NAVY CARRIER CONVERSIONS

The Royal Navy's enthusiasm to take aircraft to sea prompted the conversion of two more fast mail steamers to aircraft carriers with inclined takeoff decks. The conversions were similar to *Manxman* with heavy cranes overhanging the stern.

HMS Nairana

Purchased before completion at the Denny Shipyard, the 352 foot long overall *Nairana* was launched in early 1917 and commissioned on August 25, 1917. At 3,550 tons the 6,700 shaft horsepower steam turbine machinery drove the converted ship to 19 knots. Beam was 45 feet. Seven aircraft could be accommodated; usually a mixed bag of Sopwith Camels and Fairey Campanias. Two 3 inch guns and two 12 pounders were fitted for defense. The *Nairana* operating crew consisted of 250 officers and enlisted men. It was one of the first carriers to be fitted with an aircraft elevator. *HMS Nairana* served with the British Grand Fleet in 1918 and sailed to Northern Russia with the British Expeditionary Force in 1919.

HMS Pegasus

This conversion was very similar to *HMS Nairana*. The Admiralty purchased the mail steamer Stockholm in February 1917 and converted it into a 3,300 ton aircraft carrier capable of over 20 knots. Draft was 15 feet. Length was 332 feet overall while beam was 43

A Sopwith 1 1/2 Strutter is shown leaving the inclined ramp of HMS Pegasus in 1917. Observe the short ramp and the tall superstructure between the forward smokestack and tall crane masts. (British Aerospace, Courtesy Brendan Morrissey)

feet. Two foremasts were installed so the takeoff deck could be made as long as possible. The steam turbines developed 9,500 shaft horsepower. Crew was 260 officers and enlisted men. Twelve aircraft could be accommodated; again a mixed bag of Camels and Campanias. *Pegasus* was launched on June 9, 1917 and commissioned in late autumn. *HMS Pegasus* served with the British Grand Fleet in 1918 and was used as an aircraft transport during the immediate post-war years.

First Aircraft Elevators

The modifications were very similar to *Ben-My-Chree* except that, for the first time on any carrier, the ships were fitted with an Aircraft Elevator. Both landplanes and seaplanes were flown from the ships.

LARGE FAST CARRIER CONVERSION

It had become so obvious that landplane performance was considerably superior to seaplanes, because of the added weight and re-

A Sopwith Camel takes off from the Pegasus takeoff ramp. The ship could carry a mixed bag of 12 Fairey Campania and Sopwith Camels. The planes could not return to the ship and had to land on shore or ditch alongside the ship. (Air Ministry (Navy))

sistance of the seaplane floats, that the RNAS was determined to concentrate on landplanes. This decision was especially important regarding fighter planes because seaplanes could not reach the highflying Zeppelins which observed every movement of the British Fleet. Solving one problem only gave birth to another; the ability of landplanes to return to their ship instead of ditching in the sea or, if possible, landing shoreside, neither of which is satisfactory.

The Admiralty was aware of the landing problem and selected large and fast ships that were available hoping they could be converted into aircraft carriers able to successfully launch and recover landplanes. Several partially completed ships were acquired; cruisers *Cavendish* and *Furious*; passenger liner *Conte Rosso*; and the battleship *Almirante Cochrane*. A contract was also signed with Armstrong Shipyard to build a new ship specifically designed as an aircraft carrier!

HMS Furious

Early in 1917 the British Navy had taken the most important step in the early development of the aircraft carrier as it is known today. Arrangements were made to convert the partially completed cruiser *HMS Furious* into an aircraft carrier using Campania as the model. This cruiser was selected for conversion because the purpose for which she was being built was no longer a part of the British strategy against Germany. The First Sea Lord of the Admiralty in 1914 was Sir John Arbuthnot "Jackie" Fisher, Baron of Kilverston who, for years, had nurtured a plan to attack Germany's Baltic coast. When the war began he quickly ordered the construction of three battle cruisers; shallow draft for Baltic operations and heavily armed. The new ships were the *Furious*, *Courageous*, and *Glorious*. As fighting progressed his dream was no longer a part of the British war plans, hence the ships were available for conversion and *Furious* was selected.

HMS Furious Conversion

HMS Furious had been launched on August 15, 1916 and was in the process of fitting out when conversion to a carrier began. The forward 18 inch gun turret was removed and a hangar was erected on the forecastle. A 50 x 228 foot flying off deck was installed atop the hangar. The after half was parallel with the water while the forward half sloped downward towards the bow. A hatch in the flying off deck opened into the hangar which was to house only three seaplanes and five Sopwith Pups; far less than was intended originally. The aircraft were raised and lowered from the taking off deck and hangar by a hydraulic elevator as on *Nairana* and *Pegasus*. Workshops, 1,200 gallons of aviation fuel, and aviation ordnance magazine were arranged within the hull. Actually, the modifications were not very extensive and the Furious retained most of the features she had as a cruiser. In a way this conversion made *Furious* an aircraft carrying cruiser; which type of warship was to become very popular 70 years later.

The converted *HMS Furious* was completed in July 1917. Displacement of this 786 foot ship was 22,890 tons fully loaded. The four-geared steam turbines developed a total of 94,000 horsepower, each turbine geared to a propeller. This gave the ship a top speed of 31.5 knots. In addition to the aircraft, Furious had one 18 inch gun aft plus (10) 5 inch guns and (5) 3 inch guns; (6) torpedo tubes were also fitted.

The 31.5 knot speed of *HMS Furious* when steaming into a fresh breeze created a wind over deck (WOD) speed which approached the landing speed of the Sopwith Pup. Much of the cruiser superstructure had remained which blocked a direct landing approach to the takeoff deck, creating a most hazardous condition.

Lieutenant Edwin Harris Dunning was determined to prove that landings could be made on the Flying Off Deck of HMS Furious, and succeeded. A later attempt to improve the technique ended in his death. (The Fleet Air Arm Museum)

Officers and crew of HMS Furious rush to congratulate Commander Dunning for his accomplishment of being the first to land on a moving ship on August 2, 1917. (Peter Doyle Collection)

Dissatisfied with his first landing Commander Dunning made a second attempt to land on the forward Flying Off Deck of HMS Furious on August 4, 1917. As he approached the deck his fellow officers reached for the leather loops attached to his Sopwith Pup. (Peter Doyle Collection)

On Commander Dunning's second landing on August 4, 1917, all went well until the Sopwith Pup's starboard tire burst upon impact with the deck. This caused the Pup to veer to the right and, before the men could grab the leather loops, the Pup went over the side and Dunning drowned. (Peter Doyle Collection)

HMS Furious Landing Trials

During the summer of 1917 the ship lay at anchor in Scapa Flow and, whenever the bow was to windward, many of the pilots practiced landing approaches to the flying off deck. The usual procedure was to fly as slowly as possible alongside *Furious*, from stern to bow, and as soon as the bridge was passed a gentle sideslip brought the Pup over the deck. With sufficient wind over deck (WOD) the pilots agreed that it would be possible to land safely on the deck.

When *HMS Furious* went to sea on August 2, 1917 Squadron Commander Edwin Harris Dunning was determined to prove that it was possible to land on the flying off deck while the ship was underway. Dunning took the precaution of attaching several leather loops at strategic points of his Sopwith Pup. He planned to have his fellow officers waiting on deck ready to grab the loops as soon as

In late 1917 HMS Furious was modified to include a 70 x 285 foot Landing Deck aft of the superstructure. This was connected to the Flying Off Deck, forward of the superstructure, via an 11 foot wide taxiway on each side of the superstructure, clearly visible in this photo. Observe the blimp on the Landing Deck and the Sopwith 1 1/2 Strutter on the Takeoff Deck. (Ministry of Defence [Navy])

the Pup touched down and began to roll. The Squadron Commander made the often-practiced approach and then sideslipped over the deck and settled to a safe landing. This was the very first landing on a moving ship. The men were elated at this successful landing, except Dunning. He was not entirely satisfied with the performance because some of the catchers grabbed the loops before his wheels touched down.

Determined to try again, Dunning took off on August 4, 1917 and upon his return to *Furious* he flew alongside and then sideslipped over the deck. As his wheels touched the deck his starboard tire burst and the Pup slewed to the right. Before the catchers could grab hold of the leather loops the plane went over the side into the sea. The high speed of *HMS Furious* delayed any immediate attempts at a rescue and when the wreckage of the Pup was examined it was discovered that Commander Dunning had drowned. Further landing trials were strictly forbidden because of this accident.

The news of Squadron Leader Dunning's death resounded like an explosion in the halls of the Admiralty and it became a priority objective to devise a system that would safely retrieve landplanes on deck. It was clearly understood that Dunning's method deserved merit but it was a most difficult maneuver, to be attempted only by the most experienced pilots; therefore, the Admiralty withdrew *Furious* from sea duty for modifications to accommodate landings.

HMS Furious Modifications

Towards the end of 1917 the after 18 inch gun turret was removed and replaced by a landing deck, a hangar, workshops, elevator, and additional accommodation for six planes. The forward flying off deck and the after landing deck were separated by the superstructure, including the smokestack; therefore, two 11 foot wide taxiways were constructed around the superstructure, one on each side, to connect the two decks. This improvisation was not the ultimate solution; however, it was a step in the right direction. When *HMS Furious* left the shipyard she was able to operate 14 Sopwith 1 1/2 Strutters and two Sopwith Pups. Many of the officers as well as

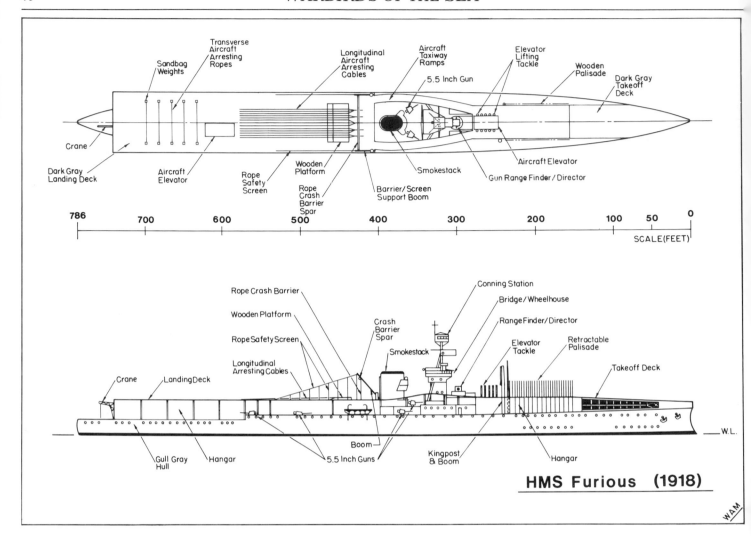

HMS Furious (1918)

HMS Furious was fitted with longitudinal ropes on the Landing Deck to keep the landing aircraft on a straight path. It was also fitted with transverse ropes to arrest the plane. The aircraft wheels were replaced with skis so the wheels would not roll over the ropes. Sharp prongs were attached to the skis and cross axle to engage the transverse ropes. (Ministry of Defence [Navy])

A Sopwith Pup nears the end of the HMS Furious Landing Deck slightly askew despite the longitudinal ropes and skis. Note the manila rope barrier to halt the plane if it does not stop on the deck. Observe the block and tackle to keep the longitudinal ropes taut. (Ministry of Defence [Navy])

This Sopwith Pup has modified skis and an arresting hook instead of the prongs. The Pup was ideal for aircraft carrier service because it had a very light wing loading and was easy to fly. (Air Ministry [Navy])

Captain Wilmot S. Nicholson, *HMS Furious* Commanding Officer, expressed doubts regarding the safety of landing on the after deck. They reasoned that the turbulence from the hot smokestack gasses and the bridge structure would buffet the light aircraft and make landings hazardous. They also argued that it would be difficult and dangerous to move the planes from the after deck to the forward deck via the narrow connecting taxiways, especially when the ship was steaming. To insure safe stopping once touchdown was ac-

complished an unusual system of cables and ropes was used. This had been tested in a shoreside installation and proved successful. It consisted of longitudinal wire cables a few inches above the landing deck, held securely at each end, which were intended to keep the plane running straight upon touchdown. An arresting system was also installed, following the transverse ropes and sandbag system used by Eugene Ely. The airplane wheels were replaced by skids so the craft could not roll over the longitudinal cables. They were also fitted with hooks to engage the arresting ropes. In the event that this system failed to stop the planes a curtain of manila ropes was stretched vertically at the forward end of the landing deck to stop the aircraft.

Second *HMS Furious* Landing Trials

Upon its completion *Furious* returned to sea in March 1918. On board was First Admiral Commanding Aircraft of the Royal Navy, Rear Admiral P.F. Phillimore, to witness the landing trials. Only 25 percent of the aircraft landings were successful. As Captain Nicholson and his officers had predicted, the light aircraft were buffeted by the superstructure-created turbulence during the approach and hardly ever touched down in a straight and level attitude. Even some of the more experienced pilots went over the side into the sea; however, none were lost. Further, the headwind disappeared as the planes lost altitude and approached the landing deck because the superstructure created a barrier that reduced the wind

On July 19, 1918 seven Sopwith Camels took off from HMS Furious, each loaded with two 50 pound bombs to drop on the Zeppelin Base at Tondern. The L 54 and L 60 were destroyed. The seven Camels are shown on the Flying Off Deck preparatory to takeoff. (Peter Doyle Collection)

over deck (WOD) to dangerous levels. The superstructure and smokestack created turbulence at the higher altitudes and blocked the wind at lower altitudes closest to the superstructure and smokestack. Many of the landing Pups wound up in the manila rope barrier, sustaining some damage. As a result of this experiment the use of the landing deck was abandoned and only the takeoff deck was used for the rest of the war.

HMS Furious Aircraft Raid
On July 19, 1918 seven Sopwith Camels, each loaded with two 50 pound bombs, took off from *Furious* to bomb the Zeppelin base at Tondern. The raid was a success with the Camels destroying two of the airships; the *L 54* and *L 60*.

HMS Vindictive
The Admiralty had such high hopes for the *Furious* landing deck that they prematurely ordered immediate conversion of the cruiser *Cavendish* to an aircraft carrier using *Furious* as the model before *Furious* had been tested. The converted ship was renamed *HMS Vindictive*. Very little flying was conducted from this ship and the vessel was soon reconverted back to cruiser configuration.

LANSING-ISHII AGREEMENT
As a result of Japan's help in the war, U.S. Secretary of State Robert Lansing and Japanese Special Ambassador Viscount Kikujiro Ishii exchanged notes regarding their respective countries' intentions towards China. Secretary Lansing's note of November 2, 1917 stated in part: "The Governments of the United States and Japan recognize that territorial propinquity creates special relations between countries, and consequently the Government of the United States recognizes that Japan has special interests in China, particularly in the part to which her possessions are contiguous." Despite Secretary Lansing's caveat that: ". . . the governments of Japan and the United States will not take advantage of the present conditions to seek special rights or privileges in China which would abridge the rights of the subjects or citizens of other friendly states," this exchange of notes is called the Lansing-Ishii Agreement and, in effect, gave Japan a free hand in China.

THROUGH DECK CARRIERS
The *Furious* experiments proved most valuable in the design of the three other aircraft carriers that had been started while *Furious* was undergoing conversion and testing. The tests proved that, to be effective, an aircraft carrier had to be constructed with a through deck from stem to stern; just as Clement Ader had described in 1895.

HMS Argus
The *Conte Rosso* conversion was originally conceived to have two separate decks divided by an amidship bridge and smokestack, not unlike *Furious*. The forward deck was to be a takeoff deck for wheeled aircraft while the after deck was to carry seaplanes that would be lowered to the water by crane for takeoff. Landplanes were to ditch while seaplanes were intended to land on the water near the ship. This concept changed when landing on carriers be-

came a primary consideration and *HMS Argus*, as the converted ship was renamed, emerged as the world's first through-deck aircraft carrier. The Flight Deck was clear of all obstructions, including the smokestacks and navigating bridge. The stacks were run horizontally under the Flight Deck and exhausted out the stern while the bridge and other operating spaces were arranged below the forward edge of the Flight Deck. The wheelhouse was mounted on a hydraulic jack so that it could be lowered when flying operations were being conducted. The Flight Deck was led to a point at the bow which, because of its appearance, quickly earned *Argus* the nickname of "Flat Iron."

Argus Data
A 68 x 350 foot Hangar 20 feet high was located under the 550 foot Flight Deck. Two electrically operated elevators were installed to move aircraft between the Hangar and Flight Decks. *HMS Argus* displaced 17,272 tons fully loaded with an overall length of 565 feet. The Flight Deck was 69 feet wide; only one foot greater than the hull. *Argus* could accommodate 20 Cuckoos and Pups. Longitudinal cables were fitted to the Flight Deck as on *HMS Furious*.

A total of 21,500 shaft horsepower was developed by four steam turbines driving four propellers. This drove *HMS Argus* to a top speed of 20 knots. *Argus* was completed as a strike carrier instead of a reconnaissance machine and entered service in the Autumn of 1918; too late to see action. She was the first of a long line of mobile airfields that were destined to change the complexion of naval warfare.

HMS Eagle
The second ship undergoing conversion into an aircraft carrier during the *Furious* experiments was *Almirante Cochrane*. As with *Argus*, *Almirante Cochrane* conversion emerged as an innovative prototype which set the basic design for all future aircraft carriers. The *Almirante Cochrane* was a battleship under construction for the Chilean Navy when the war began. As will be remembered, she was selected for carrier conversion along with *Furious*, *Conte Rosso*, and *Cavendish* in early 1917.

Renamed *HMS Eagle*, *Almirante Cochrane* was not completed until after the Armistice; therefore, she will be described in the following chapter.

HMS Hermes Purpose-Built Carrier
Armstrong-Whitworth was progressing with the world's first purpose-built aircraft carrier which would learn much from the *Furious* experiments. Here again, *HMS Hermes*, as she was named, would not be completed until long after the Armistice.

UNIFIED ROYAL AIR FORCE = DEATH OF RNAS
A total reorganization of the British military air forces on April 1, 1918 proved calamitous by bringing the development of aviation in the Royal Navy to a virtual halt.

An Air Ministry was created which combined the Royal Flying Corps with the Royal Naval Air Service into one independent air arm; the Royal Air Force. Naval pilots were given the choice of remaining in the Royal Navy and giving up flying or joining the Royal Air Force. The majority chose the latter rather than give up

HMS Argus was the world's first through deck aircraft carrier. The Wheelhouse on the Flight Deck was retractable to clear the deck during flight operations. The Bridge and other operating spaces were located beneath the forward edge of the Flight Deck. Smokestacks were run aft under the Flight Deck. Argus is shown here in standard gray and in "warpaint." (U.S. Naval Historical Center)

their flying career. RNAS uniforms were changed to RAF uniforms for those who transferred to the RAF. RNAS ranks were changed to corresponding RAF ranks.

The new independent Royal Air Force meant that the captains of aircraft carriers no longer had the ultimate responsibility for the conduct or employment of the aircraft which was far from the ideal arrangement.

With the passing of the Armistice drastic cuts were made in the Armed Forces, cuts so severe that the majority of military projects were abandoned so that the few priority programs could be kept alive. This forced the new RAF, fearful for its very existence, to reduce its expenditures on and divert its best personnel away from what it considered to be a purely ancillary function; the naval air section.

This terrible neglect of what had become the leading naval air service in the world enabled other naval powers to outstrip the Royal Navy in aircraft design and operation. Virtually no naval officers with any aviation experience remained and the primitive aircraft provided for the British Fleet were, for the most part, flown by land-based pilots lacking the skill necessary to operate shipborne aircraft. Naval aviation's importance to the Fleet was discounted and progress was very slow, intermittent and misdirected.

LAST SHIPBOARD ZEPPELIN VICTORY

During the summer of 1918 the movements of the British naval forces operating in the southern sector of the North Sea were increasingly hampered by German highflying dirigibles or airships. These are generally called Zeppelins although only those craft made by the Zeppelin Company should bear this name. As previously mentioned, the airships were virtually impossible to drive off or destroy because they operated beyond the range of land-based fighters and flew so high that the antiaircraft guns of the period proved ineffective. The British Harwich Force suffered most from the spying, which became unbearable.

Towed Flight Deck Lighters

In desperation, Commodore Sir Reginald Tyrwhitt, Commander of the Force, ordered Colonel Charles R. Samson to develop a suitable method of launching fighter aircraft from shipboard because the Harwich Force had no access to carriers or turret top platforms. Samson was in command of No. 4 Group at Felixstowe on the east coast of England, operating small flying boats. In order to extend their range he had been mounting the seaplanes on ship-shaped barges or lighters which were towed out to sea by a destroyer. The seaplanes were then lowered into the water and conducted their mission. When they returned, the flying boats were hoisted onto the lighter and the Force returned to base. Samson reasoned that by adding a flight deck to one of the lighters and by towing it at high

Squadron Commander Charles Rumney Samson poses with his Nieuport prior to takeoff on the Turkish Front. Samson was very active in the development of British Naval Aviation. (Peter Doyle Collection)

Above: U.S. born Sublieutenant Stuart Culley scored a German airship after taking off a towed lighter in the North Sea on August 11, 1918. (Official U.S. Navy Photograph) Below: Wing Commander Stuart Culley was stationed in the Middle East during World War II. (Air Ministry)

speed by a destroyer to obtain a strong wind-over-deck condition, a fighter plane should be able to take off. Landing was to be in the water and only the pilot would be saved. The sunken fighter plane was a small price to pay for the destruction of a giant dirigible.

First Takeoff Trial

Samson selected the Sopwith Camel 2F.1 for his experiments. The wheels were replaced with ski-like skids. A wooden deck was fitted atop the lighter and longitudinal cables were added to the deck as was done on *Furious*. The skids were to fit between the deck cables in order to keep the plane from sliding off the deck. Colonel Samson tested the idea himself, but it ended in failure as the Camel skidded off the deck into the sea and was run over by the speeding barge. Samson was unhurt and, upon the insistence of his staff, he selected Sublieutenant Stuart D. Culley to continue the experiments under his direction.

Second Takeoff Trial

Culley was born in Nebraska in 1895 of a Canadian mother and an English father. He was accepted in the Royal Naval Air Service at the age of 21 years. When the RAF was formed in April 1918, combining all British flying forces, Culley, as well as Samson, were integrated into the Royal Air Force. It was because of this that Commander Samson became Colonel Samson. Culley's idea was to retain the wheels on the Camel and the second trial took place off

Air Ministry Sublieutenant Culley with his crew and Sopwith Camel 2F.1. Note that the Camel still sports the cowl-mounted Vickers machine guns which were replaced with Lewis guns for the flight. (Peter Doyle Collection)

Great Yarmouth on the east coast of England in August 1918 and was a resounding success. The destroyer *HMS Redoubt* towed the lighter at a speed of 30 knots and the Sopwith lifted off the deck with a very short roll because of the high wind over deck. The plane landed on a shore airfield.

Armament Changes

Preparations for action now went ahead at a feverish pace starting with an armament change. It was necessary to fire incendiary am-

Culley's Sopwith Camel 2F.1 ready for the flight. Note the Lewis guns mounted on the upper wing. Culley made a soft landing in the sea and both man and plane were rescued. (Peter Doyle Collection)

munition in order to ignite the highly flammable hydrogen in the dirigible; however, it was also considered dangerous to fire incendiary ammunition through the propeller disc over the rotary engine of the Camel because of the flammable engine fumes and oil emmissions from this powerplant. In order to solve this problem the twin cowl-mounted Vickers machine guns were removed and two lighter Lewis guns were installed in fixed mounts atop the upper wing. This change in armament was a weight saver as well as a safety measure. Each gun was fitted with a drum containing 97 rounds of ammunition. This was considerably less than was normally supplied with the Vickers and it gave Culley fewer chances to score on the hydrogen filled airships.

Zeppelin Sighted

On August 11, 1918 the entire Harwich Force, consisting of four cruisers and 13 destroyers, went to sea before dawn to carry out an offensive sweep in the southeastern portion of the North Sea. The destroyer *HMS Redoubt* had Culley's Camel in tow while others towed lighters carrying flying boats. The cruisers carried six torpedo boats to attack German ships. As the offensive developed, the flying boats failed to take off due to calm seas and no wind, and the torpedo boats were all destroyed by German seaplanes as they neared

Colonel Samson and the crew on the Flight Decked lighter. Observe that the longitudinal ropes have been removed from earlier trials. (Royal Navy Photo)

The lighter is towed out to the North Sea at 10 knots by the destroyer Redoubt as Culley enters the cockpit. (Royal Navy Photo)

the Dutch coast. British fortune seemed to be drifting from bad to worse when, at eight o'clock in the morning, a German dirigible was reported in the vicinity. The silver cigar-shaped craft was in sight flying at about 10,000 feet 20 minutes later. It was the *L 53* under the command of *Kapitänleutnant* Proell of the Imperial German Navy who had left the base at Nordholz to report the movements of the British force to German naval units.

The Attack

With the Sopwith Camel tied down on the lighter the destroyer accellerated to a speed of about 30 knots. Culley climbed into the cockpit and the propeller was swung to start the Bentley engine. At 8:41 Culley raced the rotary full out and the crew released the Sopwith. The craft surged forward and, after rolling only five feet, it left the deck, turning neither left or right and headed directly

With the lighter towed at a speed of 30 knots (approximately 35 miles per hour) Culley's Camel rolled only five feet before it left the Deck because of the high wind over deck (WOD). (Royal Navy Photo)

Luftschiff L 53 (Airship L 53) fell into the North Sea in flames before Sublieutenant Culley's guns on August 11, 1918. (Bundesarchiv)

towards the towing destroyer. He missed the mast by a few feet and then strained the Camel in an effort to reach the airship before it could spot him and climb above the Sopwith's ceiling. At 5,000 feet the dirigible appeared no larger and the Sublieutenant realized that the Germans were also climbing. At 15,000 feet the Camel's controls became sluggish and the Bentley began to cough but Culley pressed on, flying higher and higher into the rarefied air. At 18,000 feet, which was more than tops for the Sopwith, Culley was still about 700 feet below the airship. At this time the dirigible changed course and began climbing towards Germany. The *L 53* was now heading directly toward the climbing Canadian, only a few hundred feet above him. The closing speed was at least 160 mph which gave Culley very little time to climb up to the dirigible. Soon the huge airship loomed ahead and began to pass over the tiny Camel like a dark cloud. Culley pulled the stick into his belly and began firing. One gun jammed after only a half dozen rounds but the other Lewis emptied its drum as the German Goliath rumbled overhead. Suddenly, the Sopwith shuddered and stalled, falling about 2,000 feet, completely out of control. When Culley recovered control of his plane he saw that the *L 53* had passed him and appeared unaffected by his attack, sailing majestically at about 19,000 feet. The Sublieutenant turned the Camel for a second attack when three separate spurts of flame erupted from the dirigible. Within a minute the entire airship, except the tail, was enveloped in a giant ball of flame which died out as quickly as it had started. The dirigible skeleton then dropped into the sea in one piece taking over 30 of the crew to their doom including the captain. Only one crew member survived the disaster when he bailed out as soon as Culley started his attack. This was the last Zeppelin to be shot down during World War I. The entire operation, from take off to victory, lasted exactly one hour. This was the first aerial victory in which the aircraft flew off the deck of a ship.

The Ditching

Culley's ordeal was not quite over. Now, he had to find the Harwich Force so that he could ditch his plane and be rescued from the sea. With his fuel almost depleted, Culley dropped to 5,000 feet and zigzagged across the water for what seemed an eternity until, finally, he spotted the British ships through an opening in the mist which had hampered his search. The Camel was ditched with such skill that both pilot and plane were retrieved and Culley's Sopwith Camel can now be seen on exhibition hanging in the Imperial War Museum in London. Only one pint of fuel remained in the Camel's tank when it was ditched.

The Salute

Commodore Tyrwhitt ordered Culley to stand atop *HMS Redoubt*'s gun turret while the entire force passed in line review with sailors standing on the decks cheering the man who represented a new breed: the shipborne airman.

For his achievement Sublieutenant Stuart D. Culley was awarded the Distinguished Service Order. During World War II Culley attained the rank of Group Captain and again served Britain with distinction.

Lighter/Barge Fighters Good Idea

The very idea of dedicating a lighter/barge to one fighter plane was an excellent scheme to combat the Zeppelin reconnaissance. By operating singly, dozens of fighter-laden barges could patrol hundreds of square miles and, thereby, increase the chances of sighting and destroying an airship; however, the war ended before this concept could be expanded and refined.

SOPWITH SEA CAMEL 2F.1

Samson was wise to select the Sopwith Camel for this experiment because this descendant of the Pup was a superb fighter which caused no end of trouble for the Imperial German Air Service. More Sopwith Camel fighters were built during World War I than any other airplane. A total of 5,490 Camels was constructed by at least nine manufacturers and the design was considered to be one of the best dogfighters of the 1914-1918 conflict. The Sopwith Camel was responsible for the destruction of 1,294 German airplanes, more than any other Allied design. It was the first British fighter designed for two machine guns and made its first appearance at the front in the Spring of 1917. Two basic versions were produced, the original F.1

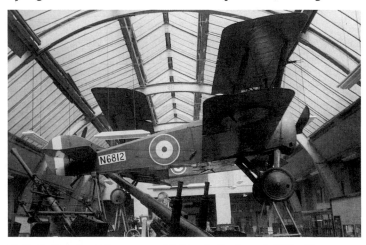

Culley's Camel now hangs on exhibition in the Imperial War Museum, Lambeth Road, London, England. (Courtesy Charles Donald Collection)

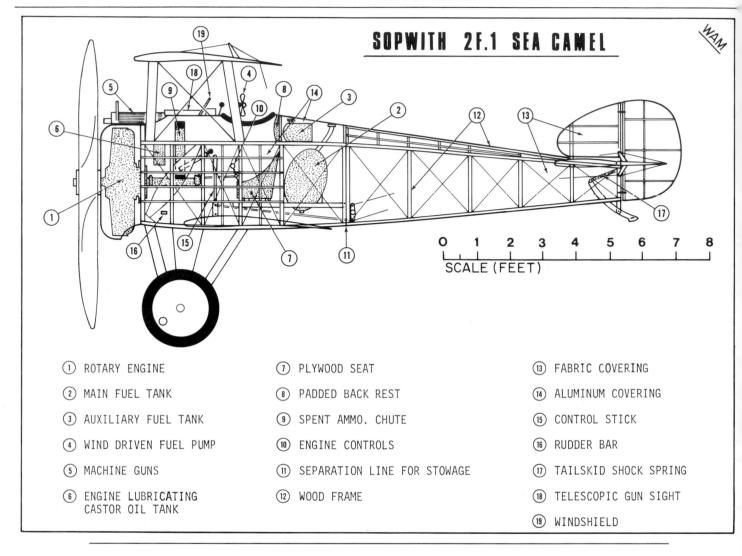

SOPWITH 2F.1 SEA CAMEL

SCALE (FEET)
0 1 2 3 4 5 6 7 8

① ROTARY ENGINE
② MAIN FUEL TANK
③ AUXILIARY FUEL TANK
④ WIND DRIVEN FUEL PUMP
⑤ MACHINE GUNS
⑥ ENGINE LUBRICATING CASTOR OIL TANK
⑦ PLYWOOD SEAT
⑧ PADDED BACK REST
⑨ SPENT AMMO. CHUTE
⑩ ENGINE CONTROLS
⑪ SEPARATION LINE FOR STOWAGE
⑫ WOOD FRAME
⑬ FABRIC COVERING
⑭ ALUMINUM COVERING
⑮ CONTROL STICK
⑯ RUDDER BAR
⑰ TAILSKID SHOCK SPRING
⑱ TELESCOPIC GUN SIGHT
⑲ WINDSHIELD

and the later 2F.1 which was prepared for the Royal Navy. The 2F.1 had shorter wings, smaller horizontal tail surfaces, more powerful engine, and the fuselage was arranged to separate just aft of the cockpit for ease of stowage on carriers. The 2F.1 Camels were powered with the 150 horsepower Bentley Rotary engine which gave the plane a 124 mph maximum speed. The craft could climb to 10,000 feet in 11 1/2 minutes. Ceiling was considered to be 17,300 feet. Many 2F.1 Camels were fitted with one Vickers machine gun mounted on the cowl while a Lewis machine gun was located atop the upper wing. Others were fitted with twin Vickers guns atop the cowl as was the F.1. The Camel got its name from the fuselage top fairing which covered the gun breeches between the cockpit and the engine cowl. This fairing formed a hump, hence the Camel nickname, which soon became official.

U.S. NAVAL AVIATION IN WORLD WAR I

During this Royal Navy pioneering activity with shipborne aircraft the United States Navy appeared to have made little progress with the development of its air service. Between 1911, when the U.S. Navy bought its first airplane, and 1916, its inventory increased to only three flying boats and 14 seaplanes, some of which were not even in flying condition. When the U.S. entered the war on the side of the Allies in April 1917 there were 48 pilots in the naval services; 10 in the U.S. Marine Corps and 38 in the U.S. Navy. Total naval aviation personnel was less than 300. Aircraft included three landplanes, six flying boats, and 45 seaplanes.

No Fighter Escorts

The first U.S. naval air units arrived in France during June, 1917 under command of Lieutenant Kenneth Whiting. During the first six months of action the U.S. units dropped almost 300 tons of bombs but 21 bombers were lost. Lieutenant John Towers, U.S Naval aviator No. 3, suggested that the slow patrol bombers would be more efficient if they had an escort of fighters to protect them Navy brass rejected the suggestion and decided that bombers were more important than fighters. Further, the U.S. Army had been given priority in the production of all war material.

Interservice Rivalries

All U.S. military forces in Europe were under the unified command of General John "Black Jack" Pershing who had decided tha the naval air forces should handle the bombing of submarine pens and should be given whatever equipment was needed. The Navy

Lieutenant Kenneth Whiting commanded the first U.S. Naval Air Units to arrive in France in World War I. He also championed a U.S. carrier force during the postwar years. (U.S. National Archives)

These officers comprised all the pilots of the U.S. Navy Aviation Corps in 1914. Photo was taken at the Naval Aeronautic Station, Pensacola, Florida. From left to right: Lieutenant V.D. Herbster; Lieutenant W.M. McIlvain, USMC; Lieutenant (jg) P.N.L. Bellinger; Lieutenant (jg) R.C. Saufley; Lieutenant J.H. Towers; Lieutenant Commander H.C. Mustin; Lieutenant B.L. Smith, USMC; Ensign G. De C. Chevalier; Ensign M.L. Stolz. (U.S. Naval Historical Center)

request was 75 bombers and 40 single-seater fighter escorts. The U.S. Army Air Service, under command of Major General Benjamin D. Foulois, protested and argued that landplanes or fighter aircraft and the bombing of land targets was their job and not the Navy's! Pershing insisted; however, no fighter landplanes ever reached the U.S. Navy. This is very reminiscent of the RAF and Royal Naval Air Service interservice problems.

The only opportunity U.S. naval personnel had to fly fighter planes in combat was to fly with RAF squadrons in their spare time. Lieutenant David Sinton Ingalls became an Ace while flying with No. 213 Squadron, RAF.

PEACE

With the passing of the Armistice on November 11, 1918 the Allies handed the German Weimar Government an ultimatum, without prior negotiations, to sign the Treaty of Versailles or face an armed occupation army in all of Germany. The German High Seas Fleet was to sail to Scapa Flow and surrender to the Allies; however, in protest to the Treaty the Germans scuttled their fleet while it was anchored in the British naval base. Germany signed the Treaty of Versailles on June 28, 1919; exactly five years to the day after Archduke Franz Ferdinand was shot in Sarajevo, starting World War I.

Peacetime Struggle for Naval Supremacy

Upon entering the interwar period Germany is found to have no naval forces, the British and American Fleets dominate the seas, with the Japanese, French, and Italian navies struggling far behind in the race for naval supremacy in which the aircraft carrier and its air group are destined to play a principal role.

CHAPTER II
EVOLUTION: 1919-1938

POSTWAR NAVAL CONDITIONS

With Germany prostrate having no army, navy or air force; and Russia in the throes of revolution and civil war, the Allies' principal concern was to rebuild their wartorn economy. The war weary populations greeted demobilization with optimism; victors and vanquished alike looked to the League of Nations to make war an impossibility, and President Wilson's impractical idealism struck a responsive chord throughout the world.

U.S. Navy and Royal Navy Become Rivals
Naval planners were not so naively optimistic. In the U.S. and Britain, armies would disappear; however, the ships remained and with them rested the foundation of their defense policy. This made the two English-speaking countries naval power rivals but it strained their economy and all expenditures had to be carefully budgeted; especially for Britain. The public mood in the two democracies refused to endure military expenditures of any sort.

Royal Navy Carriers
The war ended with the Royal Navy in possession of two operational aircraft carriers; the flush deck *Argus* and the formidable *Furious*. Two more carriers were under construction; the converted battleship *Eagle* and the first ever purpose-designed aircraft carrier *Hermes*. Work was progressing at a leisurely pace due to a shortage of funds and the end of the war emergency.

U.S. Turret Top Platforms
The U.S. Navy still had no aircraft carriers, but concentrated on the development of turret top landplane operation which the Royal Navy had pioneered late in the war. With no American fighter plane available,

PREVIOUS: USS Yorktown (CV-5), shown here in 1937, and USS Enterprise (CV-6) formed the Yorktown class aircraft carriers. The ship reflected the change in U.S. policy from smaller to larger carriers. (Official U.S. Navy Photograph, U.S. Naval Historical Center)

Eight U.S. battleships were fitted with Flying-Off platforms. The very first U.S. turret platform takeoff was on March 9, 1919 when Lieutenant Commander E.O. McDonald flew from USS Texas (BB-35) in a Sopwith Camel. This Camel on USS Texas is all wrapped up to protect it from the elements. Note the restraining lines and braces that prevent the aircraft from being blown overboard. (U.S. Naval Historical Center)

the U.S. Navy bought war surplus British Sopwith Camels and Pups, and French Nieuports and Hanriots. On March 9, 1919 Lieutenant Commander E.O. Mc Donald made the first turret platform takeoff from a U.S. warship, flying a Camel from the battleship *USS Texas* at anchor in Guantanamo Bay, Cuba. This was followed by a directive from the Secretary of the Navy on June 1 authorizing the installation of turret takeoff platforms on eight battleships.

It wasn't long before the disadvantages of this arrangement began to surface. The effective range of the fighters was severely

A French-built U.S. Navy Nieuport 28 rests on a gun turret Flying-Off platform on the battleship USS Arizona (BB-39). Observe the steel structure supporting the wooden platform. The turret turned into the wind for takeoff. (U.S. Naval Historical Center)

A British-built U.S. Navy Sopwith Camel makes the first takeoff from USS Mississippi (BB-41) with Lieutenant Commander E.L. Hammond at the controls at Guantanamo Bay, Cuba, on April 8, 1919. Launching was accomplished by having crew members hold the tail of the plane while the pilot raced the engine; then the crew released the plane and the craft leaped forward. (U.S. Naval Historical Center)

As with the Royal Navy, the U.S. Navy Turret Platforms were replaced by catapults on battleships and cruisers. Single-float seaplanes were used so they could return to the ship by landing alongside. A Vought VE-7 is shown being hoisted aboard USS Oklahoma (BB-37) after landing in the water. (U.S. Naval Historical Center)

restricted because of the landing problem with wheeled aircraft. This forced the mother ship to operate within aircraft range to shoreside airfields. The alternative was to ditch the plane at the end of every flight but this was not considered acceptable. Several devices were developed to enable the plane to ditch with relative safety. These included compressed air-inflated bags; jettisonable landing gear to prevent nose-over landings; and hydrovanes, or small wings, set at a positive angle and mounted just forward of the landing gear to prevent nose-overs by skimming on the water as a surfboard.

The demise of the battleship-based landplane was accelerated by the development of the compressed air catapult which could be traversed into the wind as the turret. Within a few years catapults were standard equipment throughout the U.S. Fleet as were seaplane scouts.

Commander Whiting and America's First Carrier

On March 8, 1919 the U.S. Navy General Board listened to Commander Kenneth Whiting, who had commanded the first U.S. Naval Air Units in France in World War I and was assistant to the Director of U.S. Naval Aviation, as he strongly recommended the construction of an aircraft carrier. Knowing that the economy-minded Congress would reject a new ship, Commander Whiting agreed to accept a conversion and the collier *USS Jupiter* (AC-3) was selected. It was slower than Whiting wanted but there was plenty of space in the hull for stowage of aviation needs. It was a compromise. Later that year Congress authorized the conversion of *USS Jupiter* into an aircraft carrier.

Concurrent with the preparation of the *Jupiter* conversion specifications, were specifications for carrier-based fighter and torpedo-bomber designs.

JAPAN: APPREHENSIVE OF THE WEST

Japan had increased spending on the Imperial Navy to nearly 250 million dollars which was about one-third of Japan's total budget. This island nation had looked on, with suspicion, as the western powers established themselves throughout Asia and the Pacific Ocean. Early on, Britain and France had secured India, Ceylon, Burma and Indo-China while the Netherlands took the East Indies. The U.S. had also moved closer to the Japanese Islands by occupying Hawaii, Midway, Guam and the Philippines.

Western Abuse

China had lost the Sino-Japanese War (1894-95) and China's defeat stimulated renewed aggression by the Western Powers. The Treaty of Shimonosiki gave to Japan: Korea, Formosa, Shantung Peninsula, strategic Liaotung Peninsula and other important areas. The aggressive Western Powers who refused to accept any Imperialism that was not their own, literally robbed Japan of its proper territorial rewards: Britain and Germany took Shantung; Portugal took Macao; Russia took Dairen (Liaotung); France took Kwangchowan and other territory as Japan looked on, helpless to stop the West from taking what was rightly hers. These coastal areas are called enclaves and although the Western countries arranged long term leases with China it appeared to be only a subterfuge to cover their actions.

Japan Helps the West; Anglo-Japanese Alliance

Despite this abuse, when China rebelled against this Western invasion four years later in the Boxer Rebellion, Japan helped Britain in this fight. Then in 1902 Japan concluded an alliance with the British Empire. The Anglo-Japanese Alliance was renewed in 191 because Japan was, by then, recognized as a first class world power She was, however, suspicious of Western intentions.

U.S. - Japan Naval Armaments Race

The naval armaments race which had existed between German and Britain prior to World War I came to an end with Germany' defeat; however, a new naval competition had replaced the former The naval armaments race between Japan and the U.S. had becom an established fact by 1921. Early that year 11 new battleships an six battle cruisers were under construction in U.S. shipyards whil Japan had commissioned two battleships. Two more Japanese battle ships plus four battle cruisers had been started in 1921. Japan ha also designed two further 18-gun, 45,000 ton battleships for futur construction. Despite crippling economic difficulties Britain strov to retain her long established sea supremacy and; therefore, fe impelled to enter this three-power naval leadership race.

WASHINGTON NAVAL DISARMAMENT CONFERENCE

In the spring of 1921, U.S. President Warren C. Harding signed naval appropriations bill and Congress asked him to call for a nava disarmament conference.

U.S. Navy Bureau of Aeronautics Created

President Harding also authorized the formation of the U.S. Nav Bureau of Aeronautics which would supervise the development an production of U.S. naval aircraft. Rear Admiral W.A. Moffett wa placed in charge, with Commander Kenneth Whiting in control o all carrier tasks. This was the same man who had proposed the *Lang ley* conversion in 1919.

Conference Begins

Anglo-American distrust was combined with the realization by bot English-speaking powers that an imbalance of power now existe in the Western Pacific. These uneasy feelings, plus Presiden Harding's request, led to the inauguration of the First Internation Conference on Limitation of Naval Armaments in Washington, D.C (Nov. 1921 - Feb. 1922). In this way Britain and the U.S. sought t limit the increase in Japanese naval power while watching eac other closely to be certain that neither gained a decisive edge in th Atlantic. During the early 1920s naval rivalry was the accepte status of Japanese-American relations. In addition to Japan, Ital and France were also invited to the conference by the U.S.

U.S. and Britain Cancel Japanese Agreements

Britain used the Conference to end the Anglo-Japanese Alliance which she no longer wanted; replacing it with the Five Power Pac (Britain, France, U.S.A., Italy and Japan) which by no means ca ried the weight and prestige of its predecessor. It was a polite wa for Britain to end the relationship. Japan felt insulted.

President Warren C. Harding had authorized the U.S. Bureau of Aeronautics in 1921 and air-minded Rear Admiral William A. Moffett was placed in command of the new Bureau. Admiral Moffett and the Bureau accelerated the U.S. aircraft carrier program. (U.S. National Archives)

Without prior discussion the U.S. cancelled the Lansing-Ishii friendship agreement that had been concluded with Japan in 1917 because Japan helped the Allies during World War I. Japan was stunned by this action.

Washington Conference Decisions

The principal discussion at the Washington Conference involved battleships or capital ships of over 10,000 tons. The U.S. called for scrapping 66 of the world's battleships displacing a total of two million tons. The U.S. was to scrap 30, two of which had just been launched and six of which were under construction; Britain was to abandon three large *Hood* class battle cruisers which had not yet been started, plus 19 older battleships; Japan was to abandon her four planned battle cruisers and to scrap three new battleships, one of which had just been launched, plus three others under construction as well as 10 older battleships for a total of 20 ships. This scheme would establish a 5:5:3 ratio in capital ships between the U.S., Britain and Japan respectively. The Anglo-Americans were quick to explain that Japan's interests were concentrated in the Pacific but Britain and the U.S. had interests worldwide and; therefore, required more capital ships. Japan was most dissatisfied with this arrangement but was overruled by the Anglo-Americans. As compensation a Non-Fortification Clause was added to the Treaty, whereby the U.S. and Britain pledged not to strengthen the fortifications of their Pacific possessions (New Zealand, Singapore and Australia excepted), while the Japanese were free to increase their Home Island defenses. Since Germany was Versailles Treaty-bound not to build battleships, the U.S. and Britain felt confident that together they could rule the waves at least until the Five Power Pact expired in 1930.

Nine Power Treaty

Japan was also forced to sign the Nine-Power Treaty guaranteeing the independence of China.

Aircraft Carriers Win

The Washington Conference unwittingly stimulated the construction of aircraft carriers because the terms of the Treaty were generous regarding the carrier tonnage allowed to each participant: Britain and the U.S. 135,000 tons each; Japan 81,000 tons; and France and Italy 60,000 tons each. A maximum carrier size of 27,000 tons was agreed upon until Commander Whiting, who was a U.S. Negotiating Team Advisor, objected and requested a 33,000 ton maximum because, rather than scrap two battle cruisers, Whiting knew it was wiser to convert the 33,000 ton ships into aircraft carriers. It was, therefore, agreed that the U.S. could build two 33,000 ton carriers but all subsequent carriers must adhere to the 27,000 ton limit.

Captain Kenneth Whiting became Admiral Moffett's assistant in control of all carrier tasks. Captain Whiting was also the first Commanding Officer of USS Langley and USS Lexington. (U.S. National Archives)

The U.S. was not alone with its intention to convert capital ships into aircraft carriers rather than destroy them. Britain and Japan also made plans to circumvent the Treaty that they had all signed, by converting capital ship hulls into aircraft carriers. Britain, Japan and the U.S. were loathe to destroy any capital ships. Yet, despite the conversions, none of the powers really understood the full potential of the carrier.

The two U.S. battle cruisers were to become *USS Lexington* (CV-2) and *USS Saratoga* (CV-3). The Japanese decided to convert the capital ships *Akagi* and *Amagi* while Britain chose to convert two near sisters of *HMS Furious*; *HMS Courageous* and *HMS Glorious*.

CARRIERS UNDER CONSTRUCTION - EARLY 1920s

In 1921 Britain had *Argus* and *Furious* in service with *Hermes* and *Eagle* under construction. The U.S. was converting the collier *Jupiter* into the carrier *Langley* while Japan was completing its purpose-built carrier *Hosho*. Neither France nor Italy was enthusiastic about aircraft carriers although France was converting the unfinished battleship Bearne into a carrier.

ROYAL NAVY FLEET AIR ARM

Other important events were happening in 1921. The Royal Air Force agreed that only naval officers would fly as observers in naval aircraft and that 70 percent of the pilots in the Fleet Air Arm, which is what the former RNAS was now called, would be naval officers holding dual naval and RAF rank. The Royal Navy Fleet Air Arm was finally receiving some well-deserved consideration.

GENERALS MITCHELL and TRENCHARD -
AIR POWER CRUSADE

Two visionary promoters of air power were working on opposite sides of the Atlantic Ocean; General Hugh Trenchard in Britain and General William "Billy" Mitchell in the U.S.A. Both were forcefully outspoken proponents of sinking battleships with bombers, but were met with equally forceful resistance from the conservative "battleship mentality" which had permeated both navies for generations.

After months of wrangling with Washington officialdom Mitchell finally received permission to conduct bombing tests using the ex-German battleship *Ostfriesland* which had been taken from Germany as a World War I reparation. On July 21, 1921 twin-engined U.S. Army bombers dropped one and two thousand pound bombs on the battleship as she lay at anchor off the Virginia Capes. The bombs were dropped from an altitude of 1,700 feet and the *Ostfriesland* sank before a very critical audience of naval experts.

OPPOSITE: One of the most vocal preponents of air power during the 1920s was U.S. Army General William "Billy" Mitchell. His ship bombing demonstrations and his feud with the U.S. Navy, plus outspoken criticism, resulted in his court marshall and resignation. Mitchell's efforts to prove that his land-based bombers could sink ships actually stimulated the construction of a carrier fleet. (U.S. National Archives)

Two months later General Mitchell repeated the test on the battleship *USS Alabama* with the same results.

Two years later Billy Mitchell's bombers sank the battleships *USS Virginia* and *USS New Jersey*. Meanwhile, he continued his feud with the U.S. Navy and his nation-wide publicity campaign for a united air force similar to the RAF. Fortunately, Mitchell's dream did not materialize.

Also in 1923, General Trenchard conducted bombing tests on the battleship *HMS Agamemnon,* dropping practice bombs from 8,000 feet. The bombing was a success; however, the results were kept secret for several years.

General Mitchell became so outspoken that he was court marshalled and he then resigned from the army. As with many prophets, 20 years later after his death, when the truth of his claims were appreciated, Mitchell was restored to service with the rank of Major General and was awarded the Congressional Medal of Honor.

It is also ironic to realize that Generals Trenchard and Mitchell, who had fought so hard to prove the effectiveness of their land-based bombers against ships, should have unwittingly provided the very evidence that was to result in the great aircraft carrier forces of their countries.

RUSSO-JAPANESE WAR AND JAPANESE
NAVAL EXPANSION

The threat of war with Russia in the early years of this century had forced the rapid expansion and modernization of the Japanese Navy. This would not have been possible without considerable technical assistance from Britain. When the Japanese Navy annihilated the Czar's Fleet at the Battle of Tsushima in 1905 Japan became a leading naval power and, by the end of World War I, she ranked third behind Britain and the U.S. The Washington Treaty was angrily regarded as a "Rolls-Rolls-Ford" ratio by the Japanese and they decided that Japan needed a navy that could dominate the Pacific in order to insure their security.

Japanese Aircraft Carrier Design

The tonnage restrictions of the Washington Treaty drove the Japanese naval designers into obtaining the highest speed and heaviest fire-power from hulls of restricted displacement. This approach often resulted in a sacrifice of structural integrity and/or a lack of suitable stability; however, the dedication did produce a range of remarkable warships. No other navy has ever approached its ship-building and tactical problems in such a doctrinaire and dogmatic manner.

Japan's carriers ignored all traditional ship design and concentrated on providing a seagoing flight deck as the all-important objective. Masts, bridge, smokestacks and defensive armament were secondary to the flight deck. The Japanese carriers appeared awkward but were most practical.

IJNS *Hosho* - First Purpose-built Carrier

Although the British were the first to design a purpose-built aircraft carrier, construction of *HMS Hermes* progressed at such a leisurely pace that it enabled the Japanese to build and commission the first purpose-built aircraft carrier, *Hosho*. The 7,470 ton ship

The world's first purpose-built aircraft carrier was commissioned on December 27, 1922. Japan's IJN Hosho had been constructed with a small island and hinged smokestacks as in this photo, however, shortly after commissioning the island was removed and stacks fixed in a horizontal position. (U.S. National Archives)

had been started in December 1919, launched in November 1921, and commissioned on December 27, 1922; roughly the same length of time spent to convert *USS Langley*.

Some researchers claim *Hosho* was really a converted oiler or, at best, adapted an oiler hull to the carrier design. The fact that the basic *Hosho* hull exhibits virtually no sheer except in the forecastle strongly suggests that the ship was contemplated as a carrier from the onset with the remote possibility of using oiler lines to reduce the design effort which is considered acceptable.

It is quite probable that the basic *Hosho* design was influenced by *HMS Argus* because much of the hull plating extended up to the Flight Deck. It is also an interesting coincidence that the smokestacks were originally hinged to assume a horizontal position during aircraft operations, as was done on *USS Langley*. As originally constructed *Hosho* had a small navigating bridge on the Flight Deck just forward of the stacks, but this was removed shortly after commissioning. The smokestacks were also fixed in the horizontal position at this time.

Hosho Data

Hosho Flight Deck measured 74 x 520 feet while the hull was 59 x 551 feet long. Draft was 20 feet. A short Hangar was installed between the Main Deck and Flight Deck. This was about 300 feet long, located just aft of amidship with an aircraft elevator positioned near the aft end. Aircraft capacity was to be about 26 of mixed types. The original air group was made up of British-built Gloster Sparrowhawk fighters. British type longitudinal arresting cables were installed on the Flight Deck.

Steam to the two geared turbines was supplied by 12 boilers. This powerplant generated 30,000 shaft horsepower which propelled the ship to a speed of 25 knots via twin screws. *Hosho* carried both oil and coal as fuel due to the scarcity of both in Japan. Both fuels could have been burned simultaneously in the same boiler if the coal was ground to a powder and mixed with the oil to a slurry. It is

also possible that separate coal and oil fired boilers were installed

Most interesting is the fact that the Japanese were able to obtain a 520 foot Flight Deck on a relatively low tonnage ship. In addition, the 30,000 shaft horsepower propulsion plant strongly suggests that IJN *Hosho* was intended to be an aircraft carrier from the onset. Also of interest is the high power and speed which indicate that the Japanese Navy recognized the value of the aircraft carrier not only as a reconnaissance vehicle but as an offensive weapon. It is in the development of this concept that the Imperial Japanese Navy led the world.

JAPANESE CARRIER AIRCRAFT - 1920s

Although the Imperial Japanese Navy was able to conceive, design and construct aircraft carriers, the development of aircraft suitable for carrier operation confounded the Japanese engineers and tacticians because, as mentioned in the Prologue, carrier aircraft are unique and a breed apart from conventional planes. Anxious to forge ahead without delay, the Japanese looked elsewhere for assistance

British Assistance To Japan

The Japanese were greatly impressed by British experience in operating aircraft from flight decks and, exercising their alliance with Britain, they had asked for the loan of an Aviation Mission in 1920 The British Government requested Colonel the Master of Sempill (later known as Lord Sempill), who had served in the Royal Naval Air Service, to lead several other ex-RNAS officers in a semiofficial Mission to Japan in the following year. Sempill's job was the "reorganization, equipment specification and training of the Imperial Japanese Naval Air Service." Included in his task was advice regarding the types of aircraft required plus the taking of orders for up to 200 planes with all spare parts and equipment necessary for their operation.

The British Gloster Mars was exported to Japan as the Gloster Sparrowhawk. Japan bought 30 single-seaters and 10 two-seaters. Note the hydrovane. Sparrowhawks served on the Carrier Hosho. (U.S. National Archives)

The British design team in Japan developed the successful Mitsubishi 1MF-1 or Type 10 fighter design which made the first flight deck operations from the carrier Hosho. Claws for longitudinal arresting cables were fitted to the axle. (Official U.S. Navy Photograph)

Britain had sold Japan numbers of the ever-popular Sopwith Pup, as well as the Gloster Sparrowhawk, Sopwith Cuckoo, and Parnall Panther. It cannot be denied that these sales bolstered the sagging British economy somewhat; however, there is a lesson to be learned here. As usually happens in these cases, Mitsubishi Internal Combustion Engine Manufacturing Company soon decided to design and build its own aircraft. Some aero designers were included in the Mission and among them was the Englishman Herbert Smith who came from Sopwith. Early in the year Mitsubishi invited designer Smith and seven engineers to its Nagoya plant to begin the design of a shipboard fighter. Meanwhile, the Imperial Japanese Naval Air Service relied upon the Gloster Sparrowhawk as their premier shipboard fighter.

Gloster Sparrowhawk
Produced by the Gloucestershire Aircraft Company the Gloster Sparrowhawk I was the second design of what the factory called its "Gloster Mars Series." The firm had purchased designs from the famous French airplane manufacturer Nieuport in 1920 and used the Nieuport Nighthawk as the basis for the Mars Series. The Sparrowhawk I was a clean single-seater biplane powered by the 230 horsepower Bentley B.R.2 rotary engine which propelled the craft to a 108 mile per hour top speed at about a 6,000 foot altitude. The 2,165 pound fighter had a service ceiling of 15,000 feet. A hydrovane was installed in front of the wheels and jaws were mounted on the axle to grip the *Hosho* longitudinal arresting cables.

Sparrowhawk was apparently the name selected by the Imperial Japanese Naval Air Service for the export version of the Gloster Mars of which 30 were delivered. Japan also purchased 10 two-seater versions which were named Sparrowhawk II.

Mitsubishi 1 MF 1 (Type 10)
Designer Smith and his engineers had developed a simple biplane fighter which prototype made its appearance in October 1922. The official trials during the following month were such a resounding success that the plane was ordered into production at once. The Mitsubishi 1 MF 1 was designated "Type 10" by the Japanese Navy in accordance with the Imperial calendar.

1 MF 1 Data
Powered by a 300 horsepower Hispano-Suiza water-cooled engine the 2,513 pound plane attained a respectable 140 miles per hour maximum speed at an altitude of 6,500 feet. Service ceiling was 23,000 feet and the craft could remain airborne for 150 minutes.

Two 7.7 millimeter machine guns were located atop the fuselage just forward of the cockpit.

Wingspan was 28 feet - 6 inches and length was 22 feet. Height was 9 feet - 6 inches. No hydrovane was installed; however, claws for the arresting cable were fitted to the landing gear.

First Japanese Flight Deck Operations
During the last days of February 1923 Mitsubishi's British test pilot, Captain Jordan, took off and landed on IJNS *Hosho* while flying a 1 MF 1. Mitsubishi awarded the Captain a 10,000 yen bonus for making the first flight deck operation such a success. A few days later the feat was duplicated by Japanese Navy First Lieutenant Shunichi Kira also flying a 1 MF 1.

1 MF 1 Production
A total of 128 aircraft had been built when 1 MF 1 production halted in December 1928. Squadron deliveries had begun in late 1923 and the fighter remained in service until 1929.

Sempill's Report
Lord Sempill made no secret of his open admiration of the Japanese as military aviators and when the mission returned to Britain his official report read in part: "The general ability in pilots is distinctly high, possibly higher than we are accustomed to find in this country, though it would seem likely that there is a smaller percentage of abnormally good pilots...The men are splendid, keen and hard-working...and will often forego leave without being asked in order to finish some work on hand."

Mitsubishi B 1 M (Type 13)
The last product of Herbert Smith's design team in Japan was the first Japanese-built plane capable of operating in full naval torpedo attack, bombing, and reconnaissance roles. This was the Mitsubishi

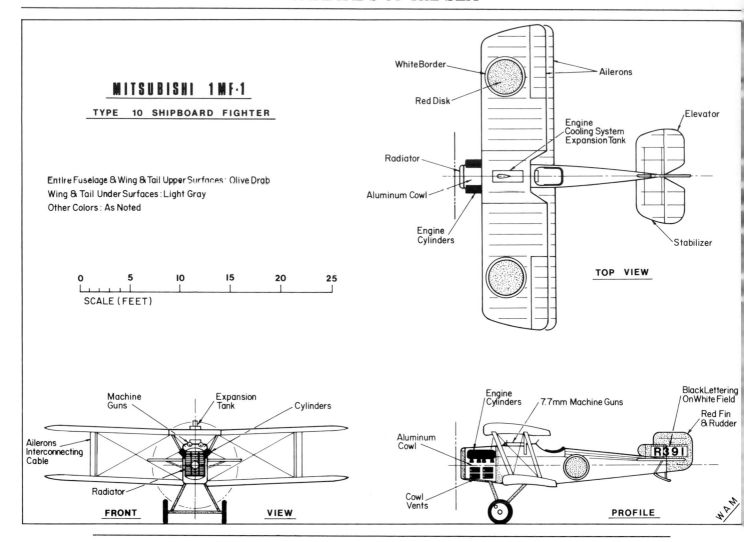

B 1 M, or Type 13 in the Imperial calendar, shipboard aircraft which remained in service as the mainstay of the Imperial Japanese carrier attack force until 1938.

B 1 M Data

The B 1 M prototype was completed in January 1923. The performance and serviceability were so good that it was rushed into production and 442 were built. Initial production units were powered by the British 450 horsepower Napier Lion water-cooled engine; however, later aircraft were equipped with the Mitsubishi-built Hispano-Suiza water-cooled engine of the same power.

The 5,945 pound torpedo bomber could carry one 18 inch 1,765 pound torpedo or 1,070 pounds of assorted bombs. Defensive armament consisted of two 7.7 millimeter machine guns on a moveable mount. Some models were also fitted with two forward firing fixed machine guns located just forward of the pilot's cockpit.

Top speed was 130 miles per hour and flight endurance was 150 minutes. The folding wings spanned 48 feet - 6 inches while overall length was 32 feet.

First Japanese Plane Used in Combat

The B 1 M was the first Japanese airplane to experience aerial combat. The location was over Soochow, China (between Shanghai and

The first Japanese-built torpedo-bombing-reconnaissance plane was the Mitsubishi B1M or Type 13. It was also the first Japanese aircraft to be used in combat. (U.S. Army Photograph)

Nanking) on February 22, 1932 when three B 1 M torpedo bombers in concert with three other Japanese aircraft engaged an American-made Boeing P-12 flown by Robert Short. The Boeing was shot down; however, it is understood that Short scored at least three of the Japanese.

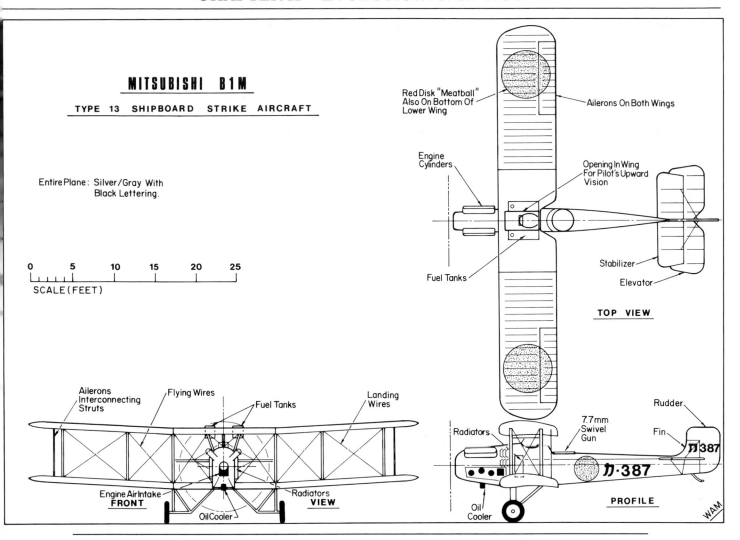

MITSUBISHI B1M

TYPE 13 SHIPBOARD STRIKE AIRCRAFT

Entire Plane: Silver/Gray With Black Lettering.

0   5   10   15   20   25
SCALE (FEET)

Red Disk "Meatball" Also On Bottom Of Lower Wing

Ailerons On Both Wings

Engine Cylinders

Opening In Wing For Pilot's Upward Vision

Fuel Tanks

Stabilizer

Elevator

TOP VIEW

Ailerons Interconnecting Struts

Flying Wires

Fuel Tanks

Landing Wires

Engine Air Intake
FRONT

Oil Cooler

Radiators
VIEW

Radiators

7.7mm Swivel Gun

Rudder

Fin

力·387

Oil Cooler

PROFILE

WAM

BRITISH CARRIERS - EARLY 1920s

Unlike the Imperial Japanese Navy the Royal Navy had not yet truly conceived the attack role for aircraft carriers.

Reconnaissance First

High ranking Royal Navy officials usually described the carriers' function as providing "An aerial reconnaissance screen", as well as "airplane spotting for capital ships." Another requirement for carriers was to carry artillery observation machines for two divisions of battle cruisers, and also as many torpedo machines and fighters as possible. The requirement for torpedo bombers and fighters almost appears as an afterthought; if there was any room left on the carrier for them.

The reconnaissance first and strike second policy dominated Fleet Air Arm strategic thought and tactical planning for almost 20 years and was to result in dreadful consequences. The Royal Navy has often been criticized for its excessive emphasis on battle-line reconnaissance and artillery spotting rather than on antiaircraft carrier tactics. It should; however, be remembered that this policy was formulated when Britain ruled the seas and the physical threat of any potentially hostile aircraft carriers did not exist. Britain alone had operating carriers in a battle fleet second to none so why worry about enemy carriers that don't exist? It seems to be a very natural

reaction; however, this complacency lasted for a decade into the 1930s.

Advanced Carriers: *HMS Hermes* and *HMS Eagle*

HMS Hermes and *HMS Eagle* were completed and commissioned seven months apart; the purpose-built *Hermes* entering service first. Her keel had been laid January 1918, launched in September 1919 and commissioned in July 1923. Although *Hermes* was the first aircraft carrier designed as such, IJNS *Hosho* was completed first because of the intentional slow pace of *Hermes'* construction.

The Island Concept

HMS Hermes was the first carrier to have the smokestack and Navigating Bridge combined into an island offset to one side of the Flight Deck. This was done because ducting the boiler uptakes aft as on *Argus* posed some very difficult problems on both *Hermes* and *Eagle*. The alternative solution of a single structure offset to one side was received with skepticism so a test was arranged. A temporary island structure was erected on the starboard side of *Argus'* Flight Deck, representing a Navigating Bridge and smokestack, for landing trials. Upon completion of the tests all participating pilots reported that the island did not produce dangerous turbulence nor did it interfere with visibility during the approach and landing. It

HMS Hermes was the first aircraft carrier to be fitted with an off-center located island containing the smokestack and operations spaces such as pilot house, chart room, etc. (U.S. National Archives)

was decided; therefore, that both *HMS Hermes* and *HMS Eagle* would be constructed with an offset superstructure; thereby, setting the standard for the vast majority of carriers constructed since that time.

HMS Hermes

The 10,850 ton *Hermes* was a comparatively small carrier and the afterthought offset island caused some stability problems. Although very narrow, the island was quite long and massive for a ship of this size. The island location forward of amidships made the ship trim by the bow (floating with the bow lower than the stern). The weight of the offset island also caused a list to starboard (starboard side lower than port side). This imbalance had to be corrected by carrying more water ballast and fuel oil in the port side and aft tanks than in the starboard side and forward tanks. It was a time of trial and error.

HMS Hermes Data

The basic hull had been built along the lines of a light cruiser which included side blisters, 3 inch armor belt protection diminishing to 2 inches at the ends, and 1 inch Main Deck armor over the forward magazines plus 1 inch Upper Deck armor over the boiler rooms and engine rooms. The shell flared sharply at the bow to fair into the Flight Deck which presaged the hurricane bow of two decades later. Although the Main Deck was the strength deck, shell plating was continued up to the Flight Deck with openings as needed. The hull measured 600 feet long with a 70 foot beam over the blisters. Full load draft was 21.5 feet.

The Flight Deck was 580 x 65 feet; the wings of which had a decided rise at the aft end. This was apparently the result of wind over deck studies which the Royal Navy pursued at length. A 400 foot long Hangar, between the Main Deck and Flight Deck, extended from forward of the island to the open space aft. One air-

In order not to interfere with hangar space the HMS Hermes elevator was located externally in the stern; aft of the Hangar. Aircraft were passed to the outdoor elevator via Hangar doors. The same philosophy was applied to the much later deck-edge elevators. (U.S. Naval Historic Center)

This aerial view of HMS Hermes reveals the deck markings and code HR. Note the Swordfish aircraft with folded wings and life rafts mounted on the Island side. (Ministry of Defence [Navy])

craft elevator was fitted in the open space between the Main Deck and Flight Deck. This location was chosen in order not to take away airplane stowage space in the Hangar; however, the arrangement made it necessary to pass aircraft through an opening in the Hangar after bulkhead in order to use the elevator. It soon became evident that another elevator was needed and this was installed in the forward end of the Hangar which reduced the aircraft complement from 20 to 15.

A standard light cruiser powerplant was installed which consisted of six boilers and two steam turbines producing a total of 40,000 shaft horsepower; divided between two propellers and developing a speed of 25 knots. A complement of 664 was required to operate *HMS Hermes*.

Armament consisted of six 5.5 inch and three 4 inch guns plus two 0.5 inch, four-barrelled pom-poms.

HMS Hermes was the victim of considerable adverse criticism such as that the elevator and Hangar size did not consider the growth in size and weight of shipboard aircraft in the future, nor was a catapult installed for the same reason. It must be remembered that at the time *Hermes* was on the drafting board there were no true carriers operating for long enough so the benefit of their experience could be adapted to *HMS Hermes* design.

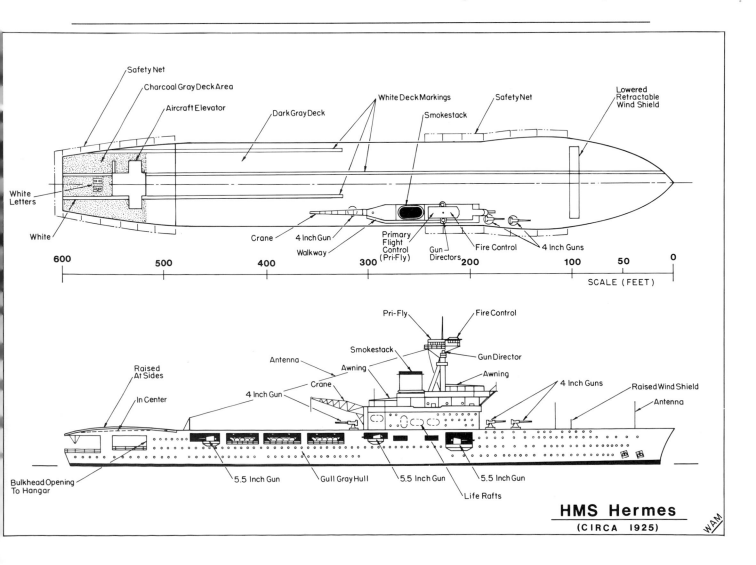

SCALE (FEET)

HMS Hermes
(CIRCA 1925)

Among the aircraft that operated from *HMS Hermes* were Fairey Flycatchers, Blackburn Ripons, and Fairey III F.

HMS Eagle

HMS Eagle followed *HMS Hermes* into service, having been launched in June 1918 and commissioned as an aircraft carrier in February 1924. It will be remembered that, unlike *HMS Hermes*, *Eagle* was a converted battleship under construction in Britain for the Chilean Navy. The *Almirante Cochrane* had been started in 1913; however, work had come to a halt when World War I started. The ship was selected because it was felt that its inherent strength and protection would make an ideal aircraft carrier; however, in fact her heavy structure proved to be an unnecessary burden.

HMS Eagle Data

The 100 ton Flight Deck measured 96 x 652 feet which included one inch armor plate. This was located about 25 feet above the Upper Deck. The 400 foot long Hangar was positioned amidships with an aircraft elevator located at each end. No catapult was installed. Although designed for an aircraft complement of 25 *Eagle's* normal complement was reduced to 18 by the time she entered service due to aircraft development. During 1929 six each of Blackburn Dart, Fairey Flycatcher, and Fairey III F were operated from *Eagle*.

The hull was armored with a 4 1/2 inch thick belt and the bulkheads were 4 inches thick. The Upper Deck, Hangar, and Main Deck were 1.5 inch thick armor plate. Armament consisted of nine 6 inch guns along the sides and stern of the Main Deck, and five 4 inch guns forward and aft of the island on the Flight Deck. The ship's complement was 748.

HMS Eagle displaced 22,600 tons with an overall hull length of 667 feet and a beam over the underwater blister of 105 feet (95 feet without blisters). Deep load draft was 26.5 feet.

Propulsion steam was generated by 32 boilers which powered the four turbines to develop 50,000 shaft horsepower; distributed to four propellers. Speed was 24 knots and range was 4,000 miles at 18 knots.

One of the factors that delayed completion of *Eagle* was the uncertainty of the Admiralty in 1920 whether to continue with the conversion or reconvert the carrier to a battleship and sell it to Chile as originally intended. The official decision was handed down on September 24 to continue with the conversion.

Self-Sufficient *Eagle*

Eagle was a formidable fighting ship and was capable of beating off attacks by light cruisers and destroyers in the event she found herself alone without a surface escort and no aircraft. This was, of course, not the intention because a carrier was never to operate far from the protection of the battle fleet in the minds of the early strategists.

HMS Furious Modifications

During the time that *Hermes* was under construction and *Eagle* was undergoing conversion *HMS Furious* was being rebuilt. It will be recalled that the separate landing and takeoff decks connected by two narrow taxiways was not successful. Experience with *HMS Argus* no doubt influenced the decision to extensively modify *Furious*. Two shipyards undertook the work starting in 1921 at the Royal Dockyard in Rosyth, Scotland and concluding in 1925 at Devonport Dockyards. The entire Navigating Bridge and smokestack were removed along with the masts and cranes. The existing Flight Decks and Hangars were extended and joined together forming a single 550 x 50 feet Hangar.

Converted from a battleship under construction, HMS Eagle was a formidable fighting ship able to defend itself from attacks by light cruisers and destroyers in the event no aircraft were available. Note the sharply pointed flight deck. Photo taken in 1922. (Ministry of Defence [Navy])

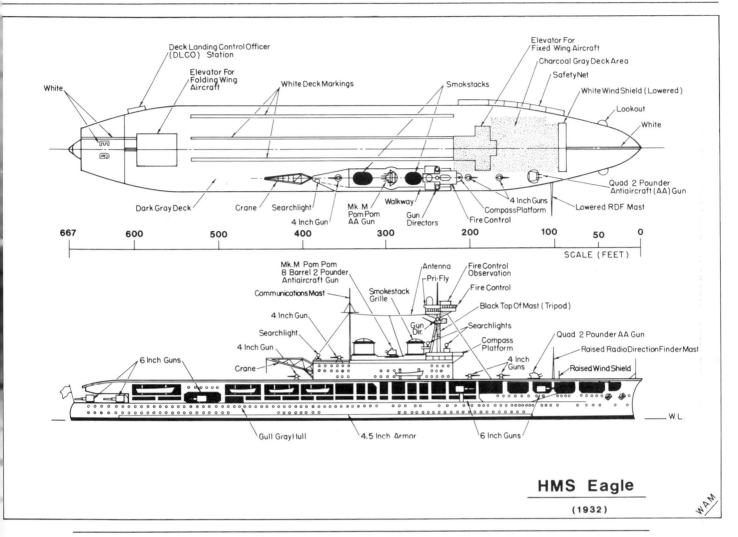

Deck Landing Control Officer
(DLCO) Station

Elevator For
Folding Wing
Aircraft

White Deck Markings

Smokstacks

Elevator For
Fixed Wing Aircraft

Charcoal Gray Deck Area

Safety Net

White Wind Shield (Lowered)

White

Lookout

White

Dark Gray Deck

Crane

Searchlight

4 Inch Gun

Mk. M
Pom Pom
AA Gun

Walkway

Gun
Directors

Fire Control

Compass Platform

4 Inch Guns

Quad 2 Pounder
Antiaircraft (AA) Gun

Lowered RDF Mast

667   600   500   400   300   200   100   50   0

SCALE (FEET)

Mk. M Pom Pom
8 Barrel 2 Pounder
Antiaircraft Gun

Communications Mast

4 Inch Gun

Searchlight

4 Inch Gun

Crane

6 Inch Guns

Smokestack
Grille

Antenna

Pri-Fly

Gun
Dir.

Fire Control
Observation

Fire Control

Black Top Of Mast (Tripod)

Searchlights

Compass
Platform

4 Inch
Guns

Quad 2 Pounder AA Gun

Raised Radio Direction Finder Mast

Raised Wind Shield

W.L.

Gull Gray Hull

4.5 Inch Armor

6 Inch Guns

HMS Eagle

(1932)

WAM

Atop this structure was added another Hangar of 530 x 50 feet. A new 630 foot Flight Deck was installed over the new Hangar covering the after four-fifths of the ship. The two elevators were extended to service the added Flight Deck. Boiler uptakes were led along the sides of the ship horizontally to exhaust at the stern. A conning station was located on each side at the forward end of the new Flight Deck and a retractable Navigating Bridge was located on the forward end of the Flight Deck at the centerline. The Navigating Bridge was lowered during flying operations. Armament consisted of five 5 inch guns on each side of the Main Deck and two 4 inch antiaircraft guns each fore and aft.

The semicircular forward end as well as the rounded forward edge of the new Flight Deck was the result of careful wind over deck studies and experiments conducted by the British National Physical Laboratory. The studies revealed that with this form steadier and more consistent aerodynamic conditions would prevail for small variations of angles of yaw of the wind.

This conversion increased the tonnage to 22,130 and increased the mean draft to 24 feet. As completed *HMS Furious* could launch aircraft from two decks simultaneously; the new Flight Deck and the Forecastle Flying Off Deck. Landing could be accomplished only on the new Flight Deck. No catapult or arresting gear had

The massive structure and heavy armor belt of HMS Eagle is shown in this photo. Bulkheads were 4 inches thick and Flight Deck weighed 100 tons. (U.S. Naval Historical Center)

Very evident in this photo is the crow's nest-type elevated pilothouse on the huge tripod mast. HMS Eagle was very advanced for its time, having been launched in June 1918. (U.S. National Archives)

The HMS Furious third modification, 1921-1925, was very extensive through the addition of a new Flight Deck atop a new Hangar. The central superstructure was replaced with a small island. (U.S. Naval Historical Center)

been fitted. The new Flight Deck was constructed with a slight upward slope about 200 feet from the forward edge of the Flight Deck just aft of the forward elevator. The purpose of this rise in the Deck was to slow the roll of landing aircraft.

Flight Deck Safety Nets
Until 1932-33 British naval aircraft landed on the decks of carriers relying only on the slowest possible deck speed and touchdown with high wind over deck speeds to bring them safely to a halt. The planes were not fitted with brakes nor steering tailwheels to help keep them running straight after touchdown. Surprisingly, the accident rate was less than it was with the longitudinal cable system. To minimize the consequences of a swerve or yaw after touchdown, wire netting set at a slight rise from horizontal and supported by steel stanchions was installed along the edges of the Landing Deck to catch any plane which would have gone over the side into the sea. *HMS Hermes* and *HMS Eagle* were the first carriers to have the deck edge safety nets installed. Safety nets are now standard

The rounded leading edge of the new Furious Flight Deck was the result of extensive studies to attain more consistent aerodynamic conditions during varying angles of yaw to the wind. Note the Fairey Flycatcher on the lower Flight Deck. (Ministry of Defence [Navy])

quipment on all aircraft carriers and helicopter landing decks sav-
ng lives as well as machines. The absence of an arresting gear
ndoubtedly delayed the development of heavy, high speed aircraft
or the Fleet Air Arm.

Longitudinal Arresting Cables Abandoned

Both *Hermes* and *Eagle* were fitted with the same longitudinal cable
system of aircraft arresting gear that was installed on *HMS Argus*,
with one modification. The cables were supported above the Deck
by a series of hinged flaps which the airplane wheels knocked down,
thereby causing deceleration of the plane from the moment of touchdown.

Agile, low landing speed, and light wing loading aircraft such
as the Sopwith Pup were able to overcome the deficiencies of the
longitudinal cable system; however, as heavier aircraft such as the
Sopwith Cuckoo, Parnall Panther, and Blackburn Dart appeared,
their greater weight and higher landing speeds made the defects of
the fore-and-aft cable system more apparent and of more consequence. The percentage of accidents varying from damaged landing gears or tail skids to unrepairable crashes grew alarmingly. The
slightest yaw on touchdown subjected the landing gear to stresses
beyond that for which it had been designed. The cables invariably
multiplied a minor error into a major accident. Finally, the longitudinal cable system was abandoned in the mid-1920s, but no alternative system had yet been substituted.

BRITISH CARRIER AIRCRAFT - 1920s

Absorbed by the RAF, the impetus gained by the Royal Naval Air
Service had been dissipated within a few months and by the end of
1919 the naval branch of the RAF was reduced to one flight of
fighters, one half a torpedo squadron, one spotter-reconnaissance
squadron, and one each of a seaplane flight and a flying boat flight.
It was lucky that the aircraft carriers, being ships, were still under
the control of the Royal Navy and the Air Ministry finally realized
that new generation carrier aircraft had to be developed for the growing carrier force.

Parnall Panther

Fortunately, the Admiralty had already prepared Specification N.2A
for a carrier-based landplane design in 1917. Following this specification, engineer Harold Bolas designed a two-seater biplane, the
prototype of which was flown later that year. Over 300 of the 230
horsepower Bentley BR.2 rotary engine powered craft were ordered
by the Admiralty; however, the signing of the Armistice forced a
reduction of the order to 150 aircraft. These were built during 1919
and 1920 and named Panther.

The Parnall Panther spotter-reconnaissance plane was the very
first landplane specifically designed for operation from aircraft carriers. Due to the limited Parnall production facilities the craft were
built by the Bristol Aeroplane Co. The Panther fuselage was made
to fold just aft of the rear cockpit in order to conserve stowage
space on carriers. Visibility was considered so important that the
cockpits were raised above the fuselage with a fairing around them.
The cockpits were so high that the pilot had to enter through a hole
in the upper wing center section. The landing gear was fitted with a

The Parnall Panther was the first landplane specifically designed for aircraft carrier operation. The wings did not fold; however, the fuselage folded just behind the cockpits for stowage. Note the hydrovane or small wing forward of the landing gear to prevent nose-overs in the event of a ditching. This spotter-reconnaissance craft was built during 1919-1920. (Ministry of Defence [Navy])

hydrovane or small wing just forward of the wheels. Hydrovanes
were used to prevent nose-overs in the event of an emergency landing at sea.

Both wings spanned 39 feet 6 inches while overall length was
24 feet 11 inches. The 2,595 pound craft attained a speed over 108
miles per hour and had a service ceiling of 14,500 feet. Endurance
was 4.5 hours. The only armament was a single Lewis machine
gun. The axle was fitted with claws which could be closed on the
carrier deck longitudinal cables to slow the roll of the plane upon
landing.

Panthers served on *HMS Argus* and *HMS Hermes* until 1926
when they were replaced by the Fairey III D.

Blackburn Swift

Towards the end of 1919 the Air Ministry issued specifications for
a Sopwith Cuckoo replacement. The Blackburn Aeroplane and
Motor Co. Ltd. which had constructed many Cuckoos for the RNAS
presented their own design, the prototype of which was completed
in five months. The Blackburn T.1 Swift, designed by Major F.A.
Bumpus, incorporated many innovations; some of which were to
become standard features for all combat aircraft. A fireproof bulkhead was installed between the engine compartment and a 66 gallon self-sealing fuel tank located in the fuselage! A wind-powered
fuel pump was arranged to distribute fuel to either the 15 gallon
upper wing center section gravity tank or to the carburetors.

The landing gear had a divided axle to accommodate an 18
inch torpedo and the landing gear was also jettisonable in order to
minimize the risk of nosing over in the event of an emergency landing on water. Flotation bags were also installed in the fuselage.
Fittings were built into the wing center section for hoisting the aircraft when necessary. The cockpit was located very high relative to
the engine to insure maximum forward visibility when landing.

Also of special interest in the design are the folding wings; this
is the first plane to solve the problem of folding a staggered wing
biplane. All previous wing folding biplanes had the wings set with
one directly above the other. In order to achieve the immense strength
required in a plane which was to carry a concentrated load and with-

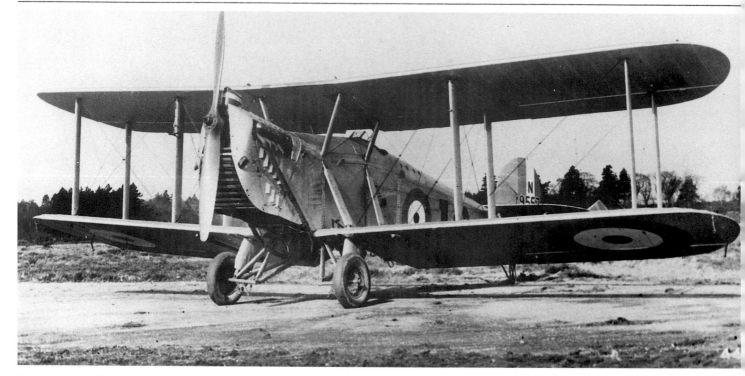

The single-seat Blackburn Dart torpedo-bomber was very innovative with a self-sealing fuel tank; fireproof bulkhead between the engine and fuel tank; flotation bags in the fuselage; a strength nucleus of a welded steel structure supporting the wings, landing gear and engine mounts; and a detachable engine mount to enable engine changes in a few hours. (Ministry of Defence [Navy])

stand the hard shocks of deck flying, the Swift was built around a nucleus in which the landing gear, forward fuselage, upper wing center section and lower wing roots were integrated into a single rigid structure made entirely of welded steel tubing. All fittings were machined from solid steel. The engine had a detachable mount so the engine could be changed in an afternoon.

Although the Swift's appearance was ordinary and uninspiring, its performance with the 1,500 pound torpedo attracted several foreign governments which placed orders for the plane. Three went to the Spanish Navy, one to Brazil, and two each to the U.S. Navy and the Imperial Japanese Navy.

With minor modifications 69 Swifts were purchased by the Air Ministry and renamed T.2 Dart. Export models were to retain the Swift appellation.

Blackburn Dart

The Blackburn Dart was powered by a 450 horsepower Napier Lion II B which propelled the 6,383 pound gross weight craft to 107 miles per hour at 1,000 feet. Endurance at 95 miles per hour was three hours. The wingspan was 45 feet 6 inches; three feet shorter than the Swift and because the wing loading was only nine pounds per square foot the Dart was easy to land on carriers. The stalling speed of only 45 miles per hour further improved the Dart's handling qualities. It was one of the first airplanes to be fitted with smokescreen making apparatus, carrying the chemical tank in the torpedo rack. The wheel landing gear was interchangeable with floats and 10 Darts were purchased with dual landing gear.

The Blackburn Dart was the first of many future Blackburn torpedo bomber designs. Darts served on *HMS Furious, HMS Eagle* and the yet to come *HMS Courageous.*

Fairey Flycatcher

From the mid-1920s to the mid-1930s every Royal Navy aircraft carrier had played host to a jaunty little popular biplane that was the Fleet Air Arm's first-line fighter for over a decade. The Fairey Flycatcher was one of the first British naval aircraft to capture the popular imagination. This was due not only to its longevity but to the thrilling demonstrations this rugged aerobatic and diving performer gave at air shows throughout Britain, especially at the great Hendon Air Displays in the 1920s. This enthusiasm was also shared by Flycatcher pilots who had nothing but praise for the plane.

Flycatcher Data

Fairey designed and produced the plane in record time; following Air Ministry Specification 6/22 of 1922 and having production machines delivered in the following year. The fuselage was of composite wood and metal structure with fabric covering.

Powered by an uncowled 400 horsepower air-cooled Armstrong Siddeley Jaguar radial engine, the Flycatcher attained a maximum speed of 133 miles per hour at 5,000 feet altitude. Service ceiling was 19,000 feet and combat range was 310 miles. The 2,980 pound biplane spanned 29 feet and length was 23 feet. Height was 12 feet. Armament consisted of two fixed forward-firing Vickers machine guns buried in the upper fuselage. Racks for four 20 pound bombs were provided under the lower wing.

Early production models were fitted with steel jaws on the axle to grasp the longitudinal arresting cables. These were omitted on most production aircraft. The Fairey Flycatcher was the first Fleet Air Arm airplane to have hydraulic wheel brakes which reduced landing runs to as short as 150 feet. The wheels were interchangeable with twin floats and an amphibian was tested.

A Fairey Flycatcher fighter at the moment of lift off reveals the jaws mounted on the axle. Actuated by the pilot, the jaws gripped the longitudinal arresting cables. The plane could be quickly disassembled for stowage on carriers. (Air Ministry [Navy])

Flycatcher Easily Disassembled

This airplane had two unconventional features well worth mentioning: unusual for a carrier plane is the fact that the wings did not fold, nor did the fuselage. Instead the entire plane was designed and constructed so that it could be easily disassembled into components not exceeding 13 feet - 6 inches long. Assembly was also easily accomplished.

Flycatcher Patented Flaps

The other unusual feature of the Flycatcher design was the Fairey Patent Camber Gear. This consisted of flaps running along the entire trailing edge of both wings. Each flap was divided into an inboard and an outboard panel. During normal flight the outer panels acted as ailerons; however, during takeoff and landing the aileron panels could be lowered simultaneously with the inner panels. This shortened the takeoff and landing runs considerably and steepened the glide path. This was the forerunner of the wing flaps used on most modern aircraft.

The Fairey Flycatcher was easy to fly, easy to land and still highly maneuverable. It has been said that pilots often performed a slow roll immediately after takeoff with complete safety. This little gem proved that the British aircraft industry could still design quality naval aircraft if given the opportunity and funding.

U.S. NAVY'S FIRST CARRIER

America's first aircraft carrier was commissioned on March 20, 1922. The 19,360 ton collier or coal carrier Jupiter conversion to the aircraft carrier *USS Langley* (CV-1) had been completed at Norfolk Navy Yard in three years. The 10 year old ship, renamed to honor aviation pioneer Samuel Pierpont Langley, was intended to be experimental; converted to learn the requirements for carrier design and operation before a purpose-built carrier would be attempted, despite the fact that Britain and Japan were each building a purpose-built carrier.

USS Langley was truly a ship of firsts. As *USS Jupiter* she was the Navy's first turbo-electric propelled ship. Steam turbines turned generators which supplied electricity to electric motors via switchboards and rheostats. The electric motors drove the two propellers. *Jupiter* was also the first U.S. Navy ship to pass through the Panama Canal from the Pacific to the Atlantic Oceans.

A Vought VE-7 has just landed on America's first aircraft carrier, USS Langley. The ship, as originally converted, was fitted with one stack that hinged outboard. (Vought Aircraft Company, Courtesy Paul Bower)

A later Langley modification resulted in two hinged smokestacks. Curtiss TS-1 fighters of VF-1 and VF-2 are lined up on deck. (Official U.S. Navy Photograph, U.S. Naval Historical Center)

USS Langley

Basic carrier design followed *HMS Argus* but the conversion was not as extensive nor as sophisticated. Most of the after superstructure was removed and a complex steel structure was erected over the Main Deck to support the 64 x 534 foot wooden planked Flight Deck. After trying port and starboard smokestacks the uptakes from the three boilers were trunked to a port side hinged cylindrical smokestack. The normal position was vertical except when planes were in operation in which case it was lowered outboard into horizontal position. A second smokestack was installed in late spring of 1922.

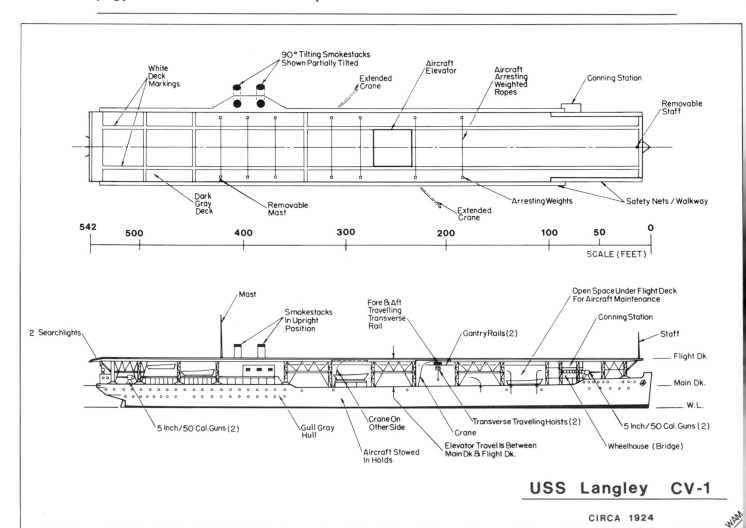

USS Langley CV-1

CIRCA 1924

Langley Aircraft Complement and Handling

The hull side plating was not raised as in *Argus*; the space between the Main Deck and the Flight Deck being obstructed only by Flight Deck supporting structure. Flight Deck had no obstructions with the pilot house located between the Forecastle Deck and the Flight Deck. In view of the above *USS Langley* really had no hangar space; however, four of the six large holds were converted into aircraft stowage spaces to carry 34 assembled planes or 55 disassembled planes. The clear spaces on the Main Deck served as maintenance and assembly areas. During normal operation the airplane complement was intended to be 12 fighters, 12 scouts or observation planes and 10 torpedo-bombers. Six of the torpedo-bombers were intended to be twin-float seaplanes which would be lowered onto the water and raised to the Main Deck by means of 35 foot cranes on each side of the ship. Apparently the concept of the seaplane carrier was still important to U.S. Naval planners. Two three-ton hoists ran on a transverse rail that rode on two longitudinal gantry rails under the Flight Deck. These were used to transport the planes from the stowage holds to the electric motor-driven elevator, which lifted the planes from the Main Deck to the Flight Deck. The space beneath the elevator was used for the stowage of aircraft ammunition which included 275 bombs and 25 torpedoes.

Langley Data

After conversion *USS Langley* displaced 12,700 tons. The hull was 542 feet long overall with a beam of 65 feet 6 inches which made the Flight Deck 18 inches narrower and eight feet shorter than the hull. Deep loaded draft was 22 feet. The powerplant developed 7,000 shaft horsepower which drove the ship to a maximum speed of 15 knots. Four 5 inch guns were mounted on the Main Deck, fore and aft, as defensive armament.

USS Langley's speed of 15 knots or just over 17 miles per hour was very slow when compared to the 20 knot *HMS Argus* and the 31.5 knot *HMS Furious*. This slow speed was; however, of some benefit because it stimulated catapult and arresting gear research due to the slow wind over deck which would have made it difficult, if not impossible, for heavy planes to take off and land on the carrier deck. Two 60 feet long compressed air powered catapults were installed in the Main Deck with the rails countersunk into the deck so as not to interfere with the normal movement of aircraft on the deck.

Commander Whiting had followed the design and conversion of *USS Langley* very closely making improvements as necessary while construction progressed.

Langley Arresting Gear Selection

Now, with the new problem taking priority the selection of the proper arresting gear design had to be made. Lieutenant Commander Godfrey De Courcelles Chevalier, usually called "Chevvy", had just completed experiments with torpedo-bombers when the arresting gear project surfaced. Commander Chevalier was one of the U.S. Navy's first naval pilots and a crack flyer; therefore, Commander Whiting assigned him the task of organizing a precommissioning detail of pilots and mechanics for *USS Langley*. During the spring of 1921 American battleships sailed northward from Cuba to unload their turret-launching pilots and equipment at

This aerial view of Naval Air Station, San Diego (North Island) reveals the Langley Practice Landing Area and the turntable-mounted wooden flight deck on which the pilots practiced landings. (Official U.S. Navy Photograph)

the Norfolk Naval Base. These were virtually the only U.S. Navy pilots who had landplane flying experience. Lieutenant Commander Chevalier, sensing the urgency of the situation, did not bother to go through formal channels and quickly put the *Langley* detail to work. The U.S. Navy Bureau of Construction and Repair had built a short wooden Flight Deck mounted on a turntable, shoreside, and equipped it with the British longitudinal cable arresting gear. Whiting and Chevalier decided to use this apparatus as the starting point for arresting gear experiments. Tests continued for the remainder of the year with all *USS Langley* pilots practicing landings on the turntable deck without any fatalities. The final decision was to install the transverse cable arresting system as was used successfully by Eugene Ely when he landed on *USS Pennsylvania* in 1911.

On March 22, 1922 Whiting became Commanding Officer of *USS Langley* in addition to his Bureau of Aeronautics duties. Six months later all was in readiness for flying off and landing trials with *USS Langley*.

First Langley Takeoff

On October 17 Lieutenant Commander Virgil C. "Squash" Griffin, Jr. made the first takeoff from the anchored *Langley* while flying a Vought VE-7 biplane.

First Langley Landing

Nine days later "Chevvy" Chevalier approached *USS Langley* for a landing while flying an Aeromarine trainer. The plane was fitted with a long Vee shaped rigid arresting hook anchored high on the landing gear struts. The hook, itself, formed the apex of the Vee. This could, of course, be lowered by the pilot at the proper moment. *USS Langley* was steaming into a 26 knot wind which, when added to the ship's forward speed through the water, produced a wind over deck velocity of about 40 knots or about 45 miles per hour. Just before 11 o'clock in the morning the Aeromarine crossed the after end of the Flight Deck at an airspeed of 60 miles per hour and when the plane was a few feet above the Deck Chevalier lowered the arresting hook and engaged the first cable. After the initial shock of reduced momentum the Aeromarine tail began to rise and although he pulled back on the stick "Chevvy" still couldn't rem-

On October 17, 1922 Lieutenant Commander Virgil C. "Squash" Griffin made the first takeoff from an American aircraft carrier, USS Langley, in a Vought VE-7SF single-seater. (Official U.S. Navy Photograph)

Lieutenant Commander Godfrey De Courcelles "Chevvy" Chevalier made the first landing on an American carrier when he alighted on USS Langley on October 26, 1922 in an Aeromarine biplane. (Official U.S. Navy Photograph)

edy the problem. As the nose dropped the whirling propeller chewed into the Flight Deck and splintered; then the tail settled to the Deck. Chevalier was unhurt but was more interested in the reason for the Aeromarine's nose-down reaction at the moment the cables were snared despite the slow plane speed over deck of only 15 miles per hour.

The force of arresting a landing airplane is tremendous at the point of hook attachment on the airframe. This force must be transmitted to and absorbed by a specially designed fuselage. The Aeromarine was, of course, not so constructed therefore, the hook was anchored to the strongest structural assembly which was the landing gear/fuselage attachment. Although a structurally sound location, this was not correct from a balance or force arrangement viewpoint because lines of force from the hook passed under the Aeromarine's center of gravity pulling the nose down. This is the sort of lesson Commander Whiting was looking for during *USS Langley* flight operations.

Chevalier never lived to see the full glory of the aircraft carrier. He died in an unrelated plane crash three weeks after his historic landing.

Ensign Alfred M. "Mel" Pride was the first to complete the first takeoff and landing cycle from *USS Langley* in October, 1922.

While Whiting and his pilots learned the art of carrier flight operations through trial and error he planned to apply this knowledge and experience to the conversion of *USS Lexington* and *USS Saratoga* which was getting underway.

U.S. NAVY CARRIER AIRCRAFT AND ENGINE DEVELOPMENT - 1920s

Naval aviation in the United States during the early 1920s was a period of impressive technical progress. Accurate bomb sights were developed; reliable radios were put to use; and instrumentation was greatly improved. The World War I bungee cord landing gear shock absorber was being replaced by the oleo strut and folding wings became commonplace for operation from aircraft carriers.

Tactics were conceived and refined such as dive bombing, torpedo attack, gunfire spotting, fighter escort, interception and combat air patrol. As the years passed the carrier and its air wing became increasingly appreciated as the ultimate naval fighting machine.

Fleet fighter activity was strictly limited. The seaplane fighters were restricted to two per capital ship and further, had to be catapulted off and land at sea; not the best arrangement. Few fighters operated at sea due to the short range except for operation from the only U.S. carrier, *USS Langley*; however, bigger and better carriers were on the way.

As was learned during the battleship turret aircraft operations period, the U.S. had no fighting planes and was forced to purchase surplus British and French aircraft during the immediate postwar years. There was a lot of catching up to be done.

Vought VE-7

The Vought VE-7 that was flown off *USS Langley* by Commander Griffin had been designed in 1917 as a trainer in competition with the Curtiss Jenny which had secured the major contract. The postwar years, however, saw 129 Voughts delivered to the U.S. Navy between 1920 and 1924.

VE-7SF Data

Performance was so good that 51 of the VE-7 were delivered as fighter planes with one instead of the usual two cockpits. A machine gun was also installed atop the fuselage just forward of the cockpit. Two fighter squadrons were supplied with the VE-7 single-seater. The Vought VE-7SF, as it was designated, had a wingspan of 34 feet 3 inches and was 22 feet 4 inches long. Height was 8 foot 7 inches. This product of the Lewis and Vought Corporation at-

The Vought VE-7 Bluebird was designed as a trainer but performance was so good that 51 were delivered as fighter planes, designated VE-7SF. This single-seater supplied two U.S. Navy fighter squadrons. The Vought VE-7 Bluebird is shown here. (U.S. Naval Historical Center, Courtesy Lt. Gustave J. Freret, USN (Ret))

tained a maximum speed of 117 miles per hour and had a range of 291 miles. Service ceiling was 15,000 feet. The Vought had but one drawback; it was powered with a water-cooled engine which proved a constant source of trouble compared with the air-cooled engine powered Sopwith Pup and Camel; Nieuport; and Hanriot Aircraft in U.S. Navy service. Hispano-Suiza or "Hisso" engines had powered several popular aircraft during World War I such as the SPAD and SE 5 and performed well for the French and British at that time.

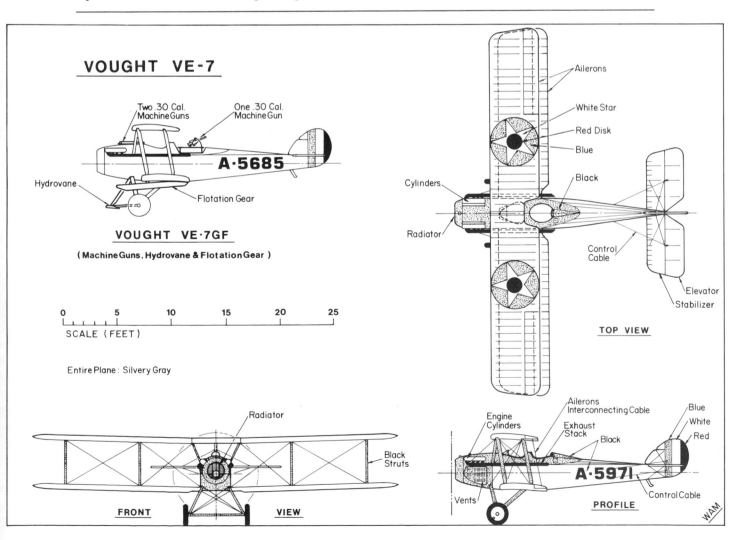

Enter The Air-Cooled Radial Engine

Actually, it was not the "Hisso" engine in particular that caused the U.S. Navy to eventually refuse to consider any new design powered by a liquid-cooled engine; it was liquid-cooled engines in general. One event greatly influenced this decision. During the immediate postwar years the Lawrence Aero Engine Company had designed a 9-cylinder air-cooled radial engine which developed 220 horsepower at 1,800 revolutions per minute and weighed only 420 pounds. The U.S. Navy became extremely interested in this powerplant and funded the refinement of the design and construction of prototype engines to the amount of 100,000 dollars. The investment brought results because the required 50 hour test run was satisfactorily completed during January 1922. The Lawrence engine was designated J-1 and ushered in a new era. The air-cooled radial engine replaced the heavier water-cooled type with its water pump and not only heavy but vulnerable radiator on all U.S. Navy aircraft.

Curtiss FC-1/Naval Aircraft Factory TS-1

The U.S. Naval Aircraft Factory went to work at once on a single-seater shipboard fighter design for the Lawrence engine, Project engineer for the TS-1 design was a 30 year old aeronautical engineer from the Scientific Section of the U.S. Navy Bureau of Construction and Repair who was to go on to supervise the designs of many classic aircraft for the U.S. Navy. After working as an aeronautical draftsman for two years Rex Beisel became one of the first true aeronautical engineers; having been certified by the U.S. Navy Bureau of Construction and Repair in 1919.

Rex Buren Beisel was born with several ailments that would discourage anyone else. He was deaf in one ear; color blind; had no sense of smell; and suffered from Parkinson's Disease, which caused a tremor that increased to an obvious shake as he grew older. Having been an aircraft and ship designer for a half-century the writer can attest to the fact that the Parkinson's ailment is a seriously disabling affliction for any designer who must perform drafting as a principal part of his chosen profession; however, Rex Beisel persevered and became one of the greatest designers of naval aircraft.

Two unusual features of this design are worthy of mention: Beisel located the fuel tank in the lower wing center section under the fuselage from where it could be jettisoned in an emergency; rigid struts which were located between the lower wing center section and the upper wing interplane strut junction replaced the normally installed landing and flying rigging wires. This single strut absorbed the flying wire load in tension and the landing wire load in compression.

Armament consisted of a single machine gun mounted atop the fuselage just forward of the cockpit. A second gun was added later.

Curtiss Awarded Production Contract

When the design was complete, Curtiss was awarded the contract to construct the new shipboard fighter. The prototype was delivered to the U.S. Navy at Anacostia for flight testing on May 9, 1922. This plane was actually designed around the J-1 engine and was the first American fighter designed expressly for aircraft carrier operation. Generally known as the Curtiss TS-1 the fighter was

Rex B. Beisel was the project engineer for designing the TS-1 at the age of 30. He continued in his career for more than a quarter century; designing innovative and classical naval aircraft for the U.S. Navy. (Courtesy Rex B. Beisel Jr.)

rushed into production because procurement of specialized aircraft for *USS Langley* had become a major priority in 1922. Curtiss constructed 34 while the Naval Aircraft Factory built an additional five airframes to experiment with various powerplants, including water-cooled types. Meanwhile, the J-1 engine became known as the Wright J-1 because Lawrence had been purchased by the Wright firm.

TS-1 Data (FC-1)

The TS-1 was a small airplane with the lower wing having a greater span than the upper wing (negative overhang). Wing span was only 25 feet with a length of 22 feet-1 inch. Height was 9 feet. Maximum speed was a respectable 125 miles per hour as was the range of 482 miles. The 1,920 pound plane had a service ceiling of 16,250 feet. A seaplane version was also tested.

U.S. Navy Aircraft Designating System

In March 1923 the U.S. Navy instituted a system of assigning designations to all procured aircraft and the various models of the TS

The Curtiss TS-1 (FC-1) was the first U.S. Navy fighter plane designed expressly for carrier operation. It was also the first U.S. Navy plane to be powered by a radial engine. It equipped Fighter Squadrons VF-1 and VF-2 on USS Langley. (Official U.S. Navy Photograph)

The Chance Vought Corporation produced the VE-9 as a development of the VE-7 with a rounded and strengthened fuselage. Navy designation of this fighter was UF-1 of which 18 were constructed. The Aeromarine liquid-cooled engine powered variant is shown here. (U.S. National Archives)

1 became known as FC-1 (Fighter, Curtiss, First Design, First Modification); F2C-1 (Fighter, Second Design, Curtiss, First Modification); F3C-1 (Fighter, Third Design, Curtiss, First Modification); F4C-1 (Fighter, Fourth Design, Curtiss, First Modification). This designating system, which revealed the type of aircraft plus manufacturer, remained in effect throughout World War II but was revised during the immediate postwar years into the present system.

Metal Structures Lighter Than Wood

Some of the experiments with the F4C-1 consisted of an all-metal framework with the conventional fabric covering. Surprisingly, the metal construction proved to be one half the weight of the original wood which improved speed, maneuverability, payload, range and altitude. This stimulated the use of metal construction for U.S. Navy aircraft. The FC-1/F4C-1 remained in service until 1926.

Vought VE-9

The Chance Vought Corporation of Long Island City, N.Y. had continued design development on the VE-7 to produce a fighter plane acceptable to the U.S. Navy and this became the VE-9. The craft had a more rounded fuselage and was strengthened as necessary for catapult launching and arresting hook installation. The U.S. Navy ordered 18 of the UF-1 as it was officially known. Vought had been assigned the letter U; therefore, the designation code read "Vought-Fighter - First Design." There was a delay in delivery caused by a conversion from the Aeromarine water-cooled engine to the Lawrence J-1 air-cooled engine. Although the UF-1 was reliable and rugged its speed was insufficient for the fighter role and; therefore, it was soon redesignated to a UO-1 or Vought, Observation - One. The craft performed so well in its new task that 141 were procured by the U.S. Navy and these remained in service until 1927.

The Vought UF-1 was too slow for a fighter so it was redesignated to UO-1 for observation duties. The UO-1 shown here is negotiating an arrested landing on USS Langley. Observe the cloth markers suspended from the elevated arresting cables. (Vought Aircraft Company, Courtesy Paul Bower)

The liquid-cooled engines in the Vought UF-1 and UO-1 were replaced with Lawrence J-1 air-cooled radial engines. This UO-1 has been so fitted. Observe the arresting hook. (Vought Aircraft Company, Courtesy Paul Bower)

Douglas DT-1

In addition to, but not secondary to fighters, the U.S. Navy stimulated the development of torpedo bombers. One of the first American torpedo bombers was the Douglas DT-1 (Douglas Torpedo-One). The craft was based upon the successful Douglas commercial Cloudster design and three prototypes were ordered by the Navy in 1921. This was the first military plane design constructed by Douglas and went through a series of evolutionary changes from DT- through DT-6 in both landplane and seaplane configuration as well as air-cooled engine tests.

DT-1 Data

The DT-1 emerged as a single-seater, as was the British Sopwith Cuckoo; however, the U.S. Navy insisted upon a two-seater so all

The first Douglas military design was the DT-1 which was also one of the first U.S. Navy torpedo-bombers. As with the Sopwith Cuckoo, the DT-1 was a single-seater; however, the U.S. Navy insisted upon a two-seater and all subsequent variants had a crew of two. (McDonnell Douglas, Courtesy Hubert K. Gagos)

ubsequent modifications had a crew of two. Thirty years were to ass before the single-seater torpedo bomber concept would be accepted by the U.S. Navy.

The 50 foot equal-span biplane wings were of the manually olded type. Fuselage length of the DT-4 was 34 feet 5 inches and eight was 13 feet-5 inches. Takeoff weight was 6,989 pounds without the 1,835 pound torpedo. The TD-4 was powered with the famous Liberty 400 horsepower water-cooled engine which propelled his big plane to a maximum speed of 108 miles per hour. Service eiling was 11,075 feet and combat range was 240 miles.

The U.S. Navy procured over 60 DT variant airframes which emained in service until 1926.

Martin T2M-1/Curtiss SC-1

The successor to the Douglas DT series appeared in 1923 as the Martin T2M-1 torpedo bomber. Curtiss and the U.S. Navy collaborated in the design which was constructed by Glenn L. Martin Co. This three-place biplane was constructed in both landplane and seaplane configuration and was the first torpedo bomber designed by Curtiss, hence the sometimes designation of Curtiss SC-1 or Scout Curtiss-First Design; Scout being used for a variety of tasks. As was the practice in the early 1920s the production contract for aircraft went to the lowest bidder and the Martin Company price was less than the Curtiss bid.

Curtiss delivered six SC-1 landplane and two SC-2 seaplane prototypes while Martin's production contract included 35 landplanes and 40 seaplanes.

SC-1 Data

Powered by the 585 horsepower Wright T-3 water-cooled engine the 8,310 pound biplane attained a maximum speed of 100 miles per hour. Service ceiling was 7,950 feet and combat range 403 miles. The lower wing had a span of 56 feet which was greater than the upper wing as in the Curtiss TS-1 fighter. Length was 38 feet - 5 inches and height was 15 feet - 3 inches. Crew consisted of the pilot, torpedo man, and gunner. Production deliveries were completed in January 1926.

U.S. NAVAL AVIATION DEFINED

After countless meetings and voluminous reports U.S. Army and Navy officials mutually agreed upon a policy for the role of naval aviation. This was confirmed in General Order No. 132 of July 7, 1924 which stated that naval aircraft would operate from carriers or from shore bases in cooperation with the Fleet as an integral arm of the Fleet; for attacks on enemy aircraft, warships, and submarines; for overwater scouting; for attacks on enemy shore installations; to protect coastal sea communications; in cooperation with the Army against enemy ships attacking the coast. By defining the role of naval aviation this order not only eliminated interservice bickering but confirmed the role of carrier-based aircraft.

Lampert Report

The two battle cruiser conversions that Commander Kenneth Whiting envisioned at the Washington Conference were launched seven months apart in 1925, but it was to require two more years before

USS Lexington and USS Saratoga were ready for commissioning. Also in 1925, USS Langley participated for the first time in the U.S. Navy annual war games. This triple U.S. carrier event stimulated intense interest in the new type warships which brought about changes in the procurement of U.S. military aircraft following the Lampert Report. This report was prepared by a special Congressional Committee to "Make Inquiry Into the Operation of the United States Air Services" which was chaired by Congressman Florian Lampert. The old system of awarding contracts to the low bidder was abolished. The U.S. Army and Navy were encouraged to survey and condemn useless equipment and cooperate with each other in the purchase of new equipment. They were also to embark upon a new five-year program for which not less than 10 million dollars was to be spent annually on aviation by each service. It is interesting to note that in the early 1920s aircraft were purchased in ones and twos; however, now in the late 1920s they were procured in lots of tens and twenties, proving that the expansion and efficiency of any military service is directly proportional to the willingness of its government to provide sufficient funds.

Aircraft Armament Stagnation

U.S. naval aviation was on the move and the next decade would witness the change from water-cooled inline engines to air-cooled radials and the evolution of biplane to monoplane. There was one important item that did not improve in this decade of progress; aircraft armament. Despite the fact that although the two cowl-mounted machine guns were the standard aircraft armament during the later years of World War I individual pilots, on their own initiative, satisfactorily increased the offensive armament of their airplanes. German Ace Max Immelmann had installed three machine guns on his Fokker E IV while French Ace Georges Guynemer scored victories with a 20 millimeter cannon that he had mounted in his Spad. Despite these proven experiments in increased fire power, two machine guns remained the standard aircraft offensive armament, synchronized to fire through the propeller arc. The U.S. Army and Navy standardized the installation of one .50 inch caliber machine gun and one .30 inch caliber machine gun which had an advantage over the other nations because only the U.S. used the .50 inch caliber gun for aircraft.

U.S. NAVAL AVIATION BOOMS

The Lampert Report enabled the Navy to discard the obsolete Curtiss TS-1 (FC-1) and converted Vought VE-7. Curtiss had been the Navy's favorite aircraft supplier until Boeing came upon the scene. There already was great rivalry between Curtiss and Boeing with designs for the U.S. Army Air Corps. Rear Admiral William A. Moffett, Chief of the U.S.N. Bureau of Aeronautics, had been watching the Army evaluation of the Curtiss and Boeing fighter plane prototypes with the thought of combining the Army and Navy procurement into a single contract, and thereby reduce the unit price and standardize the aircraft of both services. Navy pilots were permitted to fly both contenders to evaluate their applicability to naval requirements and, although the Boeing had a slight advantage over the Curtiss in maneuverability, Navy orders were placed for both machines, as had the U.S. Army, in order to encourage further development of the designs.

First U.S. Production Carrier-Based Fighters

Boeing received a Navy contract in December 1924 for 14 FB-1 fighters which were similar to the Army's PW-9. Most of the FB-1 fighters were fitted with arresting gear for operation from *USS Langley* with VF-1B and VF-6B and became the FB-2. The largest production order was for 27 Boeing FB-5 fighters which served on *USS Lexington* in VF-3B fighter squadron.

Curtiss was awarded a Navy contract for nine F6C-1 and F6C-2 fighters in March 1925. These were similar to the P-1 ordered by the U.S. Army. Production orders for 35 Curtiss F6C-3 fighters followed. The F6C designs were the first planes to bear the famous Hawk name and were the progenitors of the Curtiss Hawk line of classic fighters.

Outwardly the Curtiss and Boeing fighters appear identical at first glance; tapered wing biplanes, both powered by a Curtiss 12-cylinder Vee water-cooled engine with chin radiator, but closer inspection reveals subtle differences. Dimensions and performance were also extremely close as shown by this comparison between the Boeing FB-1 and Curtiss F6C-2:

	Curtiss F6C-2	Boeing FB-1
Wingspan:	31 feet, 7 inches	32 feet, 0 inches
Length:	22 feet, 6 inches	23 feet, 6 inches
Height:	10 feet, 11 inches	8 feet, 9 inches
Weight:	2,838 pounds	2,944 pounds
Max Speed:	159 mph	167 mph
Ceiling:	22,700 feet	21,200 feet
Range:	330 miles	325 miles
Engine:	435 horsepower	Engine: 440 horsepower
	Curtiss V-1150-3	Curtiss D-12-D

The range shown could be increased with an underbelly auxiliary fuel tank. The Curtiss engines were water-cooled inline engines and were the last of the type used by the U.S. Navy. Most later U.S. Naval aircraft would be fitted with air-cooled radial engines. The F6C design was one of the first U.S. planes to be fitted with the new landing gear oleo shock absorbers.

As the first production carrier-based fighters flown by both the U.S. Army and the U.S. Navy the FB and F6C set the pace for the immortal naval fighters of the 1930s. They were responsible not only for advancements in design but in tactics as well. One example of this took place in October of 1926 during routine maneuvers in the Pacific. As the Fleet neared the coast it received a wireless message that Navy planes would make a mock attack on the ships and the Pacific Fleet must prepare to defend itself. The exact time of the attack was stated in the message. F6C-2 Hawks of VF-2 took off from San Diego and climbed to 12,000 feet. At the prescribed time Commander F.D. Wagner led the Hawks down to the ships in an almost vertical dive and achieved complete surprise. The ships' officers and crews expected a serene horizontal bombing run and not a swift hit-and-run dive bombing attack. The admiral later admitted that defense was impossible and the attack was an unqualified success. This was not really an innovation because dive bombing had been used previously; however, U.S. naval pilots and aircraft had honed the technique to a fine edge which was to pay dividends in little more than a decade later.

Enter Pratt & Whitney

Frederick Brant Rentschler had left his post as president of the Wright Aeronautical Corporation in 1924 and formed his own company, Pratt & Whitney, in Hartford, Connecticut. In a frame garage belonging to the new company, George Mead and Andrew van Dean Willgoos combined their mechanical talent and engineering genius to create a remarkable new air-cooled radial engine, the Pratt & Whitney Wasp. Already convinced of the air-cooled radial's superior performance the Bureau of Aeronautics encouraged Curtiss and Boeing to develop new fighters around the Wasp engine. The new engine was compared to a very efficient Wright engine of 325 horsepower and, weighing the same as the Wright engine, the Wasp produced 400 horsepower with virtually the same fuel consumption.

The first production Wasp engine was tested in a Curtiss F6C airframe designated F6C-4 and the Navy ordered 31 to serve on *USS Langley*. Lieutenant Ralph Ofstie had flown this plane across the continent to San Diego and Seattle; then returned to Washington, D.C. via Salt Lake City, a distance of 7,000 miles. The new engine reaffirmed the Navy's decision to place a production order

The Boeing FB-1 was the first Boeing aircraft purchased by the U.S. Navy and was the first of many classic Boeing fighters to follow. This Marine Corps FB-1 was one of 14 ordered in December 1924. Observe the twisted steel propeller. (The Boeing Company, Courtesy Gordon S. Williams)

The Curtiss F6C Series of fighters were the first to bear the name Hawk. The U.S. Navy bought the F6C-2 in March 1925. Note the flat steel propeller twisted into shape. (Curtiss Aeroplane and Motor Co., Courtesy George Page)

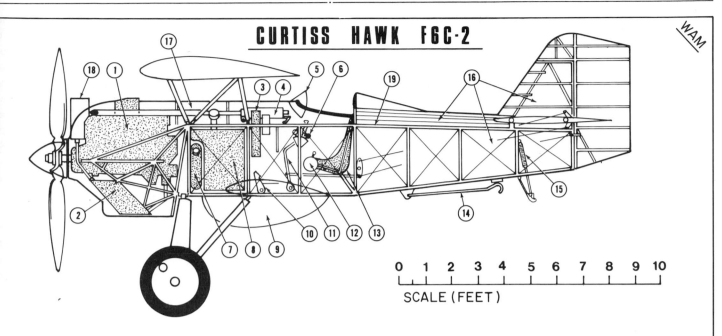

CURTISS HAWK F6C-2

WAM

SCALE (FEET) 0 1 2 3 4 5 6 7 8 9 10

① LIQUID COOLED ENGINE
② RADIATOR
③ AMMUNITION CASE
④ MACHINE GUNS
⑤ WINDSHIELD
⑥ ENGINE CONTROLS

⑦ LUB. OIL TANK
⑧ MAIN FUEL TANK
⑨ LONG RANGE TANK
⑩ RUDDER PEDALS
⑪ CONTROL STICK
⑫ STABILIZER ADJUSTMENT

⑬ ALUMINUM SEAT
⑭ ARRESTING HOOK
⑮ TAILSKID SHOCK SPRING
⑯ FABRIC COVERING
⑰ METAL COVERING
⑱ ENGINE COOLANT TANK
⑲ WELDED STEEL TUBING

---

with Pratt & Whitney. By early 1927 Pratt & Whitney was producing Wasps at the rate of 15 each month and Curtiss, Vought and Boeing were busy designing carrier planes for this engine.

First Vought Corsair

The first Navy plane designed around the Wasp engine was the Vought 02U observation series first produced in 1927. Over 250

This Curtiss F6C-4 was the first U.S. Navy plane to be powered by the new Pratt and Whitney air-cooled radial engine. The U.S. Navy ordered 31 to serve on USS Langley. Note the unusual location of the star insignia on the underside of the upper wing. (Official U.S. Navy Photograph, News Photo Division)

were procured in seaplane and landplane configuration. The single float Vought seaplanes became standard Navy equipment for observation squadrons VO-3B, VO-4B, and VO-5B which provided aircraft for the catapults of battleship divisions. The landplane configured Voughts were operated from *USS Langley* and later from *USS Saratoga* and other carriers as well.

The Vought 02U-1 through 02U-4 were the first to carry the famous Corsair name. They were also among the first U.S. Navy planes to use an all-steel tubing fuselage structure. The fuel tanks were cheek type tanks, pioneered on previous Vought designs, which flanked the pilot's cockpit forming the fuselage sides.

Corsair Data

The 3,635 pounds gross weight Corsair attained 150 miles per hour at sea level with the 450 horsepower P & W Wasp R-1340-88 engine. The 02U-1 could climb to 5,000 feet in 3.6 minutes. Service ceiling was 18,700 feet and combat range 608 miles.

Wingspan was 34 feet-6 inches and length was 24 feet-6 inches. Height was 10 feet-1 inch and wing area was 320 square feet.

Armament was one forward-firing and two flexible mounted .30 inch caliber machine guns plus assorted bombs carried under

The first U.S. Navy plane designed to use the Pratt and Whitney Wasp engine was the Vought 02U-1 observation two-seater. Note the uncowled engines. This was also the first plane to carry the Corsair sobriquet. These craft were assigned to USS Saratoga. Four world speed and altitude records were established by 02U-1 aircraft. (Ling Temco Vought, Courtesy Arthur L. Schoeni)

Vought 03U Corsairs were an improvement over the 02U design and were redesignated SU as scouts, serving aboard USS Lexington and USS Saratoga. The Vought SU-2 is shown here. Note the Townend ring cowling around the engine. (See Arrow). Also observe the gunner in the rear cockpit facing aft and the single machine gun at rest in a vertical position. (See Arrows). (Vought Aircraft Company, Courtesy Paul Bower)

the lower wing. Marine Squadron VO-7M flew four Corsairs in action against rebel strongholds in Nicaragua which first earned the Corsair public acclaim.

First Curtiss Helldiver

The U.S. Marine Corps needed a light attack plane to replace the aging World War I De Havilland DH-4B and the Navy was interested in a high performance two-seat fighter and dive bomber. Optimistically, the Bureau of Aeronautics expected one design to fulfill all the tactical roles.

As Assistant Chief Engineer of the Curtiss Aeroplane and Motor Co. Inc. Rex Beisel had developed the Hawk F6C-2 fighter and he now proceeded to lead his team to meet the U.S. Navy's requirement for a two-seat fighter/dive bomber as Chief Engineer.

In 1927 Curtiss proposed a design based on its Army 0-1 observation and A-3 attack Falcon series, using the P & W Wasp engine instead of the original water-cooled engines. The Curtiss XF8C-1 with its 38 foot wingspan did not satisfy the fighter requirement. It was redesignated OC-1 and OC-2 and assigned to land-based Marine observation squadrons. The XF8C-2 was a new design with six foot shorter biplane wings and more suited as a fighter being more compact and of cleaner design. This plane started the famous line of Helldivers; an expression which became a household word in the 1930s, synonymous with dive bomber which also caught America's imagination. Movie theatres throughout the U.S. featured a rash of films about dive bombers in general and Helldivers in particular with one film actually entitled "Helldivers." The XF8C-2 had exceptional diving qualities; however, the plane crashed during terminal velocity power dive tests. Convinced of the capabili-

Chance Vought, who had been designing naval aircraft since 1914, designed the successful VE-7 and went on to develop the first Vought Corsair 02U and 03U biplanes. The company that bears his name has produced some of the most outstanding and innovative naval combat aircraft of all time. We will meet some of these achievements in the following chapters. (Vought Aircraft Company, Courtesy Paul Bower)

ies of the Helldiver design, the Navy ordered 25 F8C-4 models with an improved Wasp engine. These equipped VF-1 "High Hat" Squadron. Another order followed for 65 F8C-5 models using the Pratt & Whitney Wasp R-1340-4 engine. This model was fitted with a collector ring exhaust pipe and improved cooling louvers plus a Townend ring cowling around the engine, which improved cooling and streamlining.

Helldiver Data

Manufactured by the Curtiss Aeroplane and Motor Co., Inc. of Buffalo, N.Y., the F8C-5 was powered with a 450 horsepower Wasp engine which propelled the 4,020 pound loaded aircraft to a top speed of 146 miles per hour at sea level. Cruising speed was 110 miles per hour at which speed the range was 720 miles. The Helldiver could climb to 5,000 feet in 5.5 minutes and had a service ceiling of 16,250 feet.

Wingspan was 32 feet with an overall length of 25 feet-7 inches. Height was 10 feet-3 inches. Wing area was 308 square feet.

Offensive armament was two fixed .30 inch caliber Browning machine guns located in the upper wing center section, firing outside of the propeller arc. One 500 pound bomb was carried under the fuselage or, alternatively, two 116 pound bombs were carried under each lower wing panel. Two .30 inch caliber Lewis machine guns were mounted on a moveable Scarff mount in the rear cockpit for defense against enemy fighters.

As had been done on the Vought Corsair, the Helldiver fuel tanks were made to form the fuselage sides in way of the cockpits.

The Helldiver suffered from the same problems of most multi-purpose aircraft designs because it could not perform all the tasks expected of it with perfection. It failed in its fighter role because the two-seat fighter concept was envisioned as a sort of mixed formation with single-seat fighters in a mutual defense system and the Helldiver could not match the speed of the single-seaters. This meant reducing the speed of the entire formation to accommodate the slower Curtiss which was intolerable. The result was a redesignation to eliminate the fighter role and convert to observation craft, thereby becoming 02C-1. Duties became observation and scouting plus dive

bombing and the Curtiss 02C-1 Helldiver proved so satisfactory in this role that 30 more were ordered for Navy and Marine squadrons. The idea of two-seater fighters surfaced repeatedly in the minds of the world's naval air tacticians only to meet with inevitable failure. The famous Helldiver remained in service until 1937.

The author worked on a Curtiss 02C Helldiver while attending Aviation school and can attest to its rugged construction.

Twin Engine Carrier-Based Aircraft

Naval aviation history was made in 1927 when a twin-engine airplane operated from an aircraft carrier for the first time. Looking for better performance than could be provided by existing U.S. Navy torpedo-bombers, the Bureau of Aeronautics designed a large twin-engine biplane torpedo-bomber. The prototype was constructed by the Naval Aircraft Factory and Douglas Aircraft Company of Santa Monica, California was given a contract for three more aircraft which were designated T2D-1.

The planes were issued to Torpedo Squadron VT-2 assigned to *USS Langley* on May 25, 1927 and it was during this time that the T2D-1 was successfully operated from the carrier.

T2D-1 Data

Powered by two 525 horsepower Wright R-1750 air-cooled radial engines the 10,890 pounds gross weight plane attained a maximum speed of 124 miles per hour at sea level and could climb to 5,000 feet in 5 minutes. Service ceiling was 13,830 feet and combat range was 422 miles.

The two equal wings spanned 57 feet and length was 45 feet. Height was 14 feet-8 inches and wing area was 886 square feet.

Crew comprised a pilot and two gunners with one of the gunners also acting as a copilot. One 1,618 pound torpedo or bomb could be carried externally under the fuselage. Defensive armament consisted of two flexible Scarff mounted .30 inch caliber machine guns, one forward and one aft.

Interservice Rivalry

Nine more planes were ordered from Douglas in late 1927, how-

The Curtiss F8C Helldiver was the first military plane to capture America's imagination and the first to exploit dive bombing. The prototype XF8C-4 is shown here. Later models were designated 02C-1. The F8C-4 served in VF-1B aboard Saratoga. (U.S. National Archives)

A twin-engine plane first flew from a carrier when a Douglas T2D-1 torpedo-bomber flew from USS Langley in 1927. U.S. Army Air Corps' objections forced the U.S. Navy to convert the twin-engine planes into seaplanes and operate them as patrol-bombers! (McDonnell Douglas, Courtesy Hubert K. Gagos)

With its arresting hook extended, a Martin T4M-1 torpedo-bomber approaches USS Saratoga (CV-3) preparatory to landing. Photo was taken from a companion T4M-1 in 1932. Note the gunner's cockpit located well aft of the pilot and navigator cockpits to give the gunner a better arc of fire. (U.S. National Archives)

ever, by the time they were delivered interservice rivalry had erupted. The U.S. Army Air Corps strongly objected to the Navy operation of large carrier-based bombers as infringing on the Army's jurisdiction. This resulted in converting the T2D-1's into twin float seaplanes for patrol bomber use and they were assigned to Patrol Squadron VP-1 at Pearl Harbor. An additional 18 were procured from Douglas with the designation P2D-1. These were powered by 575 horsepower Wright R-1820 engines and served with Patrol Squadron VP-3 in the Panama Canal Zone until 1937.

Despite its short carrier operations life, the T2D-1 proved that large heavy aircraft can be operated even from small-decked, slow speed carriers.

Last U.S. Navy Biplane Torpedo-Bomber

The U.S. Navy seemed to be in a perpetual search for the ideal torpedo-bomber in the mid-1920s. In view of this situation the Glenn L. Martin Company of Cleveland, Ohio drew from its experience in building the Navy/Curtiss designed SC-1 torpedo-bombers in 1925 and offered a new version of this plane to the Navy. Orders for 25 Martin T3M-1 and 100 T3M-2 water-cooled engine powered torpedo-bombers were placed by the Navy. Martin and the

Naval Aircraft Factory modified a T3M-2 into an XT3M-3 which included a P & W air-cooled radial engine. The Navy ordered 102 of this modification in 1927 as the Martin T4M-1.

T4M-1 Data

This 8,071 pounds gross weight torpedo-bomber attained a top speed of 114 miles per hour, powered by the 525 horsepower Pratt & Whitney R-1690-24 Hornet air-cooled radial engine. Combat range at the 98 miles per hour cruising speed was 363 miles. The T4M-1 required 14 minutes to reach 5,000 feet and its service ceiling was 10,150 feet.

Crew consisted of the pilot, torpedo man/bombardier, and gunner with a single flexible mounted .30 inch caliber machine gun.

Assigned Units

The Martin T4M-1 was issued to torpedo squadrons VT-1B and VT-2B in time to serve on *USS Lexington* and *USS Saratoga* respectively. The T4M-1 was the last in an era of U.S. Navy biplane torpedo-bombers for the all-metal monoplanes would not be long in coming.

LARGE, HIGH-SPEED U.S. CARRIERS

The world's largest aircraft carriers were commissioned in late autumn of 1927; *USS Lexington* (CV-2) on December 14 at Bethlehem Steel shipyard and *USS Saratoga* (CV-3) on November 16 at New York Shipbuilding in Camden, NJ. These beautiful ships remained the largest carriers for a decade and a half into World War II. It will be recalled that two U.S. battle cruisers under construction were selected for conversion to aircraft carriers at the Washington Naval and Disarmament Conference of 1921-22 where Commander Whiting made the suggestion. Now, conversions were a reality and the U.S. Navy had its first truly operational aircraft carriers.

Lexington Class Data

The battle cruiser hull, including armor, remained virtually unchanged. The existing armor consisted of a belt plate just below the waterline nine feet deep, about 600 feet long and with an average thickness of six inches. An armored deck over the magazines was composed of two layers of Special Treatment Steel, two inches thick. Watertight bulkheads were five to seven inches thick. An enormous Hangar measuring 450 feet long, 70 feet wide, and 21 feet high was

erected over the hull and the largest Flight Deck yet constructed was installed above the Hangar. The Flight Deck was planked with teak and measured 106 x 888 feet. A 105 foot aircraft maintenance shop was erected just aft of the Hangar. Immediately below the maintenance shop was a cavernous 120 foot hold for disassembled aircraft and spare parts. Two large centerline aircraft elevators were installed; one adjacent to the Navigating Bridge structure and the other adjacent to the smokestack structure. The *Lexington* class carriers had one feature which was popular in carriers of the Royal Navy but was not to appear on American carriers again until the post-World War II years; the shell of the ship was continued up to the Flight Deck and flared at the bow to fair into it. The island was separated into two separate components; the smokestack assembly and the Navigation Bridge structure. The smokestack supported several operating enclosures including flight control; therefore, a light catwalk connected the stack with the Bridge structure at the Wheelhouse level.

Propulsion machinery was General Electric steam turbine electric drive, which operating principal was similar to but more complex than *USS Langley*. Sixteen boilers generated steam at 295 pounds per square inch pressure. Eight propulsion electric motors

USS Lexington (CV-2) and USS Saratoga (CV-3) were the largest aircraft carriers in the world for almost two decades. USS Saratoga could be distinguished from Lexington by the wide vertical black band on the side of the stack. Planes on deck can be identified as Martin T4M-1, Vought Corsair, Curtiss F6C, and Boeing F2B. Photo taken in 1930 at San Francisco Bay. (Official U.S. Navy Photograph, News Photo Division)

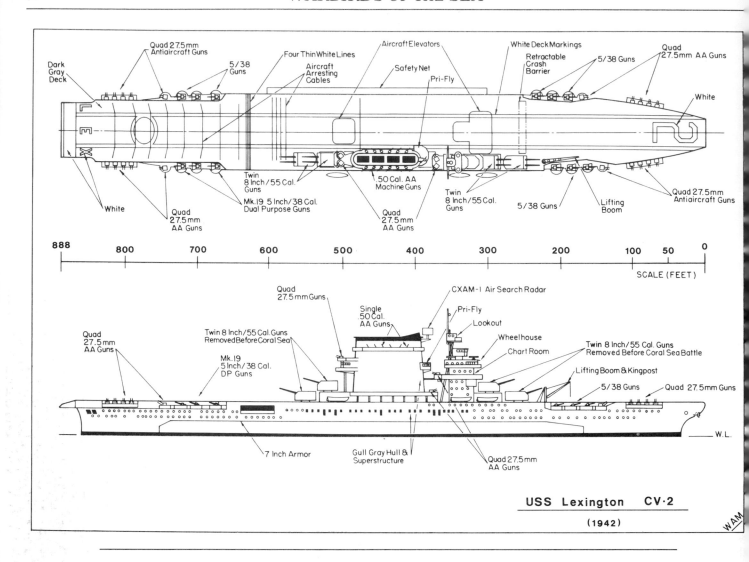

Dark Gray Deck

Quad 27.5mm Antiaircraft Guns

5/38 Guns

Four Thin White Lines

Aircraft Arresting Cables

Aircraft Elevators

Safety Net

Pri-Fly

White Deck Markings

Retractable Crash Barrier

5/38 Guns

Quad 27.5mm AA Guns

White

White

Quad 27.5mm AA Guns

Twin 8 Inch/55 Cal. Guns

Mk.19 5 Inch/38 Cal. Dual Purpose Guns

.50 Cal. AA Machine Guns

Quad 27.5mm AA Guns

Twin 8 Inch/55 Cal. Guns

5/38 Guns

Lifting Boom

Quad 27.5mm Antiaircraft Guns

888　800　700　600　500　400　300　200　100　50　0

SCALE (FEET)

Quad 27.5mm AA Guns

Twin 8 Inch/55 Cal. Guns Removed Before Coral Sea

Mk.19 5 Inch/38 Cal. DP Guns

Quad 27.5mm Guns

Single .50 Cal. AA Guns

CXAM-1 Air Search Radar

Pri-Fly

Lookout

Wheelhouse

Chart Room

Twin 8 Inch/55 Cal. Guns Removed Before Coral Sea Battle

Lifting Boom & Kingpost

5/38 Guns

Quad 27.5mm Guns

W.L.

7 Inch Armor

Gull Gray Hull & Superstructure

Quad 27.5mm AA Guns

USS Lexington　CV·2

(1942)

WAM

This overhead photograph of USS Lexington shows clearly the Flight Deck contours and the turreted twin 8 inch guns fore and aft of the smokestack. Planes on deck are Vought SBU-1. (Official U.S. Navy Photograph, Courtesy Vought Aircraft Company)

Vought 02U Corsairs of VS-2 are being arranged at the bow of USS Lexington. Note the wooden planked deck and the safety net at the edge of the deck. (Official U.S. Navy Photograph, Courtesy Ling Temco Vought)

A line up of Boeing F2B fighters warms its engines prior to takeoff from USS Saratoga in 1928. Observe the Pri-Fly (Primary Flight Control) on the forward end of the huge smokestack. Note the tapered wings on the F2B. (The Boeing Company, Courtesy Gordon S. Williams)

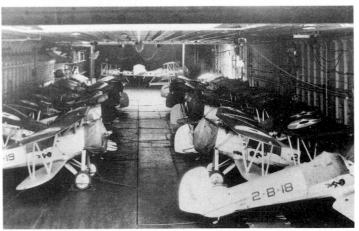

Boeing F3B fighters in the Hangar of USS Lexington (CV-2). Note the cage under the wheels to prevent the planes from rolling in rough weather. Also observe the engine and cockpit covers. (The Boeing Company, Courtesy Gordon S.Williams)

of 22,500 horsepower each were geared two to each of the four propeller shafts, turning at 317 revolutions per minute. The propulsion motors could be controlled from the Navigating Bridge as well as from the engine room control station. The 180,000 shaft horsepower powerplant was the most powerful of any ship previously built. During full power runs during the trials 209,000 shaft horsepower was actually recorded. Fuel consumption was 2,000 tons per day at full power.

The boilers were located eight on each side of the engine rooms and the uptakes were trunked together on each side. Those on the port side were led across the ship under the Hangar Deck and then all uptakes were led into an enormous smokestack which terminated 80 feet above the Flight Deck. This exceptional height was selected to eliminate smoke drift across the Flight Deck; however, the stack was shortened by 10 feet soon after entering service.

The battle cruisers, if completed, would have been 43,000 tonners, however,the elimination of the main battery of eight 16 inch guns and other items reduced the tonnage to 38,500 despite the addition of the Flight Deck. The hull length at the waterline was 850 feet and beam 104 feet-7 inches. Mean draft was 27 feet-6 inches and deep load draft was 32 feet-6 inches. Speed at 180,000 shaft horsepower was a very respectable 33.25 knots. Range was 10,000 miles at 15 knots. Complement was from 2,000 to 2,500 operating crew and officers.

Lexington Class Aircraft Complement
A total of 80 aircraft could be accommodated which capacity was not to be matched by any other carrier for more than a decade. Some of the earlier aircraft which served on the *Lexington* class aircraft carriers were Curtiss F6C, Boeing FB, Vought 02U, and Martin T4M.

Lexington Class Armament
On board armament was quite powerful because it was assumed that the carriers must be able to defend against attacking cruisers and torpedo boats in the event that no aircraft were available. Four 8 inch guns in twin turrets were mounted at each end of the Flight Deck superstructure (smokestack and Navigating Bridge structure). Twelve 5 inch guns were single-mounted along the sides in groups of three within four Flight Deck recesses. The original design included provision for torpedo tubes as well; however, these were never installed.

In operation, as with *HMS Hermes*, the *Lexington* class carriers were forced to retain 1,100 tons of fuel in the port side tanks as ballast in order to keep the ships floating on an even keel due to the tremendous weight of the offset island. The ships were unable to use this fuel as it was classified as permanent ballast. The eight 8 inch guns further aggravated this unbalanced condition. A starboard side blister was installed on *Saratoga* in 1942 to correct the imbalance by virtue of the added buoyancy on the starboard side created by the blister. *Saratoga* could then use the fuel oil ballast.

The first takeoff from *USS Lexington* was made by Lieutenant A.M. Pride on January 5, 1938 and the first takeoff from *USS Saratoga* was made by Commander Marc A. Mitscher on January 11, 1938. Both flights were made in the Vought UO-1.

USS Lexington and *USS Saratoga* were of extremely advanced design which features would not be duplicated by future U.S. Navy carriers for another two decades.

USS Lexington and *USS Saratoga* were the supercarriers of their day and the cost of 45 million dollars each was a well-spent investment in the security of the U.S. An example of their tremendous power was illustrated during the winter of 1929-30 when *USS Lexington*'s generators supplied the entire city of Tacoma, Washington with electricity for a month because a severe drought had caused the city's hydroelectric plant to fail.

New U.S. Carrier Operation Strategy
The new carriers were so capacious and extremely fast that they forced a change in carrier operations strategy. Having so many more aircraft on board resulted in the natural desire to apply them for maximum effect which resulted in the concept of mass strikes and revised flight deck procedures.

The comparatively small Royal Navy and Imperial Japanese Navy carrier Flight Decks had little room for aircraft parking during flight operations; therefore,each plane took off soon after the elevator brought it to the Flight Deck. As each plane took off it circled in a rendezvous area and waited for the rest of the squadron. Upon returning from the mission each plane was struck down to the Hangar Deck by the elevator as soon as the plane landed, meanwhile the other members of the squadron waited their turn to land and be struck down. A considerable amount of fuel was consumed with this method which reduced the effective combat range of the squadron.

A massive strike force would consume two to four times the amount of fuel lost by a small force because the wait after takeoff and before landing would be much longer. The U.S. Navy revised the deck handling as well as the takeoff and landing system by first assembling the entire strike force on the aft end of the flight deck and then having it take off as rapidly as possible. After the mission all aircraft would land in rapid succession and quickly taxi to the forward end of the flight deck. Efficient catapults, arresting gear and safety barriers were mandatory with this new operating procedure. After the entire force had landed it would be struck down. This system not only extended the range of the strike force but enabled it to apply the important element of surprise to most strikes by getting all aircraft into the air quickly.

Langley Re-Rated
Now that the huge *Lexington* class carriers were in service the Navy's original carrier, having served her purpose, was re-rated as an aircraft transport. *USS Langley* served in this capacity into World War II.

With carriers fast enough to operate as an integral part of the fleet, aircraft became recognized as both an offensive and defensive weapon. No longer were they merely the eyes of the fleet. To meet the increasing needs of taking aircraft to sea, new planes were designed and procured, new squadrons formed and revolutionary tactics formulated. Naval Aviation had outgrown its initial role and was bursting with new and varied aircraft.

CLASSIC BOEING BIPLANE FIGHTERS
Following the success of its FB series of fighters and realizing that Curtiss was continuing the development of its Hawk series, the Boeing Airplane Company of Seattle, Washington embarked on a concentrated program to design carrier-based fighters around the P & W Wasp engine. The first product was a refined version of the FB with rounded fuselage and horizontal tail,and powered by an uncowled Wasp radial engine. A production order for 32 Boeing F2B-1 fighters was received in late 1926 and these were issued to squadrons VF-1B in late 1927 and VF-6B in mid-1928.

Boeing F3B-1
Only a few months after the F2B-1 was accepted by the Navy, Boeing introduced its F3B-1. After initial teething troubles the plane was considerably modified and emerged as a refreshingly new design. Constant chord wings had been fitted; the upper wing with 6.5 degrees of sweepback. An innovation that was continued on numerous Boeing designs began with the F3B-1; corrugated dural sheet semi-monocoque tail surfaces and control surfaces. This new

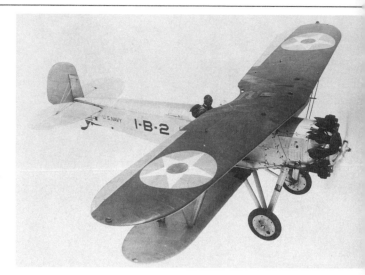

The F3B-1 was the first Boeing fighter with constant chord wings. The corrugated tail surfaces were continued on all descendants of the F3B which became classics in the 1930s. (The Boeing Company, Courtesy Marilyn A. Phipps)

design was first flown on February 3, 1928 and the U.S. Navy ordered 74 with deliveries beginning in August.

Squadrons receiving the Boeing F3B-1 included VB-2B on *Saratoga*, and VF-3B and VB-1B on *Lexington*. The plane served in front line squadrons until 1932.

F3B-1 Data
The 2,945 pounds gross weight Boeing F3B-1 attained a maximum speed of 157 miles per hour when powered with the 425 horse power Pratt & Whitney R-1340-80 Wasp air-cooled nine cylinder radial engine. Initial climb was 2,020 feet per minute and service ceiling was 21,500 feet. Range was 340 miles at 131 miles per hour. Wingspan was 33 feet and length was 24 feet, 10 inches. Height was 9 feet, 2 inches and wing area was 275 square feet.

Boeing F4B-1
The Boeing F3B-1 became a stepping stone to a series of fighter designs which are considered classics of the 1930s. The Boeing Airplane Company was greatly encouraged by U.S. Navy purchases and made a dedicated effort to capture the market for fighters. The Curtiss Aeroplane and Motor Co. Inc. was Boeing's only serious competitor; therefore, Boeing initiated a company private design project which emerged as Models 83 and 89 in the summer of 1928. The difference in the two prototypes was a rack for a 500 pound bomb installed under the fuselage of the Model 89 taking advantage of its split axle landing gear. Test flights of the Model 83 produced a top speed of 168.8 miles per hour and a rate of climb of 2,920 feet per minute on June 25.

The plane proved such an outstanding performer at the Los Angeles National Air Races that the U.S. Navy accepted delivery at the Air Races as the XF4B-1. Although enthusiastic about the new Boeing, the Navy failed to place a production order. The U.S. Army Air Corps was so impressed that General James E. Fechet placed a verbal order at the Races and confirmation from Washington followed. The Army Boeing became the P-12 and was identical to the XF4B-1 except for the absence of the arresting hook and other special naval equipment.

The U.S. Navy ordered 27 F4B-1 fighters in August 1928 and the initial production aircraft was first flown on May 6, 1929. Production models had the split axle landing gear and bomb rack plus arresting hook. Fuselage construction was unconventional in that the structure consisted of square aluminum tubing bolted in place. Wings were constant chord with no sweepback and the customary upper wing cutout in way of the cockpit was absent. The tail surfaces and ailerons were fabricated from corrugated dural as was done on the F3B-1; wings were made as a one piece structure of spruce, mahogany, and ash. All framework was fabric covered.

F4B-1 Data

Powered by an uncowled 450 horsepower P & W R-1340-8 Wasp engine the F4B-1 attained a top speed of 176 miles per hour at 6,000 feet. The plane could climb to 5,000 feet in 2.9 minutes and service ceiling was 27,700 feet. Gross weight was 2,750 pounds. Range was 371 miles. Two .30 inch caliber machine guns were fitted by this time because the Navy had stopped using .50 caliber guns.

The Boeing F4B-1 was flown as a fighter/bomber by Squadrons VB-1B, VF-5g, and VF-2. A refined version of the F4B-1 was fitted with a Townend ring cowling, spreader bar axle, tailskid replaced with a full swivelling tail wheel and provision was made underwing for carrying four 116 pound bombs instead of the fuselage bomb. The Navy ordered 46 Boeing F4B-2's and they served in Squadrons VF-6B on *Saratoga*, and VF-5B on *Lexington*.

Boeing F4B-3

Boeing did not relax despite its successes and still another company private venture emerged as its Model 218. The U.S. Navy ordered 21 examples of this highly modified F4B-2, which was designated F4B-3, on April 23, 1931.

Although the Boeing F4B fighters did not require a catapult for takeoff with sufficient WOD, catapults were often used to study their advantage to get the entire strike force airborne as soon as possible. Here an F4B-3 is catapulted off the deck of a Lexington class carrier while another waits its turn in the foreground. Note the airborne F4B-3 that had been launched moments before (see arrow). (The Boeing Company, Courtesy Marilyn A. Phipps)

The wings of the F4B-3 were basically the same as the previous F4B designs; however, the fuselage was a radical departure from the standard construction practice of the period. It was a truss-braced duralumin covered semi-monocoque structure which means that, unlike the fabric covered structures, the metal covering of the new Boeing fuselage added considerable strength to the entire structure. The tail surfaces and ailerons were corrugated dural sheet as on previous Boeing fighters. Landing gear was of the spreader bar axle design. A distinctive feature of the F4B-3 was an unusually large headrest/turtle deck. The U.S. Army Air Corps also purchase this plane as the P-12E.

F4B-3 Data

A Townend ring-cowled 500 horsepower Pratt & Whitney R-1340-D Wasp engine gave the F4B-3 a top speed of 187 miles per hour, and the ceiling of 27,500 feet was a new experience for many Navy and Marine pilots.

Boeing F4B-4

The ultimate F4B series refinement was the F4B-4 which made its appearance as Boeing Model 235 in early 1932. The U.S. Navy liked what it saw and bought 92 in three separate contracts; one of

The jaunty Boeing F4B-4 fighter was a true classic of the 1930s. In order to save deck space on USS Ranger, aircraft were parked on outriggers as shown. Note the long range fuel tank under the belly and the large headrest which housed a life raft. (The Boeing Company, Courtesy Marilyn A. Phipps)

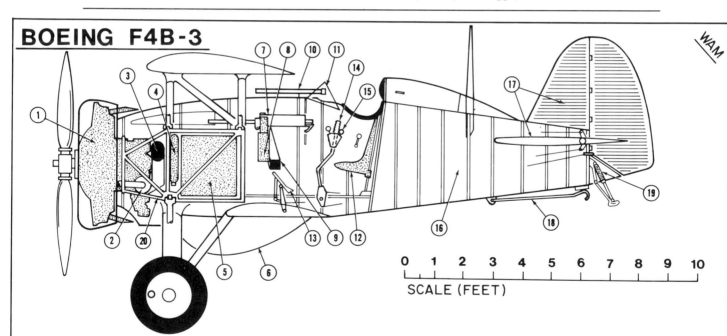

BOEING F4B-3

SCALE (FEET)
0 1 2 3 4 5 6 7 8 9 10

① RADIAL ENGINE

② CARBURETOR HEATER

③ CARBURETOR AIR INLET

④ LUB. OIL TANK

⑤ MAIN FUEL TANK

⑥ LONG RANGE FUEL TANK

⑦ MACHINE GUNS

⑧ AMMUNITION CASE

⑨ SPENT AMMO CHUTE

⑩ TELESCOPIC GUN SIGHT

⑪ WINDSHIELD

⑫ ALUMINUM SEAT

⑬ RUDDER PEDALS

⑭ CONTROL STICK

⑮ ENGINE CONTROLS

⑯ ALUMINUM COVERED FUSELAGE

⑰ CORRUGATED ALUMINUM TAIL

⑱ ARRESTING HOOK

⑲ TAILSKID SHOCK SPRING

⑳ WELDED TUBING STRUCTURE

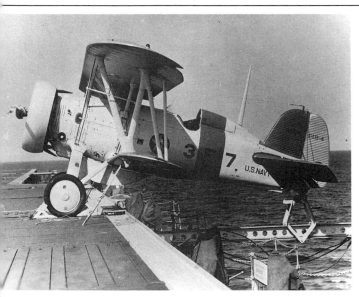

The Boeing F4B-4 featured an all-metal fuselage and tail surfaces. Wings were fabric covered. Observe the different outrigger design used on USS Ranger. This F4B-4 has an unusually tall antenna mast. (The Boeing Company, Courtesy Marilyn A. Phipps)

he largest orders for fighter planes thus far. The wings were greatly strengthened for dive bombing, and the headrest/turtle deck, which was even larger than the F4B-3, housed a life raft plus emergency and first aid supplies. The fin had also been enlarged from the F4B-3.

F4B-4 Data

The Boeing F4B-4 was powered by a 550 horsepower P & W R-1340-16 Wasp engine which produced a top speed of 188 miles per hour at 6,000 feet. Landing speed was 62.5 miles per hour. Climb to 5,000 feet required 2.7 minutes and service ceiling was 26,900 feet. Gross weight was 3,611 pounds and combat range was 370 miles. Range could be extended to over 500 miles with a 55 gallon auxiliary belly tank.

In addition to two .30 inch caliber machine guns, bomb racks were installed under the lower wing for two 116 pound bombs.

First production F4B-4's were delivered in July 1932 and the last of the type was delivered in February 1933. The F4B-4 equipped Marine Squadrons VF-9M and VF-10M, and Navy Squadrons VF-2, VF-3 and VF-6B on *Saratoga*, VF-8 and others.

The F4B-4 was a pilot's airplane. The craft was easy on the controls and always in control regardless of the situation. It was rugged and possessed unequalled all-around performance. Acceleration on takeoff was surprisingly good and the F4B-4 became airborne after a short run. It was an excellent dive bomber and equipped many bombing squadrons.

Boeing Fighter Production

Between the years 1928 and 1933 Boeing built 586 aircraft in the F4B/P-12 design series, setting a record for production of a basic U.S. military plane that was not surpassed until 1940. This series proved that the requirements for land-based aircraft and carrier-based aircraft were not always so far apart that they were incompatible and is an outstanding example of a single basic design ef-

fectively serving in two roles with necessary modifications. The F4B-4 served with front line units until 1936 and beyond when it was replaced by Grumman F2F and F3F biplanes.

FRENCH AIRCRAFT CARRIER - 1920s

As with the American, British and Japanese participants of the Washington Naval Disarmament Conference, France was also reluctant to depart with its capital ships and therefore, decided to convert a battleship then under construction into an aircraft carrier.

The keel for the battleship *Bearn* had been laid on January 10, 1914; however, when World War I began all work was halted in favor of more immediate projects with the result that by the War's end in 1918 the ship was still incomplete. After some deliberation, conversion to an aircraft carrier was authorized in 1922. The British gave the French considerable assistance based upon their own experience with *HMS Eagle* and the *Bearn* conversion began in 1923.

The hull armor was reduced considerably. Aircraft shops and a 400 foot long Hangar were mounted atop the Main Deck. The Flight Deck was one inch thick armor and mounted above the Hangar. The hull sides were extended up to the Flight Deck, British fashion, but the bow and stern were open.

Unusual Island Installation

Bearn is one of the earliest examples of an island extending beyond the boundary of the Flight Deck. This island location provided more space on the Flight Deck for aircraft and facilitated their movement. The island was supported by a large sponson of streamline shape to minimize wave impact during rough seas. The sponson enclosed the boiler uptakes and was fitted with large vents which admitted air that mixed with the boiler gases, diluting them, in an effort to prevent smoke from interfering with flight operations.

Bearn Data

The 22,100 ton carrier attained 21.5 knots with its 40,000 shaft horsepower. Range was 7,000 miles at 10 knots. *Bearn* carried 40 aircraft, and complement was 870 officers and crew.

The waterline length was 574 feet with a maximum beam of 89 feet. Flight Deck measured 580 x 70 feet. Mean draft was 27 feet-6 inches.

The *Bearn* powerplant was most unusual because steam turbines were geared to the two inboard propeller shafts while triple-

Converted from the incompleted battleship Bearn the aircraft carrier of the same name was completed for the French Navy in May 1927. Unusual features were the Island location beyond the Flight Deck edge, and covers over the elevator pits when the elevators were in the down position. (Marine Nationale/ECP Armees)

expansion reciprocating steam engines powered the two outboard shafts. Twelve boilers generated steam for the propulsion machinery. Steam engines were for economical cruising while the turbines were cut in for high speeds.

Another unusual feature of *Bearn* was the aircraft elevator design, of which three were fitted. The electrically powered elevators were covered by hinged Flight Deck covers in order that, when the elevator was below the Flight Deck, the covers closed the opening and normal flight operations could be conducted because there would be no large elevator well to interfere with aircraft movement on Deck. Transverse arresting gear cables were installed. No catapults were fitted.

By 1940 *Bearn* did not qualify for first-line duty because of her slow speed and inadequate facilities and was classified as a transatlantic airplane ferry and training carrier.

ROYAL NAVY CRUISER CONVERSIONS - 1930s

It will be remembered that at the conclusion of the Washington Naval and Disarmament Conference Britain decided to convert the two light cruisers *HMS Glorious* and *HMS Courageous* into aircraft carriers rather than scrap them as would have been required by the Washington Treaty. The ships were near sisters to *HMS Furious* and after considering the reconstruction of *Furious*, which began in 1921, the Royal Navy was convinced to convert the two light cruisers by following the reconstruction theme of *Furious*. The obvious advantages of having a squadron of three 31.5 knot through-deck carriers gave credence to the decision to convert. Redesign started in 1923.

Glorious and *Courageous* Flight Decks

The conversion was similar but not identical to the *Furious* reconstruction and was accomplished by the same two shipyards; Royal Naval Dockyard at Rosyth, Scotland and Devonport Dockyard during 1924-1930. The entire superstructure was removed including all guns, decks, bulkheads and masts. Two 550 feet long aircraft Hangars, stacked one above the other, were built onto the hull and a 100 x 591 feet Flight Deck was fitted atop the Hangars with the aft end in line with the stern. Two large cruciform shaped aircraft elevators were located well forward and well aft on the Flight Deck each measuring 46 x 48 feet. The Flight Deck was constructed with two built-in ramps. The after end of the Flight Deck sloped down toward the stern to simplify landing. The forward end of the Flight Deck sloped gently up toward the bow, as was fitted on *HMS Furious* in order to slow the roll of landing aircraft because wheel brakes were generally not used and no arresting gear was installed..

A second flying off Deck was constructed over the bow with an opening to the upper Hangar. In this way aircraft from the upper Hangar could take off over the bow at the same time operations were being conducted from the Flight Deck. This arrangement was similar to that fitted on *HMS Furious*.

Catapults and Arresting Gear

No catapults were fitted until 1935 when two hydraulic catapults were installed forward on the Flight Deck. Shortly after commissioning the longitudinal arresting cables were replaced by the now conventional transverse arresting cables and all Fleet Air Arm carrier-based aircraft were obliged to exchange their landing gear jaws for present day arresting hooks.

The boiler uptakes were led across the ship under the Hangar and emerged on the starboard side of the Flight Deck to combine with the Navigating Bridge structure to form an island as on *HMS Hermes* and *HMS Eagle*.

Armor

All existing armor remained and this consisted of a 3 inch main belt closed by 3 inch bulkheads; a 2 inch forward belt closed by inch bulkheads; 1.75 inch Main Deck; 1.5 inch longitudinal bulk

HMS Glorious and Courageous were converted cruisers. The arrangement of Flight Decks was similar to the Furious modifications. Note the hull blister at the waterline. HMS Courageous is shown here. (Ministry of Defence [Navy])

heads closed by 1.5 inch bulkheads. The existing hull blisters were deepened to improve stability and reinforced to withstand an underwater shock of 440 pounds of TNT.

Defensive Armament
The initial defensive armament was ten 5.5 inch guns, six 4 inch high angle guns, and four pom-poms. In the late 1930s defensive armament was changed to (16) 4.7 inch antiaircraft guns.

Glorious and *Courageous* Data
Each completed carrier required 748 operating personnel plus 468 FAA personnel.

The 22,000 ton vessels were powered by geared steam turbines developing 90,000 shaft horsepower. Steam was produced in 18 Scotch boilers. The quadruple screw ships had an overall length of 786 feet and a beam of 81 feet (90 feet across the hull blisters). Mean draft was 24 feet. *Glorious* and *Courageous* carried 34,500 gallons of aviation fuel and 3,840 tons of ships' fuel oil which produced a combat range of 5,860 miles at 16 knots.

Courageous keel had been laid on March 28, 1915 and she was launched on February 5, 1916. Commissioning as an aircraft carrier was held on May 5, 1928. *Glorious* keel had been laid on May 1, 1915 and she was launched on April 20, 1916. Commissioning was on March 10, 1930.

The carriers were designed to accommodate 48 aircraft: 16 each of Fairey Flycatcher fighters, Fairey III F spotter/reconnaissance planes, and Blackburn Ripon Torpedo-bombers.

HMS Glorious and *HMS Courageous* were considered the most satisfactory carriers in the Royal Navy into the late 1930s with good speed and useful aircraft capacity.

BRITISH CARRIER-BASED AIRCRAFT - EARLY 1930s
With more state-of-the-art carriers joining the Royal Navy, new and improved carrier-based aircraft were developed and procured by the Fleet Air Arm.

Blackburn Ripon
While *Glorious* and *Courageous* were under reconstruction the Air Ministry sought a replacement for the Blackburn Dart and issued Specification 21/23 for a torpedo-bomber/reconnaissance design. One of the requirements was that the plane must have an endurance in excess of 12 hours which dictated a second cockpit for a navigator/gunner. Blackburn went to work on the project at once under the direction of Major F.A. Bumpus and produced a biplane which bore a strong resemblance to the Dart. Externally, the obvious differences were a single bay biplane arrangement versus the double bay arrangement of the Dart and that the forward fuselage was more slender than the Dart. An unusual design feature was the lower wing root. This formed an inverted gull wing at the fuselage junction, not unlike the World War II Corsair fighter. The arrangement dropped the lower wing to increase the gap; thereby, lowering the upper wing to improve the pilot's visibility. It also shortened the landing gear while still providing plenty of clearance for the torpedo. The inverted gull wing was truly innovative for the period.

The Blackburn Ripon I torpedo-bomber/reconnaissance design was a replacement for the Blackburn Dart. Observe the inverted gull lower wing to shorten the landing gear, allow clearance for the torpedo and increase the wing gap. Ripon II had retractable cheek radiators instead of the shuttered nose radiator. (Air Ministry [Navy])

After flight testing the Ripon, as the new design had been named, refinements were made which included increased wing sweepback, closer fitting engine cowl, and replacement of the shuttered nose radiator with two retractable cheek radiators on either side of the fuselage under the control of the pilot. Blackburn was awarded a contract when the Ripon II emerged triumphant from competitive trials against designs by Avro and Handley Page in 1927.

The principal production version was the Ripon II A. This model featured composite construction wings with spruce spars and ribs, and Duralumin compression ribs. Duralumin is an alloy of aluminum and copper with manganese and magnesium added. It is light and stronger than pure aluminum. Wings were hinged to fold back alongside the fuselage. Fuselage construction was similar to the Dart with steel engine mount, steel tubing center structure and a tie rod-braced wooden rear section.

Ripon Data
Empty weight was 4,132 pounds and a military load of 3,150 pounds could be carried. The 570 horsepower Napier Lion XI water-cooled engine propelled the plane to the respectable top speed of 132 miles per hour. Initial climb was 800 feet per minute and service ceiling was 13,000 feet. Endurance on torpedo-bombing missions was four hours; however, for reconnaisance missions a 120 gallon auxiliary fuel tank was carried in the torpedo rack. The addition of this tank extended the endurance to 14 hours, exceeding the Air Ministry requirements. A wind-driven propeller fuel pump was built into the auxiliary fuel tank nose to maintain a flow of fuel into the main fuel system.

Wing span was 45 feet-6.5 inches and with wings folded the width was 17 feet-10 inches. Length was 36 feet-9 inches with height at 12 feet-10 inches. Wing area was 683 square feet.

To demonstrate the agility of the design, Blackburn test pilot Flight Dieutenant A.M. Blake flew a production Ripon IIA in its debut before the Press. He dropped a one-ton practice torpedo into the river and then climbed straight up into a tight loop!

Armament consisted of the torpedo or alternatively one 1,100 pound smoke canister or a bomb load of either six 250 pound bombs or three 550 pound bombs under the lower wings and fuselage. An aiming window was provided in the fuselage bottom. One forward-firing Vickers gun and one flexible-mounted Lewis gun were also installed.

The 93 Royal Navy Blackburn Ripons operated from *HMS Furious, Courageous* and *Glorious* with the Mediterranean Fleet as well as the Home Fleet in the North Atlantic.

Fairey III F

Probably the most handsome and elegant of all Fleet Air Arm aircraft during the interwar period was the three-place spotter/reconnaissance Fairey IIIF. This design has the distinction of having operated from every aircraft carrier in the Royal Navy; the number of which at this time was six. A total of 622 of III F aircraft were constructed for the Air Ministry, of which more than 340 were delivered to the FAA, making this plane the most widely used spotter/reconnaissance craft between the wars.

The Fairey III F Mark I was first produced in February 1927 and the Mark II first flew that August. The ultimate refinement was the Mark III B which had its maiden flight in June 1930. This mark had an all-metal structure which was fabric covered. The fuselage was specially strengthened to permit catapulting because this method of launching was becoming a necessity as carrier-borne aircraft grew heavier every year. Over 165 were produced for the FAA.

Fairey III F Data

The 6,300 pound Fairey IIIF Mark IIIB was powered by a 570 horsepower Napier Lion XI A water-cooled engine which propelled the craft to a top speed of 120 miles per hour at 10,000 feet. Service ceiling was 20,000 feet. Endurance was four hours. The Mark III B had a 45 feet-9 inches wingspan and was 34 feet-4 inches long. Height was 14 feet-3 inches. The craft served in Spotter/Reconnaissance Squadrons Nos. 820, 822, 823, 824 and 825. It was declared obsolete in 1940.

Hawker Nimrod

In continuing with outstanding Fleet Air Arm aircraft of the early 1930s the Hawker Nimrod deserves mention. This single-seat fighter was developed to replace the Fairey Flycatcher. The Nimrod was a carrierborne counterpart of the Royal Air Force Hawker Fury; however, it was not merely a reworked Fury because both designs, although similar, were developed separately. Although the Nimrod is very similar to the Fury in external appearance, as previously mentioned in the prologue, naval aircraft such as the Nimrod require special features and equipment. The naval gear on the Nimrod included: fuselage strengthening to permit catapulting; larger fuel tank for extended range; more comprehensive radio gear; oxygen; hoisting gear, flotation bags in the fuselage rear; and flotation boxes in the top wing.

The prototype was first flown in early 1930 and a production order for 35 aircraft was placed in the following year as Nimrod Mark I. These aircraft were not fitted with deck arresting gear and were assigned to *HMS Glorious* and *HMS Eagle*.

Nimrod Data

An improved version, Nimrod Mark II, was fitted with the more powerful 650 horsepower Rolls-Royce Kestral V water-cooled engine, swept back wings, enlarged tail surfaces and deck arresting gear. A total of 36 were constructed in 1933. Top speed of the Hawker Nimrod Mark II was 195 miles per hour at 14,000 feet. The 4,258 pound fighter had a 26,000 foot service ceiling. Wingspan was 33 feet-6 inches and length was 27 feet. Height was 9 feet9 inches. Two .30 inch caliber Vickers guns were mounted in the fuselage forward of the pilot.

Stainless Steel Structure

An item of interest is the fact that three Mark II basic structures were made with stainless steel to combat corrosion; however, these were not placed into production, possibly because of weight problems.

The last of the Nimrods served aboard *HMS Glorious* until 1939 and the plane was another example of one basic design serving naval and land requirements.

Blackburn Baffin and Sharks

Blackburn continued work on improving torpedo-bomber design by exploring the installation of an air-cooled radial engine to replace the heavy liquid-cooled Napier Lion in the Ripon. This led to the development of the new and innovative Shark.

The Fairey IIIF of 1927 operated from all six Royal Navy carriers of the period and was the most widely-used British spotter-reconnaissance aircraft between the wars. This elegant plane was a three-seater. (Air Ministry [Navy])

The Hawker Nimrod fighter was the Fleet Air Arm's counterpart to the RAF's Hawker Fury. The 75 Nimrods that were constructed served on HMS Eagle and HMS Glorious. (British Aerospace, Courtesy Brendan Morrissey)

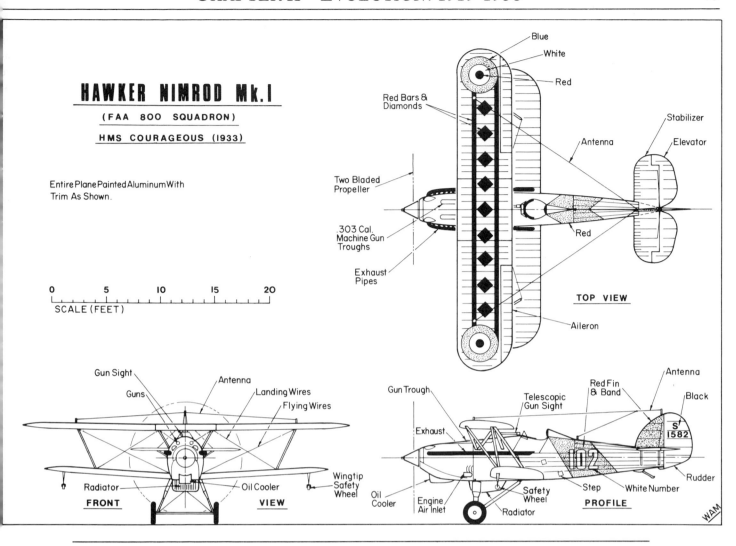

HAWKER NIMROD Mk.I

(FAA 800 SQUADRON)

HMS COURAGEOUS (1933)

Entire Plane Painted Aluminum With Trim As Shown.

SCALE (FEET)
0 5 10 15 20

Blue
White
Red

Red Bars & Diamonds

Antenna

Stabilizer
Elevator

Two Bladed Propeller

.303 Cal. Machine Gun Troughs

Exhaust Pipes

Red

TOP VIEW

Aileron

Gun Sight
Guns
Antenna
Landing Wires
Flying Wires

Radiator
Oil Cooler
Wingtip Safety Wheel

FRONT   **VIEW**

Gun Trough
Telescopic Gun Sight
Red Fin & Band
Antenna
Black

Exhaust
S 1582

Oil Cooler
Engine Air Inlet
Safety Wheel
Radiator
Step
White Number
Rudder

PROFILE

WAM

The installation of an air-cooled radial engine in the Blackburn Ripon formed the basic Blackburn Baffin which was a stepping stone to the Blackburn Shark. (Blackburn Aeroplane and Motor Co. Ltd.)

Blackburn Baffin

Two modified Ripon prototypes were built; one with a 650 horsepower Armstrong Siddeley Tiger twin-row radial and the other with a 565 horsepower Bristol Pegasus I. M3 single-row radial. The Air Ministry selected the Pegasus version which became known as the Blackburn Baffin. By 1934 the Baffin was serving on *HMS Glorious*, *HMS Courageous* and *HMS Furious*, as well as in the Royal New Zealand Air Force, forming the New Zealand General Reconnaissance Squadron.

Blackburn Shark

The operational experience and data gained with its Dart, Ripon, and Baffin designs enabled Blackburn to develop its next torpedo-bomber, the Shark. Advanced design features consisted of a buoyant Alclad covered fuselage and fin, use of a diagonal strut to serve as landing and flying wires, and a hydraulic folding wing locking and unlocking device. Blackburn engineers designed this device and had it manufactured by Lockheed Hydraulic Brake Co. Ltd. This system enabled the deck crew to withdraw or engage upper and lower wing root bolts simultaneously with only a few strokes of a small pump handle on the lower wing center section; thereby, saving considerable time and effort during wing folding and ex-

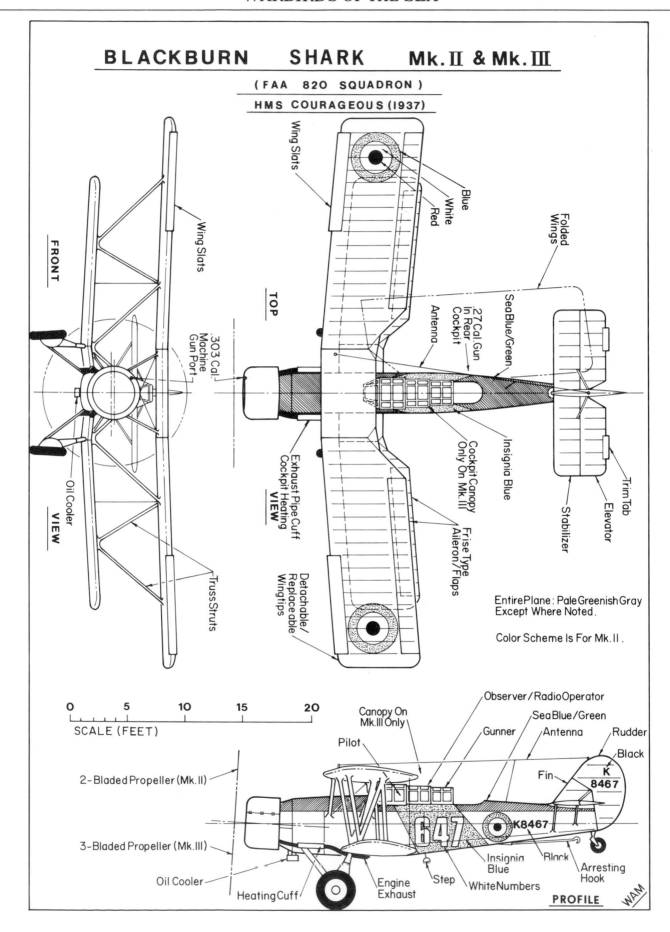

BLACKBURN SHARK Mk. II & Mk. III

(FAA 820 SQUADRON)
HMS COURAGEOUS (1937)

FRONT

VIEW

Wing Slats

Wing Slats

.303 Cal. Machine Gun Port

Oil Cooler

Truss Struts

TOP

VIEW

Blue

White

Red

Folded Wings

SeaBlue/Green

Antenna

.27 Cal. Gun In Rear Cockpit

Insignia Blue

Cockpit Canopy Only On Mk. III

Frise Type Aileron/Flaps

Exhaust Pipe Cuff Cockpit Heating

Detachable/Replaceable Wingtips

Stabilizer

Elevator

Trim Tab

Entire Plane: Pale Greenish Gray Except Where Noted.

Color Scheme Is For Mk. II.

0 5 10 15 20
SCALE (FEET)

2-Bladed Propeller (Mk. II)

3-Bladed Propeller (Mk. III)

Oil Cooler

Heating Cuff

Engine Exhaust

Step

White Numbers

Insignia Blue

Pilot

Canopy On Mk. III Only

Gunner

Observer/Radio Operator

SeaBlue/Green

Antenna

Fin

Rudder

Black

Black

Arresting Hook

K 8467

647

K8467

PROFILE

WAM

The Blackburn Shark reflected the experience with the Dart, Ripon, and Baffin. The two-bay wing structure was strut-braced instead of the conventional wire bracing which made it so strong that the wings could be folded with a full load of bombs in place. (Blackburn Aeroplane and Motor Co. Ltd.)

landing operations. The wings were so strong that they could support a full load of bombs when the plane was stowed below decks with wings folded.

Pilot, observer/wireless operator, and gunner were in open cockpits which were warmed from an engine exhaust pipe muff. The bombardier/observer lay prone under the pilot's seat during bombing runs.

Stainless Steel Spars
Wing spars were stainless steel tubes while ribs and tail structure were aluminum alloy. All open structure was fabric covered. Wingtips were easily detachable and could be replaced if damaged.

Armament
One 1,500 pound torpedo carried under the fuselage or the equivalent weight in bombs carried under the lower wing comprised the offensive armament. One Vickers air-cooled .30 inch caliber machine gun was mounted in the fuselage ahead of the pilot. The rear gunner was equipped with a Vickers-Berthier quick-firing, gas-operated gun on a ring mount.

Slats and Flaps
To improve takeoffs and landings the full span Frise-type ailerons could be lowered on both wings to become camber changing flaps. Leading edge slats were also installed to reduce the plane's stalling speed.

Shark Production
Blackburn built a total of 238 Sharks for the Fleet Air Arm: Mark I (16); Mark II (127); Mark III (95). The Mark III was fitted with a long greenhouse type sliding canopy over the cockpits.

Shark Data
The Blackburn Shark Mark II was powered with an 800 horsepower Bristol Pegasus III air-cooled radial engine which propelled the craft to a top speed of 140 miles per hour on torpedo missions and 157 miles per hour on reconnaissance missions at sea level. Initial climbing ability was 990 and 1,340 feet per minute respectively, Service ceiling was 14,600 and 19,000 feet respectively. The range was 617 miles for torpedo sorties and 829 miles for reconnaissance mis-

sions. The reconnaissance range could be extended to 1,260 miles with a 150 gallon auxiliary cylindrical fuel tank carried in the torpedo rack. The Mark II weighed 3,939 pounds and the military load for torpedo-bombing was 2,712 pounds while for reconnaissance 1,595 pounds.

Wingspan was 45 feet and folded width of the plane was only 15 feet. Length was 35 feet-3 inches while height was 12 feet-1 inch. Wing area was 489 square feet. In addition to the other advanced design features the Shark boasted pneumatic wheel brakes and a swivelling tail wheel.

In competition with designs from U.S., German, Italian and Czechoslovakian aircraft manufactureres in 1935 the Blackburn Shark won a contract to supply six aircraft to the Portugese Government.

LONDON NAVAL DISARMAMENT CONFERENCE
The London Naval Conference was called in 1930 for the signatories of the Washington Treaty to extend the expiration date for another five years, and to limit the construction of cruisers and destroyers. Japan strongly protested the proposed 10:10:7 ratio of cruisers and destroyers for the U.S., Britain and Japan respectively but was overruled. She was; however, permitted parity with the U.S. and Britain in submarines. Japan expressed her dissatisfaction with the Washington Treaty terms and the Anglo-American unwillingness to alter them. This, despite the onset of the economic crash of 1929 causing great reluctance in Britain and the U.S. to spend vast sums on naval armament. The U.S. still retained the principal of overall parity with Britain.

Carrier Definition
The U.S. delegation made the surprise statement that in order to be classed as an aircraft carrier a ship must have been designed and built primarily for carrying and operating aircraft. Conversely, a ship which was designed and built to battle with guns and happens to have a flight deck for aircraft is not, in truth, an aircraft carrier. All agreed. All participants also agreed to extend the Washington Treaty to 1935.

SHIPBOARD AIRCRAFT CORROSION PREVENTION, 1927-1935
During the late 1920s and early 1930s radical advances were being made in the materials used for naval aircraft construction. The changes were the transfer from wood and wire structures to welded steel tubing and light aluminum alloys; still fabric covered. Another technique which was gaining popularity was light alloy semi-monocoque and full monocoque fuselages.

These changes in construction required new and improved materials, and fabricating and maintenance techniques. New methods of corrosion prevention required considerable research. The red oxide primer was replaced by zinc chromate primer which was a distinct naval aircraft development and virtually eliminated corrosion of aluminum in a saltwater environment at that time.

Navy gray enamel was replaced by lacquer while cellulose nitrate and the acetate dopes were supplanted with the fire-resistant cellulose acetate butyrate dope. The U.S. Navy prepared manuals and specifications to standardize naval aircraft coatings for corrosion resistance, appearance and fire-resistance.

FIRST U.S. PURPOSE-BUILT AIRCRAFT CARRIER

Although the converted collier *USS Langley* and the converted battle cruisers *USS Lexington* and *USS Saratoga* were launched in the 1920s, the U.S. Navy did not start to construct purpose-built carriers until the 1930s. *Lexington* and *Saratoga* were the world's largest and most powerful carriers, and were available to play a decisive role in the evaluation of naval air power during fleet exercises to be used for guidance in designing America's first purpose-built aircraft carrier.

Washington Treaty Restrictions Dictate Carrier Size

It will be recalled that the Washington Treaty restricted the U.S. aircraft carrier fleet to a total of 135,000 tons and the maximum size of individual carriers to 27,000 tons. The effect of these restrictions was to influence the U.S. decision to build the smallest practical aircraft carriers in order to permit the largest number of them. It was also reasoned that when the *Lexington* class was subtracted from the total permissible tonnage only about 70,000 tons were left; just about enough to build four or five small carriers.

Construction of the small carrier began in September 1931 in Newport News Shipbuilding & Dry Dock Co.

USS Ranger

The new carrier was to displace 14,000 tons and named *Ranger* honoring the sloop commanded by John Paul Jones during the American Revolution. In view of its size *Ranger*'s design was based on *Langley* instead of the *Lexington* class; however, the new carrier's principal development was dedicated to aviation requirements. The original idea was to construct a flush decker, such as *HMS Argus* and *USS Langley*, to keep the Flight Deck unobstructed for aircraft. As with *Langley* the Flight Deck was supported over the Main Deck by a light steel girder latticework and stanchions. With the emphasis on aircraft-carrying capacity *Ranger* sacrificed seakeeping ability, defensive armament and speed.

Ranger Data

The geared steam turbine propulsion machinery was placed as far aft as possible with boiler rooms close together in order to simplify trunking the boiler uptakes and to discharge as far aft as possible. Machinery spaces were also arranged to provide as much room for aviation facilities as possible. Grouping the propulsion machinery spaces close together increased *Ranger*'s vulnerability because one good hit could conceivably deactivate the entire twin-screw pro

The first U.S. purpose-built aircraft carrier was USS Ranger. The small size was dictated by the terms of the Washington Naval Disarmament Treaty which gave birth to the U.S. Navy philosophy that many small carriers are better than a few large carriers. Notice the three horizontal smokestacks on each side of the hull. (U.S. Naval Historic Center)

ulsion system. Armor and underwater protection consisted of one inch Flight Deck protection, a band of armor at the waterline to protect the engine and boiler rooms, a double hull, and 29 underwater bulkheads below the waterline to restrict internal flooding in the event of a hit.

The Flight Deck measured 109 x 710 feet with narrow areas forward and aft measuring 87 feet across. The hull overall length was 769 feet and beam was 80 feet. Full load draft was 22 feet-6 inches. *Ranger* speed was 29 knots with 53,500 shaft horsepower and range was 10,000 miles at 15 knots.

This smaller carrier could accomodate 76 aircraft; two squadrons of fighters (36) and two squadrons of dive bombers (36) plus four utility aircraft. Unlike the Royal Navy Fleet Air Arm no provision was made for torpedo-bombers. This aircraft capacity merits comparison with the *Lexington* class regarding the amount of ship tonnage required for one airplane: *Lexington* 450 tons/plane, and *Ranger* 180 tons/plane. The intention here is not to condemn nor to praise either ship, but is merely to illustrate the widely divergent paths that can be taken in aircraft carrier design to attain specific objectives.

Initial complement was 1,788; however, this rose to about 2,000 during World War II. No catapult was fitted until 1944 when a single hydraulic catapult was installed. Initial defensive armament was eight 5 inch guns; however, this was modified several times during *Ranger*'s service life.

Island Decision
It was decided to add an island during construction when it became apparent that visibility and command must be improved. The island was kept as small as possible and located amidships which was adjacent to both aircraft elevators. This increased topside weight.

The *Ranger* (CV-4) was launched on February 25, 1933 by the First Lady, Mrs. Herbert Hoover, who smashed a bottle of grapejuice instead of champagne against the bow because Prohibition was still in force. The carrier was commissioned on the Fourth of July, 1934.

Ranger was an attempt to create a carrier force while adhering to the restrictions of the Washington Treaty. Lessons were learned.

U.S. NAVAL AVIATION EXPANSION- Early 1930s
In 1934 the U.S. Congress and the National Industrial Recovery Act funded an unprecedented expansion of U.S. Naval Aviation.

NRA Spurs U.S. Carrier-Based Aircraft Development
The depression that started with the 1929 Stock Market Crash lasted for several years. Naturally, this limited funds for naval aviation; therefore, experimentation rather than production became the rule. The principal weapon to overcome the American depression was the National Industrial Recovery Act of June 16, 1933. This Act had allotted seven and one half million dollars for the procurement of new aircraft and equipment for naval aviation. A 1,000 plane program was to become a reality.

Vinson-Trammel Act
On March 27, 1934 Congressman Carl Vinson, Chairman of the House Naval Affairs Committee, cosponsored the Vinson-Tram-

mel Act, which limited defense profits and authorized the Navy to build up to the limits allowed by the Washington and London naval treaties over an eight year period. This resulted in the construction of three new aircraft carriers and rapid advances in U.S. naval aviation.

U.S. NAVY SHIPBOARD AIRCRAFT - EARLY 1930s
The Washington Treaty limited the U.S. Navy to a nominal parity with the Royal Navy. Although both navies relied on their battle fleet as the main striking force, the Royal Navy had more carriers but fewer naval aircraft than the U.S. Navy. Unlike the Royal Navy, U.S. Naval Aviation had never been absorbed into a separate unified air force and did not lose its identity. Although naval air power was not yet fully recognized as the principal strength of the U.S. Fleet, a number of senior officers were air-minded and several well-designed U.S. naval aircraft emerged to equip America's expanding carrier force. With funds available from the NRA and Congress U.S. Naval Aviation forged ahead, outstripping the Japanese Navy and the Fleet Air Arm.

Air-Cooled Radial Engine; U.S. Navy Standard
By the early 1930s the air-cooled radial engine was the only powerplant acceptable for U.S. Navy airplanes and the Bureau of Aeronautics would consider no other. Pratt & Whitney had its Twin-Wasps and Wright had its Cyclone in production which encouraged American aircraft manufacturers, both new and experienced, to submit their new designs. Curtiss, Grumman, Great Lakes, and Douglas all produced acceptable carrier-based aircraft designs using air-cooled radial engines.

At this time the biplane was still king although its reign was about to be inherited by the monoplane. The biplane didn't give up easily and resorted to retractable landing gear, enclosed cockpits, stressed skin fuselages, and tighter cowling in order to improve performance and prolong its life.

First Grumman Navy Fighter
The fledgling Grumman Aircraft Engineering Corporation moved into the American Airplane and Engine Corporation plant in Farmingdale, Long Island when American went out of business. Grumman won a contract for a two-seat fighter prototype in April 1931; only two years after the company was founded.

Leroy Grumman had been associated with Grover Loening for six years and developed the retractable landing gear of the famous Loening Amphibian. The Grumman firm's initial contact with the Navy had been designing floats to convert seaplanes into amphibians, then Grumman submitted his fighter design for which he received the contract.

Innovative Design
Grumman's design featured several advanced and innovative features among which were: a retractable landing gear in which the wheels were raised almost vertically to lie flush with the fuselage sides just ahead of the lower wing; a telescoping canopy completely covering both cockpits; all-metal monocoque stressed skin fuselage; and fabric covered all-metal wing and tail structure.

The first Grumman plane for the U.S. Navy was the innovative FF-1 two-seater fighter. It was the first U.S. Navy plane with a retractable landing gear and a completely enclosed cockpit canopy. (Official U.S. Navy Photograph)

FF-1 Data

The prototype XFF-1 was delivered to the Navy late in 1931; the first Navy fighter with a retractable landing gear. Powered with a Wright R-1820E the XFF-1 attained 195 miles per hour and when a Wright R-1820F engine was installed the speed went up to 201 miles per hour; faster than any single-seat fighter then in service!

The production Grumman fighter was powered by the 700 horsepower Wright R-1820-78 engine which propelled the plane to a 207 miles per hour top speed at 4,000 feet. Initial climb was 2.9 minutes to reach 5,000 feet and service ceiling was 21,000 feet. Its 120 gallon fuel tank gave the Grumman a 920 mile combat range. Most of the FF-1's were modified to have duel controls in both cockpits and these were known as FF-2. Landing gear retracted by handcranked gear and chain.

Wingspan was 34 feet-6 inches, length was 24 feet-6 inches and height was 11 feet-1 inch. Wing area was 310 square feet. Empty weight was 3,250 pounds and gross weight was 4,828 pounds. Armament consisted of one fixed forward-firing and two flexible-mounted guns for the gunner. All guns were .30 inch caliber. The gun arrangement suggests that the principal offensive and defensive weapons were in the rear cockpit.

Leroy Grumman won a contract for the FF-1 only two years after he founded his company. He went on to develop many classic aircraft for the U.S. Navy. The famous designer is shown here in 1948. (Grumman Corporation, Courtesy Lois Lovisolo)

Production

Contracts for 27 FF-1 fighters and 33 scout versions, designated SF-1, were awarded. The SF-1 had increased fuel capacity for longer range.

Assigned Units

The FF-1 deliveries began in the summer of 1933 and equipped VF-5B on *USS Lexington*. The SF-1 was flown by VS-3B also serving on *USS Lexington*. The Grummans were withdrawn from Fleet service by 1937 and were assigned to Naval Reserve units.

Carrier/Dirigible-Based Fighter

In the annals of U.S. Naval Aviation the Curtiss Sparrowhawk fighter occupies a unique position being the only operational aircraft to serve aboard an airship. The Sparrowhawk served on the U.S. Navy dirigibles *USS Akron* (Z RS-4) and *USS Macon* (Z RS-5). Contracts for the construction of the dirigibles were signed with Goodyear/Zeppelin on October 6, 1928. The airships were constructed to accommodate four fighter planes each. This included a hangar with large trapdoors in the hull bottom and a retractable trapeze from which the aircraft could be launched and retrieved by means of a skyhook on the planes. In effect, the dirigibles were aircraft carriers which floated in the air rather than on water; a mere difference of fluids.

As construction progressed on the two giants the procurement of a suitable fighter did not, and lagged far behind. Meanwhile, on May 10, 1930 Bureau of Aeronautics Specification Design No. 96 had been issued. This required a very small fighter for aircraft carrier duty. Curtiss, General, and Berliner-Joyce competed; however, none of the planes was small enough to suit the Navy requirement. The Curtiss entry was; however, small enough to enter the dirigible doors, and very light as well, so the Curtiss XF9C-1 was selected for possible dirigible operation, as well as carrier duty.

First Flights and First Hook-On

After its first flights at Mitchell Field, Long Island, during March 1931 the XF9C-1 was tested at the Naval Air Station, Anacostia, followed by carrier landing tests at Hampton Roads in June. On its first landing the little Curtiss wound up on its nose, much like the first landing on *USS Langley*. The reason was also the same; arresting hook anchor point was also too far forward on the fuselage. A skyhook was installed and the XF9C-1 was transferred to N.A.S. Lakehurst, N.J. (home of the U.S. Navy dirigibles) and made its first hook-on and release from the airship *USS Los Angeles* on October 27, 1931. This was not the first time a plane had hooked on a dirigible. In the mid-1920s a Vought UO-1 had hooked on and off *USS Los Angeles* to determine if it could be done.

Meanwhile, the Bureau of Aeronautics had released a specification for an Airship Fighter in July, 1931; written around the XF9C-1. This prompted Curtiss to incorporate all the necessary changes and in 90 days a new prototype XF9C-2 was produced at company expense. A contract for six production aircraft was awarded in October, 1931 and these were delivered in September, 1932. The F9C-2 Sparrowhawks began operating from *USS Akron* at once.

Sparrowhawk-*Akron* Operations

Plans were to assign *USS Akron* to the Atlantic, based at Lakehurst, and to assign *USS Macon* to the Pacific, based at Moffett Field, California. All eight Sparrowhawks were operating with *Akron* pending the commissioning of *Macon*. After six months of successful operations disaster struck! Bad weather at Lakehurst had grounded the Sparrowhawks but *Akron* was on patrol over the Atlantic on April 4, 1933. Caught in a storm, with Commander Frank McCord in command, *USS Akron* crashed into the sea off Barnegat Light, N.J. Of the 76 men aboard, 73 were lost, including the Chief of the Bureau of Aeronautics, Rear Admiral William A. Moffett.

The diminutive Curtiss Sparrowhawk was unique because it is the only operational aircraft to serve aboard dirigible airships. Observe that the upper wing is attached directly to the fuselage, forming a gull wing, in order to allow space for a strong dirigible hook structural attachment to the fuselage. (Official U.S. Navy Photograph, Courtesy N.H. Hauprich)

In addition to dirigible airships, the Curtiss F9C-2 was designed to operate from aircraft carriers as well. The fairing under the fuselage between the tail surfaces and the fuselage band is the tailhook attachment. Note that the antenna wires are arranged to avoid passing over the fuselage in order not to interfere with the dirigible trapeze. (Official U.S. Navy Photograph, Courtesy N.H. Hauprich)

The dirigible USS Macon sails majestically as two Curtiss Sparrowhawks approach from below to hook on the trapeze extended from the bottom of the dirigible. (U.S. Naval Historical Center)

Sparrowhawk-*Macon* Operations

The Akron Sparrowhawks were transferred to California and operations with *Macon* became routine. The HTA (Heavier Than Air) unit of Sparrowwawks had the landing gear removed and depended entirely upon the skyhook/trapeze for launching and recovery. This improved performance by reducing wind resistance and weight. After seven months of operation disaster struck again. On February

This tiny Curtiss F9C-2 is caught at the moment it hooked on the USS Macon trapeze. The projecting structure will be lowered so the padded horseshoe will grip the fuselage to hold the plane steady as it is hoisted into the airship. Note the weighted flag to inform the pilot of dirigible speed and wind direction. (Official U.S. Navy Photograph, Courtesy N.H. Hauprich)

12, 1935 *USS Macon*, with Commander Herbert V. Wiley in command, crashed into the sea off Point Sur, California with the loss of two lives. Four Sparrowhawks were on board. This disaster ended the Navy's operation of rigid airships.

Sparrowhawk Data

The Curtiss F9C-2 was powered with a 438 horsepower Wright R-975-E3 air-cooled radial engine with which a 176.5 miles per hour top speed at 5,000 feet was attained. Empty weight was 2,089 pounds and gross weight was 2,770 pounds. Initial climb was 1,700 feet per minute and service ceiling was 19,200 feet. Range was 350 miles which could be increased with an auxiliary belly tank. Wing span was 25 feet-5 inches; length 20 feet-7 inches, and height 10 feet-11 inches. Wing area was 173 square feet.

Lone Sparrowhawk Survivor

After the loss of *USS Macon* the remaining Sparrowhawks served as utility aircraft. The lone survivor of this rare and interesting plane can be seen in the National Air and Space Museum, Smithsonian Institution, Washington, D.C.

Legendary Curtiss Goshawks

Naval planners have always been intrigued with multipurpose aircraft for carrier duty because of the extreme space restrictions on board. Categories such as scout/bombers, scout/fighters, fighter bombers and scout/observation were some of the types developed for operation in the U.S. Navy during the 1930s while Curtiss developed the classic Goshawk.

F11C-2 Goshawk

Light dive bombing was becoming more attractive to the U.S. Navy and the single-seat fighter was called upon to fill this dual role. In Spring of 1932 the Curtiss Aeroplane Division of the Curtiss-Wright Corporation introduced the latest of its Hawk designs: a nicely proportioned, clean, streamline biplane. On April 16 two prototypes were ordered by the Navy. The XF11C-1 was powered with a 600 horsepower Wright R-1510-98 twin-row radial engine while the XF11C-2 had a 700 horsepower Wright SR-1820-78 single-row Cyclone air-cooled radial. The XF11C-2 began trials in June 1932 and the XF11C-1 was tested a few months later. A Navy production order for 28 of the F11C-2 was issued in October, 1932. The Curtiss biplane was now named Goshawk and the first deliveries in February 1933 were assigned to the Navy's famous High Hat Squadron VF-1B operating aboard *USS Saratoga*.

BFC-2 Goshawk

One year later the Navy decided to change the Goshawk and squadron designation to better indicate their bombing fighter role. The Goshawk became the BFC-2 while the High Hat Squadron number was changed to VB-2B and then to VB-3B. Due to the diving speeds the Goshawk headrest was enlarged to a turtleback and a partial sliding canopy was installed, covering only the rear half of the cockpit. In this period of transition from open to covered cockpits many pilots disliked the new covered cockpits and perhaps the partial covering on the BFC-2 was a halfway measure intended to please everyone. A rubber life raft was stowed in the large headrest. In

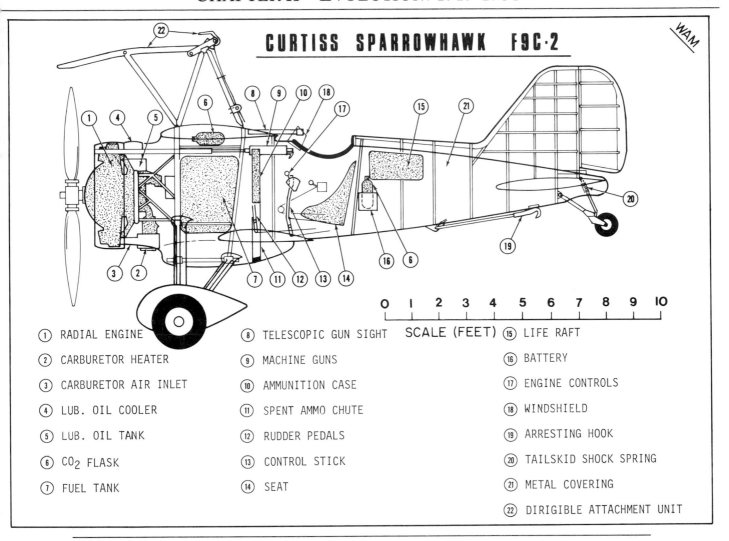

CURTISS SPARROWHAWK F9C·2

WAM

SCALE (FEET)

0 1 2 3 4 5 6 7 8 9 10

① RADIAL ENGINE	⑧ TELESCOPIC GUN SIGHT	⑮ LIFE RAFT
② CARBURETOR HEATER	⑨ MACHINE GUNS	⑯ BATTERY
③ CARBURETOR AIR INLET	⑩ AMMUNITION CASE	⑰ ENGINE CONTROLS
④ LUB. OIL COOLER	⑪ SPENT AMMO CHUTE	⑱ WINDSHIELD
⑤ LUB. OIL TANK	⑫ RUDDER PEDALS	⑲ ARRESTING HOOK
⑥ CO_2 FLASK	⑬ CONTROL STICK	⑳ TAILSKID SHOCK SPRING
⑦ FUEL TANK	⑭ SEAT	㉑ METAL COVERING
		㉒ DIRIGIBLE ATTACHMENT UNIT

Designed as a fighter the Curtiss F11C-2 Goshawk was also called upon to perform dive bombing duties. Observe the open wheel pants to facilitate wheel and tire maintainance and removal. (U.S. National Archives)

addition to the converted Goshawks the Navy procured 10 more BFC-2 models from the Curtiss factory.

The BFC-2 attained a top speed of 205 miles per hour in clean fighter condition but this dropped to 195 miles per hour as a bomber at 8,000 feet. Initial climb was 2.6 minutes to 5,000 feet and service ceiling was 24,300 feet. Range was 560 miles which could be

extended to 650 miles with a 50 gallon drop tank. Empty weight was 3,037 pounds while with full load the craft weighed 4,638 pounds. Two fixed forward-firing Browning .30 inch caliber machine guns were installed in the upper fuselage between cockpit and engine. Wingspan was 31 feet-6 inches; length 25 feet and height 10 feet-7 inches. Wing area was 262 square feet.

BF2C-1 Goshawk
Even before the BFC-2 evolved, one F11C2 had been fitted with retractable landing gear at the Curtiss plant. The wheels retracted similar to those on the Grumman FF-1 and a belly had to be added to the fuselage to accommodate the wheels. Powered by a 700 horsepower Wright R-1820-04 Cyclone the 3,329 pounds empty and 5,086 pounds gross plane attained a 225 miles per hour top speed at 8,000 feet. Service ceiling went up to 27,000 feet and range to 797 miles. This plane became the Navy's second retractable landing gear fighter.

These improved performance figures justified a contract for 27 which was placed in February 1934. This Goshawk designation was changed to BF2C-1. Production models incorporated the BFC-2 turtleback headrest and sliding cockpit cover. Delivery of the new model began in October, 1934 and these were issued to VB-5B serving on the new carrier, *USS Ranger*.

The BFC-2 Goshawk variant was fitted with a turtledeck headrest and a partial sliding cockpit canpopy for more pilot comfort during dive bombing. Designation change was for Bombing Fighter. Note the streamline drop tank, telescopic sight and High Hat Squadron insignia. (Official U.S. Navy Photograph, News Photo Division)

Armament

All Goshawk models were fitted with the same armament which consisted of one 474 pound bomb under the fuselage or four 116 pound bombs carried under the lower wing. Machine guns were as described for the BFC-2.

Goshawk Exports

Export versions of the Goshawk totalled 251 planes. The Goshawk appellation was not used for export; the old Hawk name was used instead. Hawks were sold to China, Germany, Turkey, Argentina, Bolivia, Colombia and Spain.

The Goshawk series were true classics in the annals of naval aviation and were the last Curtiss fighters to serve in the U.S. Navy.

Great Lakes Dive Bomber

The Great Lakes Aircraft Corporation had purchased the Glenn L. Martin plant in Cleveland in 1928 and its first contact with the U.S. Navy was the production of the Martin T4M-1 torpedo-bomber (previously described). By 1932 Great Lakes had produced its own design in answer to the Bureau of Aeronautics requirement for a dive bomber which could carry a 1,000 pound bomb. A prototype

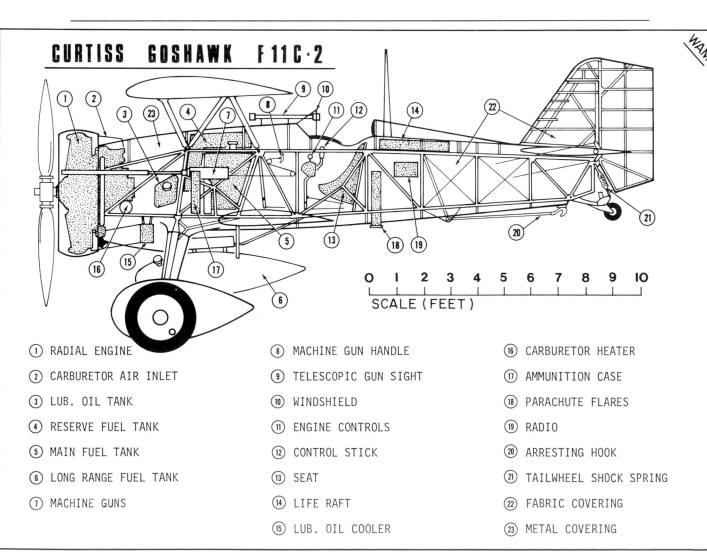

CURTISS GOSHAWK F11C-2

SCALE (FEET)

1. RADIAL ENGINE
2. CARBURETOR AIR INLET
3. LUB. OIL TANK
4. RESERVE FUEL TANK
5. MAIN FUEL TANK
6. LONG RANGE FUEL TANK
7. MACHINE GUNS
8. MACHINE GUN HANDLE
9. TELESCOPIC GUN SIGHT
10. WINDSHIELD
11. ENGINE CONTROLS
12. CONTROL STICK
13. SEAT
14. LIFE RAFT
15. LUB. OIL COOLER
16. CARBURETOR HEATER
17. AMMUNITION CASE
18. PARACHUTE FLARES
19. RADIO
20. ARRESTING HOOK
21. TAILWHEEL SHOCK SPRING
22. FABRIC COVERING
23. METAL COVERING

The final Goshawk variant was the BF2C-1 which featured a retractable landing gear. Speed increased from 205 to 225 miles per hour. Aircraft shown served on USS Ranger. (Curtiss-Wright Corporation)

was ordered in June 1932 which was in competition with a Consolidated Aircraft design. Great Lakes was the winner and production contracts in November 1933, January 1934, and February 1935 totalled 60 planes. Production models, unlike the prototype, had a telescoping sliding canopy over both cockpits.

BG-1 Data

The Great Lakes BG-1 was powered by a 750 horsepower Pratt & Whitney R-1535-82 Wasp air-cooled radial engine with which the plane attained a 188 miles per hour top speed at 8,900 feet. Initial climb was 5.5 minutes to reach 5,000 feet. Service ceiling was

The little known Great Lakes BG-1 dive bomber served on USS Ranger and could carry a 1,000 pound bomb. A total of 60 aircraft were built during 1933, 1934 and 1935. (U.S. National Archives)

The Vought Corsair was improved by Rex Beisel who added a full chord cowling with adjustable engine cooling flaps (arrow), larger rudder and a cockpit canopy. The X03U-6 was the first plane to use adjustable engine cooling cowl flaps which earned Beisel the Manley Memorial Medal and the Wright Bros. Medal. U.S. Marines received 32 03U-6 Corsairs. This design became a stepping stone to the very successful Vought SBU design. (Vought Aircraft Company, Courtesy Paul Bower)

Although the Vought SBU owed many of its design features to the 03U-6 it emerged as an entirely new airplane. One of the inherited features is the adjustable engine cooling cowl flaps (arrow) which contributed to the plane's top speed of 205 mph. Note the neutrality star on the nose of this 1940 SBU-1. (Official U.S. Navy Photograph)

20,100 feet and the range while carrying a 1,000 pound bomb-was 549 miles. Empty weight was 3,903 pounds while the weight loaded was 6,347 pounds. Wingspan was 36 feet; length was 28 feet-9 inches and height was 11 feet. Wing area was 384 square feet. Two .30 inch caliber machine guns were installed; one fixed and one flexible.

Assigned Units

The first unit equipped with the BG-1 was VB-3B aboard *USS Ranger*. Marine Squadrons VMB-1 and VMB-2 were also equipped with the BG-1 and flew them in service until 1940.

Unable to compete with the established naval aircraft manufacturers the Great Lakes Aircraft Corporation went out of business in 1936.

Last U.S. Navy Vought Biplane

Although Vought had been providing the major portion of the U.S Navy's scouting and observation aircraft it was far less successfu with its efforts to secure a fighter plane contract. Again in Spring o 1932 the Chance Vought Division of United Aircraft and Transpo Corporation responded to Bureau of Aeronautics Specificatio Design 113 for a two-seat fighter of higher power and slower land ing speed than the F8C Helldiver. Six other manufacturers submit ted proposals but Vought received a contract for a prototype desig nated XF3U-1.

From Fighter to Scout Bomber

The prototype was first flown in May 1933 and in November th Navy requested that the XF3U-1 be modified into a prototype scou

The SBU was the last Vought biplane in the U.S. Navy. Tapered wings and long cowl for the twin-row engine were the major features that set it apart from the Corsair. The U.S. Navy purchased 124 of these Vought scout-bombers. (Ling Temco Vought, Courtesy Arthur L. Schoeni)

The Curtiss SBC started life as a monoplane fighter and evolved into a biplane scout/bomber. Three flights of Curtiss SBC-3 Helldivers from Saratoga fly in a difficult tight formation in this photo. Note the trapeze bomb rack beneath the fuselage. (U.S. National Archives)

bomber. After several variants the 03U-6 evolved into an entirely new scout bomber designated XSBU-1. The necessary modifications to convert to the SB category included larger internal fuel tanks for greater range, larger and stronger wings, and provision for a 500 pound bomb under the fuselage. The XSBU-1 was, in fact, a new airplane and was delivered to the Navy for trials in June 1934.

Assigned Units and Production

During testing it was discovered that the XSBU-1, as modified, would exceed existing U.S. Navy scouts' top speed by almost 20 miles per hour and range by over 220 miles. A production order for 34 planes was placed with Vought in January 1934. Deliveries of the SBU-1 began in November 1935 and Scouting Squadron VS-3B was the first to be equipped, followed by VS-2B and VS-1B.

A second procurement of 40 planes was made. These were slightly modified and designated SBU-2.

SBU-1 Data

The Pratt & Whitney R-1535-80 Twin Wasp engine was selected because its small diameter presented less frontal area. The SBU-1 weighed 3,645 pounds empty and 5,520 pounds gross. Maximum speed was 202 miles per hour at 8,900 feet and cruising speed was 122 miles per hour-. Initial climb was 1,180 feet per minute and service ceiling was 23,700 feet. Range was 548 miles.

Construction consisted of a conventional dural structure with fabric covering. Wingspan was 33 feet-3 inches; length 27 feet-10 inches, and height 11 feet-11 inches. Wing area was 327 square feet. Armament was one fixed and one flexible mounted .30 inch caliber machine guns.

The SBU was the last Vought biplane for the U.S. Navy because monoplanes were just around the corner.

Last U.S. Navy Curtiss Biplane

Curtiss also responded to Bureau of Aeronautics Specification Design 13 for a two-seat fighter and submitted a parasol wing monoplane design. The U.S. Navy ordered one prototype, designated XF12C-1, which was tested in the Fall of 1933. The two and one-half ton plane exceeded 215 miles per hour and landed at a slow 64 miles per hour, thanks to slots and flaps; however, the monoplane's maneuverability was sluggish. With a wingspan of over 41 feet the wing was arranged to fold for stowage in carriers. No U.S. Navy plane had ever used folding wings because they had all been biplanes. Biplanes always have shorter wings because the wing area is shared by two smaller wings. Famous fighters such as the F4B and Goshawks had fixed wings because they spanned less than the arbitrary 36 feet maximum set by the Navy for stowage aboard carriers.

Monoplane Proposed

As with the Vought SBU the Navy visualized the Curtiss design as having the qualities of an observation plane. A larger engine was installed and the XF12C-1 became XS4C-1 which, in January 1934, again changed to Scout/Bomber as XSBC-1. During a test dive in September 1934 the wing collapsed and the monoplane crashed. Total reconstruction was necessary and when the rebuilding was finished the XSBC-2 emerged as a biplane. In March 1936 a still larger engine of 825 horsepower was installed and the designation became XSBC-3.

Production

In August 1936 the Navy awarded Curtiss a production contract for 83 SBC-3 Scout/Bombers which carried a single 500 pound bomb for dive bombing attacks. The wingspan was 34 feet and; therefore, no folding mechanism was required. Deliveries of the SBC-3 began in July 1937 and these were issued to Scouting Squadron VS-5. As with its Hawk series Curtiss decided to continue its Helldiver name for all dive bomber designs.

The final modification of the SBC series was designed in late 1937. An order for 174 of the SBC-4 was placed in January 1938 and deliveries began in March 1939.

SBC-4 Data

The 4,841 pounds empty and 7,632 pounds gross SBC-4 attained a maximum speed of 237 miles per hour. Range was 590 miles at 127 miles per hour with a 500 pound bomb. Powerplant was the 950 horsepower Wright R-1820-34 Cyclone radial engine which gave the SBC-4 an initial climb of 1,860 feet per minute. Service ceiling was 27,300 feet. A 1,000 pound bomb could be carried under the fuselage. One fixed forward-firing and one flexible .30 inch caliber machine guns were installed. Wingspan was 34 feet, length 28 feet-4 inches, and height 12 feet-7 inches. Wing area was 317 square feet.

Assigned Units

The SBC-3 served in VS-3, VS-5 and VS-6 while SBC-4 served in VB-8 and VS-8 on *USS Hornet*, as well as in Marine Squadron VMO-151.

The Curtiss SBC-4 Helldiver was the last biplane dive bomber to serve in the U.S. Navy, having been succeeded by monoplanes. Yet, it is ironic that this biplane started life as a monoplane.

Having failed in the quest to satisy its brief obsession with two-seat fighters, the Navy dismissed the idea for three decades until the advent of sophisticated jets.

U.S. NAVY MONOPLANE PROPOSALS

Boeing, Northrop and Curtiss had prepared designs for single-seat carrier-based monoplane fighters by 1932-1933 and these were tested by the U.S. Navy through 1935-1936.

Boeing XF7B-1

The Boeing proposal was the XF7B-1 which paralleled the U.S. Army's YP-29A which, in turn, was a development of the successful Army P-26. This low-wing, all-metal fighter featured an enclosed cockpit and retractable landing gear. A minor accident disqualified this design.

Northrop XFT-1

The Northrop prototype was a miniature of the famous record-breaking Northrop Gamma mailplane. An unauthorized flight ended in a serious crash which terminated this all-metal fighter project.

Curtiss XF13C-1

The Curtiss entry was a high-wing, cabin-type which had a definite non-military appearance. Fuselage was all-metal, but wing and tail structures were fabric covered dural frames. A retractable landing gear similar to the BF2C biplane was installed.

A Biplane/Monoplane Design

The novel and innovative aspect of this design was the fact that it could be flown as a biplane, as well as a monoplane! The prototype was ordered in November 1932; designated XF13C-1. Factory flight tests were satisfactory in both configurations so the monoplane was flown to Anacostia in February 1934 for Navy testing. The lower wing halves were shipped separately. These had a narrower chord than the upper wing. Strangely, the monoplane version was about 85 pounds heavier than the biplane and the reason was the weight of the heavy struts and fittings on the monoplane.

Performance of the two versions varied as expected: takeoff run for the monoplane was 615 feet and for the biplane 500 feet; top speed for the monoplane was 224 miles per hour, and for the biplane 205 miles per hour. The biplane landing speed was slower than the monoplane. The XF13C-1 passed all flight tests and the carrier operation tests; however, it could not escape the criticism directed at the cabin configuration because of the limited visibility. After a series of modifications the Navy decided to terminate all tests in October 1935 and gave the XF13C-1 to the Langley Field laboratories for experiments.

The possibility remains that, had the XF13C-1 been developed further, it could have resulted in a fighter with the advantages of monoplanes and biplanes as the situation demanded; however, it now seemed that the carrier monoplane fighter would be long in coming so the U.S.Navy returned to the biplane.

Grumman Single-Seat Fighter

The U.S. Navy needed a single-seat fighter to replace the aging Hawks and F4B fighters so it turned to Leroy Grumman, who had produced the very satisfactory FF-1 two-seater. On November 2, 1932 the Navy issued an order for a protype single-seat fighter designated XF2F-1. In most respects the new design was a miniature FF-1 except that, in order to locate the wheel wells, the belly had to

be more pronounced, which gave the little plane a sort of rotund or pudgy appearance. This made the XF2F-1 appear even smaller than it was.

First Flight

First flown on October 18, 1933, the little Grumman was tricky to fly and exhibited some stability problems. Navy trials were run at Anacostia and Hampton Roads and, after a few minor changes, an order was placed for 54 of the F2F-1. Construction followed the FF-1 with fabric covered dural framework wings and tail while the fuselage was Alclad stressed-skinned monocoque. The landing gear retracted as on the FF-1, with a handcranked sprocket and chain belt.

F2F-1 Data

Powered by a 700 horsepower twin-row Pratt & Whitney R-1535-72 air-cooled radial engine, the 2,691 pound empty and 3,847 pound gross fighter attained a top speed of 231 miles per hour at 7,500 feet. Initial climb was a very respectable 2,050 feet per minute and service ceiling was 27,100 feet. Range was 985 miles, which was equal to or better than many scout and reconnaissance planes.

Wingspan was 28 feet-6 inches and length 21 feet-5 inches. Height was 9 feet-1 inch. The wing area was 230 square feet.

Armament was two fixed .30 inch caliber machine guns. Bombs were also carried for dive bombing missions.

Assigned Units

Deliveries began in January 1935 and the F2F-1 was issued to Squadrons VF-2B on *USS Lexington*, and VF-3B on *USS Ranger*.

It was later flown by VF-5 and VF-7 on *Wasp* and *Yorktown*. The F2F-1 was extremely rugged and it could endure the most violent maneuvers and high speed dives. This enabled it to undertake dive bombing with no risk of structural failure.

Spin Problems

Its Achille's heel was the tendency to spin, as well as directional instability. This was, of course, undesirable, and both Grumman and the Navy undertook to solve the problem with a hands-on approach. A special F2F-1 was constructed as an experimental test

This Curtiss XF13C-1 proposal as a U.S. Navy monoplane fighter could be flown as a biplane as well as a monoplane. Although not accepted for production, the XF13C-1 demonstrated the advantages of the monoplane as well as the biplane. (U.S. Naval Institute)

With no monoplane fighter on the horizon, the U.S. Navy reverted to the biplane for a Hawk and F4B replacement. Leroy Grumman's F2F design was selected in November 1932. This plane was very rugged and maneuverable. (Official U.S. Navy Photograph, Courtesy Grant Daily)

The U.S. Navy's first monoplane was the Douglas TBD Devastator torpedo-bomber. A three-man crew was accommodated and the wings were folded hydraulically. This flight of Douglas TBD-1 Devastators are in Torpedo Five from USS Yorktown. (McDonnell Douglas, Courtesy Hubert K. Gagos)

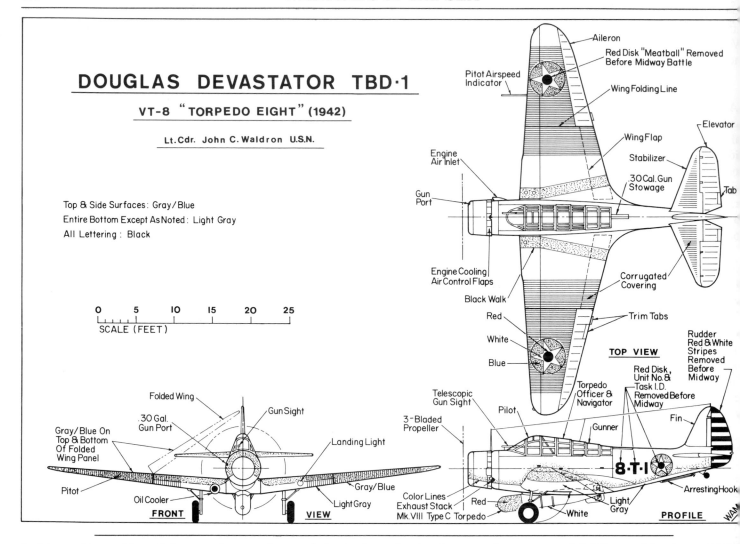

DOUGLAS DEVASTATOR TBD·1

VT-8 "TORPEDO EIGHT" (1942)

Lt.Cdr. John C. Waldron U.S.N.

Top & Side Surfaces: Gray/Blue
Entire Bottom Except As Noted: Light Gray
All Lettering: Black

SCALE (FEET)
0   5   10   15   20   25

Aileron
Red Disk "Meatball" Removed Before Midway Battle
Pitot Airspeed Indicator
Wing Folding Line
Elevator
Engine Air Inlet
Wing Flap
Stabilizer
Gun Port
.30 Cal. Gun Stowage
Tab
Engine Cooling Air Control Flaps
Corrugated Covering
Black Walk
Red
Trim Tabs
White
TOP VIEW
Blue
Rudder Red & White Stripes Removed Before Midway
Red Disk, Unit No. 8, Task I.D. Removed Before Midway
Telescopic Gun Sight
Pilot
Torpedo Officer & Navigator
Fin
3-Bladed Propeller
Gunner
Folded Wing
Gun Sight
.30 Gal. Gun Port
Landing Light
Gray/Blue On Top & Bottom Of Folded Wing Panel
Gray/Blue
Pitot
Oil Cooler
Light Gray
Color Lines Exhaust Stack
Red
Light Gray
Arresting Hook
Mk.VIII Type C Torpedo
White
FRONT
VIEW
PROFILE

bed to avoid repetition of these unpleasant characteristics in the new F3F series then in the planning stages.

First U.S. Navy Monoplane
The U.S. Navy initiated development of a new torpedo-bomber in 1934 which was intended for the new generation of aircraft carriers starting with *USS Ranger*. Prototypes were ordered from Douglas and Great Lakes on June 30, 1934. Ten months later Great Lakes delivered their XTBG-1, which was a conventional biplane, while Douglas submitted their XTBD-1, which was an all-metal low-wing monoplane. This design competition was the transition point from biplane to monoplane.

Power Operated Wing Folding
The wing-mounted landing gear retracted back into the wing, exposing one half of the wheels which, it was claimed, would provide partial protection in the event of a wheels-up landing. The corrugated wing outer panels, which folded upwards and over the fuselage for stowage on carriers, featured another first of a kind; the wing-folding was power actuated in lieu of manual.

Crew and Armament
The XTBD-1 was designed for a crew of three; pilot, torpedo of-

ficer/navigator, and rear gunner. A 1,000 pound bomb or a 15 foo torpedo of equal weight could be carried under the fuselage.

First Flight and Assigned Units
First flight of the XTBD-1 was made on April 15, 1935 and it wa delivered to the Navy on the 24th. After successful trials the ne monoplane was approved and 129 were ordered on February 1936. Deliveries began on June 25, 1937 and Torpedo Squadro VT-3 was the first to receive the TBD-1. Six months later VT-VT-5, and VT-6 were equipped in the Spring of 1937. At tim the TBD-1 was one of the finest carrier-based strike aircraft in th world. The name Devastator was adopted for this pace-setter.

Devastator Data
Powerplant of the Douglas Devastator was the 900 horsepower Pra & Whitney R-1830-64 air-cooled radial engine which produced maximum speed of 206 miles per hour at 8,000 feet. Combat rang with a 1,000 pound bomb was 716 miles at 128 miles per hour. Th initial rate of climb was 720 feet per minute and service ceiling wa 19,700 feet. Wingspan was 50 feet and length 35 feet. Height wa 15 feet-1 inch. Empty weight was 6,182 pounds and gross weig 10,194 pounds. Wing area was 422 square feet. One fixed forwar firing and one flexible-mounted .30 inch caliber machine gun we

tted. The Douglas TBD-1 Devastator remained in service into World War II where this torpedo-bomber was used extensively at the Battle of Midway.

JAPANESE AIRCRAFT CARRIERS - 1930s

As with the U.S. and Britain, Japan was reluctant to scrap its capital ships in compliance with the Washington Treaty and had decided to convert two battle cruisers then under construction, *Akagi* and *Amagi*, into aircraft carriers. Since the Washington Conference participants had permitted the U.S. to convert two large battle cruisers, *Lexington* and *Saratoga*, Britain and Japan were also permitted to do the same, as Britain had selected *Glorious* and *Courageous* for conversion.

Amagi Earthquake Disaster

By converting *Amagi* and *Akagi*, Japan saw the chance of having two carriers that could compete with America's *Lexington* class. The ships were ordered for conversion in November 1922. As the conversion design neared completion, a violent earthquake struck the Tokyo district of Japan on September 1, 1923 and *Amagi* was so badly damaged that it was beyond repair and had to be scrapped. The partially completed battleship *Kaga* was selected as the *Amagi* replacement; therefore, the two ships were not sisters, but are often wrongly classed together. Near-sisters is a better description.

Akagi Conversion

Conversion work on the *Akagi* began late in 1923. The basic hull remained intact except for a reduction in the armor thickness: waterline belt from 10 inches to 6 inches; Upper Deck armor reduced from 3.8 inches to 3.1 inches and lowered to the Main Deck. These hull weight reductions were necessary because, as with the British *Courageous* class, a very heavy double-decked Hangar arrangement was planned. A 100 x 624 feet Flight Deck was erected atop the Hangars and located over the after three-quarters of the hull. The forward end of each Hangar opened onto a Flying-Off Deck; Upper Hangar Flying-Off Deck was 50 feet long while lower Flying-Off Deck was 175 feet long, extending to the bow. This arrangement permitted aircraft to takeoff from three decks; thereby, enabling a strike force to takeoff very quickly. This arrangement gave *Akagi* a stepped profile, as had the *Furious* reconstruction and the *Courageous* class. The Flight Deck sloped down toward the bow and stern with the high point amidships. Two elevators were installed fore and aft with longitudinal arresting gear cables between them on the Flight Deck.

Akagi Uptakes and Bridge

The boiler uptakes were trunked to the starboard side and discharged out of an unusual downward and aft sloping smokestack which effectively diverted the exhaust gasses down to the water and away from the Flight Deck.

The navigating bridge was located under the forward edge of the principal Flight Deck. An auxiliary navigating station was located on the starboard side forward, also under the Flight Deck.

Akagi Data

The 29,600 ton *Akagi* was equipped with 19 boilers producing steam for turbines totalling 131,000 shaft horsepower; driving four propellers. Speed was 32.5 knots and range was 8,000 miles at 14 knots. Both coal and oil were used for fuel because the Japanese islands must import all of the oil they use. Burning coal and oil helped to conserve the scarce oil supply. Eight of the boilers were coal burning, while the remaining 11 burned oil-sprayed, pulverized coal.

Armament was 60 aircraft and ten 8 inch guns plus twelve 4.7 inch guns. Complement was 1,600 officers and enlisted personnel.

IJNS *Akagi* keel had been laid in December 1920 as a battle cruiser and was launched as an aircraft carrier. Commissioning was in March 1927.

Final Configuration

In 1929 the longitudinal arresting gear was replaced with a transverse cable system, and because the short flying-off decks became useless as planes grew larger and heavier, the lowermost Flying-Off Deck was shortened and the Flight Deck was increased by 193 feet to the end of the bow. Hangar space was also extended forward. A new aircraft elevator was added amidships and a small island was fitted on the port side, instead of the more conventional starboard side. The 8 inch guns were removed and 14 twin-mounted 25 mm antiaircraft guns added. Displacement rose to 36,500 tons and speed dropped to 31.5 knots. The aircraft complement was increased to 90, including such types as Mitsubishi A5M fighters, Aichi D1A dive bombers, and Yokosuka B4Y torpedo-bombers.

The Japanese carrier Akagi is shown in its final configuration on April 27, 1939 in Sukumo Bay. Akagi had been converted from a battle cruiser and the Flight Deck was lengthened shortly after commissioning. (U.S. Naval Historical Center, Courtesy Kazutoshi Hando, Tokyo)

Although there is a strong resemblance, Akagi and Kaga are not sister ships. Kaga, shown here at sea in 1936, was converted from a battleship. Note the downward discharge of the smokestack which was shortened in 1935. (U.S. Naval Historical Center, Courtesy Kazutoshi Hando, Tokyo)

Kaga Conversion

The battleship *Kaga* was chosen for conversion to an aircraft carrier, not because it was the best selection, but on grounds of economy! Battle cruiser sisters to *Akagi* were on shipyard ways but it was cheaper to convert the laid up *Kaga* despite its less powerful machinery and broader hull.

Conversion of *Kaga* was based on the *Akagi* specification and; therefore, the two ships appeared identical when completed. Obvious differences included the smokestacks which, on IJNS *Kaga*, were ducted aft for a distance of 300 feet on each side of the hull under the Flight Deck. In addition, transverse arresting gear cables were installed instead of the initially installed longitudinal system on *Akagi*.

Kaga Data

The Flight Deck measured 100 x 560 feet on a 782 feet long hull and a 97 feet beam. With a displacement of 29,600 tons and 91,000 shaft horsepower *Kaga* top speed was 27.5 knots. Range was 8,000 miles at 14 knots.

The number of aircraft and defensive guns were the same as *Akagi*. Complement was 1,340.

Kaga keel had been laid in July 1920 and launched as a battleship in November 1921. *Kaga* was commissioned as an aircraft carrier in March 1928.

The powerplant was combination oil/coal-fired; 12 boilers having been installed while steam turbines drove four propellers.

Kaga Modifications

Seven years after commissioning as a carrier, *Kaga* was reconstructed following the plan used for *Akagi*, except that the small island was installed on the conventional starboard side of the Flight Deck. An additional modification to *Kaga* was the rearrangement of the smokestack by eliminating the long horizontal port and starboard runs and duplicating the *Akagi* downturned exhaust duct amidships on one side of the ship only. A new 127,500 shaft horsepower powerplant was also installed which increased the speed by only one knot because the displacement had risen to 38,200 tons because of the added weight.

Kaga Aircraft

Among the aircraft that operated from *Kaga* was Mitsubishi B1M attacker, Nakajima A1N fighter, Aichi D1A and Mitsubishi A5M fighter.

Ryujo; Purpose-Built Carrier

In November 1929 Japan began the construction of a most extraordinary purpose-built aircraft carrier; *Ryujo*. Earlier in this chapter was mentioned the fact that Japanese designers were driven to pack

The Japanese Ryujo was a most extraordinary purpose-built aircraft carrier. In order to carry as many aircraft as possible, double deck hangars were fitted which created instability problems for the 8,000 ton ship. Observe that the bow wave is up to the Main Deck in the calm sea. (U.S. Naval Historical Center)

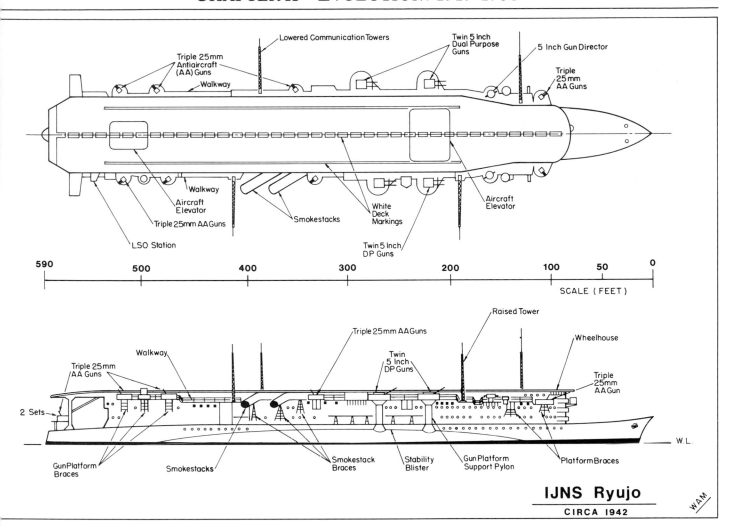

IJNS Ryujo
CIRCA 1942

the most into the smallest hull due to Treaty restrictions. *Ryujo* is an example of this overloading folly.

As with the American *Lexington* and *Saratoga*, *Akagi* and *Kaga* had used a considerable amount of Japan's allowable aircraft carrier tonnage according to Treaty restrictions. In this way it was planned to make this small ship as potent as larger fleet carriers.

Ryujo Data

The hull design was that of a light cruiser 590 feet long overall with a beam of 66 feet. As originally conceived, a full-length Hangar was to be fitted; however, this would accommodate less than 30 aircraft and more were desired. In order to meet the ambitious requirement for more planes a second Hangar was mounted atop the original. Of course, this had been done in the past, but on much larger carriers than the 8,000 ton *Ryujo*. The Hangar addition increased the aircraft capacity to 48 but the topside weight started a series of stability problems. A 75 x 513 feet Flight Deck was installed atop the upper Hangar which was in line with the hull fantail and extended forward for about seven-eighths of the hull length. The navigating bridge was located under the forward edge of the Flight Deck. Two elevators were installed; one well aft and the other just forward of midship. Transverse arresting gear cables were fitted.

The six oil-fired boilers generated steam for two geared turbines which delivered a total of 65,000 shaft horsepower to two propellers. The boiler uptakes were run to the starboard side where they terminated in two downward and aft canted smokestacks. The stacks extended out so far that they had to be supported from below with three triangular steel structures.

Speed was 29 knots and at 14 knots the range was 10,000 miles. Complement was 600 officers and enlisted crew.

Armament consisted of four twin 5 inch guns and 10 triple 25 millimeter antiaircraft guns. The dual 5 inch gun installations were mounted atop vertical pylon-like sponsons which extended from the hull blister to just below the Flight Deck, two on each side of the ship.

Ryujo was launched in April 1931 and commissioned in May 1933. Stability problems were so severe that in the following year the ship returned to the shipyard where efforts were made to remedy the problem. Ballast was added low in the hull and the blisters were enlarged, producing a beam of 68 feet. The after two dual 5 inch guns were removed along with their sponsons in a rash move to reduce topside weight. In addition, the hull was strengthened. These needed modifications improved stability somewhat; however, the displacement went up to 10,800 tons, which increased the draft from 18 feet-3 inches to 23 feet-3 inches. This reduced the

The Soryu class of Japanese carriers comprised light structured, high speed ships that carried 72 aircraft. As with Ark Royal in the Royal Navy the Soryu class was to set the pattern for future Japanese carriers. Soryu was commissioned in late 1935. (U.S. Naval Historical Center, Courtesy Kazutoshi Hando, Tokyo)

freeboard so dangerously low that Main Deck sheer was increased forward to form a forecastle, thereby raising the stem.

Ryujo Aircraft

During her career *Ryujo* operated with Mitsubishi A5M fighters, Nakajima B5N torpedo-bombers, and Mitsubishi A6M fighter-bombers.

JAPAN RENOUNCES WASHINGTON TREATY

For obvious reasons a decision was made not to repeat the *Ryujo* experiment. In desperation, Japan looked to the aircraft-carrying cruiser or the through-deck cruiser because, at the U.S.'s suggestion, the London Naval Conference had agreed that these would not be classified as aircraft carriers. The Imperial Japanese Navy reasoned that if the Washington Treaty restrictions were to be followed Japan would be forced to either repeat the *Ryujo* or opt for the aircraft-carrying cruiser. The latter was selected with designs prepared and construction funded for two 17,000 ton vessels under the 1931-1932 program. Before the project got underway Japan decided it could not live within the Washington Treaty limitations which allowed her a navy only three-fifths the size of the U.S. Navy and of the Royal Navy. Japan; therefore, decided to cancel her agreement with the restrictive terms of the Treaty, although this important decision had not yet been announced to the world.

Japanese Light-Weight Carriers

Instead of the two through-deck cruisers, a type which was to become extremely popular with the world's navies a half-century later, the Imperial Japanese Navy decided upon two light-structured, high-speed carriers with a respectable aircraft complement. The keels of

Soryu and *Hiryu* were laid in November 1934 and July 1936, respectively. It was intended that the design concept of *Soryu* and *Hiryu* should set the pattern for future Japanese aircraft carriers.

As was noted above, *Soryu* was started about 20 months before *Hiryu*. This delay appears to have been timed so the keel would not be laid until after the second London Naval Conference because construction of *Hiryu*, as the second carrier, would have pushed Japan's total tonnage above the allowed 81,000 tons, thereby violating the Treaty and risking international disgrace.

Soryu Data

The *Soryu* hull of 746 feet long x 70 feet beam was a very light structure with minimal protection which consisted of 1.8 inch belt armor and 1 inch deck armor for the machinery spaces plus 2. inches overhead armor for the magazines.

Soryu was fitted with two Hangars, one set above the other. The 420 feet long lower Hangar was recessed well into the hull thereby lowering the ship's profile and the important center of gravity. The upper Hangar was about 100 feet longer. A Flight Deck measuring 85 feet-6 inches wide x 705 feet-6 inches long was erected atop the upper Hangar. This was fitted with three aircraft elevators. A complement of 72 aircraft could be carried and 150,000 gallons of aviation gasoline tankage was installed.

Geared steam turbines served by eight boilers delivered a total of 152,000 shaft horsepower to four shafts. Speed was 34.5 knots and at 18 knots the range was 7,800 miles.

The boiler uptake ducts were led to the starboard side, amidships, terminating in two downward and aft directed smokestacks. A small island was installed on the starboard side in way of the smokestacks on this 16,000 ton carrier.

Hiryu was the other member of the Soryu class but differed from Soryu by having the island on the port side, instead of the conventional starboard side. In addition, the Soryu island was located forward of midship, while the Hiryu island was amidship. Hiryu also had more freeboard than Soryu. (U.S. Naval Historical Center, Courtesy Kazutoshi Hando, Tokyo)

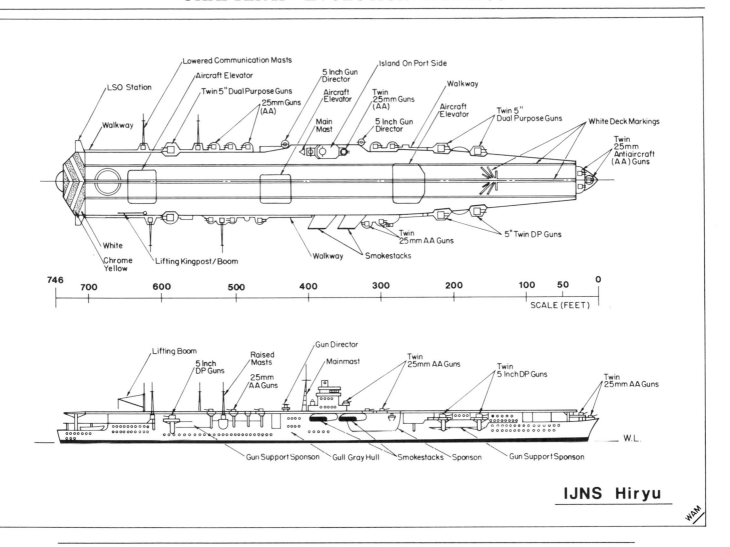

IJNS Hiryu

Armament included six twin 5 inch guns and 14 twin 25 millimeter gun installations. All guns were antiaircraft types, another progressive move for Japanese carriers.

Soryu was launched in December 1935 and commissioned in January 1937.

SECOND LONDON NAVAL DISARMAMENT CONFERENCE

Meanwhile, the Second London Conference had convened on December 9, 1935 with Britain, the U.S., Japan, France, and Italy attending. Japan had some feeling of security until the passage of the Vinson-Trammel Act because, when the program covered by this Act would be completed, the U.S. Navy would have the 67 percent margin of superiority which was so feared by Japanese strategists. Again, Japan asked for parity, and again her request was refused by the Anglo-Americans. Blocked at every turn, which was as she expected, Japan refused to renew the Naval Limitation Treaty on its expiration in 1936 and renounced her participation in the Treaty. Feeling isolated Japan looked for friends and joined Italy and Germany in the Anti-Comintern (Anti-Communist) Pact on November 25, 1936.

Second London Conference Fails

Italy remained at the Conference; however, she refused to sign the final agreement. The Conference concluded on March 25, 1936 with Britain, France and the U.S. remaining but the Treaty contained so many contingency clauses that it was meaningless. It appeared that the period of naval arms limitations had ended.

Anglo-Americans Prepare for War

Naval experts in the U.S. and Britain continued to press their governments to concentrate on naval research and construction. Contrary to the spirit of appeasement in Britain and isolationism in America, the governments began to take notice of their warnings and began preparations for the unthinkable, but apparently inevitable war.

Japan Proceeds With *Hiryu*

With the restrictions of the Washington Treaty expired, the Imperial Japanese Navy was now free to proceed with *Hiryu*.

Hiryu Data

Experience during the construction of *Soryu* revealed areas which needed improvement and these were applied to *Hiryu*: hull was strengthened and forecastie made higher; hull beam was increased to 73 feet-3 inches; armor was increased to 3.5 inches for the machinery space belt and to 5.9 inches for the magazine. *Hiryu* now displaced 17,300 tons and was about 10 feet longer. Aircraft complement was 73. The island was located on the port side as on *Akagi*. *Hiryu* was launched in November 1937 and commissioned in July 1939.

JAPANESE SHIPBOARD AIRCRAFT - 1930s

These ships were to play an important part in the fierce naval battles soon to come.

With five new aircraft carriers afloat the Japanese Navy embarked upon a program to develop a new generation of carrier-based aircraft and to encourage native Japanese designs in lieu of importing European designers and prototypes.

Nakajima A2N1 Fighter

Nakajima Hikoki K.K. introduced a very successful biplane fighter in early 1930 which had the classic lines of the Curtiss Goshawk and Boeing F4B-4. This nimble, yet easy to control, design became the standard Japanese carrier-based fighter throughout the early 1930s, having entered production in late 1930. The plane was well liked by both pilots and mechanics.

A2N1 Data

The Nakajima A2N1 or Type 90 fighter was powered by a 450 horsepower Bristol Jupiter VI which was fitted with a deep Townend ring. Nakajima built this British air-cooled radial engine under license. The 2,866 pound craft attained a maximum speed of 187 miles per hour at 6,560 feet. Service ceiling was 32,150 feet and combat range was about 400 miles. The Type 90 had a wingspan of 30 feet-10 inches and was 21 feet-7 inches long. Height was 10 feet-6 inches.

A modified version, A2N2, was strengthened and incorporated dihedral in the upper wing. Over 100 of both models were produced. Armament was two fixed forward firing 7.7 millimeter machine guns.

Operating from *Kaga*, 24 of the Type 90 saw action over northern China during the Sino-Japanese Incident in 1937.

A4N1 Variant

In 1924, the A4N1 made its appearance as a modification of and replacement, for the beloved A2N1 but was not as well received by the Japanese carrier pilots. The A4N1 or Type 95 was powered by a 750 horsepower engine and was fast and maneuverable; therefore, a production order for 300 was issued. A squadron of the Type 95, operated from the carrier *Hosho*, in the Japanese occupation in northern China in 1937; however, its limited range proved a handicap and an effort to increase the range of future Japanese carrier-based fighter planes was designated a priority project.

Mitsubishi B2M1 Torpedo-Bomber

When the Imperial Japanese Navy issued a specification for a carrier-based attack plane to Nakajima, Aichi, Kawanishi and Mitsubishi, the latter hired British aircraft design teams to prepare the preliminary design, which included Blackburn, Handley-Page, and a team headed by Herbert Smith. Mitsubishi couldn't lose with this talent!

The Blackburn design was submitted to the Japanese Naval Air Force and accepted. The prototype was built by Blackburn and delivered to Japan in February 1930. Even Blackburn's Chief Engineer went to Japan to supervise the construction of additional Mitsubishi prototypes.

The three-seat biplane was accepted in March 1932 and ordered into production as Mitsubishi B2M1 or the Navy Type 89. Blackburn had designed another winner.

B2M1 Data

The B2M1 was powered with a 600 horsepower Mitsubishi-built Hispano-Suiza water-cooled engine which gave the 7,940 pound torpedo-bomber a 132 miles per hour maximum speed. Service ceiling was 14,300 feet and range was 1,105 miles.

Wingspan was 49 feet-11 inches; length 21 feet-7 inches; and height 12 feet-2 inches. The B2M1 had a fabric covered all-metal framework. A modified version appeared in 1934 as the B2M2 and production of both models totalled 205. Armament was one fixed forward-firing and one flexible-mounted aft-firing 7.7 millimeter machine gun. These aircraft had been used in the Sino-Japanese Incident.

The Nakajima A2N1 was the first Japanese-designed and built carrier-based fighter. This handsome aircraft was very maneuverable, yet easy to fly. It saw action in the Sino-Japanese Incident. (National Air & Space Museum)

This Mitsubishi B2M1 carrier-based-attack or strike aircraft design involved at least three British design teams. Over 200 B2M airframes were built. (U.S. National Archives)

The Aichi D1A was the first Japanese aircraft specifically designed for dive bombing. Called Susie by the World War II Allies, the plane made world headlines when a flight from Ryujo sank the American gunboat Panay in 1937. (National Air & Space Museum)

Aichi D1A Susie Dive Bomber

Aichi Kokuki produced the first Japanese airplane specifically designed for dive bombing purposes. In 1933 when the Japanese Navy invited Aichi and Nakajima to submit dive bomber designs for consideration, it granted Aichi permission to offer a plane that was not an original design. The reason for this concession has never been revealed.

Aichi was inspired by the Luftwaffe's Heinkel He-50 single-seat biplane fighter despite the fact that the Navy Specification had required a 600 pound plus bombload and a two-man crew. The Aichi design proved to be superior to the Nakajima and the Type 94 carrier-based dive bomber was placed in production in late 1933. It is generally known as the Aichi D1A. An air-cooled radial engine was installed instead of the Heinkel's water-cooled powerplant and the wings were double-bay rigged, instead of the single-bay Heinkel design in order to strengthen them to endure the powerful forces of dive bombing. Allied code name for the D1A was Susie.

D1A1 Data

A 580 horsepower Nakajima Kotobuki 2-1 engine gave the D1A1 a top speed of 174 miles per hour. Range was 660 miles. Three guns were installed; two fixed-firing forward and one movable in the rear cockpit. A 680 pound bomb load could be carried.

A total of 162 D1A1's were produced and early in 1934 the type began serving aboard *Ryujo*.

D1A2 Data

An improved version was fitted with a 730 horsepower Nakajima Hikari 3 air-cooled radial engine which raised top speed to 195 miles per hour and increased the bomb load to 880 pounds. Visible external modifications included streamline wheel covers and a wider Townend cowl ring. This type was D1A2 of which 428 were constructed.

The D1A2 created an international incident when a flight from *Ryujo* mistakenly attacked and sank the American gunboat Panay on the Yangtse River on December 12, 1937.

SINO-JAPANESE INCIDENT

In 1931 Japan had announced its policy of a "Greater East Asia Co-Prosperity Sphere" which was intended to free Asian countries from colonialism and imperialism, solve Japan's over-population, and make Manchuria the bulwark against Communism in Asia. Critics accused Japan of imperialism and colonialism but, in truth, it was no more than the Europeans had been doing to Asia for hundreds of years. At least they (the Japanese) were of the same Yellow Race, was Japan's argument. By that time Japanese investment in China had reached 1.25 billion dollars, which was about one-third of the total Japanese foreign investment, yet this was less than Britain's total investment in China.

The Communist influence in China was increasing rapidly and the Chinese periodically boycotted Japanese goods. In July 1937 Japan overreacted and attacked China, capturing Shanghai and Peiping. This became known as the Sino-Japanese Incident. The Chinese surrounded the Japanese marine garrison in Shanghai and this became the Shanghai Incident as the Japanese fought to rescue the entrapped troops. The Sino-Japanese Incident and the Shanghai Incident are both used to describe this conflict. Japanese carrier aircraft were also involved in this fighting; flying from *Ryujo*, *Hosho*, and *Kaga*.

JAPANESE NAVY TURNS TO MONOPLANES

The Japanese Naval Air Service was rapidly drifting away from the British biplane influence and drawn towards the American monoplane ideal which the U.S. had not yet fully accomplished.

Mitsubishi A5M Claude Monoplane Fighter

Well aware of the fact that Japanese airplane manufacturers were still depending heavily upon European designs, the Imperial Japanese Navy issued a requirement, in 1934, for an original naval monoplane fighter which no naval power had yet satisfactorily developed and; therefore, could not be copied. Jiro Horikoshi accepted the challenge.

Jiro Horikoshi was considered by his associates as one of the world's greatest aircraft designers. He had joined the Nagoya Aircraft Works of Mitsubishi Heavy Industries in 1927 and some of Japan's finest fighter plane designs had been created on his draft-

The Mitsubishi A5M2b was the final variant of the world's first operational naval monoplane fighter. Named Claude by the Allies, the plane created a sensation in the Sino-Japanese Incident. (Official U.S. Navy Photograph, News Photo Division)

ing board. Horikoshi applied his talent to the new project and produced a remarkable step forward in Japanese aeronautical design.

The Mitsubishi A5M single-seat, all-metal monoplane fighter which he developed was of low wing configuration with flush riveting; employed for the first time in Japan. A cantilever, fairing-covered landing gear was attached to the graceful semi-elliptical wing which was fitted with full split flaps; another first for Japanese military aircraft.

The initial prototype made its first flight on February 4, 1935 and had been built with an inverted gull wing very much like the Stuka dive bomber and Vought F4U Corsair. This was done to improve downward visibility; however, control problems forced a change to a more conventional three-panel wing.

A5M Production

The first production model was the A5M1 Type 96 of which only 37 were constructed. This model was replaced by the A5M2a. Produced simultaneously with the A5M2a was the next variant A5M2b. This model was fitted with a sliding cockpit enclosure which was disliked by pilots. After a short service life production of the 2b was discontinued. The A5M3a was an experiment with a Hispano-Suiza 12-cylinder water-cooled engine which was fitted with a cannon firing through the hollow propeller shaft, but the Imperial Japanese Navy wasn't impressed. The last model to see service was the A5M4 which remained in front line service through the first six months of 1942. The Allied code-name for the A5M was Claude.

A5M2a Data

The 3,550 pound A5M2a was powered by 610 horsepower Kotobuki 2 Kai-3 air-cooled, direct drive radial engine which propelled the plane to a maximum speed of 265 miles per hour at 10,000 feet. Combat range was 460 miles and service ceiling was 14,026 feet. Wingspan was 35 feet-6 inches; length 25 feet-7 inches and height 10 feet-6 inches. One thousand Claudes were built.

Claude Action In The Sino-Japanese Incident

The A5M or Type 96 fighter received its baptism of fire in the Sino-Japanese Incident. As previously mentioned, the Japanese Marine Garrison in Shanghai was surrounded by a very large Chinese force in mid-August 1937. This force was supported by about 300 planes and threatened to exterminate the marines. Since there was no usable airfield near Shanghai the surrounded garrison had to depend upon the Japanese Carrier Striking Force.

The Carrier Striking Force consisted of the First Carrier Division under the command of Rear Admiral Shiro Takasu in *Ryujo* and the Second Carrier Division under the command of Rear Admiral Rokuro Horie in *Kaga*. The air groups included the Nakajima A2N and A4N fighters, Mitsubishi B2M torpedo-bombers, Aichi D1A dive bombers and others. These were distributed in *Kaga* of the Second Carrier Division and *Ryujo* and *Hosho* of the First Carrier Division.

The planes of *Kaga* suffered severe losses at the onset when the entire complement of (12) B2M attack planes, led by Group Commander Lieutenant Commander Iwai, headed for a raid against Hangchou on August 17. The bombers were intercepted by a mixed bag of Chinese fighters, including British Gloster Gladiator biplanes,

Curtiss Hawk 75 monoplanes (ancestor of the famous P-40), Soviet-built I-15 biplanes and I-16 monoplanes which types had seen action in the Spanish Civil War. Eleven of the Japanese attackers were shot down with the 12th so badly damaged that it barely made it back to Kaga. The carrier was then ordered to return to Sasebo immediately and load a full complement of A5M fighters. It was to return to the Shanghai theatre when fully loaded.

Among the Claude pilots were four of Japan's outstanding fighter leaders and tacticians; Lieutenant Commander Minoru Genda, Lieutenant Commander Okamura, Lieutenant Nomura and Lieutenant Nango. The first A5M raid was against Nanking on September 18 when the monoplanes escorted D1A dive bombers. This combination was repeated over and over again, even after the Shanghai Garrison was saved. The Chinese air force put up a desperate air defense against the A5M fighters but the Claudes proved their superiority. During one engagement over Nanking Lieutenant Nango's pilots destroyed 10 Soviet-built I-16 monoplane fighters without loss to themselves. A hard-to-believe incident was experienced by Flight Petty Officer Kashimura when he had just dived on a Chinese I-16 and shot it down. As he sped past the stricken plane it tumbled out of control, smashing into Kashimura's Claude. The impact tore off more than one-third of the Mitsubishi port wing but the pilot managed to return to base safely; a fitting testimonial to the A5M durability.

Despite the A5M success, its range was insufficient for naval operations in the Pacific so Jiro Horikoshi went to work on the design of a long range naval fighter to succeed Claude.

Aichi D3A Va1 Monoplane Dive Bomber

Even the dive bomber, which was the last aircraft type adopted for Japanese carrier duty, was selected for conversion to monoplane design. In 1936 the Imperial Japanese Navy requested that Mitsubishi, Aichi and Nakajima submit monoplane dive bomber designs for approval. The Aichi design was chosen and a development contract was awarded.

Aichi D3A Val

The Japanese government had, for some time, an agreement with the German aircraft manufacturer, Ernst Heinkel A.G., for the exchange of technical information and design data. In view of its elliptically-shaped low wing configuration and similar weight and dimensions the Aichi D3A dive bomber is often compared to the Heinkel He 70 and He 170 aircraft. The new design became the first Japanese all-metal low wing monoplane dive bomber when it was selected for production in December 1937.

D3A1 Data

The Aichi D3A1 or Type 99 carrier-based dive bomber was powered with a 1,075 horsepower Mitsubishi Kinsei air-cooled radial engine. The 8,047 pound plane attained a maximum speed of 242 miles per hour at 7,600 feet. Service ceiling was 31,200 feet and range 1,130 miles. Wingspan was 47 feet-1 inch and length was 33 feet-5 inches with a height of 12 feet.

The D3A design was exceptionally strong, and quite maneuverable without its bomb load. A single swing-mounted 550 pound bomb was located under the fuselage and this could be supplemented

AICHI D3A2 VAL II TYPE 99

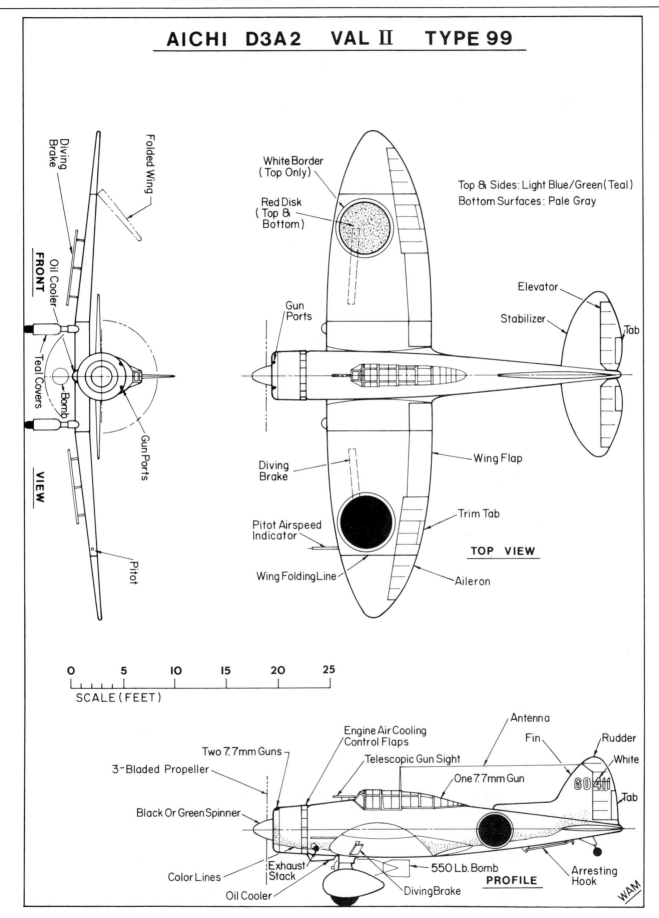

Folded Wing

Diving Brake

Oil Cooler

FRONT

Teal Covers

Bomb

Gun Ports

VIEW

Pitot

White Border (Top Only)

Red Disk (Top & Bottom)

Top & Sides: Light Blue/Green (Teal)
Bottom Surfaces: Pale Gray

Gun Ports

Elevator

Stabilizer

Tab

Diving Brake

Wing Flap

Pitot Airspeed Indicator

Trim Tab

TOP VIEW

Wing Folding Line

Aileron

```
0     5     10    15    20    25
|  |  |  |  |  |  |  |  |  |  |
SCALE (FEET)
```

Engine Air Cooling Control Flaps

Antenna

Fin

Rudder

Two 7.7mm Guns

Telescopic Gun Sight

White

3-Bladed Propeller

One 7.7mm Gun

60 411

Black Or Green Spinner

Tab

Color Lines

Exhaust Stack

550 Lb. Bomb

Arresting Hook

Oil Cooler

Diving Brake

PROFILE

WAM

The first all-metal low wing monoplane dive bomber was the Aichi D3A, named Val by the Allies. Val was one of the most successful naval dive bombers of World War II. (U.S. National Archives)

Val and the German Junkers Stuka were the only fixed landing gear dive bombers that were operational throughout World War II. Note the bomb and elliptical wing on this Aichi D3A Val. (U.S. Naval Historical Center)

with underwing bombs up to a total of 800 pounds. The bomb which is dropped by a dive bomber travels faster than the bomber because it has less resistance and if the plane continues in its dive, and does not pull out at once, there is the danger of having the bomb strike the propeller with disasterous results. The swing-mount is a rigid trapeze which swings the bomb forward and down so it clears the propeller arc prior to its release. This was standard dive bomber equipment by the late 1930s. Two fixed forward-firing 7.7 millimeter machine guns and one flexible-mount gun firing aft were fitted. The outboard six feet of the wing folded up for carrier stowage.

D3A Production

The D3A1 was the standard dive bomber of the Japanese Naval Air Service during the early years of the Pacific War and is credited with the sinking of several ships of the U.S. and Royal Navies. Its Allied code name was Val. Over 475 D3A1 airframes were produced by 1942 when it was replaced by the D3A2 of which 816 were built by 1944.

D3A2 Data

The D3A2 Val was fitted with the more powerful 1,300 horsepower Kinsei 54 engine which increased the plane's weight to 9,080 pounds. Speed went up to 266 miles per hour, but combat range dropped to 970 miles.

Vals took part in virtually every Pacific naval battle and when teamed with the Kate torpedo-bomber the pair proved most troublesome to the Allied navies.

Nakajima B5N Kate Monoplane Torpedo Bomber

The Imperial Japanese Navy was fascinated with the torpedo bomber as was the Royal Navy and both were well rewarded for their faith in this weapon. Early in 1936 the Japanese Naval Air Service had requested design submittals for a carrier-based monoplane torpedo-bomber capable of at least 207 miles per hour. Nakajima and Mitsubishi responded and although the Nakajima design was selected a small contract for the less progressive Mitsubishi design was placed as insurance against failure of the Nakajima.

The Nakajima B5N torpedo-bomber was Val's partner in attacks on Allied ships during World War II, having participated in the sinking of two U.S. battleships and four U.S. aircraft carriers. (U.S. Naval Historical Center)

Nakajima B5N Kate

The prototype Nakajima B5N1 made its first flight in January 1937. The all-metal stressed-skin, low wing monoplane was fitted with a hydraulically operated retractable landing gear which was the first installation for a single-engine Japanese plane. Other very progressive design features included mechanically folding wings, Fowler flaps, Hamilton-Standard controllable pitch propeller built under license, and NACA (U.S. National Advisory Committee for Aeronautics) long cowling. The design generally exhibited a decided American appearance.

B5N1 Data

Powered by a 770 horsepower Hikari 3 nine-cylinder air-cooled radial engine the 8,045 pounds gross B5N1 attained a maximum speed of 229 miles per hour at 6,560 feet. Service ceiling was 24,280 feet and range 684 miles. Wingspan was 50 feet-11 inches, length 33 feet-11 inches, and height 12 feet-2 inches. Wing area was 406 square feet.

B5N1 Armament

The B5N1 or Type 97 was equipped to carry an 18 inch, 1,756 pound torpedo under the fuselage. Two 550 pound bombs or six 130 pound bombs on racks under the wing center section could be carried instead of the torpedo on light bombing missions. Two fixed forward-firing 7.7 millimeter machine guns comprised the defensive armament. The Type 97 Nakajima B5N Kate carrier-based torpedo-bomber proved its superiority over the fixed landing gear fitted Mitsubishi B5M1 and; therefore, only 125 of the latter were built. The two or three-seat Nakajima was quite nimble; however, it required a fighter escort, as do most bombers.

B5N2 Variant

In 1939 the Hikari engine was replaced by the 1,000 horsepower Nakajima Sakae II 14-cylinder, twin-row air-cooled radial engine which increased the speed and weight to 235 miles per hour and 9,039 pounds. This modification changed the designation to B5N2.

Production and Service Record

Production began in late 1937. The 1,200 production Nakajima B5N's saw extensive service in the Sino-Japanese Incident as well as the coming Pacific War in which the Allied name for this torpedo-bomber was Kate. The B5N was largely responsible for two U.S. battleship and four U.S. aircraft carrier sinkings and it was in action from Pearl Harbor to the Marianas campaign.

GERMAN SEA POWER AND THE VERSAILLES TREATY

Unlike her two partners, Italy and Japan, Germany was never to be a major naval power because of her political interests and geographical location. Germany's politics were always concentrated in the European heartland, and geographically her limited Baltic and North Sea coasts are too vulnerable to a blockade by a major sea power. The only interest and need for a German naval force is commerce raiders to cut the Sea Lines of Communications of the enemy.

Versailles Treaty Repudiation

The World War I Versailles Treaty restricted Germany to an emasculated coastal defense force with no ship to exceed 10,000 tons, hence the birth of the pocket-battleship. The post-World War Weimar government embarked on a program of submarine and pocket-battleship construction in accordance with the Treaty; however, when Adolf Hitler became Chancellor in 1933 he repudiated the Treaty and accelerated naval construction of larger ships although he never appreciated the importance of sea power. By 1935 Britain felt the need to negotiate another agreement and entered into a bilateral pact with Germany in order to slow the pace of German naval construction. This pact restricted Germany to a fleet no larger than 35 percent of the British fleet tonnage. The Anglo-German naval agreement was hailed as a victory for naval disarmament although it did not restrict the size of the ships to be built.

German Aircraft Carrier

The German Kriegsmarine had been toying with the idea of some sort of air-capable ship since 1930 and had begun basic design work in 1933. The Anglo-German Treaty limited Germany to a total carrier displacement of 42,750 tons and; therefore, Germany decided to construct two aircraft carriers to absorb this allowance. Naval Constructor Wilhelm Haedeler was given the task of leading the design team, as well as supervising the actual construction of the carriers. The biggest obstacle was the fact that, unlike Britain, Japan and the U.S.A., Germany had no experience with aircraft carriers. Despite the realization that there were only two carriers in service of World Navies that had been purpose-built ships, the Germans decided to construct purpose-built carriers rather than convert existing hulls.

Research and Assistance

A carrier of about 20,000 tons was envisioned and the search began for published information about existing aircraft carriers. Articles in *Jane's Fighting Ships* and U.S. Naval Institute *Proceedings* plus technical papers presented before societies such as the American Society of Naval Engineers and the Society of Naval Architects and Marine Engineers were studied very carefully; however, many were obsolete. The design team, therefore, adapted freely from the *Courageous* class of converted cruisers; not only because it approximated the target tonnage, but because these ships were considered as state-of-the-art carriers of the period. The Japanese extended their ally the courtesy of inspecting the *Akagi* and gave the Germans about 100 blueprints as reference material. This convinced the designers to use a full length flight deck instead of a shortened deck as on the *Courageous* class.

Flugzeug Traegers "A" and "B"

The keel of the first German aircraft carrier was laid in Slip No. 1 of Deutche Werke Kiel shipyard on December 28, 1936 and was called Flugzeug Traeger "A" or Aircraft Carrier "A" because it was Kriegsmarine custom to announce the names of combat vessels at the time of launching. The Flugzeug Traeger "B" keel was laid in Germania-Werft shipyard two years later.

Graf Zeppelin

As Haedeler had suspected, the displacement rose as construction progressed. The original design in 1935 called for a displacement of 19,250 tons which increased to 24,500 tons in the following year and to 27,000 tons in 1937. By the time Flugzeug Traeger "A" was launched on December 8, 1938 the displacement had risen to 28,000 tons. Hitler, Goering and many high ranking officials watched Countess Hella von Brandenstein-Zeppelin christen the ship *Graf Zeppelin* (Count Zeppelin) in honor of her father.

Graf Zeppelin Data

The hull overall length was 862 feet with a Flight Deck 790 feet

Tens of thousands of cheering Germans watched Countess Hella von Brandenstein-Zeppelin christen the carrier Graf Zeppelin (Count Zeppelin) in honor of her father on December 8, 1938. Hitler, Goering and other high officials attended the launching. After launching, tugs move the Graf Zeppelin to the outfitting dock for completion. Observe the pointed stern which has since been abandoned. Also note the large openings in the hull at the Hangar Deck. (Bundesarchiv, Courtesy Hans Justus Meier)

Despite the fact that many Japanese carrier drawings were studied by the designers, Graf Zeppelin had a definite British flavor. Note the exceptional freeboard height. (Bundesarchiv, Courtesy Hans Justus Meier)

long and 88 feet wide. Following British practice the aft end of the Flight Deck curved downwards. The hull beam was 15 feet greater than the Flight Deck width, contrary to the growing practice of the time of having the flight deck the same size or greater than the hull dimensions. During construction the weight of the island increased considerably due to the addition of armor for the Navigating Bridge and Chart Room plus the installation of heavier antenna masts. To correct this imbalance the plating for the port side blister was made twice as heavy as that on the starboard side. Shortly before launching Chancellor Hitler made the suggestion that a ship such as Traeger "A" with sufficiently strong armament plus the aircraft capability would be a very effective weapon against enemy lines of supply. His naval architects rejected the idea after conducting studies, never imagining that ships such as the Soviet *Kiev* and the British *Invincible* would appear a half-century later.

The propulsion machinery was the same as that which had been developed for the battleship *Scharnhorst* class. This consisted of four geared steam turbines driving quadruple propellers. High pressure, high temperature steam was generated in 16 La Mont water-tube boilers. One unusual aspect of the machinery installation was the two Voith-Schneider electric motor-driven cycloidal propellers fitted in the bow. The purpose was to assist maneuvering at low speeds and when in harbors. The propellers were to retract into the hull when the ship was at sea. A total of 200,000 shaft horsepower was installed to drive the *Graf Zeppelin* to an estimated maximum speed of 33.8 knots. Range was to be 8,000 miles which was 2,000 miles under that required by the Kriegsmarine because the battleships and battle cruisers with which the *Graf Zeppelin* was to work

in concert had a 10,000 mile range. Complement was to be 1,760.

Armor consisted of a 4 inch hull belt, 2 1/2 and 1 1/2 inch deck protection, and 3/4 inch for the Flight Deck. Armament included 2 x 6 inch guns, 12 x 4.2 inch antiaircraft guns plus 22 x 37 millimeter and 28 x 20 millimeter antiaircraft guns; a formidable array of offensive and defensive armament in addition to its aircraft. The final design called for 42 aircraft; an increase from the originally proposed 30. This was another problem for the unprepared Kriegsmarine; the absence of carrier aircraft and pilots with carrier experience!

German Carrier Aircraft - Late 1930s

Germany, as with Britain, had organized a unified air force in which the Luftwaffe, under Reichsmarshall Goering, controlled not only all military aircraft development, procurement and operation, but also controlled all antiaircraft units, as well as paratroopers. The Naval Corps of the Luftwaffe was Luftkreis IV under the Command of General Zander, a former naval officer with very little influence with the overbearing Goering who had no interest in German naval aviation, which suffered even more than the Fleet Air Arm.

One year before the keel-laying of Traeger "A" at Deutche Werke Kiel the Kriegsmarine had requested Arado Flugzeugwerke GMBH to develop a combined torpedo-bomber/reconnaissance design for shipboard use; however, the prototypes of the Arado Ar-95 failed to meet the specifications. Several weeks after the Traeger "A" keel was laid the Kriegsmarine decided to try again and presented Arado and Gerhard Fiesler Werke GMBH with another speci-

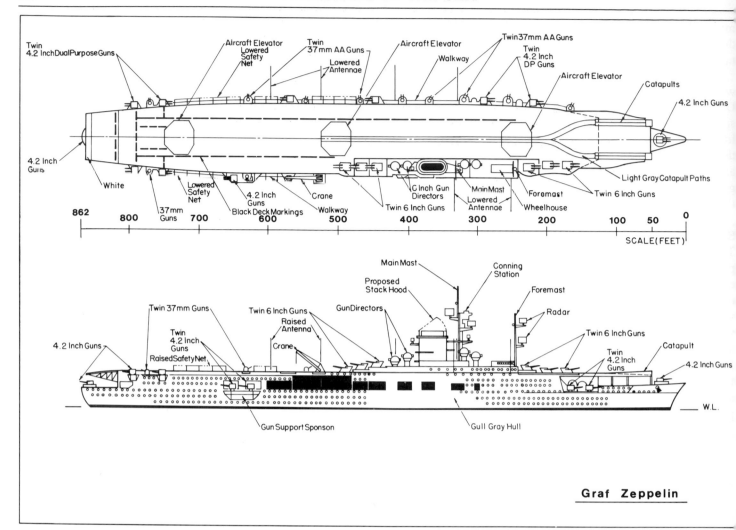

Graf Zeppelin

---

fication for a multi-purpose shipboard aircraft design to replace the unsuccessful Arado Ar-95. The principal requirements were: nonretractable, jettisonable landing gear, folding wings, flotation gear, and the ability to carry a torpedo or 1,100 pounds of bombs. Design proposals from both firms were accepted and prototypes were ordered. Arado proposed a new design Ar-195 and Fiesler offered his Fi-167.

Fiesler Fi-167 Carrier-Based Torpedo-Bomber

The Arado Ar-195 prototype failed to meet the requirements and was rejected; however, the Fiesler Fi-167 biplane project, under the direction of Reinhold Mewes, was a complete success and exceeded the requirements by such a wide margin that the third prototype requirement was replaced with an order for 12 pre-production models. Catapult fittings and arresting hook were fitted.

Fiesler Fi-167 Data

The Fiesler Fi-167 was powered by the 1,100 horsepower Daimler-Benz DB 601B, 12-cylinder, inverted Vee liquid-cooled engine turning a three-bladed propeller. Empty weight was 6,173 pounds and maximum loaded weight was 10,690 pounds. Wingspan was 44 feet-3 1/2 inches, while overall length was 37 feet-4 3/4 inches. Height was 15 feet-9 inches. Total wing area was 490 square feet.

One fixed 7.9 millimeter MG 17 machine gun was installed in th starboard side of the fuselage with 500 rounds while a similar gu was flexible-mounted in the rear cockpit with 600 rounds. The cra could carry a 2,205 pound bomb or a 1,685 pound torpedo. Rack under the lower wing could accommodate four 110 pound bomb plus a 551 pound bomb or a 1,102 pound bomb under the fuselag

Maximum speed as a bomber was 199 miles per hour while o reconnaissance missions speed increased to 202 miles per hou Cruising speed was 155 miles per hour. Combat range for bombin

The Fiesler 167 torpedo-bomber was intended to equip Graf Zeppelin. Landing gear could be jettisoned and flotation gear was fitted. (Bundesarchiv)

missions was 808 miles while for reconnaissance duty range with a drop tank was 932 miles. Service ceiling was 26,900 feet for reconnaissance missions.

The Fi-167 fuselage was all-metal monocoque design and the wings and tail had an all-metal structure. Wing center sections were Dural covered. The landing gear was fitted with a large streamline spat-type fairing and an extra long oleo strut was used to absorb the impact of carrier landings, as well as the force from sharp angle descent landings. Spring-loaded bolts held the landing gear in place and could be electrically released by the pilot to jettison the landing gear and avoid a nose-over in the event of an emergency landing in the sea.

STOL Performance

Tests during the summer of 1938 revealed that the Fiesler had superb slow speed flight characteristics. With full up elevator and engine barely idling, the plane lost altitude slowly, descending almost vertically. Gerhard Fiesler had been a World War I pilot and was one of the most accomplished pilots in Germany; therefore, he was able to demonstrate that the Fi-167 could descend slowly from almost 10,000 feet to 100 feet while constantly remaining over a fixed point on the ground. In effect, with zero ground speed! At that time Gerhard Fiesler was the world authority on STOL aircraft design, having just produced the Storch; the world's first STOL airplane. The STOL performance was the result of the judicious ap-

The Arado 197 was designed as fighter protection for Graf Zeppelin and to escort the Fiesler 167. Performance was good but monoplanes were needed. (Bundesarchiv)

plication of leading edge slats on the upper wing and full length flaps on the lower wing.

Arado Ar-197 Carrier-Based Fighter

Luftkries IV of the Kriegsmarine also needed a shipboard fighter to escort the torpedo-bombers and intercept any hostile aircraft bent on attacking *Graf Zeppelin*. During the interim between the designing of the Arado Ar-95 and the Arado Ar-195, Arado had been asked to prepare a proposal for a shipboard biplane fighter which became known as the Arado Ar-197. The design team was led by Ing. Walter Rethel under the general supervision of Dipl.Ing. Walter Blume, a World War I Ace and director of Arado. This was destined to be Germany's last biplane fighter.

Outwardly, the Ar-197 appeared to be a warmed-over version of Arado's 1935 Ar-86H fighter; however, this was not true because the wooden structure and plywood wing covering gave way to an all-metal frame and Dural covered wings for the Ar-197 design. The fuselage was of welded steel tubing covered with easily detachable Dural panels forward of the cockpit and on the turtledeck. The fuselage remainder and control surfaces were fabric covered. Catapult fittings, arresting hook and a long range belly tank were fitted. The cockpit was enclosed with a frameworked bubble canopy. As with all plane projects associated with Traeger "A" this Arado received very little encouragement from the Luftwaffe Brass and after the first Ar-197 prototype was fitted with the new Daimler-Benz engine the company was informed that the engine would no longer be available to them for this project! The second prototype was fitted with a 9-cylinder, 815 horsepower BMW 132J air-cooled radial engine. The engine was so tightly cowled that it was necessary to incorporate streamline blisters into the cowl to cover the individual engine valve rocker arms. The reduced power was reflected in a deterioration of performance so the third prototype used a BMW 132DC engine of 880 horsepower.

Arado Ar-197 Data

The BMW 132DC-powered Arado Ar-197 empty weight was 4,056 pounds while loaded weight was 5,456 pounds. Wingspan was 36 feet-1 inch; length was 30 feet-2 1/4 inches; and height was 11 feet-9 3/4 inches. Wing area was 229 square feet. Landing gear was jettisonable using explosive bolts.

In 1938 Gerhard Fiesler demonstrated his 167 by descending almost vertically. This was accomplished by pulling back on the control stick with engine barely idling as the aircraft lost altitude slowly. Note the folded wings; the ends of which have been left uncovered and unprotected. (Bundesarchiv)

Maximum speed was 248 miles per hour at 8,200 feet and cruising speed was 220 miles per hour at 4,920 feet. Service ceiling was 28,215 feet and the plane could climb to 13,120 feet in 5.3 minutes. Normal range was 432 miles; however, this could be extended to 1,018 miles with an auxiliary drop tank.

Armament included two 7.9 millimeter MG 17 machine guns in the upper fuselage just forward of the cockpit with 500 rounds per gun. In addition to this standard armament two 20 millimeter MG FF cannon were installed in the upper wing, just outboard of the propeller arc, with 60 rounds per gun.

German Monoplane Carrier-Based Aircraft
Despite the fact that the Arado Ar-197 performance compared favorably with existing shipboard fighters in service in Britain, U.S.A., and Japan the Reichsluftfahrtministerium (German Air Ministry) realized, in late 1937, that the three naval powers were busy developing production monoplane shipboard fighters. By the time *Graf Zeppelin* would have been commissioned in 1940, the biplane would be obsolete; therefore, the Arado and Fiesler projects were abandoned and further work forbidden. The Kriegsmarine looked in desperation for suitable existing monoplanes that could be converted into shipboard aircraft. Only two candidates emerged: Messerschmitt Me-109 fighter, and Junkers Ju-87 Stuka dive bomber.

By the winter of 1937-38 Messerschmitt had captured the world's headlines. During the summer of 1937 this state-of-the-art fighter plane made an outstanding showing at the Zurich Flying Meet in the climb and dive competition as well as in assorted speed courses. On the basis of this proven competence Professor Willi Messerschmitt was asked to submit proposals for a shipboard version of his monoplane fighter.

In an effort to produce a German equivalent to the Japanese Kate, Junkers was requested to propose a naval version of the standard Luftwaffe dive bomber.

In desperation for a monoplane fighter and torpedo-bomber the Kriegsmarine turned to the vaunted Messerschmitt fighter (above) and Junkers Ju 87 Stuka dive bomber (below) neither of which could meet the demands of carrier-based operations. Note the enlarged wing on the Messerschmitt and arresting hook on the Junkers. (Bundesarchiv)

German Shipboard Flight Training
The Luftwaffe finally relented and permitted the creation of a carrier operations training program. Traegergruppe 186 (Carrier Group 186) was formed on August 1, 1938 at Kiel-Holtenau, training with standard Messerschmitt Me-109B and Junkers Ju-87A Land-based aircraft.

Messerschmitt Me-109T Carrier-Based Fighter
In early 1939 Messerschmitt submitted a proposal to add two feet to each wing of the Me-109E which would increase the area by 1 square feet; incorporate a manually folding wing which required the removal of the flaps when wings were folded; and reinforce the fuselage for catapult fittings and arresting hook. The already fragile landing gear was not strengthened for carrier operations. The proposal was accepted and Fiesler was given the task of working out the details of design and production of the navalized Me-109E. The carrier version of the Me-109E was redesignated Me-109T-1. Further minor modifications and larger engine evolved into the Me-109T-2.

Me-109T-2 Data
A 1,200 horsepower Daimler Benz DB601N 12-cylinder liquid-cooled engine propelled the craft to a top speed of 357 miles per hour at 16,685 feet. Empty weight was 4,409 pounds while at maximum overload condition the plane tipped the scales at 6,786 pounds. In the loaded condition it could reach 26,250 feet in 10 minutes. The Me-109T-2 could take off and clear a 66 foot obstacle in 55 yards. Landing speed was 80 miles per hour. Inadequate range always had been the Messerschmitts's Achille's Heel and the Traeger version was no exception with a 568 mile range when using an auxiliary drop tank.

Junkers Ju-87C Carrier-Based Torpedo/Dive Bomber
Junkers adapted the Ju-87B for navalization and this became the Ju-87C. Arresting hook, catapult fittings, flotation equipment, jettisonable landing gear using explosive bolts, and electrically folding wings were the principal modifications. Provisions for carrying a torpedo were also made at a later date.

Ju-87C Data
The 12-cylinder Junkers Jumo 211 Da liquid-cooled engine produced 1,200 horsepower for takeoff and 1,100 horsepower at 4,920 feet. Maximum speed was 238 miles per hour at 13,410 feet and service ceiling was 26,250 feet. The Ju-87C required 12 minutes to reach an altitude of 12,190 feet. The plane weighed 9,560 pounds fully loaded. Total bomb load was 1,102 pounds with which the range was only 370 miles! This performance was most inferior to the U.S. Douglas SBD and the Japanese Aichi D3A2 dive bombers.

Sporadic *Graf Zeppelin* Construction
Work on the *Graf Zeppelin* was suspended in October 1939 and then continued sporadically until it was again suspended in May 1942. This caused cancellation of the aircraft conversions which were not able to produce acceptable carrier aircraft. *Graf Zeppelin* construction limped throughout World War II.

Germans Underestimate Carrier Complexity

The halfhearted cooperation of the Luftwaffe with the Kriegsmarine in the Flugzeug Traeger hindered progress for the entire project. More important was the fact that the complexity of aircraft carriers and shipboard airplanes was grossly underestimated by high ranking officials. The normally thorough and efficient Germans failed to realize that aircraft carriers are not merely ships topped with a flight deck and that shipboard airplanes are not merely land-based planes with arresting hooks and catapult fittings. These complex machines are a breed apart from the average ship and plane.

HMS ARGUS AND USS LANGLEY MODIFICATIONS

During the mid-1930s two of the earliest through-deck aircraft carriers underwent extensive modifications; the Royal Navy's *HMS Argus* and the U.S. Navy's *USS Langley.*

HMS Argus Modifications

Blister protection had been added to *HMS Argus* during 1925-26, and in a major modification during 1936-38 the forward 100 feet of the Flight Deck was rebuilt; removing the original downward slope, adding two catapults and extending the bow shell plating up to the Flight Deck. In addition, the old fire-tube cylindrical boilers were replaced with used destroyer water-tube boilers.

USS Langley Modifications

The U.S. Navy was also in the middle of a carrier building program; therefore, it was decided to convert *USS Langley* into a seaplane tender. The forward 250 feet of Flight Deck was removed and a crane installed. As a tender the designation was changed to AV-3 and due to the changes displacement dropped to 11,050 tons. *USS Langley* was assigned to the Pacific Fleet to support American seaplane operations.

Both ships demonstrated the effectiveness of aircraft carrier operation and also proved the validity of their configuration. The veterans served into World War II; assisting their more powerful and faster descendants.

HMS Argus Hangar was small by comparison with later carriers but it could accommodate these non-folding wing Sea Hurricanes quite comfortably. Photo taken 1940-1941 when the Sea Hurricane was issued to the Fleet Air Arm. (Ministry of Defence [Navy])

U.S. NAVY ABANDONS SMALL CARRIERS

While *USS Ranger* was still under construction in the early 1930s the U.S. Navy Bureau of Ships was struggling with a previous decision to build five minimum size aircraft carriers to fit within the constraints of the Washington Naval Treaty. This resulted in decisions to abandon the small *Ranger* design and that a larger 20,000 ton ship would be more efficient for the new carriers. The Treaty allowed only two carriers of that size; therefore, it was decided to use the balance with another small carrier of the *Ranger* size. The two larger carriers were to be named *Yorktown* and *Enterprise* while the smaller fill-in carrier was to be named *Wasp.*

Yorktown Class Carriers

The keels for *USS Yorktown* (CV-5) and *Enterprise* (CV-6) were laid at Newport News Shipbuilding Co. on May 16 and July 16, 1934 respectively. *Yorktown* was launched by Mrs. Franklin D. Roosevelt on April 4, 1936 and the *Enterprise* launching followed on October 3. These two famous ships were commissioned on September 30, 1937 and May 12, 1938 respectively.

During a two year major modification ending in 1938 HMS Argus had its bow partially enclosed and forward Flight Deck levelled from the original downward slope. Two catapults were also fitted. Photo taken in 1942 when Argus was equipped with Seafires. (U.S. National Archives)

Flight Deck Design Philosophies

As it has been seen, the American and Japanese philosophy on carrier design differed considerably from that of the Royal Navy regarding the flight deck and hangar.

The *Yorktown* class continued the American practice of constructing the hangar space as a light superstructure topped with a light flight deck which made no contribution to hull strength. The hangar deck was the armored deck. Hangar sides were closed off with roll-down doors. The American concept was based upon reliance on the combat air patrol to protect the carrier from enemy air attack. Advantage was that by extending the hangar to the very sides of the ship it created maximum hangar volume and; therefore, more space for aircraft stowage and maintenance. In addition, with the roll-doors in the open position aircraft preparing for a mission could run their engines while still in the hangar and emerge on the flight deck with engines warm and ready for takeoff. The principal disadvantage of the American concept was that bombs could penetrate the flight deck and explode in the hangar, starting below deck fires. This would also halt flight operations due to flight deck bomb craters.

Conversely, the Royal Navy continued the shell plating up to the flight deck which became part of the hull structure, contributing to its strength. The flight deck was armored and the hangar was an armored box, totally surrounded with compartments, which could be entered only through a fireproof air lock or lobby. Obviously, the main advantage of this scheme is that the carrier was relatively safe from extensive aerial bomb damage. Disadvantages are that fewer aircraft could be stowed in smaller hangars which had lost volume due to armor and buffer compartments. In addition, aircraft engines could not be run in the hangar space and planes had to be brought to the flight deck to warm up engines.

The following chapters will accompany carriers into action that were built in accordance with both theories.

Yorktown Class Data

The *Yorktown* class aircraft carriers displaced 19,872 tons with a deep load draft of 25 feet-11 inches. Waterline length was 770 feet and maximum beam was 83 feet-3 inches. Flight Deck measured 802 x 86 feet. Steam was generated in nine Babcock & Wilcox boilers which powered Parsons steam turbines geared to four propeller shafts. The 120,000 shaft horsepower drove the ships to a top speed of 32.5 knots. A range of 12,000 miles was attained while cruising at 15 knots. Complement was 1,890 officers and men in peacetime and 2,500 in combat. The *Yorktown* class normally accommodated 80 aircraft; 20 more than *HMS Ark Royal*, a carrier of comparable size. Three elevators were installed, each with a 15,000 pound capacity.

The Flight Deck was covered with six inches of wood planking and was fitted with two hydraulically powered catapults located at the forward end.

Unusual Catapult and Arresting Gear Installations

For the first time on a U.S. carrier a third catapult was installed. Located forward on the hangar deck it was arranged to launch aircraft athwartships or off the side of the ship at a right angle or 90 degrees to the Flight Deck. In addition, the *Yorktown* class Flight Deck was fitted with two sets of transverse arresting cables; one set of nine cables aft and one set of four cables forward. The reason for the arresting cables at the bow was because U.S. Navy requirements of that time specified that provision must be made for landings over the bow while the carrier is heading full speed astern.

Hull Armor and Subdivision

Some hull armor was installed. A 2 1/2 inch to 4 inch waterline belt, 4 inch bulkheads and 1 1/2 inches over the machinery spaces and magazines was the maximum allowed without exceeding the Treaty weight restrictions.

Outstanding in the *Yorktown/Enterprise* design was the extensive underwater compartmentation or subdivision which gave the ships a good chance of survival in the event of a hit.

Guns and Planes

Defensive armament consisted of eight 5 inch/38 caliber dual-purpose guns, mounted fore and aft at the sides of the Flight Deck. Gun directors were located fore and aft of the island.

The initial aircraft complement included Grumman F2F fighters, Douglas TBD torpedo-bombers and Curtiss SBC dive-bombers. It required about 10 pilots, mechanics, and plane handlers to keep one plane flying.

USS Enterprise (CV-6)

USS Enterprise (CV-6) was virtually identical to *USS Yorktown* and was the seventh U.S. warship to bear that name. The first was captured from the British by General Benedict Arnold; the second and third were also active in the American Revolution while the fourth was a schooner of 1831. The fifth Enterprise was a steam Corvette of 1874 and the sixth was a patrol boat during World War I. The aircraft carrier *Enterprise* (CV-6) experienced extensive action in World War II, which is covered in the following chapters.

MORE JAPANESE CARRIER CONVERSIONS

During the 1930s Japan constructed several ships that were very adaptable for conversion to aircraft carriers in the event of a war emergency. IJNS *Chitose* and *Chiyoda* were first in the program constructed as seaplane carrier/tenders but easily converted to either oilers, submarine tenders or preferably to flush deck aircraft carriers. *Chitose* and *Chiyoda*, respectively, were launched in November 1936 and November 1937, commissioned in July 1938 and December 1938. Conversion to aircraft carriers was undertaken at Sasebo and Yokosuka with completion during January 1944 and November 1943.

Blisters were added to the hull for stability because a 75ft. x 590 ft. Flight Deck was installed with two aircraft elevators. A 300 ft. long Hangar was located under the Flight Deck. Eight 5 inch/40 caliber dual purpose guns and (30) 25 mm AA guns were also fitted. The ships displaced 15,000 tons at deep load.

Both Diesel engines and steam turbines were installed. The diesel powerplant operated for cruising in order to conserve fuel however, the more powerful geared steam turbines were used for high speeds.

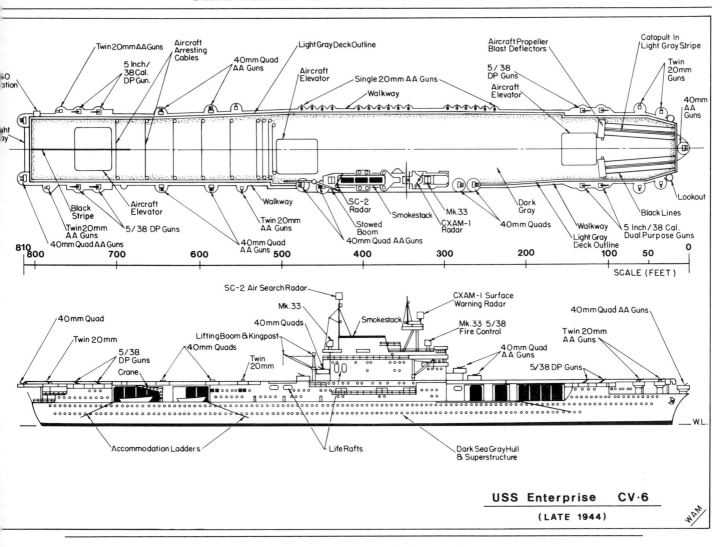

Twin 20mm AA Guns
5 Inch/38 Cal. DP Gun.
Aircraft Arresting Cables
40mm Quad AA Guns
Light Gray Deck Outline
Aircraft Elevator
Single 20mm AA Guns
Walkway
Aircraft Propeller Blast Deflectors
5/38 DP Guns
Aircraft Elevator
Catapult In Light Gray Stripe
Twin 20mm Guns
40mm AA Guns

Black Stripe
Aircraft Elevator
Twin 20mm AA Guns
5/38 DP Guns
40mm Quad AA Guns
Walkway
Twin 20mm AA Guns
40mm Quad AA Guns
SC-2 Radar
Stowed Boom
40mm Quad AA Guns
Smokestack
Mk.33
CXAM-1 Radar
Dark Gray
40mm Quads
Walkway
Light Gray Deck Outline
Black Lines
5 Inch/38 Cal. Dual Purpose Guns
Lookout

810 800   700   600   500   400   300   200   100   50   0
SCALE (FEET)

SC-2 Air Search Radar
Mk.33
40mm Quads
Lifting Boom & Kingpost
40mm Quads
Smokestack
CXAM-1 Surface Warning Radar
Mk.33 5/38 Fire Control
40mm Quad AA Guns
40mm Quad AA Guns
Twin 20mm AA Guns

40mm Quad
Twin 20mm
5/38 DP Guns
Crane
Twin 20mm
40mm Quad AA Guns
5/38 DP Guns

Accommodation Ladders
Life Rafts
Dark Sea Gray Hull & Superstructure

USS Enterprise CV·6
(LATE 1944)

After seeing action in Japanese landings and sea battles in a [sh]ort career both carriers were sunk in the Battle of Cape Engano, [O]ctober 1944.

[I]NNOVATIVE ROYAL NAVY CARRIER
[O]n January 12, 1939 a squadron of Fairey Swordfish left [S]outhampton, England, heading for the new Royal Navy carrier [H]MS Ark Royal and became the first planes to land on this most [c]elebrated carrier in the Royal Navy.

British; Carrier Experts
Unlike the German Kriegsmarine and Luftwaffe, the Royal Navy had the most experience of any nation with carriers and carrier aircraft; appreciating the special requirements of these unusual machines. It was the British who usually incorporated innovations into their carrier designs which were then copied by other nations.

While Japan and the U.S. engaged in their deadly game of aircraft carrier chess, Britain, who had laid the foundation for the development of carrier design and operations, was forced to move along at a snail's pace because of limitations in the national economy

[T]he Japanese aircraft carriers IJNS Chitose and Chiyoda were converted from seaplane carrier/tenders in late 1943 and early 1944. Each ship [d]isplaced about 15,000 tons and could operate a mixed bag of about 30 aircraft. IJNS Chitose is shown here in early 1944. (Official U.S. Navy [p]hotograph)

The innovative HMS Ark Royal saved 500 tons of weight by substituting welding for riveting. It was also the first carrier to incorporate the Flight Deck into the hull structure to add to the strength of the hull. (Ministry of Defence [Navy])

and the spread of Pacifism among the population, as well as the politicians.

Ark Royal; Trend Setter

Finally, on September 16, 1935 the keel was laid in the Birkenhead shipyard of Cammell Laird on the River Mersey for one of the most remembered and revered aircraft carriers of all time; *HMS Ark Royal.* This became the first large Royal Navy fleet carrier to be purpose-designed and built. The success of the *Ark Royal* design was such that all the aircraft carriers built for the Royal Navy during World War II were based on this trend setter.

Third *Ark Royal*

This carrier became the third ship to bear the *Ark Royal* name. The first was built at Deptford, England for Sir Walter Raleigh, who christened the vessel *Ark.* The custom in 17th Century England was that ships bore the name of the owner so the craft was named *Ark Raleigh.* As friction between Britain and Spain increased, the ship was requisitioned by Queen Elizabeth for 5,000 pounds Sterling while still in the shipyard, and was then renamed *Ark Royal.* The 1,500 ton ship played an important part in battling the Spanish Armada as the Flagship of Lord Howard of Effingham, Lord High Admiral of England. The second *Ark Royal* fought during World War I, and is described in Chapter I.

Carrier Philosophy Change

As with *HMS Hermes,* the Royal Navy's carrier philosophy had been that several small aircraft carriers were better than a few large carriers. This policy had changed abruptly in 1934 with the result that *Ark Royal* was twice the size of *HMS Hermes* but could accommodate four times the number of aircraft.

The design is of special interest because the Flight deck was made the principal strength deck with the shell of the ship extending up to it. In this way the Flight Deck was integrated into the overall structure and contributed considerably to the strength of the hull. This was diametrically opposite to the American and Japanese carrier designs in which the flight deck was a separate entity from the hull and was supported by it; contributing little or no strength to the ship. Another objective of the design was to combine the largest possible flight deck with the shortest possible hull in order to operate the highest number of aircraft with a hull affording the maximum maneuverability and propulsion economy. This resulted in a flight deck 59 feet longer than the waterline length of the hull; a truly innovative idea for that time.

The weight of the relatively small island on the starboard sid was compensated by placing as much auxiliary equipment as pos sible on the port side, as well as increasing the port side beam abov the waterline, instead of increasing the port side fuel capacity an adding blisters, as was done on previous carriers.

Ark Royal Data

The double-deck Hangar could handle 72 planes but the norma complement was 60; about five Fleet Air Arm Squadrons of Faire Flycatchers, Blackburn Darts and Fairey III-F's. The upper Hanga was 568 feet long while the lower Hangar was 452 feet long. Bot were 60 feet wide and 16 feet high.

Two new hydraulically-powered catapults were designed t handle aircraft as heavy as 12,000 pounds because the designer were looking ahead in order that *Ark Royal* could handle the heavie and faster carrier aircraft of the future. Transverse arresting ge: was installed.

Another innovative technique was welding. At a time whe standard ship construction employed riveting, Cammel Laird mad extensive use of welding and saved 500 tons of steel weight b welding 65 percent of the hull.

Ark Royal was launched on April 13, 1937 by Lady Hoar wife of the First Lord of the Admiralty Sir Samuel Hoare. The co: had been 3,215,639 pounds Sterling. Upon completing trials in Jul it was found necessary to add eight feet to the height of the smoke stack to prevent the boiler gasses from curling down onto the Fligl Deck.

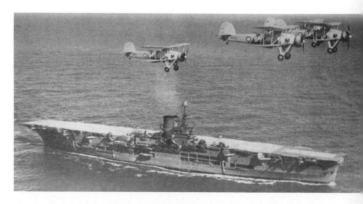

A squadron of Swordfish overflies HMS Ark Royal. This carrier was the first to combine the largest possible flight deck with the shortest possibl hull in order to operate the maximum number of aircraft. The short hull was desired to achieve maximum maneuverability. (Ministry of Defence [Navy])

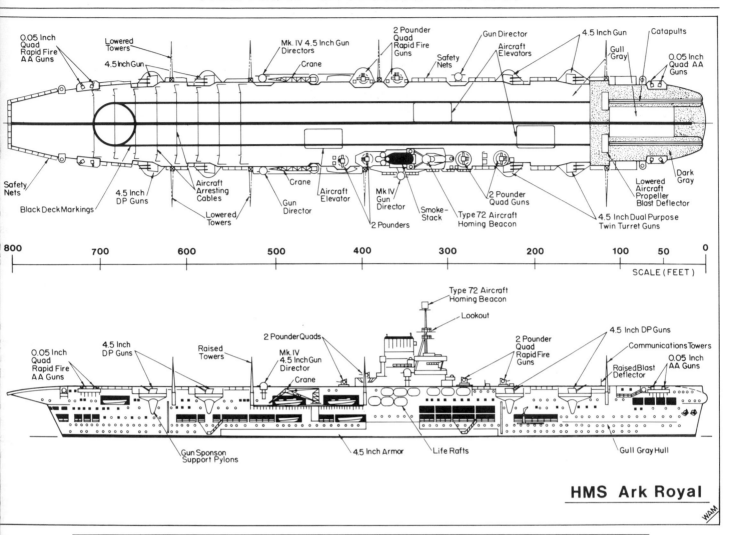

HMS Ark Royal

Displacement was 22,000 tons standard and 27,720 tons fully loaded. The Flight Deck measured 780 x 96 feet while the hull length was 721 feet and beam was 94 feet-9 inches at the waterline. Deep load draft was 27 feet-9 inches.

The powerplant consisted of six Admiralty high pressure boilers generating steam for three Parsons geared turbines which delivered a total of 102,000 shaft horsepower to three propellers. The boiler spaces and engine rooms were arranged three abreast across the hull; total of six spaces. Watertight bulkheads separated the spaces. Maximum speed was 31 knots while a range of 7,600 miles could be attained when steaming at 20 knots.

Defensive armament was (16) 4.5 inch caliber dual-purpose guns in twin mountings intended mainly to combat air attacks because the Admiralty had concluded that it was best to leave defense against surface attacks to the escorting ships. Secondary antiaircraft guns consisted of six 8-barrelled two-pounder pom-poms and eight 4-barrelled Vickers 0.5 inch caliber machine guns which were later replaced by 20 millimeter Oerlikon cannon. The guns were located as high as possible along the sides of the Flight Deck, at the Gallery Deck level, in order to improve the sky arc angles with minimal interference.

The peacetime complement of officers and enlisted men was 1,575 and the wartime complement was 1,860, almost half of which were Fleet Air Arm (FAA) personnel.

Double Hull Plus Armor

Although no underwater hull blisters were installed an innovative system of a double hull below the waterline was used for anti-torpedo protection. The magazines and aviation gasoline stowage, located forward and aft of the machinery spaces, were protected along with the machinery spaces by a belt of 4 1/2 inches thick armor. The main belts were connected with 2 1/2 inches thick bulkheads. The lower Hangar Deck over the engine rooms and boiler spaces was 2 1/2 inches thick and as the Deck extended over the magazines and aviation gasoline stowage as well as over the steering gear room it increased to 3 1/2 inches thick. Longitudinal bulkheads were 1 1/2 inches thick.

HMS Ark Royal was commissioned on November 16, 1938 under command of Captain A.J. Power, C.B., C.V.O. She heavily engaged the German and Italian Navies in the early years of World War II, as will be described in the next chapter.

1939: PLANES, CARRIERS AND WORLD WAR II

The year 1939 witnessed the introduction of innovative and classic shipboard aircraft and aircraft carriers. It was also the year in which World War II started, plunging the world into a war that was to revise traditional naval weapons and tactics with the carrier emerging as the premier naval force.

FAA STANDARD: MULTIPLACE AIRCRAFT

By 1933 the captive Fleet Air Arm was still controlled by the RAF whose loyalties were naturally directed towards land-based military aviation. Not only were the FAA relative strength and aircraft types decided by the land-doctrinated RAF, but the role to be played by the FAA, as well as its tactics, were controlled by the RAF. The majority of FAA pilots were Royal Air Force-trained and, in protest, the Fleet Air Arm insisted that all naval aircraft be two-seaters for two logical reasons: with a naval officer on board as observer/navigator, the pilot would be better able to traverse large expanses of open sea and return to the carrier safely; also to be certain that at least one naval officer was a member of the crew to guarantee proper execution of the mission, which would invariably be reconnaissance and/or spotting.

Multiplace Aircraft Disadvantage

The demand for multiplace aircraft resulted in larger and slower aircraft which necessitated folding wings for proper stowage. This added to the procurement problem because larger two-seaters cost more than smaller single-seaters with the result that fewer aircraft could be purchased with fixed funding. In 1933 the Royal Navy had only 159 aircraft compared to over 1,000 in the U.S. Navy and

PREVIOUS: The production Grumman F4F-3 Wildcat differed from the XF4F-3 in that the horizontal tail had been raised to the fin, antennae mast relocated behind the cockpit, and forward-leaning vertical tail made vertical and swept into the turtledeck. (U.S. Department of Defense [Marine Corps])

411 in the Imperial Japanese Navy. It was during this year that the Fleet Air Arm flight of six planes as the basic formation was changed to the squadron of nine or 12 aircraft. This was still a small force when compared to the 18 plane squadron of the U.S. Navy.

Despite the handicap under which it was forced to operate, the Royal Navy Fleet Air Arm was able to procure outstanding aircraft in the 1930s. One of these never-to-be-forgotten aircraft was the legendary Fairey Swordfish torpedo-bomber. This multiplace carrier-based aircraft was not hampered by the fact that it was operated by a two-man crew.

Fairey Swordfish

One of the most remarkable British naval aircraft of this period was the Fairey Swordfish carrier-borne torpedo/spotter/reconnaissance biplane. Although conceived in 1933 the craft served with distinction throughout World War II; safely landing on carrier decks that were pitching and heaving 20 to 30 feet in inky darkness, as well as being able to take off tilted decks of sinking carriers. This plane even has the unusual distinction of outliving its replacement.

The Swordfish story begins when the Fairey Company produced the TSR.1 as a private venture; however, the prototype was destroyed in a spinning accident in September 1933. A second prototype TSR.II was constructed, slightly larger than the first, to meet Admiralty Specification S.15/33 for an advanced torpedo-spotter/reconnaissance aircraft. The TSR.II completed its maiden flight on April 17, 1934 and after lengthy testing it was accepted for FAA service and the name Swordfish adopted. In the summer of 1935 the Air Ministry placed an order for three pre-production and 86 production Swordfish, the first of which flew on December 31, 1935. Further contracts followed and by 1940 Fairey had delivered 892 aircraft. At that time production was transferred to Blackburn because Fairey was occupied with new projects. The Blackburn production lines produced a total of 1,700 Swordfish.

Assignments

The Swordfish first entered service in July 1936 with No. 825 Squadron on *HMS Glorious* and by the end of the year Nos. 810, 811,

The legendary Fairey Swordfish made its first flight in 1934 and yet fought superbly throughout World War II. Rugged and dependable, the Swordfish was affectionately called "Stringbag" by both air crews and maintenance crews. (Ministry of Defence [Navy])

812, 820 and 821 Squadrons had been equipped with the new plane. By 1938 the Swordfish was the only torpedo-bomber in the Fleet Air Arm and, by September 1939, 13 squadrons of Swordfish were in service.

Swordfish Construction
The all-metal structure was fabric covered, except for the area forward of the cockpits, which was covered with quickly detachable metal panels. The fuselage had a basic rectangular structure of welded steel tubing to which were attached formers and stringers to fair the fuselage to an oval section. An arresting hook and catapult fittings were installed, although Swordfish often took off without assistance from catapults.

Ailerons were installed on both wings and Handley-Page slots were fitted to the upper wing only. The wings folded laterally aft alongside the fuselage for stowage.

Swordfish Data
Wingspan was 45 feet-6 inches and overall length 36 feet-4 inches, with a height of 12 feet-10 inches. Maximum take off weight was 9,250 pounds.

Powered with a 690 horsepower Bristol Pegasus air-cooled radial engine the Swordfish attained a maximum speed of 139 miles per hour at 4,750 feet. Service ceiling was 10,700 feet and combat range 1,030 miles.

One 1,610 pound torpedo, one 1,500 pound mine, or 1,500 pounds of bombs could be carried under the fuselage between the landing gear struts. A later modification consisted of reinforcing the lower wing to carry eight 60 pound rockets and launchers instead of the torpedo or bombs. One forward-firing Vickers machine gun was installed in the fuselage forward of the pilot and one swivel-mounted machine gun equipped the rear cockpit.

Swordfish - Loved by its Crew
This remarkable airplane was loved by its crews and all who flew it, and soon became universally and affectionately known as the Stringbag. The total of 25 first line Swordfish Squadrons and 22

second line squadrons engaged in many varied, widespread, and remarkable exploits during World War II.

Fairey Albacore
The Fairey Swordfish replacement made its initial appearance and flew for the first time on December 12, 1938. The Fairey Albacore was designed to Air Ministry Specification S.41/36, issued in February 1937, and, by May, a contract for 100 aircraft had been placed.

This biplane design presented the appearance of a harmless cabin-type civilian plane because the large greenhouse canopy extended up to the upper wing. The cockpits were entered via a hinged door on the port side of the fuselage. The three cockpits were elec-

With wings neatly folded Swordfish are brought to the Flight Deck of a British escort aircraft carrier in the Atlantic Ocean. Carriers could not function without the huge airplane elevators. (Ministry of Defence [Navy])

Two Swordfish are shown on the Flight Deck of the Merchant Aircraft Carrier (MAC) HMS Macoma which was operated by Dutch crews. MAC conversions began in the summer of 1942 and consisted of a standard merchant ship, tanker or bulk carrier, which remained a merchant vessel except for the Flight Deck. MAC conversions are described in Chapters IV and IX. The Swordfish was ideal for ASW missions by virtue of its slow speed and bomb, depth charge or rocket armament. (Royal Netherlands Navy)

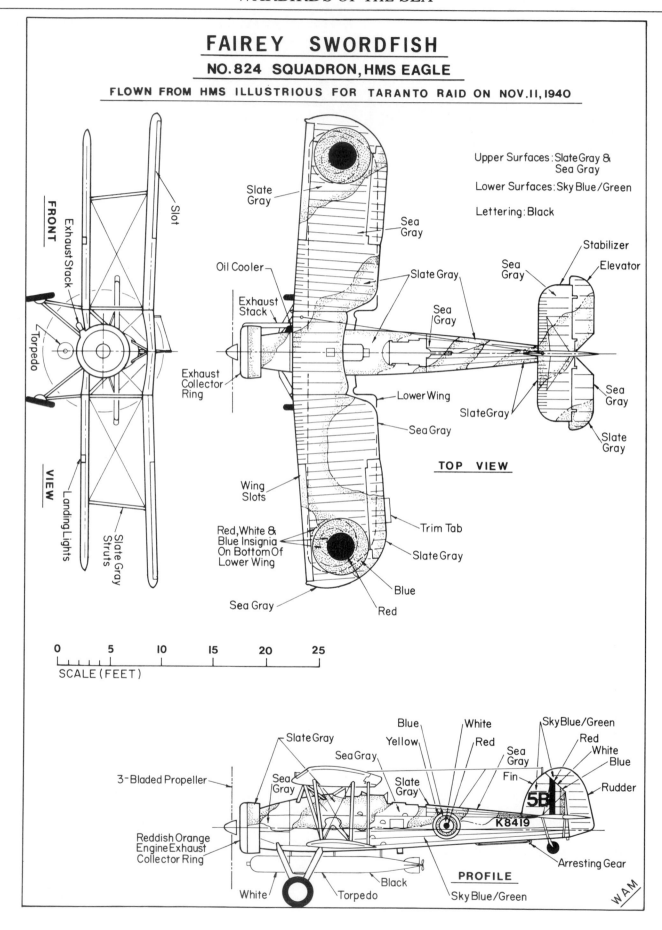

FAIREY SWORDFISH
NO. 824 SQUADRON, HMS EAGLE
FLOWN FROM HMS ILLUSTRIOUS FOR TARANTO RAID ON NOV. 11, 1940

FRONT

Exhaust Stack

Slot

Torpedo

VIEW

Landing Lights

Slate Gray Struts

Slate Gray

Oil Cooler

Exhaust Stack

Exhaust Collector Ring

Wing Slots

Red, White & Blue Insignia On Bottom Of Lower Wing

Sea Gray

Sea Gray

Slate Gray

Sea Gray

Lower Wing

Sea Gray

Blue

Red

Upper Surfaces: Slate Gray & Sea Gray

Lower Surfaces: Sky Blue/Green

Lettering: Black

Slate Gray

Sea Gray

Stabilizer

Elevator

Sea Gray

Slate Gray

Sea Gray

Slate Gray

Trim Tab

Slate Gray

TOP VIEW

0   5   10   15   20   25
SCALE (FEET)

3-Bladed Propeller

Reddish Orange Engine Exhaust Collector Ring

White

Torpedo

Slate Gray

Sea Gray

Sea Gray

Slate Gray

Black

Blue

Yellow

White

Red

Sea Gray

Fin

Sky Blue/Green

Red

White

Blue

Rudder

5B

K8419

Arresting Gear

PROFILE

Sky Blue/Green

W∧M

Fairey Albacore torpedo/reconnaissance aircraft of the Royal Navy fly in close formation over the Mediterranean Sea. The craft was ideal for carrier service and required no catapults or arresting gear; because of the slow speed and light wing loading. (U.S. Army Signal Corps)

The Fairey Albacore was intended to replace the Swordfish but became its equally efficient partner. Observe how the cockpit enclosure was integral with the upper wing, forming a cabin. Pilot sat forward of the wing. (U.S. Army Signal Corps)

trically heated and an inflatable life raft was arranged to eject and inflate automatically in the event of a ditching.

Albacore Data

The Fairey Albacore was powered by a 1,065 horsepower Bristol Taurus II 14-cylinder sleeve valve air-cooled radial engine which gave the plane a top speed of 161 miles per hour at 6,000 feet. Service ceiling was 20,700 feet and combat range 930 miles with a 1,610 pound load at cruising speed of 116 miles per hour. Empty weight was 7,200 pounds while gross takeoff weight was 12,600 pounds.

Wingspan of the Albacore measured 50 feet-0 inches and overall length 39 feet-9 inches. Height was 15 feet-3 inches. Wing area totalled 623 square feet.

The metal framework wings were fabric covered and manually folded rearward as on the Stringbag. Ailerons were installed on both wings while hydraulically operated flaps were fitted to the lower wing only. The flaps were also used as air brakes during dive

bombing. Slats were fitted to the upper wing. Fuselage was of all-metal monocoque construction.

One 18 inch, 1,610 pound torpedo could be carried beneath the fuselage. Alternatively, six 250 pound bombs or four 500 pound bombs could be fitted to racks under the lower wing. One fixed Vickers machine gun was located in the lower wing, starboard side, firing outside the propeller arc. Two Vickers machine guns were flexible-mounted in the rear cockpit.

Albacore Assignment

Albacores first went into service in March 1940 with No.826 Squadron which unit was specially created to operate the new planes. In November Nos. 826 and 829 Squadrons joined *HMS Formidable* with their Albacores.

Although the Fairey Albacore was a definite improvement over the Swordfish, many pilots preferred the Stringbag, and instead of replacing the Swordfish, the Albacore merely supplemented the venerable Stringbag. The Albacore served with distinction in World War II.

Proving that it does not require a catapult, a Fairey Albacore has left the deck of HMS Illustrious at the halfway mark and is well airborne before reaching the end of the Flight Deck. (Ministry of Defence [Navy])

FAA MULTIROLE, MULTIPLACE SHIPBOARD AIRCRAFT DILEMMA

By 1938 the Fleet Air Arm found itself with the necessity of phasing out the aging Hawker Nimrod; however, it had no single-seat fighter replacement.

This predicament was caused by an unfortunate compromise during discussions in 1934 between the Royal Air Force, which still controlled the Fleet Air Arm at that time, and the Royal Navy. The conferences centered on the question of the usefulness of single-seater fighters aboard aircraft carriers. Even some senior naval officers believed that reconnaissance and delivering attacks against enemy ships was the only value of carrier-borne aircraft and that defense of the fleet from aerial attack could be left to the naval antiaircraft guns! Some naval participants at the meetings also agreed with the Royal Air Force, which was already planning multiplace fighters such as Fairey Battle and Boulton-Paul Defiant for RAF

The FAA flew Sea Gladiators as a temporary measure to bridge the gap from the Hawker Nimrod to the two-seater multi-role aircraft under development. Sea Gladiators served from 1939 through 1941. (Imperial War Museum)

The Blackburn Skua was the first dive bomber to equip FM squadrons, and the first Royal Navy all-metal low wing cantilever monoplane with retractable landing gear. The Skua scored well early in World War II. Note the arresting cable supports. (Air Ministry [Navy])

use, that single-seat fighters would be at a disadvantage at sea because they could not venture beyond visual range of the carrier due to problems of navigation, and were not able to escort torpedo-bombers on long range missions. The compromise was; therefore, to combine the functions of two distinct types of aircraft into a multirole machine and; thereby, buy greater flexibility. The folly of this reasoning was to reveal itself in mortal combat. Economy in weapons cost can lead only to disaster; history has proven this.

Sea Gladiator Biplane Fighter
In view of the above, the Nimrod replacement was to be a temporary measure because the two-seater, multirole fighter/bomber/reconnaissance aircraft were not yet ready for production. The RAF Gloster Gladiator was, therefore, selected for carrier use and named Sea Gladiator. The first order for this smart looking biplane was placed in March 1938 for 38 aircraft which were to be converted from RAF Gladiator Mk.II planes on the Gloster production line. Modifications included reinforced fuselage frame and the addition of a Vee type arresting hook, naval T.R.9 radio, air speed indicator calibrated in knots, catapult fittings and collapsible life raft stowed in the fuselage. The main production group of 60 Sea Gladiators was ordered in June 1938.

Gladiator Assignments
Sea trials were conducted on board *HMS Courageous* during March 1939 and the Gloster biplanes embarked for front line service in *HMS Courageous, HMS Glorious, HMS Furious* and *HMS Eagle.*

Gladiator Data
The RAF Gloster Gladiator began as a private venture to replace the Gloster Gauntlet in 1934 which resulted in the first of several production orders on July 1, 1935. The Sea Gladiator had a wingspan of 32 feet-3 inches, length of 27 feet-5 inches, and height of 10 feet-4 inches. The Bristol Mercury supercharged, 9-cylinder, air-cooled radial engine of 830 horsepower, turning a Fairey three-bladed propeller, gave the craft a top speed of 210 miles per hour at sea level and 248 miles per hour at 17,500 feet. The Sea Gladiator could climb to 4,000 feet in 90 seconds and to 10,000 feet in five

minutes and 55 seconds. Stalling speed with flaps lowered was 5? miles per hour. Takeoff run into a 30 knot wind was 65 yards. Rang at 220 miles per hour was 415 miles. Wing loading was 15.4 pound per square foot and power loading was 6.05 pounds per horsepowe. Empty weight was 3,553 pounds while normal loaded weight wa 5,019 pounds. Structure was all-metal with fabric covering. Aile rons were fitted to both wings as were the flaps. The landing gea design merits attention. The single streamline strut was aerodynami cally clean with the shock-absorbing mechanism contained at th lower end of the strut and the wheels. Armament consisted of fou Browning 0.30 inch caliber machine guns; two in the forward fuse lage and two in streamline enclosures beneath the lower wings.

Although intended for temporary service the Sea Gladiator wa engaged on several fronts during World War II well into 1941 an fought alongside the multirole aircraft that had been procured t replace it.

Independent Fleet Air Arm
Six more Royal Navy carriers were in the planning stage and ai craft had to be designed and procured to serve on these ships. Fu ther, well-trained and experienced pilots were needed for carrie duty. At a time which could not have been more propitious the Flee Air Arm was given its freedom in 1937 and once again there wer two separate air forces in Britain. There was much to accomplish

Blackburn Skua Monoplane Dive Bomber/Fighter
The first of the FAA multirole aircraft completed its initial flight o February 9, 1937 piloted by Flight Lieutenant A.M. Blake. Thi was the Blackburn Skua; designed by G.E. Petty to Air Ministr Specification 0.27/34. His design was selected in preference to pro posals which had been submitted by Hawker, Vickers, Boulton Paul and Avro. The urgency for the Skua was so severe that a pro duction contract for 190 of the dive bomber/fighters was placed i July 1936; more than six months before the prototype was first tes flown! The first production Skua, named for the large northern preda tory sea bird, first flew on August 28, 1938 and engaged in carrie trials on *HMS Courageous* in December. The 190 planes were pro duced from October 1938 to March 1940.

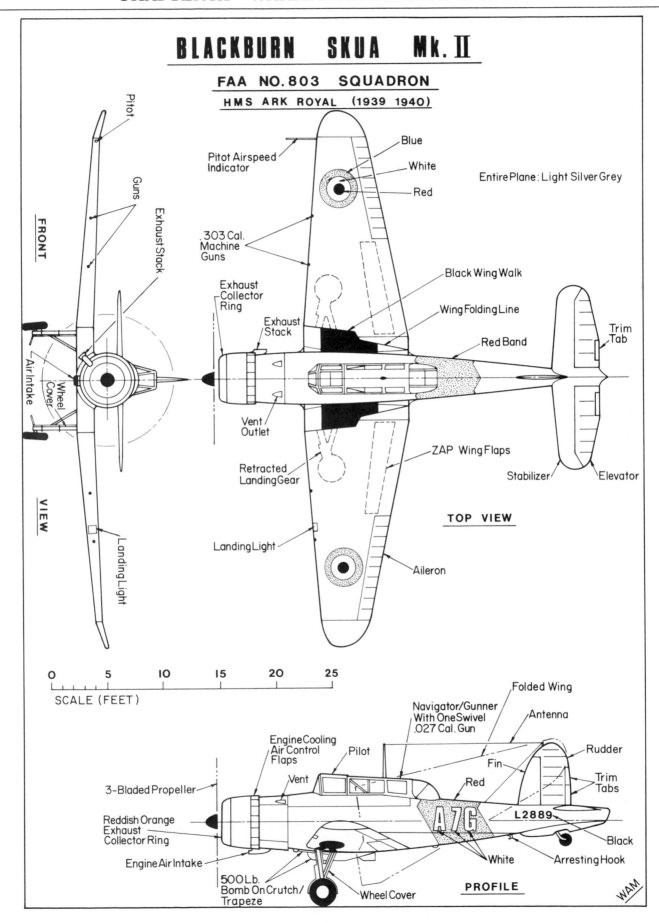

BLACKBURN SKUA Mk. II

FAA NO. 803 SQUADRON
HMS ARK ROYAL (1939 1940)

Pitot

FRONT

Guns

Exhaust Stack

Air Intake

Wheel Cover

VIEW

Landing Light

Pitot Airspeed Indicator

Blue

White

Red

Entire Plane: Light Silver Grey

.303 Cal. Machine Guns

Black Wing Walk

Wing Folding Line

Red Band

Trim Tab

Exhaust Collector Ring

Exhaust Stack

Vent Outlet

Retracted Landing Gear

ZAP Wing Flaps

Stabilizer

Elevator

Landing Light

TOP VIEW

Aileron

0   5   10   15   20   25

SCALE (FEET)

Folded Wing

Navigator/Gunner With One Swivel .027 Cal. Gun

Antenna

Engine Cooling Air Control Flaps

Pilot

Rudder

Vent

Fin

Red

Trim Tabs

3-Bladed Propeller

Reddish Orange Exhaust Collector Ring

Engine Air Intake

A7G

L2889

Black

White

Arresting Hook

500 Lb. Bomb On Crutch/ Trapeze

Wheel Cover

PROFILE

WAM

The Blackburn Skua was the first British dive bomber to equip FAA squadrons and the first British modern all-metal cantilever low wing monoplane with retractable landing gear intended for carrier service.

Flotation Compartments

In view of the fact that this naval craft was to spend most of its operational life over water, four watertight compartments were built into the structure to help keep it afloat in the event of an emergency ditching. One watertight compartment was located in each wing outer panel between the two Spars; another was under the cockpit floor, and the fourth was in the fuselage rear aft of the navigator/gunner's cockpit.

Skua Data

The wing outer panels could be manually folded by the deck crew; twisting 90 degrees as they stowed alongside the fuselage and fin, leading edge uppermost. The landing gear retracted upwards and outwards into the outer wing panels by means of an engine-driven hydraulic pump. The oversize wing flaps not only shortened the takeoff run and landing approach but also limited the diving speed to 300 miles per hour. The entire plane was covered with flush-riveted Alclad, except for fabric covered control surfaces.

Powered by a Bristol Perseus XII sleeve valve air-cooled radial engine of 890 horsepower, the production Blackburn Skua attained 225 miles per hour at 6,500 feet. Service ceiling was 20,000 feet and range about 400 miles. Empty weight was 5,490 pounds and gross weight was 8,228 pounds. Wingspan was 46 feet-2 inches and with wings folded it was 15 feet-6 inches. Wing area was 319 square feet. Length was 35 feet-7 inches.

Four Browning machine guns were buried in the wing, firing beyond the propeller arc, and one Lewis machine gun was flexible-mounted in the rear cockpit. The bomb load consisted of one 500 pound semi-armor-piercing bomb carried beneath the wing center-section. The bomb was mounted on a semi-retractable ejector swing arm which brought the missile forward and down to clear the propeller arc when released during a steep dive.

Skua Assignments

First deliveries to the Fleet Air Arm were to Nos. 800 and 803 Squadrons aboard *HMS Ark Royal* and subsequent deliveries re-equipped No. 801 Squadron aboard *HMS Furious*. By September 1939 there were 33 Blackburn Skuas on active duty and although regarded as an effective but not potent dive bomber the Skua had already been outclassed as a fighter; evidence that multirole aircraft cannot be first-rate in every role and often prove to be mediocre in all of them.

The Blackburn Skua was not a failure and scored notably in the first years of World War II. Its combat life was; however, short-lived but the Skua did enjoy a few months of glory, as is recounted in the next chapter.

Blackburn Roc Monoplane Turret Fighter

A development of the Skua dive bomber/fighter, the Blackburn Roc was to be a two-seater naval fighter. Air Ministry Specifications 0.30/35 of 1935 called for a four-gun turret armed fleet fighter with no forward-firing guns.

In order to satisfy the current British theory of multi-gun turret fitted fighters, the Skua was modified to include a four gun power turret behind the pilot. Turret can be seen projecting above the wingtip. The theory proved a failure and the Blackburn Roc was relegated to target towing. (Air Ministry [Navy])

Power Turret Theory

Despite the fact that the power turret was a lethal weapon, it was an absurd tactical theory to expect enemy aircraft to fly alongside the turret-armed fighter and exchange broadside volleys. The theory was not new. This concept had been originally applied to the Royal Air Force Boulton-Paul Defiant and the Roc was intended to be the Fleet Air Arm equivalent of the Defiant. In view of the fact that the power turret was of Boulton-Paul design that firm was awarded the contract to assemble 136 Rocs in April 1937, having been supplied with subassemblies. The first Roc flew on December 23, 1938 and Rocs were first issued to a land-based squadron in February 1940.

Poor Showing - Early Roc Retirement

On July 19, 1940 12 RAF Boulton-Paul Defiants had engaged in combat with Messerschmitt single-seat fighters from Gruppe III of JG 51. Eleven Defiants were shot down with no losses for the Messerschmitts. The handwriting was on the wall; power turrets were great defensive weapons but had no place in fighter tactics which are purely offensive. Thereafter, Rocs were withdrawn from front line service and served for target towing and various training duties. The last Roc was retired in August 1943.

Fairey Fulmar Two-Seat Fighter

A new Fleet Air Arm two-seater fighter of the period was the Fairey Fulmar designed to Air Ministry Specification 0.8/38 of 1938. Basically a development of the Royal Air Force Fairey Battle, modified for naval service, the Fulmar had a crew of two instead of three and was slightly smaller than the Battle. The first Fulmar prototype

Introduced in early 1940 the Fairey Fulmar two-seater fighter flew from many carriers and featured the heavy fire power of eight .30 caliber machine guns buried in the wing. The Fulmar's shortcoming was its relatively slow speed. (Air Ministry [Navy])

FAIREY FULMAR Mk. I

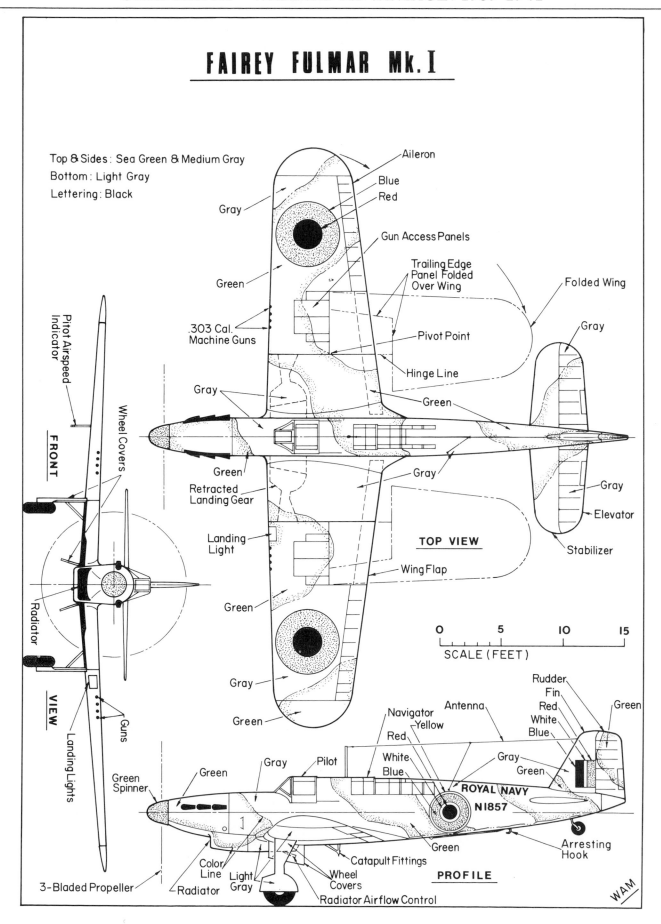

Top & Sides : Sea Green & Medium Gray
Bottom : Light Gray
Lettering : Black

Pitot Airspeed Indicator

Wheel Covers

FRONT

Radiator

VIEW

Landing Lights

Guns

3-Bladed Propeller

Green Spinner

Color Line

Radiator

Light Gray

Wheel Covers

Catapult Fittings

Radiator Airflow Control

Green

Gray

Pilot

Navigator

Yellow

Red

White

Blue

Antenna

Rudder

Fin

Red

White

Blue

Green

Gray

Green

ROYAL NAVY

N1857

Green

Arresting Hook

PROFILE

Aileron

Blue

Red

Gray

Green

.303 Cal. Machine Guns

Gun Access Panels

Trailing Edge Panel Folded Over Wing

Folded Wing

Gray

Pivot Point

Hinge Line

Green

Gray

Green

Retracted Landing Gear

Gray

Gray

Elevator

Stabilizer

Landing Light

TOP VIEW

Wing Flap

Green

Gray

Green

0   5   10   15

SCALE (FEET)

WAM

appeared on January 4, 1940 for its first test flight and Fairey was promptly awarded a production contract for 250 machines. Fulmar is a large arctic sea bird.

Assignments

No. 808 Squadron on *HMS Ark Royal* was the first to be equipped with the new fighter in June 1940 and by September Nos. 806 and 807 Squadrons were equipped to replace their Skuas.

Fulmar Data

Powered with a 1,080 horsepower Rolls-Roycc Merlin VIII 12-cylinder Vee, liquid-cooled engine, the 9,800 pound loaded Fairey Fulmar I attained a maximum speed of 256 miles per hour, which was not much more than the Gladiator biplane it was to replace. Service ceiling was 22,400 feet and combat range was 830 miles.

The principal asset of the Fulmar was its firepower, which consisted of eight fixed 0.30 inch caliber Browning machine guns located in the wing outboard of the propeller arc. A single Vickers K machine gun was swivel-mounted in the navigator's cockpit for defensive purposes.

Wingspan was 46 feet-4 inches with a length of 40 feet-3 inche Height was 14 feet-0 inches. Wing area was 342 square feet.

Hit and Run

The most serious fault was the Fulmar's lack of speed compared contemporary single-seat fighters. With its excellent fire power th meant that a surprise dive on the enemy was the only tactic to i sure victory because if the pilot failed to score with his first attac he would hardly get a second chance in the ensuing dogfight.

The Fulmar was of all-metal stressed-skin construction ar included manually folding wings, catapult fittings, arresting hoc and stowage for an inflatable life raft.

Fulmar Wing Folding

Fulmar's wing folding was a bit unusual. The outer wing pane were folded back, laterally, hinged at the rear spar. That portion the wing panel aft of the rear spar was first folded over the ma portion of the outer panel in order that the wing could be folde back laterally. Wing folding design requires a lot of ingenuity ar careful consideration because when extended it must withstand se vere stresses as the plane goes through violent maneuvers.

This close-up of the Fulmar reveals the neatly cowled engine and the wheel cover (Arrow). Wheel covers are often omitted due to damage or left off at the factory to speed construction in wartime. Pressure of the retracted wheel on the crossbar forces the levers to close the wheel cover (Arrow). (Imperial War Museum)

Fulmar Mark II

The Mark I was followed by the Fulmar Mark II powered by the 1300 horsepower Rolls-Royce Merlin XXX engine; however, the performance was only marginally improved. A total of 350 Mark II Fulmars were constructed. By 1942 Fairey Fulmars equipped 14 squadrons of the Fleet Air Arm. The Fulmar's wartime activities will be examined later in this chapter.

SUPERIOR JAPANESE CARRIER-BASED FIGHTER

Unlike the Fleet Air Arm, the Imperial Japanese Navy had no obstacles to overcome in the development of a single seat carrier-based fighter plane.

Mitsubishi A6M Zero-Sen Fighter

It will be recalled in Chapter II that Japanese aircraft designer Jiro Horikoshi began to conceive a successor fighter plane to his Mitsubishi Claude.

Just as the designer began studies for the Claude successor the Imperial Japanese Navy issued specifications for a light, fast, maneuverable and long-range carrier-based fighter in May 1937. A 311 miles per hour speed and two cannon plus two machine guns

The word Zero had become a household word in the U.S. during World War II, synonymous with all Japanese fighter planes. Jiro Horikoshi's Mitsubishi Zero-Sen fighter had caught the world by surprise because of its superlative performance. (U.S. National Archives)

were also specified. So rigid and exacting were the requirements that Nakajima did not respond to the invitation to bid. Horikoshi and Mitsubishi accepted the challenge and by March 1939 two prototype fighters were ready to fly.

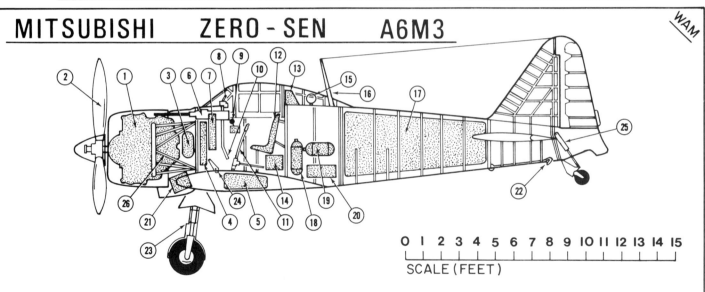

MITSUBISHI   ZERO-SEN   A6M3

WAM

SCALE (FEET) — 0 1 2 3 4 5 6 7 8 9 10 11 12 13 14 15

① RADIAL ENGINE	⑨ ENGINE CONTROLS	⑱ OXYGEN FLASK
② THREE BLADED PROPELLER	⑩ INSTRUMENT PANEL	⑲ FLOTATION BAG INFLATING FLASK
③ LUB. OIL TANK	⑪ CONTROL STICK	⑳ RADIO
④ RESERVE FUEL TANK	⑫ SEAT	㉑ OIL COOLER
⑤ MAIN FUEL TANK	⑬ HEADREST	㉒ ARRESTING HOOK
⑥ MACHINE GUNS	⑭ BATTERY	㉓ LANDING GEAR STRUT
⑦ AMMUNITION CASE	⑮ RADIO DIRECTION FINDER	㉔ RUDDER PEDALS
⑧ REFLECTOR GUN SIGHT	⑯ WOODEN RADIO MAST	㉕ OLEO STRUT
	⑰ INFLATABLE FLOTATION BAG	㉖ ENGINE MOUNT

This head-on view of the Japanese Zero fighter shows the wide track landing gear which simplified landing on a pitching carrier flight deck; especially for a mediocre pilot. The Mitsubishi Zero was an exceptionally clean design with 360 degree visibility from the cockpit. The craft was light weight, very maneuverable, and a state-of-the-art naval fighter. (U.S. National Archives)

Zero-Sen Test Flights

The new design was a clean, low wing, all-metal monoplane with retractable landing gear and was designated A6M1. The story is told that this sleek, state-of-the-art fighter plane was transported from the Mitsubishi Nagoya plant to the military airfield at Kagamigahara by means of an ox-drawn cart. With Mitsubishi test pilot Katsuzo Shima at the controls the A6M1 took off for the first time on April 1, 1939. All went well except for slight vibrations which were corrected by replacing the two-bladed variable pitch propeller with a three-bladed constant speed Sumitomo-built design. Another problem was that the top speed was six miles per hour below that specified. This was caused by the fact that Horikoshi had selected the heavier Mitusbishi Zuisei 13 fourteen-cylinder air-cooled radial engine instead of the lighter Nakajima Sakae 12 fourteen-cylinder air-cooled radial engine because he did not want to use a competitor's product. Japanese Navy officials ordered the installation of the Sakae 12 engine on the third prototype, designated A6M2, which was first test-flown in December 1939. The results were most satisfactory and the Imperial Japanese Navy decided the new fighter was ready for combat testing in China.

A6M2 Combat Debut

On July 21, 1940 two squadrons (Hikotais) with 15 preproduction A6M2 fighters left for China but did not meet with any Chinese opposition until September 13. Led by Lieutenant Saburo Shindo, 13 Mitsubishi fighters surprised 27 Russian-built Chinese Polikarpov I-15 biplanes and I-16 monoplane fighters. Within a few minutes the new fighter had shot down all of the Chinese planes with no loss to themselves. By the end of the year the Mitsubishi squadrons had shot down 59 Chinese aircraft over China and Indo-China; still suffering no losses. General Claire E. Chennault, leader of the Flying Tigers volunteer group, reported the spectacular successes of this new Japanese naval fighter to U.S. Army Air Corps brass; however, his reports were either disbelieved or ignored.

A6M2 Production and Carrier Assignments

In July 1940 the A6M2 had been placed into production as the Navy Type 0 Carrier Fighter Model II; soon to be known throughout the world as the Zero or Zero-Sen. In Japan the plane was known as the Reisen which is a contraction of Rei Sentoki which means Zero

Fighter in Japanese. As was mentioned for the U.S. Navy, the Japanese Navy also specified a maximum wingspan for carrier aircraft which was 36 feet-1 inch. This was about 39 inches shorter than the Reisen wingspan and; therefore, the Zero wing tips were arranged for manual upwards folding to meet the stowage requirements.

Over 1,000 A6M2 Reisens were constructed by Mitsubishi and Nakajima and the type saw considerable activity in 1940 and 1941 operating from the Japanese carriers *Akagi*, *Kaga*, *Soryu*, *Hiryu*, *Shokaku*, *Zuikaku* and others in actions such as Pearl Harbor, Wake Island and Midway.

Zero-Sen Variants

As war with Britain and the U.S. appeared unavoidable the Imperial Japanese Navy saw the need to further improve the Reisen in order that it could cope with the high performance planes it was expected to meet in combat. Nakajima Hikoki engineers had been improving the Sakae engine with the addition of a two-speed supercharger and bench tests were so encouraging that the engine was ordered into production as the Sakai 21 for use in the Reisen. Propeller diameter increased to 10 feet.

In addition to the more powerful engine, the A6M3 also increased the 20 millimeter wing-mounted cannon ammunition from 60 to 100 rounds per gun. The A6M3 Model 32 had the folding wingtips removed and short fairing pieces added, giving the wing a clipped appearance. U.S. observers assumed this was an entirely new design and gave it the code name of Hap, which was later changed to Hamp; however, when it was realized that the plane was really a Zero the new names were dropped. After producing about 350 Model 32 Reisens the original rounded wingtips were replaced and two internal wing tanks were added. This became the A6M3 Model 22 and had the longest range of all the Reisen models. About 600 were built.

A6M3 Data

The Nakajima Sakae 21 engine of the Mitsubishi A6M3 Model 22 developed 1,130 horsepower for takeoff but this dropped to 980 horsepower at 19,680 feet altitude. Maximum speed was 336 miles per hour at 19,680 feet. Cruising speed was 220 miles per hour which speed the range was a phenomenal 1,600 miles; very important for Pacific operations. Wingspan was 39 feet-4 1/2 inches and ength 29 feet-8 3/4 inches. Height was 11 feet-6 1/4 inches. Wing rea was 241 1/2 square feet and loaded weight was 5,906 pounds iving the Reisen an exceptionally light wing loading.

Zero-Sen Light Weight

In the design of the Zero-Sen Horikoshi and his team of Shotoro anaka, Yoshimi Hatakenaka, Teruo Tojo, Denichiro Inouye, adahiko Kato and Takeyoshi Moro concentrated on weight savings in order to produce a very maneuverable fighter.

In fact, a special aluminum alloy, developed by Sumitomo, was sed. Concentrating on lightness for performance and meeting the armament requirement forced the designers to omit pilot protection and self-sealing fuel tanks which had been in use by the Royal Air orce and the Luftwaffe in late 1939. The Japanese approach of acrificing all nonoperational weight also enhanced the combat range f the Reisen which proved invaluable during the Pacific war, where ong range was necessary.

Zero-Sen Structure

The fuselage was all-metal, semi-monocoque built in two sections. The forward section was constructed integral with the wing center ection and included the cockpit, engine mount, fuel tank, lubricating oil tank and radio equipment. This is reminiscent of the Blackburn torpedo-bomber designs of the 1920s. The rear section was detachable and included an inflatable flotation bag, arresting ook, tailwheel and fin.

The wing contained two strength spars and was all-metal except for the aileron covering which was fabric. Four fuel tanks and wo inflatable flotation bags were located between the spars. The ydraulically operated wing-mounted landing gear retracted inwardly, thereby producing a wide track, which made for safer deck peration.

Fixed tail surfaces were all-metal while the movable control urfaces were fabric covered metal structures.

Zero-Sen Drop Tank

In order to extend the combat range, a 75 gallon streamline cylindrical ventral drop tank was often carried under the wing center ection. Originally constructed of light aluminum alloy, the shortage of raw materials in Japan forced the use of alternative drop tank construction materials such as papier-mache and bamboo.

Zero-Sen Performance

The Reisen's low wing loading and high power loading gave it exeptional maneuverability and enabled it to climb in a steep angle t low speed with complete control. Most Allied fighters would have stalled if they followed a Zero-Sen into a slow speed climb. The Reisen's Achilles' heel was the absence of pilot armor and elf-sealing fuel tanks which made it very vulnerable in the event f a direct hit. Another drawback was the carburetor design which caused the engine to slow down during negative acceleration such s going into a dive without rolling into it or abruptly assuming evel flight after a steep climb.

Despite the fact that the Zero-Sen had been in action since the ummer of 1940, its outstanding performance and, in some cases,

its very existence, came as a surprise to the U.S. and Britain during the winter of 1941-42.

AMERICA'S LAST PRE-WAR AIRCRAFT CARRIERS

The keel of the 14,700 tons displacement *USS Wasp* (CV-7) was laid on April 1, 1936 at Bethlehem Steel Shipyard. A product of the Washington Naval Treaty restrictions, it is a logical assumption that she would never have been constructed were it not for that Treaty. *USS Wasp* was built with the leftover tonnage from *Yorktown* and *Enterprise*.

USS Wasp (CV-7)

The small carrier *Wasp* was a miniature *Yorktown* class carrier except that it was compressed and compromised to handle the maximum number of aircraft possible at the expense of overall efficiency. Even the horsepower of the propulsion machinery was reduced to save space which resulted in a slower speed than desired.

As with the *Yorktown* class athwartship aircraft launching capability was provided from the Hangar Deck. Two athwartship catapults were installed; one forward and one aft. These were in addition to the conventional Flight Deck catapults.

Unlike Ranger, *Wasp*'s smokestack was combined with the navigating island and, to compensate for this additional starboard side weight, the hull was made wider on the port side, as on *Ark Royal*.

Arresting cables were located fore and aft to accommodate landings from either end of the Flight Deck.

Wasp Data

The 70,000 shaft horsepower gave *Wasp* a speed of 29.5 knots. Steam was generated in six boilers and supplied to two steam turbines geared to twin-propeller shafts. Combat range was 12,000 miles at 15 knots. Waterline length was 688 with an 80 foot-9 inch beam. Flight Deck measured 727 feet-6 inches x 93 feet-0 inches. Deep load draft was 24 feet-6 inches. Peacetime complement was 1,889 officers and crew but probably increased to 2,000 during combat. The ship was designed to operate about 80 aircraft, an increase of eight planes above the *Ranger* capacity and equal to the larger *Yorktown* class! *USS Wasp* was commissioned on April 25, 1940.

Unlike most U.S. aircraft carriers in World War II USS Wasp served in the Atlantic Ocean and the Mediterranean Sea as well as the Pacific Ocean. Wasp is shown here as she completed her Atlantic service and is departing for the Pacific. (U.S. Naval Historical Center)

USS Wasp (CV-7) was a small 14,700 tons in order to meet the restrictions of the Washington Naval Treaty and is often called a miniature Yorktown carrier. It was the last of the small U.S. Navy carriers. (U.S. Naval Historical Center)

USS Hornet (CV-8)

Although planning for the new *Essex* class carriers was nearing completion the Roosevelt administration was unwilling to wait for it to be finalized before building the next carrier authorized by the Navy Expansion Act of 1938. It was; therefore, decided that this carrier would be a modified *Yorktown* class vessel to be named *Hornet*. It was the last American aircraft carrier of the pre-Pearl Harbor period. The *Hornet*'s keel was laid on September 25, 1939, at Newport News Shipbuilding & D.D. Co. only a few weeks after the invasion of Poland and the declaration of war in Europe.

The U.S. Congress was able to authorize *Hornet* construction without violating any treaty because the Washington Treaty had lapsed and the London Conferences of 1930 and 1936 had ended in virtual failure; therefore, there was no longer a restriction on total aircraft carrier tonnage.

USS Hornet (CV-8) was very similar to *USS Yorktown* and *USS Enterprise* with minor differences such as the type of gun directors, as well as other island details. *Hornet* Flight Deck was also a few feet wider than *Enterprise*. Launched on December 14, 1940, *Hornet* was commissioned on October 20, 1941, about six weeks before the Pearl Harbor attack. Her first commanding officer was Captain Marc A. Mitscher, who as Vice Admiral Mitscher was to become the best known U.S. Navy carrier commander and tactician in the soon to come Pacific carrier war.

Popular Flattops

Together with *Lexington* and *Saratoga*, *Yorktown*, *Enterprise* and *Hornet* captured the American imagination as had no other war ships and became household words during the early years of World War II. *USS Yorktown*, *Enterprise* and *Hornet* were the first U.S. Navy truly fleet-capable carriers built from the keel up as flattops. They were able to turn the tide of the war in the Pacific together with the beautiful conversions, *Lexington* and *Saratoga*. Their heroic exploits will be followed in Chapter IV as they and their air groups battle the carriers and warbirds of the Imperial Japanese Navy.

A modified Yorktown carrier, USS Hornet (CV-8) was the last American carrier of the pre-Pearl Harbor period. Hornet was commissioned on October 20, 1941. (U.S. Naval Historical Center)

carrier is shown refueling an escorting destroyer. The carrier of a VBG is responsible to refuel and replenish its smaller escorts as necessary when oilers are not available. The fueling line is a rugged 6 inch diameter hose and is very difficult to handle. (Sal Marrone Photo)

UNDERWAY REPLENISHMENT

Since the early 1920s most of the U.S. Navy was based in the Pacific because America realized that Japan was the only maritime power able or likely to challenge the U.S. The U.S. government resumed, rather openly, that the next war would be with the Japanese Empire. Despite this awareness very little was done to create new bases and build up existing bases in strategic Pacific areas. By 1939 this folly was realized, which prompted the U.S. Navy to undertake dedicated studies to develop ways of conducting long range naval actions without the need for bases. From June 11 to 13, 1939 the carrier *Saratoga* (CV-3) and the Navy oiler *USS Kanawaho* (AO-) conducted exercises off the U.S. west coast to demonstrate the concept and feasibility of underway replenishment and refueling. The experiments were very successful and this technique, pioneered by the U.S. Navy, was to prove of inestimable value during World War II. It is paradoxical that American neglect in one aspect of national defense would foster the development of a substitute technique, which not only replaced the neglected function but far surpassed its importance. Underway replenishment is a fascinating operation to witness as the two ships steam alongside each other, transferring food, munitions, fuel, and other necessities from supply ships to combat vessels or between combat vessels if no supply ship is in the area. Each ship must be equipped to handle the cables and heavy hose, and crews must be well-trained in replenishment and refueling operations.

AMERICAN TWO-OCEAN NAVY

On June 17, 1940 Admiral Harold R. Stark, Chief of Naval Operations, requested funds for a two-ocean navy. Congress and the President approved and four billion dollars was appropriated for this purpose two days later. This was a huge sum in 1940. The specter of an American Navy dedicated to the Pacific Ocean alarmed the Imperial Japanese Navy.

MORE U.S. NAVY MONOPLANES

To outfit its newer and larger carriers the U.S. Navy needed more and better shipboard aircraft. The Grumman FF-1 was being phased out of front line service, however, because no monoplane fighter was available, the F2F-1 was still entering service.

Grumman F3F-1 Biplane Fighter

Grumman had its XF3F-1 prototype ready for testing in the spring of 1935. This was an improvement over the F2F Series. After preliminary testing went well, Jimmy Collins, Grumman test pilot and well-known pilot of the 1930s, put the tiny biplane into a terminal velocity dive from which it never recovered, killing the famous pilot. In May 1935 Lee Gehlbach, also a very famous test pilot, flew the second XF3F-1 and entered the terminal velocity dive. This time the craft went into an uncontrollable spin from which Gehlbach bailed out just in time before the second crash. Leroy Grumman and his engineers would not give up and worked out all the bugs until the craft was acceptable to the U.S. Navy. A production order of 54 was placed and the first F3F-1 biplanes entered service one year later. The design underwent constant refinement up to the F3F-3 in June 1938.

Grumman F3F-3 Data

The 3,285 pound empty and 4,795 pound gross weight F3F-3 was powered by a 950 horsepower Wright R-1820-22 nine-cylinder air-cooled radial engine with which the Grumman attained a top speed of 264 miles per hour at 15,200 feet. Range with the 130 gallon internal fuel tank was 975 miles when cruising at 125 miles per hour. The initial rate of climb was 2,750 feet per minute and service ceiling 33,200 feet. Armament was the standard one .30 inch caliber and one .50 inch caliber Browning machine gun in the upper fuselage between the cockpit and the engine. Construction was basically as the previously described F2F-1. Wingspan was 32 feet; length 23 feet-2 inches; and height was 9 feet-4 inches. Wing area was 260 square feet.

Grumman F3F Assignments

The F3F-1 served with VF-5B on *USS Ranger* and with VF-6B on *USS Saratoga*. The Navy ordered (81) F3F-2 designs which

Leroy Grumman designed the F3F series to replace the F2F. The F3F was the last U.S. Navy biplane fighter because monoplanes were on the way. Note the neutrality star, and the cowl blisters to cover the engine valve rocker arms on this F3F-1. (Grumman Corporation, Courtesy Lois Lovisolo)

GRUMMAN F3F-1

VF-3 'FELIX THE CAT' Squadron·3rd Flight Leader·USS SARATOGA

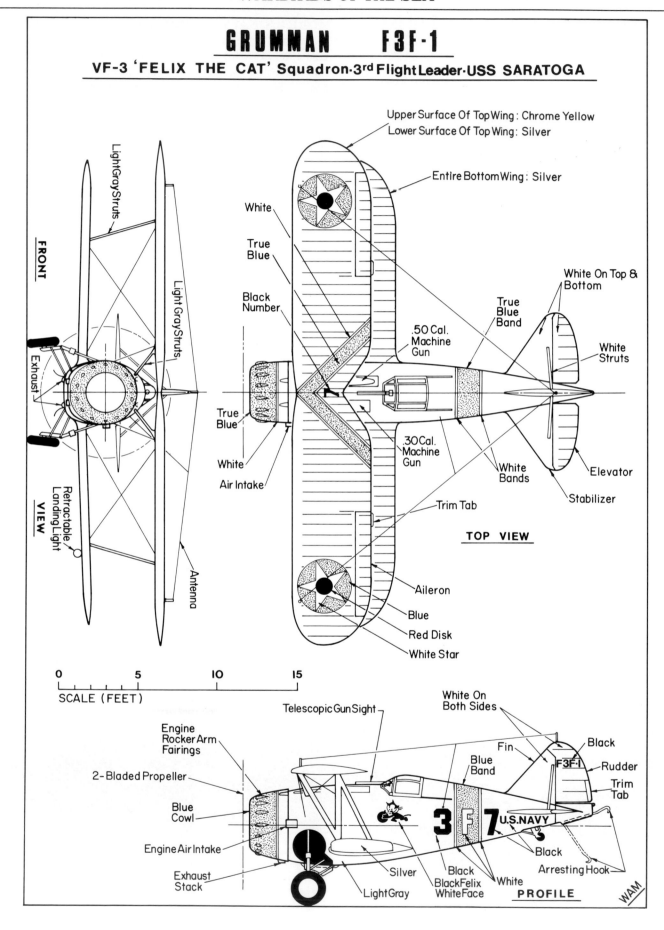

Upper Surface Of Top Wing : Chrome Yellow
Lower Surface Of Top Wing : Silver

Entire Bottom Wing : Silver

White On Top & Bottom

White

True Blue

Black Number

.50 Cal. Machine Gun

True Blue Band

White Struts

True Blue

White

Air Intake

.30 Cal. Machine Gun

White Bands

Elevator

Stabilizer

Trim Tab

TOP VIEW

Aileron

Blue

Red Disk

White Star

FRONT

Light Gray Struts

Light Gray Struts

Exhaust

Retractable Landing Light

VIEW

Antenna

SCALE (FEET)
0   5   10   15

Telescopic Gun Sight

White On Both Sides

Engine Rocker Arm Fairings

Fin

Black

Blue Band

F3F·1

2-Bladed Propeller

Rudder

Trim Tab

Blue Cowl

3 F 7 U.S.NAVY

Engine Air Intake

Black

Exhaust Stack

Silver

Black
Black Felix White Face

White

Arresting Hook

Light Gray

PROFILE

WAM

quipped VF-6 on *USS Enterprise* and Marine Squadrons VMF-1 nd VMF-2 during 1938. A contract for (27) F3F-3 aircraft was laced in June 1938. This was the last of the biplane fighters for ny U.S. Armed Service. The F3F-3 also equipped VF-5 on *USS orktown* but by 1941 none remained in operationational use. The ge of the monoplane had arrived.

After several disappointing years the U.S. Navy procured acceptable carrier-based monoplanes some of which became classics nd accomplished legendary achievements during World War II.

ought SB2U Vindicator Scout/Bomber

he U.S. Navy's first production monoplane scout/bomber (scouting dive bomber) was designed by a team led by Rex B. Beisel, hief Engineer of Vought-Sikorsky Division of United Aircraft orporation and the Navy placed an order in October 1934.The ive bomber made its initial flight on January 4, 1936. Despite the act that other navies had successful monoplanes in service and the J.S. Navy already had the successful Douglas Devastator torpedo-omber monoplane in service, the Navy insisted upon conducting omparative trials between the new Vindicator monoplane scout/omber and a new biplane scout-bomber built by the same company. The trials were conducted in spring of 1936 between two Vought designs, SB2U-1 monoplane and SB3U-1 biplane, to determine if monoplanes were really better than biplanes. The competiion clearly convinced the U.S. Navy that the monoplane scout/omber was the way to go.

indicator Variants

Vought received a contract for (54) of its SB2U-1 scout/bombers n October 26, 1936. Production deliveries began in December 1937 o Squadron VB-3. In January 1938 the Navy ordered (58) SB2U-2

monoplanes which had newer equipment installed at the request of the Navy. These were delivered by the end of the year. The next modification was the SB2U-3 which had larger fuel tanks installed, increased armor, provision for drop tanks and .50 inch caliber guns, one fixed-forward and one flexible-mount aft. In September 1939 (57) SB2U-3 monoplanes were ordered.

Vindicator Data

The Vought SB2U-3 Vindicator was powered by a 825 horsepower Pratt & Whitney R-1535-02 air-cooled radial engine which drove the 5,634 pounds empty and 9,421 pounds gross weight monoplane to a maximum speed of 243 miles per hour at 9,500 feet. Range was 1,120 miles at cruising speed of 152 miles per hour. Service ceiling was 23,600 feet and initial rate of climb 1,070 feet per minute. The two-man crew consisted of pilot and observer/gunner.

The structure was all-metal and the entire wing center section, forward one-third of the wing outer panels, fin, stabilizer, and fuselage from the nose to the rear cockpit were Alclad-covered while the remainder of the structure was covered with fabric. The outer wing panels folded upwards over the fuselage to facilitate stowage in carriers. Up to 1,000 pounds of bombs could be carried. A trapeze-type mount for 500 pound bombs was installed to swing the bomb down and forward to clear the propeller arc prior to releasing the missile.

Wingspan was 42 feet-0 inches with overall length of 34 feet-0 inches. Height was 10 feet-3 inches. Wing area was 305 square feet.

Vindicator Assignments

By 1940 SBU-1 and SBU-2 models were serving with VB-2 on *USS Lexington*, VB-3 in *USS Saratoga*, VB-4, VS-41 and VS-42

As Chief Engineer of Vought-Sikorsky Division of United Aircraft, Rex Beisel led his team to design the U.S. Navy's first monoplane scout/dive bomber in 1934; known as the SBU Vindicator. The landing gear retracted rearwards, rotating 90 degrees for the wheels to lay flat in the wing. The 169 Vindicators built saw plenty of action in 1942. Over 1,000 pounds of bombs could be carried. This is the XSB2U-3. The all-metal structure was fabric-covered except for the forward half of the fuselage, wing center section and wing leading edge which were Alclad-covered. The plane remained in production from 1936 to 1939. (Vought-Sikorsky, Courtesy Arthur L. Schoeni)

on *USS Ranger*, and VS-71 and VS-72 on *USS Wasp*. The majority of the SBU-2-3 model was issued to Marine Squadrons, including VMSB-131, VMSB-231 and VMSB-241. These units saw considerable action in 1942.

Brewster SBA-1 Scout/Bomber
Also, in 1934 Brewster Aeronautical Corporation won a Navy development contract for their XSBA-1 monoplane scout/bomber design which first flew in April 1936. During 1932 Brewster was primarily a subcontractor, constructing components for the aircraft of other manufacturers and the XSBA-1 was their first complete aircraft design. The designer, Dayton T. Brown, decided upon internal bomb stowage to reduce resistance which resulted in a top speed of 254 miles per hour at 15,200 feet for this 6,759 pound plane. Range was 1,015 miles. Brewster production facilities were limited; therefore, the U.S. Navy bought the production rights and made 30 planes at the Naval Aircraft Factory known as the SBN-1 These craft served on *USS Hornet*.

Brewster F2A and Grumman F4F Monoplane Fighters
With monoplane torpedo-bomber and scout/bomber designs in service with the U.S. Navy, it was still the Grumman biplanes that were providing the Navy's fighter strength. In response to the Navy's 1935 request for bids to replace the Grumman biplanes, four aircraft manufacturers submitted proposals. Seversky proposed a navalized version of their P-35 U.S.Army fighter (Granddad of the Republic P-47 Thunderbolt) and Curtiss did the same with their P-36 Mohawk (Daddy of the P-40 Kittyhawk/Warhawk). Grumman came up with a new biplane design while a relatively obscure New York City manufacturer, Brewster Aeronautical Corporation, proposed a specially designed all-metal shipboard midwing monoplane. The Navy concluded that carrier operations required a specially developed fighter and only the Grumman and Brewster designs met this requirement; therefore, the Curtiss and Seversky proposals were rejected. The Brewster and Grumman stories are so interwoven that they must be related simultaneously.

Monoplane and Biplane Contracts
The Bureau of Aeronautics awarded Brewster a contract for its XF2A-1 design development on November 15, 1935. Apparently

This Brewster F2A-1 Buffalo is shown in the U.S. Navy peace time pre-World War II color scheme of light gray fuselage, aluminum wing underside, chrome yellow wing upper surface, lemon yellow upper half of cowl for plane number 18, and white tail for Saratoga. Note the Felix The Cat insignia of VF-3. The F2A-1 was the first U.S. Navy production monoplane fighter. Initial deliveries to the U.S. Navy were in November 1939. (Official U.S. Navy Photograph, News Photo Division)

still not sure of monoplanes, and wanting to play it safe with a biplane in reserve in the event that the new monoplane proved a failure, a contract was simultaneously awarded to Grumman for its XF4F-1 biplane design development.

Two Monoplane Contracts
In July 1936 the Brewster XF2A-1 prototype was ordered and, one month later, the U.S. Navy cancelled the Grumman XF4F-1 biplane, realizing that the venerable biplane had reached its ultimate refinement. A new contract was issued to Grumman for an all-metal midwing monoplane, XF4F-2, similar to the Brewster configuration. Again, the Navy wanted insurance in the event the Brewster would not prove successful.

Brewster Production Facilities
The Brewster plant was a multistory loft building in the Long Island City community of the Borough of Queens in New York City. Various sub-assemblies were made on the many floors and then transported to the assembly area via large freight elevators. It was the typical 1920-1930 aircraft factory, certainly not prepared for wartime mass production. Test flights required that the plane be disassembled and crated, then loaded onto a truck and driven to a Long Island airfield where it was reassembled and then test flown. Despite this rather primitive arrangement Brewster officials apparently made extravagant promises regarding aircraft deliveries which they often failed to meet.

Grumman Production Facilities
Knowing the above conditions and realizing that the Grumman plant was a contemporary state-of-the-art production facility with access to an airfield and an efficient management team led by Leroy Grumman, it comes as no surprise that the XF4F-2 made its first flight on September 2, 1937 while the Brewster XF2A-1 did not fly until December 2, 1937. This, despite the fact that Brewster had begun construction on the prototype during March 1936, three months before the official contract for the prototype was signed.

Brewster F2A-1 assembly at the Brewster plant in Queens, New York City. This was a loft building in the center of town and the planes had to be trucked to Long Island for test flights. (Brewster Aeronautical Corporation)

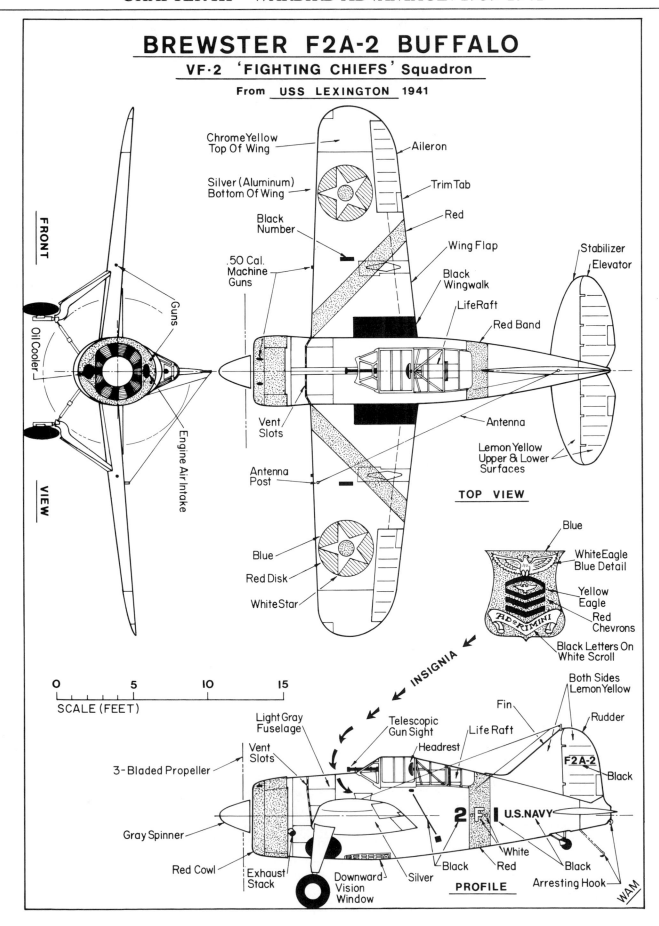

BREWSTER F2A-2 BUFFALO
VF·2 'FIGHTING CHIEFS' Squadron
From USS LEXINGTON 1941

FRONT

Oil Cooler

Guns

Engine Air Intake

VIEW

ChromeYellow Top Of Wing

Aileron

Silver (Aluminum) Bottom Of Wing

Trim Tab

Black Number

Red

.50 Cal. Machine Guns

Wing Flap

Black Wingwalk

LifeRaft

Red Band

Stabilizer Elevator

Vent Slots

Antenna

Lemon Yellow Upper & Lower Surfaces

TOP VIEW

Antenna Post

Blue

Red Disk

White Star

Blue

WhiteEagle Blue Detail

Yellow Eagle

Red Chevrons

AD·RIMINI

Black Letters On White Scroll

INSIGNIA

Both Sides Lemon Yellow

Fin

Life Raft

Rudder

F2A-2

Black

0   5   10   15

SCALE (FEET)

Light Gray Fuselage

Telescopic Gun Sight

Headrest

Vent Slots

3-Bladed Propeller

Gray Spinner

Red Cowl

Exhaust Stack

Downward Vision Window

Silver

Black

2 F

White

Red

U.S.NAVY

Black

Arresting Hook

PROFILE

WΔM

The Grumman XF4F-2 was the first Grumman monoplane fighter; the XF4F-1 having been a biplane. This rotund prototype was developed into the potent Grumman Wildcat. (Grumman Corporation, Courtesy Lois Lovisolo)

The Grumman XF4F-3 in summer of 1939 reveals the new squared wing tips and enlarged cowl from the XF4F-2. Note that the horizontal tail is mounted in the fuselage. Bombs are 100 pounders. (Grumman Corpora tion, Courtesy Lois Lovisolo)

Prototype Test Flights

The Grumman XF4F-2 initial flight with company test pilot Robert H. Hall at the controls was successful despite the engine troubles which plagued the test flights!

The Brewster XF2A-1 prototype was delivered to the Navy for acceptance trials on January 13, 1938 after Brewster test pilot Mel Gough had put the XF2A-1 through her paces. The Navy tests were disappointing but not disastrous. They revealed that the Brewster required reshaping of the various air scoops, as well as the engine cowling in order to reduce air resistance and bring the top speed up to the required 235 miles per hour. The Brewster was the first full size plane to be tested in a wind tunnel. On April 21, 1938 the prototype XF2A-1 was delivered to the Langley Memorial Aeronautical Laboratory of the N.A.C.A. for placement in the wind tunnel to determine ways to reduce the drag and improve streamlining. Not only were the air inlets revised and cowl modified, but the rudder and fin required enlargement. The revised XF2A-1 attained 304 miles per hour at 16,000 feet and had a range of 1,000 miles when powered with a 950 horsepower Wright R-1820-34 radial air-cooled engine. After trials the Navy was satisfied and placed an order for 54 production models of the F2A-1 on June 11, 1938.

XF4F-3 New Engine

The Grumman XF4F-2 had never been officially delivered to the U.S. Navy; instead, it returned to the factory for minor changes and work on the engine. In April 1938 the XF4F-2 experienced engine failure during deck landing trials with a Navy pilot at the controls and crashed causing considerable damage. Undaunted, Grumman negotiated with the Navy to install a Pratt & Whitney XR-1830-76 Twin Wasp engine in a new plane. This resulted in a new contract in October 1938 for the new model XF4F-3.

Slow Brewster Production

Several months had elapsed while Brewster prepared the tooling and jigs necessary to produce the 54 fighters. The first deliveries were to be made by May 1939; however, by that time only one F2A-1 had been delivered and that was fitted with the original small fin and rudder. This plane was exhibited at the 1939 World's Fair in New York. Delays continued and only five F2A-1 airframes had been delivered by November 1939. At this time Navy acceptance

tests revealed excessive carbon monoxide levels in the cockpit which was corrected by installing a gas venting system with small rectan gular openings at the fuselage rear, close to the fin. By December (11) F2A-1 aircraft had been officially accepted and nine of these were assigned to VF-3 (Fighter Squadron Three); the famous Felix the Cat unit aboard *USS Saratoga*. This unit became the U.S. Navy first fighter squadron to be equipped with monoplanes.

Brewsters to Finland

During 1939 war clouds were gathering over Europe and European governments began seeking foreign-made aircraft. The Brewster sales team was out in full strength, negotiating with a number of European countries, offering F2A airframes without naval equip ment. Yet, the firm didn't even have the production capacity to meet U.S. Navy needs. In September 1939 Finland had requested per mission from the U.S. Government to buy American military air craft and when the Soviet Union attacked the tiny nation on No vember 30, 1939, the U.S. quickly approved the request. Brewster with State Department approval, diverted (43) F2A-1 fighters from U.S. Navy production for export to Finland, promising that these would be quickly replaced. Individual Finnish pilots did very well with the Brewster fighter scoring as high as 34 and 39 victories against the overwhelming superiority in numbers of the Soviet Air Force. In the final tally the Finns had destroyed 15 Soviet aircraft for each Brewster fighter lost.

Brewster F2A-2

In an effort to further improve the F2A-1 performance a 1,200 horse power Wright Cyclone engine had been tried by the Navy Bureau of Aeronautics. Top speed went up to 344 miles per hour at 16,000 feet and the range was 1,015 miles on its 164 gallon internal fuel tankage at a cruising speed of 144 miles per hour. Service ceiling went up to 35,000 feet. The Brewster F2A-2 was born and the U.S. Navy promptly changed the contract from F2A-1 to F2A-2. The new engine added 350 pounds; therefore, the nose had to be short ened by 5 inches in order to maintain proper balance of the aircraft. The first of the F2A-2 fighters were issued to VF-2 aboard *USS Lexington* and to VF-3 aboard *USS Saratoga* with each carrier re ceiving nine planes.

The first few Brewster F2A-2 production models were set aside by the U.S. Navy for further evaluation tests and additional trials or combat modifications. The modifications were based on reports from the war in Europe. These included increased fuel capacity, variable pitch propeller and improved flotation gear. For the first time since the first Navy fighters in 1922, an increase in aircraft armament was specified. In addition to the standard two .50 inch caliber fuselage-mounted guns, two additional .50 inch caliber machine guns were added in the wing; one on each side. Armor protection for both pilot and fuel tanks was installed. These improvements increased the Brewster's weight about 900 pounds which reduced the ceiling by 1,000 feet and the speed by five miles per hour.

The author was a draftsman at Brewster working with Dayton Brown on F2A-2 refinements at this time.

The U.S. Navy amended its contract with Brewster to replace the (43) F2A-1 planes transferred to Finland with the new F2A-2. It also required the conversion of eight F2A-1 to F2A-2 designs.

Despite Grumman's superior production facilities, by late 1939 the Brewster design was the only American naval monoplane fighter sufficiently developed to become a front line operational fighter in the event the U.S. became involved in the war.

Grumman F4F-3

During this time Grumman had developed the XF4F-3 design, contracted for in October 1938, and the first flight was made on Feburary 12, 1939. In addition to a two-stage supercharger, the XF4F-3 had replaced the rounded wingtips of the F4F-2 with squared off blunt tips. The tail surfaces were also squared off, fin area increased, and a dorsal fin was added. Navy trials revealed a top speed of 333 miles per hour at 21,300 feet. Although engine cooling proved a problem, the plane's potential was clear and the U.S. Navy ordered (54) F4F-3's in August 1939. The U.S. Navy was fortunate to have the successful Grumman F4F-3 coupled with excellent production facilities available to meet the Navy's requirements in the face of Brewster's failure to do so. The F4F-3 production aircraft were in a constant state of improvement with strengthened landing gear, armor and improved armament.

Grumman F4F-3 fighters began rolling off the production line in early 1940 and the first production F4F-3 was flown in February, 1940. Further modifications included four wing guns and none in the fuselage; the horizontal tail was raised from the fuselage to a location on the fin; and longitudinal instability, carbon monoxide in the cockpit and inadequate tailwheel strength were quickly remedied.

New Brewster Production Facilities

In order to bolster its sagging production, Brewster moved assembly and flight testing operations to a building at Newark Airport in New Jersey, where test flights could be conducted without transporting disassembled aircraft long distances to airfields.

Brewster Buffalo

Britain ordered 120 of the Brewster Model 339, the equivalent of the Navy F2A-2 in January 1940. The British called the little monoplane Buffalo and the name was used unofficially until the U.S. Navy abandoned tradition and finally accepted the name Buffalo for the Brewster monoplane fighter. This was the first U.S. naval airplane to be given an official name, in addition to its letters and numbers designation. The U.S. naval aircraft names of the early 1930s, such as Hawk, Helldiver, and Goshawk were company trade names and not official Navy names. Since the Buffalo, every U.S. Navy plane has been given an official sobriquet.

F2A-2 Production

Brewster F2A-2 Buffaloes destined for the U.S. Navy entered production in September, 1940 with the last plane delivered in December, 1940.

Buffalo Landing Gear Problem

As with the German Messerschmitt and British Spitfire the Brewster F2A design's weakness was the landing gear. Carrier squadrons experienced very few difficulties with the Buffalo in fleet service except for landing gear failures during carrier landings. Initially, VF-2 pilots had reported that the landing gear legs were often jarred out of alignment during carrier landings. When next flown the landing leg would scrape the landing strut well and the gear fairing would not fully close. When the pilots complained, the crew chief had a simple correction made: the rivet heads on the landing gear were filed down so the fairing would close. Repeated several times, this weakened the rivets which resulted in landing gear failure. Another landing gear problem was the hydraulic retracting struts which were too weak to withstand repeated flight deck landings. Although the struts were redesigned and stronger struts were installed, the problem never disappeared. Apparently, the fault lay with Brewster management who virtually deserted the Buffalo project in preference to newer designs which Chief Designer Dayton Brown was ordered to develop. Brown really wanted to and could have refined the promising Buffalo to its ultimate potential, as had Grumman with its Wildcat design, if he had been given the opportunity.

The landing gear weakness prompted the Navy to exchange *USS Lexington* squadron VF-2 Buffaloes for Marine squadron VMF-211 Wildcats because the Wildcat landing gear was robust enough to withstand strenuous carrier landings. It had been U.S. Navy practice, for some time, to relegate unsuitable carrier aircraft to the U.S. Marine Corps because it operated from shore bases.

French And British Grumman G36A

Anxious to obtain a shipboard fighter for the two 18,000 ton carriers Joffre and Painleve then under construction, the French government had placed an order for 81 Grumman G36A fighters, the equivalent of the U.S. Navy F4F-3. The Aeronavale specified six 7.5 millimeter wing guns of French manufacture, as well as metric instrumentation and European throttle controls. The Wright Cyclone-powered G36A first flew on May 11, 1940, the day after the Germans began their French offensive. France fell the following month so the contract was picked up by the Royal Navy and the first plane was delivered on July 27. The British, who were accustomed to give all their aircraft names, called the Grumman Martlet I; the Martlet being a swallow-like European bird.

It is interesting that foreign governments were using these two pioneering U.S. Navy fighters in combat over land and sea before America's need for the fighters could be satisfied!

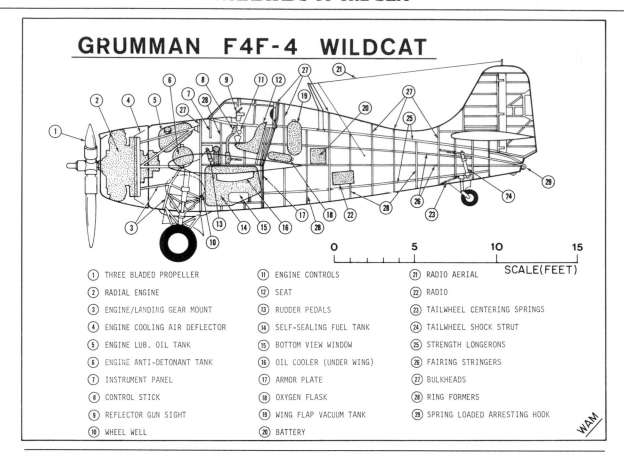

GRUMMAN F4F-4 WILDCAT

① THREE BLADED PROPELLER	⑪ ENGINE CONTROLS	㉑ RADIO AERIAL
② RADIAL ENGINE	⑫ SEAT	㉒ RADIO
③ ENGINE/LANDING GEAR MOUNT	⑬ RUDDER PEDALS	㉓ TAILWHEEL CENTERING SPRINGS
④ ENGINE COOLING AIR DEFLECTOR	⑭ SELF-SEALING FUEL TANK	㉔ TAILWHEEL SHOCK STRUT
⑤ ENGINE LUB. OIL TANK	⑮ BOTTOM VIEW WINDOW	㉕ STRENGTH LONGERONS
⑥ ENGINE ANTI-DETONANT TANK	⑯ OIL COOLER (UNDER WING)	㉖ FAIRING STRINGERS
⑦ INSTRUMENT PANEL	⑰ ARMOR PLATE	㉗ BULKHEADS
⑧ CONTROL STICK	⑱ OXYGEN FLASK	㉘ RING FORMERS
⑨ REFLECTOR GUN SIGHT	⑲ WING FLAP VACUUM TANK	㉙ SPRING LOADED ARRESTING HOOK
⑩ WHEEL WELL	⑳ BATTERY	

SCALE(FEET)

Folding Wings - F4F-4

Initially, neither plane was fitted with folding wings. The Brewster wing span was 35 feet which was within the U.S. Navy parameters, previously discussed, that did not require folding wings. The Grumman span of 38 feet also had non-folding wings until the Fleet Air Arm requested hydraulically operated folding wings on the G-36A fighters they were importing. Following the British lead, the U.S. Navy ordered a test F4F-3 fitted with this feature. The test plane, F4F-4, made its maiden flight on April 14, 1941 at the factory field in Bethpage, N.Y. In the following month the test craft was assigned to Fighter Squadron VF-42 for carrier trials aboard *USS Yorktown*. All tests with the prototype were successful; however, because the Grumman wings had to rotate 90 degrees and then fold back against the fuselage, it was decided that the hydraulically operated mechanism was unusually complex and heavy and; therefore, unnecessary. Tests had proven that the wings of the Grumman could be folded or unfolded manually by the deck crews just as fast as with the hydraulic system. This savings in weight gave the F4F-4 equal performance to the fixed wing F4F-3. Production orders were placed for the F4F-4 at once.

Grumman Wildcat

It was about this time that the U.S. Navy decided to officially adopt the name Wildcat for the F4F series because the name had been in unofficial use for some months. The Wildcat went on to become the main allied naval fighter until 1943 when new fighters appeared. Thousands of Wildcats were constructed during that time.

Brewster F2A-3

Meanwhile, Brewster continued modifications to the Buffalo accordance with Bureau of Aeronautics requirements. Fuel capa ity was increased to 240 gallons which required new fuel cells the wing leading edge and the fuselage. Additional ammunition a armor to meet the latest combat standards were fitted as well self-sealing fuel cells, bullet proof windshield, improved radio a larger engine. With all this weight added the overburdened Buffa was designated F2A-3. An order for 108 of the modified Buffa F2A-3 was placed by the U.S. Navy during January, 1941. The la F2A-3 was delivered in December, 1941.

An early production Brewster F2A-3 Buffalo reveals the Curtiss Electr cuffed propeller, and improved cockpit sliding canopy. Note absence of propeller spinner. (U.S. Naval Institute)

WILDCAT-BUFFALO COMPARISON DATA

The following technical data applies to the Grumman F4F-4 and the Brewster F2A-3:

	F4F-4	F2A-3
Powerplant	P & W R-1830-86	Wright R-1820-40
Horsepower	1,200	1,200
Wing Span	38 feet	35 feet
Length	28 feet-9 inches	26 feet-4 inches
Height	11 feet-10 inches	12 feet
Wing Area	260 square feet	209 square feet
Weights:		
Empty & Gross	5,785 & 7,952	4,732 & 7,159 pounds
Max.Speed/mph	318	321
at altitude	19,400 feet	16,500 feet
Cruising Speed	155 mph	161 mph
Initial Climb	1,950 feet per minute	2,290 feet per minute
Service Ceiling	34,900 feet	32,600 feet
Range	770 miles	1,680 miles
Armament	(6) .50 inch caliber machine guns	(4) .50 inch caliber machine guns
Location	In wings	In fuselage & wings
Wing Loading	30.6 pounds per square foot	34.3 pounds per square foot

As can be seen, the two fighters were quite evenly matched; when one was superior in a category the other excelled in a different category.

Conversations with pilots who have flown the F2A-3 and F4F-4 reveal that the Buffalo was a pilot's airplane; fast, maneuverable and fun to fly because it was very responsive to light control pressures. One U.S. Marine pilot who flew the Buffalo and Boeing F4B-4 biplane claims that the F2A-3 gave him the same exhilarating sensation as he had when piloting the jaunty Boeing F4B-4.

Pilots who flew both planes claim that the F4F-4 was not as easy on the controls as the F2A-3 and was not as maneuverable; however, the F4F-4 was very stable and required very little control retrimming. These pilots also disliked the F4F-4 manually operated retractable landing gear compared with the hydraulically operated F2A-3 landing gear. When retracting the F4F-4 landing gear during takeoff, the pilot was required to shift his left hand from the throttle to the control stick and use his right hand to turn the crank that operated the landing gear mechanism. The pilot's movement during this operation often caused the plane to wobble slightly as it became airborne. The F4F-4 had good stall warning characteristics and recovered from spins easily and quickly. Pilots found that the F4F-4 had a tendency to veer to the left on takeoff which required considerable right rudder to compensate for the slipstream effect; however, this was manageable and caused no serious problems.

Grumman Wildcat Assignments

Grumman F4F-3 fighters were initially supplied to VF-4 on *USS Ranger* and VF-7 on *USS Wasp*. Later VF-42 and VF-71 were equipped with the F4F-3, as well as Marine Squadrons VMF-121, VMF-211 and VMF-221. The F4F-3A was flown by VF-6 and

Marine Squadron VMF-111. During 1942 the F4F-4 equipped VF-5 on *USS Saratoga*, VF-6 and VF-10 on *USS Enterprise*, VF-71 on *USS Wasp*, VF-72 on *USS Hornet* and Marine Squadrons VMF-112, VMF-121, VMF-212, VMF-223 and VMF-224.

Brewster Takeover

By late 1940 U.S. Navy officials had become increasingly disenchanted with the Brewster management. Further, the Brewster Sales team made production promises that the factory could not meet. Political reasons rather than technical problems led to the Navy decision to abandon further Buffalo development, especially when the management indicated a lack of interest. The final blow came when Brewster was charged with wartime profiteering and the company was eventually taken over by the U.S. Government because of mismanagement.

Brewster Buffalo Assignments

In addition to VF-2 and VF-3 on *USS Lexington* and *USS Saratoga*, the F2A-2 also equipped VS-201 flying from the escort carrier Long Island, and Marine Squadrons VMF-211 and VMF-221 flew the F2A-3 from shore bases. Finally, the Buffalo was relegated to advanced training duties

Land-Based Buffalo Carrier Trials

The Belgian government in exile transferred several of the land-based Brewster 339B fighters to Britain. These were assigned to FAA No. 885 Squadron for shipboard trials on *HMS Eagle*. Take-offs were satisfactory; however, it required extremely talented pilots to land the planes, which had no arresting hooks fitted, so the idea was abandoned.

Northrop/Douglas Monoplane Dive Bomber

In 1934 the U.S. Navy Bureau of Aeronautics issued Specification Design 113 for a scout/bomber (scouting dive bomber) which resulted in the development of the U.S. Navy's most successful dive bomber. In response to the invitation to bid Vought, Martin, Brewster, Curtiss, Great Lakes and Northrop submitted proposals. Curtiss and Great Lakes submitted biplanes and were eliminated on that basis. Northrop won the contract for an all-metal monoplane.

The Northrop Aircraft Company was well suited to provide the airplane the Navy wanted. John K. Northrop had been a leading designer with Douglas, having developed multicellular wing construction and all-metal stressed-skin construction. When he left Douglas to start his own company in 1932, Douglas retained financial and technical links with the new company in El Segundo, California. The winning design was the XBT-1 which was the descendant of a long family of dive bombers sired by the world-famous record breaking Northrop Gamma. It was not just a matter of evolution and refinement to produce the XBT-1, a lot of designing had to go into the project, so John Northrop selected Edward Heinemann to supervise the XBT-1 design project and meet the Navy specifications.

Northrop XBT-1

Unlike previous Northrop dive bomber designs the XBT-1 featured a retractable landing gear that folded straight back into fairings under

The Northrop XBT-1 dive bomber evolved from the famous recordbreaking Northrop Gamma and was selected by the U.S. Navy in preference to designs submitted by five other aircraft manufacturers. Landing gear was semi-retractable; moving aft into fairings. (U.S. National Archives)

Edward Heinemann supervised the XBT-1 design which included innovative perforated split diving flaps to permit steep diving and stability in the dive without excessive speed. (See arrow). During the development of this design standards were established regarding control surfaces, wing shape and tail configurations for all future U.S. Navy dive bombers. (U.S. National Archives)

the wing. Split diving flaps were incorporated to provide steep diving control and stability during the dive. The split flaps opened as a clamshell; one-half lowering to below the wing trailing edge, as in a conventional flap, while the other half hinged upwards to above the wing trailing edge. First test flights in July 1935 resulted in a severe buffet caused by the opened split diving flaps. The problem was solved by perforating the flaps; thereby, allowing the compressed air to pass through the perforations instead of curling over the ends of the flaps.

The dive bomber was designed to carry a 1,000 pound bomb in a trapeze crutch mount which lowered the bomb so it would clear the propeller during a steep bombing dive.

BT-1 Production
The XBT-1 was delivered to the Anacostia Naval Air Station for acceptance trials in December 1935. The performance was so good that it passed all tests in only 60 days and Northrop received an order for 57 production BT-1 dive bombers in September 1936.

Northrop XBT-2
As the last of the BT-1 airframes came off the production line, the original XBT-1 prototype was undergoing some modifications. A larger engine was installed and, as was done with the Brewster fighter, the XBT-1 was sent to the Langley Memorial Aeronautical Laboratory for wind tunnel tests because the designers felt that improvements could be made in stalling characteristics and general aerodynamics. By the time the wind tunnel test recommendations were issued, Ed Heinemann and his designers had developed a new plane; the XBT-2. Extensive tests had been run on aileron designs and empennage configurations until the optimum proportions were discovered for the XBT-2. It was this data that established the standards for all U.S. Navy dive bombers, regarding control area ratios, wing shape, fin and stabilizer configurations and control balances (aerodynamic and static).

Douglas SBD Dauntless
John K. Northrop gave up his company in January 1938 and it became the El Segundo plant of the Douglas Aircraft Company. The XBT-2; therefore, became the XSBD-1, known throughout World

War II as the Douglas Dauntless. By this time the landing gear retracted by folding inward toward the fuselage instead of folding straight back.

SBD Production
The U.S. Navy accepted the XSBD-1 in February 1939 and orders were placed with Douglas in April for 57 SBD-1 scout/bombers for the Marines and 87 of the SBD-2 for the Navy. The SBD-2 was the same as the SBD-1 except for the addition of a .30 inch caliber machine gun in the rear cockpit, armor plate for the crew, self-sealing rubber-lined tanks and two 65 gallon fuel tanks in the outer wing panel to add 320 miles to the range plus outer wing panel bomb racks for 100 pound bombs.

Douglas Dauntless Data
Wingspan was 41 feet-6 inches, length 32 feet-2 inches, and height 13 feet-7 inches. Wing area totalled 325 square feet.

Powered by a Wright R-1820-32 9-cylinder, 1,000 takeoff horsepower air-cooled radial engine, the SBD-1 attained a maximum speed of 253 miles per hour while the SBD-2 was one mile per hour slower. SBD-1 scouting range was 1,165 miles at 142 miles per hour cruising speed, while SBD-2 scouting range was 1,370 miles at 148 miles per hour. SBD-1 service ceiling was 29,600 feet and SBD-2 service ceiling was 26,000 feet. Both models could carry a bomb load of 1,200 pounds. Maximum takeoff weight for SBD-1 was 9,790 pounds, and for SBD-2 it was 10,360 pounds.

Heinemann Research Rewarded
The painstaking research and engineering of Ed Heinemann's design team was well worth the effort because according to SBD pilots the Dauntless handled like a fighter. In fact, many SBD crews shot down numerous attacking fighters. The plane was very strong and could absorb many hits and make it back to the carrier. Knowing this encouraged Dauntless pilots to attack heavily defended targets more aggressively than if they were flying another type of plane.

Dauntless Structure
The Dauntless wing was an all-metal multicellular, stressed-skin structure using multiple Duraluminum (Dural) web spars and pressed

The famous Douglas SBD Dauntless series of dive bombers was derived from the Northrop BT design. The name changed when Douglas took over the Northrop El Segundo plant. The SBD-3 is shown here. (McDonnell Douglas Photo, Courtesy Harry Gann)

dural web ribs instead of the conventional one or two large spars and truss-type ribs. The retractable landing gear and trailing edge flaps were hydraulically operated. The wing center panel was constructed integral with the fuselage. The fuselage was an all-metal Dural, semi-monocoque, stressed-skin structure made in four separate subassemblies. A bulletproof windshield and armor plate protected the crew. Dual controls were installed so the plane could be flown from either cockpit.

The Douglas Dauntless was constantly refined into the war years when this historic airplane became famous.

WORLD WAR II BEGINS

What the world powers feared would happen appeared imminent in 1939 as war clouds moved closer and became more ominous: German troops entered Prague and Slovakia became an independent nation on March 15; the British and French governments guaranteed Poland's security on March 31; Italian troops invaded Albania on April 7; Germany and the Soviet Union signed a pact on August 25 which included an agreement to divide Poland between themselves; Germany invaded western Poland on September 1; Britain issued an ultimatum to Germany on September 2; Britain, France, Australia and New Zealand declared war on Germany on September 3; and two weeks later the Soviets invaded eastern Poland.

Allied Naval Superiority

When Britain and France declared war on Germany they held one very important trump card; naval power. They had strong navies, each of which was more powerful than the German Navy. More important was the fact that Britain had seven aircraft carriers and France had one while Germany had none in operation. Britain also had six under construction.

The Douglas Dauntless was the premier naval dive bomber of World War II. The plane handled like a fighter and shot down many intercepting fighter planes. (McDonnell Douglas Photo, Courtesy Hubert K. Gagos)

A multicellular wing and semi-monocoque fuselage gave the Dauntless ample strength to absorb enemy fire and still return to its carrier. Note the trapeze bomb launcher and tailhook (Arrows). (McDonnell Douglas Photo, Courtesy Harry Gann)

DOUGLAS SBD·3 DAUNTLESS

VS·2 Squadron — USS Lexington — Battle of the Coral Sea

Ensign J.A.Leppla & Aviation Radioman J.Liska Scored 7 Victories

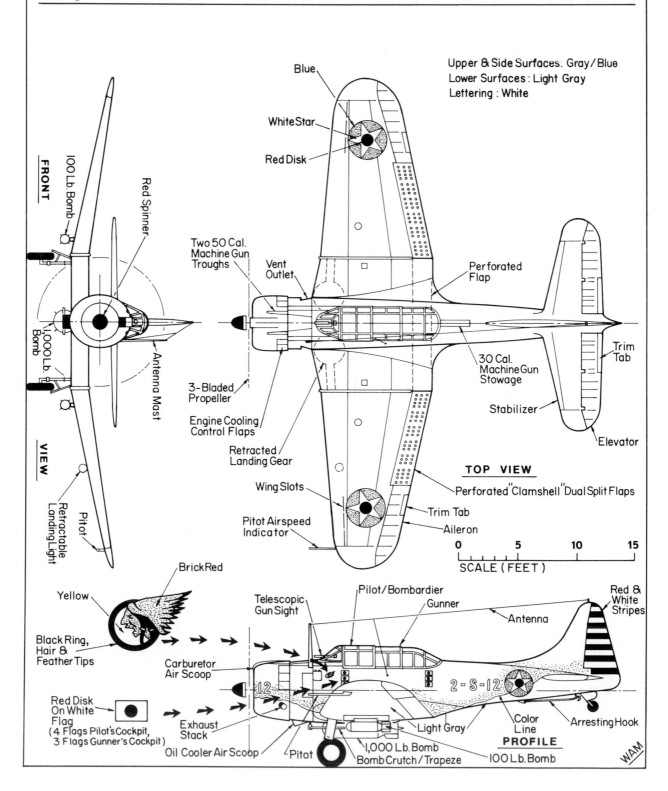

Upper & Side Surfaces. Gray/Blue
Lower Surfaces : Light Gray
Lettering : White

FRONT

100 Lb. Bomb

Red Spinner

1,000 Lb. Bomb

Antenna Mast

VIEW

Retractable Landing Light

Pitot

Blue

White Star

Red Disk

Two 50 Cal. Machine Gun Troughs

Vent Outlet

Perforated Flap

3-Bladed Propeller

Engine Cooling Control Flaps

Retracted Landing Gear

Wing Slots

Pitot Airspeed Indicator

30 Cal. Machine Gun Stowage

Stabilizer

Trim Tab

Elevator

TOP VIEW

Perforated "Clamshell" Dual Split Flaps

Trim Tab

Aileron

0   5   10   15
SCALE (FEET)

Brick Red

Yellow

Black Ring, Hair & Feather Tips

Red Disk On White Flag
(4 Flags Pilot's Cockpit,
3 Flags Gunner's Cockpit)

Carburetor Air Scoop

Exhaust Stack

Oil Cooler Air Scoop

Telescopic Gun Sight

Pilot/Bombardier

Gunner

Antenna

Red & White Stripes

2 - S - 12

Pitot

1,000 Lb. Bomb

Bomb Crutch/Trapeze

Light Gray

Color Line

PROFILE

100 Lb. Bomb

Arresting Hook

WAM

The basic strategy of the Royal Navy was to prevent German ships from breaking out of the Baltic and North Seas and to use their overwhelming power in the open seas to guard their sea lanes to bring war supplies from the U.S. and Canada as well as gather manpower from the far-flung British Empire.

Conversely, the objectives of the German Navy were to cut the lines of supply to the British Isles and destroy British warships as the opportunity presented itself. The German ships could never operate as a fleet and could only sail alone or in pairs as raiders which the Royal Navy relentlessly pursued.

Allied Naval Hunting Forces

Britain had organized the Royal Navy into striking forces and sea lane protection forces during the early months of the war. Striking forces were assembled from the main battle fleet, naval air power, and submarines whose objective was to sink or neutralize German surface warships. Forces protecting the sea lanes took the form of light antisubmarine ships and surface ship escorts. Sea lane protection forces far outnumbered the striking forces because they protected Britain's life line. The two types of hunting groups ranged from the North Sea to the West Indies and down to the Cape of Good Hope and as far as Ceylon to find German Raiders. The Hunting Forces were organized sporadically as they were needed.

The eventual Allied Hunting Groups or Forces were as follows: FORCE F- Heavy cruisers *Berwick* & *York*; FORCE G-Cruisers *Ajax*, *Exeter*, *Cumberland* and *Achilles*; FORCE H-Carrier *Eagle* and cruisers *Cornwall* and *Dorsetshire*; FORCE K-Carrier *Ark Royal* and battle cruiser *Renown*; FORCE L-French carrier *Bearne* and battle cruiser *Dunkerque*; FORCE M-Two French heavy cruisers; FORCE N-Carrier *Hermes* and French battle cruiser *Strasbourg*. Each force included attendant destroyers and other screening ships.

Royal Navy Carriers Dispersed

On September 3, 1939 the Royal Navy had seven aircraft carriers at sea. *HMS Glorious* was in the Mediterranean; *HMS Hermes* started hunting submarines in the waters around Britain and then was diverted to the South Atlantic for trade protection and to find German raiders; *HMS Eagle* was in the China Seas; *HMS Ark Royal* and *HMS Courageous* sailed with the British Home Fleet trying to prevent German warships from getting to the Atlantic Ocean and protecting the sea lanes to the British Isles; *HMS Furious* was initially used for carrier deck training in the Firth of Forth and then was kept busy ferrying aircraft and with Atlantic convoy protection; and *HMS Argus* began patrolling with the Home Fleet but was soon transferred to the Mediterranean for training duties.

Carriers Versus Submarines

At the war's beginning the German Navy had 21 submarines on station between Gibraltar and the Irish Sea and, as the days went by, British merchant shipping losses began to rise alarmingly. The Home Fleet called in aircraft carriers on September 11 to combat this unexpected force of U-boats.

The deployment and application of aircraft carriers was not yet clearly understood and in many quarters not fully appreciated. It was somewhat understood that aircraft could play an important part in fighting submarines; however, the Royal Navy's first attempt in this direction was a disaster. Deployed on antisubmarine patrols were *HMS Hermes* and *HMS Courageous* covering the southwestern sea lanes to the British Isles, and *HMS Ark Royal* covering the northwestern sea lanes. The air patrols were poorly directed and air search was rather aimless and achieved very little in return for risking valuable aircraft carriers in dangerous waters.

On September 14, 1939 the German submarine U-39 evaded the air search and got close enough to *Ark Royal* to fire two torpedoes at long range. The wakes were spotted in time for the short-hulled carrier to maneuver to safety. *Ark Royal* called on her escort, destroyers *Firedrake*, *Faulknor* and *Foxhound*, which forced the U-boat to the surface with depth charges. The entire crew were removed before the damaged submarine sank. This was the first German U-boat to be sunk in the war.

HMS Courageous Sinks

Three days later *HMS Courageous*, screened by four destroyers, was conducting air searches for U-boats when a report was received that a German submarine was attacking a cargo ship nearby. Two of the destroyers sped off to find the U-boat as *Courageous* turned into the wind to bring in her search planes which had been out most of the afternoon. In the disappearing twilight the carrier entered the torpedo station of U-29, commanded by *Kapitän* Schuhart, who fired three torpedoes in rapid succession. All three struck the carrier, which sank quickly, taking over 500 members of the crew, including the skipper, Captain Makeig-Jones, with her.

Numbers Count In ASW (Anti-Submarine Warfare)

The idea of using carrier aircraft to conduct submarine search missions was sound in principal; however, large fleet carriers were not the ships to use. Many smaller carriers would have been more effective. Also, the screening ships must remain with the carrier at all times. It should also be realized that the naval search aircraft of 1939 were not fitted with the spotting equipment or weapons necessary to be fully effective in the antisubmarine role. It was a time of learning how to use carriers; a time of trial and error in which the errors were tragic.

Carrier-Based Planes Score

The Blackburn Skua dive bomber/fighter enjoyed a few brief months of glory at the war's beginning before being replaced by faster and more potent aircraft. On September 25, 1939 all nine Skuas of No. 803 Squadron from *HMS Ark Royal* were on combat air patrol for the carrier and the battleships *HMS Rodney* and *HMS Nelson* near the German island of Heligoland only five miles from the German coast. When a German Dornier Do 18 flying boat appeared in the distance Lieutenant B.S. Mc Ewen and Petty Officer B.M. Seymour sped to the attack and sent the Dornier crashing into the North Sea. This was the first victory of World War II scored by a FAA aircraft. The Skua then returned to the patrol.

Ark Royal Bombing and *Graf Spee* Tracking

Realizing that large carriers were too vulnerable to be used independently on such hazardous duty, the Admiralty recalled *HMS Ark Royal* to port with orders to operate with the Home Fleet. On September 26 the British Fleet experienced its first air attack of the war. *Ark Royal* was steaming with battleships Nelson and Rodney when a twin-engine Heinkel He 111 high level bomber dropped a 2,000 pound bomb which exploded in the sea about 100 feet from *Ark Royal*. The explosion shook the ship violently but damage was very slight and repairs were accomplished in a short time. On October 2, 1939 FORCE K was created and *Ark Royal* assisted in the capture of several German merchantmen. The "*Ark*" spent the next two months tracking the German pocket battleship *Graf Spee*. After the quarry was spotted a running battle ensued which ended with the *Graf Spee* trapped in the Rio de la Plata in Montevideo Harbor, Uruguay. *Graf Spee* was scuttled by its crew because *Ark Royal* and FORCE K surface ships had blocked any escape.

More To Come for Royal Navy

By December 1939 the distant oceans were firmly under control of the Royal Navy; however, many dangers were to arise in the near future which would put Royal Navy aircraft carriers and Fleet Air Arm aircraft to the test.

BATTLE FOR NORWAY

By January 1940 the war had been on for four months and most of the activity had been at sea. In fact, there was so little action on the Western Front that it was criticized by both Allies and Germans; the Allies calling it the "Phoney War" and Germans saying it was a "Sitzkrieg" or Sitting War. But trouble was brewing in the far north.

Germany obtained 70 percent of its iron from Sweden. The iron mines at Galivarre, north of the Arctic Circle, supplied most of this iron. During much of the year, when the Baltic Sea was frozen, the ore was transported northwestward to the northern Norwegian port of Narvik via Swedish railroad. The nine million tons each year was then transferred to German commercial ships which made the long voyage to German Baltic ports via the Norwegian Inner Leads, or the waterway between the many Norwegian islands and the Norwegian mainland, and then through the Skagerrak and Kattegat to German Baltic ports. This set the stage for the Norwegian campaign.

Operation Wilfred/R-4

Winston Churchill often proposed and then postponed the mining of the Inner Leads which would force the ore-laden ships into international waters where British warships could capture or sink them. This plan was given the code name Operation Wilfred, and grew into a more daring plan called R-4. Should the Germans resist the mining, then R-4 was to include British occupation of the Norwegian ports of Bergen, Trondheim, Stavenger and Narvik and, if necessary, would also occupy the Swedish mines in Galivarre. This was decided at a Supreme Allied War Council on February 5, 1940. The Allies were determined to stop this flow of all-important iron ore to the Germans.

Of course, the strategic naval importance of the Norwegian coast was valued by both sides and gave impetus to the invasion preparations.

The British Admiralty knew that the minelaying would provoke the Germans and therefore prepared an invasion in the event that Germany moved. Troops, transports and escorts for the invasion of Trondheim and Narvik were assembled in the Clyde while four cruisers loaded with army units to be landed at Stavenger and Bergen were waiting in the Firth of Forth.

Weserubung

Germany also had plans to forestall any British move to cut off the iron ore supply, intending to use the Luftwaffe, paratroopers and the Kriegsmarine, code-named Weserubung.

Wilfred Detected

The Wilfred minelaying ships left Britain on April 5, 1940 to begin mining at Narvik three days later. On April 6 one of the minelaying destroyers, *HMS Glowworm,* became separated from the others and came upon the German cruiser *Hipper* with its powerful escort near Trondheim. *Glowworm* rammed *Hipper*, causing considerable damage, but was sunk by the German escorts. This incident sounded the alarm that German forces were at sea near Norway. On April the minelayers were pulled back from Narvik and, more concerned for her Atlantic lifeline than the iron ore supply route, Britain ordered the cruisers in Firth of Forth to join the Home Fleet without their army units and for the escorts waiting in the Clyde to also join the Home Fleet without their troopships. To sink the German ships was their prime objective.

Weserubung Begins

While Germany had been quite content with the neutrality of Norway, Sweden and Denmark, she could not tolerate British interference with the benefits the Fatherland derived from it; therefore, on April 9 six Kriegsmarine naval groups and Luftwaffe paratroopers invaded Narvik, Bergen, Trondheim, Oslo and Kristiansand.

Furious Sails Without Fighters

HMS Furious was the only carrier in the waters around the British Isles, undergoing refitting on the Clyde in Scotland. Not waiting for the work to be completed, *Furious* sailed for the North Sea on April 10 without her fighters, a saving of time which proved disastrous to the Anglo-French troops who needed air cover during the first two weeks of the Norwegian campaign.

First Major Sinking By Aircraft

Ark Royal was in the Mediterranean conducting exercises with *Glorious* but she had left 16 of her Blackburn Skuas with crews at Halston in the Orkney Islands, north of Scotland.

The German light cruiser *Konigsberg* had been seriously damaged by shore batteries at Bergen and was dead in the water with no propulsive power on April 9. Taking advantage of the situation, and in a brilliant opportunist attack, the *Ark Royal* Skuas, seven from No. 800 Squadron led by Captain R.T. Partridge, Royal Marines, and nine from No. 803 Squadron led by Lieutenant W.P. Lucy, Royal Navy, flew the 330 miles from Halston to Bergen to dive bomb *Konigsberg*. This round trip far exceeded the Skua range; however, due to superb navigation and judicious fuel conservation, the flight was completed and the cruiser was sunk. This was the very first occasion of a major warship being sunk by air attack during wartime.

Royal Navy Carriers Need Fighters

On April 23 *HMS Ark Royal*, Captain C.S. Holland commanding, headed for Norwegian waters to assist *HMS Furious*. While passing the Orkneys *Ark Royal* embarked Nos. 800 and 803 Squadrons. The failure of the British Naval Air Arm to develop a high performance single purpose fighter plane forced the British Fleet to operate beyond the range of land-based Luftwaffe dive bombers, leaving the German Fleet unopposed in the coastal waters of southern Norway. It was only in the far north, beyond the short range of Messerschmitt Me 109 fighters, that it was possible for unescorted Fairey Swordfish from *HMS Furious* to make some bombing raids early in the campaign. It was not until April 24-28 that Skuas and Sea Gladiators from *Glorious* and *Ark Royal* were able to provide cover for Allied ships and troops engaged in the expeditions to Andalsnes and Namsos near Trondheim.

Short Range Skuas

On April 27 five Skuas surprised two Junkers Ju 88 dive bombers attacking a convoy and set their engines afire. The same flight then shot down two Heinkel He 111 bombers and also drove off two Dornier Do 17 bombers. They then damaged a Heinkel He 111 of a 5 plane flight. The Skuas were forced to break off the fight because fuel was running low. Limited range was the Skua shortcoming. Only two Skuas had been shot down during these actions; however, eight were lost because they ran out of fuel and were unable to reach *Ark Royal*. Much of the Norwegian campaign was far enough north to experience daylight almost 24 hours a day. This meant that sorties were carried out at least 23 hours each day.

Swordfish Score

Six Swordfish attacked railroads around Narvik on May 9. The wind was so powerful that it took the biplanes two hours to reach Narvik from *Ark Royal* 100 miles away! They hit a viaduct and a train tunnel entrance near the Swedish border, tore up tracks and overturned a train, hoping to destroy the railroad which was bringing the iron ore to Narvik.

Absence Of Fighter Escort Spells Disaster

On May 24, 1940 a strike force of two formations comprising 15 Skuas, each plane carrying a 500 pound bomb, left *Ark Royal* to attack the German battle cruiser *Scharnhorst* in Trondheim Harbor, 160 miles away. The two attack formations were led by Captain R.T. Partridge and Lieutenant Commander J. Casson. When the Skuas arrived over Trondheim at 10,000 feet they were met by intense flak from two cruisers and four destroyers anchored near the *Scharnhorst*. In addition, Messerschmitt Me 109 and Me 110 fighters joined in the defense. One direct hit was scored, as well as several near-misses; however, it was learned later that the bomb scoring the direct hit had failed to explode. Eight Skuas were shot down. This was the heaviest loss ever suffered by planes from *Ark Royal* during a single operation. A fighter escort could have made this bombing attack a success.

Allies Retire From Norway

The Norwegian Campaign was turning into a fiasco for the Allies and a withdrawal was on by June 1. *Ark Royal*'s Skuas provided cover while *Glorious* embarked the eight surviving land-based Hurricanes and Gladiators. These aircraft had never landed on a carrier before, nor were they intended to, but all landed safely and all eight were stowed below deck. On June 7 *HMS Glorious* and *HMS Ark Royal*, together with a force of two heavy cruisers and 16 destroyers, were escorting troopships back to Britain when a series of events caused the convoy to disperse. The King of Norway and his staff had embarked on the cruiser *Devonshire* for exile in Britain, while an erroneous report that German ships were nearing Iceland diverted part of the escort. *HMS Glorious* claimed it was short of fuel and was given permission to sail directly to Britain with two destroyers, *Ardent* and *Acasta*. Apparently, due to a difference of opinion between the captain and the air group commander, Commander J.B. Heath, no combat air patrol was in operation, nor had Swordfish scouts been launched. Even the crow's nest lookout post was empty on this carrier which had no radar!

HMS Glorious Sinks

Meanwhile, to the northwest the German battle cruisers *Scharnhorst* and *Gneisenau*, with the heavy cruiser *Hipper*, plus four destroyers, were steaming through the Artic Sea to intercept Allied evacuation convoys. After finding and sinking some escorts and a tanker, *Hipper* and the destroyers returned to port while the battle cruiser sister-ships continued alone. Shortly before four o'clock in the afternoon on June 8 Midshipman Siegfried Goss, on watch in the crow's nest of *Scharnhorst*, sighted a plume of smoke on the horizon to the southeast. The Germans sped towards the smoke and were soon able to identify a single carrier escorted by two destroyers. By this time *HMS Glorious* was two hundred miles ahead of the main convoy and the German ships were closing fast.

At a range of 14 miles *Gneisenau* and *Scharnhorst* opened fire with their radar-directed 11 inch guns. When *Glorious* sighted the battle cruisers she fired her 4 inch guns, instead of bringing Swordfish to the Flight Deck to launch a torpedo strike at the attackers. By the time it was decided to launch an air strike shells had struck the Flight Deck and Hangar, setting some planes afire which prevented the armorers from bringing torpedoes up from the magazine. *Acasta* and *Ardent* tried to hide the carrier with a smoke screen but the radar-directed guns found their mark again and again with combined accuracy and rapidity. Such was the damage inflicted that by 5:20 PM *Glorious* was listing badly and the order given to abandon ship. The carrier sank 20 minutes later in the cold Arctic Sea.

Ardent and *Acasta* then charged the powerful battle cruisers with suicidal gallantry, firing their torpedoes. *Acasta* scored a hit on *Scharnhorst* which inflicted enough damage to make her return to base immediately. Both destroyers were sunk in this action; first *Ardent*, followed by *Acasta*.

This destroyer action discouraged the Germans from remaining in the area; thereby, saving the lightly escorted troopship convoy which was heading in that direction and could have been decimated by the battle cruisers.

In little more than an hour *HMS Glorious* and her brave escorts had been destroyed and, although several hundred men managed to escape from the sinking ships, the Arctic cold and the icy waters quickly took their toll. It took three days for rescue ships to

HMS Glorious was caught with no combat air patrol by the German battle cruisers Scharnhorst and Gneisenau in Arctic waters. By the time Swordfish torpedo planes could be launched the carrier was battered and afire. Glorious was the first aircraft carrier to be sunk by surface ships. (U.S. National Archives)

arrive at the scene and, by then, there were only 39 survivors of the 1,300 member *Glorious* crew and only one survivor each from the *Acasta* and *Ardent*! More than 1,500 brave men and three fighting ships had been lost because the basic rule that an aircraft carrier's offensive and defensive force is in her aircraft was not obeyed. The lesson learned is that a carrier which fails to use her aircraft is helpless and at the mercy of her adversary. *Glorious* has the dubious distinction of being the first carrier to be sunk by surface ships.

During the first seven months of World War II Britain had lost two fleet carriers because of misapplication and misoperation, but it was still a new weapon and only experience would teach the Royal Navy how to guide its Warbirds of the Sea to victory; and the world was watching.

FRANCE DEFEATED

With Norway secured and the flow of iron ore resumed Germany turned her attention to the phoney war on the western front. By May 10, 1940, the German army was on the move and within five days had broken through the French lines at Sedan. During this time Winston Churchill had become the Prime Minister of Britain.

By mid-June the Germans had entered Paris and then Italy joined the hostilities by declaring war on Britain and France. The Franco-German Armistice was signed on June 22 in which it was agreed that Germany would occupy about one-half of France. The southern half was to continue to function as a non-belligerent with a new government at Vichy.

France's Defeat - Royal Navy Problem

These new events created more problems for the Royal Navy. The first problem was the loss of the French Navy, creating a power vacuum in the Mediterranean Sea. The French ships were sorely missed because the Italian Navy was now a belligerent, which forced the Royal Navy to transfer ships from Atlantic duty to the Mediterranean to cope with the new situation. The second problem was that Britain was concerned about whether the French Fleet, which was mainly based at the French possessions in North Africa, would fall into German hands, or that the Vichy French Government might yield to pressure and join with the German Kriegsmarine.

Royal Navy Reinforcements in the Mediterranean

The Royal Navy Mediterranean Fleet, Admiral of the Fleet Sir Andrew Browne C. Cunningham in command, was based in Alexandria, which was too far to the east to be able to dominate the entire sea; therefore, the Admiralty decided to reinforce Gibraltar.

On June 23, 1940 *HMS Ark Royal* joined the battle cruiser *Hood*, battleships *Resolution* and *Valiant*, cruisers *Enterprise* and *Arethusa*, plus 11 destroyers to reform FORCE H, based at Gibraltar. *HMS Eagle*, formerly with the original FORCE H, was now part of Cunningham's Mediterranean Fleet. FORCE H was under the command of Vice-Admiral Sir James Fownes Somerville and was assigned to guard the western Mediterranean, plus the approaches to Gibraltar.

BRITISH ULTIMATUM TO FRENCH NAVY

The first task given to FORCE H was to negotiate with Chief of the French Naval Staff Admiral Jean Darlan and his second in command, Admiral Marcel-Bruno Gensoul, Commander in Chief of the French Fleet, in order to insure that the French Fleet would not fall into German or Italian hands. The first approach was most diplomatic; however, Admiral Darlan refused all suggestions and the British had to resort to stronger tactics. Captain C.S. Holland, who had become commanding officer of *Ark Royal* on May 1, 1940, was selected as a member of the British Naval Mission to warn Admiral Darlan of the consequences if he continued to refuse to ooperate. Captain Holland had been the Naval Attache at the British Embassy in Paris and Liaison Officer to Admiral Darlan and, when Darlan and Gensoul refused to meet with the Mission, Captain Holland was forced to issue an ultimatum to Darlan which contained the following alternatives:

1. Take the French Fleet to sea and continue to fight against Germany and now, Italy;
2. Sail the fleet with minimal crews to British ports;
3. Sail with minimal crews to a port in the French West Indies, where the ships could be demobilized;
4. Scuttle all ships within six hours.

Darlan announced he would fight to keep the fleet in French hands, consequently FORCE H gathered off the main anchorage in the Naval Base of Mers-el-Kebir near Oran and Operation Catapult was put into effect.

Operation Catapult

Captain Holland returned to Admiral Somerville's flagship and, after a brief discussion, at 5:53 on the afternoon of July 3, 1940, FORCE H began firing 15 inch shells into the congested anchorage. Swordfish from *Ark Royal* handled the spotting during the 10 minute barrage, which blew up the battleship *Bretagne* and seriously damaged *Provence* and *Dunkerque*. Five other Swordfish with a Skua escort dropped mines in the harbor entrance. *Strasbourg* skillfully broke out of the harbor at dusk with six destroyers, eluded FORCE H ships and planes, and sped for the open sea.

Six Swordfish took off from *Ark Royal* and pursued the escaping French ships. Their bombs straddled *Strasbourg* with near-misses but no direct hits were scored. A second flight of five Swordfish loaded with torpedoes gave chase and caught the French battleship at about 8:30 in the evening steaming at 28 knots off the African coast. Antiaircraft fire was intense but the Fairey Swordfish waited until sunset, when they attacked at wave top level. Torpedoes were dropped beyond the destroyer screen and although one "tin fish" struck home it did not prevent the battleship from reaching the French port of Toulon. On the following morning British reconnaissance revealed that the battle cruiser *Dunkerque* had run aground but was not permanently out of action. Two squadrons of Swordfish were sent to render the French ship impotent, taking off from *Ark Royal* at 5:15. Attacking at sunrise the Stringbags scored four direct hits which completely immobilized *Dunkerque*.

Over 1,500 French sailors had been killed and the battleship *Bretagne*, destroyer *L'Audacieux* and submarines *Ajax* and *Persee* were sunk and numerous other ships were damaged. FORCE H sustained damage to the battleship *Resolution*, cruisers *Arethusa* and *Enterprise*, as well as two destroyers.

Prior to the aforementioned naval activity, a French naval force comprising the battleship *Lorraine* and cruisers *Tourville*, *Duquesne* and *Duquay Trouin*, under the command of Vice Admiral Godfroy, had steamed to Alexandria to cooperate with Admiral Cunningham's Mediterranean Fleet; however, shortly after the French arrived, France fell and the ships had to be interned or destroyed, as with the French ships at Bers-el-Kabir. It is most significant that Cunningham was able to persuade Godfroy to immobilize his ships and the matter was settled peacefully.

The Royal Navy made subsequent strikes at the Vichy French Navy in North Africa. During one raid six Swordfish from *HMS Hermes* scored a torpedo hit on the battleship *Richelieu* in the harbor at Dakar, which put the vessel out of action.

High Level Bombing Fails

Later high level attacks by bomb-laden Swordfish biplanes on the *Richelieu* failed to score a hit. Similarly, Skuas had failed to achieve any hits when they high-level bombed other French ships. FORCE H first encountered the Italian Reggia Aeronautica on July 6 when 40 Savoia-Marchetti S.M.79 three-engine land-based bombers attacked from about 10,000 feet. No hits were scored. These operations prove the ineffectiveness of horizontal bombing against naval targets; especially when the ships are underway.

ITALIAN AND BRITISH MEDITERRANEAN NAVAL ACTIONS - 1940

Meanwhile, at the other end of the Mediterranean, the war against the Italian Navy was about to expand. Although new Royal Navy carriers were under construction the loss of *Glorious* and *Courageous* forced Sir Andrew Cunningham to operate his Mediterranean Fleet with only one old aircraft carrier, *HMS Eagle*, which was equipped with 17 Swordfish for torpedo and bombing attacks, reconnaissance, and antisubmarine patrols, plus only three Sea Gladiators for fighter cover. The Sea Gladiators were flown by one senior Fleet Air Arm officer, Commander Keighley-Peach, plus two Swordfish pilots who flew the fighters only when they were not needed for piloting the Stringbags.

On July 7, 1940 Cunningham took the fleet to sea for a sweep of the Mediterranean to cover two British convoys travelling from Malta to Alexandria. It was pure coincidence that, at the same time, an escorted Italian convoy was on its way from Italy to the Italian colony of Libya, crossing the British convoy's path. Each fleet commander was aware of the movements of the other's ships from aerial reconnaissance and submarine reports. The Italian Admiral Campioni had faster ships; therefore, he planned a running fight to draw the British Fleet into waters infested with Italian submarines and within range of land-based bombers, but Cunningham did not follow.

The following day saw Cunningham's ships heading westward past the island of Crete into what was later known as bomb alley. Italian shore-based bombers attacked the fleet incessantly from 10,000 feet, damaging but one ship, the cruiser *Gloucester*. This day was demoralizing for the ship's crews, as well as the Italian airmen because not only did the Italians realize their horizontal bombing was the wrong tactic but the British crews also became aware that their antiaircraft guns were ineffective against the attackers. *Eagle* appeared to be the favorite target of the attackers and, although receiving no direct hits, it was damaged from the explosions of many near-misses.

Italy, as with Germany, and Britain before 1937, was saddled with a unified air force which had no interest in a naval air arm and neglected the development of antiship tactics, aircraft, and weaponry.

First Carrier Fleet Actions

By July 9, 1940 the first fleet action in which carrier-borne aircraft took part was about to begin in the Ionian Sea near the Italian province of Calabria. The fleets sighted each other in early morning and nine Swordfish took off *HMS Eagle* for a torpedo attack; however, the Italian Fleet had changed course and the Stringbags never found their targets. Another raid at 3:45 in the afternoon failed to score any hits. By evening Cunningham ended the chase because it would be courting disaster to steam closer to the Italian coast, so the fleet retired to Malta.

During the evening of the next day nine Swordfish were launched from *Eagle* and attacked ships in Augusta Harbor, Sicily. The destroyer *Pancaldo* was sunk during this raid. Three more days of ineffective bombing attacks by both sides ended the Battle of Calabria. Both sides learned lessons and the most important was the British realization that aircraft carriers were extremely vulnerable without adequate fighter protection and antiaircraft batteries. Although indecisive, the Battle of Calabria paved the way for the enormous carrier battles soon to take place in the Pacific.

More Mediterranean Convoys

During September 13-14, 1940 Italian colonial troops in Libya launched an invasion of Egypt. This made both sides increase delivery of supplies to their African bases and the Mediterranean Sea became crisscrossed with convoys.

U-Boat Menace in Mediterranean

The British forces were not winning the submarine war in 1940, neither in the Atlantic nor the Mediterranean. Atlantic shipping losses from July through December totalled 280 ships when only 28 U-boats were in operation. Only one German U-boat was sunk by the Royal Navy during the autumn of 1940. During the same period in the Mediterranean Sea, despite the presence of a Royal Navy submarine flotilla at Malta and air attacks from Malta and Egypt, the Italians shipped over 690,000 tons of supplies to North African ports. Italian losses from British attacks were under two percent and Italian Navy escorts sank 10 out of 17 British submarines during that same six month period. The Royal Navy submarine failure forced the dependence, more and more, on aircraft carriers to stop the Italian convoys from reaching the Italian troops in North Africa.

Royal Navy Depends On Carriers

After a little over one year of warfare the Royal Navy began to depend increasingly on the aircraft carrier to take over the tasks normally handled by other types of naval craft. As the war expanded the carrier assumed more responsibility, including that of the dreadnaught, itself.

On October 28, 1940 Italian forces invaded Greece, fearful that the Allies would attack the Axis via Churchill's "underbelly of Europe."

HMS ILLUSTRIOUS CLASS CARRIERS ENTER SERVICE

At this most propitious time new aircraft carriers began to enter the Royal Navy. *HMS Illustrious* and her two sisters and three half-sisters were the most heavily armored aircraft carriers of their time.

After the Second London Conference of 1935-1936 the Admiralty embarked upon the 1936 program to construct two fleet carriers based upon the *Ark Royal* design; *HMS Illustrious* and *HMS Victorious*. The Second London Treaty permitted 23,000 ton carriers so it was decided to use the extra 1,000 tons above the *Ark Royal* tonnage for improvements.

In the event of war the strategic and tactical operations arena for the new carriers was to be the North Sea and the Mediterranean Sea where the ships would usually be within range of land-based bombers. In view of this threat a committee led by Third Sea Lord Admiral Henderson strongly recommended that the new carrier be extensively armored against air attack and be equipped with an extra heavy complement of antiaircraft batteries much like *Ark Royal*. All of this could not be accomplished without sacrificing something and, as with many Royal Navy carriers, the aircraft complement suffered. Another reason for this approach was that unlike the American and Japanese naval air forces, the Royal Navy's Air Arm had no first rate naval fighters with which to protect the carrier against air attack and therefore, like a mother hen, the British carrier was forced to defend itself to protect its brood of strike aircraft. Even the aviation fuel system received special attention so it would not easily erupt in the event the ship suffered bomb hits.

Illustrious Class Armor

The *Illustrious*/*Victorious* Hangar became an armored box designed to resist 500 pound bombs. It was fitted with 4 1/2 inch thick sides and ends, and a 3 inch thick overhead which was part of the Flight Deck. The rest of the Flight Deck was 1 1/2 inches thick and the Hangar Deck beyond the Hangar was 1 inch thick. Dimensions of the Hangar were 458 x 62 x 16 feet. This space could accommodate only 36 aircraft; 30 torpedo bombers and six fighter/dive bombers. The two-level Hangar of *Ark Royal* had to be abandoned due to the increased topside weight caused by the increased armor. The aircraft elevators were located at each end outside of the armored Hangar because the elevators could not be armored due to the excessive weight. Sliding armored doors separated the armored Hangar and the aircraft elevator wells. This configuration also provided more space in the Hangar.

Illustrious Class Keel Laying

The Vickers-Armstrong Barrow Shipyard laid the *Illustrious* keel on April 27, 1937 and the *Victorious* keel followed on May 4 at the Vickers-Armstrong Newcastle Shipyard.

Illustrious Class Data

Deep load displacement was over 28,600 tons with the 4,940 tons of armor plating. Waterline length was 673 feet and hull beam was 96 feet. Deep load draft was 28 feet. Flight Deck dimensions were 650 x 80 feet. Six Admiralty three-drum oil-fired boilers generated 400 pounds pressure steam for the three Parsons turbines, each geared to a propeller shaft. Total shaft horsepower was 111,000 which propelled the ships to a speed of 30.5 knots. Combat range was 11,000 miles at 14 knots. One hydraulic catapult was installed capable of launching a 14,000 pound airplane off the forward end of the Flight Deck. A transverse cable arresting gear was also fitted. Sixteen 4.5 inch guns, 48 two-pounder guns and (8) 20 milli-

HMS Illustrious was the most heavily armored carrier of its time with 5,000 tons of armor plating. An improved Ark Royal, Illustrious accommodated fewer planes because of the weight of the armor (Upper Photo). (U.S. Naval Historical Center)

Sister ship to Illustrious was HMS Victorious. Note the downward curve of the Flight Deck at the stern. In addition to armor, the class depended on gunfire as defense against air raids (Lower Photo). (Ministry of Defence [Navy])

meter guns comprised the antiaircraft batteries. The ships stowed (45) 18 inch torpedoes, (100) 500 pound bombs, (550) 250 pound bombs, (200) 250 pound armor piercing bombs, and (600) 20 pound bombs for their strike aircraft. Complement was 817 crew and officers and 394 Fleet Air Arm (peacetime).

HMS Formidable **and** HMS Indomitable

The two carriers of the 1937 construction program were to be identical with *Illustrious* and *Victorious*. *HMS Formidable*'s keel was laid at the Harland and Wolff Shipyard in Belfast on June 17, 1937 while *HMS Indomitable*'s keel was laid at Vickers-Armstrong's Walker Shipyard on November 13. Construction had barely started when the design was being criticized because the small aircraft complement of *Illustrious* and *Victorious* was being repeated. This resulted in modifications to *Indomitable* for increasing hangar volume.

A second hangar was added to *Indomitable* below the original hangar. This was half the length of the upper hangar and was located under the after portion. The travel of the after elevator was extended to serve the lower hangar. The *Indomitable* hangar side armor was reduced from 4 1/2 inches to 1 1/2 inches and hangar ends reduced from 4 1/2 inches to 2 1/2 inches. The hangar height was reduced from 16 feet to 14 feet to compensate for the added weight of the second hangar. Despite these efforts the displacement

rose by about 1,000 tons. Dimensions and performance were the same as *HMS Illustrious* except for the following: displacement (full load) 39,730 tons, full load draft 29 feet; complement 1,392 (wartime 1,592); aircraft complement 48 planes. Armament was the same as *Illustrious* plus (17) .303 inch caliber antiaircraft guns.

HMS Implacable **and** HMS Indefatigable

The Admiralty's 1938 aircraft carrier program included two more new ships of the *Ark Royal/Illustrious* class: *HMS Implacable* and *HMS Indefatigable*. In order to further increase the aircraft complement it was decided to fit the new vessels with a full length lower level hangar, much as was installed on *Ark Royal*. This limited the height of both hangars to 14 feet, as with *Indomitable*. The three engine rooms and boiler rooms arrangement of *HMS Ark Royal* was replaced with four engine rooms and four boiler rooms. This change resulted in four propellers which increased the shaft horsepower to 148,000.

Indefatigable's keel was laid in John Brown Shipyard at Clydebank on November 3, 1939; *Implacable* followed on February 21, 1940 at Fairfield Shipyard. Finding it impossible to live with the London Naval Treaty restrictions in the design of these ships, it was decided to breach the agreement in order to construct the carriers the Admiralty wanted and Britain needed, regardless of the resulting tonnage.

Problems surfaced at once. The primary objective of the full length lower-level hangar was additional aircraft capacity; however, despite the fact the hull had been lengthened to accommodate the additional engine and boiler rooms, it proved impossible to find space for the added engineering crew and shops and storerooms anywhere except the forward part of the lower hangar! Therefore, *Indefatigable* and *Implacable* began to be the same as *Indomitable* regarding aircraft stowage capacity. Determined to increase the size of the air group on the new carriers the designers borrowed an idea used by the U.S. Navy in the mid-1930s. Using outriggers extending out from the Flight Deck, aircraft were stowed with main wheels on the Deck and tailwheel on the outrigger rail. Using this system the two new carriers were operating up to 81 aircraft by the end of the war. Another item worthy of mention is the fact that, due to the Hangar structure and armor, the Flight Deck was capable of operating aircraft weighing up to 20,000 pounds and the catapult could handle the same size aircraft. Naval aircraft were not to reach that weight for several years to come. The bow was modified on the two new carriers by starting the hull flare to the Flight Deck lower on the stem, giving the bow a blunt appearance.

HMS *Implacable* and HMS *Indefatigable* Data
As completed the full load displacement of *Implacable* was 32,110 tons while *Indefatigable* displaced 32,800 tons. Flight Deck dimensions for Implacable were 770 x 101 feet and for *Indefatigable* they were 770 x 105 feet. The lengthened hull at the waterline was 761 feet. Maximum speed was 32 knots. Hangar side armor was increased to 2 inches and all other armor remained the same as *Indomitable*. Armament was also the same as *Indomitable* except for the addition of two quadruple two-pounder pom-poms and improved gun directors for the 4.5 inch guns. *Implacable* was fitted with (37) 20 millimeter antiaircraft guns while *Indefatigable* had 40 of the guns.

Complement was 845 officers and crew for the ship and 547 officers and men for Fleet Air Arm. During the war it had risen to 2,467 total.

Launching and Commissioning
Illustrious was launched April 5, 1939 and commissioned on May 25, 1940; *Formidable* was launched August 17, 1939 and commissioned on November 24, 1940; *Victorious* was launched September 14, 1939 and commissioned May 15, 1941; *Indomitable* was launched March 26, 1940 and commissioned October 10, 1941; *Indefatigable* was launched December 8, 1942 and commissioned May 3, 1944; and *Implacable* was launched December 10, 1942 and commissioned on August 28, 1944.

Sister Ships Are Not Identical
Of interest in the foregoing is how sister ships of the same class can be so different from each other. It has been the Author's experience that no two ships are identical because change orders are constantly issued to upgrade armament, powerplants, protection, electronics and many other disciplines, not only for ships in the drafting stage but ships under construction as well. Some historians insist that *HMS Indomitable, HMS Formidable,* as well as *HMS Indefatigable* and *HMS Implacable,* should be considered as separate classes from

A batsman on an Illustrious class carrier guides an incoming plane to a landing. Observe that he is using bright lights instead of the previously used paddles. This was the forerunner of the yet to come Magic Mirror and other landing aids. (British Information Service)

While an Albacore leaves the Victorious Flight Deck a good view is afforded of two of the eight twin 4.5 inch turrets on the Illustrious class carriers. (Ministry of Defence [Navy])

Further improvements over Ark Royal and Illustrious were incorporated into Indefatibable and Implacable. This included a rearrangement of machinery spaces into four engine rooms and four boiler rooms to prevent assymetrical flooding in the event of a hit. HMS Indefatigable is shown here. (U.S. National Archives)

the *Ark Royal/Illustrious* class; however, the consensus is that they are three groups of the *Illustrious* class: *Illustrious, Victorious, Formidable*; *Indomitable*; and *Implacable, Indefatatigable*.

As can be seen, no ship of this class was in service when World War II began; however, the entire class performed yeoman service in the Atlantic, Mediterranean, and Pacific naval actions, enduring one-ton bomb strikes and Kamikaze hits. Their story is unfolded later in this chapter and in following chapters.

TARANTO NAVAL BASE AIR RAID

Cunningham's Mediterranean Fleet now had the task to conduct a classic air raid from which the Imperial Japanese Navy learned the technique to attack Pearl Harbor.

The possession of aircraft carriers, although equipped with aircraft of mediocre performance, was the Royal Navy's principal advantage over the Italian Navy in the Mediterranean. It enabled the British Mediterranean Fleet to operate as it chose, despite the

HMS Implacable reveals its broad bow flare into the Flight Deck in order to obtain as much interior volume as possible and to prevent damage to the Flight Deck in very rough seas. A double deck hangar was fitted in an effort to increase aircraft capacity. (U.S. National Archives)

fact that it was closely fenced in by Italian airfields in Italy and Africa. The main thorn in the side of the Royal Navy was the Italian Battle Fleet stationed in the naval base at Taranto. By this time British and Commonwealth troops had taken the offensive against the Italian colonials in the Western Desert and a constant flow of supplies was essential. The quickest way to deliver war materiel was via the Mediterranean, but the ships at Taranto made this proposition too dangerous. In late August the new carrier *Illustrious*, the newly refitted battleship *Valiant*, plus two antiaircraft cruisers arrived in the Mediterranean. The radar-fitted carrier was equipped with Fairey Fulmar two-seat fighters. The new arrivals enabled the British to plan an ambitious attack against the Italian Fleet. It was decided to use Swordfish to torpedo the fleet at anchor in Taranto Harbor and because the Stringbag was easy prey to fighters in daylight, plans were made for a night raid.

While night takeoffs and landings were practiced in the darkness by the pilots of *Eagle* and *Illustrious* the carriers also conducted night raids on the Dodecanese Islands, using Swordfish in their new role of dive bomber. On the night of September 17 two Italian destroyers were sunk in the port of Benghazi.

Taranto was the finest naval harbor in Italy, consisting of an inner harbor called the Mar Piccolo, or small sea, and an outer harbor called Mar Grande, or large sea. The two bodies of water are connected by means of a canal which passes through the town of Taranto. A series of breakwaters partially enclosed the main Italian Fleet anchorage in the Mar Grande.

Soon the Swordfish crews were ready enough to launch a torpedo attack with 30 planes by the selected date of October 21, 1940; however, on October 19 a fire erupted in the Hangar of *Illustrious* but was quickly quenched by the sprinkler system. Nevertheless, several Swordfish were destroyed while others were damaged and saturated by the water, which forced the raid to be postponed until the next favorable phase of the moon. The new date for Operation Judgement, as the raid was named, was for the night of November 11. In many ways the delay was fortunate because it provided more time for additional aerial photo-reconnaissance, which discovered barrage balloons and antitorpedo nets protecting the Italian ships.

Eagle Damaged
Meanwhile, *HMS Eagle* began to show symptoms of structural weaknesses due to the repeated near-misses she endured during the many Italian air raids. Her aircraft fuel system was also affected, revealing traces of saltwater in the storage tanks, which forced three Swordfish to ditch at sea because of the contaminated fuel. *Eagle* was declared unfit to participate in the raid and five of her Swordfish and eight crews were transferred to *Illustrious*.

On To Taranto
The fleet sailed from Alexandria on November 6 and, in order to keep the Italians from becoming suspicious at this Royal Navy activity, the operation was also involved in covering naval reinforcements for the Mediterranean Fleet, as well as escorting several convoys between Malta, Greece and Alexandria. On November 8 the fleet was in the Ionian Sea where it had to endure Italian aerial reconnaissance and bombing. Three days later *HMS Illustrious* detached from the fleet with her escort of four cruisers and four destroyers and headed for the flying off position 175 miles from Taranto.

Incomplete Taranto Defenses
On the night of November 11 the Italian naval base was packed with prime targets for the entire Italian battleship strength was moored in the Mar Grande. This included *Vittorio Veneto, Giulio Cesare, Littorio, Caio Duilio, Andrea Doria* and *Conte de Cavour* The cruisers *Zara, Fiume* and *Goritzia*, plus seven destoyers were also moored in the Mar Grande. In the Mar Piccolo were the cruisers *Trieste, Bolzano, Trento* and *Pola*, with a half-dozen destroyers. Two thirds of the torpedo netting had not yet been installed and 60 of the barrage balloons had been destroyed in a recent storm Thus, there were gaps in the defenses above and below the surface of the water. The Italian antiaircraft defenses included about (20) inch guns and about 200 machine guns of assorted calibers intended for low-flying torpedo planes. About two dozen searchlights were stationed ashore and on pontoons, in addition to those on the ships

Reduced Torpedo-Armed Aircraft
Once the full extend of the balloon barrage and torpedo netting was known it was decided to restrict the number of torpedo-armed aircraft to six in each wave because of the limited torpedo launching spaces. The remainder of the 21 Swordfish were loaded with bombs and parachute flares.

Taranto First Wave
Shortly after 8:00 o'clock on the evening of November 11, 194 the first wave, consisting of a dozen Swordfish, began to take off from the deck of *HMS Illustrious* and by 8:40 the planes had made formation and began the 2 1/2 hour flight to the target. When the Stringbags were about 20 miles from Taranto the Italian antiaircraft guns began firing. As the planes neared the target the squadron commander, Lieutenant Commander Kenneth Williamson, gave the order to split up and the six torpedo-carrying Swordfish turned in order to make their attack from the west while the remaining six bomb and flare-laden Stringbags flew in the opposite direction to operate on the east side of the Mar Grande. The first flare illuminated the harbor at about 11:00 PM and was followed by a long line of others, which silhouetted the ships for the torpedo planes, which were diving into a hail of gunfire.

Williamson led the attack and the six Stringbags got through the balloon cables without a mishap. Flying 30 feet above the water, the torpedoes were released and Lieutenant Commander Williamson, being in the lead, bore the brunt of the intense antiaircraft fire. Just as his torpedo struck *Cavour* the Stringbag's engine was hit and the biplane crashed into the Mar Grande. Williamson and his observer/gunner, Lieutenant N.J. Scarlett, were rescued by the Italians and taken prisoner. Of the remaining torpedoes, two struck the *Littorio*. Meanwhile, the six bombers were frustrated by the failure of many bombs to explode; however, the bombers did start a huge fire by hitting the fuel storage tanks in the oil depot in Mar Piccolo and wrecked the seaplane station. More important, they proved to be an effective diversion for the torpedo attack.

The aftermath of the Taranto air raid is vividly illustrated in this aerial photograph of Mar Piccolo or the inner harbor. Observe the enormous amount of oil pouring from damaged cruisers and destroyers as the result of combined torpedo and dive bombing attacks. (Ministry of Defence [Navy])

Taranto Second Wave

The second wave of nine Swordfish had taken off one hour after the first wave. Led by Lieutenant Commander J.W. Hale, with Lieutenant G.A. Carine as observer/gunner the eight Stringbags were approaching Taranto as the first wave began the return flight. Lieutenant Commander Hale's squadron had started off nine strong; however, one Swordfish inadvertently dropped its external long range tank and was forced to return to *Illustrious*. The five torpedo planes of the second wave approached Mar Grande from the north while three bombers dropped flares along the south side of the harbor. One torpedo struck the *Duilio* and a second Tin Fish hit the

stricken *Littorio*. As the fifth Swordfish, flown by Lieutenant G.W. Bagley with Lieutenant H.J. Slaughter as observer/gunner, was making its run it was hit by a large shell and exploded, crashing near the cruiser *Gorizia*. Both men died. The bombers experienced the same problem as the first wave; many of the bombs had failed to explode.

Taranto Raid Results

All planes except the aforementioned two returned to *Illustrious* and landed safely, the last one arriving at about 3:00 o'clock in the morning of November 12.

With this relatively small loss the Italian Fleet had been crippled as though it had lost a major sea battle. The battleship *Littorio* was to be out of action for four months, *Duilio* for six months and *Cavour* for the remainder of the war.

The history-making events of that night over the Taranto Naval Base were viewed with interest by Imperial Japanese Navy Admiral Isoroku Yamamoto, who appreciated this demonstration of the effectiveness of torpedo planes against ships moored in a naval base. He would use this technique one year later against the United States Navy.

ROYAL NAVY CONTROLS MEDITERRANEAN

With *Eagle* and *Illustrious* under his command and the Italian Navy weakened at Taranto, Cunningham quickly reasserted British control over the Central Mediterranean. Fulmar and Swordfish aircraft attacked at random, dive bombing, mining and creating chaos with communications all along the Axis-held African coast.

Split Forces Spell Failure

The next major action in the Mediterranean theatre involved FORCE H which was escorting an eastbound convoy southwest of Cape Spartivento, Sardinia, on the morning of November 27, 1940. The convoy was about to make rendezvous with the old battleship *Ramillies* and two cruisers when Swordfish air reconnaissance from *Ark Royal* reported the Italian Fleet to the north. Admiral Sir James Somerville decided to challenge the superior Italian force; superior in every way except in naval air power. The convoy was sent southward; away from the impending battle.

The cruisers of both forces exchanged fire at very long range with no results but, when Italian Admiral Campioni learned that *Ark Royal* was part of the British force, he turned away at high speed and refused to fight. Campioni was only following standard orders from the Italian Ministry of Marine because, since Taranto, the two remaining battleships could not be risked. It was only because the Italian ships were faster that Campioni could make this decision.

Somerville realized that his only chance of engaging the Italian Fleet was to reduce its speed with an air attack. The order was given and *HMS Ark Royal* launched 11 torpedo-laden Swordfish led by Lieutenant Commander Johnstone. The planes found the Italian battleships *Vittorio Veneto* and *Giulio Cesare* steaming in line with a screen of seven destroyers. These were truly tempting targets and the Swordfish attacked, skillfully fishtailing through the heavy antiaircraft barrage to launch their torpedoes inside the destroyer screen! Frantic evasive maneuvering of the two battleships avoided the Tin Fish although the Swordfish crews were certain at the time that they had scored three hits. All planes returned safely to *Ark Royal*.

Split Forces Spell Failure

With the safety of the convoy his primary objective, Somerville called off the chase and turned southward towards the convoy. *HMS Ark Royal* was left free; however, to mount an attack on an Italian cruiser which had been reported damaged and dead in the water. Captain Holland ordered a torpedo strike to finish off the cruiser

and, by the time the nine Swordfish had been armed and reached a state of readiness, Holland was informed of the imagined torpedo hit on the battleships. The Captain then changed his orders for the torpedo strike to be directed against the battleships and for a flight of seven Skuas to dive bomb the cruiser. Captain C.S. Holland has been accused of making a serious tactical error with his revised orders because he violated one of the oldest and most basic rules of warfare: concentrate all your strength at the point of contact with the enemy. In later chapters it will be evident that leaders who split up their forces in combat inevitably lost the battle. Captain Holland had split his forces by sending the Skuas to bomb the cruiser and the Swordfish to torpedo the battleships, instead of ordering a coordinated dive bombing/torpedo attack on one target at a time. The Swordfish led by Commander Stewart-Moore could not find the damaged battleships so they attacked a cruiser squadron instead while the Skuas, led by Lieutenant Richard M. Smeeton, never found the crippled cruiser, so they bombed another cruiser squadron instead. Neither attack proved successful.

By nightfall FORCE H was back at Gibraltar. Regarding the criticism directed at Captain Holland's decision, it should be remembered that carrier warfare was in its infancy and many mistakes were made until the secret of successful carrier operation was discovered through trial and error.

SEA HURRICANE FIGHTER

The absence of a suitable state-of-the-art naval fighter plane forced the Fleet Air Arm to adapt land-based RAF fighters to the naval role. It has been seen how this was done with the Gloster Gladiator however, better performance was necessary. The successful operation of RAF Hawker Hurricanes from the deck of *HMS Glorious* during the Norwegian Campaign prompted the conversion of standard RAF Hurricanes for naval use. The Sea Hurricane closely resembled the RAF version; the outstanding differences being the addition of catapult fittings and arresting hook. The navalized Hurricane was converted from the Mk.IIA type and, because it was fitted with an arresting hook, it was known as Hooked Hurricane II. This type was equipped with eight .303 Browning machine guns located in the wing.

Sea Hurricane Data

The Hooked Hurricane II had a wingspan of 40 feet and length of 32 feet. Height was 13 feet-1 inch. The 8,250 pound fighter was powered by a Rolls-Royce Marlin XX 12-cylinder liquid-cooled engine of 1,280 horsepower which drove the Hawker to a maximum speed of 340 miles per hour. Service ceiling was 36,300 feet and range was 900 miles with two underwing drop tanks. The basic fuselage was a framework of welded steel tubing to which was added wooden fairing strips. Detachable metal panels covered the fuselage from just aft of the cockpit to the nose. The wing and tail surfaces consisted of a Dural structure with an Alclad-covered forward third of the wing. The fin was also Alclad-covered. The remainder of the plane was fabric-covered.

The Sea Hurricane was especially suited for carrier operation because of its wide track and strong landing gear which retracted inward. A total of 800 Sea Hurricanes were built or converted and served well on several Royal Navy carriers.

A Sea Hurricane is being serviced on HMS Argus. The navalized version of the RAF Hawker Hurricane proved very suitable to carrier operation. It was often called Hooked Hurricane, referring to the arresting hook. (Air Ministry [Navy])

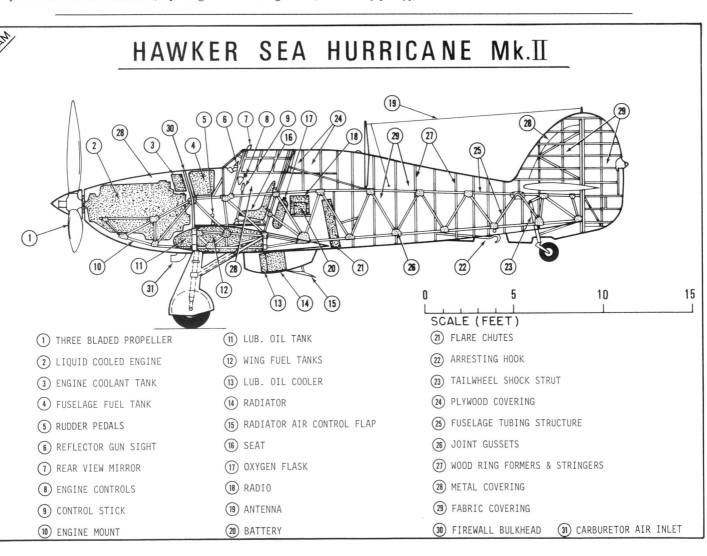

HAWKER SEA HURRICANE Mk.II

SCALE (FEET)

① THREE BLADED PROPELLER	⑪ LUB. OIL TANK	㉑ FLARE CHUTES
② LIQUID COOLED ENGINE	⑫ WING FUEL TANKS	㉒ ARRESTING HOOK
③ ENGINE COOLANT TANK	⑬ LUB. OIL COOLER	㉓ TAILWHEEL SHOCK STRUT
④ FUSELAGE FUEL TANK	⑭ RADIATOR	㉔ PLYWOOD COVERING
⑤ RUDDER PEDALS	⑮ RADIATOR AIR CONTROL FLAP	㉕ FUSELAGE TUBING STRUCTURE
⑥ REFLECTOR GUN SIGHT	⑯ SEAT	㉖ JOINT GUSSETS
⑦ REAR VIEW MIRROR	⑰ OXYGEN FLASK	㉗ WOOD RING FORMERS & STRINGERS
⑧ ENGINE CONTROLS	⑱ RADIO	㉘ METAL COVERING
⑨ CONTROL STICK	⑲ ANTENNA	㉙ FABRIC COVERING
⑩ ENGINE MOUNT	⑳ BATTERY	㉚ FIREWALL BULKHEAD ㉛ CARBURETOR AIR INLET

SHIPBOARD AIRCRAFT CORROSION PREVENTION; 1940-1945

Continuing problems and remedies surfaced to prevent shipborne aircraft corrosion. In the 1940s and 1950s airplanes were made from Specification AA 2024 and similar aluminum alloys, known as Duraluminum or Dural. These alloys were much stronger than the pure aluminum previously tried; however, they were prone to corrosion in the saltwater environment. The wing and fuselage thin skin covering was then clad with pure aluminum, commonly called Alclad, which overcame the corrosion problem. The only difficulty was that the soft aluminum scratched easily and corrosion occurred at the scratches. This presented a danger because, if undetected, the corrosion could weaken the structure of an Alclad-covered wing or a monocoque or semi-monocoque fuselage, causing structural failure. To guard against scratches on the soft aluminum many construction and maintenance personnel wore felt-soled slippers when their tasks bore the risk of scratching the surface. In addition to chemically treating the surface of magnesium alloys to prevent it from powdering and flaking, steel components were phosphate treated to improve their resistance to corrosion. Many advancements were also made with primers and surface pretreatments to improve the adhesion of organic and inorganic coatings which helped fight corrosion and improved camouflage which was becoming important for shipborne aircraft.

AXIS AND BRITISH MEDITERRANEAN NAVAL ACTIONS 1941

During the first days of 1941 the British situation in the Mediterranean appeared to be favorable with the prospect of receiving some of the new armored carriers then under construction.

Luftwaffe Versus Royal Navy

Germany decided to aid Italy in North Africa by sending General Erwin Rommel with his Afrika Corps, German convoys were then forced to run the gauntlet of British naval air power with *Illustrious*, *Eagle* and *Ark Royal* in operation, and more carriers on the way. The Germans knew that they had to knock out the Royal Navy carriers so they trained and organized a special Luftwaffe unit to do just that; Fliegerkorps X. Realizing the Luftwaffe's failure to score against naval units in the Norwegian campaign, Fliegerkorps X was given special concentrated antiship training and, by the first of the year, 150 Junkers Ju 87 and Ju 88 dive bombers, 40 twin engine Messerschmitt Me 110 fighters, 120 Heinkel He 111 long range bombers and 20 reconnaissance aircraft had arrived at Sicilian airfields and were ready to work with the Italians in bombing the British aircraft carriers in the Sicilian Narrows; the closest point between Italy and Africa.

Illustrious Damaged

On January 10, 1941 Admiral Cunningham's Mediterranean Fleet was escorting a convoy 60 miles west of Malta when it was attacked by Italian torpedo planes and German dive bombers of Fliegerkorps X. The converging dive bombing attacks concentrated on *HMS Illustrious* and, according to witnesses, the attacks were brilliantly executed. Never before had ships been subjected to such a concentrated and coordinated dive bombing attack. The Junkers Ju 87 and twin engine Junkers Ju 88 dive bombers dropped 1,100 pound and 2,200 pound armor-piercing bombs with extraordinary precision and, despite being under attack by intercepting Fulmar fighters, the Fliegerkorps X bombers scored six direct hits on Illustrious. The Flight Deck was wrecked, destroying nine aircraft, and fires were started. Her steering gear malfunctioned for a while but repairs were quickly made and *Illustrious* steamed for Malta under her own power. On the way the carrier was again under attack and another direct hit was made. *HMS Illustrious* had endured savage punishment that would have sunk any American or Japanese carrier. It was the armored flight deck and armored box hangar system plus the carefully designed aircraft fuel system that saved her from certain destruction. By nightfall *Illustrious* was in Malta undergoing temporary repairs. The attacks had killed 83 crew members and seriously wounded 60 more but, considering the ferocity of the attacks, the casualties were relatively light. Under cover of darkness Illustrious left for Alexandria where she was found to be in need of such extensive repairs that she sailed to the U.S. for an overhaul.

Before sailing, her aircraft were transferred to the British force fighting in the African desert.

FORCE H Operations

With *Illustrious* gone the Royal Navy Mediterranean Fleet was confined to the eastern end of the Mediterranean. In the meantime, at the western end, Admiral Somerville's FORCE H attacked northern Italy. On February 2, *Ark Royal* Swordfish attacked Tirso Dam on Sardinia and seven days later they bombed Genoa, the Pisa airfield and railway yard, the Azienda oil refinery in Leghorn, and laid mines in Spezia Harbor.

Battle of Cape Matapan

The new Royal Navy carrier *HMS Formidable* joined Admiral Sir Andrew Cunningham's Mediterranean Fleet in early March 1941 and he promptly resumed the offensive by escorting the British supply convoys to Piraeus, the seaport of Athens, and to the island of Crete. By this time the Germans had decided to help their Ally who wasn't doing too well in its Greek adventure, by sending troops to Greece and the crucial island of Crete. The Germans wanted the flow of Commonwealth troops to Greece stopped before they would commit German troops; therefore, they urged the Italian Navy to make bold moves to intercept and destroy the Allied convoys; promising the extensive cooperation of the land-based Luftwaffe with reconnaissance, as well as fighter cover and dive bombing.

This prodding resulted in the ordering of the Italian Commander in Chief, Admiral Iachino, to take his fleet to sea. On the morning of March 27, 1941 Italy's newest battleship *Vittorio Veneto,* six heavy cruisers, two light cruisers and a number of destroyers made rendezvous and headed for Gavdos Island, southwest of Crete; near the convoy route to Greece. A Short Sunderland reconnaissance flying boat spotted the Italian ships and reported their position to Cunningham who led his fleet out of Alexandria that evening under cover of darkness. Overnight, the Mediterranean Fleet steamed between the convoy route and the Italian Fleet, launching Albacores on reconnoitering flights from *Formidable* at first light. The Albacores located an Italian cruiser squadron which was scouting about

00 miles ahead of Iachino's main body of ships and a long-range running fire-fight erupted between British and Italian cruisers. The Italians retired to the main fleet which had not yet been located by the British but another Italian cruiser squadron was steering to cut off the British cruisers. Sir Andrew ordered a torpedo strike and, by 0 o'clock, six Albacores flew off *HMS Formidable* with two Fulmars as escorts; heading for the Italian cruisers. After flying for an hour the British aircrews were surprised to see the massive bulk of the *Vittorio Veneto* firing its 15 inch guns at the trapped British cruisers just south of Cape Matapan, sometimes called Cape Tainaron. This southernmost Greek cape is located between the Gulf of Laconia and the Gulf of Messenia. The Albacores peeled off at once and swooped to wave level into the withering fire from the battleship and her four-destroyer escort. It was during this engagement that the technique of splash barrage was first used by a defending ship during an aerial torpedo attack. *Vittorio Veneto* fired her 15 inch guns into the water in the path of the Albacores sending up geysers of sea water. This forced the Albacores to swerve because to hit a splash from the barrage would destroy or severely damage the low-flying planes so they could not continue the attack. Although the Albacores failed to score a hit, they did rescue the hard-pressed Royal Navy cruisers.

Coordinated Air Attack

When Admiral Iachino realized he was opposed by an aircraft carrier and, lacking the fighter protection he had been promised by the Luftwaffe, he turned westward and sped for safety. *Vittorio Veneto* was 60 miles ahead of Cunningham, which made it impossible to close the gap, so he ordered another torpedo strike. This time only three Albacores and two Swordfish had been serviced so they took off with two Fulmars as escorts, at about 2:15 o'clock in the afternoon of March 28. Sir Andrew coordinated his attack with the RAF, based on the Greek mainland, with the result that twin-engine Bristol Blenheims conducted a bombing attack while the torpedo strike was still 15 minutes away. Although the high level horizontal bombing scored no hits it had accomplished its purpose by diverting the attention of the ships to high altitude overhead while the Albacores and Stringbags made their attack at low altitude. Lieutenant Commander J. Dalyell-Stead led the three Albacores to attack the battleship's port bow. *Vittorio Veneto* turned hard to starboard as the torpedoes were launched. The squadron commander Dalyell-Stead pressed on to extremely close range to ensure a hit and, at the very moment of his torpedo release, he was shot down and killed. Lieutenant Commander Dalyell-Stead's torpedo ran true and struck the battleship hull near the outboard port propeller shaft. The propeller shaft had fractured, steering gear jammed, and a large hole was blown in the hull, which admitted 4,000 tons of sea water. The two Swordfish followed in quickly and both torpedoes also struck the troubled battleship.

Vittorio Veneto speed was down to 13 knots and the two cruiser squadrons fell back to escort and protect the limping battleship in her westward journey home. The Italian engineers aboard the battleship had performed the impossible by repairing the steering gear and managed to attain a steady 18 knot speed with only the starboard shafts in operation.

Admiral Cunningham ordered a third torpedo strike and *HMS Formidable* readied six Albacores and two Swordfish for the raid. Lieutenant Commander W.H.G. Gaunt led the flight into the twilight to rendezvous with two more Swordfish from Maleme Airfield on Crete. It was dark and overcast when the Italian Fleet was sighted and through the blinding searchlight beams and tracer bullets could be seen the fact that the cruisers and destroyers had formed a double screen around *Vittorio Veneto*. Gaunt split his flight for individual attacks from all directions because it would have been suicidal to attack in formation in view of the intense antiaircraft barrage that was put up by the Italian ships. It became a chaotic scene of utter confusion during the torpedo attack and all the torpedoes ran wild except that from the last Stringbag. This last torpedo struck the 10,000 ton cruiser *Pola*, stopping it dead in the water. The Albacores and Swordfish quickly turned for Crete because their fuel was dangerously low.

Thus ended the Warbirds' involvement in the Battle of Cape Matapan; however, the fighting was not yet over. Admiral Iachino had to know the location of his pursuers, Cunningham's Mediterranean Fleet. The Italian Admiral had no radar and had to depend upon shore-based aerial reconnaissance of shore-based radio direction finder stations to inform him of the British ship's position. Iachino didn't trust aerial reconnaissance so he contacted a shore station which stated that Cunningham's Fleet was 170 miles astern of the Italians when it was actually only 70 miles away! The Italian Admiral sent two cruisers, *Fiume* and *Zara*, with four destroyers, to turn back and guard the stricken Pola. In the inky black moonless night, the radarless cruisers and destroyers steamed toward Pola, not realizing the closeness of the Mediterranean Fleet, and at 10:15 that nigh passed blindly across the bows of the Royal Navy battleships. The *Pola*, *Zara*, *Fiume* and two destroyers were all destroyed within a few minutes by the British battleships' big guns at a range of only 4,000 yards.

Carrier Planes Ensure Victory

The Battle of Cape Matapan victory had been made possible by a handful of carrier aircraft and this was the first carrier-borne striking force to take part in a naval action on the open sea. The British confidence in the torpedo as the only weapon capable of sinking or damaging a capital ship was justified by the success of the Stringbags and Albacores in this encounter. It also demonstrated that simultaneous attacks by bombers and torpedo planes is very effective and this was carefully noted by American and Japanese tacticians.

Italy Needs A Carrier

Admiral Iachino also realized the effectiveness of coordinated air attacks and was certain that if he had a carrier in his fleet, the fighter planes would have given him air cover when he most needed it. There is no doubt that he included this in his battle report because only a few months later, Italy began construction of its first aircraft carrier.

ITALIAN CARRIER INTEREST

Italy's first aircraft carrier was initially conceived in mid-1930 as a conversion of the fast passenger liner *Roma*; however, the project did not receive very much official attention until the Battle of Cape Matapan in March, 1941. By June work had begun converting the liner *Roma* into the aircraft carrier *Aquila*, which means Eagle in English.

Aquila Conversion

The entire superstructure of the 32,500 ton *Roma* was removed and much of the hull interior was gutted. Two sets of cruiser machinery were installed driving four propellers, while eight boilers generated steam for the four-geared steam turbines, totalling 140,000 shaft horsepower. The hull was lengthened and two concrete-filled steel plate blisters were added at the waterline for the dual purpose of improving stability and to provide anti-torpedo protection. A conventional island and smokestack were located on the starboard side of the Flight Deck. The 83 x 700 feet Flight Deck was mounted atop the 96 feet-6 inches beam x 680 feet long hull. Maximum speed was to be 30 knots and range at 18 knots was 4,000 miles. A single 60 x 525 feet Hangar was installed to stow 36 Reggiane Re 2001 Falco single-seat fighter/bombers with nonfolding wings. These were to be converted Reggia Aeronautica fighters. A 1,410 pound bomb could be carried under the fuselage or a torpedo could be carried instead. Some Falco fighters were tested with arresting hooks. Displacement of the completed carrier was 23,300 tons at a draft of 24 feet. Defensive armament comprised (8) 3.1 inch caliber antiship guns; (12) 65 millimeter and (132) 20 millimeter anti-aircraft guns. Complement was planned at 1,420 officers and crew. The ship was virtually complete in September, 1943 when Italy capitulated. Severely damaged by air raids and torpedoes, *Aquila* was broken up for scrap in 1951.

Sparviero Conversion

Italy, again, became interested in the aircraft carrier in early 1942. Back in 1936 it was suggested that the 1927-built 30,500 gross tons passenger ship *Augustus* be converted to a carrier; however, the idea was rejected. Resurrected in 1942, conversion was to be a flush deck carrier without an island. It was to have concrete reinforced blisters added to the hull for protection and stability. Two cruciform elevators were to serve a single hangar. The Flight Deck was to be about 75 percent of the ship's length with the space from the Flight Deck to the bow used for a narrow takeoff runway. This was done to give the guns mounted on the bow a good arc of fire against aircraft. Actually it resembled a British carrier of the early 1920s. Work at the shipyard proceeded at a snail's pace due material shortages and by the time Italy was out of the war only the passenger ship superstructure had been removed. The Germans sank the hull to block Genoa Harbor. If completed the ship was to be named *Sparviero*.

LUFTWAFFE IN THE MEDITERRANEAN

On April 6, 1941 Greece was entered by German ground and air forces to assist the stalled Italian troops. Within two weeks it was all over and Commonwealth troops began to evacuate Greece. This placed an unbearable strain on the Royal Navy. Not only must the evacuation of troops and material be safely transported to North Africa but German reinforcements enroute to Greece had to be in-

tercepted, plus the primary task of escorting Allied convoys in the Mediterranean stretched the Mediterranean Fleet beyond its capability.

Luftwaffe Sinks Royal Navy Ships

By May 21 the Germans had taken Maleme Airfield on Crete and the Royal Navy could no longer use the island for a base. With *HMS Formidable* engaged in convoy escort duty the surface ships in the waters around Crete were forced to operate without air cover. On May 23 a force of Royal Navy cruisers and destroyers was heavily bombed by German planes from Crete. The attackers included many single-engine Messerschmitt Me-109 fighters fitted with bombs. The destroyer *HMS Greyhound* and the cruisers *Fi* and *Gloucester* were quickly sunk. On the following day Lord Lou. Mountbatten's famous 5th Destroyer Flotilla was attacked by the Crete-based Luftwaffe which sent *HMS Kelly* and *HMS Kashmir* the bottom of the sea; all because no Warbirds of the Sea were available to provide air cover.

Armor Saves *HMS Formidable*

The destructive Luftwaffe attacks upon the Royal Navy in the waters around Crete enticed *HMS Formidable* to move in so her warbirds could attack the German airfields on the island. This brought the carrier so close to these bases that she invited the same massed dive bombing attack which had crippled *Illustrious*. After suffering two direct hits from 1,000 and 2,000 pound bombs the carrier retired to Alexandria; however, the damage required greater facilities than were available in Egypt so *HMS Formidable* continued to the U.S.A. for repairs on July 24, 1941, via the Suez Canal. This is another outstanding example of how protective armor saved a Royal Navy aircraft carrier from total destruction.

ROYAL NAVY SINKS *BISMARCK*

Meanwhile, the German battleship *Bismarck* had entered the Atlantic Ocean from her Norwegian base on May 23, 1941. On the following day *HMS Ark Royal*, battleship Renown, and the cruiser Sheffield of FORCE H sped northward from Gibralter to cut off *Bismarck*'s route to her base in Brest, France. The Royal Navy Home Fleet was also mustered to find and destroy *Bismarck*. This included the battleships *HMS Rodney, HMS King George V, Prince of Wales*, and *HMS Ramillies*, plus the battle cruisers *HMS Repulse* and *HMS Hood*. It also included 14 cruisers with five destroyer flotillas. This most powerful assembly of capital ships would have failed in their quest were it not for two Royal Navy aircraft carriers that were on the scene. The brand-new *HMS Victorious* sailed with the Home Fleet which complimented *HMS Ark Royal* in FORCE H.

Bismarck Damaged

On May 23, 1941 *Bismarck* and her escort *Prinz Eugen* were sighted by Royal Navy cruisers northwest of Iceland. *HMS Hood* and *HMS Prince of Wales* were quickly directed to the German ships and an encounter ensued, which resulted in the sinking of *HMS Hood* and damage to *HMS Prince of Wales*. *Bismarck* received two hits, neither of which affected her performance; however, one shell pierced

ismarck's fuel tanks and this loss of fuel forced the German ship
abandon her plans for operations in the Atlantic Ocean as a raider,
she headed to Brest for repairs.

erial Torpedo Strike on *Bismarck*

MS Victorious launched seven Swordfish and two Fulmars in a
rpedo strike at *Bismarck*, 100 miles away. The Swordfish were
tted with the newly developed airborne radar which made it easier
locate their target in the overcast night. One torpedo struck the
ismarck amidships where it caused slight damage because of the
mor belt; however, the violent maneuvers at high speed in very
ugh water forced the crack in the hull to widen, thereby flooding
ne of the boiler rooms, which reduced the speed considerably. Then
ismarck disappeared! For 31 hours the large battleship was not to
e seen, despite the many ships searching the area.

ismarck Found By Catalina

t 10:30 in the morning of May 26 an American naval officer, En-
gn Leonard B. Smith, flying as co-pilot in a U.S. Navy PBY
atalina flying boat, which had been lent to the Royal Navy, sighted
e *Bismarck* heading for the coast of France and only 11 hours
om Brest. Time was of the essence because a few more hours of
avel would put the *Bismarck* within range of the land-based
uftwaffe, under whose protective umbrella she would arrive safely
Brest. The German ship had passed between Iceland and
reenland and around the southern coast of Britain in its attempt to
each Brest. The Home Fleet was about 130 miles from *Bismarck*
nd could not intercept the German ship in time.

econd Aerial Torpedo Strike

dmiral Somerville detached the cruiser *Sheffield* to join the hunt
r *Bismarck*; however, *Ark Royal* was not notified of this assign-
ent and launched 14 torpedo-laden Swordfish to attack the Ger-
an ship. Flying in the overcast, the Swordfish flight detected
heffield on their radar and assumed it was *Bismarck*! The attack
as launched; however, *Sheffield* managed to maneuver clear of
ny damage. The humiliated Swordfish pilots returned to *Ark Royal*
rearm.

hird Aerial Torpedo Strike

torpedo strike was essential to slow the *Bismarck* in order that
e Royal Navy battleships could catch the German ship. FORCE
was still in good position southwest of Ireland to launch the needed
trike and *Ark Royal* readied 15 Stringbags on the windswept Flight
eck. A fierce gale of hurricane force was blowing with torrential
ins. The sea was so rough that green water was washing over the
light Deck and *Ark* was pitching so violently that the bow and
tern moved a vertical distance of 50 feet. The Deck crews had to
old the planes fast, lest they be blown overboard. Lieutenant Com-
ander Eugene Esmonde was ready to lead the attack at 7:10 PM.

The entire flight of 15 Swordfish took off safely; some rolling
phill and some rolling downhill, depending upon the attitude of
e ship in the violent sea. After flying for two hours the Swordfish
ilots sighted *Bismarck* and Lieutenant Commander Esmonde or-
ered his men to the attack in small groups of from two to five

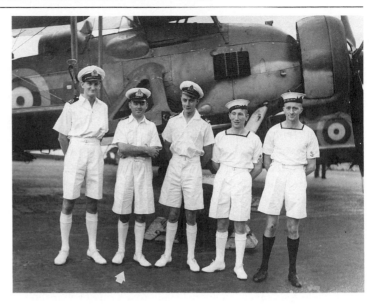

Commander Eugene Esmonde, second from left, led a Swordfish torpedo strike on the German battleship Bismarck which disabled the raider so that the Royal Navy battleships could close in and sink the German ship. The occasion was Admiral Somerville's visit to Ark Royal to congratulate and decorate the officers and enlisted men for their part in the Bismarck sinking. Observe the fine close-up of the Swordfish in the background. (Imperial War Museum)

planes from divergent angles. Two definite hits were made on the
port side and on the starboard quarter, while a possible hit on the
port quarter was also reported. *Bismarck* began running in circles
and then ran straight, albeit erratically; suggesting that the steering
gear had been knocked out and the battleship was steering with its
engines. During the night a flotilla of destroyers attacked *Bismarck*,
slamming two more torpedoes into her side.

Death of *Bismarck*

In the morning of May 27, 1941 the Royal Navy battleships *King
George V* and *Rodney* caught up with and pounded *Bismarck* un-
mercifully, turning the German raider into an unrecognizable hulk.
The cruiser *Dorsetshire* delivered the coup de grace with her torpedoes.

Germany Needs A Carrier

As with the Italian High Command after the Battle of Matapan, the
German High Command realized that the loss of *Bismarck* was directly attributed to the action of British aircraft carriers and their
torpedo-carrying Warbirds of the Sea, and the lack of same in the
German arsenal. Fearful that the remaining battleship *Tirpitz* would
suffer the same fate as *Bismarck* if it went to sea without a carrier,
interest in the *Graf Zeppelin* returned in late 1941 only to fade away
in late 1942 when all available steel was needed for the submarine
expansion program.

No More Capital Ship Raiders

As a result of this vacillation never again did the Kriegsmarine use
its capital ships for commerce raiding in the Atlantic Ocean.

CAM SHIPS PROTECT CONVOYS

From January through May 1941 German U-boats sank 1,141,175 tons of merchant shipping laden with supplies bound for Britain; a total of 202 ships. During that period an average of 27 U-boats had been operating and nine of these were sunk. German long-range reconnaissance bombers helped the submarines, considerably.

Kondor Reconnaissance Bombers

In addition to the U-boat menace, convoys were harassed by long-range Focke-Wulf FW-200 Kondor four-engined reconnaissance bombers. Operating from bases near Bordeaux-Merignac, France and Trondheim, Norway, the large Kondors ranged the Atlantic Ocean searching for convoys. When a convoy was found the Kondor reported its position to the nearest U-boats or, very often, bombed the ships with their four 550 pound bombs if no U-boat was nearby. Originally an airliner, the Kondor had been redesigned and improvised for the reconnaissance bomber role when war erupted. Kondors had not been reinforced for combat and proved fragile when hit by gunfire or when taking evasive maneuvers.

Scourge of the Atlantic

The 2,760 mile range four-engined Fock-Wulf 200 Kondor, long-range reconnaissance bombers were able to remain airborne for as long as 18 hours and flew as far as the east coast of Greenland, reconnoitering and bombing convoys. They were so troublesome that Winston Churchill referred to the Kondors as the "Scourge of the Atlantic." This situation was reminiscent of World War I when the high-flying Zeppelins over the North Sea were impossible to reach without launching aircraft from ships. Now it was Kondors over the Atlantic which had to be intercepted to save Britain's lifeline.

CAM Ships

The logical stopgap solution was for the convoy's conventional cargo ships to launch their own aircraft, and so the CAM (Catapult Aircraft Merchantman) was born. A catapult structure was constructed over the forward deck or forecastle in such a manner to not interfere with cargo loading and unloading. A rocket-propelled trolley was placed on the catapult structure rails. The trolley was designed to support a Hawker Sea Hurricane Mk.1A fighter with its landing gear retracted but high enough for the propeller to clear the rails. Once launched, the Hurricane could not return to the ship. As was done during World War I, the fighter was forced to ditch near a ship of the convoy for the pilot to be rescued while the fighter plane sank. It seemed like a fair exchange; one Kondor for one Hurricane. Very often the landing gear was removed in order not to waste this valuable mechanism and to improve performance. The rocket-powered trolley had been chosen to avoid the complexity and delays inherent with the installation of a compressed air or hydraulic system. Simplicity of operation and rapid installation were essential.

Hurricat and Catafighter

The CAM ships began operations in late spring of 1941 and the catapult Sea Hurricanes soon earned the sobriquets of Hurricat and Catafighter. Each merchant ship was equipped with only one

A Hawker Hurricane Catafighter is caught during launching from a CAM (Catapult-Aircraft Merchantman). A rocket-powered trolley was used in order to avoid the complexity of a compressed air or hydraulic system. (Air Ministry [Navy])

Hurricat which remained on the rocket trolley throughout the voyage with a pilot on the ready in the CAM. As soon as a Kondor was reported in the area the Rolls-Royce Merlin engine was started and warmed up. Many catapult Sea Hurricanes were equipped with engine heating equipment which kept the lubricating oil warm. This equipment shortened the warmup time considerably. With the Hurricat engine on full power, the solid fuel rocket was ignited and the Sea Hurricane was off. Those brave fighter pilots who were launched in this manner are among the unsung heroes of World War II.

ESCORT CARRIER CONVERSIONS; 1941

Obviously, the CAM could only be considered a stopgap measure and better convoy protection was imperative. The search continued until someone remembered the merchantman conversions of World War I; however, any new conversions had to be through-deck carriers to enable the aircraft to return and land on the ship as HMS Argus and unlike the World War I HMS Campania or the CAM conversions.

The basic idea of a trade route carrier had been considered by the Admiralty during the late 1930s but apparently was not taken seriously until it became the only solution to guard Britain's all important SLOC (Sea Lines of Communication) which stretched across the Atlantic. In view of the large number of convoy escort carriers required they had to be austere, quickly constructed, and expendable.

First Escort Carrier

In March 1940 the German Norddeutscher Lloyd Line's 5,500 gross tons cargo-passenger motorship *Hanover* had been captured in the West Indies by *HMS Dunedin* and taken to Britain as a war prize. The Admiralty decided to convert the *Hanover* into an austere carrier designed for convoy duty. Blythe Shipbuilding Co. was en

aged in the conversion by January 1941 and the carrier was com-
eted and commissioned during June 1941 as *HMS Audacity*.

udacity Data

anover's masts, superstructure and smokestack had been removed
nd a wooden Flight Deck measuring 60 x 453 feet was added. In
eeping with the austere requirements no hangar, elevators or cata-
ult were fitted. All six Grumman Martlets were to be stowed on
he Flight Deck. During takeoff operations the planes were grouped
: the aft end of the Flight Deck and during landing operations the
lanes were grouped at the forward end of the Flight Deck. Two
resting cables were fitted to the Flight Deck at the aft end.

The smokestack was diverted horizontally under the Flight
eck, Japanese fashion, and no island was fitted. Navigating sta-
ion and air control center were located on a platform below the
light Deck, protruding to starboard.

Displacement as a carrier was 10,395 tons deep load, which
ncluded solid ballast in the ship's bottom to improve stability.
verall length was 467 feet-3 inches, while deep load draft was 21
et-7 inches. Two 7-cylinder MAN diesel engines powered twin
crews, producing 5,200 shaft horsepower, which drove the small
arrier to a maximum speed of 16 knots. Range was 12,000 miles.
efensive armament consisted of one 4 inch .45 caliber dual-pur-
ose gun mounted on the stern, plus four 2 pounders at the deck
dge aft and amidships and four 20 millimeter antiaircraft guns
ounted at the deck edge forward. Anticipating the antisubmarine
le, which was sure to come, four depth charge racks were located
n the fantail.

Two more arresting cables were installed a few months after
ompletion. The new conversion was aptly renamed *HMS Audac-
y* and entered service in convoy protection duty along the west
oast of Africa to Liverpool and other British ports.

udacity Critics

o pleased with the *Audacity* concept was Air Marshal Sir Philip
oubert de la Ferte, Commanding Officer of RAF Coastal Com-
hand, that on September 29, 1941, in a letter to Vice-Admiral H.R.
Moore, he stated in part: "The convoys . . . should be accompanied
y the . . . *Audacity* class aircraft carrier." Air Marshal Joubert had
roperly recommended the escort carrier as the final solution to the
Kondors and U-boats.

Shortsighted critics of *Audacity* called her a Woolworth Car-
ier, but Sir Winston Churchill agreed with Joubert that *Audacity*
vas the model upon which many escort carriers should be based
or use in convoys.

When the Royal Navy embarked on the escort carrier program
he U.S. was requested to supply six more conversions under the
rovisions of the Lend-Lease Act.

IMS Audacity Operations

t was about this time that the Royal Navy was again spreading its
ir and surface forces dangerously thin by providing protection for
he questionable practice of sending supplies to the Soviet Union.
This diversion of fighting men, ships and planes northward left the
Bay of Biscay without sufficient air and sea escorts for the convoys
ailing to Liverpool, England from Capetown, Union of South Af-

rica, and from the African west coast ports. Gibraltar was able to
give only limited assistance using shore-based aircraft. When the
convoy sailed beyond the range of these planes an escort carrier
such as *HMS Audacity* can provide protection with its six Grumman
Martlets by intercepting the Focke-Wulf Kondor reconnaissance-
bombers.

Walmar Incident

On September 19, 1941 *HMS Audacity* pilots found a surfaced German submarine and strafed it until the U-boat submerged to escape
the attack. During the next night a submarine Wolf Pack sank several ships of the convoy, but the survivors were taken aboard the
rescue ship, *Walmar Castle*. On the morning of September 21 a
Kondor bombed the *Walmar Castle*, setting it ablaze. Sub-Lieuten-
ants G.R.P. Fletcher and N.H. Patterson took off in their Martlets
and intercepted the raider. After each pilot fired about three dozen
rounds the Kondor's tail surfaces broke off and the four-engined
Focke-Wulf 200 tumbled into the sea. This was the first Kondor to
be shot down by U.S.-built carrier aircraft and the first escort carrier victory.

Kondors Not Sitting Ducks

An incident in November proved that the Fw-200C Kondor was
not helpless and easy prey for fighter planes. Upon sighting a Kondor
the squadron leader, Lieutenant Commander J.M. Wintour led another Martlet to intercept the intruder. Wintour damaged the Focke-
Wulf; however, the Kondor gunners sent several shells crashing
through his companion's cockpit, killing the pilot, Sub-Lieutenant
D.A. Hutchinson. Then the Kondor burst into flames and crashed
into the waters of the Atlantic; apparently Wintour's victory.

On that very same November afternoon two Kondors approached the convoy; however, only one serviceable Martlet was
available and had taken off. Sub-Lieutenant E.M. Brown knew of
another Martlet on board with a badly bent propeller and was so
eager to intercept the Focke-Wulf that he begged the Commanding
Officer for permission to fly the damaged plane. Brown's takeoff
was uneventful and when the pilot reached altitude he made several firing passes at one of the Kondors and followed it into a cloud
bank. Brown circled the clouds and met the Focke-Wulf head-on as
it emerged from its cover. A short burst sent the German plane into
a spin from 10,000 feet, losing a wing before it hit the water. The
second Kondor escaped without inflicting any damage to the convoy. The escort carrier was working!

Audacity Sinks

On December 20, 1941 *Audacity*'s Grummans had flown a total of
30 hours and the last two made their landings after dark. Unknown
to the officers and crew, Lieutenant Commandant Bigalk was stalking *HMS Audacity* for the proper moment to fire the torpedoes of
his U-751. When *Audacity* and the convoy were off the Portuguese
coast the first torpedo hit on the port side amidships. The carrier
settled by the stern but the commanding officer, Commander D.M.
Mackendrick, knew he could save the ship and refused to abandon
her. About 20 minutes later a second torpedo exploded on the port
bow, followed by three more five minutes later. *Audacity*'s stern
shot up into the air as the bow structure collapsed and the planes

tumbled off the deck, destroying lifeboats on the way. Casualties were heavy as the first escort carrier sank beneath the waves, also taking with it the commanding officer and two of the Martlet pilots.

Audacity Score

Although short-lived, *HMS Audacity* proved her worth by contributing to the sinking of three U-boats and the scuttling of a fourth. Her Martlets had shot down five Focke-Wulf Kondors and damaged three more. Many more escort carriers were to follow now that it had been proven that fighter planes could successfully operate from the small carriers.

Atlantic Convoys - 1941

Despite the fact that the number of U-boats in operation in Atlantic waters quadrupled during 1941, and were supplemented by the long-range Focke-Wulf Kondors, the number of German submarines sunk during the year increased from zero in January and February to 10 in December. The number of convoy vessels sunk during the first six months of 1941 was 263, which totalled 1,451,175 tons. During the remainder of the year 169 convoy ships were sunk, totalling 719,900 tons; virtually one half the tonnage of the first half total. Much of the credit for this Allied success in fighting the German submarine and Kondor anti-convoy efforts belongs to shipborne aircraft; Warbirds of the Sea which were flown from Catapult Merchant Ships (CAM) and the new escort aircraft carrier *HMS Audacity*.

The CAM ship Hawker Hurricane fighter's rate of attrition was, of course, one Kondor for one Hurricane because it was understood that every time a CAM fighter was launched it must be considered lost. It must be appreciated that the action of the fighter by destroying the Kondor and/or spotting and reporting a nearby U-boat was saving many thousands of tons of important shipping and many lives.

Mediterranean Convoys - 1941

Greece and Yugoslavia had been lost to German forces in 1941, while the island of Crete had been more of a liability than an asset and fell under Axis control. The Royal Navy, British and Commonwealth Armies, plus the RAF and FAA were forced to retire to North Africa. There were only two paths by which war materiel could reach Egypt, the main base for all North African operations, and they were via the Mediterranean through the Straits of Gibraltar or around the Cape of Good Hope and the Red Sea. The latter route was threatened by German and Italian submarines; however, the Mediterranean route was menaced by the very efficient Luftwaffe which had supplemented and often supplanted the submarine danger. By 1941 the Italian surface fleet had ceased to be a menace and became impotent without aircraft carriers; however, under the protection of the land-based Luftwaffe, Italian merchant vessels were able to make the run to the German and Italian forces in North Africa. It was because of this that the importance of the island of Malta was most clearly defined; shining like a jewel in the scheme of the British overall defense.

American Escort Carriers

Simultaneously with the conversion of *HMS Audacity* the U.S. was engaged in its own program in the development of escort or auxiliary aircraft carriers. Apparently, President Roosevelt had ordered the conversion of merchant vessels into auxiliary aircraft carriers in Autumn of 1940. The President insisted that he would not tolerate any construction time longer than 90 days.

U.S. Navy First Escort Carriers

Posthaste, the Navy obtained two diesel-powered C3 cargo ships from Moore-McCormack Lines via the U.S. Maritime Commission; Mormacland and Mormacmail. Both ships became available in early 1940 and Mormacmail entered Newport News Shipbuilding and Drydock Company on March 18 to begin conversion. Surprisingly, because of Roosevelt's interest, the conversion was given a priority equal to the fleet carrier *Hornet*, also under construction at Newport News. The conversion to carrier was accomplished in only 77 days, and upon commissioning on June 2, 1941 the ship was renamed *USS Long Island*.

Mormacland/Archer Conversion

Mormacland entered the same shipyard and conversion was completed in early November 1941, with commissioning later in the

USS Long Island was America's first escort carrier; having been converted from a C-3 cargo ship by Newport News Shipbuilding. The ship engaged in amphibious landing maneuvers that proved the need for aerial cover. (Official U.S. Navy Photograph, News Photo Division)

...onth. This conversion was renamed *HMS Archer* and became the ...rst of the six escort carriers requested by the Royal Navy. The ...dditional five Sun Shipbuilding Corp.-built C3 type carrier con-...ersions scheduled to be delivered to the Royal Navy by the U.S. ...ecame *HMS Avenger, Biter, Tracker, Dasher,* and *Charger.* All ...vere transferred except for Charger, which was retained by the U.S. ...lavy for deck landing training of Royal Navy Fleet Air Arm air-...rews. *USS Charger* designation eventually became CVE-30.

...SS Long Island **Data**

...SS Long Island was fitted with a 78 x 360 feet wooden planked ...light Deck mounted on a lattice of steel girders not unlike that ...vhich had been installed on *Langley.* Not as austere as *Audacity,* ...ong Island was equipped with a 120 feet long Hangar aft and one ...enterline elevator. By mid-August 1941 the Flight Deck had been ...engthened to 420 feet and a hydraulically operated catapult was ...dded to the Flight Deck, running diagonally across the Deck 30 ...egrees from starboard to port. The normal aircraft complement ...onsisted of a mixed bag of Brewster F2A-3 fighters and Curtiss ...OC-3 scout planes of VS-201; totalling 16 aircraft.

Four 7-cylinder Sulzer diesel engines were geared to a single ...ropeller shaft developing 8,500 horsepower, which drove the ...4,250 tons (deep load) displacement ship to a maximum speed of ...6 knots. Hull length at the waterline was 465 feet and hull beam ...9 feet-6 inches, while draft was 25 feet-6 inches.

Armament was one 4 inch gun, two 3 inch guns and four 0.5 ...nch caliber machine guns. This was supplemented with five 20 ...nillimeter guns. Complement was almost 1,000 officers and crew.

...esignation Changes

...nitially, *Long Island* was designated APV-1 (transport and aircraft ...erry); however, this was soon changed to AVG-1 (aircraft tender, ...general purposes. She was redesignated in 1942 to ACV-1 (auxil-...ary aircraft carrier) and in July 1943 *USS Long Island* became CVE-... (aircraft carrier,escort).

...scort Carrier **Amphibious Operations**

...America's first escort carrier spent much of her time operating ex-...erimentally along the U.S. East Coast as part of Carrier Division 3 ...of the U.S. Atlantic Fleet. In August 1941 *Long Island* was en-...gaged in maneuvers which foretold one of the most important ac-...ivities in which escort carriers became engaged during World War ...I; an activity in which they were not originally intended to partici-...bate. The maneuvers in which *Long Island* became involved con-...isted of air support for troop landings on an enemy shore. VS-201 ...Curtiss Seagulls handled the gunfire spotting for the preliminary ...oombardment, while Brewster Buffaloes provided a combat air ...batrol (CAP) over the transports as they unloaded equipment and ...roops on the beach. Admiral Ernest J. King, Commander, Atlantic ...Fleet, was very enthusiastic about the idea and included escort car-...iers in the Atlantic Fleet operations manual. The remarkable per-...formance of purpose-built escort carriers during the Leyte Gulf land-...ngs in 1944 will be described in Chapter V.

Auxiliary aircraft carriers such as *HMS Audacity* and *USS Long ...sland* were not included in the Washington Treaty tonnage agree-...nent and, therefore, unlimited numbers could be built.

U.S. Navy/Royal Navy Ballasting

HMS Archer conversion was similar but not identical to *USS Long Island* despite the fact that they were initially sister ships. The U.S. Navy practice of replacing consumed fuel with seawater was not acceptable to the Royal Navy. The British insisted that permanent ballast be carried in separate tanks to maintain stability in the event of partially empty tankage. This added ballast increased the stan-dard displacement to 10,220 tons, compared to *Long Island's* 7,886 tons.

Catapult Mishaps

Both ships had catapult mishaps during initial launching operations. *USS Long Island* experienced a catapult malfunction while launch-ing an F2A-2 Buffalo. The little fighter literally dribbled off the Flight Deck and headed for the sea but the pilot managed to keep the Buffalo airborne and came so close to the water that the turbu-lence from his propeller made a large wake on the water's surface. *HMS Archer* had the same problem while launching a Grumman Martlet; however, the pilot could not pull up in time and crashed into the sea.

Mid-Ocean Gap

Until the entry of escort carriers into service for Anti-Submarine Warfare (ASW), air patrols had been undertaken by shore-based aircraft; however, even the longest range aircraft could not provide complete cover across the Atlantic Ocean. This resulted in a mid-ocean gap devoid of air cover which the U-boats were quick to exploit. Escort carriers eventually closed this gap.

HMS ARK ROYAL SINKS

Meanwhile, back in the Mediterranean theatre, *HMS Ark Royal* was operating with FORCE H, escorting convoys bound for Malta and North Africa. This continued throughout the summer and autumn of 1941. In addition, *Ark Royal* flew off reinforcement aircraft for Malta in June, September and November. While returning from Malta and approaching Gibraltar on November 13, 1941 *HMS Ark Royal* had flown off a dozen aircraft for combat air patrol (CAP) while 14 Swordfish waited to land.

HMS Ark Royal Torpedoed

As *Ark Royal* steamed westward to Gibraltar with the carrier *Argus*, battleship *Malaya*, and destroyers *Laforey, Legion* and five others, Lieutenant Guggenberger was stalking FORCE H with his U-boat U-81. When *Ark Royal* was about 25 miles from Gibraltar the *Kapitän* fired a salvo of torpedoes into the starboard side of *Ark Royal* at 3:41 P.M. All torpedoes struck the carrier amidships and she began to list immediately.

The list was caused by the centerline armored longitudinal bulkheads separating the engine and boiler rooms. This protective barrier prevented the incoming water from flooding the port and starboard sides of the hull equally, whereupon only the starboard side had flooded, creating an assymetrical weight on the hull; which caused a list to starboard.

Ark Royal List Increases

The immediate list was 10 degrees and within three minutes it had

HMS Ark Royal is shown listing to starboard after receiving a salvo of torpedoes from the German submarine U-81 in the Mediterranean on November 13, 1941. The list continued until the beloved carrier capsized and sank 14 hours later. (British Information Service)

increased to 12 degrees. Power and communications had been disrupted and a chain of seamen was formed to establish communications between the Bridge and Engine Rooms. Several aircraft had been blown overboard by the blast and the remaining aircraft waiting to land were waved off and sent to Gibraltar for landing. *Ark Royal* assumed a list of 18 degrees by 4:00 PM and the list was increasing every minute. Captain Maund ordered the port side machinery spaces to be flooded in an attempt to correct the list but this did not fully correct the condition. He then ordered all personnel to abandon ship, except for damage control parties. The destroyer *HMS Legion* was ordered to take on the *Ark Royal* crew and it was brought alongside *Ark Royal* by its captain, Commander R.S. Jessel, carefully avoiding the carrier's propeller and radio antennae.

Fourteen Hours of Agony

The destroyer *Laforey* also pulled alongside *Ark Royal* and provided water and electric power, which enabled the carrier to raise steam. At a time when expectations were at their peak fire engulfed the port boiler room at 2:15 AM, November 14, 1941 and destroyed all hope of making it to port under her own power. The list had increased to 20 degrees overnight and by 4:00 o'clock in the morning of November 14 the list was 27 degrees. The few men left were ordered to abandon ship and Captain Maund was the last to leave the ship at 4:30 as *Ark Royal*'s list went to 35 degrees. At 6:13 the beloved carrier rolled over, remained capsized for a few minutes, and then plunged beneath surface. It had taken 14 hours for *Ark Royal* to sink after the torpedo strike. Only one member of the crew was killed.

MORE JAPANESE CARRIERS

While Britain was struggling against German surface raiders and submarines in the Atlantic Ocean and North Sea and against the

Italian Navy in the Mediterranean, Japan resolutely increased he[r] carrier forces.

Two Japanese Aircraft Carrier Conversions

Two submarine tenders, *Tsurugisaki* and *Takasaki*, had been se[-] lected for conversion to aircraft carriers. The first to be complete[d] was *Takasaki*, commissioned as *Zuiho* on December 27, 194[0]. *Tsurugisaki* followed and was commissioned on January 26, 194[ ] as *Shoho*.

Shoho and *Zuiho* Data

The 9,500 ton auxiliaries had the original diesel engine propulsio[n] machinery replaced with geared steam turbine destroyer machin[-] ery in order to insure a good speed despite the increase in displace[-] ment to 14,200 tons at full load due to the conversion. A singl[e] hangar about 350 feet long with two centerline elevators was in[-] stalled which was topped by a 590.5 x 75.5 feet Flight Deck. Hu[ll] length at the waterline was 661 feet with a beam of 59.75 feet. Th[e] mean draft was 21 feet-7 inches. The 52,000 shaft horsepowe[r] powerplant was shared by two propeller shafts and drove the carri[-] ers to a maximum speed of 28 knots. Combat range was 7,800 mile[s] at 18 knots. The aircraft complement was an assortment of div[e] bombers, torpedo bombers and fighters totalling 30 aircraft. De[-] fensive armament consisted of eight 5 inch guns and eight 25 mil[-] limeter antiaircraft guns. *Zuiho* received an additional installatio[n] of six triple-mounted 25 millimeter guns, plus six 8-barrelled rock[et] launchers to bolster the air defenses. Each carrier had a crew an[d] officer complement of 785. The *Shoho* and *Zuiho* engaged the U.S[.] Navy in some of the important Pacific naval air battles to be de[-] scribed in later chapters.

New Japanese Fleet Carriers

The two most successful Imperial Japanese Navy aircraft carrie[rs]

Japanese aircraft carriers Shoho and Zuiho had been converted from submarine tenders Tsurugusaki and Takasaki. Conversion was very common practice in the Imperial Japanese Navy throughout the war because of the shortage of materials and manpower. Shoho is shown here. (U.S. National Archives)

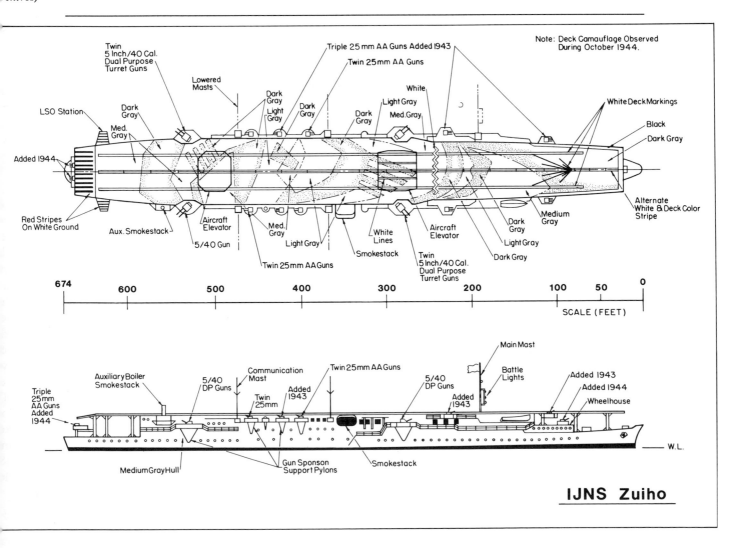

IJNS Zuiho

Launched in 1939, the most successful Japanese aircraft carriers Shokaku and Zuikaku were completed just in time to get ready for the Pearl Harbor attack. Due to a shortage of steel the Flight Deck was made from wood and no armor was fitted to the closed Hangar. Zuikaku is shown here. (U.S. Naval Historical Center, Courtesy Mr. Kazutoshi Hando, Tokyo)

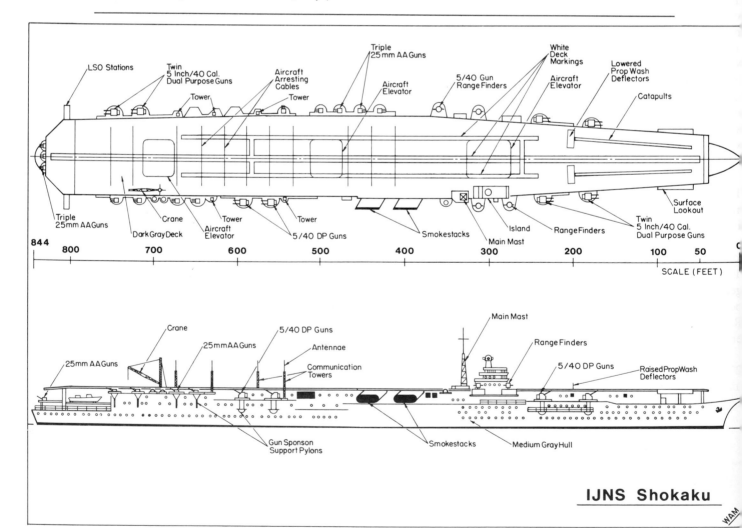

IJNS Shokaku

ere commissioned in 1941; *Shokaku* on August 8 and *Zuikaku* on eptember 25. Although not as large as the *Lexington* class, the hokaku class are considered as the direct equivalents of these U.S. arriers because of their high speed, large aircraft complement, and rmored cruiser size hull. However, unlike the *Lexington* class carers these Japanese carriers were purpose-designed, built from the eel up as carriers and not conversions as many of the world's carers had been at the time the ships were being designed.

hokaku and Zuikaku

esigned in 1936 by the Yokosuka Imperial Naval Shipyard, hokaku was built in this yard, while the *Zuikaku* was constructed a the Kawasaki shipyards. The former ship's keel was laid on December 12, 1937 and *Zuikaku*'s keel was in place by May 25, 1938. he carriers were launched on June 1, 1939 and November 27, 1939, espectively, and commissioned on August 8, 1941 and September 5, 1941, respectively.

Design Data

he hull design followed that of a heavy cruiser to permit the intallation of a 6.5 inch band of belt armor in way of the magazines nd 5 inches of armor over the magazines, plus an 8.3 inch belt in vay of the machinery spaces, including 3.9 inches deck over the nachinery spaces. A bulbous bow was worked into the clipperhaped stem below the waterline. Following the lead by the Royal Navy, *Shokaku* and *Zuikaku* used totally enclosed Hangars; howver, unlike the Royal Navy, the Hangars were unarmored. Apparntly due to the steel shortage, a wooden Flight Deck was installed ver the Hangars, except in way of the two forward catapults, as vell as over the boiler uptakes, which were steel. Three elevators vere installed in the 95 x 787 feet Flight Deck. Transverse arrestng cables were installed forward and aft on the Flight Deck.

Armament consisted of eight twin 5 inch/40 caliber guns along he sides of the Flight Deck, plus one dozen 25 millimeter triplemounted antiaircraft gun installations (36 guns total) also located along the Flight Deck edge.

The 25,675 tons deep load displacement ships were 820 feet ong at the waterline with a maximum hull beam of 85 feet. Mean draft was 29 feet. Eight boilers generated steam for four turbines geared to four propeller shafts. The total of 160,000 shaft horsepower propelled the ships to a maximum speed of 34.25 knots. Range was 10,000 miles at 18 knots. Complement was 1,660 officers and crew.

The 84 plane complement consisted of 27 Val dive bombers, 27 Kate torpedo bombers and 18 Zero Sen fighters. A dozen more aircraft were stowed in reserve.

Shokaku and *Zuikaku* experienced considerable action from Pearl Harbor into 1944, which will be described in the following chapters.

Three Japanese Aircraft Carrier Conversions

Adhering to its practice of preserving all available resources, the Imperial Japanese Navy constructed three more aircraft carriers by using existing hulls. The converted ships were the 17,100 tons, 21 knot passenger liners; *Kasuga Maru, Yawata Maru* and *Nitta Maru*. *Kasuga Maru* was converted at Sasebo Navy Yard and renamed *Taiyo*; *Yawata Maru* and *Nitta Maru* were converted at Kure Navy Yard and renamed *Unyo* and *Chuyo*, respectively.

Taiyo Class Data

As with the U.S. and British escort carrier conversions modifications were kept to a minimum. The boiler uptakes were led out the starboard side just under the Flight Deck and a 300 feet long Hangar was installed with elevators at the extreme forward and aft ends. No catapult was fitted on the 75 x 492 feet Flight Deck, nor were arresting cables installed.

The original four boilers and two turbines geared to two propeller shafts was retained producing 25,200 shaft horsepower. Despite a slight increase in tonnage the ships kept the 21 knot speed. Range was 6,500 miles at 18 knots. Up to 27 aircraft could operate from each ship. Conversions were completed in six months. *Taiyo* was commissioned on September 15, 1941; *Unyo* on May 31, 1942; and *Chuyo* on November 25, 1942.

FAST JAPANESE DIVE BOMBER

During November of 1940 an unusual Japanese dive bomber had made its first flight; the Yokosuka D4Y Suisei (Comet).

The Imperial Japanese Navy specifications of 1937 required a top speed of at least 320 miles per hour which was equal to that of the Zero fighter of that year. This high speed required a small airframe and it was decided to break Japanese Navy tradition by installing a liquid-cooled in-line engine. After its first flight the design was accepted and the plane entered production in 1941. Aichi Kokuki K.K. was selected to manufacture the plane; however, because the design had been developed by the Yokosuka Naval Air Arsenal, it retained the Yokosuka name and designation.

D4Y2 Data

The 1,200 horsepower Aichi Atsuta 21 twelve-cylinder inverted Vee engine sped the plane to a maximum speed of 360 miles per hour at 17,225 feet, 40 miles per hour faster than the required speed. The

IJNS Taiyo was converted from the passenger liner Kasuga Maru. Sister conversions were IJNS Unyo and Chuyo. No catapults or arresting cables were installed on the 75 x 492 feet Flight Deck. (U.S. National Archives)

The Yokosuka Naval Air Arsenal had designed the Yokosuka D4Y Suisei dive bomber and Aichi Kokuki K.K. was awarded the construction contract. Code-named Judy by the Allies, the craft was relegated to high speed reconnaissance due to its small bomb capacity. (National Air and Space Museum)

10,267 pound gross weight plane had a combat range of 750 miles and a service ceiling of 30,170 feet. Wingspan was 37 feet-8 inches; length 33 feet-6 inches and height of 10 feet-9 inches.

D4Y3 Data

Due to production problems with the liquid-cooled engine, later models were fitted with the 14 cylinder Kinsei 62 1,560 horsepower air-cooled radial engine which made it resemble the Zero to the point where many American pilots mistakenly identified the two-seater D4Y3 as the famous Japanese fighter. Speed of the D4Y3 dropped to 350 miles per hour but range increased to 944 miles.

Relegated to Reconnaissance

At about the same weight as the Douglas Dauntless, the D4Y Suisei had considerably less wing area in order to attain the high speed and; therefore, was able to carry only one 550 pound bomb in the fuselage, plus one 66 pound bomb under each wing. In view of this, plus certain structural weaknesses, caused the Suisei to be used more for high-speed reconnaissance duties than for dive bombing.

Judy Production

A total of 2,320 Suisei aircraft was built; 1,820 by Aichi and 500 by the Hiro Naval Air Arsenal. The Allied code name for the Yokosuka Suisei was Judy.

U.S. NAVY TORPEDO AND DIVE BOMBERS

The majority of naval aircraft developed before and after World War II carried bombs and torpedoes externally under the fuselage and/or the wings. In the years immediately preceding World War II the U.S. Navy requested designs in which the disposable armament was stowed internally. Three respondents are worthy of mention.

Grumman TBF Avenger

The second most used aircraft on American escort carriers after the Grumman Wildcat (or Martlet) was the Grumman Avenger torpedo-bomber. Initially, escort carriers were equipped only with fighter planes to combat the Focke-Wulf Fw-200 Kondors and to locate U-boats for the convoy ASW ships. Later it was decided that the escort carriers should be fitted with planes that could attack submarines and the bomb or mine-carrying Avengers were selected.

The Grumman TBF Avenger became the standard torpedo-bomber of the U.S. Navy during World War II and was the first plane of this type designed by Grumman. Photo taken in late 1942. (Grumman Corporation, Courtesy Grant Daily)

U.S. Navy Standard; Grumman Avenger

The Grumman TBF Avenger became the U.S. Navy's standard torpedo-bomber of World War II and remained in operation for years. Designed to replace the aging Douglas Devastator, the U.S. Navy ordered two prototype Avengers on April 8, 1940. Eight months later Grumman received a production contract for 286 TBF-1's and deliveries to the U.S. Navy began on January 30, 1942.

Avenger Data

The TBF-1 had a wingspan of 54 feet-2 inches, length 40 feet and height of 16 feet-5 inches. The 15,905 pound plane was powered with a 1,700 horsepower Wright R-2600-8 radial, air-cooled engine which drove the craft to a maximum speed of 271 miles per hour at 12,000 feet altitude. Service ceiling was 22,400 feet and combat range was 1,215 miles. The fuselage extended below the wing to provide an enclosure for the torpedo. Alternatively, a 2,000

The three-seat Avenger was fitted with a .50 caliber machine gun-fitted power turret and a dorsal swivel-mounted .30 inch caliber machine gun. One fixed .50 inch caliber machine gun was buried in the starboard side of the cowling. All three locations are readily apparent in this photo, taken in early 1942. (Grumman Corporation, Courtesy Grant Daily)

GRUMMAN TBF-1 AVENGER

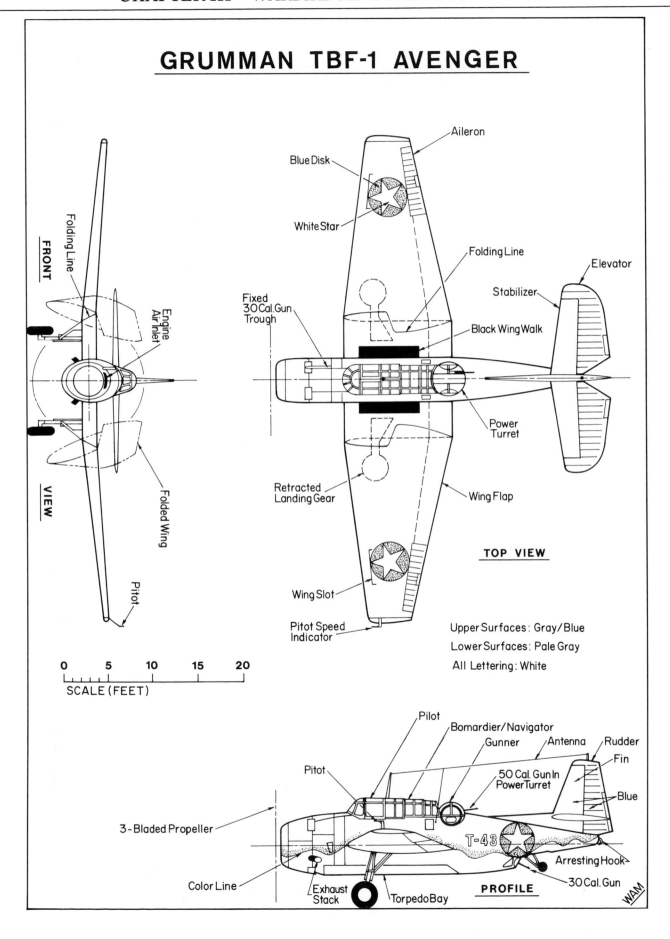

FRONT

Folding Line

Engine Air Inlet

Folded Wing

Pitot

VIEW

Blue Disk

White Star

Aileron

Folding Line

Stabilizer

Elevator

Fixed 30 Cal. Gun Trough

Black Wing Walk

Power Turret

Retracted Landing Gear

Wing Flap

Wing Slot

Pitot Speed Indicator

TOP VIEW

Upper Surfaces : Gray/Blue
Lower Surfaces : Pale Gray
All Lettering : White

```
0      5      10     15     20
|__|__|__|__|__|__|__|__|__|__|
SCALE (FEET)
```

Pilot

Bomardier/Navigator

Gunner

Antenna

Rudder

Fin

50 Cal. Gun In Power Turret

Blue

Pitot

3-Bladed Propeller

T-43

Arresting Hook

Color Line

Exhaust Stack

Torpedo Bay

30 Cal. Gun

PROFILE

WAM

The Brewster SB2A-1 Buccaneer/Bermuda carried an internal bomb load of 1,000 pounds. The U.S. Navy Buccaneer was fitted with a power turret but the British Bermuda was not. The plane saw limited service with the U.S. Navy. (U.S. National Archives)

The Vought TBU-1 Sea Wolf torpedo-bomber could attain 311 miles per hour with an internally mounted torpedo. The U.S. Navy issued a purchase order for 1,100 Sea Wolves which was reduced to 180 aircraft in 1944-45. Some Sea Wolves were fitted with a radome on the starboard wing. (Vought Aircraft Company)

pound bomb could be carried instead of the Tin Fish. An electric-powered rotating gun turret was fitted just aft of the cockpit enclosure. This was the favored arrangement for rear gunners in the late 1930s and early 1940s because it was assumed that the higher aircraft speeds would make it impossible for the gunner to man his gun in the slipstream. The turret was fitted with a single .50 inch caliber machine gun. A forward-firing .30 inch caliber machine gun was located in the engine cowling. A movable gun of the same caliber was located below the fuselage just aft of the torpedo/bomb bay, firing down and aft, and operated by the bombardier, who had to crawl to the fuselage bottom and lie prone to fire the gun. The bombardier normally sat between the pilot and the rear gunner.

General Motors Avengers

As with the Grumman Martlet/Wildcat, due to the fact that Grumman was occupied with new designs, the General Motors automobile plant in Trenton, N.J. was converted to produce Avengers. The plant became part of General Motors' Eastern Aircraft Division and mass-produced about 7,500 of the torpedo-bombers. Grumman built about 2,300 Avengers of all models. General Motors Avengers were designated TBM.

Avenger Variants

Later Avengers had two forward-firing .50 inch caliber guns in the wings while others were fitted with rockets. The Grumman Avenger TBM-3W was fitted with a huge radar pod under the belly, while others were used to hunt and kill submarines.

Brewster SB2A-1 Buccaneer (Bermuda)

While the Brewster SBA-1 was going into production at the Naval Aircraft Factory and Brewster was refining its Buffalo, the little company was also developing a larger version of the SBA-1. The U.S. Navy placed an order for this dive bomber in April 1939 and the XSB2A-1 was first flown on June 17, 1941. As with the Avenger the new Brewster was equipped with an electric power turret. It was a fairly clean design with internal stowage for a 1,000 pound bomb. The RAF placed an order for 450 and the Netherlands East Indies ordered 160. The U.S. Navy approved the RAF request which aircraft were delivered without the power turret; however, the Navy intercepted the East Indies shipment for use by U.S. forces. The British called the craft Bermuda, while the U.S. Navy gave it the name Buccaneer. Very few of the (140) SB2A-1's reached opera-

tional squadrons due to the failure of the company to meet schedules. The 14,290 pound craft attained 274 miles per hour.

Vought TBU/TBY Sea Wolf

In April 1940 the U.S. Navy issued a contract to Chance Vought for a torpedo-bomber monoplane design to be designated XTBU-1. The prototype first flew on December 22, 1941 and easily met or exceeded the specified requirements. The craft resembled a lean version of the Avenger with a dorsal turret and ventral gun position. The torpedo was internally stowed and .50 inch machine guns were installed, one each in the engine cowl and the power turret. A .30 inch caliber machine gun was provided for the ventral placement.

The 2,000 horsepower Pratt & Whitney R-2800-2 radial air-cooled engine enabled the 18,488 pound plane to reach a top speed of 311 miles per hour at 13,000 feet. Service ceiling was 27,200 feet, while range was 1,505. Wingspan was 56 feet-11 inches; length 39 feet-2 1/2 inches; height 15 feet-6 inches. The U.S. Navy decided to order 1,100 of the design, called Sea Wolf; however, Chance Vought had become fully committed to the Corsair F4U fighter therefore, the Navy made arrangements with Convair to produce the Sea Wolf at the new Convair factory in Allentown, Pennsylvania. This resulted in a change to the Sea Wolf designation from TBU (torpedo-bomber Vought) to TBY (torpedo-bomber Convair).

Neither the Buccaneer nor the Sea Wolf attained the fame enjoyed by many other airplanes of World War II.

THE BENT-WING BIRD ARRIVES

One of the planes of this period, which became a household word is the famous Vought Corsair fighter. This unusual plane is one of the best known naval fighters of World War II. After many attempts Vought finally developed a big-winning single-seat fighter.

The Corsair was created as the result of a U.S. Navy design competition issued on February 1, 1938 for a high performance naval fighter. Vought-Sikorsky responded two months later with a proposal to construct the XF4U-1. The design staff, headed by Chief Engineer Rex B. Beisel, came up with a most ingenious and efficient design.

Biggest Engine

At that time Vought was joined with Sikorsky helicopters, Pratt & Whitney engines and Hamilton-Standard propellers to form United Aircraft Corporation in Hartford, Connecticut. Pratt & Whitney had

The Vought F4U Corsair was one of the most unusual and best remembered Allied naval fighters of World War II. This is the prototype XF4U-1 which mounted two guns in the cowl and two in the wing. Landing gear twists 90 degrees as it retracts back into the wing. (Ling Temco Vought, Courtesy Arthur L. Schoeni)

just developed its 18-cylinder XR-2800-4 twin-row, air-cooled, radial, Twin-Wasp engine capable of producing 1,850 horsepower and the XF4U-1 was designed to use this huge powerplant. Power was increased to 2,000 horsepower for later variants of the Corsair.

Largest Propeller

In order to absorb the tremendous power of this engine it became necessary to design the largest propeller ever built for a U.S. Navy fighter plane until that time; a three-bladed Hamilton-Standard with a diameter of 13 feet 4 inches. To provide the needed clearance for this enormous propeller without resorting to an inordinately long and spindly landing gear strut, designer Rex Beisel hit upon the unique configuration, which was to stamp the appearance of the F4U as one of the most recognizable airplanes in the world; the inverted gull wing. This unusual design gave the plane its nickname, "bent-wing bird."

The XF4U-1 of 1941 had a forward located cockpit, and the most powerful engine and largest propeller installed on any naval fighter until that time. (U.S. National Archives, Courtesy Arthur L. Schoeni)

Inverted Gull Wing Advantages

What may have seemed as a big design concession actually had many other good features. Aerodynamically, a right angle juncture between the wings and fuselage skin results in the least possible drag and dispenses with the necessity of large wing fillets.

In addition, a much shorter and sturdier landing gear leg was possible which enabled it to fit into the wing when retracted straight back. Pilot visibility was also improved by the lowered wing. The wing outer panels folded upwards and met the maximum Hangar Deck height restrictions only because the hinge point was at the low point of the inverted gull wing. The wing panels folded hydraulically and were controlled from the cockpit.

On June 11, 1938 Vought-Sikorsky was awarded a contract for the first prototype Corsair, the XF4U-1. Work began at once, however, the Navy's Bureau of Aeronautics could not inspect the plane until February 8, 1940. On March 29 the XF4U-1 flew for the first time with Vought's Chief Pilot, Lyman Bullard, at the controls.

Corsair Exceeds 400 Miles Per Hour

A few days later Rear Admiral John Towers, the naval aviation pioneer and now Chief of the Navy's Bureau of Aeronautics, was on hand to witness the Corsair prototype race through a speed course at 405 miles per hour! In 1940 400 miles per hour was an unimagined figure, except for specially designed record breakers. Admiral Towers was very impressed and, after some modifications, a production contract for 584 Corsairs was awarded to Vought-Sikorsky on June 30, 1941.

Corsair Associate Contractors

The U.S. Navy was so impressed with the Corsair that it contracted with Brewster during November 1941 to also undertake production of the Corsair as the F3A-1. In December, 1941 Goodyear Aircraft was also named an associate contractor to produce this remarkable fighter as the FG-1.

Corsair Modifications

Some of the modifications made to the Corsair before it went into production included the relocation of the nose guns to the wing and the addition of two more guns in the wing for a total of six .50 in. caliber wing guns. This necessitated the conversion of the wing fuel tanks to a single large self-sealing fuel bag in an enclosure just forward of the cockpit which moved three feet aft to accommodate the tank. In addition, 170 pounds of armor was added to protect the pilot and oil tank; a bullet-proof windshield was added and the cockpit canopy was made jettisonable. Very important was the large number of forgings and castings used to speed up production; the tailwheel forging was the largest forging in use on any fighter at that time. The Corsair was one of the first airplanes to use spot welding instead of rivets.

Carrier Operation Delayed

It will be seen later that, despite its superlative performance, the Corsair had to overcome a bad reputation before it was permitted to operate from U.S. Navy aircraft carriers.

AMERICA/AXIS COLLISION COURSE

Relations between the U.S. and Japan had deteriorated through the 1920s and 1930s, which eventually led to a confrontation on December 7, 1941. Some of the steps that led to the U.S. entry in World War I follow.

Ambassador Nomura and the Japanese Navy

In the late 1930s Japanese Admiral Kichisaburo Nomura was not alone in firmly believing that the Imperial Japanese Navy was the only stabilizing force in Asia and, as long as it existed, no western nation would attack or economically exploit Japan or any other Asiatic country. He was against involvement in a European war and, as an attendee at the Paris Peace Conference at the end of World War I, he observed that only those powers which had powerful forces left after the fighting had the right to make proposals even though some of them had not made big sacrifices during the war; obviously referring to the U.S. Nomura was appointed Japan's Foreign Minister in 1939 and as relations between the U.S. and Japan deteriorated he was appointed the Japanese Ambassador to the U.S. in November 1940.

U.S. Naval Aircraft Build-Up

The U.S. had been inching closer to war in 1940 when, on May 14, 1940, Congress approved a naval build-up which included 4,500 naval aircraft. This was raised on the very next day to 10,000 planes.

U.S. Two-Ocean Navy

On June 17, 1940 Admiral Harold Stark, USN Chief of Naval Operations, appeared before Congress for funds to build a two-ocean navy. Congress approved and President Roosevelt signed the new Naval Expansion Act into law on June 19, 1940. It was not the intention of this Act to split the existing navy into two parts; Atlantic and Pacific. The Act called for four billion 1940 dollars to more than double the existing 1,250,000 tons of major warships, plus the addition of 15,000 naval aircraft. This expenditure put the U.S. Navy and the U.S. shipbuilding industry in good shape by the end of 1941. The Navy had an ample supply of ships and planes and the aircraft and shipbuilding industries were getting warmed up and geared for mass production.

U.S. Oil Embargo on Japan

Taking advantage of France's defeat by Germany, the Japanese moved into French Indochina on June 24, 1940 with Vichy French approval. Angered by this event, President Roosevelt froze all Japanese assets in the U.S. and halted all sales of oil to Japan two days later. This reaction by the U.S. struck Japan in its economic weak spot; the need for imported oil.

The president's action confronted the Japanese government with one of two options: reach an accommodation with the U.S. or strike out for the much needed petroleum by taking the oil fields of the European colonies in Southeast Asia, such as the Dutch East Indies.

Export Control Act

On July 2, 1940, the U.S. Congress granted President Roosevelt the authority to control the export of any and all war materiel and related commodities; known as the Export Control Act. Three days later the President placed an embargo on Japan prohibiting the sale of iron, steel, coal, lumber, scrap steel and other commodities. Having interests in the Far East, it was no surprise when Britain joined the U.S.A. in this embargo.

U.S. Destroyers To Royal Navy

President Roosevelt and British Prime Minister Churchill concluded an agreement on September 2, 1940 whereby 50 U.S. Navy World War I destroyers, urgently needed by Britain to combat the German submarines in the Atlantic, would be transferred to the Royal Navy. In exchange for the destroyers the U.S. was given 99 year leases to British bases in Bermuda, the West Indies and New Foundland.

First U.S. Peacetime Draft

For the first time in American history a peacetime military draft was inaugurated by President Franklin Delano Roosevelt on September 16, 1940, called the Selective Training and Service Act. This was tantamount to mobilizing.

Japanese Treaty With Axis Nations

On September 27, 1940 the inevitable happened. Japan, feeling rebuffed and friendless, as well as suspicious of being threatened by the U.S.A. and Britain, concluded an alliance with Germany and Italy for mutual assistance, known as the Tripartite Pact.

U.S. Neutrality Act Scrapped

On March 11, 1941 the U.S. moved still closer to becoming involved in the war when the U.S. Congress virtually scrapped the Neutrality Act of 1939 and permitted the Allied countries to obtain war materials on credit or loan. This was called the Lend-Lease Act.

ABC-1 Staff Agreement War Plan

On March 27, 1941 a meeting was held in Washington, D.C. between naval and military representatives of the U.S. and Britain. An agreement was signed which established the basis for Anglo-American cooperation in the event the U.S. entered the war. The key provisions were that both countries would concentrate their war efforts to defeat Germany and that American and British Chiefs of Staff would work together as the combined Chiefs of Staff. Effective immediately was that the U.S. Atlantic Fleet will begin assisting the Royal Navy in Atlantic convoy escort duty as soon as it is able, despite the fact that the U.S. was not officially at war This would make the U.S.A. a co-belligerent.

U-Boat Sinks U.S. Cargo Ship

The American active participation in the war led to anti-U.S. submarine actions. A German U-boat torpedoed and sank an American cargo ship, Robin Moore, in the South Atlantic on May 21, 1941. This was the first U.S. merchantman to be lost in World War II. On May 27 President Franklin D. Roosevelt proclaimed a state of Unlimited National Emergency for the U.S.

Soviets Attacked

Germany attacked the Soviet Union on June 22, 1941 which seemed to accelerate U.S. preparations for war.

U.S. Sea Frontiers Established

On July 1, 1941, the American coastline was divided into six Sea

With war with Japan imminent, USS Lexington (CV-2) sailed into the Pacific on October 11, 1941 to deliver combat aircraft to U.S. bases. Brewster Buffalo fighters are at the bow, Douglas Dauntless dive bombers are adjacent to the smokestack followed by ten Douglas Devastators and more Dauntless dive bombers at the stern. (Official U.S. Navy Photograph, Naval Photographic Center)

Frontiers whose commanders were responsible for convoy escort, antisubmarine warfare, and all patrols in their designated zone. Two additional Sea Frontiers were created for Hawaii and the Philippine Islands. Six days later an agreement with Iceland provided for U.S. naval forces to assume responsibility for that island nations's defense. Marine forces were soon landed at Reykjavik; another step closer to active U.S. involvement in the European war.

U.S. Naval Reserve
The U.S. Naval Reserve was mobilized on July 12, 1941.

U-Boat Attacks U.S. Destroyer
The undeclared shooting war between Germany and the U.S. escalated on September 4, 1941 when the destroyer *USS Greer* (DD-145J was attacked south of Iceland with torpedoes from the Kriegsmarine U-boat U-652. The torpedoes missed, as did the depth charges dropped by *USS Greer*.

President Roosevelt Orders "Shoot On Sight"
Seven days later, blaming the *Greer* incident, President Roosevelt ordered all U.S. naval vessels to attack any ship that threatens American shipping or foreign shipping under U.S. protection or escort.

ABC-1 Staff Agreement Activated
On September 16, 1941 the provisions of the ABC-1 Staff Agreement were put in force and the U.S. Navy joined the Royal Canadian Navy in escorting North Atlantic convoys to and from a Mid-Atlantic Ocean rendezvous with the Royal Navy. Now the U.S. Navy was engaged in active participation in the war on the side of Britain and France.

U.S. Refuses Summit Conference With Japan
Diplomatically and militarily the U.S. and the Axis were drawing closer and closer to war. On October 2, 1941, after spending two months considering Japanese Prime Minister Fuminaro Konoye's request for a summit conference to avoid war, President Roosevelt flatly rejected the suggestion of a summit conference. Konoye was then replaced by General Hideki Tojo.

U.S. Destroyer Torpedoed
A U-boat torpedoed the U.S. destroyer *Kearny* DD-432, Lieutenant Commander A.L. Davis commanding, on October 19, 1941, while the destroyer was patrolling off the southern coast of Greenland. The ship did not sink; however, 11 crewmen were killed.

U-Boat Sinks U.S. Destroyer
It was on October 31, 1941 that the first U.S. Naval ship was sunk by the Axis Powers. U-562 torpedoed the destroyer *USS Reuben James* DD-245, Lieutenant Commander H.L. Edwards commanding, while the destroyer was escorting a convoy from Halifax, Nova Scotia to Britain. The sinking caused the loss of 115 lives.

U.S. Navy In Control of Coast Guard
The U.S. Coast Guard was placed under control of the U.S. Navy, on November 1, for the duration of the National Emergency.

U.S. Navy Captures German Freighter
Five days later the German blockade runner *Odenwald*, disguised as the American freighter *Willmoto*, was captured by the cruiser *USS Omaha* CL-4 and the destroyer *USS Somers* DD-381 in the central Atlantic.

U.S. Arms Merchant Ships
On November 17, 1941 the U.S. Congress authorized the arming of U.S. merchant ships. War between the U.S. and the Axis powers appeared imminent.

Admiral Yamamoto Opposes War
Japanese Admirals Masamitsu Yonai and Isoroku Yamamoto, Minister and Vice-Minister of the Navy respectively, were opposed to a war with America, as was Nomura, according to Japanese Admiral Teizaburo Fukada. Because of his views a conspiracy of young army officers attempted to assassinate Yamamoto but failed. Yamamoto, like Nomura, had come to know Americans quite well in his position as Naval Attaché in Washington from 1925 to 1927 and, as with Nomura, was a veteran of international conferences and the two London Naval Conferences. In order to safeguard Yamamoto's life, which was in danger because of his views, Yonai assigned the Vice-Minister to be Commander-in-Chief of the Combined Fleet.

Although Japanese Admiral Isoroku Yamamoto opposed war with the U.S., as Commander-in-Chief of the Combined Fleet he was ordered to plan for an attack on the U.S. He worked with Commander Minoru Genda to plan the Pearl Harbor strike. (U.S. National Archives)

Why Pearl Harbor Attack?

What, then, drove Japan to attack America? According to Admiral Fukuda six important points must be taken into consideration:

(a) Japan felt that its Greater East Asia Co-prosperity Sphere policy was important to its survival in this industrialized society. Japan's industrial awakening and population explosion demanded expansion into the Asiatic mainland as a source of raw materials, as markets for finished products, and living space.

(b) The United States' repudiation of the Lansing-Ishii Agreement, by which Japan had been given a free hand in China as a neighboring country, and Britain's scrapping of the Anglo-Japanese Alliance made the Japanese believe that neither the U.S. or Britain could be trusted.

(c) The Japanese Naval General Staff believed that war with America was inevitable because of the U.S. interference and determination to stop the Japanese expansion policy.

(d) They were depressed with the results of the Washington and London Conferences which they felt were unfair to Japan.

(e) As previously mentioned, Japan also looked with suspicion at the U.S. Pacific Fleet bases moving closer and closer and she was certain that she would soon be attacked. Japan was especially alarmed about U.S. bases in Hawaii and the Philippines. The Philippines bases can be compared with the Oct. 1962 discovery of Soviet missiles in Cuba which the U.S.A. viewed with alarm and instituted a blockade. There was danger of war during both events.

(f) The strongest reason of all was the U.S. note handed to Ambassador Nomura on November 26, 1941. This was in answer to Japan's final negotiating program delivered to the U.S. Secretary of State by Japanese Special Envoy Saburo Kurusu on November 20, asking a reinstatement of the Lansing-Ishii Agreement. The American reply was drafted by one of President Roosevelt's advisors, Harry Dexter White, and it demanded that Japan withdraw from China and Indo-China, knowing full well that this was impossible because Japan was running out of oil. Upon reading the American ultimatum the Japanese Cabinet felt they had no alternative to war!

NAVAL FORCES IN THE PACIFIC

In December 1941 the naval forces in the Pacific Ocean consisted of the following warship strength:

	British Empire	U.S.	French	Dutch	Japan
Battleships	2	9	-	-	10
Aircraft Carriers	-	3	-	-	8
Heavy Cruisers	1	13	-	-	18
Light Cruisers	7	11	1	3	20
Destroyers	13	80	-	7	113
Submarines	-	56	-	13	63

A point to remember is that all of Japan's warships were in the Pacific while Britain and the U.S. had fleets in other oceans as well as the Pacific.

PEARL HARBOR ATTACK

Given orders to go to war, Admiral Yamamoto had planned well. He knew Japan could win some spectacular victories during the opening stages of a war with the U.S. and, to insure this, he knew that America's naval superiority must be reduced. Having studied the Fleet Air Arm attack on the Italian Fleet at Taranto, Yamamoto decided to use the Japanese carrier-based naval air arm to cripple the U.S. Pacific Fleet at Pearl Harbor; however, he knew that any attack would awaken a sleeping tiger.

Japanese Striking Force Sails

While the U.S. and Japan were negotiating, a Japanese naval strike force consisting of the aircraft carriers *Akagi* and *Kaga* of the First Carrier Division; *Hiryu* and *Soryu* of the Second Carrier Division; *Zuikaku* and *Shokaku* of the Fifth Carrier Division; the battleships *Hiei* and *Kirishima*; the heavy cruisers *Tone* and *Chicuma*; the light cruiser *Abukuma*, nine destroyers, tankers and submarines set sail from Etoforu Island in Hitokappu Bay of the Kurile Islands on

Vice Admiral Chuichi Nagumo was Commander-in-Chief of the Japanese First Air Fleet and placed in command of the Pearl Harbor attacking Force. He also led the Carrier Striking Force at the Battle of Midway. (U.S. Naval Historical Center)

November 26, 1941 and headed for Pearl Harbor. Vice Admiral Chuichi Nagumo was in command of this strike force and carried orders to attack the U.S. Pacific Fleet at Pearl Harbor unless negotiations with the U.S. reached a satisfactory agreement by December 5. Although negotiations dragged on, neither side expected a satisfactory outcome.

Admiral Stark's War Warning

The day after the Japanese Striking Force set sail, U.S. Chief of Naval Operations Admiral Harold R. Stark sent a warning to the commanders of the U.S. Atlantic, Pacific and Asiatic Fleets, and during November 27-28 the Fourth Marine Regiment was withdrawn from Shanghai after 14 years of duty in China.

Japanese Special Equipment

Admiral Yamamoto had pressed ahead with detailed planning and specialized training for the Pearl Harbor strike. The already superior Japanese aerial torpedoes were modified to avoid the initial deep dive in the shallow Pearl Harbor waters. Standard 16 inch armor-piercing shells had been converted into aerial bombs to be carried by high-flying Nakajima B5N bombers.

While on the subject of torpedoes, a basic weapon in the plane versus ship arsenal, we must discuss the superior Japanese aerial torpedo. The Imperial Japanese Navy Long Lance torpedo was far superior to the torpedoes of Germany, Britain and the U.S. The Type 95 M2 24 inch torpedo attained a speed of 50 knots with a range of 5,760 yards. The explosive charge weighed 1,210 pounds. The Type 93 Ml had a speed of 49 knots and a tremendous range of 22,000 yards. The Japanese torpedoes were also rugged and reliable; able to withstand release at 1,000 feet from aircraft traveling 250 knots and more!

Torpedo Propulsion System

The Japanese torpedo propulsion system was a big factor in their success. The Royal Navy had developed torpedoes using liquid oxygen with fuel during the mid-1920s and, although performance had greatly improved, a series of mishaps led the British to abandon this great idea. As a result, when World War II began the Royal Navy was still using the 20 year old steam turbine-driven torpedo, as was the U.S. Navy. During the late 1920s, early 1930s, the Imperial Japanese Navy produced an oxygen-enriched fuel which developed more power and occupied less space than the alcohol-fired steam turbine system.

Declaration of War Delayed

It is important to understand that Admiral Yamamoto and his staff had planned the Hawaiian Operation, as the Japanese called it, as a surprise attack following a Declaration of War by Nomura and not as a sneak attack preceding the Declaration of War. It was the inability of the Japanese Embassy personnel to promptly decode the message sent by the Japanese Cabinet that prevented the Declaration of War from being delivered to the U.S. State Department on time to precede the Pearl Harbor attack.

Stormy Weather For Striking Force

Admiral Nagumo's striking force ran into very fierce weather of steady gales and pounding seas at the onset. Refueling at sea was attempted on November 28 but the waves tossed the ships so wildly that the large hoses broke and whipped across the decks, hurling members of the crew overboard. The heavy weather lasted for several days but the armada maintained course and formation.

The First Pearl Harbor Raid

At six o'clock in the morning of December 7, 1941 the Japanese Fleet was 200 nautical miles north of Oahu. At that time the first attack group, led by Commander Mitsuo Fuchida of *Akagi*, was flying off carriers. This consisted of 40 Nakajima B5N2 Kate torpedo bombers from *Soryu* led by Lieutenant Commander Shigeharu Murata; 25 Aichi D3Al Val dive bombers led by Lieutenant Akira Sakamoto; 26 Val dive bombers led by Lieutenant Commander Kakuichi Takahashi; 49 high level bombing Kates with 1,760 pound armor-piercing bombs under the Pearl Harbor Attack Group Supreme Air Commander Fuchida's direct control; and 43 Mitsubishi A6M2 Zero Sen fighters led by Lieutenant Commander Shigeru Itaya. The 183 bombers, fighters and torpedo planes of the first wave began arriving over Pearl Harbor at 7:55 AM.

The American battleships, cruisers and auxiliary vessels were moored at Ford Island, the U.S. Navy Base in Pearl Harbor. As the torpedo-carrying Kates swooped in below 100 feet the high-flying Kates dropped their armor-piercing bombs on the immaculate row of dreadnaughts with devastating effect. In less than 30 minutes *USS Arizona* (BB-39) was a burning wreck; *USS California* (BB-44) was sinking; *USS West Virginia* (BB-48) had been hit with several torpedoes, plus two bombs, and went down burning; and *USS Oklahoma* (BB-37) had capsized, killing 415 of her 1,354 officers and men.

Meanwhile, the Val dive bombers attacked the neatly parked Army and Marine planes on the Pearl Harbor airfields. The Zeroes joined in with strafing attacks because they had met little opposition in the air.

USS Arizona had been hit by several torpedoes and then armor-piercing bombs rained on the burning ship. One bomb pierced the Deck beside number two gun turret and penetrated the magazine. The explosion sent flames 500 feet high. Another bomb entered a boiler room (fire room) and blew it to bits. *Arizona* sank so quickly that 1,103 of the 1,400 men aboard were killed, including Rear Admiral Isaac C. Kidd and Captain Franklin van Falkenburgh.

The only battleship to get underway was *USS Nevada* (BB-36). After a 45 foot hole had been torn in the hull by a Japanese torpedo, the senior officer on board, Lieutenant Commander Francis J. Thomas wisely decided to move the ship out of the target area.

As *Nevada* entered a relatively safe area a squadron of Val dive bombers spotted the moving battleship and changed course to attack the escaping vessel. Near-misses were causing as much damage as direct hits because of the gaping torpedo hole. With five direct hits the *Nevada* could not remain afloat so two Navy tug boats moved the stricken ship to a hard bottom where the battlewagon settled.

Battleships *USS Pennsylvania* (BB-38), *USS Tennessee* (BB-43) and *USS Maryland* (BB-46) were fortunate to escape with only minor damage.

The Second Pearl Harbor Raid

At 8:25 AM the first wave of attackers had completed its mission and returned to the carriers. A second wave of 170 Vals, Kates and Zeroes took off under the command of Lieutenant Commander Shigekazu Shimazaki 15 minutes later and began arriving at Pearl Harbor. Shimazaki was also in charge of 54 level bombing Kates from *Zuikaku* carrying two 550 pound bombs each, plus six 100 pound fragmentation bombs. Commander Takashige Egusa led 80 Vals from *Soryu* armed with two 550 pound bombs each. Fighter cover was provided by 36 Zero-Sen A6M2 fighters from *Akagi* led by Lieutenant Saburo Shindo, who had fought over China in the A6M2 six months earlier.

By the time the second wave arrived over Pearl Harbor the Americans had time to organize and the Japanese were met with fairly heavy antiaircraft fire from ships and shore installations.

One of the principal objectives of the second raid was the dockyard where the U.S. Pacific Fleet Flagship *Pennsylvania* was hit and damaged while several destroyers were wrecked by Val dive bombers. Shimazaki's Kates pounded the Pearl Harbor fighter and bomber airfields while the 36 Zeroes intercepted any U.S. fighters which managed to become airborne and conducted strafing attacks on U.S. Air Bases. The second attack ended at 9:45 AM with the Japanese aircraft returning to their carriers.

Largest Air Attack - Severe Damage

Thus ended the largest aerial operation ever attempted until that time. In a single coordinated strike a total of 353 aircraft from six carriers had sunk four battleships, a fifth had been beached and three others badly damaged. The light cruisers *Raleigh* and *Helena* were badly damaged and the light cruiser *Honolulu* suffered slight damage. The destroyers *Shaw*, *Cassin* and *Downes* were badly damaged, as was the repair ship *Vestal* and the seaplane tender *Curtiss*. The old auxiliary ship *Utah* was sunk. When it was all over 2,400 Americans had been killed and 1,178 had been wounded, which is more than the U.S. Navy lost in all of World War I.

Japanese Losses

Of the 353 planes launched by Admiral Nagumo 199 had been assigned to strafe and bomb the airfields, leaving Kaneohe Naval Air Station, Bellows Field, Wheeler Field and Hickam Field in shambles while destroying dozens of American fighters and bombers. This left only 154 Japanese planes to destroy the U.S. Pacific Fleet! Japanese losses were 15 Val dive bombers, five Kate torpedo/level bombers, and eight Zero fighters. Seven of these losses were shot down by American fighters, while U.S. antiaircraft fire got the rest.

Neglected Targets

Admiral Nagumo was very pleased with the results of the attack as one might expect; however, there were two vital flaws in the perfection of his success. First in importance was the fact that not one U.S. carrier was found in Pearl Harbor and further; the fuel storage tank farm, submarine pens, and repair facilities were overlooked and remained unscathed. Nagumo rejected the advice of his air group leaders, who urged another attack to draw in the U.S. aircraft carriers, and he turned the fleet away from Hawaii for a scheduled replenishment rendezvous with his tankers. The carriers *Soryu* and

Hiryu were detached from the main body and headed for Wake Island with the cruisers *Tone* and *Chikuma*, plus two destroyers, while the main task force returned to Japan.

No U.S. Carriers in Pearl Harbor

Where were the American aircraft carriers that Admiral Nagumo missed? Whether by design or by accident *USS Enterprise*, Captain George E. Murray commanding, was about 200 miles west of Pearl Harbor, having just completed delivery of Marine Corps Fighter Squadron VMF-211 to Wake Island; *USS Lexington*, Captain Frederick Sherman commanding, was 420 miles southeast of Midway, on its way to deliver a Marine Corps scout bomber squadron to the island; *USS Saratoga*, Captain Archibald H. Douglas commanding, was off the coast of California heading for Bremerton Navy Yard for overhaul. Several scout bombers had been launched from Enterprise and headed for Ford Island in Pearl Harbor, arriving at the moment of the Japanese onslaught in which they were destroyed. *USS Saratoga* was then ordered to steam for Pearl Harbor post-haste to become the nucleus of a new U.S. carrier striking force.

Minoru Genda

Admiral Nagumo's operations officer was the famous Minoru Genda, who was previously mentioned as a fighter leader and tactician during the Sino-Japanese Incident. Commander Genda was responsible for the rapid growth and initial success of the Japanese

Commander Minoru Genda was Admiral Nagumo's operations officer for the Pearl Harbor raid. He had been responsible for the rapid growth and successes of the Japanese Navy's carrier force. Genda initiated the mass employment of fighters for control of the air. (U.S. National Archives)

Navy's carrier force and initiated the mass employment of fighters to gain control of the air in cooperation with bombers. His innovative tactics in the Sino-Japanese conflict had won for him and his units the nickname Genda Circus and, in 1937, Genda became one of the youngest Air Group operations officers in the Japanese Navy. After graduating with honors from the Naval War College he spent two years in London as the Japanese Assistant Naval Air Attache and this assignment was followed with the position of aide to Admiral Takijiro Onishi, Chief of Staff of the 11th Air Fleet. As operations officer on Nagumo's staff Commander Genda was very concerned that no American carriers were found at Pearl Harbor because he realized that as long as an American carrier task force could be put to sea, Japan's position in the Pacific Ocean was precarious, despite the Pearl Harbor victory. Genda combined his talents and enthusiasm with the more air-minded officers in the Japanese Navy for the preparation of a new tactical doctrine which would amalgamate all available naval air groups aboard the six Japanese carriers into a single all-powerful attack force that would strike at the U.S. carrier force head-on. This plan resulted in one of the most important naval battles of the war in the Pacific.

U.S. Navy Fighter Plane Strength, 1940 - 1941
When the Japanese made their attack on Pearl Harbor the total U.S. Navy fighter plane strength was only 90 Brewster Buffaloes and 148 Grumman Wildcats. Almost one half of the units that they equipped were not fully organized, insufficiently trained, not up to strength, and pilots not familiar with their planes. It appears that this condition was the result of gross negligence on the part of the political/military leaders of the U.S., especially when it had become obvious that the U.S. and Japan were on a collision course to open warfare.

MORE JAPANESE ATTACKS
The flame and smoke at Pearl Harbor had not yet subsided when Japanese forces launched air and surface attacks on selected Western nation colonies and other targets.

Japanese Attacks In Western Pacific
The Japanese struck at Thailand and Malaya for their drive to the rubber plantations and the oil fields of the Dutch East Indies. Simultaneously, attacks were made on Hong Kong, Borneo and Guam. Wake Island was attacked on the next day.

Japanese Sink Royal Navy Battleships
During October 1941 Winston Churchill had ordered the modern battleship *Prince of Wales* and the old battle cruiser *Repulse* to Malaya in order to overawe the Japanese and prevent them from attacking Malaya. Churchill overrode the Naval Staff's objection to this ill-conceived plan. The Naval Staff had contended that only a balanced fleet with at least one aircraft carrier was worth sending to the Far East. While steaming off the eastern coast of Malaya, *Prince of Wales* and *Repulse* were caught by Japanese aircraft and sent to the bottom in rapid succession by a coordinated dive bombing and torpedo attack on December 10; three days after the Pearl Harbor attack.

Japanese Attack On Philippine Islands
On the same day the British warships were sunk Japanese force attacked the Philippine Islands; landing on Luzon. Only one Japanese aircraft carrier was available, *Ryujo*, because the bulk of Japan carrier force had been engaged in the Pearl Harbor operation. *Ryujo* was just east of Davau on Mindinao when she launched 13 dive bombers at dawn, escorted by nine Zero-Sen fighters. The force attacked the U.S. seaplane tender, William B. Preston, anchored i Davau Gulf, and sank two of her PBY flying boats which wei moored alongside. The tender escaped undamaged to a safer ai chorage.

In view of the fact that Japan had only one carrier available fo the Philippine operation most of the air raids were flown from th island of Formosa, now called Taiwan.

Japanese Attacks On Wake And Guam
The attack on Wake and Guam was conducted by Imperial Japanese Navy Vice-Admiral S. Inouye's Fourth Fleet with assistanc from the carriers *Soryu* and *Hiryu* which had just returned from th Hawaiian Operation. Guam fell quickly.

The Japanese occupied the island of Guam on December 1 and quickly completed the airfield that the Americans had left ur finished because U.S. politicians had claimed it was too expensiv to complete. This airstrip proved valuable later in the war.

Axis Declares War On U.S.
On December 11 Germany and Italy declared war on the Unite States.

Wildcat Versus Zero-Sen
The first Japanese air attack on Wake Island on December 8 d stroyed eight Grumman F4F-3 Wildcats of Marine Fighting Squa ron VMF-211 while they were at rest on the runway.

On the following day the Wildcat and the Zero-Sen met in cor bat for the first time. The combat revealed that the Zero was fast and had a better rate of climb at all altitudes above 1,000 feet. also had a longer range and higher service ceiling. Near sea lev the planes were equal in level speed. The Wildcat had the adva tage of internal protection and could endure pull-outs and-turns high speeds. The Zero engine had the tendency to lose power stop during a push-over into a dive. The Wildcat had the advanta during high speed rolls.

Japanese Repulsed At Wake Island
On December 11 the Japanese suffered their first set-back of th war when a sea-borne assault on Wake Island was repulsed by th 388 man battalion and the pilots of VMF-211. Two Japanese d stroyers were sunk; *Hayate* by the garrison's 5 inch guns, ar *Kisaragi* by 100 pound bombs in an air attack. These were the fii significant Japanese surface ship losses of the war. A troop tran port was also sunk and a light cruiser, a freighter, and two oth destroyers were damaged later.

Wake Island Captured
Since their repulse on December 11 the Japanese carrier plan bombed Wake without respite until December 22, the last two Wil

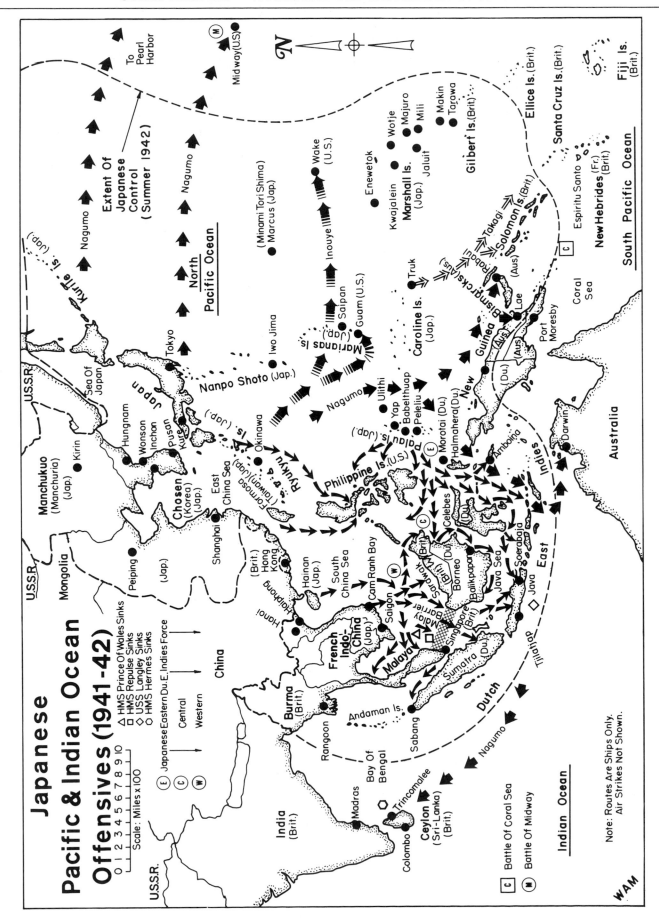

Japanese Pacific & Indian Ocean Offensives (1941-42)

Scale: Miles x 100
0 1 2 3 4 5 6 7 8 9 10

(E) (C) (W) Japanese Eastern Du. E. Indies Force
Central
Western

△ HMS Prince Of Wales Sinks
□ HMS Repulse Sinks
◇ USS Langley Sinks
○ HMS Hermes Sinks

Extent Of Japanese Control (Summer 1942)

To Pearl Harbor
Nagumo
Midway(U.S.) (M)
Nagumo
Nagumo

North Pacific Ocean

Wake (U.S.)
Minami Tori Shima (Jap.)
Marcus (Jap.)
Inouye

Enewetok
Kwajalein
Marshall Is. (Jap.)
Jaluit
Wotje
Majuro
Mili
Makin
Tarawa
Gilbert Is.(Brit.)

Ellice Is. (Brit.)
Santa Cruz Is.(Brit.)
Fiji Is. (Brit.)

Espiritu Santo
New Hebrides (Brit.)
(C)

South Pacific Ocean

Truk
Caroline Is. (Jap.)
Takagi
Solomon Is.(Brit.)
Rabaul (Aus.)
Bismarcks (Aus.)
New Guinea (Aus.)
Lae
Port Moresby
Coral Sea

Saipan
Guam (U.S.)
Marianas (Jap.)
Nanpo Shoto (Jap.)
Nagumo
Ulithi
Yap
Babelthuap
Peleliu
Palau Is. (Jap.)
Morotai (Du.)
Halmahera(Du.)
(E)
Amboina
Ceram (Du.)

Iwo Jima
Tokyo
Sea Of Japan
Hungnam
Wonson
Inchon
Pusan
Kure
East China Sea

Okinawa
Ryukyu
Formosa (Taiwan)(Jap.)
Philippine Is. (U.S.)

Manchukuo (Manchuria) (Jap.)
Kirin
Chosen (Korea) (Jap.)

U.S.S.R.
Kurile Is. (Jap.)

Mongolia
Peiping
(Jap.)
Shanghai
China

Hong Kong (Brit.)
Hainan (Jap.)
South China Sea
Cam Ranh Bay
(C)
Sarawak (Brit.)
Celebes (Du.)
Borneo
Balikpapan
Java Sea
Soerabaja
Java
East Indies
Darwin
Australia

Hanoi
Haiphong
Saigon
French Indo-China (Jap.)
(W)
Malaya
Malay Barrier
Singapore (Brit.)
Sumatra (Du.)
Dutch

Burma (Brit.)
Rangoon
Andaman Is.
Sabang
Nagumo
Bay Of Bengal

India (Brit.)
Madras
Trincomalee
Colombo
Ceylon (Sri-Lanka) (Brit.)

Indian Ocean

U.S.S.R.
U.S.S.R.
Japan

(C) Battle Of Coral Sea
(M) Battle Of Midway

Note: Routes Are Ships Only.
Air Strikes Not Shown.

WAM

On December 20, 1941 Admiral Ernest J. King was appointed Commander-in-Chief of the U.S. Fleet. (U.S. Naval Historical Center)

Admiral Chester W. Nimitz was appointed Commander-in-Chief, U.S. Pacific Fleet and Pacific Ocean Areas on December 31, 1941. (U.S National Archives)

cats had been shot down while fighting 39 Japanese carrier planes. On the following day 1,000 Japanese troops of the Special Naval Landing Force landed on the island and after several hours of hopeless fighting the island commander ordered the defenders to surrender.

Japanese Capture Hong Kong

Hong Kong was taken by Japanese forces on Christmas Day, 1941.

U.S. CARRIER TASK FORCE ORGANIZED

During December 15 to 23 a task force consisting of *USS Saratoga*, three heavy cruisers, nine destroyers and the 12 knot oiler *Neches* (AO-5), commanded by Rear Admiral Frank Jack Fletcher, had been sent to rescue Wake Island. Unfortunately, the refueling oiler dictated the speed of the entire task force during refueling operations. The oiler *USS Neches'* 12 knot top speed compelled the task force to waste December 22, which brought the faster ships no closer to Wake Island. The Japanese had foreseen this problem and designed their oilers for speeds equal to the combat ships they were intended to refuel.

Task Force Recalled

When Admiral Fletcher's task force was 425 miles from Wake Island it was recalled because of the surrender.

Admirals Nimitz and King Appointed

Meanwhile, Admiral Husband E. Kimmel had been relieved as Commander-in-Chief of the Pacific Fleet on December 17 and on December 31 Admiral Chester W. Nimitz assumed command of the U.S. Pacific Fleet. On December 20 Admiral Ernest J. King had been appointed Commander-in-Chief of the U.S. Fleet.

U.S. Search For Japanese Carriers

The main objective of the U.S. Navy was to find the Japanese carriers and destroy them. To reinforce the U.S. Pacific Fleet the Atlantic Fleet was ordered to transfer *USS Yorktown* with all aircraft and full complement of air crews, the battleships *New Mexico, Mississippi,* and *Idaho,* plus a destroyer squadron to the Pacific. In addition, three squadrons of Navy land-based bombers were transferred to the Pacific Fleet.

U.S. Army Air Corps Helps Navy

In order to assist in the search for the Japanese carriers the Army Air Corps could spare only three Boeing B-17 Flying Fortresses, 11 Douglas B-18 twin-engine bombers, and about 80 fighter and reconnaissance aircraft. Pearl Harbor had only three consolidated PBY Catalina flying boats, about 10 Douglas SBD Dauntless scout bombers and seven miscellaneous aircraft available to scout the Pacific Ocean for the Japanese carriers.

"JUNKYARD" FLEET STUNNED THE EXPERTS

The Pearl Harbor Operation of December 7 was not only a military set-back for the U.S. but was also a dramatic demonstration that a small island nation holding the short end of the Washington Conference naval ratio agreement was capable of delivering a devastating blow to a more powerful nation. This left most of the political and military world gasping; not only because the Imperial Japanese Navy had been the subject of ridicule as the "Junkyard Fleet" by western experts, but also because the weapons used were aircraft carriers and their Warbirds of the Sea! This caused a revision in the concept of capital ships which, overnight, changed from the battleship to the aircraft carrier in the principal navies of the world.

EUROPE FIRST: THEN THE PACIFIC

The U.S. had agreed to direct its principal effort into the European Theatre, leaving the Navy to contain the Japanese in the Pacific Theatre. The U.S. Marines were smarting under their initial losses and had tried to obtain fighter planes from the U.S. Army; however, none could be spared because the U.S. had been providing war materiel to any country essential to the defense of the U.S. under the Lend-Lease Act of 1941. As a result, large quantities of aircraft were shipped to Britain and the Soviet Union while the U.S. Forces were left wanting.

America knew that time was on her side and this time meant development and production which was to lead to ultimate victory.

CHAPTER IV
CONFRONTATION: 1942

Into the Southwest Pacific • Arcadia Conference • Carrier Actions In Southwest Pacific • ABDA And The Malay Barrier • Japanese Threaten Australia • King and MacArthur Appointed • U.S. Task Force Helps Royal Navy • Nagumo Enters Indian Ocean • Doolittle's Tokyo Raiders • Eastern Aircraft Wildcats • USS Wasp Delivers Spitfires • Japanese Operation "MO" • Battle of the Coral Sea • New Planes and Carriers • Battle of Midway • Japanese Seaplanes • Back to the Southwest Pacific • Back to the European War • Second Arcadia Conference • Operation Torch and Supermarine Seafires • Bent-Wing Bird Carrier Trials • U.S. Navy Escort and Training Carrier Conversions • New U.S. and Royal Navy Fleet Carriers • Japan's Carrier Construction Program • Preparing For The Carrier Battles

INTO THE SOUTHWEST PACIFIC

Only two weeks after returning to Japan Admiral Nagumo was ordered to take his Pearl Harbor striking force to sea again to support the assault on the Bismarck Archipelago and the Solomon Islands in the Southwest Pacific. The objective was to create a buffer around Japan's primary objective in the area, the Dutch East Indies. This move was to precipitate violent air, sea and land battles for the next two years.

ARCADIA CONFERENCE DECISIONS

The first wartime Washington Conference (called Arcadia) which had begun on December 23, 1941, came to a conclusion on January 14. President Roosevelt and Prime Minister Churchill agreed that, although the war was to concentrate on the defeat of Italy and Germany, Australia and the Sea Lines of Communication (SLOC) with the U.S. ie; New Caledonia, the Fiji Islands, and American Samoa, must be held against Japan and the U.S. took on the responsibility of handling the Pacific war. It was also agreed to launch an invasion of French North Africa in 1942 and to organize a joint chiefs of staff committee.

NEW U.S. CARRIER TASK FORCES

In order to locate and combat the Japanese carriers the U.S. Navy had organized three search/strike carrier task forces, two of which were to remain at sea while the third was to undergo maintenance and refuel and replenish at Pearl Harbor. Task Force 8 was organized around *USS Enterprise* with Vice Admiral William F. "Bull" Halsey in command; Task Force 14 was organized around *USS Saratoga* with Rear-Admiral Herbert F. Leary in command; and Task Force 17 was organized around *USS Yorktown* with Rear Admiral Frank Jack Fletcher in command. It had also been decided to use the new carrier groups to escort crucial convoys and conduct raids on the new Japanese bases which had been set up in the Gilbert Island and the Marshall Island chains which were at the extreme eastern limit of Japanese expansion in the Pacific Ocean. Each carrier was escorted by cruisers, battleships and destroyers.

PREVIOUS: Japanese Val dive bombers from IJNS Hiryu score a direct hit on the USS Yorktown (CV-5) Flight Deck while another Val is seen diving on the stricken ship at noon of June 4, 1942. (U.S. National Archives)

In order to locate and combat the Japanese carriers U.S. Navy carrier task forces were organized in early 1942. Vice Admiral William F. "Bull" Halsey was placed in command of Task Force 8 with USS Enterprise as the principal unit of the battle group. Later, he commanded the Solomon campaign and led the U.S. Third Fleet. (U.S. National Archives)

The first assignment for the new U.S. Navy carrier strike force was to escort a U.S. Marine force which was to be rushed to Pago Pago, American Samoa. Sailing from San Diego on January 6, 1942, the reinforcement fleet was convoyed by Task Force 17 until they approached Samoa, at which time Task Force 8 joined the convoy to insure safety in the event of a Japanese carrier attack. The convoy arrived safely at Pago Pago on January 23 without incident.

Saratoga Torpedoed

Meanwhile, on January 11 Task Force 14 was patrolling about 500 miles west of Hawaii when a Japanese submarine torpedoed

Task Force 17 was organized around USS Yorktown with Rear Admiral Frank Jack Fletcher in command. Admiral Fletcher later fought Japanese carriers in the Battles of the Coral Sea and Midway. (U.S. National Archives)

Saratoga. Three of the four firerooms or boiler rooms became flooded and six of the crew had been killed; however, the carrier was able to reach Bremerton, Washington under her own power for repairs and modernization. Task Force 14 was then disbanded and the *Saratoga* air group was distributed among the other carriers. Admiral Leary was reassigned to command an Australian/New Zealand force in the Southwest Pacific.

Manila Captured
On January 2, 1942, the Philippine capitol of Manila and the Cavite Naval Base were taken by Japanese forces.

U.S. Central Pacific Raids
Another task force was created around *USS Lexington* to replace Task Force 14. Vice Admiral Wilson Brown was placed in command of this new carrier force. Admiral Brown's first assignment was to attack the Japanese installations on Wake Island but when the task force was only about 150 miles from Pearl Harbor the oiler *USS Neches* was torpedoed and sunk by a Japanese submarine! No task force was able to operate in the vast Pacific Ocean without periodic refueling; therefore, Admiral Brown was not able to proceed and the Wake Island strike was cancelled; another set-back for the carrier groups.

Gilbert and Marshall Islands Raids
Undaunted by these reversals Admiral Nimitz gave orders to Admirals Fletcher and Halsey on January 25 to conduct raids on selected islands of the Gilbert and Marshall Archipelagoes. Task Force 8 was assigned to strike the seaplane bases at Maloelap and Wotje Atolls, as well as the concentration of Japanese aircraft and shipping at Kwajalein Atoll in the Marshall Islands.while Task Force 17 was to raid Makin Island in the Gilbert Group, and Mili Atoll, plus Jaluit Atoll in the Marshall Islands.

The two task forces sailed out of Samoa on January 31 and then split up for their individual attacks which were made on February 1. Both task forces met only with mediocre success; the absence of adequate charts of the area was a major contributor. In fact, one group used charts prepared by the Charles Wilkes Exploration Expedition of 1840! In the final tally: the Japanese transport *Bordeau Maru* and a Japanese submarine chaser were sunk; a mine layer, two transports, the light cruiser *Katori*, an ammunition ship and a submarine tender were damaged. Two Zero fighters and a four-engine bomber were shot down. The task forces lost six dive bombers and the cruiser *USS Chester* sustained a bomb hit which killed eight crew members and injured 12 more.

CARRIER ACTIONS IN SOUTHWEST PACIFIC
On the very next day Admiral Nagumo's strike force attacked Darwin, Australia. It was reported that his carrier aircraft devastated the surrounding military installations and the escorting Zero fighters shot down eight Australian interceptors and destroyed 15 more aircraft on the ground. In addition, Nagumo's carriers had supported the invasion of Amboina on the island of Ceram in the Dutch East Indies, northwest of Darwin, as well as the thrust into the Bismarck Archipelago, securing New Britain, New Ireland and the key base of Rabaul, which was to hold up the Allied advance in that area for more than two years. Four days later the U.S. destroyer *Peary* was sunk during a Japanese air raid on Darwin.

Pilots of Fighting Squadron Six (VF-6) pose on the deck of Admiral Halsey's USS Enterprise CV-6 shortly before the raids on the Marshall Islands in early February 1942. Note the Grumman Wildcat fighter behind the men. (U.S. National Archives)

Singapore Captured

Also on February 15 British Lieutenant General Arthur E. Percival surrendered Singapore to the Japanese. Singapore was often called the Gibraltar of the East and had been groomed over the years to support a powerful Royal Navy Far Eastern Fleet, but with its fall went the last hope of a unified defense of Southeast Asia.

Japanese Isolate Philippines and Dutch East Indies

With their forces well established in Rabaul and the remainder of the Bismarck Archipelago the Japanese effectively isolated the Philippine Islands and the Dutch East Indies. The powerful Japanese base in the Truk Islands of the Caroline Chain is about 800 miles due north of Rabaul and the combination of the two bases created a barrier over 1,500 miles long, running north and south! It was; therefore, expedient for America to shift the next carrier attack from the Central Pacific to the Southwest Pacific for a carrier strike on Rabaul and the intense Japanese shipping activity in the area.

Lexington Warbirds Score

Vice Admiral Wilson Brown was ordered to make the strike with his Task Force, of which *USS Lexington* was the nucleus. Seven U.S., one Australian and four Royal Navy cruisers, plus 16 U.S. destroyers comprised the remainder of the task force. Admiral Brown decided to attack Rabaul from the north side of New Ireland and this required that the ships sail along the northeastern side of the Solomon Islands. In the mid-afternoon of February 20, 1942 *Lexington* was in position to launch her warbirds when a Japanese four-engine Kawanishi H6K maritime patrol flying-boat was reported trailing the U.S. Force. Captain Frederick C. Sherman, Commanding Officer of *Lexington*, selected Lieutenant Commander John S. Thach, Commanding Officer of Fighting Squadron 3, to lead a division of four Wildcats to destroy the patrol plane before it had time to report the sighting to its base. Thach led his division through layers of cloud and he shot it down in flames from 1,500 feet. A second Kawanishi was destroyed by one of *Lexington*'s scout planes.

When *Lexington* had reached a position off the coast of Bougaineville, northernmost of the Solomon Islands, a flight of nine twin-engine Betty shore-based bombers appeared, which made it obvious that the Kawanishi crews had reported the American task force strength and location. Commander Thach already had a six plane combat air patrol in the air at 10,000 feet, while another flight of six were about to return to the carrier to refuel; however, without hesitation he recalled the flight. The F4F-3 Wildcats engaged the bombers only a dozen miles from *Lexington* and shot down six of them while the ship's antiaircraft guns accounted for two more. The last bomber was damaged and raced for home. A second wave of bombers attacked a few moments later and six more Wildcats from Fighting Squadron 3 left the carrier led by Lieutenant Edward H. O'Hare. Upon testing his guns O'Hare's wingman discovered they had failed to fire and he was given permission to return to *Lexington* and have the problem corrected.

First U.S. Navy Ace; World War II

O'Hare, who was known as Butch, sped into the bomber formation without a wingman, firing long bursts into the bombers' engines, some of which actually fell off the wings. The intrepid pilot made

The first World War II U.S. Navy Ace was Lieutenant Edward H. O'Hare, also known as Butch O'Hare. He was awarded the Medal of Honor when he shot down five Japanese bombers that were attacking USS Lexington and saved the carrier from destruction. During this action the ace was without his wingman but in sight of the squadron. (U.S. National Archives)

pass after pass as the bombers flew closer to *Lexington*. Thach and the other Wildcat pilots were too far away to help O'Hare so, without assistance of any kind, the young Lieutenant scored one after the other, with only one thought in his mind; he had to save *Lady Lex*, and he did. During a bare four minutes of frenzied activity Butch O'Hare shot down five Japanese twin-engine bombers. In fact, the victories were so rapid that, at times, he had scored his next victory before the previous victim hit the water! Thach and the other pilots arrived as O'Hare's fifth victory fell into the sea and they scored two more of the bombers while the two remaining Japanese turned tail and sped for home.

Scoring five victories made Lieutenant O'Hare the U.S. Navy's first Ace of World War II and, for his outstanding performance O'Hare was awarded the Medal of Honor. This was presented to O'Hare by President Roosevelt at a White House ceremony on April 21, 1942. The citation read as follows: "For conspicuous gallantry and intrepidity in aerial combat, at grave risk of his life above and beyond the call of duty, as section leader and pilot of Fighting Squadron Three, when on February 20, 1942, having lost the assistance of his teammates, he interposed his plane between his ship and an advancing enemy formation of nine attacking twin-engine heavy bombers. Without hesitation, alone and unaided, he repeatedly a

Commander Thach (aircraft F-1) and Lieutenant O'Hare (aircraft F-13), shown on combat air patrol from USS Lexington, were members of VF-3 Felix The Cat fighter squadron. The Felix The Cat insignia is barely visible on the fuselage side adjacent to the windshield on their Grumman Wildcats. (U.S. National Archives)

acked this enemy formation at close range in the face of their intense combined machine gun and cannon fire, and despite this concentrated opposition, he, by his gallant and courageous action, his extremely skillful marksmanship, making the most of every shot of his limited amount of ammunition, shot down five enemy bombers and severely damaged a sixth before they reached the bomb release point. As a result of his gallant action, one of the most daring, if not the most daring single action in the history of combat aviation, he undoubtedly saved his carrier from serious damage."

Butch O'Hare was advanced 30 numbers in his permanent rank of Lieutenant (Junior Grade) and promoted to the rank of Lieutenant Commander. He was also placed in command of Fighting Squadron 3 on June 19, 1942 (designation changed to Fighting Squadron 5 on July 15, 1942).

John Thach - Warbird Tactician

Lieutenant Commander Thach was awarded the Distinguished Service Medal and the Navy Cross in midsummer, 1942 which combined his heroic achievements in two other operations, in addition to those of February 20.

Lieutenant John Smith Thach was renown as an innovative tactician having developed a very effective flying formation called the "Thach Weave." In fact, it was a sort of weave: he dispensed with the tight Vee formations and had his pilots fly hundreds of feet apart and actually weave back and forth to cover a large expanse of sky to not only increase the chances of spotting enemy aircraft but, more important, reduce the chances of being surprised by the Japanese.

Lexington and *Yorktown* Join Forces

When Admiral Brown realized that the Japanese knew all about his task force and that he had lost all chances of a surprise attack on Rabaul he headed in a southeasterly direction to meet his tankers for refueling and then join with Admiral Fletcher's *USS Yorktown*.

Despite the disappointment of failing to conduct a surprise attack on Rabaul, Admiral Brown had the satisfaction of having his airmen engage in the largest air battle thus far over the Pacific; and the Americans had won this aerial engagement.

ABDA AND THE MALAY BARRIER

Late in 1941 the American-British-Dutch-Australian (ABDA) command had been organized with U.S. Admiral Thomas C. Hart, commanding officer of the U.S. Asiatic Fleet, in command. Political considerations reorganized ABDA on January 3, 1942, placing British General Sir Archibald P. Wavell in charge with Admiral Hart as naval commander. The objective of ABDA was very optimistic, hoping to stop the Japanese forces at the Malay Barrier extending from Malaya to the Dutch East Indies. Eight days later the Japanese invaded the Dutch East Indies in force. The politics of ABDA were to be the cause of more catastrophies to come! During the night of January 24 ABDA ships inflicted casualties on a Japanese invasion force off Balikpapan in Borneo, but could not deter the Japanese forces from landing.

ABDA Fiasco and Politics

On February 4 an ABDA naval force consisting of two Dutch cruisers, two U.S. cruisers, and four Dutch destroyers under the com-

Commander John S. Thach was the first U.S. naval air tactician. He developed the Thach Weave which dispensed with the rigid Vee formation. This enabled fighter formations to cover a larger expanse of sky and gave them more freedom to maneuver. (U.S. National Archives)

mand of Dutch Rear Admiral Karel Doorman was trying to intercept a Japanese invasion force off the coast of Borneo when the ABDA Group was surprised by Japanese planes. The U.S. cruiser *Marblehead* was so seriously damaged that she had to return to the U.S. for repairs; cruiser *USS Houston* had its aft 8 inch gun turret blown off; and a Dutch cruiser was seriously damaged. This was another example of the possible consequences for entering a naval engagement without proper air cover.

Politics again reared its ugly head on February 14 when, due to Dutch and British pressure, Admiral Thomas C. Hart was replaced by Dutch Vice Admiral C.E.L. Helfrich as Commander-in-Chief, Allied Naval Forces Southwest Pacific.

ABDA Fiasco; *USS Langley* Sinks

The plight of the Dutch East Indies was very dismal; Java was losing more and more ground to the Japanese who had advanced virtually unopposed, protected by the Imperial Japanese Navy. Despite the impending conquest of the Dutch possession Sir Archibald Wavell of ABDA was of the opinion that, with sufficient aircraft, the Indies' defenders could stave off defeat. The island of Timor had just been captured which cut off the island-hopping supply route to Java and this meant that aircraft could not be brought into the Java area except by sea; however, the large battle carriers could not be spared for this job. *USS Langley* CV-1, America's first carrier, was selected because she had been reassigned from front line service to that of an Auxiliary and Aircraft Transport AV-3.

The *Langley* Mission

On February 22, 1942 *USS Langley* was loaded with 32 Curtiss P-40 Warhawk fighters and 33 USAAC pilots. She set sail from Australia with the *Sea Witch*, a freighter loaded with 27 crated Warhawks in her hold. The duo joined a convoy, escorted by Task Force 5, headed for India. *Langley* and *Sea Witch* were escorted by the light cruiser *USS Phoenix*. The three ships were scheduled to leave the convoy about 300 miles southwest of Sunda Strait, which divides Sumatra and Java and then make their way to Tjilatjap on the southern coast of Java.

Fatal Orders

All went well until, without consulting U.S. Vice Admiral William A. Glassford, Jr., Task Force 5 Commander, Dutch Admiral C.E.L. Helfrich ordered *Langley* and *Sea Witch* to separate from the convoy later than planned and then for *Langley* to proceed to Tjilatjap alone without *Phoenix*! This incompetent order was issued despite the fact that Japanese shore airbases were nearby. Later, Commander Robert P. McConnell, commanding *Langley*, was promised that two U.S. destroyers, *Whipple* and *Edsall*, would escort the carrier to Java. After some confusion and lost time due to contradicting orders, the two destroyers and two Dutch PBY Catalina patrol planes began escorting *Langley* on the morning of February 27.

Langley Attacked

At about 9:00 o'clock that morning an unidentified plane was sighted in the distance and more planes were spotted three hours later. Unknown to the little convoy was the fact that Imperial Japanese Navy Admiral Nobutake Kondo and his Southern Striking Force were not far behind. Kondo had apparently relayed *Langley*'s location to shore bases of the Japanese Navy 11th Air Fleet. Shortly after noon on February 27, 1942, nine twin-engined bombers approached *Langley* at 15,000 feet. Every gun on the carrier fired at the Japanese raiders and Commander McConnell zig-zagged wildly to avoid the bombs; however, the bombers scored five direct hits on their third salvo, plus two near-misses, which buckled the plates of the old carrier.

Langley Sinks

USS Langley assumed a list to port as a half-dozen Zero Sens strafed the Flight Deck. All the planes on deck had been blown overboard or were burning out of control. McConnell had hoped to enter Tjilatjap Harbor and beach the stricken ship; however, the engine spaces soon flooded, bringing the powerplant to a dead stop. At 1:30 in the afternoon McConnell ordered the ship abandoned and all but 16 of the crew were rescued by the two destroyers, which then sank America's first carrier with torpedoes and gunfire. The venerable ship had fallen victim to petty rivalry and political infighting among the Allies, which resulted in inept leadership.

ABDA and Java Sea Battle

On the same day that *USS Langley* sank, a battle had been raging in the Java Sea. Dutch Admiral Karel Doorman led an ABDA strike force of five cruisers; *USS Houston* (CA 30), *HMS Exeter*, *HMAS Perth*, *RNN DeRuyter* and *RNN Java*, plus 11 destroyers, but without air cover, on a sortie from Surabaja, Java to intercept two Japanese invasion forces. Instead, the Allied force encountered Rear Admiral Takeo Takagi's support force of four cruisers and 13 destroyers and in the ensuing battle the Long Lance torpedo proved decisive by sinking both Dutch cruisers and three destroyers. Only one Japanese destroyer was damaged.

On February 28, the following day, the Allied survivors of the Battle of the Java Sea, headed for Sunda Strait between Java and Sumatra to intercept another Japanese landing in Banten Bay. The Allied force sank one troop transport and damaged three others; however, *Houston* and *Perth* were sunk by the Japanese force under Rear Admiral Takeo Kurita.

More ABDA Ships Sunk

On March 1 three more survivors of the Java Sea Battle, *HMS Exeter*, *USS Pope* and *HMS Encounter*, were sunk by Japanese air and surface forces off Surabaja, Java. The Allied force had no air cover.

Japanese Breach Malay Barrier

The Malay Barrier had been breached by the Japanese Navy. In a space of less than three months the Allies had lost two capital ships, five cruisers, an airplane transport, and 17 destroyers in the defense of Southeast Asia. This failure resulted from the attempt to engage a force which possesses superior weapons without using air power or at least having air cover.

JAPANESE THREATEN AUSTRALIA

The Japanese thrust into the southwestern Pacific had extended beyond Rabaul and the Bismarck Archipelago for they had made ndings on the eastern coast of New Guinea at Lae and Salamaua on March 8, 1942 with the objective of taking Port Moresby on the southern side. Good airfields at Lae and Salamaua enabled patrol flights to link up with Rabaul and Truk and posed the danger to Australia of having the Japanese totally occupy New Guinea. The harbors of Lae and Salamaua were filled with Japanese ships of all description from warships and troopships to tankers.

Lexington/Yorktown Planes Raid Salamaua and Lae

Admirals Brown and Fletcher had combined the *Lexington* and *Yorktown* forces after the aborted Rabaul raid and quickly prepared for a raid on the Japanese bases of Lae and Salamaua. Their plan was to sail along the southern side of New Guinea and launch the attack across the Owen Stanley Range of 14,000 feet high mountains. Commander W.B. Ault and Lieutenant Commander W.L. Hamilton conducted some research and learned of a 7,000 feet pass through the mountains. Over 100 planes were launched from the carriers at 8:00 o'clock in the morning of March 10, 1942. Commander Ault led the way for the Dauntless dive bombers and Devastator torpedo planes, flying figure eights over the pass to guide the other planes through.

When the main force was only 25 miles from Salamaua Harbor the engine noise alerted the Japanese and by the time the American dive bombers and torpedo planes had begun their attacks several of the target ships had started to move out of the harbor.

U.S. Heroes Commended

Only one Japanese fighter attempted to intercept the carrier-launched armada and Lieutenant Noel Gayler shot it down, which earned him a Gold Star to add to his Navy Cross. Lieutenant Commander John Thach was commended for his leadership with a Distinguished Service Medal and Lieutenant John A. Leppla earned a Navy Cross for his dive bombing attacks. Lieutenant Commander Weldon Lee Hamilton led his dive bombers to the attack and, in the face of severe antiaircraft fire, his men sank an escaping cruiser by blowing off the stern and severely damaged two others. He was awarded the Navy Cross for his leadership.

The attack proved a success by sinking two heavy cruisers, one light cruiser, one destroyer and five large troop transports and, in addition, the harbor was littered with damaged and burning ships, thanks to the Warbirds of the Sea.

Japanese Take Dutch East Indies

On the same day as the Lae and Salamaua raid the Dutch East Indies surrendered to Japanese forces.

KING AND MAC ARTHUR APPOINTED

Admiral Ernest J. King was assigned the combined post of Chief of Naval Operations (CNO) and Commander-in-Chief U.S. Fleet on March 12, 1942, and five days later General Douglas MacArthur was appointed Allied Supreme Commander in the Southwest Pacific.

U.S. TASK FORCE HELPS ROYAL NAVY

Despite the fact that the U.S. Navy was faced with great problems in the Pacific, Task Force 39 was sent to reinforce the Royal Navy in European waters on March 25, 1942. The carrier *USS Wasp* (CV-7) was escorted by the battleship *USS Washington* (BB-56), the heavy cruisers *USS Tuskaloosa* (CA-37) and *USS Wichita* (CA-45), plus a squadron of destroyers.

NAGUMO ENTERS INDIAN OCEAN

Following operations in the Dutch East Indies Admiral Chuichi Nagumo led his carriers westward into the Indian Ocean on March 26. His strike force now consisted of *Akagi, Hiryu, Soryu, Shokaku* and *Zuikaku*, while the little *Ryujo* led a force of cruisers on a commerce raiding expedition in the Bay of Bengal under the command of Vice-Admiral Jisaburo Ozawa. Nagumo's carriers were supported by the battleships *Haruna, Kongo, Hiei* and *Kirishima*, plus three cruisers and eight destroyers.

British Eastern Fleet - Admiral Somerville

The important British naval bases at Trincomalee and Colombo on the island of Ceylon presented a serious threat to the Japanese advance; therefore, Nagumo was ordered to repeat his Pearl Harbor success on these British bases. Realizing that Ceylon was a prime target, the Royal Navy organized the British Eastern Fleet under the command of Admiral Sir James Somerville, who had previously seen action in the Mediterranean Sea. His force consisted of the aircraft carriers *HMS Hermes, Formidable* and *Indomitable*, plus the battleships *HMS Warspite, Royal Sovereign, Revenge, Ramillies* and *Resolution*. These were attended by eight cruisers, 15 destroyers and five submarines. All were based at Ceylon.

Nagumo Attacks Colombo

Somerville had correctly estimated that the Japanese would approach from the Southeast and attack early in April; however, the surface search force returned after a 48 hour sortie having found no sign of Nagumo's ships. On April 4 the entire British Eastern Fleet was either refueling or taking on fresh water at the Maldive Islands when a British Catalina search plane reported the Japanese carriers heading for Ceylon, now known as Sri Lanka.

On Easter Sunday, April 5, 1942, Nagumo unleashed 54 Vals, 36 Zero Sens, and 90 Kates on Colombo. The attackers found only two dozen ships in the harbor because the Colombo shore Commander, Vice-Admiral Sir Geoffrey Arbuthnot, had ordered all shipping out to sea because of the impending Japanese attack. The Japanese concentrated on critical shore installations such as fuel depots, naval repair shops, and docks. The raiders were met by 36 RAF Hawker Hurricanes and six FAA Fairey Fulmars, which shot down 16 Japanese aircraft while losing 15 Hurricanes and four Fulmars. Colombo Naval Base guns accounted for five more of the raiders.

Two British Cruisers Sunk

Meanwhile, at sea the cruisers *HMS Dorsetshire* and *Cornwall* were steaming to join Somerville's main force when they were discovered by Nagumo's scouting planes and, in less than two hours, the cruisers were being attacked by Vals, which sent both ships to the bottom under a hail of bombs.

Admiral Somerville rushed his fleet to sea with the intention of inflicting nocturnal torpedo plane attacks on the Japanese Strike Force; however, neither fleet located the other.

Nagumo Attacks Trincomalee

On April 6, the very next day, Nagumo's planes appeared over Trincomalee when about 60 bombers attacked the harbor and the airfield at China Bay. The damage was considerable and 17 Hurricanes and six Fulmars arose to intercept the Japanese. The final score was that 15 Japanese aircraft were shot down in exchange for eight Hurricanes and three Fulmars lost. The airfield antiaircraft guns accounted for nine more carrier aircraft.

Admiral Nagumo's Strike Force again attacked Colombo two days later and lost four carrier planes in exchange for five RAF Bristol Blenheim bombers.

HMS Hermes Sinks

On April 9 the carriers *Soryu*, *Hiryu* and *Akagi* spotted the British carrier *HMS Hermes* and her Australian destroyer escort *HMAS Vampire* off the east coast of Ceylon. *Hermes* had no aircraft aboard at the time and lay defenseless as over three dozen bombs sank her in 20 minutes. More than 300 men were lost.

Nagumo's Wide-Ranging Victories

Admiral Nagumo had reached the pinnacle of his career because in four months he had scored victories in seas covering the distance of one-third of the earth's circumference. His planes had sunk five battleships, two cruisers, one carrier, and seven destroyers, plus thousands of tons of merchant ships and fleet auxiliaries.

Despite these successes the Japanese attacks on Ceylon were to have a detrimental effect on the Imperial Japanese Navy's efforts in battles of May and June due to Nagumo's depleted air groups and carriers in need of maintenance. The trained pilots and aircraft were very difficult to replace and the time consuming maintenance pulled three of his carriers out of service.

DOOLITTLE'S TOKYO RAIDERS

During the spring of 1942 most of the war news was bad for the U.S. and when the news about the fall of Bataan reached America the population was cast into the depths of despondency. Unknown to but a few was the fact that plans were already being implemented to improve the people's spirit. To bomb Tokyo was the obvious solution; but how? The necessary range far exceeded that of any U.S. bomber. Then, somebody suggested flying twin-engined North American B-25B Mitchell bombers from an aircraft carrier operating as close as possible to Japan. Credit for this brilliant idea has been variously given to Admiral Ernest J. King, Captain Donald B. Duncan (Admiral King's air operations officer), Army Air Corps General Henry H. Arnold and USAAC Lieutenant Colonel James H. Doolittle. All collaborated in preparations for the flight.

One Way Trip

The B-25B had a maximum range of 1,525 miles and its wingspan

The world's first purpose-designed aircraft carrier HMS Hermes is shown listing, afire and bow virtually under water while suffering hits from more than three dozen Japanese bombs off the coast of Ceylon on April 9, 1942. The carrier sank in 20 minutes with 300 of the crew. (Ministry of Defence [Navy])

of 67 feet-6 inches was small enough to fit on a U.S. Fleet carrie however, it was impossible for the carrier to recover the 25,0 pound bomber. It was; therefore, imperative that the planes co tinue flying westward after dropping their bombs and land in Chi as best they could. Generalissimo Chiang Kai-shek was notifi but it was too late to designate suitable landing strips.

USS Hornet Selected

Colonel Doolittle was to lead the flight and the carrier selected w the brand new *USS Hornet* under the command of Captain Marc Mitscher. The *Hornet* was part of Vice Admiral William F. Halsey new Task Force 16 which also included the carrier *USS Enterpri* The cruisers *USS Nashville, Vincennes, Northampton* and *Salt La*

Lieutenant Colonel James H. Doolittle (arrow) and members of the fli, crew pose on the Flight Deck of USS Hornet before taking off on the e flight to bomb Tokyo. Note the bomb on the deck (lower right). (U.S. Army Air Corps, Courtesy Henry Tremont)

...ight of the 16 North American B-25B Mitchell twin-engined bombers of the Doolittle Raiders are shown tied down on the Hornet Flight Deck ...n route to the takeoff point. The Mitchells would not fit in the Hangar; therefore, they were carried on the Flight Deck. (U.S. Naval Historical ...enter)

...ity under the command of Rear Admiral Raymond A. Spruance
...ere also part of TF 16. April 18 was the date assigned for the raid.

...lanes Lightened

...he B-25B bombers were modified by removing eight of the ma-
...nine guns, as well as the tail power turret to accommodate a 2,000
...ound bomb load and 1,140 gallons of fuel. With 16 of the altered
...itchells tied down on the Flight Deck, *Hornet* steamed out of San
...rancisco Harbor on April 2, 1942. It had been calculated that the
...unching had to be 500 miles from the Japanese coast in order for
...e planes to reach China. It was also agreed that 13 planes would
...omb Tokyo while the remaining three were to attack Osaka, Nagoya
...nd Kobe with incendiary bombs only.

...arly Launch

...he task force was still 700 miles from Japan when in the early
...orning of April 18 three Japanese ships were sighted. One was
...nk by *Nashville* but the two others disappeared. Rather than risk
...tack by Japanese shore-based planes in the event that *Hornet's*
...cation had been reported by the Japanese ships it was decided to
...unch at once. Colonel Doolittle was the first to take off 623 miles

USS Hornet gunners watch one of the last Tokyo raiders leave the deck. The planes were stripped of machine guns and tail power turret so they could carry 2,000 pounds of bombs and 1,140 gallons of fuel for the long trip to China and/or Soviet Asia. This raid damaged the Japanese carrier Ryuho in the Yokosuka shipyard when it was being converted from a submarine tender. (U.S. Army Air Corps, Courtesy Henry Tremont)

to nearest land and 688 miles from Tokyo at 8:24 AM. Doolittle preceded the rest of the planes by about three hours in order to provide pathfinder fires by dropping incendiaries on Tokyo.

Soviets Intern U.S. Crew

None of the planes were lost over Japan; however, one Mitchell developed engine trouble and landed on Soviet territory in Vladivostok where the plane was impounded and the crew was interned! Some who reached China were captured by Japanese troops and executed; others drowned and another brave man died when his parachute failed to open. Of the 80 heroes who embarked on this dangerous mission, 71, including Doolittle, survived and made it back to America.

Raid Impossible Without Carriers

Although the damage caused by the raid was minor compared to European standards it was met with boundless enthusiasm by the American people. It also showed that the aircraft carrier could make the impossible possible and that this operation was a wonderful example of inter-service cooperation.

The five General Motors factories that previously built automobiles were converted to construct Wildcat fighters in order to free Grumman to concentrate on the F6F Hellcat. The plants became known as Eastern Aircraft. Over 1,100 Eastern Aircraft FM-1 Wildcats were built during the first year of operation; 300 of which were supplied to the Royal Navy which called them Martlet V. (U.S. Army Signal Corps)

The Royal Navy flew Martlets from carriers and from shore bases. The latter were used for coastal defense and patrol as was this Martlet V photograph at La Senia Air Base in Algeria. Observe the installation of only four machine guns instead of the normally installed six machine guns. This was done on some of the last production FM-1 Wildcats to lighten them for better operation from the smaller escort carriers. At this time Eastern Aircraft was preparing to produce the FM-2 with more power and only four machine guns for quicker takeoffs from the converted CVE short decks. (U.S. Army Signal Corps)

With a more powerful but lighter engine and only four machine guns the Eastern Aircraft FM-2 attained a top speed of 332 mph. The fin and rudder were made taller than the FM-1 and F4F-4 to counteract the increased engine torque. Note the engine exhaust smudge on the fuselage as opposed to the downward exhaust of previous Wildcats. This beautifully reconstructed FM-2 is one of the 4,777 produced by Eastern Aircraft. (WAM Foto)

Raid Draws Japanese Into Battle

Admiral Halsey declared, "In my opinion their flight was one of the most courageous deeds in military history." Later, it will be seen how this raid influenced the Japanese to initiate a decisive naval battle.

EASTERN AIRCRAFT WILDCATS

In the spring of 1942 General Motors Eastern Aircraft was made a second source for the Grumman F4F-4. Eastern Aircraft comprised a group of five factories that previously produced General Motors automobiles in peacetime. This left Grumman free to concentrate on the F6F Hellcat. Over 1,100 Eastern Aircraft FM-1 Wildcats were constructed during the first 12 months of production; 300 of which were supplied to the Royal Navy Fleet Air Arm as the Martlet V in 1942-43.

The many new escort carrier conversions with their short flight decks and slow speed demanded planes with more power for takeoff, as well as a slower landing speed. To meet these requirements

A Fleet Air Arm Martlet V is taking off from a Royal Navy carrier in the Mediterranean Sea without use of the catapult. Observe the split flaps which shorten the takeoff run. (U.S. Army Signal Corps)

USS Wasp is loaded with a dozen Spitfires for delivery to the island of Malta enroute from Scotland. The British planes are at the aft end of the Flight Deck with the Wildcat combat air patrol in the foreground so the CAP can takeoff first to patrol the area. Note the folded wing F4F-4 Wildcats at the extreme left. (Official U.S. Navy Photograph, Naval Imaging Command)

Grumman developed the F4F-8. This was a F4F-4 fitted with the 1,350 horsepower, supercharged Wright Cyclone R-1820-56 air-cooled radial engine. This engine was 230 pounds lighter and produced 150 more horsepower than the standard F4F-4 engine. Armament was reduced to four 0.50 inch caliber guns while speed increased to 332 miles per hour at 28,800 feet. The vertical tail was heightened to counteract the increased torque of the more powerful engine. Grumman stopped constructing Wildcats in late 1942 when production of the F4F-8 was turned over to General Motors Eastern Aircraft Division which was already producing Martlet V's and Avengers. Designated FM-2, 4,437 were constructed for the U.S. Navy with an additional 340 for the Fleet Air Arm. By this time the Royal Navy no longer used the name Martlet but had adopted the Wildcat name for the Grumman design. The FM-2 was known as the Wildcat VI in the Fleet Air Arm.

USS WASP DELIVERS SPITFIRES

Upon the request of the Royal Navy *USS Wasp* was transferred from North Sea duty to that of transporting Spitfire fighters from Scotland to the Mediterranean island of Malta. The Spitfires were loaded on the carrier by crane but took off under their own power after the *Wasp*'s Wildcats had set up a combat air patrol. In two voyages on April 20 and May 7 the American carrier delivered 58 and 47 Spitfires respectively, thereby playing a vital role in keeping the island's air defenses in operation.

JAPANESE OPERATION "MO"

By this time, in the spring of 1942, Japan controlled all territory between Burma, China and the Solomon Islands plus all territory north of Australia except the southeastern coast of New Guinea, which was to be Japan's next objective. Japanese forces had been able to cut the estimated schedule of conquest in half and had lost only two dozen naval ships; the largest of which were destroyers. This rapid advance enabled the Japanese to accelerate their original timetable, therefore, Operation "MO" began.

The Japanese plan for Operation "MO" involved the occupation of Port Moresby on the southeastern coast of New Guinea, which was called Papua, and Tulagi on Florida Island in the Solomons in order to gain mastery of the air over the Coral Sea and its shores. To secure this southward expansion of the Japanese defensive perimeter the Solomon Islands would eventually have to be occupied by Japanese forces. The Coral Sea lies between Australia and the Solomon Islands. Also included in Operation "MO" was the seizure of Ocean Island and Nauru Island, west of the Gilberts, because they were a rich source of phosphorus; necessary as fertilizer for Japanese agriculture.

Japanese Grand Strategy

Operation "MO" was the second step in the Japanese Grand Strategy to immobilize U.S. interference with the Greater East Asia Co-prosperity Sphere. The first step was, of course, the attack on Pearl Harbor and the third step was to be the occupation of Samoa, New Caledonia and Fiji in order to cut off the SLOC (Sea Lines of Communication) between the U.S. and Australia. The final step was the invasion of the Western Aleutians and Midway in order to complete Japan's outer defensive perimeter and a necessary move to draw the U.S. Pacific Fleet into a decisive engagement. Japan was compelled to defeat the U.S. Pacific Fleet in 1942 or be placed on the defensive in the following year by America's irresistible counterattack which was inevitable! The Doolittle Tokyo raid stimulated this decision.

Small Japanese Force Available

Only a very small force was available for Operation "MO" because Admiral Yamamoto's Combined Fleet was being assembled for the Midway showdown. Admiral Nagumo had brought his Carrier Striking Force back to Japan in mid-April for maintenance and air group replenishment after its actions in the Indian Ocean and Ceylon. A task force was assembled under the overall command of Vice Admiral Shigeyoshi Inouye. This included the Fifth Carrier Division, led by Rear Admiral Tadaichi Hara, which comprised *Zuikaku* and *Shokaku*; each operating about 60 planes. Supporting all operations were 10 cruisers, 12 destroyers, seven submarines, light carrier *Shoho*, plus assorted minelayers, minesweepers, transports, subchasers, and 155 shore-based aircraft. The Fifth Carrier Division was part of the Striking Force led by Vice Admiral Takeo Takagi.

Japanese Code Broken

Unknown to the Japanese was the group of dedicated American cryptoanalysts, mathematicians, and linguists who labored in an anonymous windowless basement beneath the streets of Pearl Harbor. Lieutenant Commander Thomas H. Dyer and the group worked tirelessly to break the Japanese code. These unsung heroes emerged once every two or three days to receive a picnic basket of food from their wives. It was under these adverse conditions that Tommy Dyer and his staff had broken the Japanese code prior to April 17, which gave Admiral Nimitz the information that a Japanese Armada was on the move toward the Coral Sea, aiming to occupy Port Moresby. This port was scheduled to play an essential part i General MacArthur's strategy and it was; therefore, important t block this Japanese thrust.

Captain Thomas H. Dyer USN (Ret) died in 1985 at age 82. was not until 20 years after the war that his family knew of Dyer secret work that virtually assured U.S. victory in the Pacific.

BATTLE OF THE CORAL SEA

Admiral Nimitz ordered the *Yorktown* group, Rear Admiral Fran Jack Fletcher's Task Force 17, and the *Lexington* Group, Rear Ac miral Aubrey W. Fitch's Task Force 11, to rendezvous at the easter end of the Coral Sea by May 1. The combined groups became Tas Force 17 under Fletcher's command. The two carriers were sup ported by six American and two Australian cruisers, 13 destroyer: two oilers, six submarines, and one seaplane tender. Each carrie was equipped with one each of a fighter, dive bomber, scouting and torpedo plane squadron, which brought the total aircraft comple ment to just under 150 planes. The Japanese had estimated tha there was only one American aircraft carrier available in the Pa cific because when the *Saratoga* had been torpedoed on January 1 the Japanese had mistaken her for *Lexington* and assumed she ha sunk.

Rear Admiral Aubrey W. Fitch was in command of Task Force 11, USS Lexington group, during the Battle of the Coral Sea. Photo taken when Admiral Fitch became the 34th Superintendent of the U.S. Naval Academy with the rank of Vice Admiral. (U.S. Naval Historical Center, Courtesy U.S. Naval Institute Photo Collection)

Douglas Dauntless dive bombers are crowded at the aft end of the USS Lexington Flight Deck preparatory to a strike at Japanese carriers. Note the perforated dive brake flaps and the wing slots (Arrows). (U.S. National Archives)

Japanese Landing On Tulagi

Upon rendezvous, Fletcher began refueling *Yorktown* from the oiler *Neosho* and ordered Fitch to do the same from the other oiler, *Tippecanoe*. Somehow, it was not until the following day that *Lexington* began to take on fuel which was not scheduled to be completed until noon of May 4. Meanwhile, Fletcher received information from MacArthur that Japanese forces were moving east into the Coral Sea. This forced Fletcher to head for the middle of the Coral Sea without Fitch or Royal Navy Rear Admiral John G. Crace's three-cruiser force in order to ascertain the strength and location of the Japanese forces. While Fletcher was steaming north at a leisurely pace to allow *Lexington* and the others to catch up, the Japanese were landing troops at Tulagi on Florida Island. Admiral Takagi's two big carriers did not enter the Coral Sea, but were well north of Bougainville planning to sail down the northeast side of the Solomon Islands and enter the Coral Sea from the east between the Solomon and Santa Cruz Islands on May 4.

Yorktown Too Late At Tulagi

It was not until the evening of May 3 that Fletcher learned that patrol planes based in Australia had sighted the Tulagi landings. The Admiral quickly ordered *Neosho* with the destroyer *Russell* as escort to meet Fitch and Crace at the previously arranged refueling rendezvous on May 4, then for the entire force to meet him 300 miles south of Guadalcanal at daybreak of May 5. He quickly turned for Tulagi but was too late and the *Yorktown* raiders sank only one destroyer and four landing craft. The *Yorktown* group then returned south to join with the *Lexington* and cruiser groups. Three days had passed and the main Japanese forces had not yet been sighted. *Yorktown* joined *Lexington* and Crace's cruisers in the morning of May 5 and around noon one of *Yorktown*'s planes shot down a four-engine Kawanishi flying boat patrol plane which had flown from Rabaul. Task Force 17 steamed slowly on a southeasterly course while completing the interrupted refueling and changed course to the northwest on that evening, reasoning that the Invasion Group

A Grumman Wildcat of the Lexington CAP (Combat Air Patrol) is being directed on the Flight Deck prior to takeoff. Observe the large twin eight inch gun turret. (Official U.S. Navy Photograph News Photo Division)

would come from Rabaul. Meanwhile, Admiral Takagi's Carrier Striking Force was speeding down the Solomon's coast and rounded San Cristobal Island, the easternmost of the Solomons, at the same time that Fletcher had changed course. While the Anglo-American force was heading northwestward to locate the Japanese Port Moresby Invasion Group, the Japanese carriers were behind them; steering east, south and then north, hoping to find that lone American carrier. It was like a game of blindman's buff, with both participants blindfolded!

Admiral Fletcher detached *Neosho* and the destroyer *Sims* escort at about 7:30 PM on May 6 so the task force could improve its speed. At about 6:30 the following morning TF-17 had arrived about 100 miles east of the easternmost island of the Louisiade Archipelago and Fletcher ordered Crace to press ahead with his cruisers to intercept the Port Moresby Invasion Force which had to cut through the Louisiades in order to reach Port Moresby.

Sims and *Neosho* Sink

Early in the morning of May 7 Admiral Takagi sent out search planes which sighted *Sims* and *Neosho*, mistaking them for a cruiser and an aircraft carrier. At first reading this appears absurd; however, from an altitude of 10,000 feet it requires a very experienced observer to correctly identify types of ships, not to mention recognizing friend from foe! After two unsuccessful horizontal bombing attacks by Kates from Takagi's carriers, the admiral sent 36 Val dive bombers to complete the task at midday. The Japanese attacked in three waves and at the onset three 500 pound bombs made direct hits on *USS Sims*; two exploding in the engine room. Within a few minutes the destroyer literally bent in two and sank. Only 15 of the crew survived! Meanwhile, 20 Vals had concentrated on *USS Neosho* and scored seven direct hits and eight damaging near-misses. Many crew members misunderstood one of Captain Phillips' orders and began jumping overboard; very few could be rescued.

Although mortally wounded *Neosho* drifted westward for four days as the crew worked frantically to keep the tanker afloat. The derelict was found about noon on May 11 and the remaining 123 men were transferred to the destroyer *Henley* which then scuttled *Neosho*.

This incident adds more living testimony to the fact that ships are virtually helpless during an air attack without air cover in the form of a Combat Air Patrol (CAP).

First American Strike

Scout bombers from the American carriers had sighted some Japanese cruisers with *Shokaku* and *Zuikaku* at a distance of 225 miles. Admiral Fletcher launched 28 Dauntless dive bombers, 12 Devastator torpedo bombers and 10 Wildcat fighters from *Lexington* and 25 Dauntless, 10 Devastators and eight Wildcats from *Yorktown* against the Japanese ships. This was virtually the entire American aerial strike force and the carriers were very vulnerable while the planes were away. Fortunately, Hara's search planes had found *Neosho* and *Sims* and the two more expendable ships received the furious Japanese aerial attack; thereby saving *Yorktown* and *Lexington*. The U.S. attacking aircraft failed to find the Japanese carriers and returned to their ships.

Cruisers Scare Off Invasion Force

Meanwhile, Admiral Crace's cruisers scared off the Port Moresby Invasion Force, but not before the cruisers underwent severe air attacks.

Shoho Sinks

Just before noon on May 7 an aerial strike force of 93 planes from *Lexington* and *Yorktown* became the very first American planes to attack an enemy aircraft carrier. Earlier that morning Rear Admiral Aritomo Goto's Port Moresby Invasion Force Covering Group which included four cruisers and the light carrier *Shoho* equipped with 12 Zero Sen fighters and nine torpedo planes had been spotted by American scout planes. *Shoho* was about 160 miles from the U.S. carriers and in the first onslaught was hit with two 1,000 pound bombs which started enormous fires. The pounding continued until *Shoho* had been hit by 13 bombs and seven torpedoes which made the carrier sink within five minutes. Lieutenant Commander Robert Dixon, leader of Scouting Squadron Two (VS-2), reported the sinking over his radio by transmitting this well-remembered message: "Scratch one flat-top, Dixon to Carrier Scratch one flat-top."

Leppla and Liska

Virtually all of the Zero fighters had been able to take off from Shoho to defend the carrier but, by the time the attack was over eight of the Japanese fighters had been shot down by the escorting Wildcats; however, it was not only Wildcats which scored against the Japanese defenders. Ensign John A. Leppla, who had been awarded the Navy Cross during the attack on Salamaua and Lae piloted a Douglas Dauntless with Aviation Radioman 3rd Class John Liska as the gunner in the rear cockpit during the first dive bombing attack on Shoho. The pair had been attached to Dixon's squadron which was operating from *Lexington*. During the first dive the SBD was jumped by two Zeroes. Liska quickly shot down the first attacker and had just driven off the second when Leppla noticed a Zero closing in on another diving Dauntless. Without leaving his dive Leppla got into firing position and sent the Zero crashing into the sea. Upon releasing his bomb Leppla climbed for altitude and was surprised to find another Japanese fighter nearby. A quick turn

...wo heroes of the Battle of the Coral Sea were John Leppla, pilot, and ...ohn Liska, gunner, of a Douglas Dauntless dive bomber assigned to 'SS Lexington. (U.S. National Archives)

...rought the Zero in his sights and Leppla scored again! During the ...eturn flight to *Lexington* the duo came upon a Japanese biplane ...cout and Leppla got him with a burst from his twin nose guns.

Liska was 19 years old during this activity. He was a native of ...oaldale, Pennsylvania and had enlisted in the regular Navy on ...ebruary 28, 1941, Leppla was a 26 year old Naval Reservist from ...ima, Ohio.

The Battle Begins

...dmirals Fletcher and Takagi were thirsty for each other's blood ...ut neither knew the other's location nor his intention. The night of ...1ay 7-8 saw Task Force 17 heading in a southeasterly direction ...hile Hara's carriers went north to provide air cover for the Port ...1oresby Invasion Force now that *Shoho* had been sunk.

Dawn of May 8 saw the scout planes of each side take off in ...earch of the other's carriers. Task Force 17 was sailing in clear ...veather while Takagi's carriers were in an overcast with intermit-...ent rain squalls; however, the scouting parties detected each other's ...arriers almost at the same time. Each carrier launched a striking ...orce at once. Takagi sent 33 Val dive bombers, 18 Kate torpedo ...lanes, and 18 Zeroes in a southerly direction, while Fletcher sent ...6 Dauntless dive bombers, 21 Devastator torpedo planes, and 15 ...Vildcats northeastward in two separate groups. The *Lexington* group ...ollowed that of *Yorktown* by 10 minutes.

American Attack

...Vhen the *Yorktown* planes arrived over the target area Zuikaku ...lipped into a rain squall leaving *Shokaku* to bear the brunt of the ...ttack. Lieutenant Commander Joseph Taylor of Torpedo Squad-...on Five (VT-5) led the attack, with Wildcats of VF-2 providing

Ensign John Arthur Leppla shot down four Japanese aircraft, including a vaunted Zero, with his Dauntless forward firing guns in the Coral Sea battle. He is shown here in his later Lieutenant (jg) uniform. (U.S. National Archives)

...s the rear gunner of a Douglas Dauntless dive bomber, Aviation ...Radioman 3rd Class John Liska shot down three Japanese planes, ...ncluding a Zero fighter in the Battle of the Coral Sea with his single ...novable gun. (U.S. National Archives)

protection for the low and slow-flying Devastators from the defending Zeroes. The Dauntless divebombers coordinated their attack with that of the torpedo planes while the Wildcats engaged the Zeroes.

This initial sea battle of American Naval Aviation revealed some very serious defects in U.S. torpedoes: they were so slow that when dropped beyond point blank range they were easily dodged by the Japanese carrier; many failed to detonate upon impact; others ran wild and missed the target; and still others failed to reach the target. The dive bombers fared better by scoring two direct hits with 500 pound bombs, one forward and the other aft. The forward bomb damaged the *Shokaku* Flight Deck which prevented planes from taking off and also started gasoline fires. The aft bomb exploded below deck and destroyed the aircraft engine repair shops. The explosions and fires killed 108 and wounded 40; however, *Shokaku* was not mortally damaged and headed homeward as the fires were brought under control. The Japanese carrier was to engage in later battles.

Some of *Lexington*'s air group had failed to find the Japanese ships and turned back. Despite bad weather some Devastators and Wildcat escort managed to make a torpedo run; however, five torpedo planes and three Wildcats were shot down. The dive bombers were more successful.

Japanese Attack

A few minutes after *Yorktown*'s air group launched its attack on *Shokaku*, Kates, Vals and Zeroes from *Shokaku* and *Zuikaku* were descending upon Lexington and *Yorktown*. The only combat air patrol for both carriers consisted of a mere nine Wildcats so Admiral Fitch sent up 23 *Lexington* Douglas Dauntless dive bombers to help intercept the attackers. This was a very wise move because the SBD was quite maneuverable and, despite the fact that the plane was inadequately gunned for interception, of the 91 Japanese planes shot down during the Coral Sea fighting Dauntless crews are credited with 40 victories.

The Coral Sea had become a strange crisscross air battle with the Japanese air group better balanced having a larger proportion of fighters than the U.S. carriers, and more accurately directed to the target. It was just after 11:15 AM on May 8 that Japanese aircraft approached from the northeast with torpedo-carrying Kates leading the attack on the two American carriers. The more maneuverable *Yorktown* was able to avoid a total of eight torpedoes; however, the larger and less maneuverable *Lexington* was attacked using the anvil system. This is the technique in which two torpedoes are aimed at the same point on opposite sides of the hull so that, regardless of the evasive maneuver, a hit is virtually guaranteed! Thirteen torpedoes were launched at three-quarter mile range from about 150 feet altitude on both sides of *Lexington*. Eleven passed under, forward and alongside; however, two found their mark.

While the torpedoes were still generating wakes Val dive bombers began their dives from 17,000 feet and released bombs from 2,500 feet on *Lexington* and *Yorktwon*. Two 500 pound bombs penetrated *Lexington*'s Flight Deck, which jammed the aircraft elevators and started fires, while *Yorktown* was hit by a single 800 pound bomb which struck the Flight Deck just inboard of the island and plunged down to the Fourth Deck, starting fires.

Burn Victims

Of the 65 men who died or were seriously injured, many were caused by burns because most of the victims had been wearing short sleeve shirts and short pants or rolled up sleeves or pant legs. It had been proved during the Java Sea battle that short sleeves and pants exposed crewmen to terrible burns while even the thinnest and lightest covering protected the skin from radiated heat. Although abbreviated clothing was more comfortable in the tropics it was an invitation to death or serious injury in the event of fire.

Lady Lex Sinks

The Lexington and *Yorktown* fires were quickly extinguished and the Battle of the Coral Sea was considered over by 11:45 in the morning of May 8. Both sides retired. *USS Lexington* was listing seven degrees, aircraft elevators inoperable, and three fireroom partially flooded. The ship was brought to an even keel by transferring fuel oil and it appeared that the beautiful carrier would be saved. Unknown to anyone was the fact that the many near-misses, as well as the direct hits, had sent shocks through the hull and piping, which caused the aviation gasoline tanks and/or piping to fracture, allowing flammable fumes to escape. These finally reached a sparking motor generator via the ventilation system and caused a devastating internal explosion which shook the big carrier from stem to stern at 12:47 PM. Several violent explosions continued, which disrupted internal communications. An enormous explosion followed at 2:45 destroying the fire room and engine room ventilating systems. The destroyer *Morris* pulled alongside and passed fire hose to help quench the many fires; however, erupting flames hampered this assistance. As the fire approached the bomb stowage Captain Frederick C. Sherman ordered all sick and wounded personnel to be disembarked in *Lexington*'s whaleboats and all excess squadron personnel to transfer to destroyers alongside. By 4:30 the ship was dead in the water and one half hour later Admiral Fitch ordered Captain Sherman to abandon ship. It was one of the most orderly ship evacuations ever experienced and nobody drowned. Crewmen, Marines and Air Group personnel took off their shoes and placed them in an orderly line along the edge of the Flight Deck and then descended hand-over-hand on knotted lifelines into liferafts or waiting destroyers.

Captain Sherman and his executive officer, Commander M Seligman, conducted a final inspection of the stricken carrier to be certain that no wounded had been overlooked and were left behind. The two officers and a Marine corporal were the last to abandon ship. Admiral Fitch then ordered the destroyer Phelps to administer the coup de grace with torpedoes and at about 8:00 PM on May USS Lexington, affectionately called *Lady Lex*, sank beneath the waters of the Coral Sea to a depth of 2,400 fathoms, taking 36 plane down with her.

American Coral Sea Heroes

Many American Heroes emerged from the Coral Sea fighting, in addition to Leppla and Liska, who scored three more victories while intercepting the attacking Japanese air group of Vals, Kates an Zeroes. The final score for the duo was four victories for Ensign John Leppla, who was awarded a Gold Star in lieu of a second Navy Cross, and three victories for Aviation Radioman 3rd Class

BATTLE OF THE CORAL SEA; MAY 4-8, 1942

LEGEND

- ⊃ JAPANESE INVASION FORCE – ADM. GOTO
- ⇨ U.S. TF-II USS LEXINGTON – ADM. FITCH
- ‖▶ COMBINED TF-II & TF-17
- ⇒ JAPANESE AIR STRIKES
- S SHOHO SINKS MAY 7
- ◇S SHOKAKU DAMAGED MAY 8
- Ⓝ USS NEOSHO SINKS MAY II

- ➤ JAPANESE CARRIER DIV.5 SHOKAKU & ZUIKAKU –ADM.HARA
- ▶ U.S. TF-17 USS YORKTOWN – ADM. FLETCHER
- •••▶ ROYAL NAVY ADM. CRACE - TF-44 CRUISERS
- ➤ U.S. AIR STRIKES
- Ⓢ USS SIMS SINKS MAY 7
- Ⓛ USS LEXINGTON SINKS MAY 8

150°E   155°E   160°E   165°E.   0°

Admiralty Is.

New Ireland

RABAUL

New Britain

Papua

Bougainville

Choiseul

SOLOMON ISLANDS

Tulagi

Guadalcanal

Santa Cristobal

05°S

May 4

May 5

May 11

LOUISIADE

May 5

May 7

May 6

PORT MORESBY

May 7

May 7

S ARCH.

◇S

May 8

May 9

May 6

May 10

May 4

May 7

May 6

10°S

Santa Cruz Is.

C O R A L

Ⓛ

May 8

Ⓝ

Ⓢ

May 4

May 5

S E A

May 5

15°S

Espiritu Santo Is.

May 9

New Caledonia

WAM

Australia

20°S

The USS Lexington crew are abandoning the mortally damaged ship by lowering themselves to the water hand-over-hand on knotted ropes. Note the destroyer barely visible in the smoke (arrow) assisting the evacuees. (U.S. National Archives)

John Liska, for whom no record could be found of an award for his remarkable achievement.

Lieutenant Commander R.E. Dixon was awarded the Navy Cross for leading his squadron in the *Shoho* dive bombing action during which time he dived to a very low altitude to ensure a direct hit on the carrier. On May 8, having sighted *Shokaku* and *Zuikaku*, he remained on station in order to direct his dive bombers to the Japanese carriers.

Lieutenant John J. Powers was posthumously awarded the Medal of Honor for his dive bombing achievements during the Tulagi attacks in which he destroyed a gunboat with bombs and damaged another so seriously by strafing that it was forced to beach itself. He led his Douglas Dauntless Division to the attack on *Shoho* and risked his life by pulling out at a very low altitude to ensure a hit. As Squadron Gunnery Officer he often stressed the importance of releasing the bomb at the lowest possible altitude, but also warned of the potential danger. During the attack on *Shokaku* he dove so low that his SBD flew through shell and bomb fragments, flame, smoke and debris from the explosion on the carrier, which prevented Lieutenant Powers from recovering from his dive.

Lieutenant (jg) E.S. McCuskey was awarded the Navy Cross for disrupting a fighter attack on torpedo planes he was escorting and for shooting down one of the four Japanese fighters.

Coral Sea - A New Concept of Naval Warfare

The Battle of the Coral Sea introduced a new concept of naval warfare in which the opposing fleets fought battles without the ships ever coming within sight of one another. The ships had become like small nations waging wars on a frontierless landscape. The ideas of Ader, Ely, Samson, Chambers, Whiting, Moffett, Dunning and all the early pilots who risked their lives had finally come to full maturity.

Indecisive

Coral Sea was a strategic victory for the U.S. because the Japanese

Captain Frederick Carl Sherman was commanding officer of USS Lexington in the Coral Sea battle and conducted one of the most orderly abandon ship operations ever experienced. We will meet him later as Rear Admiral Sherman, task force commander, in which uniform he is shown here. (Official U.S. Navy Photograph, Naval Imaging Command)

ivasion of Port Moresby had been thwarted, which was the first Japanese setback of their planned southward expansion.

Tactically, Coral Sea was a Japanese victory mainly due to the inking of *Lexington*; however, the loss of highly trained Japanese arrier pilots kept *Zuikaku* out of action until the middle of June nd the damage to *Shokaku* kept it out of service for two months, vhich made Coral Sea a Pyrrhic victory for the Japanese because either carrier was available for the coming Midway battle. In efect, Coral Sea was an indispensable preliminary to Midway.

JEW PLANES AND CARRIERS

Vhile CAM ships and Escort Carriers fought the Battle of the Atantic, and the U.S. and Japanese carriers with their shipboard airraft continued to slug it out in the Pacific, new carriers and shipoard aircraft were making their appearance.

wordfish and Dauntless Replacements

Despite the fact that the Fairey Swordfish was still performing yeonan service for the Fleet Air Arm and the Douglas Dauntless' suerlative performance was a hard act to follow in the U.S. Navy, oth the Air Ministry and Bureau of Aeronautics had replacements nder development since the late 1930s. Both production craft first ippeared in May and June of 1942.

airey Barracuda

Designed to meet the requirements of Air Ministry Specification .24/37 of 1937 Fairey developed a three-seater monoplane toredo/dive bomber for operation from aircraft carriers. The shoulter-positioned wing folded back laterally to facilitate below deck towage. The prototype first flew during December 1940; however, roduction was delayed because other more urgently needed planes took precedence at that time. Although the Barracuda was to relace the Swordfish and Albacore, both biplanes continued to serve n the Fleet Air Arm.

Barracuda Data

The initial production order for 25 planes was delivered in May 1942. By this time the Fairey design was called Barracuda and the irst batch designated Mark I. Powered by a 1,260 horsepower Rolls-Royce Merlin 30 liquid-cooled engine, the Mk.I attained a top speed of 235 miles with 2,000 pounds of bombs and/or a torpedo. Empty weight was 8,700 pounds, while gross weight was 13,500 pounds.

The Mk.I was quickly followed by the Mk.II, which was powered by a Rolls-Royce Merlin 32 engine developing 1,640 horsepower, driving a four-bladed propeller. The Mk.II carried one 1,620 pound torpedo, four 450 pound depth charges or a 1,500 pound bomb load. Speed of the 14,100 pound plane was 228 miles per hour at 1,750 feet. Range was 524 miles fully loaded.

The Mark III was virtually identical to the Mk.II except that it was specially developed for the antisubmarine reconnaissance role. This craft carried one 1,572 pound torpedo or four 250 pound depth charges. Speed and range had increased to 239 miles per hour and 584 miles. The Mk.III was also fitted with a radar scanner in a radome under the fuselage.

Although conceived as a torpedo-bomber the Fairey Barracuda achieved fame as a dive bomber. Observe the large Fairey-Youngman wing flaps and long landing gear which retracts into the wing and fuselage side. This Barracuda just landed on HMS Furious. (Ministry of Defence [Navy])

The three-seater Barracuda was produced in three marks of which 2,572 airframes were constructed. Note the access window/doors in the fuselage sides and the air stabilizing torpedo fins. (Air Ministry [Navy])

Dimensions of Marks I, II and III were identical with a wingspan of 49 feet-2 inches; length of 39 feet-9 inches; height 15 feet-1 inch. Wing area was 367 square feet. Barracuda construction was all-metal except the control surfaces, which were fabric covered.

Although conceived as a torpedo plane the Barracuda will always be remembered for its dive bombing achievements. Total production of the three Marks was 2,572 aircraft produced by Fairey, Blackburn and Boulton-Paul aircraft companies.

Curtiss SB2C Helldiver

As the result of Bureau of Aeronautics Specification 1937 for a sturdy, high-performance dive bomber that could carry heavy loads at high speed, the Airplane Division of the Curtiss-Wright Corporation was awarded an experimental contract on May 15, 1939 for a prototype designated XSB2C-1. The new design was called Helldiver, the third and last Curtiss to bear that name, and bore a strong resemblance to the Brewster SB2A Buccaneer with which it had been in direct competition for this contract. The Helldiver had a crew of two.

At that time Curtiss-Wright's new facility in Columbus, Ohio was not yet finished, therefore, the project design staff was compelled to complete its work in a barn owned by Ohio State University. Much of the prototype was also constructed here. The initial production order for the SB2C-1 had been placed in November 1940, one month before the prototype had flown for the first time with Curtiss test pilot Lloyd Childs at the controls on December 18.

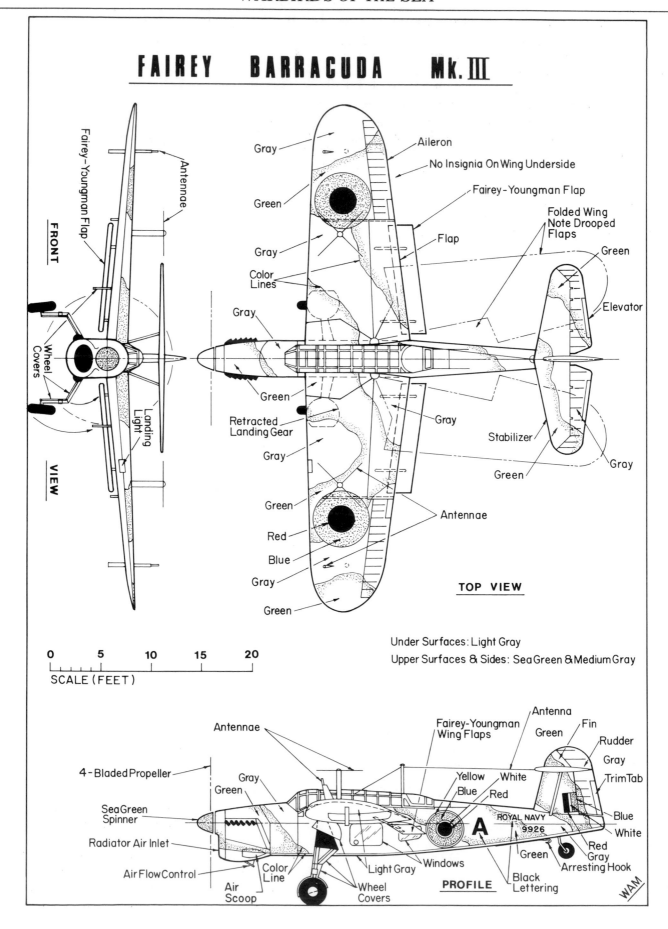

FAIREY BARRACUDA Mk. III

FRONT

Fairey-Youngman Flap

Antennae

Wheel Covers

Landing Light

VIEW

Gray

Green

Gray

Color Lines

Gray

Green

Retracted Landing Gear

Gray

Green

Red

Blue

Gray

Green

Aileron

No Insignia On Wing Underside

Fairey-Youngman Flap

Flap

Folded Wing Note Drooped Flaps

Green

Elevator

Gray

Stabilizer

Green

Gray

Antennae

TOP VIEW

Under Surfaces: Light Gray

Upper Surfaces & Sides: Sea Green & Medium Gray

0   5   10   15   20

SCALE (FEET)

Antennae

4-Bladed Propeller

Gray

Green

SeaGreen Spinner

Radiator Air Inlet

Air Flow Control

Air Scoop

Color Line

Wheel Covers

Light Gray

Windows

Fairey-Youngman Wing Flaps

Yellow   White

Blue   Red

Antenna

Green   Fin

Rudder

Gray

TrimTab

Blue

White

Red

Gray

Arresting Hook

Green

Black Lettering

ROYAL NAVY

9926

A

PROFILE

WAM

The Curtiss SB2C Helldiver was the first U.S. Navy production dive bomber to carry its bombs internally. Torpedoes and depth charges could also be accommodated on the bottom of the fuselage or wings. (Curtiss Wright Corporation)

Stability Problem

The Bureau of Aeronautics Specification had required a short overall length in order that two of the dive bombers would fit on a carrier elevator. This space requirement created an aerodynamic problem caused by the short distance between the tail surfaces and the center of gravity that produced severe longitudinal and directional instability. The prototype crashed during the subsequent tests early

Fire Control Technician Sal Marrone inspects the twin machine guns in the Curtiss SB2C-3 Helldiver rear cockpit. Observe the retracted turtledeck to improve the arc of fire and the wing slot on the folded wing (arrows). (Sal Marrone Photo)

in 1941. Enlarged tail surfaces improved the stability problem; however, the condition was never fully corrected. Despite the prototype crash and the inherent stability problem the U.S. Navy never lost faith in the design.

Refinements

The first production Helldiver was flown in June 1942. A series of refinements were incorporated as the plane entered production. One of the major changes involved the increased fuel capacity in bulletproof tanks. Another change was the wing flap mechanism which was redesigned to operate the flaps three times faster than the original speed. Split flaps were incorporated to reduce the Helldiver's landing speed. Leading edge slots were also added for improved control and stability during slow speed landings. The wing folding mechanism was modified to fold the wings more snugly against the fuselage to improve stowage. The Helldiver was a large plane and the turtledeck just behind the rear cockpit interfered with the gunner's sight and arc of fire. The turtledeck was, therefore; redesigned to telescope downward so the top of the turtledeck was only a few inches above the side of the cockpit.

Internal Bomb Bay

The Helldiver was the first U.S. Navy production dive bomber to carry its bombs completely enclosed within the fuselage where three rows of bomb racks were provided for an assortment of armament ranging from 100 to 1,600 pound bombs or depth charges of 350 to 650 pounds. A torpedo could also be carried from the centerline rack through the use of an adaptor which required that the bomb bay doors be locked open. Underwing racks could accommodate

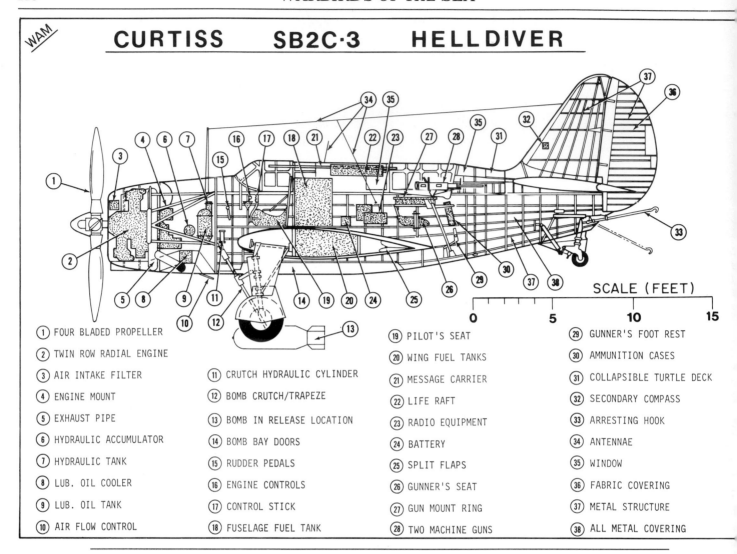

CURTISS SB2C·3 HELLDIVER

1. FOUR BLADED PROPELLER
2. TWIN ROW RADIAL ENGINE
3. AIR INTAKE FILTER
4. ENGINE MOUNT
5. EXHAUST PIPE
6. HYDRAULIC ACCUMULATOR
7. HYDRAULIC TANK
8. LUB. OIL COOLER
9. LUB. OIL TANK
10. AIR FLOW CONTROL
11. CRUTCH HYDRAULIC CYLINDER
12. BOMB CRUTCH/TRAPEZE
13. BOMB IN RELEASE LOCATION
14. BOMB BAY DOORS
15. RUDDER PEDALS
16. ENGINE CONTROLS
17. CONTROL STICK
18. FUSELAGE FUEL TANK
19. PILOT'S SEAT
20. WING FUEL TANKS
21. MESSAGE CARRIER
22. LIFE RAFT
23. RADIO EQUIPMENT
24. BATTERY
25. SPLIT FLAPS
26. GUNNER'S SEAT
27. GUN MOUNT RING
28. TWO MACHINE GUNS
29. GUNNER'S FOOT REST
30. AMMUNITION CASES
31. COLLAPSIBLE TURTLE DECK
32. SECONDARY COMPASS
33. ARRESTING HOOK
34. ANTENNAE
35. WINDOW
36. FABRIC COVERING
37. METAL STRUCTURE
38. ALL METAL COVERING

SCALE (FEET)
0   5   10   15

---

100 to 1,000 pound bombs, smoke screen cannister, twin .50 inch caliber gun containers or a 100 gallon gasoline drop tank. The SBC2-4 also had provision for eight 5 inch rockets. All Helldivers were able to carry 2,000 pounds of bombs, torpedoes, etc.

Production

The most numerous variant was the SBC2-4 of which 2,045 were built. Other production figures are: SB2C-1 (978); SB2C-2 (one experiemental seaplane); SB2C-3 (1,112); SB2C-5 (970). Canadian Fairchild built over 300 Helldivers and Canadian Car and Foundry completed almost 900 of the dive bombers.

Helldiver Data

Dimensions of the Helldiver are: wingspan 49 feet-9 inches; length 36 feet-8 inches; height 13 feet-2 inches; and wing area 422 square feet. The SB2C-4 was powered by a 1,900 horsepower twin-row, air-cooled radial Wright Cyclone R-2600-20 engine turning a four-bladed propeller. SB2C-1 and SB2C-2 variants had been fitted with three-bladed propellers. Maximum speed at 16,700 feet was 295 miles per hour and cruising speed was 158 miles per hour which gave the craft a range of 1,165 miles with a 1,000 pound bomb load. Initial rate of climb was 1,800 feet per minute and service

ceiling was 29,100 feet. Empty weight was 10,597 pounds while loaded weight was 16,616 pounds. Armament consisted of two fixe forward-firing 20 millimeter rapid fire cannon in the wings plu two .30 inch caliber or .50 inch caliber movable machine guns i the rear cockpit.

IJNS *Junyo* and *Hiyo*

The Japanese aircraft carrier *Junyo* was commissioned on May 5 1942 and was destined to take part in the sea battles soon to unfold She and her sister ship *Hiyo* were converted from trans-Pacific pas senger liners one year before the liner scheduled launching date These 24,140 ton displacement carriers were powered with geare steam turbines which developed 56,250 shaft horsepower supplied to two propeller shafts which drove the ships to a maximum spee of 25.5 knots. Overall length was 719 feet with a beam of 87 feet-inches. Draft was 26 feet-9 inches. The ships could operate 53 plane and employed a crew of 1,200. During the conversion from th *Izumo Maru* and *Kashiwara Maru* topside weight became critica therefore, the height of each of the two hangar levels was a mere 1 feet-6 inches, hardly adequate for the Zero fighter! The 690 x 9 feet Flight Deck was constructed of lumber due to a steel shortag plus economy and weight-saving reasons.

Converted from the trans-Pacific liners Kashiwara Maru and Izumo Maru respectively, the Japanese carriers IJNS Hiyo and IJNS Junyo abandoned standard Japanese carrier design by fitting an island superstructure which included the boiler uptakes. Junyo is shown here under repairs at an unidentified shipyard. (U.S. Naval Historical Center)

One unusual feature of the *Hiyo/Junyo* design is that the boiler uptakes were led through the island to a high smokestack which was canted outboard to direct the gasses away from the Flight Deck area. This gave the ships a decidedly un-Japanese look and more like a Royal Navy carrier.

Gun batteries comprised (12) 5 inch general purpose guns and (24) 25 millimeter antiaircraft guns.

JNS *Ryuho*

This aircraft carrier was converted from the submarine tender IJNS Taigei at the Yokosuka Naval Shipyard in 1942 and commissioned that November. The four Diesel engines were replaced with a twin-crew destroyer-type geared steam turbine powerplant that developed 52,000 shaft horsepower. The new powerplant was very troublesome in service. This can probably be attributed to the crew's unfamiliarity with steam turbine machinery which is more complex to operate than diesel engines. Maximum speed was 26 knots and range was 8,000 miles at 18 knots.

Ryuho displaced 16,500 tons deep load and had a mean draft of 21 feet-9 inches. The wooden 675 x 75 feet Flight Deck was set atop the single level hangar in which a mixed bag of about 30 aircraft could be accommodated.

Hull overall length was 707 feet with a beam of 64 feet-3 inches. Eight 5 inch guns were fitted. Complement was about 1,000 officers and crew.

JATO TEST

Using a Brewster Buffalo on May 26, 1942, Commander C. Finke Fischer was the first to successfully demonstrate the feasibility of JATO (jet assisted take off). Five British solid fuel rockets had been firmly attached to the Buffalo fuselage during the test, which resulted in a 49 percent reduction in takeoff distance. This device proved most useful in getting heavily laden aircraft off carriers in the shortest possible distance.

BATTLE OF MIDWAY

The turning point of the war in the Pacific loomed on the horizon as Admiral Yamamoto planned that necessary showdown with the U.S. Pacific Fleet. In the event that the U.S. Fleet didn't appear Japan would still have completed her outer defensive perimeter by occupying the western Aleutians and Midway. As previously mentioned, Japan had planned this Central Pacific offensive even before the Battle of the Coral Sea.

Yamamoto Plan Decoded

Unknown to the Japanese was the fact that the Pearl Harbor basement codebreakers, led by Commander Joseph J. Rochefort, had already decoded the Japanese battle plans and forwarded the information to Admiral Nimitz. Midway was the westernmost U.S. Naval Base in the Central Pacific at that time because the Japanese had taken Guam and the Philippines. Admiral Nagumo had correctly stated: "Midway Island acts as a sentry for Hawaii." Admiral Nimitz picked up the gauntlet thrown down by Admiral Yamamoto and both men prepared for the showdown.

Japanese Reconnaissance Plane Downed

As early as March 10 the Japanese Navy had sent long-range reconnaissance flying boats to Midway to collect data and photograph installations. On that date a four-engine Kawanishi H8K Emily was shot down by U.S. Marine Corps Brewster Buffalo fighters when it came to snoop around Midway.

U.S. and Japan Shortage of Carriers

Both leaders felt handicapped due to the shortage of operable carriers. Admiral Yamamoto had to sail without *Shokaku* and *Zuikaku* while Admiral Nimitz had to do without *Saratoga*, which was undergoing repairs after being torpedoed and was also being modernized. *Yorktown* was out of action due to damage received in the Coral Sea Battle. The *Yorktown* repairs were estimated to require

JNS Ryuho was converted from a submarine tender at the Yokosuka Naval Shipyard where its original diesel engine propulsion machinery was replaced with a destroyer-type steam powerplant. As with many Japanese aircraft carriers the flight deck was made from wood because steel was scarce in Japan. The wooden deck also reduced topside weight. (U.S. National Archives)

about three months to complete, however, the engineers and dock-yard workers in Pearl Harbor Navy Yard worked their hearts out around the clock and completed the repairs in less than three days! Now, Admiral Nimitz had one more carrier than he had planned, which still wasn't enough. *Yorktown* had lost much of her air group in the Coral Sea; therefore, she embarked most of the *Saratoga* Air Group which prepared *Yorktown* for the ensuing battle.

Japanese Midway Forces

Admiral Isoroku Yamamoto, Commander-in-Chief of the Imperial Japanese Combined Fleet, or Rengo Kantai, made his headquarters on the battleship *Yamato*, which was part of the Main Body or First Fleet, also personally commanded by Admiral Yamamoto.

The Carrier Striking Force, commanded by Vice Admiral Chuichi Nagumo, comprised the carriers *Kaga*, *Hiryu*, *Soryu* and *Akagi*. The Air Group totals were 93 fighters, 85 dive bombers and 93 torpedo bombers. The carriers were escorted by two battleships, three cruisers and 12 destroyers. This force was to neutralize Midway's defenses by means of an air attack at dawn on June 4.

The Midway Occupation Force with Vice Admiral Nobutake Kondo in command was to take 2,500 troops to invade and secure Midway. The Covering Group for this unit was made of two battle-ships, four cruisers and seven destroyers under Admiral Kondo.

A Close Support Group of four cruisers, under Rear Admiral Takeo Kurita, was to bombard the island just prior to the landing.

The Transport Group included 12 transports and other ship under command of Rear Admiral Raizo Tanaka.

The Main Body (First Fleet) under Admiral Yamamoto include the light aircraft carrier *Hosho* with eight torpedo bombers; three battleships; 13 destroyers, and two seaplane carriers. It was intende that the Main Body, plus the various cruisers and battleships th had accompanied the outlying forces were to hold back and the close in for the kill after the Carrier Striking Force had complete its mission.

The Aleutian Island Mobile Force, led by Rear Admiral Katkuta, comprised the carriers *Junyo* and *Ryujo* with a Suppo Group of four battleships, two cruisers, and four oilers under th command of Vice Admiral Shiro Takasu. This force was also to a as a decoy to lure the U.S. Forces away from Midway. Command Minoru Genda was Yamamoto's most valued air operations tactic advisor and was assigned to Admiral Nagumo's staff.

American Midway Forces

Admiral Chester W. Nimitz, Commander-in-Chief U.S. Pacific Fle and Pacific Ocean Areas, made his headquarters in Pearl Harbo about 1,100 miles from Midway. Yamamoto had fast battleship

Japanese Admiral Nobutake Kondo was in command of the Midway Occupation Force as well as the battleship/cruiser Covering Group. (U.S. Naval Historical Center)

Japanese Admiral Raizo Tanaka commanded the Midway Transport Group. (U.S. Naval Historical Center)

Rear Admiral Raymond A. Spruance commanded Task Force 16 centered around USS Enterprise (CV-6) and won the Battle of Midway. He was later promoted to Chief of Staff for Admiral Nimitz. Spruance is shown here as Commander of the U.S. Fifth Fleet. (U.S. National Archives)

that could keep up with his carriers but the U.S. Navy had none; therefore, Admiral Nimitz had no alternative but to concentrate all offensive power in his three carriers.

The Carrier Striking Force, commanded by Rear Admiral Frank Jack Fletcher, included Task Force 16 under Rear Admiral Raymond A. Spruance and Task Force 17 led by Admiral Fletcher. Admiral Spruance had commanded Admiral Halsey's heavy cruisers and was now thrust into the Task Force command because Halsey was incapacitated by illness. Nimitz had made a wise choice because Spruance, although a relatively obscure non-pilot, was extremely competent, had cool judgment, and easily adapted to carrier operations. Though he became one of the leading naval commanders of World War II, he was a quiet warrior without the flamboyance and showmanship of some other high-level commanders.

Task Force 16 comprised Task Groups TG-16.2, TG-16.4, and TG-16.5. *USS Enterprise* (CV-6) and *USS Hornet* (CV-8) were the principal elements of TG-16.5 commanded by Captain George D. Murray.

USS Enterprise (CV-6), Captain Murray commanding, operated a four-squadron air group led by Lieutenant Commander Clarence W. McClusky, Jr.: VF-6 flew 27 Wildcats with Lieutenant James S. Gray in command; VS-6 flew 19 Dauntless dive bombers

with Lieutenant Wilmer E. Gallaher in command; VT-6 flew 14 Devastators with Lieutenant Commander Eugene E. Lindsey in command; and VB-6 flew 19 Dauntless dive bombers with Lieutenant Richard H. Best in command.

USS Hornet (CV-8), Captain Marc A. Mitscher commanding, also operated a four-squadron air group led by Commander Stanhope C. Ring: VF-8 flew 27 Wildcats with Lieutenant Commander Samuel G. Mitchell in command; VB-8 flew 19 Dauntless dive bombers with Lieutenant Commander Robert R. Johnson in command; VT-8 flew 15 Devastators with Lieutenant Commander John C. Waldron in command; and VS-8 flew 18 Dauntless dive bombers with Lieutenant Commander Walter R. Rodee in command.

Task Group 16.2 included six cruisers, Rear Admiral Thomas C. Kinkaid commanding. Task Group 16.4 comprised nine destroyers and the very important Oiler Group included two oilers with two destroyer escorts.

Task Force 17 comprised Task Groups TG-17.2, TG-17.4 and TG-17.5. *USS Yorktown* (CV-5) was the principal element of TG-17.5 commanded by Captain Elliott Buckmaster.

USS Yorktown (CV-5), Captain Buckmaster commanding, operated a four-squadron air group led by Lieutenant Commander Oscar Pederson.

It was standard practice to number U.S. Navy carrier squadrons with the same number as the aircraft carrier to which they were assigned, ie; VS-8 was Scouting Squadron 8 assigned to CV-8 *USS Hornet* or, to describe it in another way, the fighting squadrons assigned to *Hornet* could have no other designation than VF-8. There were exceptions in TG-17.5 because *Yorktown* took on most of the *Saratoga* Air Group. These squadrons retained the *Saratoga* designation number CV-3; therefore, VF-3, VT-3 and VB-3 were assigned to operate from CV-5 *USS Yorktown* without a number change. VS-5 was the only original *Yorktown* Squadron.

VF-3 flew 25 Wildcats with Lieutenant Commander John S. Thach in command; VS-5 flew 19 Dauntless dive bombers with Lieutenant Wallace C. Short, Jr. in command; VB-3 flew 18 Dauntless dive bombers with Lieutenant Commander Maxwell F. Leslie in command; and VT-3 flew 13 Devastators with Lieutenant Commander Lance E. Massey in command.

TG-17.2, commanded by Rear Admiral William W. Smith, included two cruisers. TG-17.4, led by Captain Gilbert C. Hoover, comprised six destroyers.

The U.S. Navy Submarine Force of 25 boats was commanded by Rear Admiral Robert H. English. The submarines were deployed between Midway and Oahu.

As can be seen, the Japanese Force was superior to the American ships and aircraft; however, Nimitz' advantage was knowing the Japanese code which told him they were heading for Midway. The Japanese were not aware of this coup and did not expect the American Force to be waiting for them near the island.

Midway Shore-Based Forces

Marine Aircraft Group 22 of the 2nd Marine Air Wing based on Midway, led by Lieutenant Colonel Ira L. Kimes USMC, was poised to meet the overwhelming Japanese onslaught. MAG-22 included VMF-221, led by Major Floyd B. Parks, USMC, which was equipped with 21 Brewster Buffaloes and seven Grumman Wildcats; and VMSB-241, led by Major Lofton R. Henderson, USMC, which was outfitted with 11 Vought Vindicators and 16 Douglas Dauntless dive bombers.

The shore-based aircraft on Midway included 32 Catalina flying boat patrol craft, a VT-8 Detachment of brand new Grumman TBF Avenger torpedo bombers, plus Marine Aircraft Group 22. All these aircraft were under the command of Captain Cyril T. Simard, USN.

Preliminary Moves

Kakuta's Aleutian Force was the first to leave Japanese waters, followed by Nagumo's Carrier Striking Force on May 26. Yamamoto's Main Body departed two days later. The Midway Occupation Force had sailed from Saipan late on May 27 and Kurita's Close Support Group left Guam on the same day.

Admiral Spruance's Task Force 16 left Pearl Harbor for Midway on May 28 with orders to, ". . . inflict maximum damage on the enemy by strong attrition tactics." Admiral Fletcher's Task Force 17 sailed from Pearl Harbor two days later with orders to, ". . . support Task Force 16."

Action began when, on June 3, two waves of bombers from *Junyo* and *Ryujo* devastated Dutch Harbor in the Aleutian Islands; however, the news of this attack did not divert Admiral Nimitz' attention from the Midway area. The Japanese decoy had been a failure.

On the following day, June 4, search planes from Midway spotted two of Nagumo's carriers at 5:30 in the morning and one-half hour later came word that unidentified aircraft were heading for Midway and closing fast. This placed the attacking planes about 200 miles west by southwest of Task Force 16. Admiral Fletcher couldn't move in because his scout planes had not yet returned to *Yorktown* so at 6:07 AM he ordered Admiral Spruance to attack the Japanese carriers at once with this message: "Proceed southwesterly and attack enemy carriers when definitely located. I will follow as soon as planes recovered." Task Force 16 sped toward Midway although nobody knew the exact location of Nagumo's carriers but knew the direction in which they were heading.

Japanese Attack Midway

At 4:30 AM on June 4, 1942, when Nagumo's carriers had been about 240 miles from Midway, aircraft from the four Japanese carriers took off to attack Midway; 36 Kates from *Hiryu* and *Soryu*, 36 Vals from *Kaga* and *Akagi* with an escort of 36 Zeroes from all the carriers. The attack was led by Lieutenant Joichi Tomanaga, *Hiryu* flight officer. Midway search radar detected the 108 plane armada at about 6:00 o'clock when the Japanese were about 100 miles from the island and, within a few minutes, every serviceable plane began taking off except Catalinas and large Army bombers.

U.S. Fighters Versus Zeroes

Major Parks had 25 serviceable aircraft of the 28 planes in VMF-221; 20 Buffalo and 5 Wildcat fighters. Parks led the first formation of six Buffaloes and three Wildcats, while Captain Kirk Armistead led the second formation of 12 Buffaloes and one Wildcat. The U.S. fighters encountered 107 Japanese aircraft at about 6:15 AM, 30 miles from shore at 12,000 feet altitude. The Ameri-

cans had no idea how potent the Zero fighter would be. The firs[t] flight climbed to 17,000 feet and attacked a formation of Vals. The[y] were promptly set upon by the 36 vaunted Zero fighters which vir[-] tually decimated the Major's flight. By the time Captain Armistead['s] flight arrived the Zeroes had regained altitude and the carnage wa[s] repeated. A total of 13 of the 18 Brewster Buffaloes and two of th[e] four Grumman Wildcats were shot down, including Major Parks[,] in exchange for two Zeroes, one Val and seven Kates destroyed b[y] VMF-221. The Buffaloes had lost 72 percent, while the Wildcat[s] had lost 50 percent of their Force.

Captain Marion Carl, one of the VMF-221 survivors, verifie[d] that the Zero's speed and versatility was amazing. It seemed tha[t] few U.S. naval fighters could match this Japanese fighter plane[,] especially when outnumbered.

A major factor that contributed to VMF-221's heavy losses a[t] Midway was that about 30 percent of the pilots had joined the un[it] only nine days before the battle. These pilots came directly fro[m] flight training and were given no time to accumulate operation[al] experience before entering combat against veteran Japanese com[-] bat pilots.

Apparently high rate of climb and responsive controls were n[o] longer the prerequisites for a successful naval fighter in the 1940[s.] Designed in 1935, the Brewster Buffalo followed the naval comba[t] philosophies of the Thirties which included speed, maneuverabil[-] ity and long range. Firepower and rugged survival ability were n[ot] considered as essential at that time and this was lacking in th[e] Brewster design. Its principal disadvantages were inadequate a[r-] mament; the Wright R-1820-40 engine which severely limited th[e] Buffalo performance at altitudes above 16,000 feet; and most im[-] portant of all was its inability to absorb the punishment necessar[y] to make it a reasonably survivable fighter. The Japanese Zero wa[s] also plagued with the latter disadvantage.

By comparison the Wildcat was virtually indestructable an[d] was fitted with a potent array of six machine guns. The two-stag[e,] two-speed supercharged Pratt & Whitney engine enabled the F4[F-] 4 to successfully engage the Zero above 20,000 feet altitude. Th[e] Wildcat had sacrificed high rate of climb for those qualities tha[t] enabled it to survive in combat.

An interesting incident during the battle proved that the Bu[f-] falo could stand its ground against the Zero despite its poor show[-] ing. Captain William C. Humberd led a section of Buffaloes again[st] a flight of Val dive bombers and just as he shot one down, a pair [of] Zeroes jumped on his tail. Captain Humberd's description of th[e] fight is as follows: "I heard a loud noise and, turning around, saw [a] large hole in the hood of my plane, also two Jap Zeroes on m[e] about 200 yards astern. I immediately pushed over in a steep div[e] in which one Zero followed me. I descended to water level in try[-] ing to gain distance on the fighter, but the plane stayed with me. [I] stayed at water level with full throttle, gaining distance slowly unt[il] I decided the distance was great enough to turn on the plane, [in] which case we met head-on. I gave a long burst when we we[re] about 300 yards apart, and his plane caught fire and, out of contro[l,] dived into the water." The fact that Captain Humberd was able [to] outrun and then make a 180 degree turn to face the nimble Ze[ro] appears to be a feat worthy of note.

Captain Humberd destroyed the Zero while he was flying a Brewster F2A-3 Buffalo similar to that shown here. (Official U.S. Navy Photograph, News Photo Division)

erhouse was badly damaged, fuel storage tanks were destroyed, as was the seaplane hangar. The storehouses, hospital and gasoline piping system were set ablaze. The attackers were not, however, able to destroy the runways. The air raid was over in 20 minutes and not considered successful.

Torpedo Attack On *Hiryu* and *Akagi*

As VMF-221 had left Midway for its fateful interception at 6:15 AM June 4, several other flights took off at the same time and headed

U.S. Marine Corps Captain William C. Humberd shot down a Zero fighter that was on his tail by making a 180 degree turn and facing his pursuer head-on in his Brewster Buffalo fighter. (Official U.S. Navy Photograph, Naval Imaging Command)

VMF-221 Citations

Captain Humberd was awarded the Navy Cross for scoring against the Japanese as was Captain Carl, who shot down a Zero while flying a Wildcat. Major Parks was also awarded the Navy Cross because he, ". . . gallantly gave up his life in the service of his country." Other members of VMF-221 who died fighting the Japanese onslaught and were awarded the Navy Cross are: Captain John R. Alcord, Captain Robert F. Curtin, Lieutenant John D. Lucas, 2nd Lieutenant David W. Pinkerton, Jr. and 2nd Lieutenant Martin E. Mahannah.

Admiral Nimitz had ordered Captain Simard to "go all out for the carriers" and to leave the defense of Midway to its shore batteries. Momehow, this information never got to VMF-221 and if they had assumed their intended role of escorting the Marine dive bomber and torpedo bomber assault on the Japanese ships the casualties might have been considerably lower.

Kates Bomb Midway

Shortly after the VMF-221 encounter, Kate high altitude bombers began dropping their loads on Midway from about 14,000 feet at 6:30 AM June 4, followed by Val dive bombers. The Midway pow-

U.S. Marine Corps Captain Marion E. Carl scored the first of his 18 1/2 victories at the Battle of Midway when he dived away from three Zeroes, then turned to face them in his Grumman Wildcat. (U.S. Defense Dept. Photo, Marine Corps)

Major Lofton Henderson USMC led the dive bombers of VMS-241 in strikes against the Japanese carriers attacking Midway. With his plane afire he intentionally crashed his Douglas Dauntless into one of the carriers and was posthumously awarded the Navy Cross. Henderson Airfield on Guadalcanal was named in his honor. (U.S. National Archives)

for the Japanese carriers without fighter protection. These included four Army Martin Marauder B-26 twin-engine bombers fitted with torpedoes and six TBF Avenger torpedo planes which encountered *Hiryu* and *Akagi* at about 7:10 AM. The slaughter was worse than that met by VMF-221 because five of the Americans were shot down before they ever reached a launching postion. Those that did launch torpedoes were disappointed to see them porpoise or travel so slowly that gunfire from the carriers was able to explode them harmlessly far from the ships. When it was over only two Marauders and one Avenger made it back to Midway; a rather inauspicious debut for the TBF, which was to meet with great success in later actions. Two of the Marauders crash-landed, while the TBF was badly shot up. No torpedoes hit their target.

Dive Bomber Attack on Japanese Carriers

About 45 minutes after the torpedo planes left Midway, Marine Scout-Bombing Squadron VMS-241, led by Major Lofton Henderson, took off to attack the Japanese carriers. The Force led by Henderson consisted of 16 Douglas SBD Dauntless dive bombers. Another VMS-241 flight of Vought Vindicators led by Major Benjamin Norris was soon to follow. As Henderson's flight neared *Hiryu* at 7:55 AM June 4 the squadron leader decided to make a

glide-bombing attack because most of his men were inexperience in dive bombing. Zeroes swarmed all over the eight SBD's an shot down several in the initial pass with Major Henderson's plan the first to be hit. According to an eye-witness, Henderson's le wing burst into flame; however, instead of abandoning his cripple plane, he continued the attack and then intentionally smashed hi Dauntless onto one of the Japanese carriers. Captain Elmer G "Ironman" Glidden, Jr. quickly took command of the flight an continued the attack, dropping about a dozen bombs, all of whic missed *Hiryu* because of the fierce fighter attacks. Only half of th VMS-241 Dauntless flight returned to Midway.

Major Norris' VMS-241 flight of 11 Vought SB2U Vindica tors, which had left Midway soon after Henderson's flight, cam upon the Japanese carriers at 8:20 AM; however, when the fligh leader spotted countless Zero fighters protecting the carriers, h shifted the attack to the nearest target, *Haruna*, which was one c the three battleships supporting the carriers. Ten Vindicators mad a dive bombing attack at 8:30 AM; however, all bombs missed the mark due to the withering antiaircraft fire. Nine Voughts returne safely.

Major Lofton Henderson was posthumously awarded the Nav Cross and the famous Guadalcanal airfield was named in his hono Captain Elmer Glidden was also awarded the Navy Cross for hi heroism.

Midway Planes Delivered By Carriers

The foregoing operations by the Midway-based carrier aircraft, a though not successful against such staggering odds, harasse Nagumo at a time when he was making crucial decisions and als forced his carriers to conduct violent evasive maneuvers when the should have been preparing their aircraft for important operation These shore-based Marine carrier aircraft would probably not hav been available on Midway for this important mission had not *Le ington* and *Saratoga* previously flown them to shore after a lon

U.S. Marine Corps. Captain Elmer G. "Ironman" Glidden promptly to command of the Dauntless flight upon Major Henderson's sacrifice. He continued the attack on the Japanese carriers and was awarded the Na Cross. Glidden is shown here watching bombing raid credits painted on his Douglas Dauntless. (U.S. National Archives)

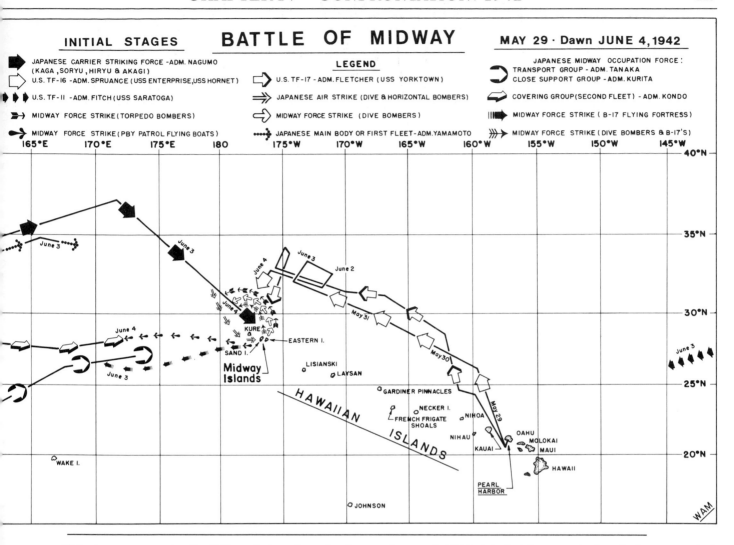

ea voyage. This demonstrates the flexibility of aircraft carriers' Warbirds to not only operate on the open sea but be quickly transported where and when needed to shore bases at short notice, especially in emergency situations.

Spruance Launches Early

With his Task Force 16 steaming in a southwesterly direction Admiral Spruance had decided to launch his strike at 9:00 o'clock in the morning June 4; however, as reports were received about the Japanese strike on Midway, he decided to launch his planes two hours earlier in an effort to catch Nagumo's carriers in the act of retrieving aircraft or refueling and reloading the planes for a second strike. It was a very difficult decision because to launch earlier meant Task Force 16 would be further away from Nagumo and the SBD's, TBD's and F4F's would be required to fly further; nearer the limit of their range. At 7:02 AM planes began taking off from *Hornet* and *Enterprise*; however, before launching was complete a Japanese scout plane spotted the task force but got away. Although he had lost the element of surprise Spruance decided to attack, planning to catch Nagumo in a defenseless position. The American Strike Force consisted of 72 Dauntless dive bombers, 29 Devastator torpedo bombers, and 20 Wildcat fighters. A combat air patrol of 18 Wildcats was retained with 18 more held in reserve to relieve or

supplement the CAP. Admiral Spruance had made the correct decision to launch an all-out strike force and his timing was perfect.

Nagumo's Dilemma

Admiral Nagumo had wisely withheld, from his Midway strike force, one half the Val dive bombers of *Soryu* and *Hiryu*, plus one half the Kates from *Kaga* and *Akagi*, in the event that an American fleet threatened his carriers while the Midway raid was underway. These aircraft had been armed to attack ships with torpedoes and armor-piercing bombs in the event that a U.S. Task Force appeared.

As Lieutenant Joichi Tomanaga led his planes back to the carriers from the Midway bombing, he informed Admiral Nagumo at 7:00 AM June 4, that a second strike against Midway was required.

While the Japanese admiral was pondering the incompatibility of the two tasks upon which he had to decide; prepare to attack ships or prepare to launch a ground attack on Midway, the Midway planes had launched the attack on his ships. This attack made Nagumo decide to launch a second strike against Midway. At 7:15 AM Nagumo ordered the Kates struck down into the hangars and exchange the torpedoes for bombs; an operation that would take one hour. Fifteen minutes later Admiral Nagumo received word from his scout plane that had sighted Task Force 16, which was 300 miles away. While Midway aircraft were making their futile attacks Nagumo was trying to rethink his weighty problem now that he knew an American Force was near. He finally decided upon a compromise; something warriors should never do. Nagumo decided to make the second strike against the American ships using only those Kates which still had torpedoes installed; however, for the next half hour it was impossible to launch any aircraft from the Japanese carriers because they were forced to zig-zag in order to avoid the bombs and torpedoes from the Midway Americans.

Nagumo Changes Course
By 8:35 AM the Japanese carriers began recovering planes from the first Midway strike, and because Nagumo continued to receive reports about the U.S. carriers, he made a wise decision at 9:05 AM to change the course of his carrier striking force from southeast to northeast. The course change was completed at 9:17 AM June 4 and the carriers were in the exact condition in which Spruance wanted to find them; refueling and rearming planes.

The Search For Nagumo
The Task Force 16 aircraft which had been launched from Hornet and Enterprise at 7:02 AM comprised the following units, planes and leaders:

From the deck of *USS Enterprise* rose 10 Grumman Wildcat fighters led by Lieutenant J.S. Gray (VF-6): 37 Douglas Dauntless dive bombers led by Lieutenant W.E. Gallaher and Lieutenant R.R. Best (VS-6 and VB-6 respectively); and 14 Douglas Devastator torpedo planes led by Lieutenant Commander E.E. Lindsey (VT-6). Lieutenant Commander C.W. McClusky was the Air Group Commander.

USS Hornet launched 10 Wildcat fighters led by Lieutenant S.G. Mitchell; 35 Dauntless dive bombers led by Lieutenant Commander R.R. Johnson and Lieutenant Commander W.F. Rodee (VB-8 and VS-8), and 15 Devastators led by Lieutenant Commander J.C. Waldron (VT-8). Lieutenant Commander S.C. Ring was the Air Group Commander. Torpedo Squadron Eight with its 30 pilots and gunners was about to go down, literally, in the air-history books.

The American force, not aware of Nagumo's change in course, continued in a southwesterly direction towards a point where the Japanese ships would have been had they not changed course; all, that is, except Lieutenant Commander Waldron.

Lieutenant Commander Waldron and Torpedo Eight
John Charles Waldron of Fort Pierre, S.D., had remained a Navy man since his graduation from Annapolis on June 4, 1924 (precisely 18 years before this fateful June 4). After his stint at the U.S. Naval Academy, he instructed at the Naval Air Station in Pensacola and then served with Torpedo Squadron Nine, Scouting Squadron Three, and Patrol Squadron Six. While working at the Naval Proving Ground and Bureau of Ordnance in Washington, Waldron secured a law degree. Thus equipped, he became commanding officer of Torpedo Squadron Eight in August 1941. Waldron, always efficient, demonstrated sound judgment; almost intuition. His men attributed this to one of the Commander's grandparents, a Sioux Indian.

When Waldron had first learned that his squadron would see service in the Pacific, he accumulated a collection of hunting knives,

Lieutenant Commander John Charles Waldron found the evasive Japanese carriers and led Torpedo Eight to the attack without fighter plane protection. Observe the non-regulation two guns (hip and shoulder holsters) and hunting knife which Waldron felt were necessary in the event that squadron members were stranded in the jungle. Waldron stands in front of one of Torpedo Eight's Devastators. (U.S. National Archives)

extra side arms, machetes, and pocket compasses which he distributed to his men. This equipment, he figured, would be a vital necessity should any of his men be forced down on a jungle island. Thus, the men of Torpedo Squadron Eight usually carried one .4 caliber automatic in a shoulder holster and another on their hip. In addition, machetes and hunting knives, plus extra ammunition dangled from their belts. Waldron also collected steel plate which he had installed in Devastator cockpits as improvised armor.

The role of the torpedo squadron was not an easy one. Enemy ships had to be approached at low altitude, usually through smoke screens, against overhead fighter protection. The pilot could fly a zig-zag course to dodge antiaircraft fire until he began his run in on the target at wavetop level. Then no deviation was possible and he could expect to meet the full fury of the enemy's guns. Waldron trained his men hard. He made his pilots fly long hours low over the water and had their rear gunners practice incessantly with the single movable gun.

As the mechanics and armorers prepared his planes for action early that morning of June 4, 1942, Waldron looked at his aging Douglas TBD torpedo bombers and regretted not having received

, Commander Waldron (arrow) and the pilots of Torpedo Eight (VT-8) se on the USS Hornet Flight Deck in early 1942 just before the Battle Midway. The men are top row, left to right: Squadron Executive fficer Lieutenant James C. Owens; Lieutenant John Porter Gray; quadron Commander Lieutenant Commander John C. Waldron rrow); Lieutenant Raymond Austin Moore; Ensign William Robinson ans; Ensign Grant W. Teats; Ensign Harold J. Ellison. Bottom row, ft to right: Lieutenant George M. Campbell; Ensign William W. ercrombie; Ensign Henry R. Kenyon, Jr.; Ensign George H. "Tex" ay, Jr.; Lieutenant Jeff D. Woodson; Ensign William W. Creamer, Navy lot Robert B. Miles. Ensign Gay (circled) was the only survivor of rpedo Eight's heroic attack on the Japanese carriers. (U.S. Naval istorical Center, Courtesy U.S. Naval Institute Collection)

The aging TBD-1 Devastator, a fine torpedo plane for its time, had been designed in 1934.

The 130 Devastators that were built saw service aboard the *Saratoga, Yorktown, Enterprise* and *Hornet* and they had already taken part in the fighting at Wake Island, Coral Sea, Tulagi Harbor and New Guinea.

Before takeoff on that June 4th Waldron conferred with his men and Executive Officer Owens. He decided to use two-man, instead of three-man crews because of the extreme danger involved and instructed the pilots to fly in pairs; Waldron would lead a "vee" formation of three planes. He assigned Ensign George H. "Tex" Gay, Jr. to fly the tail-end Charlie position at the rear of the formation.

At 8:00 o'clock that morning Torpedo Eight was the last squadron to take off and was to be escorted by *Enterprise* Wildcats. Waldron did not follow the *Hornet*'s fighters and dive-bombers, which were on their way to a hypothetical meeting with the Japanese carriers. Instead, he led his men on a course about 18 degrees farther north. Waldron's Naval War College training in strategy and tactics convinced him that Nagumo would not maintain his course once he sighted U.S. ships. The Commander figured that the Japanese would turn northward in order to be in position to attack the U.S. task force's flank. His Devastators flew at an altitude of only 300 feet under a cloud cover, thus undetected by high-flying Zero patrols. Ten Wildcats from *Enterprise*, led by Lieutenant Gray, were at 20,000 feet; but the radio frequency used by *Enterprise*'s fighters could not pick up calls from *Hornet*'s torpedo planes. As Torpedo Eight droned toward the enemy, fighting a strong headwind, the dive bombers and fighters from *Hornet* were many miles to the south, well out of sight. *USS Enterprise*'s high-flying Wildcats soon lost sight of Waldron because of the clouds so they went off to find their own dive bombers and torpedo planes.

e Grumman TBF Avenger replacements. He had been told that x Avengers, belonging to Torpedo Eight, were at Midway waiting or him. What he did not know was that these craft had already ken off from the island with four B-26 Army bombers and were, this very moment, engaging the carrier *Akagi* in what was to be e Avenger's baptism of fire.

)ouglas Devastator torpedo-bombers of Torpedo Squadron Eight at Norfolk Naval Air Station await the flight to USS Hornet. Note the wing folding nd the corrugated or ribbed wing covering. (U.S. Navy Photo in U.S. National Archives)

These Torpedo Eight Devastator torpedo-bombers are carrying two 500 lb. bombs instead of a torpedo (arrow). Observe the black 8-T-2 on the fuselage sides (Eight-Torpedo Squadron-Plane No.2). This system of aircraft marking as well as the red dot in the national insignia were discontinued shortly after hostilities began with Japan. Note the Devastator just after takeoff (arrow). (U.S. Navy Photo in U.S. National Archives)

Waldron and his men were alone now, headed directly toward the enemy whose ships were bristling with antiaircraft guns and protected by high-flying Zero patrols.

Torpedo Eight Attacks

When Waldron sighted the enemy carriers he closed in on the target and checked his fuel gage, Waldron saw he was approaching the point of no return. Headwinds had forced the heavy Devastators to consume more fuel than planned. If he attacked the Japanese his squadron would be forced to ditch in the lonely Pacific. Waldron ordered the attack because only Torpedo Eight stood between the Japanese and Task Force 16. He noted that the Japanese were preparing to launch another air strike. The Americans were still 10 miles from their target when Mitsubishi Zeros dived upon the lumbering Devastators. The four carriers, with their cruiser and destroyer escort, maneuvered sharply to evade the attack. Torpedo Eight was now down to wavetop level with canopy hatches open for quick escape and heading for *Kaga*. Japanese fighters tore into the TBD formations. In a few seconds five Devastators, including Waldron's two wingmen, plunged into the Pacific. It was now 9:28 as Waldron led his remaining men in their closing run in on the carriers. Pure hell broke loose as antiaircraft fire concentrated on them from the Japanese ships. This was indeed a "mission impossible", but determined pilots held their course while brave gunners fired furiously at the Japanese fighters. As the planes of Torpedo Eight were riddled with cannon and machine guns one by one they slammed into the choppy sea.

When Waldron reached his torpedo release point only a few Devastators remained, including Ensign Gay.

Just as the commander was about to release his tin fish Zeroes sprayed his plane with cannon shells. The TBD's fuel tanks erupted in a ball of flame. Waldron tried to hold the huge plane on course but searing flames engulfed the cockpit and his Devastator smashed into the waves and sank in a pool of burning gasoline. One by one the remaining members of Torpedo Eight shared their leader's fate, except for tail-end Charlie.

Ensign Gay: Only Survivor

As Ensign Gay line up his sights on the nearest carrier he knew there was no turning back. He could feel the Zero machine gun bullets slam against the improvised armor that Waldron had installed. When the chatter of his rear firing gun stopped, Gay glanced over his shoulder and was met by the open-mouthed, open-eyed stare of what had been his comrade. He was all alone now.

Did the Ensign's life swiftly pass before his eyes? Did he recall his youth in Waco, Texas, where he was born on March 8, 1917? And of his years at Texas A & M College? And his first meeting with Waldron on November 3, 1941 when Gay reported for duty with Torpedo Eight - was that in his mind at this moment? Here he was on his first assignment; he was certain that it would be his last.

As the huge Japanese carrier loomed before him Gay noticed that it was swerving to starboard in an effort to elude his attack. As he was about to release his torpedo Gay was hit in the left arm and left leg. Although stunned, he pressed the torpedo release button but nothing happened. He was now on a collision course with the carrier and knew he could not clear the giant hull with the one-ton torpedo strapped to his plane's belly. He groped frantically for the emergency torpedo release wire and yanked with all his strength. When the TBD rose gently Gay knew that the torpedo was on its way. He quickly pulled back on the control column and soared over the deck of the carrier with only a few feet to spare. During all this time Gay's Devastator was being peppered full of holes; now its rudder controls were gone. The engine was rapidly losing power.

Ensign Gay was the only survivor of the Torpedo Eight attack on the Japanese carriers during the Battle of Midway. He floated in the water among debris for 20 hours witnessing the carnage of the battle after which a Navy flying boat rescued the pilot. He is shown here shortly before the battle. (U.S. Naval Historic Center, Courtesy U.S. Naval Institute Photo Collection)

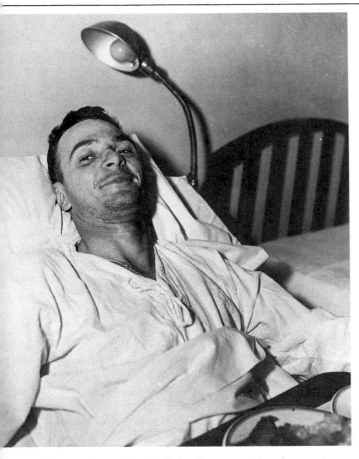

Exhausted Ensign George H. "Tex" Gay forces a smile as he rests in hospital recovering from arm and leg wounds as well as from exposure that he received on the morning of June 4, 1942. (U.S. National Archives)

forcing the ensign to ditch the plane as soon as he crossed over the carrier. When the crippled TBD struck the water the starboard wing tore off and the huge craft began to sink at once. Gay swam clear, inflated his life jacket, and hid among floating debris. The only survivor of the Torpedo Eight attack drifted for over 20 hours. During this time he witnessed the remainder of the Battle of Midway. After the battle a Navy patrol plane rescued him.

Radio Alert
Waldron's radio instructions to his men during the attack had been picked up by an aircraft farther south. The news that Torpedo Eight had located the enemy was relayed to the other squadrons; most all turned toward the Japanese carriers.

Torpedo Six Attacks
During Torpedo Eight's run in against the carriers Lieutenant Commander Lindsey turned his VT-6 outfit northward where he launched a torpedo attack on the enemy a few minutes later. Again the Japanese gunners and Zero pilots massacred the unescorted Devastators. Only four out of 14 planes escaped; Lindsey died with his men.

Below: Immediately after the Torpedo Eight strike, Lieutenant Commander Eugene E. Lindsey led his Torpedo Six (VT-6) Squadron to the attack on the Japanese carriers in the Battle of Midway. Of the 14 unescorted Douglas TBD-1 Devastator Torpedo bombers in the strike, only four planes escaped the withering antiaircraft fire and deadly Zero fighters. Lindsey died with his men. A Torpedo Six Douglas Devastator is shown launching its torpedo. (McDonnell Douglas Photo, Courtesy Harry Gann)

Dive Bombers Attack *Kaga* and *Akagi*

It was 40 minutes after Torpedo Eight's initial attack that Lieutenant Commander McClusky appeared over the Japanese carriers, leading two squadrons of Dauntless dive bombers; three dozen planes. McClusky had flown past the point where Nagumo was estimated to be and, when the Japanese Fleet was not in sight, he turned north, as had Waldron. As McClusky approached the carriers he ordered Lieutenant Gallaher's VS-6 to attack *Kaga* with its 500 pound bombs and Lieutenant Best's VB-6 to attack *Akagi* with its 1,000 pound bombs. Both squadrons made 70 degree dives at about 325 miles per hour and met no resistance from the Zeroes because the fighters were operating at very low altitudes to intercept the two torpedo bomber squadrons that had finished their attack only moments before the dive bombers began their dives.

Combined Attack On *Soryu*

Just before the *Enterprise* dive bombers attacked, Massey's (12) VT-3 Devastators arrived on the scene and made its run on *Soryu*. The *Yorktown* Devastators suffered the same fate as those from *Hornet* and *Enterprise* with only two planes surviving. Lieutenant Commander Massey was killed in this attack. While VT-3 was engaged in its run on *Soryu*, Leslie's (17) VB-3 Dauntless dive bombers arrived at 20,000 feet and promptly attacked *Soryu* from 14,000 feet. Of the (41) Douglas TBD torpedo bombers that attacked the enemy's carriers only six survived. While it was all over in only half an hour, their sacrifice was not in vain. Although there is no verification of torpedo hits, the action of Torpedo Eight and VT-3 and VT-6 forced the Japanese ships to engage in evasive maneuvers which prevented them from launching an air strike against the U.S. Task Forces. In addition, the gallant men drew the Japanese fighter cover down to their low altitude; thereby, enabling the high-flying Douglas SBD Dauntless dive bombers to strike at the enemy virtually unmolested.

The three Dauntless squadrons caught the Japanese carrier crews in the midst of refueling and rearming their planes. Their decks were full of aircraft when 500 and 1,000 pound bombs rained down on the *Akagi*, *Kaga* and *Soryu*. Flaming gasoline from ruptured fuel tanks poured over the decks and into the bowels of the ships resulting in enormous fires and many deaths. The *Hiryu*, farther north, escaped this particular attack.

U.S. Fighter Victories

Lieutenant Commander Thach's VF-3 Wildcats had been very busy during the attack on the three Japanese carriers. After seeing one of his Wildcats shot down by Zeroes, and two others chased out of the area, Thach and the two others climbed to above 3,000 feet. Then, applying the "Thach Weave", the three Wildcats beat off 15 to 20 Zeroes, shooting down six! The Wildcats also escorted damaged Devastators out of the battle. When he returned to *Yorktown* Thach brought Admiral Fletcher the first visual evidence that the three Japanese carriers were on fire and were being battered to pieces by the Douglas Dauntless dive bombers.

U.S. Warbirds' Losses

By the early afternoon the three Japanese carriers were in a sinking condition and the American carriers had not been hit. There were, however, losses of American Warbirds of the Sea: *Yorktown* had lost 10 out of 12 Devastators, two Dauntless dive bombers and three Wildcats; *Enterprise* had lost 14 out of 37 Dauntless dive bombers, 10 out of 14 Devastators, and one Wildcat; *Hornet* had lost all 15 of her Devastators in the battle. The *Hornet* Wildcat fighters and Dauntless dive bombers had not found the Japanese carriers at the estimated location and assumed they had steamed to Midway. By the time the three *Hornet* squadrons came within sight of Midway their fuel had been virtually depleted with the result that several Dauntless dive bombers ditched into the Midway Lagoon, while the Wildcats splashed into the Pacific. Actually, the losses were very low considering the damage they had inflicted on the Japanese carriers.

Kaga, *Soryu* and *Akagi* Sink

Kaga and *Soryu* sank between 7:00 and 7:30 o'clock that evening, but *Akagi* remained afloat until she was given the coup-de-grace by Japanese torpedoes 10 hours later. Now, Nagumo had only one carrier left, *Hiryu*, with a complete air group.

Torpedo Eight Citations

The following citation was awarded to Torpedo Squadron Eight by President Roosevelt for its outstanding achievement: "For extreme heroic and courageous performance in combat during the Air Battle of Midway June 4, 1942. Flying low without fighter support, Torpedo Squadron Eight began the perilous mission, 'Intercept and attack!' First to sight the enemy, the squadron attacked with full striking power against crushing enemy opposition, scoring torpedo hits on Japanese forces. Realizing to a man that insufficient fuel would prevent a return to the carrier, the pilots held doggedly to their target, dropping torpedoes at point-blank range in the face of blasting antiaircraft fire that sent the planes, one-by-one, hurtling aflame into the sea. The loss of 29 lives, typifying valor, loyalty, and determination, was the price paid for Torpedo Squadron Eight's vital contribution to the eventual success of our forces in this epic battle of the air."

Each of the 30 men of VT-8 who participated in the attack was awarded a citation and a medal for his heroism. The pilots were decorated with the Navy Cross; each radioman/machine-gunner received the Distinguished Flying Cross.

Navy Cross citations read as follows: "For extraordinary heroism and distinguished service beyond the call of duty as a pilot of Torpedo Squadron Eight in the Air Battle of Midway, against enemy Japanese forces on June 4, 1942. Grimly aware of the hazardous consequences of flying without fighter protection, and with insufficient fuel to return to his carrier, he resolutely, and with no thought of his own life, delivered an effective torpedo attack against violent assaults of enemy Japanese aircraft and against an almost solid barrage of antiaircraft fire. His courageous action, carried on with a gallant spirit of self-sacrifice and a conscientious devotion to the fulfillment of his mission, was a determining factor in the defeat of the enemy forces and was in keeping with the highest traditions of the United States Naval Service."

The above citation with the Navy Cross was awarded to the following Torpedo Eight pilots: Lieutenant Commander John Charles Waldron; Lieutenant James Charles Owens, Jr.; Lieutenant (JG) Raymond Austin Moore; Lieutenant George M. Campbell

Lieutenant (JG) Jeff Davis Woodson; Ensign William W. Abercrombie; Ensign Ulvert M. Moore; Ensign William W. Creamer; Ensign George H. Gay, Jr.; Lieutenant (JG) John Porter Gray; Ensign Harold J. Ellison; Ensign Henry R. Kenyon, Jr.; Ensign William Robinson Evans; Ensign Grant W. Teats; and Navy Pilot Robert B. Miles.

Distinguished Flying Cross citations read as follows: "For heroism and extraordinary achievement while participating in an aerial flight as radioman and free machine-gunner of an airplane of Torpedo Squadron Eight during an attack against enemy Japanese forces in the Air Battle of Midway on June 4, 1942. Grimly aware of the hazardous consequences of flying without fighter support, and with insufficient fuel to return to his carrier, he resolutely, and with no thought of his own life, pressed home his attack with utter disregard for his own personal safety and in the face of tremendous antiaircraft barrage and overwhelming fighter opposition. His gallant spirit of self-sacrifice and his conscientious devotion to the fulfillment of a vastly important mission contributed materially to the success of our forces and were in keeping with the highest traditions of the U.S. Naval Service."

The above citation with the Distinguished Flying Cross was awarded to the following Torpedo Eight radiomen/gunners: Aviation Radioman Benerd P. Phelps; Aviation Radioman William F. Sawhill; Aviation Radioman Amelio Maffei; Aviation Radioman Tom H. Pettry; Chief Radioman Horace F. Dobbs; Aviation Radioman Orway D. Creasy, Jr.; Seaman Francis Samuel Polston; Aviation Radioman Max A. Calkins; Aviation Radioman Darwin L. Clark; Aviation Radioman Ross H. Bibb, Jr.; Aviation Radioman Hollis Martin; Aviation Radioman Robert Kingsley Huntington; Aviation Radioman Ronald J. Fisher; Seaman Aswell Lovelace Picou; Aviation Radioman George A. Field.

Additional Citations

The following brave U.S. Navy pilots were awarded the Navy Cross for their bravery and leadership in the destruction of the Japanese carriers: Commander Clarence W. McClusky; Lieutenant Commander Eugene E. Lindsey; Lieutenant Commander Lance E. Massey; Lieutenant Commander Maxwell F. Leslie; Lieutenant Commander Wallace C. Short, Jr.; Lieutenant Richard H. Best and Lieutenant Wilmer E. Gallaher.

Lieutenant Commander Robert R. Johnson was awarded the Distinguished Flying Cross.

Hiryu Warbirds Attack Yorktown

Admiral Nagumo had abandoned his flagship *Akagi* and transferred temporary tactical command to Rear Admiral Hiroaki Abe, his cruiser and battleship commander. Unknown to the Americans, assorted Japanese scout planes had followed the homeward-bound U.S. Navy planes and sighted *Yorktown* in the distance; about 240 miles from Midway. As soon as Rear Admiral Tamon Yamaguchi of *Hiryu* heard of the American carrier location he lost no time to launch 18 Val dive bombers with a six-Zero escort at 11:00 AM June 4 because he had witnessed the fatal results of Nagumo's vacillation. The raiders were led by Michio Kobayashi, a very experienced veteran of aerial attacks in the Pacific and Indian Oceans. Meanwhile, Yamamoto had ordered the two Aleutian raiders, *Ryujo*

and *Junyo*, to head south and back up *Hiryu*. A second flight left *Hiryu* at 1:30 in the afternoon comprised of 10 Kate torpedo bombers with a six-Zero escort.

Yorktown CAP Scores

Meanwhile, *Yorktown* had one CAP (Combat Air Patrol) of 12 Wildcats in the air while refueling the relief CAP. The pilots of the CAP were part of Lieutenant Commander Thach's VF-3 and as soon as the Japanese raiders appeared on radar the Wildcats intercepted and tore into the Val formation. Ten of the dive bombers were shot down or forced to jettison their bombs and retreat.

Lieutenant (JG) Elbert Scott McCuskey (not to be confused with Commander McClusky) was in the midst of the fighting, during which he shot down three Val dive bombers and damaged three others.

Yorktown Hit

Eight Vals broke through and, although antiaircraft fire shot down two, the remaining six scored three direct hits on *Yorktown*. One of the bombs tumbled from a Val that had disintegrated under heavy antiaircraft fire and struck the Flight Deck, killing many of the crew and starting serious fires below deck. Another bomb hit the smokestack and ruptured three boiler uptakes, extinguishing the fires in five of the six boilers. *Yorktown*'s speed dropped to six knots and by 20 minutes after noon the ship was dead in the water. The third bomb had penetrated down to the Fourth Deck and exploded, starting fires near a magazine and gasoline stowage. Damage Control parties worked so well that by 1:40 PM June 5 four boilers had been fired up, enabling the ship to exceed 18 knots.

Lieutenant Elbert Scott McCuskey scored in the Battle of the Coral Sea and repeated his victories during the Battle of Midway while flying a Grumman Wildcat. He is shown here in his Wildcat. Note the seven victory flags. (U.S. Naval Historical Center, Courtesy U.S. Naval Institute Photo Collection)

Damage Control Teams hasten to repair the bomb crater in the Yorktown Flight Deck caused by Hiryu dive bombers. Note the wounded being tended in the background and the gunners on the catwalk ready for another attack. (U.S. National Archives)

As *Yorktown* began refueling her Wildcats, *Hiryu*'s torpedo attack was detected 40 miles away. The carrier had time to launch only eight Wildcats which joined four other Wildcats that had been on patrol. The 10 fast Kates and six Zeroes approached from 7,000 feet at 2:30 PM on June 4 and, as *Yorktown* zig-zagged, the torpedo planes dropped to about 300 feet and split into four groups attacking from different directions. When the Kates closed to 3,000 yards the American heavy cruisers fired their guns into the water just ahead of the torpedo planes, which created a splash barrage that the Italian Navy had developed during the Battle of Cape Matapan. Four Kates got through, launching their torpedoes as close as 500 yards from Yorktown, and as the carrier was dodging the four torpedoes two struck the hull on the port side and exploded.

Yorktown Captain: Abandon Ship!

Fuel tanks ruptured; rudders jammed; all power lines damaged; the ship took an immediate list of about 17 degrees to port. This in

USS Yorktown is caught at the moment that two torpedoes explode into the port side of the hull in the afternoon of June 4, 1942. This was the death blow for Yorktown at Midway. (U.S. National Archives)

Instrumental in Admiral Spruance's Task Force 16 success at the Battle of Midway was USS Enterprise (CV-6) from which he dispatched dive bombers to sink the Japanese carriers Akagi, Hiryu and Kaga. (U.S. Naval Historical Center)

creased to 26 degrees within 20 minutes. Fearful that the ship was about to capsize Captain Buckmaster gave the order to abandon ship one half hour after the torpedo attack began.

More CAP Victories

During the torpedo attack Lieutenant Commander Thach's Wildcats did the best they could against the attackers but the fast Kates managed to score despite their efforts. Lieutenant McCuskey shot down two more Zeroes while Thach got one Kate before it could release its torpedo. Both pilots were awarded a Gold Star in lieu of a second Navy Cross in appreciation for their efforts and accomplishments.

Spruance Launches Attack On *Hiryu*

Even before the dive bomber attack on *Yorktown*, Admiral Fletcher estimated that there was one more Japanese aircraft carrier that the Americans had missed. He had the foresight to send 10 scout bombers on a search mission; Lieutenant Wallace C. Short, Jr. and his VS-5. It was 2:45 PM when Lieutenant Samuel Adams reported

that he had sighted a Japanese carrier, two battleships, three cruisers and four destroyers heading north about 100 miles northwest of *Yorktown*'s location.

At 3:30 PM June 4 Spruance ordered 24 Dauntless dive bombers launched from *USS Enterprise* to attack *Hiryu*. Led by Lieutenant Gallaher, VS-6, along with some *Yorktown* Dauntless dive bombers, dived on the Japanese carrier and its cruiser escort at 5:00 PM. *Hiryu* was speeding at 30 knots when it received four direct hits, one of which blew off the forward elevator and smashed it against the island; such was the force of the explosion. The impact of the heavy elevator platform destroyed all communications and control, killing many on the bridge, including Admiral Yamaguchi, who had often been mentioned as Admiral Yamamoto's successor. The other bombs penetrated deep into the hull, starting uncontrollable fires, which sealed the carrier's fate. Three SBD's and their crews were lost in this operation. Major Benjamin White Norris, who had succeeded Major Henderson as C.O. of VMS-241, led five Vindicators and six Dauntless' in a takeoff from Midway at 7:00 PM to make a nocturnal attack on the burning *Hiryu*. Weather was overcast and

Pounded by Enterprise dive bombers the Japanese aircraft carrier Hiryu was a burning wreck on June 4, 1942. Observe the aircraft elevator that was blown into the air and landed against the island (arrow) which disrupted communications and killed many officers on the bridge including an admiral. (U.S. Naval Historical Center, Courtesy Mr. Kazutoshi Hando)

Douglas Dauntless dive bombers were principally credited for sinking four Japanese aircraft carriers during the Battle of Midway. This Dauntless has just released a 1,000 pound bomb, which often penetrated Japanese carrier flight decks and exploded in the bowels of the hull. Note the perforated diving brakes. (McDonnell Douglas photo, courtesy Harry Gann)

nightfall came quickly with the result that the stricken carrier could not be found. Among those who did not return to Midway was Major Norris, who was last seen making a steep right turn as he began to let down about 40 miles from Midway. Major Norris was awarded the Navy Cross, posthumously.

Yamamoto Cancels Midway Invasion

At 2:55 AM on June 5 Admiral Yamamoto ordered a retreat and 20 minutes later *Hiryu* was abandoned. At 5:10 AM two Japanese destroyers tried to sink the carrier with torpedoes; however, *Hiryu* remained afloat, burning fiercely until 9:00 AM, when she capsized and sank. Yamamoto was very depressed and could only ask: "Is Genda alright?" Commander Minoru Genda was the Admiral's only hope with which to recover Japanese Naval air power.

Split Forces Lose Battles

With the sinking of *Hiryu* the last of Nagumo's operable, powerful, fast carriers perished; a victim, like the others, to Yamamoto's faulty plan which violated the two major principles of war: always concentrate one's forces, and always maintain the objective in any conflict. Admiral Yamamoto had assigned two incompatible objectives, which caused Nagumo to fail in both. The Japanese force was spread out over thousands of square miles of the Pacific which spelled defeat. Had all six carriers and the battleships moved as a coordinated mass, it is quite possible that the Japanese could have won this critical battle. Even in the throes of defeat Yamamoto planned a final encounter with the Americans, using the powerful Japanese 18 inch gun battleships in a night engagement. The canny Spruance suspected Yamamoto's plan and, having no intention of being drawn

into a night fight on Japanese terms, he headed east. In deep humiliation Admiral Yamamoto set sail for Japan because, even with the most powerful battleship force in the world, he dared not follow Spruance without air cover.

Sub Sights Kurita's Cruisers

While *Hiryu* was being abandoned as she burned, Admiral Kurita's line of four cruisers, *Kumano, Suzuya, Mogami* and *Mikuma* had been sighted 90 miles from Midway by the U.S. submarine *Tambor* at 2:15 AM June 5. The boat tracked the ships heading west in the moonlight when, at 3:40 AM, Kurita saw the submarine and ordered a sharp left turn. The cruiser *Mogami* had been the last in line and apparently had failed to get the order soon enough because it rammed the port quarter of *Mikuma*, which had been next ahead. The ships hit with great force because *Mogami* caught fire and tore away so much of her bow that the best speed she could make was knots! *Mikuma*'s fuel tanks had ruptured and she was losing oil. Kurita continued full speed, leaving two destroyers to screen the cruisers.

Captain Fleming's Sacrifice

At daybreak of June 6 a Midway Catalina spotted the two cruisers and reported them as two battleships. Captain Marshall Tyler, who had become the third commanding officer of VMS-241 within 24 hours, led six SBD's and assigned six SB2U's to Marine Captain Richard E. Fleming. A 50 miles long oil slick made the ships easy to find 170 miles west of Midway. Captain Tyler led his Dauntless in a dive from 10,000 feet and the flight scored some very close near-misses on *Mogami*. Captain Fleming led the Vindicators in glide bombing from 4,000 feet into intense antiaircraft fire. As his plane neared the cruisers it was hit in the engine area and thick smoke poured out of the cowling but Fleming kept going and

Midway based and Enterprise based dive bombers pounded the Japanese heavy cruiser Mikuma to a hulk. U.S. Marine Captain Richard E. Fleming intentionally crashed his Vought Vindicator onto the aft gun turret, starting a large fire. The wreckage can be seen on the turret. He was posthumously awarded the Congressional Medal of Honor. (U.S. National Archives)

dropped his bomb on *Mogami*. When he pulled out of the steep glide, his Vought burst into flames and, although VMS-241 pilots and the official wartime report contradicted the evidence, Fleming's plane levelled off and headed for *Mikuma*, where it dived into the aft gun turret, setting off a large fire! This was described by Japanese Admiral Akira Soji, commanding officer of *Mogami* at Midway, during postwar interrogation: "I saw a dive bomber dive into the last turret and start fires. He was very brave." Captain Fleming was awarded the Medal of Honor, posthumously.

Spruance Chases Midway Remnants

The submarine Tambor's report described Admiral Kurita's force as many unidentified ships, which made Admiral Spruance feel that a Japanese invasion of Midway might still be attempted. He changed course to southwest to render air support to Midway, if necessary. After receiving confused and conflicting reports about the burning *Hiryu* and the cruiser collision, plus the retiring Japanese Fleet 200 miles to the northwest, Spruance again changed course to due west at 9:30 AM on June 5 and passed about 50 miles north of Midway. After serious consideration, Admiral Spruance decided to attack the large Japanese force to the northwest, reasoning that if any aircraft carriers survived they would be in that fleet. Another change in course to northwest by west at 11:25 AM and the chase began.

By 3:40 PM June 5 Spruance had launched a search and attack group of Dauntless dive bombers, 26 from *Hornet* and 32 from *Enterprise*, but due to the heavy overcast they could not locate the Japanese ships after flying 315 miles from the task force.

Meanwhile, Yamamoto had consolidated his scattered ships into a large fleet of 11 battleships, eight heavy cruisers, several destroyers, and two light carriers, most of which had not engaged the American forces, nor even sighted an American plane!

Spruance Pounds Japanese Cruisers

At dawn of June 6 *Enterprise* launched a scouting flight which found *Mogami* and *Mikuma* and by 8:00 AM the first attack flight of eight Wildcats and 26 Dauntless dive bombers took off from *Hornet*. The second flight of 12 Wildcats, three Devastators and 31 Dauntless' left *Enterprise* at 10:45, while *Hornet* launched a third flight of eight Wildcats and 24 SBD's at 1:30 PM. The two cruisers were helpless targets, except for some antiaircraft fire. *Mogami* received two bomb hits during the first attack, one of which pierced an aft turret and exploded. Two more direct hits came from the second strike which started fires and a third hit sealed up a burning engine room! Despite this battering *Mogami* was able to sail to Truk for temporary repairs and was back in action a little over a year later. The *Mikuma* crew was ordered to abandon ship after the second

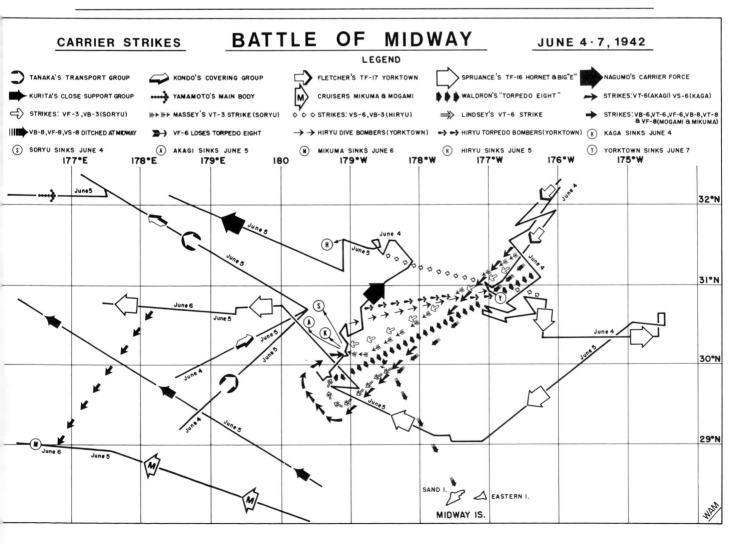

Right: These excerpts from the Admiral Nimitz report of the battle of Midway reveal the bomb sizes used, number of U.S. Aircraft, and names of the Japanese carriers. Note the references to Torpedo Eight and Ensign Gay. (Official U.S. Navy Photo)

strike and were rescued by a destroyer. Other bombs scored direct hits, one of which detonated the cruiser's torpedoes. The screening destroyers abandoned the wreck and *Mikuma* sank that night.

Midway Was First Japanese Defeat

The Battle of Midway was over and victorious Spruance headed eastward to rendezvous with the oilers for refueling. After six months of repeated victories the Japanese Navy was not only stopped but actually beaten at Midway. The cream of their carrier pilots perished in the four sunken fleet carriers and these skilled flyers could not be replaced; yet, they would be in increasing demand as the war continued. The Battle of Midway verified that all the lessons learned at Taranto, Matapan, the Bismarck sinking and Coral Sea were valid and showed that a fleet of fast and powerful battleships were no match for a fleet of aircraft carriers. The Warbirds of the Sea reigned supreme and the strategic situation had changed overnight, in which the ultimate fate of the Pacific War would be decided. Midway had been the first Japanese defeat in three centuries!

Yorktown Sinks

Lest it be forgotten, *Yorktown* was still afloat but had been abandoned. By the morning of June 5 the stricken carrier had corrected its list and pilots who had flown over the ship claimed it appeared seaworthy. Admiral Nimitz, himself, ordered ships in the area, including a fleet tug, minesweeper and a destroyer, to *Yorktown's* assistance. A towline was secured to the carrier; however, by 3:30 PM June 5 *Yorktown* was listing 25 degrees and was trimming down by the bow.

Admiral Fletcher and Captain Buckmaster finally decided to organize a proper salvage party. This comprised the Captain, 29 selected officers and 141 volunteers who boarded the destroyer

Severely damaged by bombs plus aerial and submarine torpedoes on June 4 and June 6, 1942, the abandoned USS Yorktown lists to port before she capsized and sank to a depth of 12,000 ft. at dawn on June 7, 1942. (U.S. Navy Photograph)

COMMANDER-IN-CHIEF
FLAG OFFICE
RECEIVED

Cincpac File No.   UNITED STATES PACIFIC FLEET   A16
A16   FLAGSHIP OF THE COMMANDER-IN-CHIEF

No1699   JUN 28 1942

SECRET   DECLASSIFIED

From: Commander-in-Chief, United States Pacific Fleet.
To: Commander-in-Chief, United States Fleet.

Subject: Battle of Midway.

Reference: (a) CincPac A16/(90) Ser. 01693 of 6/15/42.

Enclosures: (A) Track of the Battle of Midway - Composite of
                   All Reports.
               (B) Copy of Cincpac A8/(37)/JAP/(26.2)(no date)
                   and Cincpac A8/(37)JAP/(26) Ser. 01753 dated
                   21 June 1942.
               (C) ComCru,Task Force SEVENTEEN A16-3/(013) dated
                   12 June 1942.
               (D) Copy of Comtaskforce SEVENTEEN A16-3/A9(0029N)
                   dated June 26, 1942.
               (E) Copy of NAS Midway NA38/A16-3 Serial 075 dated
                   18 June 1942 with ComHawSeaFron. 1st End. thereon.
               (F) Summary of Army Aircraft Attacks at Midway,
                   ComGen.Haw.(8672).

     1.   In numerous and widespread engagements lasting from
the 3rd to 6th of June, with carrier based planes as the spearhead
of the attack, combined forces of the Navy, Marine Corps and Army
in the Hawaiian Area defeated a large part of the Japanese fleet
and frustrated the enemy's powerful move against Midway that was
undoubtedly the keystone of larger plans. All participating personnel, without exception, displayed unhesitating devotion to duty,
loyalty and courage. This superb spirit in all three services made
possible the application of the destructive power that routed the
enemy and inflicted these losses:
               (a) 4 CV sunk - AKAGI, KAGA, SORYU, HIRYU - with
                   the loss of all their planes and many of their
                   personnel. Estimated 275 planes, 2400 men.
               (b) 2 probably 3 BB damaged, 1 severely.
               (c) 2 CA sunk - MOGAMI, MIKUMA - 3 or more others
                   damaged, some severely.
               (d) 1 CL damaged.
               (e) 3 DD sunk, 1 other possibly sunk.
               (f) 4 AP and AK hit, 1 or more possibly sunk.
               (g) Estimated total number of personnel lost 4800.
     2.   These results were achieved at the cost of the
YORKTOWN and HAMMANN sunk and about 150 planes lost in action or
damaged beyond repair. Our total personnel losses were about
ninety-two(92) officers and two hundred and fifteen (215) men.

---

     27.   This was the situation when our carrier attack
began. Task Force 16 and 17, ready about 200 miles to the northeast of the Japanese carriers, had intercepted the first contact
reports by the Midway scouts. At about 0700 launching commenced
of the following attack groups, YORKTOWN's being temporarily held
in reserve until her scouts returned (majority of fighters retained
for combat patrol):

               HORNET   - 35 VSB, 15 VTB, 10 VF
               ENTERPRISE - 35 VSB, 14 VTB, 10 VF

(Bombers carrying 1-1000 lb, or 1-500 lb, or 1-500 and 2-100 lb bombs)

These two groups proceeded independently to attack.

     32.   Not a plane survived this magnificent devotion to
purpose. One pilot, after attacking and probably hitting the KAGA
at close range, with his gunner already killed, crashed near the
AKAGI, ducked under his seat cushion to prevent being machine
gunned, and from this reserved position observed the fierce attacks
that followed.

     35.   When the HORNET torpedo squadron attacked, there were
4 carriers dispersed in a wide roughly circular formation. AKAGI,
KAGA and SORYU were in the same general vicinity, probably having
just landed planes. SORYU was smoking, showing signs of heavy
damage, as was also a ship some distance away that resembled a
battleship. The surviving HORNET VT pilot, Ensign Gay, USNR, had
been in the water only a few minutes when the ENTERPRISE and YORKTOWN
dive bombers struck hard and most effectively. Both KAGA and AKAGI,
between which he lay, were hit repeatedly, the planes on deck that
they sought to launch being ignited until the two ships burned fiercely
from stem to stern. SORYU was also hit again and continued to burn.

     90.   The performance of officers and men was of the
highest order not only at Midway and afloat but equally so among
those at Oahu not privileged to be in the front line of battle. I
am proud to report that the cooperative devotion to duty of all
those involved was so marked that; despite the necessarily decisive
part played by our three carriers, this defeat of the Japanese Arms
and ambitions was truly a victory of the United States' armed forces
and not of the Navy alone.

                                              C. W. Nimitz
                                          C. W. NIMITZ

Hammann and headed for *Yorktown* over 24 hours after she had been abandoned. Before daybreak of June 6 Hammann secured to *Yorktown's* starboard side and salvage work began. Five destroyers circled *Yorktown* on antisubmarine patrols; however, despite this precaution the Japanese Submarine I-168 carefully penetrated the destroyer screen and, at 1:30 PM, fired four torpedoes. The first missed but the second and third traveled under Hammann and exploded against *Yorktown's* hull. The last torpedo struck the destroyer midships, breaking it in half, and she sank in less than four minutes with heavy loss of life.

During the night *Yorktown's* list increased and by dawn of June 7 the carrier capsized and sank to a 12,000 feet depth. Admiral Nimitz was most unhappy and issued the following order: "In the event a ship receives such severe battle damage that abandonment may be a possibiliiy, a skeletonized crew to effect rescue of the ship shall be ready either to remain on board or to be placed in an attendant vessel."

Spruance Promoted
On June 18, 1942 Admiral Chester Nimitz selected Rear Admiral Raymond Spruance to serve as his Chief of Staff.

JAPANESE SEAPLANES
When the Pacific War began one of the major weaknesses of the Japanese Armed Forces was its engineering corps, which was not only too small but so poorly equipped that it was impossible to construct airfields quickly in newly acquired areas. Further, it was impossible to provide carriers for all encounters in areas with no airfields. In order to take advantage of the preponderance of water and lengthy coastlines in the battle area, attention shifted to seaplanes.

Although seaplanes existed and new designs were in the development stage, time was so short that only a conversion could meet the Japanese timetable. Nakajima was instructed to develop a high performance seaplane version of the Zero Sen or Reisen fighter and designers Tajima and Nitake added a single float to the A6M2 Model II to produce the A6M2-N. The landing gear had been re-

The A6M2-N Rufe high performance seaplane fighter was a conversion of the A6M2 Zero Sen fighter. This plane was necessary because the Japanese were slow in building airfields in newly acquired areas and were forced to use seaplanes due to a shortage of carriers. (U.S. National Archives)

moved, rudder enlarged, small ventral fin added and an auxiliary fuel tank built into the float. The craft made its combat appearance in the summer of 1942. It was called Rufe in the Allied code system.

Despite the resistance and weight of the float and the relatively small 950 horsepower engine, Rufe earned the respect of Allied pilots because it was able to shoot down some of the better U.S. Army fighters such as the Lightning. The A6M2-N also conserved the Japanese carrier force by covering beachheads and other coastal operations without the use of airfields. The 5,423 pound plane attained a top speed of 270 miles per hour, had a range of 1,108 miles and proved exceptionally maneuverable. The U.S.Navy was so impressed with Rufe that experiments were conducted with seaplane versions of the Wildcat and, in late 1943, with seaplane versions of the Hellcat and Helldiver. Tests were successful; however, by that time there was no need for seaplane versions of these aircraft. Under some conditions seaplane tenders were provided to service the Rufes which was reminiscent of the early days of shipboard aircraft.

BACK TO THE SOUTHWEST PACIFIC
Although the Battle of the Coral Sea thwarted the Japanese thrust to Port Moresby and the decisive Battle of Midway inflicted a serious blow to the Imperial Japanese Navy, Admiral Yamamoto did not lose the hope and confidence to try once more to gain a foothold in Port Moresby. He realized that in the next effort he must guard his left flank to ensure that the Coral Sea Battle would not repeat itself. It was decided to establish an air base on the swampy, fever-infested island of Guadalcanal in the Solomons chain. This island was chosen because it had a long area of level ground that was ideal for an airstrip. As soon as the seaplane base at Tulagi on Florida Island was complete a construction battalion was sent to Guadalcanal to begin work on the airstrip.

Operation Watchtower
Simultaneously with the Japanese Guadalcanal decision was the American Chiefs of Staff decision to occupy the Santa Cruz Islands, which are east of the Solomons, and to establish an air base near Tulagi, just north of Guadalcanal. When Allied aerial reconnaissance discovered the activity on Guadalcanal it became clear that this obscure island was the key to control the Southwest Pacific. Vice Admiral Robert L. Ghormley's South Pacific Command was assigned the capture and retention of the Guadalcanal airfield site as its primary and most urgent task because control of the adjacent seas, through which the land forces must pass and be supplied, was of paramount importance. In the absence of shore air bases Nimitz called upon three of his four aircraft carriers to provide air cover; *Saratoga*, having recently completed its repair and modernizing; *Enterprise*; and *Wasp*, which had just been transferred from Atlantic duty. Admiral Fletcher was placed in command of this carrier force.

The Guadalcanal invasion code was "Operation Watchtower" and began on August 7 when the American invasion force, which had left New Zealand on July 22, landed on the island. This marked the change in America's role in the Pacific War from that of a de-

Vice Admiral Robert L. Ghormley was in charge of the South Pacific Command and was assigned the capture of the Japanese-held Guadalcanal airfield soon to be known as Henderson Field. As Commander Ghormley he was Director of War Planning for the U.S. Military in 1938. (U.S. National Archives)

fensive posture to the offensive it was to maintain throughout the conflict. During the landing operation, Japanese bombers arrived from Rabaul, 560 nautical miles from the beachhead, but were driven off by Fletcher's Grumman Wildcats. The troop transports escaped serious damage and landed 17,000 U.S. Marines, who captured the incomplete airstrip; hereafter, called Henderson Field in honor of the heroic Marine dive bomber squadron leader at Midway. Japanese troops still occupied parts of Guadalcanal.

Simultaneously with the Guadalcanal landing were landings at Tulagi and small nearby islands of Tanambogo and Gavutu.

Battle of Savo Island

When Admiral Yamamoto learned about the U.S. landings he ordered Vice Admiral Gunichi Mikawa to break up the invasions with his heavy cruisers from Rabaul. At noon of August 7 Mikawa led five heavy cruisers, two light cruisers and one destroyer out of Rabaul's Simpson Harbor and arrived at Savo Island, a small island north of Guadalcanal, at about 1:30 AM on August 9. The flotilla passed between Savo and Guadalcanal undetected by the American destroyers guarding the area. Minutes later the Japanese cruisers pounded the Allied Fleet guarding the beachhead. First to feel the fury of the attack was the Australian cruiser *Canberra*, which received two torpedo hits as well as concentrated eight-inch shells.

Ablaze, the *Canberra* sank that day. Mikawa then turned northward and the U.S. cruisers *Quincy*, *Astoria* and *Vincennes* met the same fate as *Canberra*.

Mikawa Retires - Task Incomplete

Surprisingly, instead of attacking the remaining three cruisers, destroyer squadron and, most important, the troop transports, Mikawa returned to Rabaul. The only possible explanation is that the Japanese admiral feared the U.S. carriers in the area and thought it prudent to save his ships before dive bombers appeared; perhaps not realizing that night carrier operations were not normally conducted by the U.S. Navy in 1942. One can only contemplate the destruction carrier planes would have wrought on Mikuma's ships had night combat operations been routine in the U.S. Navy.

Air Support Necessary

Admiral Mikawa was wise to realize that, without air support, he would be at the mercy of U.S. carriers; therefore, in effect, U.S. aircraft carriers saved Allied cruisers, destroyers and troop transports by merely existing and posing a threat to Mikawa's cruisers without firing a shot.

Battle Of The Eastern Solomons

Henderson Field became fully operational on August 17, 1942 however, U.S. Marines were forced to beat off relentless attacks from Japanese forces that were still on Guadalcanal. Both sides continued to land troops on this valuable bit of real estate.

On August 21 Admiral Yamamoto's Combined Fleet was escorting three transports with 1,500 troops from Rabaul to Guadalcanal. The fleet comprised the carriers *Zuikaku*, *Shokaku* and *Ryujo* with 177 planes; four heavy cruisers; 17 destroyers; seaplane carrier *Chitose*; scouting submarines; two battleships; and three light cruisers. This was the fleet with which Yamamoto still hoped would engage in that "final" naval battle with the U.S. Navy.

The Combined Fleet was intercepted by Admiral Fletcher's Task Force 61, which included *Wasp*, *Enterprise* and *Saratoga* with 259 fighters, dive bombers and torpedo planes; battleship *South Carolina*, plus cruisers and destroyers.

Ryujo Sunk - Enterprise Damaged

Saratoga's dive bombers and torpedo planes sank *Ryujo* on August 24, while *Shokaku* was lightly damaged by *Enterprise* dive bombers. Fletcher had retained three squadrons of Wildcats to protect *Enterprise*; however, while they were decimating a Japanese torpedo plane attack, Val dive bombers were diving on the Big E from 18,000 feet and scored three direct hits. The bombs plunged through the unarmored Flight Deck, then exploded, starting enormous fires. Thanks to efficient damage control the fires were under control within an hour. The Flight Deck was then quickly patched and steaming at 24 knots, *Enterprise* was able to recover her planes and make it to Pearl Harbor for repairs.

One transport had been sunk and so many Japanese planes and pilots had been lost, which Japan could ill-afford, that Nagumo retired to obtain replacements, if possible. Fletcher sailed south to meet *Wasp* and refuel.

The battle was a tactical standoff; however, the Japanese troop landing had been turned back, which was Fletcher's objective.

USS Hornet was ordered to the Solomons to replace *Enterprise*.

Torpedo Junction

At this time the waters east of Guadalcanal were called "Torpedo Junction" because, although only few Japanese submarines were operating around the Solomons, they were extremely active and successful.

Saratoga Torpedoed

On August 31, 1942, *Saratoga* and *Hornet* were patrolling at about 13 knots near Guadalcanal when Japanese Submarine I-26 fired several torpedoes at *Saratoga*. Only one torpedo struck the carrier and she was able to steam the 3,000 miles to Pearl Harbor for repairs.

Wasp Sunk

American carrier strength was now down to two serviceable ships, *Hornet* and *Wasp*. On September 6 *Hornet* was narrowly missed by torpedoes fired by the Japanese Submarine I-11.

It seems lessons were not learned; for on September 15, the Japanese Submarine I-19 pumped three torpedoes into the small carrier *Wasp*, Captain Forrest P. Sherman commanding, as she was screening a troop convoy. It was impossible to save the flaming wreck and the coup-de-grace was administered by an attending destroyer. Over 190 crewmen were killed and 366 wounded of the 2,247 complement.

Halsey Replaces Ghormley

Admiral Nimitz had become dissatisfied with Admiral Ghormley's handling of the Solomon's Campaign and replaced him as Commander, South Pacific Area and South Pacific Force, with Vice Admiral William F. Halsey, on October 18.

Battle of Santa Cruz

The struggle for control of Guadalcanal continued into autumn with both sides pouring men and materiel into the area. Finally, once again on October 22, Admiral Yamamoto sent his entire Combined Fleet south to the area just north of the Santa Cruz Islands, southeast of the Solomons.

By the summer of 1942 the waters east of the Solomon Islands were called Torpedo Junction because Japanese submarines were successful in this area. On September 15 USS Wasp was torpedoed south of the Solomon Island of San Cristobal by the Japanese submarine I-19 and burned fiercely until sunk by U.S. destroyers. (U.S. National Archives)

Japanese Forces

As had been done in previous battles, the Combined Fleet was divided into groups. Vice Admiral Nobutake Kondo was in command of the entire fleet and he remained with the Advance Force comprising two battleships, four cruisers, carrier *Junyo* and a destroyer screen. The Striking Force was 120 miles to the southeast comprising the aircraft carriers *Shokaku*, *Zuikaku* and *Zuiho*, plus their destroyer screen, led by Admiral Nagumo. Sixty miles south of the Striking Force was the Vanguard Force of two battleships, three heavy cruisers and a destroyer screen.

U.S. Forces

The ships at Admiral Halsey's disposal comprised Task Force 17 centered around *USS Hornet*, and speeding to join it was Task Force 16 with *USS Enterprise*. In addition to the carriers was battleship South Dakota, six cruisers, and 14 destroyers.

The two U.S. forces made rendezvous on October 24, 1942 near the Santa Cruz Islands where Vice Admiral Thomas C. Kinkaid was placed in command of the entire force. On the following day patrolling Catalinas sighted the Japanese carriers but Nagumo turned northward and was lost to Kinkaid's scout planes. Vice Admiral Kinkaid sent out 16 Dauntless scouts at dawn of the 26th and, although he had received orders from Admiral Halsey to attack, Kinkaid waited until the Japanese force's strength and location were verified by his own scouts. When, at 6:50 AM the Imperial Japanese Navy Combined Fleet was located by a pair of SBD's about 200 miles to the northwest, Kinkaid ordered a strike against Nagumo.

Vice Admiral Thomas C. Kinkaid commanded Task Force 16 centered around USS Enterprise and Task Force 17 centered around USS Hornet in the Battle of Santa Cruz. Mrs. Kinkaid said this was the Admiral's favorite photo of himself. (U.S. Naval Historical Center, Courtesy Mrs. Thomas C. Kinkaid)

Kinkaid Launches Strike

It was 7:30 AM on October 26 when 15 Douglas Dauntless div bombers, six Grumman Avenger torpedo planes and an eigh Grumman Wildcat escort took off from *Hornet*. One half hour late *Enterprise* launched three SBD's, eight TBF's and eight F4F's. second *Hornet* strike followed at 8:15 AM, which included nin Dauntless dive bombers, nine Avenger torpedo bombers and nin Wildcat fighters.

Nagumo Launches Strike

Admiral Nagumo learned the presence and location of Halsey's forc simultaneously with Kinkaid and ordered a strike at once. By 7:0 AM the Japanese had launched about 65 planes, of which rough half were Zero Sen Fighters.

Zuiho Hit

No sooner had the planes left Nagumo's carriers than two c *Enterprise*'s Dauntless scouting detail dived on the small *Zuiho* an dropped two 500 pound bombs on the Flight Deck; penetrating th unarmored deck and exploding below. This started enormous fire which put *Zuiho* out of action. Lieutenant Commander S.B. Stron and Ensign C.B. Irvine are credited with this timely attack.

Striking Forces Meet

Something was about to happen which had never before been re corded in the annals of naval air history. Both Japanese and Amer can aerial strike forces were in the air at the same time, heading fc a strike on each other's carriers, when they began to pass each othe in opposite directions. A dozen Zero fighters sped toward the *Er terprise* formations and shot down four Avengers and an equal num ber of Wildcats, in exchange for the loss of three Zero fighters. Th chance meeting of the two strike forces alerted both carrier force to the impending attack.

Attack on *Hornet*

The Japanese strike force arrived at their target before the Amer cans reached theirs by virtue of the fact that the Japanese starte earlier. Upon their arrival the dive bombing Vals were intercepte by the *Enterprise* Wildcats; however, the torpedo-carrying Kate charged the carrier at low altitude with impunity. At that moment tropical rain squall engulfed *Enterprise*, which forced the Kates t transfer their attention to *Hornet*. Although about half of the Kate were shot down, two torpedoes found their mark on *Hornet*'s sta board side. In addition, one of the Kates which had been critical hit continued against *Hornet*'s bow in an enormous explosio Meanwhile, Vals began their dives from 17,000 feet into a barrag of gunfire. As three were hit and falling out of control they mar aged to drop their 500 pound bombs before their Vals crashed int the sea. Two of the bombs plunged through the unarmored Fligh Deck and penetrated several decks below before detonating. Th third bomb exploded upon impact. One Val, which appeared to b flown by the squadron leader, was fatally hit; however, it turne into *Hornet*'s island, destroying the bridge and starting furious fire It only required a few minutes to convert the powerful *Hornet* int a motionless, burning wreck!

Attack On *Shokaku*

By this time the American striking force had arrived at the Japanese Combined Fleet. The Hornet force appeared uncoordinated and had difficulty finding the Japanese carriers but succeeded in finding the Vanguard Force, which they proceeded to attack. The TBF Avengers were severely handicapped by the antiquated torpedoes they were forced to use; however, a Dauntless managed to score a direct hit on the cruiser *Chikuma*. The dive bombers continued forward despite the fact that their fighter escort had been drawn away by a Zero attack from *Junyo*. Lieutenant Commander Widheim pressed on and led his Dauntless squadron until *Shokaku* had been sighted. Despite fierce antiaircraft fire and Zero attacks which disabled four of Widheim's dive bombers, including his own, Lieutenant J.E. Vose led the squadron to the attack which scored four direct hits with 1,000 pound bombs. *Shokaku*'s Flight Deck had been turned into a mass of jagged metal and fires consumed the hangar. *Shokaku*'s speed was reduced to 20 knots and the once proud carrier left the battle with *Zuiho*.

Attack On *Enterprise*

It appears that Admiral Halsey's carriers had exhausted their offensive power; but Nagumo still had 44 planes on *Zuikaku* which he launched against *Enterprise* at 8:22 AM of October 26, 1942. Two bomb hits were registered which put the forward elevator out of commission. As the crew worked frantically to repair the Flight Deck so that the orbiting returning strike force could land before the planes ran out of fuel, a Japanese strike force of 29 planes from *Junyo* appeared. They failed to score a hit on *Enterprise*; however, direct hits were made on *South Dakota* and the cruiser *San Juan*. Soon thereafter, *Enterprise* was able to recover her waiting planes, thanks to her efficient damage control planning.

Hornet Sinks

With American offensive and defensive air power spent, six Japanese torpedo-carrying Kates attacked the crippled *Hornet* which was being towed by the cruiser *Northampton*. One torpedo struck the hull, causing severe damage, which forced the abandonment of the American carrier. During the abandon ship operation, dive bomb-

The sky is full of FLAK over USS Enterprise as planes from the Japanese carrier Zuikaku launch an attack in the morning of October 26, 1942 during the Battle of Santa Cruz. Damage from two bomb hits was quickly repaired. (Official U.S. Navy Photograph, Naval Imaging Command)

ers from *Junyo* scored two more hits, but *Hornet* refused to sink! Even after everyone had left the gallant ship and U.S. destroyers attempted to administer the coup-de-grace with torpedoes and a five inch gun barrage *Hornet* refused to give up. After the American forces had retired from the area, Japanese destroyers moved in and sank the carrier with torpedoes.

No U.S. Navy Operational Carriers

The Battle of the Santa Cruz Islands was a tactical victory for the Japanese forces because now the only operational aircraft carriers in the Pacific were Japanese and they were in possession of the "field." Of course, the American occupation of Henderson Field, somewhat offset the Japanese carrier superiority but reinforcements and supplies to the Americans on Guadalcanal had to breach the Japanese carriers.

Japanese Aircrew Losses Are Severe

On the other side of the coin was the fact that, again, Japanese air-

Crippled by torpedo planes and dive bombers from the Japanese carrier Junyo, USS Hornet is dead in the water as a destroyer takes off survivors to abandon ship. The abandoned carrier was sunk by Japanese destroyers. (Official U.S. Navy Photograph)

The Battle of Santa Cruz left the U.S. Navy with no serviceable carriers. HMS Victorious was transferred to the U.S. Pacific Fleet and operated in concert with the recently repaired USS Saratoga in the Coral Sea and Southwest Pacific. Both ships exchanged aircraft and crews as necessary. Saratoga pilots posed for this photo aboard Victorious with the British carrier's crest and British White Ensign. (British Information Service)

crews suffered severe losses, which left Admiral Yamamoto with only enough carrier aircrews to equip his two smaller carriers which could operate less than 100 planes. Losses were so severe that only 30 Zero fighters could be spared for the Solomons area.

Leppla and Liska

John Leppla and John Liska, who figured so prominently in the Coral Sea battle, also fought in the Santa Cruz battle. Leppla had since transferred to fighters and, while piloting a Wildcat, was jumped by Zeroes. Apparently, the Wildcat received critical damage because Leppla bailed out; however, his parachute failed to open and he fell one mile into the Pacific. At that time John Liska was the radioman/rear gunner for Ensign Johnson in VS-6 and during an interception by Zero fighters Johnson shot down two and Liska scored one Zero in their Dauntless on October 26, 1942.

Ozawa Replaces Nagumo

Admiral Isoroku Yamamoto replaced Admiral Chuichi Nagumo with Vice Admiral Jisaburo Ozawa as Commander of the Striking Force after the Battle of Santa Cruz Islands.

U.S. Navy Asks Royal Navy For Carriers

The U.S. Navy had been reduced to the partially effective *Enterprise* which was badly in need of repair, so the U.S. turned to the Royal Navy for assistance. This appeal resulted in the transfer of *HMS Victorious* to the Pacific Fleet to serve with the U.S. Navy. As previously mentioned, Fleet Air Arm aircraft had been neglected by the unified air force and could never have stood up to the superlative Japanese carrier planes. *HMS Victorious* had to be re-equipped with American carrier aircraft. By the time this had been accomplished *USS Saratoga* had completed repairs and the two ships operated as a team in the South Pacific while *Enterprise* underwent badly needed repair.

BACK TO THE EUROPEAN WAR

Lest it be forgotten, the war at sea was still raging in the Atlantic and Mediterranean with aircraft carriers and Warbirds of the Sea playing leading roles. The majority of Royal Navy fleet carriers were employed in the Mediterranean Sea and in the Atlantic Ocean along the coast of Portugal escorting the all-important convoys from the British Isles to the strategic island of Malta and North Africa. Although the British carriers had no competition from enemy carriers, as did the U.S., they were forced to operate within range of shore-based bombers. Trans-Atlantic and Soviet Union convoys were being left more and more to the new expendable escort carrier merchant ship conversions while fleet carriers *HMS Indomitable, HMS Furious, HMS Eagle* and *HMS Argus* plied the waters of the eastern Atlantic and Mediterranean with Grumman Martlets, Fairey Swordfish and Fulmars, Sea Hurricanes and Grumman Avengers operating from their flight decks.

Merchant Aircraft Carriers (MAC)

The admiralty anticipated an increase in submarine activity in the summer of 1942 and conceived another stopgap measure as it had with the CAM. This time it was the MAC (Merchant Aircraft Carrier) which was a considerable improvement over the CAM because the aircraft could land on the through flight deck. Externally, the MAC resembled an ordinary escort carrier; however, no hangar, elevators or catapults were fitted and the hull interior remained that of a merchant ship. In operation it not only carried its cargo but also handled four to six Fairey Swordfish which were stowed on deck. The MAC conversions were restricted to tankers or bulk grain carriers because the flight deck could prohibit access to the hatches of a conventional freighter. Tankers and grain ships are loaded and unloaded via large hoses; the oil is pumped and the grain is moved by a flow of air in the hose. The average topside weight increase created by the added flight deck was about 700 tons. About 5,000 gallons of aviation gasoline was carried; however, the only cargo carried was heavy bunker oil in order to reduce the risk of explosion and fire in the event of a hit. MAC ships entered service in the spring of 1943.

Malta Convoy

By August 1942 the unsinkable Island "aircraft carrier" Malta was at the end of its endurance and would have been starved into surrender if supplies were not forthcoming. A convoy was quickly organized, which was no easy task, to make another desperate and dangerous attempt to break through to the blockaded outpost. This was coded "Operation Pedestal" and its principal objective was to reinforce the Malta air defense by having *Furious* transport 38 Spitfires to that isolated island.

The main convoy, which included 13 cargo ships and one tanker, left Scotland on the night of August 2 and reached Gibraltar seven days later, where it met its escort. This included *Eagle, Victorious, Argus,* and *Indomitable,* plus battleships *Rodney* and *Nelson,* six cruisers, 32 destroyers and four corvettes, which is a clear indication of the importance of the Malta lifeline. As soon as the convoy passed Gibraltar Italian scout planes shadowed the ships and, when the convoy passed Majorca, the Luftwaffe took over.

Eagle Sinks

When all eyes were looking skyward, an enormous explosion rocked Eagle. The German U-boat U-73, *Kapitän* Rosenbaum commanding, had sent four torpedoes into the venerable carrier. In less than 10 minutes Eagle took on a list and sank with 200 of her crew and most of her aircraft.

The loss of Eagle reduced the convoy's fighter defense to 16 Fulmars and six Hurricanes on *Victorious* and 10 Martlets and 24 Hurricanes on *Indomitable*. This force had to fight off 36 German dive bombers and torpedo planes at dusk. No hits were scored and the ships' guns shot down three attackers. It was a different carrier war than in the Pacific but just as harrowing and dangerous.

Escort Carrier Operations

HMS Avenger, which had been one of five escort carrier conversions produced in the U.S. for the Royal Navy, had its first chance to demonstrate escort carrier value in early August when it was selected as part of the escort for Convoy PQ18 to northern Russia. The previous convoy on this route, PQ17, had met with disaster from German torpedo planes and dive bombers that were stationed in Norway. The basic objective of *HMS Avenger* was to launch intercepting fighters when German aircraft appeared; therefore, its aircraft complement consisted of 12 Sea Hurricanes with six spares, plus three Fairey Swordfish for antisubmarine operations.

Poor Beginning

The handful of Hurricanes started poorly in the fighter defense role when, on September 12, they concentrated on the shadowing German shore-based scouts which drew them away from the convoy as six twin-engine Junkers 88 dive bombers plunged on the ships. In a coordinated attack four dozen twin-engine shore-based Heinkel 111 bombers swooped in at low altitude, each carrying two torpedoes. Eight ships of the convoy were sunk before the Hurricanes returned in time to shoot down one Heinkel, driving off the remainder.

New Tactics

The following day saw a change in tactics for the carrier's fighters. Only two Hurricanes were kept aloft for routine patrols and for chasing reconnaissance aircraft while the main force remained on HMS Avenger ready for takeoff on short notice. The shore-based Heinkels returned in two waves of 22 and 25 aircraft; all torpedo fitted. High level bombing Heinkels joined in but the Sea Hurricanes were ready. They tore into the attackers and scattered their formations, discouraging any more attacks. One merchant ship was sunk but tactics were being refined. During attacks on September 13 and 14 several shore-based German planes fell victim to the Hurricanes, while others fell before the ship's antiaircraft guns. In exchange, three Hurricanes were shot down; however, the pilots were rescued from the cold water.

ASW Swordfish

The antisubmarine work of the Swordfish also paid dividends. Since September 10 German U-boats had been following the convoy and sank three ships; but, in turn, had lost three of their own thanks to the Stringbags which spotted, dropped depth charges and actually led an escorting destroyer to the U-38 which sank the submarine.

Operations Near Shore - Disaster

Aircraft carrier operations within range of shore-based aircraft is veritable suicide and to be avoided in any strategic or tactical situation because, unlike carrier aircraft, shore-based aircraft are not confined to a sinkable aircraft carrier and usually have access to a variety of sources for fuel, pilots, ammunition and bombs.

Multi-Role Escort Carriers

Escort carriers appeared in greater numbers and their role was enlarged to covering beachheads during amphibious operations. In the following chapter it will be seen how these little expendable ships saved an important amphibious landing with unbelievable bravery.

SECOND ARCADIA CONFERENCE

The Second Arcadia Conference was held to confirm the decision for Allied Forces to invade North Africa despite arguments to the contrary.

It has been seen that an overwhelming responsibility of the Royal Navy was keeping the sea lanes open for materiel and personnel to Malta and North Africa. The second wartime Washington Conference was held during June 19-25, 1942 as a continuation of

While defending against a German air attack in the Mediterranean Sea, the converted battleship HMS Eagle was struck by four torpedoes from the German U-Boat U-73. Within ten minutes the venerable carrier assumed a list and sank with 200 of her crew. The dying carrier is shown afire and listing while still making speed on August 11, 1942, when it sank on its way to the island of Malta. (U.S. Naval Historical Center)

the Arcadia Conference of January. Despite the objections of General George C. Marshall, the previously agreed upon invasion of North Africa by U.S. and Commonwealth Forces was upheld. The invasion of North Africa by the Allies would relieve many British naval forces for other duties because shore-based aircraft would protect Allied convoys.

OPERATION TORCH AND SUPERMARINE SEAFIRES

As agreed at the Second Arcadia Conference American ground forces made a series of landings on the coast of French North Africa on November 8 under the overall command of Major General Dwight D. Eisenhower. Admiral Sir Andrew Cunningham was in command of the Allied naval forces, which included the Royal Navy carriers *Furious*, *Formidable*, and *Argus*. The landings, which were code-named "Operation Torch", were covered by Seafires operating from the three carriers; No.885 Squadron on *HMS Formidable*, Nos. 801 and 807 Squadrons on *HMS Furious* and No. 880 Squadron on *HMS Argus*. Interestingly, the British Seafires flew with American star markings instead of the British cockades during the action. These were removed when the Seafires left the operation.

Seafires also saw action in the Pacific where they confronted the nimble Zero Sen. Even the maneuverable Seafire was no match for the Zero when it attempted to dogfight as the Spitfire was doing with the Messerschmitt 109. New Tactics had to be developed, such as "hit and run" maneuvers, in order to succeed against the Japanese fighter.

A Seafire IIC nearing touchdown on HMS Furious. Observe the squared off wingtips and long arresting hook attached well forward on the fuselage. (Air Ministry [Navy])

Supermarine Seafire; Carrier-Based Aircraft

The successful adaptation of the Hurricane to carrier operation led to experiments to do the same with the superior Spitfire. Tests with a converted RAF Spitfire began on *HMS Illustrious* late in 1941 by Lieutenant Commander Bromwell. The trials were so successful that 48 RAF Spitfires were converted into Seafires or Hooked Spitfires. The major alterations included a strengthened fuselage for the addition of a Vee frame arresting hook and catapult fittings. The conversion work was ordered in mid-1942. On September 11, 1942 Lieutenant E. Brown made successful landing trials on Avenger's sister escort carrier, the U.S. converted *HMS Biter* which Flight Deck was only about 60 percent as long as the *Illustrious* Flight Deck.

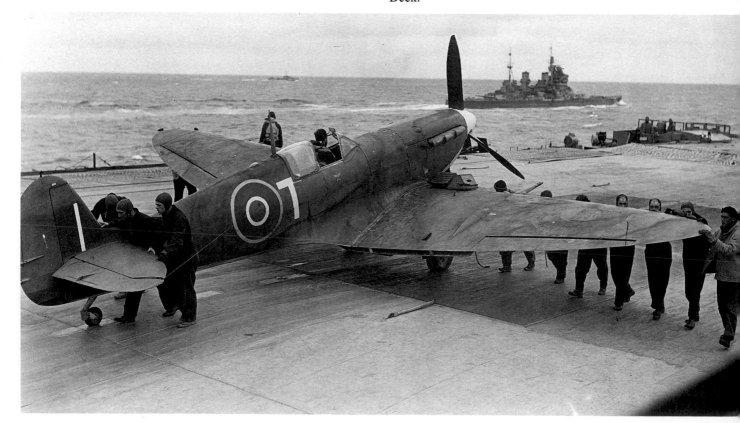

Many RAF Spitfires were converted into Seafires for aircraft carrier service. This converted Spitfire Vb operated from HMS Furious which was the first carrier to take Seafires into combat. (Ministry of Defence [Navy])

Difficult Adaptation

As mentioned in the Prologue, carrier aircraft are a breed apart, far more complex and rugged than even the most sophisticated shore-based type. So it was with the vaunted Spitfire; although successful, the trials revealed that the poor visibility caused by the long nose and low cockpit forced the pilot to make a nose-down approach or fish-tail until the point of touch down which had to be a three point, nose-up landing. Experience showed that if the Spitfire, or Seafire as it was called, made a normal two wheels, tail-up landing it would bounce dangerously, miss the arresting cables and either flip over the side into the sea or wind up in the crash barrier.

Landing Gear Weakness

The landing gear was also delicate by carrier plane standards and could not withstand repeated hard landings.

Takeoff and Landing Advantage

The Seafire did, however, have a distinct advantage over many heavier purpose-designed carrier aircraft. Its rapid takeoff characteristic did not warrant the use of catapults because unassisted takeoffs could be made 90 seconds apart which was an improvement over catapult launching in the early 1940s. Safe takeoffs could be made with as little as a five miles per hour WOD. A fast landing recovery rate was another Seafire advantage with elapsed time between touchdowns as little as 40 seconds; superior to most purpose-built shipboard aircraft of that period. This takeoff and landing advantage can be attributed to the Seafire's high power loading and relatively low wing loading.

Seafire Production

The first of 402 Mark II Seafires was delivered in September 1942. By this time 166 Seafires had been converted from RAF Spitfires and many had seen quite a bit of action in the RAF and were, in fact, used aircraft. The Mark II was the first version to be delivered directly from the factory as Seafires. Westland built 870 Seafires

and Cunliffe-Owen completed another 350 under subcontracts. About 1,700 Seafires were delivered to the FAA.

Folding Wings

The final version of the Seafire was the Mark III. This was fitted with manually folding wings which reduced the span to 13 feet-6 inches. Folding was up and over the wing roots and held in place by a special strut. The folding added 125 pounds and reduced the wing strength by about 10 percent.

Seafire Data

Top speed of the 7,100 pound Mark III fighter was 352 miles per hour at 12,250 feet. Range was 465 miles which could be extended to 725 miles with an auxiliary drop tank. Service ceiling was 36,000 feet. Powerplant was a 12-cylinder Vee liquid-cooled Rolls-Royce Merlin 55 which produced 1,470 horsepower. Armament comprised eight .303 inch caliber machine guns or two 20 millimeter cannon and four .303 inch caliber machine guns all mounted in the wing. The all-metal plane had an extended wingspan of 36 feet-10 inches and a folded span of 13 feet-6 inches. Wing area was 242 square feet. Length was 29 feet-11 inches with a height of 11 feet-2 inches.

BENT-WING BIRD CARRIER TRIALS

The U.S. fighter that was destined to stop the apparently invincible Zero was rolling off the production line in mid-1942. The first production Vought F4U-1 Corsair (Bureau of Aeronautics No. 02153) flew on June 25, 1942.

F4U-1 Data

The 2,000 horsepower, 18-cylinder Pratt & Whitney R-2800-88 (B) twin-row radial engine gave the 12,060 pound F4U-1 a top speed of 415 miles per hour at 19,000 feet and a sea level rate of climb of 3,120 feet per minute. Service ceiling was 37,000 feet and combat range was 1,015 miles. Wingspan was 41 feet and overall length 33

This Supermarine Seafire Mark III illustrates the manually folding wing. Note the downturned wingtips and the strut holding the wing panel in position. Folding mechanism added 125 pounds and reduced wing strength by 10 percent. (Air Ministry [Navy])

The first Vought Corsair production variant was the Vought F4U-1 which had the cockpit moved aft three feet to make space for a large self-sealing fuel tank. A small bubble was also fitted to the cockpit canopy to house a rear view mirror (arrow). Note the cutout behind the cockpit to improve rearward visibility (arrow). (Official U.S. Navy Photograph, Courtesy Vought Aircraft Company)

VOUGHT F4U-1D CORSAIR

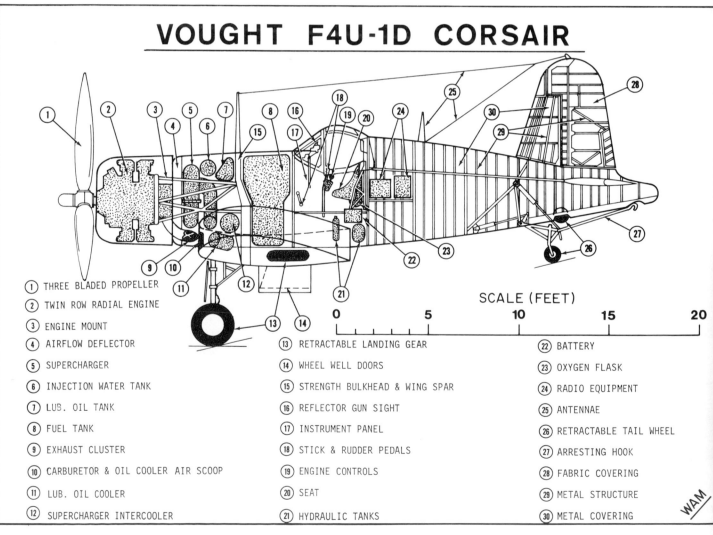

① THREE BLADED PROPELLER
② TWIN ROW RADIAL ENGINE
③ ENGINE MOUNT
④ AIRFLOW DEFLECTOR
⑤ SUPERCHARGER
⑥ INJECTION WATER TANK
⑦ LUB. OIL TANK
⑧ FUEL TANK
⑨ EXHAUST CLUSTER
⑩ CARBURETOR & OIL COOLER AIR SCOOP
⑪ LUB. OIL COOLER
⑫ SUPERCHARGER INTERCOOLER

⑬ RETRACTABLE LANDING GEAR
⑭ WHEEL WELL DOORS
⑮ STRENGTH BULKHEAD & WING SPAR
⑯ REFLECTOR GUN SIGHT
⑰ INSTRUMENT PANEL
⑱ STICK & RUDDER PEDALS
⑲ ENGINE CONTROLS
⑳ SEAT
㉑ HYDRAULIC TANKS

㉒ BATTERY
㉓ OXYGEN FLASK
㉔ RADIO EQUIPMENT
㉕ ANTENNAE
㉖ RETRACTABLE TAIL WHEEL
㉗ ARRESTING HOOK
㉘ FABRIC COVERING
㉙ METAL STRUCTURE
㉚ METAL COVERING

SCALE (FEET)
0   5   10   15   20

WAM

ABOVE OPPOSITE: The second Vought Corsair production variant was the F4U-1A which improved visibility for the pilot by raising the cockpit and installing a one piece cockpit bubble canopy. The F4U-1D was a basic F4U-1A with provision to carry two large bombs. (Vought Aircraft Company, Courtesy Paul Bower)

feet-4 inches. Height was 16 feet-1 inch. Maximum fuel capacity was 361 U.S. gallons. The armament was (6) .50 inch caliber Browning MG 53-2 machine guns buried in the wing with 2,350 rounds of ammunition.

Corsair Carrier Trials

Carrier trials were undertaken aboard *USS Sangamon* in Chesapeake Bay on September 25 by Lieutenant Commander S. Porter flying the seventh production F4U-1. After only four takeoffs and landings were made it was decided that the Corsair was not qualified for carrier operation because the fighter had the tendency to swing badly upon touchdown and was prone to bounce due to the rigidity of the landing gear oleo struts. Until the problem was corrected all Corsairs were diverted to the U.S. Marine Corps since their operations were confined to shore bases. The 700 Corsairs flown by the Fleet Air Arm had been flying from carriers since the onset and experienced no operational problems. Royal Navy Corsairs were operating from aircraft carriers a full nine months before the U.S. Navy approved the "bent wing bird" for carrier operation.

On October 3, 1942 (10) Corsairs were delivered to Navy Fighter Squadron 12 (VF-12), then temporarily assigned to *USS Saratoga* for service test evaluation and the F4U-1 failed! The plane was found to be very difficult to land because the huge nose obscured the Landing Deck Signal Officer at the crucial moment of touchdown. By the end of October, VF-12 transferred their Corsairs

to the Marine Corps for operation from shore bases in the Solomons at a time when the U.S. Navy was experiencing a severe shortage of aircraft carriers. The carrier rejection problem was a severe blow to Vought designers who worked very hard to solve the problem.

As 1942 drew to a close, 178 F4U-1's had left the production line at Vought's Stratford, Connecticut plant. The first planes allocated to combat units had gone to land-based Marine Fighter Squadron 124 (VMF-124) in late September. VMF-124 was also to be the first unit to take the Corsair into combat.

U.S. NAVY ESCORT AND TRAINING CARRIER CONVERSIONS

Pleased with the Royal Navy's favorable experience with escort carrier conversions, the U.S. Navy requested the conversion of additional cargo ships and tankers into escort aircraft carriers and training carriers.

Paddle Wheel Training Carrier

Although they never fired a shot or ventured into a combat area the *USS Sable* and *USS Wolverine* are two aircraft carriers that must be mentioned. They were the only side paddle wheel-driven aircraft carriers and the only carriers that operated on the Great Lakes. Both had been built before World War I.

Carrier pilots require extensive training before they can fly from the moving airfields; however, the U.S. Navy was reluctant to assign combat carriers to training duties. German submarines were operating off the U.S. East Coast and even entered Long Island Sound, which made training along the coast extremely hazardous. The obvious answer was in the conversion of two Great Lakes

USS Sable and USS Wolverine were the only paddle-wheel aircraft carriers ever built. The carriers were used on the Great Lakes to train pilots for aircraft carrier operations. Wolverine is shown here. (U.S. Naval Historical Center)

USS Charger (CVE-30) had been converted from the C-3 cargo ship Rio de la Plata and was commissioned in March 1942. The ship was used in the U.S. as a training carrier for the Fleet Air Arm. Unlike USS Long Island, Charger was fitted with a 190 foot long Hangar, 16 feet high, and a full length Flight Deck. The six-cylinder 8,500 brake horsepower Sun Doxford diesel engine drove the carrier at 17 knots. Flight Deck was 78 x 440 feet. Charger's original designation was BAVG-4 (Royal Navy), then AVG-30 and ACV-30. Finally, CVE-30 was adopted in mid-1943. (Official U.S. Navy Photograph)

paddle-steamers, *Seeandbee* and *Greater Buffalo* on Lake Erie. The steamer conversions would not only free combat carriers to fight but would operate in the safety of the Great Lakes.

The paddle-steamer *Seeandbee* was converted to *USS Wolverine* in Buffalo, New York in early 1942. The huge superstructure was removed and a 98 x 500 feet wooden flight deck was installed. No elevators or hangars were fitted because it had no complement of aircraft. A small island was constructed around the four stovepipe stacks which had been rerouted to the starboard side. The island also gave the trainees a feel for realistic flight deck conditions. Eight arresting cables were fitted but no catapults were installed. All aircraft which operated from Wolverine were shore-based.

The powerplant was a 4-cylinder inclined steam-driven compound reciprocating engine which developed 8,000 indicated horsepower. Steam was generated in four cylindrical "Scotch" boilers. *USS Wolverine* attained a speed of 16 knots. Complement was 270. It was commissioned on August 22.

Greater Buffalo was converted to *USS Sable* in similar fashion as was *Seeandbee*. Both ships were sold and scrapped after the war ended. Unglamorous as they were, the paddle wheel carriers performed a sorely needed service and freed combat carriers, which were in short supply in 1942.

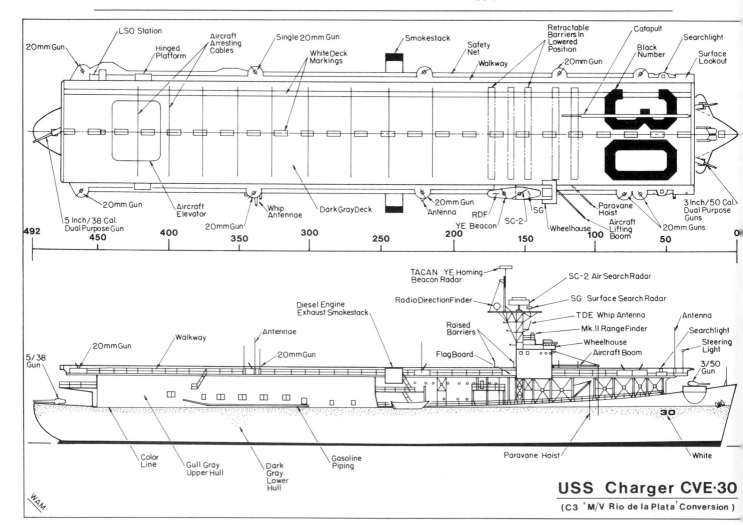

USS Charger CVE-30

(C3 'M/V Rio de la Plata' Conversion)

Bogue Class Escort Carriers

The successful conversions of the escort carriers *Long Island*, *Charger*, *Archer*, and *Audacity*, plus President Roosevelt's enthusiasm for the expendable little aircraft carriers, led the U.S. Maritime Commission to release (11) C-3 size merchant ships for conversion during the last days of 1941. Experience with the operation of the previous conversions led to slight design modifications to correct the shortcomings, such as increasing the size of the air group and improving aircraft handling facilities.

Design Improvements

The 18 feet high hangar was lengthened and the sides enclosed for its entire length. Two elevators were installed, each capable of handling a 6 1/2 ton load. The wood-planked Flight Deck measured 82 x 440 feet, which was a bit shorter than the hull length of 496 feet overall. A catapult was installed, which could handle a 3 1/2 ton plane. A small island was erected well forward on the starboard side, while the smokestacks terminated amidship, port and starboard, at the Flight Deck level, similar to Japanese carriers, except that they discharged upwards, rather than downward or horizontally as was the Japanese custom.

USS Card (CVE-11) was a Bogue class C-3 cargo ship conversion. The Flight Deck was located closer to the hull than Charger and Long Island, which improved stability. (U.S. National Archives)

USS Ranger (CV-4) spent most of World War II in the Atlantic Ocean operating with the Royal Navy Home Fleet. Grumman Avengers at the bow and Douglas Dauntless dive bombers are preparing to raid German shipping off the coast of Norway. Ranger was also in action during Operation Torch. (McDonnell Douglas Photo, Courtesy Harry Gann)

Improved Stability

The Flight Deck was installed closer to the hull than on *Charger* and *Long Island*, which improved stability; however, it was still difficult to land on the *Bogues* in choppy seas or on windy days.

Bogue Data

Specifically, the hulls were C3-S-A1 designs contracted for construction to the Seattle-Tacoma Shipyard in the U.S. Northwest. As with the majority of C-3 cargo ships, the conversions were powered by an 8,500 horsepower steam turbine geared to a single propeller which drove the ships to a top speed of 18 knots. The range was 26,000 miles at about 14 1/2 knots.

Two 5 inch guns were mounted on the fantail or stern, while (10) 40 millimeter and (27) 20 millimeter antiaircraft guns were mounted on either side of the Flight Deck. Aircraft complement was 28 fighters and torpedo planes.

The 11 ships were: *Bogue* CVE-9, *Card* CVE-11, *Copahee* CVE-12, *Core* CVE-13, *Nassau* CVE-16, *Altamaha* CVD-18, *Barnes* CVE-20, *Block Island* CVE-21, *Breton* CVE-23, *Croatian* CVE-25, and *Prince William* CVE-31. Commissioning began in September 1943 with *Prince William*. *Bogue*, *Card*, *Block Island* and *Croatian* operating in the Atlantic during most of their service.

Sangamon Class Escort Carriers

When it was realized that no more C-3 hulls could be spared for conversion to escort carriers the U.S. Navy turned to four Navy oilers, which had been converted from commercial T-3 tankers during 1940 and 1941. *USS Sangamon* AO-28 (former Esso *Trenton*), *USS Santee*, AO-29 (former *Seakay*), *USS Chenango* AO-31 (former Esso *New Orleans*), and *USS Suwannee* AO-33 (former *Markay*) were very valuable as oilers; however, the U.S. Navy was so desperate for sea-going flight decks that it was willing to sacrifice the important oilers for more important aircraft carriers.

Escort Carriers/Oilers

The four oilers were converted in 1942 and became the largest converted escort aircraft carriers. In view of the enormous tankage left in the hull after conversion the carriers' ability to serve as oilers

USS Sangamon (AO-28) was one of four U.S. Navy oilers that became the largest converted escort carriers. Sangamon became CVE-26 after conversion. The Sangamon class saw considerable action during World War II. (Official U.S. Navy Photograph)

was preserved so they could replenish ships of the fleet when called upon to do so.

Sangamon Data

The basic hull was 556 feet long overall with a 75 feet beam. Atop this was constructed the Flight Deck measuring 85 x 503 feet, which was mounted lower than the *Bogue* class, making the *Sangamon* class even more stable, which is very important for an aircraft carrier. Propulsion machinery was four boilers and two geared steam turbines driving twin-screws. Turbines totaled 13,500 horsepower, giving the carriers a top speed of 18 knots. Range was about 24,000 miles at 15 knots. Displacement was 12,000 tons.

The aircraft complement was 30 fighters and torpedo planes (Wildcats and Avengers). As with the *Bogue* class, (2) 5 inch guns were mounted on the fantail plus (22) 40 millimeter and (20) 20 millimeter antiaircraft guns were installed around the Flight Deck.

CVE Operations

Although conceived for convoy duty the escort carrier soon became a jack-of-all-trades, performing tasks such as antisubmarine warfare (ASW), aircraft transport (carrying planes to distant bases or to fleet carriers), and providing air cover for amphibious assault operations. In the latter role, during Operation Torch in North Africa, *HMS Dasher*, *HMS Biter*, and *HMS Avenger* provided air cover over the beaches, while *HMS Archer*, *USS Sangamon* (CVE-26), *USS Suwannee* (CVE-27), *USS Chenango* (CVE-28), and *USS Santee* (CVE-29) escorted American troopships to the beachhead.

NEW U.S. AND ROYAL NAVY FLEET CARRIERS

Thus far, all eight of the prewar-built U.S. carriers had distinguished themselves in the war. Five of the eight had already been lost in the first year of the war; however, newer and better carriers were on the way to more than replenish the losses.

Essex Class Carriers

By the end of 1942 the Imperial Japanese Navy and the U.S. Navy had large programs of aircraft carrier construction under way; not only to recoup their losses, but to prepare for the battles to come. The U.S. had started planning in 1939 with the *Essex* class and the light cruiser hull *Independence* class, with the result that nine each of *Essex* and *Independence* class carriers were under construction during December 1942. On the other hand, the Japanese had only

started their program after the Battle of Midway, which put them at a decided disadvantage with aircraft carrier construction.

While *USS Hornet* CV-8 was still under construction, the final design for the next class of American aircraft carriers was approved in early 1940. The CV-9 Class was to feature alternate fire and engine rooms for the four propellers. Two catapults were proposed, one on the Flight Deck and the second in the Hangar Deck, much like some of the early Royal Navy designs. The design was intended to have a capacity for 82 aircraft, which surpassed contemporary Japanese and British carriers and reflected the U.S. Navy principal design objective to operate as many aircraft as possible from its carriers.

Also proposed was the ability of launch and recovery over either end of the Flight Deck. The CV-9 Class carriers became the world's first to be fitted with a full deck-edge elevator, thereby clearing the Hangar Deck for faster spotting of aircraft on the Flight Deck. Designing and planning continued through 1940 and into 1941 with the first keel laid in April 1941, *USS Essex*.

Improved *Yorktown*

Basically an enlarged and modernized *Yorktown* class carrier, the *Essex* class had no restrictions in tonnage. A specified 10 percent increase in aircraft capacity and improved defensive measures resulted in a constantly growing design. More planes required additional accommodations and larger aviation fuel tanks, plus more munitions. The added armor totalled 100 tons. Anti-torpedo protection was improved over *Yorktown* and hull subdivision was increased. More powerful propulsion machinery was then needed which, in itself, added 500 tons to the ship. By the time the design was finalized, the displacement had increased to almost 30 percent above that of the first scheme.

First Construction Program

The initial order for *Essex* class carriers was for 11 ships in 1940. Newport News Shipbuilding & Drydock Co. was awarded the first seven ships: *Essex* (CV-9), *Yorktown* (CV-10), *Intrepid* (CV-11), *Hornet* (CV-12), *Franklin* (CV-13), *Ticonderoga* (CV-14), *Randolph* (CV-15), Bethlehem Steel Co. Quincy Shipyard constructed the remainder: *Lexington* (CV-16), *Bunker Hill* (CV-17), *Wasp* (CV-18), *Hancock* (CV-19). Notice that several ships bore the names of carriers lost during the first year of the war in order to commemorate those valiant ships and their crews.

Improved Construction Program

Additional *Essex* class carriers were ordered as the war progressed until the total reached 24. Never before or since has such an ambitious construction program been undertaken for capital ships; especially so many ships of the same class. The lead ship, *USS Essex* (CV-9) was launched on July 31, 1942, only 15 months after construction began, and was commissioned on December 31, 1942. Sixteen more *Essex* class carriers would be commissioned by the end of the war; some to be constructed by New York, Philadelphia and Norfolk Navy Yards. Newport News delivered eight *Essex* class carriers in 30 months. The officially estimated cost was to average 68 million dollars per ship; however, costs varied from 76 million dollars to 90 million dollars.

The Essex class carriers became the standard U.S. Navy aircraft carriers of World War II. USS Essex, shown here at Hampton Roads, was commissioned in late 1942. Observe the deck edge elevator in its vertical raised position. Also note the absence of Deck catapults which were installed in late 1943. (Official U.S. Navy Photograph, Naval Imaging Command)

Naturally, the number of modifications worked into such a large class of carriers are almost beyond recording. The newer ships were heavier and longer with stronger Flight Decks, plus more powerful elevators and catapults for heavier aircraft. In view of the foregoing, the specifications that follow are for the typical wartime *Essex* class aircraft carrier.

Wartime *Essex* Class Data

Standard displacement was 27,100 tons, while deep load displacement reached 33,000 tons. Hull length was 872 feet overall with a beam of 93 feet. Flight Deck measured 96 x 860 feet. Geared steam turbines totalling 150,000 horsepower turned four propellers, which drove the ship to a top speed of almost 33 knots. Range was 15,000 miles at 15 knots. Eight boilers generated high pressure steam for the turbines. Aviation fuel tanks contained 240,000 gallons and ships' fuel tankage was 6,300 tons.

This unusual photograph shows an Avenger torpedo bomber landing on the bow of an Essex class carrier as the ship runs full speed astern. In all probability the aft end of the Flight Deck was blocked due to bomb damage or aircraft wreckage. (Official U.S. Navy Photograph)

Normal air group consisted of two squadrons of fighters (36), two squadrons of dive bombers (36), and one squadron of torpedo planes (18); however, *Essex* class carriers are known to have operated 110 planes during combat conditions. Complement was 2,700 officers and crew. Armament comprised (12) 5 inch guns, (32) 40 millimeter and (46) 20 millimeter antiaircraft guns. Armor included a four inch belt, two and three inch bulkheads, one and one-half inch Main Deck and, for the first time on an American carrier, a 3 inch armored Hangar Deck.

The Flight Deck remained unarmored, as was the U.S. Navy custom. For additional safety the fire rooms (boiler rooms) and engine rooms were arranged staggered across the ship.

Pacific Fleet Backbone

This fleet of carriers became the backbone of the U.S. Naval Forces in the Pacific and, in cooperation with the Independence class carriers, became a virtually irresistible naval force for the next three years.

The remaining 13 improved *Essex* class carriers had been ordered from various shipyards: Newport News; *Bennington* (CV-20), *Boxer* (CV-21), *Leyte* (CV-32) – New York Naval Shipyard; *Bon Homme Richard* (CV-31), *Kearsarge* (CV-32), *Oriskany* (CV-34) – Philadelphia Naval Shipyard; *Antietam* (CV-36), *Princeton* (CV-37), *Valley Forge* (CV-45) – Norfolk Naval Shipyard; *Shangri-La* (CV-38) – *Lake Champlain* (CV-39); *Tarawa* (CV-40); Bethlehem Steel Co.; *Philippine Sea* (CV-47).

Independence Class Light Carriers

Realizing there would be an inevitable gap between the *Hornet* launching in 1941 and the 1944-45 launchings of the second group of *Essex* class carriers, President Roosevelt was taking no chances, knowing that big aircraft carriers were essential, and insisted upon an emergency carrier construction program. The President strongly

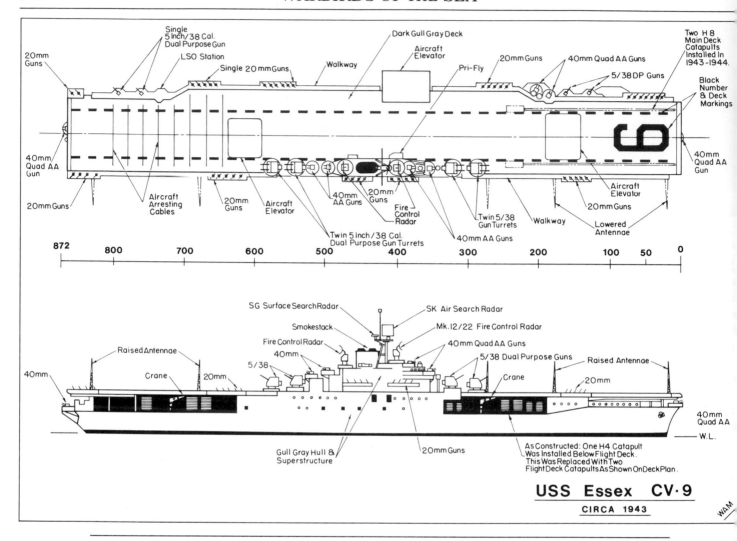

USS Essex CV·9

CIRCA 1943

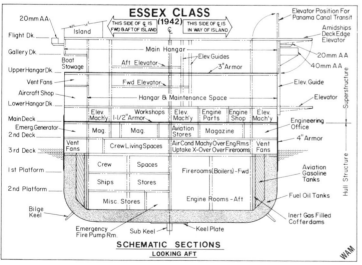

recommended that a number of *Cleveland* class light cruisers, the
being constructed at New York Shipbuilding Corp. in Camden, N.J
be converted to aircraft carriers at once.

Navy Objects

The Navy was quick to point to the difficulties inherent in conver
ing high length/beam ratio hulls into aircraft carriers but Presider
Roosevelt was adamant.

Nine hulls were selected for conversion to light aircraft carr
ers (CVL). The cruiser names were changed and the new carri
names and designations were as follows: *Independence* (CVL-22
Princeton (CVL-23); *Belleau Wood* (CVL-24); *Cowpens* (CVL-25
Monterey (CVL-26): *Langley* (CVL-27); *Cabot* (CVL-28); *Bata*
(CVL-29) and *San Jacinto* (CVL-30). Notice that the *Independenc*
class numbers fill the gap between the two groups of *Essex* clas
numbers.

Independence Class Data

The hull was 622 feet overall with a beam of 71 feet. The 5 inc
armor belt was removed and blisters were added for stability. Ato
this hull was constructed a 73 x 544 feet Flight Deck. This narrow
Flight Deck on a fleet carrier allowed no space for the island an
forced a bulge in the port side Flight Deck in way of the forwar

Converted from Cleveland class light cruisers, Independence class carriers were able to operate as an effective team with Essex class carriers by virtue of their high speed. USS Cowpens (CVL-25) is shown here with Hellcats and Avengers on the Flight Deck. (U.S. National Archives)

elevator in order that aircraft could taxi around the elevator. The island was located to starboard off the edge of the Flight Deck, supported by braces extending upwards from the hull. The uptakes from the four boilers were trunked to the starboard side just aft of the island, but a good distance further outboard, into four smoke-stacks. The stacks were located so far outboard that each was indi-vidually braced from the hull. Standard displacement was 10,660 tons, while deep draft displacement was 15,000 tons.

The four Babcock & Wilcox boilers and four General Electric steam turbines produced 100,000 shaft horsepower, distributed to four propellers, which drove the carriers to a maximum speed of 31 knots. Range was 13,000 miles at 15 knots. The light carriers could accommodate an aircraft complement of 30 planes. Officers and crew totalled 1,500 men. Two 5 inch guns and (16) 40 millimeter and (10) 20 millimeter guns were initially installed.

Two catapults were installed in the unarmored, wood-planked Flight Deck, which was also fitted with about eight arresting cables.

The *Independence* class carriers were able to operate with the *Essex* class by virtue of their high speed.

New *Eagle* Class Carriers

By mid-1942 Britain had developed a new carrier design which incorporated lessons learned from the war to date. Actually, the initial idea was conceived in 1940 when the *Illustrious* class was under construction. The plan was to build an improved *Implacable* design; however, with British resources stretched to the limit in 1940, the project had to be cancelled.

Following Japan's entry into the war, Britain desperately needed new carriers for the Pacific and; therefore, revived the new carrier program. Instead of an improved *Implacable*, an entirely new "*Eagle*" class design emerged, which was to set the pace for all postwar carriers. Four ships were planned: *Ark Royal, Audacious, Africa* and *Eagle*.

The conventional Royal Navy hangar height of 14 1/2 feet had been planned for each of the two hangar levels when it was realized that the Royal Navy was dependent on the U.S. for naval aircraft, which required more hangar height. A major redesign to increase hangar height to 17 1/2 feet resulted in an increase in beam to com-pensate for the increased depth, which made the hangar wider. The 78 plane complement increased to 100 which, in turn, required ad-ditional accommodations and stores. One of the major changes in

Royal Navy practice was the aviation gasoline tanks. Up to this time it was British practice to store aviation fuel in cylindrical tanks separated from the hull structure and mounted inside of structural rectangular tanks which were filled with sea water. This was an extremely safe method but one in which the aviation fuel tanks had a very limited capacity. The increase in aircraft complement as well as aircraft size escalated the demand for more aviation fuel stow-age. This forced the designers to adopt the U.S. Navy system of stowing aviation fuel in rectangular structural hull tanks, surrounded by seawater-filled cofferdams or narrow tanks. This method pro-vided more stowage volume; however, it was not as safe as the former Royal Navy practice of locating cylindrical gasoline tanks within a water-filled compartment, especially from underwater ex-plosions that could cause structural fractures.

Twelve directors controlled 64 antiaircraft guns; however, as will be seen during extensive modifications in later years, the num-ber of guns dropped dramatically.

Despite the fact that contracts were awarded to four different shipyards in 1942-43 in order to avoid delays, very little progress had been made at the war's end. *Eagle* and *Africa* were to be can-celled; therefore, *Audacious* was renamed *Eagle*. The new *Eagle* and *Ark Royal* will be covered in later chapters.

JAPAN'S CARRIER CONSTRUCTION PROGRAM

In stark contrast to the vast American aircraft carrier program was the overly ambitious Japanese plans which, although meager in comparison to the U.S. Navy, had little chance of being realized. The Imperial Japanese Navy planned the construction of six fleet carriers of the 29,000 ton *Taiho* class, 15 of the 17,000 ton *Unryu* class, plus conversion of the giant battleship *Shinano* of the *Yamato* class. Seaplane tender and merchant ship conversions were also planned but Japan's wartime production capacity could not hope to compete with that of the United States.

PREPARING FOR THE CARRIER BATTLES

The year 1943 would be spent by both Pacific combatants in re-building their carrier and Warbird forces for the impending battles of 1944.

MRS. ROOSEVELT SAVES *YORKTOWN*'S REPUTATION

The second Essex class carrier, *USS Yorktown* (CV-10), was launched by Mrs. Franklin D. Roosevelt on January 21, 1943. Mrs. Roosevelt had launched the first *Yorktown* (CV-5) in 1936 and returned to Newport News Shipbuilding to launch the new *Yorktown*. During the launching ceremonies the big carrier began to slide down the ways seven minutes ahead of schedule. Mrs. Roosevelt quickly jumped up, interrupting the speaker, and managed to smash the champagne bottle against the bow seconds before the ship had moved beyond reach. Had the ship been launched without breaking the bottle on its bow, this would have been considered a bad omen, according to the lore of the sea, and the ship would have to bear the reputation of being cursed. It was wartime and the incident was considered good luck for *USS Yorktown* because it represented "snatching victory from the jaws of defeat." Sailors are very superstitious and sailing a ship that has the reputation of being cursed would have destroyed the *Yorktown* crew's morale.

SEVERE LOSSES

The Imperial Japanese Navy and the U.S. Navy had suffered severe losses in men, planes and carriers during the opening battles of the Pacific fighting and had fought to a virtual standstill. Both navies had to rebuild depleted carrier strength, replace lost aircraft, and organize and train new air groups. Neither side had sufficient operable carrier strength to engage in battle.

BREAKING THE BISMARCK BARRIER

As America switched from the defensive to the offensive phase of the war General MacArthur's forces were to advance westward along the coast of New Guinea to the Philippine Islands while the

Mrs. Franklin D. Roosevelt had christened the first Yorktown (CV-5) in 1936. She returned to Newport News Shipbuilding to launch the second Yorktown (CV-10) in January 1943 and jumped up to smash the bottle of champagne on the bow when the ship began to slide down the ways seven minutes early. To the right of Mrs. Roosevelt are Mrs. Homer Ferguson and Rear Admiral O.L. Cox. (Newport News Shipbuilding)

naval effort under Admiral Nimitz was to batter the Japanese-he[ld] Central Pacific Islands. The Japanese base of Rabaul blocke[d] MacArthur's advance.

Primary Objective; Rabaul

Rabaul is on the northeastern tip of the island of New Britain in th[e] Bismarck Archipelago; 800 miles south of the Japanese base [at] Truk, 560 miles northwest of Guadalcanal and 445 miles northea[st] of Port Moresby, The Japanese planned to dominate the Solomon[s]

PREVIOUS: Task Force 38 conducted air strikes on and around the Philippines during the preliminary moves for the Philippines invasion. Hellcats and Helldivers are shown on USS Enterprise (CV-6) getting ready for a raid on Japanese installations. (U.S. National Archives)

USS Yorktown (CV-10) was the second Essex class carrier and saw plenty of action in the Pacific. Hellcats, Avengers and Helldivers are shown on deck. Note the deck edge elevator in normal working position. (U.S. Naval Historical Center)

New Guinea, and the coast of Australia from Rabaul; therefore, it was imperative that the "Bismarck Barrier" be broken if the war was to be won.

Stepping Stones to Rabaul

The offensive against Rabaul had to be accomplished without the active participation of aircraft carriers. Fortunately, the Solomon Islands were arranged as stepping stones in a northwesterly path to Rabaul. An island-hopping strategy had to be adopted with shore-based planes operating from island airstrips. The Vought Corsair, rejected for carrier operation, was flown to victory by the U.S. Marines in the Solomons Campaign and this offensive became the Corsair's "Shining Hour."

Carriers: Mobile Air Replacement Depots

The only contribution that the few carriers could make was to furnish aircraft for the many strikes against the enemy strongholds and airstrips. In effect, the aircraft carrier had become a mobile aircraft depot for this campaign.

CASABLANCA CONFERENCE

From January 14 through 23, 1943 President Roosevelt and Prime Minister Churchill, plus the Allied combined Chiefs met in Casablanca, Morocco to formulate Allied strategy for 1943. Against the American's wishes, it was agreed that the British plan to defer cross-channel invasion in order to maintain momentum in the Mediterranean by landing in Sicily would be acceptable. Admiral King obtained approval for his proposal to advance against Japan through the Central Pacific while maintaining pressure on Rabaul, which was a continuation of Operation Watchtower. President Roosevelt surprised the attendees by announcing his decision, contrary to the Clausewitz doctrine, to demand "unconditional surrender" of the Axis Powers.

WAR PLAN ORANGE

Since 1897, four decades before the Pearl Harbor attack, the U.S. Navy had been formulating its strategy to defeat Japan. Modified and updated periodically by input from George Dewey, Alfred T. Mahan, Douglas MacArthur, Robert L. Ghormley, Ernest J. King and other prominent military strategists, the scheme to defeat Japan was known as War Plan Orange.

Although modified and refined by each successive War Plans Board, the basic scheme included two routes: across the Central Pacific through the Marshall Islands, Mariannas Islands, Iwo Jima, Okinawa and Japan itself; and a drive through the Solomons to the Philippine Islands and up to Japan. General MacArthur and Admiral Nimitz adhered to these basic concepts in their strategy to defeat Japan during World War II.

BATTLE OF RENNELL ISLAND

Another of the many outstanding examples of the importance of naval air cover was the little known Battle of Rennell Island during January 29-30, 1943. Rear Admiral Robert C. Giffen, Commander of Task Force 18, had detached his two escort carriers because their slow speed was making it difficult for him to make a scheduled rendezvous with other American ships near Guadalcanal. Leaving the two "Baby Flattops" behind, Giffen pressed on with seven cruisers and six destroyers. At dusk Japanese shore-based planes attacked the task force and torpedoed the heavy cruiser *Chicago* (CA-29). The Japanese returned on the following morning and finished their work, sinking *USS Chicago* near Rennell Island. The escort carriers could have saved the cruiser.

YAMAMOTO KILLED

Imperial Japanese Fleet Admiral Isoroku Yamamoto was ambushed, while he was a passenger in a transport plane, by 16 Lockheed Light-

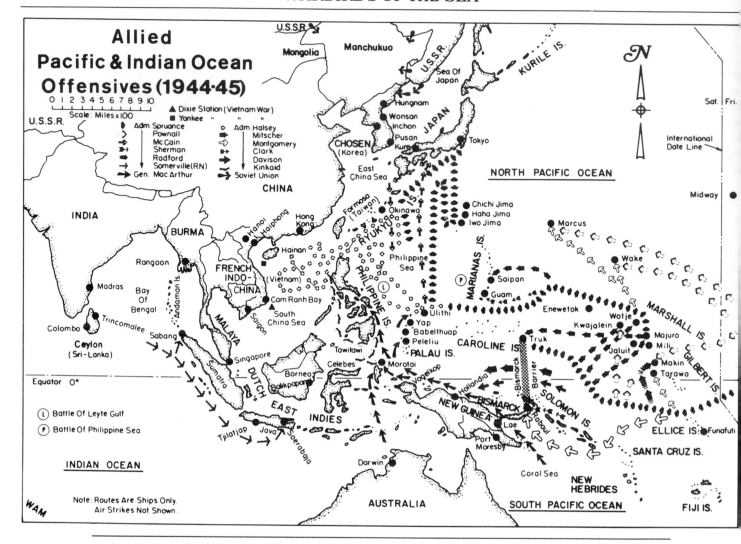

ning fighters just south of Bougainville, and was shot down and killed on April 18, 1943. He had been the most talented officer ever to command the Rengo Kantai, or Combined Fleet. Admiral Mineichi Koga was his successor.

TRIDENT CONFERENCE

May 13 saw the German and Italian troops surrender in North Africa, and only four days later, the British and American leaders began meetings in Washington called the Trident Conference, to plan the next moves in this worldwide conflict. General George C. Marshall still proposed a cross-channel invasion of Europe; however, the British suggestion of an invasion of Italy was approved with the proviso that Britain agree to intensify the war against Japan. It was also agreed to invade the Gilbert Islands first, instead of the Marshalls, so as not to divert as many troops far from the Southwest Pacific. The target date for beginning the Central Pacific offensive was November 15, 1943. The Marshalls would follow on February 1, 1944. This was to be a Navy show so a formidable naval force had to be organized. Admiral Nimitz began at once to plan his campaign, covering thousands of square miles of the Pacific Ocean.

ESCORT CARRIERS WINNING U-BOAT BATTLE

As the escort carriers were coming into service the U-boat wolfpacks had been wreaking havoc in the Atlantic, having sunk 85 Allied ships during the first three weeks of March, 1943. Convoys sank only six U-boats during that period. On March 5 *USS Bogue* (CVE 9) became the first escort carrier assigned specifically to antisubmarine operations. Convoy escort groups organized around these little carriers were destined to make a major contribution to winning the Battle of the Atlantic. *USS Bogue*, Captain Giles E. Short commanding, achieved the first U-boat kill when one of her Grumman Avengers sank U-569 on May 22. On the following day a Fairey Swordfish from *HMS Archer* sank U-752 with rocket projectiles. This was the first submarine to be sunk by rockets.

During the month of May 1943, over 40 German submarines had been sunk; 25 by convoy air and surface escorts, thereby forcing Admiral Karl Doenitz, Commander of the German Navy submarine force, to recall his U-boats from the North Atlantic. No Allied ships were sunk by U-boats from May to September, 1943.

NEW PLANES AND CARRIERS

Several planes and carriers, which had been under development

...ade their appearance in time for the Central Pacific battles soon ...unfold.

...ew U.S. Carriers On The Way

...he *Essex* class carrier *Lexington* (CV-16) was commissioned on ...ebruary 17; eight days later the light carrier *Princeton* (CVL-23) ...as also commissioned; and March 31 saw *Belleau Wood* (CVL-...) commissioned. These were followed by commissioning of ...rktown* (CV-10) on April 15; *Bunker Hill* (CV-17) on May 25; ...d *Cowpens* (CVL-25) on May 28.

...rumman F6F Hellcat

...y 1943 the F4F Wildcat was scheduled to be replaced aboard the ...S. Navy's principal aircraft carriers by the Grumman F6F-3 ...ellcat. On June 30, 1941, the same day that the Vought Corsair ...d been ordered into production, a contract was awarded to ...rumman for the design of a Wildcat replacement, designated XF6F. ...lthough larger and more powerful than the Wildcat, the F6F ...ellcat, as it became known, bore more than a casual resemblance ...its ancestor.

...ellcat Development

...vo prototypes were ordered and the first XF6F-1 had its maiden ...ight on June 26, 1942, three weeks after the Battle of Midway. ...he design team had been led by Leroy R. Grumman and William ... Schwendler and, by the time they had met the specification re... ...uirements of increased fuel and ammunition capacity, the weight ...f the new fighter had increased 60 percent above that of the Wild... ...at. In order to maintain a light wing loading for maneuverability ...d good carrier landing characteristics, a larger wing was required, ...hich was to have the largest area of any World War II U.S. single... ...gine production fighter plane.

The XF6F-2 was to use a turbo-supercharged engine but de... ...ys with engine development cancelled this project.

The second basic airframe was fitted with the Pratt & Whitney ...-2800-10W 2,000 horsepower 18-cylinder engine, instead of the ...right R-2600 Cyclone 1,600 horsepower 14-cylinder engine, ...hich had powered the XF6F-1, in order to attain more speed and ...te of climb to combat the Zero. This became the XF6F-3, which ...ew for the first time on July 30, 1942.

The Grumman Hellcat proved to be one of the most successful carrier-based fighters of World War II. By virtue of the largest wing area of any fighter of the war, the Hellcat had a very light wing loading and was pleasant to fly. The pilot has just received the signal to takeoff from the carrier as the 2,000 horsepower engine screams. Note the crewmen in the catwalk protecting their ears from the engine noise. (Official U.S. Navy Photograph, News Photo Division)

Initial flights were satisfactory except for excessive trim changes when lowering the flaps, as well as excessive longitudinal stability. Airspeed in a dive had to be kept below 525 miles per hour due to a flutter. These problems were all corrected.

Production had been ordered on May 23, 1942 and the first F6F-3 production model made its first flight on October 4.

The Navy acceptance trials revealed some tail buffeting and during carrier arrester tests in November an arresting hook was pulled out of the fuselage. In December a complete fuselage failure occurred during landing; however, the problem was quickly corrected and the acceptance trials were completed to the Navy's satisfaction.

New Grumman Hellcat Factory

A new factory had to be constructed in which to produce the Hellcat; however, it was wartime and steel girders were in short supply. Grumman President Leon A. Swirbul knew that Hellcat production could not be delayed so he bought the steel girders from New York City's dismantled Second Avenue elevated rapid transit railway for use in the new factory construction.

...his lineup of Grumman F6F-5 Hellcats are fresh from the assembly line and ready for delivery to the U.S. Navy. A new factory was built especially ...r the Hellcat production and, in fact, the planes were rolling off the assembly line before the plant was finished! Notice the line of Hellcats with ...lded wings. (Grumman Corporation, Courtesy Grant Daily)

F6F-3 Production

Hellcats were moving down the assembly line even before the plant was finished. A U.S. Navy order for 184 planes was soon followed by another contract for 252 by the Royal Navy, and then a U.S. Navy request for 3,139 more of the F6F-3.

Hydraulic Operation

The 42 feet 10 inches wingspan could be reduced to 16 feet-2 inches when wings were folded for carrier stowage. Unlike the Wildcat the wings were folded hydraulically against the fuselage and the landing gear was hydraulically retracted. Control surfaces and flaps were all controlled hydraulically as well. Two backup hydraulic systems were fitted in the Hellcat.

F6F-3 Data

Overall length was 33 feet-7 inches and height was 11 feet-3 inches. Empty weight was 9,042 pounds, while normal loaded weight was 12,186 pounds. Maximum overloaded weight was 13,221 pounds.

   Maximum speed (at 11,381 pounds) was 376 miles per hour at 22,800 feet and 324 miles per hour at sea level; (at 12,186 pounds) 373 miles per hour at 23,700 feet and 303 miles per hour at sea level; (at 13,221 pounds with a 150 gallon drop tank) 359 miles per

This Grumman Hellcat is being serviced on the Flight Deck of USS Essex (CV-9) while the carrier was in a friendly port. Of interest in this photo are the drainage troughs and wooden planking atop the steel Flight Deck (arrows). Note the aircraft elevator at lower right (arrow). (U.S. National Archives)

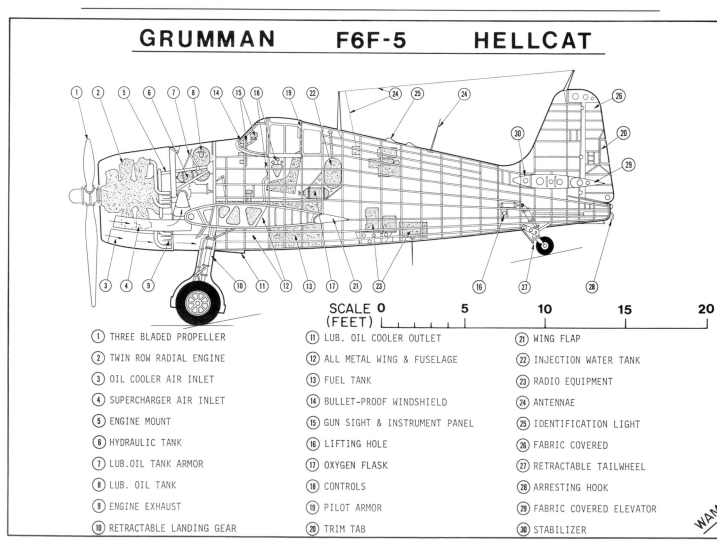

GRUMMAN   F6F-5   HELLCAT

SCALE 0   5   10   15   20
(FEET)

1. THREE BLADED PROPELLER
2. TWIN ROW RADIAL ENGINE
3. OIL COOLER AIR INLET
4. SUPERCHARGER AIR INLET
5. ENGINE MOUNT
6. HYDRAULIC TANK
7. LUB.OIL TANK ARMOR
8. LUB. OIL TANK
9. ENGINE EXHAUST
10. RETRACTABLE LANDING GEAR

11. LUB. OIL COOLER OUTLET
12. ALL METAL WING & FUSELAGE
13. FUEL TANK
14. BULLET-PROOF WINDSHIELD
15. GUN SIGHT & INSTRUMENT PANEL
16. LIFTING HOLE
17. OXYGEN FLASK
18. CONTROLS
19. PILOT ARMOR
20. TRIM TAB

21. WING FLAP
22. INJECTION WATER TANK
23. RADIO EQUIPMENT
24. ANTENNAE
25. IDENTIFICATION LIGHT
26. FABRIC COVERED
27. RETRACTABLE TAILWHEEL
28. ARRESTING HOOK
29. FABRIC COVERED ELEVATOR
30. STABILIZER

WAM

our at 23,700 feet and 294 miles per hour at sea level. The maximum range (with the internal self-sealing 235 gallons fuel cells, located under the pilot) was 1,085 miles at 179 miles per hour; with the addition of the 150 gallon drop tank) 1,620 miles at 177 miles per hour.

Initial rate of climb was 3,240 feet per minute. The Hellcat could reach an altitude of 15,000 feet in 7.7 minutes and to 25,000 feet in 14 minutes. Service ceiling was 37,500 feet.

Armament was six 0.50 inch caliber Colt-Browning machine guns buried in the wing just outboard of the fold joint. Containers for 400 rounds per gun were provided. Armor to protect the pilot, oil tank and oil cooler weighed 212 pounds.

Hellcat structure was all-metal with fabric covered control surfaces. The fuselage consisted of two vertical keels straddling the centerline. Aluminum alloy pressed flange frames were riveted to the keel and stringers completed the basic structure. The stressed Alclad covering was applied in longitudinal strips and flush-riveted. The wing had three main spars and several sub-spar stringers, Alclad covered. The landing gear rotated 90 degrees and folded back into the wing much as the Corsair. There was some criticism about excessive tire wear; however, that seemed to be a minor problem. An outstanding feature of the Hellcat was its exceptional visibility by virtue of the high cockpit location.

Initial Deployment
The first production F6F-3 Hellcats were delivered to U.S. Navy Fighter Squadron VF-9 aboard *USS Essex* on January 16, 1943.

F6F-3 Versus Zero
In combat with the Zero Sen, the Hellcat had superior speed, altitude and diving capabilities; however, despite the agile qualities of the F6F-3, it could not match maneuverability of the Zero at low altitudes. Generally, the Hellcat had no trouble in staying on the tail of a Zero, but the F6F-3 could not follow the Japanese fighter into a loop or into a tight turn. Very often, when performing the latter, the Hellcat was forced to roll out to avoid a stall. When following the Mitsubishi in a turn the F6F-3 usually managed a fatal burst; however, it could not continue for more than 90 degrees of the turn before breaking away. It was no contest in fire power; the fragile Zero disintegrated upon being hit by a short burst from the sextet of .50's of the Hellcat.

Hellcats quickly replaced the Wildcats on U.S. carriers, with 2,555 F6F-3 airframes completed by the end of 1943, and quickly became the standard U.S. Navy carrier fighter. Hellcats were destined to be in the midst of the coming air battles as Admiral Nimitz sent his new carriers into the Central Pacific in late 1943 and throughout 1944 and 1945. Then it will be discovered why the Hellcat is called the "Ace Maker", having destroyed over 5,000 enemy aircraft.

Nakajima B6N Tenzan (Jill)
A new Japanese torpedo bomber made its initial appearance in combat in 1943. Its development was contemporary with the Grumman Avenger and the Fairey Barracuda and, in fact, the Nakajima B6N Tenzan was superior in many respects to its Allied counterparts. Tenzan means "Heavenly Mountain" and it had been reported that

The Japanese Nakajima B6N1 Tenzan torpedo bomber was a superb design that played an important role in the Central Pacific battles. (U.S. National Archives)

the plane was named after a mountain in China. Its Allied code-name was "Jill."

Engine Development Problem
Design of the Tenzan began in 1941 and the prototype was first flown in March, 1942. Considerable trouble was experienced with the Nakajima Mamori engine development because of overheating and excessive vibration. This delayed and finally cancelled production of the Nakajima B6N1 or Type 11.

B6N2 Data
The B6N2 or Type 12 was basically the same plane with an engine change. The reliable Mitsubishi Kasai 25 twin-row air-cooled radial engine of 1,850 horsepower was selected and, although it had 20 less horsepower, it was much lighter than the Mamori engine. Top speed of the B6N2 Tenzan was 299 miles per hour at 16,076 feet and 259 miles per hour at 8,200 feet. Cruising speed was 207 miles per hour at 13,120 feet. Combat range at cruising speed was 1,084 miles. The Nakajima B6N2 could climb to 9,842 feet in 5 1/2 minutes and to 19,685 feet in 19 1/2 minutes. Empty weight was 6,636 pounds and loaded weight was 12,456 pounds, which indicates that the plane could carry a load almost equal to its own weight. Standard load was a 1,765 pound torpedo, plus bombs.

Wingspan of this torpedo bomber was 48 feet-10 inches with a length of 35 feet-7 1/2 inches. Height was 12 feet-5 1/2 inches. The projected wing area was 400 square feet. Construction was all-metal except for fabric covered control surfaces.

The Tenzan (Heavenly Mountain) was a state of the art torpedo bomber that could carry its own weight in munitions. Tenzan's Allied code name was "Jill." This is the B6N2. (U.S. National Archives)

NAKAJIMA B6N2 TENZAN (JILL)

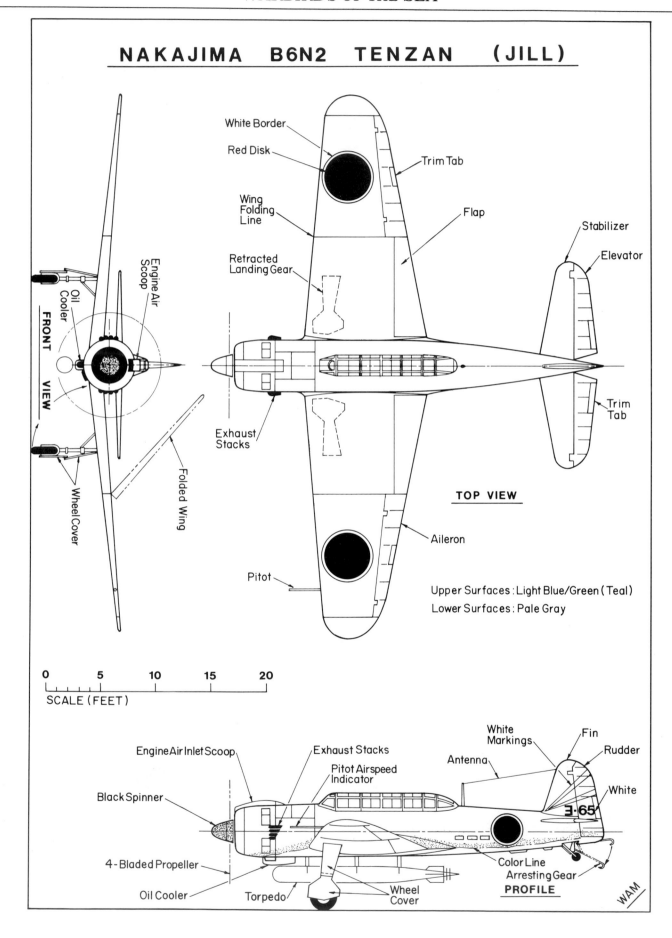

FRONT VIEW

Oil Cooler

Engine Air Scoop

Wheel Cover

Folded Wing

White Border

Red Disk

Trim Tab

Wing Folding Line

Flap

Stabilizer

Elevator

Retracted Landing Gear

Exhaust Stacks

Trim Tab

TOP VIEW

Aileron

Pitot

Upper Surfaces : Light Blue/Green (Teal)
Lower Surfaces : Pale Gray

SCALE (FEET)
0   5   10   15   20

Engine Air Inlet Scoop

Exhaust Stacks

Pitot Airspeed Indicator

White Markings

Fin

Antenna

Rudder

White

Black Spinner

ヨ-65

Color Line

4-Bladed Propeller

Arresting Gear

Oil Cooler

Torpedo

Wheel Cover

PROFILE

WAM

Tenzan Production
By the war's end a total of 1,268 Tenzan torpedo bombers had been completed by the Nakajima plants at Koizumi and Handa.

Tenzan Deployments
Tenzans were assigned to the Imperial Japanese Navy 601, 652 and 653 Air Corps, which formed the air complement of the First, Second and Third Carrier Divisions. The B6N2 played an important role in the carrier battles of the next two years, including the Mariana Islands, and also fought against the U.S. ships covering invasions, such as Iwo Jima and Okinawa.

Nakajima C6N Saiun (Myrt)
Another excellent Nakajima design, following closely on the heels of Tenzan, met with the same production delays because of engine design problems. This time it was the Nakajima Homare 9-cylinder radial engine which Nakajima tried to join in tandem to double the power. After many futile attempts a more orthodox approach met with success as a single compact 18-cylinder twin-row engine.

The Nakajima C6N Saiun (Colorful Cloud) was designed as a carrier-based reconnaissance plane by Yasuo Fukuda in 1942. Performance was so remarkable that it could outrun and outclimb most Allied fighters in the Pacific! Normal armament was a single 7.92 millimeter movable machine gun in the rear cockpit for defense against interceptors.

C6N1-S Night Fighter
In later years, during the U.S. bombing of Japan, several Saiuns (called Myrt in the Allied code names) were converted into night fighters. These were equipped with two fixed 20 millimeter cannon buried in the fuselage aft of the rear cockpit. These were set to fire obliquely upward and forward at a 60 degree angle similar to German "Schragmusik" installations. The tactics were to fly into the bomber stream and pump cannon shells into the bellies of B-29 bombers. This Saiun version was designated C6N-S. Other Myrts were adapted to torpedo bombers as the C6N1-B.

C6N1 Reconnaissance Data
The standard C6N1 had a wingspan of 41 feet-1/2 inches and length of 36 feet-1 inch. Height was 13 feet. Maximum takeoff weight was 11,630 pounds. The 1,990 horsepower, 18-cylinder air-cooled twin-row radial Nakajima Homare 21 engine drove the craft to a maximum speed of 378 miles per hour at 19,685 feet. Service ceiling was 35,236 feet and range was a very respectable 1,914 miles.

This all-metal plane, except for fabric covered control surfaces, was a very slender and clean design uslng a Nakajima Type "K" laminar-flow airfoil or wing section. Laminar-flow is the continuous, nonturbulent movement of air past the wing, thereby improving efficiency. The U.S. Army Air Force Mustang fighter also employed a laminar-flow wing design. The basic C6N1 was still in production near the end of the war, 498 having been constructed by Nakajima at Handa and Koizumi. Japan's shortage of aircraft carriers in 1945 spelled the end of this fine aircraft's career.

Fairey Firefly
The Royal Navy Fleet Air Arm was steadily emerging from its troublesome lack of modern carrier aircraft; however, in its eagerness to accumulate as many as possible new designs for every task, the FAA concentrated on multi-purpose aircraft requiring two or three crew members.

Often considered to be the finest Royal Navy specialized carrier-based plane produced during World War II, the Fairey Firefly was a fighter-reconnaissance two-seater having excellent all-around performance, especially at lower speeds because of the Fairey-Youngman wing flaps. These behaved as secondary airfoils when extended beneath the wing, parallel with the wing, by means of struts. The flaps could, of course, be depressed at an angle in the conventional manner for landing and takeoff. The Fairey-Youngman flaps improved cruising speed, as well as maneuverability for the Firefly.

Firefly Mark I Data
Although the Firefly was designed and constructed in accordance with Royal Navy Specification N.5/40 of 1940, the Mark I did not go into service until 1943. Powered with the 1,730 horsepower, 12-cylinder liquid-cooled Rolls-Royce Griffon II B engine the Firefly Mark I attained a top speed of 316 miles per hour at 14,000 feet. Combat range was 1,070 miles and service ceiling was 28,800 feet. Wingspan was 44 feet-6 inches with length 37 feet-7 inches. Height was 13 feet-7 inches. The Firefly was all-metal.

Designed as a carrier-based reconnaissance plane, the Nakajima C6N Saiun (Colorful Cloud) also served as a night fighter and torpedo bomber. Known by the Allied code name of Myrt, the Saiun could outrun and outclimb many Allied fighters. (U.S. National Archives)

The Fairey Firefly F.MK.1 was fitted with large Fairey-Youngman flaps, shown lowered in this photo, and a chin radiator. Note the Vee type arresting hook and four 20 millimeter cannon protruding from the wing. The Deck Landing Control Officer (DLCO) is at right, directing the plane. (Ministry of Defence [Navy]).

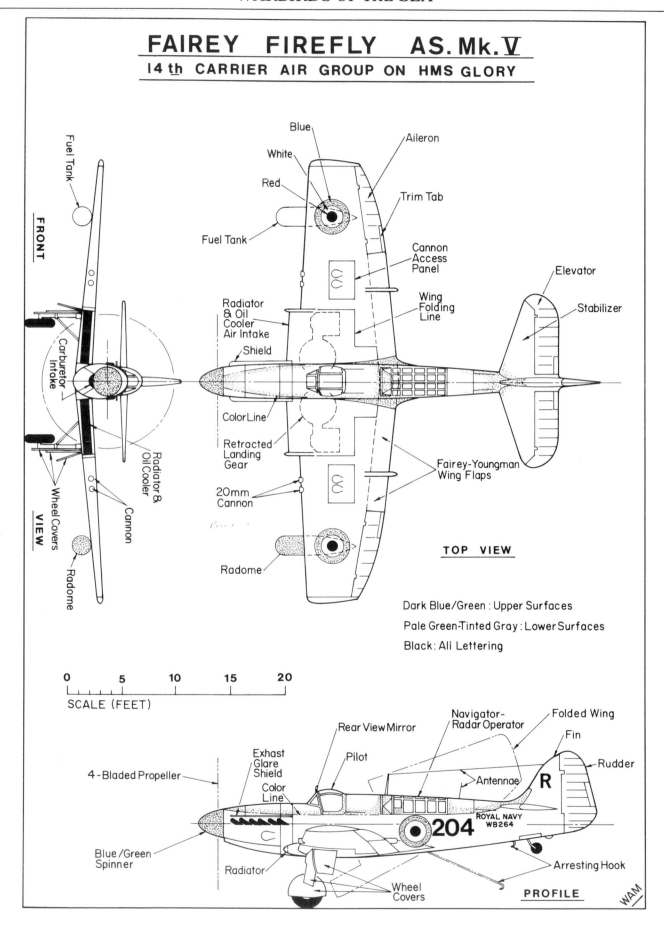

FAIREY FIREFLY AS. Mk. V
14 th CARRIER AIR GROUP ON HMS GLORY

FRONT

Fuel Tank

Carburetor Intake

VIEW

Wheel Covers

Radiator & Oil Cooler

Cannon

Radome

Blue

White

Red

Fuel Tank

Aileron

Trim Tab

Cannon Access Panel

Wing Folding Line

Elevator

Stabilizer

Radiator & Oil Cooler Air Intake

Shield

Color Line

Retracted Landing Gear

20mm Cannon

Radome

Fairey-Youngman Wing Flaps

TOP VIEW

Dark Blue/Green : Upper Surfaces

Pale Green-Tinted Gray : Lower Surfaces

Black : Ali Lettering

0   5   10   15   20

SCALE (FEET)

4-Bladed Propeller

Exhast Glare Shield

Color Line

Blue/Green Spinner

Radiator

Rear View Mirror

Pilot

Navigator-Radar Operator

Folded Wing

Fin

Rudder

Antennae

R

ROYAL NAVY
WB264

204

Wheel Covers

Arresting Hook

PROFILE

WAM

This multi-mission two-seater was arranged by placing the pilot in a raised cockpit and semi-bubble canopy and the observer/navigator/bombardier was seated several feet behind the pilot in a spacious framed greenhouse-enclosed office. The Firefly was armed with four 20 millimeter cannon, which was the heaviest concentration of firepower for any carrier-borne fighter at that time. In addition to the cannon, the wings were stressed to carry up to 2,000 pounds of bombs or eight 60 pound rockets.

Wing Folding

Every designer seems to have his own ideas about how best to fold airplane wings for stowage aboard aircraft carriers. This is not an easy task; probably the most dIfficult design problem on carrier aircraft. The Firefly separation line was a jagged cut with four 90 degree bends. The outer panels hinged on the rear spar and, to fold, the flaps were disconnected and the wing was manually rotated 90 degrees so the leading edge was uppermost; it was then folded against the fuselage with the disconnected flaps extending under the wing roots between the landing gear.

Firefly Mark IV

The Mark IV replaced the chin radiator with radiators built into the wing roots and had the wingspan reduced to 41 feet-2 inches by squaring off the wingtips. Top speed was 386 miles per hour at 14,000 feet, and range increased to 1,300 miles.

Firefly Mark V Variants

The Mark V featured power-folding wings and was variously produced as FRV fighter/reconnaissance; NVF night-fighter, equipped with a radar pod on the wing leading edge and a shroud over the exhaust stacks to avoid detection by the enemy; and ASV anti-submarine patrol, fitted with a radar pod under the left wing and long-range tank under the right wing. The 20 millimeter cannon barrels were removed from the anti-submarine variants.

The purpose-designed/built Casablanca class mini-carriers were smaller than converted escort carriers but carried the identical air group, were faster, steadier, and more maneuverable. USS Manila Bay (CVE-61) is shown here with its Deck filled with Dauntless dive bombers, Avenger torpedo-bombers and U.S. Army Airacobra fighters at the bow for delivery to Pacific air bases. Note the pilot boat guiding the carrier through dangerous shoals as it nears land. (U.S. Department of Defense [Navy])

Firefly Operations

The multi-purpose Fireflies were very active in the Far East and the Pacific Theatre of operations during World War II and played a very important role in the Allied aerial activities of the Korean War.

Firefly Production

Variations continued into the postwar years when the total number of Fireflies produced reached 1,638 and remained in service until 1956.

Casablanca Class Mini-Carriers

The CVE escort aircraft carriers had been performing such a commendable job that more were needed; not only to fill the gap left by sinkings, but to be available to assist in the big Pacific battles which were on the horizon. The escort carrier conversions had proven themselves worthy by providing air cover over beachheads and many invasions were planned in the drive through the Central Pacific.

No Commercial Hulls Available

The supply of suitable commercial hulls for conversion had dwindled and purpose-built improved "Baby Flattops" appeared to be the only solution to satisy the demand for these useful carriers. After a lot of waffling about by the military, as well as politicians, one man made a profound suggestion after consulting with a prominent naval architect.

This element of ASW Firefly A.S.MK.5 reveals the large "office" for the observer/navigator/electronics operator and the underwing pods for auxiliary fuel tank and radar scanner. Fuel tank is under right wing of nearest Firefly. The MK.5 was the first Firefly with power folding wings. (Imperial War Museum)

White House Approval

It all started when industrialist Henry J. Kaiser, a U.S. west coast shipbuilder who had made his fortune in aluminum, proposed the construction of mini-carriers to the U.S. Navy, who rejected the offer. Kaiser then took his scheme to Admiral Emory S. Land, head of the U.S. Maritime Commission, who got the White House interested, This resulted in a Maritime Commission contract to Kaiser in June 1942 for the construction of 50 mini-carriers. In view of the fact that Kaiser's contract for the ships was with the Maritime Commission, which was involved only with commerical and not naval ships, the U.S. Navy remained aloof of any involvement with the design or construction.

Design and Coordination

Henry J. Kaiser selected prestigious New York Naval Architect George G. Sharp and his staff to design the new carriers and to prepare the shipyard construction drawings, coordinate construction, and order all material and equipment as well. The Sharp organization was to later design the famous Victory ships, of which several hundred were built.

In order to save time, which was of paramount importance, it was agreed to use the hull shape of the S4 special naval hull, sometimes called the Maritime Commission P-1 hull. The structure and compartmentation was redesigned to meet carrier requirements an all sheer was eliminated except in the Forecastle. As design an construction progressed the Navy had to participate in the areas naval concern, such as arresting gear, catapults, guns and ammun tion.

Better Than *Bogues*

This large class of escort carriers is known officially as th *Casablanca* class, but is sometimes erroneously referred to as th Kaiser class. The ships were lighter than the *Bogue* class but ca ried the identical air group. They were steadier than the converte CVE's; far more maneuverable and faster as well.

Author's Involvement

The author, as a member of the George G. Sharp design staff, pr pared the basic design concept for these unusual carriers and the went on to work on the many fluid-flow systems; continuing on the shipyard drawings.

Produced In Record Time

This new class of 50 purpose-built mini-carriers was produced the short space of two years from the start of design drawings to th launching of the final 50th carrier on June 8, 1944. The first carri

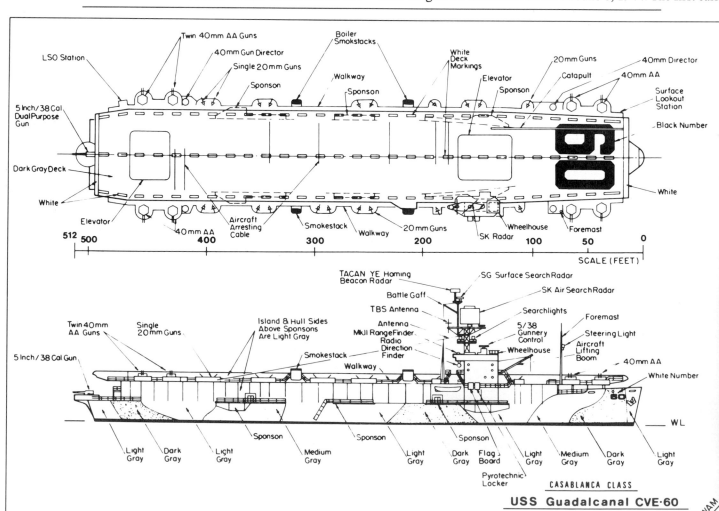

CASABLANCA CLASS

USS Guadalcanal CVE·60

The 50 Casablanca mini-carriers were designed and built in the short space of two years despite the fact that they had to be constructed with non-strategic materials and equipment. These photos show USS Guadalcanal (CVE-60) with a load of Avengers and Wildcats. This ship was the only carrier to capture a submarine. Although designed primarily for convoy escort and ASW duty, the Casablanca class carriers proved their ability to conduct offensive operations in the Pacific. (Official U.S. Navy Photographs, News Photo Division)

The author is shown designing the Casablanca class carrier basic arrangement in late 1942. (WAM Fotos)

had been launched on April 5, 1943, only 10 months after the beginning of the project.

Non-Strategic Materials and Equipment

It was a time when America was conserving all critical material such as: chromium, tin, copper, rubber, aluminum, molybdenum and many other resources; therefore, the use of these materials was restricted on the mini-carriers. In addition, the mini-carriers were limited in their use of electric motors, propulsion gears, large turbines,etc. because these were needed for combat weapons such as fleet carriers, submarines, combat aircraft, tanks and so forth. This forced the 50 flattops to use nonstrategic materials and machinery, which compelled many auxiliary pumps, compressors, and blowers to be steam-driven. The other inescapable problem was to select material and equipment, such as pumps, heat exchangers, boilers, engines, coolers, blowers, etc., which were not only not needed for fleet carriers, but which would be available for the shipyard in quantity when required so that not one day would be wasted. This problem was multiplied by 50 with a myriad of manufacturers providing identical equipment.

Steam turbines and Diesel engines were also not available to power the *Casablancas* so the designers turned to relatively low pressure steam-driven reciprocating Skinner Uniflow poppet valve engines. These engines were reliable and a considerable advancement over the much earlier triple and quadruple expansion steam engines; however, they could not compete economically with steam turbines or Diesel engines; requiring a higher fuel consumption. The main problem with the Uniflow engines was the inadvertent leakage of lubricating oil into the expended steam. This exhausted steam was to be condensed and the water pumped back into the boilers, but the entrained lubricating oil had to be removed before the water entered the boilers. A system of filtration using diatomaceous earth-coated terrycloth filter beds, as well as loofagourd sponges required skillful maintenance and operation.

Machinery Spaces

Two engines were installed; each directly connected to a propeller. Two boilers generated steam for each engine. Two machinery spaces were provided, separated by a compartment containing the fresh water tanks, fuel oil settling tanks and miscellaneous stores. Two boilers and one engine were located in each machinery space.

Uptake Dampers

All boiler uptakes terminated upward in port and starboard stacks outboard of the Flight Deck level; four stacks total. A new feature in the uptakes was the addition of a damper in each athwartship set. The damper was arranged to divert the fumes and smoke to the downwind side of the Deck so that no smoke would drift across the Flight Deck, regardless of wind direction.

Casablanca **Data**

The U.S. Navy Hulls No. CVE-55 through CVE-104 each displaced 6,730 tons standard and 10,200 tons full load. Overall length was 490 feet with a 65 foot hull beam. Flight Deck dimensions were 85 x 475 feet. The engines produced a total of 11,200 indicated horsepower which drove the mini-carriers to a maximum speed of 19 knots. Combat range at 15 knots was 15,000 miles. Tankage for about 2,200 tons of fuel oil and 100,000 gallons of aviation fuel was provided. The originally estimated complement was 764; however, under many service conditions this doubled to 1,500 officers and crew. Fighters and torpedo planes were the basic aircraft carried; nine Wildcats and 18 Avengers. At times nine each of Wildcats, Avengers and Dauntless dive bombers were deployed on board, depending upon the assigned mission.

Defensive armament comprised one 5 inch .38 caliber gun mounted off the fantail, plus (16) 40 millimeter and (18) 20 millimeter antiaircraft guns. This armament varied as the war progressed. Radar included air and surface search, plus the standard homing beacon for aircraft.

Production

All 50 ships of this never-to-be-duplicated achievement were constructed in the Kaiser Shipyards in Vancouver, Washington and, upon launching, the carriers were sailed down the Columbia River to Astoria, Oregon by some of the shipyard personnel and ships' officers. Here the mini-carrier received its final outfitting and the crew got their first look at that huge, silent mass of steel that they would soon turn into a living, breathing, noisy, fighting monster.

Casablanca Class Ships

The *Casablanca* class included the following mini-carriers: *Casablanca* (CVE-55); *Liscome Bay* (CVE-56); *Coral Sea/Anzio* (CVE-57); *Corregidor* (CVE-58); *Mission Bay* (CVE-59); *Guadalcanal* (CVE-60); *Manila Bay* (CVE-61); *Natoma Bay* (CVE-62); *Midway/St. Lo* (CVE-63); *Tripoli* (CVE-64); *Wake Island* (CVE-65); *White Plains* (CVE-66); *Solomons* (CVE-67); *Kalinin Bay* (CVE-68); *Kasaan Bay* (CVE-69); *Fanshaw Bay* (CVE-70); *Kitkun Bay* (CVE-71); *Tulagi* (CVE-72); *Gambier Bay* (CVE-73); *Nehenta Bay* (CVE-74); *Hoggatt Bay* (CVE-75); *Kadashan Bay* (CVE-76); *Marcus Island* (CVE-77); *Savo Island* (CVE-78); *Ommaney Bay* (CVE-79); *Petrof Bay* (CVE-80); *Rudyerd Bay* (CVE-81); *Saginaw Bay* (CVE-82); *Sargent Bay* (CVE-83); *Shamrock Bay* (CVE-84); *Shipley Bay* (CVE-85); *Sitkoh Bay* (CVE-86); *Steamer Bay* (CVE-87); *Cape Esperance* (CVE-88); *Takanis Bay* (CVE-89); *Thetis Bay* (CVE-90); *Makassar Bay* (CVE-91); *Windham Bay* (CVE-92); *Makin Island* (CVE-93); *Lunga Point* (CVE-94); *Bismarck Sea* (CVE-95); *Salamaua* (CVE-96); *Hollandia* (CVE-97); *Kwajalein* (CVE-98); *Admiralty Islands* (CVE-99); *Bougainville* (CVE-100); *Matanikau* (CVE-101); *Attu* (CVE-102); *Roi* (CVE-103); and *Munda* (CVE-104).

USS Coral Sea was later known as *USS Anzio* and *USS Midway* was later known as *St. Lo* because the names *Coral Sea* and *Midway* were to be given to large battle carriers yet to be built.

The ships were originally designated S4-S2-BB3 Auxiliary Aircraft Carriers.

Unfair Criticism

Unarmored and inadequately armed because they were to depend on the destroyer screen for protection, escort carriers in general and *Casablanca* class in particular, have been criticized and ridiculed by misinformed or uninformed writers over the years, calling them, among other epithets, "Kaiser Coffins." This will be for the reader

to decide while the *Casablanca* service record unfolds, sometime as part of "Doug MacArthur's Navy", in late 1943 and 1944. Only six of the 50 *Casablancas* were sunk by enemy action.

Essex Class Catapult Change

The American arsenal was launching and placing into service an increasing number of carriers at a pace never before imagined. The light carrier *Monterey* (CVL-26) was commissioned on June 17, 1943, followed by the *Cabot* (CVL-28); six days later, with *Langley* (CVL-27) commissioned on August 31. On August 16 the *Essex* class carrier *Intrepid* (CV-11) was commissioned. *Intrepid* was the first of this class to have two catapults on the Flight Deck and omitting the seldom used Hangar Deck catapult. A 40 millimeter quad antiaircraft installation replaced the Hangar Deck catapult on the port side.

Royal Navy Abandons Armored Flight Deck

The Royal Navy ordered three new fleet carriers in the summer of 1943 from three different shipyards. This was to be the Malta class which included *HMS Gibraltar* and *HMS New Zealand*. The design was to be a follow-up to the new Eagle class, previously described, and is worthy of mention if only for the fact that the Royal Navy's long-standing practice of armored flight decks and hangars was abandoned. Instead, the U.S. Navy practice was adopted in order to be able to warm up the aircraft engines below the Flight Deck. The British were willing to sacrifice the armor protection in exchange for rapid deployment of strike forces. The *Malta* class was also to be faster, more powerful, able to handle 30,000 pound aircraft, plus improved underwater protection; in effect, a supercarrier with a 900 foot long flight deck and almost 60,000 tons full load. Only the keel of *HMS Malta* had been laid and all were cancelled at the war's end.

Japanese Navy Adopts Armored Flight Deck

The Imperial Japanese Navy, on the other hand, abandoned their long-standing practice of unarmored flight decks to adopt the British practice of employing an armored flight deck and enclosed bow on their next carrier project; the *Taiho* class. In general, *Taiho* bore a striking resemblance to the typical Royal Navy carrier and was of a size similar to the American Essex class. The Japanese plan was to construct six of this class but the overly ambitious project could never materialize. *Taiho* means Giant Phoenix in Japanese, an apparent reference to a resurrection of the once-powerful Imperial Japanese Navy carrier force.

Taiho Data

Construction had started in July 1941 and *Taiho* was launched in April 1943 at the Kawasaki Jyuko Company Shipyard in Kobe. Standard displacement was 29,300 tons, while the full load displacement was 36,809 tons. Hull measured 855 feet overall x 90 foot beam and the Flight Deck measured 843 x 98 feet. Eight boilers generated steam for the turbines, which delivered 160,000 shaft horsepower to four propellers. These could drive the ship to a maximum speed in excess of 33 knots. Combat range was 8,000 miles at 18 knots. Fuel tanks were sized for about 5,700 tons.

HMS Searcher was a Bogue class C-3 conversion operated by the Royal Navy under the terms of Lend-Lease. Designated AVG-22 by the U.S. Navy, the ship was built by Seattle-Tacoma Shipyard and converted by Commercial Iron Works. The Royal Navy modified the aviation gasoline tank arrangement to include a sea water cofferdam around the tank which reduced the aviation gasoline (Avgas) capacity. HMS Searcher operated in British Home Waters during 1943 and participated in the attack on Tirpitz in 1944, as well as conducting ASW operations during the Normandy Invasion. (U.S. Naval Historical Center)

The 4 inch thick steel plate Flight Deck was designed to withstand bombs in excess of 1,000 pounds and the hull belt armor was 6 inches thick. Almost 1/3 of *Taiho*'s displacement was made up of armor. The island was rather large for a navy that preferred unobstructed flight decks and the island even incorporated a smokestack in lieu of the usual deck edge exhausts. The stack was canted outboard to direct the flue gasses away from the Deck.

Aircraft complement was 53; however, a maximum of 74 planes could be operated. Normal crew complement was 1,700.

Defensive armament was (12) 3.9 inch and (51) 25 millimeter antiaircraft guns.

Most Advanced Japanese Carrier

Taiho was not only the most unusual, but the most advanced Japanese carrier of World War II. *Taiho* will next be met in the Battle of the Philippine Sea where she will experience her baptism of fire.

Unryu Class Japanese Carriers

Unlike the armored *Taiho*, the next important Japanese carriers followed conventional Japanese construction with lightweight structures and unarmored flight decks. The *Unryu* class of six proposed carriers was Japan's last effort to produce an effective carrier class. Strongly resembling the *Hiryu/Soryu* class, *Unryu* is often called an economy version of an improved *Hiryu*.

The first of the six hulls was started in August 1942 with the last keel laid about one year later. The carriers were to be named *Unryu*, *Amagi*, *Katsuragi*, *Kasagi*, *Aso* and *Ikoma*. In order to accelerate production, standard cruiser machinery was to be installed; however, the powerplant production could not conform to the schedule and *Katsuragi* and *Aso* were fitted with destroyer machinery instead. This reduced the speed by one third.

Unryu Data

Unryu displacement was about 17,000 tons and 22,000 tons at deep load draft. Overall length was 746 feet with a beam of 72 feet. Flight Deck measured 88 feet-6 inches x 712 feet. The cruiser steam turbine machinery developed 152,000 shaft horsepower, which propelled the *Unryu* to a maximum speed of 34 knots. Steam was generated in eight boilers and geared turbines connected to four propellers. Range was 8,000 miles at 18 knots.

Converted from the passenger liner Argentina Maru into an aircraft carrier during 1943 IJNS Kaiyo became a 13,600 ton, 52,000 shaft horsepower ship attaining a top speed of 24 knots. The diesel propulsion machinery was replaced with destroyer-type machinery and a 72 x 490 feet wooden Flight Deck without catapults was added. No island was fitted so the boiler gasses discharged downward on the starboard side. Only 24 aircraft could be accommodated in this 546 feet long carrier. Kaiyo was damaged by aircraft from HMS Victorious, Formidable and Indefatigable in July 1945 in Beppu Bay, Kyushu and ran aground to avoid sinking. It is shown here being dismantled after the war. (U.S. Naval Historical Center)

Resembling the typical Royal Navy carrier with the smokestack incorporated in the island structure, IJNS Taiho was the first Japanese aircraft carrier to feature an armored Flight Deck. In fact, the ship was so heavily armored that armor accounted for about one third of the entire weight of the carrier. The shell plating also extended to the Flight Deck, Royal Navy style. Taiho was launched in April 1943 and commissioned March 1944. (Official U.S. Navy Photograph, News Photo Division)

Armor was held to a minimum with 1.8 inches for magazines, 6 inches for the hull belt and 1 inch for the Hangar Deck. Defensive armament consisted of about (90) 25 millimeter antiaircraft guns, plus two dozen single swivel mounts. Six 8-tube rocket launchers were also installed. About 60 aircraft could be carried; however, it is questionable if, by the time the carriers were launched from September 1943 to November 1944, the Imperial Japanese Navy had the trained pilots or the planes to meet the carrier's needs. Only *Unryu*, *Amagi* and *Katsuragi* were completed.

The ships were not used in combat due to the shortage of aircraft. *Unryu* was torpedoed and sunk by a U.S. submarine, *Amagi* was sunk during the bombing of Kure, and *Katsuragi* was damaged in the Kure bombing raids and taken by the Allies as a war reparation only to be scrapped.

SPRUANCE COMMANDS U.S. FIFTH FLEET

On August 4, 1943 recently promoted Vice Admiral Raymond Spruance had been detached as Admiral Nimitz' Chief of Staff to become Commander of the U.S. Fifth Fleet. On the following day he assumed command of a powerful force that contained the majority of the combatant ships that would be used as the U.S. Navy's striking force in the Central Pacific; making long-range strikes on Japanese-held islands, as well as supporting amphibious landings on these islands.

IJNS Katsuragi was an Unryu class carrier based upon the Soryu design. Three ships of the class were constructed: Unryu, Aso and Katsuragi. Unryu and Aso were fitted with cruiser machinery but a shortage of equipment left Katsuragi with destroyer machinery. This photo shows the many defensive gun emplacements on Katsuragi sponsons. (U.S. National Archives)

Rear Admiral Charles A. Pownall commanded Task Force 50 which was the most powerful carrier force ever assembled until that time. TF-50 included ten carriers, six battleships, six cruisers and 21 destroyers. (U.S. National Archives)

Task Force 50

The Fifth Fleet had been specially created for this purpose and the planned attack against the Gilbert Islands was to be made by Task Force 50 of the Fifth Fleet. TF-50 was commanded by Rear Admiral Charles A. Pownall and was the most powerful carrier force ever assembled until that time. It included five of the new light carriers, three *Essex* class carriers and the veteran *Saratoga* and *Enterprise*. Six new battleships, three heavy cruisers, three antiaircraft cruisers and 21 destroyers made up the carrier screen.

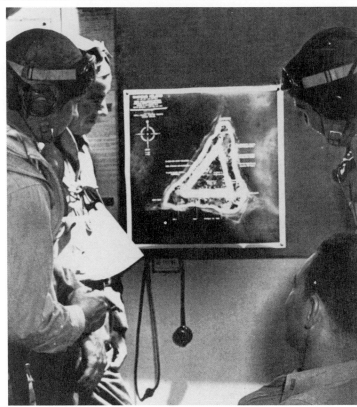

eft: Captain Joseph J. "Jocko" Clark was commanding officer of USS Yorktown (CV-10) in Task Force 50. The captain was a popular, hard-driving
ipper who was proud of the fact that he had Cherokee Indian blood running through his veins. Right: Pilots on USS Yorktown (CV-10) study an
rial photograph of Marcus Island (Minami Tori Shima) to plan the daring raid on this target that is less than one thousand miles from Japan. (U.S.
aval Historical Center)

The 10 carriers of TF-50 were divided into four groups: 1.
arrier Interceptor Group - *Yorktown*, *Lexington* and *Cowpens*; 2.
orthern Carrier Group - *Monterey*, *Enterprise* and *Belleau Wood*;
 Southern Carrier Group - *Independence* and *Bunker Hill*; 4. Re-
ef Carrier Group - *Saratoga* and *Princeton*.

Escort carriers were also included to support the big carriers,
cort the convoys and cover amphibious assaults.

.S. Navy Training Raids

he new U.S. carriers coming into service had only partly-trained
r units, while the escort carriers, which had proven their value in
e Atlantic and Mediterranean, had not yet found their true place
 the actions in the Pacific. The air groups and ships needed much
am training; therefore, a series of training raids was devised to
ve the men combat experience before sending them into the Cen-
al Pacific offensive. The raids were to have no strategic or tactical
urpose, but were merely training exercises to gain combat experi-
ice.

On September 1, 1943 the *Essex* class carriers, *Essex* and
orktown*, plus the light carrier *Independence* launched Dauntless
ve bombers and Avenger torpedo planes in a raid on Marcus Is-
nd, less than 1,000 miles from Japan. Six strikes were made that
y with negligible results, but lessons were learned. Two and a
alf weeks later the *Essex* class carrier *Lexington* and light carriers,
elleau Wood* and *Princeton*, launched strikes against Makin and
arawa. Four U.S. planes failed to return to the carriers but the raid

Commander Charles L. Crommelin, commanding officer of Fighting
Squadron Five (VF-5) on USS Yorktown led his squadron on many
Pacific island raids. While strafing Mili Airfield in the Marshall Islands
a Japanese 40 millimeter antiaircraft shell crashed through his cockpit
and exploded. With instruments gone, windshield shattered and impos-
sible to see through, eyes injured which made eyesight virtually non-
existent, wounded face and chest and broken wrist, this intrepid pilot
flew 120 miles over open sea back to USS Yorktown and landed!
Commander Crommelin had four brothers in the U.S. Navy, three of
which were naval aviators; John, Richard and Quentin. The fifth brother,
Henry, became a famous destroyer captain. (U.S. National Archives)

Rear Admiral Frederick C. Sherman, Task Force 38 Commander, welcomes good news from Commander Joseph "Jumpin Joe" Clifton who led his fighter group on raids against Rabaul. During the twelve-day assault more than 130 Japanese carrier-based planes were destroyed. The men are on board USS Saratoga (CV-3). (Official U.S. Navy Photograph, News Photo Division)

caused considerable damage, including nine Japanese planes. Wake Island was next on October 5-6, 1943, when planes from *Essex, Yorktown, Lexington, Independence, Belleau Wood* and *Cowpens* made over 700 combat sorties against a strong aerial defense. About 12 U.S. planes were shot down in combat and 14 more were lost due to faulty takeoffs, landings or ditched at sea for a variety of reasons, but 22 Japanese planes were destroyed. The carrier and air crews were now ready for Admiral Nimitz' large-scale offensive into the Central Pacific.

CARRIERS IN THE BISMARCKS
Essex class and Independence class carriers were being commissioned so quickly that, by autumn of 1943, U.S. carriers had arrived in the Southwest Pacific to help Admiral Halsey's island-hopping to Rabaul. On November 5 Admiral Frederick Sherman's Task Force 38 with *Saratoga* (CV-3) and *Princeton* (CVL-23) raided Rabaul's Simpson Harbor with 97 planes and six days later Admiral Alfred Montgomery's force of *Essex, Bunker Hill* and *Independence* repeated the raid but met increased fighter resistance in the form of 68 Zero fighters.

Despite very heavy shore-based attacks on the carriers they escaped undamaged which was contrary to what had been expected based upon Royal Navy experience in the Mediterranean Sea. There are two basic reasons for this good fortune. One is the fact that the Wildcat was being replaced by the newer, more potent Hellcat on carriers. The other factor is that Navy and Marine Corsairs based on the Solomon Islands not only participated in the raids but also flew Combat Air Patrol duty for the American aircraft carriers.

Corsairs Operate From Carriers
It is important to relate two very interesting activities that occurred on November 11, 1943 when F4U-1A Corsairs of VF-17 "Jolly

Rogers", based on New Georgia, shot down an entire attacking force of 18 Japanese torpedo planes; thereby, saving *Essex* and *Bunker Hill* from serious damage or destruction.

During the course of this lengthy mission, far from their base many VF-17 Corsairs landed on the two carriers to refuel and re-arm by pilots who had no carrier training at all. When replenishment was complete the Corsairs took off without incident, despite the fact that this was not officially permitted by the U.S. Navy.

Japanese Carrier Warbirds Weakened
Although the Rabaul raids were not overly effective against shore or naval targets, they had the far-reaching effect of weakening Japanese carrier aircraft strength at the moment of the Central Pacific assault. Admiral Mineichi Koga had frittered away his carrier aircraft and crews by transferring them to shore bases where they suffered steady attrition trying to stem the U.S. drive. When the Japanese aircraft returned to Shokaku and Zuikaku in mid-November they had lost three-quarters of the original 175 planes during a period of 12 days. They returned to Japan to rehabilitate and rest while Nimitz had embarked on his Central Pacific offensive.

Rabaul Neutralized
By December 17, 1943 Rabaul had been neutralized and it was eventually decided to bypass the Japanese base. The Bismarck Barrier had been breached and the route to the Philippines was open.

CENTRAL PACIFIC AGENDA
In the Central Pacific, American preparations were nearing completion for the naval and air assault on the Gilberts, Marshalls, Carolines and Marianas; collectively known as Micronesia. These chains of islands are strategically arranged across the main sea lanes which link the U.S. with the Philippines, China and Japan. Kwajalein in the Marshalls, Tarawa in the Gilberts, Saipan in the Marianas and Truk in the Carolines had each become part of the Japanese defensive network; therefore, it had become imperative that these outposts be wrested from Japanese control.

Long Distance Between Bases
A major problem was the enormous expanse of ocean between and around these islands. Distances of 1,000 miles and more between U.S. and Japanese bases were commonplace. In the Solomon Islands U.S. aircraft very seldom ventured more than 300 miles from the nearest Allied airfield. When covering an amphibious assault the planes usually operated within 150 miles of a friendly airfield; therefore, the Central Pacific drive was not going to be easy. If it wasn't for the growing fleet of U.S. aircraft carriers and the Warbirds it would have been impossible.

Leap Frogging
In order to overcome the long distances between Allied bases and target islands, as well as between target islands, a new technique was developed called "leap frogging." The basic concept was to bypass powerful Japanese island bastions to outflank and cut them off from supplies. This proposed activity demanded the mobility and heavy punch that only aircraft carriers could deliver.

ice Admiral Richmond Kelly Turner was in command of the Makin and
arawa (Operation Galvanic) assault groups which included six escort
ircraft carriers. (U.S. National Archives)

Operation Galvanic (Tarawa)

The first objective was Tarawa Atoll in the Gilbert Islands; code-
amed Operation Galvanic. Simultaneous landings were planned
or Makin Island and Abemama Island, also in the Gilberts.

Admiral Raymond Ames Spruance had divided his force into
hree main divisions: the landing forces under Rear Admiral Rich-
mond Kelly Turner; the carrier forces under Rear Admiral Charles
A. Pownall; and the shore-based air forces, which included U.S.
Marine as well as the U.S. Army Seventh Air Force aircraft, under
Rear Admiral John H. Hoover.

Admiral Pownall assigned a carrier group led by Rear Admiral
Alfred E. Montgomery to stand off Tarawa and another carrier group
ed by Rear Admiral Arthur W. Radford to stand off Makin. Two
ther carrier groups led by Rear Admiral Frederick C. Sherman and
Admiral Pownall himself guarded the open sea area in way of the
andings.

Assault Group

Rear Admiral Richmond Kelly Turner was in command of the as-
ault group; V Amphibious Force. Six escort carriers to cover Op-
ration Galvanic were part of Admiral Turner's command and com-
rised two task groups; a Southern Attack Force and a Northern
Attack Force.

Admiral Turner took charge of the Northern Attack Force directed at Makin while he assigned the Southern Attack Force directed at Tarawa and Abemama to Rear Admiral Harry W. Hill.

Task Group 53.6, Rear Admiral Van H. Ragsdale commanding
Carrier Division Division 22, included the converted escort carri-
ers *Sangamon*, *Suwannee* and *Chenango* as part of the Southern
Attack Force. Five destroyers screened the *Sangamons*.

Task Group 52.3, Rear Admiral Henry M. Mullinnix commanding Carrier Division 24, included the new Kaiser-built *Liscome Bay*,
Coral Sea and *Corregidor* as part of the Northern Attack Force.
The latter had been commissioned in August and had little time for
a shakedown cruise before she had been rushed to Pearl Harbor,
loaded with planes, and then set sail for the Gilberts. Seven destroyers screened the *Casablancas*.

The *Sangmons* were equipped with a mix of 27 to 30 Hellcats,
Dauntless and Avengers, while the *Casablancas* carried 21 to 28
Wildcats and Avengers.

Steaming with the *Casablancas* were the battleships *Mississippi* and *New Mexico*, plus the cruiser *Baltimore*; forming TG-
52.3 to cover the Makin Island invasion in the north.

USS Independence Torpedoed

The carriers *USS Essex*, *USS Bunker Hill*, and *USS Independence*
launched dive bombers against Betio, a fortified island located in
the lagoon of Tarawa Atoll, which included a very important airfield that had to be neutralized.

During this operation a Japanese shore-based torpedo plane
broke through the combat air patrol and scored a direct hit on the
light carrier *Independence*, damaging the steering gear. This put
the light carrier out of action until the summer of 1944.

Makin Island Landings

The Makin invasion had begun on November 20, 1943, and because of unexpected delays, had not yet been completed four days
later. This forced the covering ships to steam in the same general
area much longer than planned, which became an open invitation
to Japanese submarines that had begun to congregate in the area.
USS Liscome Bay was Admiral Mullinnix' flagship, Captain Irving
D. Wiltsie commanding, and acted as the guide of the formation. It
was just before dawn on November 24, 1943 that flight quarters
had been sounded on *Liscome Bay* as the carrier was about to turn
to the northeast. The formation was quite ragged because two destroyers were missing and the others were trying to close the gaps.
Destroyer *Hoel* had been sent to Makin, while destroyer *Franks*
went to investigate a distant light. Both destroyers had been screening the starboard side of *Liscome Bay* which left a gap that was
difficult to close.

USS Liscome Bay Disaster

Lieutenant Commander Sunao Tabata found that gap most inviting
and fired several torpedoes from his Imperial Japanese Navy submarine I-175. The torpedoes entered the gap and one struck *Liscome
Bay* (CVE-56) on the starboard side just aft of the after machinery
space, which was the bomb stowage magazine. The resulting explosion was unbelievable as 200,000 pounds of bombs blew up en
masse.

During the Makin Island landing escorting destroyers had left the starboard side of USS Liscome Bay (CVE-56) exposed which enabled IJN submarine I-175 to send a torpedo into the bomb stowage magazine setting off a thunderous explosion. Debris rained down on ships of the task group as far as three miles away. (U.S. National Archives)

Captain John G. Crommelin Jr. was the highest ranking survivor of the Liscome Bay sinking. He was Chief of Staff to Admiral Mullinix and brother of Charles on the Yorktown. Fortunately for himself the captain had been taking a shower in a part of the ship not immediately affected by the torpedo hit but was cut off from his clothes by the flames. Although suffering severe burns the naked Crommelin helped members of the crew get off the burning ship until he was also rescued. He is shown here preparing his report of the Liscome Bay sinking. We will meet Captain Crommelin again during the post-World War II years when he will be deeply involved in the Revolt of the Admirals; fighting for carriers in the U.S. Navy. (U.S. National Archives)

Debris from the stricken carrier rained down on the other ship as far as three miles away. White hot pieces of steel, planes, flam ing oil, molten drops of metal, clothing, flesh and bones, and fligh deck planking showered the sea for miles around. Flame from th explosion erupted 1,000 feet in the air as the entire stern was blow off! The Hangar Deck was a mass of fire and smoke, while tongue of flame from floating oil licked at the bow. According to eye wi nesses on *USS Corregidor*, *Liscome Bay*'s island was so hot that glowed cherry red.

About 20 minutes after the explosion *USS Liscome Bay* bega to sink into the Pacific, gurgling and hissing as the hot steel quenche itself, creating clouds of steam which hid the final plunge to th depths of the sea!

This catastrophic explosion resulted in the deaths of 53 offi ers, including Admiral Mullinnix and Captain Wiltsie, and 591 crew men. Only 55 officers and 217 crewmen survived, many of who were maimed, seriously burned, or suffered from severe concu sion because of the enormous explosion.

The *Liscome Bay* sinking resulted in much unwarranted crit cism of the *Casablanca* class carriers, despite the fact that eve fleet battle carriers such as *Lexington*, *Ark Royal* and *Wasp* explode burned or flooded and sank with loss of life when hit in a vulne able location.

Betio and Abemama Island Landings

Marines landed on Betio in Tarawa Atoll and Abemama Islands the Gilbert Chain and earned a quick victory after 76 hours of fier fighting.

Makin Surrenders

Makin Island surrendered on the day of the *Liscome Bay* disaste Tarawa Atoll was next but, despite concentrated dive bombing an strafing, the target held out until late in November.

Commander O'Hare And Night Fighting

As previously mentioned, the Japanese were proficient at nig operations in the air and on the sea. To counter this the U.S. Nav Bureau of Aeronautics issued contracts to develop radar-equippe Corsairs in 1942 and Hellcats during the summer of 1943. The r dar-equipped Hellcats were not yet available during Operation Ga vanic; however, Lieutenant Commander Edward "Butch" O'Ha could not wait until they were issued and conducted the U.S. Navy first nocturnal hunter-killer operation. Using a radar-equippe Grumman Avenger as the hunter, O'Hare led two standard Grumma F6F-3 fighters as the killers. When the Hellcats took off from *E terprise* on November 24 it was the first time night fighters ha operated from U.S. carriers. No contact was made but the exper ence prepared the crews for operations two nights later. On the nig of November 26 the hunter-killer combination intercepted attac ing Japanese torpedo planes. Although no planes were lost by e ther side, the torpedo planes were dispersed and routed before an damage could be inflicted on Task Force 50.

Operation Flintlock (Marshalls)

The U.S. carriers had been playing the part of mobile airfields attack land targets in the Gilbert Islands because there were no Jap ese carriers in the area to challenge them. Admiral Pownall's TF-50 was now turned towards Kwajalein Atoll in the Marshalls.

Kwajalein and Roi Raids

At 6:00 o'clock in the morning of December 4, 1943 the light carriers *Cowpens* (CVL-25) and *Belleau Wood* (CVL-24) each launched a Combat Air Patrol (CAP) for the two groups that were assigned to raid the atoll. One half hour later *Lexington* (CV-16) and *Yorktown* (CV-10) began launching aircraft for torpedo strikes in Kwajalein Lagoon; however, the absence of accurate charts caused endless confusion and wasted effort. Of 36 torpedoes launched by Avengers, only five found their mark. Hellcats were sent out to beat up the airfield at Roi in the northern end of the atoll; however, they were deceived by the camouflage and missed 40 parked Japanese planes.

Second Strike Cancelled

A second strike was to have been launched against these targets; however, Admiral Pownall cancelled it because of the meager results which had been obtained in the first strike.

The Admiral was fully aware of the Japanese night fighting capability and realized that his close proximity to the target area was an invitation to disaster. Pownall apparently decided to place as much distance as possible between his carriers and the Japanese shore bases. Surprise is the only factor in favor of the fast carrier strike and once the enemy shore-based air force is enticed into the air it will be in the more advantageous position. Kwajalein was a case in point because it was the center of the Japanese outer defensive complex and the longer the carriers remained in the area, the greater would be the risk. Carriers cannot slug it out with well-armed shore-based air power. The first strike was recovered at 10:30 AM. of December 4, 1943 and one last strike was planned.

Wotje Atoll Raid

At about noon *Yorktown* launched 30 planes for an attack on Wotje Atoll, which accomplished little more than some excellent photographic reconnaissance.

Japanese Torpedo Attacks

Shortly after this raid three Kate torpedo planes from Maloelap Atoll, just southeast of Wotje in the Ratak Chain of the Marshalls, launched an attack on the new *Lexington*; however, all three were splashed by flying into geysers made by the 5 inch guns. Four more Kates attacked *Lexington* that afternoon flying very low to evade the high-flying combat air patrol but, before they could release their torpedoes, the four Kates were shot down by the combined fire from a screening cruiser and two destroyers.

Japanese Night Attack

By nightfall Task Force 50 was steaming northeastward, hoping to sail beyond range of shore-based bombers before it got too dark because it had no carrier fighters trained in night operations. Japanese reconnaissance planes had already been sighted, which later dropped flares from high altitudes in the darkness. Torpedo-armed Kates and twin-engine Bettys roared in from all sides now that the ships were clearly silhouetted by the flares.

New Japanese Tactics

The Japanese raiders initiated a new tactic on this night of December 4-5, 1943. After dropping flares the reconnaissance planes flew across the battle area from all directions. In addition, the Kate and Betty torpedo planes continued to fly over the American ships after launching their torpedoes; criss-crossing *Lexington* and her screen, instead of returning to their bases. As can be imagined, this heavy traffic fouled the U.S. Navy radar screens, which resulted in electronic chaos and made it impossible to determine which of the blips were the attacking planes. It was estimated that from 30 to 50 Japanese planes took part in the attack, which lasted about 45 minutes. Fourteen torpedo and bomb hits were scored; however, no sinkings were achieved.

Lexington Torpedoed

One torpedo penetrated *Lexington*'s Steering Gear Room, which jammed the rudders over hard and broke one of the propeller shafts. Crewmen specialists managed to jack the rudders into neutral position so the ship could be steered by the engines. *Lexington* arrived at Pearl Harbor on December 9, 1943 where temporary repairs were accomplished. The ship then continued to Puget Sound Navy Yard for complete repairs.

Task Force 50 wisely retired from its limited success in the assault on the Gilbert and Marshall Islands. With Tarawa Atoll taken by U.S. troops, an uninterrupted effort was underway to develop the Atoll as a base to support further U.S. carrier action in the area.

Still more carriers had joined the U.S. Pacific Fleet with the commissioning of USS *Hornet* (CV-12) on November 29, 1943 and the last of the nine *Independence* class light carriers, USS *San Jacinto*, commissioned on December 15, 1943.

JAPAN STILL SEEKS SHOWDOWN BATTLE

Ever since the Pearl Harbor attack Admiral Yamamoto had tried to convince the Imperial General Staff in Tokyo that Japan must engage the U.S. Navy in one great battle and defeat the Americans in this battle. Then, he reasoned, the politicians could negotiate a peaceful settlement which would assure the existence of the Japanese Empire.

Yamamoto's successor, Admiral Mineichi Koga, was a devoted believer in Yamamoto's theory and managed to do what his predecessor could not; convince the Imperial General Staff that this was the best solution to Japan's predicament.

Combined Fleet Deployment

Koga reorganized the Combined Fleet and deployed the main body, Mobile Fleet, to a line running from the Marianas south to the Carolines, and then west to the Philippines.

Japan's Carrier Force

Japan still had *Zuikaku* and *Shokaku*, plus the three light carriers *Junyo*, *Zuiho* and *Hiyo*. *Taiho* was nearing completion and the world's largest carrier, *Shinano*, was scheduled for completion in 1945. In addition, two battleships, *Ise* and *Hyuga*, were being converted into aircraft carriers. Meanwhile, America was producing

On the night of December 4-5, 1943 Japanese torpedo planes used a new tactic to confuse U.S. carriers in the Marshall Islands. USS Lexington (CV-16) was torpedoed in the steering gear room which jammed the rudders over hard and fractured a propeller shaft. Damage control made partial repairs so the ship could reach the U.S. for complete repairs. Lexington is shown in March 1944 after the repairs were completed. (Official U.S. Navy Photograph, News Photo Division)

fleet carriers, light carriers and escort carriers at a phenomenal rate, which Japan could never hope to approach.

Koga Plan to Double Carrier Strength

Admiral Koga realized this problem and devised a plan to double his effective aircraft carrier strength. His solution was to use the many islands within the perimeter of the empire inner boundary as substitute carriers. The great naval battle would rely on the Japanese Navy Air Force to operate efficiently from the island bases, as well as from the remaining carriers. Saipan was selected as the headquarters of the Combined Fleet, while Tinian was chosen to be the principal base of the shore-based naval air force, Koga's plan was to place 500 planes on the remaining Japanese carriers and, during the battle, have the carrier-based planes shuttle with 500 planes based in the Marianas Islands, as well as the Palau Islands in the Carolines, southwest of the Marianas. It was planned that the Japanese planes from the island bases would attack the U.S. Force and land on the Japanese carriers, refuel and rearm, and take off to attack the American ships a second time on the way back to their shore bases. Meanwhile, the planes from the Japanese carriers were to continue on to the island bases after the first attack on the U.S. Navy ships and, after refueling and rearming, to strike again at the Americans on the way back to their carriers.

Admiral Koga planned an intelligent application of his available resources and intended to use the Japanese Pacific Island air bases as aircraft carriers while the Americans were using aircraft carriers as floating air bases. Meanwhile, Spruance continued the Marshall assaults.

U.S. Third and Fifth Fleet Identity

Before continuing into the carrier battles of 1944-45 it is important to mention the unusual U.S. Navy system in use for numbering the Pacific Fleets, which often confuses the researcher and layman alike. Often mentioned in descriptive material about the Pacific war are Admiral William F. Halsey and his Third Fleet, as well as the Fifth Fleet commanded by Admiral Raymond Spruance. Similarly, the exploits of Task Force 58 led by Vice Admiral Marc Mitscher and Task Force 38 commanded by Vice Admiral John McCain are widely admired.

The Third Fleet and the Fifth Fleet were, in fact, one and the same; same carriers, cruisers, battleships, destroyers and so forth. Likewise, TF-38 was physically the identical entity as TF-58. The very same fleet and all task forces merely changed numbers when the Fleet Commanders and their staffs relieved one another. While one commander was leading the fleet into battle the other was studying past battles and planning future moves against the Japanese. This had the advantage of keeping constant pressure on the Japanese Forces. When Admiral Halsey was in charge it was the Third Fleet and all task force numbers began with the number three, such as 33, 38, etc. When Admiral Spruance was in command it became the Fifth Fleet and all task force numbers began with the number five, such as 53, 58, etc.

USS Franklin Commissioned

On January 31, 1944 the *Essex* class carrier *Franklin* (CV-13) was commissioned. This ship was to be in the midst of the violent battles to come.

Marshalls Strikes and Landings

From January 29 through February 6 Admiral Spruance's Fifth Fleet Task Force 58 under Vice Admiral Marc A. Mitscher joined shore-based planes from Tarawa in strafing and bombing Japanese positions at Kwajalein, Eniwetok, and Wotje in the Marshall Islands; Operation Flintlock. The assault force was commanded by Rear Admiral Richmond Kelly Turner, who was America's foremost amphibious expert. Undefended Majoro Atoll, southeast of Kwajalein Atoll was quickly occupied and converted into a large fleet anchorage but the coral islands of Kwajalein Atoll took a bit longer to secure.

Task Group 53.6 led by Rear Admiral Ragsdale, Commander Carrier Division 22, covered the northern landings at Roi-Namur, while Task Group 52.9, led by Rear Admiral Ralph E. Davison, Commander Carrier Division 24, covered the southern landings on Kwajalein Island, from which the Atoll got its name. TG-53.6 comprised the escort carriers *Sangamon* (Air Group 37); *Suwannee* (Air Group 60); and *Chenango* (Air Group 35). TG-52.9 included the Kaiser-built escort carriers *Manila Bay* (Air Group VC-7); *Coral Sea* (Air Group VC-53) and *Corregidor* (Air Group VC-41).

The *USS Manila Bay* Air Group VC-7 Avengers were the first planes in the Pacific to be equipped with rockets, later to also be known as missiles. On February 1, 1944 two Avengers made rocket attacks against installations on Bigej, just north of Kwajalein Island in the Atoll, and made hits on a camouflaged ammunition dump. Later, another pilot launched his rockets at what appeared to be an ordinary camouflaged building but turned out to be a fuel depot.

The atoll was secured on February 8 when *USS Coral Sea* (CVE-57) entered the enormous lagoon to refuel and rearm, having the honor to be the first American carrier to anchor in former Japanese waters.

Operation Catchpole

Many troops from Kwajalein Atoll moved in on Eniwetok for Operation Catchpole on February 17, 1944. Eniwetok is about 360 miles northwest of Kwajalein and only 700 miles from the key Japanese base at Truk Islands, (pronounced Trook, as in kook or spook). The Truk Islands are often called the Japanese Pearl Harbor and consist of several mountain peak islands surrounded by a coral ring about 30 miles in diameter. If Eniwetok became secured the U.S.

Fleet Admiral Mineichi Koga, Commander of the Imperial Japanese Navy Combined Fleet, reorganized the Fleet and prepared its Mobile Fleet for a showdown with the U.S. Pacific Fleet which was to become the Battle of the Philippine Sea. (U.S. Information Agency)

Vice Admiral Marc A. Mitscher, one of America's early naval pilots, commanded Task Force 58 during the Battle of the Philippine Sea and his pilots scored heavily in the Marianas Turkey Shoot. Admiral Mitscher was one of the U.S. Navy's finest carrier task force commanders. (U.S. Naval Historical Center)

Above: Fleet Admiral Chester Nimitz (center) and his Chief of Staff Rear Admiral Forrest Sherman (right) listen to Admiral "Bull" Halsey aboard a U.S. Navy ship in the Pacific as Halsey presents his views about the impending Philippine invasion. At this time Admiral Spruance was busy winning the Battle of The Philippine Sea.

Below: Rear Admiral Forrest Sherman (left) and Vice Admiral John H. Towers, Chief of U.S. Naval Air Operations in the Pacific, confer with carrier officers aboard a ship in the Pacific to coordinate aerial and surface activities. It will be recalled from Chapter One that John Towers was a prominent naval aviation pioneer. (U.S. Naval Historical Center, Courtesy Fleet Admiral Nimitz)

Navy would have a base from which to strike at Truk but Admiral Spruance did not wait for the Kwajalein or Eniwetok Islands occupation which, in fact, did not happen until May 22, 1944.

SPRUANCE RAID ON TRUK

In a brilliant decision Spruance gathered units of the Fifth Fleet to strike at Truk during February 17-18, 1944. The Admiral flew his flag from the fast battleship *New Jersey* (BB-62) and was in overall command of the operation. Spruance dedicated nine aircraft carriers, 10 cruisers, six battleships and over two dozen destroyers to the Truk raid and Spruance, himself, commanded Task Group 50.9. This was a surface action force assembled around the fast battleship *USS Iowa* (BB-61) and his flagship *USS New Jersey*.

Admiral Mitscher's Task Force 58

Rear Admiral Marc A. Mitscher was in command of Task Force 58 which consisted of three carrier task groups. TG-58.1: *USS Enterprise* (CV-6), *USS Yorktown* (CV-10), and *USS Belleau Wood* (CVL-24). TG-58.2: *USS Essex* (CV-9), *USS Intrepid* (CV-11), and *USS Cabot* (CVL-28). TG-58.3: *USS Bunker Hill* (CV-17), *USS Monterey* (CVL-26), and *USS Cowpens* (CVL-25).

Two Day Raid

Admiral Spruance planned a two-day raid using the task force Grumman F6F-3 Hellcats to gain aerial superiority during the first day by beating up Truk's three airfields and destroying as many fighter planes as possible on the ground and in the air. On the sec-

ond day the task force dive bombers and torpedo planes were scheduled to bomb shore installations, as well as bomb and torpedo any ships in the area. Aerial resistance was expected to be negligible in the second attack because of the Hellcat raids in the first day.

On the morning of February 17, 1944 the carriers arrived at the launch point, 90 miles east of Truk, two hours before dawn. The Hellcats began leaving the carriers in darkness at about 6:30; 12 each from *Enterprise*, *Intrepid*, and *Yorktown*, 11 from *Essex*, and 22 from *Bunker Hill*. The light carriers remained with the task force to provide combat air patrol and to act as a reserve back-up. Lieutenant Commander William R. Kane, often known as "Killer Kane", of the *Enterprise*, led the 69 Hellcats in this audacious attack on the Japanese fortress.

Vraciu Shoots Down Four

The fighters reached Truk's big lagoon at about 8:00 o'clock and were flying at 13,000 feet when a couple of Betty twin-engine bombers were seen taking off just as Kane was leading the planes down to strafe the field. Ten VF-6 Hellcats from *USS Intrepid* followed except one section of fighters whose leader sighted Japanese fighters at about 15,000 feet. He called to his squadron mates but his warnings were ignored. This section leader was Lieutenant (JG) Alex Vraciu, who had been "Butch" O'Hare's wingman in 1942 and had just become an Ace with five victories to his credit. Vraciu led his wingman, Ensign Lou Little, into the attack head-on. The lead Zero broke off the attack and dived below the Americans, but before they could go after him more Zeroes surrounded the two Hellcats. Vraciu shot down two of the Japanese fighters when they tried to dive away from his F6F-3. His third victory was a Rufe seaplane, which had tried the same tactic. Ensign Little also scored a Zero. After regaining altitude Vraciu played hide-and-seek with another Zero, darting in an out of a bank of fluffy clouds, until the Japanese pilot made a false move and Vraciu scored his fourth kill of the day.

Lieutenant (jg) Alexander Vraciu of VF-6 aboard USS Intrepid (CV-11) shot down four Japanese aircraft on the February 17, 1944 Task Force 58 air raid on the Japanese bastion of Truk. He became the U.S. Navy's fourth ranking ace with 19 victories to his credit. Vraciu is shown here with his Grumman Hellcat on February 19, 1944. Observe the Felix the Felix The Cat insignia. Plane number at this time was 99. (U.S. National Archives)

During the afternoon Admiral Mitscher ordered his Hellcats to bomb the airfield runways so they would be of no use to the Japanese should they decide to transfer replacement aircraft to Truk from carriers or other island bases. *USS Enterprise* launched five F6F-3's of VF-10, each loaded with a delayed fuse 1,000 pound bomb to be planted on the Moen Island bomber runways. While the Hellcats of VF-10 were destroying the single runway, other F6F-3's strafed parked aircraft. By the end of the day all Japanese aerial resistance had been obliterated and Truk was ready for the bombers and torpedo planes.

Intrepid Torpedoed

During the night of February 17-18, 1944, a Japanese Kate slipped past the destroyer screen and launched a torpedo into the stern of the carrier *Intrepid*. The explosion severely damaged the steering gear and this *Essex* class carrier was put out of action for six months.

Dauntless and Helldiver dive bombers left the carriers of Task Force 58 in the morning of February 18 with Avenger torpedo planes and headed for Truk. There is no record of any Japanese planes having taken off to intercept the Americans. Virtually all of Koga's Combined Fleet had left Truk before Task Force 58 arrived but the raiders scored heavily against naval auxiliaries and cargo ships.

Truk Raid Results

A total of 47 noncombatant ships were sunk, which totalled 137,000 tons. The light cruiser *Naka* and three destroyers were the only warships sunk by carrier aircraft.

The attack on Truk was a resounding success with Task Force 58 planes flying more than 1,200 sorties. Approximately 365 Japanese aircraft were destroyed on the ground and in the air by Hellcats. Despite the success of this well-planned and executed operation the carrier planes did experience some losses. Six Avengers, eight Hellcats and three dive bombers were lost due to enemy action and about 10 other aircraft were lost due to operational accidents. This was a small price to pay for the damage wrought to this key Japanese base. The operation also illustrated the fact that without shore-based air support a carrier attack on enemy shore-based installations must depend upon surprise for success.

U.S. CARRIERS STRIKE MARIANAS

On February 23, 1944 six carriers from Task Groups 58.2 and 58.3 launched attacks on Guam, Tinian, Rota and Saipan in the Marianas in preparation for an invasion.

NEW JAPANESE STRATEGIES; KOGA KILLED

In March the Japanese Fleet was reorganized to replace battleships with aircraft carriers as the dominant weapons of the force. Vice Admiral Jisaburo Ozawa who had commanded all Japanese carriers and their destroyer screens was now in tactical command of the battleships as well.

Koga Leaves Plan Z

Admiral Mineichi Koga, Commander-In-Chief of the IJN Combined Fleet, was killed in an airplane accident near the end of March

These members of a Hellcat division (four-plane formation) were deeply involved in the Central Pacific air raids. Lieutenant Eugene A. Valencia scored three victories in the Truk raid and continued to become the U.S. Navy's third ranking ace with 23 victories. Valencia was the division leader that included, from left to right, Lieutenant (jg) Harris Mitchell 10 victories; Lieutenant Clinton L. Smith six victories; and Lieutenant (jg) James B. French 11 victories. Note that the censor has blocked out the unit's squadron insignia on their flight jackets. (Official U.S. Navy Photograph, News Photo Division)

Many Planes Fall Into Lagoon

Japanese aircraft were taking off in rapid succession but many were stopped by the strafing Hellcats before they left the ground. Others were destroyed on the tarmac or in revetments and so many were destroyed in the air that it seemed that Japanese planes were falling into the lagoon at the rate of one each minute. Many Japanese ships also sank in the lagoon. In fact, so many planes, including some Hellcats, plunged into the lagoon that it has been dedicated as an underwater memorial park by the Federated States of Micronesia where scuba divers can visit to view the many planes and ships which rest on the bottom and pay their respects to the many pilots who perished during the raid of February 17, 1944. The F.S.M. has changed the name Truk to Chuuk.

Lieutenant J.E. Reulet of VF-6 from Enterprise had scored a Zero and a Rufe, while four pilots of VF-10 from *Yorktown* scored 10 victories; Lieutenant Commander Edward M. Owen shot down two Japanese interceptors, Lieutenant Robert W. Duncan got three Zeroes, Lieutenant (jg) Theodore Schofield destroyed two, one of which crashed into several parked Japanese planes, and Lieutenant (jg) Thomas McClelland scored three Japanese. Lieutenant Commander William R. Kane of VF-10 and his wingman Lieutenant (jg) Vernon Ude shot down five planes in five minutes.

Lieutenant Eugene A. Valencia of VF-9 from *Essex* became separated from his flight and soon found himself attacked by six Zeroes. The Japanese chased Valencia several miles out to sea, firing constantly but scoring no hits. The American abruptly swung the Hellcat into a 180 degree turn and shot down three of his pursuers! Eugene Valencia went on to become the U.S. Navy's third-ranking Ace with 23 official victories.

Imperial Japanese Navy Vice Admiral Jisaburo Ozawa commanded the First Mobile Fleet in the Battle of the Philippine Sea and suffered a humiliating defeat from Admiral Spruance's Fifth Fleet carriers. (U.S. Naval Historical Center)

Fleet Admiral Soemu Toyoda succeeded Admiral Koga as leader of the IJN Combined Fleet and commanded the Japanese forces in the Battles of the Philippine Sea and Leyte Gulf. (U.S. Naval Historical Center, Rear Admiral Samuel E. Morison Files)

at the very time that Admiral Nimitz was planning the Marianas invasion. Koga left behind an important strategic battle plan which was based upon Admiral Yamamoto's desire to confront the U.S. Navy in one enormous and decisive battle. Koga's plan was known as Plan Z, which called for a Japanese strike against the U.S. Navy with all available ships and aircraft as soon as the Americans entered the Philippine Sea.

Toyoda Succeeds Koga
Koga's successor was Admiral Soemu Toyoda, who was a battleship/cruiser advocate, rather than an aircraft carrier type. He, therefore, made greater use of battleships than Koga's plan intended. Much of Toyoda's Combined Fleet was confined to Japanese waters where it was relatively immobile due to the lack of fuel oil because U.S. submarines had been sinking Japanese tankers as they made the run from the East Indies to Japan.

Japanese Fuel: Dangerous and Scarce
The Japanese fuel oil problem was manifold. In addition to the U.S. submarine actions, the oil from Borneo proved to be a hazard because, although it was light and pure enough to use in boilers without refining, it contained highly volatile elements which created dangerous fire hazards. Despite the fact that the fuel oil was strained and filtered it still contained impurities which fouled the boiler

burner tips. These problems limited the Japanese naval operation to a very short distance from the Yap Islands and Woleai Atoll the western Caroline Chain.

Operation A-GO Conceived
Admiral Toyoda and the entire Japanese General Staff decided adopt a revised Plan Z because of the fuel oil situation. The ne strategy, called Operation A-GO, was devised to entice the U. Pacific Fleet into waters south of a line connecting Woleai, Yap ar Palau, and north of New Guinea, where Admiral Ozawa would l able to engage the U.S. ships and be well within his fuel oil rang Simultaneously, the island bases to the south of Palau were to pr vide shore-based aircraft that would also attack the American ship

Spruance Attacks
In apparent anticipation of Toyoda's plan, Admiral Spruan launched a lightning raid on the Palau Islands from March 30 throu April 1, 1944.

CORSAIRS JOIN HELLCATS ON U.S. CARRIERS
In the meantime, entering its second year of combat, the Voug Corsair was still not acceptable for U.S. Navy carrier deploymen Even the Royal Navy reports on carrier suitability did not sway t

Vought F4U-2 Corsair night fighters of VF(N)-101 ready for takeoff from USS Intrepid (CV-11). Note the radome on the starboard (right) wing. (U.S. Navy Photograph, Courtesy U.S. Naval Institute Photo Collection)

U.S. Navy. Finally, Jack Vospers, Vought's tireless service manager instituted "Project Dog" immediately to cure the "built-in-bounce." He went directly to the heart of the problem and improved the oleo characteristics of the landing gear strut and by April 1944 the problem was solved. Any remaining doubts about the Corsair's ability to serve from carriers were dispelled when VF-301, flying Corsairs with modified oleo struts, completed 113 landings on the *Casablanca* class escort carrier *USS Gambier Bay*. The Navy immediately ordered all Corsairs on the West Coast of the U.S. to undergo the strut modification. At last the F4U was accepted for carrier service.

Corsair Versus Zero Sen

A U.S. Navy intelligence report states: "The Zero is far inferior to the F4U-1 in level and diving speeds at all altitudes. It is inferior in climb at sea level and above 20,000 feet. Between 5,000 and 19,000 feet the Zero is slightly superior in average maximum rate of climb...However, the Zero cannot stay with the F4U-1 in high speed climbs. The superiority of the F4U at 30,000 feet is very marked." Of course, the six guns of the Corsair were far more lethal than the two 7.7 millimeter machine guns of the Zero, which had difficulty in penetrating the armor plate of the Allied planes. Even the Zero's 20 millimeter cannon had a low rate of fire and a slow muzzle velocity, which was only partially corrected later in the war. Regardless, the Corsair was the first Allied plane to surpass the performance of the Zero.

Vought Corsair Variants

Also in April 1944, the Navy accepted the Vought F4U-1D, which was fitted with pylons for carrying two 1,000 pound bombs. The

The U.S. Navy finally gave the Vought F4U Corsair approval to operate from aircraft carriers in the spring of 1944; about one year after it had entered service. Shown here are Corsairs with their characteristic upturned wing folding on CV-37 USS Princeton preparing for takeoff. Just forward of the Island are a pair of Grumman Avenger torpedo-bombers. (Sal Marrone Photo)

F4U-4 also appeared in early 1944 with a top speed of 446 miles per hour at 26,200 feet, service ceiling of 40,200 feet and a 4,400 feet per minute rate of climb. The F4U-4C was fitted with four 20 millimeter cannon having 924 rounds per gun. Rocket launchers were fitted under the outer wing panels for 5 inch HVAR rocket. An armored bucket seat was also installed. Now that the F4U had been cleared for carrier duty many Corsairs began to sail the seas as a companion to the Hellcat.

Grumman F6F-5 Hellcat

The last Grumman F6F-3 had been delivered to the U.S. Navy in the spring of 1944 and production began on the F6F-5 Hellcat in April. This was basically a cleaned up version of the F6F-3 in order to develop a higher top speed. The windshield was streamline, the landing gear fairing was improved, engine cowling reshaped for less air resistance, and armor was increased to 240 pounds. Some F6F-5's were fitted with 20 millimeter cannon; however, the majority retained the six machine guns. Maximum speed went up to 380 miles per hour at 23,400 feet and rate of climb was 2,980 feet per minute.

F6F-5 Versus Zero

Comparison with the Zero revealed the F6F-5 faster from 10,000 to 25,000 feet. The Hellcat's climb rate was inferior to the Zero up to 9,000 feet but was equal to it at 14,000 feet and the Hellcat climb rate was superior to the Zero at higher altitudes. The A6M-5 Zero was generally more maneuverable than the F6F-5 at slow speeds, especially in turns at low or medium altitudes. At 30,000 feet maneuverability was about equal for the two adversaries; however, at 10,000 feet the Zero gained one 360 degree turn in three and one half turns at slow speeds. In general, the Hellcat was the superior fighter plane by a large margin.

Coincidentally with the introduction of new models of the Hellcat and Corsair, April 1944 was a time of varied carrier activity on opposite sides of the earth.

BOMBING THE *TIRPITZ*

The German battleship *Tirpitz* had been in Kaafjord at the northern tip of Norway undergoing repairs of damage caused by Royal Navy midget submarines in September 1943. By March 1944 it was known that repairs had been completed and *Tirpitz* was ready to move out. The German battleship had posed a serious threat to convoys to the Soviet Union and forced the British to maintain a large naval force in the area. It was, therefore, decided to bomb the ship in order to cause enough damage which would prevent its leaving the fjord. It was impossible to sink the ship with dive bombing because of *Tirpitz'* heavy armor. An aerial torpedo attack was out of the question because the mountains that surrounded the ship prevented torpedo planes from making their low-level runs. Further, *Tirpitz* was encased in steel mesh torpedo nets.

The Attacking Force

Admiral Sir Michael Denny was in command of the raid with a force comprised of the two fleet carriers *HMS Victorious* and *HMS Furious*, plus the escort carriers *Searcher*, *Fencer*, *Pursuer* and

Royal Navy fleet carriers HMS Victorious and HMS Furious launched Fairey Barracuda dive bombers while Royal Navy escort carriers Searcher, Fencer, Pursuer and Emperor launched Vought Corsairs and Grumman Hellcats against the German battleship Tirpitz which was moored in Kaafjord at the northern tip of Norway on April 3,1944. Corsairs flew top cover while Barracudas bombed and Hellcats strafed. This Fleet Air Arm Corsair II has just landed on an escort carrier. (Royal Navy Photo, Courtesy Ling-Temco-Vought)

Emperor. A total of 42 Fairey Barracuda dive bombers were deployed on the fleet carriers while Vought Corsairs and Grumman Hellcats were deployed on the escort carriers. Rehearsals had been conducted in Loch Eriboll on the northern coast of Scotland before the carriers assembled about 250 miles northwest of *Tirpitz* on the afternoon of April 2.

The Attack

Surprise was essential to the success of this attack and, although the mountains surrounding the Fjord helped in this respect, it was not an easy task for the Barracuda pilots to skim over the mountains as low as possible and then abruptly attack *Tirpitz*, which would appear suddenly as the Barracudas passed over the last mountain peak.

At dawn of April 3, 1944, the carriers were 120 miles from *Tirpitz* and 21 Barracudas left *HMS Victorious* while 40 Corsairs and Hellcats were launched from the escort carriers. The planes skimmed the wave tops until they reached landfall and were forced to climb to clear the mountains. The Barracudas carried a variety of bombs: 1,600 pound armor-piercing; 500 pound semi-armor-piercing; and fragmentation anti-personnel bombs. The Corsairs flew top cover in the event that Luftwaffe Messerschmitts appeared while the Hellcats flew in ahead of the Barracudas, strafing *Tirpitz* and shoreside antiaircraft batteries. As the Fleet Air Arm planes arrived *Tirpitz* was weighing anchor to leave the fjord. Smoke generators from the ship and shore covered *Tirpitz* with dense clouds. The Barracudas followed and attacked with such efficiency that it lasted only one minute. Several hits were scored, leaving the superstructure in shambles and injuring the *Kapitän*. One dive bomber was shot down while the remainder escaped unharmed. As the first strike began its return to the carriers, the second strike of 19 Barracudas

om both fleet carriers and 39 fighters from the escort carriers were
 their way to *Tirpitz*. By the time the second strike arrived the
ip was completely enshrouded with smoke; however, it hindered
e antiaircraft batteries more than it did the attacking planes. Four-
en hits were made which put the battleship out of commission for
veral months and after that it was suitable only for coastal dense duty. One more dive bomber was shot down but all the fight-
s and remaining dive bombers of the second strike returned safely.

he Carrier Advantage

he *Tirpitz* attack was another example that the aircraft carrier had
placed the battleship as the capital ship of all major naval forces.
 would have been virtually impossible for battleship/cruiser types
 inflict the damage that the Warbirds of the Sea wrought on *Tirpitz*.
he trajectory of their guns would have been too shallow to clear
e mountains and still strike *Tirpitz*; further, the ships would have
ad to sail much closer to the fjord to be within range of the target.

*oyal Navy Admiral Sir James Somerville was in command of a task
rce comprising carriers HMS Illustrious, USS Saratoga (CV-3), HMS
hah, HMS Begum and battleships HMS Valiant, HMS Renown and
MS Queen Elizabeth for an attack on the Dutch East Indies. The
dmiral (left) talks with Saratoga's commanding officer Captain John H.
assidy while conducting conferences on Saratoga at Trincomalee,
eylon. Observe the Douglas SBD-5 Dauntless dive bomber behind the
en. (U.S. National Archives)*

CARRIER STRIKES IN DUTCH EAST INDIES

Planes from the U.S. carrier *USS Saratoga* (CV-3), Captain John
Howard Cassidy commanding, joined planes from the Royal Navy
carrier *HMS Illustrious* in a strike against the Japanese-occupied
Netherlands East Indies on April 19. The task force was commanded
by Admiral Sir James Somerville and included Royal Navy escort
carriers *Shah* and *Begum*, plus the battleships *Queen Elizabeth*,
Valiant and *Renown*.

Carrier Raid on Java and Sumatra

The targets were Sabang, an important Japanese naval base at the
northwestern tip of Sumatra, which faces the Bay of Bengal and
guarded the strategic Strait of Malacca; and Soerabaja, Japan's largest oil refinery in the East Indies at the eastern tip of Java on the
shores of the Java Sea.

Sabang Raid

Commander Joseph "Jumpin Joe" Clifton's Air Group Twelve which
included fighters, dive bombers and torpedo/bombers was assigned
to this task on *USS Saratoga*. This oldest active carrier in the U.S.
Navy was still a potent weapon and affectionately called "Saracobra"
by its officers and crew.

Early in the morning the task force arrived undetected at a point
about 100 miles from Sabang, and began launching 83 fighters and
dive bombers. The surprise was so perfect that it is reported that
FLAK did not start until after the first bombs were exploding. The
Barracuda and Helldiver dive bombers made many direct hits with
big bombs on hangars, runways, dockyards, repair shops, wharves
and power stations at Sabang. Airfields at nearby Lho Nga were
also attacked and many parked planes were destroyed, in addition
to large fuel storage tanks. Despite the fact that Admiral Somerville
held the task force no closer than 100 miles from shore, three Japanese torpedo planes managed to reach the ships, but all were shot
down by the Combat Air Patrol. In addition to shoreside damage,
two Japanese destroyers, an escort patrol ship and two cargo ships
were hit and left burning. Only one Allied plane was shot down and
this was by antiaircraft fire.

Sabang Raid Results

The success of this raid had far-reaching effects. The Allies had an
overwhelming superiority in aircraft carriers and this made Japan
depend, increasingly, on land bases to assist their dwindling carrier
force. Sabang had been used to support Imperial Japanese Navy
action in the Indian Ocean and, with its destruction, the Japanese
never again fought in the Indian Ocean. The attack on Sabang also
cut off communications between Japanese forces in Burma and the
East Indies.

Soerabaja Raid

After the Sabang raid the task force sailed in a southeasterly direction along the southern coast of the East Indies towards Soerabaja.

Oil from the Dutch East Indies was essential to the operation
of the Japanese Navy and the objective of the raid on Soerabaja
was to deprive the Japanese of most of this fuel. Commander
Clifton's three squadrons teamed up with those from *HMS Illustrious* to raid the huge refinery, oil storage tanks and tankers in the

The Supreme Allied Commander of the Southeast Asia Command Vice Admiral Lord Louis Mountbatten congratulates Commander Joseph Clifton for the outstanding performance of his Air Group Twelve in the attack on a Japanese naval base and oil refinery in the Dutch East Indies (Indonesia). (U.S. National Archives)

river and harbor. The ships were bombed and strafed from masthead level while the refinery was bombed from higher altitudes for the safety of the attacking planes. The refinery complex was entirely destroyed and left in flame and smoke. A nearby railroad yard was also destroyed.

Soerabaja Raid Results
The destruction of the Soerabaja refinery, pumping stations and oil storage tanks was a devastating blow to the Japanese war effort because it cut off a large portion of the Japanese Navy's oil supply with which it could not operate. This loss could not be replaced.

U.S. Carriers Raid New Guinea
Close on the heels of the Sabang and Soerabaja raids, more carrier action was happening three days later when Rear Admiral Daniel E. Barbey's Seventh Amphibious Corps landed two U.S. Army Divisions at Hollandia on Humboldt Bay on the north coast of Netherland New Guinea. This area is generally called Hollandia despite the fact that it is really only the name of a tiny village on an arm of Humboldt Bay.

Other landings were being made on Tanahmerah Bay and Aitape further east. This was one of General MacArthur's most brilliant operations; trapping the Japanese 18th Army at Wewak between the new landings, and the Australian troops advancing up the coast further east. Vice Admiral Mitscher's TF-58 carriers had been loaned to MacArthur to support the landings.

Mini-Carriers Take Over
Fast carriers could not be loaned for any length of time; therefor eight escort carriers quickly replaced the TF-58 fleet carriers. The escort carriers made up Task Force 78 under the command of Re Admiral Ralph E. Davison, which was divided into two task group TG-78.1, Rear Admiral Van H. Ragsdale commanding Carrier D vision 22, comprised of the carriers *Sangamon, Suwanne Chenango,* and *Santee.* and TG-78-2, Rear Admiral Davison con manding Carrier Division 24, comprised of the *Casablanca* cla carriers *Coral Sea, Natoma Bay, Manila Bay,* and *Corregidor.* T *Sangamons* were flying Hellcats and Avengers while t. *Casablancas* were equipped with Wildcats and Avengers. Each ta group included seven destroyers as a screen.

Casablancas Show Off Maneuverability
After the TF-58 carriers left, the escort carrier air groups were bu bombing, strafing and, most important, they took pictures of lan ing areas for MacArthur's next moves. It was during this operati that the *Casablanca* carriers got to show off their maneuverabili The *Casablanca* Polo-Pony characteristic of being able to turn o dime was put to good use during the execution of maneuvers d ing the Hollandia/Aitape operation. The four *Casablancas* of T 78.2 deftly wove through the four carriers of TG-78.1 with th respective courses at near right angles, passing bows across ster in an exciting display of amazing ship maneuverability.

Escort Carrier Captures U-Boat
While on the subject of *Casablanca* carriers it is of interest that t only U-boat captured by the U.S. Navy in World War II was June 4, 1944 when *USS Guadalcanal* (CVE-60) and its screen five destroyers captured U-505 off the Atlantic coast of Afri Forced to the surface by aircraft, the U-boat was boarded by a pa that the carrier's Captain Daniel V. Gallery had organized in anti pation of just such an occasion. The U-505 is now an exhibit in t Chicago Museum of Science and Industry. Conversely, on May 2 1944 the escort carrier conversion *USS Block Island* became t only American carrier sunk in the Atlantic when it was torpedo by U-549 northwest of the Canary Islands.

The only submarine captured by the U.S. Navy during World War II wa taken by the Casablanca Class mini-carrier USS Guadalcanal on June 4, 1944. This was the first U.S. Navy wartime boarding operation sinc the War of 1812. Note the carrier in the background with folded wing Grumman Avengers on deck (arrow). (Official U.S. Navy Photograph, News Photo Division)

USN GROWING STRONGER - IJN GETTING WEAKER

It was becoming increasingly obvious that Japan would not win the war because the Japanese could not hope to compete with America's industrial production. In less than two and one-half years of war U.S. Navy carriers had demolished the greater proportion of Japan's sea and air power and the U.S. Navy was recognized as the greatest sea power the world had ever seen. Yet, there were fiercer battles to be fought by the carriers and their Warbirds before Peace could be declared.

Essex Long Hull Carriers Commissioned

America's carrier strength increased rapidly as more Essex class ships were commissioned. On April 15 the Essex class carrier Hancock (CY-19) was commissioned. Ticonderoga (CV-14) joined the Pacific Fleet on May 8. This was the first long hull Essex carrier which had a longer hull and a shortened flight deck in order that four 40 millimeter antiaircraft mounts could be installed fore and aft with wide arcs of fire. This change was repeated in 14 later Essex class carriers.

Second Truk Strike

In order to ensure Truk's impotence Admiral Spruance ordered units of the Fifth Fleet to repeat the bombardment of February during April 29-May 1, 1944. Admiral Mitscher's carriers made their strike on the fleet base at Truk and the port facilities at Ponape, east of Truk. Ponape was also shelled by Rear Admiral Willis A. Lee's battleships. The airfield on Satawan, southeast of Truk was shelled by Rear Admiral Jesse B. Oldendorf's cruisers.

Forrestal Becomes Navy Secretary

Meanwhile, James V. Forrestal was sworn in as the 48th Secretary of the Navy on May 19, 1944. He was one of the most dedicated holders of that important office and carried his fight for bigger and better aircraft carriers in the U.S. Navy into the postwar years which ended tragically.

BATTLE OF THE PHILIPPINE SEA

Two huge Japanese and American Fleets were preparing for separate operations, A-GO and Forager, in May 1944. The opposing fleets engaged in one of the decisive confrontations of the Pacific War; Battle of the Philippine Sea which included the Marianas Turkey Shoot.

Operation A-GO Preparations

During early May, in preparation for Admiral Toyoda's Operation A-GO, Admiral Ozawa sailed his First Mobile Fleet, which included nine carriers, to the naval anchorage at Tawitawi. This is one of the southernmost islands of the Philippines just east of northern Borneo. Tawitawi is a strategic island in the Celebes Sea less than 200 miles from the Borneo oil depot at Tarakan from where the Japanese Fleet could obtain quick deliveries of Borneo's unprocessed petroleum. The disadvantages of Tawitawi were that it had no airfield on which to train new carrier air groups and that it was located in waters infested with American submarines.

James V. Forrestal, with hand on Bible, takes the oath of office as Secretary of the Navy on May 19, 1944. Among the attendees shown here in uniform are General Eisenhower, U.S. Army; Admiral Nimitz, U.S. Navy; and General Spaatz, U.S. Army Air Corps. (U.S. National Archives)

MacArthur Finds Operation A-GO Plans

As the Fates would have it, a copy of the preliminary outline of Operation A-GO was captured during General MacArthur's invasion of Hollandia. This important information lost no time in reaching Admirals Nimitz, Spruance and Kinkaid. The discovery remained unknown to the Japanese.

Operation Forager (Marianas Invasion)

Admiral Nimitz ordered Admiral Spruance to plan and schedule an invasion of Saipan and Guam in the Marianas. This was to be the first American attack within the Japanese inner defensive perimeter and the coming battle was to be 1,000 miles from the closest American base. The new fleet carriers were to play their most important role thus far. Saipan was needed as a base for Boeing B-29 bombers so they could reach Japan. Spruance led units of the Fifth Fleet to anchor in Majura Lagoon in the Marshalls where he met with his staff and admirals to plan the attack.

Wake and Marcus Island Strikes

In the meantime, Admiral Mitscher ordered Rear Admiral A.E.

Units of the Fifth Fleet are shown at anchor in Majuro Lagoon at Majuro Atoll in the Ratak Chain of the Marshall Islands in early June 1944 prior Operation Forager. USS Essex is in the foreground while other Essex class carriers and Independence class carriers are in the background with battleships and smaller ships. (U.S. National Archives)

Montgomery to lead his Task Group 58.6 comprised of fleet carriers *Essex* and *Wasp* and the light carrier *San Jacinto* to raid Wake Island, north of the Marshalls, and Marcus Island, northwest of Wake Island.

Lieutenant Commander David McCampbell, air group Commander on *USS Essex*, led 11 Hellcats, eight Avengers, and 15 Helldivers into the air at 6:30 AM on May 19 for the first strike on Marcus Island. While the Hellcats strafed and flew top cover, the Avengers dropped 500 pound bombs and the Helldivers dropped 500 and 1,000 pound bombs. Three more raids that day dropped bombs weighing 2,000 pounds, which destroyed the runways and other important installations. The carriers steamed away but returned on May 20 to raid Marcus twice more to finish the job.

During the May 19 attack on Marcus Island, McCampbell was flying an F6F-3 Hellcat named Monsoon Maiden. Early in the strike, his plane was hit by antiaircraft fire that damaged the after fuselage and controls, also setting the auxiliary fuel tank afire. Instead of turning back he remained over the target until all bombs and ammunition were expended. McCampbell then nursed the severely damaged Hellcat back to *Essex* and, as soon as he clambered to

safety, the plane was pushed over the side as a total wreck. He w awarded the Distinguished Flying Cross for this act of bravery a dedication.

Commander McCampbell was to become the U.S. Navy's lea ing Ace with 34 official victories to his credit. McCampbell h won his wings in April 1938. He organized Fighting Squadron in September 1943 and in February 1944 McCampbell took co mand of Air Group 15. The air group comprised fighters, dive bom ers and torpedo bombers, and it was McCampbell's job to lead the squadrons into battle and coordinate the attacks. Under his co mand, Air Group 15 became known as Fabled Fifteen and duri its seven months of action the unit destroyed 315 Japanese aircr in aerial combat, and 348 on the ground. Fabled Fifteen also sa 296,000 tons of Japanese shipping.

Task Group 58.6 again raided Wake Island on May 23 and turned to Majura Lagoon by the 26th.

U.S. Navy Marianas Preparations

Admiral Spruance prepared his Marianas forces at once, which co sisted of a vast collection of diverse task groups and units.

A Curtiss Helldiver is brought up on a deck edge elevator for a bombing strike. Although the plane appears crowded on the elevator, the Helldiver was designed to enable two to fit on Essex class elevators. (Sal Marrone Photograph)

Task Force 58 Reorganized

Admiral Mitscher had been reorganizing his Task Force 58 to be prepared, not only to support Operation Forager (the Marianas assaults) but to also be able to meet Ozawa's force head-on and inflict a crushing defeat: Task Group 58.1, Rear Admiral J.J. "Jocko" Clark commanding, comprised the *Essex* class carriers *Hornet* and *Yorktown* with the light carriers *Belleau Wood* and *Bataan*, cruisers *Boston*, *Baltimore* and *Canberra*; antiaircraft light cruisers *Oakland* and *San Juan*, plus 14 destroyers; Task Group 58.2, Rear Admiral Alfred E. Montgomery commanding, comprised the *Essex* class carriers *Bunker Hill* and *Wasp*, light carriers *Cabot* and *Monterey*, light cruisers *Mobile*, *Biloxi* and *Santa Fe*, plus 12 destroyers; Task Group 58.3, Rear Admiral John W. Reeves commanding, comprised the prewar *Enterprise* (still going strong) and the *Essex* class carrier *Lexington*, light carriers *San Jacinto* and *Princeton*, cruiser *Indianapolis*, antiaircraft light cruisers *Cleveland*, *Reno*, *Montpelier* and *Birmingham*, plus 13 destroyers; Task Group 58.4, Rear Admiral W. K. Harrill commanding, comprised *USS Essex*, light fleet carriers *Cowpens* and *Langley*, antiaircraft light cruisers *San Diego*, *Miami*, *Houston* and *Vincennes*, plus 14 destroyers; The support group was Task Group 58.7, Vice Admiral W.A. Lee commanding, comprised of battleships *Iowa*, *North Carolina*, *Washington*, *New Jersey*, *Alabama*, *South Dakota* and *Indiana*, cruisers *Wichita*, *San Francisco*, *New Orleans* and *Minneapolis*, plus 13 destroyers; It required about 100,000 men to man the ships and planes of TF-58.

Fifth Fleet Commander-In-Chief, Admiral Raymond A. Spruance, chose *USS Indianapolis* as his flagship, while Task Force 58 Commander, Vice Admiral Marc A. Mitscher, had selected *USS Lexington* as his flagship.

Admiral Turner and the Invasion Forces

Vice Admiral Richmond K. Turner was in command of the Joint Expeditionary Force, Task Force 51, and was in overall command of the amphibious landings on Saipan, Tinian and Guam. He was also in personal command of the Saipan-Tinian invasion force TG-52, which he was training in Hawaii, while Rear Admiral Richard L. Conolly was in command of the Guam invasion force TF-53, which he was training in Guadalcanal. Task Force 52 was known as

the Northern Attack Force, while Task Force 53 was known as the Southern Attack Force.

Mini-Carrier Forces

In addition to Task Force 58, three task groups of escort carriers had been assigned to Operation Forager: Task Group 52.14, Rear Admiral Gerald F. Bogan commanding, consisted of two task units of *Casablanca* class carriers; Task Unit 52.14.1, Rear Admiral Bogan commanding, comprised *Fanshaw Bay* and *Midway* (later renamed *St. Lo*); four destroyers provided the screen; Task Unit 52.14.2, Captain Oscar A. Weller commanding, included *White Plains* and *Kalinin Bay*; Task Group 52.11, Rear Admiral Harold B. Sallada commanding, consisted of two task units of *Casablanca* class carriers; Task Unit 52.11.1, Rear Admiral Sallada commanding, comprised *Kitkun Bay* and *Gambier Bay*, three destroyers provided the screen; Task Unit 52.11.2, Rear Admiral Felix B. Stump commanding, consisted of *Corregidor* and *Coral Sea* (later renamed *Anzio*), three destroyers provided the screen.

Each *Casablanca* class carrier operated from 20 to 28 Wildcats and Avengers. Task Unit 53.7.1, Rear Admiral Van H. Ragsdale commanding, consisted of three converted tankers: *Sangamon*, *Suwannee* and *Chenango*. Each carrier operated 31 Hellcats and Avengers. Four destroyers provided the screen.

Operations Forager and A-GO Collide

All units involved in Operation Forager had converged on Majuro Lagoon in the Marshall Islands and on June 6, 1944, which was the D-Day invasion of Normandy on the other side of the world, the American Armada set sail for the Marianas. By June 11, 1944, Task Force 58 was about 300 miles east of Guam and launched over 200 Hellcats and Avengers against Saipan and Tinian in order to reduce Japanese aerial resistance. During that night TG-58.1 headed for Guam, while TG-58.2, TG-58.3 and TG-58.4 went for Saipan and Tinian.

The Japanese order to prepare for Operation A-GO had been issued on May 20, 1944, and all shore bases of the Japanese First Air Fleet were alerted because the island bases were to work in cooperation with the Japanese carriers. Additional planes had been

A Grumman F6F-5 Hellcat is about to have its engine started for a raid to reduce Japanese aerial resistance on Saipan and Tinian. The Hellcats strafed airfields and shot down any Japanese aircraft that were able to takeoff. (U.S. National Archives)

sent to Saipan, Guam and Tinian in the Marianas, plus Truk, Yap and Palau. Several less important bases were also alerted and bolstered with aircraft. Admiral Ozawa expected the First Air Fleet to destroy at least one third of Spruance's carriers and most of any amphibious operations launched by the Americans. Apparently, he was not aware of the destruction wrought by the U.S. Fifth Fleet carrier forces on key Japanese bases.

During an extended raid on the Marianas Island of Pagan, on June 11, 1944, Air Group 15 leader, Commander David McCampbell, scored the first of his 34 victories. On June 13 his Air Group destroyed 50,000 tons of Japanese shipping and Commander McCampbell was awarded the Navy Gold Star for this action.

U.S. Submarines Harass Mobile Fleet
Admiral Ozawa's optimism began to fade because of the continual U.S. submarine attacks in the Tawitawi anchorage. Two tankers had been sunk by *USS Puffer* a few days after the Mobile Fleet arrived at Tawitawi and during the night of June 6-7 *USS Harder* sank the destroyers *Minazuki* and *Hayanami*. On the night of June 8, 1944 the Japanese destroyer *Tanikazi* was sunk by a salvo of four torpedoes from *USS Harder*.

I.J.N. First Mobile Fleet Departs
When Admiral Toyoda learned of the air attacks against the Marianas on June 11, he ordered Admiral Ozawa to destroy the American Fleet. Operation A-GO was now underway and the First Mobile Fleet departed Tawitawi on June 13, 1944.

First Mobile Fleet Units
The Imperial Japanese Navy First Mobile Fleet under Commander-In-Chief Vice Admiral Jisaburo Ozawa comprised the following forces: Van Force - Vice Admiral Takeo Kurita commanding in *Atago;* light fleet carriers *Zuiho, Chitose* and *Chiyoda*; battleships *Yamato, Haruna, Kongo* and *Musashi*; cruisers *Atago, Maya, Chokai* and *Takeo*; plus nine destroyers. Force A - Vice Admiral Ozawa commanding in *Taiho*; fleet carriers *Taiho, Zuikaku* and *Shokaku*; cruisers *Haguro* and *Myoko*; light cruiser *Yahagi*; plus nine destroyers. Force B Rear Admiral T. Joshima commanding; fleet carriers *Hiyo* and *Junyo*; light fleet carrier *Ryuho*; battleship *Nagato*; cruiser *Mogami*; plus 10 destroyers.

U.S. Submarines Tracking First Mobile Fleet
As the First Mobile Fleet weighed anchor at Tawitawi the U.S. submarine *Redfin* was watching and reported the move. Two days later the U.S. submarine *Flying Fish* saw the Japanese ships entering San Bernardino Strait, the water passage between the Philippine Islands of Luzon and Samar, and the U.S. submarine *Seahorse* reported the fleet exiting on the eastern side. Admiral Ozawa then split his ships into two forces.

U.S. Saipan Invasion
In the early morning of June 15, 1944 American troops began the Saipan invasion but, by nightfall it was apparent that conquest of Saipan would be very difficult and reserves had to be called. The slow progress of the troop invasion, coupled with the submarine reports on the Mobile Fleet movements forced Admiral Spruance to cancel the planned assault on Guam.

Spruance Protects Invasion Force
Although some of his admirals pressed Spruance to search and destroy the Japanese force, the prudent Commander-In-Chief refused to be lured away from the Saipan invasion force, the protection of which he correctly regarded as his primary objective.

Mitscher's TF-58 Strikes Marianas Bases
By June 13 Task Groups 58.1 and 58.4 had headed north for air raids on Pagan, in the center of the Marianas, as well as on Iwo Jima and Chichi Jima, north of the Marianas. Task Groups 58.2 and 58.3 continued to cover the Saipan landings and conducted air raids on Tinian, Rota, and other islands in the Marianas.

Ozawa Heads For TF-58
When Admiral Ozawa learned of the strikes on the three northern islands and the state of the fighting on Saipan, he reasoned that a large American Fleet must be in the vicinity of the embattled island. Ozawa was determined to find the American Fleet and strike the first blow because he understood that the failure of the Japanese Force to locate the Americans at Midway and make the first strike contributed to the Japanese defeat. Ozawa did not know that the island airfields and planes of the First Air Fleet under Vice Admiral Kakuji Kakuta, on which he had depended so heavily, had been decimated by the Fifth Fleet. His concern was to locate the American Task Force and he sent his scouts out to find it. Admiral Ozawa planned to keep his heavy punch Force A about 400 miles away from Task Force 58 and beyond its range. He planned to use the Van Force as a decoy by sailing it 300 miles from the American carriers. He reasoned that the Americans would be lured by the Van Force at which time his Force A planes would attack TF-58 from their distant carriers because they had a longer range than the heavier American planes. By using this tactic Ozawa expected his Force A to attack the American carriers of TF-58 with complete surprise knowing that the U.S. planes could not reach his Force A carriers.

Spruance Refuses Strike On Mobile Fleet
On the night of June 18 Ozawa broke radio silence to send a message to Admiral Kakuta on Tinian. This brief transmission was enough for Spruance to establish the Japanese Fleet's location. He did not, however, know their strength, which was information Spruance desperately needed. With the First Mobile Force location known, Admiral Mitscher urged Admiral Spruance to give him permission to head full speed westward toward the Japanese Fleet so that by dawn TG-58 would be in position to launch a strike against the Japanese ships. Admiral Spruance was aware of the Japanese tactic of using decoy forces to lure the U.S. Navy away from the primary target and he feared that the other half of the Japanese Fleet would attack the beachhead as soon as TF-58 departed. Admiral Spruance, therefore, refused to approve Admiral Mitscher's request.

Spruance's tactic for guarding the beachhead was to steam westward during the day and eastward at night in order to reduce the possibility of the Japanese Fleet passing TF-58 in the darkness.

Japanese Snoopers Out In Force

It was during the early morning hours of June 19, 1944, while TF-58 was still heading eastward, that a Japanese reconnaissance plane from Guam located the American ships, dropped a flare to verify its discovery, and returned to base with the news. *Enterprise* quickly launched 15 radar-equipped Avengers to find the Japanese Fleet but the search was a failure. By dawn's light another Japanese reconnaissance plane scanned the task force but was shot down only 37 miles from the U.S. ships. Ozawa was moving in fast and was eager to strike with hslp from Admiral Kakuta's planes and airfields on Guam to implement the shuttle tactic. Hellcats were launched at once to reconnoiter Guam and observed planes landing from some of the other Japanese-held islands because Admiral Kakuta was getting ready for Operation A-GO. About 50 of the Japanese planes were shot down by the Hellcats between 7:00 and 8:00 o'clock that morning while others were destroyed on the runway and tarmac by strafing. This rendered the airfield temporarily useless. Meanwhile, *USS Langley* aircraft shot down about six Japanese snoopers.

Ozawa Attacks

Admiral Ozawa's Force A launched the first strike at 9:30 in the morning of June 19, which comprised 45 new Aichi D4Y3 radial engine Judy dive bombers on their first raid, eight new torpedo-carrying Jills, and 16 Zero fighter escorts. The Judy was initially mistaken for a Zero by the American airmen. Ozawa's strike planes were picked up on battleship radar at a range of 150 miles. Task Force 58 carriers turned into the wind to launch their Hellcats at once. The carriers had been preparing for an offensive operation and there was no time to strike down the dive bombers and torpedo planes that were arranged on the decks. In order not to duplicate the Japanese dilemma at Midway these planes were ordered to take off to clear the decks and, while airborne, the dive bombers finished the job on Guam while the torpedo planes circled until the 300 Hellcats were in thc air.

The intercepting Hellcats began leaving the carriers at about 10:15 AM of June 19 and climbed to 24,000 feet in order to be well above the Judy dive bombers which were flying at 18,000 feet. Lieutenant (JG) George R. Carr as leader of the second division of four Hellcats scored well against Ozawa's first strike. At the onset he flamed a Judy which exploded seconds later, forcing Carr to fly through the debris. As he sped under the Judy formation the lieutenant maneuvered onto the tail of another Judy and his six guns sent it spiraling into the sea. While Carr was scoring his second victory of the day a Zero fighter got on his tail and, as he evaded his attacker, he saw another Zero coming at him dead ahead. Both pilots fired and the Zero burst into flames. One of the Mitsubishi bullets lodged in Carr's windshield impairing his vision somewhat, but despite this obstruction, he sighted two more Zero fighters ahead. He got on the tail of the nearest fighter and a short burst set the Zero afire. It appeared that the pilot bailed out but no parachute opened. Lieutenant Carr quickly shifted to the second Zero and set it smoking, but before he could fire a second burst the Zero exploded. Five victories in one morning within 10 minutes is quite an achievement.

Lieutenant (jg) George R. Carr shot down five Japanese planes while he was intercepting an air attack on the Saipan invasion force. Carr scored 11 1/2 victories during the war. He was a member of Air Group 15, known as Fabled Fifteen. (Official U.S. Navy Photograph, News Photo Division)

Ozawa's First Strike Results

By 11:00 AM the raid had broken up and, of the 69 planes in Ozawa's first strike, only 27 returned, but not all the planes of the Japanese force were successfully driven off. Several Japanese planes broke through and scored a direct hit on the battleship *South Dakota*, which killed 27 crew and injured 23. A badly damaged Jill rammed the battleship *Indiana* but the torpedo did not explode. The cruiser *Minneapolis* received a near-miss but sustained no damage.

Admiral Ozawa's second strike left at about 9:55 AM and consisted of 53 Aichi Judy dive bombers, 27 Nakajima Jill torpedo bombers, and 48 Zero fighters.

Taiho Torpedoed - A Hero Saves Her

While Ozawa's second strike was taking off, the U.S. submarine Albacore had managed to penetrate Ozawa's Force A defenses and fired six torpedoes at the new Japanese carrier *Taiho* as it was launching aircraft. One struck the hull and a second torpedo was heading for a direct hit when Warrant Officer Sakio Komatsu, who had just taken off, spotted the tin fish and saved his carrier by diving onto the torpedo. The torpedo exploded, his plane disintegrated and the *Taiho* escaped with minor damage. Although *Taiho* was well-armored and the torpedo hit was not lethal, she did suffer internal

USS Bunker Hill (CV-17) suffered several near misses from Admiral Ozawa's dive bombers on June 19, 1944. Although near misses appear harmless the underwater explosion can send damaging shocks through the ship which will fracture piping, split tanks and hull plating, break access ladders and jam elevators if repeated near misses are in the same general area. Bunker Hill escaped serious damage from the explosions of June 19. Observe the Japanese plane tumbling out of control with its tail shot off (arrow). (U.S. National Archives)

Commander David McCampbell shot down seven Japanese aircraft in two sorties on June 19, 1944 during the Battle of the Philippine Sea. The Commander went on to become the U.S. Navy's top Ace of World War II. (Official U.S. Naval Photograph, News Photo Division)

injuries that were not readily apparent. The shock of the explosion had cracked one of the aviation gasoline tanks, which would reveal itself later in a most deadly manner. Damage control parties discovered that the forward aircraft elevator had jammed and when they went below to repair the elevator they found gasoline in the elevator pit. The ventilating system was then turned on full blast to dissipate the fumes but this actually distributed the fumes throughout the ship.

Ozawa's Second Strike

The second Japanese Force A strike was detected when the raiders were 120 miles away. This gave the Hellcats plenty of time to make the interception well before the Japanese planes reached the American ships.

Commander David McCampbell led a dozen Hellcats from *Essex* in the second interception wave at 11:40 AM of June 19, 1944. He quickly latched onto a Judy and blew it apart with a short burst from the Hellcat's six guns. The Commander scored four more Judy dive bombers that morning. The scene was one of carnage as Japanese planes streaked through the sky in flames, smoking, or shedding wings or tails and the sea became pock-marked with foam as the planes splashed onto the water. Of the 119 planes in the second strike only 41 returned to the First Mobile Fleet because of the almost impenetrable defense put up by the Grumman Hellcats.

Ozawa's Second Strike Results

About 20 strike planes managed to break through the Hellcats only to face the overwhelming massed antiaircraft fire of the battleships, destroyers and cruisers. The Japanese attackers managed to shoot up some destroyers, inflicted minor damage on *Bunker Hill* and *Wasp*, bounced a torpedo off *Indiana*'s hull which failed to explode, and dropped two near-misses on *Alabama*. This poor performance by the Japanese pilots was probably due not only to the antiaircraft fire and the harassing Hellcats, but also their lack of training and experience.

Shokaku Sinks

In order to afford the maximum protection for his precious fleet carriers Admiral Ozawa arranged his Mobile Fleet with the three light carriers of the Van Force leading up front of the force with the destroyers. This tactic was intended to stop any American air attack before it could reach the six fleet carriers at the rear of the formation. Apparently Ozawa did not consider the possibility of a submarine attack because he left the rear of the formation virtually unguarded. June 19, 1944 saw American submarines out in force near Saipan and among them was *Cavalla*, which had followed the First Mobile Fleet doggedly through the night until it found the ideal attacking position at 12:20 PM. As the Japanese carrier *Shokaku* was recovering its air group, Lieutenant Commander H.J. Kossler fired six torpedoes; three of which hit the big carrier. Smoke and flames erupted from below decks as the aviation gasoline tanks ignited, forcing the carrier out of action. The crew fought the fires for over two hours as they became progressively worse. At 3:00 PM the *Shokaku* rumbled with an enormous explosion as the bomb stowage ignited, setting off torpedoes in a chain reaction. The ship literally came apart and the flaming wreck sank with hundreds of her crew.

Taiho Sinks

Within the hour after *Shokaku* sank, the *Taiho* damage control officer informed Ozawa that his crew could not repair the damage; whereupon, the Admiral and his staff transferred to the cruiser *Haguro* and later switched to *Zuikaku* because of communication problems on *Haguro*. It will be recalled that an aviation gasoline tank had cracked and the ventilating fans were turned on to dissipate the fumes on *Taiho*. The fumes travelled throughout the ship and eventually entered an electric generator compartment or other sparking electrical equipment which set off a series of violent explosions. The Flight Deck buckled, the sides bulged and large holes were blown into the ship bottom. Only 500 of the 2,100 man crew survived as the flaming *Taiho* sank beneath the waves.

Ozawa's Third Strike

Force B carriers had launched 47 planes in midmorning, which arrived at the American ships about 1:00 PM. Hellcats from *Hornet* and *Yorktown* broke up the raid in its early stages without TF-58 suffering any damage. Some of the Japanese escaped to Guam and Tinian, putting the shuttle system to good use.

Mitscher Discovers Shuttle System

When Admiral Mitscher learned that the various island airfields

Lucky pilot! When a Hellcat pilot was waved off from a landing on USS Enterprise his arresting hook accidently caught a cable as he gunned the engine. This spectacular crash resulted. What appears to be the pilot making a miraculous escape is really Lieutenant Walter Chewing, Jr. climbing onto the flaming plane to save the pilot, which he did! Lieutenant Chewing was awarded the Navy and Marine Corps Medal for his outstanding bravery. (Official U.S. Navy Photograph, News Photo Division)

were being used by the raiding carrier planes, he ordered more strikes to insure the airfields would be useless. At 2:25 PM Commander McCampbell led a dozen Hellcats to a raid on Guam; bombing and strafing the airfield.

Ozawa's Fourth Strike Decimated

A fourth strike had been launched by Force B just before noon, using up *Zuikaku*'s reserve aircraft to bring the attacking force to a total of 87 aircraft. This force failed to find Spruance's ships; therefore, the pilots decided to spend the night on Guam and resume the attack on the following day. The planes of the fourth strike arrived over Guam at 2:30; just in time to meet McCampbell and his dozen Hellcats, which were joined by 15 more Hellcats. All but 19 of the

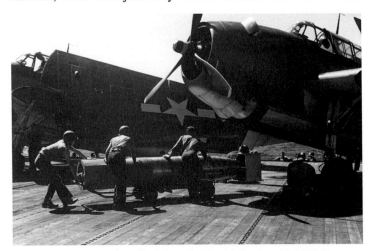

Grumman Avengers were fitted with bombs and/or torpedoes for the attack on the Japanese First Mobile Fleet in the Battle of the Philippine Sea. A torpedo is being rolled under an Avenger to be installed in the bomb bay. (Official U.S. Navy Photograph, News Photo Division)

Japanese were shot down as they desperately looked for an airstrip. Many fought back but were outclassed by the well-trained and experienced Hellcat pilots. McCampbell shot down two more Japanese aircraft in this melee to bring his score for June 19, 1944 to seven victories.

Ozawa Retreats

Admiral Ozawa, located as he was so far from the action, had no idea of the overwhelming defeat suffered by his pilots and he rejected Admiral Kurita's suggestion to return to Japan. When very few planes returned to the carriers Ozawa assumed that they had landed on the island airfields assigned to the shuttle bombing operation. He was refueling for another strike when Admiral Toyoda, having heard of the damaging island airfield raids, ordered Ozawa to return to Japan. The First Mobile Fleet then steamed slowly northwestward.

Spruance Attacks Mobile Fleet

Meanwhile, Spruance was planning his next move and this would be to attack Ozawa's Mobile Fleet; except that its location was unknown. Finally, at 3:40 on the afternoon of June 20, Lieutenant R.S. Nelson, an Avenger pilot from *USS Enterprise*, found the Japanese Fleet. Admiral Mitscher estimated the Mobile Fleet to be 275 miles away, which would be a long strike for the American planes. Further, it was getting late, which would force the pilots to return in the dark; but tomorrow would be too late. Mitscher, on the flag bridge of *USS Lexington*, Captain Arleigh A. Burke commanding, sent a message to Spruance requesting permission to launch a strike, which was quickly granted.

It was 4:21 PM when Task Force 58 turned into the wind and launched 77 Helldivers, 54 Avengers, and 85 Hellcats from *Lexington*, *Wasp*, *Enterprise*, *Bunker Hill*, *Hornet* and *Yorktown*. The Hellcats and Helldivers carried drop tanks to extend their range.

Mitscher's planes reached the Japanese ships about 7:00 o'clock in the evening. Ozawa's carriers were well out in front, followed by the battleships and cruisers, while the oilers and destroyers were far astern. The first Japanese ships to be sighted were the oilers and destroyers, but very few Americans attacked them because the prime targets were Ozawa's seven carriers.

Hiyo Sinks

Lieutenant (JG) George B. Brown led his five torpedo-armed Avengers from *Belleau Wood* in an attack on *Hiyo*. The antiaircraft fire was devastating and part of Brown's port wing was shot off and fires started as he began his approach. Brown ordered his gunner and radio man to bail out, then continued on alone. As he neared the carrier the fire burned itself out. The brave and determined lieutenant completed his attack and scored a direct hit on *Hiyo*. His wingman launched but missed; however, a third torpedo, launched by Lieutenant (JG) Warren R. Omark, blew up against the carrier's hull and started a thunderous explosion. Two Japanese battleships attempted to assist the stricken carrier but all was in vain as the still smoking *Hiyo* made her final plunge to the depths of the sea.

Lieutenant Brown's wingman, Lieutenant (JG) Benjamin C. Tate, found his leader at about 10,000 feet and reformed alongside. Brown's Avenger was badly damaged and it was flying erratically which suggested that the hero was seriously wounded. They were separated in the action and Lieutenant Brown disappeared.

The Avenger crews in other squadrons could not duplicate the achievement of Lieutenant Brown and Lieutenant Omark because their Avengers were fitted with 500 pound bombs. Although these were courageously dropped with precision, the 500 pounders failed to cause any vital damage, except that *Enterprise* Helldivers started fires on *Zuikaku*, which were quickly extinguished. It appears that the U.S. Navy had less confidence in the aerial torpedo than either the Fleet Air Arm or the Imperial Japanese Navy.

Chiyoda, *Haruna*, *Ryuho*, and *Maya* were hit with 500 pound bombs, causing damage that was quickly repaired in time for the next battle.

Night Landings

The returning Hellcats, Helldivers and Avengers were forced to make the long trip in the darkness, where all manner of perils taunted them. Almost half of the returning aircraft landed on the wrong carriers and, on at least one occasion, planes from seven or eight different carriers found themselves on one deck! About 3[?] Helldivers, 17 Hellcats and 28 Avengers were destroyed by ditching at sea or crashing on flight decks; however, only 16 pilots and 33 crewmen had been killed in these mishaps.

Resounding Japanese Defeat

So ended the Battle of The Philippine Sea, often called the Mariana Turkey Shoot because of the resounding defeat inflicted upon the Japanese airmen by the American pilots of Admiral Spruance's Fifth Fleet. The victory becomes more vivid when we realize that the First Mobile Fleet carriers started the battle with 473 aircraft and after eight straight hours of combat Admiral Ozawa was left with only 35 operable planes. Only 23 U.S. planes were shot down. This had been one of the greatest carrier battles of all time and one of the most decisive battles of the war that even dwarfed the size of the Battle of Midway. After his defeat Ozawa tried to resign but Admiral Toyoda refused to accept the resignation.

Spruance Remained On The Job

Admiral Spruance, in his hour of victory, came under undue criticism because of his cautious strategy, particularly from U.S. naval aviators who had wanted to abandon the beachhead and sail to attack the Japanese carriers once they had been sighted. If the two sides had exchanged simultaneous attacks, more Japanese carriers would have been destroyed, but conversely, U.S. casualties would have also been heavy. In that event Spruance would not have been able to put up that impenetrable wall of fighters to repel the Japanese attacks. The Spruance tactic proved correct because, while conducting his primary operation of guarding the Saipan invasion, he managed to destroy the trained Japanese carrier air crews, which could not be easily replaced. Without air crews the Japanese carriers became useless.

Fighter Directors Deserve Credit

Unsung heroes of the air battles of June 19, 1944 were the fighter directors whose job it was to deploy and direct fighter aircraft to meet the various Japanese attacks. The fighter director had to quickly

This unusual photograph of USS Enterprise (CV-6), the Big E, was taken by the crew of a Douglas SBD Dauntless that has just taken off for a strike at Tinian Island. Note the remaining Dauntless dive bombers on the Flight Deck. USS Lexington (CV-16) can be seen in the right background. (U.S. Naval Historic Center)

estimate how many interceptors would be needed to stop each consecutive Japanese strike and still hold enough in reserve for future raids. Each fighter group was controlled by its own fighter director who controlled the planes until the missions had been accomplished. In addition to talking to their pilots, they also conferred among themselves in order to cooperate and coordinate their aircraft interceptions, which worked exceedingly well. It was not an easy task.

Guam Invasion and Tinian Strikes Resumed

Although Task Force 58 of the Fifth Fleet had given the First Mobile Fleet a conclusive defeat by keeping it away from Saipan the job was far from complete. Spruance had reinstated the Guam invasion and scheduled it for the last week in July; therefore, the island had to be prepared for the landings. In addition, the troops fighting on Saipan needed air support and the impending invasion of Tinian required more preparation by the squadrons of TF-58. Softening up the three principal islands plus some ancillary islands

began on June 21, the day following the Philippine Sea Battle, with raids on Agana Airfield in the middle of Guam, as well as supporting the troops on Saipan. Guam bore the brunt of the attacks and Rota, just north of Guam, was hit on the 27th and 29th. On July 4 and 5 Japanese installations on Chichi Jima Retto, Haha Jima Retto, and Iwo Jima were bombed and strafed. By July 9 Saipan had fallen to the American troops, thanks to the dedicated air support. On July 21 American Forces made landings on the beaches of Guam at three points (Operation Stevedore). Two days later American troops invaded Tinian Island.

By July 29 American troops were in control of Guam's Orote Peninsula and the airfield plus other strategic areas. To celebrate the heartening progress, on the afternoon of the 29th Admiral Spruance, General Holland Smith, Marine Lieutenant General Roy Geiger and Army Brigadier General L.C. Shepherd attended a ceremony on the former American parade grounds to celebrate the recapture of the former American possession.

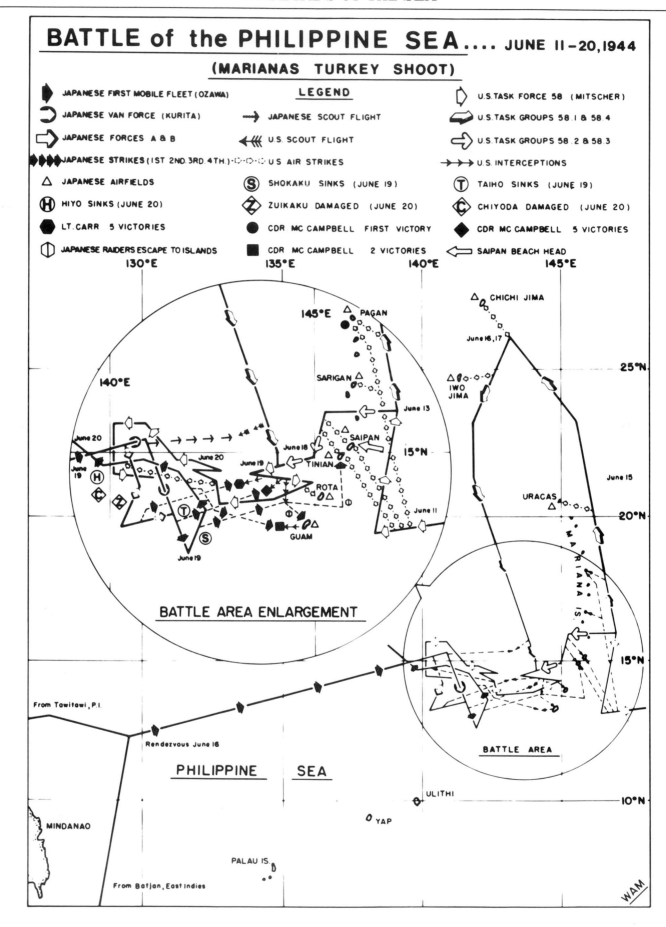

BATTLE of the PHILIPPINE SEA.... JUNE 11–20, 1944

(MARIANAS TURKEY SHOOT)

LEGEND

- JAPANESE FIRST MOBILE FLEET (OZAWA)
- JAPANESE VAN FORCE (KURITA)
- JAPANESE FORCES A & B
- JAPANESE STRIKES (1ST 2ND.3RD.4TH.)
- JAPANESE AIRFIELDS
- HIYO SINKS (JUNE 20)
- LT. CARR 5 VICTORIES
- JAPANESE RAIDERS ESCAPE TO ISLANDS

- JAPANESE SCOUT FLIGHT
- U.S. SCOUT FLIGHT
- US AIR STRIKES
- SHOKAKU SINKS (JUNE 19)
- ZUIKAKU DAMAGED (JUNE 20)
- CDR MC CAMPBELL FIRST VICTORY
- CDR MC CAMPBELL 2 VICTORIES

- U.S. TASK FORCE 58 (MITSCHER)
- U.S. TASK GROUPS 58.1 & 58.4
- U.S. TASK GROUPS 58.2 & 58.3
- U.S. INTERCEPTIONS
- TAIHO SINKS (JUNE 19)
- CHIYODA DAMAGED (JUNE 20)
- CDR MC CAMPBELL 5 VICTORIES
- SAIPAN BEACH HEAD

130°E   135°E   140°E   145°E

145°E PAGAN

CHICHI JIMA

June 16,17

25°N

SARIGAN

IWO JIMA

June 13

140°E

June 20

SAIPAN

15°N

June 20

June 18

June 19

TINIAN

June 19

ROTA

June 15

June 11

June 19

June 20

June 19

GUAM

URACAS

20°N

MARIANA IS.

BATTLE AREA ENLARGEMENT

15°N

BATTLE AREA

From Tawitawi, P.I.

Rendezvous June 16

PHILIPPINE   SEA

ULITHI

10°N

MINDANAO

YAP

PALAU IS.

From Batjan, East Indies

WAM

Admiral Raymond A. Spruance, Admiral Ernest J. King and Admiral Chester W. Nimitz meet on Saipan after that Japanese bastion had fallen. (U.S. National Archives)

U.S. Takes Tinian and Guam

Tinian surrendered to U.S. troops on August 1, and nine days later Guam was secured by U.S. Forces.

More Carriers For The U.S. Fleet

The *Essex* class carrier *USS Bennington* (CV-20) joined the growing U.S. carrier fleet on August 10, 1944. *USS Randolph* (CV-15) followed on October 9.

PHILIPPINE INVASION - BATTLE OF LEYTE GULF

Back in May the U.S. Joint Chiefs of Staff prepared, as did the Japanese, for the operation to be selected after the Marianas fighting. It was decided to secure a line connecting the Palau Islands, Yap and Ulithi in the Carolines with Morotai and Halmahera in the Moluccas. The principal reason for taking the island of Ulithi was to establish a forward base of naval operations to facilitate the invasion of the Philippine Islands, which was to be the next big operation of the Pacific War. The central Philippine Island of Leyte was to be invaded in late December, following a Mindanao landing two months before. In the meantime, several smaller island stepping stones had to be captured by U.S. Forces. The carriers of TF-58 had already launched air raids on the Palau Islands, Yap, Ulithi and Ngulu during late July.

Halsey Relieves Spruance

Early in August Admiral Halsey relieved Admiral Spruance; therefore, the Fifth Fleet then became the Third Fleet and Mitscher's TF-58 became TF-38. While Spruance and his staff began planning the next operation, Halsey was to lead the Third Fleet with his staff against the stepping stone islands and the Philippines.

U.S. At Sea Logistics Service Group

While Task Force 38 pounded the Bonin Islands, the Palaus, Visayan Sea islands, Cebu and other islands in or near the Philippines a new U.S. development appeared in the Pacific during the summer of 1944. As the Pacific fighting moved westward logistics became more difficult because the task forces operated increasingly further from U.S. bases. This also shortened their time at sea because more fuel, ammunition and provisions were consumed for every operation. In an effort to keep U.S. Navy ships at sea longer Task Group 30.8, the Fleet Oiler and Transport Carrier Group, was formed. It was better known as the At Sea Logistics Service Group and enabled the fast carriers to remain at sea much longer, thereby putting more pressure on the Japanese Navy. At its full strength the At Sea Logistics Service Group comprised about 35 fleet oilers, 20 destroyers, 25 destroyer escorts, seagoing tugboats and about a dozen escort carriers; quite a large task group. The ships were divided into a number of task units, which operated near the task force, fueling and replenishing food and ammunition plus aircraft from some of the escort carriers. Each task unit included at least one CVE escort carrier, not only for replacement aircraft and pilots from the replacement pools at Guam, Eniwetok or Manus, but also to provide combat air patrols and antisubmarine patrols as protection for the precious but vulnerable oilers.

Japanese SHO Strategy

Preliminary activities for the scheduled Philippine invasion had to begin months in advance of the invasion to secure surrounding islands and other strategic areas. The Japanese realized that the U.S. would soon begin another offensive; therefore, both sides prepared for the ultimate confrontation.

The Imperial General Staff realized that the American forces would continue their thrusts westward very soon but did not know where the next move would be. Japan still envisaged a final decisive battle and made plans for four alternative battle fronts. Sho 1

Commander Charles L. Crommelin congratulates Lt. Hamilton McWhorter III who received the Gold Star. Lt. McWhorter scored eleven victories with his carrier-based Hellcat. (Official U.S. Navy Photograph, Naval Imaging Command)

prepared for a U.S. attack in the Philippines; Sho 2 anticipated U.S. landings on the Ryukyu Islands (Nansei Shoto) and on Taiwan (Formosa) south of Japan; Sho 3 foresaw U.S. landings on all Japanese home islands, especially Kyushu; Sho 4 assumed a U.S. attack in the north on Hokkaido or Sakhalin. The Japanese word Sho means victory.

The Japanese Army, air forces and navy were all to take part in the impending battle. The four remaining aircraft carriers were useless in this battle because they had no trained air crews and only about 100 planes. The experienced Japanese pilots and carrier aircraft had been decimated by Spruance's Fifth Fleet carrier planes; therefore, the Japanese were forced to offer their carriers as sacrificial decoys in all their Sho planning. Also, the Imperial General Staff was well aware of the U.S. Navy's preoccupation with carrier warfare; however, as the fighting came closer to Japan, the need for Japanese carriers dwindled because shore-based aircraft could be used. The remaining Japanese carriers were to be used as lures to entice the U.S. carriers away from the central point of operations. The new slogan was Zemmetsu Kokugo (readiness for complete annihilation, in self-sacrifice for the nation).

Japanese Conserve Air Forces

When TF-38 planes raided the Philippine Island of Mindanao on September 8 and 9 they were unchallenged by Japanese fighters, nor were U.S. planes challenged on subsequent raids on the Viscayan Islands. A feeble defense was put up on September 12 and 13 and, when Commander David McCampbell shot down four defenders on the first day and three more on the second day, this brought his score to 21 victories, for which he was awarded the Silver Star and Gold Star.

Admiral Halsey's airmen had flown a total of 2,400 sorties, or individual flights, during the raids of September 11 and 12 but there was a general absence of opposition from the Japanese. On the evening of September 13, Halsey decided that the Japanese air forces in the Philippines were so weak that the preliminary assaults on the Palau Islands, Yap and Mindanao should be cancelled. Instead, he felt the invasion forces should attack Leyte directly as soon as possible, and he presented his plan to Admiral Nimitz on that night. Nimitz, MacArthur, Admiral King and the Joint Chiefs of Staff all agreed and the invasion of Leyte was advanced two months to October 20; only Halsey was wrong! The Japanese air forces in the Philippines were only holding their planes back and conserving them for the U.S. landings they expected to take place very soon. The invasion of the Palaus was still on because Nimitz wanted the islands for forward airfields and another anchorage for the fleet.

Another reason for the weak Japanese aerial defense in the southern Philippines was that a report had been received in the Japanese Air Operations Center at Clark Field near Manila that U.S. carriers were heading north. The natural assumption was that the landings would be on Luzon; therefore, many air groups and air divisions had been transferred to Luzon to fight the invasion.

U.S. Forces Take Ulithi, Palau, and Morotai

Nimitz' Central Pacific Forces and MacArthur's South Pacific Forces were brought together for the Philippine operation as the Palaus and Morotai were invaded on September 15. Six escort carriers covered the Morotai landings as part of the U.S. Seventh Fleet sometimes called Doug MacArthur's Navy. The Palau landings were covered by 11 escort carriers, plus Task Group 30.8; the largest contingent of escort carriers yet assembled. The escort carrier was coming into its own and was to really prove itself in the impending battle.

Unyo Sinks

On September 16 the Japanese aircraft carrier *Unyo* was torpedoed and sunk by the U.S. submarine *Barb* in the South China Sea, which further reduced the already ineffective Japanese carrier strength.

The undefended atoll of Ulithi, between the Palaus and the Carolines, was occupied by U.S. forces on September 23. Ulithi was to replace Eniwetok as the principal advanced base of the U.S. Pacific Fleet.

U.S. Carriers Raid Okinawa And Kamikaze Begins

The Third Fleet's Task Force 38 kept pressure on the Japanese with air raids on and around the Philippines as far as Okinawa and Formosa during late September and early October. The U.S. objectives of these raids was to reduce Japanese air power so it could not protect Japan's oil supply route through the South China Sea and into the Philippine Sea; and to also cut Japan's Air Pipe Line with which Japan could supply the Philippines with airplanes to oppose the U.S. landings on Leyte by using Formosa and Okinawa as flying-off bases. The Japanese fought back by launching shore-based aircraft from the Philippines. These included torpedo-carrying Bettys, Jills and Kates, but the Task Force 38 combat air patrol repulsed every Japanese raid which resulted in very slight damage to the American ships. The defending American carriers also engaged in the Italian Navy-developed splash barrage, which destroyed several Japanese torpedo planes.

As previously mentioned, the vast majority of Japanese pilots were so untrained and inexperienced that they could not effectively bomb or torpedo the American ships. The last of Japan's trained and experienced aircrews had been destroyed by Spruance's Fifth Fleet and Japan had neither the manpower nor the training program to replace them. There was only one solution left to stop the American juggernaut.

Suicide Missions A Personal Decision

Totally frustrated by their failure to penetrate the Task Force 38 combat air patrols, a small group of dedicated Japanese pilots decided to immolate themselves to get at the American carriers. The decision was apparently a personal one, devoid of official sanction. On Sunday, October 14, this group of dive bomber pilots took off for their scheduled sortie and, when confronted by the Hellcats, made suicidal attacks by plunging their bomb-laden airplanes into the American ships.

The Divine Wind

Obviously the success of the immolated pilots came to the attention of high-ranking officials in the Imperial Japanese Navy, some of which felt that the suicide tactics should be adopted as the only way the American carriers could be destroyed.

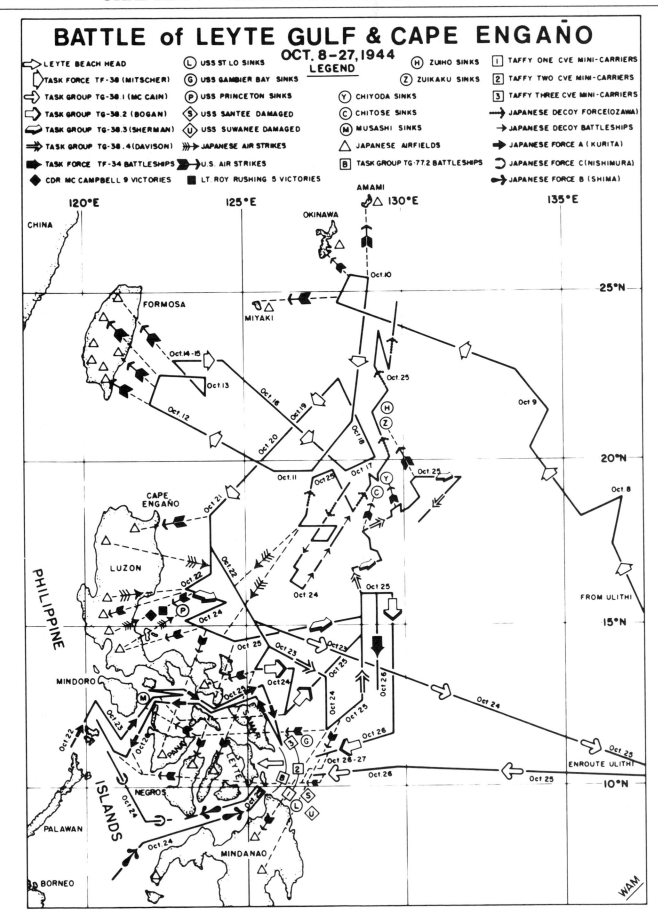

BATTLE of LEYTE GULF & CAPE ENGAÑO
OCT. 8-27, 1944
LEGEND

→ LEYTE BEACH HEAD
→ TASK FORCE TF-38 (MITSCHER)
→ TASK GROUP TG-38.1 (MC CAIN)
→ TASK GROUP TG-38.2 (BOGAN)
→ TASK GROUP TG-38.3 (SHERMAN)
→ TASK GROUP TG-38.4 (DAVISON)
→ TASK FORCE TF-34 BATTLESHIPS
◆ CDR. MC CAMPBELL 9 VICTORIES

Ⓛ USS ST LO SINKS
Ⓖ USS GAMBIER BAY SINKS
Ⓟ USS PRINCETON SINKS
Ⓢ USS SANTEE DAMAGED
Ⓤ USS SUWANEE DAMAGED
→ JAPANESE AIR STRIKES
→ U.S. AIR STRIKES
■ LT. ROY RUSHING 5 VICTORIES

Ⓗ ZUIHO SINKS
Ⓩ ZUIKAKU SINKS
Ⓨ CHIYODA SINKS
Ⓒ CHITOSE SINKS
Ⓜ MUSASHI SINKS
△ JAPANESE AIRFIELDS
Ⓑ TASK GROUP TG-77.2 BATTLESHIPS

① TAFFY ONE CVE MINI-CARRIERS
② TAFFY TWO CVE MINI-CARRIERS
③ TAFFY THREE CVE MINI-CARRIERS
→ JAPANESE DECOY FORCE (OZAWA)
→ JAPANESE DECOY BATTLESHIPS
→ JAPANESE FORCE A (KURITA)
→ JAPANESE FORCE C (NISHIMURA)
→ JAPANESE FORCE B (SHIMA)

On October 17 the very innovative Vice Admiral Takijiro Onishi, who had developed the Japanese Special Attack Corps, arrived in the Philippines to assume command of the First Air Fleet, which was responsible for the air defense of the islands. Onishi felt that the only way to stop the U.S. Navy steamroller was to duplicate the October 14 suicide attacks and many Japanese pilots volunteered for this patriotic duty. By October 20, 1944 suicide attack bases had been established at Mabalacat near Manila and at Davao on Mindanao. The objective was for the pilot to dive his bomb-laden plane onto American ships, especially carriers. This scheme was called Kamikaze or Divine Wind, which appears to have two conflicting derivations. Both involve an ancient enemy about to invade Japan when a Divine Wind destroyed the enemy fleet. One story involves the Mongols of the 13th Century and the other involves the Koreans of roughly the same period. Admiral Onishi felt that this new Divine Wind or Kamikaze would also destroy Japan's modern-day enemy.

Divine Wind to Wreak Havoc
The Kamikaze caught the U.S. Navy by surprise and struck with devastating effect. It became a weapon of death and destruction that was virtually impossible to combat. Organized Kamikaze attacks made their debut during the Battle of Leyte Gulf.

SHO 1 Activated
By October 17 General MacArthur's invasion fleet had moved toward the entrance to Leyte Gulf which made it clear to Admiral Toyoda that the Americans planned to attack the Philippines. Sho 1 was put into operation at once, which included the practice of Kamikaze, or Divine Wind.

Two Mighty Fleets Ready For Showdown
Two massive fleets converged on the Philippine Islands, not only because U.S. recovery of the Philippines would block Japan's access to Borneo's oil, but because this was Japan's last chance to avoid defeat.

U.S. Philippine Invasion Units
The U.S. Navy Forces for the Philippines invasion were as follows: The U.S. Navy Third Fleet, Commander in Chief Admiral William F. Halsey, Jr. commanding in *USS New Jersey*. Task Force 38, Fast Carrier Task Force Pacific Fleet, Vice Admiral Marc A. Mitscher commanding in *USS Lexington*, consisted of the following units: Task Group 38.1, Vice Admiral John S. McCain commanding, carriers *Hornet*, *Hancock* and *Wasp*; light carriers *Monterey* and *Cowpens*; plus six cruisers and 13 destroyers. Task Group 38.2, Rear Admiral G.F. Bogan commanding, carrier *Intrepid*; light carriers *Cabot* and *Independence*; plus two battleships, three light cruisers and 16 destroyers. Task Group 38.3, Rear Admiral Frederick C. Sherman commanding, carriers *Essex* and *Lexington*; light carriers *Langley* and *Princeton*; plus two battleships, four light cruisers, and 15 destroyers. Task Group 38.4, Rear Admiral R.E. Davison commanding, carriers *Enterprise* and *Franklin*; light carriers *Belleau Wood*, and *San Jacinto*; plus two light cruisers, and 13 destroyers.

Task Force 34 Heavy Striking Force was scheduled to be formed in the morning of October 25, 1944, by Admiral Halsey, and to be commanded by Vice Admiral Willis A. Lee, Jr. This force was t comprise four task groups which, collectively, was to consist of fiv battleships, seven cruisers and 18 destroyers. The formation of thi Task Force was to be fraught with confusion.

The United States Navy Seventh Fleet, Commander-in-Chie Vice Admiral Thomas C. Kinkaid, was to defend the Leyte beach head. The Seventh Fleet comprised Task Force 77 Covering Forc Command, Vice Admiral T.C. Kinkaid commanding in *USS Wasatc* which included Task Group 77.2, Rear Admiral Jesse B. Oldendor comprised six old battleships, three heavy cruisers, two light cruis ers, and 10 destroyers; Task Group 77.3, Rear Admiral R.S. Berkle was equipped with two light cruisers, one heavy cruiser, and si destroyers; Task Group 77.4, Escort Carrier Group, Rear Admira Thomas L. Sprague commanding, included Task Unit 77.4.1, als known as Taffy One, Rear Admiral Thomas L. Sprague command ing, which operated converted tanker carriers *USS Sangamon*, *US Suwannee*, *USS Chenango*, and *USS Santee*, plus the *Casablanc* class mini-carriers *USS Petrof Bay* and *USS Saginaw Bay*; Tas Unit 77.4.2, also known as Taffy Two, Rear Admiral Felix B. Stum commanding, operated the *Casablanca* class mini-carriers *US Manila Bay* and *USS Natoma Bay*, while in the same Task Uni Rear Admiral William D. Sample commanded *Casablanca* clas mini-carriers *USS Marcus Island*, *USS Savo Island*, *USS Kadasha Bay*, and *USS Ommany Bay*, with a screen of eight destroyers an destroyer escorts; Task Unit 77.4.3, also known as Taffy Three, Rea Admiral Clifton A.F. Sprague commanding, included *Casablanc* class mini-carriers *USS St. Lo*, *USS Fanshaw Bay*, *USS White Plain* and *USS Kalinin Bay*, while in the same Task Unit Rear Admira Ralph A. Ofstie commanded *Casablanca* mini-carriers *USS Gam bier Bay* and *USS Kitkun Bay*, plus eight destroyers. Taffy One car riers were equipped with Hellcats and Avengers, while Taffy Tw and Taffy Three carriers were equipped with Wildcats and Aveng ers. Task Group 30.8, At Sea Logistics Group, was attached to TF 77 with 11 escort carriers.

Doug MacArthur's Navy
Admiral Kinkaid's U.S. Seventh Fleet had worked so often in Gen eral MacArthur's campaigns that the Seventh Fleet was often unof ficially referred to as Doug MacArthur's Navy.

Operation Reno Command Confusion
The Leyte landings, including sea and air cover, was called Opera tion Reno and involved one of the most complicated and bewilder ing command arrangements of World War II. Admiral Halsey wit his Third Fleet had been assigned to cover the supporting forces i order to assist in the seizure and occupation of objectives in th Philippine Islands. Halsey was responsible to Admiral Nimitz an was to cooperate with the Seventh Fleet. Nimitz and MacArthu were to share the responsibility for the invasion; MacArthur for th ground forces and Nimitz for the fast carrier units. Under thes men were the combat field commanders, Kinkaid with his Sevent Fleet and Halsey with his Third Fleet; however, the problem wa that Halsey reported to Nimitz and Kinkaid reported to MacArthu with very little communication between the two combat leader Kinkaid was concerned with getting the troops ashore and protec ing them, while instead of being concerned with protecting the in

asion force, Halsey appeared to be interested in a carrier battle. As he story unfolds it will become evident that the operation would ave worked smoother and saved lives if the leaders had coordinated their plans and actions more closely. About 1,000 American hips and 200,000 men were involved in this operation and their ate was in the balance.

apanese SHO-1 Units And Leyte Strategy

Vith Imperial Japanese Navy Commander in Chief Vice Admiral Soemu Toyoda commanding, the Japanese Naval Force of Sho 1 ncluded: Carrier Force, Vice Admiral Jisaburo Ozawa commanding, comprised *Zuikaku, Zuiho, Chiyoda* and *Chitose*, with a total aircraft complement of about 100 Zero fighters and fighter-bombers, Val dive bombers, Jill and Kate torpedo bombers, and Aichi ake float planes, plus two battleship/carriers which had the after urrets replaced with a flight deck. Three light cruisers and eight destroyers provided the screen. Force A, Vice Admiral Takeo Kurita commanding, comprised five battleships, 10 cruisers, two light cruisers, and 15 destroyers. Force C, Vice Admiral Shoji Nishimura commanding, comprised two battleships, one cruiser and four destroyers. Second Striking Force, Rear Admiral Kiyohide Shima commanding, comprised two cruisers, one light cruiser and four destroyers.

Toyoda's plan was for Force C to enter the Mindanao Sea and hread its way through the Surigao Strait, between the islands of Mindanao and Leyte, then enter Leyte Gulf from the south on October 25 to attack the Seventh Fleet. Force A would, at the same ime, pass through San Bernardino Strait, between the islands of Samar and Luzon, then turn south to attack the Seventh Fleet from he north. These attacks were to be supported by the Second Striking Force. The Japanese forces were powerful and quite capable of engaging the Seventh Fleet's aging battleships and small escort carriers; however, they could not survive the overwhelming, forceful attacks of Mitscher's TF-38 Warbirds of the Sea. In order to avoid the crushing air strikes a plan was developed to lure Task Force 38 away from Leyte Gulf so that the Japanese battleships could safely attack the Seventh Fleet, using the remaining feeble Japanese carriers as the bait!

Admiral Ozawa was to take his impotent Carrier Force into the Philippine Sea and head south toward Leyte with the hope that Halsey would abandon the Leyte beachhead and send his carriers north to engage the decoy of Japanese carriers. This was to be an gnominious role for the once-powerful Japanese carrier force.

The Battles For Leyte Gulf

American assault troops hit the beaches of Leyte on October 20, which was destined to start the climactic, as well as the biggest naval battle of World War II. Hundreds of American ships filled Leyte Gulf and these vulnerable transports, landing ships, and landing craft had to be guarded against a Japanese attack. This was done by assigning ships to one of three concentric arcs fanning out to the sea. The innermost arc was to comprise destroyers, destroyer escorts, cruisers, and battleships. The center arc to comprise the escort carriers, often called Baby Flattops or Jeeps, which were about 70 miles from the beachhead. The outermost arc was to be Admiral Halsey's Third Fleet, spread over 300 miles of ocean. Task

Force 38 planes were busy engaging Japanese shore-based planes to prevent them from reaching the troops while fighters from the Baby Flattops engaged those planes that broke through. Everything was under control and considered safe enough for General MacArthur to wade ashore.

U.S. Submarines Torpedo Force A
Two days later, as Kurita led his Force towards the San Bernardino Strait, the ships were sighted by two U.S. submarines. *USS Darter* torpedoed Kurita's flagship *Atago* and the cruiser *Takeo*, while the submarine *USS Dace* torpedoed the cruiser *Maya*. *Atago* and *Maya* sank, while *Takeo* limped away to Borneo. Despite this activity, neither Kinkaid or Halsey knew of the Japanese forces approaching the Philippines.

Force A Sighted
Meanwhile, Admiral Halsey ordered Vice Admiral John S. McCain to sail his TG-38.1, which was the largest task group of the fleet, to Ulithi for rest and supplies! With more than one-fourth of Task Force 38 absent, a Helldiver pilot, Lieutenant (JG) Max Adams, had picked up a radar contact at 7:45 AM on October 24 that was Kurita's Force A. The entire Third Fleet was alerted at once and McCain's TG-38.1 was called back from Ulithi, over 1,000 miles away.

Force C Sighted
At this time another search plane had reported Nishimura's Force C in the Mindinao Sea, approaching Surigao Strait. Admiral Kinkaid immediately ordered Rear Admiral Jesse Oldendorf to close the strait with his old battleships of TG-77.2.

TG-38.3 Under Air Attack
Admiral Halsey ordered Rear Admiral Sherman to attack Kurita's force with TG-38.3 but he could not because the task group was too busy beating off massive air raids of swarms of dive bombers and torpedo planes from Luzon, north of Leyte. Many of the raiders had also flown from Ozawa's carriers; however, the Americans did not realize it at the time because the presence of the Japanese carriers was not yet known.

The *Princeton* Tragedy
During the Japanese raids on TG-38.3 in the morning of October 24, 1944, a lone Aichi Judy dive bomber cleverly dodged landing Hellcats and planted a 500 pound bomb squarely on the *USS Princeton* (CVL-23), which pierced the Flight Deck, plus three lower decks, before exploding in the bakery. The blast blew through the Hangar Deck where it started several gasoline fires that were fed by ruptured fuel piping. When the flames reached Avengers loaded with torpedoes, the explosions lifted the huge elevators off the Deck, only to have them come crashing down again. At 10:10 AM, all hands, except about 500 damage control personnel, were ordered to abandon ship and 10 minutes later 250 more crewmen were ordered off the stricken ship.

The cruiser *Birmingham* and a couple of destroyers pulled in close to evacuate personnel and to pass fire hoses and jumper cables to the carrier. An air raid and a submarine scare delayed the salvage operation until, at 3:25 PM, a tremendous explosion blew away

Four days after U.S. troops began the Philippine invasion, a dive bomber hit USS Princeton (CVL-23) with a 500 pound bomb which started fires below deck. The cruiser USS Birmingham (CL-62) is closing with the stricken carrier to help extinguish the fires and provide emergency electricity. (U.S. National Archives)

Rear Admiral Jessie B. Oldendorf commanded Task Group 77.2 at Leyte Gulf. His battleships, cruisers and destroyers decimated Japanese Force C in Surigao Strait. He is shown here after his promotion to Vice Admiral. (U.S. National Archives)

battleship to be sunk by air attack alone and the largest ship ever sunk in wartime. So ended the Battle of Sibuyan Sea, which was another classic example of the vulnerability of surface ships to air attack without protective air cover.

Hellcat Pilots Score

During the action-packed day of October 24 Commander David McCampbell had been leading a mission east of the island of Luzon with his wingman, Lieutenant Roy Rushing, and an escort of five Hellcats, when 20 shore-based Japanese dive bombers were sighted flying directly toward TG-38.3 carriers *Langley*, *Essex* and *Lexington*. McCampbell ordered the five Hellcats to intercept the Japanese formation while he and his wingman maintained altitude to act as top cover for his men. As he suspected, a formation of 40 shore-based Zeroes appeared overhead. This was the dive bomber

Princeton's stern and tore up the aft section of Flight Deck as though it was made from cardboard. The Deck section then came crashing down on the hull amidst mangled bodies. The bomb and torpedo stowage exploded from the heat, raining death and destruction on *Birmingham*, killing many of the rescuers. This was truly one of the most horrible sights in the history of naval warfare.

Princeton's casualties were seven dead, 290 wounded, and 101 missing. *Birmingham*'s casualties from the *Princeton* explosion were twice that of the carrier's, although the cruiser was only slightly damaged. *Princeton* remained afloat and was given the coup de grace by the light cruiser *USS Reno*.

Giant Battleship *Musashi* Sinks

Throughout the morning and afternoon of October 24 Rear Admiral Bogan's TG-38.2 and Rear Admiral Davison's TF-38.4 pounded Kurita's Force A in the Sibuyan Sea with Helldivers and Avengers.

Although many hits were scored, damage to the battleships was generally slight. The 60,000 ton, 18 inch gun battleship *Musashi* was hit with eight torpedoes by Avengers from the TG-38.2 carriers *Cabot* and *Intrepid*. The big ship dropped out of formation and, although crippled, turned back to head for base. That evening a concentration of Avenger strikes from the three active task group carriers *Intrepid*, *Cabot*, *Enterprise*, *Essex* and *Franklin* sent 10 more torpedoes into the side of *Musashi*. Four hours later the Japanese battleship rolled over and sank. This was the first Japanese

With Birmingham alongside, a series of explosions buckled Princeton's Flight. The carrier crew was evacuated except for 250 Damage Control personnel. (Official U.S. Navy Photograph, News Photo Division)

Commander David McCampbell shot down four Japanese aircraft on September 8 and three more on September 9, 1944 during raids on the Philippine Island of Mindanao in his Hellcat "Minzi II." Then McCampbell shot down 9 Japanese Zero fighters in one running dogfight on October 24, 1944; a feat never equalled by any U.S. pilot. He is shown in his Hellcat F6F-5, Minzi III, in which he scored the latter victories. (Official U.S. Navy Photograph, Courtesy Albert L. Lewis)

escort and it was preparing to dive on the five Hellcats. McCampbell and Rushing climbed to the attack and, in their first pass, each man scored a victory. After a few minutes the Zeroes regrouped and turned for home; then McCampbell attacked! The sky was full of planes and the commander seemed to be everywhere at once; twisting, turning, climbing, and diving. He scored again, then again, and still more! The Japanese pilots realized that they were no match for the Hellcat and its expert flyer and they continued heading west towards Luzon. The running battle lasted for over one hour and a half, during which time McCampbell and Rushing pressed the attack without respite until fuel and ammunition were dangerously low.

Lieutenant Rushing's tally was five victories and Commander McCampbell destroyed an unbelievable nine Zeroes in this single dogfight. He also had two probables which could not be confirmed. This achievement will probably never be equalled by a U.S. pilot and it earned McCampbell the Medal of Honor, which was presented to the Ace by President Roosevelt at a White House ceremony in January, 1945. Rushing was awarded the Gold Star by Admiral Sherman on Nov. 16, 1944.

The final result of this interception was the destruction of 24 Japanese aircraft without the loss of a single Hellcat. The carriers had been saved because the dive bombers were helpless without their escort so they turned tail and sped for home pursued by the five Hellcats. Not a single enemy bullet touched McCampbell's plane and the only damage to his Hellcat was caused by striking debris from his exploding victims. Later in the day the Ace was

kept busy directing air attacks against Kurita's Force A and the huge battleship *Musashi*.

Admiral Kurita was most disappointed that his expected shore-based air cover never materialized, so he reversed course to a westerly direction until darkness fell, in order to keep out of range of

Photographers swamp Commander McCampbell after his amazing multiple victories of October 24. Note the increase in victory flags on Minzi III. The ace scored his last four victories on November 8 and 11, 1944 making him the U.S. Navy's top scorer with 34 victories. (Official U.S. Navy Photograph, News Photo Division)

Rear Admiral Frederick C. Sherman, commanding officer of Task Group 38.3, presents a Gold Star in lieu of a second Air Medal to Lt. Roy Warrick Rushing on the Flight Deck of USS Essex during a ceremony on November 16, 1944 after the Battle of Leyte Gulf. The presentation was made for Rushing's feat of scoring five Japanese aircraft in one dogfight. He scored 13 victories for his World War II total (left). During the same ceremony Admiral Sherman awarded the Distinguished Flying Cross to Lt. Jg. Arthur Singer who scored 10 victories during World War II (right). (Official U.S. Navy Photograph, News Photo Division)

the American planes. He intended to return to San Bernardino Strait and make his way to Leyte Gulf under cover of darkness.

Decoy Carriers Sighted - Halsey Leaves Beachhead

Just before 5:00 o'clock in the afternoon of October 24 a search plane from TG-38.3 had spotted Ozawa's carriers about 250 miles off the northern tip of Luzon. This information was relayed to Halsey at the same time that he learned of Kurita's turn westward. Amidst glowing reports by TF-38 pilots of the destruction inflicted upon the Japanese Force A Halsey erroneously assumed that Kurita was limping away, having been mortally wounded.

TF-34 Not Formed

On the afternoon of October 24 Halsey amended the original battle plan to create Task Force 34 Heavy Striking Force composed of battleships, cruisers and destroyers. This order had stated in part that TF-34 would be formed "if the enemy sorties . . . when directed by me." This order was transmitted via TBS, or Talk Between Ships, and neither Admiral Mitscher nor Admiral Kinkaid received this important message. Both of the admirals thought that Task Force 34 had been created and was guarding the eastern approaches of San Bernardino Strait.

Admiral Mitscher's staff had worked out a battle plan to keep Task Force 34 off San Bernardino Strait with one group of carriers to provide air cover and to send two more battleships north against Ozawa's carriers with carriers providing air cover. This plan had already been dismissed by Halsey and his staff before Mitscher could propose it.

Halsey Takes The Bait

Halsey was apparently obsessed with the Japanese carriers and he wanted, so much, to be the victor in a carrier vs. carrier duel. By 8:00 o'clock that evening, Admiral Halsey had advised Admiral Kinkaid that he was "proceeding north with three groups to attack enemy carrier force. . ." Kinkaid still thought Halsey had formed TF-34 and would leave it guarding the strait. Mitscher, who was Halsey's chief subordinate, shared Kinkaid's opinion! Halsey had

no intention of leaving any ships to provide protection for the Seventh Fleet. He was taking every carrier and battleship at his disposal north to attack the impotent decoy carriers. The Japanese scheme had developed exactly as they had planned and Halsey fell for it! The Third Fleet headed north in the early morning darkness of October 25, not even waiting for McCain's TG-38.1, and left the Leyte beachhead to its own fate.

Battle of Surigao Strait

While Halsey was preparing to head north the surface action had begun in Surigao Strait. At 3:41 AM on October 25 Admiral Nishimura led his Force C into Admiral Oldendorf's trap. U.S. destroyer torpedoes and battleship guns tore the Japanese Force apart and only the rear guard escaped destruction. The Japanese attack on the Leyte Gulf landings from the south via Surigao Strait had been successfully aborted.

Halsey Ignores Kinkaid Question

At 4:12 AM Kinkaid had informed Halsey of the successful Battle of Surigao Strait and then asked if the fictitious Task Force 34 was guarding San Bernardino Strait. Halsey did not reply, but Japanese Force A gave the answer about 150 minutes later.

Battle of Samar

At 6:42 AM on October 25 the escort carrier Fanshaw Bay detected a ship on radar that was 18 miles to the northwest, which was about midway between San Bernardino Strait and Leyte Gulf, but no ship was supposed to be at this location. A few moments later scout pilots reported that the Japanese Fleet was coming and by 6:53 the men of Taffy Three could see the ships of Kurita's Force A on the horizon. This event set the stage for the Battle of Samar; so-called because Taffy Three was the northernmost CVE unit off the coast of Samar Island.

Kurita's Force A In Leyte Gulf

Admiral Kurita had achieved a singular feat by successfully sailing his Force A 150 miles from Sibuyan Sea to Leyte Gulf undetected

Left: Imperial Japanese Navy Vice Admiral Takeo Kurita commanded Force A which battleships and cruisers pounded the abandoned minicarriers of Doug MacArthur's Navy during the Battle of Leyte Gulf. (U.S. Naval Historical Center, Courtesy Rear Admiral Samuel E. Morison U.S.N. (Ret.))

until the ships reached their destination. He was now in the ideal position to disrupt the Leyte invasion but lacked important information that would have given him more confidence. The principal weapon that stood between Kurita's battleships and the troop transports, landing craft, supply ships, military headquarters, supply dumps and landed troops were Rear Admiral Clifton Sprague's CVE mini-carriers or Baby Flattops, which had been derisively called CVE-*Combustible*, *Vulnerable* and *Expendable*.

Mini-Carriers Counterattack

The first battleship salvoes thundered from a distance of 17 miles at 6:59 AM. The mini-carriers made smoke screens for each other and tried to keep out of range of the 14 and 18 inch shells; however, this proved futile because their speed was little more than half that of their pursuer's! As many planes as possible were launched at once, carrying depth charges, torpedoes, bombs, antipersonnel bombs, or with whatever else they happened to have been loaded.

Below: When the Third Fleet abandoned the Leyte Beachhead, Admiral Kurita's Force A battleships pounded the escort mini-carriers with 14 and 18 inch shells at a range of 17 miles. Kurita's ships can be seen on the horizon (arrows). Photo taken from USS Kitkun Bay (CVE-71). (Official U.S. Navy Photo in U.S. National Archives)

USS Gambier Bay (CVE-73) was beaten to a wreck by Kurita's shells and sank shortly after the big guns opened fire on October 25. Shells are straddling the carrier as it generates smoke in an attempt to hide. (U.S. National Archives)

Nimitz Disturbed

Admiral Clifton Sprague called Kinkaid for help but Oldendorf's battleships were short of ammunition and three hours steaming away from the battle. Kinkaid realized the worst had happened, as he had feared, and pleaded for battleship support. In Hawaii, Admiral Nimitz was quite disturbed over this turn of events and sent this message to Admiral Halsey: "All the world wants to know where is Task Force 34?" This was obviously intended to be criticism for Admiral Halsey's abandonment of the Leyte Gulf operation; especially leaving San Bernardino Strait unguarded.

Taffy Three's Gallant Stand

The six carriers and their destroyer screen made one of the most gallant efforts of its kind in the entire war. In fact, Kurita was actually suffering losses from the desperate action fought by Admirals Clifton Sprague's and Ralph Ofstie's Taffy Three. When it seemed that the carriers couldn't last another few minutes Sprague ordered the destroyers *Hoel* and *Johnson*, and the destroyer escort *Samuel B. Roberts*, into the attack. With superb suicidal gallantry the trio sped against the powerful battleships and cruisers and launched all their torpedoes. The cruiser *Kumano* was crippled and was forced to retire. Three more destroyer escorts joined the fight and their torpedoes forced Kurita's ships to turn away, giving Taffy Three a little time to rearm their Avengers with bombs and torpedoes.

Taffy Two to the Rescue

Meanwhile, Taffy Two arrived and launched its Avengers with those of Taffy Three in raids on Kurita's Force A. The gallant *USS Hoel*, *USS Johnson* and *USS Samuel B. Roberts* had been sunk by Kurita's big guns and the three destroyer escorts were damaged but escaped destruction. The rain of bombs and torpedoes from the Taffy Two and Taffy Three Avengers sank the cruisers *Chikuma*, *Chokai* and *Suzuya*. They also distracted the gunnery of the other ships in Force A.

Kurita Turns Back

USS Gambier Bay (CVE-73) had been hammered to a wreck by Kurita's big guns and sank at about 9:00 o'clock that morning. Three

more carriers had been severely hit while others experienced damage from near-misses. The Japanese cruisers were closing in for the kill and had come to within five miles of the carriers when Kurita suddenly turned away at 9:25 AM, consolidated his forces, and pondered for three hours whether to return into Leyte Gulf, but finally headed for San Bernardino Strait.

Although Admiral Kurita was aware of the total destruction of Force C in Surigao Strait, he did not know whether Halsey had fallen for the decoy carriers in the north. It seems that Ozawa's radio transmitter was inoperative at that crucial moment when he tried to tell Kurita that Halsey's carriers had left Leyte! The courageous fight put up by the *Casablanca* class carriers and the considerable damage they inflicted on Kurita's cruisers made the Japanese admiral believe that the carriers in the distance were the battle carriers of the Third Fleet. Remembering the pounding Force received from the Third Fleet carriers in Sibuyan Sea, Kurita decided to retire and headed back for San Bernardino Strait not knowing how close he had come to victory.

Kamikaze Attacks

In the meantime, Taffy One, the southernmost CVE unit, had launched Hellcats and Avengers against the remnants of Nishimura's Force C at 5:45 on the morning of October 25 and, before this strike had returned, Kurita was pounding Taffy Three about 200 miles to the north. Admiral Thomas Sprague ordered Taffy One to assist the beleaguered Taffy Three, but before all was in readiness, Kamikaze planes attacked from Davao on Mindanao.

USS Santee was caught with several Avengers being rearmed in the Hangar, nor did the gunners have time to man their guns in time. A Kamikaze smashed into the Flight Deck amidships and continued through into the Hangar, where the small bomb it was carrying exploded, starting a few fires, but causing little damage to the ship except for a 5 x 10 yard hole in the Flight Deck. The blast injured 27 and killed 16 crewmen. Another Kamikaze dived at *Sangamon* but was hit by a 5 inch shell and the doomed plane hit the water so close to the ship that bomb and plane fragments killed one and wounded two crewmen on the forecastle.

Seconds later another Kamikaze aimed at *Petrof Bay* which, thanks to the *Casablanca* class maneuverability, was able to dodge the Japanese plane long enough to give *Petrof Bay*'s gunners time to shoot it down.

USS Suwannee was the next target as a Kamikaze slammed through the Flight Deck into the Hangar, where the bomb exploded. This made a big hole in the Hangar Deck through which the plane's engine plunged to the Main Deck below! The Hangar was a mass of flames with dense smoke billowing through the hole in the Flight Deck. however, remarkably prompt action by the crew extinguished the fires before they got out of control. Within a few hours the Flight Deck was patched with lumber and *Suwannee* was again conducting flight operations.

Mini-Carriers Sink Cruiser

Kurita's Force A was barely out of sight when Admirals Clifton Sprague and Ralph Ofstie decided to launch strikes against the retreating ships. At 10:30 AM torpedo-carrying Avengers and Wildcat escorts left *St. Lo*, *Kitkun Bay*, and *White Plains*. Heading north

After a Kamikaze hit, USS St. Lo (CVE-63) burns fiercely following a series of bomb and torpedo stowage explosions. The carrier sank 30 minutes after the hit. Another mini-carrier can be seen on the horizon (arrow). Admiral Halsey and TF-38 were many miles away. (U.S. National Archives)

he strike planes found the Japanese cruiser *Tone*. The Avenger torpedo planes attacked from both sides so that no matter how the cruiser maneuvered the odds for a hit would be good. Two torpedoes struck amidships on the port side, which sank the cruiser.

More Kamikaze Attacks

While the Taffy Three strike planes were away more Kamikaze planes attacked *Kalinin Bay, Kitkun Bay, Fanshaw Bay* and *White Plains*. All escaped damage; however, *St. Lo* was hit and sank in 30 minutes after a series of internal bomb and torpedo explosions. Of the 900 man crew 114 sailors were killed. The Kamikaze terror had begun!

Halsey Turns Southward - Too Late

After receiving Nimitz' Task Force 34 message Halsey had continued heading north at high speed for another hour before he decided

Indispensable to any carrier air strike are the many armorers and weapons handlers who are shown here loading Avengers with bombs preparatory to a strike on Japanese ships. (Official U.S. Navy Photo)

to send help to the beleaguered forces in Leyte Gulf. Finally, at 11:15 AM he organized Task Force 34 and took it south with carrier Task Group 38.2. Admiral Halsey had also sent a message to Admiral McCain, who had been refueling his TG-38.1 far to the east, to attack Kurita's Force A in San Bernardino Strait. McCain, however, appreciated the seriousness of the situation and was already rushing to the rescue at 30 knots because he knew his mission was to protect the Seventh Fleet. Neither Task Force 34 nor Task Group-38.1 arrived in time to destroy Kurita's Force A before it escaped through San Bernardino Strait.

Battle of Cape Engano

It was just before 6:00 o'clock in the morning of October 25 that Halsey's carriers had launched air strikes against Ozawa's helpless decoy carriers. Commander McCampbell led the first TG-38.3 strike of 101 planes and Ozawa was able to launch only 20 planes to intercept the American strike force. The day-long massacre of the helpless Japanese carriers had begun. The carrier *Chitose* was the first target and was sunk by the same strike force which also torpedoed Ozawa's flagship *Zuikaku*, reducing her speed to 18 knots. The carrier *Zuiho* was damaged by a bomb, while the cruiser *Tama* was torpedoed. The following strike concentrated on the carrier *Chiyoda*, which was left afire and helpless. Continued pounding sank Zuikaku at 2:10 o'clock that afternoon, while *Zuiho* followed at 3:26 PM. The drifting *Chiyoda* was sent to the bottom by Third Fleet cruiser gunfire. In addition to the carriers, the destroyer *Hatsuzuki* was also sunk by the cruisers. The battleship/carriers *Ise* and *Hyuga* were bombed and torpedoed without respite and despite holed decks, damaged superstructures and punctured hull blisters, they sailed off westward. In this action, known as the Battle of Cape Engano, Ozawa lost four carriers, one cruiser and two of his eight destroyers, but he had accomplished his mission. He had drawn Admiral Halsey away from San Bernardino Strait and had given Kurita his chance to destroy the Leyte invasion. The winning of the Battle of Cape Engano was an empty victory; however, it cannot be denied that it further weakened Japan's naval combat ability.

The converted Japanese aircraft carrier Zuiho is shown here on October 25, 1944 during the Battle of Cape Engano. Note the attempt to camouflage the carrier to resemble a battleship. Observe the smoke billowing from the deck edge smokestack as the carrier maneuvers to avoid the TF-38 dive bomber and torpedo attacks. (U.S. Naval Historical Center)

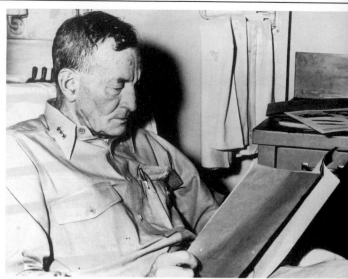

Admiral Halsey replaced Admiral Mitscher with Vice Admiral John S. McCain, Sr. as Commander of Task Force 38 after the Battle of Leyte Gulf. Admiral McCain is shown in his quarters aboard the carrier USS Hancock (CV-19). (U.S. National Archives)

Jeeps Sink More Ships

On the very next day, October 26, Taffy Two carriers launched strikes at a Japanese force that was retiring through the Visayan Sea, west of Leyte, after having landed reinforcements on Leyte. This effort resulted in the sinking of the cruiser *Kinu* and the destroyer *Uranami*.

Task Force 38 Planes Harass Force A

Task Group 38.1 and 38.2 planes harried Kurita's Force A as it transited Mindoro Strait, between Palawan and Mindoro, on October 26-27 and sank the Japanese destroyers *Noshiro* and *Hayashimo*, plus the cruiser *Abukuma*. The giant battleship *Yamato* was pounded mercilessly but survived. The mini-carriers had inflicted more damage to Kurita's Force A than had Halsey's Third Fleet.

Leyte Gulf - Greatest Naval Engagement

Leyte Gulf was one of the greatest naval engagements in all history and the climactic Pacific battle of World War II. It was, however, overshadowed at the time by MacArthur's return to the Philippines and Eisenhower's reaching the Rhine River and only appreciated after the war when historians researched the facts. Between October 22 and 27, 1944 over 230 warships of all types and almost 2,000 aircraft took part in this enormous battle which, as with most battles, was actually a series of multiple encounters. The Leyte Gulf Battle covered a distance of 500 miles in an east-west direction and 700 miles in a north-south direction in a half dozen seas.

The Japanese Fleet, which had been carefully hoarded for this final do-or-die showdown, was soundly beaten, despite the Third Fleet's dash to the north. It took only 96 hours to reduce the world's third most powerful fleet into impotence. Once again the value and supremacy of the aircraft carrier was proven beyond any doubt, witness the Battle of Samar, in which the Taffy Two and Taffy Three CVE Baby Flattops scored against powerful cruisers that had tremendous fire power and speed.

Halsey Replaces Mitscher With McCain

At this time Admiral Halsey had replaced Admiral Mitscher wi Admiral McCain as commander of Task Force 38. Some historia believe that Mitscher was relieved because he did not fully agr with Halsey's tactics at Leyte Gulf.

Japanese Leyte Losses

Of the 65 Japanese ships that had taken part in the Leyte Gulf a tion, 26 had been sunk. The U.S. Navy lost six ships of the 1(fighting ships it had committed.

Taffy Losses

Admiral Sprague's little force had suffered about 1,500 casualti and lost five ships as the price for their brave and determined d fense that saved the abandoned invasion fleet.

The Bull's Run Argument

The one aspect of the Leyte Gulf Battle which will always spaw differences of opinion is Admiral Halsey's dash north after the d coy carriers without at least forming Task Force 34 to guard Sa Bernardino Strait. Many argue that the Third Fleet's primary fun tion was to protect the Seventh Fleet; however, the aviators gene ally feel that Halsey was right because they focus their view on t carrier's offensive power, which cannot be denied, but abandonir the Leyte Gulf area leaves Halsey open to plenty of criticism. I addition to Nimitz' alarm regarding Halsey's run north, Fleet A miral Ernest J. King demanded that Halsey submit detailed ev dence so he could form his own judgment. It is of some interest th three-star Vice Admiral Kinkaid was promoted to four-star rar about five months after the battle and that two-star Rear Admir Oldendorf was promoted to three-star Vice Admiral shortly aft the battle; however, Halsey was not given another star until he r quested retirement in November, 1945. The pro and con of Bull Run, as it is called, will go on forever.

USS Intrepid (CV-11) was the most frequently hit carrier in the U.S. Fleet during World War II. Today this Essex class carrier is open for inspection in the Hudson River in New York City. (U.S. Naval Historical Center)

Kamikaze Raids Increase

Even after the beachhead was secured the Kamikaze attacks continued with Task Force 38 as the prime target. On October 29, 1944 USS Intrepid (CV-11) of TG-38.2 was hit by a Kamikaze and suffered 16 casualties. On the following day, 70 casualties resulted from a severe hit on *USS Franklin* (CV-13) of TG-38.4, which destroyed 33 of her planes in the explosion and fire. The Kamikaze that struck *Franklin* made a direct hit and plunged through the Flight Deck and Gallery Deck, exploding in the Hangar. Damage Control was excellent and, as fires were extinguished below, the crew slid steel plates over the Flight Deck holes and shored them with timbers from below. The damage was repaired so efficiently that planes were landing 75 minutes after the Kamikaze hit. The carrier was eventually sent to Puget Sound Naval Shipyard for complete repairs, especially to the aircraft elevator machinery. *USS Belleau Wood* (CVL-24) also of TG-38.4 was hit by another Kamikaze, los-

Many aircraft were destroyed by the fires in the USS Intrepid Hangar. Sodden crewmen check the damage while water from hoses and sprinklers continues to pour on them. (U.S. Naval Historical Center)

ing 12 planes and suffering 146 casualties. Kamikaze strikes on the first day in November hit three destroyers, sinking *USS Abner Reed*.

Kamikaze Not Always Lethal

The Kamikaze attacks were not always lethal but one in every four caused considerable damage and casualties. Records show that about one in 30 hits sank a ship. As Task Force 38 mopped up the area Kamikaze activity increased in intensity.

Task Force 38 Reorganized

McCain had inherited a can of worms because of the feverish Kamikaze activity and he promptly reorganized TF-38 to better combat the suicide planes. He reduced the number of task groups from four to three with more carriers and a heavier screen for each group. The three fast carrier groups comprised the following: TG-38.1 included the carriers *Yorktown* and *Wasp*, light carriers *Monterey* and *Cowpens*, two battleships, four cruisers, and 18 destroyers; TG-38.2 comprised the carriers *Hornet*, *Lexington* and Hancock, light carriers *Independence* and *Cabot*, two battleships, five cruisers and 20 destroyers; TG-38.3 included the carriers *Essex* and *Ticonderoga*, light carriers *Langley* and *San Jacinto*, battleships *South Dakota* and *Washington*, four cruisers and 18 destroyers. The carriers *Franklin* and *Intrepid*, and light carrier *Belleau Wood* were under-

On November 25, 1944 USS Intrepid was hit by a Kamikaze which started numerous fires below deck. Smoke from the fires is seen seeping through the Flight Deck expansion joints. (U.S. Naval Historical Center)

USS Belleau Woods (CVL-24) was hit by a Kamikaze on October 30, 1944 off the Philippine coast. Flight deck crews are moving TBM Avengers away from the flames which kept the loss down to 12 planes. USS Franklin burns in the distance from another Kamikaze hit. (U.S. Naval Historical Center)

going major repair due to Kamikaze damage. The carrier *Enterprise* and light carrier *Independence* were being modified for nocturnal operations at this time.

The counter-Kamikaze operation of TF-38 was to include a drastic revision in the makeup of the aircraft complement of the carriers. Previously, the standard complement had been 36 fighters, 18 torpedo planes and 36 dive bombers, but the new arrangement increased fighters to 73, reduced dive bombers to 15 and cut down torpedo bombers slightly to 15. McCain's idea was to use his Corsairs and Hellcats as fighter-bombers so they could carry up to 2,000 pounds on bombing missions unescorted, and could also intercept Japanese strikes, as well as fly combat air patrols; thereby, adding considerably to the carriers' efficiency and effectiveness. Task Force 38 was thus able to spread a blanket of fighters over Philippine airfields all around the clock, which prevented the Japanese from taking off to attack the American ships.

The new TF-38 commander also formulated new tactical innovations to be used by the screening ships. Radar picket destroyers, fitted with the latest in electronic gear and aircraft homing devices, were to be stationed about 75 miles out on either side of the protected carriers. These would provide early warning of approaching Japanese aircraft and would also screen U.S. Navy aircraft returning to their aircraft carrier. All returning aircraft had to circle directly over the pickets to be certain that no Kamikaze had joined the U.S. flights returning to the carrier, which had been a favorite Kamikaze tactic.

Persistent Kamikaze strikes sank the destroyers *Mahan* and *Reid* on November 7 and 11 respectively as they covered the Ormoc

Bay Beachhead on the west coast of Leyte; however, plans were being completed to nip this menace in the bud.

Admiral McCain's order for continuous fighter sweeps over Kamikaze bases resulted in two smart interceptions on December 14 and 16, 1944. On the first day eight Corsairs from *Ticonderoga* were making their last sweep of the day when they spotted a mixed bag of 27 Army Nakajima Oscar fighters and Navy Mitsubishi Zero fighters, off the northeast coast of Luzon, heading for Task Force 38 carriers. The Corsairs attacked at once and, in the ensuing melee, 20 of the Japanese planes were shot down with the remaining seven scurrying back to base. On the second interception Hellcats from *Hancock* and *Lexington* shot down 11 Japanese planes that had just taken off and were heading for the carriers.

First B-29 Raid

U.S. Army Air Corps Boeing B-29 bombers made their first air raid on Tokyo on November 24 from the newly developed airfields in the Marianas Islands, which had been secured by Spruance's Fifth Fleet.

U.S. Production Miracle

The American Marine industry was breaking all production records and another *Essex* class carrier, *Bon Homme Richard* (CV-31), was commissioned on November 26. It was fleets of fighting ships such as this that made the U.S. Navy, in 1944, the most powerful naval force the world had ever seen.

HALSEY GUARDS PHILIPPINES

The U.S. Third Fleet patrolled the waters east of the Philippines as TF-38 aircraft bombed and strafed shore installations preparatory to U.S. amphibious landings.

GIANT CARRIER *SHINANO*

It must be admitted, however, that despite its limited resources and labor shortage, Japan did produce some spectacular naval designs such as the largest aircraft carrier in the world, *Shinano*. The 64,800 ton displacement of this giant was not to be surpassed for 16 years.

Construction of the *Shinano* began in 1940 as a *Yamato* class battleship and was converted to a carrier before it was completed. It retained virtually all the battleship armor and included a 3 inch thick armored Flight Deck. It was to carry 120 aircraft and was to be fitted with (16) 5 inch guns, 300 missile launchers, and (150) 25 millimeter antiaircraft guns! On the night of November 29 *Shinano* was being moved from its shipyard to an outfitting yard some miles away across Tokyo Bay. The U.S. submarine *Archerfish* (SS-311) lookout spotted the giant carrier but, as the story is told, the *Archerfish* skipper Commander J.F. Enright, took a quick look and discounted the enormous mass as an island. The lookout is reported to have replied: "Your island is moving, Sir." Four torpedoes slammed into the hull of the unfinished *Shinano* and the world's largest carrier sank seven hours later. Apparently pumps, piping, watertight doors and other critical items had not yet been fitted, whereupon unrestricted flooding spread throughout the ship.

The *Shinano* was the *Archerfish*'s only kill of the war; however, because of the enormous tonnage, this single sinking made S-311 the most successful U.S. submarine of the entire war. Submarine successes were measured by the total tonnage destroyed and not by the number of ships sunk.

New U.S.N. Rank

The new U.S. Navy rank of Fleet Admiral or Five Star Admiral was created on December 14, 1944 and the first naval officers to be promoted to this exalted rank were Admirals Chester W. Nimitz, Commander of the Pacific Fleet; William D. Leahy, Chairman of the Joint Chiefs of Staff; and Ernest J. King, Chief of Naval Operations or CNO. The promotions were executed on December 15, 1944.

Third Fleet Carriers Strike Luzon

The Philippine island of Luzon was to be the next important landing for U.S. Forces and Admiral McCain's Task Force 38 bombed ships and shore installations in and around the island preparatory to the landings. On November 13, 1944 U.S. carrier aircraft sank the Japanese cruiser *Kiso* and destroyers *Hatsubaru*, *Akebono*, and *Okinami* in Ormoc Bay.

Third Fleet carriers were hitting Luzon without respite and on November 25 aircraft from Task Force 38 sank the Japanese cruisers *Yashojima* and *Kumano*.

Mindoro Landings

On December 15 U.S. Forces landed on the Philippine Island of Mindoro, west of Luzon. The only opposition was from Kamikaze attacks, some of which slipped through U.S. combat patrols and damaged several U.S. ships.

Halsey China Sea Sortie Refused

Admiral Halsey had harbored a longstanding desire to take the Third Fleet into the South China Sea, west of the Philippines, where Japanese ships that had escaped the Leyte Gulf fighting had sought shelter. This move away from the Leyte area was rejected by Admiral Nimitz and Admiral King because they felt that U.S. shore-based aviation was not yet strong enough to combat the Japanese in the Philippines without the Third Fleet carriers.

Halsey And The Typhoon

On December 18 one of the worst Philippine Sea typhoons hit the Philippine east coast. Although it gave adequate warning Halsey failed to move the Third Fleet out of the storm's path. Never, in the annals of nautical history, had a naval force suffered such losses due to natural forces as had the Third Fleet in the typhoon of 1944.

Three destroyers capsized, *USS Hull* (DD-350), *USS Spence* (DD-512), and *USS Monaghan* (DD-354) while others had their smokestacks torn off, superstructures crushed and masts toppled. The carriers of Task Force 38 had been dispersed over a 100 mile area and few ships were in visual or radio contact with each other. They pitched and rolled to dangerous angles sending Flight Deck aircraft overboard and Hangar Deck planes crashing into each other, starting fires due to spilled aircraft fuel.

USS Monterey (CVL-26) caught fire, lost 18 planes, and lost all steering. Gun emplacements were torn away as she lay dead in the water while the steering gear was repaired.

USS Kwajalein (CVE-98) was rolling 39 degrees so that her catwalks scooped up green water and three of her aircraft had to be jettisoned from her Flight Deck. Three other escort carriers lost a total of 86 planes.

Langley (CVL-27) rolled 70 degrees, which injured a large number of the crew and broke valuable and necessary equipment.

And so it went, as nature wrought its fury upon the helpless fleet. Numerous vessels were lost or damaged, 146 planes were destroyed, and 765 men had drowned while many more had been injured and maimed. A U.S. Navy Court of Inquiry had found Admiral William F. Halsey principally responsible for this disaster by failing to get the Third Fleet out of the way of the typhoon.

On December 18, 1944 Admiral Halsey led his Third Fleet into one of the worst Philippine Sea typhoons to hit the Philippine east coast. Among the many ships and aircraft that were destroyed or damaged was the carrier USS Langley (CVL-27) which rolled 70 degrees. This destroyed many aircraft and important equipment, and injured many of the crew. (Official U.S. Navy Photo)

MARINE CORSAIRS ON CARRIERS

Just after Christmas, Navy Hellcats serving on U.S. carriers were joined by Marine Corsair squadrons for the first time ever when VMF-124 and VMF-213 landed on *USS Essex*. The important invasions proposed for 1945 required not only considerable air cover but also needed fighter/bomber activity, with which the Marines had plenty of experience. Carriers were the only way to get the Marines within striking distance of the Japanese-held islands. An example of how important the fighters had become is that the *USS Wasp* and *USS Essex* aircraft complement comprised over 90 fighters and only 15 Avenger torpedo planes each. Fighters now doubled as dive bombers.

Fighter Planes Reign Supreme

The carrier fighter had developed into a very potent weapon to a point never before imagined, thanks to napalm (jellied gasoline), rocket launchers, and more powerful designs that could carry loads up to 4,000 pounds. With this improved armament and performance, plus better instrumentation, a single crew member could now perform the tasks which, at one time, required a two or three-man crew.

Carrier Improvements

Aircraft carriers also underwent improvement with rapid advances in radar which enhanced the efficiency of the ship's Combat Information Center (CIC). Damage control techniques and fire-fighting practices, plus the use of screening vessels as fireboats for carrier fires were refined as the result of experience. *USS Enterprise* and *USS Independence* had been modified for night operations and formed the first night-fighting carrier task group early in 1945.

KAMIKAZES ATTACK LINGAYEN FORCE

By the first of January 1945 Admiral Halsey had led the Third Fleet, reorganized and repaired since the typhoon disaster, out of Ulithi and west to the Philippines to support the Luzon landings. During the week of January 3-9, Admiral McCain's Task Force 38 carriers launched over 3,000 sorties, dropped almost 10,000 pounds of bombs and lost less than 90 planes.

On January 2, 1945 Admiral Oldendorf led his Task Group 77.2, comprising six battleships, six cruisers, 33 destroyers and 12 escort carriers from Leyte Gulf to Lingayen Gulf in northwestern Luzon to bombard the area preparatory to landing troops. Kamikazes were out in force and sank the *Casablanca* class mini-carrier *Ommany Bay* (CVE-79) and the destroyer *Hovey* (DD-208) while seriously damaging two dozen other ships. A Kamikaze dive on the cruiser *Louisville* (CA-28) killed the commanding officer of Cruiser Division 4, Rear Admiral Theodore E. Chandler, while another Kamikaze impact on the battleship *New Mexico* (BB-40) killed Lieutenant General Herbert Lumsden, the British liaison officer at General MacArthur's headquarters. The Kamikaze was proving itself more lethal every day that passed so that even heavily armored cruisers and battleships could not escape the Divine Wind.

Admiral Kinkaid's Seventh Fleet escaped severe Kamikaze attacks on the way to Lingayen Gulf because the Japanese were concentrating on Oldendorf's group. Despite the light attacks, Kamikaze hits on *Casablanca* class carriers *Kitkun Bay* (CVE-71) and

Kadashan Bay (CVE-76) disabled, but did not sink the ships. The Seventh Fleet landed about 70,000 troops on Luzon on January as Oldendorf's battleship barrage and strikes from the CVE's dro the 250,000 Japanese troops into the mountainous interior. T Australian cruiser *HMAS Australia* was seriously damaged by Kamikaze that evaded the combat air patrols.

HALSEY RAIDS IN SOUTH CHINA SEA

On January 9, 1945 Admiral Halsey received his long-awaited pe mission to take the Third Fleet into the South China Sea. Arrang ments had been made with the China and India-based Boeing B-2 Superfortress bombers to bomb Formosa (Taiwan) daily to preve supplies and reinforcements from reaching Luzon and the U.S. Arm Air Corps Fifth Air Force, based on Mindoro and Leyte, also too over so Halsey could leave the Philippines for the South China Se

The Third Fleet sailed westward and by January 12 it ha achieved spectacular successes along the Indochina coast by sin ing over two dozen Japanese merchant ships and about 12 nav vessels, totalling over 130,000 tons. The Third Fleet then turne north and raided Japanese shipping off the Chinese Coast near Hor Kong, Canton, Hainan Island, Formosa and the Pescadores Island between China and Formosa, on January 15 and 16. The America torpedo planes took a beating. It seems that the U.S. Navy torpe was still a failure despite the addition of fins and drag rings. I addition, the torpedo depth settings were adjusted too deep and t tin fish buried themselves in the mud or went under the target. O freighter and one small tanker were sunk and 13 Japanese plan were destroyed. Third Fleet operational losses totalled 27 plane while combat losses were 22 planes; the majority from intense a tiaircraft fire.

Task Force 38 then led the way eastward through Balinta Channel, north of Luzon, for strikes on the east coast of Formo and the Japanese Ryukyu Islands. Hellcat and Corsair fighter swee were launched by all three task groups, in the early morning January 21, against airfields on Formosa. Over 1,000 sorties we flown, resulting in over 100 Japanese planes destroyed on th ground. Later strikes were directed against shipping, in which fi freighters and five tankers were sunk and the destroyer *Haruka* was damaged.

While the Warbirds were engaged in their successful strike the carriers and screening ships were struggling against fierce K mikaze attacks. The task groups were arranged in a north/south ro with TG-38.1 the farthest north and closest to Formosa; followe by TG-38.2 and TG-38.3 in a southerly direction. TG-38.3 bore t brunt of the Kamikaze with attacks on battleships refueling destroy ers, *USS Langley* and *USS Ticonderoga* in rapid succession. T refueling operation broke up, Langley was back in operation thre hours later, but *Ticonderoga* (CV-14) was the hardest hit.

Ticonderoga Damaged

A Kamikaze carrying a 550 pound bomb crashed through th *Ticonderoga* Flight Deck with the bomb exploding in the Hanga Flaming gasoline from the serviced planes in the Hangar start fires below on the Second and Third Decks, too. A second Kam kaze evaded the antiaircraft fire and crashed into the island, star g more fires; however, all fires were brought under control two ours later. The nine degree list was reduced to three degrees and e ship was saved, but the price paid was 143 killed or missing and 02 wounded, including the commanding officer Captain Dixie iefer who was seriously wounded but recovered much later. Two uisers and three destroyers escorted *Ticonderoga* back to Ulithi.

Admiral McCain then sailed his task force northward for at-cks on the Ryukyu Islands (Nansai Shoto) with Okinawa as the incipal target on January 22, 1945. The Third Fleet then returned Ulithi.

hina Sea Results

uring its 13 day sortie Halsey's Third Fleet sank over 300,000 ns of shipping and destroyed 615 Japanese planes by strafing and mbing. Task Force 38 lost over 200 carrier aircraft and 167 pilots nd crewmen. A total of 205 seamen were killed during the Kami-aze attacks.

pruance Relieves Halsey

dmiral Raymond A. Spruance relieved Admiral William F. Halsey, :. as Commander of the Third Fleet, which was redesignated to ifth Fleet, on January 26, 1945. Simultaneously, Vice Admiral Marc .. Mitscher relieved Vice Admiral John S. McCain as Commander f Task Force 38, which was redesignated Task Force 58.

SS Antietam Commissioned

wo days later more power was added to the U.S. Navy aircraft arrier fleet when the *Essex* class carrier *Antietam* (CV-36) was ommissioned.

leet Air Arm Destroys Refineries

he 10 Royal Navy Fleet Air Arm Hellcat II (F6F-5) squadrons ere very busy in January 1945 when they struck at Japan's Achil-s' heel by destroying oil refineries on the Dutch East Indies is-and of Sumatra. Without oil, Japan's dwindling number of ships nd aircraft would be unable to move or fire a shot.

ALTA CONFERENCE

he infamous Yalta Conference was held from February 4 to 11 vith Churchill, Stalin and Roosevelt attending. At Roosevelt's urg-ng Stalin agreed to enter the war against Japan, for which there vas no necessity, in exchange for Japanese real estate. It was here hat Stalin also agreed to hold free elections in the occupied East-rn European countries; a promise he totally disregarded, thereby recipitating the Cold War!

PERATION DETACHMENT (IWO JIMA)

dmiral Mitscher's Task Force 58 aircraft struck at Japanese in-tallations around Japan on February 16 and 17, then shifted to Iwo ima from February 19 to 23, and back to Japan on February 25, 945. TG-58 then turned to the Ryukyu Islands. Mitscher's force ncluded *Essex* class carriers *Bennington* (CV-20), *Franklin* (CV-3), *Essex* (CV-9), *Hancock* (CV-19), *Bunker Hill* (CV-17), *Hornet* CV-12), *Lexington* (CV-16), *Randolph* (CV-15), *Wasp* (CV-18),

British Prime Minister Churchill, U.S. President Roosevelt, and U.S.S.R. Premier Stalin met in Yalta, U.S.S.R. from February 4 to 11, 1945. Roosevelt urged Stalin to declare war on Japan, and Stalin promised to have free elections in occupied Eastern European countries, which promise was not kept and led to the cold war. Attending the conference (first row standing) are Admiral William Leahy (1), advisor to President Roosevelt and Admiral Sir Andrew Cunningham (2). (U.S. Army Photo)

and *Yorktown* (CV-10), plus the two veteran prewar carriers *Saratoga* (CV-3) and *Enterprise* (CV-6). Four escort carriers, 8 battleships, 18 cruisers, and 75 destroyers completed Task Force 58. Over 300,000 tons of Japanese shipping and 648 airplanes were destroyed during this 14-day sortie.

During the time TF-58 spent clearing the seas around Iwo Jima from February 19 to 23, Operation Detachment was in full force as Vice Admiral Richmond K. Turner's Task Force 51 landed U.S. Marines on the island. The Kamikaze was very active during Op-eration Detachment and one of the victims was the escort carrier *Bismarck Sea* (CVE-95). The carrier was hit at dusk of February 21 and sank in three hours.

Saratoga Hit

The venerable *USS Saratoga* (CV-3) was also hit on February 21, 1945 by not just one, but by several Kamikaze and set afire. Cor-sairs on the Flight Deck burst into flames and the burning gasoline seeped through fractured Flight Deck expansion joints, causing more problems; however, quick and efficient response by the damage control teams saved the ship from debilitating damage.

James Forrestal on Iwo Jima

Although not generally known, the famous February 23 flag-rais-ing by Marines on Mount Suribachi was witnessed by Secretary of

Several Kamikaze planes smashed into USS Saratoga (CV-3) on February 23, 1945 off Iwo Jima. Burning Corsairs spilled flaming fuel on the Flight Deck which seeped below deck through damaged expansion joints. Quick and dedicated action by the firefighters, using foam, held the damage to a minimum. (U.S. National Archives)

Burning gasoline and firemain water pour from the ship's side as smoke billows from the hull of USS Franklin. Many planes were burned on deck; note the collapsed Corsair almost hidden by the smoke (arrow). (Official U.S. Navy Photograph, Courtesy U.S. Naval Institute Photo Collection)

the Navy James V. Forrestal, who was standing on the beach at Iwo Jima at that historic moment.

USS FRANKLIN DISASTER

As it sailed 90 miles off the coast of Japan on March 19, 1945 a Japanese dive bomber from *Kyushu* penetrated the picket ships and combat air patrols and dropped two 550 pound bombs through the *USS Franklin* (CV-13) Flight Deck. One of the bombs penetrated the Hangar Deck, which ignited not only armed planes in the Hangar but also set off ready ammunition and aviation gasoline, which turned the ship interior into a raging inferno. Quick and efficient action by the valiant Damage Control crews prevented a total disaster. Most of the crew was quickly disembarked onto attending destroyers and cruisers with only a skeleton crew remaining to save the ship. The cruiser *Pittsburgh* took the blazing carrier in tow to get it beyond range of Japanese bombers and then headed for Ulithi at six knots. The men struggled to save their ship for several days and finally, by March 28, all the fires had been extinguished and one boiler was operating. On April 3 *Franklin* limped into Pearl Harbor for temporary repairs and then sailed 12,000 miles to New York under her own power, listing heavily and with her open wounds waiting to be dressed. The carrier was greeted with a tumultuous welcome as she entered New York Harbor.

Franklin Heroes

A total of 393 decorations were awarded to *Franklin*'s crew in a ceremony on the Flight Deck, the most ever presented on a single ship in the history of the U.S. Navy and, possibly of any navy. The brave crew had saved the ship against tremendous odds and surely deserves the lion's share of the credit. One must not forget the designers of the ship who worked endless hours planning a carrier that could endure punishment and control damage; also the ship-

Explosions on Big Ben send a shower of debris into the air as the topmast assumes a dangerous tilt. Of the 3,450 crew, 724 were killed and 265 were wounded. Franklin was commanded by Captain Leslie H. Gehres and was the flagship of Rear Admiral R.E. Davison's TG-58.2. (Official U.S. Navy Photo, News Photo Division)

USS Franklin (CV-13) before the fateful dive bomber strike that sent two bombs crashing through her Flight Deck on March 19, 1945. Note that camouflage differs on starboard side (above) from port side (below). (Official U.S. Navy Photo, Courtesy U.S. Naval Institute Photo Collection)

With smoke billowing from flaming fuel in its hull, Big Ben appears to be a doomed ship. Observe the crew members forward of the collapsed aircraft elevator (arrow). The stricken ship is beginning to list to starboard. (Official U.S. Navy Photo)

An escorting cruiser USS Santa Fe (CL-60) pulls alongside to evacuate most of the crew with only a skeleton crew remaining to save the ship. Note the men assembled on the Flight Deck and Franklin listing dangerously to starboard. (Official U.S. Navy Photo)

USS Santa Fe (CL-60) circles the crippled USS Franklin, ready to render any assistance as the carrier lays dead in the water. Note the life rafts floating alongside the carrier. Photograph was taken from USS Santa Fe. (Official U.S. Navy Photograph)

The cruiser USS Pittsburgh towed the smoldering USS Franklin beyond range of Japanese bombers and then headed for Ulithi at a speed of six knots while the crew worked hard to correct the starboard list. The carrier received temporary repairs at Pearl Harbor and then travelled 12,000 miles to New York under its own power. (Official U.S. Navy Photograph, Courtesy U.S. Naval Institute Photo Collection)

OPERATION ICEBERG (OKINAWA)

Task Force 58 now turned its attention to Okinawa, Operation Iceberg, to destroy the airfields preparatory to the American landing on this Ryukyu island. On March 26 the British Pacific Fleet joined TF-58 and the U.S. Fifth Fleet to help in the assault on Okinawa. British Admiral Sir Bernard Rawlings placed his entire fleet, comprising the carriers *Illustrious*, *Victorious*, *Indomitable*, and *Indefatigable* with an escort of battleships, cruisers and destroyers under Admiral Spruance's supreme command. This British Force was so equivalent to a U.S. task group that it was designated Task Force 57 and assigned a separate group of targets from TF-58. The first assignment was the airfields of Sakashima Gunto, a cluster of islands between Formosa and Okinawa.

Range Versus Armor

The Royal Navy carriers were not as combat-effective as the American carriers in the broad expanse of the Pacific Ocean. Designed for the European and Mediterranean Theatres, the British carriers lacked the range of the U.S. carriers because they did not need it in the confines of the North Sea or Mediterranean Sea however; they did have a feature that was lacking in U.S. Navy carriers; armor. On April 1, 1945 a Kamikaze had scored a direct hit on the Flight Deck of *HMS Indefatigable*, but within a few hours the carrier was operating normally as soon as the rubble had been cleared away. *Indefatigable* was able to continue its support of the Okinawa landings, which had begun on that day, despite the impact and explosion of the Kamikaze.

Whistling Death

The last great amphibious landing of World War II was on Okinawa in which 1,200 warships participated. The carrier plane most associated with the Okinawa campaign was the Vought Corsair. Apparently, its ground support activities were so invaluable that the U.S. troops called the Corsair "Sweetheart of Okinawa," while the Japanese troops cursed it as the "Whistling Death" because of the whistle created by the airflow through the wing root oil coolers as it strafed and bombed their positions.

yard workers of Newport News Shipbuilding who built the best ship they could, realizing the bombs and torpedoes that would be hurled at it.

Of the original 3,450 crewmen, 724 were killed and 265 were wounded. No other American aircraft carrier has ever survived such punishment and no other American warship has sustained such casualties and remained afloat.

Operation Ten-Go

On April 6 the Japanese inaugurated Operation Ten-Go as their response to the invasion of Okinawa. Admiral Toyoda had developed the concept of coordinated massed Kamikaze attacks to smash the Okinawa invasion supporting fleets. Toyoda had planned to concentrate 4,500 planes in the raid but could muster only 699; 355 of which were Kamikaze. The Divine Wind came on like a tornado, sinking two destroyers, one destroyer minesweeper and two ammunition cargo ships. The raid also damaged 12 other ships, including four destroyers that had to be scrapped. The Japanese called these raids Kikusui, or Floating Chrysanthemums.

Cannon-fitted Corsairs went into action for the first time on April 7, 1945 with Marine Air Group 31, which was catapulted from the carriers *Breton* (CVE-23) and *Sitkoh Bay* (CVE-86) to intercept Kamikaze attacks.

BATTLE OF EAST CHINA SEA

April 7 also witnessed the last naval action of World War II, known as the battle of East China Sea. On the afternoon of April 6 the Japanese 72,000 ton battleship *Yamato* sailed from Kyushu, the southernmost Japanese home island, and headed for Okinawa on a suicide mission. Escorted by one-light cruiser and eight destroyers, *Yamato*'s purpose was to disrupt the American amphibious fleet at Okinawa, even at the cost of its own destruction. In fact, the ships did not have enough fuel oil for the return trip back to Japan. Admiral Toyoda had assumed that his Ten-Go had been more successful than it was and that Task Force 58 would be too busy licking its wounds to interfere with *Yamato*'s mission.

No air cover was provided because planes were being set aside in the event that the Americans invaded the Japanese home islands.

Yamato had been sighted by American submarines on the evening of April 6 and, at 8:22 AM on April 7, a TF-58 scout plane spotted the Japanese ships. At 10:00 o'clock an aerial armada of 386 planes was launched from TF-58 carriers; Curtiss Helldivers with two 1,000 pound bombs each; Grumman Hellcats with one 500 pound bomb, and Grumman Avengers with one torpedo. The objective was to punch holes in the sides of the ship to let in the water and to punch holes in the top of the ship to let out the air. It has been variously estimated that the giant battleship had been hit with five to 17 bombs and 11 to 20 torpedoes. After two hours of uninterrupted pounding the world's largest warship capsized, taking all but 269 of the original complement of 2,767 with her as she sank. The force commander, Vice Admiral Seiichi Ito and *Yamato*'s captain, Rear Admiral Kosaku Ariga, went down with the ship. Task Force 58 lost 10 planes and 12 airmen to antiaircraft fire. The light cruiser and four of the destroyers were also sunk by TF-58 planes.

President Roosevelt Dies

On April 12, 1945 America's president died and was succeeded by Vice President Harry S. Truman.

KAMIKAZE RAMPAGE

While all this activity was going on one Kamikaze evaded the picket ships and the Hellcat combat air patrol to dive into the *USS Hancock*

The Battle of East China Sea was the last naval action of World War II. It centered on the 72,000 ton Japanese battleship Yamato (above) which conducted a suicide mission against the U.S. Okinawa invasion force. Below: Yamato is shown receiving direct bomb hits from U.S. carrier aircraft. Yamato was sunk on April 7, 1945 when it was hit by approximately 10 bombs and 10 torpedoes from 386 planes of Task Force 58. (both - U.S. Naval Historical Center)

Flight Deck, causing about 800 casualties and putting the carrier out of action.

The second and third Kikusui raids took place on April 13 and 16, 1945, sinking and damaging several destroyers. The *Essex* class carrier *Intrepid* (CV-11) was also hit and damaged in the third raid.

USS Sangamon (CVE-26) was severely damaged by a Kamikaze on May 4. Several picket destroyers were also sunk and damaged in this fifth Kikusui.

Kamikaze And Royal Navy Armor

The Kamikaze had become the most effective and feared anti-ship weapon of the war and had taken its toll of American aircraft carriers and other surface ships, as well as wounding and killing hundreds of U.S. Navy personnel. It will be remembered that the design philosophy for Royal Navy carriers was to armor the flight deck, as well as the entire hangar, despite the fact that this resulted in a lower airplane complement and prohibited running aircraft engines below deck. Britain did not have the production capacity of the U.S.; therefore. could not afford to lose any carriers. Royal Navy carriers depended upon their armor to protect themselves from aerial bombing and this served them very well, as experiences in the Pacific proved, without question.

While Admiral Rawlings' battleships were shelling the island of Miyako, southwest of Okinawa, on May 4, 1945 two of the Royal Navy carriers were hit by the Kamikaze. The first Kamikaze exploded upon impact with *HMS Formidable*'s Flight Deck, destroying parked aircraft and causing 56 casualties. Although the Flight Deck had been pierced and many parked planes were ablaze, the carrier was back in action in six hours when the Flight Deck had

Royal Navy carriers operating in the Pacific fared better than U.S. carriers under Kamikaze attack by virtue of their armored flight decks. Victorious, Formidable, Indomitable and others were back in action in a matter of hours after Kamikaze hits. The crew of this British carrier is clearing the Deck of damaged planes after a Kamikaze bounced off the Deck. (British Information Service)

been repaired. Later in the day another Kamikaze struck *HM Indomitable*'s Flight Deck and actually bounced off the Deck and caromed into the sea. Five days later *Formidable* was again a victim of Kamikaze, as was *Victorious*, but the results were the same as in most attacks. Within a few hours the Royal Navy carriers were in operation again. *Formidable* lived up to her name by enduring direct hit during the sixth Kikusui on May 11 and was back in action within a few hours. *Victorious* was also hit a short time later and, despite a punctured Flight Deck, escaped serious damage. Were it not for their armor the entire British Pacific Fleet carrier force would have been lost. This fact was well recognized by U.S. Navy officials.

Over 150 Kamikaze planes staged the sixth Kikusui on Okinawa on May 11, hitting two U.S. destroyers, a landing ship and *USS Bunker Hill* (CV-17). One Kamikaze is capable of sinking a ship, but two planes hit *Bunker Hill*, Admiral Mitscher's flagship. The carrier was badly damaged and out of action with 396 crewmen killed and 264 wounded. Mitscher was ordered to transfer his flag to the venerable *Enterprise*, which was quickly accomplished.

USS Enterprise (CV-6) had been damaged near Okinawa in March by a direct bomb hit and was hit again by a Kamikaze in

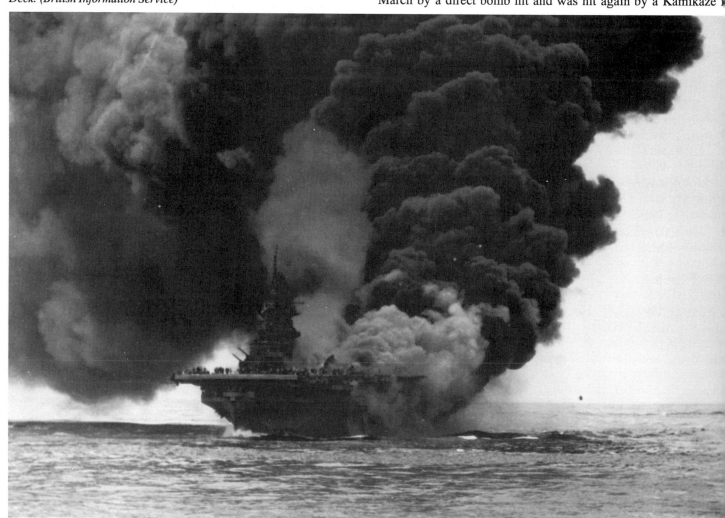

Admiral Mitscher was sailing his flagship USS Bunker Hill (CV-37) off Okinawa on May 11, 1945 when two Kamikaze planes hit the ship, turning it into an inferno and killing 396 of the crew with 264 wounded. The carrier was so badly damaged that it was put out of action. (U.S. National Archives)

pril, but the worst was yet to come. Three days after Admiral itscher transferred to *Enterprise*, the carrier was seriously damged by a Kamikaze attack, killing 14 crewmen and injuring 34. *nterprise* endured 21 more attacks on this day and was put out of tion, never again to return to active service.

The seventh and eighth Kikusui were made by 165 and 158 amikaze planes respectively from May 23-25 and May 27-30.

The damage caused by Japanese bombing and Kamikaze atcks on ships was on the wane because, by the end of May, the merican forces on Okinawa were advancing and required less aborne air and bombardment support, which reduced the need r so many U.S. support forces off the beach. Further, the constant mbing of Japanese airfields in the area by TF-58 had reduced pan's ability to organize air strikes.

ermany Surrenders

n the other side of the world, Germany surrendered unconditionly on May 7.

alsey Relieves Spruance

'hile the eigth Kikusui was underway Admiral Halsey relieved dmiral Spruance, whereupon the Fifth Fleet became the Third Fleet n May 27. On the next day Admiral McCain relieved Admiral litscher.

APANESE HOME ISLANDS BOMBED

'ith Okinawa virtually secured the U.S. turned its attention to the panese home islands. From this time until the end of the war it as to be Japan itself that would feel the might of the U.S. Navy as ask Force 38 bombed airfields, factories and oil depots on land d the remnants of the Japanese Navy were to be sunk or severely maged in their very own harbors. This next and probably last ase of the Pacific war began on June 2 when Task Group 38.4, ear Admiral Arthur W. Radford commanding, launched an air atck on Kyushu from the carriers *Yorktown*, *Intrepid*, *Independence* d *Langley*. This attack on Kyushu airfields was repeated by TG-8.4 on June 8.

alsey And The Second Typhoon

isaster hit the Third Fleet on June 5 when it was again caught in a phoon off Okinawa. A total of 36 U.S. Navy ships were damged; one of which was *USS Hornet* (CV-12). The violent storm rapped her Flight Deck down around her bow, but after the tyhoon was passed, *Hornet* continued to operate despite the damye, by running full speed astern and launching planes over the aft d of the Flight Deck! A Navy Court of Inquiry decided that Adiral Halsey and Vice Admiral McCain had used poor judgment hen the storm approached.

he Miracle of *USS Natoma Bay*

he ninth Kikusui of June 3-7, 1945 comprised only 50 Kamikaze lanes, which achieved very meager results. The Japanese Empire ppeared on the verge of collapse; however, it was still capable of flicting damage on the American ships.

Italy's only aircraft carrier of World War II, Aquilia, was converted from the passenger liner Roma and was close to completion by the time of the Italian capitulation in 1943. The ship was then taken over by the Germans but was soon damaged by Allied air raids and torpedoes whereupon the hulk was scuttled. Aquilia was raised, postwar, and moved to La Spezia for reconstruction but was broken up during 1951-1952. The carrier is shown shortly after the German acquisition. (U.S. National Archives)

The German aircraft carrier Graf Zeppelin was still unfinished at the end of World War II and was then scuttled in the Stettiner Haff, an inlet of the Baltic Sea, to prevent the advancing Soviets from seizing the ship. The Soviets did, however, raise Graf Zeppelin and loaded it with booty. As the carrier was being towed to a Soviet port it capsized because of an overloaded flight deck and sank in 1947. It now lies at the bottom of the Baltic Sea. (Bundesarchiv, Courtesy Hans Justus Meier)

On the morning of June 7 the *Casablanca* class escort carrier *USS Natoma Bay* (CVE-62) was operating about 50 miles east of Sakishima Gunto, one of the southernmost Ryukyu Islands (Japanese Nansei Shoto). At about 6:35 AM a Kamikaze appeared and approached the carrier from the stern, flew over *Natoma Bay*, and dived into the extreme forward end of the Flight Deck. It smashed through the Deck and struck the anchor windlass in a ball of fire and explosion which blew a 15 x 30 feet hole in the Flight Deck.

USS Hornet (CV-12) had sunk or damaged 1.3 million tons of Japanese shipping and her aircraft and antiaircraft guns shot down 1,410 Japanese planes without damage to herself. The carrier was, however, severely damaged when led into the second Pacific typhoon by Admiral Halsey. (Official U.S. Navy Photograph)

The Kamikaze made a 15 x 30 foot hole in the Flight Deck adjacent to the port side catapult before smashing into the Natoma Bay anchor windlass. (Official U.S. Navy Photo, Courtesy Lt. Col. O.K. Williams, USMC (Ret.))

A Wildcat that had been spotted on the catapult caught fire and had to be catapulted off the Deck. A short time later all fires above and below Deck were extinguished, and the Flight Deck repair began. By 3:00 o'clock in the afternoon the Deck repairs had been completed, using heavy timbers, plywood and steel plate; however, aircraft were already being launched as the work progressed.

U.S. Navy Okinawa Losses

Okinawa was declared secured on June 21. The bitter battle for the island cost the U.S. Navy almost 5,000 killed and 4,824 wounded officers and crew. The U.S. Navy lost 32 ships and 368 were damaged; mostly by Kamikaze. This was the bloodiest battle for the U.S. Navy in its entire history because of the Divine Wind.

Kamikaze Killer Needed

An important lesson had been learned since the early Kamikaze attack on *USS Franklin* and this was that the Close In Weapons System (CIWS) of 20 and 40 millimeter close-range antiaircraft

With the fires extinguished, members of the crew repair the Deck with heavy timbers, steel plate, and plywood. The repair is temporary but useable and will be reconstructed in a shipyard. (Official U.S. Navy Photo, Courtesy Lt. Col. O.K. Williams, USMC (Ret.))

Caught at the moment of impact, the Kamikaze sends up a cloud of black smoke from the explosion as it crashes through the forward end of the USS Natoma Bay (CVE-62) Flight Deck. (Official U.S. Navy Photo, Courtesy Lt. Col. O.K. Williams, USMC (Ret.))

A Grumman Avenger is catapulted off USS Natoma Bay while repair work is still underway. The 15 x 30 foot hole was repaired in eight hours. (Official U.S. Navy Photo, Courtesy Lt. Col. O.K. Williams, USMC, (Ret.))

ns, including the vaunted 40 millimeter pom-pom, did not have e necessary stopping power against the Kamikaze. Until 1945 tacking aircraft could be forced to take violent evasive action and ight even break off the attack due to a carrier's antiaircraft fire. In dition, a damaged aircraft or wounded pilot would turn and limp r home. Not so with the Kamikaze because body wounds or air- aft damage only made the pilot press the attack with increased gor. In order to solve this problem a low altitude, powerful and avily armed Kamikaze interceptor was needed. Time was short d existing equipment had to be utilized.

oodyear F2G Corsair

ratt and Whitney had just developed and tested their R-4360 Wasp, -cylinder, four-row, 3,000 horsepower air-cooled radial engine d, on March 22, Goodyear Aircraft was asked to adapt the FG-1 orsair to this new engine in order to develop a Kamikaze inter- eptor and the F2G-1 was born. The design had a nonfolding wing, own-bubble canopy, and (8) .50 inch caliber machine guns or ur to six machine guns, plus (8) 5 inch rockets. A water injection ystem was to boost the engine horsepower to 3,650, which was to rive the plane to 450 miles per hour. As Kamikaze activity sub- ded, the order for 400 planes was reduced to 10 in May 1945. An 2G-2 carrier version with folding wings and tail hook had attained speed of 431 miles per hour at 16,400 feet.

he Last Kamikaze Raid

he last Kikusui attack was conducted on June 21, using only 45 lanes with negligible effect. By this time the Japanese war effort ad exhausted itself.

llied Air Raids Meet Little Resistance

n July 1 Admiral McCain led his Task Force 38 into Japanese ome waters for continuous attacks on the Japanese Home Islands nd remained there until the end of the war. The air raids met with ery little aerial interference because the Japanese were conserving eir planes for use in the event of an Allied invasion of the Home lands. Airfields, steel mills, and other lndustrial and military tar- ets were hit as far north as Hokkaido, the northernmost Home sland.

The Royal Navy joined the U.S. Navy on October 17 in an ttack on the Tokyo area. The task force sailed as close as 50 miles om shore which, against a strong enemy, would have been sui- ide. On that day Royal Canadian Navy Lieutenant R.H. Gray sank destroyer with his Corsair at Shiogama before being shot down y antiaircraft fire. He was awarded the Victoria Cross, Britain's ighest honor, for this brave deed.

The vast Allied Fleet, which included more than 20 fleet carri- rs and 1,500 combat planes, continued to range the length and vidth of Japan with less opposition as each day passed. Between uly 24 and 28 heavy raids were launched against the Japanese Navy ases at Kobe and Kure in Japan's Inland Sea, north and west of hikoku Island. These raids scored heavily by sinking the battle- hips *Haruna*, *Ise* and *Hyuga* a *Tone* class heavy cruiser plus the leet carrier *Amagi*. The carriers *Ryuho* and *Katsiragi* were heavily amaged.

An Allied Fleet of over 20 fleet carriers and 1,500 aircraft pounded Japan during the summer of 1945. Task Force 38 aircraft sank a Japanese Tone-class heavy cruiser on July 24, 1945 at the Kure Naval Base on Honshu, by entering Japan's Inland Sea. The cruiser (arrow) is surrounded by bomb explosions and what appears to be a direct hit. (U.S. Naval Historical Center)

In Desperation; The Baka Bomb

Japan was in desperate straits by 1945 and could no longer afford the use of standard fighters, dive bombers and torpedo planes for the Kamikaze program. One of the alternatives was the develop- ment of a purpose-built piloted missile; Ohka (Cherry Blossom), known to the Allies as Baka which means "fool" in Japanese. Built by the Yokosuka Naval Arsenal as the MXY8 the flying bomb was powered by a solid fuel rocket which drove the 4,850 pound craft to a 535 miles per hour top speed. The Ohka was designed to be carried to within a few miles of the target under the belly of a Mitsubishi Betty bomber. Upon its release the rocket motor started

Japanese pilots discuss their next mission with the Ohka piloted missile shown under the belly of a Mitsubishi bomber. This rocket powered flying bomb was carried to within a few miles of the target and then released. The pilot then flew the missile into the target. (U.S. Naval Historical Center, Courtesy U.S. Naval Institute)

A16-3(2●-A)   COMMANDER FIFTH FLEET   7 JUL 1945
UNITED STATES PACIFIC FLEET
FLAGSHIP OF THE COMMANDER

Serial: 00232

S E C R E T   DECLASSIFIED

FIRST ENDORSEMENT to:
CTF 58 A16-3 Serial
00222, dated 18 June
1945.

From: Commander FIFTH Fleet.
To: Commander in Chief, United States Fleet.
Via: Commander in Chief, U.S. Pacific Fleet.

Subject: Report of Operations of Task Force FIFTY-EIGHT in Support
          of Landings at OKINAWA, 14 March through 28 May (East
          Longitude Dates), including Actions against KYUSHU, NANSEI
          SHOTO, Japanese Fleet at KURE, the YAMATO, and Operations
          in Direct Support of Landings at OKINAWA.

    1.   Forwarded.

    2.   This excellent report briefly and succinctly summarizes one
of the most remarkable and most successful naval operations ever conducted.
For the first time in history a fleet steamed to the threshold of an enemy
homeland and, with its own air force embarked, stayed there, at sea, for a
period of months until our own land and air forces were firmly established
on the enemy's doorstep. Despite the most desperate and fanatical resistance that the Jap has yet conducted, not one ship of this force was sunk.

    3.   The enemy was decisively defeated; a large part of his air
force was destroyed; his fleet was further decimated and he was prevented
from reinforcing his forces on OKINAWA or interfering effectively with our
operations there. It is no disparagement of the efforts of land based air
which are now hastening the end to say that the carriers of Task Force 58
and their planes have made possible the victory which is now in sight.

                                        R. A. SPRUANCE.

UNITED STATES PACIFIC FLEET
AND PACIFIC OCEAN AREAS
HEADQUARTERS OF THE COMMANDER IN CHIEF

                                        24 September 1945.

        The story of the escort aircraft carriers is like
a story with a surprise ending. When the United States
began to build them, there was a definite purpose in
view — fighting off submarines and escorting convoys.
But as the war progressed, the small carrier demonstrated surprising versatility. It became a great
deal more than its name implies.

        From a purely defensive measure, the escort
carrier emerged as an offensive weapon. In each of
our operations from Tarawa to Okinawa, naval aircraft were over our amphibious forces continuously.
Many of these planes came from the decks of the escort carriers — the so-called "jeeps" — which stood
offshore for long periods in the most difficult circumstances. In heavy weather, against heavy enemy
aircraft attack, and even in the face of the heaviest
guns of the enemy fleet at Leyte, the escort carriers
of the Pacific Fleet bore a heavy responsibility for
the safety of our beachheads and the air support of
our forces ashore during the critical days after the
landings.

        To the officers and men who made such success
possible, I send a hearty "Well Done".

                                        C. W. NIMITZ
                                Fleet Admiral, U. S. Navy
                        Commander in Chief, U. S. Pacific Fleet
                              and Pacific Ocean Areas

---

and because of its high speed it was extremely difficult to identify
or hit. The rocket motor had a duration of about 30 seconds. The
2,200 pound warhead was very lethal. Very few Baka bombs were
fabricated before the war ended and there is little verification of
their success in combat.

Japan's Fuel Supply Cut

Borneo had fallen in early July which eliminated Japan's only remaining source of oil. Although Japan had battleworthy ships and
several thousand planes at the Home Islands, Korea and Manchuria, they could not be used for lack of fuel.

*Above: This official report on the Okinawa Campaign was prepared by
Admiral Spruance on July 7, 1945. It is interesting that the Admiral
credits the carriers and shipboard aircraft of Task Force 58 with this
victory. (Official U.S. Navy Photo)*

*Above right: Fleet Admiral Chester W. Nimitz lauded the small carriers
(AKA escort carriers, "Jeeps", mini-carriers) and he congratulated the
officers and men who sailed the escort mini-carriers in the Pacific
campaigns with this open letter on Sept. 24, 1945. (Official U.S. Navy
Photo)*

*Right: Admiral "Bull" Halsey prepared this Action Report of the Third
Fleet operations against Japan on October 11, 1945. Note that he
describes the power of the Japanese air forces as "largely depleted",
thanks to naval air power. (Official U.S. Navy Photo)*

A16-3/(11)   UNITED STATES PACIFIC FLEET   lrb
                      THIRD FLEET
Serial   OCT 1 1 1945
    00322

S-E-C-R-E-T
        DECLASSIFIED   1st Endorsement on
                        C2CTF Secret ltr.
                        Serial 00242, dated
                        31 August 1945.

From: Commander THIRD Fleet.
To :   Commander-in-Chief, United States Fleet.
Via :   Commander-in-Chief, U. S. Pacific Fleet.

Subject: Action Report - Operations Against JAPAN; 2 July - 15   1945

    1.   Forwarded.

    2.   The operations of Task Force 38 during the period covering
this report will ever be remembered in the annals of naval history. The naval
power of the enemy was not only made impotent but was, for all intents and purposes, exterminated. An enemy air force hampered by lack of fuel, necessarily
wide dispersal, and disorganized by continued defeat was hunted out and its
effective striking power largely depleted. The shores of the enemy homeland
for the first time felt the stinging blows of naval bombardment. In consequence
the offensive of the great task force even abruptly ended on August 15, 1945
with the collapse of the enemy.

    3.   The near perfect defensive record of Task Force 38 during this
period is most worthy of comment and commendation. Though termed defensive,
such is more accurately described as offensive - defense. Employing enemy air
field "blanket" together with concentrated attacks against enemy installations
in nearly every circumstance reduced air reaction before it could be effectively
organized. What relatively minor enemy air strength that did threaten the task
force was in most every case quickly eliminated by intelligent stationing of
pickets, effective stacking of combat air patrols, exceptional fighter direction
and aggressive fighter tactics.

    4.   Noteworthy operational planning combined with excellent photo-
graphy, meticulous pilot briefing and good pilot technique made possible the
destruction of enemy air power on the ground, even though protected by wide dispersal and typical, effective oriental camouflage methods.

    5.   The destruction of the major enemy naval strength which was
operable at the beginning of this offensive was a most difficult and trying
task. The successful accomplishment of this task is most gratifying — the
photographs, and consequent record, speak for themselves.

                                        W. F. Halsey

POTSDAM DECLARATION

The Japanese Government sent out peace feelers to the Allies which were answered with the Potsdam Declaration. On July 25 a statement was issued by Britain, Soviet Union and the U.S. after a conference in Potsdam, Germany, which called upon Japan to surrender unconditionally or face utter destruction, an obvious reference to the atomic bomb, which existence was not known to Japan or the rest of the world. Clausewitz was turning in his grave!

Atomic Bombs Dropped On Japan

In reply to the Potsdam Declaration the Japanese refused to agree to an unconditional surrender with the result that a Boeing B-29 dropped an atomic bomb on Hiroshima on August 6. This city of 300,000 near Kure on southern Honshu suffered 70,000 deaths and thousands of disfigurements and injuries. Two days later the Soviet Union declared war on a prostrate Japan, the only promise it made at the Yalta Conference that it kept!

A second atomic bomb was dropped on Japan on August 9. Nagasaki on Kyushu was the target where 20,000 inhabitants were killed.

Third Fleet Continues Attacks

Strangely, the news of the Hiroshima bomb did not stop Halsey's offensive against Japan; nor did it halt Japanese military activity against the Allied Fleet. In fact, on the same day as the Nagasaki bombing, Task Force 38 carriers launched air strikes on airfields of northern Honshu which destroyed 251 Japanese planes and damaged another 141 planes. The air strikes continued on the following day.

JAPAN SURRENDERS

The Japanese Government agreed to an unconditional surrender on August 15. Planes of TF-38 that were approaching the Japanese coast for an air strike were recalled when Admiral McCain received news of the surrender. The last operation for the Third Fleet was to provide cover as the U.S. occupation troops began landing in Tokyo Bay on August 30. Japan's surrender was signed in that bay aboard *USS Missouri* three days later.

Admiral McCain Dead

Vice Admiral John S. McCain died only three weeks after the Japanese surrender for which he deserves much credit as commander of Task Force 38. His passing was caused by Coronary Thrombosis on September 6, 1945 at San Diego, California.

CARRIER CONSTRUCTION AT WAR'S END

The approaching cessation of hostilities caught the three principal naval powers, Britain, Japan and the U.S. in the midst of carrier construction programs, several of which had their inception near the war's beginning. Many of the later aircraft carriers had been completed too late to see action in the war but are worthy of mention because of their interesting designs.

Royal Navy *Colossus* Class Carriers

In late 1941, after the Pearl Harbor attack, the British Admiralty foresaw an increasing role for aircraft carriers in the expanding war and envisaged the production of about one dozen identical carriers in much the same manner as the U.S. Navy *Essex* class carrier program was developed. Britain, however, did not have the productive capacity of the U.S. and the few specialized naval construction shipyards that were able to build large fleet carriers were fully occupied with other warship construction. It was, therefore, expedient to have the hulls of the new carriers constructed to commercial standards at the merchant shipbuilding division of naval construction shipyards, as well as merchant ship specialists, such as the escort carriers. In fact, the construction of escort type carriers was considered but discarded in favor of an Intermediate Aircraft Carrier or Light Fleet Carrier design. Other factors that prompted this decision was the production difficulty to supply the usual fleet carrier turret guns, armor plate, and gun fire control equipment. These inexpensive and easily constructed carriers were designed to be propelled by standard destroyer machinery. The initial aircraft complement was to be hooked Sea Hurricanes and Seafires. These were to be converted from RAF supplies which could be spared at this time because the Battle of Britain was winding down.

Colossus/Majestic Classes

A total of 16 carriers was ordered from nine shipyards with the first two keels laid on June 1, 1942. The lead ship was named *Colossus*

The Royal Navy Colossus class Intermediate Aircraft Carriers were constructed in merchant shipyards rather than in naval shipyards because the latter were fully occupied with other warship construction. The first and last hulls of the 16 ship class were commissioned about three years apart; 1943-1946. (Ministry of Defence [Navy])

and the remaining 15 members of the class were *Perseus, Glory, Ocean, Vengeance, Pioneer, Warrior, Venerable, Theseus, Triumph, Majestic, Terrible, Magnificent, Hercules, Leviathan,* and *Powerful.* The last six were modified to handle 20,000 pound high speed aircraft by reinforcing the Flight Deck. Hull subdivision was also improved but less fuel was carried to compensate for the additional steel weight. Modifications to the original *Colossus* class design were so extensive within the hull that the last six ships are considered to be a new *Majestic* class.

The basic design appeared to be a scaled-down version of the *Illustrious* class, especially in the concept of blending the Flight Deck into the hull in such a manner as to obliterate the exact point where one began and the other ended. This technique had been diametrically opposite to that used by the U.S. and Imperial Japanese Navy aircraft carriers in which the flight deck appeared to have been an afterthought.

Colossus Class Data
These unarmored, twin-screw carriers attained a maximum speed of 25 knots with 40,000 shaft horsepower geared steam turbines. Steam at 400 pounds per square inch pressure was generated in four boilers. In order to provide greater resistance to damage, auxiliary machinery rooms were arranged alternately with boiler or fire rooms and engine rooms arranged abreast but daigonally opposed or staggered to each other. The 31,000 tons of fuel oil gave the ships a range of 12,000 miles at 14 knots.

Displacement of 18,000 tons full load was maximum for this class which varied almost 2,000 tons from heaviest to lightest ship because of the different roles assigned, such as: night-fighter carrier, strike carrier, combat air patrol carrier, and maintenance carrier. The overall length was 695 feet and Flight Deck dimensions were 80 x 695 feet. Beam was also 80 feet. The initial complement was estimated at 854 ships' personnel plus 222 Fleet Air Arm personnel; however, this increased to 1,300 in service. Full load draft was 23 feet. Two elevators and one hydraulic catapult and a single 17 foot-6 inches hight Hangar were installed.

Defensive armament comprised six quad-mounted two-pounders and (21) 40 millimeter antiaircraft guns. After the initial Seafires and Sea Hurricanes more potent and adaptable shipboard aircraft were fitted. Mixed bags of Hellcats and Fireflies, Corsairs and Fireflies, plus Barracudas and Fireflies were carried, depending upon the assigned role.

Colossus was the first to be launched, September 30, 1943, and commissioned December 16, 1943, while *Triumph* was the last to be launched, October 2, 1944, and commissioned May 6, 1946. None of the class saw operational service in World War II; however, the design did become the model for many postwar carriers.

Colossus Class Disposals
Several were retained by the Royal Navy while many others were sold to members of the Commonwealth and to eager foreign governments. *Colossus* became the French Navy Arromanches in 1946; *Hercules* became the Indian Navy *Vikrant* in 1957; *Powerful* became the Royal Canadian Navy *Bonaventure* in 1952; *Terrible* became the Royal Australian Navy *Sydney* in 1948; *Majestic* became the Royal Australian Navy *Melbourne*; *Venerable* became the Royal

Netherlands Navy *Karel Doorman* in 1948 and then became t Brazilian Navy *25th de Mayo* in 1968; *Warrior* became the Arge tinian Navy *Independencia* in 1958; and *Vengeance* became t Brazilian Navy *Minas Gerais* in 1957 after service in the Roy Australian Navy. The remainder were sold for scrap and broken after their service in the Royal Navy.

Japanese Army Aircraft Carriers
It was the Imperial Japanese Army instead of the Imperial Japane Navy that acquired two 10,000 ton tankers and arranged to ha flight decks installed so that Japanese Army Air Force fighters, su as the Nakajima Ki 84 "Frank", could protect troop convoys fro air attack. Essentially, the converted tankers were to be floating strips with no elevator, hangar or catapult. Commissioned on Jan ary 27, 1945 the first conversion, *Yamashiro Maru*, was not able sortie due to the lack of fuel and was sunk by U.S. Navy planes Yokohama Harbor on February 17, 1945. The 75 x 410 foot Flig Deck had been supported over the 516 foot long hull by heavy ve tical stanchions. The ship was to have operated eight planes, have crew of 220, and her 4,500 horsepower geared turbine was to dri the ship to 15 knots. *Yamashiro Maru*'s sister ship *Chigusa Ma* conversion never materialized.

Japanese Navy Aircraft Carriers
The Imperial Japanese Navy also ordered two tankers to be co verted into escort carriers, *Shimane Maru* and *Otakisan Maru*. T former was commissioned on March 30, 1945; however, t *Otakisan Maru* conversion was never completed and she was su by a mine after the war's end. *Shimane Maru* was 526 feet lo overall with a 500 x 75 feet Flight Deck mounted on an amidshi Hangar with vertical stanchions fore and aft. The 8,600 shaft hors power geared turbine drove the ship to 18.5 knots. One elevator b no catapult or arresting gear was fitted. As with *Yamashiro Mar Shimane Maru* was never used operationally and was sunk on Ju 24, 1945, during a U.S. Navy air raid.

Japanese Amphibious Assault Ship
A third Japanese carrier conversion was the first example of amphibious assault ship; a type which was to be in favor with t U.S. Navy well after the war. The twin-screw ship's 10,000 sha horsepower geared turbines enabled *Kumano Maru* to attain a knot top speed. The converted cargo ship was 500 feet long over topped with a 360 x 70 feet Flight Deck. Although not verified, it assumed that at least one elevator was installed to handle the p posed complement of almost 40 Japanese Army Air Force plan The planes were to protect beachhead landings but could not retu to the ship due to the high landing speeds and absence of arresti hooks. A dozen landing craft could be discharged into the water inclined ramps through stern doors. *Kumano Maru* never saw o erational service.

Unfortunately, there are no known photographs of these uniq Japanese Spartan designs.

Commencement Bay Class CVE Carriers
Although used mainly for transport and training duties during t war, the U.S. Navy *Commencement Bay* class escort carriers form

The Commencement Bay carriers formed the nucleus of the U.S. Navy's immediate postwar ASW Fleet. This is USS Mindoro (CVE-120) which was in service from 1946 to 1955. The carrier is shown here with five helicopters deployed on Deck during October 1953. (Official U.S. Navy Photograph)

the nucleus of the Navy's antisubmarine warfare (ASW) fleet during the postwar years. By the time the keels were laid, from late 1943 through 1945, critical machinery and materials had become more readily available than when the *Casablanca* class CVE was conceived; therefore, a geared steam turbine powerplant plus electric motor-driven pumps and other ancillary equipment were fitted in this new CVE class.

The originally proposed 35 ships was reduced to 19 carriers constructed with 17 actually commissioned; eight of which were completed after Japan's surrender. The hull design and general arrangement followed those of the *Sangamon* class tanker conversions with the machinery spaces well aft. This twin-screw design was, however, an improvement over the *Sangamon* conversions by placing the engine rooms and fire or boiler room in a staggered arrangement to provide more safety in the event of a torpedo hit in way of the machinery spaces.

Commencement Bay Class Data
Designed by the firm of Gibbs and Cox, the *Commencement Bay* carriers had a full load displacement of 21,700 tons. Overall length was 555 feet with the Flight Deck measuring 80 x 495 feet. The 16,000 shaft horsepower propelled the ships to a maximum speed

of 19 knots. The aircraft complement was 33 planes compared to the 28 planes of the *Casablanca*. The entire class was built by Todd-Pacific Shipyard.

The numbers CVE 105 to CVE 123 were assigned to this class. Each ship required a complement of 138 officers and 996 crew plus the air group.

Defensive armament included two 5 inch guns on the fantail plus 36x40 millimeter and 20x20 millimeter antiaircraft guns distributed around the perimeter of the Flight Deck.

First All Marine Aircraft Carriers
USS Cape Gloucester (CVE-109) was one of the first all U.S. Marine carriers. Heretofore, Marine Aviation had been shore-based; partially due to the ban on Corsairs flying from carriers and, when this was lifted, Marine Corsair squadrons operated on carriers along with the regular Navy squadrons. As small task groups were organized to cover amphibious assault and ASW activities off the China coast and Okinawa, Marine-only squadrons were deployed on some *Commencement Bay* class escort carriers, *Cape Gloucester* being one of the first. VMF-351 flew Corsairs and VMTB-132 flew Avengers from *USS Cape Gloucester*.

The 19 ships of the Commencement Bay class escort carriers (CVE-105 to 123) were constructed near the end of World War II. USS Cape Gloucester (CVE-109), shown here, was one of the first all U.S. Marine aircraft carriers and saw action in the assault on the Japanese home islands. (Official U.S. Navy Photograph, Courtesy U.S. Naval Institute)

The Allies lost no time to analyze the design, construction and performance of captured Japanese aircraft. This Mitsubishi A6M2 Zero is being tested by British forces in South East Asia. Observe the British insignia and special codes of the Allied Technical Air Intelligence Unit, S.E. Asia (ATAIU-Insignia-SEA). (U.S. Naval Historical Center)

At the war's end many Japanese naval aircraft were found at the Yokasuka Naval Arsenal. These had been experimental models of operational types and included: (1) Liquid-cooled engine-powered Judy dive bomber; (2) Air-cooled engine-powered Judy dive bomber; (3) Myrt undergoing conversion to B-29 interceptor; (4) Nakajima Irving study for Gekko naval night fighter; (5) Irving undergoing conversion to naval assault fighter and B-29 interceptor. (6) Betty land-based twin-engine bombers which made many torpedo attacks on U.S. Navy ships. (U.S. National Archives)

Nimitz Becomes CNO

In September 1945 Fleet Admiral Chester W. Nimitz issued a hearty "Well Done" to the officers and men of the Pacific escort aircraft carriers citing the operations at Tarawa, Leyte and Okinawa. He became U.S. Navy Chief of Naval Operations (CNO) on December 15, 1945.

CARRIER RELATED ACTIVITIES

As the end of 1945 approached a few significant carrier related activities are of interest. The battle carrier *U.S.S. Franklin D. Roosevelt* (CVB-42) was commissioned on October 27, 1945 and the *Essex* class carrier *Princeton* (CV-37) was commissioned on November 18, 1945.

The first carrier landing was made by a jet-powered aircraft when a Ryan FR-1 Fireball alighted on the escort carrier *U.S.S. Wake Island* (CVE-65) on November 6, 1945. On December 3, 1945 Royal Navy Lieutenant Commander F.M. Brown became the first pilot to land a purely jet-propelled plane on the deck of an aircraft carrier, *HMS Ocean*. The plane was a DeHavilland Vampire specially modified for carrier operation, and designed by Sir Geoffrey DeHavilland, who was awarded the Elmer A. Sperry Award in 1959 for his work with jet engines and jet-propelled aircraft.

As World War II came to an end, carrier aviation found itself on the threshold of a new and exciting era. The jet-powered plane had proven it could operate from carriers and this stimulated the development of imaginative jet and propeller designs; many of which have become timeless classics.

Carrier designs also underwent unimagined development to meet the requirements of the new aircraft.

Damaged Japanese aircraft were found at many Japanese repair depots after the war. Among the aircraft found at the Atsugi Airfield are: (11)Mitsubishi "Zero" naval fighter; (12) Nakajima "Myrt" reconnaissance plane; (13) Nakajima "Gekko" naval night fighter (14) Aichi "Judy" dive bomber/reconnaissance plane; (15) Mitsubishi "Jack" naval interceptor fighter. (U.S. Air Force Photo)

Warbirds Dictate Carrier Design • Shipboard Aircraft Development at War's End • Exciting Shipboard Aircraft • Operation Crossroads • Colossus Class Innovations • First U.S. Carrier Jet Squadron • U.S. Navy Wants Supercarrier and Atomic Bomb • The Cold War Begins • U.S. Navy Protests Unification • James Forrestal Promotes Supercarrier • Revolt of the Admirals • U.S. Shipboard Aircraft Development Continues • U.S. Sixth & Seventh Fleets and Missile Test • Communist Confrontation • Douglas Skyraider Variants • Unpainted Carrier Aircraft Experiments • Blended Jet Fuel • U.S. Navy Adopts Steam Catapults • Royal Navy Eagle Class Carriers • U.S. Supercarriers At Last • The Productive Decade

---

WARBIRDS DICTATE CARRIER DESIGN

The demobilization that followed the Japanese surrender in 1945 rendered U.S. and British naval aviation virtually impotent along with the other military services. The one redeeming factor, as it had been after World War I, was research. Now the quest was to create the optimum jet-powered and propeller-driven naval shipboard warplanes. So great and successful was this development of shipboard Warbirds that aircraft carrier design found itself lagging behind the naval aircraft design explosion but was quick to adapt to the faster and heavier aircraft. Heretofore, the carrier Warbirds had been developed for service aboard existing or planned carriers; however, the postwar years ushered in a new set of rules in the development of carriers and carrier aircraft. The tables had been turned and the carrier was now forced to meet the requirements of the rapidly developing carrier aircraft. This was to be the most momentous change in naval shipboard aviation; a veritable revolution.

Midway Class Battle Carriers

The most outstanding aircraft carriers constructed too late to participate in World War II were the three *Midway* class battle carriers, which are often called the first of the postwar American supercarriers. The class was named to commemorate the great naval battle of 1942 and the three carriers were ordered one month after the battle.

Midway Class Design

The *Midway* class proved a radical departure from standard U.S. Navy aircraft carrier design philosophy by adopting the Royal Navy practice of armored flight decks because of the British carriers' ability to endure direct hits from heavy bombs. It is important to recall at this time, that each of the three naval powers appeared to be groping for the ideal aircraft carrier recipe. The previously mentioned Japanese carrier *Taiho* broke with tradition and embraced the Royal Navy armored flight deck concept, yet the British *Malta* class abandoned the armored flight deck and hangar in favor of the U.S. Navy practice of open hangar sides, as was previously described. Apparently, in their anxiety to achieve perfection, each navy imagined something better in foreign carrier designs and emulated the admired features.

PREVIOUS: Grumman Panther jet fighters are catapulted from the deck of USS Bon Homme Richard (CVA-31) for a mission over the Korean mainland. Panthers were employed in fighter and ground support missions. (Official U.S. Navy Photograph, News Photo Division)

The Midway class U.S. battle carriers were America's first Supercarrie[rs] and were the world's largest at the time of their completion. USS Midw[ay] (CVB-41) (below), USS Franklin D. Roosevelt (CVB-42) and USS Cora[l] Sea (CVB-43) (above) featured armored Flight Decks. USS Coral Sea [is] shown with Corsairs and Skyraiders on deck. (Official U.S. Navy Photograph, News Photo Division)

This battle carrier design was prepared to operate twin-engi[ne] carrier aircraft capable of carrying the atomic bomb in order to gi[ve] the U.S. Navy a nuclear capability. This requirement, alone, w[as] enough to enlarge the *Midway* class over the *Essex*; however, the 1/2 inch Flight Deck armor plus 2 inch armor for both Main De[ck] and Hangar Deck, 8 inch armor belt along the waterline, and 6 [1/2] inch bulkheads up to the belt reducing to 2 1/2 inch above the belt [and] Hangar Deck added thousands of tons, which further increased t[he] size of the ship. *USS Midway (CVB-41), USS Franklin D. Roosev[elt]*

USS Midway plows through rough seas and gale force winds in the eastern Mediterranean Sea. Observe the seven gun turrets along the side of the hull. Note the Corsairs in the foreground on the carrier from which this photograph was taken. (U.S. National Archives)

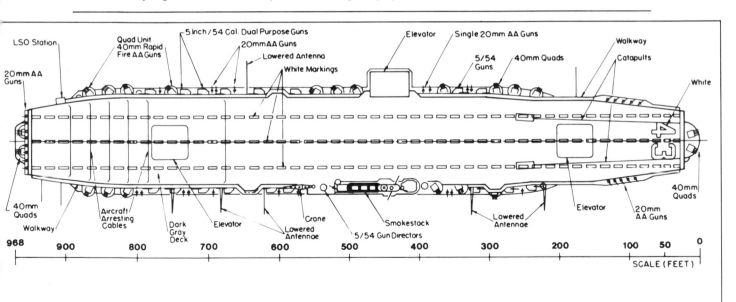

USS Coral Sea   CVB·43

CIRCA 1947

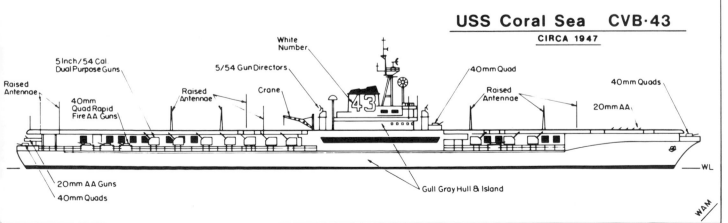

(CVB-42), and *USS Coral Sea* (CVB-43) attained a deep load displacement of 60,858 tons, then the largest carriers in the world.

USS Franklin D. Roosevelt Name Breaks Tradition

This aircraft carrier is the first U.S. aircraft carrier to be named after a person. It had been more rule than custom to name U.S. Navy aircraft carriers to commemorate battles in which America had been involved or to honor famous U.S. warships, but now that rule had been broken and *Franklin D. Roosevelt* was the first of the many pro-Navy, especially pro-aircraft carrier military and civilian personalities, as well as naval leaders, to have been so honored except, of course, *USS Langley* (CV-1).

Shipyards and Construction Time

Newport News Shipbuilding constructed *Midway* and *Coral Sea*, while the New York Naval Shipyard, also known as the Brooklyn Navy Yard, built *Franklin D. Roosevelt*. Elapsed time from the keel laying of the first ship, *Midway*, to the commissioning of the last ship, *Coral Sea*, was four years; October 1943 to October 1947.

Midway Class Data

Overall length was 968 feet with a 113 x 932 feet Flight Deck. Hull beam was the same as the Flight Deck, 113 feet. Loaded draft was 34 feet - 6 inches. The four propellers were driven by geared steam turbines, which had been built for the cancelled *Montana* class battleships. Developing a total of 212,000 shaft horsepower, the powerplant drove the huge ships to a maximum speed of 33 knots. Range was 15,000 miles at 15 knots. The proposed aircraft complement was 137, which was to include a number of twin-engine bombers; however, the initial complement comprised Corsairs, Hellcats and Helldivers. A total of 350,000 gallons of aviation fuel was carried.

The operating complement was about 2,500 officers and crew. The air group complement of about 1,600 increased the total number of officers and men on board to 4,100.

SHIPBOARD AIRCRAFT DEVELOPMENT AT WAR'S END

In addition to aircraft carriers, several promising shipboard aircraft were under development when Japan surrendered but they were not ready in time for use in World War II.

Grumman F8F Bearcat

In order to continue the development of the Wildcat/Hellcat fighters, the U.S. Navy placed an order with Grumman for two prototypes of a new shipboard fighter design on November 27, 1943. The XF8F-1 Bearcat reversed the apparent trend that bigger was better and followed the Messerschmitt design philosophy of designing the smallest possible airframe that could handle the largest possible engine and be able to contain the necessary fuel and armament.

Bearcat Production

The first prototype made its initial flight on August 21, 1944 and met the specified performance, especially the rate of climb which was a phenomenal 4,800 feet per minute! This was ideal for a fighter

First flown in August, 1944 the Grumman Bearcat reversed the trend of increasingly larger fighter aircraft and was the smallest possible airframe that could handle the largest possible engine, fuel and armament. (Official U.S. Navy Photograph, Naval Imaging Command)

whose intended primary role was to be as an interceptor from smaller aircraft carriers. The U.S. Navy ordered 2,033 production Bearcats from Grumman on October 6, 1944. Eastern Aircraft Division of General Motors received a contract to produce 1,876 more Bearcats designated F3M-1. Production deliveries began in February 1945.

Bearcat Data

Wingspan of the F8F-1 Bearcat was 35 feet - 10 inches, which was smaller than that of the Wildcat and about the same as the Brewster Buffalo. Wing area was 244 square feet, which was 90 square feet less than the Hellcat and also less than the Wildcat. Overall length was 28 feet-3 inches, with a height of 13 feet-10 inches. Empty weight was 7,070 pounds and gross weight was 12,947 pounds which was 2,466 pounds lighter than the Hellcat. A 2,100 horsepower Pratt & Whitney R-2800-34W Twin Wasp, 18-cylinder, air cooled, radial engine drove the F8F-1 to a top speed of 421 miles per hour; faster than the Hellcat. Cruising speed was 163 miles per hour, at which speed the range was 1,105 miles. The production F8F-1 initial rate of climb was 4,570 feet per minute and service ceiling was 38,700 feet.

Armament was four .50 inch caliber machine guns located in the wing. This little plane could also carry 2,000 pounds of bombs, two drop tanks or four 5 inch rockets.

In view of the light structure a very unusual design feature had been incorporated in the wing but was eventually discontinued. Break points were located near the tips so that if the plane was maneuvered too violently the wing tips would break off at selected locations, thereby relieving the excessive strain on the wings. Explosive bolts enabled the pilot to jettison the remaining wingtip in the event that only one tip broke away during the maneuver.

Aerobatic Bearcat

The Bearcat was apparently very maneuverable because the world famous aerobatic expert Major Al Williams selected the Bearcat as his Gulfhawk 4 and performed very intricate aerobatics with the plane during the postwar period.

Folding Wing Despite Short Span

Unlike the previous Grumman monoplane fighters, the Bearcat wing

Ided upwards and towards the fuselage. The hinge-point was at
e aileron/wing flap junction, further outboard than on most air-
aft because of its short wingspan.

arcat Production

pon the Japanese surrender the Eastern Aircraft contract was ter-
inated and Grumman production reduced to 899 planes. Many
rplus Bearcats, designated F8F-1D, were used by France to com-
t the revolutionaries in the Indo-China War. The Vietnam and
lai Air Forces also used Bearcats to help the French.

ngle-Seat Strike Fighters

s single-seat fighters began to bear the brunt of aerial combat,
cluding interception, ground attack and dive bombing in 1944
d 1945, new purpose-built designs appeared. The trend towards
ry large single-engine multipurpose craft operated by a crew of
e produced some very interesting planes that made their appear-
ce too late for World War II.

awker Sea Fury

Ithough one of the cleanest and best looking of all Fleet Air Arm
ciprocating engine-powered aircraft, the Hawker Sea Fury was
scended from the brutish but devastatingly efficient RAF Tem-
st design.The Hawker Sea Fury was developed from studies to
oduce a lighter version of the Tempest for the RAF in 1942. Six
ototypes were ordered, powered by a variety of engines, includ-
g air and liquid-cooled types of radial, vee, and "H" configura-
on. Tests were also conducted with three-bladed contra-rotating
opellers. The 2,480 horsepower, 18-cylinder, twin-row, air-cooled
ristol Centaurus XVIII sleeve-valve radial engine was selected
cause it was the most readily available. This Sea Fury flew for
e first time on February 21, 1945.

a Fury Data

he Royal Air Force Hawker Fury and the Fleet Air Arm Sea Fury
d been developed simultaneously, sharing as many construction
atures as possible in order to facilitate production. Top speed of
e Mark XI was a respectable 460 miles per hour at 18,000 feet
d range was 1,040 miles using a drop tank. The maximum take-
f weight was 12,500 pounds and service ceiling was 35,800 feet.
'ingspan was 38 feet-5 inches with a length of 34 feet-8 inches

*e Fleet Air Arm Hawker Sea Fury was the fastest and most efficient
rrier-based propeller driven fighter/bomber developed for the Royal
avy. The author examines the wing-folding installation of this Sea
ury. (WAM Foto)*

*Of interest in this photograph of a Hawker Sea Fury, shown at the
moment of impact with the HMS Glory flight deck, is the compressed
starboard (right hand) landing gearstrut. Apparently the craft was in a
slight bank to starboard upon touchdown, hence the lowermost landing
gear was forced to bear the force of the initial impact but compressed
enough until the port side strut touched down to share the shock without
a bounce. It is for this reason that long stoke oleo struts are usually
selected for carrier aircraft. Also of interest are the tailhook/arresting
cable contact and the fitting that keeps the cable suspended above the
deck. (Imperial War Museum)*

and a height of 15 feet-10 inches. Wing panels were folded hydraulically.

The Sea Fury was armed with four 20 millimeter Hispano Mark
V cannon in the outer wing panels with 145 rounds per gun, plus
(8) 60 pound rockets under the wing. Alternatively, two 1,000 pound
bombs could be carried instead of the rockets.

This all-metal stressed skin construction single-seater was the
end of an era for the Royal Navy because it was the last reciprocating or piston engine-driven fighter to serve with the Fleet Air Arm.
Its service life extended from 1947 to 1957 when it was finally
phased out by the equally beautiful jet-powered Sea Hawk, which
will be described later in this chapter.

Sea Fury Production

When the war in Europe ended, the Royal Air Force cancelled the
Fury program; however, Sea Fury development continued for Fleet
Air Arm operations in the Pacific. When production ended in 1952,
65 Furies and 860 Sea Furies had been constructed. The first unit to
receive Sea Furies was 802 Squadron in 1948, followed by 801,
804,.805, and 807 Squadrons, all of which served on the *Colossus*
class carriers *HMS Theseus, Glory* and *Ocean* as of 1949.

Sea Fury Exports

Hawker Sea Furies were exported to the German Federal Republic,
Netherlands, Cuba, Burma, Egypt and Pakistan, as well as serving
with the Royal Australian and Royal Canadian Navies; a good indication that this fine design was in great demand. Although the Sea
Fury arrived too late to become operational in World War II it became one of the most successful propeller-driven fighter/bombers
of the Korean Conflict. Surplus Sea Furies have been much sought
after for civilian air race competition.

HAWKER SEA FURY F.B. Mk. II
ROYAL CANADIAN NAVY SQUADRON NO. VF-870

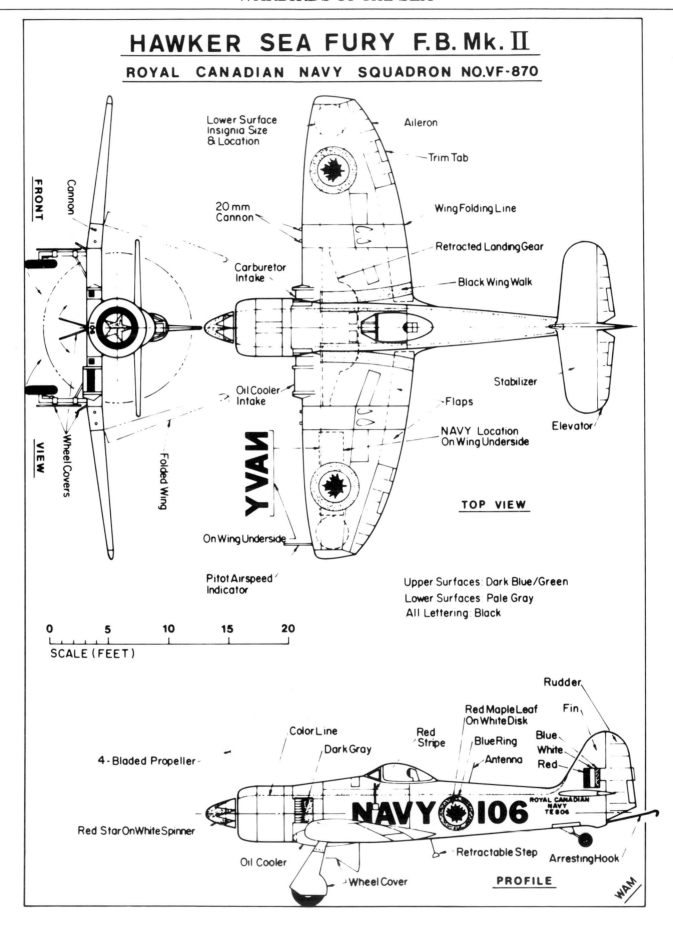

FRONT

Cannon

VIEW

Wheel Covers

Folded Wing

Lower Surface Insignia Size & Location

20 mm Cannon

Carburetor Intake

Oil Cooler Intake

NAVY

On Wing Underside

Pitot Airspeed Indicator

Aileron

Trim Tab

Wing Folding Line

Retracted Landing Gear

Black Wing Walk

Stabilizer

Flaps

Elevator

NAVY Location On Wing Underside

TOP VIEW

Upper Surfaces: Dark Blue/Green
Lower Surfaces: Pale Gray
All Lettering: Black

0   5   10   15   20
SCALE (FEET)

4-Bladed Propeller

Color Line

Dark Gray

Red Stripe

Red Maple Leaf On White Disk

Blue Ring

Antenna

Rudder

Fin

Blue
White
Red

Red Star On White Spinner

NAVY ◉ 106

ROYAL CANADIAN NAVY TE 806

Oil Cooler

Wheel Cover

Retractable Step

Arresting Hook

PROFILE

WAM

BLACKBURN FIREBRAND T.F. Mk. V

FAA NO.827 SQUADRON - HMS EAGLE

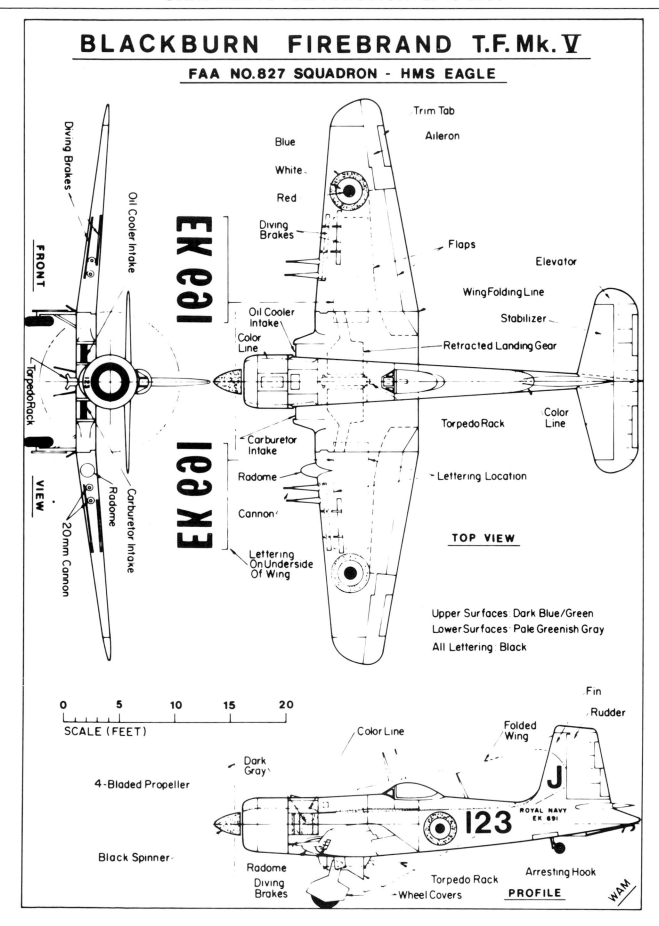

FRONT

VIEW

Diving Brakes

Oil Cooler Intake

Torpedo Rack

20mm Cannon

Carburetor Intake

Radome

EK691

EK691

Oil Cooler Intake

Color Line

Carburetor Intake

Radome

Cannon

Lettering On Underside Of Wing

Trim Tab

Aileron

Blue

White

Red

Diving Brakes

Flaps

Elevator

Wing Folding Line

Stabilizer

Retracted Landing Gear

Torpedo Rack

Color Line

Lettering Location

TOP VIEW

Upper Surfaces: Dark Blue/Green
Lower Surfaces: Pale Greenish Gray
All Lettering: Black

0   5   10   15   20

SCALE (FEET)

4-Bladed Propeller

Black Spinner

Radome Diving Brakes

Color Line

Dark Gray

Wheel Covers

Torpedo Rack

Folded Wing

Fin

Rudder

J

ROYAL NAVY
EK 691

123

Arresting Hook

PROFILE

WAM

The Fleet Air Arm Blackburn Firebrand started as a carrier based interceptor but was developed into a torpedo/bomber strike aircraft. A Firebrand Mark IV is shown with torpedo in 1945. (Ministry of Defence [Navy])

Blackburn Firebrand

One of the largest single-seaters of its time, the Royal Navy Blackburn Firebrand, required a five year gestation period before becoming operational at the war's end. The Firebrand design started as a single-seat, short-range, carrier-based interceptor, in accordance with Royal Navy Specification N.11/40. The Firebrand prototype first flew on February 27, 1942, powered by a Napier Sabre III liquid-cooled, 24-cylinder, sleeve valve, H-type engine of 2,300 horsepower.

Conversion To Strike Aircraft

By early 1943 the Supermarine Seafire was fully operational and the Ministry of Aircraft Production decided that another fighter was not necessary. The MAP took advantage of the Firebrand's enormous load-carrying capability, as well as Blackburn's vast experience with torpedo aircraft and requested that the Firebrand be developed into a single-seater, hard-hitting, torpedo-carrying, carrier strike aircraft.

Firebrand Torpedo Installation

Provisions were made to carry and launch an 1,850 pound, 18 inch torpedo. A specially designed torpedo mount was developed that could change the torpedo angle relative to the fuselage. In the air, the torpedo was parallel to the fuselage; however, on the ground the torpedo nose was lowered and the fins raised so the torpedo would clear the ground without the necessity of lengthening the landing gear. The Firebrand made its first flight with a torpedo on April 2, 1943.

Engine Change

The Strike Fighter Specification S.8/43 was finalized and issued on October 3, 1943. This document required, as with the Hawker Sea Fury, that the neatly cowled Sabre be replaced by the Bristol Centaurus engine which necessitated a reworking of the Firebrand fuselage forward structure. The prototype T.F. Mark III first flew on December 21, 1943.

Dive Bombing Added

This remarkable plane's ability was extended to include dive-bombing by installing two 2,000 pound bomb racks under the wing outer panel. Four 20 millimeter cannon were mounted in each wing outer

panel with 200 rounds per gun. Alternatives to the torpedo and bombs were (16) 60 pound rockets or two 45 gallon drop tanks for long-range work. Diving speed was limited to 300 miles per hour for dive-bombing assignments by means of retractable spoilers located in recesses in the upper and lower surfaces of the wing.

Firebrand Data

The fin and rudder were enlarged on the Mark IV, which entered service with No. 813 Squadron during September 1945. The extended wingspan of 51 feet-3 1/2 inches could be reduced to feet-10 inches by manually rotating the wing outer panels 90 degrees so the leading edge is uppermost and folding them back alongside the fuselage. Overall length was 38 feet-9 inches and height feet-3 inches. Wing area was 383 square feet. The bare weight was 11,689 pounds and loaded weight was 15,671 pounds. The Mark IV could attain a top speed of 342 miles per hour, which dropped 320 miles per hour when carrying the torpedo or bombs. At a cruising speed of 256 miles per hour the Firebrand had a range 745 miles. The initial rate of climb was 2,440 feet per minute, and service ceiling was 34,000 feet. A total of 220 Blackburn Firebrand of all Marks were constructed.

Aerobatics With a Torpedo

In September 1946 the amazing Firebrand put on an unforgettable and astounding display of low altitude aerobatics while carrying torpedo! The pilot was P.G. Lawrence, a former Fleet Air Arm pilot who had become a Blackburn test pilot.

Firebrand Deployment

Firebrands served on *HMS Illustrious*, *Eagle* and *Implacable* although *Illustrious* and *Eagle* were engaged in the Korean conflict, Firebrands did not fight in that war mainly because there were no North Korean ships that were so large to require a torpedo attack to sink them.

U.S. Navy Single-Seat Strike Aircraft

Apparently the new concept of combining dive bombing and torpedo operations into one single-seater design, as the Blackburn Firebrand, influenced the U.S. Navy to abandon its two and three-seat specialized dive bomber and torpedo planes. On December 31, 19 the U.S. Navy placed an order with Curtiss for a single-engine single-place attack plane that could combine dive bombing and torpedo launching, and carry a big ordnance load. A similar order was given to Kaiser-Fleetwings on March 31, 1944 while Martin received an order on May 31, 1944. A fourth order was awarded Douglas on July 6, 1944 and the competition was on. All designs had to be carrier-based, single-seaters.

The Curtiss and Kaiser-Fleetwings designs never passed prototype stage; however, the Martin and Douglas designs received production orders.

Martin AM-1 Mauler

The Martin Model 210, Navy designation XBTM-1 (Experimental Bomber Torpedo Martin-One) had made its first flight on August 26, 1944. Flight trials were successful, resulting in a U.S. Navy production order on January 15, 1945 for 750 Martin BTM-

The Martin AM-1 Mauler weighed 14,500 pounds empty and could carry a payload equal to its empty weight. This strike/attack plane could takeoff with three torpedoes and six large bombs. The XBTM-1 Mauler experimental prototype is shown. (Official U.S. Navy Photograph, News Photo Division)

Meanwhile, the U.S. Navy simplified its designation code to combine the Bomber and Torpedo into Attack for all strike aircraft; therefore, by the time the first production Martin BTM-1 had made its initial flight on December 16, 1946, it had become Martin AM-1 (Attack Martin-One). The name Mauler was also adopted for this plane.

Mauler Data

The Martin AM-1 Mauler was powered by a 2,975 horsepower, 18-cylinder, air-cooled Pratt & Whitney R-3350-4 radial engine which gave the plane a top speed of 367 miles per hour at 11,600 feet. Cruising speed was 189 miles per hour at which speed the range was 1,800 miles. Initial rate of climb was 2,780 feet per minute and service ceiling was 30,500 feet.

With a wingspan of 50 feet, length of 41 feet-2 inches and height of 16 feet-10 inches, the 496 square feet wing area Mauler weighed 14,500 pounds empty with a gross weight of 23,386 pounds. The AM-1 demonstrated a prodigious load-carrying capacity. Although the normal ordnance load was about 5,000 pounds, the Mauler performed the remarkable feat of flying with 10,689 pounds of ordnance, plus 3,940 pounds of fuel, for a gross takeoff weight of 29,129 pounds!

Fixed armament was (4) 20 millimeter cannon in the wing outer panels. Strong points under the wing were intended for three torpedoes; one under each outer panel and one under at the center section, plus six large bombs under each wing outer panel. Rockets could be installed, instead of the bombs.

Mauler Productions

When 152 Maulers had been completed the U.S. Navy stopped production and the last Martin AM-1 was delivered in October 1949.

ECM Maulers

Special electronic gear was installed on six Maulers for electronic countermeasures; these craft being designated AM-1Q, were one of the first production aircraft to be so fitted.

Douglas AD-1 Skyraider

The fourth and most satisfactory plane in the U.S. Navy single-seater attack plane competition was the Douglas design. Ed Heinemann, of Douglas Dauntless fame, and his design team had developed the XBT2D-1 into one of the most successful of all Douglas aircraft produced for the U.S. Navy. This plane was to become known as the famous AD-1 Skyraider, which enjoyed 22 years of service in the U.S. Navy through two wars.

The prototype XBT2D-1 made its first flight on March 18, 1945 and one month later the U.S. Navy ordered 548 production Skyraiders as the AD-1. Production deliveries began in December 1946; however, the contract had been cut back to 277 planes after the Japanese surrender in World War II. The AD-1 entered service with Attack Squadron VA-19A based on the carrier *Midway*.

Skyraider Variations

While the AD-1 was being produced and delivered to Marine and Navy squadrons, six of the XBT2D-1 prototypes were being converted to test new configurations which included: nocturnal operations with an enormous searchlight under the port (left) wing and a radome (radar dome) under the starboard (right) wing, plus two radar operators in the fuselage; reconnaissance version with cameras mounted in the fuselage at various angles; electronic countermeasure (ECM) with the equipment and an operator located in the fuselage; airborne early warning version with a large bulbous radome under the fuselage; and one was converted into the AD-2 prototype which had a strengthened wing, increased fuel capacity and the installation of the 2,700 horsepower Wright R-3350-26W twin-row, 18-cylinder, air-cooled radial engine to replace the original 2,500 horsepower Wright R-3350 engine.

AD-2 Data

The AD-2 wingspan was 50 feet with a length of 38 feet-2 inches and height of 15 feet-5 inches. Wing area was 400 square feet. Empty weight was 10,546 pounds and maximum takeoff weight was 18,263 pounds; however up to 8,000 pounds of ordnance could be carried.

The Douglas Skyraider single-seater strike/attack plane enjoyed 22 years of service in the U.S. Navy. A squadron of AD-1 Skyraiders is shown here in echelon formation. (McDonnell Douglas, Courtesy Harry Gann)

It is interesting to note that the Martin and Douglas attack plane could carry the same weight in bombs and torpedoes as the World War II Boeing B-17E Flying Fortress four-engine bomber! The AD-2 Skyraider's maximum speed was 321 miles per hour at 18,300 feet. Cruising speed was 198 miles per hour, at which speed the range was 915 miles. Initial rate of climb was 2,800 feet per minute and service ceiling was 32,700 feet.

Armament consisted of (2) 20 millimeter cannon in the wings with 15 strong points under the wings and fuselage for torpedoes, bombs or rockets. Later modifications were able to also carry napalm, mines, and depth charges and the wing armament was increased to four cannon, starting with the AD-4B.

Production

The last of 3,180 Skyraiders was completed in 1957; 177 of which were AD-2 models. The Skyraider was very active in the Korean and Vietnam fighting.

U.S. Navy Interest In Turbojets

German and British turbojet engine-powered fighters had been developed by 1943 and the Messerschmitt Me 262 had already been flown in combat by 1945; however, the U.S. Navy was taking a cautious approach to jet-powered aircraft.

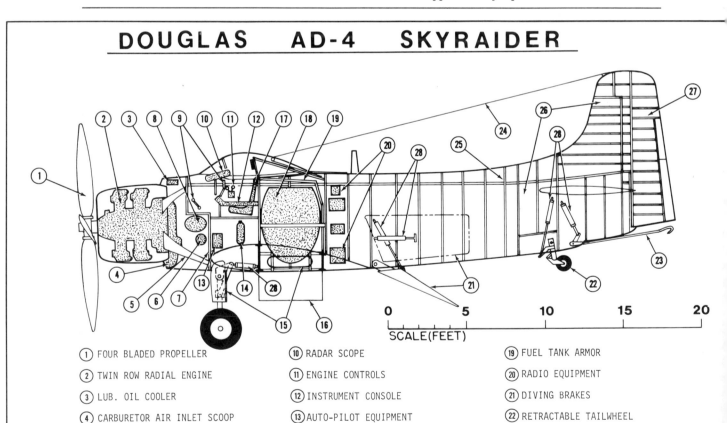

DOUGLAS AD-4 SKYRAIDER

SCALE (FEET)
0   5   10   15   20

① FOUR BLADED PROPELLER
② TWIN ROW RADIAL ENGINE
③ LUB. OIL COOLER
④ CARBURETOR AIR INLET SCOOP
⑤ ENGINE MOUNTS
⑥ OXYGEN BOTTLE
⑦ FIREWALL BULKHEAD
⑧ LUB. OIL TANK
⑨ RUDDER PEDALS & STICK

⑩ RADAR SCOPE
⑪ ENGINE CONTROLS
⑫ INSTRUMENT CONSOLE
⑬ AUTO-PILOT EQUIPMENT
⑭ HYDRAULIC TANK
⑮ RETRACTABLE LANDING GEAR
⑯ WHEEL WELL DOORS
⑰ SEAT
⑱ FUEL BLADDER (TANK)

⑲ FUEL TANK ARMOR
⑳ RADIO EQUIPMENT
㉑ DIVING BRAKES
㉒ RETRACTABLE TAILWHEEL
㉓ ARRESTING HOOK
㉔ ANTENNA   ㉘ HYDRAULIC CYLINDERS
㉕ METAL STRUCTURE
㉖ METAL COVERED
㉗ FABRIC COVERED

WAM

...kyraiders could carry the same weight in bombs, rockets and auxiliary tanks as the four-engine Boeing B-17E Flying Fortress bomber. This ...kyraider is armed with an assortment of rockets. Skyraiders were also designed for nocturnal operations; reconnaissance with several cameras; and ...r electronic counter-measures (ECM) with electronic equipment in the fuselage. Nocturnal versions included two radar operators in the fuselage ...hile ECM versions included one electronics specialist in the fuselage. (McDonnell Douglas, Courtesy Hubert K. Gagos)

...ight: The Ryan FR-1 Fireball (top) was the first U.S. Navy composite-...owered fighter. A total of 66 were constructed; powered by a recipro-...ating radial engine driving a propeller and a turbo-jet engine exhaust-...g out of the fuselage rear. Jet engine air intake opening was in the ...ing root (arrow). An improvement over the Fireball was the Ryan ...F2R-1 Darkshark which used a turboprop engine to drive the propeller ...enter). Jet engine was same as the Fireball. The combine horsepower ...as 4,800 which drove the plane to a 500 miles per hour top speed. ...urboprop exhaust (arrow) added to the plane's speed and climb. The ...st U.S. Navy fighter composite combined powerplant experiment was ...e Curtiss XF15C-1 (bottom). Note turbojet exhaust beneath fuselage ...rrow). (U.S. Naval Historical Center)

One concept for the use of turbojet powerplants in U.S. Navy ...ircraft was to augment the propeller drive for bursts of high speed ...r for rapid climbs.

Ryan FR-1 Fireball: Composite-Powered Fighter

...n February 1943 the U.S. Navy placed an order with the Ryan ...eronautical Company of San Diego for a composite-powered ...ighter which was powered by a 1,425 horsepower Wright R-1820-...2W air-cooled radial engine in the nose and a 1,600 pounds of ...rust General Electric J-31 turbojet engine buried in the fuselage ...nd exhausting out the tail. Air inlets were located in the wing roots. ...he plane could fly on either engine alone and when operating on ...e turbojet alone the propeller automatically full-feathered so the ...lades were parallel to the slip stream. Top speed was 400 miles ...er hour and loaded weight was 9,960 pounds. Production was 66 ...ircraft. Wingspan was 40 feet-0 inches and length was 32 feet-4 ...ches. The first FR-1 was delivered in February 1945.

Composite-Powered Corsair

...While the Ryan Fireball was under development composite-power ...nstallations continued when the Naval Air Material Center at Phila-...elphia installed a Westinghouse Model 19A turbojet engine be-...eath the fuselage of a Goodyear FG-1 Corsair in October 1943. ...light tests with composite-power were conducted in early January ...944; however, the test instrumentation malfunctioned and the tests ...vere abandoned by June.

Curtiss XF15C-1: Composite-Powered Fighter

...n an effort to obtain more speed and highter altitude, the U.S. Navy ...rdered three composite-powered fighters from Curtiss on April 7, ...944, designated XF15C-1. Powered by a 2,100 horsepower Pratt

& Whitney R-2800-34W air-cooled radial engine in the nose turn-ing a four-bladed propeller and an Allis-Chalmers-built 2,700 pounds static thrust DeHavilland turbojet in the fuselage exhausting under the fuselage behind the wing. Wingspan was 48 feet-0 inches and length was 44 feet-0 inches. The 16,650 pound plane attained a top speed of 450 miles per hour. The first prototype was delivered in March 1945. It was the last of the Curtiss fighters for the U.S. Navy.

The Grumman Guardian started as a composite-powered torpedo-bomber but was produced as propeller-driven ASW Hunter/Killer team members. The composite-powered Grumman XTB3F-1 is shown here. This design was later redesignated AF-1 and AF-2. (Official U.S. Navy Photograph, News Photo Division)

Observe the large torpedo bay on the original Guardian design. Also note the wing located air inlets for the jet engine. The single cockpit accommodated a two-man crew; sitting side-by-side to improve communication. (Grumman Corporation, Courtesy Grant Daily)

Composite-Power: No Advantage

Tests with the Ryan Fireballs and the Curtiss XF15C-1 proved that composite-power had no advantages and that pure jet propulsion was the answer to speed and simplicity. It seems that one of the major problems was fuel. The turbojet engine did not require the high octane gasoline necessary for the piston engine and, rather than carry two different fuels, a compromise gasoline was used that was not ideal for either engine.

Grumman AF Guardian

Intended as a replacement for the TBF Avenger torpedo-bomber, Grumman designed their G-70 in late 1944 for the U.S. Navy. The single cockpit was arranged for side-by-side seating for two. No defensive armament was provided because high speed was to be used to evade attackers.

Guardian Composite-Power

High speed was attained with composite-power, which comprised a 2,300 horsepower Pratt & Whitney R-2800-46 Double Wasp radial air-cooled engine in the nose turning a four-bladed propeller, plus a 1,600 pounds static thrust Westinghouse 19 XB turbojet in the fuselage exhausting out the tail. The U.S. Navy ordered two prototypes in February 1945 with the designation XTB3F-1.

The prototype made its first flight on December 19, 1945; however, shortly thereafter, the turbojet augmentation was abandoned, despite the 350 plus miles per hour speed. This decision was probably influenced by the Fireball and XF15C-1 experiments.

Antisubmarine Warfare Guardians

The torpedo-bomber role was dropped by the U.S. Navy in preference to the growing importance of ASW (AntiSubmarine Warfare) and the design developed into two versions in order to operate as the components of Hunter-Killer teams. The Grumman Hunter version was designated AF-2W Guardian. This was fitted with a large radome under the fuselage and provision for two additional radar specialist crew members in the fuselage.

When a submarine was sighted by the Hunter, the Grumman AF-2S Guardian Killer version was to attack it with one or a vari-

ety of two 1,600 pound depth charges, two 2,000 pound bombs or 2,000 pound homing torpedo, which were carried internally in bomb bay. Underwing launchers were also fitted for six rocket. The AF-2S Hunter version was able to pinpoint the submarines exact location with the help of APS-30 radar under the starboar wing, which was operated by a radar specialist in the fuselage.

The first AF-2 flew on November 18, 1948 and the Guardia entered service with Navy Squadron VS-25 in October 1950.

Guardian Data

The 14,580 pounds empty and 25,500 pounds loaded AF-2S had wingspan of 60 feet-8 inches, length of 43 feet-4 inches and heigl of 16 feet-2 inches. Wing area was 560 square feet. The 2,400 hors power Pratt & Whitney R-2800-48W air-cooled radial engine gav the AF-2S a maximum speed of 317 miles per hour at 16,000 fee Service ceiling was 35,500 feet and range was 1,500 miles.

Guardian Production

A total of 156 AF-2W and (19) AF-2S were constructed. Produc tion continued into 1953 when (16) AF-3W and (25) AF-3S we built. These Grummans have the distinction of being the first pu pose-built ASW Hunter-Killer team aircraft and were replaced b the Grumman S2F Tracker several years later.

EXCITING SHIPBOARD AIRCRAFT

The postwar period was very exciting for naval aircraft designe who were experiencing the same enthusiasm, frustration and dete mination of those naval aircraft designers of the 1920's and 1930 who created many outstanding classics in their unquenchable thir to conceive the ideal shipboard aircraft; experiencing the transitio from biplane to monoplane designs. Now, it was the problems (high speeds, swept wings and turbojet powerplants, which behav ior was not always predictable.

Into the Unknown

Many excellent jet aircraft with straight and swept wings were a cepted designs that saw service with Navy and Marine squadror

Four early single-seat jet powered naval fighters from the U.S. Naval Air Test Center (NATC) fly in formation. From top to bottom these pioneers are: Vought F6U Pirate; Grumman F9F Panther; McDonnell F2H Banshee; and Vought F7U Cutlass. (Official U.S. Navy Photograph, News Photo Division)

for several years, but had restrictions imposed upon their operation. Spins were especially troublesome with many early jet fighters because these speedy craft could lose 2,000 to 3,000 feet of altitude in only one 360 degree turn of a spin! More surprising was the fact that, at times, it required 6,000 to 8,000 feet of altitude for complete recovery from a spin. The standing order was for crewmen to eject in the event of going into a spin below 8,000 feet. Needless to say, intentional spins were forbidden. Very often, a skidding turn would throw a swept-wing jet into a spin. Much had to be learned and the myriad of designs developed during this period led to the technically fascinating present day supersonic jets.

U.S. Navy's First Jet: McDonnell FH-1 Phantom
The U.S. Navy was also interested in the pure turbojet; therefore, on August 30, 1943, the U.S. Navy had approved a jet-propelled

fighter design prepared by McDonnell Aircraft Corporation of St. Louis and ordered two prototypes.

McDonnell completed the two prototype turbojet fighters in the Autumn of 1944 and the first flew successfully in October, but crashed during the following month at the McDonnell plant. The second prototype McDonnell FH-1 Phantom was delivered to the Navy for trials after successful test flights by company test pilots. The U.S. Navy did not wait for the sea trials and ordered 130 Phantoms on March 7, 1945; however, after the Japanese surrender the contract was reduced to 60 planes. As with many early turbojet-powered aircraft, production was delayed due to engine design problems; therefore the engines were slow to reach the production stage. It was not until January 1947 that the FH-1 Phantom was ready for squadron service.

Phantom Data
The U.S. Navy's first jet fighter was powered by two 1,600 pounds static thrust Westinghouse J30-WE-20 turbojet engines buried in the wing roots. Top speed was 479 miles per hour at sea level. Cruising speed was 248 miles per hour with a range of 980 miles. Service ceiling was 41,100 feet. Empty weight was 6,683 pounds and gross weight was 12,035 pounds. Wingspan was 40 feet-9 inches, with a length of 38 feet-9 inches and height of 14 feet-2 inches. Initial rate of climb was 4,230 feet per minute.

McDonnell Phantom Operates From Carrier
History was made in the U.S. Navy on July 21, 1946 when Lieutenant Commander James Davidson made a series of landings and take-offs with a McDonnell XFH-1 Phantom on the *USS Franklin D. Roosevelt* (CVB-42). This was the first operation from a carrier by an all jet-propelled plane in the U.S. Navy and accelerated interest in carrier-based jet aircraft.

Vought Pirate: Innovative
The Chance Vought Division of United Aircraft had made such an outstanding reputation with the F4U Corsair that a U.S. Navy con-

The McDonnell FH-1 twin-engine Phantom was the U.S. Navy's first jet powered fighter, making its first flight in October 1944. It entered squadron service in January, 1947. (McDonnell Douglas, Courtesy Harry Gann)

The Vought XF6U-1 Pirate single-engine jet-powered interceptor/fighter made its test flight on October 2, 1946. Although the plane was lightly constructed the jet engine did not produce enough power for the Pirate prototype to attain the desired performance. (Vought Aircraft Company, Courtesy Paul Bower)

The F6U-1 Pirate is shown in the Vought shop with an afterburner installed in order to get more power from the jet engine. Note the five access doors to electronics and hydraulic components; a vast improvement over removable panels (arrows). (Vought Aircraft Company, Courtesy Paul Bower)

tract was awarded for the development of a light weight jet-powered interceptor/fighter on December 29, 1944. This design was the first U.S. Navy plane to use wingtip drop tanks, jet engine afterburner and Metalite construction. Metalite was a Vought development consisting of a balsa wood core bonded between two thin aluminum alloy sheets. This provided a light, strong and smooth covering material.

The first of three prototypes flew on October 2, 1946; however, performance was a disappointment to both the Navy and Vought. The plane proved to be difficult to handle at slow speeds and maneuverability fell short of expectations. Unlike the FH-1 Phantom the Vought XF6U-1 Pirate was fitted with only one engine, which made the plane underpowered. A large dorsal fin was added to improve handling and, although not intended for that pur-

pose, the wingtip fuel tanks also improved stability and handling. In order to increase the power of the 3,000 pounds static thrust J24 WE-22 Westinghouse jet engine, one of the first afterburners was added in the engine tailpipe and this boosted the thrust to 4,22. pounds. Speed and rate of climb were improved; however, a tim limitation of five minutes was imposed on the afterburner use be cause of the excessive consumption of fuel. The afterburner tech nique is to lengthen the tailpipe and inject fuel into the exhaus gasses before they exhaust out of the tailpipe, thereby increasing thrust.

F6U-1 Pirate Data

Wingspan of the F6U-1 fighter was 32 feet-10 inches, while lengt with afterburner was 37 feet-7 inches. Height was 12 feet-11 inche

The addition of an afterburner to the Vought F6U-1 altered the shape of the fuselage rear and demanded that heat resistant steel be used. Note also the new wingtip fuel tanks. The Pirate was the first jet to use afterburner and tip tanks. (Vought Aircraft Company, Courtesy Paul Bower)

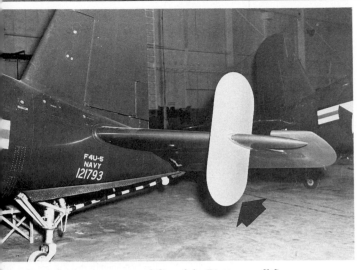

In order to further improve stability of the Pirate, small fins were installed on the stabilizer of a Corsair F4U-5 to test their effectiveness. The fins proved successful and it was decided to install them on the Pirate. (Vought Aircraft Company, Courtesy Paul Bower)

Test pilot Boone Guyton gets ready to flight test the F6U-1. The plane was very innovative. In addition to the afterburner and wing tip tanks, the Pirate was constructed of Metalight; a Vought development consisting of a balsa wood core bonded between two thin aluminum alloy sheets. Note the small fins on the stabilizer. (Vought Aircraft Company, Courtesy Paul Bower)

Pirate Production
The U.S. Navy purchased 30 production F6U-1 craft and these were soon relegated to various research units. Although not accepted for first-line service the Vought F6U-1 Pirate did contribute to the advancement of aeronautics by virtue of the wingtip tanks and afterburner.

Bare weight was 9,200 pounds and gross weight was 12,571 pounds. Top speed of the F6U-1 was 564 miles per hour at 20,000 feet. Range was 730 miles while service ceiling was 49,000 feet. A Westinghouse J34-WE-3 turbojet engine with afterburner was installed. Despite increased power performance did not measurably improve.

North American Fury
Using the same Bureau of Aeronautics specification that spawned the Vought Pirate, North American Aviation had submitted a single-engine jet fighter design in May 1945 for operation from carriers. Utilizing its experience with the U.S. Air Force XF-86 Sabre, North American's naval design featured a more rounded fuselage and straight wings. Three prototypes were ordered and designated XFJ-1, this being North American's first naval design. The company named the design Fury, which the Navy accepted.

Harrowing Fury Test Flight
The first Fury prototype had been completed during February 1946; however, the engine was not ready until July. During Navy acceptance trials in September, with test pilot Al Conover at the controls, the Fury cockpit canopy blew off during spin tests. Conover's head was slammed against the cockpit and, despite the strong protective helmet, he lost conciousness and recovered at 16,000 feet during a climbing slow roll. Conover was semiconcious, battered and bleeding as he brought the Fury back to Patuxent for a safe landing!

Rex B. Beisel, General Manager of Chance Vought (left), reviews Pirate construction with Factory Manager Bert Taliaferro. Note the F6U-1 Pirate under construction in the background. (Courtesy Rex B. Beisel Jr)

Fury Production and Deployment
Before acceptance trials were finished the Navy ordered (100) FJ-1 Furies on May 18, 1946, but this was soon reduced to 30 in keeping with postwar needs. The first production models were issued to VF-5A aboard USS Boxer in the Pacific in November 1947.

The North American FJ-1 Fury of 1946-1947 was one of the earlier U.S. Navy carrier-based jet powered aircraft. The 30 production Furies were assigned to USS Boxer (CV-21) in the Pacific. Fuselage and fin markings were needed for observers during test flights. (North American Rockwell, Courtesy J.M. Syverson)

The 364 McDonnell F2H-2 Banshee fighters purchased by the U.S. Navy were almost twice the weight and had twice the power of the McDonnell FH-1 Phantom with only a slight increase in overall dimensions. A total of 347 gallons of fuel was carried in the permanent wing tip tanks. (McDonnell Douglas, Courtesy Timothy J. Beecher)

Fury Data

The North American FJ-1 Fury wingspan was 38 feet-1 inch, while overall length was 33 feet-7 inches. Height was 14 feet-6 inches. Wing area was 275 square feet. This all-metal aircraft had an empty weight of 8,843 pounds, while gross weight was 15,600 pounds.

Armament comprised six 0.50 inch caliber machine guns in the nose, three on each side of the engine air inlet. This was to be the last installation of machine guns on a U.S. Navy airplane.

The 4,000 pounds static thrust Allison J-35-A-2 turbojet engine enabled the Fury to attain a top speed of 547 miles per hour at 9,000 feet. Initial rate of climb was 3,300 feet per minute. Service ceiling was 32,000 feet and ferry range was 1,500 miles.

Larger Carriers Needed

Furies remained with VF-5A for a short time because, as with the Phantom, the Fury proved the need for larger carriers with more powerful catapults and arresting gear. Furthermore, faster and heavier jets were under development, which would soon render the pioneers obsolete. Shipboard aircraft were being developed at such a rapid pace that they had forged ahead of the carrier's capabilities. In April 1949 the VF-5A Furies were assigned to Naval Reserve units.

McDonnell Banshee

Shortly after the McDonnell FH-1 Phantom made its first flight the U.S. Navy authorized the company, on March 2, 1945, to develop a larger, more powerful design based upon the FH-1. The two XF2H-1 prototypes, called Banshee, were ready in early 1947 and the maiden flight was made on January 11. Following successful trials a production order for (56) F2H-1 Banshees was placed four months later.

Naval aircraft development was moving at a rapid pace and it appeared that by the time a design left the production line it was almost obsolete. As the F2H-1 production neared completion, the

Navy requested a more powerful version with larger fuel capacity. The F2H-2 featured a longer fuselage and fixed wingtip tanks in order to carry 347 additional gallons of fuel. Inflight refueling capability was also installed. Night-fighter versions with nose radomes, F2H-2N, and reconnaissance models with lengthened nose for cameras, F2H-2P, were also produced from late 1949 to September 1952.

Banshee Data

The F2H-2 Banshee was powered by two 3,250 pounds static thrust Westinghouse J34-WE-34 turbojet engines which propelled the plane to a top speed of 532 miles per hour at 10,000 feet. Cruising speed was 501 miles per hour with a range of 1,475 miles. Initial rate of climb was 3,911 feet per minute and service ceiling was 44,800 feet.

Wingspan of the F2H-2 was 44 feet-10 inches, length 40 feet-2 inches and height 14 feet-6 inches, while wing area was 294 square feet. Empty weight was 11,146 pounds with gross weight 22,312 pounds. Armament comprised four 20 millimeter cannon in the nose.

It is interesting to note that the F2H-2 had twice the power of the FH-1 and was almost twice as heavy with only a slight increase in overall dimensions.

Banshee Production

McDonnell F2H-2 Banshee production totalled 364 aircraft, plus (14) F2H-2N night-fighters and(58)F2H-2P photo-reconnaissance variants. Two further all-weather variants had been produced as (250) F2H-3 and (150) F2H-4 models, which ended the Banshee line.

First U.S. Use of Ejection Seat

The British-designed Martin Baker aircraft ejection seat was used for the first time by an American pilot when Lieutenant J.L. Furia successfully ejected from his Banshee at 575 miles per hour on August 9, 1949.

The Grumman TBF-3E Avenger was the principal immediate postwar operational submarine hunter flown by the U.S. Navy, Royal Navy, Canadian Navy and French Aeronavale. (Official U.S. Navy Photo, News Photo Division)

The Grumman TBF-3W-2 ASW Avenger was fitted with the powerful APS-20 search radar which required a big radome beneath the fuselage. The rear portion of the canopy and the gun turret were replaced with an aluminum cover. Observe the added vertical fins to compensate for the side area of the radome. (Gruman Corporation, Courtesy Lois Lovisolo)

Grumman Avenger: Still In Demand

The end of World War II did not terminate the life of the U.S. Navy torpedo-bomber workhorse of that war; the Grumman TBF Avenger. Many special purpose variants were developed between 1945 and the mid-1950's. Special antisubmarine search equipment produced the TBF-3E, which was the main postwar U.S. Navy carrier-based operational submarine hunter. One Hundred of these craft served with the Fleet Air Arm as the Grumman AS Mk.4. The Royal Canadian Navy operated about 115 and the French Aeronavale also used this ASW Avenger. The TBF-3W variant was developed later and was fitted with APS-20 search radar which required a huge radome beneath the fuselage.

Still later was the TBF-3W-2, which featured a further revision of the electronic equipment and had the rear portion of the cockpit canopy and the mechanized rear gun turret replaced with an aluminum cover. Radar office was in the fuselage. This version also served in the French Aeronavale, Japanese Maritime Self Defense Force and the Royal Netherlands Navy.

Other variants were fitted with equipment intended specifically for antisubmarine strike duties. The TBF-3S and TBF-3S-2 were flown as a team with the Grumman TBF-3W. The TBF-3S and TBF-3S-2 were also flown by the Netherlands and Japan. Two of the last versions of the Avenger were a target-towing variant TBM-3U, and a COD (Carrier Onboard Delivery) seven-seat Avenger used to deliver vital supplies and priority personnel to carriers.

The Grumman Avenger was retired from U.S. Navy front-line service in 1954 after performing yeoman service for more than a decade.

The prototype Westland Wyvern was powered by a Rolls-Royce Eagle 22 Vee 24-cylinder engine because the turboprop engine had not yet been developed in 1944. The engine drove two four-bladed 13 foot diameter contra-rotating propellers. Note the torpedo and bombs. (Westland Helicopters Ltd., Courtesy P.D. Batten)

Westland Wyvern: Unique Turboprop

One of the most innovative and interesting combat planes to make its appearance in the postwar period was the Westland Wyvern.

Although conceived during the same period as the Martin Mauler and Douglas Skyraider this single-seater strike torpedo plane/bomber/fighter did not enter squadron service until 1952 due to powerplant development and propeller improvements.

The author examines the wing folding mechanism of the prototype Westland Wyvern Mark 1. In order to clear Royal Navy hangars, the wingtips also folded downward. (WAM Foto)

The production Westland Wyvern S.4 was powered by a 4,110 horse-power Armstrong Siddeley Python turboprop engine. Notice the turbojet engine exhaust on the fuselage side below the cockpit (arrow). Observe the auxiliary fins on the stabilizer (lower photo). (Westland Helicopters Ltd., Courtesy P.D. Batten)

Turboprop Powerplant

The Fleet Air Arm awarded a contract to Westland Aircraft in April 1944 for a shipboard turboprop-powered strike/fighter without the usual competitive design evaluation stage. Turboprops have a lower fuel consumption than turbojets and consist of a modified turbojet engine with an added power turbine which is geared to a propeller to drive the plane. Instead of directing the hot gasses only through the compressor turbine and then out of the tailpipe for thrust, as on a turbojet, the gasses on a turboprop also drive a power turbine which turns the propeller. The gasses are then directed out the tailpipe, which exhausts toward the rear of the plane, contributing to the speed. Although Naval Specification N.11/44 called for a turboprop, none was yet available for service at that time. Rather than delay the project, it was decided to install the new and untried powerful 2,690 horsepower, 24-cylinder, liquid-cooled Vee, Rolls-Royce Eagle 22 piston engine. This engine was geared to a pair of 13 feet diameter contra-rotating four-bladed propellers.

The Royal Air Force had also become interested in the Wyvern and shared the 6 prototypes that were ordered in November 1944; however, during 1945 Britain was rapidly converting engine development from piston reciprocating engines to rotary gas turbine turbojets. The Rolls-Royce Eagle was the last of the firm's piston reciprocating engines and the Wyvern was the only airplane to use this engine. Rolls-Royce attention then concentrated on the gas tur-

bine engine. In August 1946 a contract for (20) Rolls-Royce Eagle powered Wyverns was placed with Westland; however, only 10 were delivered.

Turboprop Engines Developed

The Eagle engine powered Westland Wyvern Mk.1 made its first flight on December 12, 1946, which proved successful. Meanwhile Rolls-Royce and Armstrong Siddeley were feverishly working on their respective turboprop engines, the Clyde and the Python. It was not until January 18, 1949 that the Rolls-Royce Clyde-powered Wyvern TF.2 made its maiden flight. The Armstrong Siddeley Python-powered Wyvern maiden flight followed in March. The Admiralty decided to power the Westland Wyvern with the 4,110 horsepower Python ASP-3 turboprop which released Rolls-Royce to pursue development of turbojet engines; however, prototype Wyverns were powered with Clyde as well as Python engines.

Many Wyvern Technical Problems

In addition to its own prototype design and development, the Westland Wyvern had to act as a test bed for the development of three engines. No sooner had the many problems been solved when the largest problem of all cast its shadow over the project. Unlike piston reciprocating engine, the gas turbine turboprop or turbojet

While the Westland Wyvern was under development the U.S. Navy and Douglas Aircraft Company were experimenting with a similar project. The Douglas A2D Skyshark was powered by two 2,300 horsepower turboprop engines; each driving one of the two contra-rotating propellers. This single seat strike/fighter was a spin-off from the Douglas Skyraider but could carry a 50 percent greater bomb load. Range could be extended by cruising on one engine; driving a single propeller and feathering the idle propeller. The Skyshark project was terminated before the craft went into production. (McDonnell Douglas Photo, Courtesy Chet Miller)

WESTLAND WYVERN S.4

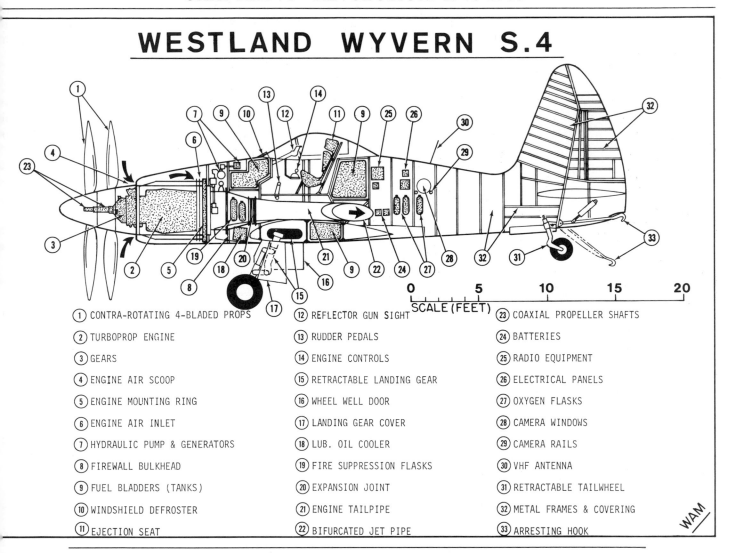

① CONTRA-ROTATING 4-BLADED PROPS
② TURBOPROP ENGINE
③ GEARS
④ ENGINE AIR SCOOP
⑤ ENGINE MOUNTING RING
⑥ ENGINE AIR INLET
⑦ HYDRAULIC PUMP & GENERATORS
⑧ FIREWALL BULKHEAD
⑨ FUEL BLADDERS (TANKS)
⑩ WINDSHIELD DEFROSTER
⑪ EJECTION SEAT

⑫ REFLECTOR GUN SIGHT
⑬ RUDDER PEDALS
⑭ ENGINE CONTROLS
⑮ RETRACTABLE LANDING GEAR
⑯ WHEEL WELL DOOR
⑰ LANDING GEAR COVER
⑱ LUB. OIL COOLER
⑲ FIRE SUPPRESSION FLASKS
⑳ EXPANSION JOINT
㉑ ENGINE TAILPIPE
㉒ BIFURCATED JET PIPE

㉓ COAXIAL PROPELLER SHAFTS
㉔ BATTERIES
㉕ RADIO EQUIPMENT
㉖ ELECTRICAL PANELS
㉗ OXYGEN FLASKS
㉘ CAMERA WINDOWS
㉙ CAMERA RAILS
㉚ VHF ANTENNA
㉛ RETRACTABLE TAILWHEEL
㉜ METAL FRAMES & COVERING
㉝ ARRESTING HOOK

SCALE (FEET)   0   5   10   15   20

WAM

ngine does not react promptly to changes in throttle position. The very high rotating speed builds up tremendous inertia in a turbine nd, not having pistons compressing air in cylinders to slow it, the urbine tends to rotate at high speed even when all fuel is cut off nd loses speed very slowly. In turboprops it means that the propel-er keeps turning when the engine is shut down. This condition can e tolerated when operating from shore bases; however, the "en-ine cut" carrier landing technique was still being used during the ostwar period. When the landing control batsman signalled the Vyvern pilot to cut his engine and settle to the deck the plane con-inued at speed, passing the touch-down point and either hit the rash barrier or smashed into the planes on the bow. Lucky pilots vere able to pick up speed and circle for another try.

ropeller Control

t became obvious early in the carrier trials that controlling the en-ine with the speed control was not the way to go in this unusual lane. It is interesting to note at this point, that the U.S. Navy was truggling with exactly the same problem in a turboprop powered ersion of the Douglas Skyraider, called the Skyshark, and eventu-lly had to abandon the project. Westland continued with the Wyvern roject and decided to control the propeller pitch with the throttle

lever while the turbine engine ran at a constant speed. In order to obtain a sufficiently sharp thrust cut-off when closing the throttle the propeller pitch was given a very rapid motion so that it fol-lowed the pilot's hand on the throttle proportionally. This solution solved the deck approach problem; however, at high speeds the same system produced undesirable characteristics; the quick pro-peller pitch change had the tendency to release the kinetic energy that was stored in the rapidly rotating system. This had a violent effect on the pilot because big changes of thrust following in rapid succession caused his head to be thrown forwards and backwards with great violence! Some of these surges could be quite dangerous and at one time all Fleet Air Arm testing was discontinued and only Westland test pilots were allowed to continue test-flying the Wyvern.

Finally, through a combined effort between Armstrong Siddeley and the propeller manufacturer, Rotol, a new propeller device was designed and developed. This was an inertial controller which was sensitive to engine acceleration, rather than just engine speed. This also included a device that enabled the propeller blades to antici-pate the new throttle lever position so they would begin changing pitch before the signal is actually transmitted. It required two years of dedicated designing, plus dangerous and difficult flight-testing to arrive at the propeller pitch solution.

This Wyvern has just engaged the arresting cable as it lands on a Royal Navy aircraft carrier. Note the large Youngman flaps (large arrow) and air brake flaps (small arrow). (Westland Helicopters Ltd., Courtesy P.D. Batten)

Wyvern Production

Production resumed and on February 1, 1953 the first Wyvern squadron was formed, No. 813, under the command of Lieutenant Commander C.E. Price. R.N. Wyverns also equipped Nos. 830 and 831 squadrons; the former serving on *HMS Eagle*. A total of 127 Westland Wyverns were produced.

Wyvern Data

Westland Wyvern wingspan was 44 feet which was reduced to 20 feet when folded. Wing area was 355 square feet. Height was 15 feet-9 inches and with the wings folded upwards and over the fuselage the height was increased to 18 feet-1 3/4 inches. Empty weight was 15,608 pounds, gross weight 21,200 pounds and maximum flying weight was 24,500 pounds.

Armament comprised four 20 millimeter cannon in the wing plus provision for a 20 inch torpedo, three 1,000 bombs, mines or depth charges. A total of 16 rocket projectiles could also be carried.

Wyvern's maximum speed at sea level was 383 miles per hour and at 10,000 feet it was three miles per hour slower. Cruising speed at 20,000 feet was 348 miles per hour at which speed the range was 904 miles. Initial rate of climb from sea level was 2,350 feet per minute and service ceiling was 28,000 feet.

Wyvern; World's First Military Turboprop

The successful conclusion from the years of dedication and perseverance in the development of the world's first operational military turboprop aircraft and the only naval turboprop strike/fighter to ever reach squadron service was a considerable contribution to aeronautical science.

The Westland Wyvern became the Fleet Air Arm's standard strike aircraft and served in Squadrons No. 764, 813, 827, 830 and 831.

Spruance: Naval War College President

Admiral Raymond Spruance, one of America's greatest Admirals, began his two year term as President of the U.S. Naval War College on March 1, 1946.

Reduced Aircraft Carrier Inventories

Before demobilization began, the U.S. Navy had 99 aircraft carriers in operation. These included the original prewar carriers *Saratoga*, *Ranger* and *Enterprise*; 17 *Essex* class fleet carriers; 7 escort carriers; and eight *Independence* class converted cruiser light carriers. The U.S. Navy also had 39 more carriers under construction, either on the ways or already launched and fitting out. By the end of 1947 the U.S. Fleet had been reduced to 20 aircraft carriers. Some had been deactivated (mothballed) or sunk in tests while several *Essex* class carriers had been scheduled for extensive modification and rebuilding to enable them to handle the faster and heavier jet-powered planes.

The Royal Navy had started an extensive carrier construction program to follow the *Illustrious* class. In addition to the previously described *Collosus/Majestic* class, Britain had planned three *Gibralter* class 45,000 ton carriers which would have been similar to the U.S. *Midway* class; four *Audacious* class of 36,800 tons carriers; and eight *Hermes* class light carriers. This program was cut back considerably, leaving only a few ships that were dedicated to AntiSubmarine Warfare (ASW).

OPERATION CROSSROADS

The atomic bomb could devastate cities and ravage the countryside but its effect upon ships at sea was unknown. Vice Admiral W.H. Blandy, Chief of the U.S.N. Bureau of Ordnance, had proposed in October 1943 that a number of enemy ships and surplus U.S. ships be used as target ships to test the effect of new weapons. After V Day it was decided to conduct atomic bomb tests in July 1946 with a 2,000 yard diameter test site in a corner of the 10 x 20 mile Bikini Atoll lagoon of the Marshall Islands. The test was given the name Operation Crossroads, and the bombs to be used were the same as the one dropped on Nagasaki, having the explosive force of 23,000 tons TNT.

Aerial Explosion Test Able

Two U.S. aircraft carriers were included in the tests, *USS Saratoga* and *USS Independence*. During the first test, Able, on July Saratoga was located about 500 yards from the blast center, while *Independence* was located near the test center. Able was an aerial explosion and resulted in sinking a destroyer and two transports immediately. *Independence* was severely damaged and heavily contaminated, while *Saratoga* received superficial damage.

Underwater Explosion Test Baker

In the second test, Baker, on July 25 the bomb was detonated 9 feet below the water surface. *Saratoga* was relocated to 300 yards from the blast center and *Independence* to the 500 yard location. The armored *Saratoga* was so severely damaged that the ship sank in less than eight hours, while *Independence* was so "hot" that she had to be sunk by gunfire. Other ships that sank in test Baker were the battleship *USS Arkansas*, which went down at once, and the Japanese battleship *Nagato*, which took over four days to sink.

Operation Crossroads Conclusion

The tests proved that even the most rugged and armored warship

USS Saratoga (CV-3) is shown sinking in Bikini Lagoon after having been located 300 yards from the center of the underwater atomic bomb explosion during Test Baker of Operation Crossroads on July 25, 1946. Constructed with 1,000 watertight compartments, the armored carrier was blown to 800 yards from the explosion and thrust upward 43 feet, then fell into a deep wave trough. Twenty-seconds later a 94 foot wave washed over the deck, sweeping the smokestack and all aircraft and vehicles into the sea. The carrier drifted back to 600 yards from the blast center and began to sink, stern first. About eight hours later the venerable carrier settled into a watery grave, finally resting upright on the lagoon bottom in 180 feet of water. Almost 100,000 aircraft landings had been made on the flight deck of "Sara" during her 19 year lifetime, and rather than be scrapped, the beautiful Saratoga was sacrificed on the altar of science. (U.S. Navy Photograph, Courtesy U.S. Naval Institute Collection)

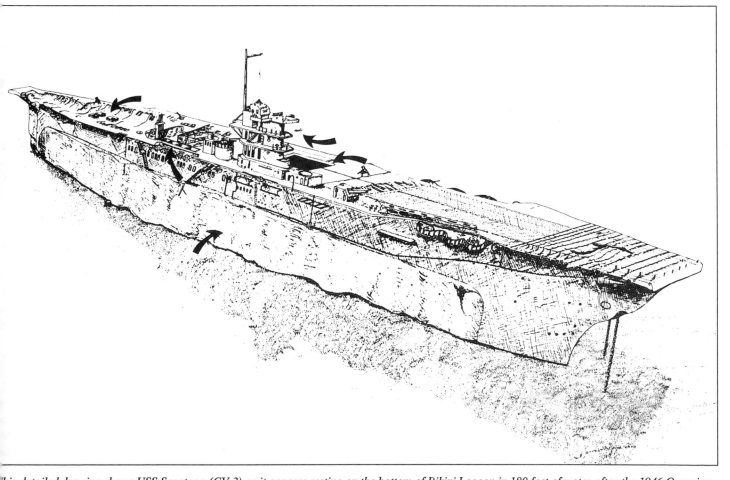

This detailed drawing shows USS Saratoga (CV-3) as it appears resting on the bottom of Bikini Lagoon in 180 feet of water after the 1946 Operaion Crossroads underwater nuclear explosion of Test Baker. The drawing was made by Jerry Livingston and Larry Nordby after this archaeologcal diving team had carefully mapped the sunken carrier in 1989. Observe the following damage as reported by Livingston and Nordby: 1. Aft flight deck ushed to a depth of twelve feet. 2. Missing elevator platform crashed to bottom of shaft. Platform bent 90 degrees. 3. Hull blister and 6 inch armor attened and bent. 4. Stack is blown away. Note the Scuba diver underwater archaeologist mapping "Sara" who could very well be Principal nvestigator Dan Lenihan, Chief of the Submerged Cultural Resources Unit, U.S. National Park Service. (Courtesy National Park Service)

were not impervious to an atomic explosion. All target ships within 500 yards of the explosion had been sunk, or seriously damaged, but those beyond 750 yards from the explosion suffered little damage or contamination. Most important was the fact that many of the target ships that showed no signs of damage were too contaminated with nuclear radiation to be boarded for inspection. In wartime these ships would be out of action because the entire crew would be either dead or incapacitated by heavy doses of radiation. The most surprising aspect of the tests was that the underwater explosion generated much more radiation than the air explosion and Baker contaminated more than 90 percent of the target vessels.

Operation Crossroads Benefits

The tests helped to create improved and safer ships, which could better ward off the effects of an atomic blast; washdown systems which spray the entire exterior of the ship with water; decontamination stations for the crew; fewer openings to the atmosphere; and smooth, uncluttered superstructures without spaces where contaminated water or dust could be trapped. Hull structure plus rudders, propellers, and propeller shafts have been more carefully designed to endure an underwater blast of great magnitude.

Saratoga Damage Surveyed

In August 1989 and May 1990 underwater archeologists/divers of the submerged Cultural Resources Unit, National Park Service, United States Department of the Interior examined and mapped the sunken USS Saratoga (CV-3) and other ships of Operation Crossroads in Bikini Lagoon.

Under serious consideration is the dedication of Bikini Lagoon as an underwater park to be available for scuba diving by naval history enthusiasts.

Admiral Mitscher Dies

Vice Admiral Marc A. Mitscher died in the U.S. Naval Hospital, Norfolk, Virginia on February 3, 1947. Admiral Mitscher had been one of the earliest U.S. Navy pilots and commanded Task Force 58 during World War II.

COLOSSUS CLASS INNOVATIONS

Those *Colossus* class aircraft carriers that remained in Royal Navy service during the postwar years proved to be most effective, economical and efficient. They were also employed in many innovative carrier modifications and experiments.

Flexideck

In late 1948 *HMS Warrior* was engaged in flexideck trials. The aft end of the Flight Deck was fitted with an inflated rubber landing deck not unlike a huge mattress. The objective was to test the concept of landing jet planes which have the landing gear removed. The basic thought was that once relieved of the weighty wheels, struts, foundations, hydraulic system and so forth the plane would increase its range and exhibit improved all-around performance. Using a converted deHavilland Sea Vampire the landing trials were a success, however, the system was not considered practical nor workable in wartime and the idea was abandoned.

Steam Catapult

HMS Perseus had the newly invented steam catapult installed f trials in 1950. The steam catapult was much more powerful th the hydraulic type and was necessary for the heavier aircraft beir designed at that time. The steam catapult was also much safer th the hydraulic because it was less prone to start and feed fires. T steam powered catapult had been invented by C.C. Mitchell, Brown Brothers & Co., Ltd., of Edinburgh, who used a slotted cy inder with a large piston driven by steam from the ship's boilers. rod attached to the piston connects to the aircraft pick-up points

Angled Flight Deck

Also in 1950, *HMS Triumph* tested the concept of the angled flig deck so that planes could land without interfering with the launc ing operation; thereby, eliminating the necessity for the crash ba rier, which had been used to protect the planes waiting to be launch from overshooting landing aircraft. Instead of undergoing stru tural modifications a line was painted on the Flight Deck angled 10 degrees from the ship centerline. Trial takeoff and landing c erations proved successful. This simple but clever idea has becor an integral part of every U.S. aircraft carrier design built since 19!

FIRST U.S. CARRIER JET SQUADRON

On May 6, 1948 the first all-jet U.S. Navy Squadron VF-17A qua fied for carrier operation aboard the light carrier *Saipan* (CVL-4 off the U.S. Atlantic coast. Once fully qualified and assigned, V 17A became the first in service carrier jet fighter squadron in t world. The squadron flew the McDonnell FH-1 Phantom whi was the U.S. Navy's only jet fighter because the Vought Pirate w not in production and the FJ-1 Fury was not yet in service.

U.S. NAVY WANTS SUPERCARRIERS
AND ATOMIC BOMBS

It had been previously mentioned that the faster and heavier turt jet-powered aircraft demanded larger aircraft carriers; setting of revolution. There is a second reason for this large carrier requi ment; the atomic bomb.

The largest weapon carried by carrier aircraft during Wo War II was the Mark 13 torpedo of 2,200 pounds; whereas, t Hiroshima atomic bomb weighed 9,000 pounds and the Nagas; bomb weighed 10,000 pounds. It became obvious that to ca bombs of this weight would not be feasible with the current U carrier aircraft. Bigger Warbirds were needed.

The first recorded discussions regarding the U.S. Navy carr aircraft capability to deliver atomic bombs of that size took place late 1945 between Vice Admiral Marc Mitscher, Deputy CNO (A and two U.S. Navy officers who were involved in the atomic bor development and delivery. The three officers concluded, withr any doubt, that the U S. Navy must have a nuclear strike capabili

By 1946 the U.S. Navy feared that the supremacy of its carr forces, built up during World War II, was threatened by the n weapon and had become determined to acquire its own nuclear pability. The 12,000 pound weight of the new Mark VI atomic bor plus the long range dictated by the strategic role, required a pla of enormous weight and proportions for carrier operations. T meant bigger carriers would also be needed.

...e North American Savage strategic strike aircraft was designed to ...liver the atomic bomb while operating from aircraft carriers. Two ...ston engines and one turbojet engine were fitted. The AJ-1 is shown ...re. (North American Rockwell, Courtesy J.M. Syverson)

...orth American Savage

...order to attain this nuclear strike capability, the U.S. Navy or-
...red three prototypes of a strategic strike aircraft design from North
...merican Aviation on June 24, 1946. The design was required to
...liver the atomic bomb and, due to the weight of the bomb and the
...ng range necessary, the plane evolved into a twin-engine propel-
...r-driven craft, which was the largest plane intended to operate
...om carriers on a regular basis.

...avage Composite Powerplant

...s with the Grumman AF-2, the North American XAJ-1 Savage
...as fitted with a turbojet engine in the aft fuselage. This time it was
...e more powerful 4,600 pounds static thrust Allison J33-A-19 tur-
...ojet which was intended to boost the Savage speed while over the
...rget and provide additional power during takeoff.

...avage First Flight/Production Contract

...he first prototype Savage made its initial flight on July 3, 1948.
...his resulted in a production contract for 43 planes, the first of
...hich was delivered in the spring of 1949. Composite Squadron
...C-5 was the first to receive the Savage in September 1949.

...avage AJ-2 Data

...n order was awarded for an improved variant, AJ-2, which had
...lded fuel tanks, taller fin and eliminated the stabilizer dihedral.
...owered by two 2,400 horsepower 18-cylinder Pratt & Whitney R-
...800-44W air-cooled, twin-row radial engines, the AJ-2 attained a

...he AJ-2 Savage was an improved AJ-1. Many were converted to ...fueling tankers by replacing the jet engine with a hose reel and fuel ...nks. The tanker version is shown here. (Official U.S. Navy Photograph, ...ews Photo Division)

A North American Savage AJ-2 tanker is shown refueling a Vought F7U-3 Cutlass in this unusual overhead photograph. (Vought Aircraft Company, Courtesy Paul Bower)

maximum speed of 425 miles per hour with the turbojet fired up as well. The range without the wingtip tanks was 2,200 miles. The wing and top of the fin folded for stowage on carriers.

Wingspan with the standard equipment wingtip tanks was 75 feet and without the tanks it was 71 feet. Length was 65 feet with a height of 21 feet-5 inches. Gross weight was 55,000 pounds. The plane had no defensive armament.

Existing Carriers Too Small

The *Essex* class carriers could not accommodate the Savage; there-fore, only the Midway class CVB's were able to handle the large planes. This could be accomplished only by sacrificing two con-ventional carrier aircraft for each Savage that was taken aboard. In addition, Savage-equipped squadron commanders stated that Flight Deck captains complained that these large craft were upsetting the deck spotting and pattern of operations for which the carrier crew had been carefully trained.

With no carrier available to properly operate planes the size of the Savage, plus the fact that the U.S. Navy was already planning a turbojet-powered successor to the Savage spelled the end of this propeller-driven nuclear bomber.

Production continued into 1954 when the 143rd Savage was delivered to the U.S. Navy. Many Savages were converted into re-fueling tankers by replacing the turbojet with a hose reel and add-ing fuel tanks in the bomb bay. Others were converted into recon-naissance planes fitted with up to five sophisticated cameras. The North American Savage not only provided plenty of valuable infor-mation regarding large carrier aircraft but proved, beyond ques-tion, that large supercarriers were necessary for nuclear strike planes.

THE COLD WAR BEGINS

The Western Powers' shortsighted patronizing of Soviet expansionist ambitions at the Yalta Conference was beginning to worry the West, especially the U.S. This prompted President Truman, on March 12, 1946, to proclaim that it must be the policy of the U.S., "...to support free peoples who are resisting attempted subjugation by armed minorities or outside pressure." This declaration became the principal concept for American foreign policy during the Anti-Communist Cold War and was to lead the U.S. into two more wars in which American carriers and Warbirds proved themselves.

Counterforce Containment

In July 1948 an article appeared in Foreign Affairs magazine titled "Sources of Soviet Conduct" written by George F. Kennan, a foreign service officer at the American Embassy in Moscow and a veteran observer of Soviet-American relations. In view of his official position, Kennan had signed the Article "X." The profound text concluded that the U.S. must adopt a policy of, "...patient but firm...containment" of Soviet expansionism by the "Application of counterforce at a series of constantly shifting geographical and political points corresponding to the shifts of...Soviet policy." Kennan later admitted his authorship of the article which contents, together with the Truman Doctrine and the Marshall Plan, became the foundation of American strategy in the Cold War. Most of the containment was to be the task of the U.S. Navy; especially the carriers and their Warbirds. George F. Kennan is the author of many outstanding books on international diplomacy and history.

U.S. NAVY PROTESTS UNIFICATION

Ignoring the words of Royal Navy Fifth Sea Lord Sir Arthur Lumley St. George Lyster, Commander of all British Naval Aviation, who had stated that unification virtually destroyed the Fleet Air Arm, President Truman transmitted a special message to Congress in December 1945 outlining a unified Army, Navy, and Air Force! On June 15, 1946 Truman followed this with a specific plan that resulted in the National Security Act of 1947 which also created the U.S. Air Force as an equal to the Army and Navy.

Many high-ranking members of the three armed services criticized this unification because they claimed it would work against the national security interests of the U.S. Interservice rivalry was also brewing, which would jeopardize the future of U.S. carrier aviation, as well as the security of the U.S.

During the summer of 1947 the U.S. House of Representatives Finance Committee held hearings on the Unification Act. Captain John Gevaerdt Crommelin Jr. asked to be called as a witness. It will be recalled that John had four brothers who also served in the U.S. Navy during World War II and that he was the highest ranking survivor of the *USS Liscome Bay* sinking. Crommelin had also been assigned as an aide to Sir Arthur Lumley St. George Lyster when Sir Arthur visited the U.S. in 1941. The British naval officer had been commanding officer of *HMS Illustrious* during many actions in the Mediterranean Sea and Atlantic Ocean. He related his experiences to the eager Crommelin and also volunteered the fact of how Royal Navy Aviation was virtually destroyed by unification of the air services. Crommelin had served as wartime air officer and executive officer of *USS Enterprise* (CV-6) as well as Chief of Staff for a carrier division commander. At this time he was the first commanding officer of *USS Saipan* (CVL-48). Crommelin influenced

Captain John G. Crommelin precipitated the Revolt of the Admirals and was elected into the Carrier Aviation Hall of Fame because he "saved carrier aviation." (U.S. National Archives)

a Committee member to have Admiral Gerald F. (Gerry) Boga and Admiral Joseph J. (Jocko) Clark testify at the hearings. Capta Crommelin testified after the admirals that carrier aviation, beir highly mobile, embodied the Navy's most effective offensive stri ing power and to destroy this effective force would endanger U. national security. All other testimony concurred with Crommelin opinions.

Media Is Anticarrier

Soon the opinionated media got into the act with obviously plant misinformation, which lauded the giant B-36 bomber and cor demned carrier aviation. Publications went as far as to write a ticles in cooperation with the U.S. Air Force which would, of cours be derogatory towards carrier aviation and in favor of the lon range bomber as the only weapon able to guarantee U.S. nation security. Everyone had forgotten the poor record of General Geor C. Kenney's Fifth Air Force B-17 Flying Fortresses when they tri to bomb Japanese ships. Carrier-based dive bombers were far mo successful, naturally.

Unification Becomes Law

The specter of U.S. Army, Air Force, and Navy unification becan a reality on September 18, 1948 when the National Security Act 1947 (NSA 47) took effect. NSA 47 combined the three milita

...mes V. Forrestal, a leading Supercarrier advocate, became America's ...st Secretary of Defense on September 18, 1948 when NSA 47 took ...ect. His term of office ended in tragedy. (U.S. National Archives)

...rvices under the aegis of a single Department of Defense with the ...fices of Secretary of the Army, Navy, and Air Force as subcabinet ...osts. On that day John L. Sullivan became the 49th Secretary of ...e Navy, replacing James V. Forrestal, who had been appointed ...merica's first Secretary of Defense. Little did Forrestal realize ...e fuss and fury that was to mar his term of service; ending in ...agedy.

...AMES FORRESTAL PROMOTES SUPERCARRIER

...early 1948 the U.S. Navy carrier force consisted of three 45,000 ...n *Midway* class, eight *Essex* class, two *Independence* class, and ...ven escort carriers. Except for the *Midway* class the U.S. carriers ...ere inadequate to handle the heavier and faster operational jet ...rcraft that were being developed.

As previously mentioned, the two developments that influenced ...rrier aviation during the immediate postwar years were jet-pow-...ed aircraft and the atomic bomb.

Experience with the North American AJ-1 Savage pointed to ...e fact that the existing U.S. Navy aircraft carriers were not ad-...quate to accommodate a multi-engine, atomic bomb carrying, long-...nge strategic bomber. This led to the inescapable conclusion that ...large supercarrier that would be capable of operating long-range ...uclear-armed aircraft was desperately needed to give the U.S. Navy ...e capability of atomic strategic attack on the enemy. Secretary ...orrestal had proposed the carrier to Congress, of which four were ...o be built. Congress approved and funded the project in the au-...umn of 1948.

Supercarrier Data

The supercarrier was to be a 65,000 ton ship designed for flushdecked flight operations. The proposed retractable island was deemed necessary in order to enable a multi-engine 2,000 mile range, 80,000 pound strategic bomber, carrying nuclear weapons, to oper-ate from the flight deck without interference from the island. Dou-glas Aircraft Company had been awarded a contract in 1947 to de-sign a turbojet-powered carrier-based strategic bomber. The 1,090 feet long supercarrier, to be named *USS United States*, was to be the largest warship built to that time. Four catapults were planned; two forward and two amidship. The ship was to be fully armored with the Flight Deck integrated into the hull structure. Deck edge elevators were to lower to a 28 feet high Hangar.

Forrestal Attacked By U.S. Air Force and Media

Secretary Forrestal had fought hard for the important supercarrier and the first to criticize the idea of a new carrier was the fledgling U.S. Air Force, which had been recently created by NSA 47. The USAF objected to giving the Navy strategic attack capability. It argued that only the U.S.A.F. should have the means of strategic attack and claimed the Convair B-36 bomber was the only weapon capable of this mission. The Air Force openly defied the Defense Secretary on appropriations and the fair-minded Forrestal even per-mitted Air Force Brass to present their views before Congress. The family fight burst into the open, with the news media accusing Forrestal of not being able to control the Air Force insubordination.

On February 11, 1949 Assistant Secretary of the Navy for Air, John N. Brown, resigned because of the way Naval Aviation was being abused.

Forrestal In Hospital

Secretary of Defense Forrestal fought for his carrier as long as he was able, but on March 4, 1949 he resigned his post, effective March 31. He was awarded the Distinguished Service Medal on March 29 and entered Bethesda Naval Hospital on April 2 suffering from ner-vous exhaustion.

Supercarrier Cancelled

On March 28, 1949 Louis Johnson had been selected to succeed Forrestal.

The keel of *USS United States* had been laid at Newport News Shipbuilding and Drydock Co. on April 18, 1949 with a minimum of ceremony and a good deal of secrecy. With Forrestal out of the picture, five days later Secretary of Defense Johnson announced the cancellation of the supercarrier *United States* (CVA-58) with-out consulting with or informing Secretary of the Navy Sullivan or Chief of Naval Operations, Admiral Louis E. Denfield! Johnson instructed Newport News Shipbuilding to discontinue construction ". . . at once and at the least possible cost to the Government." News of this abrupt dictatorial cancellation resounded like a thun-derclap throughout the U.S. Navy and those officers who had pro-tested unification now realized that U.S. Navy carrier aviation was doomed to share the fate of the Royal Navy Fleet Air Arm. Secre-tary of the Navy John L. Sullivan resigned at once in protest to this underhanded and unwarranted cancellation.

The Forrestal Tragedy

In the early morning of May 22, 1949 James V. Forrestal sat in his room on the 16th floor of Bethesda Naval Hospital writing a passage by Sophocles. Despite the fact that he was hospitalized on the 16th floor, Forrestal, somehow, was transported to the 13th floor and, at 2:00 o'clock in the morning, he either fell, jumped, or was pushed from a 13th floor window, from which the screen had been carefully removed. Forrestal's tragedy was officially recorded as suicide.

President Truman called him a war casualty and blamed excessive work during and after the war. Military affairs analyst Hanson Baldwin blamed the news media.

It seems that nobody thought about the probability that Forrestal might have been despondent about the supercarrier cancellation and concerned over the future of U.S. Navy carrier aviation and his country.

REVOLT OF THE ADMIRALS

Forrestal's death and the supercarrier cancellation infuriated Navy Brass and a series of events began which led to the Revolt of the Admirals. From June 3 to August 25, 1949 controversy raged over the B-36 bomber with accusations and reports that this plane had been selected by Secretary of Defense Johnson and Secretary of the Air Force Stuart Symington for political and personal profit reasons. The U.S. House Armed Services Committee cleared everyone of all charges after a two-month investigation.

On May 25, 1949 Francis P. Matthews, a Nebraska businessman and lawyer who had very little experience in naval affairs, was sworn in as Secretary of the Navy.

Frustrated over the steamroller tactics in these dangerous turns of events, Captain Crommelin called a press conference on September 10 and assumed the mantle of spokesman for the entire U.S. Navy. He warned that the Joint Chiefs of Staff, acting as a "General Staff", could be controlled by "landlocked concept" members which is "intolerable." Captain Crommelin stated that the NSA-49 (National Security Act of 1947 that had been amended) was a dangerous piece of legislation and that the Secretary of Defense was making dangerous decisions which were stripping the Navy of vital offensive power and greatly imperiling the security of the United States.

Admirals Back Crommelin

Crommelin's statements created a sensation in the Sunday papers and Secretary Matthews quickly sent confidential messages to senior Navy commanders asking for their comments on Crommelin's news releases. This was Matthew's big mistake because all of the Naval officers he contacted agreed with Crommelin.

Admiral Ernest J. King warned that seapower would not receive its proper recognition and reminded the Secretary that the absorption of Britain's crack Royal Naval Air Service into the RAF destroyed that service and made the Royal Navy a second-rate power by 1940.

Admiral Arthur W. Radford, Commander in Chief, U.S. Pacific Fleet, said that the majority of officers in the Pacific Fleet concur with Captain Crommelin.

Admiral Louis E. Denfield, CNO, stated that his naval office are convinced that a Navy stripped of its offensive power means nation stripped of its offensive power.

Vice Admiral Gerald F. Bogan, commanding First Task Fle in Pacific, declared hearty and complete agreement wi Crommelin's statements and said there was a genuine fear in th Navy for the security of the U.S. if the Department of Defense do not change its policies.

A copy of the admirals' letters stamped "Confidential" ha reached Crommelin on October 1, 1949; obviously classified keep it hidden from the population and the media. Capta Crommelin believed it should be made public and doctored the le ters to conceal the fact that they were classified documents. gave them to the press which featured the story under banner hea lines throughout the nation, such as: "Morale Shot, U.S. in Per Admirals Say."

House Naval Affairs Committee Hearings

Prompted by the sensational revelations, Congressman Carl Vinso Chairman of the House Naval Affairs Committee, announced th hearings on national defense policy would be started the followin week regarding how unification was affecting morale.

With his objective attained, Captain Crommelin notified t media that the source of the letters could now be revealed. Secr tary Matthews moved swiftly and suspended Crommelin from du and restricted him to the city of Washington, calling the Captain . . faithless, insubordinate and disloyal." The Revolt of the Adm rals had begun as the 10 day hearings opened.

Air Force Secretary Symington denied any plans to abso Naval and Marine aviation into the USAF, contradicting Air For Chief of Staff General Carl "Tooey" Spatz. The Commandant the Marine Corps, General Clifton B. Cates, personally attack Secretary of Defense Johnson and the Chiefs of Staff of the Arn and Air Force! The Navy and Marine witnesses asserted that t needs of the seaborne services had been ignored, specifically cri cizing the cancellation of the *USS United States*. The most force presentation at the hearings was by Admiral Denfield. Admira Halsey, Spruance, Nimitz, Kincaid, King, Radford and Blandy al testified for the Supercarrier at the hearings.

Admiral Denfield Fired

On October 27, 1949 Secretary of the Navy Francis P. Matthe recommended that President Truman remove Admiral Denfield CNO, which Truman did on November 1; thereby effectively en ing the Admirals' Revolt.

Committee Report

The House Naval Affairs Committee report on March 2, 1950 su ported the Navy's position; however, the Supercarrier was not rei stated. It appears that back-room politics and personal vindictiv ness had reared its ugly head and played games with America National Security.

Revolt Not Widely Publicized

Very few Americans realize how close the U.S. Navy came to sha ing the fate of the Royal Navy Fleet Air Arm had it not been f courageous and dedicated officers who risked their careers to save the carrier force and shipboard aircraft of the U.S. Navy.

Unification Can Be Absurd

The outstanding example of how absurd unification can become was the German Luftwaffe, which not only controlled the Air Force but also operated naval aviation, paratroopers, and antiaircraft batteries as well.

Captain Crommelin Honored

Captain John G. Crommelin retired from the Navy with the rank of Rear Admiral on June 1, 1950. In 1987 he was elected into the Carrier Aviation Hall of Fame aboard the the preserved and restored *USS Yorktown* (CV-10) at Patriot's Point, South Carolina. The last line of the citation reads: "In 1949 sacrificed his 4.0 career by precipitating the Air Admirals' Revolt that saved carrier aviation."

U.S. SHIPBOARD AIRCRAFT DEVELOPMENT CONTINUES

Although America's sorely needed Supercarrier had been scuttled by interservice rivalry and high-ranking politicians, the development and production of turbojet-powered shipboard aircraft continued with enthusiasm and without interruption.

Grumman Panther

One of the most successful carrier jet fighters of the early 1950s

Chief of Naval Operations Admiral Louis E. Denfield was fired by President Truman because of Denfield's participation in the Revolt of the Admirals. (U.S. National Archives)

Below: The successful Panther was Grumman's first jet-propelled design. This F9F-2 was powered with a Pratt & Whitney-built Rolls-Royce Nene turbojet engine. The plane has just landed and the wing is beginning to fold. Note the extended arresting hook. (Grumman Corporation, Courtesy Lois Lovisolo)

was the Grumman F9F Panther. Grumman's first jet fighter design originated in 1946 from a Bureau of Aeronautics preliminary specification for a night-fighter. Douglas was also contracted for night-fighter prototype designs at that time. As with many jet-propelled designs of the period, engine design and production had become the stumbling blocks which interfered with and delayed aircraft design and production.

Panther - A Four-Engine Night-Fighter?

The original Grumman XF9F-1 was to be powered by four Westinghouse 24C turbojet engines; each rated at 2,700 pounds static thrust. This engine was under development as the Panther was being designed. The design nightmare of a four-engined fighter was finally abandoned, as was the night-fighter requirement, in October 1946. Instead, attention was concentrated on a day-fighter to be powered by the Rolls-Royce Nene turbojet of 5,000 pounds static thrust. Two of the British engines were sent to the U.S. however, Pratt & Whitney eventually produced the engine under license as the J42 series.

Rolls-Royce Engine Superior

Grumman's new single-engine day fighter was designated XF9F-2 and the first of two prototypes made its initial flight on November 24, 1947. A third prototype flew on August 16, 1948 as the XF9-3, powered by a 4,600 pounds static thrust Allison J33-A-8 engine. Production contracts were immediately placed for (47) F9F-2 and (54) F9F-3 Panthers. Both production variants flew in November 1948 and the P & W-made Rolls-Royce Nene-powered F9F-2 proved superior; therefore, F9F-3 Panthers were re-engined and converted to F9F-2.

Panther Production and Deployment

The first production deliveries were made to VF-51 in May 1949

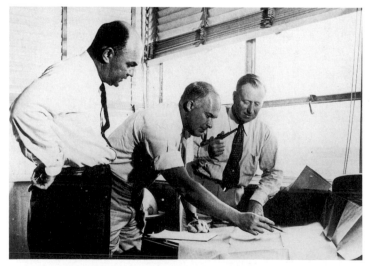

The driving force behind the Grumman design effort was, for many years, embodied in these three former Loening Aeronautical Engineering Corporation engineers. The founders of the Grumman Corporation are, left to right: Production Manager Jake Swirbul; practical, disciplined engineer William T. Schwendler; and incisive, creative design engineer Leroy Randle (Roy) Grumman. (Grumman Corporation, Courtesy Lois Lovisolo)

Many Grumman F9F-3 Panthers were converted into the F9F-2 by replacing their Allison J-33-A-8 engines with the P & W-built Rolls-Royce Nene turbojet. This F9F-3 is dumping fuel from its permanent wingtip fuel tanks. (Grumman Corporation, Courtesy Lois Lovisolo)

and these differed from the prototype in that they mounted permanent wingtip tanks as pioneered by the defunct Vought Pirate. The F9F-4 was absorbed into the 655 production F9F-5 Panthers which were powered by improved P & W J48-P-2. J48-P-4 or J48-P-6 turbojets producing 6,250 pounds of static thrust. The F9F-5 had two feet added to the fuselage, sported a higher fin, and first flew on December 21, 1949. Panthers became the first U.S. Navy jet powered fighters to be used in combat and would soon be seen in action.

Panther Data

The all-metal stressed skin Panther was armed with (4) 20 millimeter rapid-fire cannon in the nose and production also included the F9F-5P camera-equipped reconnaissance version. The F9F-5 attained a maximum speed of 575 miles per hour at 40,000 feet. Cruising speed was 481 miles per hour with a range of 1,300 miles. Initial rate of climb was 5,090 feet per minute and service ceiling was 42,800 feet. Wingspan was 38 feet and length was 10 inches longer. Height was 12 feet-3 inches and wing area 250 square feet. Empty weight was 10,147 pounds, while gross weight was 18,721 pounds. The craft could take off in 800 feet with no wind or in 430 feet with a 35 mile per hour wind over deck.

Panther Deployment

The vast majority of Panthers were supplied to U.S. Navy Squadrons; however, at least three U.S. Marine Squadrons (VMF-115, VMF-311, and VMF-451) received the planes. Most of the Navy Panthers saw service on aircraft carriers, including *USS Valley Forge* and *USS Philippine Sea.*

Douglas Skyknight

Anticipating a development contract for a carrier-based night-fighter, Ed Heinemann and his Douglas design team started work on the XF3D-1 Skyknight as early as September 1945. The contract was signed on April 3, 1946 for a two-seater airborne radar-equipped turbojet-powered interceptor night-fighter.

Skyknight Unusual Crew Escape System

The U.S. Navy decided that operation of the radar equipment re

The Douglas F3D Skyknight night fighter destroyed more planes in the Korean War than any other U.S. Navy and Marine aircraft that were in action during the war. This Marine Skynight is a F3D-2. (McDonnell Douglas, Courtesy Harry Gann)

Edward H. Heinemann, for many years Chief Designer at Douglas El Segundo, led his design team in developing classic aircraft such as the Dauntless, Skyraider, Skyknight, Skywarrior, Skyhawk and many others. (McDonnell Douglas, Courtesy Harry Gann)

quired a second crew member and side-by-side seating was selected as the most effective arrangement. This seating arrangement made escape in the event of an emergency in the normal manner, such as ejection upward or downward, impractical and dangerous. An ingenious method was devised, whereby the crew members slid down a chute out the bottom of the aircraft. By operating the evacuation lever, the seats moved aft and to the sides of the fuselage, while a door opened at the bottom of the chute. The crew slid down the chute feet first.

The first of three prototype XF3D-1 Skyknights made its maiden flight on March 23, 1948 powered by two 3,000 pounds static thrust Westinghouse J34-WE-22 turbojets faired into each side of the lower fuselage and exhausting at the wing trailing edge.

Skyknight Engine Problems
An order for 28 production F3D-1's was received and the first off the line flew on February 13, 1950, powered by two Westinghouse J34-WE-32 engines, which proved underpowered for the Skyknight.

The F3D-2 was then developed to use the new 4,600 pounds static thrust Westinghouse J46-WE-3 turbojet; however, the engine was cancelled due to development and production problems. This forced the F3D-2 to accept the 3,400 pounds static thrust Westinghouse J34-WE-36 turbojet, which engine was installed on all the 237 F3D-2 Skynights that were produced. The first F3D-2 flew on February 14, 1951 and almost missed seeing action in the Korean conflict because of turbojet-engine delivery problems.

Skyknight Data

The F3D-2 Skyknight attained a maximum speed of 600 miles per hour at 20,000 feet, while cruising speed was 350 miles per hour and range was 1,200 miles. Initial rate of climb was 4,500 feet per minute.

Armament comprised four 20 millimeter rapid-fire cannon located in the underside of the nose so that the pilot would not be blinded by the muzzle flash when the guns were fired at night. Some Skyknights were fitted with air-to-air missiles.

Wingspan was 50 feet, which could be halved when the wings were folded. Length was 45 feet-6 inches and height was 16 feet. Wing area was 400 square feet. Empty weight was 18,160 pounds while gross weight was 26,850 pounds.

The Skyknight was equipped with air conditioning, auto-pilot, bulletproof windshield, wing spoilers for a better rate of roll, and "barn door" air brakes fitted to each side of the fuselage. These opened into the slipstream, which slowed the plane in order to reduce the landing speed while permitting the engine to produce adequate thrust. Douglas Skyknights scored heavily in the Korean War.

U.S. SIXTH & SEVENTH FLEETS AND MISSILE TESTS

Two U.S. Fleets became especially important during the post-World War II years.

USS Midway Launches Missile

The carrier *USS Midway* (CVB-41) successfully launched a captured German V-2 ballistic missile at sea on September 6, 1948, which foreshadowed future naval warfare; the use of missiles at sea, which would threaten even the most powerful warships, as well as shore installations.

U.S. Sixth Fleet

On October 1, 1946 a new command had been created; U.S. Naval Forces, Mediterranean. It soon grew in importance, giving the volatile Mediterranean a measure of stability with carriers playing the dominant role. This force was designated Sixth Task Fleet in 1948 as its importance grew, and in February 1950, it earned full recognition as the U.S. Sixth Fleet. The Fleet now comprises two carrier battle groups (CVBG) which are constantly deploying to a trouble spot at one or more of the 14 Mediterranean countries and has become one of the busiest of the U.S. Fleets.

U.S. Seventh Fleet

The World War II Seventh Fleet, often called Doug MacArthur's Navy, had been created in 1943 to cover the many Allied island invasions. It had comprised old battleships and the many CVE escort carriers and destroyers that won the Battle of Leyte Gulf by attacking the Japanese battleships and cruisers.

The Seventh Fleet had fully matured by the 1950s with fleet carriers, cruisers, destroyers and other types patrolling the Western Pacific and Indian Oceans; covering about 30 million square miles! The countries bordering this vast area contain about half of the world's population. The U.S. Seventh Fleet has been the only American Fleet to fight since World War II and the first conflict to draw this fleet into action occurred in the early morning during the summer of 1950.

COMMUNIST CONFRONTATION

The Western Powers' former Ally began showing its true colors by blocking all access to occupied Berlin on June 19, 1948. The Soviets continued to block access for nearly one year, while the Allies were forced to institute the Berlin Airlift. This was only the first of many confrontations with expansionist Communism that would eventually call the carrier Warbirds into action.

KOREAN WAR

In 1910 Japan had annexed Korea, which it called Chosen, after defeating Russia who also coveted the peninsula. As World War II came to an end in 1945 Soviet troops occupied the northern half and American forces moved into the southern part of Korea resulting in a standoff. The Soviets refused to permit free elections and refused to admit U.S. Observers in the northern portion of Korea. Then the politicians took over and repeated the mistakes of the Yalta Conference by surrendering to Communist demands. Soviet and U.S. troops withdrew in 1949; the tragic result being the virtual partition of an ethnically indigenous people into two diametrically opposite political spheres of influence, both of which wanted to control the entire country. This paved the way for a future conflict which burst on the scene as the Korean "Police Action"; a polite word for war coined by the same politicians.

North Korea Attacks The South

Six North Korean Communist infantry divisions and three Border Constabulary Brigades with 100 Soviet-made tanks invaded the Republic of South Korea before dawn of June 25, 1950. The United Nations Security Council immediately condemned this attack but was ignored by the Communists. U.N. Forces were dispatched.

The Grumman Panther was one of the U.S. Navy's principal air weapons used in the Korean War. This trio of Panthers is preparing for a carrier landing. Observe the extended arresting hooks. (Grumman Corporation. Courtesy Lois Lovisolo)

Vought Corsair production lines had to be re-opened to meet U.S. Navy orders for new models needed for the Korean War. One contract called for 215 F4U-5N types from which the F4U-5NL was developed for nocturnal missions in severe cold weather. It included wing and tail de-icers plus extra oxygen for the pilot, and radar. The Vought Corsair had also become the Basic U.S. Navy and Marine Corps close support ground attack plane in the Korean War. (Official U.S. Navy Photo, News Photo Division)

Two days later President Harry S. Truman authorized General Douglas MacArthur, Commander-in-Chief, Far East, to use the American naval and air power to support the unprepared South Korean forces, but by June 28 North Korean forces had occupied the South Korean capital of Seoul. Now, desperately needed for the U.N. Forces, was an adequate Navy and, above all, its air forces. A blockade of the Korean coast was essential. On July 4, 1950 President Truman proclaimed a blockade of the North Korean coast and the U.S. Seventh Fleet was in business with its aircraft carriers and Warbirds of the Sea. Three days later General MacArthur was appointed Supreme Commander of all U.N. Forces in Korea.

Multi-National Carrier Force

Among the many aircraft carriers that were active in the Korean War were the following: Royal Navy; *HMS Glory, HMS Triumph, HMS Theseus, HMS Ocean*. Australian Navy; *HMAS Sydney*. United States Navy; *USS Boxer, USS Princeton, USS Bon Homme Richard, USS Philippine Sea, USS Shangri-La, USS Oriskany, USS Valley Forge, USS Leyte, USS Sicily, USS Badoeng Strait, USS Bataan*.

First Carrier Strikes And Victories

The first air strikes into North Korea took place on July 3-4 from two units of Vice Admiral Arthur D. Struble's Task Force 77; the aircraft carriers *USS Valley Forge* (CV-45), Captain L.K. Rice, commanding; and *HMS Triumph*, Captain A.D. Torless, DSO, commanding. The strikes began when *HMS Triumph* launched a dozen Fairey Firefly fighter/bombers of No. 827 Squadron plus nine Supermarine Seafire 47 fighters of No. 800 Squadron, armed with rockets, at 5:45 a.m. on July 3. Targets were Haeju airfield, about 70 miles south of Pyongyang, plus railroads and bridges in the area.

Fifteen minutes later, sixteen Vought Corsairs of VF-54, loaded with five inch rockets, plus twelve Douglas Skyraiders, armed with 100 and 500-pound bombs, were launched from *USS Valley Forge* to attack Pyongyang airfield at the North Korean capitol.

A short time later the air group commander, Commander Harvey P. Lanham, led eight Grumman Panthers from *USS Valley Forge*. The jet fighters overtook the Corsair/Skyraider flights in time to provide air cover for the strikes and became the first U.S. Navy jets to enter combat. The Panthers shot down two intercepting propeller-driven Yak-9 fighters when Lieutenant (JG) L.H. Plog and Ensign E.W. Brown each scored one. These were the first post-World War II jet victories.

Panther And Corsair Teamwork

The Grumman Panther was one of the U.S. Navy's principal air weapons during the Korean War. The other was the Vought Corsair. The Panther was still under development during the war and the last F9F-5 was delivered in December 1952 when a total of 1,388 Panthers had been built. Corsairs and Panthers often worked as a team with the Grummans flying top cover while the Voughts flew in low for close air support work.

Corsair Production Reestablished

The Vought Corsair had become the basic close support plane for the U.S. Navy and Marines during the Korean War; forcing Vought to reestablish the Corsair production lines at its plants in Connecticut and Texas to meet the U.S. Navy orders for new models then being designed. Korean War orders for Corsairs included (111) AU-1's, (223) F4U-5's, (315) F4U-5N's, and (40) F4U-5P's, which kept the Corsair in production until December 1952.

Corsair Cold Weather Modifications

It had been found that Corsairs needed special modifications to endure the Korean severe cold weather and the F4U-5NL was developed for nocturnal missions in cold weather. More pilot comfort was provided with a more efficient heating system, extra oxygen supplies, plus windshield defrosters for improved visibility. Also fitted were rubber boot de-icers to the wing and tail surface leading edges, plus a propeller liquid de-icing system. Dual radio equipment insured communication under the most adverse conditions.

Special Close Support Corsairs

The close support role required different performance characteristics than fighters because high altitude and top speed had to be sacrificed for a heavy punch and the AU-1 Corsair was born. This was developed from the XF4U-6 which, in turn, was a converted F4U-5. The AU-1 gross weight increased to 19,398 pounds when fitted with 4,000 pounds of bombs, 10 missiles, or napalm.

North Korea Blockaded

By July 25 multi-national Task Force 96.5 was blockading the Korean coast with the U.S. Navy covering the east coast and British Commonwealth forces handling the west coast. Also on that day Task Force 77 carriers began providing tactical air support for the hardpressed Eighth Army Forces holding the Pusan Perimeter.

Carriers Fill In For Missing Airfields

U.S. Marines began fighting in Korea on August 7 with valuable close air support from VMF-214 and VMF-323 flying from the escort carriers *Badoeng Strait* (CVE-116) and *Sicily* (CVE-118) of Rear Admiral Richard W. Ruble's Carrier Division 15. *USS Philippine Sea* (CV-47) had begun launching close support missions for the Eighth Army two days earlier and without these carrier-based close support sorties the heroic ground forces could not have been able to hold out against the Communist onslaught. U.N. Forces had

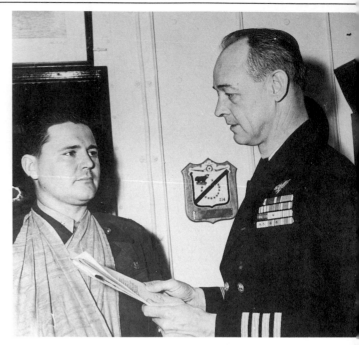

Captain John S. Thach, World War II combat tactician and now the Commanding Officer of USS Sicily (CVE-118), presents the Purple Heart to Major K.J. Reusser USMC. Reusser, Executive Officer of Marine Fighter Squadron 214 (VMF-214) Black Sheep, was forced to ditch his Corsair in Korean waters after a catapult launch on January 18, 1951. (Official U.S. Navy Photograph, Courtesy Dave Ekstrand)

very few airfields in Korea because the Communists had overrun much of the peninsula; therefore, the aircraft carriers became the front-line air bases until airfields such as Kimpo were captured.

Yalu Bridges Bombing is Restricted

On September 27, 1950 MacArthur was authorized to pursue the North Koreans north of the infamous 38th Parallel, which he did on October 9. This resulted in Chinese troops, tanks and aircraft entering North Korea by crossing the Yalu River to engage United Nations Forces. On November 1, Russian-built Chinese MiG-15 jet fighters based in Manchuria crossed into North Korea to attack United Nations planes. Seven days later aircraft from Carrier Task Force 77 bombed the Yalu River Bridges to stop the Chinese entering North Korea. This assignment was complicated by the fact that for political reasons, the Navy pilots were forced to restrict their attack to the Korean end of the bridges!

First Jet-To-Jet Victory

Lieutenant Commander W.T. Amen, Commanding Officer of VF-111, from *USS Philippine Sea*, shot down a MiG-15 jet fighter with his Grumman F9F-2 Panther on November 9, 1950. This was the first jet-powered plane to be shot down by a U.S. Navy pilot while flying a jet.

U.S. Carriers Cover Evacuation

U.S. Navy carriers again proved indispensable during December 24 when, after 300,000 Chinese troops had poured into North Korea and attacked United Nations Forces, carrier aircraft from Rear Admiral James H. Doyle's Task Force 90 provided air support

This view of USS Valley Forge (CV-45) clearly illustrates the brutal weather conditions that was endured by the carrier crews in Korean waters; even in mid-spring. Photo was taken on May 8, 1951. Observe the rockets mounted under the Corsair wings. (U.S. National Archives)

McDonnell Banshees were very active in the Korean War; escorting B-29 bombers and conducting ground support missions. This F2H-2 is flying over snow-covered Korean mountains. (McDonnell Douglas, Courtesy Harry Gann)

cover the evacuation of 105,000 troops, 350,000 tons of supplies and 91,000 civilian refugees from the North Korean Port of Hungnam. Carriers involved were *USS Leyte* (CV-32), *USS Valley Forge* (CV-45), *USS Princeton* (CV-37), *USS Philippine Sea* (CV-47), *USS Bataan* (CVL-29), *USS Badoeng Strait* (CVE-116), and *USS Sicily* (CVE-118).

Truman Fires MacArthur

General Douglas MacArthur, Supreme Commander of United Nations Forces in Korea, complained bitterly because the politicians had forbidden him to lead his forces across the Yalu River in pursuit of Chinese troops or to conduct air attacks across the Chinese border. When his protests were made public, and backed by many Americans, President Truman relieved MacArthur of his command for political expediency and replaced him with General Matthew B. Ridgeway on April 11, 1951.

Banshees Escort Superfortresses

Flying high and low altitude missions, the McDonnell Banshee had been in operational service with several Navy Squadrons when it entered the Korean War. *USS Essex* (CV-9) arrived in Korea during August 1951 loaded with fresh supplies, equipment, men and F2H-2 Banshees. These were flown by VF-172 of Task Force 77 alongside F9F-5 Panthers on August 25, while escorting Boeing B-29 Superfortresses for a high-altitude bombing raid on the Rashin rail center in the northeast corner of North Korea. Later, on October 8, Banshees, alone, escorted B-29's on a raid. The Banshee was also very active in the ground support role.

Panther Fighter/Bombers

By midsummer 1951 Panthers were routinely used for the pinpoint bombing of bridges and other important targets. This had its beginning on April 2 when two F9F-2 Panthers of VF-191 were fitted with four 250 pound and two 100 pound general purpose bombs.

They had been catapulted from *USS Princeton* and attacked railroad bridges near Songjin. This had been the first time the U.S. Navy had used jets as fighter-bombers. The Panther fighter/bomber had been designated F9F-2B and, by the following year, VMF-311 had been fully equipped with the F9F-2B.

Sea Fury And Corsair Jet Victories

The Hawker Sea Fury was performing yeoman's service in the ground attack role in the Korean fighting. Used throughout the conflict, the craft often engaged Soviet-built MiG-15 jet fighters and succeeded in destroying several of the faster jets in combat. The first of these kills was made on April 9, 1952 by Lieutenant P. Carmichael of FAA 802 Squadron. Sea Furies started in Korea with 807 Squadron and served on the carriers *Theseus*, *Ocean* and *Glory*; flying thousands of sorties.

America's ground attack mainstay of the Korean War, the Vought Corsair, scored its first jet fighter victory when Marine Captain Jesse G. Folmar shot down a MiG-15 on September 9, 1952. The Sea Fury and Corsair were certainly a breed apart from all other contemporary propeller-driven fighters.

Meanwhile, United Nations naval aircraft continued the pounding of Communist positions and facilities in North Korea.

Coordinated Attacks On North Korea

On June 23, 1952 three dozen Douglas Skyraiders and an equal number of Grumman Panthers from the carriers *USS Boxer* (CV-21), *Philippine Sea* (CV-47), and *USS Princeton* (CV-37) joined U.S. Air Force Republic Thunderjets in an attack on the huge hydro-electric powerplant at Suiho, North Korea. The plant was put out of commission, as were several others during the two-day raid.

Over 40 targets were destroyed around the North Korean capital of Pyongyang when over 90 planes from *USS Bon Homme Richard* (CV-31) and *USS Princeton* (CV-37) joined British carrier planes and Australian aircraft in a fierce raid on July 11, 1952.

The biggest bombing raid of the Korean War was launched on August 29 when planes from U.S. carriers *Boxer* and *Essex* joined 1,000 other United Nations aircraft in attacks on selected targets around Pyongyang.

The largest carrier plane raid of the war followed on September 1 when 144 planes from the carriers *Boxer*, *Essex* and *Princeton* destroyed the oil refinery at Aoji, North Korea, only eight miles from the Soviet border.

Cherokee Strikes

The Seventh Fleet Commander Vice Admiral J.J. "Jocko" Clark initiated a battlefront bombing campaign against Communist positions that were beyond the range of United Nations artillery. The campaign lasted from October 9, 1952 through July 1953 and was named after the admiral's American Indian ancestry; Cherokee Strikes.

Soviet MiGs Tangle With Panthers

A dangerous international incident was barely avoided only a few miles from the Soviet border, southwest of Vladivostok, when seven Soviet MiG-15 jets engaged three F9F-5 Panthers from *USS Oriskany* on November 18, 1952. Two MiG's were shot down but none of the Grummans were lost.

Corsair Night-Fighters and "Bed Check Charlie"

A Korean War record was established when, on June 16, 1953, *USS Princeton* (CV-37) launched 184 sorties against Communist targets during that single day.

USS Princeton was again in the news exactly one month later when night-fighting Corsairs tackled Communist "Bed Check Charlies." In view of the fact that much of the Korean Conflict naval air war was fought by high-speed jets high above the front and by low-level ground support aircraft such as the Corsair and Sea Fury, not much has been written about the unsung heroes who fought the "Bed Check Charlies." In an effort to destroy American and other United Nations forces' morale and efficiency, the cunning Communists resorted to nocturnal nuisance raids by slow single-engine propeller-driven planes over United Nations installations in South Korea. These "Bed Check Charlies" relied on their noisy engines and by dropping small bombs to keep the troops awake at night running to shelters. They were often called "Washing Machine Charley" because of the noisy engine. The Soviet-built Lavochkin LA-11 and Yakovlev YAK-18 were too slow and too maneuverable for the U.S. Air Force jet fighters to shoot down so they asked the Navy for help.

In response to Fifth Air Force requests, four night-fighter pilots were ordered to Kimpo Airfield on June 25, 1953; their mission being the destruction of the "Washing Machine Charlies." Lieutenants Donald Edge and "Zolly" Stevens flew their Vought F4U-5N Corsairs from *USS Philippine Sea* (CV-47) while Lieutenant Guy P. Bordelon and another officer flew their Corsairs from *USS Princeton* (CV-37). The night-fighting Corsairs had been performing yeoman service against North Korean supply columns, trains and truck caravans which the enemy activated under cover of darkness. Now, they were called upon to rid the skies of the North Korean nocturnal nuisance.

Lieutenant Guy Bordelon was one of four Corsair F4U-5N nightfighter pilots who transferred from their carriers to Kimpo Airfield to intercept North Korean Bed Check Charley nocturnal air raiders. Observe the exhaust shield (No.1) and gun muzzle cone (No.2) on Lt. Bordelon's Vought F4U-5N which were necessary to keep the glare of the muzzle flashes away from the pilot's eyes during nocturnal operations. Bordelon is shown here discussing his Corsair with crewmen. (U.S. Naval Historical Center)

After several weeks of night patrols in the inky blackness, the four F4U-5N pilots dampened the Communists' enthusiasm for any more nocturnal nuisance raids.

Had the carriers *Princeton* and *Philippine Sea* not been available and not been in the immediate area it would have been very difficult and time consuming to find and relocate suitable night fighters to deal with the "Washing Machine Charlies." Even when aircraft don't operate directly from their aircraft carrier during a specific assignment, the carrier must be credited for having its planes near a shoreside sector where they are most needed. Without carriers this assignment could not have been completed in such short notice.

Korean War Data

On July 29, 1953 a cease-fire agreement, effective at 10:00 o'clock in the morning, was signed by United Nations and Communist negotiators in the village of Pannmunjon, leaving Korea still divided into two diverse political spheres of influence.

The Korean Police Action had involved 16 nations; however 90 percent of the United Nations' effort was borne by the United States. U.S. Navy and Marine planes flew more than one-third of all the combat sorties flown by U.S. Air Forces in Korea with carrier-borne aircraft playing an indispensable role in pushing the North Korean troops out of South Korea. Combat use of carriers in Korea was on a more continuous basis than carrier use in World War II.

It is interesting to note at this time that, of all the U.S. Navy and Marine aircraft in action during the Korean War, Douglas F3 Skyknights destroyed more enemy aircraft than any other type.

DOUGLAS SKYRAIDER VARIANTS

As with the Vought Corsair, the Douglas Skyraider was saved from extinction by the demands for propeller-driven workhorses in the Korean War. Since the introduction of Skyraiders at the end of World War II, the plane had undergone constant refinement to fit the multipurpose roles to which it was being assigned. The first Douglas AD-5's were delivered to the U.S. Navy as the Korean Armistice was being signed.

Skyraider Conversion Kits

With the AD-5 came a cleverly innovative concept which amplified the already broad multipurpose capability of the Skyraider design. Developed by Ed Heinemann, Douglas El Segundo Chief Designer, and his team, were seven 500 pound conversion kits built by Douglas which could convert the AD-5 from the basic day attack plane into a variety of other specialized aircraft in from two to 12 hours by squadron mechanics and plane handlers on an aircraft carrier. The kits could convert the AD-5 into a VIP transport by installing four backward-facing plush seats behind the pilot; into an ambulance plane by installing four litters or stretchers and a hoist; into a high-density transport by installing two bench-type seats along the fuselage sides which could seat 10 passengers; into a cargo transport which includes heavy plywood flooring and a cargo hoist; into a photographic plane with five giant cameras and the cartographer in a comfortable chair; into a target tow plane which includes a belly-pod for the target, towing-line and reel; into a long-range reconnaissance or bomber with the addition of two 150 gallon fuel tanks in the fuselage, which doubled the normal internal tankage of the Skyraider. This rapid conversion procedure was called the Multi-plex system.

Larger Cockpit

The most obvious external difference in the AD-5 from the original AD-1 was the enormous size of the cockpit canopy. It was wider and much longer and could accommodate a crew of two sitting side-by-side. The fin and rudder are also larger.

Radar and Sonar Fitted

The radar-equipped AD-5N night-attack version could also be used for night interdiction, all-weather operation and ASW (Anti Submarine Warfare). This model was fitted with sonar equipment and a searchlight for submarine detection. Another version, AD-5W, was an airborne early-warning and antisubmarine search aircraft with highly sophisticated radar equipment.

Skyraider activities will be examined at a later time when it wreaks havoc in another Asian war.

UNPAINTED CARRIER AIRCRAFT EXPERIMENTS

Carrier aircraft corrosion continued to be a problem, but not without its remedy. Beginning in 1950 new refinements by Harold Acker of the Philadelphia Naval Aircraft Factory consisted of zinc chromate as the inhibitive pigment dispersed in a varnish-type vehicle. This new primer was a vital contribution to corrosion inhibition of aluminum in a marine atmosphere. Unfortunately, at that same time, U.S. Navy Fleet units and commands had started a campaign requesting carrier aircraft without exterior paint because, at that time,

The U.S. Navy's experiment with unpainted carrier aircraft resulted in failure because it required too much time and effort to polish out corrosion pits and corrosive engine exhaust smudges. The consensus was that unpainted aircraft do not belong on aircraft carriers. Photo shows unpainted Vought Cutlass fighters. (Vought Aircraft Company, Courtesy Paul Bower)

U.S. Air Force planes were being flown in their natural aluminum exterior. The U.S. Navy Bureau of Aeronautics gave in against its better judgment; listening to the arguments of weight savings and excessive manhours required to touch-up chipped and worn paint.

About 250 unpainted carrier aircraft were procured in early 1952 and quarterly maintenance reports were requested from all U.S. Naval Unit recipients. Over 1,000 reports were received by the Bureau of Aeronautics during the first 18 months and all agreed on the basic points. Photographs of U.S. Navy carrier planes of the 1950's, unpainted and in their polished, natural aluminum finish are fairly common. It always seemed that they were incomplete and awaiting their coat of paint, which is not the case. These were the subjects of the corrosion reports.

For the first three months of carrier duty most units reported a slight improvement in speed for the unpainted aircraft.

Reports during the second three-month period agreed that considerable time and effort had been spent polishing out corrosion pits and removing exhaust gas deposits and stains. Many units requested a better cleaner/wax in order to reduce the time spent keeping the planes polished and bright. The third three-month period produced so many complaints and requests to end the entire program that the Bureau of Aeronautics cancelled the balance of the unpainted planes and reverted back to the painted aircraft.

The short-lived program proved that unpainted airplanes do not belong on aircraft carriers and saved the U.S. Navy many millions of dollars worth of maintenance manhours.

During World War II and subsequent conflicts, unpainted U.S. land-based aircraft were ferried to the war zones on the decks of merchant ships. These natural aluminum-finished planes were either sprayed with a grease-like preservative or enclosed within hermetically sealed cocoons to ward off the corrosive effects of the marine environment. On the other hand, naval aircraft required no protection from the environment during ferrying operations because their paint prevented corrosion problems from developing.

BLENDED JET FUEL

During 1951-1954 the U.S. Navy modified the *Essex* class carriers *Hancock*, *Ticonderoga* and *Intrepid* to blend fuel for the turbojet-powered planes. In view of the fact that turbojet-powered planes could use low-grade fuel similar to kerosene and that these were flown in conjunction with gasoline fueled propeller planes, it was decided to save tankage by mixing the aviation gasoline and ship's heavy fuel oil to form jet fuel. Despite the fact that the fuel was well-purified and filtered it caused serious impingement on the turbine blades by vanadium and other minerals in the fuel oil due to the intense heat of the engine. The blending was soon abandoned in favor of specialized jet fuels such as JP-4 and the later JP-5.

U.S. NAVY ADOPTS STEAM CATAPULTS

Essex class carriers had been undergoing necessary modifications since 1948 and by the time the first two, *Essex* and *Wasp*, had completed modernization they were returned to the shipyard because additional alterations were required in the early 1950s. It had become difficult for the carriers to keep up with the Warbirds' rapid development. The heavier and faster planes required stronger elevators and arresting gear, plus more powerful catapults. The U.S. Navy was in the process of developing a more powerful catapult, using gunpowder, as had been done in the pioneering days of shipboard aviation, when the Royal Navy demonstrated the steam-powered catapult. Proven in use on Royal Navy carriers, the steam catapult was soon adopted as the standard U.S. Navy catapult with the initial installation on *USS Hancock* (CV-19) in 1952.

ROYAL NAVY *EAGLE* CLASS CARRIERS

Btween October 1, 1951 and February 25, 1955 the Royal Navy had commissioned two state-of-the-art carriers, which had been started a decade before. In 1940 the Royal Navy had proposed the construction of four carriers as an improvement of the *HMS Implacable* design; however, the British war machine had other urgent priorities at that time, and the program was cancelled. With the advent of the Japanese seizure of colonies in Asia and the Pacific, Britain suddenly needed more carriers and, by early 1942, a new design had been formulated, based upon aircraft carrier war experience to date. The four carriers were to be named *Ark Royal*, *Audacious*, *Africa* and *Eagle*.

Eagle Class Two-Level Hangar

A two-level hangar with a 14 feet-6 inches height for each level was originally planned; however, because of the U.S. aircraft that were used extensively by the Fleet Air Arm, plus the realization that its own Warbirds would grow to immense proportions, the hangar heights were raised to 17 feet-6 inches. This single development increased the hull depth and beam which, in turn, widened the

The Eagle class aircraft carriers' armor protection accounted for about one-fifth of the weight with portions of the Flight Deck designed to withstand 1,000 pound bomb direct hits. Hawker Sea Hawks and Fairey Gannets line the deck of HMS Eagle. (Ministry of Defence [Navy])

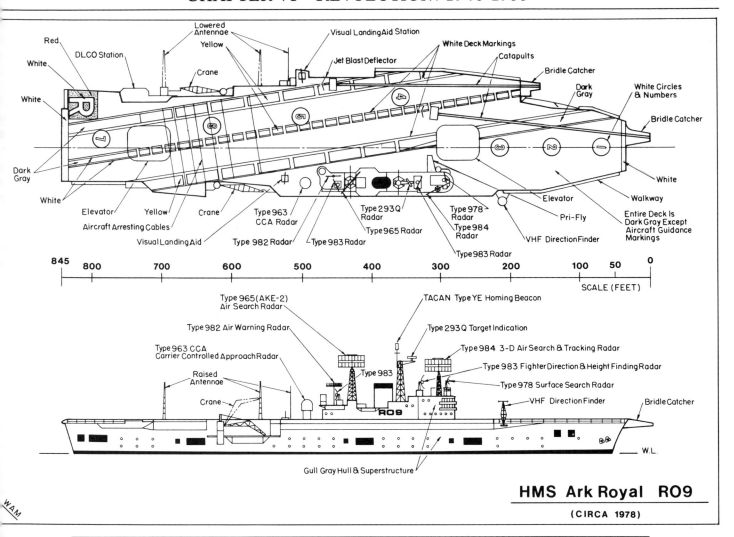

Red
White
DLCO Station
White
Lowered Antennae
Yellow
Crane
Visual LandingAid Station
Jet Blast Deflector
White Deck Markings
Catapults
Bridle Catcher
Dark Gray
White Circles & Numbers
Bridle Catcher
Dark Gray
White
White
Elevator
Yellow
Crane
Aircraft Arresting Cables
Visual Landing Aid
Type 963 CCA Radar
Type 293Q Radar
Type 982 Radar
Type 965 Radar
Type 983 Radar
Type 978 Radar
Type 984 Radar
Type 983 Radar
Elevator
White
Walkway
Pri-Fly
VHF Direction Finder
Entire Deck Is Dark Gray Except Aircraft Guidance Markings

845 800   700   600   500   400   300   200   100   50   0
SCALE (FEET)

Type 965(AKE-2) Air Search Radar
TACAN Type YE Homing Beacon
Type 982 Air Warning Radar
Type 293Q Target Indication
Type 963 CCA Carrier Controlled Approach Radar
Type 984 3-D Air Search & Tracking Radar
Type 983 Fighter Direction & Height Finding Radar
Type 983
Type 978 Surface Search Radar
Raised Antennae
VHF Direction Finder
Bridle Catcher
Crane
R09
W.L.
Gull Gray Hull & Superstructure

HMS Ark Royal R09

(CIRCA 1978)

hangar, which enabled it to accommodate 80 planes. An additional 20 aircraft could be stowed on the Flight Deck.

Eagle Class Armor

Armor protection accounted for about one-fifth of the carrier's weight and this was distributed as follows: waterline hull belt was 4 1/2 inches thick with an additional 1 1/2 inch underwater curtain for protection from torpedo hits. Flight deck was four inches thick over the hangar to withstand direct hits of 1,000 pound bombs. The remainder of the flight deck was 1 1/2 inches thick. Hangar sides were 1 1/2 inches thick, while the ends were 2 1/2 inches thick. The lower hangar deck was 2 1/2 inches thick between the hangar and ship's side. The deck over the steering gear was 3 inches thick. Transverse bulkheads were 2 1/2 inches, while longitudinal bulkheads were 1 1/2 inches thick.

Leisurely Progress

Although the keels were laid in 1942-43 very little progress had been made by the end of the war in 1945. *HMS Africa* had been cancelled earlier and its name given to a Malta class carrier and now, at the war's end, *Eagle* was cancelled and scrapped at the shipyard. Work on the two remaining carriers of the class was stopped for about three years and then construction was reinstated.

Audacity gave up her name in order that the name *Eagle* could be perpetuated; therefore, the two remaining carriers were to be *HMS Eagle* and *HMS Ark Royal* to honor the two gallant carriers of World War II.

Eagle Follows Wartime Design

HMS Eagle was the first to be launched on March 19, 1946 at the Harlan & Wolf Yard in Belfast, Ireland, and the ships became known as the *Eagle* class. As completed, *Eagle* followed the wartime design as an axial deck carrier with improved radar. Two catapults or accelerators were installed. The term accelerator was gaining acceptance because the larger and faster aircraft were not actually tossed into the air but sped along the deck to attain flying speed before the end of the flight deck was reached. Two aircraft elevators, eight arresting cables, and six aircraft barriers were also fitted; all designed to handle planes as heavy as 30,000 pounds.

Eagle Class Data

Standard displacement was 36,800 tons while full load displacement was 45,720 tons. Hull length at the waterline was 750 feet with a beam of 113 feet. The flight deck dimensions were 775 x 112 feet. Draft was 33 feet standard and 36 feet full load.

This aerial view of HMS Ark Royal in 1955 reveals the diagonal landing runway to forming a 5 1/2 degree angled deck. Note the large radius corners on the aircraft elevator openings in order to reduce the stress on the armored Flight Deck. (Ministry of Defence [Navy])

This interesting view of the new Ark Royal clearly shows the "motor boat" transom stern which has become common in aircraft carrier design as opposed to the sharp cruiser stern of earlier carriers. (Ministry of Defence [Navy])

Eight Admiralty boilers delivered 400 pounds per square inc steam pressure to four Parsons steam turbines geared to four pr peller shafts. This powerplant developed 152,000 shaft horsepowe driving the carrier to a speed of 30.5 knots full load and 32 kno standard. Range was 5,000 nautical miles at 24 knots. Fuel oil tank age was 6,500 tons and aviation fuel tankage was over 100,00 gallons. The Royal Navy had abandoned its practice of stowin aviation fuel in cylindrical tanks located in compartments filled wit seawater because of the increasing amount of aviation fuel that ha to be stowed due to the heavier and faster aircraft with fuel-gulpin jet engines. *HMS Eagle* class was the first Royal Navy carrier clas in many years to stow aviation fuel in structural tanks. Structura tanks provided more volume for the fuel.

Normal ship operating officers and crew was 2,250 with pr visions for 2,800 in wartime, plus an equal number of FAA person nel. *HMS Eagle* was commissioned on October 1, 1951.

Ark Royal More Advanced

Ark Royal was launched over four years after Eagle on May 3, 195 at the Cammel Laird Yard in Birkenhead, England, and incorpo rated many advancements in aircraft carrier technology. *HMS A Royal* was fitted with a 5 1/2 degree angled Flight Deck, two stean powered catapults (accelerators), and a deck edge elevator, simil to the *Essex* class, which was subsequently removed, plus the ne mirror landing assist. The Flight Deck dimensions increased to 80 x 112 feet.

Eagle Class Aircraft

The initial aircraft complement included the Blackburn Firebran and Supermarine Attacker, followed by the Westland Wyver Hawker Sea Hawk, Douglas Skyraider, DeHavilland Sea Venon Fairey Gannet, Blackburn Buccaneer and others, plus helicopte such as the Westland Sea King, Westland Lynx and Westland Drag onfly. From 80 to 100 aircraft could be accommodated.

U.S. SUPERCARRIERS AT LAST

Prior to the Korean War U.S. politicians and some military leade believed that America's premier weapon was the atomic bom however, U.S. involvement in that war demonstrated the value aircraft carriers in the conventional power projection role. As w related, by mounting sustained pressure on the Communists wi endless air strikes in support of U.N. troops, the aircraft carrier an its Warbirds proved a formidable and indispensable weapon.

Supercarriers Funded

Armed with this indisputable evidence, the Supercarrier proponen in the U.S. Government managed to gather enough support to ha funds appropriated for four Supercarriers, and *USS United Stat* like the Phoenix rose from the ashes to become a reality.

USS Forrestal Construction Begins

Ordered in July 1951, the keel of the Supercarrier was laid at Ne port News Shipbuilding on July 14, 1952. The new carrier was a signed the name *USS Forrestal* to honor the former U.S. Secreta of the Navy and the first U.S. Secretary of Defense, who had foug

The new HMS Ark Royal had been started in 1943 but was not launched until 1950. By that time it had been fitted with steam catapults, mirror landing device, and 5 1/2 degree angled Flight Deck. Among the planes on deck are Supermarine Scimitars and de Havilland Sea Vixens. (U.S. Naval Historical Center)

hard for the Supercarrier's existence. The first *Forrestal* design schemes generally followed that of the cancelled *USS United States*; however, with the advent of the angled Deck, which had been tested in the *Essex* class carrier *Antietam* (CV-36) in January 1953, the design was altered during construction to include an eight-degree angled Flight Deck on the port side. The angled Flight Deck replaced the two CVA-58 amidship catapults. As with *USS United States*, *USS Forrestal* was designed to operate the 80,000 pound Douglas Skywarrior strategic bomber, which was to give the U.S.

Navy its own nuclear strike capability. This plane, under development since 1947, governed many of the new carrier's characteristics. In turn, the large size of the plane was dictated by the 12,000 pound atomic bomb.

USS Forrestal Data
USS Forrestal (CVA-59) displaces 59,650 tons standard and 78,000 tons full load. Hull length at the waterline is 990 feet with a beam of 129 feet-6 inches. Flight Deck dimensions are 1,039 x 252 feet.

The second carrier of the Forrestal class was USS Saratoga (CVA-60). Note the catapult bridle arrestors just forward of the catapults. This was a new concept that became a standard installation on all carriers. (Official U.S. Navy Photograph, News Photo Division)

PPOSITE: USS Forrestal (CVA-59) set the pattern for all future U.S.
vy Supercarriers and was the largest warship of its time. It was also
e first U.S. aircraft carrier to be constructed with an angled deck. The
rcraft on deck include the Phantom II, Skywarrior, and Skyhawk.
fficial U.S. Navy Photograph, News Photo Division)

eep load draft is 37 feet. This huge quadruple-screw warship is
wered by eight boilers, which deliver 1,200 pounds per square
ch steam pressure to four geared steam turbines developing a to-
l of 260,000 shaft horsepower. This powerplant drives the
percarrier to a maximum speed of 33 knots. The combat range is
,000 miles at 20 knots. Ships' complement is about 2,790 offic-
s and crew, plus 2,150 members of the air wing, for a total of
940 souls on board.

In order to accommodate the Douglas Skywarrior the Hangar
ight was increased about 50 percent from the Midway class to 25
et. The very wide Flight Deck, which was necessary to accomodate the Skywarrior, created exceptional overhang, which fa-
litated the installation of four deck-edge elevators, without en-
oaching on Hangar space. This enabled the enormous Hangar to
ow more than half of the 85 plane complement.

Original armament comprised (8) 5 inch guns in single-turret
ounts; however, these were replaced two decades later with
aytheon Sea Sparrow SAM (Surface-to-Air) missile launchers.

USS Forrestal's aviation fuel stowage tanks total 750,000 gal-
ns while ship's fuel tankage consists of 7,800 tons. Two thousand
ns of ammunition, bombs, and missiles are also stowed in the
agazines deep in the bowels of the ship.

orrestal Features

SS Forrestal was not only the largest warship of its time but also
cluded features never before incorporated in purpose-built U.S.
rcraft carriers. These included the hurricane bow; steam catapults

For many years all U.S. Navy ship dimensions were governed by the clearance under New York's Brooklyn Bridge and the width of the Panama Canal locks. USS Saratoga was built in the New York Naval Shipyard (Brooklyn Navy Yard) and, in order to clear the Brooklyn Bridge, the main mast was made to be lowered as shown. (Official U.S. Navy Photograph)

of (2) C7 and (2) C11 types; angled Flight Deck; and a Flight Deck
that was constructed as an integral structural member of the entire
hull, which contributed considerably to the carrier's longitudinal
strength. The Flight Deck was 3 inches thick armor plate, which
served the dual purpose of adding strength to the ship, as well as
armor protection from aerial attack. It will be remembered that these
new ideas had been conceived by the Royal Navy. USS Forrestal,
with these features plus the distinctive configuration of enormous
Flight Deck area with generous overhang and small island incorporating the smokestack, had set the standard which has been adopted
by all subsequent U.S. Supercarrier designs.

learly shown in this side view of the third Forrestal class carrier, USS Ranger (CVA-61), are the three large hangar openings in the starboard side. he center opening just aft of the island has been closed. Deck edge elevators are directly over the hangar openings. (U.S. Naval Historical Center)

The *Forrestal* Class Supercarriers

The three other carriers built under this initial appropriation were *USS Saratoga* (CVA-60); *USS Ranger* (CVA-61); and *USS Independence* (CVA-62). It required three-and-one-half years from keel laying to commissioning for *USS Forrestal* to enter service with the U.S. Atlantic Fleet. *USS Forrestal* was launched on December 11, 1954 and commissioned on October 1, 1955.

Forrestal Aircraft

Aircraft which have served on *USS Forrestal* include Panther, Skyraider, Banshee, Skywarrior, F-4 Phantom II, Intruder, Skyhawk, Prowler, Hawkeye, Viking, Corsair II, Sea King helicopter and others. Some have been described on previous pages, while others will be described later as they appear on the historic scene. *Forrestal's* CVA designation was changed to CV in the 1970s.

THE PRODUCTIVE DECADE

The 1950s witnessed a prolific blossoming of imaginative and innovative shipboard aircraft designs that incorporated numerous aerodynamic and engineering advances which, truly, made it a decade of progress for Warbirds of the Sea.

Supermarine Attacker

After having made significant advances in turbojet engine and aircraft carrier design Britain issued the first Fleet Air Arm single seater carrierborne jet-powered fighter to frontline Squadrons No. 800, 803 and 890 in 1953.

Designed Around Rolls-Royce Turbojet

By 1944 the Rolls-Royce Nene turbojet engine had been proven successful; therefore, Air Ministry specification E. 10/44 was prepared for a fighter design using this engine. Supermarine, the firm that built the famous Spitfire and Seafire, had been working on the ultimate Spitfire/Seafire development known as the Spiteful/Seafang. The firm proposed that the very advanced laminar flow Spiteful/Seafang wing, complete with landing gear, be mated to a new fuselage which would house the 5,000 pounds static thrust engine. This was accepted and the Supermarine Type 392 prototype was first flown on July 27, 1946; however, because World War II was over, the new design was met with little or no enthusiasm by the RAF.

Attacker Adapted to Carrier Operation

The second and third prototypes were quickly adapted to carri

The fourth Forrestal class carrier is USS Independence (CVA-62). Observe the four McDonnell Douglas F-4 Phantom II fighters about to be launched at the catapults and the walkways at the Flight Deck edge. (U.S. Naval Historical Center)

he Supermarine Attacker was designed around the successful Rolls-oyce Nene Turbojet engine. A total of 145 Attackers was ordered by the leet Air Arm after the RAF lost interest in the design which became the rst British jet powered carrierborne single-seat fighter. (Ministry of efence [Navy])

The Grumman Cougar was basically a swept-wing version of the Grumman Panther. The prototype Grumman XF9F-6 is shown here on a test flight. The Cougar was the first swept-wing aircraft to see service on U.S. carriers. (Grumman Corporation, Courtesy Lois Lovisolo)

peration being fitted with a long stroke landing gear, spoilers and anding arresting hook by following Specification No. E. 1/45. This as now the Supermarine Type 398 and, after the first flight in une 1947, a production order was awarded for the Attacker as the ew design was named. The first production Attacker made its inial flight on April 20, 1950 and when production ended in 1953 a tal of 145 Attackers had been delivered to the Fleet Air Arm.

The plane was of exceptionally clean and uncluttered design. arly production craft F.1 did not have a dorsal fin; however, this as fitted to the two subsequent modifications FB.1 and FB.2. hroughout the three year production run the two-wheel "tail draging" landing gear was retained, rather than convert to tricycle deign which was more adaptable for jet aircraft operation. Apparntly, the Fleet Air Arm was so pleased to get this jet fighter that it esitated to insist upon expensive refinements. The fact that the ailpipe directed the exhaust gasses onto the flight deck during taxing caused considerable deck erosion and corrosion.

Attacker Data

he Supermarine Attacker F.1 weighed 8,434 pounds empty while ross weight was 11,500 pounds. The 5,100 pounds static thrust Rolls-Royce Nene 3 turbojet engine gave the Attacker a maximum peed of 590 miles per hour at sea level. At the cruising speed of 55 miles per hour the range was 590 miles. Service ceiling was 5,000 feet. The straight tapered wing spanned 36 feet-11 inches while overall length was 37 feet-6 inches. Height was 9 feet-11 nches and wing area was 226 square feet.

By 1954 Attacker squadrons were being refitted with Sea Hawks nd Sea Venoms in which case the Supermarines were relegated to eserve units. Although in frontline service for only three years, the Attacker initiated the FAA into jet-powered fighters and provided nuch useful data for future operations.

Grumman Cougar

Proposals to develop a swept-wing version of the F9F Panther had een made by Grumman to the U.S. Navy in 1949. When the plane egan to prove itself and Soviet-built swept-wing fighters appeared n the Korean War, a contract was awarded in March 1951.

An entirely new 35 degrees swept-back wing was mated to the Panther fuselage and tail with the installation of the more powerful Pratt & Whitney J48-P-8 of 7,250 pounds static thrust. This was

known as the Grumman G-93 and the Navy designation became XF9F-6, which suggested that it was another variant of the Panther; however, the Panther popular name was dropped in favor of Cougar.

Cougar Test Flights and Mods

First flight was made on September 20, 1951 and Navy evaluation was completed during the following year. Deliveries of the F9F-6 totalled 706, while 168 of the F9F-7 were produced, which was identical, except that it was powered by the Allison J33-A-16A turbojet engine.

The F9F-8 Cougar conducted its maiden flight on December 18, 1953. This variant had 8 inches added to the fuselage in order to accommodate more fuel and the wing chord was increased about 15 percent. The wing leading edge now sported some camber and a small radome had been installed under the nose.

Cougar F9F-6 Data

Fixed armament comprised four 20 millimeter cannon in the tip of the nose which had become the U.S. Navy standard armament. Underwing pylons could accommodate four Sidewinder missiles or 2,000 pounds of bombs.

Maximum speed at sea level was 690 miles per hour; initial climb was 9,000 feet per minute and 40,000 feet could be reached in seven minutes; service ceiling 50,000 feet; and range was 1,000 miles.

The photographic-reconnaissance version of the Grumman Cougar was the F9F-8P, shown here. Note the lengthened and reshaped nose to accommodate photographic equipment. (Grumman Corporation, Courtesy Lois Lovisolo)

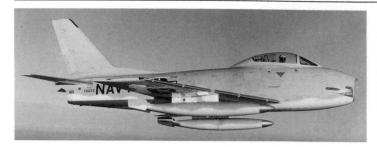

The North American FJ-2, FJ-3, and FJ-4 Fury jet powered carrierborne fighter were developments of the successful U.S. Air Force North American F-86 Sabre. Over 500 of the FJ-3s, shown here, were constructed and served on USS Bon Homme Richard and USS Bennington. An FJ-3 was the first plane to land on USS Forrestal. A total of 17 Navy and four Marine squadrons flew the FJ-3. (North American Rockwell, Courtesy J.M. Syverson)

Gross weight was 20,000 pounds; wingspan 36 feet-5 inches and overall length 41 feet-7 inches. Height was 15 feet. Wings folded up and over the fuselage, hinging just outboard of the engines which are buried in the wing root as on the Panther.

Production was completed at the end of 1959 when 1,985 Cougars had been delivered. The Cougar had been the first swept-wing design to see service on U.S. Navy carriers.

Sabre Jet Adapted To Carriers

Flushed with the success of the swept wing Cougar the U.S. Navy decided to try what the Fleet Air Arm had been forced to do; convert an existing land-based Air Force jet fighter to meet the rigid requirements of shipboard operation. The Air Force North American F-86 Sabre had made a good showing in Korea and was selected for naval use. On March 8, 1951 the Navy ordered a prototype F-86 with the minimum necessary modifications for shipboard operation. Although this design was considerably different from the previous FJ-1 Fury, it was designated XFJ-2 and named Fury; in effect, a design modification. This subterfuge is often used when funds are available for modifications but not available for new designs, as with the Panther/Cougar.

Sabre Naval Modifications

The first two prototypes were essentially Sabres with lengthened nose wheel strut, British-type Vee frame arresting hook, folding wing (outboard seven feet); improved gunsight; four 20 millimeter cannon replacing the six Air Force .50 inch caliber machine guns, a completely redesigned cockpit and catapult fittings. Test flights in December 1951 resulted in a production contract for 300 FJ-2 Furies on February 10, 1951. As a Sabre second source North American Aviation had bought the Curtiss-Wright Corporation plant in Columbus, Ohio, where the first Fury emerged in Autumn 1952. By the end of 1953 only 25 Furies had been completed because of the F-86 priority; therefore, when the Korean War ended the contract was reduced to 200 planes, all of which went to Marine squadrons; VMF-122, VMF-235; VMF-232; VMF-312; VMF-334 and VMF-451.

The FJ-2 Fury had been powered by the 6,000 pounds static thrust General Electric J47-GE-2 turbojet engine and attained a maximum speed of 676 miles per hour at sea level. Curtiss-Wright had just acquired the license to manufacture the Rolls-Royce Saffire turbojet engine of 7,800 pounds static thrust and it was decided to use this powerplant in the next Fury variant, FJ-3 Fury.

In addition to the more powerful engine the FJ-3 was fitted with extended leading edges to replace the wing slots; redesigned rudder; additional fuel tanks in the wing; some were equipped for firing AAM Sidewinder missiles; in-flight fueling probes were installed in the port or left wing; and the air intake nose opening was enlarged slightly. A total of 538 FJ-3 Furies were ordered and deliveries began in September 1954. VF-173 took the FJ-3 aboard *USS Bennington* in May 1955 and an FJ-3 from VF-21 was the first plane to land on *USS Forrestal* on January 4, 1956. A total of 17 Navy and four Marine squadrons flew the FJ-3.

FJ-4 Variant

The final variant was, in fact, a new design, although it bore a strong resemblance to the FJ-2 and FJ-3. The objective was to increase the range without sacrificing overall performance; therefore, the FJ-4 was designed to carry 50 percent more fuel than the FJ-3, which required a reshaping of the fuselage. Wing area was also increased by 51 square feet, coupled with a thinner airfoil. A wider track landing gear with redesigned oleo struts had improved safety in high speed carrier landings because speeds of over 140 miles per hour had to be maintained for normal landings, despite the addition of large slotted flaps and inboard aileron action to supplement the flaps. Air brakes were also fitted under the fuselage. The fin was taller and thinner with a large dorsal.

Hydraulic Safety

The North American FJ-4 Fury featured an innovative emergency power control pump system. Hydraulic power had become an essential part of high speed aircraft as a booster for flight controls plus slots and flaps, as well as landing gear operation. The pilot could not fly the plane if hydraulic pressure dropped or was lost entirely. In order to maintain hydraulic pressure in the event of power failure a wind-driven emergency hydraulic pump could be manually extended into the airstream on the starboard or right side of the fuselage just aft of the air intake. The air turbine drove the emergency pump which pressurized the standby flight control system with the same pressure as that normally produced by the engine driven pump.

FJ-4 Fury Data

Powered by the 7,700 pounds static thrust Wright J65-W-16A turbojet the FJ-4 Fury had a top speed of 680 miles per hour at sea level and the range at the 534 miles per hour cruising speed was

020 miles. Initial rate of climb was 7,660 feet per minute, and
mbat ceiling was 46,800 feet. Weight was 13,210 pounds empty
d 23,700 pounds loaded.

Wingspan was 39 feet-1 inch with a length of 36 feet-4 inches.
eight was 13 feet-11 inches. Wing area was 339 square feet.

Armament was the Navy standard four 20 millimeter cannon.
ur underwing pylons were fitted for 3,000 pounds of bombs or
 to four AIM-9A Sidewinder missiles. Ground attack versions
uld carry five Martin ASM-N-7 Bullpup missiles plus a guid-
ce transmitter.

rumman Tracker: ASW Hunter/Killer

espite the apparent obsession with turbojet-powered aircraft there
mained a definite need for propeller-driven carrier planes. The
oviet Union's rapidly growing submarine fleet during the early
950s had a far-reaching effect upon the design and deployment of
.S. Navy antisubmarine aircraft. It was decided to replace the
unter-killer teams of Grumman Avengers, Grumman Guardians,
d Douglas Skyraiders, which were often affectionately called
urkey or Pregnant Guppy, with a single design to handle the com-
ined search, detect, and destroy roles of antisubmarine warfare
SW). The development of a wide range of sophisticated detec-

*Grumman Trackers housed 16 sonabuoys in each engine nacelle which
were ejected into the sea via a tube in the nacelle. Panels have been
removed for maintenance. Author inspects the Wright Cyclone engine.
(WAM Foto)*

*he Grumman Tracker was the U.S. Navy's first Search and Strike ASW aircraft which combined the operation of a hunter-killer team into a single
lane that could handle the combined search, detect and destroy roles. Note the MAD boom protruding from the fuselage rear. (Grumman Corpora-
ion, Courtesy Lois Lovisolo)*

tion equipment, coupled with onboard computers, plus advancements in ASW weaponry, had rendered the existing ASW hunter-killer teams obsolete and larger planes were necessary.

New ASW Requirements

The principal requirements for the new hunter/killer plane were the ability to carry all the necessary search electronics, weapons, sufficient fuel for long search missions and accommodations for electronics technicians plus pilots. Neither high speed nor high altitude performance were necessary for the hunter/killer mission. These requirements led to a large carrier-based, multireciprocating engine-powered, propeller-driven plane with a spacious fuselage.

Tracker Arrangement

Grumman design G-89 was selected and the prototype, Navy designation XS2F-1, made its initial flight on December 4, 1952. The U.S. Navy's first Search and Strike ASW aircraft emerged as a twin-radial engine-powered shoulder wing monoplane. The wing was of exceptionally high aspect ratio (long span and narrow chord) for stability, good slow speed control, optimum weight-carrying capability and long range. An enormous weapons bay in the midbody housed homing torpedoes or depth charges, while six underwing pylons were fitted for 5 inch missiles or bombs. Pilot and copilot/navigator sat side-by-side with two electronics technicians located directly behind the pilots in a spacious cockpit.

Electronic Equipment - Primary Payload

The S2F-1, which was called Tracker, was loaded with electronic equipment more than any previous aircraft had been so fitted; up to 16 sonobuoys were stowed in the aft section of each engine nacelle. Sonobuoys are cylindrical containers holding sensitive sound-sensing instruments which transmit information back to the Tracker. Once the submarine's presence has been detected the sonobuoys are ejected via a tube at the rear of the nacelle into the water in a large circular pattern with one sonobuoy in the center. When the sonobuoy hits the water it floats upright, half-submerged, and lowers a microphone that will pick up any sound, whether it be engines, propellers or even interior sounds from the submerged submarine. Each sonobuoy transmits on a different frequency so that any noise will be detected by at least three sonobuoys; the center and two on the circumference of the circular pattern, forming a segment of the disk. Any submarine movement will be detected by other sonobuoys covering another segment or "slice of the pie." The sonobuoy sensors can remain active for several hours.

The Tracker is also fitted with APS-38 search radar housed in a retractable cylindrical enclosure or radome located in the fuselage bottom just aft of the weapons bay.

A long-range sound detection system called Julie was also carried in the Tracker. This system made use of an explosive echo-ranging technique for detection and location of submarines. Julie is based upon the principle that the accurate timing of a sound of known speed and the sensing of its echo permits a calculation of the distance between the submarine that reflected the sound and the initial source of the sound. Julie was used in association with the Jezebel AQA-3 passive long-range acoustic search equipment.

An ASQ-10 Magnetic Anomaly Detector, MAD, was installed in a retractable boom in the fuselage rear just above the carrier arresting hook.

Despite this impressive array of electronic equipment the S2F-1 was fitted with a 70 million candle-power searchlight under the right wing to depend upon normal vision, or Mark-8 Eyeball as it was often called, to help find the hidden enemy!

Tracker Data

The S2F military designation was soon simplified to S-2. The S-2 Tracker was powered by two 1,525 horsepower, 9-cylinder Wright R-1820-82WA Cyclone air-cooled, radial engines which propelled the Tracker to a maximum speed of 265 miles per hour at 1,500 feet, at which speed the range was 1,150 miles. Service ceiling was 22,000 feet and initial rate of climb was 1,800 feet per minute. This sedate performance befits the Tracker's function.

Tracker wingspan was 72 feet-7 inches, while overall length was 43 feet-6 inches. Height was 16 feet-7 inches. Wing area was 499 square feet. Empty weight was 19,033 pounds and gross weight was 26,867 pounds. The maximum weapons load was 4,810 pounds.

"Willie Fudd" Tracer: Advanced Early Warning

By 1954 the U.S. Navy had announced its need for a carrier-based airborne electronic surveillance aircraft with a primary mission for Advanced Early Warning (AEW) to detect targets beyond the line of sight or radar of surface ships. The secondary mission was to be ASW. Grumman modified the Tracker design to meet the Advanced Early Warning requirements and the resulting WF-2 Tracer made its first flight on March 1, 1957. The obvious external changes were a huge, bulbous radome located three feet above the fuselage and the increase of from one to three vertical fins. Only the two outer fins were fitted with rudders, while the center fin assisted in supporting the radome. The radome was cleverly designed with an airfoil shape so it would help lift the weight of the large rotating APS-82 radar and its radome.

This interesting photo of a Grumman Tracer being catapulted off USS Oriskany (CV-34) reveals the equipment laden catwalk and gun sponsons. Note the lowered whip antennae and the white safety stripe around the aircraft elevator. (Grumman Corporation, Courtesy Lois Lovisolo)

"Willie Fudd" comes in for a landing with flaps, tailhook and landing gear in the down position. The Grumman Tracer is a flying information center that transmits Advanced Early Warning and other important information to the surface flagship, including the exact radarscope image as seen by the Tracer crew. (Grumman Corporation, Courtesy Lois Lovisolo)

The Grumman Tracer radome airfoil shape is readily evident in this photo of the plane in flight. This assists in lifting the weight of the radome and the internal rotating antenna. Observe the heavy center fin that helps support the radome. (Grumman Corporation, Courtesy Lois Lovisolo)

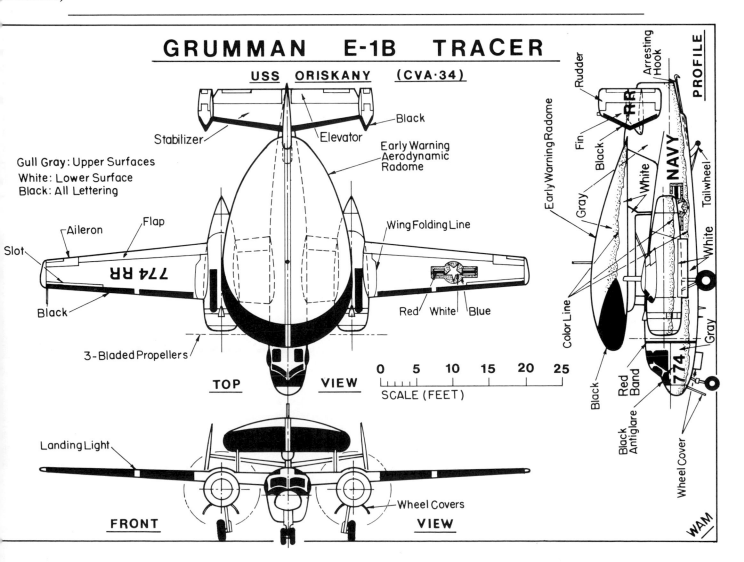

GRUMMAN E-1B TRACER
USS ORISKANY (CVA·34)

Gull Gray: Upper Surfaces
White: Lower Surface
Black: All Lettering

Stabilizer
Black
Elevator
Early Warning Aerodynamic Radome

Aileron
Flap
Slot
Wing Folding Line
Black

774 RR

Red   White   Blue

3-Bladed Propellers

TOP   VIEW

0   5   10   15   20   25
SCALE (FEET)

Landing Light

Wheel Covers

FRONT   VIEW

PROFILE

Rudder
Fin
Arresting Hook
Black
RR
White
Early Warning Radome
Gray
NAVY
Tailwheel
Color Line
White
774
Black
Gray
Red Band
Black Antiglare
Wheel Cover

WAM

This Grumman Tracer on a carrier deck edge elevator illustrates the 90 degree twist and fold back method of wing folding necessitated by the large radome which prohibits overhead wing folding. (Grumman Corporation, Courtesy Lois Lovisolo)

Grumman Tracker and Trader wing folding is directly overhead with offset hinging in order that each wing folds flat over the fuselage. The hydraulic folding system is under the pilot's control. A Trader is shown here after a carrier landing. (Grumman Corporation, Courtesy Lois Lovisolo)

Tracer: Mobile Information Center

The Grumman WF-2 Tracer was affectionately called "Willie Fudd" because of the WF designation and the nickname continued even after the designation was changed to E-1. The craft was a veritable mobile information center with two Combat Intelligence Center-trained Navair observation controllers seated behind the pilots. One of the pilots serves as the tactical director and both pilots are also trained observation controllers. The actual image seen on Willie Fudd's radarscope can be transmitted to the surface flagship; thereby, increasing the surface vessel's visible horizon well beyond its own radar antennas.

Crew Comfort for Long Flights

Unlike the S-2 Tracker, the E-1 Tracer is unarmed and, for reasons of seeing further over the horizon, it flies much higher with the crew on oxygen most of the time. Missions are to last six hours and longer; therefore, the team is self-sufficient with warm food, plus toilet and sanitation comfort. Tracers also participate in rescue missions; however, once the object of the search is found, as with the enemy target, Tracers cannot make the rescue or attack the enemy. The E-1 Tracer searches and relays vital information and, until it does, nothing can be accomplished until Willie Fudd paves the way.

Grumman Trader: COD

A noncombatant version of the Tracker was also developed by Grumman for the U.S. Navy as the C-1 Trader. This transport/cargo plane had accommodations for nine passengers and was intended as a Carrier Onboard Delivery transport (COD).

Wing Folding

The folding wings on the Tracker and Trader were hinged to move upwards and over the fuselage, thereby reducing the span to about one-third of the extended span. The Tracer could not use this folding system because of the large overhead radome and resorted to the 90 degree twist and fold-back system.

Tracker, Tracer and Trader Production

Grumman built 1,281 S-2 Trackers, 88 Tracers and 87 Traders. D Havilland Canada constructed 100 Trackers for the Royal Can dian Navy. Brazil flew 13 Trackers from its aircraft carrier Min Gerais, while the Royal Netherlands Navy operated 17 Trackers

DeHavilland Vampire, Vixen and Venom

After having developed successful turbojet-engines and numero advancements in aircraft carrier design, it was inevitable that so interesting jet-fighter designs would be developed for the FAA d spite the serious British economic situation which imposed auste measures in all sectors of government spending.

The yardstick with which to measure any truly successful co bat aircraft is its suitability for development by accepting heavi armament, more powerful engines, higher speeds and new sophi ticated equipment without requiring extensive redesign of its bas airframe or fundamental components. This was true of the Hawk Siddeley (de Havilland) Sea Vixen.

Sea Vampire

Developed during the latter part of World War II, the de Havillar Vampire entered service in the Royal Air Force in 1946 with N 247 Squadron as the second British jet-fighter in front-line servic This progenitor of the Sea Vampire was of unusual configurati with a pod-like fuselage containing the cockpit and engine, a twin-booms extending from the wing to support the tail surface This arrangement was selected to shorten the distance between t jet-engine air inlet ducts and jet tailpipe to improve efficiency a achieve maximum thrust. The twin-boom arrangement also i proved rearward visibility.

Wooden Fuselage

Vampire construction was all-metal except for the fuselage/p which was of wood. The de Havilland designers were well-expe

The de Havilland Sea Vampire was a development of the RAF Vampire fighter and was the first jet powered plane to takeoff and land on an aircraft carrier. The Sea Vampire shown here is the French-built version for the Aeronavale, known as the SNCASE Aquilon, landing on HMS Bulwark. (Imperial War Museum)

enced in wood construction, having used it for such outstanding planes as the 1934 de Havilland Comet long-distance racer and the famous de Havilland Mosquito of World War II fame. The pod/fuselage/nacelle was of monocoque design with the shell consisting of two preformed halves made from balsa sandwiched between two thin plywood skins. The half-shells were shaped in a powerful press and joined along a top and bottom seam. The use of wood was apparently a wartime conservation measure.

RAF Vampire Adapted to Carriers

Early production Vampires were powered by one 2,700 pounds static thrust de Havilland Goblin turbojet-engine, while later production variants used an uprated Goblin engine of 3,100 pounds static thrust.

The Royal Navy had acquired a navalized version of the Vampire in mid-1945 which required a reinforced airframe to withstand the shock and stress of high acceleration takeoffs and arrested landings. The standard FAA Vee-type arresting hook was also installed, as were catapult fittings. The Sea Vampire became the first jet-powered plane in the world to take off and land on an aircraft carrier and was used in the air mattress experiments on *HMS Warrior*; previously described. About 2,000 Vampires and Sea Vampires were built. The design was such a fine-handling plane that it was used as a jet trainer for RAF and FAA pilots. Top speed was 526 miles per hour.

Sea Venom

Constant improvement of the Vampire design evolved into the de Havilland Venom, in 1949, of which three principal variants were produced; two-seat night-fighter, single-seat fighter/bomber, and a two-seat carrierborne all-weather strike fighter for the FAA. Principal improvements from the Vampire were a slight wing sweepback and a thinner airfoil section.

Power increased to 5,300 pounds static thrust with the installation of the new de Havilland Ghost turbojet engine which increased the speed to 575 miles per hour.

The Sea Venom retained the gentle slow-speed handling qualities and high-altitude maneuverability of the Vampire and it became the Royal Navy's first all-weather jet-fighter. It was the only all-weather jet-fighter in the world with side-by-side seating for the crew. This proved very popular because of the ease of cockpit communication which was extremely important. This seating arrangement has been used in many subsequent designs throughout the world. Power-operated folding wings were incorporated in the Sea Venom design for carrier stowage.

The Sea Venom made its first flight on September 2, 1949 and entered service with the Royal Navy in March 1954. The design introduced the Martin Baker ejector seats and power-jettisoning cockpit canopy.

Sea Venom Armament

Basic armament comprised four 20 millimeter Hispano cannon and, despite the fact that the Sea Venom was intended for the all-weather fighter role, provision was made to carry eight 60 pound underwing rockets, thereby giving the plane anti-shipping strike capabil-

With more power, slightly swept wing and a thinner airfoil the de Havilland Sea Venom became an improved Sea Vampire with an increase in top speed. It was the first side-by-side seating all-weather fighter. (Air Ministry)

ity. Alternatively, two 1,000 pound bombs could be fitted. A total of 256 Sea Venoms were constructed, many of which were flown in the Royal Australian Navy and France's Aeronavale. The Fleet Air Arm flew the Sea Venom from *HMS Eagle*, *HMS Albion* and *HMS Illustrious*.

Sea Vixen

The ultimate refinement and the largest, most powerful of the de Havilland twin-boom and pod designs was the Sea Vixen. Although the craft was first proposed in 1946 in Naval Specification N. 40/46 as an all-weather fighter, the project was delayed, revised, cancelled and reconsidered until the prototype made its first flight on September 26, 1951. Powered by two 7,500 pounds static thrust Rolls-Royce Avon RA-7 turbojet-engines the prototype achieved supersonic speed during a shallow dive in April, 1952. In fact, five months later at the popular air show at Farnborough, England, the same prototype broke up in air during a demonstration, killing the pilot, John Derry, and the test flight observer, plus several spectators. It was heavily rumored at that time that the plane had attained supersonic speed which tore the plane apart. This had been a belief held by many aeronautical experts at that time.

The second Sea Vixen prototype underwent several structural changes and made its first flight in July 1952; followed with sea trials aboard *HMS Albion* in September 1954. After a production order in January 1955 the Hawker Siddeley Sea Vixen F(AW) Mk.1 emerged two years later powered by two 11,230 pounds static thrust Rolls-Royce Avon 208 turbojet-engines, mounted side-by-side in the pod/nacelle. During this troublesome period many British aircraft manufacturers had joined forces, with the result of fewer but larger British aircraft companies. Blackburn and de Havilland were but two famous names that had disappeared in this amalgamation.

Sea Vixen Innovative Armament

The Sea Vixen armament was advanced, potent and innovative. No machine guns or cannon were installed. Instead, the primary armament was two rocket packs which retracted into the plane's belly when not in use. Each pack was loaded with (14) 2 inch rockets. In addition, a wide variety of underwing weapons could be carried such as (4) 500 pound bombs, (18) 3-inch air-to-surface missiles, (48) 2-inch rockets, (4) Firestreak infra-red homing air-to-air missiles or U.S. Bullpup air-to-surface missiles. Two 180 gallon external drop tanks could also be carried on underwing pylons just outboard of the booms; the wingtip tank location of the Sea Venom having been abandoned. Also abandoned was the rounded nose of the Sea Vampire and Sea Venom. Instead, the Sea Vixen sported a long, sharply pointed radome which housed the scanner for airborne interception radar.

Sea Vixen Trim Change Compensation

Large wing flaps were fitted to the wing trailing edge and, in order to prevent trim changes when the flaps were extended, the horizontal stabilizer was designed to operate in conjunction with the flap position. When the flaps were extended the stabilizer leading edge moved downward to compensate for any trim changes caused by the dynamic effect of the flaps.

Sea Vixen Machined Wing Covering

The swept-back wing was built on three spars; however, the wing skin was not the conventional Alclad aluminum sheets, riveted to the structure. Instead, the wing covering was machined from aluminum planks.

Pilot's Canopy

The canopy was for the pilot only and was offset to port or the left side with the radar operator/navigator inside the pod/nacelle on the right or starboard side. An overhead hatch was used to enter the navigator's compartment.

The twin-engine, two-seater Vixen became the ultimate refinement of the de Havilland twin-boom designs. The prototype disintegrated at an air show when it attained supersonic speed or, as it was called in 1952, "breaking the sound barrier." (Ministry of Defence [Navy])

Sea Vixen Data

The Sea Vixen Mk.1 had a maximum speed of 645 miles per hour at 10,000 feet. Service ceiling was 48,000 feet. Initial rate of climb was 10,000 feet per minute and the craft could climb to 40,000 feet in about seven or eight minutes. Gross weight was 35,000 pounds.

Wingspan was 51 feet-0 inches, while overall length was 55 feet-7 inches. Height was 10 feet-9 inches. Wing area was 648 square feet. The wing halves fold upwards hydraulically for stowage aboard carriers.

The Sea Vixen went into FAA service in the summer of 1959 with No. 892 Squadron and served aboard *HMS Victorious*, *HMS Ark Royal*, *HMS Hermes* and *HMS Centaur*. The Sea Vixen was the end of the line for the twin-boom designs; possibly because, despite its superb flying qualities, this configuration is not the ideal for supersonic flight. The design had reached its limit for refinement.

Hawker Sea Hawk

Maneuverable, easy to fly, long range, and reasonable speed made the Hawker Sea Hawk the favorite naval fighter of three European countries during the mid-1950's. It was during the last weeks of 1944 that Hawker Aircraft completed the design of a turbojet-powered single-seat, interceptor fighter. This company project became known as the P.1040 and, when presented to the RAF, it was rejected, despite its superlative performance, because the RAF was already heavily committed to the Vampire and another jet-fighter. In December 1945 the Royal Navy invited bids for the design of a carrierborne interceptor fighter and the P.1040 was selected with an order for three prototypes.

Sea Hawk Bifurcated Trunk

Although the Hawker P.1040 Sea Hawk was powered by a single-engine, two-inlet ducts were provided in the wing leading edge and the exhaust tailpipe was also divided into twin-ducts, discharging out near the wing trailing edge on each side of the fuselage. This was done to shorten the tailpipe and improve efficiency, as had

Hawker Sea Hawks with folded wings line the deck of HMS Ark Royal during a 1958 Fly Past. The single engine plane was fitted with two engine air inlets and two exhaust tailpipes (arrows). Sea Hawks were flown by the Navies of four countries. Three Sea Vampires can be seen along the deck edge at the right. (Imperial War Museum)

been done in the Sea Vampire, Venom and Vixen. This arrangement reaped the additional benefit by leaving the fuselage aft of the wing free of the engine tailpipe and available for the installation of large fuel tanks. This novel arrangement of engine ducting was called the bifurcated trunk system.

Sea Hawk Test Flight and Production

The beautifully shaped, elegant P.1040 was given the name Sea Hawk. After the first prototype flight on September 2, 1947 a contract for 150 planes was awarded in November 1949. After completing 35 Sea Hawks, Hawker transferred further production and development to the Armstrong Whitworth Company in order to be able to concentrate on their next jet fighter. The production Sea Hawk F.1 first flew in November 1951 but did not enter service until March 1953 when 806 Squadron was so equipped. The squadron took their Sea Hawks aboard *HMS Eagle* one year later.

Sea Hawk Variants

Power-assisted aileron controls were the major modification to the Sea Hawk F.2; however, the next variant underwent a change from its original tactical role. As previously seen, it appears that the fate of many fast-climbing single-seat interceptor fighters is to be laden with underwing attachments for carrying a wide assortment of destructive hardware, which thrusts them into the fighter/ground attack role. This is what happened to the Sea Hawk F.B.3. The wing had been strengthened and fitted with attachments for two drop fuel tanks, two 500 pound bombs, 3 inch or 5 inch rockets, mines, napalm, or sonobuoys. The design was modified further with additional underwing attachments for (20) 3 inch, 60 pound rockets and two more 500 pound bombs, in addition to the standard (4) 20 millimeter cannon. This became the FGA.4.

More Power

The original 5,000 pounds static thrust Rolls-Royce Nene Mk.101 engine was replaced by the up-rated Nene Mk.103 turbojet of 5,400 pounds static thrust on F.B.3 and FGA.4 Sea Hawks. The re-engined planes were then designated F.B.5 and FGA.6. About 100 early Sea Hawks were re-engined and 86 new FGA.6 aircraft were constructed.

FGA.6 Sea Hawk Performance

Top speed of the Hawker Sea Hawk FGA.6 was about 630 miles per hour at sea level and it could reach up to 84 percent of the speed of sound at 36,000 feet. Combat range was 575 miles which could be extended to 1,400 miles with the use of drop tanks. The initial rate of climb was 8,000 feet per minute while service ceiling was 44,500 feet.

Wingspan was 39 feet-0 inches with an overall length 39 feet-10 inches. Height was only 8 feet-9 inches. Wing area was 278 square feet. The Sea Hawk weighed 9,560 pounds empty but the gross takeoff weight was 16,200 pounds.

Sea Hawk Structure

In the summer of 1954 a Sea Hawk FB.3 flew from London to Amsterdam in 24 minutes, averaging 571 miles per hour. Construction was all-metal with a stressed heavy-gauge wing skin. The fuselage was semi-monocoque to just aft of the engine with an internal steel structure. The remainder was full-monocoque with the skin or shell absorbing all stresses. The wing stub,as far out as the main landing gear,was built integral with the fuselage for greater strength. The cockpit was fully pressurized and fitted with a Martin-Baker ejection seat.

First Blow-In Doors

As far as is known, the Sea Hawk was the first jet-powered plane to be fitted with spring-loaded air-augmenting trap doors; now known as "blow-in" doors. The doors are located on the fuselage skin and open automatically to admit air to the jet intake in the event that the turbojet is starving for air.

Wing Folding

The wing outer sections are folded upwards hydraulically, thereby reducing the stowage span to 13 feet-4 inches.

Foreign Demand

Over 550 Sea Hawks were built for the FAA. The Netherlands, Australia and the German Kriegsmarine purchased the Sea Hawk because it met their specific requirements. Germany contracted for 68 Sea Hawks on February 20, 1957 when the craft was no longer a new design; however, the Kriegsmarine demanded a plane which could successfully combine ground attack duties with long-range reconnaissance flights plus an easy-to-fly aircraft with excellent maneuverability. The Sea Hawk was the plane that met these requirements!

Supermarine Scimitar

After the pioneering work with the Attacker, Supermarine emerged with a state-of-the-art turbojet fighter that incorporated numerous innovative features which have been used on most subsequent military turbojet aircraft. The Supermarine Scimitar was the Fleet Air Arm's first swept-wing fighter having made its first flight on August 31, 1951; however, it did not enter service until almost six years later. After the initial flight of Supermarine Type 508 the Admiralty ordered three prototypes; VX133, VX136, and VX138, the first of which flew on April 27, 1954. Then, a new Naval Specification N.113D was prepared which required some redesigning and three more prototypes; the first of which flew on January 19, 1956.

Scimitar Innovative Structure

Construction was all-metal with extensive use made of milled, high-strength aluminum alloy components. Almost 300 pounds of titanium was also used in the Scimitar structure. The wing was a three-spar structure using high-tensile steel and a preformed wing-skin milled from a slab.

Standby Hydraulic System

Another feature was the first time that two separate hydraulic control systems had been fitted to an airplane with two pumps to each system. This was an important advancement at a time when all high-speed aircraft required power-actuated flight controls, including the slots and flaps. There was no manual reversion, except for the rud-

The Supermarine Scimitar incorporated many innovative features such as high tensile steel, titanium, milled aluminum alloys, blown flaps, standby hydraulic system, sawtooth leading edge and coke bottle fuselage which have been used on many subsequent military turbojet aircraft. (Ministry of Defence [Navy])

der; therefore, flight instructions were to return to base in the even of failure of one entire system.

Scimitar Blown Flaps

Among the many innovative features in the Scimitar design we blown flaps often called super-circulation. With blown flaps high pressure air is ducted from the turbojet-engine compressor to th upper surface of the wing flaps; the effect being to delay turbulenc over the wing at high angles of attack and/or low speed during take offs and landing. Blown flaps energize the wing boundary laye and prevent flow breakaway, which could cause a fatal stall. Land ing speeds can be reduced as much as 10 percent, using only abou 5 percent of the engine air flow.

In order to assist the blown flaps effort to maintain the bound ary layer at slow speeds and high angles of attack, the leading edg slats and stabilizer were made to coordinate their position in co junction with the trailing edge flaps. As the main trailing edge flap were lowered and extended, the leading edge slats moved dow and forward during the first 10 degrees of main flap deflection an simultaneously, the tailplane automatically adjusted to a four-de gree positive angle to prevent aircraft trim changes due to the win camber increase made by the slats and flaps.

"Sawtooth" Leading Edge

In order to reduce or eliminate the pitch-up tendency at high spee and high altitudes with a heavy load, the outer 20 percent of th wing leading edge was extended forward so it jutted ahead of th main wing. A small wing fence was installed at the point where th outer panel jutted forward, which point is often called the Sawtoot

"Coke Bottle" Fuselage

Another term of interest was the Scimitar Coke bottle fuselage shap In September 1952 the result of three years of intensive research b Richard T. Whitcomb of N.A.C.A. on the subject of wing-to-fus lage interface resistance was announced by the National Adviso Committee for Aeronautics in Washington, D.C. The result was th formulation of the Area Rule principle as it relates to aircraft. Th consisted of gently contouring the fuselage inward in way of th wing attachment area. Mr. Whitcomb's study revealed that the total cross-section area of the fuselage and airfoil at this point should not exceed that of a normal well-streamlined fuselage. The Area Rule fuselage was soon known as the Coke bottle because it somewhat resembled the well-known Coke bottle shape with a pinched midbody. Tests had proven that by applying the Area Rule to fuselages drag was reduced by as much as 25 percent.

It is not certain whether Supermarine designers used Mr. Whitcomb's formulation, or if they developed the pinched fuselage independently.

Scimitar Data

The Supermarine Scimitar F.1 was powered by two 11,250 pounds static thrust Rolls-Royce Avon 202 turbojet-engines mounted side-by-side in the fuselage. Twin-cheek air intakes were installed, one on each side of the fuselage, while the engine tailpipes protruded just aft of the wing trailing edge. Maximum speed was 710 miles per hour at 10,000 feet. The range was well over 1,300 miles which was proven when a Scimitar had flown the 1,298 miles from London to Malta nonstop, averaging 588 miles per hour. Surely, had the plane flown at its slower, more economical cruising speed the range would have been greater. In addition to the nine internal fuel tanks, up to four 100 to 250 gallon drop tanks could be mounted on the wing pylons for extreme range missions. The Scimitar was fitted with refueling equipment so that, not only could it receive fuel replenishment but could act as a buddy tanker and refuel other Scimitars with a refueling pack and retractable drogue mounted on the starboard inner pylon.

The 40,000 pound interceptor/strike fighter had a wingspan of 37 feet-2 inches and a length of 55 feet-4 inches. Height was 15 feet-3 inches. Although 100 were ordered, only 76 were built.

Basic armament was four 30 millimeter Aden rapid-fire cannon mounted on the lower half of the jet-engine air intakes. The Scimitar was the first FAA aircraft capable of carrying a nuclear bomb, which had become lighter and smaller since its inception. Four 500 or 1,000 pound bombs, or (24) 3 inch rockets are typical strike hardware. For interception activities 96 unguided air-to-air rockets, or four Sidewinder infra-red homing missiles could be carried under the wing. An interchangeable nose fairing was available with oblique cameras for reconnaissance missions.

The sliding canopy was jettisonable in an emergency and the cockpit was fitted with a Martin-Baker ejector seat. The cockpit was pressurized and air-conditioned for maximum comfort on long missions. The Scimitar F Mk 1 entered FAA service in June 1958.

The Supermarine Scimitar proved a potent medium and high altitude interceptor, as well as a spectacular low-level strike aircraft, skimming the waves with an assortment of conventional or nuclear weapons at speeds approaching Mach One; the speed of sound.

Douglas Skywarrior

The U.S. Navy's turbojet-powered atomic bomb-carrying strategic bomber, which had governed the size and many other features of the *USS Forrestal*, joined the Fleet on March 31, 1956, just five months after the first supercarrier had been commissioned.

McDonnell Douglas Skywarrior, the U.S. Navy's atomic bomb carrying jet powered bomber, governed the size of USS Forrestal on which it is shown landing. (McDonnell Douglas, Courtesy Harry Gann)

DOUGLAS A-3A SKYWARRIOR
USS FORRESTAL (CVA-59)

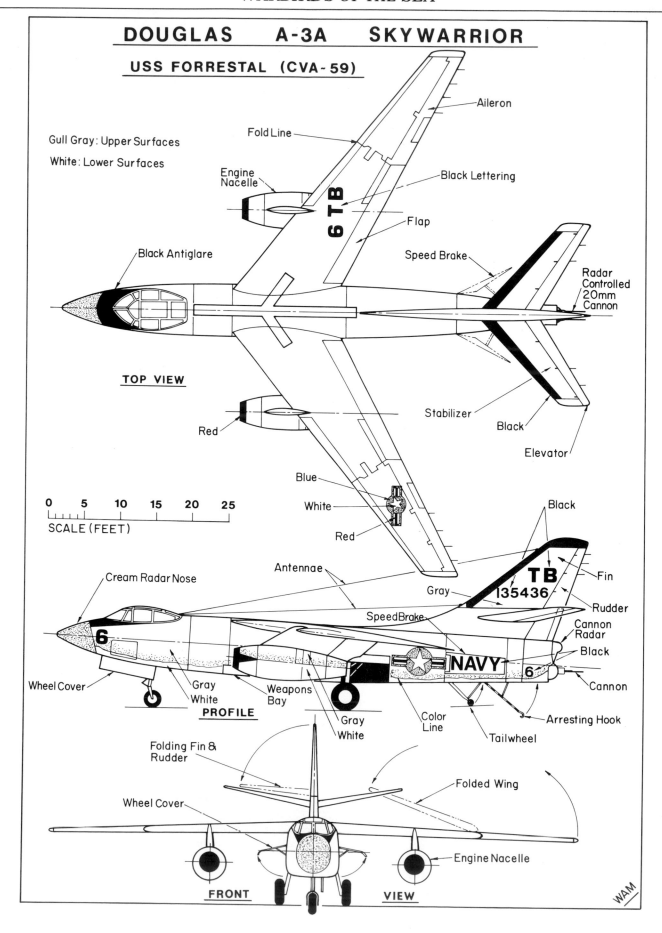

Gull Gray: Upper Surfaces

White: Lower Surfaces

Aileron

Fold Line

Engine Nacelle

Black Lettering

6 TB

Flap

Black Antiglare

Speed Brake

Radar Controlled 20mm Cannon

TOP VIEW

Stabilizer

Black

Red

Elevator

0 5 10 15 20 25

SCALE (FEET)

Blue

White

Red

Black

Antennae

TB 135436

Gray

Fin

Cream Radar Nose

Speed Brake

Rudder

Cannon Radar

6

Black

Wheel Cover

Gray White

Weapons Bay

NAVY

6

Cannon

PROFILE

Gray White

Color Line

Arresting Hook

Tailwheel

Folding Fin & Rudder

Folded Wing

Wheel Cover

Engine Nacelle

FRONT   **VIEW**

WAM

In 1947, the Douglas design, prepared by Ed Heinemann and s El Segundo design team, was up against fierce competition from her aircraft manufacturers. Curtiss, Martin, Republic, Consoli- ated and Fairchild all submitted proposals; however, Douglas El egundo was awarded the contract.

esigned Around the Bomb Bay

he Douglas A3D Skywarrior was designed around a box measur- g 5 x 5 x 15 feet, as specified by the U.S. Navy Bureau of Aero- autics. This governed the size of the bomb bay, which was located the center of gravity. The 36 degree swept-back wing was shoul- er-mounted in order to not interfere with the specified bomb bay. he Douglas designers had proposed a gross weight of 78,000 ounds compared to the Navy estimate of 100,000 pounds.

A contract for two prototypes, designated XA3D-1, was warded on March 31, 1949 and the first flight was made on Octo- er 28, 1952. The prototype was powered by two 7,000 pounds atic thrust Westinghouse XJ40-WE-3 turbojet-engines; however, evelopment problems with this series of engines made Douglas vitch to the 9,700 pounds static thrust Pratt & Whitney J57-P-6 urbojet-engine. The first Douglas YA3D-1 flew with the P & W ngines on September 16, 1953 and production began on the kywarrior. The definitive production variant of this attack bomber as the A3D-2 which included more powerful engines, redesigned omb bay to include provision to handle mines, in-flight refueling it with a 1,300 gallon fuel tank, and assorted military stores. Bomb ay could handle 12,800 pounds.

kywarrior Crew and The Bomb

he Douglas A3D-2 Skywarrior was operated by a pilot, bombar- ier, and navigator/tail gunner; all in a pressurized cockpit. The ilot and bombardier sat side-by-side, while the navigator sat back- o-back with the pilot. Ejection seats were not installed; apparently save weight. Instead, the escape chute scheme used in the kyknight was installed in the Skywarrior. The crew had access to ie bomb bay because the atomic bomb was still to be armed en oute to the target, as it was in the Hiroshima and Nagasaki bomb- igs. The radar-controlled twin 20 millimeter M3 cannon with 500 ounds per gun, located in the tail barbette, could be manually op- rated by the navigator/gunner as desired or when necessary.

kywarrior Data

he A3D-2 was powered by two 12,400 pounds static thrust Pratt Whitney J57-P-10 turbojet-engines which drove the 82,000 pound raft to a maximum speed of 610 miles per hour at 10,000 feet. ervice ceiling was 41,000 feet. Normal range was 1,050 miles, hich could be extended to over 2,000 miles with a 750 gallon uxiliary tank in the bomb bay. Empty weight of the A3D-2 was 9,409 pounds.

The 73 feet-6 inches wingspan was reduced to 45 feet when ie wings were folded with the outer panels virtually flat atop the iner panels. The overall height of 22 feet-9 1/2 inches could be alved when the vertical fin and rudder were folded over the star- oard or right side stabilizer. Overall length was 76 feet-4 inches. Ving area was 812 square feet. Aspect ratio was an efficient 6.75.

The Skywarrior structure was simple, compact and strong to endure the rough handling of aircraft aboard carriers. High strength 7075 S aluminum alloy was used for the fuselage. Two deep keels extended from the nose bulkhead to the end of the bomb bay (some- times called the weapons bay) and supported the nose wheel, cock- pit floor and formed the weapons bay doors hinge beams. Heavy fuselage skin is used between the keels to reinforce the fuselage bottom to provide strength for the catapult fittings. Other keels con- tinue to the tail to support the tail bumper and the huge arresting hook.

The wing structure consists of two main spars covered with a single layer of 7075 S alloy skin of constant thickness from the fuselage to the folding joint. Much of the nose is a fiberglass enclo- sure for the bombing radar antenna. All flying controls and wing and tail folding are hydraulically operated with manual control in the event of loss of hydraulic pressure.

New Squadrons

Twelve newly designated Heavy Attack Squadrons had been formed for the Douglas Skywarrior: VAH-1,2,5,7,9 and 11 were organized in November 1955, while VAH-3,4,6,8,10 and 13 were formed in July 1956. Some AJ Savages shared VAH squadrons with Skywarriors until 1959 when the last of the reciprocating piston engine-powered planes were phased out of the attack/strike role. In view of its large size Skywarrior squadrons aboard the *Forrestal* and *Midway* class carriers comprised only three Skywarriors.

U.S. Air Force Procures Skywarriors

It is amusing to note that the U.S.Air Force, which was strongly opposed to the Navy having any nuclear weapon carrying aircraft, actually procured 294 modified versions of the Skywarrior as the B-66 Destroyer.

Overtaken By Technology

Advances in aircraft and nuclear weapon design were progressing at an unbelievable pace with the result that the Skywarrior was soon overtaken by technology. The Navy had decided that it needed su- personic aircraft to deliver nuclear weapons. Further, the atomic bomb had become considerably reduced in size and weight, which no longer required large planes such as the Savage or Skywarrior. Another possible factor was the growth of missile submarines in the early 1960's which had begun to assume the primary naval nuclear strike role at the expense of the carrier Warbirds.

Skywarrior Production

In addition to 213 strike/attack A3D-1 (A-3A) and A3D-2 (A-3B) Skywarriors, Douglas El Segundo produced (30) A3D-2P (RA-3B) photo-reconnaissance versions, (24) A3D-2P (EA-3B) electronic surveillance variants, and (12) A3D-2T (TA-3B) attack trainer air- craft. The designations in parenthesis are the new U.S. Navy Skywarrior designations effective in 1962. As of 1989 some Skywarriors were still in U.S. Navy service after 33 years of active fleet duty; a truly remarkable longevity. The Skywarrior was fi- nally retired in 1991.

Douglas Skyhawk

Edward H. Heinemann and his Douglas El Segundo design team reversed the apparently inexorable trend to the bigger is better philosophy in the design of combat fighters and strike aircraft by turning their collective talents to a design less than one-fifth the size of the Skywarrior. This effort in 1950 was bent upon designing a successor to the legendary propeller-driven Skyraider and it became a study in miniaturization with a return to the simple basics of aircraft design. As the Douglas concept developed, the U.S. Navy issued an invitation to bid on the design of a turbojet shipboard attack plane that would be capable of delivering nuclear bombs and perform interdiction missions as those which had been undertaken by the Skyraider. The top speed of the new plane had to be at least 575 miles per hour with the loaded weight not to exceed 30,000 pounds and the minimum range was to be not less than 600 miles.

Lighter and Faster

As with the Skywarrior, Heinemann stunned the Bureau of Aeronautics with the Douglas proposal which stated that the proposed design would exceed the specified speed by 100 miles per hour and the range by 100 miles. More astounding was the claim that the Douglas design would be half the weight of the specified maximum!

One-Piece Wing

The first full size mock-up of this radical and innovative design was inspected in February 1952, resulting in a contract for preproduction airplanes being awarded four months later. The aircraft was designated A4D-1. The normal practice of ordering experimental aircraft for testing had been bypassed and the first planes had to be constructed on production tooling. The wingspan was so short that the wing did not require folding. This enabled the designers to employ one-piece continuous spars from tip to tip, as had been done on the prewar Brewster Buffalo. In fact, the span of the nonfolding wing was shorter than the folded wings of many contemporary shipboard aircraft.

Heinemann's Hot Rod Sets Speed Record

The first preproduction A4D-1 made its initial flight on June 22 1954 and, on October 15, 1955, a preproduction model had bee flown at an average speed of 695.127 miles per hour over a 30 mile closed course to establish a new world speed record in th Federation Aeronautique International (FAI) Class C. By this tim the official name for this spectacular craft was Skyhawk; howeve the diminutive plane became known as Heinemann's Hot Rod b the workers at the El Segundo plant.

Skyhawk Structure

The Skyhawk structure consisted of three basic subassemblies, eac of which was completed with all equipment, wiring, control run and tubing before mating with the other subassemblies. The thre subassemblies were the forward fuselage, wing, and the rear fuse lage. The wing subassembly was attached to the forward fuselag by 10 steel tension bolts while the rear fuselage was attached to th forward fuselage by only six steel bolts. The fuselage had a detach able plastic nose cone which housed the integrated avionics pac of communications, navigation and identification equipment; a mounted on the forward bulkhead.

The delta-shaped wing was a three-spar box structure with high hat stringers and a continuous Dural covering. The spar box struc ture formed an integral fuel tank, thereby earning further weigh reduction. The modified delta plan-form had a 33 degree sweepbac for two-thirds of the chord with a straight trailing edge. One half the trailing edge length was devoted to split flaps while 70 percen of the leading edge length sported an enormous wing slat whic required no actuating mechanism. These were actuated aerodynam cally according to the flight attitude and other flight condition

Known as Heinemann's Hot Rod, the Douglas Skyhawk is less than one fifth the size of the Skywarrior yet has a takeoff weight of almost 25,000 pounds. This strike/fighter was half the empty weight specified by the U.S. Navy. The single-seat A-4M Skyhawk is shown here. (McDonnell Douglas, Courtesy Harry Gann)

The Douglas TA-4F Skyhawk is a two-seat training version of the Strike fighter. Of interest is the long Skyhawk landing gear, necessary for sufficient ground clearance to fit bombs, missiles and fuel tanks on the wing pylons. (McDonnell Douglas, Courtesy Harry Gann)

e rudder was single thickness dural with external stiffeners, while
e fin was constructed as part of the rear fuselage subassembly.

el Tanks

self-sealing fuel bladder was located immediately behind the
ckpit and, together with the wing tanks, the fuel capacity totalled
0 gallons. This could be supplemented by two 250 gallon auxil-
ry fuel tanks carried on underwing pylons.

nding Gear Design

o emergency or backup hydraulic system was provided; there-
re, the landing gear was cleverly arranged so that all three struts
tracted with the wheels forward. In the event of a hydraulic mal-
nction the landing gear legs could be released and would lower
d swing backwards by means of gravity and be pushed into place
 the airstream until they locked in the down position for a safe
nding.

mergency Generator

e Skyhawk also had no battery for electrical backup; however, a
tractable wind-driven generator was installed. This was located
 the forward fuselage subassembly on the starboard or right side;
imediately ahead of the wing. The generator was released manu-
ly at any speed below 450 miles per hour. A constant speed gov-
nor maintained proper speed by automatically adjusting the gen-
ator blade pitch.

ISS

s is readily apparent, the Skyhawk was well designed for light
eight and efficiency by following the KISS principle: "Keep It
mple, Stupid."

kyhawk Data

he Douglas A4D-5 strike/fighter is powered by an 8,500 pounds
atic thrust Pratt & Whitney J52-P-6A turbojet-engine which drives
e craft to a maximum speed of 675 miles per hour at sea level.
ervice ceiling is 47,900 feet and range 700 miles. The empty weight
 9,853 pounds while gross weight with pylons filled is 24,500
ounds.

rmament

rmament comprises two 20 millimeter cannon in the nose and
rovision for 8,200 pounds of externally mounted ordnance. In fact,
 first glance the Skyhawk appears a bit awkward on the ground

A Douglas A-4C Skyhawk is ready to launch on a USS America (CVA-66) catapult. Note the Douglas Skywarrior in the background (curved arrow). SPS-52 3-D Air Search Radar Antenna is just above the Skyhawk while the smaller SPS-43 Sea Search Radar Antenna is mounted on the mast (straight arrow). (Official U.S. Navy Photograph, News Photo Division)

because of the unusually long landing gear for the plane's small size. This was done to raise the wing high enough off the ground to provide clearance for the three multipurpose underwing racks for high energy bombs, air-to-air rockets, infrared air-to-air missiles, air-to-surface missiles, double-barrelled 20 millimeter cannon packs, torpedoes, or auxiliary fuel tanks.

Production

Over 2,000 Skyhawks had been delivered to the U.S. Navy by mid-1967; 500 of which were the A4D-5 which designation was changed to A4-F in 1962. This variant comprised the most important modifications which included re-engineered structure to increase the underwing load with the addition of two more pylons. A more economical fuel consumption engine was also installed.

The Skyhawk enjoyed a long service life, having served well in Viet Nam and seeing action in the Falklands War. It was a well designed, functional combat plane.

Having witnessed the astounding revolution in aircraft carrier design caused by the remarkable advances in carrier-based aircraft during the post-war decade, it is difficult to envision further technological development in carrier aircraft design that will stimulate aircraft carrier development to an even greater degree. The following chapter will cover these fascinating technical advances.

CHAPTER VII
NEW CONCEPTS:
1956-1972

Vertical Takeoff and Landing (VTOL) Breakthrough • Innovative Carrier-Based CTOL Aircraft New and Modernized U.S. Carriers • New Royal Navy Auxiliary Fleet Carriers • Helicopters and Assault Helicopter Carriers • Unusual Fixed-Wing ASW Aircraft • U.S. Carriers Busy World-Wide • New Kitty Hawk Class Supercarriers • Nuclear-Powered USS Enterprise • USS John F. Kennedy • French Postwar Carriers and Shipboard Aircraft • Soviet ASW Helicopter Carrier/Cruisers and Carrier Aircraft • Eagle Class Carriers Updated • Shipboard Aircraft Corrosion Prevention (1960s) • Hi-Tech SAM's Spawn Super Strike Planes • Warbirds of the 1960s • Cuban Missile Crisis • Vietnam War • Innovative Technology On The Way

VERTICAL TAKEOFF AND LANDING (VTOL) BREAKTHROUGH

One of the most spectacular historic flights of the previous half-century was made on September 12, 1961 when a single-engine, jet-powered aircraft took off vertically while in a normal horizontal flight attitude and, when the proper altitude was reached, it transitioned into high-speed horizontal flight. The plane then returned to its starting point, slowed to a hover, and settled vertically to the ground. Test pilots Hugh Merewether and Bill Bedford had made several flights on that day and proved that high-speed fixed-wing aircraft could take off and land vertically, as well as hover over one spot, rotate on its vertical axis, and transition into speeds exceeding 650 miles per hour! This remarkable aircraft was to prove a blessing for ground attack tacticians and would, eventually, force a radical change in aircraft carrier design and seaborne naval aviation. The Hawker Siddeley P.1127 Kestral, which was to be known as the British Aerospace Harrier GR and the McDonnell Douglas AV-8 Harrier, was not the first attempt to create a VTOL (Vertical Take Off and Landing) aircraft.

German VTO Operation
The Luftwaffe had experimented with VTO during World War II. The Bachem Natter was designed as a bomber interceptor that was launched from a vertical ramp but had to be landed in two sections via parachutes.

U.S. Navy VTOL Experiments
After World War II the U.S. Navy had embarked on a program to develop VTOL fighter aircraft. Contracts were awarded to Convair at the end of March,1951 and to Lockheed in mid-April, 1951. The Navy's objective was to operate strike/fighter planes from nonmilitary cargo ships in order to protect convoys from air or submarine attack, and to enable destroyer and light cruiser types to embark a fighter plane for protection from enemy air attack.

Lockheed and Convair Designs
Both Lockheed and Convair were to use the same engine. Turbojet-engines had been considered; however, none in the U.S. had suffi-

PREVIOUS: A Kaman UH-2A Seasprite Utility helicopter hovers over the bow of the U.S. Navy oiler USS Chipola (AO-63) during refueling of the carrier USS Yorktown (CVS-10) on December 22, 1964. The helicopter is most useful in this activity to transfer key personnel, carry leader lines and monitor the operation. (Official U.S. Navy Photograph, Naval Imaging Command)

The U.S. Navy Lockheed XFV-1 experimental VTOL fighter was designed to takeoff and land on its tail but required this apparatus to s[et] it on its tail initially. (Lockheed Aircraft Corporation, Courtesy Alex. L[ ] Anderson)

cient power to lift the planes. Therefore, turboprop power was spe[ci]fied. Allison Division of General Motors Corporation combin[ed] two T38 turboprop-engines to produce 5,800 shaft horsepow[er] which permitted the engines to operate separately or in uniso[n.] Curtiss-Wright designed and built special gears and contra-rotati[ng] six-bladed, large diameter propellers for the two experiment[al] planes.

It was 1954 before the Convair XFY-1 and Lockheed XF[V-1] were ready for flight. The XFY-1 made a 20 minute flight on N[o]vember 2 and became the world's first VTOL fighter. The XF[V-1] did not fly until late 1955. The Navy program was terminated [in] January 1956; however, the U.S. Air Force had become interest[ed] in VTOL aircraft as the result of the Navy's experiments and ins[ti]tuted its own research.

with the Lockheed XFV-1, this Convair XFY-1 VTOL experimental ghter was designed to rest on the ground on its tail. Both planes were dison turboprop powered. (Convair Corp.)

The U.S. Air Force turbojet powered Ryan X-13 Vertijet experimental VTOL aircraft also operated from a nose-high position and required an apparatus to raise the plane to its vertical position. (Ryan Aeronautical Co., Courtesy James J. Mulvey)

.S. Air Force VTOL Experiments
yan Aeronautical Company had been conducting VTOL research r the U.S. Navy since 1947 and, in August 1953, with the coop- ation of the Navy, the U.S. Air Force awarded Ryan a contract to esign and construct two turbojet-powered VTOL research planes esignated X-13 Vertijet. The first transitional flight was made on ovember 28, 1956 when the Ryan turbojet demonstrated transi- on from level flight to hovering and then back to level flight for a onventional landing.

TOL Tail Landing Disadvantage/Multi-Engine Remedies
he XFY-1, XFV-1 and X-13 had been designed to rest on their ils in a vertical position, nose pointing upward, and required a round service trailer to elevate the plane to this position from the ormal horizontal attitude. The planes took off vertically; then ansitioned to horizontal flight. Landing required a transition back vertical position in order to land on their tails in the vertical nose- p position. The pilot's seat was gimbal-mounted to remain upright uring vertical/horizontal transition.

ell Aircraft Multi-Engine Horizontal VTOL
ell Aircraft Corporation had flown an experimental turbojet-pow- red VTOL aircraft on November 16, 1954, which remained in a

horizontal position during all aspects of flight. The wingtip-mounted jet engines rotated 90 degrees from vertical to horizontal in order that the plane could remain in a horizontal position throughout the flight. A refined version of this scheme was unveiled by Bell in 1960 as the D188A fighter/bomber, developed under joint contract with the U.S. Navy and U.S. Air Force. The D188A was powered by eight turbojet-engines; two pivoting engines at each wingtip, two in the tail for forward thrust and two vertically-mounted in the fuselage for lift. The German aircraft firm Entwicklungsring-Sud constructed a similar aircraft which was destroyed in a crash on September 14, 1964.

First British VTOL: Multi-Engine Horizontal Short S.C.1
Meanwhile, on October 25, 1958, the first British fixed-wing VTOL aircraft made its initial vertical ascent and transition. The Short S.C.1 remained in horizontal position throughout the flight without using pivoting engines. This VTOL was powered by five Rolls-Royce turbojet-engines; two vertically-mounted for lift and three horizon- tally-mounted for forward flight. Stability and control during tran- sition from vertical lift to level horizontal flight and return was governed by an onboard computer acting as an autostabilizer.

The Bell D188A experimental VTOL fighter/bomber was powered by eight turbojet engines and remained in a horizontal position throughout the flight. Wingtip engines were to rotate 90 degrees to lift and then transform the plane into horizontal flight. Two jet engines in the tail provided forward thrust while two more in the fuselage provided lift. (Bell Aerosystems)

The Wibault Concept

Although the foregoing experiments contributed considerably to VTOL science, none was suitable for practical use because of tail takeoff and landing positions or multiple jet-engine installations; however, someone had the answer.

During the mid-1950s, the eminent French aircraft designer, Michel Wibault, had developed a VTOL design using only one horizontally installed turbojet-engine. This engine was to power four centrifugal compressors, which were to force cold air out of four rotatable nozzles for both horizontal and vertical thrust. This concept of vectored thrust appeared to be the remedy for all previous VTOL ailments. Wibault called his concept Le Gyroptere.

The Wibault concept came to the attention of U.S. Air Force Colonel John Driscoll, Chairman of the MWDP (Mutual Weapons Development Program), which was a U.S.-sponsored organization established to examine and encourage European military projects which would have become extinct without adequate funding. Driscoll ordered the MWDP to evaluate Wibault's theory in March

This Short S.C.1 was the first British VTOL. The five Rolls-Royce turbojet engines enabled this craft to rise vertically in a horizontal position and transition to horizontal flight without rotating engines. Two engines were dedicated for lift while the remaining three were for forward flight. (Air Ministry)

1956, which resulted in a favorable report. This prompted the Colonel to meet with Wibault and Dr. Stanley Hooker, Technical Director of Bristol Aero-Engines, at the MWDP offices in Paris.

Bristol Pegasus Vectored Thrust Turbofan Is Born

Several meetings were held during July 1956 which resulted in a new engine design for the MWDP in January 1957. This engine design, B.D.52, was the light and powerful Bristol Orpheus turbofan which simplified Wibault's basic concept. The new engine eliminated the centrifugal air compressors and the associated shafting gears and clutches. A dedicated axial flow compressor/fan directed its flow from the first three stages through two rotatable nozzles, one on each side. The turbine-jet exhaust was directed to two more rotatable nozzles, one on each side. The nozzles could be vectored to exhaust downward, slightly forward, and aft. Vertical lift plus forward or rearward thrust could be experienced in any desired proportion by properly vectoring the nozzles. Some major improvements were the addition of a low pressure gas turbine at the aft end of the Orpheus to drive the nozzle compressor. The connecting shaft was run through the tubular main compressor/turbine shaft and the shafts were designed to contra-rotate in order to reduce the effect of gyroscopic action; especially during the hovering mode. The dedicated lift compressor was changed to a bypass design so that a portion of its airflow would supercharge the main compressor. The new engine project was designated B.E.53 and became known as Bristol Pegasus turbofan.

With the propulsion and lift problems solved it appeared that the stage was set for work to begin on the development of a practicable VTOL design; however, Dr. Hooker's parent company, British Aeroplane, was not the least bit interested in the project.

Duncan Sandys' White Paper

At this crucial moment the United Kingdom Minister of Defence, Duncan Sandys, had published his infamous White Paper, which stated, albeit erroneously, that missiles could perform the tasks of

r. John Fozard was the Hawker Senior Project Designer assigned to e Kestral V/STOL design which was ready in a few months. This was bsequently refined into the unique Harrier V/STOL strike/fighter hich proved itself in combat. (U.S. Naval Institute)

anned fighter planes and; therefore, the fighter plane was no longer ecessary and would not be procured for the British armed forces! e went so far as to direct the RAF to not even consider fighter roposals.

ir Sidney Camm and the P.1127 Kestral

ortunately, Sir Sydney Camm, Technical Director of Hawker Air- raft and designer of the World War II Hurricane fighter and many ther famous aircraft, took an interest in the orphaned VTOL con- ept and decided to take on the design as a private venture. He ssigned his Senior Project Designer Dr. John Fozard with Ralph ooper to the project and urged them to keep the design simple and let the pilots do the flying. A workable design was ready in a few onths, designated Hawker P.1127. The Hawker program increased scope when, in 1959, the MWDP agreed to pay 75 percent of the evelopment expenses. The first turbofan engine, now named Pe- asus I, was run at Bristol in September 1959 and Sir Sydney then ecided to construct two prototype aircraft.

American enthusiasm for the project had grown so that, by 960, NACA (National Advisory Committee for Aeronautics) had onducted wind tunnel tests at Langley Field, Virginia with a one- ixth scale model of the Hawker design, which verified the aircraft's apability to conduct VTOL operations. This American interest in ie P.1127 finally stirred the British Ministry of Supply into action reimburse Hawker Aircraft for the two prototypes, although the MWDP was still funding the engine development.

Amalgamations in the British aircraft industry, previously nentioned, formed Hawker Siddeley Aviation with Hawker Air- raft known as its Hawker Blackburn Division.

Kestral Tripartite Evaluation Squadron Proposed

In January 1962 the U.S. Kennedy Administration persuaded the U.S., British, and German governments to fund a Tripartite Evalu- ation Squadron (TES) of nine P.1127 aircraft, now known as the Kestral. The name was well-selected because the Kestral is a Euro- pean hunting hawk noted for its ability to hover. The squadron was to be composed of pilots and ground personnel from the RAF, Ger- man Luftwaffe, U.S. Air Force, U.S. Navy, and U.S. Army. For some unknown reason, the U.S. Marines, who had been the most enthusiastic proponent of the P.1127, were not represented in the TES.

Engine and Airframe Improvements

Although successful, the original P.1127 Kestral had insufficient thrust to lift the necessary weapons load. Close cooperation be- tween Hawker and Bristol Aero-Engines (which had now become Bristol Siddeley Engines, Ltd.) resulted in constant refinement and redesign of the Pegasus turbojet to increase thrust. Pegasus 3 made its appearance in March 1962, rated at over 13,000 pounds of static thrust and, two years later, the 15,200 pounds static thrust Pegasus 5 was installed in the last of six Kestral prototypes.

Meanwhile, by mid-1963, a number of design changes and re- finements in the airframe had become evident; the horizontal tail was given pronounced anhedral, two ventral fins had been added; the vertical fin area was increased; full sweepback wing; and stream- line raked wingtips had been fitted. Minor modifications had also been made to the tail parachute installation, mainwheel door, outrigger wheels and rear-lift thrust nozzle.

Kestral Carrier Deck Trials

Test pilots Bedford and Merewether had conducted Kestral deck landing and takeoff trials aboard *HMS Ark Royal* in early 1962 at sea and in the English Channel. The trials were conclusively suc- cessful and the importance of the demonstration induced the Admi- ralty to authorize the preliminary design for a transonic/supersonic Kestral designated Hawker Siddeley P.1154. This vectored thrust aircraft was designed to use a new plenum chamber burning con- cept and several other novel design features. Dr. John Fozard had been designated Chief Designer for this project.

By this time the Kestral had been classified as a V/STOL (Ver- tical/Short Take Off and Landing) design because, unlike the very early experiments, the Kestral is able to negotiate conventional take- offs and landings although the ground roll can be shortened by vec- toring the thrust nozzles.

Ryan XV-5A Is Abandoned

Meanwhile, the U.S. Army-sponsored Ryan XV-5A VTOL made its first flight on May 25, 1964. This fixed-wing aircraft obtained its vertical lifting force from fans imbedded in the wing. The fans were driven by two General Electric turbojets located in the fuse- lage. Smaller fans were located, horizontally, in the nose for longi- tudinal control during the hovering mode. As with previous Ameri- can experiments, this project was abandoned.

British Abandon V/STOL Naval Fighter

During 1964 the British Government made a momentous decision based upon economic restraints and its predilection for highly supersonic aircraft. It decided to equip Fleet Air Arm squadrons with the American Phantom II instead of proceeding with the P.1154 V/STOL naval fighter. The P.1154 was cancelled in its entirety in the following year and Dr. Fozard was then made Chief Designer of the entire V/STOL project. Apparently Duncan Sandys had changed his mind regarding fighter aircraft.

U.S. Marines Save the Kestral

The last of the six prototype Kestrals flew in February 1964 and became representative of the Tripartite design. Three weeks later, on March 7, the first TES Kestral was flown by Bill Bedford as the eight additional aircraft were under construction for the multinational evaluation. All TES craft were marked with a distinctive and most unusual insignia on both wingtips; a disk that combined the British cockade, German cross, and American star and bar insignia.

The Tripartite Evaluation Squadron made 940 flights, totalling over 600 flying hours, from April to November 1965 and the pilots were very enthusiastic over the Kestral. As with the Admiralty, the U.S. Navy and U.S. Air Force showed no interest in a fighter that did not operate at supersonic speeds. The Germans gave their TES planes to the Americans.

Although no U.S. Marine flew in the TES, the U.S. Marine Corps followed the evaluation closely and it was the U.S. Marine Corps that proved most enthusiastic when it realized the Kestral's potential as a strike/fighter. In close support action the Kestral would be able to mount continuous attacks against the enemy by virtue of its ability to land close to the front lines to refuel and rearm. The U.S. Marines had rescued the Kestral!

Kestral Becomes Harrier

In 1967 the British Ministry of Technology (formerly Ministry of Supply) announced that the P.1127 will be called Harrier, instead of Kestral.

U.S. Firms Join the Harrier Project

One year later the Pegasus 6 was born with a rating of 19,000 pounds static thrust and by January 1969 the U.S. Marine Corps had obtained funding for 14 Harriers. Total procurement of Pegasus 6-powered Harriers was to be 114; however, a substantial number had to be constructed in the United States. McDonnell Douglas was interested and signed a 15-year license agreement with Hawker Siddeley, while Pratt & Whitney made a similar arrangement with Rolls-Royce Ltd., which had absorbed Bristol Siddeley Engines Ltd. During October 1969 the U.S. and British governments announced the welcome news that they had signed a memorandum of understanding to jointly undertake further Harrier development.

Home of the Harrier

The RAF had founded No. 1 (F) Squadron at Wittering, England, in 1969 as the vanguard of its first Harrier GR (ground/reconnaissance) Group. The author experienced the pleasure of living in Stamford, only a few miles from RAF Wittering, in 1982-1983. I very often bicycled over to the field and never tired of watching these amazing aircraft go through their paces. Wittering was called "The Home of the Harrier."

The Hawker Siddeley P.1127 Kestral was the prototype V/STOL (Vertical/Short Take Off and Landing) design which became the unique world famous Harrier strike/fighter. The P.1127 shown here is one of the Tripartite evaluation aircraft. Note the combined U.S., German and British insignia. (British Aerospace, Courtesy Brendan Morrissey)

U.S. Marines Fly the Harrier

Hawker Siddeley (soon to become part of British Aerospace, Lt had constructed 110 U.S. Marine AV-8A Harriers, based on the R. GR.3 Harrier, but modified to U.S. Marine Corps specificatio: One of the principal changes was the ability to fire AIM Sidewinder air-to-air missiles. The first Harrier was accepted the U.S. Marine Corps on January 6, 1971, and the Marines op ated the AV-8A regularly from *Tarawa* class LHA's. The Marir had also flown from *USS Guam* (LPH-9) in 1972 which was se ing as the interim Sea Control Ship at that time. The SCS aircr carrier will be met in Chapter VIII.

The Kestral/Harrier design underwent continuous developm by British Aerospace and McDonnell Douglas until it was refin into the superb carrierborne V/STOL strike/fighter that proved self in battle. This story will be continued in the following chapt

INNOVATIVE CARRIER-BASED CTOL AIRCRAFT

Just when it appeared that nothing new could be conceived Conventional Take Off Landing (CTOL) carrier-based aircraft, n and revolutionary ideas were developed in bomb bay design, fu lage shape, in-flight adjustable wing incidence, radical conce; for flight control surfaces, and tailless fighters to meet the ch lenge of ever increasing power and speeds. A description of t outstanding aircraft that successfully applied these new conce follows.

North American Vigilante

As was mentioned in the Skywarrior narrative in Chapter VI t U.S. Navy had decided it wanted a supersonic attack/bomber deliver the atomic bomb. The requirements were announced in 19 for a supersonic aircraft of all-weather capability and better perf mance than any previous Navy attack/bomber. The North Ame can Aviation proposal was accepted and two prototypes were dered in August 1956; the first of which made its initial flight tv

The sleek North American Vigilante atomic bomb-carrying attack/bomber attained the amazing service speed of 1,385 miles per hour at 40,000 feet in 1962. Note the bomb bay extension beneath the fuselage which was part of the innovative bomb ejection system (arrow). (North American Rockwell, Courtesy J.M. Syverson)

years later. Here was another innovative carrier plane at the other end of the size scale from the Skyhawk.

Mach 2.1

Designated A3J-1, which became A-5 in 1962, the North American Vigilante attained the amazing speed of 1,385 miles per hour at 40,000 feet or Mach 2.1, a truly supersonic aircraft.

Unique Control System

No ailerons were installed; blown flaps were used for low speed control while a combination of wing spoilers and differential all-moving horizontal tail provided lateral control at high speeds. There was no separate elevator and stabilizer. Instead, the entire surface not only pivoted on its transverse axis with the two surfaces pivoting in unison to control pitching for climbing and diving, but the two horizontal tail surfaces could also be made to pivot in opposite directions to cause the plane to roll along its longitudinal axis. Aileron flutter had been experienced by many high speed planes and

Another advanced feature of the Vigilante was the variable geometry engine intake which comprised an adjustable louver-like arrangement that restricted the air amount entering the inlet duct based upon the speed and altitude of the plane. Note the shutters in the upper portion of the huge engine air inlet (arrow). (WAM Foto)

this novel approach might have been North American's way of avoiding that problem, considering the Vigilante's extremely high speed.

Controlled Engine Intake

Another advanced feature of the Vigilante was a variable geometry engine intake which employed a shutter-like arrangement that could restrict the amount of air that enters the inlet duct based upon the speed and altitude of the aircraft.

Unique Bomb Bay

The Vigilante pioneered the linear bomb bay concept, which extended almost the entire length of the fuselage between the two

The Vigilante's supersonic speed inspired a unique control system in which no ailerons were fitted; blown flaps were used for low speed control while a differential all-moving horizontal tail provided lateral control at high speeds. In effect, the horizontal tail could twist to roll the aircraft. Observe the drooped leading edge as this Vigilante enters a landing approach. (North American Rockwell, Courtesy J.M. Syverson)

engines. Because of the very high speed this was developed to eject the bomb rearward, clear of the aircraft. The atomic bomb was attached to two fuel tanks in the bomb bay and these tanks were emptied before any other during the flight to the target. When the bomb was released the two attached fuel tanks remained with the bomb, acting as aerodynamic stabilizers as the weapon fell toward the target.

Production deliveries of the A-5A began in 1960. VAH-7 became the first Vigilante squadron in June 1961 and served on the nuclear-powered carrier *USS Enterprise* in the following year.

U.S. Navy Ends Strategic Bombing Dream

The linear bomb bay was presenting difficulties with its operation but, before the problems could be solved, a major shift in U.S. Navy policy ended its interest and activities in the strategic bombing role! This surprising decision spelled the end of the Vigilante attack-bomber and all efforts were directed to the development of an unarmed reconnaissance version for which this North American design was eminently qualified. The two crew members became pilot and observer/radar operator.

Reconnaissance Variant

The RA-5C high speed electronic and visual reconnaissance variant was fitted with additional fuel tanks in a deepened fuselage which resulted in a humped back. A full-blown boundary layer wing, larger flaps, and four, instead of the former two, underwing pylons were features of the RA-5C. A wide variety of electronic equipment and a large assortment of special cameras occupied the former bomb bay. In addition to active and passive ECM (Electronic Counter Measure) equipment the visual reconnaissance equipment included vertical, split image, and oblique cameras. In addition, side-looking airborne radar was housed in a ventral fairing under the fuselage. The prototype RA-5C Vigilante first flew on June 3,

1962 and over 100 were produced, including conversions from oth[er] RA-5 variants.

Vigilante Data

The futuristic and innovative North American Aviation RA-5C Vig[i]lante weighs 61,730 pounds gross. Wingspan is 53 feet with a[n] overall length of 73 feet-2 1/2 inches. Height is 19 feet-4 3/4 inche[s] Projected wing area is 700 square feet which produced a wing loa[d]ing of 88 pounds per square foot.

The maximum speed is more than twice the speed of sou[nd] (1,385 miles per hour) made possible by outstanding aircraft d[e]sign and two 10,900 pounds static thrust General Electric J79-G[E]8 turbojet-engines with afterburners. Cruising speed is 1,254 mile[s] per hour and range is 3,000 miles. Operational ceiling is a phenom[e]nal 64,000 feet.

The four underwing pylons could carry bombs, rockets, air-t[o-]ground missiles, or auxiliary fuel tanks to extend the already gene[r]ous range. Among the carriers from which the RA-5C operated w[as] the Supercarrier *USS Ranger* (CVA-61).

McDonnell Demon

After an inauspicious beginning and protracted gestation th[e] McDonnell F3H Demon emerged as a high performance shipboar[d] fighter serving on seven U.S. carriers and outperforming mar[y] shore-based fighters. It became America's first real missile fight[er] and the standard U.S. Navy shipboard fighter.

Navy's Answer to Soviet MiG

The Demon was designed to meet the U.S. Navy requirement for [a] high performance interceptor that would be able to equal the pe[r]formance of shore-based contemporaries; therefore, two prototyp[es] were ordered on September 30, 1949. The Korean War impelle[d] the Navy to issue a 56 plane production contract in early 1951 b[ut]

The McDonnell Demon was the U.S. Navy's first missile fighter, fitted with four Sparrow air-to-air missiles. Demons served on seven U.S. aircraft carriers and became the standard U.S. Navy ship board fighter. The F3H-1 is shown here. (Official U.S. Navy Photograph, News Photo Division)

A McDonnell F3H-2 or F3-B strike/fighter is about to lift off a carrier deck. Note the high angle of attack of the plane and the drooped leading edge to increase lift during takeoff. Of interest is the forward tailpipe location relative to the tail surfaces. (McDonnell Douglas, Courtesy Timothy J. Beecher)

fore the XF3H-1 prototypes had been completed. The Navy also decided that the high performance interceptor should be changed to a general purpose, all-weather fighter; all this before the prototype had flown. This change in mission capability increased the gross weight of the production models from 22,000 to 29,000 pounds. Apparently, the Demon was expected to be the Navy's answer to the Soviet MiG-15.

Engine Development Problems

The prototype finally flew on August 7, 1951, powered by a single experimental Westinghouse XJ40-WE-6 turbojet-engine of 7,200 pounds estimated static thrust; however, the engine failed to live up to the designers' expectations. Both prototypes proved to be seriously underpowered, which is more of a danger for high speed jets than for slower flying propeller planes. The plane had been designed to be powered by the 9,500 pounds static thrust Westinghouse J40-WE-24 turbojet, which never materialized! Despite the fact that the plane was seriously underpowered the Navy, under pressure from the Korean War, ordered 146 more Demons on August 29, 1952.

Serious Crashes

Delivery of the first Demons began in 1953; however, only 11 had flown by 1955, of which a half-dozen had crashed, killing two of the test pilots. Existing planes were grounded and McDonnell was instructed to redesign the Demon for the 9,700 pounds static thrust Allison J71-A-2 turbojet, which could develop 14,250 pounds static thrust when the afterburner was fired up.

F3H-2 Is Born

Wing area was also increased slightly in the new variant; designated F3H-2 and classified as a strike/fighter. The F3H-2M was fitted to carry four AIM-7C Sparrow III missiles while the F3H-2N was tailored for the all-weather role. These became known as the F-3B, MF-3B and F-3C, respectively, in 1962 when all designations were changed by the U.S. Department of Defense in order to eliminate all distinction between U.S. Air Force and U.S. Navy aircraft designations.

Demon Data

The McDonnell F3H-2 or F3-B Demon wingspan was 35 feet-4 inches and wing area was 519 square feet. Length was 58 feet-11 inches with overall height of 14 feet-7 inches. The empty weight was 22,133 pounds while gross weight was 33,900 pounds.

The Allison engine drove the Demon to a maximum speed of 647 miles per hour at 30,000 feet. Range was 1,370 miles. The initial climb rate was 12,795 feet per minute, while service ceiling was 42,650 feet.

Four 20 millimeter rapid-fire cannons were installed; two on each side of the fuselage just under the engine air inlets, while underwing pylons carried bombs, rockets or auxiliary fuel tanks. The engine air inlets were very carefully designed to be as small as possible and still provide the proper air supply to the engine.

Over 500 Demons were delivered to the U.S. Navy and the well designed plane had temporarily fallen victim to the absence of a reliable American turbojet-engine, as had many other Warbirds of

This closeup of an F3-B Demon shows the nose details of the craft to good advantage such as: (1) Nose radome housing for Hughes APG-51 radar; (2) Carefully designed jet engine air inlet duct to fair into the fuselage contours; (3) Single port for two 20 millimeter cannon; (4) Sturdy nose wheel landing gear strut. (WAM Foto)

the Sea, during this period. Demons remained in service until the summer of 1964 and much design and operational data was provided for the phenomenal McDonnell F4H design, which was under development as the Demon had begun to enter U.S. Navy service. All Demons were equipped with Hughes APG-51 radar.

Tailless Warbirds

Two very unusual shipboard fighters joined the U.S. Navy squadrons in the 1950s. The planes were devoid of a horizontal tail, hence tailless aircraft, but not of true delta plan-form. This illustrates the willingness of the usually conservative U.S. Navy to invest time and money in the most unorthodox designs in its quest for more efficient and high performance turbojet-powered carrier planes. The postwar years were, indeed, a time of great progress for carrier aviation.

Vought Cutlass

When data on German wartime aeronautical research became available in 1945 Chance Vought designers studied the tailless and delta designs of Arado Flugzeugwerke and those of Dr. Alexander Lippisch, who had designed the only operational tailless fighter of World War II; the Messerschmitt 163. Vought then began design studies for a very unconventional tailless design.

Vought Wins Navy Contract

From April to June 1946 the U.S. Navy Bureau of Aeronautics invited bids for an interceptor fighter in the 600 miles per hour at 40,000 feet performance class. Grumman, Douglas and Curtiss submitted designs and Vought proposed its tailless project. Vought was selected and an order for three experimental prototypes was placed on June 25. The design was stressed for 12 "G" maneuvers.

The first XF7U-1 prototype made its initial flight on September 29, 1948 powered by two Westinghouse J34-WE-32 turbojet-engines. It was the first U.S. Navy fighter designed from the outset to employ engine afterburners for added power and drag 'chutes during landing.

Rigorous Trials

U.S. Navy and Vought test pilots flew the prototypes through grueling trials which ended with successful carrier landings and take-

Two Vought Cutlass tailless fighters await launching on the Flight Deck of USS Hancock. Observe the vertically folded wing of the Cutlass in the foreground (No.1) and the interesting squadron insignia on the fin in which the bones of the Skull and Crossbones are cutlasses (No.2). Note also the extended wing slats (No.3). (Official U.S. Navy Photograph, Courtesy Arthur L. Schoeni)

The most obvious external difference between the Vought F7U-1 (below) and the final F7U-3 variant (above) is the cockpit. The high angle of attack of the Cutlass on the ground and during takeoff and landing hindered forward visibility; therefore, the entire nose was redesigned to improve the pilot's visibility. (Vought Aircraft Company, Courtesy Paul Bower)

duction models were ordered. These equipped fighter squadrons VF-81, VF-83, VF-122 and VF-124.

Cutlass Data

Powered by two 4,600 pounds static thrust Westinghouse J46-WE-8A turbojets, which power increased to 6,000 pounds static thrust with the Solar afterburners operating, propelled the Cutlass to 680 miles per hour at 10,000 feet and 700 miles per hour at 40,000 feet. The rate of climb was a fantastic 13,000 feet per minute, a truly awe-inspiring sight! The F7U-3 was not only capable of flying on one engine but could accelerate and climb away on one engine plus afterburner in the event of a wave-off during a carrier landing. The wingspan was 38 feet-8 inches which was halved when folded. Length was 44 feet-3 inches and height 14 feet-7 1/2 inches. Wing area was 496 square feet. Empty weight was 18,210 pounds and gross weight was 31,642 pounds, despite the use of Metalite in the Cutlass construction. Range was 660 miles.

Armament included four fixed 20 millimeter cannon installed in the upper lip of the air intakes and four Sparrow I air-to-air missiles. Provision was also made for 5,000 pounds of bombs or external fuel tanks.

Tailless Characteristics

The elimination of the conventional horizontal tail reduced the weight and wind resistance but longitudinal stability and control suffered. The wing control surfaces served as both ailerons for banking and elevators for climbing and diving. Vought called these "ailevators." Watching the Cutlass takeoff was a breathtaking event. With the plane at a 10 degree angle on the runway as it gained speed, the nosewheel left the ground and the plane reared up to a 15 degree angle before the main wheels lifted from the runway and the craft became airborne, heading skyward at an unbelievable angle and climbing speed. It was, indeed, the ideal interceptor.

Rex B. Beisel was General Manager and Vice President of United Aircraft Corporation (parent company of Chance Vought) when he decided to propose the tailless Cutlass design to the U.S. Navy Bureau of Aeronautics. The plane won the Navy contract against contending designs from Curtiss, Douglas and Grumman. It will be remembered that Beisel designed famous classics such as the Curtiss Navy Hawks, original Curtiss Helldiver and Vought F4U Corsair, among others. (Courtesy Rex B. Beisel Jr.)

As two FJ-3 Furies await launching from the deck of USS Forrestal, a Vought Cutlass completes a touch-and-go takeoff during carrier tests of the plane. The Vought F7U-3 had a 13,000 feet per minute rate of climb. Note the catapult steam from a previous launching. (Official U.S. Navy Photograph, Courtesy Arthur L. Schoeni)

offs. Meanwhile, an order for 14 preproduction F7U-1 Cutlass fighters had been placed in June 1948; however, it was not until February 1950 that the first plane was delivered because of the intricate tooling for this revolutionary fighter. The F7U-1 Cutlass first flew on March 1, 1950 and all 14 aircraft were assigned to the Advanced Training Command at Corpus Christi Naval Air Station for intensive evaluation. Meanwhile, the Westinghouse J34 turbojet program ran into difficulties and F7U-2 was cancelled before the prototype had been completed.

F7U-3 Mods

The F7U-3 emerged late in 1951 with redesigned fins and rudders plus a drooped nose which tilted the reshaped cockpit canopy downward for vastly improved forward visibility; especially in view of the nose-high attitude on the ground and during takeoff. The F7U-3 Cutlass made its first flight on December 20, 1951 and 162 pro-

A Vought Cutlass F7U-3M shows off its four Sperry beam-riding Sparrow I missiles. One hundred of the F7U-3M variant were constructed for the U.S. Navy. The plane that had been designed as an interceptor could also be used in the strike/fighter role. (Vought Aircraft Company, Courtesy Paul Bower)

Cutlass Assigned to Attack Role

Unfortunately, the Cutlass was assigned to newly formed attack squadrons and composite squadrons such-as VC-3, tested for high speed mine laying and loaded with missiles and bombs. Some were fitted with radar while others had cameras installed as reconnaissance planes. It was the first U.S. naval aircraft to be armed with missiles and equipped attack squadron VA-83 on *USS Intrepid* in the Mediterranean. It appears that, after specifying an interceptor and receiving a very potent interceptor fighter, the U.S. Navy made the Vought Cutlass spend most of its service life as an attack plane which did not take advantage of the F7U-3 capabilities.

Cutlass Production

Production ended in 1955 after 290 Cutlass fighters had been constructed. The last F7U-3 in active service was retired in March 1959 and so ended another pioneering Vought design that had provided considerable design and test information which made possible future Warbird designs.

Douglas Skyray

Shortly after the Cutlass completed its maiden flight, the U.S. Navy Bureau of Aeronautics ordered a tailless design from the Douglas El Segundo plant. Conceived by Ed Heinemann and his design team with Charles S. Kennedy as the project engineer, the XF4D-1 was designed as a defensive interceptor for about five minutes of combat at full power after skyrocketing to 50,000 feet in about three minutes! As with many other superb designs this Douglas tailless project suffered delaying modifications during its development due to the ever-present U.S. turbojet-engine problems of the 1950s.

Modified Delta Wing

The U.S. Navy initially approached Douglas Aircraft Company in 1947 to investigate the feasibility of the delta wing as a fast-climbing, carrier-based, short-range interceptor. After considerable investigation it was determined that the true delta wing was far from ideal for carrier service and an unusual wing with a very low aspect-ratio was developed, featuring leading edge sweepback of about 52 degrees and fully rounded wingtips. In effect, the wing appeared to be a modified delta except that the trailing edge had 15 degrees of sweepback and the wing was so well-faired into the fuselage as to make the fuselage virtually nonexistent except for the cockpit and radome nose. In plan-form the shape was not unlike that of the family of cartilaginous fish called rays; hence, the name Skyray was selected for the Douglas XF4D-1. The wing outer panels folded upwards for stowage.

Engine Delays

The first prototype experienced its maiden flight on January 23 1951, powered by a single 5,000 pounds static thrust Allison J35-A-17 turbojet-engine instead of the specified Westinghouse XJ40-WE-8 turbojet which was not ready for installation in the plane it was to power. Obviously underpowered, the Skyray was re-engined with another interim engine, the 7,000 pounds static thrust Westinghouse XJ40-WE-6. The specified 11,600 pounds static thrust XJ40-WE-8 engine was finally installed in 1953; however, by that time it had already been decided to drop the Westinghouse turbo

The Douglas Skyray tailless fighter had a swept wing that blended into the fuselage. Skyrays set world records of 758.4 miles per hour and by climbing to 9,842.5 feet in 44.39 seconds. (McDonnell Douglas, Courtesy Harry Gann)

et-engine from the program and switch to the Pratt & Whitney J57-P-2 turbojet-engine of 9,700 pounds static thrust and 13,500 pounds static thrust with afterburning. These constant engine changes required extensive modifications that affected about 80 percent of the structure, equipment installation, specifications and drawings which underwent engineering changes without stopping the production line.

Skyray Speed Records

During the intervening time world speed records were being broken by the Skyray. On October 3, 1953 the second XF4D-1 prototype, powered by the afterburner-fitted Westinghouse XJ40-WE-8, established a world air speed record with an average speed of 758.4. Piloted by U.S. Navy Lieutenant Commander James Verdin, the XF4D-1 made four passes over the Salton Lake shoreline in southern California, which were in sequence: 746.075, 761.414, 746.503 and 759.499 miles per hour. The runs were made at altitudes between 100 and 200 feet. This Skyray was loaded with 700 gallons of fuel and used 575 gallons during the four passes which required 20 minutes of flying time. Takeoff weight of the record-breaking Skyray was 20,000 pounds. Fuel cells were in the wing center section.

Another speed record was established on October 16, 1953 when Douglas test pilot Robert O. Rahn captured the 100 kilometer closed circuit world speed record in the XF4D-1 with a speed of 728.11 miles per hour.

More Trials

During October 1953 the first XF4D-1 completed its carrier trials aboard *USS Coral Sea*.

The first production Skyray accomplished its initial flight on June 4, 1954 and subsequent flight testing revealed that the interceptor's performance and maneuverability at extreme altitudes had no equal. One of the problems encountered during the testing was the tendency for the craft to stall at high altitudes during supersonic speeds. This was caused by the engine air intakes which required modification in order not to impede the airflow to the engine under these unusual conditions.

More Records Broken

More world records tumbled during May 22-23, 1958 when a Pratt & Whitney J57-P-8 turbojet-powered production F4D-1 was flown by U.S. Marine Corps Major Edward E.N. Le Faivre when he established five Federation Aeronautique International (F.A.I.) climb records. The F4D-1 climbed to 9,842.5 feet in 44.39 seconds; 19,685 feet in 1 minute-6.13 seconds; 29,527.5 feet in 1 minute-29.81 seconds; 39,370 feet in 1 minute-51.23 seconds and 49,212.5 feet in 2 minutes-36.05 seconds; a truly superlative climbing ability.

These records resulted in Skyrays being assigned to VFAW-3 (All-Weather Fighter Squadron Three)-for service at the San Diego base of the North American Air Defense Command. This was a singular honor for Douglas as well as the Navy because this command normally uses only U.S. Air Force units and aircraft.

Douglas Skyray Data

The Skyray was armed with four 20 millimeter rapid-fire cannon in each wing plus six underwing mounts for two 300 gallon auxiliary fuel tanks, two 2,000 pound bombs, pods containing six 2.75 inch unguided air-to-air rockets, larger pods containing 19 unguided air-to-air rockets, Sidewinder infrared missiles, or any 4,000 pound combination as was required by the assigned mission. As can be seen this fast-climbing interceptor was made to double as a strike fighter as well. The nose cone radome contained an Aero 13F fire control system which included APQ-50A radar and a MK 16 sighting system which works with the four cannon.

The Douglas F4D-1 Skyray (redesignated to F-6A in 1962) attained a maximum speed of 720 miles per hour at sea level and 695 miles per hour at 36,000 feet when powered by the 10,500 pounds static thrust and 14,500 pounds static thrust with afterburning Pratt & Whitney J57-P-8 turbojet-engine. Initial rate of climb was 18,000 feet per minute with a service ceiling of 55,000 feet. Tactical radius as an interceptor was 200 miles; however, the range could be extended to 950 miles with the maximum external tankage.

The interceptor loaded weight was 20,000 pounds while the maximum permissible takeoff weight was 25,000 pounds. Wingspan was 33 feet-6 inches with a wing area of 557 square feet. Length was 45 feet-8 1/4 inches and height was 13 feet.

Production

Total production of the Skyray was 419 planes with the last leaving the El Segundo line in December 1958.

As the last of the Skyrays were leaving the production line two new carrier-based air superiority fighters had been joining U.S. Navy squadrons as replacements for the Skyray. The Grumman Tiger and Vought Crusader had been developing concurrently since 1953 when both prototypes were ordered.

Grumman Tiger

Officially announced as an attempt to extract the maximum possible performance from the basic Panther design, the Grumman G-98 was, in fact, an entirely new state-of-the-art shipboard jet fighter in both design and construction. It will be remembered that the swept-wing Cougar F9F-6 through F9F-8 had already improved on the straight-wing Panther. Despite the obvious, the U.S. Navy designated the new fighter F9F-9; possibly to facilitate the appropriation of funds for the project.

Innovative Wing

The Grumman Tiger, as it was named, featured a very thin wing in order to attain the highest speed possible and, in order to simplify production, it was machined or milled from a solid slab of aluminum. The wingtips were folded manually downward to reduce the span for stowage. The landing gear retracted into the fuselage because there was no room for it in the slender wing.

"Coke Bottle" Fuselage

The area rule principle was applied to the fuselage design and the Tiger was the first American plane to use the Coke bottle concept to reduce drag in the supersonic mode.

The vertical fin had been designed to take part of the fuel load because the wings were so thin!

The Grumman Tiger air superiority fighter was a light weight, high speed plane which production models attained 890 miles per hour. The Grumman F11F-1 was the first American plane to have a "coke bottle" fuselage. Note the retractable refueling probe extended on the right or starboard side of the cockpit. Observe the depressed wing leading edge to increase lift during takeoffs and landings. (Grumman Corporation, Courtesy Lois Lovisolo)

Tiger Prototype Trials

Ordered on April 27, 1953, the first of six prototype YF9F-9 lightweight air superiority fighters made its initial test flight on July 30, 1954 with Grumman test pilot Corwin Meyers at the controls. Early test flights revealed control and stability problems at both high and low speeds; however, this was improved through the addition of a leading edge fillet at the wing root. Considerable effort had been made to keep the Tiger as light as possible and a measure of this success is the fact that the Tiger prototype gross weight was more than 6,000 pounds lighter than the Cougar gross weight!

Powered by one 7,800 pounds static thrust Wright J65-W-4 turbojet, which produced 11,200 pounds static thrust with afterburning, the Tiger was credited with 825 to 950 miles per hour at various altitudes during the first speed trials.

By April 1955 the U.S. Navy had corrected the Tiger designation to F11F-1 and the initial production order for 39 planes was issued.

Speed and Altitude Records

In 1957 two Grumman Tigers were fitted with the 12,000 pound static thrust General Electric J79-GE-3 turbojet, which produced 15,000 pounds static thrust with afterburning. These were designated F11F-1F and were planned to be prototypes for future variants in heavily loaded strike and ground attack roles. When the F11F-1F had completed tests at Edwards Air Force Base test center, the Tiger's performance was so promising that the U.S. Navy decided to smash some World Records.

In order to attain the highest speed possible, the Grumman Tiger was fitted with a very thin wing and to simplify production it was machined from a solid slab of aluminum. The wing was so thin that the landing gear retracted into the fuselage because there was no room in the wing. Tigers set a world speed record of 1,220 miles per hour and an altitude record of 76,939 feet. (Grumman Corporation, Courtesy Lois Lovisolo)

On April 13, 1958 the Grumman F11F-1F established an unofficial World Speed Record of 1,220 miles per hour. Three days later Lieutenant Commander G.C. Watkins smashed the World's Altitude Record when he took the F11F-1F up to 72,000 feet and then increased the altitude two days later when Watkins flew the F11F-F to 76,939 feet.

Tiger Data

The sleek F11F-1 Tiger production models attained maximum speeds of 750 miles per hour at sea level and 890 miles per hour at 40,000 feet when powered by one 7,450 pounds static thrust Wright J65-W-18 turbojet. Cruising speed was 577 miles per hour at 38,000 feet. The initial climb rate was 5,130 feet per minute and service ceiling was 50,500 feet. Range was 700 miles.

Wingspan was 31 feet-7 1/2 inches with a wing area of 250 square feet. Length was 46 feet-11 1/4 inches, while height was 13 feet-2 3/4 inches. The weights were: empty 13,428 pounds; gross 22,160 pounds; and maximum takeoff of 24,078 pounds.

Armament comprised the standard four 20 millimeter cannon located in the lower portion of the jet intakes plus four underwing Sidewinder 1A or 1C air-to-air missiles located near the wingtips. Provision was also made to carry underwing auxiliary fuel tanks.

Most of the 199 Grumman F11F-1 Tigers produced served in attack squadrons despite the fact that it was basically an air superiority fighter. Perhaps the reason is that it performed well in the attack role; however, as has been related in previous narratives, several fine interceptor and air superiority fighters have been assigned to multipurpose strike/fighter roles. Perhaps the days of the single-purpose fighter were numbered.

The last Tiger rolled off the production line in 1958. It equipped two squadrons in AIRLANT (Naval Air Force, Atlantic Fleet) and four squadrons in AIR PAC (Naval Air Force, Pacific Fleet). The U.S. Navy Blue Angels aerobatic team also flew the Grumman F11F-1 Tiger.

Vought Crusader

Developed simultaneously with the Tiger was the revolutionary Vought Crusader supersonic air superiority fighter. Vought had left United Aircraft Corporation (which originally included Hamilton Standard Propellers, Pratt & Whitney, Sikorsky Aircraft and Chance Vought) and formed an independent Chance Vought Aircraft, Inc., in Dallas, Texas. It had gambled its entire existence on the Crusader and won. In competition with seven other designs, the Chance Vought proposal was chosen for development and the U.S. Navy ordered two prototypes, designated XF8U-1, on June 29, 1953.

Supersonic Test Flight

The first prototype experienced its maiden flight with John Konrad at the controls on March 25, 1955 and virtually flew off the drawing board. Powered by a single 10,900 pound static thrust and 13,200 pounds with afterburner Pratt & Whitney J57-P-4, the prototype left the ground after a short run at Edwards Air Force Base test center; climbed quickly and surpassed the speed of sound before returning to the runway for a slow, soft landing. Having passed the tests at Edwards, the XF8U-1 engaged in carrier trials in October on *USS Forrestal* and the *Essex* class *Bon Homme Richard*, which was a much smaller carrier. The landing amazed the trials board with its slow approach and short run. Quantity production had been ordered by December 1955 and almost 600 Crusaders were ordered a short time later.

Crusader Innovations

The Crusader employed some innovations in its design to ensure that it would meet the requirements of the Navy specifications. The one-piece wing was shoulder-mounted atop the fuselage and sported a saw-tooth leading edge in the 42 1/2 degree sweepback. The most interesting innovation was that the wing incidence could be adjusted in flight by the pilot via a hydraulic system. The wing hinged at the rear spar junction with the fuselage; thereby, enabling the wing to tilt upwards into the airstream. This adjustable angle plus the large trailing edge flaps and adjustable leading edges enabled the wing airfoil to be changed from a high speed, low drag wing section to a slow speed, high lift undercambered airfoil while in flight. This also had the advantage of keeping the fuselage parallel to the deck during landing while the wing assumed the high angle of attack; thereby, assuring the pilot of an excellent line of sight to the carrier flight deck. In the average carrier-based plane, the fuselage must tilt upwards to maintain a high angle of attack during

Three Vought Crusaders fly in formation over USS Forrestal. Production Crusaders had a top speed of 1,100 miles per hour while the F8U-2N or F-8D rate of climb was 22,000 feet per minute. The Crusader earned the coveted Collier Trophy for the U.S. Navy and Vought in 1957. (Official U.S. Navy Photograph, Courtesy Arthur L. Schoeni)

landing; thereby, restricting the pilot's view of the deck. The adjustable wing incidence enabled the supersonic Vought Crusader to land at a mere 115 miles per hour.

Titanium was used as much as possible in the Crusader structure which included a large portion of the midfuselage, as well as the fuselage rear at the afterburner.

The standard bubble-type cockpit canopy was not used; instead, the canopy was well-blended into the fuselage contours for minimal resistance and maximum visibility for the pilot.

The Stabilator Story

On the majority of high speed jets the horizontal tail is in one movable surface rather than in the common fixed stabilizer and movable elevator. It may be of interest to know why this change was necessary. During the early days of high speed flight several mysterious crashes were experienced when the planes dived into the

ground beyond the pilot's control, especially when they placed the elevator in the full "up" position. In one such mishap the pilot, in desperation, shoved the stick forward for a dive and the plane recovered from the dive and zoomed up to level flight. As the plane slowed for a landing the controls returned to normal. After considerable investigation, tail surface inspection, and review of the forces involved at high speeds, the fault and the solution became evident.

The force of the air against the elevator at very high speed acted upon the fixed stabilizer which supported it. The slipstream force against the upturned elevator resulted in a downward pressure along the hinge line. The stabilizer was held firmly at the fuselage; therefore, this downward pressure twisted the stabilizer, which raised the leading edge. It is easy to understand how this increased stabilizer positive incidence overcame the force of the upturned elevator and put the plane into a dive. The immediate proposed solution was to design stronger stabilizers but the final decision

VOUGHT   F-8D   CRUSADER   (VF-111)

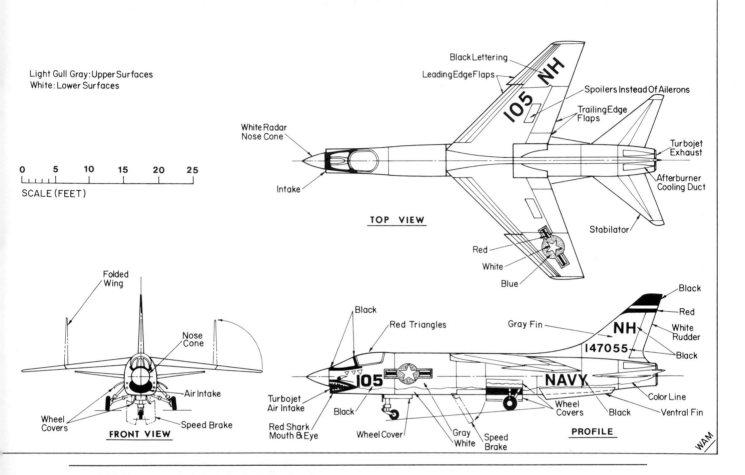

Light Gull Gray: Upper Surfaces
White: Lower Surfaces

0   5   10   15   20   25
SCALE (FEET)

TOP VIEW

Black Lettering
Leading Edge Flaps
Spoilers Instead Of Ailerons
Trailing Edge Flaps
Turbojet Exhaust
Afterburner Cooling Duct
Stabilator
White Radar Nose Cone
Intake
Red
White
Blue

FRONT VIEW

Folded Wing
Nose Cone
Air Intake
Speed Brake
Wheel Covers

PROFILE

Black
Red Triangles
Gray Fin
Black
Red
White Rudder
Black
Turbojet Air Intake
Black
Red Shark Mouth & Eye
Wheel Cover
Gray White
Speed Brake
Wheel Covers
Black
Color Line
Ventral Fin
NAVY
147055
NH
105

WAM

A Crusader trainer approaches touchdown on USS Independence. Note that the fuselage is virtually level and not in the usual nose-up attitude; thereby, improving landing visibility. This is attributed to the innovative adjustable wing incidence which is shown at a positive angle. (Official U.S. Navy Photograph, Courtesy Vought Aircraft Company)

Having landed, the Crusader trainer clearly reveals the adjustable incidence of the one-piece wing which is in the positive or raised position, note gap (No.1). Observe the folded wing tip in the vertical position (No.2) and the ventral fins under the fuselage (No.3) (Official U.S. Navy Photograph, Courtesy Ling-Temco-Vought)

On July 16, 1957 this Vought F8U-1P Crusader established a supersonic transcontinental speed record across the U.S. averaging 723.5 miles per hour. Onboard cameras had been preset to take photos from an altitude of 35,000 feet. The flight was code named "Project Bullet." (Vought Aircraft Company, Courtesy Paul Bower)

was to install an all-movable horizontal tail surface, much as those used on pioneering aircraft in pre-World War I years.

Speed Records Fall

The first production Crusaders were delivered in the summer of 1956. On that August 21 Commander R.W. Windsor established the first U.S. national speed record over 1,000 miles per hour when he attained 1,015 miles per hour over a nine mile course in a standard production F8U-1 with full naval equipment on board and fully loaded as a combat craft except for external armament or stores.

Operation Bullet

On July 16, 1957 Major John H. Glenn, Jr., U.S.M.C., earned the Distinguished Flying Cross by flying a F8U-1P photo reconnaissance Crusader from Los Angeles to New York in three hours and 26 minutes. This set a supersonic transcontinental speed record averaging 723.5 miles per hour with three inflight refuelings from AJ-1 Savage tankers. The flight was made at an altitude of 35,000 feet and, throughout the run, onboard cameras had been preset to take photographs during predetermined intervals. The pilot is the same John Glenn who was the first American astronaut to orbit the earth and who also became a U.S. Senator from Ohio.

Crusader Data

Production Crusaders are fitted with the 11,200 pounds dry static thrust (13,500 pounds static thrust with afterburner firing) Pratt & Whitney J57-P-12 turbojet which drives the 27,000 pound F8U-1 to a maximum speed of 1,100 miles per hour at 40,000 feet. Service ceiling is 60,000 feet and range is 1,200 miles. The Crusader gives

U.S. Marine Major John H. Glenn Jr. was awarded the Distinguished Flying Cross for his accomplishment in "Project Bullet." Major Glenn was the first American astronaut to orbit the earth which he circled three times on February 20, 1962. (Official U.S. Navy Photograph, Courtesy Paul Bower, Vought Aircraft Company)

Major Glenn's Vought F8U-1P Crusader received three inflight refuelings from North American AJ-1 Savage tankers during "Project Bullet." Shown here is a "Project Bullet" inflight refueling practice. (Vought Aircraft Company, Courtesy Paul Bower)

the impression of being a larger plane than it actually is. Wingspan is 35 feet-8 inches, which can be reduced to 22 feet-6 inches by folding the wingtips up to a vertical position. Overall length is 54 feet-3 inches and height is 15 feet-9 inches.

The standard U.S. Navy Armament of four 20 millimeter cannon was installed, two on each side of the air intake. These were retained long after most fighters had abandoned guns for missiles. The cannon were supplemented by two Sidewinder missiles on each side of the fuselage. In addition, a retractable missile tray with (32) 2 3/4 inch Mighty Mouse rockets was located just aft of the nose-wheel opening.

An inflight retractable fueling probe was located in a streamline housing on the port (left) side of the fuselage between the cockpit and the wing.

A point of interest is the nonretractable ram air turbine that is located inside the fuselage. Air scoops lead the air to the turbine which drives the hydraulic pump that provides the hydraulic power upon which much of the plane's mechanical equipment depends.

Deployment

The first F8U-1 Crusaders went into squadron service on March 25, 1961, starting with VF-32 in the Atlantic Fleet, and as production increased, this landmark fighter had become the standard first line equipment in over 28 Navy and Marine squadrons by 1961. By this time the first F8U-2 kept the same overall dimensions as its predecessor and the only external difference was the addition of two ventral fins between the wing and tail surfaces. These were deemed necessary in order to maintain stability at the high speed in the upper rarified atmosphere. Less visible improvements were the installation of a more powerful 13,000 pounds static thrust Pratt & Whitney J57-P-16 turbojet-engine (17,500 pounds of static thrust with afterburner). This increased the top speed to 1,155 miles per hour at 36,000 feet which, at that altitude, was Mach 1.75. The initial rate of climb rose to 16,500 feet per minute.

Crusader II also featured improved fire control systems, including infrared rocket control.

F8U-1P (later redesignated RF-8A) was the reconnaissance/photographic variant of the Vought Crusader. Observe the flattened fuselage bottom. Cameras are located in the fuselage between the nose wheel and wing leading edge. Note the angle of the stabilator as the plane is ready to lift off the runway. (Vought Aircraft Company Courtesy Paul Bower)

The most spectacular Crusader variant was the F8U-2N (F-8D) which had a top speed almost twice the speed of sound. The automatic pilot could not only maintain altitude but could select a new course and orbit over the target. Observe the cannon ports on the fuselage side and the Sidewinder missiles. (Vought Aircraft Company, Courtesy Paul Bower)

A revised automatic pilot system was also installed to reduce pilot fatigue on long flights.

Spectacular F8U-2N

Of the eight Vought Crusader variants, the F8U-2N is probably the most spectacular performer with a 20,000 pounds static thrust with afterburner Pratt & Whitney J57-P-20, boosting the top speed to Mach 1.95. Loaded weight had increased to 29,000 pounds. Service ceiling was 55,000 feet, while the initial rate of climb jumped to 20,000 feet per minute! In addition, the automatic pilot was further improved to maintain a predetermined altitude, select a new course, and orbit over the target. This night fighter had increased fuel capacity by deleting the Mighty Mouse rocket tray.

In 1962 the F8U-1 was redesignated to F-8A, F8U-2 to F-8C, and F8U-2N to F-8D.

While the Crusader was in production, Vought joined with other firms to form Ling Temco Vought and became Vought Aeronautics Division of LTV Aerospace Corporation, Dallas, Texas; hence the F8U is often referred to as the LTV Crusader.

Collier Trophy Recipient

The Collier Trophy, one of America's most prestigious aviation awards, was presented to the U.S. Navy and Vought for the most significant achievement in Aviation of 1957; the 1,000 miles per hour fighter plane.

Trans-Pacific Mass Flight

Probably the most spectacular feat accomplished by Crusaders occurred on January 11, 1962 when an entire Marine Corps Squadron flew their F8U-1 fighters nonstop from El Toro, California to Atsug[?] Japan. Inflight refueling extended the squadron's normal range.

In Smithsonian Institution

The production F-8 Crusader was the world's fastest single-engin[?] naval fighter of which 1,261 were constructed. Some we[?] remanufactured for the U.S. Navy to extend the fleet life of 4[?] planes. The French and Philippine Navies have purchased sever[?] Crusaders. The first XF8U-1 can be seen in the Smithsonian Ins[?] tution National Air and Space Museum, Washington, D.C., as [?] historic aircraft. The Crusader also proved itself in battle as will [?] discovered later in this chapter. Having made its mark in peacetim[?] and destined to do the same in war, the Crusader also spawned [?] equally historic plane for a diametrically different military role whi[?] became just as successful as its progenitor.

NEW AND MODERNIZED U.S. CARRIERS

During 1955-1960 several U.S. carriers underwent modernizatic[?] to meet the demands of operating the new carrier-based aircraft.

Essex Class Modernization

On May 27, 1954 the U.S. Navy Chief of Naval Operations (CN[?] had approved a program to thoroughly modernize about 18 Ess[?] class carriers, which was to include enclosed hurricane bows, angl[?] flight decks, steam catapults, and stronger arresting gear.

Midway Class Modernization

USS Midway CVA-41, USS Franklin D. Roosevelt CVA-42 and U[?]

Designed in response to a 1953 U.S. Navy design competition for a new supersonic carrier-based strike/fighter the Vought F8U-3 Crusader III was[?] powered by a 23,500 pounds thrust Pratt & Whitney J75 turbojet engine which was augmented by a 6,000 pounds thrust Rocketdyne rocket engine [?] increase rate of climb, provide more rapid acceleration from cruising to combat speed and to aid maneuverability at 90,000 feet altitude. Span was[?] 39 feet-11 inches with a length of 58 feet-9 inches. Speed was about 1,500 miles per hour and range was about 2,000 miles. The turbojet air inlet featured a Ferri-type swept-forward design with a variable angle to meet the requirements of the turbojet engine at supersonic speeds. The ventral fins (arrow) extend sharply downward in flight and retract to a horizontal pasition for landing and ground operation. Eighteen Crusader III's were constructed by 1957; however, the craft never entered production. (Vought Aircraft Company, Courtesy Paul Bower)

nly USS Oriskany (CV-34) of the Essex class carriers had been fitted with the steam catapult, therefore, the remaining postwar Essex carriers were ?elegated to ASW service because faster and heavier aircraft made them unsuitable as attack carriers. USS Randolph (CVS-15), shown here, reveals ?ome of its postwar modifations, raked smokestack to keep corrosive gasses away from new radar antennae; bow anchor to clear the new sonar ?ome; and enclosed "hurricane" bow, with six portholes for the back-up conning station. (Official U.S. Navy Photograph, News Photo Division)

?oral Sea CVA-43 were reclassified from CVB to CVA in October ?952. During the late 1950s and 1960s the class was updated with ?ngled Flight Deck; steam catapults; stronger arresting gear; im-?roved electronics; closed bow; and the Magic Mirror landing aid ?ystem. All aircraft elevators were converted to deck-edge types.

?he Magic Mirror

JSS Bennington (CV-20) had been severely damaged by an explo-?ion and fire; killing 103 and injuring 201 officers and crew on *?lay 26, 1954. While it was undergoing the necessary repairs, it ?ecame one of the first *Essex* class carriers to undergo the class *modernization. The first British-designed Mirror-Sight Landing Aid ?nstallation on a U.S. carrier was made on *USS Bennington* in the ?ummer of 1955. On August 22, 1955 the first U.S. Navy mirror-?ight landing was made on *USS Bennington* by a North American *'J-3 Fury and, two days later, it was another first for *USS Bennington* *when Lieutenant Commander H.C. MacKnight led Grumman F9F-

8 Cougars to the first naval aircraft night landings using the Mirror Sight Landing Aid.

The Mirror Landing Aid, originally conceived by Commander H.C.N. Goodhart R.N., was often called the Magic Mirror and re-placed the paddles and lights of the deck landing officer. The U.S. Navy version consisted of an optical glass mirror, approximately four feet high and three feet wide, surrounded by about two dozen lights. These were carefully arranged in order that one bright red light was reflected by the mirror to the incoming pilot who must adjust his rate of descent and gliding angle so that he can always see the reflected red light. The mirror had to be specially adjusted for each different plane, taking into consideration factors such as the height of the pilot in the cockpit as well as the pitch and roll of the carrier. The high speed approach of the jet-powered aircraft made the Magic Mirror a welcome improvement over the hand-held paddles and lights. The Royal Navy uses green and white lights.

JSS Boxer (CVS-21) was completed too late for action in World War II but served four tours of duty in Korean waters where it experienced an avgas ?aviation gasoline) fire in the hangar. Converted to LPH-4 (Helicopter Assault Ship) in January 1959 USS Boxer saw action in Viet Nam waters in ?arly 1966. Photo taken on January 15, 1959. Helicopters on deck are Sikorsky HUS Seahorses. (Official U.S. Navy Photograph, News Photo ?ivision)

Some of the postwar modifications on USS Hornet (CVS-12) are the angled Flight Deck; replacement of the aft elevator with a deck edge elevator just aft of the island, and the addition of the Mirror-Sight Landing Aid (magic mirror) platform (arrow). Note Grumman Trackers and helicopters o deck. (Official U.S. Navy Photograph)

Supercarriers and World War II Admirals
While the remarkable foregoing aircraft and carrier types were being developed, important things were happening; some happy and some sad.

The British Mirror-Sight Landing Aid, often called the Magic Mirror, was first installed on a U.S. carrier during the summer of 1955. This remarkable apparatus could be used day or night to guide aircraft to safe carrier landings and replaced the deck landing officer's paddles and lights. (Official U.S. Navy Photograph)

Admiral Spruance Appointed Ambassador
In early January 1952 Admiral Raymond Spruance was accord another peacetime honor; President Truman had appointed the he as U.S. Ambassador to the Philippines.

USS Saratoga Commissioned
The second *Forrestal* class Supercarrier, *USS Saratoga*, (CVA-6 constructed at the New York Naval Shipyard (Brooklyn Navy Yar was commissioned on April 14, 1956.

USS Ranger Commissioned
On August 10, 1957 the third *Forrestal* class carrier, *USS Rang (CVA-61), built at Newport News Shipbuilding, was commissione

USS Independence Commissioned
The fourth and last original *Forrestal* class carrier, *USS Indepe dence* (CVA-62), built at New York Naval Shipyard (Brooklyn Na

Opposite below: Although classed as an ASW aircraft carrier, this pho shows the USS Shangri-La (CVS-38) Flight Deck loaded with Skyhawl and Skywarriors plus two Tracers. Only one helicopter is in view. Note the exceptionally long bridle arrestors. (Official U.S. Navy Photograp News Photo Division)

USS Intrepid (CVS-11) has an earlier design "hurricane" bow than some of the other Essex class conversions. Of interest is the new deck edge elevator (arrow) and the bridle arrestors at the end of the catapults. A new taller mast and improved radar antennae were also part of the Essex class modifications. Intrepid was one of the Essex carriers that was equipped with a jet fuel blending system that mixed ship's fuel oil with gasoline for use in turbojet aircraft. Note the bow anchor. (Official U.S. Navy Photograph, News Photo Division)

During the 1950s and 1960s USS Franklin D. Roosevelt (CVB-42) received an angle deck, steam catapults, stronger arresting gear, improved electronics and the Mirror-Sight Landing Aid. The carrier is shown here in 1975. (Official U.S. Navy Photograph, News Photo Division)

The Centaur class of Royal Navy fleet carriers was a vastly improved Colossus class. HMS Bulwark, shown here in 1971, was constructed with a 5 3/4 degree angled Flight Deck and two hydraulic catapults. A Magic Mirror was added in 1954. (Ministry of Defence [Navy])

Yard), was commissioned on January 10, 1959. Four more supercarriers had been funded and two of these improved *Forrestals* were already under construction at this time.

Admiral King Dead
June 25, 1956 Fleet Admiral Ernest J. King died in Portsmouth, New Hampshire at the age of 77.

Admiral Halsey Dead
Admiral William F. "Bull" Halsey died on August 16, 1958 at age 76.

NEW ROYAL NAVY AUXILIARY FLEET CARRIERS
Between 1953 and 1959 four Royal Navy carriers were commissioned; one of which, *HMS Hermes*, was to undergo revolutionary modifications and prove itself in battle. The ships were designed in 1943, when World War II was at its height, and were intended as an improved *Colossus* class of eight auxiliary fleet carriers. The class ships were to be named *Albion, Arrogant, Bulwark, Centaur, Elephant, Hermes, Monmouth* and *Polyphemus*.

The designers doubled the *Colossus* shaft horsepower to 80,000 and added a respectable amount of armor; one inch hull belt and machinery spaces; two inch magazine overhead decks; two inch Flight Deck amidships and one inch at ends; one inch boiler uptakes and hangar. In addition, the Flight Deck was strengthened for 30,000 pound aircraft and the Hangar was a single-level structure, 17 feet-6 inches high to accommodate the larger planes that were envisioned for the future. Despite this added weight the displacement increased only about 5,000 tons to 18,300 standard.

Half of Class Cancelled
In 1945 *Arrogant, Monmouth, Hermes* and *Polyphemus* were cancelled; however, in order to perpetuate the name *Hermes, Elephant* was renamed *Hermes* at the Vickers-Armstrong Barrows Yard. The first of the class to be completed was *HMS Centaur*; launched on April 22, 1947 and commissioned on September 1, 1953; hence the name of the class, *Centaur*. Disregarding the official name, this group of carriers is often called the *Hermes* class, although *Hermes* was the last to be completed on February 16, 1953.

HMS Centaur
Only *HMS Centaur* was commissioned without modifications, being constructed to the original designs as an axial deck carrier; however, she did have a 5 1/2 degree line painted along the landing area of the Flight Deck as an early form of the angled deck. Later, the two hydraulic catapults were replaced with steam types.

HMS Bulwark and Albion
Bulwark and *Albion* were constructed with a 5 3/4 degree angle deck which increased the Flight Deck beam from the originally designed 100 feet to 123 feet. Two hydraulic catapults were installed. *HMS Bulwark* received a mirror landing device after commissioning in 1954.

HMS Hermes
HMS Hermes had been completed to a much modified configuration from the original plans; hence its long time under construction of almost nine years. The *Hermes* modifications during construction included a 6 1/2 degree angled Flight Deck which increased the beam to 144 feet from the axial deck design of 100 feet; a po-

HMS Hermes, photographed in 1960, was built with a 6 1/2 degree angled Flight Deck and two steam catapults. A Magic Mirror was also fitted (arrow No.1). Observe the large three-dimensional radar antenna which combined tracking, surveillance, elevation sighting and fighter plane direction (arrow No.2). (Vickers Armstrong Ltd.)

The former Casablanca class escort carrier, USS Thetis Bay, was converted into the first Assault Helicopter Aircraft Carrier (CVHA-1) in 1955. It was then redesignated to LPH-1. Note the twin engine North American AJ-2P Savage on deck (arrow). (U.S. Naval Historical Center)

By 1963 USS Thetis Bay had been redesignated LPH-6. During conversion the catapult and arresting gear had been removed. Notice the helicopter landing circles. Also note the relocated elevator to the aft end of the Flight Deck. (Official U.S. Navy Photograph, News Photo Division)

ide deck edge elevator was installed; island was enlarged and a huge three-dimensional radar antenna was installed that combined tracking, surveillance, elevation sighting and fighter plane direction; the new mirror landing device was fitted; and two steam catapults were installed.

Hermes Data

As commissioned, *HMS Hermes* displaced 23,000 tons standard and 27,800 tons deep load. Overall length was 744 feet-3 inches and mean or average draft was 28 feet. Flight Deck length was 710 feet. Ship's complement was about 1,800 officers and men plus about 350 FAA personnel. The geared steam turbines drove two propellers while the turbines were supplied with steam from four boilers. Maximum speed was 29.5 knots. About 20 planes could be accommodated in the Hangar, depending on their size. These included the Fairey Gannet, Supermarine Scimitar and de Havilland Sea Vixen.

HELICOPTERS AND ASSAULT HELICOPTER CARRIERS

As with the supercarrier *Forrestal*, aircraft development once again dictated the design of aircraft carriers. The postwar development and application of helicopters for assault as well as ASW detection and attack demanded specialized carriers and these, in turn, stimulated further helicopter development.

The development and initial application of Amphibious Assault Helicopter Carriers began in 1956 when the U.S. Navy and Royal Navy experimented with this new concept.

The First Assault Helicopter Carrier

During the postwar 1940s the U.S. Marine Corps conceived the vertical envelopment amphibious assault technique employing helicopters and initiated realistic experiments to test and develop this concept. The success of the experiments generated enthusiasm to refine the vertical envelopment operation; however, an assault helicopter carrier was needed. One of the few remaining *Casablanca* class CVE escort carriers was selected for conversion to a never before built Assault Helicopter Aircraft Carrier and *USS Thetis Bay* (CVE-90) entered San Francisco Naval Shipyard in June 1955 for conversion.

Catapult and arresting gear were removed and the two elevators were replaced by a single enlarged elevator located at the aft end of the Flight Deck. Quarters were installed to accommodate a Marine battalion of 2,000 men plus stowage for battle equipment ranging from tanks to small arms. Provision was also made for the operation of 20 to 40 helicopters. Defensive armament consisted of (16) 40 millimeter antiaircraft guns in eight twin-mounts. *USS Thetis Bay* was redesignated CVHA-1 and commissioned on July 20, 1956 as the very first Assault Helicopter Aircraft Carrier of any navy. It was later redesignated LPH-1 and finally became LPH-6.

Displacement had increased to 8,000 tons standard and 11,000 tons full load while Flight Deck beam grew to 108 feet. Range dropped to 11,900 miles at 15 knots. Complement dropped to 930 due, in part, to automation.

The *Thetis Bay* conversion was so successful that a second conversion was requested for 1957; however, appropriations were refused and the project was subsequently cancelled. The U.S. Navy then looked to the construction of purpose-built amphibious assault ships based upon commercial freighter design hulls.

Suez Crisis: Assault Helicopter Carriers and Aircraft Carriers

On October 29, 1956 fighting flared in the Middle East, involving Royal Navy carriers and the Fleet Air Arm, in what is known as the

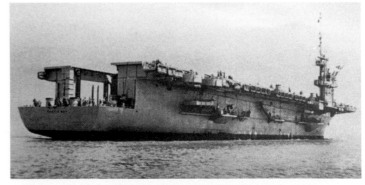

An interesting view of USS Thetis Bay with the elevator in the lowered position. The elevator was needed, not only for the 20 to 40 helicopters, but for the tanks and other military hardware of the 2,000 man U.S. Marine battalion on-board as well. This materiel was lifted to deck for the helicopters to ferry ashore along with the troops during the assault. (Official U.S. Navy Photograph, News Photo Division

Suez Canal Crisis. Britain and the U.S. had withdrawn their promised aid to Egypt for the Aswan Dam Project on July 18, which prompted President Nassar of Egypt to nationalize the Suez Canal eight days later, planning to use the canal revenue for the dam. On October 24 Britain and France reached a secret agreement with Israel for a covert attack on Egypt! Israeli troops attacked on October 29 while the Anglo-French invasion flotilla left Malta for Egypt. Included in the task force were the R.N. aircraft carriers *HMS Eagle*, *Bulwark* and *Albion*; Commando carriers (Assault Helicopter Carriers) *HMS Ocean* and *Theseus* plus the French Navy aircraft carriers *Lafayette* (former *USS Langley*) and *Arromanches* (former *HMS Colossus*).

On October 31 *HMS Eagle* and *HMS Albion* launched Westland Wyverns, de Havilland Sea Venoms and Hawker Sea Hawks to bomb and strafe Egyptian airfields in order to assist the Israeli troops.

During these attacks the U.S. Sixth Fleet was evacuating over 2,000 American citizens from Israel, Egypt and Syria.

The author was sailing with the U.S. Sixth Fleet planning ship modifications as a civilian marine designer during this crisis and had a grandstand view of the activity via long-range binoculars. U.S. disapproval of the attack revealed itself when ships of the U.S. Sixth Fleet sailed so close to the Royal Navy and French ships that it appeared the U.S. intended to disrupt the attack. Eventually the British Task Force Commander Admiral Durnford-Slater requested the U.S. Sixth Fleet Commander Vice Admiral Charles R. Brown to distance his ships from the British and French ships. Admiral Brown held fast and even illuminated his ships at night!

Egypt accepted a U.S. call for a cease-fire with Israel on November 2; however, the Anglo-French bombardment of Egyptian airfields continued unabated. Four days later Anglo-French amphibious forces landed at Port Said using *HMS Theseus* and *HMS Ocean* as makeshift Assault Helicopter Carriers. More and more Soviet ships began appearing in the Mediterranean and, using the Sixth Fleet for subtle intimidation, President Eisenhower joined with the Soviets in pressuring an Anglo-French cease-fire and withdrawal.

Commando Carrier Conversions

The success of the ad hoc Assault Helicopter Carriers *HMS Ocean* and *HMS Theseus* during the Suez Crisis proved the advantages of combined helicopter and amphibious assault. This success induced the Royal Navy to embark on a program to convert *HMS Albion* and *HMS Bulwark* into Amphibious Assault Helicopter Carriers, known in the Royal Navy as Commando Carriers.

Catapults, arresting gear and half the 40 millimeter antiaircraft guns were removed. Accommodation for 700 to 900 Commando Troopers and their battle equipment was provided. Sixteen Westland Whirlwind helicopters, later replaced by Westland Wessex types, could be stowed below deck. The ship's complement was reduced to 1,000 plus the FAA crew of about 200. Upon completion the displacement was 22,300 tons standard and 27,300 tons deep load.

ASW and Assault Helicopters

The threat posed by Soviet submarine activity to Western control of the North Atlantic had become readily apparent in the early postwar years. This grew to crisis proportions when nuclear-powered submarines entered service with the Soviet Navy in the mid-1950s.

A Hawker Sea Hawk of No. 802 Naval Air Squadron lands aboard HMS Albion after a mission over Egypt during the Suez Crisis in autumn 1956. Observe the damaged long range fuel tank under the starboard wing. (Imperial War Museum)

Surface antisubmarine ships had lost their speed advantage over the newer submarines resulting in the transfer of the antisubmarine role to carrierborne ASW helicopters using long range standoff weapons such as homing torpedoes, and long range underwater sensors. Troop-carrying, SAR, and utility types were also developed.

U.S. Navy DASH System

The U.S. Navy concentrated on developing an unmanned antisubmarine drone helicopter which was fitted with homing torpedoes. The Drone Anti Submarine Helicopter (DASH) system was controlled by the mother ship and was strictly a torpedo delivery system with no detection sensors. The project was eventually abandoned in favor of manned helicopters.

Westland Dragonfly

In 1947 British Westland Helicopters Limited foresaw the military uses of the helicopter and acquired a license to build the two-seat

Egyptian anti-aircraft fire brought down several Royal Navy aircraft during the Suez Crisis. This late variant de Havilland Sea Venom strike fighter from No. 893 Squadron was forced to make a belly landing on HMS Eagle because of a damaged landing gear hydraulic system. (Imperial War Museum)

The Westland Dragonfly was a military version of the Sikorsky S-51 intended for rescue of downed airmen and for air patrol during carrier air operations. A prototype is shown here. (Westland Helicopters Ltd., Courtesy P.D. Batten)

Sikorsky S-51, to be known as the Westland Dragonfly. This military version was a utility type for the rescue of ditched plane crews and for patrols over carriers during air operations. The Dragonfly was fitted with a pulley-fitted swing arm which could be extended off the side of the fuselage to hoist rescued personnel aboard.

Dragonfly main rotor was 49 feet in diameter and overall length was 57 feet-6 1/2 inches. Height was 12 feet-11 inches. The 550 horsepower engine propelled the 5,870 pound gross weight craft to a top speed of 103 miles per hour.

Westland Wasp and The MATCH System

As with the U.S. Navy, the Royal Navy had adopted the concept of using the helicopter as a weapons launcher without onboard detection equipment and it was, therefore, incapable of independent search operations. The Westland Wasp HAS.1 made its first flight on October 28, 1962, having been developed from the original P.531 which first flew in July 1958. Unlike the U.S. DASH helicopter, the Wasp was manned by a crew of two. The MATCH (MAnned Torpedo-Carrying Helicopter) concept was based on the speed of reaction and maneuverability of the helicopter to deliver homing torpedoes against fast nuclear submarines.

This Royal New Zealand Navy Westland Wasp HAS.1 antisubmarine light helicopter was designed to launch homing torpedoes against nuclear submarines. Observe the castoring four-wheel landing gear which wheels can be locked in place. (Westland Helicopters Ltd., Courtesy P.D. Batten)

Three Westland Dragonfly helicopters and two Westland Whirlwind helicopters perform a simultaneous takeoff from HMS Ocean. Whirlwinds are in the distance (arrow No.1). Note the swing arm hoist on the nearest Dragonfly (arrow No.2). (Westland Helicopters Ltd., Courtesy P.D. Batten)

The Westland Wasp light helicopter fuselage length was 30 feet-4 inches and the four-bladed rotor diameter was 32 feet-3 inches. Overall height was 11 feet-8 inches. Empty weight was 3,452 pounds while maximum flying weight was 5,500 pounds. The single 720 shaft horsepower Bristol Siddeley Nimbus turboshaft engine propelled the Wasp to a maximum speed of 120 miles per hour. Service ceiling was 12,200 feet and range was 263 miles. The normal weapons load comprised two Mk 44/46 homing torpedoes or two AS.11 ASM (Anti Submarine Missiles). Two stretchers or three passengers could be carried behind the cabin.

Over 70 Westland Wasps were delivered to the Royal Navy, where it remained the standard light ASW helicopter until replaced by the Westland Lynx. The Wasp was also exported to the Netherlands (12), Brazil (3), New Zealand (2) and South Africa (10).

Sikorsky HRS

Several versions of the Sikorsky S-55 commercial helicopter were used by the U.S. Army, Navy and Marine Corps during the early 1950s. The most renown and numerous variants were the HRS-1, HRS-2 and HRS-3 troop-carrying helicopters for the U.S. Navy and Marine Corps. The carrying capacity was eight battle-ready troops plus the pilot. Self-sealing fuel tanks were fitted.

The HRS-2 was built by the Sikorsky Aircraft Division of United Aircraft Corporation. It was powered by a 550 horsepower Pratt & Whitney R-1340 9-cylinder, air-cooled, radial engine which gave the helicopter a 101 miles per hour speed at 1,000 feet. Service ceiling was 10,500 feet and range was 370 miles. Empty weight was 4,590 pounds while maximum loaded weight was 7,900 pounds. The three-bladed main rotor diameter was 53 feet-O inches and fuselage length was 42 feet-2 inches. Overall height is 13 feet-4 inches. A total of 235 HRS variants were ordered by the U.S. Navy and Marine Corps with deliveries starting on April 2, 1951, in time to see action in the Korean War.

The Sikorsky HRS troop carrying helicopter could carry eight battle-ready troops plus the pilot and was capable of landing in the roughest terrain to discharge or pick up the troops. An HRS-1 is shown here. (United Technologies/Sikorsky Archives)

Westland Whirlwind

Westland Helicopters Limited made arrangements with Sikorsky to construct its own version of the S-55 in Britain. Instead of a troop carrier, Westland envisioned an ASW (Anti Submarine Warfare) helicopter. Designated Whirlwind HAS Mark 7, the helicopter was to combine the search and destroy roles as did the Grumman Tracker. Westland modified the fuselage bottom to provide an open bay to house a homing torpedo and equipped the Whirlwind with a submarine detection suite.

The four-wheel Westland Whirlwind had a rotor diameter of 54 feet-0 inches. Fuselage length was 41 feet-8 1/2 inches, while overall height was 15 feet-4 1/2 inches. Weighing 5,170 pounds empty and 7,800 pounds loaded, a 750 horsepower Alvis Leonides

This Sikorsky HRS hovers as it lowers supplies for Marine Troopers. The helicopter was capable of lifting a load of over 3,300 pounds. The radial engine is mounted in the nose. Ship-based helicopter beachhead support can ensure victory. (United Technologies/Sikorsky Archives)

Major radial engine propelled the aircraft to a top speed of 10 miles per hour. Range was 335 miles at 86 miles per hour. The piston engine was later replaced by a turboshaft engine, which improved performance.

The Westland Whirlwind HAS Mark 7 entered service with the Royal Navy in 1957.

Sikorsky Seabat/Seahorse

Meanwhile, the U.S. Navy requested that Sikorsky prepare a new ASW helicopter, based upon the Sikorsky Model S-58 commercial design.

The U.S. Navy ordered a prototype on June 30, 1952, designated XHSS-1. First flight was made on March 8, 1954, after which

Britain's Westland Whirlwind was an ASW version of the Sikorsky HRS. This is the Whirlwind Series 3 in which the piston engine was replaced by a 1,050 shaft horsepower Bristol Siddeley Gnome turboshaft engine. The new engine was installed in the nose. Note the large turbine exhaust and the longer nose than the Sikorsky HRS. (Westland Helicopters Ltd., Courtesy P.D. Batten)

The U.S. Navy ordered Sikorsky HSS Seabat helicopters for antisubmarine warfare in 1954. Seabats operated in pairs as a hunterkiller team. Because of the official designation HSS, the Seabat became widely known as "Hiss." (U.S. National Archives)

a production contract was issued. The Marine Corps ordered a transport and utility variant seven months later. The Navy ASW production model was designated HSS-1 Seabat while the Marine assault variant was designated HUS-1 Seahorse.

Sikorsky Seabat

Despite the official name of Seabat, the HSS-1 became known as "Hiss" because of the official designation letters.

Seabats planted sonobuoys, towed passive sonar "fish" and dipped ASDIC search equipment to detect and locate submarines. Since the load-carrying capability of the HSS-1 was limited, Seabats could only operate either as search/hunters or destroy/killers. The type was forced to operate in pairs as a hunter/killer team; however, it had become customary for the Seabats to search and to call upon destroyers or other ships to make the kill. Seabat killers had two externally mounted homing torpedoes.

HSS-1 was equipped with a Sikorsky automatic stabilization system, AN/APN-97 Doppler navigation equipment and an automatic hover coupler. The Seabat was operated by a crew of four. Delivery of the 350 Seabats to antisubmarine squadrons began in August 1955. In order to facilitate stowage aboard ships, the rotor blades could be folded back and the tail rotor pylon/fin folded 180 degrees against the fuselage side.

A single experimental Seabat was fitted with two General Electric T58 turboshaft engines instead of the reciprocating radial engine in order to evaluate gas turbine power for helicopters.

The U.S. Marine Corps ordered assault versions of the Seabat called the Seahorse HUS. A Seahorse is shown delivering a jeep to USS Hornet (CVS-12). (Official U.S. Marine Corps Photo, Courtesy United Technologies/Sikorsky Archives)

Sikorsky Seahorses could deliver troops from ships to the battlefield and are shown here taking off after discharging U.S. Marines and war materiel. The Seahorse could accommodate 12 fully equipped infantrymen. (Official U.S. Marine Corps Photo)

This unusual photo shows a Sikorsky Seahorse with inflated pontoons used for water operation. The doughnut-shaped floats encircle the wheels so the wheels need not be removed when operating with the floats. The floats can also be used for land operation. (Official U.S. Marine Corps Photo)

Sikorsky Seahorse

The Sikorsky HUS-1 Seahorse was powered with one 1,525 horsepower Wright R-1820-84 radial engine giving the aircraft a top speed of 123 miles per hour. Service ceiling was 9,500 feet and range was 182 miles. Empty weight was 7,900 pounds, while fully loaded weight was 14,000 pounds. The four-bladed main rotor diameter was 56 feet-0 inches. Fuselage length was 46 feet-9 inches and over-all height was 15 feet-11 inches. The Seahorse could carry 12 troops plus two pilots.

Marine Corps Seahorse production totalled 384 aircraft with deliveries starting in February 1957. During 1962 HSS-1 was re-designated SH-34 and HUS-1 became UH-34.

Westland Wessex

As with the Whirlwind, Westland obtained a license to build the Seabat and modified the design to meet Royal Navy requirements. The Prototype Westland Wessex, as the craft was called, was an imported Sikorsky HSS-1 that Westland re-engined with a 1,450 shaft horsepower Rolls-Royce Gazelle Mk. 161 turboshaft engine. This replaced the American piston reciprocating engine original equipment. The conversion first flew on May 17, 1957 and proved so successful that several other helicopter manufacturers took note and the gas turbine soon became the favorite helicopter powerplant.

In addition to its submarine detection equipment the Wessex HAS Mk.1 was well-armed to assume the combined hunter/killer role. Two externally mounted homing torpedoes were carried on the fuselage sides.

These could be supplemented or replaced with four Nord AS-11 wire-guided missiles, multi-barrel machine guns, rocket launchers or four depth bombs.

Sikorsky Seahorse assault helicopters are shown approaching an advanced base. Of interest are the louvers on the fuselage top (arrow). (Official U.S. Marine Corps Photo, Courtesy United Technologies/Sikorsky Archives)

This Royal Australian Navy Westland Wessex reveals the engine tailpipes exhausting out the fuselage below the cockpit and the air inlet near the rotor hub. (Westland Helicopters Ltd., Courtesy P.D. Batten)

The Westland Wessex HAS.3 was an improved hunter/killer fitted with a 1,600 horsepower Rolls-Royce Gazelle Mk. 165 turboshaft engine. A new search radar was installed with the antenna in a dorsal radome located just behind the cabin. Next, was a troop-carrying version, HU.5, powered by two 1,350 horsepower Rolls-Royce Mk. 110/111 Gnome gas turbines. This variant could carry large external loads such as military vehicles and artillery and land them while in a hovering mode.

The Wessex served aboard the carriers *HMS Albion*, *HMS Bulwark* and *HMS Hermes*.

Wessex Data

The Westland Wessex had a main rotor diameter of 56 feet; fuselage length of 48 feet-4 1/2 inches; and height of 16 feet-2 inches.

Empty weight (HAS.3) 7,850 pounds and (HU.5) 8,657 pounds, while maximum flying weight was (HAS.3) 12,570 pounds and (HU.5) 13,500 pounds. Maximum speed was 134 miles per hour and service ceiling was about 12,000 feet. Range was 290 miles.

The HAS.3 and HU.5 were the Royal Navy's standard ASW and assault helicopters, respectively, for over 20 years!

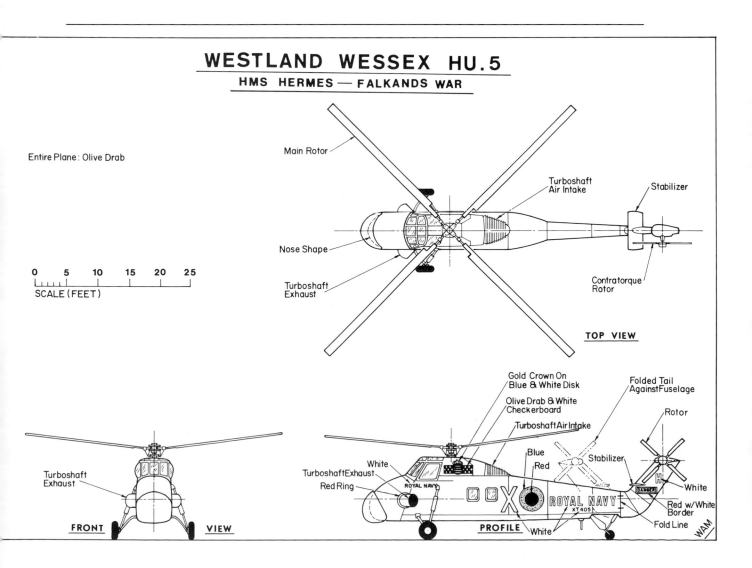

WESTLAND WESSEX HU.5
HMS HERMES — FALKANDS WAR

Kaman Seasprite

During July 1959 the Kaman Aircraft SH-2 Seasprite made its maiden flight and was accepted by the U.S. Navy in 1962 as its first standard LAMPS (Light Airborne Multi-Purpose System) helicopter. The Seasprite was configured for the ASW and antimissile defense roles, carrying two tons of special equipment including a powerful search radar, sonobuoys, MAD and advanced avionics. As LAMPS-I the Seasprite was also called upon to conduct Search and Rescue missions (SAR); assume the assault role by carrying 11 fully equipped troops; complete VERTREP (VERTical REPlenishment) tasks with 4,000 pound loads on its cargo hook; and engage in tactical strikes using fixed machine guns, rockets or grenade launchers. Antisubmarine armament included two externally mounted Mk.46 homing torpedoes.

Probably the outstanding feature of the Kaman Seasprite was the low vibration rotor design which was able to absorb the energy input of two 1,350 horsepower General Electric T58-8F turboshaft engines with an airframe that weighed only 7,000 pounds.

Seasprite Data

Maximum speed was 165 miles per hour with service ceiling a respectable 22,500 feet. Range was 367 miles and mission endurance was 2 hours-30 minutes. Main rotor diameter, which folded for stow-

The Kaman SH-2 Seasprite became the U.S. Navy's first standard LAMPS (Light Airborne Multi-Purpose System) helicopter in 1962. It was a combination assault, search and rescue, ASW, and vertical replenishment helicopter. (Kaman Aircraft)

age, was 44 feet-0 inches and fuselage length was 40 feet-6 inche Height was 13 feet-7 inches. The maximum flying weight wa 12,800 pounds.

The LAMPS Seasprite helicopters served on carriers as we as cruisers, destroyers, and frigates, plus other warships that we

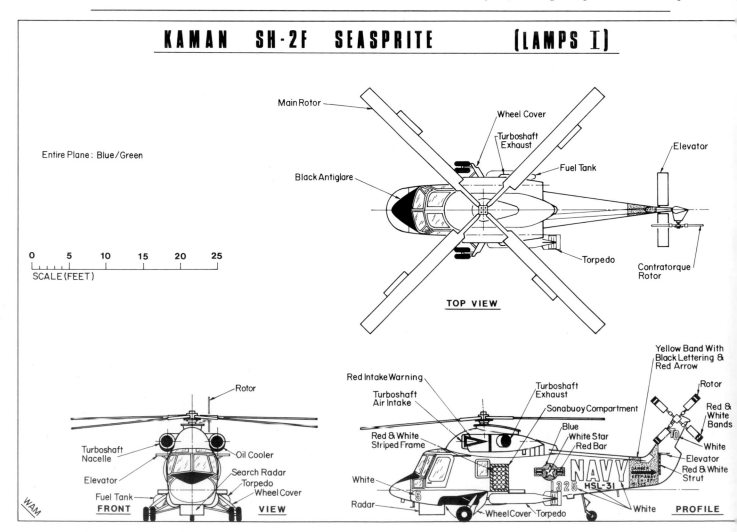

Two 1,350 horsepower turboshaft engines drove a low vibration main rotor on the Seasprite LAMPS I. The Kaman SH-2 shown is planting an ASW sonabuoy. Note the ASW torpedo on the fuselage side. (Official U.S. Navy Photograph, News Photo Division)

beginning to provide accommodations for helicopter operation and stowage. LAMPS-I system was the embarked air arm for a number of ships, especially the *Knox* DE 1052 class of dedicated ASW Destroyer Escorts.

U.S. Navy New Assault Helicopter Carriers

The success of the converted *Casablanca* class escort carrier USS *Thetis Bay* (LPH-1) as the first assault helicopter carrier in 1956 plus the performance of *HMS Theseus* and *HMS Ocean* during the Suez Crisis convinced the U.S. Marine Corps of the overwhelming advantages of having ships capable of bringing troops and military equipment to assault beaches by air to implement its Vertical Envelopment concept. After modifying three *Essex* class carriers as interim helicopter assault ships, it was decided to develop a class of purpose-built specialized helicopter assault ships.

Design Requirements

Although constructed with full flight decks and resembling aircraft carriers, these new ships were to be part of the amphibious forces. They were not fleet units intended for conventional carrier functions. In addition, because assault forces seldom move at more than 20 knots, high-powered machinery was not necessary. The assault helicopter carrier required a capacious hull to carry the necessary helicopters, troops and equipment to the beach as well as retrieve the troops and equipment as necessary, plus provide care for the wounded. These requirements led to the design of a voluminous merchant hull rather than a sleek naval hull.

LPH *Iwo Jima* Class Data

This new class comprised seven ships constructed at three different shipyards: *Iwo Jima* (LPH-2) Puget Sound shipyard, *Okinawa* (LPH-3) Philadelphia Navy Yard, *Guadalcanal* (LPH-7) Philadelphia Navy Yard, *Guam* (LPH-9) Philadelphia Navy Yard, *Tripoli* (LPH-10) Ingalls Shipbuilding, *New Orleans* (LPH-11) Philadelphia Navy Yard, and *Inchon* (LPH-12) Ingalls Shipbuilding.

The chin-mounted Radar Dome (Radome) on this Kaman HH-2D Seasprite is collapsible. With a diameter of 6 feet-8 inches the Radome can be expanded downward from 12 inches to a fully extended 52 inches and can be collapsed to 12 inches again when the helicopter is to land. (Official U.S. Navy Photograph, News Photo Division)

This Kaman UH-2A Seasprite spreads U.S. Navy "Purple K" Sodium Bicarbonate type fire extinguishing powder in way of flaming fuel from a crashed plane while fire fighters approach the wreck to recue the pilot in this exercise. (Official U.S. Navy Photograph, Naval Imaging Command)

The rounded Flight Deck of the Iwo Jima class helicopter assault ships is clearly evident in this photo. Sikorsky Sea Stallion helicopters are shown on the Deck of USS New Orleans (LPH-11). (Official U.S. Navy Photograph)

The *Iwo Jima* class vessels have an overall length of 592 feet and a hull beam of 84 feet, while the flight deck width is 105 feet. Displacement is 17,000 tons standard or light and 18,300 tons deep load while the respective drafts were 25 feet and 26 feet-7 inches. Four boilers generate steam for a steam turbine unit geared to a single propeller shaft. The 22,000 shaft horsepower propels the ship to 20 knots maximum. The helicopter hangar is 230 feet long and 20 feet high with space to stow and service about 25 helicopters. This is served by deck edge elevators, one each port and starboard. At their lowermost position the elevators can be folded upward against the hull to close the hangar openings. Accommodation for U.S. Marine battalion of about 2,000 troops is provided forward and aft of the hangar. A fully equipped hospital with 300 beds was also installed in the hull. Ship command and amphibious operations command facilities were located in the island. The originally installed defensive armament was four twin 3 inch, .50 inch caliber guns; two at each side of the stern and two on the flight deck just forward of the island. These have been replaced with two Mk.25 Basic Point Defense Missile System (BPDMS) Sea Sparrow eight shot launchers and directors.

Iwo Jima keel was laid on February 13, 1959, launched on September 17, 1960, and commissioned on October 30, 1961 as the first vessel to be built from the keel up as an assault helicopter carrier. *USS Inchon* was the last of the class to be started on April 8, 1968.

UNUSUAL FIXED WING ASW AIRCRAFT

As relations became increasingly strained between the Eastern and Western Allies during the postwar years, the ever-growing Soviet

Sikorsky Sea Stallion helicopters have become standard equipment on Iwo Jima class LPH ships. In order to accommodate a hospital, Marine battalion, equipment and helicopters a broad commercial hull was used instead of a sleek, high-speed naval hull. Observe the Hangar doors beneath the deck edge elevator and the four 3 inch-.50 caliber guns forward of the island (arrows). (United Technologies/Sikorsky Archives)

SS Okinawa (LPH-3) is shown steaming with Boeing Vertol Sea Knight *licopters ranged on Deck. Note the Sea Sparrow missile launcher *rward of the island that has replaced the four 3 inch guns. (Official *.S. Navy Photograph, News Photo Division)

Fairey Gannet AS.1 ASW hunter/killer aircraft of No.805 Squadron from HMS Eagle are shown flying over the Mediterranean. The Gannet was powered by two turboprop engines, arranged side-by-side in the fuselage, each driving one of the two four-bladed co-axial contrarotating propellers. Note the three separate cockpits for pilot and two radar operators. (Imperial War Museum)

*bmarine fleet caused such consternation among NATO members *at the French Aeronavale and the Fleet Air Arm busied them- *lves with the development of potent shipboard ASW aircraft, both *f which were unusual and innovative. The German Federal Navy *ad also indicated an interest to purchase ASW aircraft from either *rance or Britain.

airey Gannet

*he British antisubmarine hunter/killer three-seat Gannet was Fairey *viation Company's last naval design; thereby, ending a long line *f distinguished Fleet Air Arm aircraft. The prototype was ordered *1 August 1946, based upon Admiralty Specification GR.17/45, in *reference to a competing Blackburn design. A twin-engine craft *as necessary in order to extend the range by flying on one engine *uring the hunter phase and on two engines for the killer phase of *1e operation. Single-engine performance of typical twin-engine *lanes often tends to force the plane to yaw in the direction of the *topped engine, but the Fairey designers found an innovative solu- *on to this problem.

*his underside view of a Gannet AS.1 reveals the retractable cylindrical *adar dome (arrow No.1) and the turboprop engine exhaust (arrow *Jo.2). Also of interest are the co-axial contrarotating propellers (arrow *Jo.3) and the supplementary tail fins (arrow No.4). (Fairey Aviation)

Novel Engine Installation

Inspired by the 440 miles per hour Italian World Speed Record hold-ing Macchi Castoldi MC-72 of 1933, the Fairey design placed both engines within the fuselage; however, unlike the tandem-arranged reciprocating engines of the Macchi, the Fairey Gannet mounted the two turboprop engines side-by-side. Each engine was geared to one of two co-axial, contrarotating propellers and each engine was controlled independently so that one engine could be shut down and its propeller feathered for the economy of single-engine opera-tion. The power unit consisted of two Armstrong Siddeley Mamba turboprop engines mounted together as a single unit with the re-duction gears. This was called the Double Mamba 100 and deliv-ered 2,950 horsepower. The new engine arrangement began testing in 1948, while the Gannet prototype was under construction.

Fairey Gannet Features

The prototype first flew on September 19, 1949 and featured an exceptionally large fuselage weapons bay which was sized to ac-commodate either two homing torpedoes, or depth charges, or para-chute mines. This cavernous bay forced the wing location upwards to clear the prodigious amount of internal stores, which created two problems: an unusually long landing gear and overhead clearance in carrier hangars for the large wing, when folded. These were, somewhat, relieved with a slight inverted gull wing arrangement. Despite this configuration, when the wing outer panels folded up-wards over the fuselage almost half of the outer panels had to fold again outward to clear the relatively low hangar height of Royal Navy carriers; thus requiring two main folding hinge points for each wing half. A cylindrical retractable radar dome was located on the fuselage bottom, aft of the weapons bay.

Gannet AS.1 Production and Deployment

After an intensive flying development program a production order for 100 Fairey AS.1 Gannets was issued in March 1951. The first AS.1 production craft experienced its initial flight in June 1953 and the type equipped Nos. 824, 825 and 826 Squadrons.

A T.2 training, dual-control Gannet made its appearance in

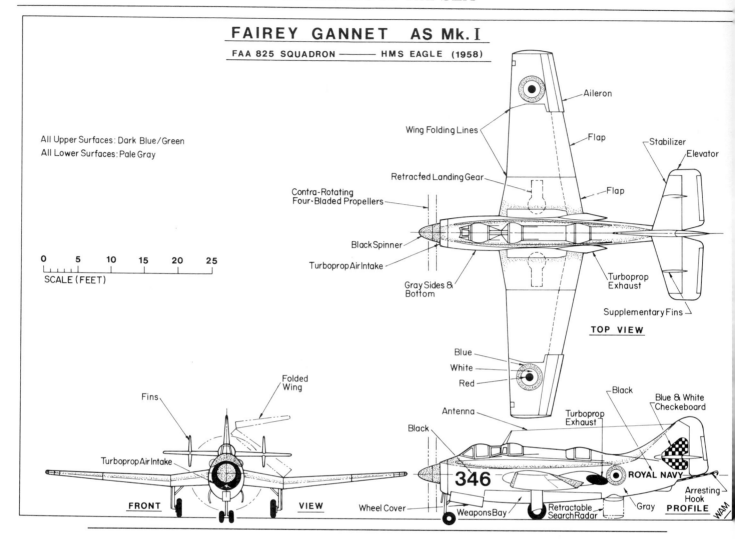

FAIREY GANNET AS Mk. I

FAA 825 SQUADRON ———— HMS EAGLE (1958)

All Upper Surfaces: Dark Blue/Green
All Lower Surfaces: Pale Gray

SCALE (FEET)
0   5   10   15   20   25

Aileron

Wing Folding Lines

Flap

Stabilizer

Elevator

Retracted Landing Gear

Flap

Contra-Rotating
Four-Bladed Propellers

Black Spinner

Turboprop Air Intake

Gray Sides &
Bottom

Turboprop
Exhaust

Supplementary Fins

TOP VIEW

Blue
White
Red

Antenna

Black

Turboprop
Exhaust

Black

Blue & White
Checkeboard

Fins

Folded
Wing

Turboprop Air Intake

FRONT   **VIEW**

346

ROYAL NAVY

Arresting
Hook

Wheel Cover

Weapons Bay

Retractable
Search Radar

Gray

PROFILE

August 1954, of which 36 were produced. Radar was omitted on this variant.

Airborne Early Warning Gannet AEW.3
The next version represented a radical departure from the AS.1. Designated AEW.3, this variant was designed to replace the Douglas Skyraider as the Fleet Air Arm's standard Airborne Early Warning (AEW) aircraft. The fuselage had been redesigned to eliminate the two radar operator cockpits; housing the two electronics crew members in a cabin within the fuselage. A new tail with a squared off fin and rudder had also been fitted. A huge belly radome replaced the retractable radome of the AS variant.

The 43 production AEW.3 Gannets served only with No. 849 Squadron, entering service in late 1960. This squadron's four flights were assigned separately aboard the Royal Navy aircraft carriers *Hermes, Centaur, Victorious, Eagle,* and *Ark Royal,* at various times until 1979 when this Gannet variant was retired.

Gannet AS.4
The next antisubmarine variant of the Gannet was the AS.4 which first flew on April 13, 1956. This variant was virtually identical with the AS.1 except for the more powerful 3,035 horsepower Armstrong Siddeley Double Mamba 101 engine. A total of 90 AS.4

Gannets were procured and, together with the AS.1, formed the backbone of the Fleet Air Arm's antisubmarine operations until the were gradually phased out and replaced with the Westland Whirlwind helicopter by the mid-1960s.

Gannet AS.4 Data
The AS.4 Gannet had a wingspan of 54 feet-4 inches and a length of 43 feet-0 inches. Height was 13 feet-8 inches. The 22,506 loaded weight plane had a top speed of 300 miles per hour. Cruising speed was 150 miles per hour with a range of 662 miles. Empty weight of the all-metal craft was 15,069 pounds. Service ceiling was 25,000 feet.

In addition to the internal stores, provision was made to carry (16) 60 pound rockets in underwing launchers on the AS.1 and AS.4

Specialized electronic equipment was often fitted to the AS.4 in which case it was redesignated AS.6 and AS.7.

Exports
Fairey Gannets were exported to the navies of the German Federal Republic, Australia, and Indonesia.

The Fairey Gannet will be remembered forever as one of the most remarkably innovative and unusual naval aircraft of all time.

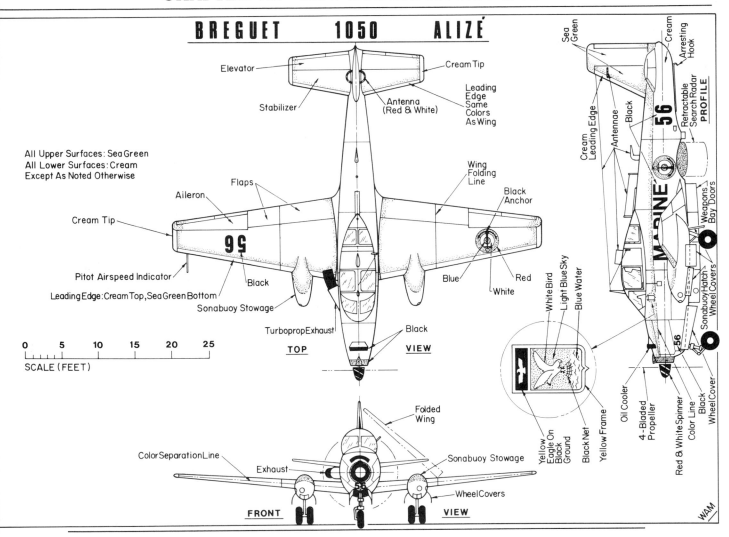

BREGUET 1050 ALIZÉ

Elevator

Cream Tip

Leading Edge Same Colors As Wing

Stabilizer

Antenna (Red & White)

Wing Folding Line

Black Anchor

All Upper Surfaces: Sea Green
All Lower Surfaces: Cream
Except As Noted Otherwise

Flaps

Aileron

Cream Tip

Pitot Airspeed Indicator

Leading Edge: Cream Top, Sea Green Bottom

Black

Sonabuoy Stowage

Turboprop Exhaust

Blue

Red

White

Black

TOP   **VIEW**

0 5 10 15 20 25
SCALE (FEET)

Sea Green

Cream

Arresting Hook

Retractable Search Radar

PROFILE

Cream Leading Edge

Antennae

Black

MARINE 56

Weapons Bay Doors

Sonabuoy Hatch Wheel Covers

56

White Bird

Light Blue Sky

Blue Water

Yellow Eagle On Black Ground

Black Net

Yellow Frame

Oil Cooler

4-Bladed Propeller

Red & White Spinner

Color Line

Black

Wheel Cover

Folded Wing

Color Separation Line

Exhaust

Sonabuoy Stowage

Wheel Covers

FRONT   **VIEW**

WAM

The French Aeronavale's Breguet Br. 1050 carrier-based antisubmarine aircraft was powered by a single turboprop engine driving the propeller. The wing nacelles housed the retractable landing gear and stowed sonabuoys. Note the lowered tailhook (arrow). (WAM Foto)

Breguet Alize

Concurrent with the Gannet development, the French Aeronavale prepared its own ASW design. The French Breguet Br.1050 Alize (Trade-wind) three-seat carrier-based antisubmarine aircraft was derived from a previous Breguet design begun in 1948 as a strike aircraft. The Breguet Br. 960 Vultur strike plane had made its first flight on August 8, 1951. The craft was fitted with a composite powerplant consisting of an Armstrong Siddeley Mamba turboprop engine in the nose plus a French-built Rolls-Royce Nene turbojet in the fuselage rear. This enabled the plane to cruise economically with the propeller and attain high speeds with the turbojet. Two prototypes of the Vultur were completed; however, no production orders were forthcoming for this company project. When the Aeronavale indicated an interest in ASW aircraft, Breguet adapted the Vultur design to meet the French Navy requirements. Since high speed was no longer necessary, the turbojet-engine was replaced with a retractable cylindrical radar scanner.

Engine Change + Third Seat = Contract

The Mamba powerplant was replaced by the more powerful Rolls-Royce Dart turboprop and the side-by-side seating was supplemented with a third radar operator's seat behind the original seats. The Aeronavale was impressed by the Alize potential and ordered two prototypes and three preproduction aircraft in late 1954. The first Br. 1050 flew on October 26, 1956 and it proved so successful that a contract for 70 production aircraft was awarded.

Alize Data

The 12,570 pounds empty and 18,190 pounds loaded plane was powered with a single 2,100 horsepower Rolls-Royce Dart R.Da.21 single-shaft turboprop engine which gave the plane a 285 miles per hour top speed at sea level. Range was 1,350 miles which gave the Alize a 4 1/2 hours endurance flight. Service ceiling was 20,500 feet. Wingspan was 51 feet-2 inches while overall length was 44 feet-10 1/2 inches. Height was 15 feet 9 inches.

Principal armament consists of one torpedo or three 350 pound depth charges stowed in the fuselage weapons bay. Racks under the inboard wing panels can accommodate two more depth charges. The outer wing panels are fitted with six 5 inch rocket launchers or Nord SS.11 air-to-surface missiles. Breguet solved the sonabuoy stowage problem by designing two streamline nacelles to fit over the wing leading edge and under the wing in way of the landing gear. The nacelles serve the dual purpose of stowing the sonabuoys and housing the landing gear when retracted. The wing folded upwards and over the fuselage.

The last Alize was delivered to the Aeronavale in 1961 and the planes served on the aircraft carriers *Clemenceau* and *Foch*. India purchased 17 for use with the Indian aircraft carrier *Vikrant*. As with the Gannet, the Alize was gradually replaced by helicopters.

Hawker Hunter

Although not used in the combat role by the Fleet Air Arm, the Hawker Hunter T.8 and GA.11 were used for advanced training purposes. The Hawker Hunter was designed for the RAF as a single-seat subsonic day-fighter and exhibited such excellent handling qualities at all speeds that it remained in first line service with many air forces for over a quarter-century.

The Hunter Mk.1 went into RAF service in July 1954 and th T.Mk.7, a two-seat trainer variant for the RAF, appeared in 1957. navalized version of the T.Mk.7 was developed for the FAA throug the addition of an arresting hook, the T.Mk.8. This aircraft entere service with the Fleet Air Arm in July 1958.

Hunter Variants and Data

The Hawker Hunter T.Mk.8 featured side-by-side seating with du controls. The Aden cannon and radar ranging equipment were r placed with TACAN (TACticAl Navigation) for its advanced train role. Three Royal Navy squadrons were equipped with the (4 T.Mk.8 trainers delivered. A small number of these craft were i sued as communications and command aircraft to Flag Officers an these aircraft remained in service into the 1980s.

The (40) Hawker GA.Mk.11 Hunters were single-seat al weather strike/fighter trainers for pilots who graduated from th T.Mk.8. First delivery to FAA squadrons was in 1962 where th GA.Mk.11 was used extensively for weapons training.

A single 7,550 pounds static thrust Rolls-Royce Avon 122 gav the T.Mk.8 a top speed of Mach 0.92 at 36,000 feet, which is ju under supersonic speed. Service ceiling is 47,000 feet. Empty weig is 13,360 pounds while loaded weight is 17,200 pounds. The T.Mk. wingspan is 33 feet-8 inches and overall length is 48 feet-10 inche Height is 13 feet-2 inches. Projected wing area is 349 square fee

Production and Export

A total of 1,985 Hawker Hunter day fighters were constructed i Britain, Holland and Belgium and the aircraft is used by the arme forces of Denmark, Iraq, Sweden, Rhodesia, India, Jordan, Swi zerland, Lebanon, Saudi Arabia, Peru and Kuwait.

Many navalized Hawker Hunter T Mk.8 were issued to the Fleet Air Arm as advanced trainers and as communications and command aircraft for Flag Officers. A Hawker Hunter T.8 (foreground) and two Harrier variants from 809 Naval Squadron are shown flying in formation. Compare the muted markings on the Harriers with the bright markings on the Hunter. (British Aerospace, Courtesy Brendan Morrissey)

The first of the three so-called "Improved Forrestal" class Supercarriers was USS Kitty Hawk (CVA-63); however, they are officially known as the Kitty Hawk class. Note the Vought Crusaders forward; Grumman Tracker on the elevator; Grumman Intruders forward of the island and McDonnell Douglas Phantom II fighters aft. (Official U.S. Navy Photograph by PH1 D.B. Wood)

U.S. CARRIERS BUSY WORLD-WIDE

U.S. aircraft carriers and their Warbirds were called upon for U.S. power projection in trouble spots throughout the world in the 1950s.

U.S. Navy Skyraiders Score Chinese Planes

Conditions in the Far East were still in turmoil, placing Vice Admiral A.M. Pride's U.S. Seventh Fleet on constant alert. On July 26, 1954 two Communist Chinese LA-7 fighters attacked two U.S. Navy Skyraiders near the South China Sea island of Hainan. The Americans fought back and shot down both Chinese planes. Then the Communist Chinese government declared, on August 11, that Nationalist-held Formosa (Taiwan) must be liberated by Communist China but President Eisenhower replied that it will be necessary to run over the Seventh Fleet to do so! On September 13 President Eisenhower ordered the Seventh Fleet to provide logistic support in the defense of the islands of Matsu and Quemoy against Communist Chinese aggression.

Lebanon

American carriers and their Warbirds were busy in the Mediterranean to maintain the peace with Sixth Fleet carriers *Essex* (CV-9), *Wasp* (CV-18) and *Saratoga* (CVA-60) covering three Marine battalion landings in Lebanon on July 15, 1958 when Lebanese President Chamoun requested U.S. aid to quell the threat of imminent war.

China

Another crisis involving U.S. carriers developed on August 23, when Communist China launched an intensive artillery bombardment of Nationalist Chinese islands of Matsu and Quemoy. President Eisenhower deployed a Seventh Fleet six-carrier task force around the large island of Formosa (Taiwan) to warn the Communists. All was quiet by the end of the year.

Cuba

Closer to the U.S. on October 24, 1958 the carrier *Franklin D. Roosevelt* (CVA-42) covered the evacuation of Americans and foreign nationals from Nicara, Cuba as Castro and his Communist revolution approached a climax.

NEW *KITTY HAWK* CLASS SUPERCARRIERS

By 1961, the three so-called "Improved *Forrestal*" class Supercarriers were under construction. Despite this most used description, there were significant differences from the *Forrestal* class because of the demands imposed upon them by the dramatic development in shipboard aircraft design; nor were the ships identical sisters. The three new supercarriers are *Kitty Hawk* (CVA-63), *Constellation* (CVA-64), and *America* (CVA-66). Although originally designated CVA, the *Kitty Hawk* class was redesignated to CV in the early and mid-1970s.

USS Constellation (CVA-64) was the second ship of the Kitty Hawk class. One of the most obvious changes from the Forrestal class was the relocation of the island aft so that two elevators were forward of the island and only one aft of the island. Observe the large sponson supporting the island. (Official U.S. Navy Photograph, News Photo Division)

Kitty Hawk Class Mods

USS Kitty Hawk and *USS Constellation* were launched on May 21, and October 8, respectively in 1960. They differed from *USS Forrestal* in that the Flight Deck of the new ships had increased area and the port side elevator had been relocated from the forward to the aft end of the Flight Deck. All four elevators were enlarged to accommodate bigger aircraft through the addition of a triangular area at the forward outboard corner. This scheme was used on all subsequent U.S. carriers because it enabled the handling of larger aircraft without adding excessive weight to the elevator platform structure. The island was moved aft which resulted in a rearrangement of the starboard side elevators; two elevators forward of the island and one elevator aft of the island. Aviation fuel stowage was more than doubled to 1,900,000 gallons due to the increased fuel consumption of heavier, more powerful planes. Aircraft were influencing carrier design more than ever.

First Missile-Armed Carriers

The *Kitty Hawk* class were the first U.S. Navy carriers armed with missiles; two Mk.10 Terrier missile launchers having been initialy installed. This required the installation of an SPG-55 missile guidance radar antenna and when surveillance antennae were added it was necessary to install a lattice-type mast for this new equipment just aft of the island.

Kitty Hawk Class Data

Complement was the same as *Forrestal* at 4,950 crew and air wing. Displacement had increased to 60,100 tons standard and 80,800 tons deep load. The new carriers attained a higher speed of 35 knots with a larger steam powerplant of 280,000 shaft horsepower. Range was the same; however, the aircraft complement was three planes less, possibly because planes had grown in size since *Forrestal* construction had started. Overall length of *Kitty Hawk* was 1,062 feet-6 inches while *Constellation* was 10 feet longer. Beam of both ships was 129 feet-6 inches and Flight Deck width was 249 feet. As with *Forrestal*, four steam catapults were fitted. Deep load draft is 35 feet-9 inches, which is 15 inches less than *Forrestal*.

USS America

USS America was completed basically as the first two carriers except that it was equipped with SQS-23 sonar; the first Navy carrier to be so fitted. *America* also had a narrower smokestack to reduce turbulence which often carried the uptake gasses downwards onto the deck. The overall length of *USS America* was slightly less than that of her sisters at 1,047 feet-6 inches; however, the standard displacement was greater at 60,300 tons. Hull beam was 6 inches greater than *Kitty Hawk* and *Constellation* at 130 feet.

The SQS-23 sonar installation required a fair size Sonar Bulb below *America*'s bow. In order not to damage this large underwater protrusion when lowering side anchors, a single anchor was installed in the stem at the front of the bow, instead of the conventional two-anchor side locations. A beak was installed to lead the anchor chain further forward so the anchor would fall clear of the forward edge of the Sonar Bulb. This beak also seats the anchor against the hull when at sea. All other characteristics were as CV 63 and CV-64.

Kitty Hawk Class Radar and Shipyards

All three *Kitty Hawks* have SPS-43 search radar antenna and three dimensional SPS-52 search radar antenna on the island plus an SPS 30 search radar antenna on the new latticework mast. The ships are also fitted with TACAN (TACtical Airborne Navigation) aids.

CVA-63 was built by New York Shipbuilding Corp., Camden N.J.; CVA-64 by New York Naval Shipyard, Brooklyn, N.Y.; and CVA-66 by Newport News Shipbuilding & Dry Dock Co., Newport News, Virginia.

The numbers gap between CVA-64 and CVA-66 had been assigned to the world's first nuclear-powered aircraft carrier, *USS Enterprise* (CVAN-65) which was started on February 4, 1958 by Newport News and commissioned on November 25, 1961 while *Kitty Hawk*, *America* and *Constellation* were under construction.

NUCLEAR-POWERED *USS ENTERPRISE*

USS Enterprise (CVAN-65) was designed as a modified *Kitty Hawk*

The third and last Kitty Hawk class carrier was USS America (CVA-66). Notice the beak for the stem anchor which was necessary to make the anchor clear the SQS-23 Sonar Bulb below the bow, also the large sponson to support the angled Deck. A Douglas Skywarrior and a Grumman Hawkeye await launching on the forward catapults (arrows). (Official U.S. Navy Photograph by PH3 L.J. Lafeir)

class aircraft carrier in order to reduce costs, which, it was hoped, would offset the added expense of the nuclear powerplant. The U.S. Navy and Congress had vacillated since 1949 whether to fund and build a nuclear-powered carrier and finally authorized the project in 1956 for the 1958 construction program on the basis of the many technological advances in nuclear science up to that time.

Enterprise Power Plant

Eight Westinghouse A2W pressurized-water-cooled reactors provide heat to 32 heat exchangers which generated steam for the four turbine units, each geared to a propeller shaft. Total shaft horsepower is 300,000 which drives the ship to a maximum speed of 35 knots. This particular powerplant occupied much more space in the hull than the more conventional fossil-fired powerplant; however, the fuel oil normally carried was omitted and some of this tankage was used to increase the aviation fuel capacity by 50 percent. The principal advantage of nuclear power is the extremely long range afforded by the reactor, enabling *Enterprise* to sail 300,000 miles between refuelings. This gave the ship the capability of cruising in continuous operation to any troubled location in the world.

USS Enterprise (CVAN) was not only the world's first nuclear powered aircraft carrier but upon its completion was the world's largest warship and the "largest moving structure ever built by man." The flat "billboards" on the island sides are search radar and tracking beam radar antennae. (Official U.S. Navy Photograph by PH 1 O.V. Williams)

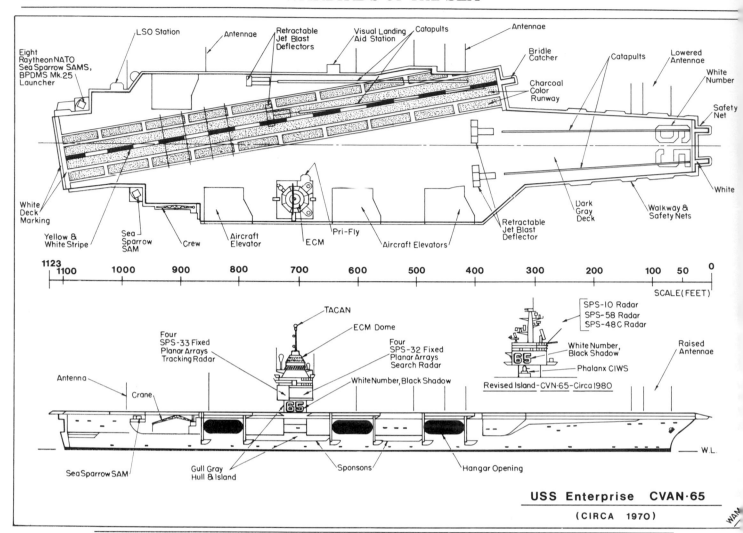

Eight Raytheon NATO Sea Sparrow SAMS, BPDMS Mk.25 Launcher

LSO Station

Antennae

Retractable Jet Blast Deflectors

Visual Landing Aid Station

Catapults

Antennae

Bridle Catcher

Catapults

Lowered Antennae

White Number

Charcoal Color Runway

Safety Net

White Deck Marking

White

Yellow & White Stripe

Sea Sparrow SAM

Crew

Aircraft Elevator

ECM

Pri-Fly

Aircraft Elevators

Retractable Jet Blast Deflector

Dark Gray Deck

Walkway & Safety Nets

1123 1100 1000 900 800 700 600 500 400 300 200 100 50 0

SCALE(FEET)

TACAN

ECM Dome

Four SPS-33 Fixed Planar Arrays Tracking Radar

Four SPS-32 Fixed Planar Arrays Search Radar

SPS-10 Radar
SPS-58 Radar
SPS-48C Radar

White Number, Black Shadow

Raised Antenna

Antenna

Crane

White Number, Black Shadow

Phalanx CIWS

Revised Island-CVN-65-Circa 1980

Sea Sparrow SAM

Gull Gray Hull & Island

Sponsons

Hangar Opening

W.L.

USS Enterprise CVAN-65

(CIRCA 1970)

Enterprise Data

The loss of interior volume due to the space required by the powerplant, plus the fact that added stores and munitions were necessary to sustain the crew and air wing for a longer period due to *Enterprise*'s range, increased the size of the ship beyond that of the *Kitty Hawks*.

USS Enterprise (CVAN-65) displaces 75,700 tons standard and 89,600 tons full load which made her the world's largest warship which has been aptly described as the "largest moving structure ever built by man." The carrier is 1,123 feet long overall, with a Flight Deck measuring 1,100 x 257 feet and covering four and one-half acres. Complement comprises 3,157 ship's officers and crew plus 2,628 air wing personnel. The cavernous Hangar, measuring 860 feet long x 107 feet side x 25 feet high, can store, repair, and service most of the 70 to 100 aircraft (depending on type) that can be accommodated aboard *USS Enterprise*.

Fixed Planar Radar and ECM

Nuclear power dispensed with the necessity for a smokestack with the attending problems caused by the corrosive boiler gasses. It also gave the designers freedom when locating the island which, on fossil-fueled carriers, is governed by the location of the boilers and uptakes. The island location followed the *Kitty Hawk*'s as did the

aircraft elevators. The *Enterprise* island was the most distinctive of all carriers with its dome and flat "billboard" sides. The absence of a smokestack unleashed the designers' imagination and eight huge fixed planar radar arrays (billboards) were installed on the four sides of the island. Four were SPS-32 search radar antennae and four were SPS-32 tracking beam radar antennae. These were selected because large fixed antennas have a greater range than the rotating types. Electronic countermeasure (ECM) antennae were installed all around the ring-shaped upper levels of the island dome.

No Defensive Armament

In order to partially offset the fact that *Enterprise* cost about 70% more than *Constellation*, which was under construction at the same time, it was completed without any defensive armament other than its aircraft in order to save money! It was planned to retrofit two Mk.10 Terrier missile launchers at a later date.

Clean Sweep on Trials

Enterprise left Newport News for builders' trials on the morning of October 29, 1961 and returned on November 3 with a big broom tied to her masthead, signifying a clean sweep in her trials. The carrier had performed so well during the first trial that the scheduled second trial was cancelled because no modifications were re

This is the view seen by a pilot making his final approach to land on USS Enterprise (except for the planes on the deck). Observe that the island is located outboard of the hull on the deck overhang. This huge carrier can sail 300,000 miles between refuelings. (Official U.S. Navy Photograph)

quired. Admiral George W. Anderson, Jr., CNO, exclaimed: "I think we hit the jackpot!" This was the truth; however, the high cost of 451.3 million dollars forced the cancellation of the five additional ships that had been planned. National Security was again measured in dollars and cents, and another decade would pass before nuclear carriers were to be funded by the U.S. Congress.

In the mid-1970s the attack designation was eliminated from all supercarriers, whereupon CVAN-65 became CVN-65 multipurpose aircraft carrier.

Enterprise Refit Mods

Armament in the form of Mk.25 Sea Sparrow BPDMS launchers were retrofitted in late 1972 instead of the originally planned Terrier missile system. During the *Enterprise* refit in 1979-1982 the Sea Sparrow was replaced with three Mk.57 NATO Sea Sparrow launchers. Three Phalanx Mk.15 20 millimeter multibarrel CIWS (Close In Weapon System) were also fitted at that time. The Phalanx is a self-contained detecting, directing and destroying system that can detect the incoming missile, aim the gun, and fire to destroy it. Three Mk.68 20 millimeter systems were also installed at this time.

The four SPS-32 and four SPS-33 billboard antennae were not only extremely expensive but also not very successful because the enormous size created severe maintenance problems; therefore, these were removed and a complete reshaping of the island was undertaken during this refit. The mast and dome were also removed because the ECM system had become obsolete since its installation. A simple, more conventional island was the result with air/surface search SPS 48C, 49 and 65 plus low level SPS 58 and search SPS

10 antennae on a central mast. An OE-82 communications satellite antenna was installed and two Mk.115 missile fire control systems were replaced with three Mk.91 systems. Three Mk.36 Chaffroc RBOC were also installed to confuse incoming homing missiles.

After the refit, the complement was reduced to 3,100 ship's crew and officers plus 2,400 members of the air wing.

The success of *USS Enterprise*, which was the eighth ship of that name in the U.S. Navy, set the stage for the current U.S. nuclear-powered aircraft carriers which have almost become commonplace and have proven themselves very safe.

USS JOHN F. KENNEDY (CVA-67)

During 1963 the U.S. Navy decided that the new supercarrier scheduled to be started in the autumn of 1964 would be nuclear-powered based upon the outstanding success of the *Enterprise* powerplant. Secretary of Defense Robert McNamara and the U.S. Congress balked at the cost and refused to provide funds for a nuclear-powered *USS John F. Kennedy*. This aircraft carrier was, therefore, destined to be constructed as an oil-fired (fossil-fuel) Supercarrier.

CVA-67 Particulars

Internally as well as externally *USS John F. Kennedy* differs considerably from the *Kitty Hawk* class and is officially recognized as a separate single-ship class. The forward end of the angled landing deck has revised contours and the smokestack is canted outboard, in the manner of some World World II Japanese carriers, to direct the smoke and boiler gasses away from the Flight Deck. As with *USS America* an anchor was installed at the stem. The stem was fitted with a long beak to guide the anchor chain and to secure the anchor when hoisted. The beak also held the anchor clear to prevent it from damaging the SQS-23 Sonar Bulb, which extends outboard beyond the hull bottom. This sonar was intended to enable the carrier to participate in ASW operations.

On May 27, 1967 Caroline Kennedy, daughter of the late president, launched the aircraft carrier USS John F. Kennedy. Photo was taken seconds after Caroline smashed the bottle against the Supercarrier's stem. President Johnson (arrow) and Mrs. Kennedy applaud the perfect launch as the spectators roar approval. (U.S. Department of Defense, Courtesy Henry Tremont)

USS John F. Kennedy (CVA-67) is a single-ship class Supercarrier. It has a conventional oil-fired power plant because the U.S. Navy's request for nuclear power plant funds was rejected by Congress and the Secretary of Defense in 1963. Note the bow anchor beak. (Official U.S. Navy Photograph, News Photo Division)

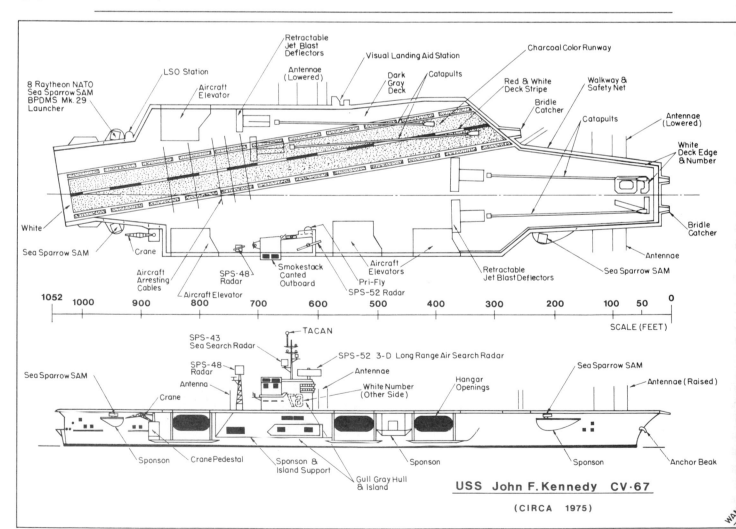

USS John F. Kennedy CV·67

(CIRCA 1975)

This view of USS John F. Kennedy clearly shows the smokestack canted outboard to direct the hot gasses away from the Flight Deck. Notice the crane on the sponson for heavy lifting, including ditched aircraft (arrow No.1) and a Sea Sparrow antiaircraft installation (arrow No.2). (Official U.S. Navy Photograph, News Photo Division by Donald D. Deverman)

The pattern of the landing runway, Flight Deck contours, and smoke drifting away from the Deck are clearly evident in this aerial view of USS John F. Kennedy. (Official U.S. Navy Photograph, News Photo Division)

CVA-67 Dimensions

The Flight Deck was three feet wider than the three *Kitty Hawk* carriers at 252 feet but her standard displacement remained at 61,000 tons while full load displacement increased to 87,000 tons. Overall length is 1,052 feet and hull beam is 130 feet. Flight Deck area is about 4 1/2 acres.

CVA-67 Electronics

USS John F. Kennedy was fitted with a SPS-43 sea search radar antenna and a three-dimensional SPS-52 air search radar antennae on the island while a SPS-48 antennae was installed on the new latticework mast. The ship was later fitted with SPS-58 search radar to detect low-flying missiles and planes. A TACAN navigation pod was also installed.

Author's Involvement

The author supervised the preparation of the all-important *USS John F. Kennedy* Damage Control Books and drawings which contain the essential information to minimize the effect of enemy-inflicted damage or for survival in the event of other serious damage. He can therefore attest to the overwhelming size and complexity of the supercarrier with its thousands of doors, hatches, valves, ventilation closures and electrical devices; a veritable self-sufficient mobile fortress that must survive the onslaught of enemy ships, aircraft and missiles.

CVA-67 Chronology

USS John F. Kennedy keel was laid on October 24, 1964; launched on May 27, 1967; and commissioned on September 7, 1968.

FRENCH POSTWAR CARRIERS AND SHIPBOARD AIRCRAFT

Throughout World Wars I and II, France had not shown as much enthusiasm for aircraft carriers as Britain and the U.S. The French attitude towards the aircraft carrier changed when the light fleet carrier *HMS Colossus* was lent to the Marine Nationale in August 1946. The British aircraft carrier was purchased five years later and renamed *Arromanches*. Flying a mix of 24 U.S.-built Corsairs, Hellcats and Helldivers, *Arromanches* was fitted with a four-de-gree angled Deck and mirror landing device in 1958. After seeing action in the Suez Crisis and Southeast Asia, she was scrapped in 1978.

A Decade of Indecision

Meanwhile, a new carrier had been proposed, called the PA 28 design. This 20,000 tons deep load displacement carrier was authorized in 1947 but was eventually cancelled due to monetary restrictions; however, the gap was filled in 1950 when the U.S. lent two *Independence* class carriers to the Marine Nationale; *Langley* and *Belleau Wood*. *Belleau Wood*, renamed *Bois Belleau*, was returned to the U.S. in 1960. *Langley*, renamed *Lafayette*, was employed as a strike carrier in the Suez Crisis and was then returned to the U.S. in 1963. Finally, in 1954 and 1955, the French government approved and funded the construction of two new light fleet aircraft carriers.

French *Clemenceau* Class Carriers

The carriers *Clemenceau* (R-98 and *Foch* (R-99) evolved from the PA 28 project and the many postwar studies that were made to de-

Vought Corsairs were flown from carriers in the Aeronavale for many years until jet fighters became available. A French F4U-7 is shown after landing on a Marine Nationale carrier. (U.S. Naval Institute Photographic Collection)

The French light fleet carrier Foch (R-99) was the second carrier of the two-ship Clemenceau class. Super Etendard strike/fighters can be seen on the forward Flight Deck while Alize ASW aircraft are on the after Flight Deck. Four of the eight multi-purpose guns are clearly evident in this photo. (U.S. Naval Historical Center)

velop the optimum Marine Nationale aircraft carrier for the Aeronavale. Apparently, greatly influenced by British and American carrier designs, the *Clemenceau* class island closely resembled the modified postwar *Essex* carriers, while the hull and flight deck showed considerable *Colossus* class shape and style except for the eight degree angled landing deck. The carriers were named to honor a French World War I politician and a general, respectively.

Clemenceau construction began in November 1955 and she was launched in February 1957 when *Foch* was started. The *Foch* launching took place in July 1960 and the carriers were commissioned in November 1961 and July 1963, respectively.

Clemenceau Class Data

The carriers displaced 22,000 tons standard and 31,000 tons deep load when commissioned. Overall length was 870 feet, while the Flight Deck measured 843 x 150 feet. Hull beam was 98 feet while deep load draft was 28 feet-3 inches. Two British Parsons steam turbine units are geared to two propeller shafts and total 126,000

Clemenceau is shown steaming at speed with Etendards on the port side and Alize aircraft on the starboard side of the Flight Deck. U.S.-built Crusaders can be seen at the after end of the Deck. Observe the 97 mm gun turrets on the hull sponsons. (Marine Nationale/ECP Armees)

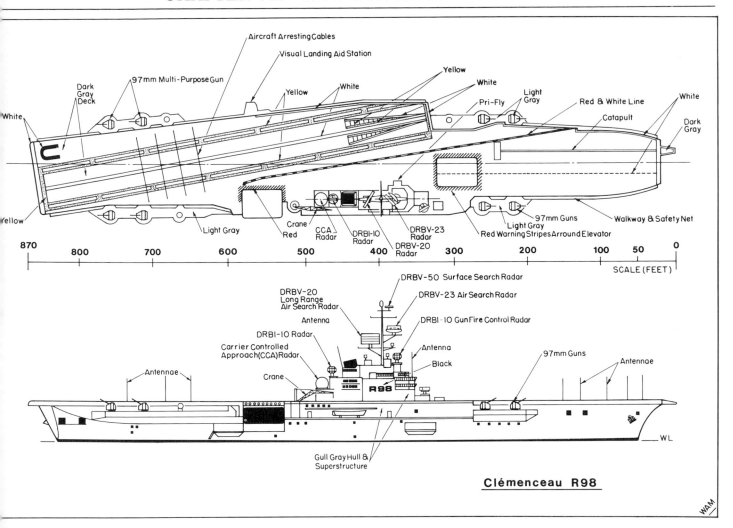

Clémenceau R98

haft horsepower which drives the ships to a maximum speed of 32 nots. Range is 7,500 miles at 18 knots.

About 40 aircraft can be accommodated consisting of Alize SW turboprops, F-8 Crusaders, and the Etendard IV which had een under development concurrent with the two carriers' construc- on. Each of the two aircraft elevators have a capacity of 44,000 ounds which restricted the size of the aircraft the carriers were apable of operating. Two British Mitchell-Brown 170 foot steam atapults, of the same capacity as the elevators, were also installed. he aircraft hangar is 590 feet long, 78 feet wide and 23 feet high. he hangar is offset slightly to the port side.

leavy Defensive Armament

)ne unusual aspect of the ships was the heavy antiaircraft battery f eight turreted 97 millimeter (4 inch) multipurpose guns; a rever- ion to the armament of pre-World War II carrier designs. It is quite ossible that this topside weight had contributed to the stability roblems experienced with the design because *Foch* had underwa- er blisters added to each side of the hull while under construction. *lemenceau* had hull blisters retro-fitted at a later date which in- reased the hull beam to 104 feet.

Clemenceau **Class Upgraded**

Both carriers were modified during the 1970s in order to operate the Super Etendard strike/fighters. A new tactical data system was also installed at that time. *Clemenceau* and *Foch* are very well equipped with SQS-503 sonar, DRBV-23 air search radar, DRBV-20 long range air search radar, and DRBV-50 surface search radar; however, it appears that they do not employ Airborne Early Warn- ing (AEW).

The 1970s modifications increased the displacement to 27,000 tons standard and 32,780 deep load.

Clemenceau was built by Arsenal de Brest and Foch was con- structed by Chantiers de l'Atlantique.

Jeanne D'Arc **Helicopter Carrier**

Jeanne D'Arc was originally intended to be a training ship but evolved into a multipurpose helicopter carrier; however, she re- tained her training capability with accommodations for over 190 cadets. This 10,000 ton standard displacement and 13,000 tons deep load displacement vessel is 590 feet long overall with a hull beam of 79 feet. Flight Deck beam is 85 feet. Mean draft is 20 feet. Four boilers generate steam for two steam turbine units, each of which is geared to a propeller shaft. The 40,000 shaft horsepower propels the ship to a 25 knots maximum speed. Range is 6,000 miles at 15

The French Marine National multipurpose helicopter carrier Jeanne D'Arc combines the Flight Deck of an aircraft carrier with the Main Deck of a cruiser with six Exocet ASUW missile launchers and four 4 inch multipurpose guns. (Marine National/ECP Armees)

knots. The superstructure is well forward to provide a large Flight Deck to accommodate 8 helicopters. The aircraft elevator is at the aft end of the Flight Deck similar to that pioneered by the defunct American SCS. Complement is 1,050 plus 700 troops. Fixed armament comprises four 4-inch multipurpose guns plus six Exocet launchers forward of the superstructure. *Jeanne D'Arc* construction began on July 7, 1960 and the ship was launched on September 30, 1961. She was upgraded in 1975 and 1982.

Dassault Etendard Carrier-Based Fighter

The Dassault Etendard IV was the first French supersonic carrier based fighter and was produced expressly for operation from *Clemenceau* and *Foch*. The Etendard IV was derived from a private venture by Societe des Avions Marcel Dassault, now known as Marcel Dassault/Breguet. The venture was stimulated by the NATO tactical strike/fighter competition of the mid-1950s in which all NATO members were invited to enter. The contestants were to be lightweight, low-cost, single-seaters. The experienced Marcel Dassault, who had designed many 1930s fighters as Marcel Bloch, drew upon his successful Mystcrc and Mirage jet fighter designs to develop several widely differing variants of the Etendard.

Early Etendard

The first to fly was Etendard II on July 23, 1956. This craft featured a 45 degree swept-wing and was powered by two Turbomeca Gabizo turbojets. The 2,400 pounds static thrust engines were mounted side by-side in the fuselage. The Armee de l"Air demonstrated its interest by ordering three prototypes; however, the plane failed to enter production.

Etendard IV was the Dassault entry in the NATO competition which was won by the Italian Fiat G91: however, NATO was sufficiently impressed with the Etendard IV to order three prototypes which first flew on March 15, 1957. No production orders were received for this variant.

The French Aeronavale's Dassault Etendard was deployed on Clemenceau and Foch in 1962 and remained in service through the 1980s. The Etendard IV-P all-weather photo-reconnaissance variant is shown. Note the extended Vee arresting hook. (WAM Foto)

Dassault Super Etendard is stowed in the Foch Hangar with its ingtips in folded vertical position (arrow). The Super Etendard was an pdated Etendard IV with excellent low-level performance in the strike ple. (Marine Nationale/ECP Armees)

laval Etendard

Most important of all was the fact that the Aeronavale was attracted y the Etendard's outstanding qualities as a naval strike/fighter with nterceptor capabilities. The first navalized prototype, Etendard IV M-01, made its test flight on May 21, 1958 resulting in a contract

for seven preproduction aircraft. One was fitted with an 11,200 pounds static thrust Rolls-Royce Avon 51 turbojet and blown flaps for experimental purposes.

Etendard IV M Data

The production Etendard IV M was powered by a single SNECMA Atar 8 turbojet of 9,700 pounds static thrust which drove the plane to a top speed of 677 miles per hour at 36,000 feet (Mach 1.02). In clean condition the Etendard IV M could attain 713 miles per hour at 36,000 feet (Mach 1.08). At sea level the aircraft top speed was 686 miles per hour (Mach 0.9). Initial rate of climb was 19,685 feet per minute and 40,000 feet altitude could be reached in 4 1/2 minutes. The 12,790 pounds empty plane had a normal catapult weight of 19,400 pounds and a maximum takeoff weight in overload condition of 23,000 pounds. Service ceiling is 49,200 feet.

Wingspan is 31 feet-5 3/4 inches with overall length of 47 feet-3/4 inches and a height of 13 feet-7 1/2 inches. The aircraft is of conventional all-metal construction. The 871 gallons internal fuel tanks can be supplemented with two 217 gallon drop tanks to attain an endurance of three hours and 45 minutes at 510 miles per hour for a range of 1,912 miles for ferrying purposes. The Etendard IV M has a sea level tactical radius of action of 186 miles which is extended to 400 miles at 36,000 feet.

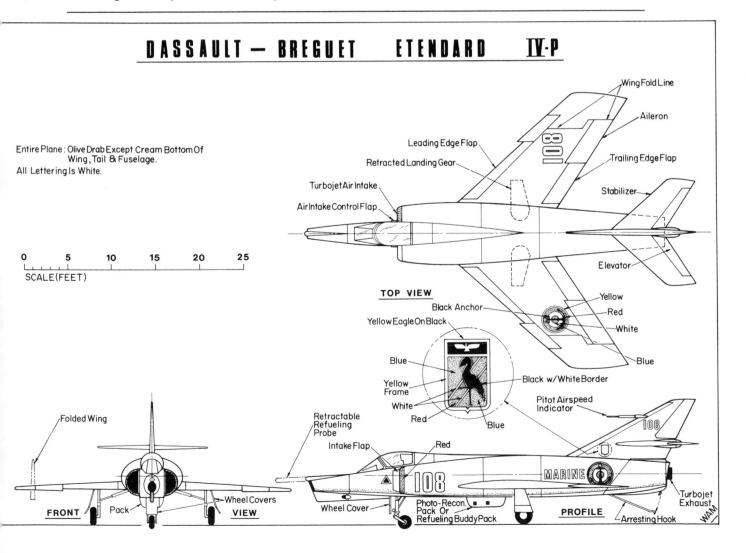

DASSAULT — BREGUET   ETENDARD   IV-P

Entire Plane : Olive Drab Except Cream Bottom Of Wing, Tail & Fuselage.
All Lettering Is White.

SCALE (FEET)

Wing Fold Line
Aileron
Leading Edge Flap
Retracted Landing Gear
Trailing Edge Flap
Turbojet Air Intake
Air Intake Control Flap
Stabilizer
Elevator

TOP VIEW

Black Anchor
Yellow
Red
White
Yellow Eagle On Black
Blue
Blue
Black w/White Border
Yellow Frame
White
Red
Blue
Pitot Airspeed Indicator

Folded Wing
Retractable Refueling Probe
Intake Flap
Red
MARINE
108
FRONT   Pack   **VIEW**   Wheel Covers
Wheel Cover
Photo-Recon. Pack Or Refueling Buddy Pack
PROFILE
Turbojet Exhaust
Arresting Hook
WAM

Built-in fixed armament consists of two 30 millimeter (1 3/16 inches) DEFA rapid-fire cannon plus four underwing mounts for the following loads: two 1,000 pound and two 500 pound bombs or two JL-100 rocket pods each loaded with 72 SNEB rockets, plus two 1,000 pound bombs or two 158 gallon drop tanks; four Sidewinder infra-red homing missiles; two Nord 5103 beam-riding air-to-air missiles; or two Aerospatiale Exocet Antiship Missiles. An Aida radar scanner is located in the nose to locate seaborne or airborne targets.

Originally 100 Etendards were ordered; however, this was soon reduced to 69 aircraft. Simultaneously, 21 Etendard IV P all-weather photo-reconnaissance variants, with cameras installed in a redesigned nose and in a fairing under the fuselage were also ordered. All Etendard IV models are equipped with inflight refueling probes and a pressurized and air conditioned cockpit plus a Hispano-built Martin-Baker Type AM.4 lightweight ejector seat.

Etendard Deployment

Dassault Etendard IV lightweight strike/fighters/interceptors were delivered to Flottille 15 F in late 1962 and in the following year the Etendard IV replaced the SNCASE Aquillon all-weather fighters (de Havilland Venom built in France under license) of Flottille llF. By early 1964 the Vought F4U-7 Corsairs of Flotilles 14F and 17F were being replaced by the Etendard IV. Each naval squadron or Flotille included eight IV M and two IV P Etendards.

Super Etendard

In the early 1970s several studies were conducted to update the Etendard and, by 1974, three modified Etendard IV aircraft had begun flight testing. The final redesign concentrated on low-level performance for the surface attack role; however, the interceptor performance was not neglected in order that the new design could replace the Aeronavale Crusaders as well as the Etendard IV. The most obvious external change in the Super Etendard was the shorter and more rounded nose which replaced the needle-nose of the Etendard IV.

The French Aeronavale operated Potez (Air Fouga) Zephyrs which wer navalized versions of the Potez (Air Fouga) Magister; the world's first jet-powered basic trainer. A Zephyr is about to be catapulted from a Royal Navy carrier. Note the bridle attachment and the carrier's antenn mast (arrow). A Potez (Air Fouga) Zephyr has just landed on HMS Eagle (RO-5). Observe the unusual Vee or butterfly tail. Armed version of the Zephyr or Magister have been used by Morocco, Cambodia, Congolese Republic and Israel. Note the Pri-Fly aircraft traffic control station projecting from the carrier's island (arrow). (Marine National/ ECP Armees)

Super Etendard Data

One 11,265 pounds static thrust SNECMA Atar 8K-50 turboj enabled the 14,220 pounds empty and 25,350 pounds loaded Sup Etendard to attain a maximum speed of 733 miles per hour at se level. Although the power, speed and weight had increased, the se vice ceiling dropped to 45,000 feet as did the range to 1,080 mile Combat radius had increased to 350 miles at sea level as had th weapons load to 4,630 pounds. Fuselage was shortened to 46 fee 11 1/2 inches and height reduced to 12 feet-8 inches, but the win span remained the same. The Super Etendard structure was su stantially strengthened to withstand the higher speeds at low alt tude. An inertial navigation system was installed as well as a ne multi-mode radar developed by Thompson CSF in cooperation wi Electronique Marcel Dassault which was essential to the low-lev attack role. The lethal Exocet AM.39 missile is carried in the stri role.

The Dassault Super Etendard is flown by the French Aeronava and the Argentine Air Forces.

This Marcel Dassault/Breguet Super Etendard has just left the Clemenceau catapult with the bridle about to drop away from the aircraft. The Super Etendard proved itself in the strike role with Exocet missiles during the Falklands War. (Marcel Dassault/Breguet, Courtesy Shirley Manfredi)

SOVIET ASW HELICOPTER CARRIER/CRUISERS AND CARRIER AIRCRAFT

While the U.S. Navy continued its interest in AEW, the Soviet Navy's interest in antisubmarine warfare took a radical turn. The deployment of the U.S. Navy *Polaris* ballistic missile-equipped submarines in 1961 threatened the Soviet citadel; the important urban industrial triangle formed by Moscow, Kiev and Leningrad. This prompted the Soviet development of the helicopter-equipped Kresta-class large antisubmarine ship (Bolshoy Protivolodochny Korabl or BPK). As the American submarine threat increased, the Soviet Navy was forced to counter it with a more dramatic warship development which no nation believed it would ever undertake. This was the antisubmarine cruiser (Protivolodochny Kreyser).

Heavily Armed *Moskva* Class

The Soviet design could have been inspired by the French *Jeanne D'Arc* and developed into a well-armed novel configuration. Wedge-shaped, the narrow forward end was a guided missile ship while the broad aft end was devoted to a helicopter deck. Two ships were constructed between 1962 and 1968, *Moskva* and *Leningrad*, which represent the first attempt by the Soviets to build a significant air-capable ship. Although armament comprised four 57 millimeter guns, (10) 21 inch, ASW torpedoes plus twin SA-N-3 (AAW) launchers, twin sonar-controlled SUW-N-1 (ASW) launchers, and two 12-tube RBU 6,000 ASW rockets, the principal offensive weapon of the *Moskva* class was the 15 to 20 Kamov Ka-25 Hormone A ASW helicopters. The torpedoes were removed shortly after the ships entered service.

Moskva Class Data

Standard displacement is 15,000 tons standard and 18,000 tons full load. Overall length is 645 feet with a beam of 92 feet. Flight Deck length from the superstructure is 295 feet with a maximum width of 115 feet. Average draft is 24 feet-9 inches.

The unusual deck contour of the Moskva class is evident in this aerial shot. Observe the conventional bow, laden with missiles, and the unusually broad Flight Deck aft for the helicopters, four of which can be seen on Deck. Note the folded rotor blades. (Ministry of Defense (Navy), Courtesy Nicholas Sampsidis)

The twin-screw ship is powered by geared steam turbines developing a total of 100,000 shaft horsepower. The steam is generated in four watertube boilers. Maximum speed is 30 knots and range is 9,000 miles at 18 knots.

The helicopter Hangar measures 220 x 80 feet and can accommodate a maximum of 30 Hormone helicopters. Two 15 x 50 feet aircraft elevators, in staggered arrangement, serve the Hangar and four helicopter spot locations on the Flight Deck.

Construction, Operation and Deployment

Both ships were constructed at Nosenko Shipyard, launched one year apart; *Moskva* in 1965 and *Leningrad* in 1966. The ships were commissioned in 1967 and 1968, respectively. It is unusual that only two ships of this class have been constructed, despite the on-going American submarine missile threat. Quite possibly the Soviet Navy was overwhelmed at that time and had shifted the responsibility to killer submarines and Kresta-II vessels.

The antisubmarine cruisers were apparently designed to operate as flagships in ASW hunter/killer groups with the SSM (Surface-to-Surface Missile) function performed by escort vessels, al-

The unique Soviet ASW cruiser Leningrad is caught by a U.S. Navy photographer as she speeds on maneuvers. This Moskva class ship is a hybrid guided missile cruiser and helicopter carrier. (U.S. Naval Historical Center)

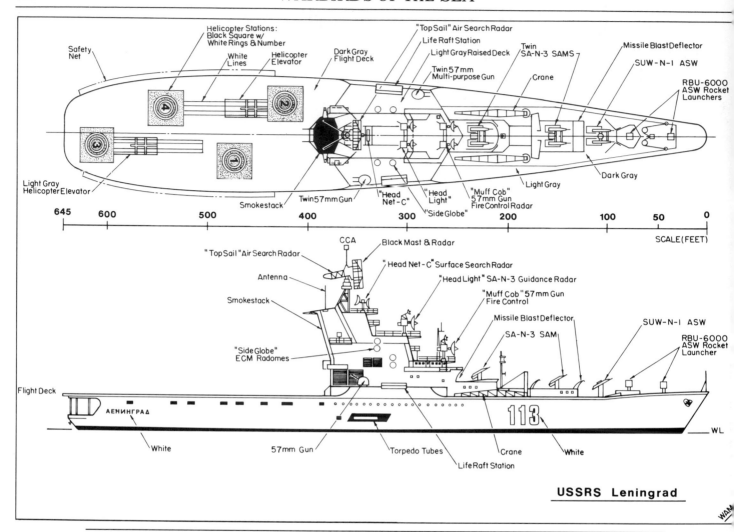

USSRS Leningrad

though few photographs of either *Moskva* or *Leningrad* show them with other ships.

Initial deployment was in the Black Sea and the Mediterranean Sea; however, the ships have been seen in all European waters. The *Moskva* class was only the first Soviet surprise for the Western world regarding air-capable ships. More were to come.

Soviet *Kiev* Class Carriers

When the U.S. Navy Polaris submarines began operating in the Mediterranean and the Norwegian Seas, it placed American submarine missiles closer to the Soviet "Citadel" and the *Moskva* class antisubmarine cruiser was not enough to combat this threat.

Most Powerful Warship Class

Apparently the Soviet Navy felt that the *Moskva* had to be supplemented because in December 1972 another unusual air capable ship was launched in the Nosenko Shipyard at Nikolayev on the Black Sea. This design bears no resemblance to the *Moskva* class because it has a 4 1/2 degree angled through-flight deck capable of handling fixed-wing aircraft, although there are no catapults or arresting gear. The angled Flight Deck terminates at the forward end of the island, thereby freeing the forward portion of the Flight (Main) Deck to be filled with lethal antiaircraft, antisubmarine and antisurface arma-

ment. This multi-purpose ship has many of the capabilities of a entire U.S. Navy task force, including the aircraft carrier plus es corting destroyers and cruisers; all contained in this single air-ca pable ship! The Soviet *Kiev* class has been called the most powe ful warship class because, unlike the U.S. aircraft carrier, the *Kie* class can mount offensive and defensive action without using i aircraft!

Kiev Armament

Fixed armament includes the following array of missiles and gun two 12-compartment MBU-2500A ASW missile launchers at th extreme bow and one twin SUW-N-1 launcher is immediately af which can selectively launch about (20) ASW FRAS-1 or SS-N-1 missiles fitted with either a nuclear depth charge or rocket-booste ASW torpedoes. Between this launcher and the island are two sta tions of four "Sandbox" SS-N-12 surface-to-surface cruise missil launchers each, which missiles have a range of 260 miles and speed of almost three times that of sound. The shipboard helicop ters can be used as relay stations to guide the SS-N-12 missiles t their targets. Located between the four forward SS-N-12 launche is a 76 millimeter dual-purpose twin-gun mount while another located aft of the island. An SA-N-3 twin-rail missile launcher fi ing 72 "Goblet" SAM missiles having a range of 13 miles up t

The Soviet Kiev class aircraft carriers have been called the most powerful warships because they can mount offensive and defensive actions without using their aircraft. The Kiev class carrier Novorossiysk is shown here. During mid-April 1994 a five-member delegation from the U.S. House of Representatives returned from Russia where they met with Russian officials and inspected the Russian Pacific Fleet. After boarding the aging aircraft carrier Kiev, the delegation agreed to have this ship plus about another 150 Russian naval vessels sail to the United States where they will be dismantled and cut into scrap at the Philadelphia Naval shipyard. (Official U.S. Navy Photograph by PH1 Loveall)

70,000 feet is located between the aft SS-N-12 launchers. A second SA-N-3 launcher is installed aft of the islands. Two twin-rail SA-N-4 launchers firing 36 "Gekko" SAM missiles are stowed in covered silos below deck and emerge for firing missiles that have a range of 10 miles at an altitude of 40,000 feet with a speed five-times that of sound. Located beneath the aft SS-N-12 missile launchers are two groups of 21 inch torpedo launchers, five on each side, which can be used against surface ships or submarines. Finally,

Although the Soviets classified the Kiev class as aircraft carrying cruisers, the U.S. Navy insists that it is an aircraft carrier. This splendid aerial view clearly shows the extensive flight deck of the Kiev Class ships which tends to give credence to the American classification. This difference of opinion will make it most difficult for future U.S.A./Russia disarmament negotiations to agree on which ships will be scrapped. (U.S. Navy Photograph, Courtesy U.S. Naval Institute Collection)

six-barrel 23 millimeter CIWS rapid-fire guns, capable of firing 3,000 rounds per minute, are distributed in eight locations on the ship. As can be seen the *Kiev* class mounts a truly formidable array of fixed armament.

Kiev Aircraft Complement

The air group comprises 18 Ka-25A "Hormone A" helicopters and 12 Yak-36 jet-powered VTOL fixed-wing aircraft. The Ka-25A helicopters can deliver ASW torpedoes as well as provide long-range missile guidance, while the Yak-36 can drop depth charges, launch antiship missiles and also fire AAM missiles at intruding aircraft.

The SS-N-12 missiles are intended to play the same role for the *Kiev* as do U.S. Navy attack/strike aircraft for Supercarriers.

Kiev Class Data

Four of the Soviet multi-purpose through-deck cruisers, *Kiev, Minsk, Novorossiysk* and *Baku*, have been constructed at the Nicolayev Shipyard. The ships displace 36,000 tons standard and 42,000 tons full load with a draft of 25 to 30 feet. Overall length is 899 feet and hull beam at waterline is 105 feet. Overall width over Flight Deck is 157 feet-6 inches, while Flight Deck length is 607 feet. Four steam turbines are geared to four propeller shafts and total 180,000 shaft horsepower. Maximum speed is 32 knots, while the range at 18 knots is 13,000 miles. Complement is 2,500.

Kiev Electronics

The unusually large combined island and boiler uptake/stack was dictated by the ship's extensive search and fire control radar such as: "Top Knot" advanced precision-approach radar; "Vee Bar" high frequency communications traffic; "Top Sail" air search radar; "Top

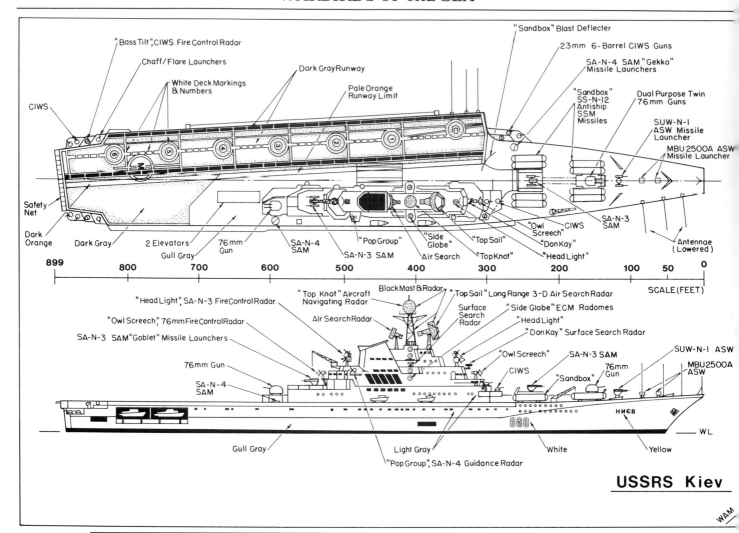

USSRS Kiev

Steer", "Top Pair" and "Head Net-A" air and surface search plus missile system target acquisition and Ground Controlled Intercept (GCI); "Head Light" radars, mounted at the forward and aft ends of the island, plus a rotatable "Trap Door" dish antennae is also used for missile guidance; "Owl Screech" 76 millimeter gun fire control radars are located under the "Head Light" radars; "Pop Group" radar for the SA-N-4 guidance; "Punch Bowl" dish antennae within a radome used for SS-N-12 missile target data acquisition; four "Bass Tilt" 23 millimeter CIWS fire control radars; one "Don Kay" radar and two "Palm Frond" units serve both navigation and surface search; "Bob Tail" radio sextant is used to control VTOL landings; and "Side Globe" ECM radomes are strung vertically, four on each side of the mast. The names given to the foregoing electronic equipment are those coined by NATO. A bulbous bow houses a low frequency bow sonar transducer or a large passive sonar array, while variable depth sonar (VDS) is housed behind two transom doors.

The fourth *Kiev* class carrier, *Baku*, was fitted with more advanced electronics including a large drum-shaped radar antenna and billboard array panels on the sides of the island.

FOD Vacuum

The Soviet Navy has developed a large self-propelled vacuum cleaner to clear the Flight Deck of FOD (Foreign Object Damage).

Kiev Class Power Projection

The multipurpose *Kiev* class carrier/cruiser ships possess a limite aviation capability when compared to a U.S. Navy carrier of simi lar size; however, the Soviet ships have an abundance of ship-re lated weaponry. The *Kiev* class is capable of independent strik cruiser operations that would normally require a multipurpose tas force. Although initially called a "Bolshoi protivolodochny kreyser or large antisubmarine cruiser, the *Kiev* class aircraft carrier/cruise is potent enough to challenge the western powers' control of SLO(because this innovative design is much more than a home defens antisubmarine cruiser. Deployment of these ships in internationa waters would have provided Soviet surface forces protection fron air attack which they did not have in the past.

Soviet Kamov Helicopter

The principal weapon of the *Moskva* class antisubmarine cruisei made its initial appearance in 1960 as the Kamov Ka-20 prototype This was refined into the ASW Ka-25, known as Hormone by NAT(Entering Soviet Navy service in 1966, the Kamov Ka-25 Hormon(remained the standard Soviet shipborne helicopter for many year:

Kamov Ka-25 Description

The unusual co-axial, contra-rotating rotors gave the small cra

The Kamov Ka-25 Hormone helicopter is the principal weapon of the Moskva class ASW cruisers. The co-axial, contra-rotating rotors produce exceptional lifting ability and obviate the necessity for a tail rotor. Observe the unusual twin rudder tail. (Ministry of Defence [Navy], Courtesy Nicholas Sampsidis)

exceptional lifting power for its size. The counter rotation eliminated torque and, therefore, the customary tail rotor was replaced with a conventional twin-rudder tail assembly which gave the Hormone a very distinctive appearance. The two three-bladed rotors fold flat over the tail so it occupies the minimum space in the Hangar and on the Flight Deck. The major disadavantage in stowing the Ka-25 was the exceptionally high Hangar required to clear the double rotors. This made it difficult for small ships to operate the Hormone.

Hormone A ASW

The ASW Hormone A can carry a maximum armament load of 2,200 pounds in its internal weapons bay. This can consist of one or two 16-inch homing antisubmarine torpedoes, conventional or nuclear depth charges or assorted weapons.

Electronics includes surface search radar, the antenna for which is housed in a large flat chin radome; a towed MAD (Magnetic Anomaly Detector); and a dunking sonar. Sonabuoys can also be carried in an add-on box under the fuselage rear.

Hormone B Missile Guidance

In addition to the ASW Hormone A, a missile guidance Hormone B variant contains sophisticated electronics to provide mid-course guidance for long range cruise missiles launched by Soviet surface ships. One Hormone B helicopter is carried by *Kresta* class missile cruisers and large missile destroyers.

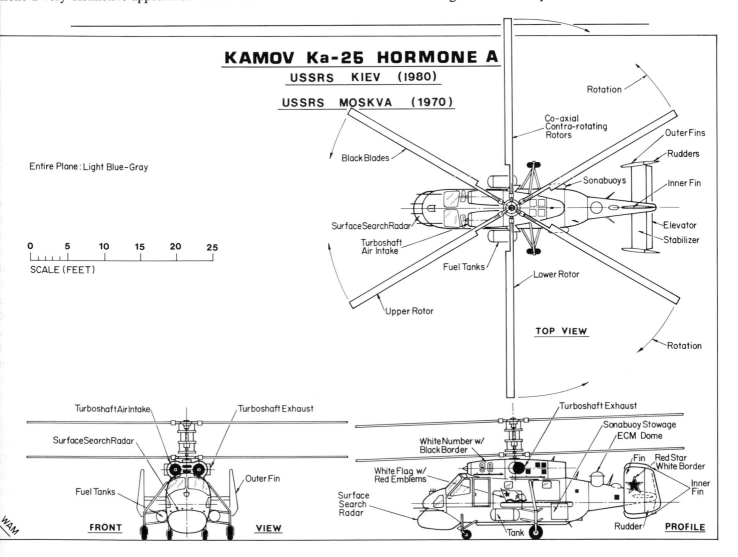

KAMOV Ka-25 HORMONE A

USSRS KIEV (1980)

USSRS MOSKVA (1970)

Entire Plane: Light Blue-Gray

SCALE (FEET)
0 5 10 15 20 25

Rotation

Co-axial Contra-rotating Rotors

Outer Fins

Rudders

Black Blades

Sonabuoys

Inner Fin

Surface Search Radar

Turboshaft Air Intake

Fuel Tanks

Elevator

Stabilizer

Lower Rotor

Upper Rotor

TOP VIEW

Rotation

Turboshaft Air Intake

Turboshaft Exhaust

Turboshaft Exhaust

Sonabuoy Stowage

ECM Dome

Surface Search Radar

White Number w/ Black Border

Fin   Red Star White Border

Fuel Tanks

Outer Fin

White Flag w/ Red Emblems

Surface Search Radar

Inner Fin

FRONT   **VIEW**

Tank

Rudder   **PROFILE**

Hormone C Utility/SAR

The Hormone C is a utility and SAR (Search And Rescue) helicopter, employed in VERTical REPlenishment (VERTREP) operations, plane guard, and general transport work. It also assumes photo-reconnaissance duties. All variants have a crew of two.

Kamov Ka-25 Data

The Kamov Ka-25 Hormone rotor diameter is 51 feet-8 inches, fuselage length is 34 feet-0 inches, and overall height is 17 feet-8 inches. Empty weight is 10,500 pounds while loaded weight is 16,500 pounds. Two 900 shaft horsepower Glushenkov GTD-3 turboshaft engines give the Hormone a maximum speed of 130 miles per hour. Range is 350 miles with a mission endurance of two hours. Service ceiling is 11,000 feet.

In addition to the USSR, the Kamov Ka-25 was flown by the armed forces of Yugoslavia, Syria and India.

An improved Hormone A antisubmarine helicopter was viewed in public for the first time in 1981. This is the Kamov Ka-32, named Helix by NATO. Following the same basic configuration as the Ka-25, the Ka-32 has the added power of two 1,000 shaft horsepower Glushenkov GTD-350 BM turboshaft engines and appears to be a slightly enlarged version of the earlier Hormone.

The Kamov Ka-32 Helix has a rotor diameter of 54 feet-11 inches, fuselage length of 37 feet-0 inches, and overall height of 18 feet 0 inches. The more spacious fuselage suggests a greater payload of ASW weapons and more sophisticated electronics than those on the Hormone can be installed.

Yak-36 Forger

The Yak-36 VTOL strike/fighter, deployed on the *Kiev* class ships, was the first shipboard fixed-wing aircraft to be based on board a Soviet ship. It was also the first USSR attempt at a production fixed-wing VTOL aircraft.

Soviet Technology Gathering

In the worldwide technology race, the Soviet Union did not compete, as do the Western nations. The USSR objective of interna-

A Yak-36 Forger VTOL is photographed landing on Kiev. Unlike the Harrier, the Forger requires three jet engines to operate VTOL; one engine for horizontal flight and two vertical lift engines. This craft is unable to STOL, it must land and takeoff vertically. (U.S. Navy)

tional dominance, which has saturated the Russian psyche since the year 1453, had spawned a unique system of acquiring technology. They gathered technology from others, instead of developing it themselves; thereby saving countless years of R & D and financial expenditure. Once acquired, Western designs were adapted to enhance USSR's capacity to produce military weapons which suit the Soviet Union's needs. The Yak-36 is a case in point which is why NATO has given this aircraft the sobriquet of "Forger."

Soviet VTOL Development

Once the Harrier proved a success the Soviets produced the vectored thrust Yak-34 "Freehand" which proved a failure because Soviet jet engine technology had lagged behind the Western nations. This is especially true of high bypass turbofan engines which power the Harrier. The Yak-36 followed quickly, making its first flight in 1971. This craft bore a remarkable resemblance to the German Federal Republic VFW-191B V/STOL tactical reconnaissance fighter and entered service with the Soviet Navy in 1978.

Forger Data

In view of the Yak-34 failure, the vectored thrust concept was replaced by a three-engine installation in the Yak-36; one 17,500 pounds static thrust vectored exhaust turbojet for horizontal flight plus two 8,000 pounds static thrust lift turbojets located vertically in tandem in the fuselage between the cockpit and the wing. The two lift turbojets exhaust directly downward and cannot be vectored; therefore, the Yak-36 is unable to STOL (Short Takeoff and Landing) and can only VTOL (Vertical Take-Off or Landing) which is a decided disadvantage because the aircraft must expend vast quantities of fuel in full load takeoffs and cannot take advantage of Ski-Jump Decks.

A later version of the Forger, Yak-38, is reported to have had STOL (Short Take-Off and Landing) capabilities. It is not known whether this was accomplished by vectoring thrust as in the Harrier or by pivoting the lift engines.

The four underwing pylons of the Yak-36 can carry about 2,500 pounds of external stores which can consist of AA-8 "Aphid" IR Air-to-Air Missiles (AAM), GS-23 23-millimeter gun pods, drop tanks, AS-7 "Kerry" Air-to-Surface Missiles, 57-millimeter rocket pods, free-fall bombs, and depth charges. Maximum speed is about 800 miles per hour at 36,000 feet.

Combat radius is limited to from 100 to 200 miles. Service ceiling is about 40,000 feet. Empty weight is 16,500 pounds while maximum weight is 25,500 pounds. Wingspan is 24 feet with a wing area of approximately 170 square feet. Overall length is 50 feet while height is 13 feet-3 inches. Despite the short wingspan the Forger wing outer half folds upwards to a vertical position to facilitate stowage on the *Kiev* class carrier/cruisers.

Forger Capabilities and Missions

The Yak-36 has very limited AAW capability and would not hope to win duels against the Tomcat, Super Etendard, or Hornet, nor could the mere dozen Forgers on the *Kiev* ever expect to overwhelm an incoming strike force, even by applying superior numbers. The Yak-36 could be effective to drive off or destroy Western maritime surveillance aircraft such as the Hawkeye, Prowler and British

YAKOVLEV YAK-36M FORGER

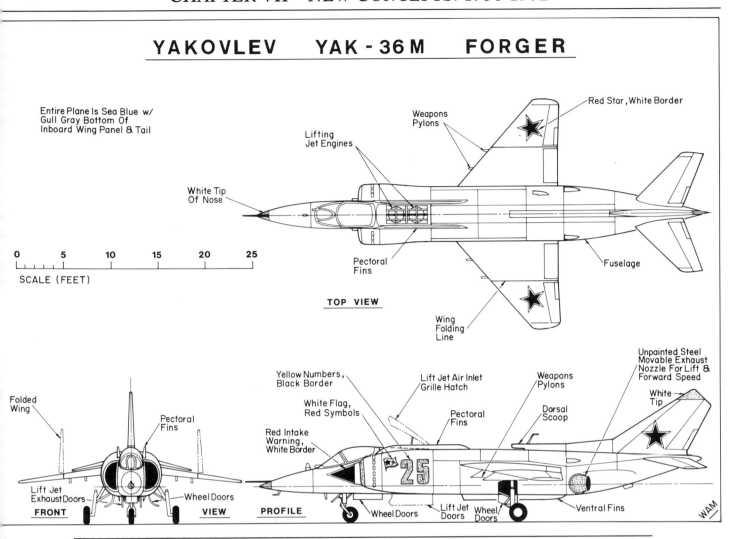

Entire Plane Is Sea Blue w/
Gull Gray Bottom Of
Inboard Wing Panel & Tail

Weapons
Pylons

Red Star, White Border

Lifting
Jet Engines

White Tip
Of Nose

Pectoral
Fins

Fuselage

SCALE (FEET)

0   5   10   15   20   25

TOP VIEW

Wing
Folding
Line

Folded
Wing

Yellow Numbers,
Black Border

Lift Jet Air Inlet
Grille Hatch

Weapons
Pylons

Unpainted Steel
Movable Exhaust
Nozzle For Lift &
Forward Speed

Pectoral
Fins

White Flag,
Red Symbols

Dorsal
Scoop

White
Tip

Red Intake
Warning,
White Border

Pectoral
Fins

Lift Jet
Exhaust Doors

Wheel Doors

Wheel Doors

Lift Jet
Doors

Wheel
Doors

Ventral Fins

FRONT   **VIEW**   **PROFILE**

WAM

Forgers are at rest on the Kiev Flight Deck aft of the island. Observe the folding wingtips in the vertical position. The plane was to protect the Soviet submarine fleet by attacking Western ASW aircraft. (Official U.S. Navy Photograph, News Photo Division)

Nimrod as well as patrol/ASW aircraft such as the Viking, Nimrod, LAMPS helicopters, Sea King, Lynx and so forth.

These Forger missions would not only help the Kiev SAG (Surface Action Group) avoid detection and; therefore, possible destruction, but could also assist the *Kiev* SAG in its primary role of protecting the large submarine fleet by attacking Western ASW aircraft. The Forger's apparent secondary mission was intended to be ASUW (Anti SUrface Warfare) by attacking patrol boats, missile boats, torpedo boats or surfaced submarines and other relatively low-value targets with free-fall bombs, 57 millimeter rockets or AS-7 Kerry missiles. This would have freed the *Kiev*'s SS-N-12 cruise missiles for bigger game such as carriers, cruisers and so forth. The Forger's use in providing close air support to landing forces during amphibious operations could have met with success.

Forger Operations

During its initial deployment on the *Kiev* class ships, fueling, arming and other servicing operations of the Yak-36 were conducted below deck in the hangar; however, these operations have been gradually transferred to the Flight Deck.

The Forger takeoff and landing was accomplished without assistance from Flight Deck personnel. After the wheel chocks and hold-down cables were removed and engines started, the flight deck

HMS Ark Royal RO-9 underwent extensive modifications during the four year period ending in 1970 which included an angled deck, more powerful catapults, stronger arresting gear and bridle catcher. Observe the Blackburn Buccaneer leaving the new angled deck catapult. (Ministry of Defence [Navy])

HMS Eagle RO-5 was also modified from 1966 to 1970 to include an angled deck catapult and stronger arresting gear for heavy strike aircraft operation. ASW helicopters were combined with the fixed wing aircraft complement to increase the carrier's versatility. (Ministry of Defence [Navy])

crew moved clear of the aircraft, Forger pilots were cleared for takeoff via radio and received very little landing guidance. Take-offs and landings were usually conducted into a 15 to 17 miles per hour wind-over-deck.

Despite the fact that the Forger is not an outstanding aircraft it has proven to be a capable mate to the *Kiev* SAG weapons systems. In addition, the plane did provide experience for pilots and ship personnel to produce a trained team for the new Soviet carriers which were being planned at that time.

Armament Remains Despite Soviet Demise
It must be remembered that the above-described carriers and air-craft remain intact notwithstanding the end of the Soviet Union.

EAGLE CLASS CARRIERS UPDATED
Royal Navy carriers *HMS Eagle* and *HMS Ark Royal* underwent extensive revisions during 1966-1970.

Ark Royal Modifications
Ark Royal had an 8 1/2 degree angled deck added along with new, more powerful catapults including a new angled deck catapult. New arresting gear and catapult bridle catchers were also fitted. The is-land was modified and RN Type 965 air warning plus 982/983 fighter direction radar was added. The addition of a flight of Westland Sea King ASW helicopters reduced the fixed wing aircraft capacity to 30 planes. *Ark Royal* was also modified to operate McDonnell-Douglas Phantom II fighters. The displacement went to 50,800 tons deep draft.

Eagle Modifications
Eagle had been modified for Buccaneer operation and an angled deck catapult was added. ASW helicopters were also added to the aircraft complement.

After modernization HMS Eagle (near) and HMS Ark Royal (far) were photographed steaming together in this unusual photo of 1970. Note the catapult bridle catcher fitted to Ark Royal. (Ministry of Defence [Navy])

This HMS Ark Royal photo taken just before its retirement shows the two bridle catchers and the revised deck markings. Observe the latticework masts which replaced the original tripod masts (arrows). (Ministry of Defence [Navy])

Sophisticated Weapons Too Expensive

Eagle was decommissioned in 1972, and *Ark Royal* in 1979 because their maintenance and operation in the Royal Navy had become financially prohibitive. Weapons had become so sophisticated and expensive that only the most prosperous nations could afford an adequate arsenal without straining their economy.

SHIPBOARD AIRCRAFT CORROSION PREVENTION (1960s)

Experiments had continued through the 1960s in the search for the ideal aircraft corrosion inhibitors in the saltwater environment of aircraft carriers. An epoxy-based primer, containing strontium chromate as the inhibitor, was developed and the two-component catalyzed product demonstrated excellent adhesion to metal.

When it was decided to omit the lacquer top coat to obtain a better scuff-resistant surface, the result was that epoxy top coats chalked badly and, being quite brittle, cracked unacceptably. The problem lay in the fact that the violent forces upon an airplane in flight bend and twist the structure to the point where perfectly fine finishes flake, crack and peel due to this movement and vibration!

The Royal Navy had been experimenting with the newly developed polyurethane finishes near the end of World War II and had obtained encouraging results. Trials on commercial aircraft in the U.S. also proved promising for polyurethane which resulted in its adoption as the top coat for carrier planes in the late 1960s.

Lockheed-California applied and service-tested the epoxy-based primer and polyurethane top coat combination on 10 Lockheed Vikings with success and the U.S. Navy CNO authorized this as the standard finish for virtually all naval aircraft on December 20, 1969.

Extended service revealed that the use of polyurethane for touch-up required special precautions to avoid health hazards to personnel in the immediate vicinity when exposed to the polyurethane spray which contained toxic and allergenic isocyanate compounds. The alternative was to fall back on the use of acrylic lacquer for the top coat.

The endless search for an ideal corrosion inhibitor for naval aircraft has been related in various stages to illustrate only one of the many problems inherent in the development of carrier planes; a very important problem given very little thought by the casual observer.

HI-TECH SAMs SPAWN SUPER STRIKE PLANES

From the advent of combat aircraft to the end of World War II the primary danger to tactical attack/strike aircraft and strategic bombers was from interceptor/fighter planes. Ground and sea air defenses lacked the range and accuracy to seriously challenge the attacking aircraft; therefore, both high-flying strategic bombers and low-flying attack/strike aircraft enjoyed three decades of dominance over ground forces and ships at sea.

SAM's Create Havoc

This came to an abrupt end with the development of radar-guided Surface to Air Missiles (SAM) and air defense radar systems. This lethal coverage was soon extended to such great distances that attacking aircraft were detected and imperiled far from their target.

Element of Surprise is Gone

Radar detection and tracking plus radar-controlled SAM missile coverage soon extended beyond 30 miles in range and from a few hundred to 90,000 feet in altitude. The large Soviet Sverdlov class cruisers employed this high-technology radar plus electro-optical systems to detect and destroy approaching aircraft and missiles at great range and altitude. This eliminated the attacking aircraft's primary advantage, which is surprise.

The Solution

This rapid advance in antiaircraft technology forced the high-flying bomber to fly even higher, which eventually rendered it eneffective. The solution appeared to be low-flying, high-speed aircraft that could penetrate the objective's radar curtain by flying under it at about 200 feet altitude. These aircraft would need to be heavily armed with bombs and missiles as well as loaded with sophisticated electronics.

Admiralty Prepares Specifications

By 1950 British military strategists decided that it was time to develop that low-level, high-speed radar-penetrating attack/strike aircraft to conduct hit and run operations. The Admiralty issued Specification M.148T in 1952 for such an aircraft which resulted in a competition that included more than a dozen aircraft manufacturers.

All-Weather, Low-Level, Shore or Carrier-Based

The Royal Navy had also foreseen the necessity for an agile turbojet strike aircraft to counter the Soviet Navy's Sverdlov class cruiser. The new jet-powered plane was to replace the Wyvern on carriers and the Canberra (Martin B-57) at shore bases. The new design must also be able to operate from all existing Royal Navy carriers. It was to have the capability of locating and destroying major surface ships of the growing Soviet Fleet regardless of darkness or weather conditions. In addition, the structure must not be subject to fatigue due to the strenuous buffeting from low-level high-speed flight.

Blackburn Buccaneer

After three years of carefully eliminating competitors the Admiralty selected the design prepared by Blackburn's Chief Designer Barry Laight and his team in July 1955. An order for 20 preproduction aircraft was quickly placed with Blackburn and General Aircraft Ltd. for extensive testing.

It has been generally conceded that the Blackburn N.A.39 design had put Britain at least three years ahead of the rest of the world in the field of high-speed, low-level strike aircraft with the result that stringent security precautions were applied to this project. The N.A. 39, soon to be named Buccaneer, was first flown in public in September, 1958 at the Farnborough SBAC Air Show but was not available for public inspection until June 1959.

Buccaneer Wing

The Blackburn Buccaneer appears larger than it is. Wingspan is 44 feet-0 inches with a wing area of 515 square feet. The wing design had to meet contradictory requirements: low-speed operation, heavy

With Blackburn Chief Test Pilot Lieutenant Commander Derek Whitehead at the controls, an early Blackburn NA.39 Buccaneer is steam catapult-launched from HMS Victorious. Observe the coke bottle fuselage. (British Information Service)

weight lifting, and long range demanded a high aspect ratio wing with thick airfoil, very small sweepback angle, and high lift devices; conversely, the attainment of long range at high-speed and low-level, high-speed operation subject to severe buffeting from gusts required a low aspect ratio wing with a thin airfoil and a large sweepback angle. The small wing area was necessary to alleviate the gust response problem when flying at near sonic speeds at an altitude of only 200 feet. A thin, compound sweepback wing was designed to incorporate 40 degrees at the root, then 38 degrees, with the remainder at 30 degrees. This geometry not only met the requirements but also created a deep section at the wing root for much needed structural strength at that point. It also provided stowage depth for landing gear retraction.

The structural strength necessary to withstand the violent low-level turbulence that the Buccaneer would encounter demanded a new approach to wing structures. The wing panels were machined from aluminum slabs complete with integral stiffening while the ribs and spars were machined from steel forgings. This structural technique provided the Buccaneer with the same length of service life as conventional naval aircraft operating under far less strenuous conditions.

The outer wing panels were folded upwards, hydraulically, reducing the span to 19 feet-11 inches for aircraft carrier stowage. Super circulation or boundary layer control, often called blown, was provided for the wing, flaps, ailerons and horizontal tail. This system could also provide heated air for thermal de-icing for the wing. The blown concept had been originated by John Attinello of the American NACA.

Buccaneer Fuselage

The fuselage was 63 feet-5 inches long which included the nose radome and the tail air brake or drogue. When using blown flaps an aircraft often needs extra drag in order to reduce the minimum landing drag speed while enabling the turbojet engines to be run at full power. The Buccaneer designers provided this extra drag by means of clamshell air brakes or drogue at the aft end of the fuselage. When closed they formed the tail cone and hinged open horizontally 90 degrees to create the necessary drag. Fuselage length was too long for British carrier elevators so the Buccaneer radome nose-cone was hinged to fold to port and, with the drogue wide open, the fuselage length was reduced to 51 feet-10 inches, which fit the elevators.

The Buccaneer's near-sonic speed required an area-rule or Coke bottle fuselage contour in order to compensate for the loss of wing cross-sectional area as the air flows aft and also to provide a smoother run during low-level flight at high speeds. The designers kept the pinch as large as they could in order to make the weapons bay as spacious as possible. The Coke bottle effect was retained by bulging the fuselage aft of the wing and in way of the cockpits. The area rule fuselage bulge housed Ferranti navigation/attack equipment which is integrated with the flight instruments, autopilot, radio and radar to provide a complete control, navigation and terrain clearance system. This integrated system solves the problem, electronically, of navigating to the target accurately without striking obstacles in the hedge-hopping flight path while flying at about 12 miles a minute. The nose-cone radome houses Ferranti ground mapping, terrain warning and range data for the weapon release computer. It also contains the master reference gyro and head-up display.

The all-metal semi-monocoque fuselage is built in three main sections; nose with cockpit, center section in way of wing with engine mounts, and the fuselage rear. This is reminiscent of the Blackburn Swift previously described, in which the three sections

uselage with parts machined from solid metal originated. The first uselage section of the Buccaneer was assembled from components machined from solid metal.

Crew and Fuel Tanks

The crew of two sit in tandem under a single sliding canopy in Martin Baker ejection seats. Integral fuel tanks totalling 1,872 gallons are fitted throughout the upper fuselage beginning just behind the cockpit and running over the weapons bay.

Weapons

No doors are fitted to the weapons bay. Instead, the entire weapons bay is rotated hydraulically to expose the weapons to be dropped. The bay can accommodate four 1,000 pound bombs or a single large device. The bay can also be fitted with a temporary fuel tank or a wide range of cameras for reconnaissance missions. Each of four wing pylons can accept a 1,000 pound bomb; two 500 pound bombs; one 18-tube 68 millimeter rocket pod; one 36-tube 2 inch rocket pod; 3 inch rockets; one Martel missile with launcher; or two 8 inch reconnaissance flares.

Toss Bombing Technique

In view of the fact the Buccaneer was designed to head for its target

In order to accommodate the ever growing size of combat aircraft on its small carriers the Royal Navy adapted the planes to suit the available space. This interesting photo illustrates the folding wings, nose and tail drogue of a Blackburn Buccaneer on the HMS Ark Royal elevator. (Ministry of Defence [Navy])

at virtually wave-top level, a new tactic had to be devised to safely and accurately score on the target. This was called the Toss Bomb technique in which the pilot sped towards the target and, assisted by the on-board electronics, pulled up into a loop at a predetermined distance from the target, governed by the altitude and ground speed of the aircraft. The bomb is released when the plane is from

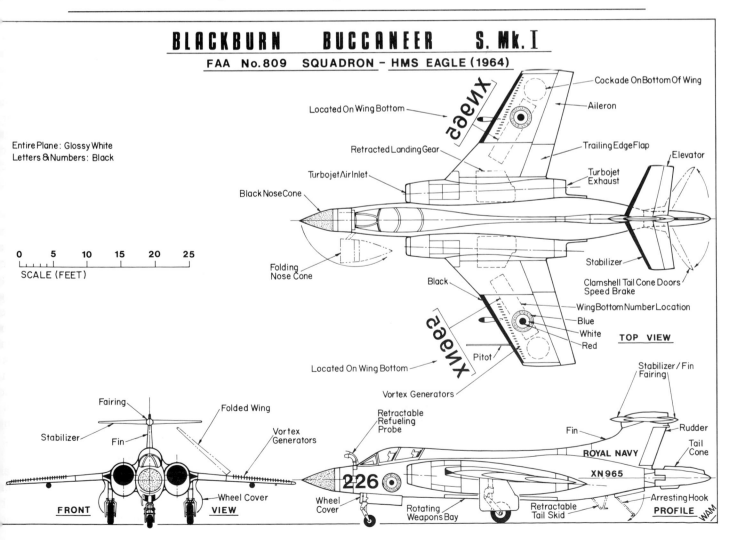

45 to 90 degrees into the loop; governed by the Buccaneer's speed and altitude, and the distance to the target. Upon release the bomb follows a ballistic trajectory to the target. The pilot continues into the loop and rolls into level flight at the top, making his escape back to the carrier using this "Immelmann Turn."

Buccaneers Bomb Tanker

On March 28, 1967 eight Buccaneers from Fleet Air Arm No. 736 Squadron and No. 800 Squadron were called upon to destroy the supertanker Torrey Canyon which had run aground off the southernmost tip of Britain. Of the 42 high-explosive 1,000 pound bombs dropped by the Buccaneers, 30 bombs scored direct hits which was a good showing of almost three out of four bombs hitting the target.

Turbojet Engines

In aircraft carrier operation it is the catapult which determines the launching speed of the aircraft at the end of the catapult run. The thrust of the plane's engine contributes very little in lauching the aircraft. It was because of this reasoning that Barry Laight and his team selected two rather low-powered turbojets for the Buccaneer. Strike aircraft require the smallest economical powerplant that meets the cruise thrust demand with adequate reserve power. Passing up the powerful Saphire and Avon turbojets Blackburn selected the 7,100 pounds static thrust de Havilland (now Bristol Siddeley due to Amalgamation) Gyron Junior which was a scaled down version of the big de Havilland Gyron. These engines enabled the 45,000 pound Buccaneer S.Mk.1 to attain a maximum speed of 720 miles per hour at sea level.

Buccaneer Deployment

The first unit to be equipped with the Blackburn Buccaneer S.Mk.1 was No. 801 Squadron on July 17, 1962.

A Blackburn Buccaneer demonstrates the Toss Bombing technique of LABS (Low Altitude Bombing System). The bomb is released and lobbed to the target while the plane is in a high speed climb and, as the missile arcs toward the target, the attacker makes its escape. (Air Ministry)

The second unit to receive the S.Mk.1 was No. 809 Squadro in January 1963, while the third and final Buccaneer S.Mk.1 un was No.800 Squadron on March 19, 1964. The Blackburn Bucca neer S.Mk.1 served on the carriers *Eagle, Ark Royal* and *Victor. ous.*

Buccaneer S.Mk.2 Mods.

In order to improve upon the S.Mk.1 8,000 pound weapons pa load the Buccaneer was modified in 1963 for the installation of tw 11,200 pounds static thrust Rolls-Royce Spey turbojet engines. Th Buccaneer S.Mk.2 could carry up to 16,000 pounds of armamer and fly 3,000 miles on a ferry mission. Weight and overall dimer sions remained the same as the S.Mk.1. In order to accelerate th perfection of the S.Mk.2 advanced radar systems, one Buccanee was lent to Ferranti Ltd. The aircraft was maintained and flown b Ferranti until it was returned about three years later with an entirel integrated electronics system.

Demonstrated in U.S.A.

Three Buccaneers were flown to the U.S.A. and operated from US Lexington. They also demonstrated low-level flying in hot and tu bulent conditions.

Foreign Orders

South Africa bought 16 Buccaneer S.Mk.2 strike aircraft fitted wit two rocket engines to assist overload takeoffs from hot airfields high altitudes.

Hawker Siddeley Buccaneer

During the Buccaneer's development and production Blackbur became part of the Hawker Siddeley group with the result that th aircraft is often referred to as the Hawker Siddeley Buccaneer i stead of the original Blackburn Buccaneer.

Grumman Intruder

The Buccaneer's U.S. Navy counterpart is the Grumman A-6A Ir truder which is fitted with the most comprehensive electronics sy tems ever installed in an aircraft of this size. Based upon its exper ence in the Korean War the U.S. Navy announced a competition, 1956, for a high-performance, carrierborne, all-weather, long-rang attack/strike aircraft with high-speed at wavetop level capabilit The competition produced 11 designs from eight aircraft manufac turers and, in December 1957, the U.S. Navy announced th. Grumman Corporation was the winner with its G-128 design. contract was placed in March 1959 for eight development and evalu ation craft designated A2F-1 and named Intruder. This designatio was eventually changed to A-6A.

Vectored Tailpipes

The Intruder was a midwing design with gentle, unaggressive co tours that belied its potent military capabilities. The first of the eig flew on April 19, 1960 and, as with all of the test planes, it wa fitted with adjustable jet engine tailpipes that could be vectore downward hydraulically to a maximum angle of 23 degrees shorten takeoffs and landings. This feature was abandoned for th production models in which tailpipes were permanently fixed at

The Grumman Intruder was fitted with the most comprehensive electronics systems ever installed on a combat aircraft of its size. Four members of this Intruder flight from USS Independence carry various armament while the two center aircraft are fitted with auxiliary fuel tanks (arrows). This suggests that they are serving as tankers for the strike aircraft on a long range mission. (Grumman Corporation, Courtesy Lois Lovisolo)

even degree downward tilt. The first production Intruders were delivered by autumn 1962 and 83 had been received by the U.S. Navy by the end of 1964.

Intruder Data
The Grumman A-6A Intruder was powered by two 9,300 pounds static thrust Pratt & Whitney J52-P-8A turbojets in side nacelles neatly faired into the fuselage sides and wing fillets. The aircraft weighs 25,684 pounds empty and 60,626 pounds gross. Wingspan

A detailed shot of the Intruder reveals the jet engine intake neatly faired into the wing/fuselage joint, (No.1); the landing gear which retracts into the wing fillet, (No.2); and the folded wing (No.3). (WAM Foto)

is 53 feet-0 inches, length 54 feet-9 inches and height 16 feet-2 inches. Maximum speed is 647 miles per hour at sea level. The combat radius on internal fuel only and without refueling is 300 miles. With maximum external fuel drop tanks plus internal fuel the range is 2,818 miles. Service ceiling is 45,500 feet.

Weapons
The entire weapons load of 18,000 pounds is carried externally on five stores pylons, each with a 3,600 pound capacity. A typical weapons menu includes two Martin Bullpup missiles and three 2,000 pound bombs or (30) 500 pound bombs arranged in clusters of three. Intruders can also fire Harpoon anti-ship missiles as well as the HARM antiradiation missile.

Two electronic equipment pods are also carried under the wing outboard of the stores pylons, one under each outer panel.

Crew Arrangement
The Intruder is of conventional all-metal construction employing a semi-monocoque fuselage structure. The pilot and radar officer sit side-by-side under a large sliding canopy forward of the wing in Martin Baker GRU5 ejector seats. The radar officer is located slightly behind and below the level of the pilot.

Intruder Wing
The controls are interesting because no ailerons are fitted. Full span wing leading and trailing edge flaps were deemed necessary; therefore, spoilers were installed in the wing upper surface for lateral control. The wing has a moderate amount of sweepback, however,

GRUMMAN A-6E INTRUDER
SQUADRON VA-34 "BLUE BLASTERS" — USS JOHN F. KENNEDY (1980)

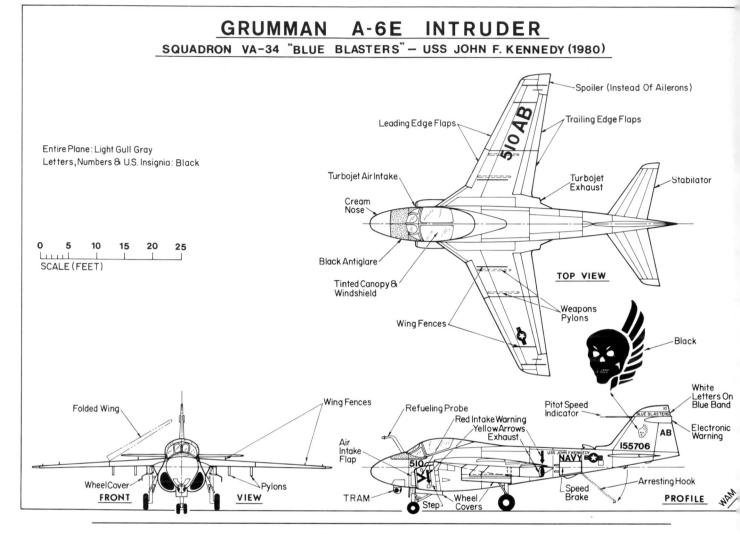

Entire Plane: Light Gull Gray
Letters, Numbers & U.S. Insignia: Black

SCALE (FEET) 0 5 10 15 20 25

Spoiler (Instead Of Ailerons)
Leading Edge Flaps
Trailing Edge Flaps
Turbojet Air Intake
Cream Nose
Turbojet Exhaust
Stabilator
Black Antiglare
Tinted Canopy & Windshield
Weapons Pylons
Wing Fences
TOP VIEW

Black
White Letters On Blue Band
Electronic Warning

Folded Wing
Wing Fences
Refueling Probe
Pitot Speed Indicator
Red Intake Warning
Yellow Arrows Exhaust
Air Intake Flap
Wheel Cover
Pylons
FRONT   **VIEW**
TRAM
Step
Wheel Covers
Speed Brake
Arresting Hook
PROFILE
155706
NAVY
USS JOHN F KENNEDY
510
AB
BLUE BLASTERS

the wing root is swept at a far greater angle which, in effect, produced a compound sweepback wing.

Electronics

The extensive electronic equipment of the Intruder includes DIANE (Digital Integrated Attack Navigation Equipment) system which includes search and track radar, inertial and Doppler navigators, high-speed digital computer, communications, navigation and identification package, automatic flight control system, electronic countermeasures systems and integrated cockpit displays.

Basically, this system made it possible for the pilot and radar officer to preselect the course of action prior to takeoff and, once in the air, DIANE will fly the plane through the complete mission including all maneuvers to clear obstacles and for weapons delivery. After discharging the weapons DIANE directs the aircraft to leave the target area immediately. The pilot lands the aircraft.

The integrated cockpit display system enables the crew to view geographical features as well as the target under all weather conditions and in total darkness by means of two viewing screens in the cockpit which furnish a visual representation of the ground or water below and ahead of the Intruder.

Precision Standoff Attack

When proven MRASM (Medium Range Air to Surface Missiles) such as Tomahawk, Harpoon and others became available and a deliverable, they gave rise to the tactical concept of a precision standoff attack. As previously related, the Fleet Air Arm Buccaneer used the Toss Bomb technique to discharge its lethal cargo as far from the target as possible in order to avoid flying over the target and/or its escorting destroyers. The precision standoff attack carries this tactical technique a step further by employing ultra-sophisticated electronics and MRASM. Standoff attack means that the attacker need not endanger itself in order to deliver its weapon but can launch the weapon at a relatively safe distance from the target to avoid facing the lethal surface-to-air missiles it will surely encounter, once detected.

The Grumman Corporation joined forces with Norden Systems of the famous World War II bombsight and a leader in airborne radar design, to develop the electronics required for the AWSACS (All Weather Standoff Attack Control System) which was sponsored by the U.S. Navy. The system involves the use of high resolution image-forming radar and high-speed digital radar signal processing for fixed and moving target detection, acquisition, classification, and tracking. The standoff missile is controlled after launch

This ECM (Electronic Counter Measures) EA-6A Prowler shows the lever fold-down ladder for crew access to the cockpit, (No.1); undering electronic pods (No.2);and the refueling probe, (No.3). (Grumman Corporation, Courtesy Lois Lovisolo)

with the same technology by transmitting periodic targeting updates to its guidance unit during midcourse and terminal attack phases. AWSACS provides the attack/strike aircraft's radar with the ability to classify ships and other targets from longer standoff ranges in adverse weather and then to attack the target with precision guided weapons from a longer standoff range.

The system also comprised SAR (Synthetic Aperture Radar) which, when combined with a relative angle measurement unit, can make the three feet diameter SAR antenna operate as though it was hundreds of feet wide! The SAR antenna collects the mass of energy reflected back from the target area and then performs a very fine grain division of the energy into individual velocity elements, using the information to create a picture of photographic quality. The relative angle measurement produces an image which visually illustrates the true closing speed with the target.

Grumman Prowler

Further development of the Intruder to provide Electronic Counter Measure (ECM) facilities for A-6A squadrons resulted in the EA-6A Prowler which was originally designated A2F-1Q.

EA-6A Electronics

Much of the DIANE was deleted to make way for over 30 different systems necessary to detect, locate, monitor, classify, record, jam and deceive enemy radar transmissions. The EA-6A also retains limited strike capability. Two ALQ-99 tactical jamming pods are carried under the wing, one on either side. The first Grumman EA-6A Prowler flew in 1965.

EA-6B Electronics

The EA-6A Prowler was succeeded by the EA-6B which was a completely reworked design, incorporating even more advanced ECM systems. As many as five ALQ-99 high-power tactical jamming pods can be carried by the EA-6B Prowler, each of which is powered by a windmill generator at the forward end of the pod. Two additional radar operators are seated side-by-side behind the pilot and the ECM radar officer. The new crew members monitor and counter enemy radar transmissions while the ECM officer manages navigation, communications, defensive ECM and dispenses chaff as necessary. The addition of two crew members resulted in a lengthened fuselage to 59 feet-5 inches. Weights increased to 32,162 pounds empty and 65,100 pounds gross. Service ceiling with five electronic pods is 38,000 feet and range is 2,085 miles. Combat radius with five pods is 470 miles. The EA-6B entered production in 1966.

WARBIRDS OF THE 1960s

Although not as prolific as the 1950s, the 1960s saw the introduction of shipboard aircraft that had become classics in their time. In

The Grumman EA-6B Prowler electronic countermeasures aircraft can carry five high-powered tactical jamming pods. Windmill generators at the nose of each pod provide electrical power for the electronic jamming equipment (arrows). (Grumman Corporation, Courtesy Lois Lovisolo)

The LTV (Vought) A-7 Corsair II light attack plane design was based upon the successful F-8 Crusader. This Vought A-7E Corsair II has just landed on USS America and is a member of the Blue Diamonds Squadron (VA-146) which fought in Vietnam. (Ling-Temco-Vought, Courtesy Arthur L. Schoeni)

An innovative feature of the Corsair II is the unusual air brake which comprises the entire fuselage bottom between the nose landing gear and the main landing gear. The brake is hinged forward and is used for speed control during bombing runs. (Ling-Temco-Vought, Courtesy Arthur L. Schoeni)

addition to the aforementioned Intruder/Prowler and Buccaneer, three outstanding designs have been selected for our narrative: a light attack plane; a strike/fighter; and a computer-laden airborne early warning aircraft (AEW).

Vought A-7E Corsair II

The U.S. Navy issued design requirements and invited proposals for a single-seat lightweight attack plane on May 17, 1963. The purpose was to find a replacement for the aging Douglas A-4 Skyhawk and the Navy was hoping to find a plane following the great tradition of U.S. Navy attack aircraft such as the SBD Dauntless, AU Corsair, A-1 Skyraider and A-4 Skyhawk. Proposals were received from four companies including LTV (Vought) which offered a design based upon the proven F-8 Crusader. LTV was declared the winner on February 11, 1964 and, on March 19, the U.S.

A retractable refueling fitting is another advanced feature of the Vought Corsair II. The receiving probe folds into the recess to become flush with the fuselage side when not in use. (Ling-Temco-Vought, Courtesy Arthur L. Schoeni)

Navy awarded LTV a contract for seven A-7A test aircraft which design became known as the Corsair II.

Corsair II Description

The new design had less sweepback, shorter fuselage, fixed incidence in order to utilize wing pylons, non-afterburning engine and lighter structure when compared with the Crusader. The Navy VAL (light attack aircraft) specification required the plane to carry more than 10,000 pounds externally and the Corsair II exceeded this requirement by 50 percent. Six underwing pylons were fitted; four with a 3,500 pound capacity and the remaining two with a 2,500 pound capacity. A 500 pound load can also be carried on each side of the fuselage. The first A-7A test aircraft completed its initial flight on September 27, 1965 which resulted in an order for 199 production A-7A Corsair II attack planes. The A-7A was powered by one 11,350 pound static thrust Pratt & Whitney TF30-P-6 turbofan jet engine. This was followed by the more powerful A-7B with a Pratt & Whitney TF30-P-8 turbofan jet engine and 196 were ordered. Later variant features improved avionics which provided all weather and nocturnal capabilities.

U.S. Air Force Interested

In 1966 the U.S. Air Force realized that the Navy had a superior attack craft in the A-7 and ordered production of an Air Force version with USAF modifications. These included the installation of the more powerful Rolls-Royce Spey turbofan jet engine and substitution of the two 20 millimeter cannon with a rotating six-barrel M-61 Vulcan 20 millimeter cannon and all-weather avionics. This was designated A-7D. The U.S. Navy soon realized the wisdom of the USAF refinements and adopted the A-7D as the A-7E. This became the definitive Corsair II of which 596 were delivered to Navy and Marine squadrons, starting in July 1969.

A-7E Corsair II Data

The LTV (Vought) A-7E Corsair II carrier-based light attack aircraft is powered by a single 15,000 pound static thrust Allison TF

Three Vought A-7E Corsairs of VA-195 await launching from USS Kitty Hawk for a strike at Vietnam. Observe the six Mark 82 general purpose 500 pound bombs mounted on each underwing pylon. Wingtips fold upwards to a vertical position to reduce the wingspan when planes are stowed. (Ling-Temco-Vought, Courtesy Arthur L. Schoeni)

1-2 turbofan jet engine which is a derivative of the Rolls-Royce Spey turbofan. With a wingspan of 38 feet-9 inches, and 23 feet-9 inches when folded, the wing area is 475 square feet. Length is 46 feet-1 1/2 inches, with a height of 16 feet-1 inch. The A-7E empty weight is 19,781 pounds with a maximum weight of 42,000 pounds. Top speed is 690 miles per hour at sea level and service ceiling 42,600 feet while range is 2,485 miles.

Corsair II Weapons

The multi-barrel cannon that replaced the two installed cannon is located inside the fuselage on the left side with only the firing barrel exposed. The 15,000 pound plus external load includes TV-guided bombs, general purpose bombs, laser-guided bombs, Rockeye free-falling bomb clusters, AP/AM (AntiPersonnel/AntiMaterial bomb clusters), flares, antiradiation missiles, chaff to confuse radar and incoming missiles, mines, Sidewinder air-to-air missiles, cluster and unit rockets, sonobuoys or antiship missiles, which covers almost every weapon in the naval aviation inventory.

Corsair II Electronics

The A-7E Corsair II is equipped with an Automatic Flight Control System (AFCS) which provides ground-controlled bombing, automatic carrier landings and control stick steering. It also has an advanced Navigation/Weapon Delivery System (NWDS) which continuously computes the navigation to the target as well as the attack; including weapon release, pullout and safe return from the target area. The A-7E also carries a Doppler radar system. Also installed is a forward-looking radar (FLR) that provides the pilot with 10 modes of operation. Among these is providing the slant range to target information to the tactical computer. The FLR also gives the pilot ground map displays; thereby, enabling him to follow the terrain and provides safe low-level all-weather navigation.

Deployment

All active U.S. Navy aircraft carriers were equipped with two squadrons of LTV A-7E aircraft each with 12 planes to a squadron. Four reserve squadrons of earlier A-7 aircraft also served on carriers. The Corsair II began phasing out of service in the mid-1980s and 60 USAF Corsair II's have been sold to Greece.

Not only was the McDonnell Douglas F-4 Phantom II the standard U.S. Navy and U.S. Air Force strike/fighter but it has also set a total of 15 world speed and altitude records. The Phantom II remained in service for more than a quarter century. (McDonnell Douglas, Courtesy Harry Gann)

McDonnell Douglas Phantom II

The author experienced the extreme pleasure of attending the International Air Tattoo at Royal Air Force Greenham Common, England in the summer of 1983 where one of the many attractions was a line-up of Phantom II fighters flown by the world's leading air forces. The reason for this extraordinary display was to celebrate the 25th anniversary of one of the most significant combat aircraft in service during the quarter-century following the end of World War II.

When the U.S. Navy initiated a design competition for a new supersonic fighter/attack aircraft in September, 1953, Vought and McDonnell were the principal competitors. McDonnell proposed an aggressive-looking twin-turbojet fighter while Vought offered a highly redesigned Crusader as the Mk.III which employed a Rocketdyne rocket engine in the fuselage rear to provide rapid acceleration and to assist maneuvers at 90,000 feet. The U.S. Navy ordered 23 preproduction McDonnell F4H-1 aircraft and 18 preproduction Vought Crusader III examples by the end of 1957. The F4H-1 first flew on May 27, 1958 while the Crusader III maiden flight was on June 2, 1958.

Phantom II Selected

Following a comprehensive evaluation of the two candidates during the summer of 1958, the F4H-1 emerged as the victor in December and was selected as the standard Navy and Marine all-weather missile fighter. All 23 preproduction Phantom II aircraft were redesignated F-4A and a further 24 were ordered in late 1959. Successful carrier suitability trials on *USS Independence* and *USS Intrepid* during February 1960 resulted in the awarding of a contract, in October, to increase production of the Phantom II to 192 planes, most of which were the F-4B definitive production version.

Phantom II Record Breakers

Even before entering service in February 1961 the Phantom II had begun establishing world speed and altitude records; demonstrating its brute power and maneuverability; on December 6, 1959 U.S. Navy Commander L.E. Flint set a world altitude record when he reached 98,560 feet over California. This accomplishment was not registered with the Federation Aeronautique Internationale (F.A.I.) therefore, it was not recognized as an official record.

U.S. Marine Lieutenant Colonel T.H. Miller established a new world speed record in a F-4A on September 5, 1960 when he attained a phenomenal 1,216.78 miles per hour at 45,000 feet over a 300 mile close circuit course. It is reported that during the 15 minute flight the F-4A burned 23,000 pounds of fuel! This record was officially approved by the F.A.I.

Twenty days later U.S. Navy Commander John F. Davis sped around a 60 mile closed circuit course at the record speed of 1,390.24 miles per hour at 46,000 feet altitude. He had attained Mach 2.25 in a continuous 3G turn in a 30 mile diameter circle!

The first Phantoms were assigned to VF-121 and VF-101 where they were used to train future crews and the record breaking continued.

U.S. Marine Lieutenant Colonel Robert B. Robinson established an F.A.I. approved world speed record of 1,606.324 miles per hour at 45,000 feet over the official 1/15 mile course on November 22, 1961. The record was flown at Mach 2.57.

This amazing plane has zoom-climbed to over 100,000 feet altitude, reaching 98,425 feet in six minutes-11.43 seconds! The Phantom has reached 49,212.5 feet in one minute-54.54 seconds and 65,617 feet in two minutes-58.5 seconds; establishing still more world records.

In December 1961 a Phantom II set a new world sustained altitude record of 66,443.8 feet over a measured course of 9/15 miles. Speed was over Mach 2.

A flight of five F-4B Phantoms from VF-101 raced across the American continent from Los Angeles to New York on May 24, 1961 to celebrate the 50th Anniversary of U.S. Naval Aviation. With three subsonic in-flight refuelings the winning Phantom made the 2,449.5 miles in 167 minutes-17.75 seconds; about the running time f a feature movie! Pilot Lieutenant Richard Gordon and radar officer Lieutenant (j.g.) B.R. Young averaged 869.739 miles per hour. Their winning F-4B was even loaded with missiles and carried a 00 gallon drop tank during the flight. The Navy team was awarded the prestigious Bendix Trophy for this outstanding achievement.

Multiple Mission Phantom II

The McDonnell F-4 Phantom II has set a total of 15 world speed and altitude records which are evidence of its superior performance. Initially conceived as a long-range all-weather attack/fighter to succeed the McDonnell Demon, the Phantom II was soon employed in a total of five major roles: air defense or interception; air superiority or fighter; photo-reconnaissance; long-range attack or strike; and tactical support or naval and ground target attack. In each of its varied roles the Phantom II provided its own air cover by virtue of its speed and maneuverability.

One Versus Two-Man Crew

The single-seater versus multi-member crews argument has raged since the first naval aircraft; however, the two-man crew has been credited as one of the reasons for the efficient and versatile mission performance of the Phantom II. McDonnell human engineering analysts studied every monitoring and control function required to operate the F-4 throughout its flight envelope and multiple mission assignments. Countless test missions were flown in the McDonnell Flight Simulation Laboratory, where control and monitoring responsibilities were defined as either manual or electronic. Those tasks that were best accomplished by using the mental reasoning and manual capabilities of the pilot and/or the radar officer were so assigned; however, those tasks that required instant, split-second, predetermined responses were assigned to the electronic computers. The crew and computer capabilities were then integrated with fire control, advanced radar, communication, and instrumentation systems which resulted in maximum efficiency in each mission performance. The conclusion of these extensive studies resulted in the decision that the full potential of an all-weather multiple mission aircraft can only be realized with a two-man crew. Combat aircraft had become so sophisticated in performance and electronic equipment that the proper operation of these complex machines had to be divided between the thinking crew and the programmed electronic equipment.

Phantom II Configuration

The McDonnell Phantom II was exceptionally bold in both aerodynamic and structural design and, as with most advanced concepts, underwent constant refinement in order to attain its ultimate configuration.

The original thin five percent thickness airfoil, 45 degree swept-wing, without dihedral revealed serious problems of pitch-up because of wingtip stalling at high angles of attack. More than 5,000 hours of wind tunnel testing with over 100 different tail designs and 75 wing shapes solved the problem which resulted in the addition of 12 degrees of dihedral in the outer wing panels to improve coordinated turns and lateral stability. In addition, a 10 percent increase in the outer wing panel chord formed a sawtooth leading edge in order to cure the low-speed pitch-up problem, as was previously described for the Supermarine Scimitar. The solution for the improvement of the high-speed pitch-up problem, which was caused by downwash from the wing disturbing the stabilator, was to slope the stabilator halves downward 23 degrees so the tips were lower than the stabilator attachment point to the fuselage. The outer wing panel dihedral is called polyhedral while the reverse dihedral of the stabilator is called anhedral.

The fuselage has a slight area rule or Coke bottle shape and the space above the side-by-side turbojet-engines is filled with five huge fuel cells. Another fuel cell is positioned immediately aft of the cockpit and supplementary fuel cells fill the leading one-third of the wing. Total internal fuel capacity is about 2,000 gallons which is 100 times more than the fuel tank capacity of a large luxury automobile. To this enormous tankage can be added a 22 feet long 600 gallon under-fuselage drop tank plus two 370 gallon underwing drop tanks. The pointed nose-radome houses the scanner dish of the APQ-72 long-range radar.

Air Inlet Control

Supersonic speeds around Mach 2 have an adverse effect on the turbojet air compressor inlet; therefore, a variable geometry configuration was devised for the turbojet inlet.

A deflector was installed against the fuselage at the air inlet scoop and this is automatically controlled through a 10 to 14 degree travel, according to engine power setting and airspeed, to deflect the supersonic shock wave at the engine air inlet and admit a subsonic airflow to the compressor.

Structure

In order to absorb the tremendous power, Mach 2.4 speed, and violent maneuvers the McDonnell F-4 Phantom II employed a sophisticated and dense structure; making extensive use of a machined aluminum skin, stainless steel honeycomb, and titanium.

As had been done for the Douglas Skyhawk, a minimum number of large airframe subassemblies was used to reduce bolting and the resulting stress concentrations. The Phantom II major subassemblies included: three fuselage sections (forward, center and aft); one-piece wing structure as on the Brewster Buffalo and Douglas Skyhawk; two outer folding wingtip panels; and one-piece stabilator (combination STABILizer and elevATOR).

In order to meet the restricted stowage space of Royal Navy carriers, Fleet Air Arm Phantoms were fitted with folding nose radomes as shown by this Phantom on a Royal Navy carrier elevator. (Ministry of Defence [Navy])

McDONNELL DOUGLAS F·4N/S PHANTOM II
SQUADRON VMFA-333 — USS NIMITZ

Entire Plane: Gull Gray
All Lettering: Black

Leading Edge Flaps
Retracted Landing Gear
Aileron
Trailing Edge Flaps
Turbojet Variable Air Intake Flaps
White Nose Cone
Black
Turbojet Exhaust
Titanium
Intake Flaps, Partially Closed
Turbojet Air Intake
White Star
Blue Background
Red Bar
Stabilator

TOP VIEW

0 5 10 15 20 25
SCALE (FEET)

One-Piece Wing
Stabilator
Folded Wing
Air Intake
FRONT
Fuel Tank
VIEW

Open Canopies
Green Bands & Shamrocks
Intake Flaps
Unpainted Titanium (Brownish Gray)
USS NIMITZ
VMFA-333
3869
136
MARINES
Red Intake Warning Symbol, White Border
Wheel Covers
600 Gal. Fuel Tank
Arresting Hook
PROFILE

Temperature Restricts Speed

Performance of the Phantom II is restricted by the temperature limits of the outer structure due to the air friction on its surfaces.

This becomes critical at about Mach 2.4, which is approximately 1,580 miles per hour above 36,000 feet, when the aluminum outer structure, cockpit canopy, wing leading edges, and titanium stabilator undersurface (due to the exhaust gasses) all reach their maximum allowable temperatures.

Hydraulic Systems

Rudder, stabilator, ailerons, spoilers, airbrakes, engine air inlet deflector and landing gear operation are all hydraulically actuated. Three 3,000 pounds per square inch hydraulic systems were installed to provide adequate backup for these important operations.

Slow Landing Speed

One of the most remarkable aspects of the F-4 performance is that, despite its phenomenal top speed, the landing speed is as low as 1/12th of the top speed! This 12 to one ratio can be attributed to the leading and trailing edge flaps which alter the airfoil; leading edge flaps depressing 30 degrees while the trailing edge flaps depress 60 degrees. In addition to the flap movement, boundary layer control

is provided for both flaps; thereby reducing the approach speed to 135 miles per hour with an angle of attack of about 10 degrees.

USAF and Foreign Orders

In addition to the U.S. Navy and U.S. Marine Corps, the U.S. Air Force and several foreign air forces flew the Phantom II: U.S.A.F. 1,383; Israel 50; German Federal Republic 88; Japan 104; Iran 32 and Britain 168 (powered by two 20,515 pound static thrust Rolls Royce Spey 25R turbo-fan jet engine).

F-4B Data

The U.S. Navy ordered 635 F-4B variants; more than any other model. The F-4B Phantom II was powered by two 10,900 pound static thrust dry (17,000 pounds static thrust with afterburner) General Electric J79-GE-8 turbojet-engines which gave the aircraft a maximum speed of 1,584 miles per hour at 48,000 feet or Mach 2.4, and an initial rate of climb of 28,000 feet per minute. The service ceiling was 71,000 feet and combat radius 900 miles. The ferry range was 2,300 miles. Wingspan was 38 feet-4 7/8 inches and wing area 530 square feet. Overall length was 58 feet- 3 1/8 inches and height 16 feet-3 inches. The empty weight was 28,000 pounds while maximum takeoff weight was 56,000 pounds.

This Grumman E-2A Hawkeye airborne early warning aircraft of Attack Carrier Wing CVW-15 from USS Coral Sea (CVA-43) exhibits its 24 foot diameter Rotodome which rotates at six revolutions per minute in the airstream. The Rotodome can be lowered 28 inches to the level of the fins for stowage on the smaller carriers. (Official U.S. Navy Photograph, News Photo Division)

Armament for the interception role consists of four 450 pound AAM-N-6 Sparrow III semi-active radar-homing missiles recessed beneath the fuselage plus two more of the same on underwing pylons. Alternatively, AAM-N-7 Sidewinder IA infrared homing missiles can be carried. For long-range attack or strike missions the McDonnell Phantom II can carry such loads as (22) 500 pound bombs.

McDonnell joined forces with Douglas during the refinement and production of the Phantom II to become the McDonnell Douglas Corporation. The U.S. Navy and U.S.Marine Corps F-4 Phantoms were gradually phased out of service after more than a quarter century of supremacy and eventually replaced by the technologically advanced Grumman Tomcat and McDonnell Douglas Hornet.

Grumman Hawkeye

Prior to 1956 Airborne Early Warning (AEW) aircraft had been adaptations of existing designs such as Avengers, Guardians and Trackers. By this time the U.S. Navy decided that a purpose-designed aircraft was necessary to implement the new concept of Airborne Tactical Data System. This electronic system was to provide a task force commander with all the information regarding the disposition of all friendly and enemy ships and aircraft necessary to properly control his forces. The principal role to be played in this concept was by an Airborne Early Warning (AEW) picket aircraft equipped with digital computers which automatically detect targets and select the best available interceptor to be directed to each target. This selection is based upon the location of the target as weil as the range and armament of the interceptor.

Grumman Hawkeye Selected

The U.S. Navy conducted an industry-wide design competition for the new AEW aircraft and Grumman Aircraft Engineering Corporation (now known as Grumman Corporation) emerged as the winner on March 5, 1957. The new plane, designated W2F-1, was soon known as the famous Hawkeye. First flight without electronic systems was on October 21, 1960, and with fully operative electronic

systems the first flight was on April 29, 1961. The plane went into production as the E-2A of which the last of 59 was delivered in the spring of 1967.

Hawkeye E-2A Data

The Grumman E-2A is powered by two 4,050 shaft horsepower General Motors Allison T56-A-8A turboprop engines which gave the plane a maximum speed of 370 miles per hour. Cruising speed was 315 miles per hour and service ceiling was 31,700 feet. Empty weight was 36,063 pounds while gross loaded weight reached 49,638 pounds. Wingspan was 80 feet-7 inches, length 56 feet-4 inches while overall height was 18 feet-4 inches. Wing area was 700 square feet. Unloaded range was 1,900 miles.

Radar Rotodome

An outstanding feature of the Hawkeye was the distinctive 24 feet diameter saucer-shaped radome that housed the AN/APA-143 an-

With landing gear, arresting hook and flaps extended a turboprop-powered Hawkeye lands on USS Constellation (CVA-64) under the watchful eyes and instructions of the Landing Signal Officer. (Official U.S. Navy Photo, News Photo Division)

tenna for the AN/APS-96 search radar. This Rotodome was mounted high above the fuselage and rotated in the airstream at six revolutions per minute. It could be lowered 28 inches to the level of the tail fins for stowage on the smaller aircraft carriers. The complex airflow over and around this giant disk compelled the designers to devise tail surfaces comprising four stationary fins and two rudders on the outboard fins, with slight dihedral in the horizontal stabilizer.

The Hawkeye had an all-metal high aspect ratio tapered wing mounted atop the fuselage while the fuselage was all-metal monocoque with a long parallel midbody and sharp taper at the tail.

Hawkeye Crew

A crew of five, which included three electronic technicians, was needed to operate the Hawkeye.

E-2B Hawkeye

A modified version of the E-2A was announced in 1967 and first appeared in February 1969. This E-2B variant had been fitted with even more advanced avionics plus provision for inflight refueling. The outboard fins had also been slightly enlarged.

E-2C Hawkeye

Meanwhile, the most capable carrier-based Airborne Early Warning aircraft yet to be produced was under development at the Grumman plant. The E-2C variant of the Hawkeye had been offered as an alternative to the more expensive E-3 AWACS which operated from land bases. Fitted with Loral ASPRO (ASsociative PROcessor) computers, a single E-2C Hawkeye could keep track of thousands of targets and possible targets over a scanning area of over a million cubic miles! The Grumman E-2C operating station is about 200 miles from the carrier, flying high to extend the radar horizon of the task force, where hostile surface units and aircraft can be detected before they enter missile range.

The APS-125 UHF radar can detect ships and aircraft as far as 240 miles away from the E-2C and is able to track, determine friend or foe, analyze all data in the plane's Combat Information Center (CIC) and then simultaneously direct strike and interception forces against 250 ships and aircraft.

The E-2C prototype made its first flight in January 1971 and production order of 95 aircraft was completed in 1986. Four Grumman E-2C Hawkeyes are assigned to each carrier air wing.

The E-2C dimensions were the same as the E-2A except for the fuselage length which was 15 inches longer. Increased power of two 4,910 shaft horsepower Allison T56-425 turboprops enabled the heavier E-2C (51,817 pounds gross) to attain 375 miles per hour. Service ceiling was less at 30,800 feet, but unloaded range had increased to 1,394 miles. Operationally, the Grumman E-2C remains on station for six hours which gives the E-2C a radius of 200 miles from the carrier, based upon its fuel consumption.

The Airborne Tactical Data System (ATDS) on board the E-2C Hawkeye incorporates Ferranti or similar data links providing real time communications with ships of the task force which works both ways, enabling the flagship to issue decisions on strikes and intercepts without delay.

The Grumman C-2A Greyhound was a military transport version of the Hawkeye, specializing in COD (Carrier On-board Delivery). Observe the method of wing folding. (Grumman Corporation, Courtesy Lois Lovisolo)

C-2A Greyhound

Early in the E-2A program, Grumman engineers realized that the basic configuration would make a good military transport for Carrier On-board Delivery (COD) with selected modifications. The U.S. Navy reacted to the Grumman proposal with an order for three prototypes of the concept which as designated C-2A and became known as Greyhound.

The E-2A wings, engines and nacelles were used; however, a longer main landing gear was necessary because the fuselage of the C-2A was much deeper and wider. The outboard fins and rudder were enlarged below the stabilizer which remained the same except that the dihedral was eliminated because no radome dish was fitted. The Greyhound was designed to carry about 40 passengers, 20 stretchers or cargo. A rear loading ramp/door was installed under fuselage rear. The prototypes first flew on November 18, 1964 and production began in the following year.

Empty weight was 31,250 pounds while fully loaded the C-2A weighed 54,382 pounds. Maximum speed was 352 miles per hour at 30,000 feet and cruising speed was 296 miles per hour at the same altitude. Service ceiling was 28,800 feet. Range was a respectable 1,655 miles.

The wing panels folded just outboard of the engines by twisting 90 degrees and folding back parallel with the fuselage, trailing edge up, on all carrier-based Hawkeyes and Greyhounds.

CUBAN MISSILE CRISIS

An international crisis erupted on October 14, 1962, which required the support of American aircraft carriers and their Warbirds, when a U.S. Lockheed U-2 reconnaissance plane photographed a Soviet nuclear missile site under construction in Cuba. Also discovered were Soviet I1-28 bombers being assembled on Cuban airfields. Ten days later a quarantine (peacetime blockade) was imposed on he island using the aircraft carriers *Wasp* (CVS-18), *Essex* (CVS-*), *Independence* (CVA-62), and *Enterprise* (CVAN-65) plus the helicopter assault ship *Boxer* (LPH-4). By October 28 the Cuban Crisis had been resolved when the Soviets agreed to remove the missiles and bombers; another job well done with the assistance of aircraft carriers.

VIETNAM WAR

One year after the Cuban Crisis ended, a more serious crisis began which was to require far greater involvement for aircraft carriers and their Warbirds. On November 2, 1963 South Vietnam President Ngo Dinh Diem was assassinated during a Buddhist-led military coup d'etat which resulted in 18 months of political instability. This hampered American efforts to aid the country in resisting the Viet Cong insurgency. U.S. President John F. Kennedy was assassinated 20 days later.

U.S. Navy Pilots Shot Down

Problems began on June 6, 1964 when Lieutenant Charles F. Klusmann was flying his RF-8 Crusader reconnaissance plane from *USS Kitty Hawk* (CVA-63), over the Plaine des Jarres, Laos. Shot down by Communist insurgent antiaircraft fire, Lieutenant Klusmann parachuted to safety, landing near the Communist Camp. When a U.S. rescue helicopter approached, Klusmann waved it away, fearing that it would also be shot down. Captured by the Communists, the Lieutenant escaped on September 1, 1964, and was awarded the Distinguished Flying Cross.

On June 7 an F-8 Crusader fighter from *USS Kitty Hawk* was also shot down by ground fire while escorting a reconnaissance aircraft over the Plaines des Jarres.

Tonkin Gulf Incident

The infamous Tonkin Gulf Incident occurred in the afternoon of August 2, 1964 when the U.S. Navy destroyer *Maddox* (DD-731)

A Douglas A-1H Skyraider is undergoing preparation on USS Intrepid (CVS-11) for a sortie over Vietnam. The A-4 Skyhawk in the background has its wing leading edges depressed to increase lift for takeoff. (Official U.S. Navy Photograph, News Photo Division)

Three Douglas EA-1E Skyraiders from Airborne Early Warning Squadron 33 (VAW-33) fly in formation over USS Forrestal (CVA-59) during the Vietnam fighting. Skyraiders engaged in many diverse roles over Vietnam. (Official U.S. Navy Photograph, News Photo Division)

was attacked by three North Vietnamese patrol boats in international waters 30 miles from the North Vietnam coast. Captain Herbert L. Ogier engaged the attackers and called on the carrier *Ticonderoga* (CVA-14) for assistance. Four F-8E Crusaders entered the fight, during which the *Maddox* evaded two torpedoes. One of the North Vietnamese boats was destroyed. The destroyer *Turner Joy* (DD-951) had also been attacked in a separate incident on that day.

Carriers Retaliate

In retaliation for the attacks on U.S. ships, President Lyndon Johnson exacerbated the growing crisis by ordering aircraft from *Constellation* (CVA-64) and *Ticonderoga* (CVA-14) to attack North Vietnamese naval bases, oil depots and patrol boats. On August 5 Commander James B. Stockdale led the first American strike against North Vietnam in his Vought F-8 Crusader; directing other Crusaders against oil storage facilities at Vinh. Commander Stockdale became one of the most highly decorated officers in the history of the U.S. Navy, serving three combat tours in Vietnam until he was shot down in 1965. He went on to attain the rank of Vice Admiral and became president of the Naval War College.

Other strikes on August 5 included Douglas A-1H Skyraiders and A-4E Skyhawks from *USS Constellation*. A total of 64 sorties was flown during which 25 patrol boats were severely damaged or destroyed and nine out of 10 oil storage tanks were burned out. One Skyraider was shot down, whose pilot, Lieutenant (jg) Richard A. Sather was the first U.S. Navy pilot to be killed in action in Viet-

nam. Lieutenant (jg) Everett Alvarez was flying a Skyhawk whe he was also shot down and became the first U.S. Navy prisoner c war in Vietnam.

Tonkin Gulf Resolution

Two days later the U.S. Congress passed the Tonkin Gulf Resolu tion in which it gave away its war-making powers to the Presiden thereby, unwittingly causing a great calamity. Congress empow ered the President to "take all necessary measures to repel any arme attack against the forces of the U.S. . . . and to assist any member c protocol state "of SEATO (South East Asia Treaty Organization). is on the basis of this ill-advised legislation that President Johnso committed U.S. Forces to an ever-expanding role in Vietnam with out a Declaration of War.

Operation Flaming Dart I

In the morning of February 7, 1965 eight American serviceme were killed and 128 wounded by a Viet Cong attack on a barrack in Pleiku, South Vietnam. The Viet Cong (Viet Nam Cong Sar were militant South Vietnamese Communist guerrillas who wer seeking national independence and were fully supported by Com munist North Vietnam. In retaliation for the attack, the U.S. Nav initiated Operation Flaming Dart I which was a strike on barrack and other facilities near Dong Hoi, North Vietnam by 83 plane from the carriers *Coral Sea* (CVA-43), *Ranger* (CVA-61) an *Hancock* (CVA-19). This took place on the very afternoon of th Viet Cong attack. One plane failed to return.

Operation Flaming Dart II

Three days later a Viet Cong bomb killed 23 Americans and wounded 21 in the enlisted men's barracks at the Qui Nhon helicopter base. Retribution was swift on the following morning, February 11, when 99 aircraft from the carriers *Hancock*, *Coral Sea* and *Ranger* launched Flaming Dart II by attacking military installations around Chan Hoa, North Vietnam. One *USS Coral Sea* F-8D Crusader was lost in this operation.

Carriers = Power Projection

Flaming Dart II ignited a blaze of U.S. aerial activity and escalated the air war. This continued, unabated, throughout the Vietnam Conflict which had become a prime example of the use of aircraft carriers for power projections. American aircraft carriers sailed the length of Tonkin Gulf, launching their Warbirds on strikes as they pleased, because military targets in both Vietnams were conveniently within reach and the Communists did not have the capability to retaliate in force. From this time onward, U.S. carriers were constantly waging war in Southeast Asia.

Operation Rolling Thunder

This bombing offensive was planned on March 2, 1965. U.S. Navy and U.S. Air Force aircraft were to begin sustained bombardment of military targets in North Vietnam with the hope that the North's endurance would collapse and its support of the Viet Cong would diminish and eventually terminate.

The new operation started on March 15, 1965 when *Hancock* and *Ranger* aircraft attacked an ammunition dump at Phu Qui, south of Hanoi. One plane and its pilot failed to return. Eleven days later 40 planes from *Hancock* and *Coral Sea* destroyed four radar sites in North Vietnam; losing two planes in this action. Both pilots were rescued.

The tempo increased and, by the end of March, 1965, up to 100 planes were flown almost every day from carriers in Tonkin Gulf. Primary targets were power stations, transportation facilities, oil depots, ammunition dumps and radar sites in North Vietnam.

A Douglas A-1E Skyraider attack aircraft returns to USS Constellation (CVA-64) in the Gulf of Tonkin after completing a mission over North Vietnam. Skyraiders performed yeoman service in the fighting. (Official U.S. Navy Photograph, News Photo Division)

Dive Bombing Skywarriors

The Douglas Skywarrior played a big role in the Vietnam fighting with bombing, reconnaissance, tanker, electronic countermeasure and electronic surveillance assignments. These large craft were often called "whales" because of their size. Douglas A-3B Skywarriors made their bombing debut on March 29, 1965 when six aircraft from VAH-2, based on *USS Coral Sea*, attacked Bach Long Vi island in Tonkin Gulf during a heavy foggy haze. Visual target sighting was impossible so the Skywarriors used radar sighting to bomb the unseen target.

From three to five Skywarriors were carried by *Essex* class carriers while the *Forrestal* class embarked a full squadron. It was reported that Skywarriors aboard *USS Oriskany* were fitted with spare Skyhawk gunsights and improvised multiple module bomb racks in the weapons bay. Thus equipped, these large twin-engine aircraft actually conducted successful dive bombing missions in Vietnam.

Skywarrior Tankers

As the burden of air strikes shifted to smaller planes such as fighters and attack aircraft, the large Skywarrior concentrated in the tanker role plus electronic and photographic reconnaissance.

Virtually every strike launched from the U.S. aircraft carriers on Yankee Station was accompanied by a Douglas KA-3B Skywarrior tanker to refuel aircraft losing fuel due to combat damage or to assist if the carrier landing cycle was slow or delayed for any reason by refueling those planes in the landing pattern that were running low on fuel. It has been conservatively estimated that about 500 planes were saved by Skywarrior tankers.

Skywarrior Reconnaissance

On photo-reconnaissance missions the RA-3B handled cartographic assignments as well as tactical reconnaissance. This was most valuable by providing information to update maps necessary for Vietnam operations. One RA-3B could shoot the equivalent of more than 3,000 rolls of commercial camera film in a single mission.

The RA-3B also conducted nocturnal reconnaissance fitted with infra-red sensors, as well as a real-time visual display. Painted black, the Skywarrior flew at 500 feet altitude or less, looking for "hot spots" produced by trucks on the Ho Chi Minh Trail and other supply routes. Orbiting strike planes were then called down to halt the traffic. Using infra-red film, the cameras could detect dead foliage from the live; thereby, enabling them to detect foliage that was being used for camouflage.

MiG's Over Vietnam

The American raiders had met no aerial resistance until April 9, 1965 when four McDonnell F-4 Phantoms, flying cover for a strike on North Vietnam, were attacked by several Soviet-built MiG-17 (Mikoyan-Gurevich) fighters about 40 miles south of Hainan Island. The MiG nationality could not be determined; however, it was generally suspected that they were Communist Chinese aircraft. One MiG appeared to fall out of control and one Phantom did not return to the carrier.

Another first occurred six days later when Warbirds from the carriers *Midway* (CVA-41) and *Coral Sea* (CVA-43) attacked Viet

Starting in April 1965 U.S. Naval aircraft began strikes against North Vietnam from U.S. carriers in Yankee Station in the South China Sea. The U.S. Navy flew 55,000 sorties of 5 to 100 aircraft raids over Vietnam. Skyhawks are shown on a U.S. carrier in Yankee Station preparing for a raid. Another carrier can be seen in the background. (U.S. Naval Historic Center)

Cong positions in South Vietnam. This was the first time U.S. Navy aircraft had attacked targets inside South Vietnam. On that same day 10 aircraft from the two aircraft carriers flew the first reconnaissance mission over North Vietnam.

Dixie Station

Dixie Station had been established in the South China Sea, 100 miles southeast of Cam Ranh Bay, in order that a single U.S. carrier at that location could launch strikes in support of U.S. and Allied Forces fighting inside South Vietnam. The new station had been placed into operation on May 16, 1965, as the U.S. became increasingly involved in the Vietnam fighting.

First Aerial Victories

The first confirmed aerial victories of the Vietnam War were made on June 17 over North Vietnam when two F-4B Phantoms of VF-20 from *USS Midway* were attacked by four MiG-17 fighters about 50 miles south of Hanoi. Two of the Soviet-built aircraft were shot down with Sparrow air-to-air missiles. Three days later two jet-powered MiG-17's attacked four propeller-driven A-1H Skyraiders from *USS Midway* and a Skyraider shot down one of the attackers with its 20 millimeter cannon. The MiG-17 was code-named Fresco by U.S. Forces.

Dangerous SAM's

The lethal quality of antiaircraft fire proved itself in North Vietnam on August 13, 1965 when a Skyraider, two Skyhawks and two Phantoms from *USS Midway* and *USS Coral Sea* were shot down by ground fire while on a search and destroy mission for SAM sites.

This was the worst day for the U.S. naval air war in Vietnam to date; however, it increased the Navy's resolve to eliminate the menacing North Vietnamese SAM sites. The first successful attack on an enemy antiaircraft missile site occurred on October 17 when an A-6 Intruder and four A-4E Skyhawks from *USS Independence* destroyed a site without any loss to themselves.

Industrial Targets

USS Enterprise (CVAN-65) launched 118 planes against targets in South Vietnam on December 2, 1965 which was the first time a nuclear-powered ship had engaged in hostilities. Enterprise joined the carriers *Ticonderoga* and *Kitty Hawk* on December 22, 1965 in launching 100 planes in an attack on the North Vietnamese powerplant at Uong Bi. This was the first raid on a purely industrial target. Two planes failed to return.

First Crusader Victory

The first ever victory scored by an F-8 Crusader was on June 12, 1966 when Commander Harold L. Marr, flying from *USS Hancock* destroyed a MiG-17 over North Vietnam with a Sidewinder air-to-air missile. The LTV F-8 Crusaders were destined to shoot down 18 of the first 29 enemy aircraft credited to U.S. Naval aircraft in the Vietnam War.

Oil Storage Targets

Near the end of June 1966 it was decided to cripple Vietnam's war effort by striking at the petroleum storage and distribution system. The first strike came on June 29 when 46 planes from *Ranger* (CVA-61) and *Constellation* (CVA-64) struck oil storage tanks in Hanoi and Haiphong suburbs. Other notable raids were made on August in which 64 planes from Constellation hit oil tanks near Haiphong and on July 21, 1967 when three MiG-17 fighters were shot down by F-8 Crusaders from *USS Bon Homme Richard* (CVA-31) during a strike at the Ta Xa oil storage depot, north of Haiphong.

Warbirds Bomb, Mine and Score

U.S. Navy carrier aircraft were kept busy in a wide variety of assignments during the Vietnam fighting; on August 29, 1966 Skyhawks and Intruders severely damaged two enemy patrol boats and sank a third; and on October 9, 1966, while bombing the Phu Ly Bridge near Hanoi, a Skyraider from *Intrepid* (CVS-11) shot down a vaunted MiG-21 jet fighter while a second MiG-21 was destroyed by an escorting Crusader from *Oriskany* (CVA-34). In addition, the aerial mining of North Vietnamese harbors and rivers was instituted on February 26, 1967 when seven VA-35 Grumman A-6 Intruders from *Enterprise* (CVAN-65) dropped mines into the Song Ca and South Giang River estuaries. Two months later, on April 24, 1967, air attacks on North Vietnam airfields began when Intruders, Skyhawks and Phantoms from *Bon Homme Richard* and

Grumman A-6A Intruders from USS Constellation (CVA-64) release general purpose bombs over North Vietnam. Intruders played a big part in the Vietnam air war. (Official U.S. Navy Photo, News Photo Division)

Vought Corsair II strike aircraft and McDonnell-Douglas Phantom II strike/fighters aboard the USS Forrestal (CVA-59) are engulfed in flame and smoke in Yankee Station. Explosions and fires that killed 134 officers and crew, destroyed 21 aircraft and damaged the ship were caused by an accident as the Airdales prepared planes for a strike on July 29, 1967. (Official U.S. Navy Photograph)

While USS Enterprise (CVAN-65) was conducting flight exercises near Hawaii on January 14, 1969 a missile on a Phantom II strike/fighter was accidently launched into other aircraft on the flight deck. The ensuing conflagration killed 28 and injured 65 crew members. Burned-out wreckage of Phantoms shown here are part of the 21 planes that were destroyed in the blaze. (Official U.S. Navy Photograph)

Kitty Hawk raided the jet base at Kep, north of Hanoi. Two MiG-17 fighters were shot down as they took off. A second sweep at the Kep airfield was made on May 1, 1967 in which six MiG-17 Fresco fighters were destroyed.

Aircraft Carrier Fires
Serious fires plagued the U.S. carriers off Vietnam. On October 26, 1966 a parachute flare's accidental ignition started a fire on the Hangar Deck of *USS Oriskany* (CVA-34) which resulted in the loss of 44 officers and enlisted men.

Three days after *Forrestal*'s deployment in Vietnam, planes were being readied on the Flight Deck for a strike on July 29, 1967. Undetected leaking fuel from one of the aircraft was accidentally ignited and the flaming fuel on the Deck set off missiles on the parked aircraft. The explosions and fires accelerated among the planes causing considerable damage to the Deck. The flames were battled for over eight hours before they were extinguished. This major disaster killed 134 officers and crew and destroyed 21 planes. *USS Forrestal* sailed to Norfolk, Virginia where the $72 million damage was repaired.

A third calamitous fire occurred on the nuclear-powered *Enterprise* January 14, 1969 while she was sailing near Hawaii. An aircraft missile accidently ignited on the Flight Deck, starting a large fire within seconds. Fortunately, the blaze was brought under control in about three hours; however, 28 members of the crew were killed and 65 injured. The foregoing incidents demonstrate the dangers inherent in the operation of these huge, complex ships even in the absence of enemy action. Safety is no accident.

Smart Bombs
The very first use of a television-guided air-to-surface bomb in combat took place on March 11, 1967 when a Walleye glide bomb was employed by planes from *Oriskany* (CV-34) in an attack on barracks at Sam Son, North Korea.

U.S. Navy Victories Increase; Then Stop
The increasing appearance of Soviet-built aircraft of the North Vietnamese or Communist Chinese forces accelerated the aerial encounters and consequential victories over Vietnam; Crusaders from *USS Bon Homme Richard* (CV-31) were flying cover for Skyhawks during a raid on a powerplant at Hanoi when MiG-17 fighters intervened. The Crusaders shot down four of the enemy planes on May 9, 1967; an F-4 Phantom from *Constellation* shot down a MiG-21 south of Hanoi on October 26, 1967 and, four days later another MiG-21 was destroyed by an F-4 air-to-air missile; on December 14, 1967 another MiG-21 was shot down by a missile launched by an F-8 Crusader. On the other side of the coin during January 1-5, 1968 five U.S. Naval aircraft were shot down by antiaircraft fire making this one of the worst weeks of the air war since 1965. Victories continued on June 26, 1968 when another MiG-17 was shot down by a Crusader from *Bon Homme Richard*. This was repeated when a Crusader from *USS Intrepid* shot down a MiG-21 over Vinh on September 19, 1968 which was the Navy's 29th victory and the last for Crusaders. Sixteen months was to elapse before a U.S. Navy plane scored another victory when an F-4 Phantom from *USS Constellation* shot down a MiG-21 near Thanh Hoa, North Vietnam on March 28, 1970. U.S. politicians had imposed severe restrictions on the airspace in which U.S. aircraft could operate with the result that enemy aircraft seldom ventured into the airspace in which U.S. aircraft were authorized to fly. It was because of this unnatural restriction that this victory by Lieutenants Jerry Beaulier and Steve Barkely of the Ghost Riders VF-142 off *Constellation* was the last naval air victory until 1972!

Peace Talks
Returning to 1969; representatives of the U.S. and North Vietnam began formal negotiations in Paris on January 25 in an effort to end the war which was to continue for three more years with accelerated ferocity.

U.S. Reduces Carrier Inventory

Despite the fact that the U.S. was engaged in a war that it was not winning and needed a strong naval presence in Vietnamese waters, especially aircraft carriers,the U.S. government reduced the number of ships in the Navy from 886 in July 1969 to only 600 by July 1971, which included the reduction of carriers such as *USS Shangri-La* (CVS-38).

Tonkin Gulf Resolution Repealed

On June 24, 1970 the U.S. Senate approved Repeal of the Tonkin Gulf Resolution and the U.S. House of Representatives did the same on December 31. President Nixon signed the bill into law on January 14, 1971; however, this had no immediate effect on the course of the war.

Warbird Losses Increase

The American aircraft carriers returned to Southeast Asia again and again with their brood of Warbirds. *USS Ticonderoga* and *USS Coral Sea* began their fifth tour of duty off Vietnam on March 5 and October 26, 1969 respectively, while *USS Constellation* sailed from San Francisco on October 1, 1971 for her sixth tour of duty in Vietnamese waters amidst a well-organized antiwar campaign to "Keep Connie Home." The growing intensity of the Vietnam air war became evident when 10 American planes had been shot down over Vietnam and Laos during the last three weeks of 1971 with 13 flyers missing and six rescued.

Enterprise Diverted

Notwithstanding the fact that carriers were needed in Vietnam waters, the nuclear-powered *Enterprise* (CVAN-65) was sent to the Indian Ocean and Bay of Bengal with an eight-ship escort in December 1971. This was necessary to counter a rapid build-up of Soviet naval forces in that area due to the Indo-Pakistani War which had just erupted. The presence of a formidable aircraft carrier and its Warbirds was crucial in this show of force to the 26 Soviet warships operating near Indian naval bases.

Harbor Mining

The year 1972 was most eventful for the U.S. Navy in general and aircraft carrier forces in particular.

Since the initial aerial mining of small rivers and estuaries in 1966, high civilian authority would not authorize the mining of deep water ports such as Haiphong because, ". . . it would escalate the war and risk confrontation either with Russia or Red China or both", according to Vice Admiral Malcolm W. Cagle. By May 8, 1972 the American negotiators at the Paris peace talks reported the intransigence of the North Vietnamese participants to President Nixon. This, coupled with the enemy's huge spring offensive, influenced the President to announced the mining of the important harbors of Than Hoa, Cam Pha, Haiphong, Dong Hoi, Vinh, Hon Gai and Quang Khe. Within two hours after Nixon's announcement, the initial phases of the mining had already been completed by carrier-based Grumman A-6 Intruders. The mines had been fitted with 72 hour delayed activation fuses to allow neutral shipping to leave the harbors before the mines became active.

Three Generations in the Carrier Navy

As 1972 began, three carriers were on Yankee Station; *Coral Sea* (CVA-43), *Constellation* (CVA-64) and the newly arrived *Hancock* (CV-19) which was the oldest carrier in the fleet. *Hancock* was the flagship of Admiral John S. McCain II, CINCPAC (Commander IN Chief PACific) whose father was deeply involved in Pacific battles of World War II as Commander of Task Force 38 in the Philippines campaign. Almost a quarter-century later Lieutenant Commander John S. McCain III was shot down by the North Vietnamese on October 26, 1967 and taken prisoner. Three generations of McCains; father, son and grandson had served their country in the finest tradition of the U.S. Navy.

The three carriers had accumulated a total of 64 years of service and were to add two more years to that figure before the war was over. *Kitty Hawk* (CVA-62) arrived on station April 3, 1972 because of the accelerated fighting caused by the fierce Communist spring offensive.

More Soviet Planes Over Vietnam

Heavy raids against missile sites in North Vietnam began in earnest on April 6 and the targets quickly expanded to include roads, bridges, airfields and storage depots. The carrier planes were busier than they had ever been and this is best illustrated by comparing SAM and AAA raids of all of 1971, which totalled 108, with those of the first three months of 1972, which totalled 90 raids. This amounted to a yearly increase of over 300 percent and it was no surprise when North Vietnamese aerial interceptions grew proportionally to the American raids. Not only did aerial encounters increase but a new Soviet-built fighter made its debut in Vietnam alongside the customary MiG-17 Fresco and MiG-21 Faceplate. The newcomer was a Mikoyan design, code-named Fishbed, that had a speed twice that of sound. MiG-19 Farmers also appeared in the Vietnam skies during this active period.

Operation Linebacker

By April 1972 developments in Vietnam, specifically the mass invasion of the south by North Vietnamese troops, upgraded the U.S. aircraft carrier's Warbirds' objectives to harassing and disrupting enemy military operations; destroying all North Vietnamese aggression-supporting resources; and reducing and impeding the movement of troops and materials through southern North Vietnam. It was relatively easy to double the Navy's Vietnam air potential in a matter of days because aircraft carriers are self-contained, floating mobile fortresses with integral fuel, ordnance, personnel, maintenance and other crucial self-sustaining supplies and services. The usual delay for follow-up logistics is nonexistent in carrier warfare. *USS Saratoga*, *USS Oriskany* and *USS America* had been ordered to Vietnam waters for Operation Linebacker; the effort to halt the Communist offensive which was instituted while peace talks were underway. Vice Admiral J.L. Holloway III relieved Vice Admiral W.P. Mack as Commander, Seventh Fleet, during this crucial period. President Nixon's orders in Operation Linebacker were to bomb North Vietnamese targets north of the 20th parallel which, heretofore, had been prohibited by previous administrations.

Cunningham and Driscoll of VF-96 Fighting Falcons from USS Constellation (CVA-64) pilot their F-4J Phantom II in October 1971; about three months before scoring their first victory over Vietnam. (Official U.S. Navy Photograph, News Photo Division)

First U.S. Aces in Vietnam

On January 19, 1972, before aerial activity between American and North Vietnamese aircraft had reached its crescendo, Lieutenant Randall F. Cunningham, pilot, and Lieutenant (JG) William Driscoll, radar intercept officer, of VF-96 Fighting Falcons from *USS Constellation*, had shot down a MiG-21 while flying a McDonnell F-4 Phantom II. This was their first victory. The team destroyed a MiG-17 with their Phantom II using a Sidewinder air-to-air missile on May 8, 1972 and shot down three MiG-17 Frescos two days later, which made Cunningham and Driscoll the first American Aces of the Vietnam War.

Busy Month For the Phantom II

May 10, 1972 had been a busy dogfighting day for American fighter

Lieutenant (jg) Driscoll (rear cockpit) and Lieutenant Cunningham (forward cockpit) smile in the cockpits of their McDonnell Douglas F-4J Phantom II after scoring their eighth victory in the Vietnam War. (Official U.S. Navy Photograph, News Photo Division)

Pilot Lieutenant Randall H. Cunningham (left) and radar intercept officer Lieutenant (jg) William P. Driscoll became the first American aces of the Vietnam War when they shot down their fifth enemy plane on May 10, 1972. Randy Cunningham was elected to the House of Representative in the U.S. Congress in the 1990s. (U.S. Naval Historic Center)

pilots in Vietnam skies. In addition to the three Cunningham/Driscoll victories on that day, Lieutenants Matt Connelly and Tom Blonski of VF-96 scored two Frescos with their Phantom II while Lieutenants K.L. Cannon and R.A. Morris of VF-51 shot down another MiG-17. The seventh Fresco of the day was sent crashing by the team of Lieutenant Curt Dose and Commander Jim McDevitt flying a Phantom II of VF-92. By the end of May two more Frescos and two new MiG-19 Farmers were shot down by the VF-161 Phantom II teams of Lieutenant J.C. Ensch and Commander Ron McKeown plus Lieutenants Henry Bartholomay and Oran Brown, and Lieutenants Pat Harwood and Mike Bell. The U.S. Navy total for May was 16 enemy aircraft shot down.

May 1972 proved a busy month for pilots flying the Phantom II in the skies of Vietnam and the men of VF-96 Fighting Falcons were in the midst of the action. Commander Wagner (center) poses with his men. Lieutenant Cunningham is standing fifth-from left (arrow). (Official U.S. Navy Photograph, News Photo Division)

Hot 'N Heavy Air Strikes

The tempo of carrier-based air strikes in Vietnam continued through the summer into the autumn of 1972. By July the U.S. Navy had six aircraft carriers on station. On July 4, the American Independence Day, planes from *USS Midway*, *USS Saratoga*, *USS Hancock*, and *USS Oriskany* struck at Kep Airbase, truck convoys, and storage depots. They also assisted ground troops with bombs, missiles and strafing. During the night of August 27 a plane from *USS Midway* sank a North Vietnamese PT-Boat.

Leathernecks Fly From Carriers

For many years U.S. Marine Squadrons had been relegated to shore-based activities and it was only during the closing actions of World War II that Marine Squadrons began serving on carriers; however, Marine units did operate from carriers during the Vietnam War. VMA-224, based on *USS Coral Sea*, and VMA-333 Shamrocks, based on *USS America*, flew Grumman A-6 Intruders and EA-6A Prowlers. The units concentrated on enemy SAM sites, which success had significantly reduced Warbird losses. Helicopters flown by HMA-369 from *USS Cleveland* (LPD-7) Amphibious Transport Dock made nocturnal sorties to search out enemy supply barges trying to slip past the American ships.

U.S. Helicopters In Vietnam

The helicopter truly proved its worth in Vietnam as both an offensive weapon and to rescue downed and stranded airmen. The Search And Rescue (SAR) helicopters were called Fleet Angels by the appreciative airmen. Helicopter Composite Squadron Seven (HR-7) had completed many SAR missions and detachments of this unit served on 10 different carriers during the war. From March to September 1972 the Nomads of the Tonkin Gulf, as this unit was affectionately called, made 22 rescues which included six stranded U.S. Air Force pilots. Proud of their motto: "Combat SAR Prevents POW's", the men of HC-7 had been serving on Yankee Station and Dixie Station for almost 2,000 days, risking their own lives to save the lives of downed and stranded airmen.

On August 7, 1972 Lieutenant William Young of Helicopter Composite Squadron Two (HC-2) based on *USS Saratoga* took off on a SAR mission and, "...although his aircraft was repeatedly hit by enemy groundfire, he continued the search until the downed airman was visually located and picked up. Lieutenant Young then flew back to the safety of Saratoga at treetop level with his crippled aircraft"." On that night Lieutenant Harry Zinser, USNR of the same unit flew, "...nearly five hours of coordinated search...in the face of intense enemy fire...turned on his landing lights... carried out a skillful landing, picked up the downed airman..." Both heroes were awarded the Navy Cross, the U.S. Navy's second highest honor. The preceding quotations are taken from the award citations.

More Peace Talks

The enemy again showed a willingness to make peace by October 1972 and a temporary halt was ordered in the bombing north of the 20th parallel. This U.S. gesture of sincerity was wasted because, by December, the Peace Talks had become bogged down again on various unresolved matters. The bombing was reinstated on December 18, 1972 and the carrier Warbirds resumed Operation Linebacker which brought the North Vietnamese running back to the Peace Talks by January 3, 1973.

Last Victory

The last MiG kill was made on January 12, 1973 when Lieutenant Walter Kovaleski, pilot, and Lieutenant James Wise, radar intercept officer off *USS Midway* scored the last victory of the Vietnam War when they shot down a MiG-17 with Sidewinder missiles over Tonkin Gulf. It was an unusual twist of fate that, two days later Lieutenant Kovaleski, with Ensign Dennis Plautz as radar intercept officer, became the last Americans to be shot down in the Vietnam fighting when their F-4 was hit by antiaircraft fire. Both men ejected safely and were rescued from the water by a Navy helicopter Fleet Angel.

Peace Agreement Signed

Le Duc Tho, chief North Vietnamese peace negotiator, and Henry Kissinger, the U.S. representative at the Peace Talks, formally signed an agreement in Paris ending American participation in the Vietnam War. The terms consisted of a cease-fire throughout South Vietnam and the withdrawal of all U.S. Forces. In addition, all American prisoners of war were to be released within 60 days. This was a far cry from the Unconditional Surrender imposed upon the Axis Powers in 1945 and united Vietnam became a Communist state.

Admirals Criticize Politicians

The U.S. military establishment was enraged at the "sell out" peace agreement. It was also angry because the war effort had been hampered by civilian politicians. The U.S. Navy was especially angry and it appeared that another Revolt of the Admirals would erupt. Shortly after the Paris Peace Accord, four respected U.S. Navy admirals had been invited to speak in the Naval Air Station auditorium at Pensacola, Florida about lessons learned in the air war over

OPPOSITE: Just plucked from his liferaft, a downed Belgian pilot is hoisted to a Westland Sea King SAR helicopter. The helicopter is indispensable to Search And Rescue operations in most of the world's navies. (Westland Helicopters Ltd., Courtesy P.D. Batten)

A Sikorsky Sea King SAR helicopter is lifting an injured seaman from the U.S. Navy ocean escort destroyer USS John Willis to rush him to a location where he can receive proper medical treatment. Helicopters can hover for long periods and need not land to pick up or discharge cargo or personnel (United Technologies/Sikorsky Archives)

Vietnam. Sponsors of the session were the U.S. Naval Institute and the Naval Aviation Museum. The honored speakers were Admiral Thomas Moorer who was soon to be the Chairman of the Joint Chiefs of Staff; Vice Admiral Robert F. Dunn who commanded Attack Squadron 146 and had been made Deputy Chief of Naval Operations for Air Warfare; Admiral M.F. Weisner, who was in command of the Seventh Fleet during the latter part of the war; and Admiral Wes McDonald who was a task group commander during Operation Linebacker in the Vietnam War.

The admirals were understandably upset over the conduct of the war by the politicians and spoke reliably about a subject with which they were most cognizant.

Admiral Moorer was the most outspoken and is quoted: "No man in his right mind would conduct a war like the Vietnam War." He is also reported to have stated that the U.S. could have won the war without difficulty: "If we'd done the same thing to Hanoi in 1965 that we did in 1972 . . . and we could have polished those clowns off in six months."

Admiral Weisner is reported to have observed: "I think we knew how to fight the war. I think we knew how to win the war, had we not been micromanaged from . . . Washington." He also said that if there is one lesson our nation's leadership should learn from the

Vietnam War, it is this: "Don't enter a conflict unless you've got the will to win." Admiral McDonald strongly agreed with Admiral Weisner's statement and said it was the most important lesson of the war. He also observed that despite the numerous frustrations imposed upon those fighting the naval air war by the politicians, "across the board, morale was high." This was a wonderful tribute to the U.S. naval forces.

Admiral Dunn outlined his experience in following rigid strike tactics and stated that "you must be flexible, you must plan for, and you must train and practice a variety of delivery methods, a variety of navigation methods, using a variety of weapons." He criticized the political restrictions that forbade using the tactical necessity of "Rollback", which is the practice of launching a series of strikes against the same target over and over again until the target defenders either run out of ammunition or are so pulverized that they can no longer offer any resistance. Admiral Dunn said "Rollback" was used successfully against Vinh, where, ". . . the first few strikes in took their share of AAA and SAM fired at them; but by the end of the day . . . we could get into the racetrack pattern and do what we wanted. We must remember that lesson." He said that only once during two cruises to Vietnam, was permission given to employ the practice of "Rollback."

Essex Class Carriers In Three Wars

Vietnam had been the third major war in which the *Essex* class aircraft carriers participated. A total of 12 fought in the war compared to 14 in World War II and 11 in the Korean War. Unable to handle supersonic heavyweights, the *Essex* carriers operated Douglas Skyraider and Skyhawk, Vought (LTV) Crusader and Corsair. Among the *Essex* class Vietnam veterans – not previously mentioned were *Yorktown* (CVS-10), *Intrepid* (CVS-11), *Shangri-La* (CVS-38) and *Ticonderoga* (CVS-14).

There are at present no *Essex* class carriers in U.S. Navy service; however, two have been rescued from scrapping and are now floating museums open for inspection. *USS Intrepid* is on the Hudson River in New York City, while *USS Yorktown* is at Patriot's Point in Charleston Harbor, Charleston, South Carolina.

Six Supercarriers In Vietnam War

Six *Forrestal* type supercarriers saw action in the Vietnam war: *Saratoga* (CV-60), *Ranger* (CV-61), *Independence* (CV-62), *Kitty Hawk* (CV-63), *Constellation* (CV-64), and *America* (CV-66.

Year of the Carrier

The year 1972 was the U.S. Navy "Year of the Carrier", not only because the aircraft carrier had proven itself to be an indispensable weapon, but because it was the 50th anniversary of *USS Langley*, the first American aircraft carrier. Three new nuclear-powered carriers were under construction and the U.S. Congress was about to authorize a fourth, despite criticism of the cost.

While the Vietnam War held the attention of the world, many noteworthy events were happening.

Skyraider Retired

On April 10, 1968 it had been decided to remove the venerable and versatile propeller-driven Douglas Skyraider from the Navy's aircraft inventory. The plane that had fought two wars in various capacities had entered service in 1945 and served well for over a quarter-century. It was to be superseded by a new generation of aircraft.

Nimitz And Spruance Dead

Two great American naval heroes had died while the Vietnam War raged. The news was met with great sadness when it was learned that Fleet Admiral Chester W. Nimitz, the U.S. Navy's last five-star admiral, had died at the age of 81 at his home on Yerba Buena Island in San Francisco Bay on February 20, 1966. The naval community also mourned the passing of Fleet Admiral Raymond A. Spruance, Commander of the U.S. Fifth Fleet and hero of the Midway and Philippine Sea battles, where he dealt the Japanese Navy devastating blows. He died at his home in Pebble Beach, California, on December 13, 1969, at the age of 83.

INNOVATIVE TECHNOLOGY ON THE WAY

The next two decades were to witness amazing advances in shipboard aircraft, carrier design and electronics, as will be related in the following chapters.

Sophisticated Electronics

Undreamed of advances in high-tech electronics for detection, defense, communications and strike direction will make it impossible for any naval force to engage the enemy without the most sophisticated electronics suites to react quickly to enemy strikes and to guide tactical decisions.

Soviet Carrier Surprises

The military world had been taken by surprise when the Soviet Union, a historic land power, suddenly realized the advantages of the aircraft carrier and developed the *Moskva*, and *Kiev*, most unusual and efficient designs ; however, a bigger surprise was in store for world navies because a "Supercarrier" size aircraft carrier was soon to be unveiled by the Soviet Navy.

Amazing Warbird and Carrier Developments

Even more outstanding innovations were under development that would place aircraft carriers within the reach of nations that could never before afford them. These new ideas will not only threaten the supremacy of the supercarrier but will also resurrect the old idea of using merchant vessels as carriers with many novel refinements. The carrier and its Warbirds were destined to reach new heights in design and importance in the years to come.

CHAPTER VIII
HI-TECH WARBIRD/CARRIER WARFARE:
1973-1990

Remarkable Harrier Development • Ski-Jump Launch For Jump Jets • Royal Navy Ski-Jump Carriers • Enhanced Harrier • Sea Control Ship • Amphibious Assault Ships • Helicopters Into the 1980s • RAST • Fixed Wing ASW Aircraft • New Nuclear-Powered Supercarriers • Potent Fighters Demand Supercarriers • Mid-Air Refueling • Aircraft Launch and Recovery Operations • New Royal Navy Ski-Jump Carriers • Troubles Erupt In The Far East • The Falklands War • U.S. Carriers Protect American Interests • Operation Desert Storm Carrier Actions • Multi-Purpose Amphibious Assault Ship • Night Attack and Supersonic Harrier

REMARKABLE HARRIER DEVELOPMENT

As was seen in Chapter VII the British Aerospace V/STOL Harrier was ready to enter a period of refinement and eventual development into a carrier-borne aircraft. This was to spawn another revolution in aircraft carrier design. It must be remembered that the Harriers of this period were intended only for shore-based operation and had not yet been developed for shipboard operation; however, these shore-based Harriers were to prove suitable for carrier operation, even before the Sea Harrier was developed.

British Aerospace Harrier

The Harrier evolved into a diminutive single-seat strike/fighter of all-metal construction. The wing is constructed in one piece as was Brewster Buffalo, Vought Crusader, McDonnell Douglas Skyhawk and Phantom II. Access to the engine is facilitated by lifting off the lightweight wing. The main landing gear is of the bicycle design with twin wheels on the aft strut to accommodate the engine weight. Retractable wheeled wingtip struts balance the craft while on the ground.

Harrier Simple Controls

No complex cockpit controls are necessary to fly the Harrier. The only additional control is a lever to rotate the lift-thrust nozzles. Stability during slow speed flight and hovering is maintained by air bleed from the engine compressor and ejected through downward exhausting nozzles in the wingtips, nose and tail. These are called "Puffer Jets" which operation is actuated by the normal rudder and stick controls. This Puffer Jet System is necessary because at slow speeds and hovering the airflow over the stabilator, rudder and ailerons is insufficient to make these normal controls effective.

Turbojet Air Inlet and Exhaust

Although the Harrier is a single-engine aircraft it is fitted with two air inlet scoops and two exhaust tailpipes very similar to the bifurcated trunks of the Hawker Sea Hawk, previously described. The divided intake trunk affords an ideal location for the cockpit, while the divided exhaust trunk is necessary in order to discharge through the aft lift/thrust nozzle on each side of the fuselage.

The British Aerospace Sea Harrier FRS was a redesigned Harrier GR Mk.3 which included a raised cockpit, anticorrosion measures, rocket-powered ejector seat, and comprehensive electronics suite. Observe the Sea Eagle antiship missile on the underwing pylon. (British Aerospace, Courtesy Brendan Morrissey)

This Sea Harrier rests on an elevator of HMS Ark Royal (RO-9) shortly before the carrier's retirement. Observe the temporary closure in the jet engine air intake duct to prevent the entry of foreign objects when the craft is at rest for long periods of time. The jet engine air inlet lip could be inflated during slow speeds of hovering and deflated for high speed efficiency. (British Aerospace, Courtesy Brendan Morrissey)

PREVIOUS: A Hornet leaves the deck of a Supercarrier. Hornets were used extensively in Operation Desert Storm in the strike attack role during the 1991 Persian Gulf War; using smart bombs and missiles. Observe the depressed ailerons that assist the flaps during this critical period of takeoff. (McDonnell Douglas, Courtesy Timothy J. Beecher)

Jet aircraft air inlet scoops must be carefully designed for the operating speed of the plane. High speeds require sharp intake lips with small radii while low speeds need blunt intake lips with large radii. The Harrier operates from hover or zero speed to 735 miles per hour which posed a dilemma. These contradictory requirements were met by cleverly installing an inflatable rubber-like collar around the intake lip. At slow speeds the collar is inflated by air bleed from the engine, forming a blunt bellmouth lip, while at high speeds the collar is deflated to lie flat against the intake lip, thereby being capable of satisfying a wide range of speeds.

Harrier Data

The British Aerospace/McDonnell Douglas AV-8A Harrier, based on the RAF GR. Mk.3 is 45 feet-6 inches long and the wing has a span of 25 feet-4 inches with an area of 201 square feet. Height is 11 feet-3 inches. Empty weight is 12,200 pounds while maximum takeoff weight is over 25,000 pounds. Powered by one 21,500 pounds static thrust Rolls-Royce Pegasus 103 vectored thrust turbofan engine, the AV-8A can attain a maximum speed of 736 miles per hour at low altitudes. Service ceiling is 50,000 feet. Maximum range is 1,600 miles; attack/strike combat radius is 200 miles; and fighter combat radius is 400 miles.

Armament consists of two 30 millimeter Aden cannon housed in streamline pods under the fuselage between the landing gear struts; two AIM-9 Sidewinder air-to-air missiles; and five 500 pound bombs or three 1,000 pound bombs externally mounted. The maximum armament load is 5,950 pounds. Fuel tanks are located in the wing center-section and in the fuselage between the forward and aft nozzles.

Harrier Auxiliary Power Unit

Unusual in many respects, the Harrier also has a self-contained Auxiliary Power Unit (APU) which enables the engine to start without any external assistance. This is most important for remote site operations, shipboard starting and quick turn-arounds from outlying fields.

Harrier Avionics

The AV-8A is equipped with an inertial navigation and attack system and Head Up Display (HUD) which provides the pilot primary instrument references coupled with navigation and weapons release information. Integrated into the inertial system is a moving map display which continuously enables the pilot to monitor his position via microfilm maps.

Harriers Future In Question

Prospects for further Harrier development continued to oscillate between the bright and the dark as projects were influenced by economics, indifference, and enthusiasm. Britain's Fleet Air Arm was in danger of having no fixed wing aircraft because its Phantoms and Buccaneers had been transferred to the RAF by the Ministry of Defence. The Harrier was the Fleet Air Arm's only hope of fixed wing-aircraft and carrier operations.

Three Harrier Projects Underway

Optimism was at its height in 1973 when the U.S. Marine Corps presented McDonnell Douglas with a formal request for a second generation Advanced Harrier with specific improvements. In order to make the request for appropriations more palatable to Congress the Marines insisted upon RAF participation. The Advanced Harrier program was stalemated until March 1975 because Britain had declined to enter the program; however, in May 1975, the British Government agreed to proceed with the Sea Harrier design which had been under development since 1971 but delayed due to official apathy.

Actually, three momentous Harrier programs were underway simultaneously; the Sea Harrier; the Ski-Jump takeoff ramp; and the Advanced Harrier AV-8B.

Spanish Matadors

Spain showed an early interest in the AV-8 Harrier and 11 AV-8S Matadors plus two TAV-8S two-seat trainers had been delivered to the Spanish Navy for the aircraft carrier *Dedalo*. The Marina or Armada Espanol prefers to call its Harriers Matadors.

British Aerospace Sea Harrier

The Royal Navy received permission to award British Aerospace a contract to study and design a carrier variant of the Harrier GR Mark 3 in 1971. This design had to be developed at minimum cost with only cost-effective or essential modifications; such was the British economy. Design studies were completed in early 1972.

Anticorrosion Measures

The constant exposure to a hostile salt water environment dictated that all magnesium aircraft components be changed to aluminum alloys to retard corrosion. Material substitutions were also necessary in the Rolls-Royce Pegasus 103 engine, redesignated Pegasus 104, in order to retard corrosion. This is a vivid example of the corrosion problem faced by carrier aircraft; a problem that their land-based counterparts don't experience.

Multi-Mission Sea Harrier

The Sea Harrier was intended to include missions from close support to fleet air defense and surface ship strike which gave it the designation of FRS (Fighter/Reconnaissance/ Strike). In the fighter role the Sea Harrier was required to have a radius of action of 400 miles at operating altitude (800 mile range), while on a reconnaissance mission plus sea search, 20,000 square miles had to be covered in one hour. Strike and ground support actions required a 280 mile range.

Sea Harrier New Cockpit and Avionics

A new cockpit was raised 11 inches to provide more panel and console space plus improved visibility via a bulbous canopy. The raised cockpit also provided more space below for additional weapon and navigation electronics. This included a Ferranti self-aligning attitude and heading reference platform which achieves inertial navigation accuracy and has an 8,000 word digital computer. Ferranti Blue Fox radar is also fitted. A Smiths head-up display with a 20,000 word digital computer provides a very flexible air-to-air and air-to-surface weapon aiming assist. A simple autopilot provides attitude, heading and height-holding capability which reduces the pilot's work

The Sea Harrier includes a complete radar suite: Fire Control radar antenna in nose cone (No.1); Electronics Countermeasures antenna in fin (No.2); and External Radar Illumination antenna in tail cone (No.3). This Sea Harrier is assigned to No.809 Naval Air Squadron. (British Aerospace, Courtesy Brendan Morrissey)

load; reducing his fatigue and freeing him to concentrate on other operations of the moment. A relaxed pilot is more likely to cope with deviations and emergencies.

The Sea Harrier is fitted with the latest Type 10 Martin-Baker zero speed/zero altitude rocket-powered ejector seat. The elapsed time from ejection to parachute deployment is only one and one-half seconds compared to the two and one-quarter seconds for the RAF seat. Explosive cord is used to fragment the canopy in the event of an emergency escape.

Sea Harrier Data

When compared to the RAF GR.Mark 3, the Sea Harrier FRS-1 empty weight increased to 12,300 pounds while loaded weight decreased to 22,500 pounds. Overall length increased to 47 feet-7 inches and wing span and area remained the same at 25 feet-4 inches and 201 square feet. Height increased to 12 feet-2 inches. Speed and service ceiling remained at 736 miles per hour and 50,000 feet.

Armament comprises two 30 millimeter Aden rapid-fire cannon for all missions; two AIM-9 Sidewinder AAM's on the outer wing pylons plus two 190 gallon drop tanks on the inner pylons for the fighter role; one centerline and four wing pylons for strike missions; and drop tanks as required for reconnaissance flights. A total maximum load of 8,000 pounds can be accommodated.

About 90 percent of the FRS-1 structure and mechanical systems are identical with the GR.Mark 3, while the weapon systems and avionics are about 90 percent new. The structure did not require extensive modification because, unlike conventional carrier aircraft which require them, no fuselage reinforcement was necessary for arresting hook and catapult fittings. The upgrading of electronics systems reflects the need for ultra-sophistication in carrier aircraft.

The Sea Harrier FRS-1 made its first flight on August 20, 1978 and the first production aircraft was delivered in June 1979. Deck

trials were conducted on *HMS Hermes* during November 1979. Four FAA squadrons have been equipped with Sea Harriers; Nos. 800, 801, 809 and 899.

Viffing

No other aircraft has the ability to suddenly change its flight attitude with rapid deceleration or climbs as can the Harrier by Vectoring In Forward Flight or VIFF. The idea started in the early 1970s when NASA experimented with one of the early Kestrals to investigate if maneuverability could be improved by vectoring the thrust nozzles during normal forward flight.

Shortly thereafter, test pilot Hugh Merewether also experimented with Viffing in the very first Harrier. Flight trials in mock combat with Hawker Hunter and Phantom II fighters were then conducted by Britain's Royal Aircraft Establishment.

Many Harrier kills were attributed to the added lift, deceleration and upward pitch created by Vectoring In Forward Flight. The U.S. Marine Corps conducted additional combat trials with their AV-8A's against such potent and varied aircraft as U.S. Navy F-14 and F-18, as well as the U.S. Air Force F-15. Not only was the Harrier pilot able to evade his opponent but to actually score numerous "victories" by Viffing.

Vectoring In Forward Flight is most applicable in evasive maneuvers as well as during dogfighting which is still considered a viable possibility in jet-powered combat engagements.

Sea Harriers For India

Six FRS/51 Sea Harriers have been purchased by India for operation from the aircraft carriers *Vikrant* and *Viraat*.

American AV-8A Carriers Operations

While the Sea Harrier was under development, the U.S. Navy integrated U.S. Marine Corps shore-based AV-8A Harriers into the nor-nal operations of a CTOL (Conventional Take Off and Landing) aircraft carrier from August 1976 to April 1977. Although U.S. Marine Harriers had flown from LPH and LPD assault ships, they had never taken part in the cyclic operations of an Operational Readiness Evaluation (ORE).

USS Franklin D. Roosevelt (CV-42) sailed from Italy with Phantom II, Corsair II, Hawkeye and helicopter squadrons plus AV-8A Harrier Squadron VMA-231 in late August 1976. The ORE required a minimum of 90 minute flight periods for CTOL aircraft. Despite the fact that the AV-8A Harriers were launched last and recovered first, they averaged 98 minute flight periods; above the required minimum. This was possible because the Harrier engine is self-starting and requires no external power source for starting. In addition, Harriers do not need catapults and; therefore, don't experience the delays caused by catapult hook-ups. Further, only a small area of flight deck is required for vertical landing which increases the amount of deck space available for deck spotting. Probably, the most important reason is the fact that the Harrier needs no arresting gear nor does it ever experience bolters or waveoffs because the craft can hover off the side of the flight deck until it is approved to land; adhering to the V/STOL principle that, "...it is better to stop and land, than to land and try to stop."

The final examination of the carrier's ORE included a scenario in which the ship had to traverse an imaginary minefield with a fixed course and a slow speed. This produced a WOD of only 15 knots at a 40 degree angle to starboard which conditions prohibited launching or recovering the Corsair II or Phantom II jets; however, the Harriers left the Flight Deck only three minutes after they were ordered to takeoff, regardless of WOD velocity and wind direction. After completing their strike against the fictitious enemy, the Harriers recovered 20 minutes later regardless of wind direction or speed.

USS Franklin D. Roosevelt passed the ORE and the Harriers of VMA-231 took top honors among the jet squadrons on board!

During the exercise, VMA-231 flew to *USS Guam* (LPH-9) in Agusta Gulf, Sicily and operated as far as the Indian Ocean, spending Christmas in Egypt. The Marines flew back to *USS Franklin D. Roosevelt* when *USS Guam* returned to Sicilian waters.

In mid-March *USS Franklin D. Roosevelt* conducted war-at-sea exercises against *USS John F. Kennedy* during which the *Roosevelt* Harriers flew 75 minute strike or reconnaissance missions; taking off and landing while *USS Franklin D. Roosevelt* sailed downwind and crosswind. The carrier was ultimately forced to turn into the wind for CTOL operations.

The advantages of the Harriers over the CTOL jets were immediately obvious, especially when it is realized that the AV-8A was not a shipboard aircraft and was flown by pilots who were untrained in aircraft carrier operations.

SKI-JUMP LAUNCH FOR JUMP JETS

It is impossible for any aircraft to takeoff with its maximum load within its minimum takeoff run. The heavier the load, the longer the run in order to attain flying speed. The Sea Harrier is no exception to this rule and is further handicapped because it operates from carriers and amphibious assault ships which have limited deck length

After two years of about 250 Ski-Jump launches, a 15 degree SkiJump ramp was built for the 1978 Farnborough International Air Show. Harriers demonstrated the Ski-Jump daily for a total of 71 ramp launches before an international assemblage of military observers and civilians. (British Aerospace, Courtesy Brendan Morrissey)

available for STO (Short Take Off) operations. This restricts the Harrier payload of fuel and/or weapons because they must be diminished to enable the takeoff within the short available run; however, there was to be a remedy.

Ski-Jump Ramp Invented

In 1973, Lieutenant Commander Douglas R. Taylor, Royal Navy, described a solution for this vexing dilemma in his University of Southampton thesis, "The Operation of Fixed-Wing V/STOL Aircraft From Confined Spaces." Commander Taylor's theory was that by curving the forward end of the flight deck upward, as in a ski jump, so that a V/STOL aircraft such as the Sea Harrier using thrust vectoring, can be launched into an upward trajectory and, thereby, realize tremendous performance improvement in the takeoff mode of its flight. In fact, the Commander, himself, is said to have coined the phrase "Ski-Jump Launch."

The upward momentum created by the ramp launches the Harrier at a high angle of attack into a ballistic trajectory at about 70 miles per hour, during which time the aircraft is not yet supported by the wing and must use the vectored nozzles to keep the Harrier airborne. After the first five seconds the nozzles are rotated to exhaust further aft which brings the plane into a shallow climb with airspeed increasing to about 110 miles per hour. Still climbing, but at a still lower angle, after about 8-10 seconds the nozzles are vectored further aft and airspeed increased to about 125 miles per hour; then, the Harrier is in full aerodynamic flight.

The reduction in takeoff run is realized because, with the Ski-Jump ramp, much of the takeoff distance to reach flying speed takes place in the air after leaving the Ski-Jump; whereas, in normal flight deck takeoff the aircraft must remain on the deck until it has reached flying speed.

Ski-Jump Only For Vectored Thrust

Conventional naval fighters such as the Tomcat and Hornet cannot utilize the Ski-Jump because they do not possess vectored thrust which is an absolute necessity during the ballistic phase of the Ski-Jump takeoff. In the event that these sophisticated fighters, with full afterburner power, were accelerated to 70 miles per hour by a short catapult inclined upwards at 20 degrees; what would support these formidable fighters during the trajectory phase of the take-off? The Ski-Jump and vectored thrust V/STOL are synergistic and the Ski-Jump is not compatible with any other aircraft type.

Ski-Jump Ramp Trials

Three years after Commander Taylor's Ski-Jump Launch theory was made public, the Ministry of Defence awarded British Aerospace a contract to design and build a Ski-Jump ramp to flight test the Jump-Jet theory. The structural steel ramp was cleverly designed to incorporate a variety of launch angles ranging from six to 20 degrees.

Trials began on August 5, 1977 with a conservative ramp angle of six degrees, on which 116 launches were completed by September 7. Launching speeds varied from 60 to 130 miles per hour.

About 250 Ski-Jump Launch trials were conducted between October 1977 and June 1979 on 12, 15 and 20 degree ramp angles with launching speeds ranging between 48 and 104 miles per hour.

In September 1978 British Aerospace demonstrated the Ski-Jump Launch at the Farnborough International Air Show. The 15 degree Ski-Jump ramp was built using British Army Medium Girder Bridge components. The Harriers performed public demonstrations daily during the show, completing a total of 71 ramp launches before a most enthusiastic audience of civilians and an international assemblage of military observers.

ROYAL NAVY SKI-JUMP CARRIERS

As a result of the six degree tests it was decided to install a seven degree Ski-Jump ramp on the Command Cruiser *HMS Invincible*, then under construction at Vickers (Barrow) Shipyard.

HMS Hermes: First Jump-Jet Carrier

HMS Hermes, had been modified in 1964-66 and 1971-73 to be capable of operating Buccaneers and Sea Vixens by widening the Flight Deck to starboard of the island to an overall width of 160 feet. It was then converted to an amphibious assault ship to replace *HMS Albion* (with catapults and arresting gear removed) including necessary modifications for Harrier operation which incorporated strengthening the Flight Deck. Delays in the *Invincible* class construction program, which will be described later in this chapter prompted further modifications in 1976-77 to enable *Hermes* to operate as an ASW carrier with a squadron each of Wessex and Sea King helicopters. During her 1979 shipyard modifications *Hermes* became the first ship to be fitted with a Ski-Jump launching ramp for Sea Harriers. The 12 degree ramp was carefully faired into the bow, giving *Hermes* an easily identifiable appearance.

Only the first 57 feet of the ramp, which rises only two feet above the Deck, was erected on board the ship. The remaining 93 feet of the ramp, including the bullnose which rises about 35 feet above the Deck, was constructed at Her Majesty's Dockyard in Plymouth, England and then installed on *HMS Hermes*. Sea Harriers of No.800 Naval Air Squadron embarked *HMS Hermes* in 1980.

ENHANCED HARRIER

When, in March 1975, Britain declined to join with the U.S. Marine Corps to support the Advanced Harrier development program McDonnell Douglas undertook the work as a private venture as Hawker had done with the P.1127 Kestral prototype. About eight months later McDonnell Douglas demonstrated to the U.S.Naval Air Systems Command (Nav Air) that the AV-8A payload and range could be doubled by airframe modifications alone. There was no

HMS Hermes (R-12) became the world's first Ski-Jump ramp aircraft carrier in 1979 in order to accommodate the Sea Harrier. British Aerospace Sea Harriers occupy the forward end of the Flight Deck. (Mininstry of Defence [Navy])

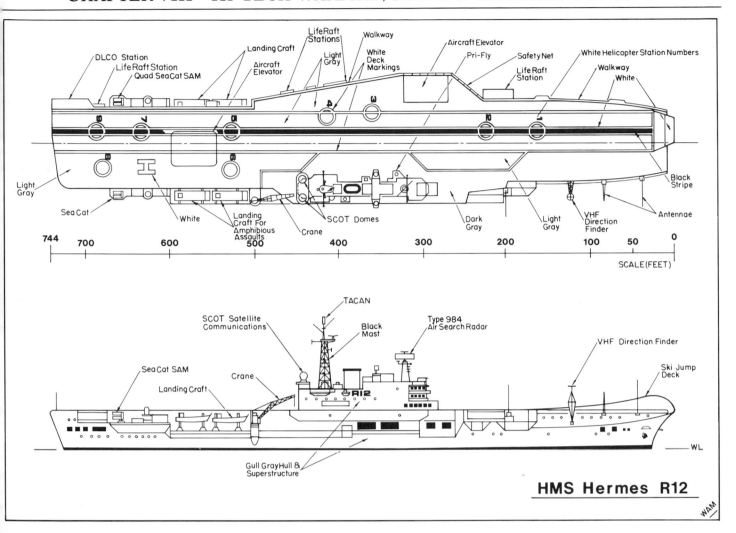

HMS Hermes R12

This shot of the HMS Hermes bow shows off the 15 degree Ski-Jump ramp shape to good advantage. Along with the angled deck and Hurricane bow, the Ski-Jump ramp is one of the outstanding carrier innovations; all British. (British Aerospace, Courtesy Brendan Morrissey)

need to upgrade the Pegasus engine above its 21,500 pounds static thrust rating with the McDonnell Douglas redesign.

The principal change in the Harrier II is an entirely new wing design of longer span to 30 feet-4 inches with area increased to 230 square feet. The leading edge sweepback was decreased from 40 to 36 degrees. The airfoil was thicker and supercritical while the aspect ratio was increased. The outrigger wheels were moved inboard from 22 feet to 17 feet to improve handling on crowded amphibious assault ship decks. This enabled the wing "Puffer Jets" to be relocated closer to the tips and become more effective.

The outstanding Harrier II innovation is the composite carbon-fiber/epoxy structure used for the wing and tail. Strong points such as leading edge, tips, pylon attachments and outriggers were of the more traditional aluminum alloys and titanium. The entire nose was also constructed from composite carbon-fiber/epoxy.

The U.S. Navy designation for the Harrier II is AV-8B and the first AV-8B made its initial flight on November 9, 1978. It underwent shipboard trials aboard *USS Saipan* (LHA-2) during October 1979. Earlier in 1979 the Ski-Jump ramp built at Farnborough had been purchased by Nav Air and installed at the Patuxent River Naval Test Center. More than 100 launches were made during the spring and summer at ramp exit speeds of from 57 to 84 miles per hour.

A Sea Harrier is ready for takeoff from the USS Hermes Flight Deck with no need for a catapult assist; nor does this amazing aircraft require arresting cables for landing. These takeoff and landing installations had been removed from HMS Hermes. (British Aerospace, Courtesy Brendan Morrissey)

U.S. Marine McDonnell Douglas AV-8A Harriers operated from USS Guam (LPH-9) during 1972-1974 in order to evaluate the feasibility of the Sea Control concept. Although the experiment proved successful, no funds were allocated for the Sea Control project. (British Aerospace, Courtesy Brendan Morrissey)

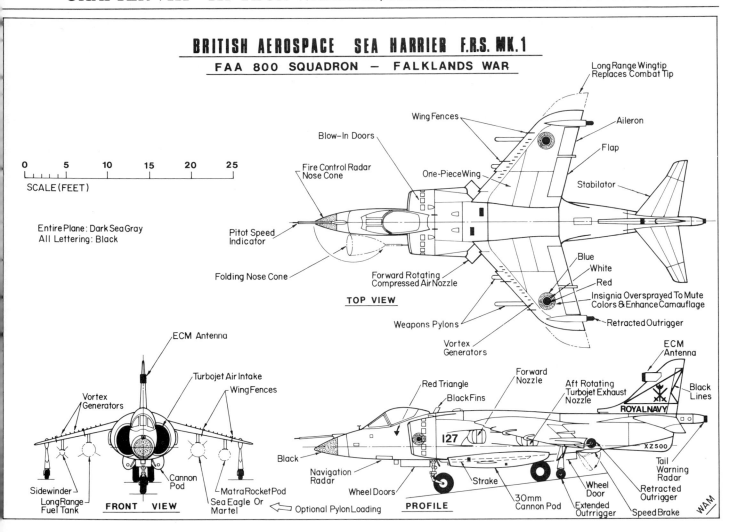

BRITISH AEROSPACE SEA HARRIER F.R.S. MK.1

FAA 800 SQUADRON — FALKLANDS WAR

SCALE (FEET)
0 5 10 15 20 25

Entire Plane: Dark Sea Gray
All Lettering: Black

Long Range Wingtip Replaces Combat Tip

Wing Fences

Blow-In Doors

Fire Control Radar Nose Cone

Aileron

Flap

One-Piece Wing

Stabilator

Pitot Speed Indicator

Folding Nose Cone

Blue
White
Red

Insignia Oversprayed To Mute Colors & Enhance Camauflage

Forward Rotating Compressed Air Nozzle

Retracted Outrigger

TOP VIEW

Weapons Pylons

Vortex Generators

ECM Antenna

ECM Antenna

Turbojet Air Intake

Wing Fences

Vortex Generators

Red Triangle

Black Fins

Forward Nozzle

Aft Rotating Turbojet Exhaust Nozzle

Black Lines

ROYAL NAVY

127

XZ500

Black

Sidewinder

Navigation Radar

Tail Warning Radar

Long Range Fuel Tank

Wheel Doors

Strake

Wheel Door

Retracted Outrigger

Cannon Pod

FRONT VIEW

Matra Rocket Pod
Sea Eagle Or Martel

Optional Pylon Loading

PROFILE

30mm Cannon Pod

Extended Outrrigger

Speed Brake

WAM

By 1981 Britain agreed to enter into a production arrangement with McDonnell Douglas to share construction of AV-8B's for the U.S. Marines and GR.5's for the RAF. The RAF Harrier GR.5 featured an even larger wing than the AV-8B having a span of 32 feet-0 inches with a 250 square foot area.

The Harrier II was developed in parallel with the Sea Harrier and there was continuous liaison across the Atlantic Ocean so that many features were common to both aircraft. One of the major advantages of the Harrier is that operations have proven that land-based pilots have had no difficulty taking off or landing on flight decks with land-based Harriers.

SEA CONTROL SHIP

During the early 1970s the aging ASW carriers of the *Essex* class were in need of replacement which ended the CVS designation. *Forrestal* attack carriers were forced to shoulder the antisubmarine role, combining two separate missions into one; although, this capability was enhanced by embarking a squadron of S-3 Vikings and a squadron of SH-3 Sea Kings. The Supercarrier designation was changed from CVA to CV; thereby eliminating specialized carrier roles. The Soviet underwater fleet numbered almost 400 sub-

marines which is more than the dozen or so supercarriers could ever track. World War II records indicate that it requires two to three ASW ships to effectively attack a submerged submarine; numbers are important, but size is not.

Sea Control Ship Mission

Taking heed of Admiral Mahan's teachings that command of the sea and protection of one's Sea Lines of Communication (SLOC) are imperative for any naval power, a new class of air capable ship was conceived by the U.S. Navy in 1971. This fresh concept, according to the Chief of Naval Operations Admiral Elmo Zumwalt, was to secure and retain Sea Control. He defined this as one of the major Navy missions including: Strategic Deterrence, Projection of Forces, and Presence. The two major functions were to provide a moving sanctuary for any convoy, underway replenishment at sea group, or amphibious force, and to provide sufficient force to sanitize any desired area above, below and on the sea. This would, in effect, provide a protective cylinder extending from the depths of the sea to the altitudes of high-flying aircraft. The mission of the Sea Control Ship was to detect, destroy or render impotent any hostile planes, ships or submarines that enter this protective cylinder. If the hostile force could not be persuaded to retreat, the Sea Control Ship and its escort of destroyers and frigates were to force the antagonists into action earlier than they had planned with a resultant higher failure rate for their efforts. The Sea Control Ship was to be low-risk and inexpensive, costing less than 100 million dollars each and, although it was to resemble a miniature aircraft carrier, it was not classified as such; however, it was to relieve the CV's from many ancillary duties. The Sea Control idea must be seen with regard to the missions for which the ship was to be created and must be examined as a total system concept and not merely as a ship.

Small, Austere and Innovative

The author assisted the U.S. Navy with the design of the Sea Control Ship in 1972 at the U.S. Naval Ship Engineering Center (NAVSEC) in Hyattsville, Maryland. The basic SCS design philosophy was for a ship that is small and austere, using innovative solutions to solve problems rather than being unduly influenced by past practices. Acquisition cost, manning, and producibility were the basic controlling factors. I suddenly had the feeling of deja vu because the SCS requirements seemed to describe a modernized, high-tech *Casablanca*-type design on which I had worked exactly 30 years before! I also remembered how well the *Casablancas* performed at Leyte Gulf.

Sea Control Ship Data

Displacement was to be about 15,000 tons with a mean draft of 21 feet-4 inches. Flight Deck was 580 x 95 feet and ship overall length was 646 feet. Two 30 x 60 feet aircraft elevators were to be installed. The aft elevator was to be located at the aft end of the Flight Deck and, when in the lowered position, would have allowed aircraft to takeoff directly from the Hangar Deck. The Hangar was to be 80 x 325 x 20 feet; quite large for a ship of this size.

It was planned to operate Harrier AV-8A VTOL's for air interception, surface attack and protection of the SCS surveillance air-

This artist's rendering is one of several Sea Control ship designs. The aft elevator was intended for AV-8A Harriers while the midship elevator was for helicopters. No catapults or arresting gear were necessary. If constructed today, a Ski-Jump would be fitted. (U.S. Navy Historic Center)

craft. Airborne Early Warning (AEW) and Anti Submarine Warfare (ASW) Sikorsky SH-3 Sea King plus LAMPS helicopters were to form the principal aircraft complement. The Harriers were to operate as V/STOL's (Vertical/Short Take Off and Landing).

The SCS was to have no defensive armament except for two Phalanx CIWS (Close-In Weapon System) one each mounted fore and aft of the island. Defense was left to its air group and the escorting ships as was sensing equipment and offensive armament.

Propulsion was to consist of two 30,000 horsepower General Electric gas turbines, each geared to a controllable/reversible pitch propeller (CRP). This propeller was necessary because gas turbines are nonreversible. The gas turbine, which is akin to the aircraft turboprop engine, uses the same basic fuel as aviation turbojet and turboprop engines, thus permitting a common fuel system for both the ship and its aircraft. Each propulsion gear train was designed to accommodate up to 45,000 horsepower. Ship speed was to be between 20 and 30 knots because average convoy speeds were estimated at 20 knots.

Eleven watertight bulkheads formed 12 watertight hull sections which were divided into hundreds of watertight compartments. Although unarmored, the Flight Deck, Hangar Deck in way of the Hangar Bay area, and the Hangar Bay forward bulkhead were to be high tensile steel. The entire island plus the mast was to be aluminum.

The Hangar was sized to accommodate 14 Sea Kings and three Harriers plus 24 containerized aviation shops and stores called MILVANS. The fully equipped 8 x 8 x 20 feet MILVAN containers represented a very innovative approach to the problem of revising aviation shops and stores spaces every time aircraft are replaced by other types and/or manufacturers. With container MILVANS, the entire shop can be easily replaced by another without laying up the ship in a shipyard for several weeks or months due to expensive retrofits. MILVANS also reduce the initial cost of the ship.

Total manning, including air group personnel was only 700 however, living accommodations were to be provided for 750 officers and men.

The major threat to sea control is submarines and the SCS was to combat this danger with an Anti Submarine Classification Analysis Center (ASCAC) which was to be combined with the Combat Information Center (CIC).

The embarked aircraft had no need for catapults or arresting gear, nor was there any need for excessive maneuvering of the SCS for launching and recovering aircraft. The ship design incorporated roll stabilization tanks in order to permit flight operations during most weather conditions.

U.S. Congress Refuses SCS Funding

It had been planned to eventually mass produce the SCS and the Navy expected funding in the 1974 budget with delivery of the first SCS in 1978; however, the U.S. Congress deleted all funds for the Sea Control Ship in 1974 despite the fact that commercial ship yards could build the Sea Control Ships.

No Substitute For the SCS Ship

Despite the fact that the class seems to be dead, the concept is not. The persistent suggestions from tacticians and strategists to use

The Tarawa class LHA amphibious assault ships combined the horizontal and vertical assault capabilities of the LSD and LPH designs. This is USS Tarawa (LHA-1). Note the Sea Knight helicopters on deck. (Official U.S. Navy Photograph, News Photo Division)

existing classes of ships such as LPH, LHA, LHD and so forth as substitute Sea Control Ships proves that the concept is alive and well; however, none of the recommended substitutes qualify for the SCS role. It is true that *USS Guam* (LPH-9) was employed in the SCS role while the Sea Control Ship design was formulated, but Guam was evaluating the feasibility of the Sea Control concept and was not an attempt to use the LPH design as a permanent SCS.

SCS Is Unique

The Sea Control Ship is unlike anything done before. It is an important concept of the future, aimed at undertaking the Navy's responsibility of control of the seas. Dozens of these simple, inexpensive platforms for the operation of sophisticated aircraft were to roam the seas and protect America's SLOC with AEW, AAW, ESM, ASW and ASM planes and helicopters.

AMPHIBIOUS ASSAULT SHIPS

The Sea Control Ship and *Iwo Jima* class ships were not the only through deck aircraft operations ships not classified as carriers. A large general purpose amphibious assault ship, that combined the horizontal and vertical assault capabilities of the LSD and LPH designs, was commissioned on May 29, 1975. *USS Tarawa* (LHA-1) was the first of five ships of this new class which was developed to overcome the *Iwo Jima* class limitations in launching a seaborne assault of heavy guns and armor.

Tarawa Data

The *Tarawa* class incorporates a 78 x 265 x 20 feet aircraft Hangar located aft, over the floodable docking well that is necessary for the landing craft and amphibious armor. The Flight Deck measures 118 x 800 feet and is fitted with two elevators; one at the aft end of the Flight Deck and the other as a deck edge type on the port side about 200 feet from the stern of the ship.

The four following ships of the *Tarawa* class are: *USS Saipan* (LHA-2) commissioned on October 15, 1977; *USS Belleau Wood* (LHA-3) commissioned September 23, 1978; *USS Nassau* (LHA-4) commissioned on July 28, 1979; and *USS Pelilieu* (LHA-5) commissioned on May 3, 1980. All were constructed by Litton/Ingalls Shipbuilding.

The *Tarawa* LHA is much larger than the *Iwo Jima* class; approximating the size of the *Essex* class carriers. Full load displacement is 39,300 tons at a 27 feet-6 inches draft. Overall length is 820 feet and hull beam is 106 feet. The twin-screw ships are powered with two Westinghouse-geared steam turbines developing a total of 140,000 shaft horsepower. Steam is generated by two Combustion Engineering boilers, the largest in any ship afloat at that time. The speed of 24 knots was a disappointment to many strategists who expected a higher speed so the *Tarawa* class could react more swiftly to world problem areas. Range is 8,500 miles at 20 knots. Operating complement is 900 officers and enlisted crew.

Aircraft Complement

Aircraft normally operated are V/STOL AV-8A Harriers, AH-1 Sea Cobra gunship helicopters, CH-53D Sea Stallion assault helicopters, CH-46 Sea Knight assault helicopters, and UH-1 Huey utility helicopters.

Amphibious assault ships are very complex and extremely important, many-faceted craft. As with the LPH the LHA is highly dependent on its V/STOL planes and the ubiquitous helicopters which serve in a wide variety of assignments. AEW and ASW helicopters are also operated from the escorting destroyers and frigates.

Tarawa Armament

The *Tarawa* class is equipped with three lightweight 5 inch/54 caliber guns for fire support. Air defense consists of 16 Sea Sparrows plus six single 20 millimeter rapid fire guns. Two Mk.25 Basic Point Defense Missile Systems (BPDMS) are located forward of the island and at the aft port corner of the hull.

Electronics Suite

The radar suite comprises SPS-40B and SPS-52B air search, SPS-10F surface search, SPG-50 fire control, and Mk.115 tracker/illuminator for the Sea Sparrow missiles.

Large Island

The island is abnormally large compared to a CV because it includes command and control ITAWDS (Integrated Tactical Amphibious Warfare Data System) including the Commander Amphibious Task Group (CATG) and the Landing Force Commander (LFC) plus their staffs. The LHA generally serves as the Flagship of Marine amphibious squadrons. Provision for 2,000 troops is provided in the spacious commercial type hull.

HELICOPTERS INTO THE 1980s

The helicopter has become increasingly important for navies, big and small, throughout the world with its many duties endlessly multiplying. The assignments are so varied that it has become difficult to imagine a military naval operation without having helicopters involved.

Early Warning Needs Aviation
Aviation is vital to AAW/AEW/ESM (Anti Air Warfare/ Airborne Early Warning/Electronic Surveillance Monitor) because the sensor is limited by a line of sight and it is only with altitude that wave-skimming missiles can be detected in time.

Early helicopters were not considered ideal for AEW service because they could not reach sufficient altitude to detect intruders early enough to take prompt action. The vibration from the rotors also had a detrimental effect on the radar performance. These deficiencies have been overcome with improved rotor materials and helicopter designs.

U.S. Navy's First Hunter/Killer ASW Helicopter
In 1957 the U.S. Navy decided to use combined hunter/killer ASW helicopters instead of the customary two-unit team in which one helicopter specialized in search or hunter while the other helicopter specialized in the destroy or killer role. Sikorsky Aircraft Division of United Aircraft Corporation designed the S-61 to meet the U.S. Navy's requirements for a hunter/killer helicopter. This was to be a

replacement for the Sikorsky Seabat or "Hiss" which had been flown only on search or hunter missions. The S-61 was a completely new design, first appearing on March 11, 1959, and given the U.S. Navy designation SH-3 Sea King. After entering U.S. Navy service in September 1961 the designation was changed to SH-3A due to minor modifications. Some Sea Kings were designated HSS-2.

Sikorsky Sea King Data
The Sikorsky SH-3A Sea King helicopter is powered by two 1,050 shaft horsepower General Electric T58 turboshaft engines.

The five-bladed rotor diameter is 62 feet-0 inches and overall length is 72 feet-5 inches. Height is 16 feet-8 inches. The maximum takeoff weight is 17,768 pounds. Maximum speed is 159 miles per hour and range is 540 miles. The service ceiling is 12,800 feet. The SH-3A has a crew of four.

The rotor blades fold back for stowage and the tail rotor pylon folds flat against the fuselage. Fuselage length is 55 feet-10 inches.

A new version SH-3D was introduced in 1965, powered with two 1,400 shaft horsepower General Electric T58-GE-10 turboshaft engines. It was this variant that Westland Helicopters was to adapt to the Royal Navy's requirements. The Sea King performed yeoman service in both navies for many years.

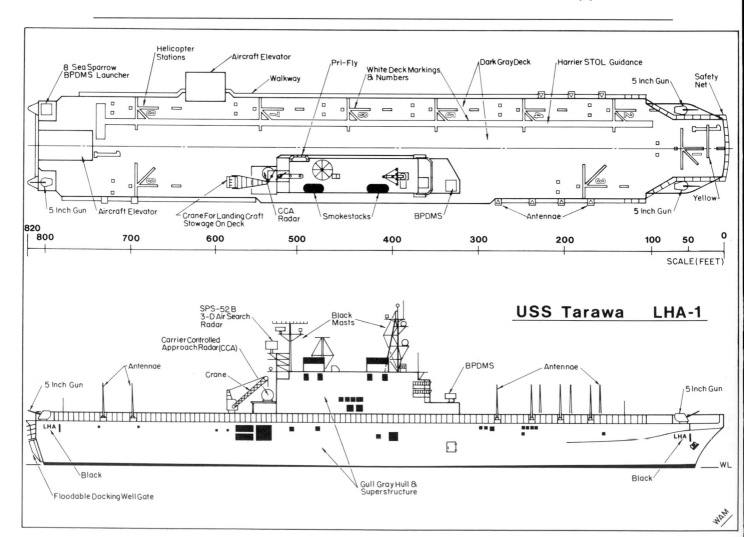

The Sikorsky HSS-2 ASW Hunter-Killer helicopter is often referred to as the Super Sea King. A principal feature is automatic stabilization and automatic altitude hold developed by Hamilton Standard. Twin 1,250 shaft horsepower General Electric T58-8 turboshaft engines feature inlet de-icing and drive the craft to a 200 miles-per-hour maximum speed. Gross weight is 17,300 pounds. This 1961 design is called "hiss Two" and can hover with 46% of its gross weight as useful load. Empty weight is 9,953 pounds. Main rotor diameter is 62 feet. Crew consists of pilot, co-pilot and two sonar operators. Fuel capacity is 663 gallons, giving the craft a four-hour duration. (Official U.S. Navy Photograph, U.S. Naval Photographic Center)

Sea King Amphibian

The Sea King is an amphibian with a hull-shaped fuselage. Outrigger floats, into which the main landing gear retracts, provide stability to prevent capsizing when the craft is afloat.

Royal Navy Prefers ASW Helicopters

The Royal Navy preferred helicopters over fixed-wing aircraft for the ASW role because they occupied less space in the limited hangar capacity of British carriers, and because of its faith in the rotary winged craft.

Left: Westland Sea King helicopters were based upon the Sikorsky S-61 and are constructed for a variety of specialized operations in addition to the basic ASW role. These HAS.2 variants are troop and cargo carrying types of 814 Naval Air Squadron and were photographed during an assault operation. Note the dorsal radome and engine-inlet foreign object deflector (arrows). (Westland Helicopters Ltd., Courtesy P.D. Batten)

The amphibious Sikorsky HSS-2 is demonstrating a taxi run during water-based operations (left). This craft is fitted with Bendix AQS-10 sonar equipment equal to the listening ability of a submarine searching on an 18 degree beam width scanning forward and aft. In order to get into listening position, the helicopter must transition from cruising speed to hover as quickly as possible; therefore, the Sikorsky designers have made this transition automatic, which also lowered the helicopter from a 300 feet cruising altitude to a 50 feet hovering altitude. The pilot could, however, override the automatic system as necessary. The hydraulically folding rotor blades and tail are necessary for stowage on aircraft carriers (right). (Official U.S. Navy Photograph courtesy United Technologies/Sikorsky Archives)

Westland Sea King

In 1966 Westland Helicopters Limited made arrangements with Sikorsky to construct Sea King helicopters which it intended to modify to meet the Royal Navy's requirements for a sophisticated ASW Wessex replacement.

The Fleet Air Arm continued to prefer independent ASW operations and; therefore, loaded the large Westland HAS.1 Sea King with sophisticated sensing and control equipment; search radar in a dorsal radome; dunking sonar; doppler navigation; and an autopilot and weapon system which controlled automatic hovering at a predetermined height plus several other automatic maneuvers in any weather. The first unit to receive the HAS.1 was 824 Squadron embarked on *HMS Ark Royal*. A total of 56 were built.

Westland Sea King Variants

The Sea King HAS.2 was first flown on June 18, 1976 with a number of improvements. A Royal Navy shipboard troop-carrying version, Sea King HC.4 made its initial flight on September 26, 1979. This variant can carry 28 fully armed troops on assault missions or 8,000 pounds of cargo. The HC-4 equipped Nos. 845 and 846 (Naval Air Commando) Squadrons. Many operated from *HMS Hermes*.

Westland HAS-5 Data

The final Royal Navy ASW variant is the Westland HAS.5 Sea King which has more powerful search radar, a new tactical navigation system, and a passive sonabuoy dropping installation working with the associated Marconi Avionics Lightweight Acoustic Processing And Display System (LAPADS) sonabuoy processor. The dunking sonar operator monitors LAPADS equipment at a fifth crew station. First delivery to the Royal Navy was in October 1980.

This AEW (Airborne Early Warning) Westland Sea King is fitted with the conventional dorsal radome plus the AEW radome on the fuselage side. This is rotated downward 90 degrees for AEW operation and is retracted to the position shown for takeoff and landing. (Westland Helicopters Ltd., Courtesy P.D. Batten)

The HAS.5 Sea King has a 62 feet-0 inches diameter rotor. Overall length is 72 feet-8 inches while fuselage is 55 feet-10 inches long. Height is 16 feet-10 inches. Two 1,660 shaft horsepower Rolls-Royce Gnome H.1400-1 turboshaft engines give the HAS.5 a top speed of 122 miles per hour. Range is 815 miles which converts to a mission endurance of 3 hours-15 minutes. Service ceiling is 10,000 feet.

Sea King Armament

Sea King ASW helicopters can be armed with two homing torpedoes or four depth bombs.

Sea King Exports

In addition to the U.S. and Britain, several other countries operate Sea Kings in a variety of roles: the German Federal Republic Marineflieger and the Norwegian Air Force operate Sea Kings in Search And Rescue (SAR) operations; the Pakistani Navy has fitted AM.39 Exocet Anti Ship Missiles (ASM) to its Sea Kings for attacks on surface ships; the Indian Navy and Australian Navy operate ASW Sea Kings from ships and the carrier Melbourne. Egypt and Belgium also operate Westland Sea Kings.

Westland Lynx

This outstanding Westland-developed helicopter is covered by a cooperative Westland/Aerospatiale manufacturing agreement. The Westland/Aerospatiale WG.13 Lynx is a multimission helicopter built by both companies.

Lynx Exports

The Lynx is flown in the armed forces of Brazil, Denmark, Argentina, Germany,Nigeria, Norway and the Netherlands.

Royal Navy Lynx

The Royal Navy Lynx is fitted with Sea Spray search radar and a passive sonabuoy processor. During antiship strike missions four homing Sea Skua ASUM's or four AS.12 wire-guided ASM can be carried on launchers at the fuselage sides. The Lynx ASW armament comprises two Mk.44, Mk.46 or stingray homing torpedoes, or two Mk.11 nuclear depth bombs.

The Westland HAS.5 Sea King ASW can be adapted to ASUW. This advanced Sea King is fitted with two British Aerospace Sea Eagle antiship missiles plus the necessary electronics. (Westland Helicopters Ltd., Courtesy P.D. Batten)

This German Kriegsmarine Westland Lynx MK.88 ASW/ASUW Helicopter is dunking its Bendix AQS18 ASW sonar. Nine countries include the Lynx in their helicopter inventory. (Westland Helicopters Ltd., Courtesy P.D. Batten)

The small size of the potent Westland Lynx enables it to operate from the smallest surface combatants as illustrated by this Royal Danish Navy Lynx landing on the fantail of a patrol frigate. (Westland Helicopters Ltd., Courtesy P.D. Batten)

Aeronavale Lynx

The 26 Lynx helicopters delivered to the Aeronavale during 1978-80 are fitted with French radar and Alcatel dunking sonar. French communications equipment was also installed. Strike armament comprises AM.39 Exocet (ASM) Anti Ship Missiles. Homing torpedoes can also be carried for ASW missions.

Lynx Data

Although the Lynx is designed for a two-man crew this antisubmarine/strike helicopter is equipped with avionics tailored to a one-man operation in all weather conditions. The tricycle landing gear has castoring wheels to facilitate deck handling. The four-bladed rotor folds back and the tail rotor fin folds against the fuselage for shipboard stowage.

Either two 900 shaft horsepower Rolls-Royce Gem 1001 or two 1,120 shaft horsepower Gem 41-1 turboshaft engines give the Lynx maximum speed of 166 miles per hour. Range is 418 miles or a mission endurance of about 2 hours 50 minutes. Hover ceiling is 8,450 feet while service ceiling is 12,000 feet. The four-bladed main rotor diameter is 42 feet-0 inches while overall length is 49 feet-9 inches. Fuselage length is 39 feet-1 1/4 inches and overall height is 11 feet-5 inches. The Lynx empty weight is 6,040 pounds and maximum weight is 10,500 pounds.

Super Lynx

In the early 1980s the Aeronavale received 14 and the Royal Navy received 20 more Lynx helicopters with upgraded Rolls-Royce Gem 42 engines and improved search radar. The Super Lynx was selected as NATO's standard light shipborne helicopter. The 360 degree chin radar and advanced dipping sonar enable the Westland Super Lynx to detect, localize and attack targets up to 100 miles away; operating autonomously in any weather, day or night.

Aerospatiale Super Frelon

The largest helicopter to be designed and built in Western Europe at that time made its first flight in December 1952. The Aerospatiale Super Frelon was a development of Aerospatiale's SA 3200 Frelon with increased power and lifting capacity. This ambitious program was completed with assistance from America's Sikorsky for the

NATO selected the Westland Super-Lynx as its standard light shipborne helicopter. Four British Aerospace Sea Skua ASM's are carried for strikes against surface ships. Note the radar antenna radome under the nose. (Westland Helicopters Ltd., Courtesy P.D. Batten)

The French Aeronavale's Aerospatiale SA 321 G Super Frelon ASW and ASUW helicopters are among the largest designed and built in Western Europe. A transport/assault variant was also developed. (Aerospatiale)

The Aerospatiale SA 316 Alouette III ASW Killer helicopter was armed with two homing torpedoes or two wire guided missiles. The craft became the French Navy's standard light shipborne helicopter. (Aerospatiale)

main and tail rotor design as well as their drive systems. Italy's FIAT provided technical assistance for the power transmission and main gearbox design.

Super Frelon Variants

The Aerospatiale Super Frelon was constructed in two principal versions: an all-weather antisubmarine variant SA321G, and a transport/assault variant SA321 Ja.

The SA321G was also constructed as a subvariant for SAR (Search And Rescue) operations, in which case the ORB 32 Heracles 1 nose radome is omitted.

Super Frelon ASW/Assault/ASUW Variants

The SA 321G ASW variant weighs 15,130 pounds empty and 28,660 pounds maximum takeoff condition. Three 1,570 shaft horsepower Turbomeca Turmo III Co turboshaft engines provide a maximum speed of 170 miles per hour. The six-bladed main rotor diameter is 62 feet-0 inches and fuselage length 63 feet-7 3/4 inches. Overall height is 16 feet-2 1/2 inches. The service ceiling is 10,325 feet and range is 440 miles. Mission endurance is about four hours.

This large helicopter is an amphibian with a hull-shaped fuselage. Two outrigger floats stabilized the craft when on the water and the landing gear retracted into the floats.

The Aeronavale operates 24 SA 321G Super Frelons, some of which are based on the carriers Foch and Clemenceau. The Super Frelons also conduct antisubmarine operations which support France's ballistic missile submarines. The SA 321G ASW Super Frelons usually operate in teams of four helicopters. While one helicopter uses its Sylphe panoramic dunking sonar to locate the quarry, the other helicopters conduct the attacks with homing torpedoes.

The SA 321G is equipped with two AM.39 Exocet ASM Anti Ship Missile mounted on the fuselage sides for surface strikes.

Four Mk.44/46 homing torpedoes are carried for ASW missions.

Super Frelon Transport/Assault Variant

The SA-321 Ja can carry 27 to 31 fully armed troops or 11,000 pounds of cargo, plus the crew of two. Service delivery to the Aeronavale began in 1963.

Super Frelon Exports

Libya operates nine Super Frelons for ASW/SAR missions; Iraq operates 10 of the helicopters armed with AM.39 Exocet ASM's for surface attack; and China uses 13 Super Frelons as transport/assault helicopters.

Aerospatiale Alouette III

The Aerospatiale SA-319 Alouette III multi-purpose light helicopter made its first flight in February 1959 and became the standard light shipborne helicopter in the French Navy.

Alouette III Data

The single-seat Alouette III was built with two different engines the Aerospatiale SA-316 Alouette III was fitted with one externally mounted 592 shaft horsepower Turbomeca Astazou turboshaft engine, while the later SA-319 Alouette III had one externally mounted 600 shaft horsepower Turbomeca Artouste XIV turboshaft engine installed. The Alouette III was not fitted with search/hunter sensors but was equipped only for destroy/killer missions against surface craft as well as submarines. In its ASW role the Alouette III was armed with two Mk.44 homing torpedoes, and for surface strikes was equipped with two AS.12 wire-guided ASM Anti Ship Missiles.

The Aeronavale Alouette III SA-319 fuselage is 32 feet-10 3/4 inches long and the four-bladed rotor diameter is 36 feet-1 3/4 inches. Height is 9 feet-10 inches. Maximum speed is 130 miles per hour. Range is 260 miles and service ceiling is 10,500 feet. Empty weight is 2,520 pounds and maximum weight is 4,850 pounds.

Alouette Exports

In addition to the French Aeronavale, the single-seater Alouette III was purchased by Argentina, Ecuador, Mexico, Peru, Chile, Pakistan, India, Indonesia, Greece, Sweden, Libya, Belgium and Denmark.

With the advent of the Lynx, the Alouette III has been relegated to liaison missions and for plane guard duties on the French aircraft carriers.

Westland/Aerospatiale Gazelles

Bearing a strong resemblance to the Alouette III, the Gazelle reverted to a skid landing gear instead of wheels. As with the Alouette, the Gazelle was equipped only for surface destroy/killer role and was not fitted with search sonar or radar.

In 1967 Westland Helicopters and Aerospatiale of France entered into an agreement to share technology and production on a 70/30 basis. One of the first helicopters developed under this agreement was the Westland/Aerospatiale Gazelle. The first prototype, designated SA.340, made its initial flight on April 7, 1967 followed by a second prototype in the following year. The first production Gazelle flew in August 1971.

The Gazelle is aptly named because it is a light, handsome, streamlined design which attained the high speed of 164 miles per hour. Its missions were training and surface attack. The Royal Navy ordered 30 Gazelle HT.2 variants to replace the Whirlwinds and the type entered Royal Navy service in December 1977.

Gazelle Description

The 592 shaft horsepower Turbomeca Astazou turboshaft engine is externally mounted. The most innovative feature of the Gazelle is that the tail rotor is encased in a duct or shroud, called the Fenestron, built into the vertical fin. Skids were fitted instead of wheels. The crew of two sits in a compound curvature glass-enclosed cockpit.

Fenestron Improves Efficiency

The shrouded tail rotor was much more efficient than unshrouded tail rotors because the shroud reduced rotor tip losses considerably. This improved efficiency required less power from the engine; therefore, more power was available for lifting and forward speed.

Gazelle Data

The four-bladed rotor diameter is 34 feet-5 1/2 inches and overall length of the craft is 39 feet-3 1/2 inches. Fuselage length is 31 feet-3 1/2 inches. Empty weight of this small helicopter is 2,022 pounds while loaded weight is 3,970 pounds. Cruising speed is 144 miles per hour with a range of 416 miles. The hover ceiling is 9,350 feet.

The Gazelle has no sensors but is armed with Anti Ship Missiles for surface attacks. It is flown by the Royal Navy and the Aeronavale.

Aerospatiale Dauphin II

The Aerospatiale SA 365F Dauphin II is a companion for surface ships of the French Navy; operating as a surface light shipborne helicopter. The Dauphin III incorporates the Fenestron of the Gazelle and features anti-vibration composite main rotor blades. The Dauphin is also intended for Search And Rescue missions. The first flight was made in January 1975.

A Dauphin III is photographed launching an AS-15TT antiship missile during a test. Observe that the anti-torque tail rotor is enclosed in a shroud in the rudder called a Fenestron. This improves the tail rotor efficiency and offers ground crew safety. (ECP Armees)

Dauphin II Data

Two 710 shaft horsepower Turbomeca Arriel 1C turboshaft engines drive the 8,598 pound craft to a top speed of 195 miles per hour. Service ceiling is 15,000 feet and empty weight is 4,720 pounds. Range is 300 miles. Four AS.15TT antiship missiles are carried; controlled by Thompson Agrion 15 fire control radar. A Thompson-CSF pulse-doppler radar is also fitted to permit midcourse guidance of Ottomat SSM's fired by friendly surface ships. Fuselage length is 39 feet-8 3/4 inches and the four-bladed rotor diameter is 39 feet-1 3/4 inches. Overall height is 13 feet-1 inch.

Export Dauphins

The U.S. Coast Guard operates Dauphins as the HH-65A for SAR missions and Saudi Arabia operates two dozen in surface attack and SAR operations.

Bell Helicopter Textron Huey

Bell Helicopter Textron first flew a new helicopter design in 1963, which was so successful that it spawned three other prominent designs for diverse missions during the next quarter-century. The Bell UH-1 Iroquois was designed using the experience gained with the

The Aerospatiale SA 365F Dauphin III is a surface attack shipborne helicopter that can fire four antiship missiles. The disk under the nose is the Agrion 15 fire control radar antenna that provides missile guidance. (ECP Armees)

The progenitor of the popular Huey and Sea Cobra military helicopters was this Bell Textron commercial HTL-7 design. Unusual feature of the design is the two-bladed main rotor. (Bell Helicopter Textron)

Affectionately called "Huey" by troops in the field, pilots, and mainte-nance personnel, the Bell UH-1 Iroquois is rarely called by its official name. The "Huey" performed yeoman's service in the Vietnam War. (U.S. Marine Corps)

The Bell Sea Cobra shipborne ground support helicopter is a direct descendant of "Huey." The pilot sits behind and above the gunner who operates the movable three-barrelled 20 millimeter cannon. The AH-1 is shown here. (Bell Helicopter Textron)

earlier HTL-3 (1951), HUL-1 (1956), HTL-7 (1958) plus the dozen various Bell designs that served in the Korean War. The Iroquois was first designated HU-1 (Helicopter Utility No.1) which led to the affectionate nickname "Huey" by phonetically pronouncing the designation letters and converting the number one into the letter I; hence HUI or "Huey." Troops in the field, pilots, and maintenance personnel have known the UH-1 as "Huey" for so long that the official name Iroquois has almost been forgotten. The UH-1 entered Marine Corps service in 1964.

The Bell Huey is one of the most versatile and widely used helicopters giving the U.S. Marine Corps support in the ship-to-shore phase of an amphibious assault. Early models were used extensively in the Vietnam War for command and control missions, plus medical evacuation operations.

Bell UH-1N Huey Data

Among the final variants of Huey is the UH-1N of which about 225 were delivered to the U.S. Marine Corps and U.S. Navy during 1971-1978. Marine Hueys often fly from LPH and LHA amphibious assault ships while U.S. Navy Hueys operate with Sikorsky SH-3 Sea Kings and Boeing Vertol CH-46 Sea Knights in helicopter support operations. The UH-1N can carry 8 to 10 combat-loaded Marines and/or supplies while for medical evacuation missions Huey has space for six litter patients plus one attendant. The normal complement comprises two pilots and one crew member.

The Bell UH-1N can be armed with 2 3/4 inch rockets, a 7.62 millimeter M60 machine gun, a .50 caliber machine gun, and a 7.62 GAU-2 B/A mini-gun. The helicopter is powered with a United Aircraft of Canada (Pratt & Whitney) twin turboshaft PT6T-3B propulsion unit which develops 1,800 shaft horsepower and drives the UH-1N to a maximum speed of 126 miles per hour. The two-bladed rotor diameter is 48 feet-2 inches and fuselage length is 45 feet-10 inches. Overall length is 57 feet-3 inches while height is 14 feet-10 inches. Service ceiling is 14,200 feet with a hovering ceiling of 12,900 feet. Range is 250 miles. Empty weight is 5,549 pounds with a maximum weight of 10,500 pounds.

Huey Exports

Huey has been exported to Norway, Thailand and Peru.

Bell Textron Sea Cobra

A direct descendant of Huey was the Bell AH-1 Sea Cobra shipborne ground support helicopter. This gunship provides fire support and fire support coordination to the landing force during amphibious assaults as well as subsequent operations ashore. The crew of two is seated in tandem with the pilot behind and above the gunner which created a very narrow fuselage.

Armament consists of a three-barrelled 20 millimeter XM197 cannon in an electrically driven turret under the nose. Stub wings protrude from each side of the fuselage with four strong points to mount 2 3/4 and 5 inch rockets, Sidewinder air-to-air missiles, 20, TOW and Hellfire antitank missiles, or gun pods.

Bell AH-1J Sea Cobra Data

The U.S. Marine Corps is the principal user of the Sea Cobra; however, some AH-1J variants had been exported to Iran in 1973. Between 1970 and 1975 about 70 of the AH-1J variant were delivered to the Marines. The AH-1J is powered with a United Aircraft of Canada (Pratt & Whitney) twin turboshaft T400-CP-400 propulsion unit of 1,800 shaft horsepower which drives the AH-1J Sea Cobra to a maximum speed of 207 miles per hour. Service ceiling is 10,550 feet. Range is 310 miles or a mission endurance of two hours. Empty weight is 7,260 pounds while loaded weight is 10,000

The Bell AH-1W Sea Cobra stub wing strong points can mount antitank missiles, air-to-air missiles, or gun pods. Sidewinder AAM's are installed on this Sea Cobra. (U.S. Marine Corps)

BELL AH-1W SEA COBRA

Entire Plane : Olive Drab

Steel Tubing Skids
Landing Gear

Turboshaft
Air Intake

Stub Wing Weapons Carrier

Yellow Band

Turboshaft
Exhaust

Stabilizer

Main
Rotor

Black Blades

SCALE (FEET)

0 5 10 15 20 25

TOP VIEW

Air Intake

WeaponsRack

3 - Barrelled
Rapid Fire 20mm
Turreted Gun

Rotating Turret

FRONT VIEW

White Star

Blue Background

Red Bar

MARINES

59228

White Numbers & Letters
(Can Also Be Black)

Countertorque
Rotor

Stabilizer

Tailskid

PROFILE

WAM

---

pounds. The two-bladed rotor diameter is 44 feet-0 inches while fuselage length is 44 feet-7 inches.

Larger Attack Squadrons

Two of the most recent upgraded variants are the AH-1T and AH-1W. U.S. Marine attack squadrons have enlarged from the former 18 Sea Cobras to a mix of 12 Sea Cobras and 12 Hueys for a 24 helicopter squadron using the AH-1T and AH-1W variants. About six composite squadrons have been activated.

Bell AH-1W Sea Cobra Data

The AH-1W Sea Cobra has a maximum-weight of 14,750 pounds, overall length of 58 feet-0 inches, fuselage length of 44 feet-10 inches, and a height of 14 feet-2 inches. Range is 203 miles and speed is 219 miles per hour. This variant is powered with a General Electric T-700-GE-401 twin turboshaft propulsion unit.

Agusta-Bell 204

In the early 1960s Bell Helicopter Textron and Agusta of Italy had entered into an agreement, similar to the Westland/Aerospatiale arrangement, to share production and technology. The first project from this understanding was a development of the Bell 204 which had made its first flight in 1961. As with the Sea Cobra, the Agusta-

The Italian-built Agust-Bell 204 shipborne ASW helicopter is another relative of the "Huey" as a militarized Bell 204 commercial design. The Italian Regia Aeronautica operates the AB 204 in hunter/killer pairs; each helicopter dedicated to one of the roles. (Regia Aeronautica)

Bell 204 shipborne antisubmarine helicopter is a close relative to the basic Bell Iroquois or Huey.

Agusta-Bell 204 Data

The AB204AS was powered with either one Rolls-Royce Gnome or one General Electric T58-3 turboshaft engine. The 1,300 shaft horsepower gave the AB204 a maximum speed of 120 miles per hour. Range is 220 miles with a service ceiling of 10,500 feet. Empty

AGUSTA - BELL 212 ASW

Entire Plane: Dark Blue-Gray

SCALE (FEET)
0   5   10   15   20   25

Surface Search Radar
Rescue Life Raft
Black Antiglare Panel
Red Nose
Stabilizer
Countertorque Rotor
Turboshaft Exhaust
Pitot Speed Indicator
Oil Coolers
Red Tail
Turboshaft Air Intake
Black Blades

TOP VIEW

Intake
Radar
Life Raft
Radar

FRONT VIEW

Intake Scoop
White Disk, Black Anchor
Oil Cooler
Surface Search
White
7-20
Antiglare
MARINA
7-20
Tailskid
Radar
Green
White
Stabilizer
Steel Tubing Skids Landing Gear
Red

PROFILE

WAN

---

weight is 4,600 pounds while loaded weight is 9,500 pounds. The two-bladed main rotor diameter is 48 feet-0 inches and the fuselage length is 40 feet-5 inches. Overall height is 14 feet-5 inches. The AB-204 has a crew of three.

Italian Navy Operations

The Italian Navy operates its AB204 antisubmarine helicopters in pairs as a hunter/killer team. The hunter is fitted with AOS-13B dunking sonar while the killer helicopter is armed with two Mk.44/46 homing torpedoes. Agusta-Bell 204 helicopters in the Italian Navy also engage in antisurface strikes on which missions they are armed with four AS.12 wire-guided ASM's (Anti Ship Missiles).

About 30 AB204 aircraft have been flown in the Regia Aeronautica since 1964; howevever, these have virtually all been replaced by the more advanced Agusta-Bell 212.

Agusta-Bell 212

The Agusta-Bell 212 shipborne antisubmarine helicopter is basically an upgraded AB204 with a larger powerplant, expanded electronics, and increased mission capabilities. The aircraft made its first flight in 1969 as the Bell 212 and (48) AB-212's began service delivery to the Regia Aeronautica in 1978.

AB-212 ASW Operations

In its ASW role the AB-212 is equipped with sonobuoys and AQS-13B dunking sonar for the search phase and is armed with two Mk.44/46 homing torpedoes for the destroy phase after the submarine has been located. The Agusta-Bell 212 successfully combined search and destroy capabilities in a very small airframe.

The Agusta-Bell 212 ASW and ASUW shipborne helicopter combines all the functions of antisubmarine and antisurface operations in a relatively small airframe. The cylinder above the four-man crew cockpit is the surface radar scanner. (Regia Aeronautica)

The unusual Piasecki HU-2 tandem-rotor helicopter flown by the U.S. Navy in the early post-World War II years was the brainchild of Frank Piasecki. This design became the ancestor of the Boeing Vertol Sea Knight. (Official U.S. Navy Photograph, News Photo Division)

AB-212 ASUW Operation

On ASUW missions the AB-212 is equipped with a surface search radome atop the three-or-four-crew member cabin plus Sea Killer ASM's.

AB-212 Missile Guidance Operation

In addition, the AB-212 is fitted with TG-2 guidance equipment with which the aircraft can provide midcourse guidance for surface ship-launched Ottomat SSM's (Surface-to-Surface Missiles).

AB-212 Data

The Agusta-Bell 212 is powered with a United Aircraft of Canada (Pratt & Whitney) twin turboshaft PR6T-3 propulsion unit which develops 1,875 shaft horsepower. Top speed is 122 miles per hour. Range is 315 miles and service ceiling is 14,200 feet. Empty weight is 7,540 pounds and maximum takeoff weight is 11,200 pounds. The two-bladed main rotor diameter is 48 feet-0 inches and fuselage length is 45 feet-11 inches. Overall height is 12 feet-10 inches.

Export AB-212

In addition to the Italian Navy, Agusta-Bell 212 ASW helicopters have been purchased by Turkey, Iraq, Venezuela, Peru, and Greece.

The longevity and flexibility of Huey descendants is fitting tribute to the basic Bell design of the early 1960s.

Boeing-Vertol CH-46 Sea Knight

Another outstanding helicopter design that has seen active service for over a quarter-century is the Boeing-Vertol CH-46 Sea Knight. This very innovative design features two contra-rotating main rotors, one at each end of the fuselage; thereby, eliminating the problems of torque and the necessity for a tail rotor.

CH-46 History

This tandem-rotor arrangement was favored by designer Frank Piasecki who had delivered 20 Piasecki HRP-1 helicopters to the U.S. Marines in 1945-46. Meanwhile, Piasecki became Vertol Aircraft Corporation which delivered (32) HUP-1, (165) UH-25B, and (50) UH-25C utility helicopters from 1949 into the early 1950s. The Vertol tandem rotor UH-25B and UH-25C were powered with a 550 horsepower Continental R-975-42 engine and had a 105 miles per hour top speed. The rotor diameters were 35 feet-0 inches and the fuselage length was 32 feet-0 inches. Maximum weight was

This U.S. Navy Boeing-Vertol Sea Knight is dunking ASW sonar on an antisubmarine assignment. This is only one of the many capabilities of this unusual aircraft. (Official U.S. Navy Photograph, News Photo Division)

5,440 pounds. The Vertol Aircraft Corporation then became the Boeing Company's Vertol Division and continued the development of the efficient tandem-rotor designs. Entering a design competition for a U.S. Marine Corps assault helicopter, Boeing-Vertol was declared the winner and received an initial order for 14 aircraft of the successful design.

Boeing-Vertol CH-46 Variants and Service

Designated CH-46A Sea Knight, the prototype made its first flight on October 16, 1962 and acceptance trials were completed in November 1964. By the summer of 1965 five Marine squadrons had been equipped with Sea Knights. Annual production orders brought the total number of CH-46A Sea Knights procured to 462 by the end of 1966.

In the summer of 1966 a more powerful variant of the Sea Knight had been developed and was designated CH-46D. This variant also featured cambered rotor blades and improved electronics. About a dozen U.S. Marine Corps squadrons were each equipped with 12 to 18 CH-46A/D Sea Knights which became the Marines' principal assault helicopter. The Sea Knight transports troops ashore during an amphibious assault, or from one area of the beachhead to another during shore operations. Also, it not only carries weapons, ammunition, equipment and other logistic necessities to shore but serves as a search and rescue aircraft as well. Sea Knights were the Marine's main assault helicopter during the Vietnam War.

Beginning in 1977, 273 of the 624 Boeing-Vertol CH-46A/D Sea Knights in service with the U.S. Marine Corps underwent modernization/reconstruction which included more powerful engines, improved navigation system and a damage-resistant fuel system installation. This became the CH-46E, the ultimate Sea Knight.

Boeing-Vertol CH-46E Data

The Boeing-Vertol CH-46E Sea Knight has an overall length of 58 feet-0 inches. Fuselage length is 44 feet-10 inches. Overall height is 16 feet-8 inches. The three-bladed rotors are 51 feet-0 inches in diameter. Empty weight is 15,835 pounds while a loaded Sea Knight weighs 24,300 pounds. The two General Electric T58-GE-16 turboshaft engines drive the aircraft to a 166 miles per hour top speed. Cruising speed is 140 miles per hour. Service ceiling is about 14,000 feet. Combat range is 206 miles while ferry range with three internal tanks is 578 miles. In addition to the two pilots and one crew-

man the CH-46E can handle up to 25 assault troops or 10,000 pounds of cargo. Troops and cargo embark and disembark via a rear loading ramp.

Helicopter VERTREP Operations

The U.S. Navy purchased six utility versions of the CH-46A, designated UH-46A, which were delivered in July 1964. This aircraft became the Navy's standard VERTical REPlenishment (VERTREP) helicopter and flew with Hueys and Sea Kings in four-helicopter combat support flights. After 24 more UH-46A's were delivered, all subsequent Navy Sea Knights were UH-46D's which were based upon the CH-46D.

The UH-46D can accommodate 25 passengers or 15 litters with two medical attendants or 10,000 pounds of cargo carried externally below the fuselage in a sling. Its primary function is the transfer of munitions, provisions, fleet freight and other logistic necessities from naval replenishment ships such as AE(ammunition), AF(provisions) and AOE and AOR (munitions and fleet freight) to combat ships such as aircraft carriers, destroyers and so forth. Sea Knights are also involved in the recent replenishment concept of keeping the naval replenishment ships on station and using ordinary freighters, fitted with helicopter VERTREP platforms, to shuttle the replenishment cargo to the naval replenishment ships from U.S.

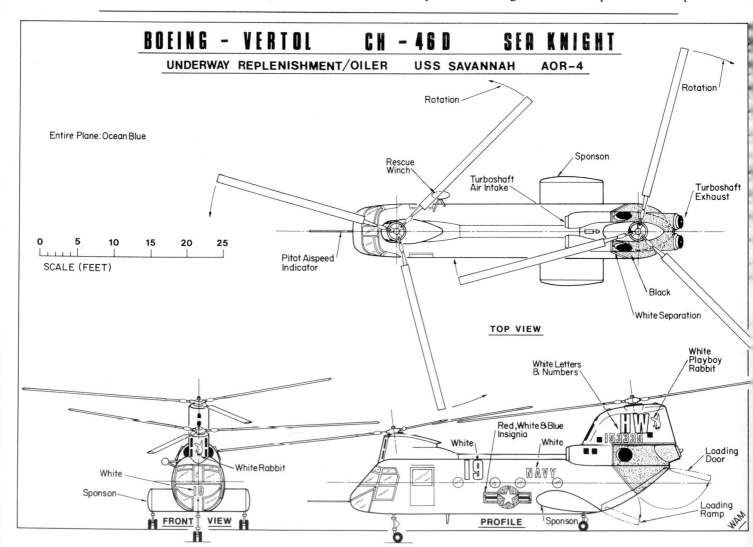

A Sea Knight helicopter from the fast combat support ship USS Sacramento (AOE-1) lowers munitions, fleet freight or provisions to the Flight Deck of the carrier USS Ranger (CVA-61) during an underway VERTREP (VERTical REPlenishment) operation. VERTREP operations are the life's blood of the fleet and Sea Knights do most of this work. (Official U.S. Navy Photograph, News Photo Division)

friendly ports. The UH-46 Sea Knights have the dual task of transferring cargo from the freighters to the naval replenishment ships and then transferring this cargo to the combat ships as required. Before this operation was conceived, naval replenishment ships were forced to leave their station and return to port to reload.

The author was deeply involved in designing the conversion of freighters into VERTREP capable ships which had hover/loading decks and cargo shuttle runways fitted so the Sea Knights could pick up cargo for delivery to naval replenishment ships.

Export
In addition to the U.S. Navy and U.S. Marine Corps, the U.S. Army and the Air Forces of Sweden and Canada operate Sea Knight helicopters.

Sikorsky Sea Stallion
The Sikorsky CH-53 Sea Stallion is another successful helicopter design developed specifically for the U.S. Marine Corps and then found adaptable to U.S. Navy requirements as well. The CH-53 Sea Stallion was designed to meet the Marines' need for a large assault helicopter. This huge shipborne assault helicopter made its first flight in October 1964 and the CH-53A was delivered to the

U.S.M.C. in May 1966. An improved variant, CH-53D, made its appearance in 1969. A total of 265 of both variants were delivered.

CH-53 Sea Stallion Lifting Capability
Sea Stallions are capable of carrying 38 combat-ready troops or 24 litter patients and four attendants in addition to the two pilots and one crewman. As an equipment transport the CH-53A/D can deliver an entire Hawk Missile System, an Honest John missile on its trailer, a 105 millimeter Howitzer or a half-ton jeep with a half-ton trailer, and a 1 1/2-ton truck and trailer. Loading and unloading is accelerated through the use of a rear ramp which permits the roll-on and roll-off of the vehicles. The Sea Stallion lifts 8,000 pounds internally or externally which can be increased to 12,000 pounds when necessary.

The CH-53A/D Sea Stallions were used extensively by the Marines during the Vietnam War.

CH-53A/D Sea Stallion Data
Two 3,925 shaft horsepower General Electric T64-GE-413 turboshaft engines power the CH-53A/D, driving the aircraft to a top speed of 196 miles per hour. Cruising speed is 173 miles per hour. Service ceiling is 24,200 feet while hovering ceiling is 13,400 feet. Range is 250 miles and ferry range is 450 miles. The six-bladed rotor diameter is 72 feet-3 inches and overall length is 88 feet-6 inches. Fuselage length is 67 feet-6 inches and overall height is 24 feet-11 inches. Empty weight is 23,628 pounds while maximum loaded weight is 42,000 pounds.

RH-53D Sea Stallion MCM Variant
The U.S. Navy Sea Stallion MCM (Mine Counter Measures) variant is designated RH-53D. Its primary mission is airborne mine countermeasures, which includes mine sweeping, spotting and neutralization, plus the destruction of floating mines, channel marking, and surface towing. The Sea Stallion's secondary utility mission consists of the movement of cargo and equipment plus the transportation of passengers. The RH-53D is deeply involved in

Developed specifically for the U.S. Marine Corps, this huge Sikorsky CH-53 Sea Stallion assault helicopter shows off its maneuverability with a sharp banking turn. Observe the six-bladed main rotor. (United Technologies/Sikorsky Archives)

The U.S. Navy operates this Sikorsky RH-53D Sea Stallion in the airborne MCM (Mine Counter Measures) role. Note that the retractable three-sectional tail strut has been extended as this RH-53D prepares to land. This strut protects the tail in the event of a rough landing. (U.S. Naval Institute Photo Collection)

mine countermeasures in trouble spots throughout the world and assisted in the clearance of mines in the Persian Gulf during 1987-1988.

The RH-53D was fitted with upgraded General Electric T64-GE-415 turboshaft engines. A minimum crew of three is required; however, additional crew members are often on board to operate

the variety of Mine Countermeasures equipment such as Mk.103 mechanical, Mk.104 acoustic, Mk.105 magnetic, and Mk.106 magnetic/acoustic. Due to a strengthened fuselage and various attachment points for MCM equipment, the empty weight had risen to 25,583 pounds; however, the maximum weight remained at 42,000 pounds. Top speed was 150 miles per hour. Basic dimensions remained about the same. Service ceiling is 21,000 feet while the hovering ceiling is 13,400 feet. The operating range is to perform a 25 mile radius of action Mk.103 minesweep mission, including 45 minutes for streaming gear, 131 minutes for towing, 45 minutes for retrieving gear, and return to ship with a 20 minute power reserve.

The first Sikorsky RH-53D's were delivered in September 1973; however, the first U.S. Navy MCM (Mine Counter Measures) squadron had been previously supplied with modified and reconstructed CH-53A's. Two active duty and one reserve squadron fly the MCM RH-53D.

Sikorsky Super Stallions

The need for even larger helicopters led to the development of the Sikorsky Super Stallion CH-53E assault/heavy lift and the MH-53E mine countermeasures helicopters. These derivatives of the Sea Stallion are the largest and most powerful helicopters that had been placed into production outside of the Soviet Union. The CH-

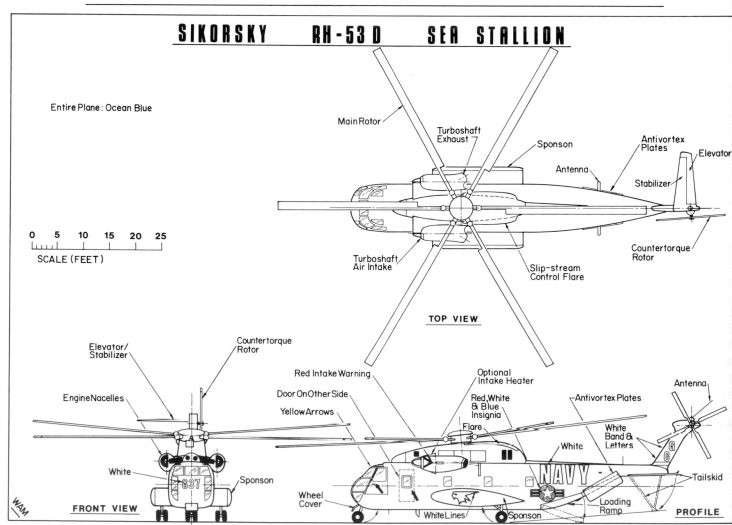

A Sikorsky MH-53E Sea Dragon MCM (Mine Counter Measures) helicopter is shown towing a mine sweeping sled. Airborne mine countermeasures have proven their worth for fleet protection. (United Technologies/Sikorsky Archives)

53E was designed to U.S. Marine Corps requirements and is also flown by the U.S. Navy while the MH-53E meets the Navy requirements for a dedicated MCM helicopter.

CH-53E Super Stallion Data

The Sikorsky CH-53E is capable of transporting 56 combat-ready Marines or 16 tons of equipment on assault missions. The Marines' most powerful helicopter can lift the Light Armored Vehicle (LAV) and the 155 millimeter Howitzer, plus its towing machine, the MN-923 five-ton truck. The CH-53E was also designed to lift all current U.S. Navy and Marine Corps fighter, attack and electronic warfare aircraft so it can recover damaged and stranded aircraft.

Three 4,380 shaft horsepower General Electric T64-GE-416 turboshaft engines power the Marine Corps CH-53E to a top speed of 196 miles per hour. Cruising speed is 173 miles per hour.

Empty weight is 33,236 pounds with a maximum loaded weight of 73,500 pounds. Service ceiling is 27,900 feet with a hovering ceiling of 16,700 feet. Combat range is 480 miles while ferry range

extends to 990 miles. The six-bladed main rotor diameter is 79 feet-0 inches while the fuselage length is 73 feet-4 inches. Overall length is 99 feet-0 inches with an overall height of 28 feet-6 inches.

As with the CH-53D, the crew comprises two pilots and one crewman. The Marines began receiving the CH-53E in December 1980 and four squadrons of 16 aircraft each or six squadrons of 12 aircraft each is the current Marine Corps inventory.

The U.S. Navy CH-53E serves in several roles. It is used for VOD (Vertical On-board Delivery) of personnel, supplies and equipment; removal of damaged aircraft from aircraft carrier decks; support mobile construction battalions; and support the Marines during assault operations by transporting troops, equipment, and cargo. The Navy received their first CH-53E in 1981 and operates three squadrons.

MH-53E Sea Dragon (Super Stallion MCM Variant)

The Sikorsky MH-53E MCM (Mine Counter Measures) version is heavier (36,745 pounds) and has a greater fuel capacity than the

CH-53E which increases its range to 1,120 miles. It is also fully equipped with sophisticated mine countermeasures equipment. The MH-53E made its first flight in 1983 and deliveries began three years later. Top speed is 185 miles per hour. Basic data the same as the CH-53D unless mentioned otherwise. Only seven MH-53E MCM Sea Dragons were funded by U.S. Congress in 1989 which prompted the Navy to advise the politicians that the 1987-88 Persian Gulf minesweeping operations confirmed "the valid requirements for organic, rapidly deployable, airborne mine countermeasures systems for fleet protection." It is a known fact that, with the world's largest navy, America has one of the smallest MCM surface fleets! The responsibility for fleet protection from the aquatic mine menace has, therefore, become the responsibility of MCM helicopters like the Sea Dragon.

Sikorsky UH-60 B/F Seahawk LAMPS III

During the development of the Stallions, Sikorsky designers were also busy creating the LAMPS (Light Airborne Multi-Purpose System) Mk. III helicopter. This was not intended as a replacement nor a substitute for the LAMPS-I helicopter and the surface combatant from which it operates in the U.S. Navy. LAMPS-III was developed to complement and exploit the long-range detection capability of the SQR-19 TAC-TAS (TACtical-Towed Array Sonar system). LAMPS-III was designed to provide the small surface warship with an independent ASW capability. It also gives frigates, destroyers and cruisers extensive ASUW (Anti SUrface Warfare) capabilities because it can detect and attack menacing surface warships as well as provide OTH (Over The Horizon) targeting for warship-launched Harpoon ASM missiles.

From Black Hawk to Seahawk

Initially the new LAMPS-III helicopter was to be similar in size and capability to the LAMPS-II lightweight helicopters in service with West European Navies; however, the U.S. Navy had eventually specified a greater lifting capacity and longer mission endurance. The U.S. Army's Sikorsky UH-60A Black Hawk was selected as the basis for the new LAMPS-III helicopter and the Sikorsky SH-60B Seahawk was born, making its first flight in 1979.

Sikorsky Seahawk Data

Many changes in the basic UH-60A were required to produce the SH-60B. Among them was a redesigned and strengthened landing gear; folding main rotor with blades gathered over the fuselage; hinged tail rotor pylon which folds 180 degrees against the fuselage side; rotor and engine intake de-icing; plus a watertight fuselage bottom in the event of emergency water landings. The Sikorsky SH-60B Seahawk is powered with two 1,690 shaft horsepower General Electric T700-401 turboshaft engines which give the aircraft a top speed of 150 miles per hour at 5,000 feet. The ASW range is two hours and the rescue range is 3 1/2 hours. Empty weight is 13,648 pounds while maximum loaded weight is 21,884 pounds. The four-bladed main rotor diameter is 53 feet-8 inches and fuselage length is 50 feet-0 inches. Overall length is 64 feet-9 inches while overall height is 17 feet-2 inches. Service ceiling is 18,500 feet. Armament consists of two Mk.50 homing torpedoes or two

The Sikorsky SH-60B Seahawk is the U.S. Navy's LAMPS III (Light Airborne Multi Purpose System) helicopter and was a development of the U.S. Army's Black Hawk helicopter. (Official U.S. Navy Photograph, News Photo Division)

Penguin antiship missiles, mounted externally on the fuselage sides plus a door-mounted M-60 machine gun.

Seahawk Deployment

The SH-60B is deployed on the newer U.S. Navy cruisers, destroyers, and frigates to provide all-weather capability for detection, classification, localization, and interdiction of ships and submarines. Secondary missions include search and rescue, medical evacuation, vertical replenishment, fleet support, and communications relay. The Seahawk SH-60B entered squadron service in 1984.

The initial procurement of 204 aircraft was increased in order to operate two LAMPS-III, instead of the originally planned single aircraft for the *Spruance* and *Kidd* class destroyers which were being modified to accommocate two LAMPS-III helicopters.

OPPOSITE: In addition to its extensive electronics dnd data link that enables every ship in the carrier battle group to share its data and tactical information, the Sikorsky SH-60B Seahawk LAMPS can be armed with two Penguin ASM's or two Mk.50 homing torpedoes. Note the radar arrays on the nose. (United Technologies/Sikorsky Archives)

The Seahawk LAMPS III helicopter gives cruisers, destroyers and frigates extensive ASUW capabilities. A Sikorsky SH-60B is shown landing on the helicopter deck of a small surface combatant. (United Technologies/Sikorsky Archives)

LAMPS-III Data Link

As with its predecessors, LAMPS-I and LAMPS-II, the LAMPS-III system is essentially ship-based because overall control remains with the surface ship. The mother ship processes data from the SH-60B's own sensors. All Seahawk operations are monitored by an Acoustic Sensor Operator (ASO) in the ship's Combat Information Center (CIC). An Air TActical Control Officer (ATACO) on the ship coordinates the activities of the three operators and is the tactical mission commander. In effect, these "guys in the tunnel" plus the three-man crew of the Sikorsky SH-60B provides the LAMPS-III with an effective crew of seven because the four shipboard operators are tactically interconnected with the helicopter through a secure, digital, directional data link. The data link functions as an intersystem conduit in exactly the same way as a larger electronics warfare aircraft's intercommunications system operates. The wealth of raw sensor data and tactical information shared simultaneously by the ship and helicopter is system unique; however, it is selectively available throughout the CVBG (Carrier Battle Group).

The LAMPS-III data link is secure and directive which means it can be used during modified EMCON (EMissions CONtrol) condition which forbids all CVBG radio emissions. This feature significantly enhances battle group operations. The data link has extended the eyes and ears of the surface warship, enabling the battle group's antisurface and antisubmarine commanders to function more effectively as scene-of-action commanders and yet be geographically removed from the hostile force.

The SH-60B is fitted with RAST (Recovery Assist, Secure and Traverse) haul down and handling which enables the Seahawk to take off and land from ships during extremely rough sea conditions.

CVBG Inner Zone ASW Seahawk SH-60F

Intended to replace the venerable and still effective Sikorsky SH-3 Sea King, the Sikorsky SH-60F was first delivered to the U.S. Navy late in 1986 as a CVBG Inner Zone CV-ASW helicopter.

CVBG Defensive Zones

A carrier battle group (CVBG) averages about one hundred miles between the outermost escorts while a carrier task force averages about 300 miles between the outermost escorts. The major threat to the aircraft carriers in these naval forces is the hostile submarine. The U.S. Navy's response to this threat has been to use multi-faceted ASW forces, that have complementary capabilities, deployed in layers around the carriers. The immense mid to outer ASW defense layer of the CVBG is patrolled and defended by attack submarines operating in direct support; carrier-based Viking S-3 ASW aircraft; LAMPS-equipped cruisers, destroyers and frigates plus other craft which depend upon passive acoustics because they operate near the fringes of the CVBG where the waters are not cluttered with noises which could mask the sounds of an intruder. These forces can detect and destroy the vast majority of hostile attack submarines that attempt to reach the carrier; however, submarines have become extremely silent, consequently the percentage of hostile submarines that will be able to penetrate the outer ASW barrier and reach the carrier is on the increase. Should the unthinkable happen and the silent intruder enters the inner zone, that no-man's-land

between the carrier and the innermost escorts, what are the search and destroy options in this arena in which the carrier is invariably within torpedo range? Here, there are no second chances!

The underwater world of the inner zone is full of noise and audible confusion. The noises made by the CVBG's ships seem to be concentrated in the inner zone, severely limiting the overall effectiveness of passive sonar sensors. Active sonar sensors are not affected by these high background noise levels; therefore, with its ability to bring an active sonar to play in the inner zone, the carrier base, sonar-dipping ASW helicopter is essential for hunter/killer activities to combat the critical inner zone submarine threats. This is the purpose for which the Sikorsky SH-60F was created; carrier based inner zone ASW and SAR capable of prompt response to any emergency in the immediate vicinity of the carrier.

Seahawks Share Maintenance

In effect, the SH-60F is an ASW variant of the SH-60B and both airframes were constructed on the same production line. Deployment of both SH-60 variants in the same CVBG enables the SH-60B to share the SH-60F supply and repair facilities on board the carrier. This arrangement greatly improves the combat readiness of at least a dozen or more SH-60B LAMPS-III because this aircraft normally relies on shore-based supply and maintenance facilities.

SH-60F Electronics

The SH-60F is fitted with the AN/ASN-123 tactical navigation system and the AQS-13F Tethered Sonar which includes a high speed reeling machine which can lower the transducer to a depth of 1,500 feet, plus a concurrent sonar transducer processing capability. A MIL-STD-1553B multiplex bus integrates avionics subsystems and provides a digital interface display for the four crew members; pilot, co-pilot, tactical sensor operator, and acoustic sensor operator.

An Automatic Flight Control System (AFCS) features altitude hold and airspeed hold plus automatic approach and departure for the dipping mission. The efficient flight pattern with AFCS results in a much reduced elapsed time between dippings, which improves the chances for detection and kill.

SH-60F Data

Other features of the Sikorsky SH-60F CV-ASW helicopter are 4.3 hour mission endurance, sea level top speed of 177 miles per hour, dual, redundant mission computers, tactical data link to other ships and aircraft, accommodation for two passengers and five rescuees, plus armed with two Mk.50 homing torpedoes. Rotor vibration is minimized through the use of a bifilar absorber and the tail rotor is of all composite construction. With a maximum loaded weight of 21,880 pounds the SH-60F compares favorably with the Sea King and SH-60B in size and weight except that it has a greater useful load in a hover mode than the Sea King.

The principal advantage of the SH-60F is in its ability to arrive quickly at the dipping station, locate the intruding submarine at extended range, and fire the homing torpedoes.

LAMPS-III; Force Multiplier

Throughout the history of civilization the main purpose of government has been and should continue to be the security of the nation

The Lockheed S-3 Viking was developed to detect and destroy enemy submarines that have penetrated the CVBG mid to outer zones or defensive layers. (Lockheed-California Company)

Lockheed Viking

Lockheed produced a carrier-borne fixed-wing antisubmarine aircraft that made its first flight in January 1972. The ultra-sophisticated Lockheed S-3 Viking was equipped with such advanced detection and data processing capabilities that more than half of the Viking's cost was for the electronics systems.

Viking Electronics

Designed to replace the venerable Grumman S-2 Tracker, the Lockheed S-3 Viking's sensors include APS-116 high resolution radar, AQS-81 MAD (Magnetic Anomaly Detector), FLIR (Forward Looking Infra Red), plus tube launchers for 60 sonobuoys. The sensor data are processed by a 65,000 word on-board AYK-30 digital computer.

In order to reduce resistance which will enhance speed and range, the MAD boom, FLIR, and the fuel probe fitting are all retractable.

All U.S. Navy Supercarrier air groups include a squadron of 10 ASW Vikings. The 518 miles per hour speed helps the Lockheed Viking react quickly and effectively to a distant submarine. (Lockheed-California Company)

The Sikorsky SH-60F protects the aircraft carrier by guarding the carrier battle group against intruding enemy submarines; detecting and destroying them if they enter the CVBG inner zone. A SH-60F Seahawk is shown dunking a sonar transducer which can be lowered to 1,500 feet below the surface. This helicopter is attached to the USS Nimitz. (United Technologies/Sikorsky Archives)

yet military spending is the first to be reduced when politicians are forced to economize. If the U.S. Navy becomes any smaller and still retains its commitments, individual ships must be capable of performing the work that once required several ships. LAMPS-III is a force multiplier that can increase the potential of destroyers, frigates and cruisers.

RAST

Operating helicopters from small combatants' landing area can be hazardous in stormy weather due to the violent rolling and pitching of the wet deck. In order to assure safe contact with the proper location on deck without lateral bouncing off target, the U.S. Navy developed the RAST (Recovery Assist Securing and Traverse) system which cables the helicopter to the landing target. The Royal Navy has designed a similar system called Harpoon; not to be confused with the U.S. Navy ASM.

FIXED WING ASW AIRCRAFT

Helicopters are indispensable for close-in short range ASW detection/destruction missions; however, the CVBG mid-to-outer defensive layer submarine detection/destruction role requires fixed-wing aircraft with good speed. long range, and a weighty payload.

The Lockheed Viking payload includes: tube launchers for 60 sonabuoys; four homing torpedoes; four depth charges; long range fuel tanks; bombs; rockets; 65,000 word computer and assorted electronics systems. (Lockheed-California Company)

The pilot and co-pilot are seated alongside each other while immediately behind them are consoles for the SENSO (SENSor Operator) and the TACCO (TACtical COordinator).

Viking S-3A Data
The Lockheed-California Company production S-3A is powered with two 9,275 pounds static thrust General Electric EF34-400 turbofan engines which give the aircraft a maximum speed of 518 miles per hour at sea level. The mission range is over 2,000 miles with a mission endurance of nine hours. Service ceiling is 40,000 feet. Empty weight is 26,783 pounds while loaded weight is 52,539 pounds. Wingspan is 68 feet-8 inches, length is 53 feet-4 inches, and height is 22 feet-9 inches.

Offensive armament comprises four Mk.50 homing torpedoes and four depth charges stowed in the internal weapons bay plus a pylon under each wing for either fuel tanks, bombs, or rockets.

Viking S-3B Variant
Although the S-3A has proven its ability to react quickly and effectively to a distant submarine, even faster reaction was desired, which resulted in the upgrading of (146) S-3A's to S-3B. This modification involves not only improvements in acoustic and radar processing capabilities, but added provision for firing Harpoon antiship missiles from the underwing pylons, plus the installation of a new sonobuoy receiver system. The U.S. Navy is confident that the Lockheed S-3B Viking will be able to counter the submarine threat into the year 2,000.

Viking Deployment
All U.S. Navy Supercarrier air groups include a squadron of ASW Vikings which average about 10 planes per squadron. It is one of the most widely used planes in the U.S. Navy. Initial Viking service delivery was in October 1973.

Versatile Viking
Lockheed has converted 16 S-3's into ES-3A electronic reconnaissance aircraft. The Viking's low fuel consumption and its ability to bring unused fuel back to the carrier has also pressed the versatile

craft into the in-flight refueling role. It is also used for COD (Carrier Onboard Delivery) duty because of its long range and ample payload.

NEW NUCLEAR-POWERED SUPERCARRIERS
While the Harrier, various helicopters, and flight deck-fitted noncarriers were being designed and produced, the U.S. was building a new class of nuclear-powered Supercarriers.

Nimitz Class Supercarriers
The lead ship, and hence the class name, was *USS Nimitz* (CVN-68) which keel was laid on June 22, 1968 at Newport News Shipbuilding and Drydock Co. and commissioned on May 3, 1975.

Other ships in the *Nimitz* class are: *USS Dwight D. Eisenhower* (CVN-69) commissioned on October 18, 1977; *USS Carl Vinson* (CVN-70) commissioned on March 13, 1982; *USS Theodore Roosevelt* (CVN-71) commissioned on October 25, 1986; *USS Abraham Lincoln* (CVN-72) commissioned on November 11, 1989; and *USS George Washington* (CVN-73) commissioned on July 4, 1992.

USS John C. Stennis (CVN-74) and *USS United States* (CVN-75) are future U.S. Supercarriers planned for delivery in December 1995 and December 1997 respectively.

Nimitz Data
Basically, *USS Nimitz* is a developed *USS John F. Kennedy* (CV-67) with a nuclear powerplant. The *Nimitz* full load displacement is

USS Dwight D. Eisenhower (CVN-69) was the second Nimitz class carrier and is shown here shortly after completion. It requires about two additional years to complete a Supercarrier after it has been launched. (Newport News Shipbuilding)

The cavernous hangar of USS Nimitz (CVN-68) is evident in this photo. Although the Nimitz class is basically a modified USS John F. Kennedy, the Hangar height had been increased to 25 feet-6 inches. (Official U.S. Navy Photograph)

Underwater explosions can wreak havoc with ships, even those as large and durable as Supercarriers. Hull seams and bulkheads can split open; piping can fracture releasing flammable fluids; ladders break and tumble, cutting off escape; valve operating rods jam; machinery shifts on foundations, causing misalignment; and plenty of other shipboard equipment can break or malfunction, causing death and injury and possible destruction of the ship. USS Nimitz is shown here undergoing a shock test. These tests can actually move the entire ship sideways a foot or more. Shock tests prove the durability of the ship before it enters service. (Official U.S. Navy Photograph, News Photo Division)

,400 tons more than *Kennedy* which can be attributed to the nuclear powerplant and attending shielding, plus more shops, a 30 feet longer Flight Deck, increased Hangar height to 25 feet-6 inches, and additional armor.

The powerplant of the *Nimitz* class was generations ahead of USS *Enterprise*. It will be recalled that eight reactors were installed in CVN-65, each producing about 35,000 shaft horsepower; however, the *Nimitz* class requires only two reactors, each generating about 130,000 shaft horsepower. The two reactors provide the equivalent of 11 million barrels of fuel; thereby, enabling the *Nimitz* class ships to operate for 13 years or 800,000 to 1,000,000 miles before refueling. This range is estimated at an average speed of 20 knots. The Westinghouse A4W reactors generate steam for four General Electric geared turbine units, each driving one of the four propellers.

The total of 260,000 shaft horsepower propels the *Nimitz* carriers to a maximum speed of 33 knots. Standard displacement is 81,600 tons and full load displacement is 91,400 tons. The absence of ship's fuel tankage, not needed due to the nuclear powerplant, made possible an increase of aviation fuel tankage to 260,000 gallons which is necessary because of the extended range of the carriers created by the nuclear powerplant. The class also has stowage facilities for 2,600 tons of bombs, missiles, shells and other ordnance. The ship's crew consists of 3,150 officer and enlisted personnel while the air wing had risen to 2,625 pilots, mechanics and plane handlers to operate and maintain the 89 Tomcats, Corsair II's, Intruders, Hawkeyes, Prowlers, Vikings and Sea Kings. A little arithmetic reveals that it requires about 29 Navy personnel to keep one plane flying.

Armament
In addition to the Tomcats the *Nimitz* class depends on three eight-cell NATO Sea Sparrow antiaircraft missile launchers for defense against air attacks. The carriers are also fitted with three Phalanx CIWS (Close In Weapon Systems) for antimissile and antishellfire defense. Surface search radar consists of SPS-43A and SPS-48 while SPS-10F is installed for surface search.

Four steam-powered catapults or accelerators and four deck edge elevators are installed.

Supercarriers Criticized
The supercarriers of the U.S. Navy have been criticized because of their cost; over one billion dollars for *USS Nimitz*, and the critics go on to insist that these huge craft are "sitting ducks" in a coordinated attack. Apparently the Carter administration believed these accusations because it attempted to block authorization of funds for *USS Theodore Roosevelt* and later supercarriers in favor of the much smaller and far less expensive fossile fuel VSS carriers, capable of operating only V/STOL aircraft. This attempt failed and the Reagan administration committed itself to the continuation of the CVN program.

POTENT FIGHTERS DEMAND SUPERCARRIERS
Two outstanding examples of electronics-laden, ultrasophisticated, high-performance, carrier-based combat aircraft which demand large fleet carriers from which to operate are Grumman F-14 Tomcat fleet air defense fighter and McDonnell Douglas F/A-18 Hornet strike/fighter. They are the world's most advanced production carrier-based combat aircraft and have no equal, anywhere. It is awe-inspiring creations from the ultimate technology of the period, such as these progressive machines, that have forced the navies of the world to abandon the large fleet carriers and adopt the through-deck cruiser/Ski-Jump ramp/cruiser-carrier configurations as their primary air capable naval vessel because of budgetary restraints. Only the U.S. Navy has continued to acquire these most useful mechanical marvels in order to fulfill America's world-wide commitments.

The Grumman F-14 Tomcat is the most technologically advanced carrier-based fighter in the world. It normally operates as part of an integrated Maritime Air Superiority (MAS) force. The Phoenix air-to-air missiles are unique to the Tomcat and can destroy hostile intruders at a 100 mile range (Grumman Corporation, Courtesy Lois Lovisolo)

Grumman F-14 Tomcat

The Grumman Tomcat was the natural outgrowth from the 1950s Douglas F-6D Skyray Missileer program plus the General Dynamics F-111B swing-wing design of the 1960s, neither of which filled the U.S. Navy requirement for a long-range, heavily armed fighter to meet the growing Soviet cruise missile, longrange reconnaissance aircraft, and bomber threat. Meanwhile, the fighting in Southeast Asia revealed that modern fighter aircraft must retain the close-range air superiority performance and armament and not rely only on long-range aerial combat. This spelled the end of the F-111B which had been constructed by Grumman under subcontract from General Dynamics.

Grumman Tomcats work in combination with a Grumman Hawkeye E2-C. The Hawkeye's tons of data processing equipment compliments the Tomcat's own electronics suite to identify, select and strike the target within seconds. Grumman Tomcats can track up to 24 targets and attack up to six enemy aircraft at the same time with their own electronics. (Official U.S. Navy Photograph, News Photo Division)

In 1968 Grumman proposed a new fighter to meet all the Navy's requirements and, to shorten the gestation period, suggested that the F-111 engines and swing-wing plus the Missileer weapons system be adapted to a more capable airframe. This program was known as the VFX and, when the F-111B was cancelled, Grumman received a contract for a VFX prototype which became the F-14A. Two years later the F-14A made its first flight in December, 1970 and began deployment to U.S. Navy squadrons in October, 1972.

Tomcat + Hawkeye = Success

The Grumman F-14 is the most technologically advanced carrier-based fighter in the world and normally operates as part of an integrated Maritime Air Superiority (MAS) force. When the Tomcat works in combination with the Grumman E2-C Hawkeye, the result is truly synergetic. With the Hawkeye stationed about 200 miles from the CVBG in the direction of the hostile force and Tomcats patrolling about 150 miles from the carrier, a two way data link is shared which has made their combined operations particularly effective.

The Hawkeye receives everything seen by the Tomcat radar and relays this data back to the carrier's CIC (Combat Information Center). Both the Hawkeye and CIC can follow what the Tomcat is doing and will evaluate the prevailing conditions before action is taken. The Hawkeye's advanced surveillance radar, with several tons of automatic data processing equipment monitored by the dedicated AEW system operators, plus the CIC team, determine what action the Tomcat should take. Explicit recommendations on how and what it should engage and, even when target designation is given, the Tomcat crew often waits for the order to fire. This appears to be a time consuming operation; however, in reality it is completed within a few seconds. The above capability is very welcome in the heat of battle.

The most outstanding feature of the Tomcat is the variable geometry wing in which the sweepback angle of the wing is computer-controlled in order to attain the optimum performance under any combat situation. The Tomcat on the catapult has wing extended for slower speeds while the Tomcats in the foreground have wings at full sweep. (Grumman Corporation, Courtesy Lois Lovisolo)

Tomcat Independent Decisions

Despite the Hawkeye and CIC recommendations the Tomcat's own weapons control computer can also decide which targets pose the most serious threat to the CVBG and must be hit first. The two-man Tomcat crew can also take complete control of its own air battle because the Naval Flight Officer (NFO) in the rear cockpit has the option of overriding the system and attack targets other than those selected by the computer or he can decide to follow the CIC or Hawkeye recommendation.

Tomcat Armament

The AWG-9 doppler-pulse fire control radar, located in the nose cone of the Tomcat, can track up to 24 targets and attack up to six enemy aircraft at the same time; simultaneously watching other hostile aircraft. This system can detect enemy bombers, such as the Backfire which will be described later, more than 150 miles away and can pick up antiship cruise missiles as far away as 75 miles. Meanwhile, the Tomcat can launch its Phoenix AAM (Air-to-Air Missiles), which are unique to the F-14, at the oncoming bombers at a range of over 100 miles.

The infra-red, heat-seeking, homing Sidewinder missiles will be fired at the hostile cruise missiles at a much shorter range, as will the Vulcan cannon.

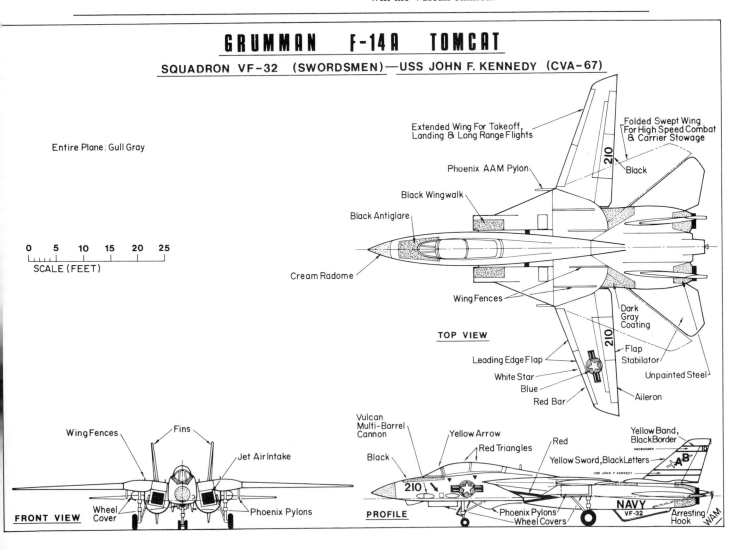

GRUMMAN F-14A TOMCAT
SQUADRON VF-32 (SWORDSMEN)—USS JOHN F. KENNEDY (CVA-67)

Entire Plane: Gull Gray

0 5 10 15 20 25
SCALE (FEET)

Extended Wing For Takeoff, Landing & Long Range Flights
Folded Swept Wing For High Speed Combat & Carrier Stowage
Phoenix AAM Pylon
Black Wingwalk
Black Antiglare
Black
Cream Radome
Wing Fences
Dark Gray Coating
TOP VIEW
Leading Edge Flap
White Star
Blue
Red Bar
Flap
Stabilator
Unpainted Steel
Aileron

Wing Fences
Fins
Jet Air Intake
FRONT VIEW
Wheel Cover
Phoenix Pylons

Vulcan Multi-Barrel Cannon
Yellow Arrow
Red Triangles
Red
Black
Yellow Band, Black Border
Yellow Sword, Black Letters
PROFILE
Phoenix Pylons
Wheel Covers
NAVY
VF-32
Arresting Hook

The Tomcat wing folding consists of a strong wing root stub to which the wing outer panel is hinged. A portion of the folded outer panel slips between the wing root and the fuselage. The dark portion of the fuselage is covered by the wing when it is in the full sweep position. (Official U.S. Navy Photograph, News Photo Division)

This means that a single Grumman Tomcat is capable of engaging a massed enemy attack of long-range bombers, approaching altitudes from sea level to 80,000 feet, that are launching cruise missiles at the CVBG. The lone Tomcat can perform this task without intercept control from CIC or the Hawkeye.

The F-14A is fitted with four strong points under the fuselage, one under each engine, and a pylon under each fixed-wing root to carry a maximum total load of 14,500 pounds. In addition to the fixed multi-barrel, 20 millimeter Vulcan M-61 cannon, the following weapon combinations can be fitted: four Phoenix AIM-54 long-range AAM's under the fuselage and two Phoenix missiles with two infra-red homing Sidewinder AIM-9AAM's on the wing root pylons; four Phoenix under the fuselage plus two Mark 83 1,000 pound bombs on the wing root pylons; or four Phoenix missiles under the fuselage plus two Sidewinders and two Sparrow AIM-7 AAM's on the wing root pylons, and two drop tanks under the engines. Each wing pylon can carry one or two missiles as required.

F-14A Tomcat Data

The Grumman F-14A Tomcat is powered by two 20,900 pound static thrust Pratt & Whitney TF30-412A afterburning turbofa engines which give the plane a maximum speed of 1,563 miles pe hour at altitude and 913 miles per hour at sea level. The 39,76 pounds empty and 74,350 pounds maximum weight F-14A has service ceiling of 56,000 feet. Maximum range is 2,000 miles an combat radius is 500 miles. Overall length is 62 feet-8 inches. Spa with wings extended at 20 degree sweepback is 64 feet-2 inche while with wings fully swept at 68 degrees, the span is 38 feet-inches. Overall height is 16 feet-0 inches.

Tomcat Swing-Wing

The most outstanding feature of the Tomcat is the variable geom etry or adjustable sweep-wing. The sweepback angle of the wing i computer controlled in order to attain the optimum angle for th best performance under any combat situation. The wing panels ar extended to a minimal sweepback angle for long range flight, take off and carrier landings, while they are retracted to a maximur sweepback angle for high-speed maneuvering. The swing wing plu the application of flaps and slots in aerial combat maneuvering hav made this huge fighter one of the most agile naval fighters in th world.

Tomcat Engine Problems

Despite the phenomenal performance of the F-14A, several short comings had to be corrected; the most important of which was th fact that the F-14A was seriously underpowered because the P&V TF30 was merely intended as an interim powerplant to be installe only in the first few Tomcats. Insufficient power appears to hav been the major deficiency in many U.S. naval jets. The principa powerplant for the Tomcat was to be a much more powerful Gen eral Electric engine in the main production run of the F-14B. Thi variant was never produced because of the military hardware bud get austerity of the late 1970s; therefore, the F-14B fell victim t the U.S. Congressional system of budgetary priorities. In view o this lack of foresight, the underpowered F-14A was placed int production with engines that were prone to compressor stall, pro duced inadequate thrust, smoked excessively and exhibited poo throttle response; all of which contributed to numerous F-14A ac cidents. This resulted in loud but unwarranted Congressional criti cism of the Tomcat design when the Grumman design was not a fault.

Grumman F-14C

Although the F-14B was never built, the next variant was the F 14C which included engine shrouds to restrain the effect of cata strophic engine failure, strengthened landing gear to endure highe loads during carrier landings, TCS (Television Camera Set) to en able the aircrew to identify hostile aircraft at longer ranges whe this is required by the rules of engagement, plus miscellaneous elec tronics and engine improvements. The F-14C entered productio in 1983 and up to that time over 500 Grumman F-14A Tomcats ha been constructed including 80 sold to Japan.

With wing panels fully extended, a Grumman Tomcat leaves the catapult of USS Carl Vinson (CVN-70). The Grumman F-14D has the added capability of launching Harpoon ASM's and HARM missiles plus the AMRAAM. (Official U.S. Navy Photograph, News Photo Division)

Super Tomcat

In the mid-1980s General Electric F110-GE-400 turbofan engines were retrofitted into F-14A airframes. These engines gave the Tomcat a 30 percent increase in installed combat rated thrust which produced quicker acceleration and a higher top speed plus a greater fuel economy despite the increased power. The new engine's compressor is also less prone to FOD (Foreign Object Damage). After (32) F-14A's had been retrofitted into Super Tomcats, (38) more Super Tomcats came off the production line as scratch-built Super Tomcats. The first Super Tomcats became operational in early 1988 with the designation remaining F-14A.

Grumman F-14D Tomcat

The outstanding success of the early Super Tomcats initiated design work on an improved Super Tomcat because the Super Tomcat only partially satisfied the aircraft's future needs in its role with the Maritime Air Superiority force. Fortunately, the original Tomcat was designed with plenty of growth potential. The new Tomcat was designated F-14D and proved to be virtually a new plane, designed from scratch. The combination of a proven airframe, advanced engine technology, and state-of-the-art digital avionics, make the F-14D a tremendous asset to U.S. naval aviation's ability to do its part in the maritime strategy. The F-14D's increased capability over the F-14A equals the increased capability that the F-14A had over its predecessors.

One of the major improvements is the Hughes APG-71 radar which replaces the AWG-9 because the APG-71 is twice as reliable and features a 40 percent increase in detection and tracking ranges plus better tracking accuracy. An Airborne Self-Protection Jammer (ASPJ) was added because of the F-14D's large radar signature.

Multi-Function Displays (MFD) enable both F-14D aircrew members the opportunity of seeing any electronic display available in the aircraft upon demand.

Hands On Throttle And Stick (HOTAS) enables the pilot to perform most tactical functions without moving his hands away from the basic flight controls.

Two novel additions will enable the F-14D to operate more easily from flight decks. An on-board oxygen generating system will draw aircrew oxygen from the atmosphere, thereby eliminating dependence on the carrier-based servicing units. The other addition is an on-board Auxiliary Power Unit (APU), similar to that on the Harrier, which can start the engine without assistance from the flight deck crew. A fatigue/engine monitoring system is distributed throughout the aircraft to indicate points of impending failure.

AMRAAM Added

A new weapon was added to the F-14D arsenal; the Hughes AMRAAM (Advanced Medium Range Air to Air Missile). Six of the missiles can be fitted and all six can be fired in rapid succession at multiple targets. AMRAAM greatly enhances the Tomcat's firepower, particularly in power projection strike support operations in which it must maintain aerial superiority.

Multi-Role F-14D

Unlike the F-14A and F-14-C, the F-14D is not strictly an air-to-air platform but has the ability to launch the Harpoon ASM (Anti-Ship Missile) as well as HARM (High-Speed Anti-Radiation Missile).

Improved Phoenix Missile

In 1986 Hughes began deliveries of an improved Phoenix missile, AIM-54-C plus. This variant eliminated the need for the Tomcat to provide liquid coolant for the missile which had been necessary on the previous variants. Consequently, the F-14D omitted the liquid coolant feature. This illustrates the complexity of the modern fighter in which numerous necessary subsystems must be installed in order for the aircraft to perform its functions properly.

F-14A Converted Into F-14D

The first of 127 production F-14D Tomcats was delivered to the U.S. Navy in March 1990 while about (400) F-14A Tomcats were remanufactured into the F-14D.

CVBG Needs Fighters to Survive

CVBG survival is a preconditon for power projection and that survival is dependent upon the awe-inspiring carrier-based fighters.

McDonnell Douglas F/A-18 Hornet

Since the inception of carrier-based aviation, the discussion still continues whether a one, two or three-man crew is best for naval fighter and strike aircraft. The principal argument for multiple crew members had been the problem of navigation and then the need for a radar officer. Those who favor the opposite view claim that today's high-tech data processing, displays and sensors obviate the second or third crew member and that the single crew member can make quicker decisions when not encumbered by a partner with whom he must share information. Single-seat proponents also point to the fact that it is a lesser risk to expose a single-crew member to enemy action, especially when it costs over five million dollars to train each crew member.

Single-Seat Decision

The single-seat McDonnell Douglas F/A-18 Hornet did, in fact, disturb the hornet's nest of the old argument: "Is one seat better than two?"

The escalating costs of the F-14 program, due to the need for the more powerful engines and electronic equipment, induced the

The McDonnell Douglas F/A-18 Hornet was conceived in cooperation with Northrop Corporation and developed from the F-5 Freedom Fighter because the U.S. Navy had specified a small, inexpensive fighter. (McDonnell Douglas, Courtesy Timothy J. Beecher)

U.S. Navy to prepare specifications for a new, smaller and less expensive fighter designated VFAX. McDonnell Douglas joined forces with Northrop Corporation to develop the experimental YF-17, evolved from the single-seat F-5 Freedom Fighter, into a VFAX contender. This was not the first time that Douglas and Northrop had cooperated in a project. It will be recalled that the pre-World War II Northrop BT-1 had been developed into one of the finest aircraft of the war, known as the Douglas Dauntless, and history repeated itself when the U.S. Navy and Marine Corps selected the McDonnell Douglas/Northrop entry for the VFAX contract in 1975 and the F-18 was born.

Multiple Roles Added

As has happened to many U.S. Navy fighters in the past, the attack

The McDonnell Douglas Hornet started life as the F-18 fighter; however, U.S. Navy added multiple roles which made the Hornet a strike/fighter F/A-18. These Hornets are attacking ground installations with heavy casing 500 pound bombs. (McDonnell Douglas, Courtesy Thomas J. Downey)

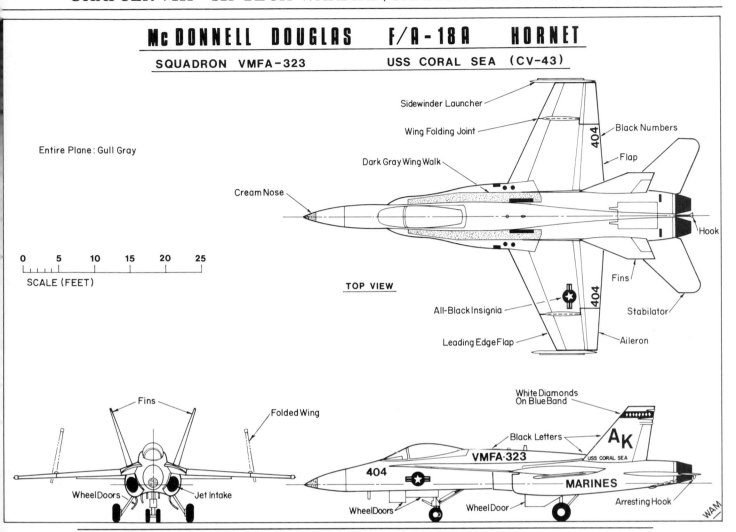

McDONNELL DOUGLAS   F/A-18A   HORNET

SQUADRON VMFA-323 **USS CORAL SEA (CV-43)**

Entire Plane : Gull Gray

Sidewinder Launcher
Wing Folding Joint
Dark Gray Wing Walk
Cream Nose

Black Numbers
Flap
404
404
Hook
Fins
Stabilator
All-Black Insignia
Leading Edge Flap
Aileron

TOP VIEW

0 5 10 15 20 25
SCALE (FEET)

Fins
Folded Wing

Wheel Doors
Jet Intake

White Diamonds On Blue Band
Black Letters
VMFA·323
AK
USS CORAL SEA
404
MARINES
WheelDoors
Wheel Door
Arresting Hook

WAM

Only half of the Hornet's weight is aluminum which includes fuselage sides, wing leading and trailing edges and ailerons. Remaining materials of the Hornet are carbon epoxy, titanium, and high impact space-age plastics. The various shades on the planes in this photo indicate the different materials. (McDonnell Douglas, Courtesy Thomas J. Downey)

role was added to the F-18 which, not only changed the designation to F/A-18 but, increased the weight and power, and raised the cost to the level of the F-14. McDonnell Douglas is the prime contractor with Northrop the principal airframe subcontractor for the F/A-18 Hornet strike/fighter.

The Hornet made its first flight in November 1978 and the first service deliveries started in February 1981 replacing the U.S. Marine Phantom II and the U.S. Navy Corsair II of VMFA-314 and VFA-113 in January and October, 1983.

Hornet Advanced Structural Materials

Only one-half of the F/A-18's weight is aluminum which includes fuselage sides, wing leading and trailing edges and ailerons. Steel consists of about 16 percent of the airframe weight which is used principally in the landing gear struts and jet tailpipes. Carbon epoxy composites are used in about 10 percent of the airframe weight for the wing skins, horizontal and vertical tail surfaces, flaps, and fuselage top and bottom. About 13 percent of the structure is titanium which is primarily used at the wing, stabilator and fin root attachment to the fuselage. The remaining 11 percent is high impact space-age plastic used for the nose cone radome, vertical tail surface tips, cockpit canopy and miscellaneous removable panels. The careful selection of construction materials has kept the weight

of the Hornet to the minimum; thereby, improving its performance. Of special interest is the use of carbon epoxy materials which comprise 40 percent of the aircraft surface area. These materials are lightweight, extremely strong plus fatigue and corrosion resistant.

Hornet Data

The F/A-18A single-seat carrier-based strike/fighter is powered by two 16,000 pound static thrust General Electric F404-400 two-shaft turbofan engines which give the aircraft a maximum speed of 1,189 miles per hour at operating altitude. Combat radius as a fighter is 633 miles while in the attack mode it is 460 miles. Ferry range is 2,070 miles. The 23,939 pounds empty weight and 56,000 loaded weight Hornet has a combat ceiling of 50,000 feet. It can carry 1,620 gallons of fuel internally and an additional 2,356 gallons of fuel in externally mounted drop tanks. Overall length is 56 feet while overall height is 15 feet-4 inches. Wingspan is only 37 feet-6 inches with a wing area of 400 square feet.

Up to 17,000 pounds of weapons can be mounted on nine stations or strong points: for strike operations – two AIM-9 Sidewinder heat-seeking AAM on the wingtips, Harpoon ASM, Mark 82, 83 or 84 low drag general purpose or laser-guided bombs, AIM-7 radar-guided Sparrow AAM missiles, fuselage-mounted laser detector tracker, AGM-88A HARM guided missile, Maverick air-to-ground missile or 315 gallon external fuel tanks, and for fighter operations two Sidewinders and four Sparrows or six Sidewinders and two Sparrows can be installed plus the fixed 20 millimeter M61-Al Vulcan multi-barrel cannon in the fuselage.

Hornet Electronics

A Hornet upgrade in 1986 included provision for AMRAAM and ASPJ systems.

Some key features that enable single-seat operation of the Hornet are the extensive use of on-board digital computers that rapidly perform mission and flight related functions. Human engineering features built into the cockpit including HOTAS (Hands On Throttle And Stick) with which the pilot can access radar features and control weapons systems at the throttle and control column, plus the integration of electronic warfare equipment with the weapons systems. The fly-by-wire flight control system uses electronic impulses, with a backup system of mechanical rods or cable, to actuate control surfaces from the cockpit controls. This system has the advantage of sensing the physical strain on the structure during violent maneuvers as well as the aerodynamic attitude of the aircraft and can override the pilot's actions if the plane is overstressed or about to become uncontrollable.

Hornet Features

An APU (Auxiliary Power Unit) allows the pilot to start the engines without any external power. Also installed in the Hornet is a fire extinguishing system, self-sealing fuel tanks and fuel lines, plus hydraulic system leak detection which automatically isolates the

OPPOSITE: The relatively short Hornet wingspan required only minimal wing folding for carrier hangar stowage. The fold line is at the aileron/flap junction and the tips need fold only to a vertical position. Observe the Sidewinder launchers on the wingtips. (McDonnell Douglas, Courtesy Timothy J. Beecher)

The Navy required many more tasks from the Hornet – jobs that previously required five different aircraft. The two-seat Hornet F/A-18D Hornet was born and is shown in the foreground. A single-seat F/A-18A escorts. (McDonnell Douglas, Courtesy of Thomas J. Downey)

section of the system that is leaking in order not to affect the remainder of the system. Landing gear problems were experienced during hard carrier landings but this has been corrected.

Export Hornets

In addition to the U.S. Navy and U.S. Marine Corps the McDonnell Douglas F/A-18 has been delivered to the governments of Canada (1982), Australia (1984) and Spain (1986).

Two-Seater Hornet

Despite the Hornet's fine performance in the strike/fighter role it seems the U.S. Marine Corps wanted more. Studies had indicated that during a nocturnal amphibious assault, from five to eight different fixed-wing aircraft would be required to support the night assault: the predarkness SEAD (Suppression of Enemy Air Defense) missions would be the responsibility of A-4M Skyhawks; the follow-up reconnaissance duty would fall to the RF-4B Phantom; FAC (Forward Air Controller), TAC(A) (Tactical Air Coordinator (Air), and SAC(A) (Supporting Arms Coordinator (Air) would be handled by OA-4M Skyhawks; night CAS (Close Air Support) would be the job of A-6E TRAM (Target Recognition Attack Multisensor) Intruders; strike/fighter, CAP (Combat Air Patrol), and escort missions would be flown by F-4S Phantoms or F/A-18A Hornets. It was realized that the second cockpit plus multiple technological additions to the proven Hornet airframe would produce a truly multimission aircraft capable of completing a myriad of assignments and, by 1987, the F/A-18D two-seat Hornet was in production.

McDonnell Douglas F/A-18D

The expanded missions thrust upon the F/A-18D comprised the interception and destruction of enemy planes that threatened Marine bases, support systems, and ground forces in all weather conditions; attack and destroy enemy airfields, seaports, plus supply and communications lines in nocturnal and all weather conditions; escort strike aircraft against hostile interceptors under all weather

In order to fly missions under all weather conditions and around the clock the F/A-18D was updated for night attack capability. A test plane is shown here. (McDonnell Douglas, Courtesy Thomas J. Downey)

conditions; operate from aircraft carriers to provide fleet defense against high and low altitude aerial attacks; conduct CAS (Close Air Support) and deep air support around the clock and under all weather conditions; conduct armed reconnaissance plus aerial multisensor imagery and target damage assessment under all weather conditions; and provide FAC, SAC(A) and TAC(A) as required.

All this requires a pilot and an NFO (Naval Flight Officer) to share in the work load of these task-saturating missions. Gone are the dive bombers and torpedo planes that scored heavily in World War II. The basic naval fighter plane has become so powerful that it evolved into the strike/fighter; able to fight off enemy air attacks as well as sink hostile ships, destroy land installations and troop concentrations while protecting friendly troops, ships and aircraft. The complex and almost intelligent on-board electronics is an important member of the crew without which these supersonic "Jack of All Trades" could not function. There is a price to pay for this high speed, heavy payload and extensive electronics, and that is fuel consumption which has made aerial refueling a dire necessity to maintain and extend sea-based airpower.

MID-AIR REFUELING

The demand for more available airborne fuel has become increasingly important in order to maintain and extend the defensive shield around the CVBG. With the deadly accuracy of air-launched ASM's it is imperative that hostile aircraft be stopped beyond missile range of the CVBG or SAG. Conversely, strikes on enemy ships should be made as far from the CVBG defensive shield as possible. More often than not, aircraft returning to carriers from missions have barely enough fuel to land and are often forced to ditch after a wave-off because every bit of fuel had been consumed to make a new approach. In 1965 the U.S. Navy decided to standardize refueling tankers and sought a replacement for the EKA-3B tanker version of the Douglas A-3 Skywarrior.

Grumman KA-6D Tanker

Grumman modified an A-6A Intruder as the KA-6D tanker prototype which made its first flight in May 1966. Pleased with the result, the Navy ordered a modification program to convert 62 early A-6A Intruders into KA-6D tankers. The fleet of KA-6D tankers

A Grumman KA-6D tanker refuels a Grumman A-6 Intruder at the rate of 350 gallons per minute. Aircraft carrier Intruder squadrons comprised 10 Grumman A-6 Intruders and four Grumman KA-6D tankers. (Grumman Corporation, Courtesy Lois Lovisolo)

each have a transfer fuel capacity of 3,000 gallons, half of which is carried externally in five 300 gallon drop tanks. The Grumman tankers are equipped with pumps and a hose reel which can extend 65 feet of hose into the airstream. A cone-shaped drogue is attached to the end of the line to keep it steady and prevent whipping. The receiving aircraft is fitted with a probe which the receiving pilot inserts into the open end of the drogue by maneuvering his plane into position. When filled he then reduces his speed to disengage from the tanker. Fuel is transferred at 350 gallons per minute and that one minute of refueling is enough to enable a starving fighter to re-enter the landing pattern and make a safe approach and landing on the carrier deck. Very often carrier aircraft have their tanks topped off immediately after takeoff in order to extend their range to the target area. On long range missions the tanker flies part of the way with the strike planes and refuels them before they reach the target.

KA-6D tankers are an integral part of carrier Intruder squadrons; (10) A-6 Intruders and (4) KA-6D tankers. Further, there are no dedicated tanker pilots because all of the squadron pilots fly either type of aircraft as required. The tankers can also be used for visual or daytime bombing missions because only sophisticated navigation and high-tech bombing systems had been removed during the conversion from attack plane to tanker.

AIRCRAFT LAUNCH AND RECOVERY OPERATIONS

It is axiomatic that an aircraft carrier's primary reason for existing is to launch and recover her aircraft which are the weapons that deliver her fighting punch. On the U.S. Navy Supercarrier, aircraft are launched and retrieved in such rapid succession that the amazingly choreographed operation never ceases to astound the viewer. The four aircraft elevators and four powerful catapults plus a well-trained operating crew enable four planes to be launched in less than a minute and when they return, the arresting cables can stop a 60,000 pound airplane, that touches down at more than 150 miles per hour, in less than 200 feet. Few of us who admire aircraft carriers and carrier aircraft stop to think about and marvel at the organization of "squires" who work so diligently in close cooperation with each other to launch the "knights" and their airborne chargers quickly and safely; then retrieve them with equal rapidity and safety.

Three distinct groups are involved with launching and retrieving aircraft.

Primary Flight Control

Primary Flight Control (Pri-Fly) is a glazed bubble on the inboard side of the island, overlooking the Flight Deck. This is the carrier's air traffic control center. It is under the command of the Air Officer who is often called AIRBOSS, which title is often emblazoned on his yellow jersey. The Air Officer is in charge of the entire Flight Deck and Hangar Deck including the four catapults, four to six sets of arresting gear machinery, pilot landing aids, television, and optical light landing guidance as well as the Landing Signal Officer (LSO) platform. He is in charge of the entire aviation deck crew which can number about 700 for each operation.

The Air Boss is invariably a former carrier pilot which adds credence to his authority over both pilots and aviation deck crew.

Second in command is the Assistant Air Officer, often called the MINIBOSS, which is also frequently inscribed on his yellow jersey. The Mini Boss also is usually a former carrier pilot. The Air Boss and Mini Boss normally have the rank of commander.

In addition to the bosses, the Pri-Fly crew includes: the optical light landing system officer who checks the arrangement of the lights to be certain that they have been set up for the type of plane scheduled to land; the status board writer who stands behind a transparent plastic panel and plots the impending arrivals with a grease pencil in mirror writing so the Air Boss can read it from the front side and the arresting gear petty officer who verifies that the energy absorbing mechanism is set to be compatible with the type of aircraft that is scheduled to land and which depends on the cables to stop safely.

The Airdales

The hundreds of specialists that comprise the aviation deck crew, called Airdales, must work quickly, accurately, and cooperatively. Members of the many divisions wear an identifying color jersey, protective headgear, ear noise protectors and life vests so the outgoing and incoming pilots will recognize the Flight Deck crewmen's specialty when they need assistance. The color codes are as follows:

Red: Top off fuel tanks; check installation of fuel drop tanks; safety checks; crash crew; FOD checks; armament checks.
Yellow: Direct taxiing aircraft to catapults, etc.
Blue: Plane handlers; bring planes to flight deck; secure parked planes to deck; rearrange planes on deck for quick launch; return planes to hangar.
Green: Catapult operators; connect bridle; adjust catapult.
Purple: Fuel handlers; perform principal aircraft fueling.
Silver: Fire and rescue in heat resistant suits; speed to deck fires in small open vehicles.
Tan: Deck catapult officer.
White: Inspect the aircraft before it is connected to the catapult.

CATCC

Carrier Air Traffic Control Center (CATCC) is a radar room inside the hull in which the carrier's aircraft are tracked.

Personnel in the CATCC advise incoming aircraft that they are too high or too low and lead them into the carrier approach guide path.

Aircraft Launching

Now that the cast of characters has been introduced it should be of interest to see how each division contributes to a typical carrier launch and retrieval production. This is a capsulized description:

(a) The Air Officer (Air Boss) orders the aviation deck crew on deck and they promptly appear in the proper color attire with life jackets, goggles in place, and head and ear protectors also in place because the Flight Deck can be a very dangerous and noisy place during air operations. The Air Boss also orders the carrier brought into the wind.

When the Blue-clad plane handlers have brought a plane to the flight deck, Red-clad crewmen top off the fuel tanks and check the deck for FOD (Foreign Object Damage). Others stand ready with fire extinguishers and fire hose applicators (arrows). Plane is a F4U-5 Corsair on USS Princeton (CV-37). (Sal Marrone Photo)

Armorers of the ordnance department check all bombs and missiles, correcting faulty installations. Safety pins are then carefully removed from the weapon. Mark 82 Snakeye bombs on a VS-192 Vought A-7E Corsair II are being checked aboard USS Kitty Hawk (CVA-63) during the Vietnam War. (Ling Temco Vought, Courtesy Arthur L. Schoeni)

(b) As the elevators bring the aircraft up to the Flight Deck, the Blue-clad plane handlers take the planes in tow and position them on the Deck in the best location for quick and direct access to the catapults.

(c) If the planes are armed a Red-clad armorer inspects the installation of externally mounted bombs and missiles and carefully removes the safety pins from these weapons.

(d) Red-clad crewmen top off the fuel tanks and check the drop tank installations. They also check the Deck for FOD (Foreign Object Damage) which is any loose object on the deck that can be drawn into a jet engine intake causing damage or total destruction of the engine.

(e) With pilots in the cockpits and engines started, the planes then taxi to the proper catapults following the hand signals of the yellow-clad directors.

(f) Blue-clad plane handlers then remove temporary chocks and any other restraining device from the plane.

(g) White-clad inspectors check the planes and then water-cooled jet blast deflectors rise out of the Deck behind the planes at the catapults.

(h) Green-clad catapult crewmen carefully and quickly install the 200 pound, 2 1/2 inch diameter steel cable catapult bridle to the catapult shuttle, the plane, and to the bridle recovery lines.

(i) The tan-clad catapult officer,complete with radio headset, supervises the launch preparations and then exchanges salutes with the pilot. When the rest of the catapult crew (green) confirm that the launch can proceed, the catapult officer crouches and points towards the bow with his left arm in a dramatic stance to order the aircraft launch.

(j) The catapult shuttle pulls the aircraft along the Deck with neck-snapping acceleration, bringing the plane to takeoff speed in three seconds. Steam continues to belch from the catapult

A Grumman Greyhound is directed to the catapult by the hand signals of a Yellow-clad plane director (arrow). Note the Green-clad catapult crewmen in the foreground walkway. (Grumman Corporation, Courtesy Lois Lovisolo)

With the pilot in the cockpit and his Vought A-7E Corsair II in position on a USS Independence (CVA-62) catapult, a Blue-clad plane handler removes temporary chocks from the plane's wheels. This plane is loaded with 19,000 pounds of ordnance for a raid during the Vietnam War. (Ling Temco Vought, Courtesy Arthur L. Schoeni)

White-clad plane inspectors carefully check a McDonnell Douglas Hornet as clouds of steam escape from the catapult slot. The inspector's approval is mandatory prior to a launch. (McDonnell Douglas, Courtesy Thomas J. Downey)

As the Green-clad catapult operator signals the pilot, Green-clad catapult crewmen install the 200 pound, 2 1/2 inch diameter steel cable catapult bridle. Note the water-cooled jet blast deflector behind this Vought F8U-1 Crusader. (Ling Temco Vought, Courtesy Arthur L. Schoeni)

OPPOSITE TOP: Aviation deck crewmen stand clear as this Vought F-8 Crusader is ready to launch from USS Forrestal (CVA-59). The catapult crewman in the deck edge walkway adjusts his headset as he waits the catapult officer's signal to activate the catapult. (Ling Temco Vought, Courtesy Arthur L. Schoeni) BOTTOM: The tan vest-clad catapult officer orders the launch of this Vought F-8H Crusader from USS John F. Kennedy (CVA-67) with a dramatic gesture. Of interest is the Primary Flight Control (Pri-Fly) glazed bubble protruding from the island structure (arrow). (Ling Temco Vought, Courtesy Arthur L. Schoeni)

The 2 inch diameter steel arresting cables are supported above the flight deck by bowed steel flat bars. Here, two arresting gear crewmen adjust an arresting cable aboard USS Dwight D. Eisenhower (CVN-69). (Official U.S. Navy Photograph, Department of Defense by PH2 Tracy Lee Didas)

The Landing Signal Station is a busy place during landing operations with continuous radio conversations with incoming planes. The Landing Signal Instrument Console (arrow) is integrated with the Fresnal Lens. (Official U.S. Navy Photograph, U.S. Department of Defense by PHAN Charles R. Solseth)

Right: A landing signal officer makes an adjustment on the Landing Signal Instrument Console at the Landing Signal Station. The console adjusts the Fresnal Lens Optical Landing System to match the particular plane making the landing. (Official U.S. Navy Photograph, U.S. Department of Defense)

track as the next plane moves into position on the catapult.

(k) The entire operation is under the watchful eyes of the Mini Boss who can abort the launching if he feels that a dangerous condition exists. By pressing a button on his console, the Mini Boss can prevent a catapult from firing.

(l) Once airborne and in stable flight, control of the flight is turned over to the CATCC.

Aircraft Recovery

The Deck must then be prepared for the arrested landings when the aircraft return to the carrier. Recovery operations demand the same trust, timing and training that is needed for launching operations. As the returning aircraft literally fall from the sky, they must be guided, arrested, and quickly led out of the path of the following plane. A brief scenario of the landing operation and an equally short description of some of the necessary equipment follows:

(a) The LSO (Landing Signal Officers) stand on a platform at the after port side of the flight deck and talk directly to the pilots. They can wave off an approach that they don't feel is safe.

(b) Once the pilot is in his final approach he sights on a set of optical lights located at the forward port side of the flight deck. The lights have been adjusted for the particular type of aircraft that he is flying and the pilot must keep his plane on a path from which he can view a specific light pattern. If the pattern changes, he must alter course to bring the proper pattern into view; this is called the Fresnal Lens Optical Landing System. The lens was named after Augustin Jean Fresnel (1788-1827), a French physicist who studied lenses and, in 1820, invented the lens that was used in lighthouses for almost two centuries. The lens used in the Landing System is patterned after that of Fresnel's experiments. The Boston (Massachussetts) Museum of Science has a large display of Fresnel's work. Little did this scientist imagine that his work would, someday, assist flying machines to land on ships.

(c) With the plane's arresting hook lowered, the pilot usually tries to engage the second or third cable. The steel cables are

This is a Vought A-7E Corsair II pilot's view of the USS Dwight D. Eisenhower (CVN-69) Flight Deck during a landing approach. Note the Fresnal lights at the distant arrow and the Landing Signal Station at the near arrow. (Official U.S. Navy Photograph, U.S. Department of Defense by Lt. Cmdr. Leenhouts)

All aircraft that land on U.S. Navy carriers use the Fresnal Lens Optical Landing System to guide them to a safe landing. The optical lights are adjusted for the approaching aircraft type and the pilot must maneuver to keep a fixed pattern of lights in sight. (Official U.S. Navy Photograph, U.S. Department of Defense by Don S. Montgomery, USN (Ret.))

supported several inches above the deck by bowed steel flat bars resembling automobile leaf springs. Once the two inch diameter cable has been caught by the aircraft arresting hook, the plane's enormous momentum pulls the cable from 200 to 250 feet of deck length before the plane comes to a halt. This means that about 500 feet of cable has been dragged along the flight deck because the tug of the plane has transformed the straight 125 feet athwartship cable into a Vee measuring almost 300 feet on each leg. From where does all this extra cable come?

The approximately 125 feet length of each of four to six steel cables stretched across the flight deck, one of which the

incoming pilot tries to engage with his hook, is only a very small portion of each cable. Each end of the Flight Deck cable runs down into the bowels of the ship, through fairleads in the deck, where it is guided by pulleys and is wound around tension-measuring reservoir drums. The cable is then connected to hydraulic pistons in long arresting gear snubber chambers. The total length of each cable is actually over 1,000 feet. This complex system must permit the cable to play out on deck at very high speed as well as quickly reel in the extra cable in preparation for following landings for which pilots have already begun the final approach.

The cable mechanism not only compensates for the weight

A Grumman Trader approaches the flight deck as landing signal officers in the Landing Signal Station (arrow) help to guide the plane to a safe landing. (Grumman Corporation Courtesy Lois Lovisolo)

The LSO (Landing Signal Officer) walks onto the flight deck to talk an F/A-18 Hornet pilot to a landing. The pilot of a landing aircraft usually attempts to engage the second or third arresting cable. (McDonnell Douglas, Courtesy Thomas J. Downey)

and speed of the landing aircraft but also adjusts to keep the plane from veering off the runway during touch-down.

(d) As soon as the plane stops, Blue-clad plane handlers swarm around it to be certain the plane is free of the cable and can proceed.

(e) Yellow-clad plane directors lead the plane to an elevator or its prearranged stowage location on deck.

(f) If the plane is to remain on deck, once it is in its proper spot the Blue jersey plane handlers secure the plane to the deck and chock the wheels.

Aircraft land in as rapid succession as they takeoff from modern carriers, and they do appear to fall from the sky rather than alight gently as a large bird. A carrier pilot acquaintance told the author that every landing felt like a controlled crash because the rate of descent was so rapid and steep through necessity.

Every landing is under the watchful eye of the Air Officer (Air Boss) who is in contact with the LSO and can abort a landing on the spot if it appears in danger of crashing.

In the event that all cables are missed, the plane's hook invariably scrapes along the deck creating a shower of sparks, and the aircraft climbs away for another try. Missing all cables is called a bolter.

The noise and vigorous activity on the flight deck is in direct contrast with the quiet tension in Pri-Fly except, of course, the constant telephone conversations of which the Air Boss often conducts three simultaneously. Even when one is familiar with the basic activities, to witness the procedures on deck and in Pri-Fly during simultaneous takeoff and landing operations fills the spectator with awe and admiration. The work is done so quickly, like a well-oiled machine, that one can hardly keep tabs of the various activities.

The Invincible class Through-Deck Cruisers are the first new carriers to be constructed with Ski-Jump ramps. Note the Harrier leaving the HMS Invincible seven degree Ski-Jump. (Ministry of Defence [Navy])

NEW ROYAL NAVY SKI-JUMP CARRIERS

With each generation of jet-powered planes growing larger and heavier than its predecessor, aircraft carriers required stronger flight decks, larger size and capacity elevators, plus more powerful catapults. This forced many nations to abandon all hope of operating fleet carriers due to budgetary restraints. The smaller countries that had purchased the former Royal Navy light fleet carriers were operating Alize or Tracker ASW aircraft and Skyhawk light attack aircraft; nothing heavier.

Britain Abandons Fleet Carriers

Even the Royal Navy eventually succumbed and gave up the large fleet carrier. Britain had made a last attempt to construct a fleet carrier in the 1960s. This was to be the CVA-01 which, together with a companion ship TDC (Through Deck Cruiser) operating large ASW helicopters, was due to be ordered in 1965 but was cancelled due to economic pressures.

Other than the U.S., only the French Marine Nationale persisted with the attack carrier; however, it has had to be content with operating relatively small and increasingly obsolescent aircraft from the decks of *Foch* and *Cemenceau*.

Royal Navy Through Deck Cruiser

Having divested itself of most of her overseas responsibilities Britain altered its naval policy when it abandoned its worldwide strike capabilities and decided to concentrate on ASW operations in the Atlantic Ocean as a dedicated member of NATO. This change in policy prompted the decision to construct the Through Deck Cruiser (TDC) which had been originally planned to escort the cancelled CVA-01. Three ships were contracted: *HMS Invincible* (R 05) with Vickers Shipyard (Barrow); *HMS Illustrious* (R 06) and *HMS Ark Royal* (R 07) with Swan Hunter Shipyard (Tyne). *HMS Invincible*

keel was laid on July 20, 1973 while Illustrious and Ark Royal were started on June 6, 1976 and December 14, 1978, respectively. The ships took as long as seven years to complete from keel laying to commissioning because of doubtful political direction and constant modifications to their operational function and design.

Invincible Class Data

The *Invincible* class has a rather handsome and unaggressive appearance which belies its naval potential. The initial design was

Aircraft complement of the Invincible class is 11 Sea King helicopters and eight Harriers. The ships also operate as commando or assault carriers and can accommodate 1,000 troops plus their combat equipment. Note the helicopter landing deck marker rings. (Ministry of Defence [Navy])

prepared for the class to operate only helicopters; however, about midway during construction, instructions were received for the ships to also operate the Harrier. Requirements were also issued for the *Invincible* class to be capable of functioning as amphibious assault or commando carriers which required accommodations for about 1,000 troops and their combat equipment. A third late requirement was the addition of a Ski-Jump flight deck which was inclined seven degrees on *Invincible* and *Illustrious*, while *Ark Royal* sported a 15 degree Ski-Jump ramp based upon experience with the *HMS Hermes* ramp conversion. In 1988 the *Illustrious* Ski-Jump ramp angle was increased to 12 degrees and the Harrier complement increased to eight planes although 12 can be embarked. The slender island runs about half the ship's length because considerable volume is taken by the gas turbine powerplant air intake and combustion exhaust ducts plus electronics equipment.

Standard displacement is 16,000 tons while full load displacement is 19,500 tons. Overall length is 677 feet with a 600 x 44 feet runway area. Hull beam is 105 feet and mean draft is about 21 feet. Maximum speed is 28 knots while the 18 knot cruising speed gives the class a range of 5,000 miles. Crew is about 1,000 with a 320 air group complement.

The original aircraft complement comprised nine Sea King HAS.5, two Sea King AEW, and five Sea Harrier FRS.1. This ar-

The two Invincible class aircraft elevators are of a new, innovative design. Instead of pulleys and cables the elevators are raised and lowered by hydraulically operated steel beams in a "scissors" type action. (British Aerospace, Courtesy Brendan Morrissey)

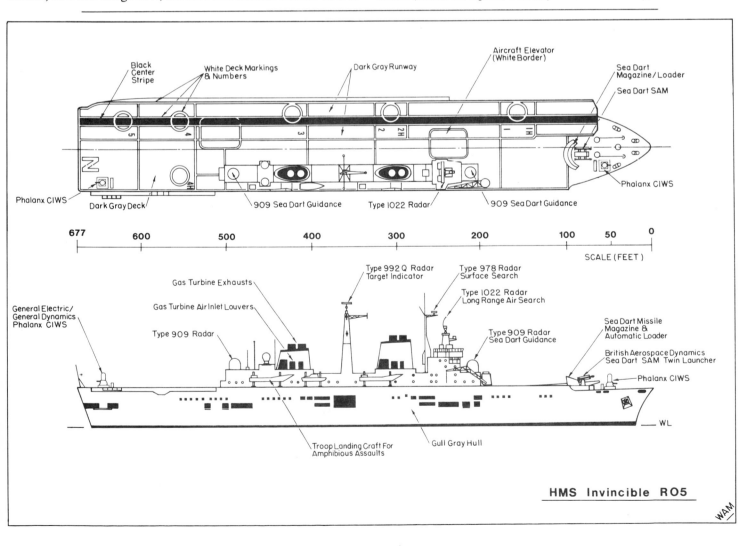

HMS Invincible R05

This head-on view of HMS Invincible shows off the bow-located Sea Dart SAM launchers. The curved magazine contains 22 Sea Dart missiles which are automatically loaded onto the launchers. (Ministry of Defence [Navy])

mament is supplemented by two Sea Dart SAM launchers in the bow, alongside the Ski-Jump ramp. A curved magazine, aft of the launchers, contains 22 Sea Dart missiles which are automatically loaded onto the launchers as required. *Illustrious* and *Ark Royal* were launched with two added Phalanx CIWS systems each on the bow and stern.

Innovative Aircraft Elevators
Two aircraft elevators are installed but the ships have no catapults or arresting gear. The McTaggart Scot elevators are of a most innovative design. Instead of the conventional multitude of cables and pulleys which normally occupy two sides of the elevator, the new design employs hydraulically operated steel beams beneath the elevator platform, lifting the elevator with a scissors type operation. This installation enables the elevators to be loaded and unloaded from three or four sides; thereby, simplifying aircraft handling.

Invincible Powerplant
Another outstanding feature of the Invincible class is the powerplant. *HMS Invincible* was the largest naval ship, at that time, to be fitted with gas turbines which are powerful marinized versions of aircraft turboshaft and turbojet engines. The advantage gained by using these engines is the quick getaway after start up because there is no waiting to generate steam nor is a warm up time, that is usually required for diesels, necessary. The compact, light weight gas turbine can be removed from the ship in its entirety as a module for overhaul and repair while another gas turbine is installed to take its place. Although the gas turbine is smaller and lighter than other powerplants of equivalent power, it requires a prodigious volume of air for combustion. Unlike its aeronautical counterpart, which speeds through the air forcing air into the jet intake, the shipboard installation must draw all its air through long ductwork from openings high in the superstructure down to the engine room without assistance from the ship's movement. This requires enormous ducts to reduce the air velocity and pressure drop or the gas turbines will starve for air. The large air intake ducts plus the turbine exhaust ducts often dis-

rupt the topside arrangement as happened with the Invincible class design in which the hangar was pinched in the middle to allow passage for the ducts.

After the *Invincible* class gas turbine installation the navies of Italy, U.S., German Federal Republic, Australia, Peru, Spain, and Venezuela also installed gas turbines to power some of their fighting ships; a few of which will be described later in the next chapter.

Four 28,000 shaft horsepower Rolls-Royce TM3B Olympus gas turbines produce 112,000 shaft horsepower. Two engines are geared to each of the two propeller shafts. Unlike commercial tankers and container ships, naval ships do not operate at full speed all the time in order to extend their range and reduce wear on the engines. Steam-powered naval ships are fitted with a cruising turbine while the Invincible class has small cruising gas turbines installed to extend range and conserve the principal powerplant. The acronym for this system is COGAG (COmbination Gas turbine And Gas turbine). The turbines can be clutched and declutched from the gears as necessary.

What's In a Name?
In view of the decision to operate fixed-wing aircraft the ships were officially redesignated "ASW Aircraft Carriers" in 1980; however, they are still generally known as "Through Deck Cruisers" or "Through Deck Command Cruisers" despite the fact that they are really aircraft carriers.

TROUBLES ERUPT IN THE FAR EAST
Two years after American forces had evacuated Vietnam all hell broke loose in Southeast Asia as the Communists returned to their program of ruthless conquest.

North Vietnamese Attack
It began on March 5, 1975 when the North Vietnamese launched a powerful invasion of the central highlands of South Vietnam. The small South Vietnam army was forced back by this surprise attack until two-thirds of the country was in North Vietnamese hands.

Communists Attack in Cambodia and Laos
On April 1, 1975 the Communist Khmer Rouge attacked the Cambodian capitol Phnom Penh, forcing the government to flee the country. Eight days later heavy fighting broke out between the Communist Pathet Lao and the government forces of Laos.

U.S. Refuses to Intervene
U.S. Army Chief of Staff General Frederick C. Weyland returned from an evaluation tour of Vietnam and reported to Congress that without U.S. military assistance Southeast Asia will fall to the Communists. Congress refused to become involved.

Carriers Evacuate Americans
Sikorsky CH-53 Sea Stallions rescued U.S.Embassy personnel from Phnom Penh which fell to the Communists on April 17 and, when North Vietnamese artillery shelled the last evacuation airfield, the U.S.Seventh Fleet took charge as Navy and Marine helicopters from U.S. carriers evacuated 9,000 people from Saigon. Grumman A-6,

Vought A-7 and Grumman F-14's provided air support for the evacuation.

Mayaguez Incident

The period May 12-15, 1975 is known as the Mayaguez Incident during which the American container ship Mayaguez was fired upon and captured by a Communist Khmer Rouge gunboat. American reaction was swift and positive.

While planes from *Coral Sea* (CVA-43) pounded naval and air bases in Cambodia, 60 Marines boarded Mayaguez and forced the Communists to return the crew and release the ship.

The foregoing incidents clearly illustrate the importance of the aircraft carrier and its warbirds to protect victimized nationals and force the release of property by hostile forces, big or small.

Spruance Class Destroyers

America's greatest fleet admiral of World War II was honored on September 20, 1975 when the lead ship (DD-963) of a new class of 30 destroyers was named for Admiral Raymond Spruance. The 7,000 ton *Spruance* class ships are the U.S. Navy's first gas turbine-powered destroyers.

U.S./Libyan Dogfight

On August 19, 1981 two Grumman F-14 Tomcats from *USS Nimitz* (CVN-68) shot down two Libyan Sukhoi-22 Fitter fighters over the Gulf of Sidra after the Soviet-built planes opened fire on the Americans. This incident was the result of a dispute regarding sovereignty over the Gulf and was to escalate into a more serious confrontation.

THE FALKLANDS WAR

By 1981 the British Ministry of Defence Command Number 8288 had made decisions to reduce the Royal Navy's already meager carrier force. It had decided to scrap the venerable *HMS Hermes*, last of the old fleet carriers, intending to replace it with the new *HMS Illustrious* in 1982. *HMS Invincible* was to be sold to Australia in 1983 and replaced by the new *HMS Ark Royal* upon its commissioning in 1984. This drastic reduction was to leave the Royal Navy with only two carriers, barely enough to meet its NATO responsibilities.

Argentine Forces Capture the Falklands

Argentina had, for many years, considered that the Islas Malvinas, popularly known as the Falklands Islands, were part of Argentina, despite the fact that the Islands had belonged to Britain for about 150 years. The proximity of the Falklands to Argentina (about 400 miles) exacerbated this feeling. On April 2, 1982 Argentine Armed Forces landed on the Falklands and quickly captured the Islands.

British Task Force Sails

Although it is over 8,000 miles away, Britain announced it would defend the Islands and organized a British Naval Task Force on the following day. By April 5 the Task Force, code-named "Operation Corporate" was on its way to the Falklands! The Force included *HMS Hermes* as the flagship and *HMS Invincible*. The carriers

Prior to embarking for the Falklands War, Fleet Air Arm Sea Harriers received a new all-over dark sea gray color scheme with muted national insignia. This Sea Harrier was photographed at British Aerospace Dunsfold just before leaving for the South Atlantic. (British Aerospace, Courtesy Brendan Morrissey)

stowed a total of 20 Westland Sea King helicopters of No. 820 and 826 Squadrons, 20 Sea Harriers of Nos. 800, 801 and 899 Squadrons plus six RAF GR.3 Harriers which had landed on the carriers for the long trip. Weapons, stores and a battalion of Royal Marine Commandoes were also a part of this vanguard force, as were escorting destroyers and submarines. This was the largest British naval force organized since World War II. Following closely was the requisitioned commercial containership *M.V. Atlantic Conveyor* carrying Sea Harriers of 809 Naval Harrier Squadron, RAF GR.3 Harriers and about a dozen troop-carrying and armed helicopters. The ship also carried spare Rolls-Royce Pegasus 104 engines.

Shortage of Harriers

It had been realized that the very small numbers of Sea Harriers would be overworked if the dual role of providing air cover for the Task Force plus assisting the troops with ground attack missions were imposed upon them. In fact, there were hardly enough Sea Harriers to accomplish the Task Force air cover Combat Air Patrol undertaking; especially when it became evident that the Sea Harriers were facing an adversary with air superiority composed of land-

Sea Harriers of No.800 Naval Air Squadron, shown flying in echelon formation, saw considerable action in the Falklands War. The 28 Fleet Air Arm Sea Harriers and 10 Royal Air Force Harriers in the war shot down 28 Argentine aircraft in aerial combat, yet no Harriers had been lost in aerial combat. (British Aerospace, Courtesy Brendan Morrissey)

A British Aerospace Sea Harrier speeds up the Ski-Jump ramp of HMS Hermes as it leaves for a mission in the Falklands War. The Royal Navy carriers had to operate well east of the Falklands to avoid the Exocet missile-fitted Argentine Super Etendard strike/fighters. (British Aerospace, Courtesy Brendan Morrissey)

based Argentine Dassault Mirage supersonic fighters as well as Douglas Skyhawk and Dassault Super Etendard strike/fighters. It was almost a repeat of the naval air situation in the Mediterranean Sea during 1940-1941 when the carrier-based Fleet Air Arm fought the shore-based Italian Regia Aeronautica.

In order to relieve the pressure on the Sea Harriers it was decided to assign RAF No. 1 Squadron GR.3 Harriers to the ground attack role in the Falklands campaign and have the Sea Harriers concentrate on the defense of the Task Force. Of course, when conditions demanded, the assignments were to become flexible.

Argentina's Carrier Out of Service

Vienticinco de Mayo, Argentina's only aircraft carrier, had accompanied the Argentine invasion force; however, the former *HMS Venerable* experienced problems with its single catapult; therefore, the Argentine Armada (Navy) could not fly aircraft from the ship because it had no Harriers so its CTOL planes were forced to operate from the southern Argentine air base of Rio Grande.

First Air Raids

The Sea Harrier first saw combat on May 1, 1982 when Lieutenant Commander Andy Auld, C.O. of No. 800 Squadron, led his pilots from *HMS Hermes* in a strafing and bombing raid on the airfield at Port Stanley. Despite heavy antiaircraft fire, which included SAM's, only one Sea Harrier was slightly damaged by small arms fire.

While the raid on Port Stanley was underway, Argentine Skyhawks, and Mirages, plus Canberra bombers were intercepted by Sea Harriers and turned back after one of each type of Argentine aircraft had been shot down with Sidewinder missiles.

Sea Skua Scores

On May 2, 1982 two Westland Lynx helicopters of the Royal Navy Task Force sank an 800 ton armed patrol boat and damaged another with Sea Skua antiship missiles north of East Falkland.

The *Sheffield* Sinking

Argentina's biggest naval loss was the sinking of the cruiser *General Belgrano* by the Royal Navy submarine *Conqueror*. It was 4:0 o'clock in the afternoon of May 2 when two Tigerfish homing to pedoes tore into the cruiser's side. Of the 1,040 crew members, 30 were killed. Admiral Jorge Anaya, Chief of the Argentine Armada vowed revenge, and aerial attacks on British ships were accelerated to avenge the cruiser's loss.

The first target in Admiral Anaya's program was a lightly armed Type 42 destroyer. In view of the fact that all Fleet Air Arm fixed wing aircraft, except Harriers, had been transferred to the RAF deactivated, the Royal Navy had no AEW (Airborne Early Warning) aircraft such as the Fairey Gannet, which fact was to prove disastrous in the Falkland Islands campaign. It had also become distinct disadvantage for the British aerial tactics and strategy to be forced to keep the carriers well east of the Falklands so as to be beyond the range of Argentine aircraft. Yet, it was necessary for destroyers and other ships to operate beyond the established carrier area of operations. On May 4, 1982 three French-made Super Etendard strike fighters, fitted with an AM.39 Exocet ASM under one wing and a long-range drop-tank under the other, were stalking the Royal Navy destroyer *HMS Sheffield* which was engaged in picket duty (spotting hostile aircraft headed for the task force and shooting them down) southeast of Lafonia Island. Two missiles were fired and one struck the 4,100 ton ship amidships causing sever damage. Of the 270 man crew, 20 were killed with 24 injured Westland Sea King helicopters quickly transferred the wounded to *HMS Hermes*. The French-made Exocet had penetrated deep into *Sheffield* before the 363 pound warhead exploded, sending flame throughout one-third of the ship. *HMS Sheffield* was taken in tow on May 9 in hopes of eventually bringing the hulk back to Britain however, on the following morning it capsized and sank in heavy seas.

First Harrier Loss

The very first Sea Harrier to be shot down was destroyed by sur face-to-air missiles as it made a low level attack at Goose Green on May 4. The pilot, Lieutenant Nick Taylor, did not survive.

Harriers Sink Ships

Five days later Flight Lieutenant David Morgan of No. 800 Squadron sighted an intelligence-gathering Argentine trawler. Following orders, the Harrier pilot bombed and strafed the ship, which sank the next day.

In order to extend their range on missions over the Falklands, Argentine pilots armed their Super Etendards with only one Exocet missile (arrow) and carried a fuel drop tank under the other wing. A French Aeronavale Super Etendard demonstrates the technique. (Marcel Dassault/Breguet, Courtesy Shirley Manfredi)

Replete in the new color scheme, two No.899 Naval Air Squadron Sea Harriers enter a banking turn to reveal the four Sidewinder AAM's and the two 190 gallon long range drop tanks. Note the two 30 millimeter cannon pods on the fuselage with the antiship missile pylon between them. These craft saw action in the Falklands. (British Aerospace, Courtesy Brendan Morrissey)

Two more Argentine ships were attacked by *Hermes* Sea Harriers on May 16 in Falkland Sound, between East Falkland and West Falkland Islands, sinking one of the supply ships.

Harriers Disappear
Two Sea Harriers flying CAP (Combat Air Patrol) for the CVBG in dense fog on May 6, 1982 suddenly disappeared and never returned to the carrier. It is presumed that the two planes collided in the pea soup visibility. This accident reduced the CVBG air cover to an unacceptably low number.

Harriers Land On Containership
Atlantic Conveyor arrived on May 18, and its cargo of Sea Harriers and Harriers took off and landed on *Invincible* and *Hermes*. The containership performed yeoman service for the Task Force because Harriers and Sea Harriers were able to land on its Deck in an emergency.

Operation Sutton
As a British invasion force was being assembled for Operation Sutton, which consisted of a May 21 landing in San Carlos Water on the western side of East Falkland Island, Argentine aircraft made several attempts to attack the ships but were driven off by Sea Harriers. Three air patrol stations were established: north of the islands; southern end of Falkland Sound; and over West Falkland Island.

Two Sea Harriers were assigned to each station and the British carriers launched a flight every 20 minutes to relieve each other on station.

The San Carlos bridgehead was successful and 5,000 troops were landed under cover of the Royal Navy; however, the following week was to be filled with air attacks on these ships with serious losses.

Accelerated Aerial Activity
The morning of May 21, 1982 began with the Falkland Sound air patrol scoring two Argentine helicopters with cannon fire; a Boeing-Vertol Chinook and an Aerospatiale Puma. Later, two Harriers of No. 899 Squadron shot down four Skyhawks, while still later, Lieutenant Clive Morell and Flight Lieutenant John Leery each scored a Skyhawk; one with a Sidewinder and the other with cannon fire at a range of 300 feet. A seventh Argentine aircraft was shot down by a Sea Harrier on that morning.

Although the design of the Sea Harrier was not intended primarily as a fighter plane, it proved equal or superior to the best aircraft in the Argentine Arsenal. This was demonstrated without resorting to the Harrier's unique ability to VIFF. The aircraft of both sides were operating at the limit of their range and could not tarry to dogfight which would have given the Harrier pilots an additional advantage by Viffing in dogfights, as well as in evasive maneuvers.

Royal Navy Ships Hit

Despite the Sea Harrier's good showing on May 21, 1982, several Argentine strike/fighters broke through to attack British warships in 12 waves comprising a total of 72 aircraft.

Just before noon, Skyhawks dropped 10 bombs at the 3,200 ton *Leander* class frigate *HMS Argonaut*; however, only two struck the ship, setting a missile magazine afire and blowing up one of the ship's boilers. A Westland Wasp helicopter from the frigate *Yarmouth* sped to *Argonaut* to evacuate the wounded.

HMS Ardent, a 3,250 ton Type 21 frigate was the next victim while *Argonaut* was saving herself from sinking. *Ardent* was among the several frigates in Falkland Sound covering the San Carlos landing with gunfire when Skyhawks dropped two 1,000 pound bombs on the stern of the unarmored ship. More bombs and missiles followed. The blasts killed 24 crewmen and wounded 30 more. Helicopters evacuated the remaining 180 officers and men. *HMS Ardent* sank that night.

The morning activity of May 23 began when a Westland Lynx helicopter from *HMS Antelope* crippled an Argentine freighter with a Sea Skua ASM. At noon all hell broke loose when four Argentine Skyhawks closed in on *Antelope*, a sister ship of *Ardent* that had also been covering the beachhead. The ship's Sea Cat SAM caught one Skyhawk; however, the others made two 500 pound direct hits on *Antelope*; just below the bridge and crashing into the engine room. Neither bomb exploded; however, as a bomb disposal team worked on the engine room bomb, it exploded, causing enormous fires. Landing craft from the beach rushed to the burning ship to evacuate survivors. *HMS Antelope* sank in the morning, broken in two from the explosion.

Carriers Remain Far Off Shore

Captain Jeremy Black of *HMS Invincible* and Captain John Coward of the destroyer *HMS Brilliant* implored Rear Admiral John "Sandy" Woodward, Flag Officer First Flotilla (FOFF) to bring his carriers closer to shore to increase the Harrier's endurance and in order that more Harriers could be kept on station. They suggested a distance of about 50 miles from shore for the carriers. After giving the matter serious consideration, Admiral Woodward refused because if one or both carriers were sunk the Task Force would be destroyed by the Argentine strike/fighters. The carriers had to remain in a safe haven to provide a base for the Sea Harriers, without which the expedition would be virtually defenseless. It appears that even if the carriers had moved closer to shore, the small number of Harriers available could never stop every single Argentine raider.

Harriers Still Scoring

On May 24, 1982 Lieutenant Commander Andy Auld shot down two supersonic Mirage V fighters while his wingman, Lieutenant David Smith, scored another Mirage V. Sidewinders had been used to destroy all three Argentine aircraft. The Mirage V fighters were flying cover for Skyhawks.

More Attacks On the Royal Navy

Also on May 24 Argentine Skyhawks attacked the 6,000 ton Landing Ships, *Sir Lancelot* and *Sir Galahad*. Two bombs hit the former and one bomb hit the latter ship but none of the bombs exploded.

Five Sea Harrier FRS Mk 1 strike/fighters of No.800 Naval Air Squadron head for the Falkland Islands to act as Combat Air Patrol for the logistics ships near shore. Note the long range tanks and sidewinder missiles to intercept any Argentine Skyhawk, Etendard or Mirage intruders. (British Aerospace, Courtesy Brendan Morrissey)

In the following morning *HMS Coventry*, a sister ship of the ill-fated *Sheffield*, was engaged in picket duty north of West Falkland Island. Two Mirages appeared in the southern sky but posed no threat to the destroyer because they were being chased out of Falkland Sound by Sea Harriers. *Coventry's* Sea Dart SAM's destroyed both Mirages and scored a third a short while later. Shortly after lunch two Skyhawks sped towards *HMS Coventry* and her escort, the frigate *HMS Broadsword*. The Argentine attackers came in at wave-top level so the *Coventry* Sea Dart system failed to lock on the Skyhawks. In desperation, *Coventry* fired every available automatic weapon at the duo forcing them to change course toward Broadsword. The frigate's Sea Wolf AAM locked on the two Skyhawks; however, because they were flying so close together, the Sea Wolf could not electronically differentiate the proper target in the double image. Then the bombs were dropped and a single bomb pierced *Broadsword's* starboard side, deflected upwards by the ship's steel structure and emerged through the helicopter platform failing to explode. It did, however, destroy the Lynx helicopter on the platform.

Without respite, a second pair of Skyhawks came into view and headed for *HMS Coventry* which had turned into the direction of the attack in order to project the smallest possible target to the Argentine pilots. Four 1,000 pound bombs were released; three penetrating the port side of the hull in fierce explosions while the fourth exploded as a near-miss astern. *HMS Coventry* began to list at once and was dead in the water as the crew began to abandon ship. Sea Kings and Wessex helicopters were vectored to *Coventry* to rescue the wounded from the red hot hull. Miraculously, only 19 men had died in the explosions and fire, while 280 survived the ordeal.

Carriers - Prime Targets

Still later in the day of May 25, realizing that the source of British air power in the Falklands Campaign was in the two carriers cruising off the east coast of East Falkland, the Argentine Air Force decided to eliminate the two Sea Harrier bases, *Hermes* and *Invincible*. Two Super Etendards, loaded with the last three air launch Exocet missiles in the Argentine inventory, flew over the South Atlantic Ocean, north of the Falklands, refueled, and headed for the carriers, which were located about 70 miles northeast of East Falkland Island. This was the most vital Argentine mission of the war.

The attackers were detected by the Type 21 frigate, *HMS Ambuscade* radar and the ship alerted the entire Battle Group. Every Royal Navy warship in the area fired chaff radar decoys to confuse the missiles that the planes had just launched; however, the containership *M.V. Atlantic Conveyor*, which was only a few miles from the carriers, had no chaff. Two of the Exocet missiles veered erratically from the warships and struck the 15,000 ton containership although they had originally headed for the carriers. Witnesses on *HMS Ambuscade* claim they saw at least one Exocet turn sharply away from the warships to the defenseless *Atlantic Conveyor*. Also, in the air at that time was a Lynx helicopter operating an active missile decoy.

The missiles struck *M.V. Atlantic Conveyor* in the engine room which started enormous fires. The ship sank, taking extremely important equipment and supplies with it. Among the lost material were thousands of tents, more than a dozen helicopters, and spare navalized Rolls-Royce Pegasus 104 engines which were the greatest loss. Twelve crew members, including Captain Ian North, perished in this tragedy. In effect, the inadvertent *Atlantic Conveyor* sacrifice had spared *Hermes* and *Invincible*.

What made the Exocet missile change course? One can only speculate that the great quantity of radar missile decoy activity might have influenced the missile to head for *Atlantic Conveyor*.

The commercial containership M.V. Atlantic Conveyor accompanied the British Naval Task Force laden with Harriers, helicopters, and spare Sea Harrier engines. On several occasions Harriers accomplished landings and takeoffs from the ship during the fighting; thereby, proving the value of commercial aircraft-capable ships during wartime. M.V. Atlantic Conveyor was sunk by Argentine Exocet missiles that were launched against British Navy carriers. (Ministry of Defence [Navy])

This incident reinforced Admiral Woodward's decision to conserve the carriers and, from that time, *Hermes* and *Invincible* rarely approached closer than 150 miles from the Falkland coast.

The High Cost of War

Argentina had entered this war with only five air launch AM 39 Exocet missiles. This appears absurd until it is realized that each of these missiles costs about one million dollars, which is an enormous expenditure for a non-superpower nation. Modern weapons have become so sophisticated and expensive that only superpowers or extremely rich countries can afford them. No longer can village boys cut the arrows which their mothers and sisters feathered in order that their fathers/husbands had enough arrows for their longbows, as was done in England during the Hundred Years War.

It is pathetic to learn that Argentina had expended the last of the Exocet missiles in the May 25 raid. Countries with limited resources, such as Argentina, are forced to purchase war materiel from others rather than try to make their own. This places them at the mercy of the arms provider in times of need. As mentioned in the Prologue, wars are usually fought with weapons accumulated in peacetime.

Argentina had purchased planes and bombs from the United States, and planes and missiles from France. When Exocet inventory dropped to a dangerously low level, Argentina could get no more. Further, Argentina never received the manual describing the method of fusing the U.S. bombs, hence the reason why so many bombs failed to detonate upon impact.

The lessons to be learned are to ensure that materiel stockpiles are sufficient to last throughout the conflict, and not to depend upon others to provide arms, even on a partnership or treaty basis. Any nation that has the ability to forge its own weapons should do so and not depend, to any degree, upon others to assist in the design or manufacture of weapons as does a prominent western superpower because "it is less expensive."

British Air Cover Strained

Disaster struck the Royal Navy at two opposite shores of East Falkland Island on June 8 which proved that the number of Sea Harriers in the South Atlantic war was grossly insufficient to provide air cover for all the ships of the Task Force. In the early morning the 6,000 ton Landing Ship Logistic (LSL) *Sir Galahad* entered Bluff Cove on the Eastern shore of East Falkland and anchored near another LSL, *Sir Tristram*. The two ships, laden with troops and war materiel, had arrived unannounced, without naval escort and were unloading.

In the early afternoon the Rothesay class frigate *HMS Plymouth* was busy in Falkland Sound bombarding Mount Rosalie on West Falkland when five Mirage V strike/fighters attacked. The Sea Harrier Combat Air Patrol which had been the only protection for the Landing Ships in Bluff Cove was ordered to help *Plymouth* in her need. Two Mirages were downed by the ship's antiaircraft fire; however, of the (10) 1,000 pound bombs released, four struck the hull. One of the bombs hit a depth charge which explosion caused major damage, while another hit the smokestack. *Plymouth* limped into San Carlos Water and eventually put out the raging fires.

When Argentine 1,000 pound bombs set the Landing Ship Logistic HMS Sir Galahad ablaze, Westland Wessex and Sea King helicopters moved in close to pluck survivors from the water and the flaming decks. A Sea King drops down to the water so the downdraft from the rotor will push survivors' rafts and boats away from the ship and flaming oil. The ship sank later. (Ministry of Defense [Navy])

By the time the Sea Harrier CAP arrived over Falkland Sound the raid was over and the Mirages were gone; however, only a few moments after the Sea Harriers had left Bluff Cove two Skyhawks and a pair of Mirages attacked *Sir Tristram* and *Sir Galahad* so the CAP was ordered back to Bluff Cove. The Argentine attackers were laden with 1,000 pound bombs because the Argentines had no more Exocets.

The first bomb to strike *Sir Galahad* ignited boxes of small arms ammunition as well as stores of gasoline needed for the troops' portable generators and, within seconds, flames had engulfed the entire midship area. Westland Wessex and Sea King helicopters rushed from shore and the brave crews winched survivors from the water, the flames, and from liferafts. Other helicopters hovered low over the water so the rotor downdraft would push survivors' rafts and boats towards the shore and away from the flaming oil on the water.

Sir Tristram did not escape the raid and at least one bomb struck the hull amidship, below the waterline. Many of its crew launched the ship's boats only to head for *Sir Galahad* in an effort to rescue survivors, instead of saving themselves.

As the Eastward-bound Sea Harrier CAP sped to Bluff Cove it chanced to meet the returning Westward-bound Mirages and Skyhawks which it promptly engaged. Flight Lieutenant David Morgan shot down two of the Argentine raiders while Lieutenant David Smith scored the third. The fourth plane had probably been damaged because it was seen to crash a short time later.

Sir Galahad sank that evening but *Sir Tristram* survived the attack. A total of 51 soldiers and seamen perished while 46 were injured, mostly due to the fire.

Britain Wins - No Political Interference

By June 14 the Argentine troops had surrendered and the war was won by Britain after seven weeks of actual fighting against constant adversity. In addition to the valor and professionalism of the British fighting men, Admiral Woodward and other British commanders in the South Atlantic War attributed the successful conclusion of the conflict to the lack of interference by politicians in the prosecution of the fighting. Unlike another western country's "mi-

nor" wars of this century, the British military were given a job and they won because they were not fettered by meddling and incompetent politicians.

Harrier Losses Very Low

The British Aerospace FAA Sea Harriers and RAF GR.3 Harriers had surpassed British military tactician's highest expectations in every assigned task, whether it be air combat or ground support and in all weather conditions which can be fierce in the Falklands. Harrier losses were expected to be as high as 50 percent; however in over 1,700 missions, the Harrier attrition was about one-half per cent which deserves to be compared to the acceptable five percent loss during World War II. The 28 Sea Harriers and 10 RAF Harrier destroyed about 28 Argentine aircraft in aerial combat, yet no Harrier type had been lost in aerial combat. Harrier losses comprised two Sea Harriers and three GR.3 Harriers shot down by SAM's or ground gunfire. Four Sea Harriers were lost in accidents. Despite the loss of the spare Pegasus 104 engines, the Harriers achieved an overall serviceability rate of better than 90 percent.

Low Altitude Combat

British Harrier and Argentine Skyhawk pilots fought each other at very low altitudes because it offers the element of surprise and relative sanctuary from SAM's and aerial attacks. In World War II aerial combat was conducted at different altitudes on each German front 15,000 to 20,000 feet in the west; 10,000 to 15,000 feet in North Africa; and the relatively low below 5,000 feet on the Russian front. Mission altitudes in Vietnam were even lower and it has been estimated that the next air war might be fought at even lower altitudes. Dogfights conducted at altitudes under 5,000 feet require a new set of fighting rules because the aircraft don't have the same performance as they did at 20,000 feet.

Increased Harrier Production

British Defence Minister, Sir John Nott, emphasized the high regard generally expressed for the Sea Harrier when he announced that additional Sea Harriers and helicopters were to be procured to replace those lost in the Falklands as well as to increase the standing squadron strength.

Unique Harrier Operations

Never before had shore-based, non-naval fixed-wing aircraft been cross-operated from aircraft carriers, nor had fixed-wing combat aircraft been able to operate from commercial freighters as was done by the Harrier and Sea Harrier. The Falklands adventure had been witness to another naval air combat revolution.

Royal Navy Carriers Indispensable

Britain could not have beaten Argentina in the Falklands nor even challenged the seizure of the islands without *HMS Hermes* and *HMS Invincible* with their Harriers and helicopters. It is a safe hypothesis to state that had the Royal Navy possessed a fleet carrier in 1982, such as the discarded *Eagle* class or the proposed CVA-01 which was aborted in 1966, Argentina would not have dared risk the Falklands invasion.

U.S. CARRIERS PROTECT AMERICAN INTERESTS

U.S. aircraft carriers and Assault Helicopter carriers were busy, world wide during the 1980s, protecting American interests; however, without carrier protection tragedy struck!

Carriers at Grenada

Aircraft capable ships had made it possible for British forces to rescue a colony from foreign domination in 1982, while 1 1/2 years later, aircraft carriers made it possible for U.S. Forces to rescue a former British colony from insurgent Communist domination. On October 19, 1983, a radical Marxist military coup overthrew the government of Grenada; a 130 square mile island in the eastern Caribbean Sea. Cubans, Soviets, North Koreans and several Eastern European nations had troops, advisors and diplomats on Grenada to help the Communists. There were about 1,000 U.S. citizens on the island.

U.S. Task Force in Action

On October 22, 1983 the Organization of Eastern Caribbean States formally asked the U.S. to intervene. The carrier *Independence* (CV-62) led a 12-ship task force, commanded by Vice Admiral Joseph Metcalf III, to the Caribbean. The task force included *USS Guam* (LPH-9) carrying 1,900 members of the 22nd Marine Amphibious Unit. Helicopter-borne Marines, SEAL teams and paratroopers landed on the island under efficient air cover from the carrier on October 25, 1983 and two days later it was all over. Over 600 Cuban troops were captured along with warehouses full of arms and military equipment. Again, air capable ships ensured the success of a military operation.

The Syrian Incident

Two months later, December 3, 1983 U.S. naval reconnaissance aircraft from carriers in the Mediterranean Sea flew over the Lebanese Bekaa Valley near Syrian positions. America's avowed support of Israel stimulated the Syrian antiaircraft batteries to fire on the planes. On the following day (16) A-6 Intruders and (12) A-7 Corsairs from the carriers *USS Independence* (CV-62) and *USS John F. Kennedy* (CV-67) struck six Syrian positions in the mountains overlooking the valley in retaliation for the Syrian attack; another example of how the aircraft carrier and its Warbirds can project power and influence thousands of miles from home with all-out attacks or with limited response.

Confrontation With Libya

America's continued political, military and financial support for Israel prompted many Moslem countries to regard the U.S. as their enemy. Among the foremost that considered the U.S. as its enemy during the 1980s was Libya.

Relations Reach Breaking Point

Following a long series of accusations and counteraccusations, U.S. embargoes, and Freedom of Navigation challenges since 1981, the U.S. severed all ties with Libya on January 7, 1986 and ordered U.S. citizens to leave Libya. This was based upon the Italian cruise ship Achille Lauro highjacking and the Rome and Vienna airport killings which were attributed to Libyan support.

U.S. Plans Attack

The U.S. Joint Chiefs of Staff were directed to prepare a list of military options for military action against Libya while more U.S. carriers were sent to the Mediterranean.

On the surface, the problem appeared to be Libya's 1981 claim that its territorial waters included the Gulf of Sidra as far north as a line drawn between points north of Misratah and Benghazi. Libya named it the "Line of Death." Claiming this line of demarcation exceeded the internationally accepted "12 mile limit", U.S. naval ships and aircraft repeatedly challenged Libya's claim as part of the U.S. Freedom of Navigation (FON) program. This resulted in a series of armed clashes between U.S. aircraft and Libyan Army Air Force (LAAF) planes and missile corvettes. The Soviet-built aircraft such as MiG-25 Foxbats, Su-22 Fitters, Il-76 Candid, and naval craft such as Soviet-built Nanuchka missile boats did not fare well against U.S. Navy aircraft.

Libya-First Stage

OVL-1 (Operations in Vicinity of Libya) extended from January 26 to 30, 1986 and consisted of extensive preparations for confrontation with Libya. The carriers *Coral Sea* (CV-43) and *Saratoga* (CV-60) were to operate just north of the Line of Death. A Combat Air Patrol consisting of at least three fighter sections of Tomcats were to patrol between the carriers and Libya 24 hours a day, armed with Sidewinder and Sparrow missiles. Hawkeye E-2C early warning and air control aircraft were already on station. SUCAP (SUrface CAPs) comprised of Intruders, Corsair II's and Hornets were flown from both carriers to provide armed surveillance of hostile surface craft, and were armed with a variety of ordnance including Harpoon ASM's, Rockeye cluster bombs and High speed Anti Radiation Missiles (HARM). The SUCAP Hornets were armed with complete air-to-air armament in order that they could cover the SUCAP and reinforce the carrier CAP when necessary.

Vice Admiral Frank B. Kelso II, Commander, Sixth Fleet, ordered all pilots and aircrew members to perform their task professionally within the guidelines of ROE (Rules of Engagement). The traditional Cold War ROE required that pilots must not fire unless fired upon; however, this made the air war a paradox because the hostile pilot can launch a missile beyond visual range. Realizing this, the admiral also urged his pilots to exercise exceptional restraint.

Only one real encounter was made during OVL-1 when, on January 26, 1986, a section of Foxbats headed toward one of the Hornet CAP stations. A Hawkeye from *Coral Sea* directed the Hornets into a classic six o'clock intercept and, after flying under escort by the Hornets for about 10 minutes, the Foxbats broke formation and sped for home. During following days *USS Saratoga* Tomcats were dogged by a wide variety of LAAF fighters but no threatening moves were made by the Libyans.

Libya-Second Stage

OVL-II extended from February 12 to 15, 1986 and included more than 150 encounters in which the Americans always gained the controlling position. The Hawkeye's surveillance and data link coordination capabilities enabled the fighter pilots to follow the entire operation as well as their own situation. Some Libyan pilots tried to lure Navy fighters over the Line of Death without success. A few Foxbats flew over *USS Coral Sea* with Hornets flying escort; however, they made no hostile moves.

Libya-Third Stage

OVL-III was the most daring exercise with the intention to sail and fly south of the Line of Death. This operation extended from March 23 to 29, 1986 and included the carrier *America* (CV-66) which had just joined the Sixth Fleet. On the morning of March 24, 1986 the ships crossed the line supported by CAP's and SUCAP's. Around noon SAM missiles were fired at Hornets from *Coral Sea* but missed by a wide margin because of the extreme range. Several more SAM's were launched in the afternoon; all missed their mark. A French-built missile patrol boat headed for the U.S. ships that evening; however, before it got close enough to fire, it was sunk by Harpoon missiles launched by SUCAP Intruders from *USS America*. After nightfall, Corsair II's from *USS Saratoga* destroyed the SAM missile site with HARM missiles and, by morning, Intruders from *USS Saratoga* and *USS Coral Sea* had sunk another missile boat and damaged a second with Rockeye bombs and Harpoon missiles.

No further Libyan action was encountered so the Task Force sailed northward across the Line of Death, having made its point.

Discotheque Bombing Blamed on Libya

On April 5, 1986 a bomb exploded in the La Belle discotheque in West Berlin, killing two U.S. soldiers and wounding 78 Americans plus almost 200 others. President Reagan blamed this bombing on Libya and, three days later, he ordered air strikes against Libyan airfields, military barracks, and training camps.

France Refuses F-111 Passage

The *Saratoga* CVBG had already left the Mediterranean so the brunt of the strikes fell on *USS America* and *USS Coral Sea* in cooperation with U.S. Air Force F-111F's of the 48th Tactical Fighter Wing based at RAF Lakenheath, England and EF-111's of the 20th Tactical Fighter wing based at RAF Upper Heyford, England. Britain approved the use of its bases for the operation; however, France refused to allow the F-111's to fly over its territory. This refusal increased the proposed 1,240 miles direct flight over France to a 2,800 miles circuitous route, over water, around France and Spain, via Gibraltar; thereby, requiring increased aerial refueling support and unquestionably affecting the final degree of success in the operation.

Close Cooperation

In order to ensure surprise, reduce risk to U.S. aircraft, and fully occupy Libyan defenses, all of the targets had to be struck simultaneously. Only one pass over each target would be permitted and any target that was not positively identified must not be attacked. These were the ROE given to the American aircrews.

Nocturnal Attack Preparation

A night strike was imperative in order to ensure surprise. Many of the Libyan defensive measures would be useless in the darkness because visually sighted SAM's could not be employed while U.S. electronic countermeasures (ECM) would totally confuse any radar-guided SAM systems. Another important reason for a nightraid was that the LAAF had very limited capability in nocturnal engagements.

The U.S. Armed Services operated only two types of aircraft which had the capability to attack with precision at night; the Navy A-6E Intruder and the Air Force F-111F. The total *USS America* and *USS Coral Sea* complement of the A-6E was only 18; therefore, it was imperative that the England-based F-IIIF's be used in order to strike the planned targets simultaneously. The A-6E was scheduled to arm with CBU-59 antipersonnel/antimateriel cluster bombs and Mark-82 500 pound general purpose (GP) bombs while the F-111F was to arm with BSU-49 500 pound GP bombs which permit a high-speed, low altitude pass over the target and the GBU-10 Paveway II Mark-84 2,000 pound laserguided bomb which is directed by the AN/AVQ-26 Pave Tack FLIR electro-optical target acquisition, laser target designation and weapons delivery system. This permits all-weather, low-level, high-speed accurate bombing of nocturnal targets.

Libya-Fourth Stage (The Attack)

OVL-IV began as preparations were being made for the night raid and covered the period April 10 to 18, 1986. *USS Coral Sea* was in the western Mediterranean and had to speed to its launching position east of the Gulf of Sidra. *USS America* was positioned slightly west of *USS Coral Sea*. Target time was 2:00 o'clock in the morning of April 15 Libya time and, on that night, three dozen aircraft were catapulted into the darkness of a new moon, as the F-111 approached from the west.

While SAR helicopters hovered near the carriers, two Hawkeye E-2C command and control aircraft coordinated the raid, Tomcat and Hornets were flying CAP at 2,000 feet, and EA-6B Prowler were jamming Tripoli and Benghazi defenses. *Coral Sea* launched six Hornets and eight Intruders, while *America* launched six each of Corsair II and Intruders. The A-7 Corsair II and F/A-18 Hornet went into their SAM suppression missions using HARM and Shrike missiles in the Benghazi, Benina, and Tripoli areas, clearing the way for the F-111 and A-6E strikes.

It was an amazing feat of mission timing when the F-111F and EF-111 force arrived at the planned time-on-target, although it started 2,800 miles away. The EF-111's quickly joined *USS America*'s A-7's suppressing the SAM sites around Tripoli and then the F-111F's took over. Three Air Force planes struck the Sidi Bilal naval base with GBU-10 bombs, causing light damage; three other F-111F's attacked the Bab al Aziziya Barracks, which included Moammar Gadhafi's headquarters, with GBU-10 bombs, causing moderate damage; and the Tripoli Military Airfield was bombed by five F-111F's using BSU 49 high-drag bombs to destroy two Soviet-built Ilyushin 76 aircraft and several buildings. One F-111F inadvertently dropped its bombs near the French Embassy causing numerous civilian casualties while another F-111F caught fire and fell into the sea, killing the two airmen. It is not known whether the fire was caused by a mechanical malfunction or by antiaircraft fire.

The usual F-111F method of attack was to streak in at 500 feet altitude, which is lower than the height of the Washington Monument in Washington, D.C., and lock onto its target with lasers and infra-red sensors. The plane then zooms up sharply and tosses the bomb toward the target for a standoff attack. As the plane banks away its sensors remain locked on the target and guide the bomb to a hit.

Meanwhile, two of the eight *Coral Sea* Intruders were forced to abort and returned to the carrier; however, the remaining six pressed the attack on Benina Airfield, south of Benghazi. Five were armed with CBU-59 APAM (Anti Personnel Anti Materiel) bombs while the sixth A-6E carried Mark 82 GP bombs. Three or four MiG-23 Floggers, two helicopters, one transport plane and one propeller-driven plane were destroyed while a helicopter, two Boeing 727 transports, and three propeller-driven planes, as well as hangars and storage buildings were damaged.

A half-dozen A-6E Intruders from *USS America* hit the Benghazi military barracks with Mark 82 bombs. Also hit was a MiG assembly warehouse and MiG shipping crates. No LAAF fighters rose to intercept the raiders.

Aircraft Carriers Made Raid Possible
The show of force in Libya could not have been a success without the use of carriers and carrier aircraft because the element of surprise was so important in this mission; further, the carriers brought their Warbirds within range of the targets, leaving the pilots refreshed as they went into battle.

Conversely, 37 American sailors were killed one year later because they had no air cover in the war zone in which they served, with the closest carrier about 2,000 miles, or over three days sailing away.

Iraq-Iran War
In 1987, war raged between two oil-producing Moslem nations bordering the Persian Gulf; Arab Iraq and Aryan Iran. Each belligerent was bent on attacking tankers that traded with its adversary which impelled the U.S. to dispatch Navy ships to the Persian Gulf to defend the tankers from attack by either side.

United States; The Policeman
America assumed this "Policeman" role to ensure a flow of oil to the industrialized nations of the world which was bound to result in tragedy!

USS Stark Attack
On the morning of May 17, 1987 the austere U.S. Navy frigate *USS Stark* was slowly patrolling in the middle of the 600 miles long Persian Gulf, across from the Bahrain Islands. At 9:00 o'clock that morning an American-manned AWACS aircraft based in Saudi Arabia spotted a French-built Iraqi Mirage strike/fighter as it left Iraq and headed south over the Persian Gulf at 2,000 feet altitude. One hour later the Mirage was also detected by *Stark*'s radar at a 200 mile range and radioed two warnings for the plane to identify itself. Despite receiving no reply, the *Stark* crew adopted no defensive measures.

At a range of 10 to 12 miles the Mirage F-1 launched two French-made Exocet ASM's from 2,000 feet. The missiles dropped to the water's surface and levelled off at 8 to 10 feet above the waves aiming headon for *Stark* at about 500 miles per hour. Only at the last moment was the Exocet finally detected by a lookout on the bridge who, with his bare eyes, saw the missile bearing down on the ship. The alarm was sounded and *Stark* was put into a high-speed right turn to enable the stern-mounted automatic Phalanx CIWS to fire at the oncoming missile, but all was in vain.

The Exocets tore a 15 foot hole in the port side of the hull, just below the bridge, killing 37 members of the crew and setting 1,800 degree fires which burned most of the day as *USS Stark* limped to port in Bahrain. Two Saudi pilots patrolling nearby in two U.S.-made F-15's asked the AWACS for permission to give chase and force the Mirage to land at a Saudi airfield; however, by the time the AWACS plane asked its ground controller for authority, it was too late. Later, the Iraqi Mirage pilot claimed he confused *USS Stark* with a tanker from Iran.

Five separate radar systems on *USS Stark* could have detected the Exocets, but none did. Without air cover, small ships as *Stark* will always remain conspicuously vulnerable to air attack. Only aircraft can detect a potentially hostile approaching plane or ship hundreds of miles away and determine its intentions. The Exocet missile that put *USS Stark* out of action is basically the same as that which sank *HMS Sheffield*. It is not a particularly sophisticated missile; however, the 15 feet long Exocet, which costs about 1,000,000 dollars, can inflict mortal damage to ships that have no air cover. This aerial protection need not be provided by a battle group Supercarrier because a Throughdeck Cruiser or Sea Control Ship is ideally suited for this singular task and can free the Supercarrier for fleet duties. The closest U.S. carrier to *USS Stark* had been in the Indian Ocean at the time of the attack.

Operation Sharp Edge
In late May 1990 the helicopter assault ship *USS Saipan* (LHA-2), Sea Knight and Sea Stallion helicopters, AV-8B Harriers, the 22nd Marine Expeditionary Unit, plus other surface units of the Sixth Fleet left Mediterranean waters for Liberia, on the west coast of Africa. Designated Task Force 61 and Task Force 62, the units' missions were: the protection and evacuation of noncombatants; a show of force; and security operations to protect American area telecommunications sites. Operation Sharp Edge was necessary because a revolution had erupted in Liberia, and Americans and other foreign nationals were threatened.

USS Saipan Too Slow
During preliminary moves by U.S. Forces, the situation in Liberia deteriorated and it became imperative to get a security force to the U.S. Embassy in Monrovia at once; however, the 22 knot speed of *USS Saipan* was insufficient to reach a launching point for helicopters in time. Alternatively, a CH-46 Sea Knight and a 75-man force rifle platoon plus a SEAL team from *USS Saipan* were embarked on the destroyer *USS Peterson* which reached the designated launching point off Monrovia on June 2; 24 hours earlier than *Saipan*. This incident illustrates a disadvantage of the relatively slow speed of some assault ships that are in service.

Americans Threatened - Helicopters Land
By August 4, 1990 a rebel leader threatened to take U.S. hostages which resulted in all ships of Task Forces 61 and 62 closing to within six miles of Monrovia by the morning of August 5. Five Sea

USS Saipan (LHA-2) spearheaded the rescue of noncombatants from Liberia during Operation Sharp Edge in August 1990. Observe the McDonnell Douglas AV-8B Harrier and Boeing-Vertol CH-46 Sea Knight on deck. This unusual photo shows the entrance to the hangar and the well deck. (Official U.S. Navy Photograph, Department of Defense by JO1 Kip Burke)

Knights landed Marines at Landing Zone Dove, a telecommunications site, and then evacuated 18 U.S. citizens to *USS Saipan*; a flight of Sea Knights and Sea Stallions landed 230 Marines in Landing Zone Magic at the U.S. Embassy and established defensive positions while over 40 U.S. citizens and foreign nationals were evacuated to *USS Saipan*; and two more Sea Knights and a Sea Stallion landed more Marines at Landing Zone Condor and evacuated three U.S. citizens.

Hueys, Sea Cobras and Harriers Provide CIFS
Meanwhile, Bell UH-1N Huey command and control helicopters plus Bell AH-1T Sea Cobra attack helicopters from *USS Saipan* circled all three Landing Zones to provide Close-In Fire Support (CIFS). In addition, McDonnell Douglas AV-8B Harriers maintained a five-minute alert on *USS Saipan*'s Flight Deck. U.S. citizens and foreign nationals continued to be evacuated from U.S. Embassy grounds until a total of more than 1,600 noncombatants had been removed by August 21.

Logistic Operations
In addition to landing Marines and evacuating noncombatants, the helicopters had flown in over 35,000 gallons of JP-5 jet fuel for the

U.S. Embassy's generators; 28 pallets of food; two pallets of medical supplies and almost 5,000 gallons of drinking water to the Embassy's Landing Zone Magic.

Forward Deployed Marine Task Force
The value of maintaining a forward deployed Marine task force of assault ships and helicopters for rapid reaction to limited objective operations was proven beyond doubt in Operation Sharp Edge. A Marine Air-Ground Task Force operating helicopters and Harriers from amphibious air capable assault ships is uniquely suited for employment in low intensity conflicts; the ideal application for an SCS.

OPERATION DESERT STORM CARRIER ACTIONS
Once again, U.S. aircraft carriers contributed significantly to an overwhelming victory with strikes against Iraq in Operation Desert Storm during the early months of 1991. Six carrier battle groups (CVBG) operated from the Persian Gulf and the Red Sea to wrest Kuwait from Iraq's grip.

USS John F. Kennedy (CV-67) operated with carrier wing No. 3 (CVW-3) and *USS Saratoga* (CV-60) operated with (CVW-17) from the Red Sea which was from 700 to 900 miles from Baghdad. *USS Midway* (CV-41) operated with CVW-5, *USS Ranger* (CV-61) operated with CVW-2, *USS America* (CV-66) operated with CVW-1, and *USS Theodore Roosevelt* (CVN-71) operated with CVW-8 in the Persian Gulf which was from 600 to 700 miles from Baghdad. The six carrier wings comprised about 60 squadrons which consisted of Grumman F-14A Tomcats, McDonnell Douglas F/A-18A and F/A-18C Hornets, Grumman A-6E Intruders, Lockheed S-3A and S-3B Vikings, Vought A-7E Corsair II, Grumman EA-6B Prowlers, Sikorsky SH-3H Sea Kings, McDonnell Douglas F-4 Phantom II, Grumman KA-6D Tankers, Grumman E-2C Hawkeyes, Boeing-Vertol CH-46 Sea Knights, and MCM Sikorsky MH-53E Sea Dragons.

Joint Interservice Operation
During the early hours of January 17, 1991 Operation Desert Storm began with a concentrated air campaign in which U.S. Navy, Marine, Army and Air Force fighters, bombers, electronics warfare, fighter/bombers, and strike aircraft flew as many as 1,000 sorties per day; pinpointing targets in Iraq with smart bombs as well as laser-guided and radar-guided missiles. The close cooperation and integration of the various air services in this operation was exceptionally well choreographed by U.S. Air Force Lieutenant General Charles Horner, Joint Force Air Component Commander (JFACC) and his staff of air planners. Not only were the many sorties well coordinated but, in the long flights from the Red Sea, U.S. Air Force Boeing KC-135 tankers refuelled Navy and Marine aircraft over Saudi Arabia. Desert Storm would not have been so effective without the JFACC.

U.S. Aerial Activities
Aircraft flying from Red Sea carriers concentrated on targets in western Iraq and the Baghdad area while aircraft operating from Persian Gulf carriers concentrated on targets in southeastern Iraq

USS John F. Kennedy (CV-67) bottom, USS Saratoga (CV-60) left, and USS America (CV-66) top, steam in the Red Sea with support elements during Operation Desert Storm. USS America later joined other carriers in the Persian Gulf. The appearance of U.S. carriers in these waters was a good example of power projection. (Official U.S. Navy Photograph, Department of Defense by PH2 William A. Lipski)

such as the naval installations at Umm Qasr and bridges near Basra. Working with both Navy and Air Force strike aircraft Navy Grumman EA-6B Prowlers jammed Iraqi radar installations; thereby, enabling the strikes to proceed with relative impunity.

U.S. Navy aircraft flew 415 missions on the first day of Desert Storm, January 17, 1991, and Grumman F-14 Tomcats began flying MiGCAP (MiG Combat Air Patrols) to suppress Iraqi interceptors, searched for mobile Scud missile launchers, and conducted reconnaissance missions.

Grumman A-6E Intruders lased Iraqi targets while McDonnell Douglas F/A-18 Hornets dropped laser-guided bombs on the objectives. RAF British Aerospace Buccaneers and Panavia Tornadoes also used the same tactic against Iraqi targets.

Two McDonnell Douglas F/A-18C Hornets of VF/A-81 from *USS Saratoga* were enroute to the target during a bombing mission on January 18 when they engaged and shot down two MiG-21 fighters, while still carrying their heavy bomb load!

Vought A-7E Corsair II's and Grumman A-6E Intruders from *USS John F. Kennedy* and *USS Saratoga* respectively, successfully launched ground attack versions of the McDonnell Douglas Harpoon missile SLAM (Stand-off Land Attack Missile) for the first time.

On January 22 four Grumman A-6E Intruders severely damaged an Iraqi T-43 minelayer and, on the following day, other Intruders disabled an Iraqi tanker that was being used to gather intelligence.

Minesweeping Problems

Although the Iraqi naval mines were low-tech, low-cost affairs, they were a thorn in the side of the U.S. Navy. This was due to the fact that U.S. Mine CounterMeasures (MCM) capabilities were grossly inadequate. *USS Tripoli* (LPH-10) and *USS Princeton* (CG-59) both struck mines as they entered waters previously swept by U.S. minesweepers. Minesweeping helicopters from the Persian Gulf carriers were called upon to assist the hard-pressed minesweepers to provide safe passage for the CVBG's and battleships.

Absence of Iraqi Air and Naval Resistance

Early in the fighting the Iraqi Air Force ended its feeble resistance and, on January 30, the Iraqi Navy left its ports and tried to break through the U.S. ships to the safety of Iran. In the Battle of Bubiyan 19 Iraqi ships were sunk and the Soviet built OSA missile boat that got through was damaged before it could fire its Styx missiles.

With air and naval resistance eliminated, the air war concentrated on strikes against communication centers, and ground attack missions. Chinese-built shore-based Silkworm missiles were the principal remaining threat against the Persian Gulf Fleet.

Sea Darts Versus Silkworms

On February 23 the battleship *USS Missouri* shelled Iraqi positions. As this was repeated on the next day, two Silkworm missiles were fired at the battleship from Iraqi shore installations. One Silkworm fell harmlessly into the water while the other headed for *USS Missouri*. A U.S. Navy Grumman EA-6B Prowler detected the missile and alerted the Royal Navy destroyer *HMS Gloucester* which fired

Five A-7E Corsair aircraft from Attack Squadron 72 (VA-72) and an A-6E Intruder aircraft from Attack Squadron 75 (VA-75) rendezvous with the KC-135E Stratotanker for in-flight refueling. The A-7E aircraft third from the top is carrying AGM-88 HARM highspeed anti-radiation missiles; the others carry Mark 83 1,000 pound bombs and AIM-9 Sidewinder missiles. (Official U.S. Navy Photograph, Department of Defense by Cmdr. John Leenhouts)

two high altitude Sea Dart SAM's at the Silkworm, destroying the oncoming missile. International cooperation such as this proved most effective in securing victory in the Persian Gulf War.

MULTIPURPOSE AMPHIBIOUS ASSAULT SHIP

While nuclear-powered Supercarriers were under construction the U.S. Navy continued its interest in amphibious warfare ships. Developed from the LHA-1 *Tarawa* class, the LHD-1 *Wasp* class multipurpose amphibious assault ship brought the U.S. Navy much closer to its long term objective of having a power-projection fleet that is capable of landing a completely equipped Marine Amphibious Force on almost any shore on earth in a matter of hours in the event of an emergent international crisis. The *Wasp* keel was laid on May 30, 1985, as the first of a 12-ship LHD Fleet, and was launched on August 4, 1987. Ingalls Shipbuilding was awarded the contract to build the first four ships of the class which are *Wasp* (LHD-1), *Essex* (LHD-2), *Kearsage* (LHD-3) and *Boxer* (LHD-4).

LHD Operations Scenario

The *Wasp* class is intended to be the Navy's first over-the-horizon capable amphibious assault ships. The primary mission is the amphibious embarkation, deployment, and support of a Marine landing force in an assault by aircraft, helicopters, amphibious vehicles and high speed landing craft.

During an over-the-horizon amphibious operation the LHD remains beyond the line of sight of the shore defenders when it launches its 60 miles per hour LCAC's (Landing Craft Air Cushion) and assault helicopters. As the LCAC's near the shore they move beyond the LHD line of sight which limits the CATF's (Commander of the Amphibious Task Force) ability to monitor the assault's progress and direct the assault waves. Some of the six LAMPS III helicopters must assist the CATF to manage the extended amphibious operations with their long-range air/surface radar ESM (Electronic Surveillance Measures) and data link. The Sikorsky LAMPS III tracks the LCAC with its radar, maintains communications with the LHD and also transmits the LCAC's progress to the LHD via data links. The LAMPS III can even pro-

The USS Wasp (LHD-1) class multipurpose amphibious assault ships are intended to remain out of sight of the shore, beyond the horizon, when conducting assault operations. The Wasp class can also assist the CVBG by serving as an extra flight deck when necessary. (Official U.S. Navy Photograph, Courtesy U.S. Naval Institute Photo Collection)

vide an ultra-high-frequency autocat communication relay capability between the LHD and the LCAC's. It can also detect hostile air and surface units for the entire amphibious group with its radar and even defend the LCAC force with its Penguin ASM's.

Amphibious Assault Air Complement
In addition to the Sikorsky LAMPS III, a mix of 30 Bell AH-1T Sea Cobra ground support helicopters, Bell UH-1N Huey utility helicopters, Boeing CH-46 Sea Knight, Sikorsky CH-53D Sea Stallion and CH-53E Super Stallion assault helicopters, plus eight AV-8B STO/VL Harriers are also part of the aircraft complement for amphibious assault missions.

Supplement CVBG Air Complement
The *Wasp* class LHD can also serve as an extra flight deck in a CVBG by revising its air wing to 20 Harriers and six LAMPS III helicopters which could release carrier aircraft to concentrate on AAW and strike missions. The Harriers and LAMPS III can perform CAP plus surface and subsurface close-in surveillance, as well as ASW killer missions.

The LHD's air wing appears to be the key to success for the *Wasp* class multipurpose role and, to accommodate the variety of aircraft, the *Wasp* class has a 2 1/2 acre Flight Deck running almost the entire length of the ship.

Wasp Data
Wasp displacement is 40,532 tons. Overall length is 844 feet with a beam of 106 feet. Two boilers generate 600 pounds per inch pressure steam for two turbine units, each geared to a propeller. The

70,000 shaft horsepower drives the ship in excess of 24 knots which is adequate for the amphibious assault role but insufficient to fully support a CVBG.

Complement consists of 98 officers and 983 crew members.

Accommodations for 1,900 Marines is also provided. With a 600 bed hospital and six fully equipped operating rooms the *Wasp* class can also serve as a hospital ship when required to do so and to assist in relief of disaster areas after storms or floods. In addition, the LHD must be able to evacuate American nationals and other personnel from countries where U.S. citizens might no longer be welcome.

Fixed defensive armament comprises two eight-cell NATO Sea Sparrow SAM launchers and three Phalanx CIWS weapons systems.

NIGHT ATTACK AND SUPERSONIC HARRIER
On June 26, 1987 an experimental AV-8B Harrier with night attack capability made its first flight. It was fitted with FLIR (Forward-Looking Infra Red) radar that can see in the dark and provides the pilot with a video picture of the scene ahead of the aircraft on a wide-angle head-up display. Night vision goggles are also used. Instrument lighting is blue-green to enhance the effectiveness of the goggles.

The operation of the McDonnell Douglas AV-8B Harriers is STO/VL (Short Take Off/Vertical Landing) in order to conserve fuel in the takeoff phase of the mission and accelerate the landing rate of these fixed-wing aircraft.

It was on January 23, 1986 that Britain and the U.S. signed a memorandum of understanding for the development of a supersonic STO/VL fighter/attack aircraft. A technology demonstrator was to fly by 1993 with the STO/VL entering service by the year 2,000. The RAF then withdrew its supersonic STO/VL requirement because it became deeply involved in the European Fighter Aircraft development for NATO. The Royal Navy picked up the idea and issued Naval Staff Target 6464 for a Harrier supersonic replacement. This will lead to a joint enterprise with the U.S. as was done in the development of the AV-8B Harrier. Actually, a supersonic STO/VL had been designed in 1963, designated Hawker Siddeley P.1154; however, this was cancelled by the Admiralty.

The supersonic STO/VL will be a remarkable development. Good ideas don't die!

A night-fighting, all-weather Harrier made its first flight in March, 1993. This was developed cooperatively by the U.S.A., Italy and Spain. The three nations have placed orders for the aircraft from McDonnell Douglas.

The next chapter will reveal how thw world's navies discharge their national security obligations using aircraft/ship combinations. Many nations fail to use the aircraft carrier due to budgetary restraints and other reasons, such as political; however, others, whom we least expect to do so, have embraced the aircraft carrier and a comprehensive maritime stategy.

CHAPTER IX
WORLD AIRCRAFT CARRIERS
JUMP-JETS OR GIANTS:
1991-FUTURE

WORLD NAVIES AND THE AIRCRAFT CARRIER

Until the demise of the Soviet Union the threat section of any naval staff in democratic countries concentrated on the Soviet Fleets in the Pacific Ocean, Black Sea, Baltic Sea, Indian Ocean, Mediterranean Sea, Northern or Norwegian Sea and the Atlantic Ocean, regardless of the openness of Soviet leaders or Glasnost. It must be remembered that the Soviets fooled the West, in the years prior to World War II, into believing that USSR was weaker than Poland, when actually the Soviets were more powerful than Germany, Britain and France combined. Defense spending in the West for the past half-century had been directed to deter Soviet expansionist aspirations, despite the articulate objections of politicians who had an inherent distast for "wasteful" spending on naval forces. The military establishment of the Free World has, in many cases, been able to gather such unambiguous facts about the USSR and its satellites that some nations have voted just about enough money to maintain a measurable naval force. Most have forsaken the carrier because of budgetary problems.

SOVIET MARITIME STRATEGY

As a preeminently continental power, the Soviet Union was not as dependent upon the sea to win a war as was Japan and Britain during World War II. The Soviet Navy's principal post-World War II task was the destruction of U.S. submarines and aircraft carriers far enough from the Soviet shore line so as to be beyond the range of U.S. missiles and aircraft.

Soviet Maritime Strategy concentrated on the protection of its coastline from the sea-based assaults by a maritime enemy. By destroying this enemy far from its shoreline, the Soviet Union planned to avoid the necessity for stationing large garrisons along the coast, sitting idle and waiting for an attack when they might be needed for more critical activities. Soviet carriers and long-range strike aircraft were the principal weapons to execute this strategy; the former against U.S. submarines and the latter against U.S. carriers. Of course, Soviet submarines were also to be sent against U.S. carriers in the event of hostilities.

SOVIET NAVY SUPERCARRIERS

Until the early 1970s the Soviet Union exhibited no interest in through-deck aircraft carriers; however, once the Soviets felt en-

PREVIOUS: The Spanish Armada or Navy flew British Aerospace Sea Harriers Mk.55S or AV-8S from Dedalo and Principe de Asturias. Harriers were called Matadors by the Spanish Armada. Colors are glossy light gray and white. (British Aerospace, Courtesy Brendan Morrissey)

dangered by the Western Powers she progressed through three classes of unusual aircraft carrier designs; the latest of which pose a threat to U.S. carrier superiority. This radical change in maritime strategy by a land-mass continental power reveals that even the Soviet Union had become aware of the inescapable importance of the aircraft capable ship for both offensive and defensive operations.

When the Soviet Navy produced the *Moskva* class helicopter carriers, the world's naval planners and tacticians were surprised and when the heavily armed *Kiev* class VTOL/helicopter aircraft carriers made their appearance, observers were amazed at these powerful air-capable ships. The two classes were aimed at the U.S. submarine fleet. Soviet attention was soon directed to the construction of Supercarriers which threatened the U.S. supremacy in that weapon.

Kuznetsov Class Supercarriers

In 1990 the largest warship ever constructed in the USSR was completed. This is the 65,000 ton aircraft carrier *Admiral Flot Sovetskogo Soyuza Kuznetsov* (Fleet Admiral of the Soviet Union Kuznetsov) which includes a six degree angled Flight Deck and 12 degree Ski-Jump bow ramp. The *Kuznetsov* class is not merely an ASW air-capable cruiser, but a full fledged through-deck aircraft carrier, which startled observers because it gave the Soviet Navy the balanced forces needed to accomplish the carrier philosophies of the late Soviet Admiral of the Fleet, Sergei Gorshkov. The new carriers combined the large size of the Supercarrier with the Ski-Jump of the Through-Deck Cruisers.

Having studied the secret of America's successful Pacific amphibious landings, which was air superiority, Admiral Gorshkov concluded that the basic role of a modern navy is operations against shore targets and covering amphibious landings. The *Kuznetsov* class could disrupt Western SLOC's; establish air and sea supremacy in localized regions to support troops, and/or to defend Soviet submarines on the open seas far from Soviet bases; and can conduct operations against U.S. carriers, submarines and cruise missiles in an all-out naval war. The Soviet Navy did not have this capability before the *Kuznetsov* class made its appearance.

This is not to say that the *Kuznetsov* class can openly challenge the American carrier force, but with a dozen of this type carrier the U.S. Navy would be hard-pressed to control the seas.

Kuznetsov Class Construction Schedule

The *Kuznetsov* keel was laid in January 1983, launched in December 1985, completed in early 1990 at which time it passed its sea trials with air trials following, and commissioned in January, 1991 *Admiral Flota Sovetskogo Soyuza Gorshkov* (Fleet Admiral of the

The 65,000 ton Kuznetsov class Soviet Supercarrier is a full-fledged through-deck aircraft carrier with a 12 degree Ski-Jump bow ramp. These carriers could revise the U.S. Maritime Strategy. (Official U.S. Navy Photograph, News Photo Division)

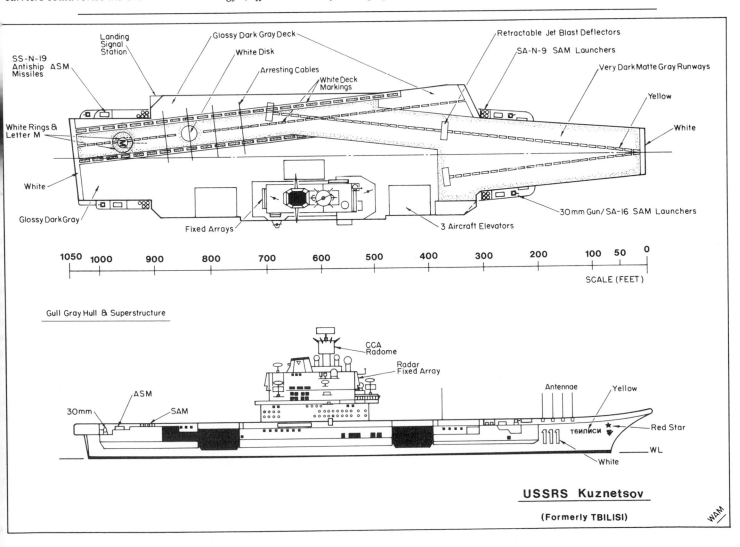

Landing Signal Station

Glossy Dark Gray Deck

White Disk

Retractable Jet Blast Deflectors

SS-N-19 Antiship ASM Missiles

Arresting Cables

SA-N-9 SAM Launchers

White Deck Markings

Very Dark Matte Gray Runways

Yellow

White Rings & Letter M

White

Glossy Dark Gray

Fixed Arrays

3 Aircraft Elevators

30mm Gun/SA-16 SAM Launchers

SCALE (FEET)

1050 1000 900 800 700 600 500 400 300 200 100 50 0

Gull Gray Hull & Superstructure

CCA Radome

Radar Fixed Array

ASM

SAM

30mm

Antennae

Yellow

Red Star

ТБИЛИСИ

WL

White

111

USSRS Kuznetsov

(Formerly TBILISI)

Soviet Union Gorshkov), is the second carrier of the class and was started in December 1985, launched in November 1988 and was scheduled for completion in late 1992. The intended third *Kuznetsov* class carrier, *Ul'yanovsk*, was started in December 1988 but has evolved into an entirely new class. The *Kuznetsov* class was built at the Nikolayev South Shipyard on the Black Sea where the *Kiev* class was constructed. It is interesting to note that the Gorshkov and *Ul'yanovsk* keels were laid after Mikhail Gorbachev became the USSR leader. The fate of the unfinished carriers is questionable and left to decisions made by the successors of the Soviet Union.

Kuznetsov Data

The 65,000 tons displacement *Kuznetsov* Flight Deck dimensions are about 240 x 1,050 feet while the hull at the waterline measures about 125 x 920 feet. Mean draft is about 35 feet. Eight oil-fired boilers generate steam for four steam turbine units, each of which is geared to a propeller shaft. The total of over 200,000 shaft horsepower propells *Kuznetsov* to a speed over 30 knots. Range is about 10,000 miles. As can be seen, the *Kuznetsov* class aircraft carriers compare favorably with early U.S. Navy Supercarriers.

Following the precedent set by the *Kiev* class, *Kuznetsov* is more heavily armed than U.S. Supercarriers, which includes (6) 30 millimeter six-barrel CIWS AK-630 Gatling-type rapid-fire guns, (24) SA-N-9 vertical SAM missile launchers, (12) SS-N-19 antiship ASM launchers, and (4) dual-purpose 30 millimeter gun/SA-16 SAM launchers.

Kuznetsov Aircraft Complement

In addition to Helix helicopters, the *Kuznetsov* class has (4) fixed-wing aircraft candidates from which to select its complement. The Sukhoi Su-27 "Flanker B" STOL long-range interceptor has made the initial Ski-Jump takeoffs and arrested landings on *Kuznetsov* with Sukhoi design bureau test pilot, Victor Pugachev, at the controls. Other STOL aircraft that have completed flight trials are the Sukhoi Su-25 UT "Frogfoot-B" strike/fighter and the Mikoyan-Gurevich MiG-29 "Fulcrum" medium range strike/interceptor. The Soviets observed the vulnerability of the Royal Navy to air attack during the Falklands War due to the absence of AEW aircraft; therefore, the Antonov An-74 "Madcap" AEW aircraft was developed

A STOL Sukhoi Flanker is about to touch down on the Kuznetsov Flight Deck. Note the Flight Deck markings with circles and a spot for helicopters and the arresting cables. (Official U.S. Navy Photograph, News Photo Division)

from the An-72 "Coaler" twin-engine jet transport with STOL capabilities. The Madcap is scheduled to fly from the Kuznetsov class carriers. The Yakovlev Yak-38 "Forger" and Yak-41 V/STOL aircraft are also available for service on the *Kuznetsov* carriers. The *Kuznetsov* class can accommodate about 30 aircraft.

No catapults were to be installed on the carriers; however, experiments with shore installations have been observed.

Name Changes

Kuznetsov was formerly named *Tbilisi* and *Gorshkov* had initially been named *Riga*.

Ul'Yanovsk Class Nuclear Supercarriers

A spinoff from the fossile fuel-powered *Kuznetsov* class, the *Ul'yanovsk* class carriers were to be nuclear-powered, however, the Soviet collapse left *Ul'yanovsk* unfinished.

Ul'yanovsk Data

The *Ul'yanovsk* class design is very similar to the *Kuznetsov* except that displacement will increase about 10,000 tons due to the heavy reactor shielding. From 25 to 50 aircraft will be accommodated. These can be the same types flown from *Kuznetsov*. The ship was expected to be fitted with a (CONAS) COmbined Nuclear And

This superb photo of Kuznetsov shows the through Flight Deck and the six degree angled Deck. An Su-27 Flanker STOL approaches for an arrested landing. (Official U.S. Navy Photograph, U.S. Department of Defense)

A Grumman Tomcat of VF-84 from USS Nimitz (CVN-68) intercepts a Soviet Tupolev Tu-20 "Bear" long-range reconnaissance, target surveillance, and missile mid-course guidance aircraft. Carriers were and still are important deterrents to the intruding, intelligence-gathering "Bears" and others that infringe upon international boundaries for hostile purposes. (Official U.S. Navy Photograph by LCDR David Vanasdlen and Lt. Dale Snodgrass)

Steam) propulsion powerplant which is similar to that installed in the Soviet *Kirov* class battle cruisers. The powerplant comprises four nuclear-fueled steam-generating plants that develops 180,000 shaft horsepower plus four fossil fuel-fired boilers that develop 120,000 shaft horsepower. Steam from either plant is directed to steam turbines that drive four propellers. When operating on the reactor speed is 35 knots and on the fossile-fired boiler speed is 30 knots. From 250,000 to 300,000 shaft horsepower can be generated by the combined CONAS powerplant.

The 75,000 tons full load displacement carrier construction schedule was for launching in 1991 and completion in 1996 at the Black Sea Nikolayev South Shipyard. Length is slightly longer than the *Kuznetsov* class at about 1,040 feet overall.

Soviet Carriers: Change In U.S. Maritime Strategy?
It is stimulating to reflect on the fact that not since the defeat of the Imperial Japanese Navy in 1945 had the U.S. Navy been confronted by a carrier-equipped adversary. The U.S. Navy had lost interest in sea control and has been concentrating on force projection, air strikes against the shore, and air defense against bombers carrying ASM missiles. The *Kuznetsov* and *Ul'yanovsk* could have forced the U.S. Navy to rethink its Maritime Strategy and increase its potential to confront a battle fleet once again in the struggle for sea control.

SOVIET AIR FORCES
The Soviet Union's five air forces had included: Frontogaya Aviatsiya (Frontal Aviation); Deistviya dal'nevo Aviatsiya (DA) (Long Range Aviation); Voeeno-transportnaya Aviatsiya (Transport

Aviation) Protivo-vozdushnaya Oberono (Strany) (Air Force of the National Air Defense); and the Aviatsiya Voennon-Morskovo Flota (AV-MF) (Soviet Naval Aviation or SNA).

Soviet Naval Aviation (SNA)
In contrast to America's Supercarriers and superbly efficient crews, Soviet Union naval aviation had taken a very different course during the 1950s and 1960s. During that time the Soviet Navy's primary concern was the defense of Soviet territory and not control of the sea lanes. The emergence of NATO carrier task forces alarmed the USSR and, to counter this threat, a largeforce of shore-based long-range patrol bombers, armed with stand-off antiship missiles, was organized from the 1960s through the 1970s.

Despite the Soviet Union's apparent current interest in developing an aircraft carrier force, a major threat to American carriers was the Soviet submarine Fleet; however, even more threatening was the fleet of Soviet very long-range surveillance and missile mid-course guidance planes plus the very long-range strike aircraft armed with standoff antiship missiles.

The SNA was one of the largest Soviet Air Forces and received most of the very long-range surveillance and strike aircraft that were produced. The SNA was larger than the Royal Air Force.

Soviet Long-Range Surveillance Tu-20 Bears
The most troublesome Soviet plane to Western Nations was the Tupolev Tu-20 Bear maritime reconnaissance aircraft. Approximately 200 Bears were in service with the Soviet DA and SNA; regularly intruding the sovereign airspace of many nations in their quest to glean military information. Hardly a week passed that U.S.

fighter planes did not intercept a prowling Bear in the vicinity of a U.S. Naval Base or CVBG to escort it out to sea.

Tupolev Bear Data

Bears were produced in seven variants; Tu-20 through Tu-20F with Soviet bureau designations ranging from Tu-95 through Tu-142. The Tupolev Tu-20F Bear wingspan is 167 feet-8 inches with an overall length of 162 feet-5 inches. Height is 39 feet-9 inches. Empty weight is 178,571 pounds while loaded weight is 414,462 pounds. The four 15,000 shaft horsepower Kuznetsov NK-12M turboprop engines drive contrarotating four-bladed propellers. Maximum speed is 525 miles per hour and, at the 435 miles per hour cruising speed, range is 6,775 nautical miles with a flight endurance of about 28 hours. Service ceiling is 44,300 feet. The crew consists of two pilots plus from five to 10 electronics technicians, depending upon the mission.

The Bear's first flight was in 1954 while service delivery of the Tu-20A was in 1956. Service delivery of the Tu-20F was in 1973.

Long-Range Missile Guidance

In addition to long-range surveillance operations, Bears were used for ASW patrol missions and provide mid-course guidance for ship-launched antiship missiles such as the SS-N-12 and SS-N-3. Over-the-horizon (OTH) targeting for Soviet warships could also be accomplished by Bears.

Backfire ASUW Strike Aircraft

The Tupolev Tu-25M Backfire ASUW Missile Strike aircraft began serving in the Soviet Naval Aviation force during 1975 and had become the most dangerous threat to U.S. aircraft carriers. With a speed of twice that of sound, a range of over 6,000 miles, a service ceiling of over 60,000 feet, and the release point of its Anti Ship Missile (ASM) 150 miles from the target, it is easy to understand why Admiral James L. Holloway III, former U.S. Navy Chief of Naval Operations (CNO), warned in 1976 that America's deployed ships must have the strength to properly defend themselves against the attacks of shore-based aircraft because increased development and production of Soviet long-range aircraft armed with antiship missiles had become a threat to the U.S. Navy that can extend to almost any location on the globe.

Backfire Covers All SLOC's

Taking off from Murmansk, the Backfire could fly the Atlantic Ocean as far as 500 miles east of New Foundland; 400 miles west of Gibralter; 300 miles northwest of the Azores and into the Bay of Biscay; Morocco; and return to Murmansk. In the Pacific the Backfire could takeoff from Petropavlovsk on the Kamchatka Peninsula and reach points as far as 500 miles from California; the Hawaiian Islands; Guam; the Philippines; Alaska; Marianas and Marshall Islands; and 300 miles east of Vietnam, and return to base! Mid-air refueling adds 2,000 miles to the range.

It was impossible for ships to travel to Japan or to Europe from the U.S. without sailing within the combat radius of the Backfire. This would have made it dangerous for any convoy that attempts the trip. The Soviet Blackjack bomber is said to be even more formidable than the Backfire.

Backfire Data

The Tupolev Tu-22M Backfire is 132 feet long, not including the refueling probe. The outboard wing panels have variable geometry capability from 20 degrees to 55 degrees sweepback. At 20 degrees the span is 113 feet while at 55 degrees the span is 92 feet. Empty weight is 119,930 pounds and maximum weight is 287,000 pounds. The maximum speed at sea level is 683 miles per hour but at 30,000 feet it can reach 1,319 miles per hour. Service ceiling is 62,355 feet. Range is 6,500 nautical miles.

Backfire Armament

Armament consists of two remotely operated 23 millimeter cannon in the tail for defense while the offensive armament comprises one AS-4 Kitchen cruise missile or an AS-6 Kingfish missile in a recess under the fuselage or two AS-4 or AS-6 ASM's on underwing pylons. Both missiles have speeds up to 3 1/2 times that of sound and

The Soviet Tupolev Tu-25M Backfire long-range strike aircraft was a serious threat to U.S. carriers because it can reach almost any location on the globe with antiship missiles and then return to base. Observe the variable sweep wing in the left photo and the long-range antiship missile under the fuselage in the right photo. (U.S. Naval Historical Center)

a guaranteed range of 150 miles, although they are capable of far greater distances. The AS-6 can be fitted with a nuclear warhead.

Stopping the Backfires

U.S. Navy carrier battle groups (CVBG) play a very critical role in seizing the initiative in wartime and fighter aircraft such as the Tomcat are most important in flying Maritime Air Superiority (MAS) or power projection missions; day or night and in all weather conditions. The CVBG must be able to create a sanctuary for its own operations in hostile areas and this MAS operation will be the predominant fighter mission. The Backfire is not only armed with long-range antiship cruise missiles but is also fitted with passive and active Electronic Counter Measures (ECM) for defense penetration. In order to be effective in this environment fighter aircraft must have supersonic speeds, very sophisticated avionics, powerful radar and a long-range homing multishot weapon capability such as the Tomcat.

In order to expect any measure of success, the fighters must engage the Backfires before the attackers reach the 150 mile missile release point. This means that, to save the CVBG or convoy, the Backfire must be detected at least 350 to 400 miles away in order to give the interceptor adequate time to intercept the strike aircraft before it reaches the missile launch point. At its 22 mile per minute speed the Backfire will be about 220 miles closer to the target in 10 minutes; therefore, at least 17 minutes warning would be mandatory. Of course, this is only a hypothetical example but it does illustrate the problem inherent with intercepting the Backfire. Actually, 17 minutes is not so generous for a jet fighter to start engines, catapult-launch, climb to altitude and reach its quarry.

It appears imperative that Airborne Early Warning (AEW) Grumman E-2C Hawkeyes be employed to detect the oncoming strike aircraft in time for successful interception.

Another possibility is the addition of small expendable carriers to the U.S. Navy inventory. It would be very effective to not only detect the oncoming Backfire (or Blackjack) and alert the CVBG but to also attempt an intercept with its own fighters. The small carriers can operate with the CVBG picket ships or be stationed in preassigned zones, with escorts, to act as Sea Control Ships. The small carriers would be in addition to the U.S. Navy Supercarriers.

The principal difficulty in detecting the Backfire is the fact that it is not shipborne to the engagement area and; therefore, there is no hostile carrier to alert the target that an attack is imminent. Tne Backfire's big advantage is surprise because it has begun its attack from a base that could be over 3,000 miles away. It quickly drops down to wavetop level to evade radar until it is clear of hostile shorelines and then resumes altitude to the target. Backfires do not travel as a group to the target. They fly diverse routes and then rendezvous, which makes them more difficult to detect.

A continuous CAP (Combat Air Patrol) of a half-dozen fighters for the CVB, or convoy vould also be most effective and shorten the interception time. They must, however, fly well ahead of the ships to be certain that interception is made in time. Closing speed for interception would be about 2,700 miles per hour unless the Backfire turns and runs, in which case it is only about 250 miles per hour!

This excellent photo of a Su-27 Flanker clearly shows the forward control surface and the rectangular jet engine air inlet. A Kamov Ka-32 Helix helicopter is shown on deck. (U.S. National Archives)

Regardless of which combination of detection/interception remedies are selected, the aircraft carrier, big or small, had to be involved with its brood of Warblrds from F-14's to E-2C's to combat the Soviet Naval Aviation maritime strike force.

SU-27 Flanker

The Sukhoi Su-27 Flanker is a large carrierborne strike/flghter of unusual design, giving the viewer a first impression of a miniature Concorde supersonic transport because of its low rectangular air inlets and long, sharp, drooping nose. Maximum speed is estimated as Mach 2.5 or two-and-one-half times the speed of sound at normal operating altitude and Mach 1.1 at sea level. Range is about 1,500 miles. Each engine in the twin-engine plane is estimated to develop more than 30,000 pounds static thrust with afterburners. An unusual feature of the Flanker is the installation of small stub wings just forward of the main wing. It appears that they are movable and provide an assist to control and maneuverability. Underwing pylons have been provided for eight beyond visual range AA-10 radar homing AAM's. The wings fold upwards for carrier stowage, reducing tne span by about 50 percent. Flankers are based on the Soviet *Kuznetsov* class Supercarriers and scheduled for tne *Ul'yanovsk* nuclear Supercarrier.

The large size of the Flanker is evident as the plane is being serviced on Kuznetsov. Observe the folded wings and unusual fuselage shape. (U.S. National Archives)

SOVIET-NATO MUTUAL DISTRUST

The Soviet Navy flexed its muscles worldwide in 1984 since it had transformed itself from a basically coastal/defensive organization into a deep ocean naval force with aircraft-capable ships. Soviet fleets entered the world's oceans in a worldwide command and control operation.

Soviet Exercise Alarms NATO

At least 30 Soviet warships, accompanied by submarines, ASUW Backfire bombers, support ships, amphibious vessels and long-range reconnaissance Bears had spread out in the area between Norway, Greenland and Scotland. Norwegian and British government sources claimed that a large number of Soviet submarines had been tracked and Soviet aerial activity was intense. The NATO commander in chief for the Eastern Atlantic, Admiral Sir William Staveley, ordered an immediate monitoring operation comprising AWACS (Airborne Warning And Control System) aircraft as well as Phantom II fighters and Panavia Tornado multi-role strike aircraft.

World-Wide Operation

Other Soviet ships also appeared in the Indian Ocean and Mediterranean Sea while the helicopter carrier Leningrad left Cuba with an escort and headed northward, leaving the Carribean area.

Still another force left the Vladivostok naval base for maneuvers in the Western Pacific Ocean.

Although NATO and SEATO surface and air patrols had been increased, it was unlikely that more than a fraction of the total number of Soviet ships had been sighted, according to NATO officials.

Unannounced fleet actions such as these Soviet maneuvers were always regarded with suspicion with the result that Eastern European and Western navies began shadowing each other with increasing intensity and belligerence.

Minsk Incident

In one incident in 1984 the Soviet aircraft carrier *Minsk* was dead in the water in the South China Sea when the frigate *USS Harold Holt* passed the carrier about 300 yards to starboard to learn if the carrier required assistance. Without provocation, the carrier fired eight signal flares at the frigate, three of which struck the hull and superstructure. Naval signal flares are very large and the heat is so intense that a burning flare can ignite any flammable material or cause serious injury or death. Fortunately for world peace there were no injuries and damage was minor.

U.S. Carrier Collision

So intense had the shadowing become that, on March 21, 1984, the U.S. carrier *Kitty Hawk* collided with a submerged Soviet *Victor* class nuclear-powered attack submarine in the Sea of Japan. The carrier sustained minor damage; however, the submarine had to be towed back to the Vladivostok naval base for repairs.

Bumping

The animosity demonstrated by Soviet crews towards U.S. ships had grown to abnormal proportions when Soviet frigates and destroyers began "bumping" American naval vessels. One such incident in the Arabian Sea during November, 1984 warranted mention in the press when a Soviet frigate bumped a U.S. destroyer; however, the mishap was described as a "minor collision."

Meetings End Tensions

This irresponsible behavior and other potentially explosive incidents at sea between U.S. and Soviet ships prompted high level meetings of U.S. and Soviet admirals in Moscow, which calmed this volatile situation.

Soviet Navy Grew More Powerful

Despite the proclaimed reductions of Soviet military potential, the Soviet Navy's capability actually increased in 1990. Although the overall size of the Soviet Navy did not increase, the Soviets replaced obsolete ships with newer, more potent types. Soviet Tactical Aviation at Sea strength was amplified during 1990 when MiG-29 and Su-27 strike/fighter aircraft operated with the new Soviet Supercarrier during her sea and air trials.

A statement by Soviet General of the Army Mikhail A. Moiseyev declared that, of all the Soviet military services, no reduction was planned in the strength of the Soviet Navy. In addition, several regiments of shore-based fighters and strike aircraft were transferred from the Soviet Air Force to the new Tactical Aviation at Sea operation of Soviet Naval Aviation; thereby, providing the SNA with outstanding capabilities it would have not possessed.

SOVIET UNION COLLAPSE

The disintegration of the U.S.S.R. has made most Western nations heave a sigh of relief and plan drastic measures for virtual complete disarmament. Outstanding contracts for submarines, aircraft and nuclear weapons have been cancelled while aircraft carriers are targeted for early retirement by gullible and shortsighted Pollyanna politicians vying for the popular acclaim of naive voters.

Soviet Carriers Still Exist

Despite the demise of the political aspect of the Soviet Union the previously described Soviet aircraft carriers and naval aircraft plus other weapons have not disappeared and remain under the control of the heirs of the Soviet complex. It is foolhardy to assume that these will not be used against the Western bloc because Russia has been engaged in expansionist activities since 1453; centuries before Communist rule.

The aircraft carriers in the Black Sea shipyards are still under construction and the former Soviet ships are still operated at sea despite dispute of ownership among the nationalistic factions that have sprung out of the Soviet rubble. In fact, minor collisions at sea between former Soviet ships and Western ships have been reported in the post-Soviet period.

Carriers Still Necessary Peace-Keepers

In this uncertain world, in which it is very difficult to determine who is friend or foe, the aircraft carrier is the principal peace-keeping weapon. Carriers must not be discarded as unnecessary by Western nations because the Communist faction in the former Soviet Union is still active and powerful at this writing.

Danish helicopters such as this Westland Lynx conduct multiple operations when flown from naval ships as well as customs patrol craft in coastal waters. (Westland Helicopters Ltd., Courtesy P.D. Batten)

Although it has no aircraft carriers the German Navy manages to conduct surveillance flights from destroyers and similar naval ships in a variety of important security operations. A Kriegsmarine Westland Lynx is shown over the North Sea. (Westland Helicopters Ltd., Courtesy P.D. Batten)

Crisis such as the Serbian, Croatian and Bosnian fighting could escalate into an unwanted war between Eastern and Western Europe. The West must keep its premier peace-keeping weapon – the aircraft carrier.

NATO NAVIES

The North Atlantic Treaty Organization (NATO) members had many diverse naval responsibilities with regards to NATO and their own national maritime strategies. Few could afford or had an interest in aircraft carriers.

Britain's Naval Dilemma

Britain, once the world's greatest naval power, is still dependent upon the sea which should be reflected in her maritime strategy; however, because of economics and the continenial demands of NATO, it has placed the political significance of uncertain alliance ahead of national naval requirements. The Royal Navy is still the most important non-superpower navy; however, only three through-deck/cruiser/Ski-Jump carriers comprise the Royal Navy through-deck air-capable ships; *HMS Invincible, HMS Illustrious* and *HMS Ark Royal*, previously described.

France Forges Ahead With Carriers

Although the Admiralty should be pressing forward wlth new carriers, it is the French who are planning new carriers to satisfy their nationalistic maritime strategy. With the carriers *Foch* and *Clemenceau*, and the *Jeanne D'Arc* helicopter/ASW/Assault ship in service, France began work on a new 32,000 ton nuciear-powered carrier design of which it planned to construct two. France is the only country that is a member of NATO civil organization but is not a member of NATO military organization, which gives it a free hand to serve only its national naval interest.

Scandinavian Navies

The Norwegian and Danish Naval Strategy is concerned with the defense of their coastlines and have no carriers.

German Navy

The German Navy strategy relates to Baltic Sea, coastal defense, and North Sea operations and has no carriers.

Royal Netherlands Navy

As with Britain, the Netherlands is dependent upon the sea for trade and many necessities. Although no aircraft carriers flew the Neth-

Norway employs Westland Sea King helicopters for Antisubmarine Warfare, Search and Rescue and Coastal Patrol. The Sea Kings are operated from shoreside as well as from Frigates and other naval craft. (Westland Helicopters Ltd., Courtesy P.D. Batten)

The former Royal Navy Colossus class HMS Venerable was purchased by the Royal Netherlands Navy in 1946 and fitted with an eight-degree angled Flight Deck, steam catapult and mirror landing system. Named HNLMS Karel Doorman, the ship was damaged in a fire, repaired, and sold to Argentina in 1968. (U.S. Naval Historical Center)

With aircraft carriers beyond its budget the Netherlands Konigsmarine operates Westland Lynx helicopters for ASW, SAR and coastal patrol work from flight decks on its fleet of aviation capable ships (Lower Photo). (Westland Helicopters Ltd., Courtesy P.D. Batten)

erlands flag during World War II, Dutch crews manned two MAC's (Merchant Aircraft Carriers) of the British *Rapana* class; *Gadila* and *Macoma*. The 16,000 ton displacement *Rapanas* were powered by single, slow-speed, 6-cylinder, 4,000 brake horsepower Diesel engine that was directly connected to the propeller shaft. Speed was about 13 knots. Complement was four aircraft and 118 crew. Armament was one 4-inch gun plus two 40 millimeter and six 20 millimeter rapid-fire antiaircraft guns. Both ships sailed in Atlantic escort duty and survived the war. They were reconverted postwar but were scrapped in 1958.

The Royal Netherlands Navy entered the Postwar era with a firm maritime strategy and its first aircraft carrier was the escort carrier *HMS Nairana*, bought from Britain in March 1946. This diesel-powered ship was renamed *HNLMS Karel Doorman*. It was returned to Britain in 1948 as a trade-in toward the purchase of another Royal Navy aircraft carrier of the *Colossus* class, *HMS Venerable*. This ship became the second *HNLMS Karel Doorman* and, during 1955-1958, it was fitted with an eight-degree angled Flight Deck, steam catapult, mirror-landing system and stronger elevators in order to qualify for jet aircraft. Hawker Sea Hawks, and Grumman Avengers served on the carrier until they were displaced by S-2 Trackers and helicopters. After a boiler room fire in 1968 *HNLMS Karel Doorman* was repaired in Rotterdam and sold to Argentina on October 15. The carrier's name was again changed to *Vienticinco de Mayo* (25 of May). The RNLN did not replace the *Colossus* class carrier that it sold to Argentina.

Belgian Navy
The Belgian Navy operates mainly minesweepers and frigates to protect English Channel shipping.

Portugese Navy
Portugal protects its coast plus the strategic Azores and Madeira but has no carriers; however, Vought A-7 Corsairs are operated from shore bases.

Spanish Navy Aircraft Carriers
Spain's maritime strategy is to help maintain sea control in the Atlantic Ocean between Spain and the Canary Islands; the waters around Gibralter; plus in the Mediterranean Sea between Spain and the Balearic Islands in cooperation with NATO. Spain has taken its responsibility very seriously. In order to accomplish these tasks, Spain has operated two aircraft carriers.

Aircraft Carrier *Dedalo*
Actually, the Spanish Navy experimented with a seaplane carrier in 1917; however, she did not have an acceptable aircraft carrier until it borrowed an *Independence* class light fleet carrier from the U.S., *USS Cabot*, in 1967. Spain then bought the ship from the U.S. in 1973 and changed the name to *Dedalo*. The principal modifications were improved radar and reducing the four stacks to two. Normal aviation complement comprised six V/STOL AV-8A Matadors (Harriers) and about 20 assorted helicopters which included Westland Sea Kings. Apparently, the combination of the carrier's age, quadruple screws and 100,000 shaft horsepower steam powerplant requiring a crew of 1,100 plus air group did not meet the Spanish Navy's requirements and operating costs were prohibitive. Spain then decided to construct a new high-tech carrier to suit its sea control needs.

Principe de Asturias Ski-Jump Carrier
With technical and financial aid from the U.S. a design was formulated, closely based on that of the U.S. Sea Control Ship which failed to be funded by the U.S. Congress. The major change from the Sea Control Ship design was the addition of a 12 degree Ski-Jump flight deck. The new carrier was ordered by the Spanish Government on June 29, 1977 and its keel was laid on October 8, 1979 at the Bazan of Ferrol shipyard.

Spain bought the U.S. Independence class carrier USS Cabot in 1973 and renamed it Dedalo. Radar was improved and the four stacks were reduced to two. (Official U.S. Navy Photograph)

After operating Dedalo for nine years Spain could no longer afford the high operating costs of the former U.S. light fleet carrier and decided to replace it with a more contemporary and more economical design. (U.S. National Archives)

Launched as *Principe de Asturias* on May 22, 1982 the new carrier is 640 feet long overall with an 80 feet beam. The Flight Deck is 105 x 575 feet and deep load draft is 22 feet. As with the defunct Sea Control Ship, *Principe de Asturias* is powered with two gas turbine engines geared to a single controllable/reversible pitch (CRP) propeller. The propulsion system is COGAG (COmbined Gas turbine And Gas turbine) in which gas turbines are used for low speed cruising as well as high speeds. The General Electric LM-2500 gas turbines develop 40,000 shaft horsepower which gives the ship a maximum speed of 26 knots. Aircraft complement comprises 15 Sea King LAMPS type helicopters and four Matadors. No catapults or arresting gear are installed. In addition to the SCS after flight deck-edge location, another aircraft elevator is installed just forward of the island. The hangar is full beam wide extending through the after two-thirds of the hull. Ships crew consists of 774 not including the air group personnel. *Principe de Asturias* was completed in 1985. It has a standard displacement of

14,500 tons and 15,250 tons deep draft. Defensive armament comprises four 12-barrel Meroka 20 millimeter CIWS units mounted on the island. The radar suite includes SPS-52C/D hemispheric search, SPN-35A CCA and SPS-55 surface search.

Royal Canadian Navy Aircraft Carriers
After operating three aircraft carriers over a 24 year period, the Royal Canadian Navy unexpectedly decommissioned its latest carrier in 1970 and had apparently abandoned carriers in favor of destroyers and frigates for ASW operations which is its primary concern.

HMCS Warrior
Canada's first carrier was the *Colossus* class *HMS Warrior*, which name was retained. It entered Royal Canadian Navy service directly upon completion in 1946 but was returned to Britain in late 1948 when it was commissioned into the Royal Navy.

HMCS Magnificent
Canada's second aircraft carrier was the *Majestic* class *HMS Magnificent*. This was lent to the Royal Canadian Navy in 1948 to replace *HMS Warrior* because *Magnificent* was capable of handling heavier and faster aircraft. *HMS Magnificent* was commissioned into the Royal Canadian Navy as *HMCS Magnificent*. Among the aircraft flown from *Magnificent* were Fairey Fireflies.

HMCS Bonaventure
In 1952 Canada purchased another *Majestic* class carrier, *HMS Powerful*, while it was still under construction at Harland and Wolff shipyard. Prior to completion an eight degree angled deck was installed as was a steam catapult and mirror-landing system. The tripod mast was replaced with a lattice structured mast and American radar was installed. She was the only *Majestic* class carrier to mount four twin 3-inch guns on four hull sponsons. The completed carrier was commissioned into the RCN as *HMCS Bonaventure* on January 17, 1957; 2,000 tons greater in displacement due to refinements. The initial air group comprised McDonnell Banshee interceptors

The state-of-the-art carrier Principe de Asturias replaced Dedalo. It was closely based upon the U.S. Sea Control Ship design with the addition of a 12 degree Ski-Jump ramp Flight Deck. The new carrier was launched at Bazan of Ferrol shipyard in May 1982. (Bazan of Ferol)

HMCS Bonaventure was the Royal Canadian Navy's most recent aircraft carrier, having been decommissioned in 1970. The former Majestic class HMS Powerful had been purchased while still under construction in 1952. An eight degree angled deck, steam catapult, and lattice mast were a few of the improvements. Grumman Trackers are shown on deck. (Canadian Armed Forces)

Although officially described as an aircraft-carrying cruiser, the Italian Navy Giuseppi Garibaldi is also called a light aircraft carrier, a through-deck cruiser, and a helicopter carrier. In fact, the ship can monitor hostile forces, defend SLOC's, manage a Task Group Naval Force, conduct ASW, and participate in amphibious landings. (Fincantieri-Cantieri Navali Italiani)

and Grumman Tracker ASW aircraft. *Magnificent* was returned to Britain when *Bonaventure* entered Canadian service and was eventually sold and scrapped in 1965. By 1961 *Bonaventure* had become a dedicated ASW carrier and the Banshees were replaced with Sikorsky Sea King helicopters. Shortly after its major overhaul to extend the *Bonaventure* service life it was suddenly decommissioned in July 1970 and eventually sold and scrapped. It has been suggested that RCN aircraft operate from U.S. carriers as a solution to this dilemma.

Italian Navy Aircraft Carrier

Although Italy had never completed an aircraft carrier for World War II, she has learned the importance of these valuable and essential ships. This led to a carrier keel-laying in June 1981 and on July 31, 1985 the Monfalcone yard of Fincantieri Cantieri Navali Italiani delivered *Giuseppi Garibaldi* to the Italian Navy. The ship, named for the famous Italian patriot, is officially described as an aircraft-carrying cruiser; however, *Giuseppi Garibaldi* is also called a light aircraft carrier, a through-deck cruiser, and a helicopter carrier. In fact, the ship is capable of functioning in many diverse roles. *Garibaldi* has replaced two old cruisers and fulfills the maritime strategy of defending the NATO southern region and the central

Mediterranean SLOC's: conduct international security, civil protection, and peacekeeping duties; participate in amphibious landings; engage in ASW operations; and monitor or engage any hostile moves by belligerent naval forces. *Giuseppi Garibaldi* can manage the operation of a Task Group Naval Force by virtue of her high-tech command and control electronics.

Garibaldi Advanced Electronics

The telecommunications systems (TLC) allows an exchange of information, messages, and orders with other air and surface units plus data on all targets. The high traffic capacity of the TLC system is a major reason for the ship's capability to be the center of coordination and control of a complex surface/air operation. In addition to AN/SPS-52C, MM/SPS-774 and MM/SPS-768 air search radar; *Giuseppi Garibaldi* is equipped with a DE 1160 LF Sonar in the bulbous bow for submarine detection; MM/SPS 702 sea search radar; MM/SPN-749 navigation radar; TACAN and MM/SPN-728vl aircraft landing radar; and an Electronic Warfare system (EW) that is capable of detecting and intercepting the hostile force's electromagnetic emissions and effectively countering those that pose a threat to the ship. The Passive sector of the EW includes equipment for the interception, the angular radiogeometry and the analysis of the hostile force's emissions while the Active sector (ECM) consists of equipment that can jam, confuse and decoy the opposition's most dangerous radars; including the active guidance equipment of incoming ASM's. The *Garibaldi* EW system also has an underwater noise producer that can confuse the homing sensors of incoming torpedoes.

Garibaldi Data

The 10,000 tons standard displacement and 13,370 tons full load displacement *Garibaldi* is 591 feet long overall with a beam at the waterline of 77 feet. The Flight Deck measures 100 x 570 feet and is fitted with a Ski-Jump. The maximum draft is 26 feet while mean draft is 22 feet. Maximum speed is over 30 knots while the range at 20 knots is 9,000 miles.

The powerplant consists of four TAG Fiat General Electric LM 2500 gas turbines which develop a total of 80,000 shaft horsepower in a COGAG (COmbined Gas turbine And Gas turbine) arrangement. Two separate propulsion sets, each made up of two gas turbines and reduction gears are located in two separate engine rooms not adjoining each other to minimize damage in the event of a hit. Each set of two turbines is geared to a propeller shaft and each shaft is fitted with a five-bladed fixed pitch propeller. Gas turbines are not reversible; therefore, normal practice dictates a complex controllable/reversible pitch propeller in which the blades can be rotated to increase or decrease propeller thrust or reverse the thrust by changing the pitch of the blades and not change the direction of rotation. Each pair of the Italian Navy light aircraft carrier *Giuseppe Garibaldi* turbines is connected to a propeller shaft via Tosi triple-reduction/single articulated gears and a Tosi hydraulic reversible converter coupling for speed changing and reversing plus an SSS clutch for full ahead power. The gears and converter couplings were designed by Franco Tosi and obviate the necessity for controllable pitch propellers. The two propellers are fitted with a Prairie system that discharges compressed air into the water to silence propeller noise. With the new Tosi converter coupling, *Garibaldi* can go from full speed ahead into full speed astern in less than three ship-lengths; an amazing capability for a 10,000 ton warship. For long distance cruising, one gas turbine can be disconnected from each shaft for fuel economy (longer range) and to conserve engine wear.

Aircraft Complement

Initially, the air group comprised 18 Agusta-made Sea King helicopters, 12 of which can be accommodated in the 49 x 360 feet hangar. In 1989 *Garibaldi* conducted cross-deck operations with Spain to evaluate the performance of the new Spanish AV-8B Matadors.

In addition, Royal Navy FRS.1 Sea Harriers and McDonnell Douglas AV-8B Harrier II's have been evaluated by the Italian Navy with flight tests from *Garibaldi* in its quest for the best STO/VL aircraft to serve on the carrier. The delay in procuring the Harriers was caused by Italian inter-service rivalry in a long dispute over which service was to fly the fixed-wing aircraft. The Italian Navy came up the winner and was given permission to purchase and fly its own planes. Six to eight Harrier STO/VL aircraft is the normal complement; however, up to 20 can be embarked as the mission requires.

An Agusta-built Sea King helicopter is shown on a Giuseppi Garibaldi elevator. Of interest is the main rotor folding system in which two of the five rotor blades fold against the fuselage side. Also note the octagonal shape of the aircraft Elevator which has the structural effect of a large radius deck cut without the complexity of forming the radius. Observe the folding tail (arrow). (Fincantieri-Cantieri Navali Italiani)

Fixed Armament

Garibaldi is well armed against hostile surface craft, aircraft and submarines. The Teseo SSM system comprises four double-launchers, two on each side of the hull just forward of the transom, which fire Otomat Mk.2 surface-skimming missiles. Two Albatros system 8-cell SAM launchers which fire Aspide missiles are located forward and aft on the island. The CIWS consists of three twin Breda/Bofors 40 millimeters turreted cannon, each controlled by a

Four Agusta Sea Kings line up on the Giuseppi Garibaldi Flight Deck preparatory to takeoff. This photo affords a good view of the island. Note the eight shot Albatros/Aspide SAM launcher. (Fincantieri-Cantieri Navali Italiani)

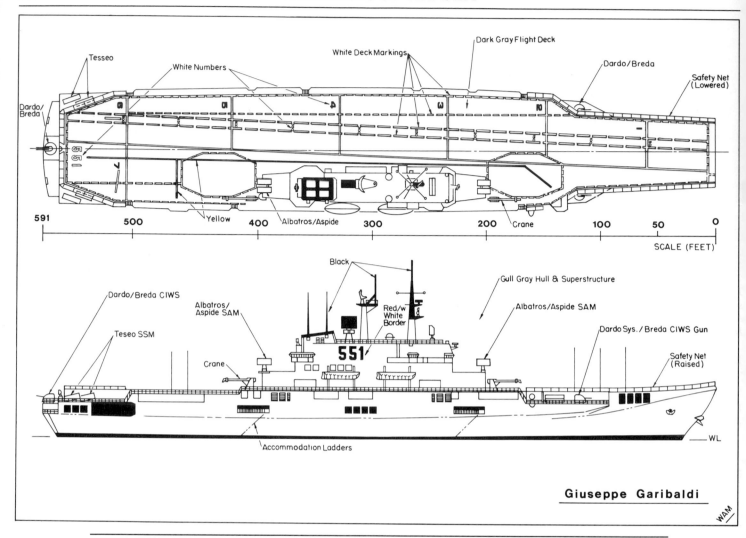

Tesseo

White Numbers

White Deck Markings

Dark Gray Flight Deck

Dardo/Breda

Safety Net (Lowered)

Dardo/Breda

551

591 500 400 300 200 100 50 0

SCALE (FEET)

Yellow

Albatros/Aspide

Crane

Black

Gull Gray Hull & Superstructure

Dardo/Breda CIWS

Albatros/Aspide SAM

Red/w White Border

Albatros/Aspide SAM

Teseo SSM

Crane

551

Dardo Sys./Breda CIWS Gun

Safety Net (Raised)

Accommodation Ladders

WL

Giuseppe Garibaldi

WAM

Dardo antiaircraft/antimissile system. The fixed antisubmarine armament comprises two 324 millimeters Mk.32 triple-torpedo launchers. Two 105 millimeters rocket launchers are installed for short-range antiaircraft defense.

None of the foregoing missile and gun systems operates independently. Each system is connected to a network of detection, evaluation, alarm and fire control electronic equipment that provides the selected weapon with all the necessary data to enable it to successfully perform its function.

No catapults or arresting gear are installed on *Giuseppi Garibaldi*.

The crew consists of 105 officers, 186 petty officers, 138 senior ratings, and 396 ratings for a total of 825, which includes the air wing.

In addition to advanced electronics, Giuseppi Garibaldi has sonar in the bulbous bow which required a centerline anchor and beak as was fitted to USS America and USS John F. Kennedy. SSM launchers are located at the ship's side near the stern (arrow). (Fincantieri-Cantieri Navali Italiani)

SAM launchers are located forward and aft on the island (arrows) and three twin 40 millimeter turreted CIWS guns are also fitted; one on the transom and one on each side of the hull, forward (arrows). The ship also fires antisubmarine torpedoes from the side of the hull, amidships. (Fincantieri-Cantieri Navali Italiani)

Third World nations have turned to the helicopter for their offshore security. Helicopters such as these Westland Lynx of the Nigerian Navy Air Arm 101 Squadron operate from Meko class frigates. (Westland Helicopters Ltd., Courtesy P.D. Batten)

Middle East nations such as Egypt and Qatar, have also turned to the helicopter. This Qatar Westland Commando development of the Sea King can carry 30 fully armed troops. These craft also patrol the Suez Canal and Persian Gulf. (Westland Helicopters Ltd., Courtesy P.D. Batten)

EASTERN MEDITERRANEAN NAVIES

The Greek and Turkish Navies' strategy is that of preserving their territorial integrity while Turkey also has the Bosporus and Dardanelles to guard. Neither country has aircraft carriers, but Greece operates shore-based Vought A-7 Corsairs.

SOUTH AMERICAN NAVIES

Only two Latin American countries have operated aircraft carriers; Argentina and Brazil. Both nations have the largest navies in South America.

Argentine Carriers

Argentina's immediate maritime strategy is the protection of its 200 mile fishing zone and claims to disputed territory south of the continent. Her first aircraft carrier was the *Colossus* class vessel *HMS Warrior*; purchased from Britain in 1958, and renamed *Independencia*. Subsequent modifications had increased the displacement more than 4,000 tons by 1962.

The Netherlands' Navy *Karel Doorman* boiler room fire in April 1968 led to the sale of another *Colossus* class carrier to Argentina six months later. Replacement boilers from the retired *Majestic* class carrier *HMS Leviathan* were installed by NV Dok en Werf Mij Wilton Fijinoord. The radar suite was also upgraded during this time. Renamed *Vienticinco De Mayo* (25 of May) the reconstructed carrier was commissioned in August 1969 at which time it was decided to withdraw *Independencia*, which had flown Vought F4U Corsairs and North American AT-6 propeller-driven aircraft until its retirement in 1971. By 1975 *25 De Mayo* was operating Sikorsky Sea Kings and Grumman Trackers for ASW, plus McDonnell Douglas A-4Q Skyhawks. When the U.S. refused to sell Argentina replacement parts for the Skyhawks because of political reasons, the South Americans turned to France and ordered 25 Super Etendard strike/fighters which were used with considerable success in the Falklands War.

Brazil's Aircraft Carrier

Brazil's maritime strategy centers on the protection of the SLOC's because all of her foreign trade is transported on ships. With a strong U.S. Navy influence, Brazil's naval concentration is on ASW operations. Her only aircraft carrier is the *Colossus* class light fleet carrier *HMS Vengeance* purchased from Britain in 1956 and renamed *Minas Gerais*. The ship spent three years in Verolme shipyard in Rotterdam where it was extensively updated with steam catapult, new elevators and arresting gear, mirror-landing system; a strengthened Flight Deck and an 8 1/2 degree angled landing deck. Island modifications included a raked smokestack, and a lattice mast replaced the original tripod mast. The radar suite was also updated with American SPS-4 surface-search, SPS-12 air-search and others. *Minas Gerais* underwent a major overhaul in 1981 to extend its service life for at least 10 more years. The combined modifications added almost 2,000 tons to the original displacement.

AUSTRALIAN AIRCRAFT CARRIERS

As with Canada, Australia has close ties with U.S. and Britain despite the fact that it is an island at the opposite side of the globe and

The Argentine Navy flew Vought F4U-5 Corsairs until 1971. A Corsair is shown taking off from Argentina's first carrier Independencia (former HMS Warrior). (Official U.S. Navy Photo)

Brazil's only aircraft carrier is Minas Gerais, which was the Colossus class HMS Vengeance. Modifications include 8 1/2 degree angled Deck, steam catapult with bridle catcher, new elevators and arresting gear, and mirror landing system. Observe the Grumman Trackers and Sikorsky Sea Kings on deck. (Official U.S. Navy Photo)

Brazil flies Westland Lynx helicopters from Minas Gerais as well as smaller aviation-capable craft such as frigates. (Westland Helicopters Ltd., Courtesy P.D. Batten)

in the southern hemisphere; isolated from Europe and the Americas. This makes the island nation heavily dependent upon naval forces.

HMAS Albatross

The Royal Australian Navy's first involvement with shipboard naval aviation was *HMAS Albatross*. This seaplane carrier was constructed in the Cockatoo Shipyard and proved one of the largest indiginous Australian shipbuilding projects completed between the wars. The keel was laid on May 5, 1926 and *Albatross* was launched on February 23, 1928. Commissioning was in January 1929. The ship was intended to protect the SLOC and take part in coastal defense. In order to have the takeoff deck as high above the water as possible in the event of rough seas, a long forecastle extended for about one-half the hull length and was two deck levels above the main deck. A compressed air catapult was installed on the Forecastle, or Fo'c'sle Deck and three cranes were fitted to lift the seaplanes from the water, lower them into the below decks hangar, and place aircraft on the catapult. The hangar could accommodate nine seaplanes. A blister had been fitted to the hull to improve stability. The 4,800 ton *Albatross* was 440 feet long overall with a beam of 61 feet and mean draft of 16 feet. Four boilers generated steam for two turbine units each geared to a propeller shaft. The 12,000 shaft horsepower propelled *Albatross* to a speed of 22 knots. Complement was 450; armament consisted of four 4.7 inch and four 2 pounder guns. The aircraft complement of nine planes included Fairey IIIF three-seat spotter/reconnaissance seaplanes. At the onset of World War II, *Albatross* was transferred to Britian where the catapult was replaced with a gunpowder-type. *Albatross* was operated as a CAM (Catapult-Aircraft Merchant) ship, previously described in Chapter III, operating in the Indian Ocean. She was scrapped in 1964.

HMAS Sydney

Australia did not operate another air-capable ship until February 16, 1949 when the RAN received the Majestic class carrier *HMS*

Terrible; name changed to *HMAS Sydney*. The carrier saw action in the Korean War and was in service during the Australian activity in Malaya in 1962. *HMAS Sydney* was also employed in the Vietnam War. She was taken out of service in 1973 and scrapped in 1975. Her aircraft complement had included Hawker Sea Furies and Fairey Fireflies.

HMAS Vengeance

HMAS Vengeance, a *Colossus* class carrier, overlapped service with *HMAS Sydney* very briefly, starting in early 1953 and returned to the Royal Navy two years later. *Vengeance* was then sold to Brazil in 1956 and renamed *Minas Gerais*.

HMAS Melbourne

Another *Majestic* class carrier, *HMS Majestic*, was purchased from Britain in 1949; however, because of numerous specified refinements while the ship was still under construction at the Vickers Armstrong (Barrow) Shipyard, *Majestic* did not arrive in Australia until May 1956 when it was renamed *HMAS Melbourne*. Some of the refinements were a new arresting gear, 5 1/2 degree angled landing deck, mirror-landing system, and a steam catapult. Later modifications comprised a refit during 1967-1969 to give *Melbourne* the capability of handling McDonnell Douglas Skyhawks and Grumman Trackers. In 1971 the Flight Deck was strengthened and catapult renewed. The initial aviation complement consisted of ASW Fairey Gannets and DeHavilland Sea Venom fighters but by 1963 ASW Westland Wessex helicopters were included. In 1976 Grumman Trackers, McDonnell Douglas Skyhawks, Westland Sea Kings (ASW) and Westland Wessex (SAR) comprised the air group. *HMAS Melbourne* had been the Flagship of the RAN but became scheduled for replacement in 1985.

Indecision Re Carriers

The Australian pro-carrier faction appeared inclined to purchase a V/STOL or STO/VL Ski-Jump carrier and had considered the Italian *Garibaldi* class as well as the *Principe De Asturias* class. Inter-

Royal Australian Navy Westland Mk.50 Sea King helicopters are employed primarily in ASW operations and were flown from Australian carriers as well as from shore bases and other surface combatants. Note the kangaroo in the Australian national insignia. (Westland Helicopters Ltd., Courtesy P.D. Batten)

Two Royal Australian Navy McDonnell Douglas Skyhawk strike/fighters fire missiles at surface targets. With no aircraft carriers in service Australian fixed wing naval aircraft are shore-based or flown from U.S. aircraft carriers in cooperation with the U.S. Navy. (Official U.S. Navy Photograph)

The former HMS Majestic was bought for the Australian Navy from Britain and renamed HMAS Melbourne. While it was still under construction the Royal Australian Navy had the carrier modernized with the addition of a 5 1/2 degree angled deck, steam catapult and bridle catcher, and mirror landing system. Grumman Trackers are shown on the Flight Deck in both photos while a Sea King rests at the aft end of the Flight Deck in thephoto below. (Official U.S. Navy Photo)

est in the Royal Navy's Invincible was very high until the Falklands War cancelled the sale. The most recent replacement scheme is to convert a merchant ship into a V/STOL carrier; however, the proponents of shore-based air power in preference to shipboard aircraft greatly influenced this island nation to replace its navy in the third rank of military appropriations. All this in the face of expanding Far Eastern navies which might become antagonistic to Australian interests. This included the Soviet Pacific Fleet which had also consolidated its foothold in the Indian Ocean.

As had been suggested for Royal Canadian Navy aircraft, it has been proposed that Australian Navy squadrons operate with a U.S. Navy carrier air wing. The Australian squadrons would normally be based in Western Australia as a force multiplier.

INDIAN NAVY AIRCRAFT CARRIERS

Alfred Thayer Mahan predicted that the Indian Ocean would be the key to the seven seas and that, in the 21st century, the destiny of the world will be decided on its waters. India's 3,000 miles of coastline extends southward into the Indian Ocean. It is bordered on the west by the Arabian Sea and on the east by the Bay of Bengal. This places the subcontinent in a very strategic location adjacent to the oil tanker traffic lanes from the Persian Gulf and, to fulfill its maritime strategy, India maintains a strong balanced Navy with two aircraft carriers, as opposed to other nations bordering the Indian Ocean that have none.

INS Vikrant

India's first carrier is the former *Majestic* class *HMS Hercules*, built by Vickers Armstrong and purchased from Britain in 1957. The ship was completed by Harland and Wolff in March 1961 to include a single hangar, angled Flight Deck, steam catapult, electric aircraft elevators and air conditioning in essential spaces. The twin-screw carrier was powered by two 20,000 shaft horsepower geared steam turbine units which drove the ship to a maximum speed of 24.5 knots. Flight Deck measured 680 x 128 feet with a hull beam of 80 feet. Mean draft was 24 feet and full load displacement was

The angled Flight Deck is readily apparent in this overhead aerial view of INS Vikrant. Note that the crew standing on the Flight Deck have arranged themselves to spell "VIKRANT." This aircraft carrier saw considerable action in the India-Pakistan War of December 1971 and it is possible that this was a celebration of India's victory. (U.S. National Archives)

19,500 tons upon completion. A mixed bag of Hawker Sea Hawks and Dassault Breguet Alizes comprised the aircraft complement. Peacetime complement is 1,075. In wartime this increases to 1,345 which includes the air wing.

The carrier was commissioned in March 1961 at which time it was delivered to India. Ten years later *INS Vikrant,* as the carrier had been renamed, received its baptism of fire in the India-Pakistan War. *Vikrant's* Hawker Sea Hawks and Breguet Alizes neutralized the East Pakistan (Bangladesh) ports of Khulna, Cox Bazar, Mongla and Chittagong as well as the river ports of Barisal and Naravanganj. This would have been impossible without the versatility and mobility of carrier aircraft operating from their moving air base in international waters. The Sea Hawks are popularly known as White Tigers, while the Alize is known as Cobra in the Indian Navy. These aircraft significantly ensured victory in the Bay of Bengal.

Vikrant underwent extensive overhaul in 1973-1974 while the Indian Navy sought a replacement for the aging Sea Hawks, and it was not until October 10, 1977 that the Indian government gave the Indian Navy permission to order six British Aerospace FRS Mk.51 Sea Harriers. Two Harrier trainers were also acquired. A Ski-Jump was added to *INS Vikrant* in mid-1980 after which more Sea Harriers were purchased. About a dozen Sea Harriers then became the normal aircraft complement aboard *Vikrant.*

INS Viraat

In 1986 India bought the Royal Navy's venerable *HMS Hermes,* the world's first Ski-Jump deck aircraft carrier that had performed yeoman service in the Falklands War. The ship was modified in Britain for Indian service and delivered in 1987 as *INS Viraat. Vikrant's* modernization and the acquisition of *Viraat* drew considerable criticism from the Indian media, which is the position taken by the media, world-wide.

India's Aircraft Carrier Program

The Indian Navy carriers operate Sea Harriers, Alizes and Sea King helicopters. Indian Navy Admiral R.H. Tahiliani has stated that future Indian carriers will be constructed in an Indian shipyard and that India's needs are for five aircraft carriers as flagships of an eastern and a western fleet.

India has clearly defined the role of the aircraft carrier in its maritime strategy and is a rare example of how a country with internal problems, burdened by poverty and with a limited industrial

India's aircraft carrier Vikrant received a Ski-Jump foredeck in mid-1980 and has operated FRS Mk.51 Sea Harriers since that time. This 19,500 ton displacement aircraft carrier plays an important role in India's maritime strategy. (U.S. National Archives)

base can acquire aircraft carriers and resulting sea power to insure the integrity of its maritime frontier.

UNITED STATES NAVY CARRIER BATTLE GROUPS (CVBG)

In order to adhere to the U.S. Department of Defense strategic philosophy of being able to fight simultaneously in two major regional theatres, twelve CVBG's will be required: five for the Arabian Sea, Indian Ocean and Persian Gulf region; three for the Western Pacific; and four for the Mediterranean Sea. This will require at least 12 fleet carriers, probably more. As can be seen, U.S. national security planning depends on the carrier battle group.

U.S. Geography Demands Need For Carriers

As with India, by virtue of its geography the U.S. is a maritime nation whose welfare and global role depends on unimpeded access to the world's SLOC's. There are always a number of regional conflicts in key world theatres that could escalate into open warfare posing a threat to the commercial and strategic interests of the Free World. A carrier force on the scene can prevent local warfare from spreading.

Post-Cold War CVBG Operations

U.S. Navy post-Cold War CVBG planning is directed toward littoral "brown water" (coastal region) operations instead of open ocean "blue water" warfare because open ocean threats to the U.S. no longer exist for the moment, at least; however, open ocean warfare has not been discounted.

"Gunboat Diplomacy" Is Not Dead

The aircraft carrier is uniquely qualified to support political interests and diplomatic initiatives, as well as contributing to crisis management in a manner that no other persuasion can.

MARITIME STRATEGY AND CARRIER SELECTION

In the foregoing, maritime strategy has been mentioned several times. This is a broad concept of how a nation or alliance will use the sea in support of national policy during peace and war. In general, it controls the application of naval forces which, in turn, governs the ships and aircraft to be procured. The formulation of a maritime strategy is not an exact science. It requires a study of the nation's needs and how and where command of the sea will reap rewards whether it be freedom of passage, blockades, coastal defense, invasion or power projection.

Planning strategy is not an easy task as I learned at the Naval War College when the U.S. Secretary of the Navy and Admiral Ronald J. Kurth invited the author to participate in the 1989 Current Strategy Forum. The divergent opinions of how to solve each of the many problems proved very stimulating to all participants which resulted in excellent conclusions, after exhaustive debate.

Command of the sea does not always result in victory; witness the Korean War and the Vietnam War. The U.S. Navy had the advantage of uncontested sea control during both conflicts and the carrier's Warbirds inflicted considerable punishment on the enemy; however, both Asian antagonists received most of their support overland from other nations, which contributed to the enemy's endurance. Had Korea and Vietnam been islands, an American vic-

Indian Navy British Aerospace FRS Mk.51 Sea Harriers peel off from a formation during exercises. These craft operate from India's two aircraft carriers; INS Vikrant and INS Viraat. (British Aerospace, Courtesy Brendan Morrissey)

tory would have been assured. Maritime strategy, whether offensive or defensive, and any other military plan that is prepared in anticipation of the actual engagement does not assure success. This brings to mind the observations of two prominent military personalities who have commented on advanced planning. Count Helmuth von Moltke, Chief of Staff of the Prussian General Staff 1858-1888 made this comment: "No plan survives contact with the enemy." The U.S. Navy's "Enfant Terrible" Admiral Hyman G. Rickover had this to say regarding planning: "A war, small or large, does not follow a prescribed scenario laid out in advance. If we could predict the sequence of events accurately, we could probably avoid war in the first place." With these astute observations before us, one can easily visualize the perplexing problems that face naval planners. The maritime strategy, in turn, exerts a strong influence on those who must select the best weapons for the armed forces.

SUPERCARRIER CRITICS

More often than not naval planners harbor divergent opinions regarding weapons selection. One argument that has been raging for many years in the U.S. Navy is Supercarriers versus small carriers and V/STOL strike/fighters versus sophisticated supersonic superiority fighters. Another faction claims that carriers are useless in this missile age. Senators, Secretaries of Defense and Presidents have all abused the Supercarrier.

Some experts claim the submarine is the best naval weapon because it sank many carriers during WWII and we salute this achievement; however, this fine weapon cannot intimidate the enemy by its very presence. Nor can it fire a "warning shot" because it is an "all or nothing" weapon; firing an atomic warhead or a devastating torpedo. A submarine cannot meet the von Clausewitz doctrine of a measured strike nor can it surgically remove a landing craft or pillbox as can carrier aircraft. Each weapon has its purpose but only the aircraft carrier is flexible.

Supercarriers More Important Than Ever

The description of Supercarriers from *USS Forrestal* (CVA-59) through *USS Nimitz* (CV-68) covered in Chapters VI, VII and VIII leaves one in awe over these marvelous ships. With their high speed and hundred-plane punch they are truly the symbol of American interest and determination in all the major oceans of the world. There is no other naval unit that can compare with the scope and scale of the Supercarrier's capabilities which, by its very presence, can fill an adversary with terror. *USS Nimitz'* nuclear reactors can operate for 13 years, the equivalent of traveling 800,000 to 1,000,000 miles before refueling. The energy expended during this time is estimated as equivalent to 425 million gallons of fuel oil.

The closing of many U.S. shoreside air bases beyond the continental U.S. increased the importance of the U.S. Supercarrier; often called, "...the one thousand mile airstrip" because of its ability to move about in contrast to the fixed shoreside air bases. Carriers are less vulnerable to attack than shoreside air bases by virtue of their mobility.

Criticism Is Not Constructive

After the Revolt of the Admirals the Korean War aircraft carriers were in favor; however, criticism of aircraft carriers and Supercarriers in particular has been revived during the past quarter-century. In 1970 a U.S. senator told the U.S. Joint Senate-House Armed Services Subcommittee that, ". . . rapid technological advances in missile development have made the carrier unusable in all but the most limited conflicts." Other critics argue that the aircraft carriers' "time has come", yet they have no viable alternative.

Must Carriers Follow History?

Five major warship types have ruled the seas at various times during recorded history: ancient galleys for about 2,000 years; sailing ships of the line for about 400 years; steam-powered ironclads for about 60 years; turreted battleships for about 60 years; aircraft carriers for more than a half-century. Each consecutive reign became shorter; however, does this prove that the aircraft carrier must follow the pattern? The esteemed philosopher/author George Santayana wrote, "He who fails to learn the lessons of history is doomed to repeat them", and this observation is worthy of our attention, but there are those who would use it to erroneously prognosticate the demise of the aircraft carrier as the premier naval weapon on the basis of the foregoing data without an indepth analysis of the carrier's future role.

Carriers Support Air Power

The fact that the carrier exists only for its aircraft is overlooked or ignored. The aircraft carrier is a highly complex mobile airfield, supply dump, maintenance depot, and living quarters for a potent air wing; therefore, why not condemn air power as well?

Supercarriers Dehumanizing?

Then there are those who call the Supercarriers a "people-eating weapons system" because of the 6,000 trained crew required for its operation. They also insist that, "the dehumanizing effect of having 6,000 souls 'stuffed' into one hull wouldn't seem to be the best environment for good order and discipline, even under the most enlightened leadership." Contrary to this accusation, aircraft carrier crew morale is extremely high, and living and working conditions are better than on the smaller ships.

ICBM's To Replace Carriers?

It was like 1949 all over again when two U.S. Secretaries of Defense brought the aircraft carrier's rationale sharply into question. In February, 1975 the Secretary of Defense prepared a defense posture statement that claimed the submarine should be regarded "as the Navy's main contribution to nuclear deterrence", and although carriers are able to launch nuclear weapons "their main justification should be nonnuclear."

Three years later another U.S. Defense Secretary in a secret memorandum, made it very clear that the key function of U.S. Navy aircraft carriers will be restricted to provide protection for critical waterways, bases and SLOC's. The memo sharply eliminated any carrier role in strikes against the Soviet mainland or covering invasion beachheads. It also deemphasized the carrier's power projection role and proposed a reduction in the U.S. Navy carrier force from 12 to 10 carriers. It was plain that carriers were being relegated to serve as a policing force, rather than a frontline, sophisticated fighting force and Supercarriers were to be wasted as Sea

Control Ships. It was a time when Intercontinental Ballistic Missiles with nuclear warheads were considered as the only first line of defense/offense for the U.S. Contrary to von Clausewitz, it was to be all-out war or nothing! The Secretary of Defense also made a decision to cut back on F-14 Tomcat production in favor of the "relatively low-cost F-18's, which are cheaper than F-14's." These are two very different fighting machines.

Admirals' Advice Ignored

Another Secretary of Defense ignored the professional judgment of the Chairman of the Joint Chiefs of Staff Admiral William J. Crowe, Jr. and the CNO Admiral Carlisle Trost, in 1989, by ordering *USS Midway* (CVB-41) and *USS Coral Sea* (CVB-43) decommissioned when the two replacement Supercarriers *USS Abraham Lincoln* and *USS George Washington* had not yet been commissioned. This unfortunate decision dashed the U.S. Navy's hope for 15 Carrier Battle Groups (CVBG) which it considered necessary.

Secretary Lehman Champions Carriers

Former Navy Secretary John F. Lehman, who had been a naval aviator, defended the carriers with statements such as, ". . . carriers enable smaller ships to survive", and, "The modern U.S. Navy carrier battle group . . . would never have allowed Mirages . . . and Exocets...the opportunities permitted in the Falklands against the British Force." Secretary Lehman told a congressional committee that carriers are, ". . . far less vulnerable than an Air Force base that can't move at 31 knots, far less than an Army Division which only travels about four knots, and less vulnerable than this building (Rayburn House Office Building) because they are made of HY-80, HY-100 (steel) armorplate, rimmed armor decks, multiple hulls and so forth. Yes, they are vulnerable, but not as vulnerable as anything else in the world."

In 1984 the U.S. Congress was concerned about a 240 billion dollar defense budget and feared it would go over 300 billion dollars in 1985. The Supercarrier was singled out for investigation, questioning its unnecessary high cost, as was the need for 15 carrier battle groups. A CVBG covers a 600 mile diameter area on the sea, below the sea, and in the air and is a formidable force. Even "Navytown" newspapers joined the U.S. Congress in its witchhunt with headlines such as "Carrier armadas run up budget."

The foregoing attacks on aircraft carriers in general and Supercarriers in particular are masked under the heading of "Cost Effectiveness." It is foolish to choose the cheapest weapon when it can't do the job. In 1978, the U.S. administration tried to scuttle nuclear-powered Supercarriers in favor of smaller fossil fuelfired substitutes. Germany made many weapon decisions on the basis of economy before and during World War II, which helped the Allied victory.

JUMP-JETS OR GIANTS

An examination of the smaller alternatives to Supercarriers must be made to properly evaluate any small carrier proposal. Among the possibilities are the following approximate viable smaller carrier sizes: 35,000 to 60,000 ton medium size carrier (CVV) capable of operating current and proposed Conventional Take-Off and Landing (CTOL) aircraft; 15,000 to 25,000 ton (VSS) V/STOL carrier or through-deck cruiser operating only V/STOL planes and helicopters; 13,000 ton Vickers Versatile Aircraft Carrier (V-VAC) which would operate a mix of STO/VL and V/STOL aircraft and helicopters; and the smallest of all are the 9,000 ton Litton/Ingalls Flight Deck DD-963 destroyers built on *Spruance* class hulls and the Frigate-size Vosper Thornycroft Harrier Carrier, each of which would be able to operate STO/VL and V/STOL aircraft and helicopters.

Big Carriers Do More For Less

At the outset it is important to mention that, in the design of aircraft carriers, one objective is to determine the ship cost per embarked aircraft and it has been found that this cost per aircraft actually decreases as the ship size increases. In addition, the installed shaft horsepower per displacement ton also decreases as the ship size increases. A *Spruance* class destroyer requires about 10 1/4 shaft horsepower per ton while a *Nimitz* class Supercarrier needs only about 3 1/2 shaft horsepower per ton. These are important facts about Supercarriers worth remembering.

Aircraft Control Carrier Design

When preparing an aircraft carrier design, the major factor to consider is the aircraft it is intended to operate. During the immediate pre-World War II years few strategists and tacticians foresaw the fighter plane's ability to score so effectively against dive bombers and torpedo planes, and eventually assume many of their functions. It was the same with the emergent V/STOL Harrier which, although not considered equal to contemporary CTOL aircraft, surprised everyone with its high performance when it engaged nearly every type of U.S. Air Force, Navy and Marine Corps aircraft in mock combat below 20,000 feet and proved a formidable and worthy opponent; often superior.

A V/STOL fixed-wing aircraft must be as small and light as possible in order to satisfy the necessary high thrust to weight ratio. Conversely, the U.S. Navy's F-14 Tomcat, one of the finest fighter planes in the world, is fitted with an extremely sophisticated electronics and weapons suite enabling it to engage several adversaries simultaneously. This makes the Tomcat a very large fighter, almost the same physical size and weight as the Douglas A-3 Skywarrior on whose behalf the Supercarrier was created. The large size of Supercarriers is necessary in order to launch and recover aircraft such as the Tomcat; however, the fixed-wing V/STOL or STO/VL can operate from the minimum length flight deck. Each aircraft has an important place in naval aviation; hence the difficulty in carrier selection.

Flight Deck Governs Hull Size

It is axiomatic that the flight deck governs the hull size, and the flight deck size is controlled by the number and/or type of aircraft to be embarked.

The minimum flight deck length required to land all current U.S. Navy CTOL aircraft is about 680 feet, assuming a minimum WOD (Wind-Over-Deck) velocity of about 20 knots and a recovery glide angle of about 3 1/2 degrees. This will not permit simultaneous launching or aircraft parking; therefore, an 8 1/2 degree angled deck and increased flight deck length to about 920 feet is necessary to permit a simultaneous launching and recovery capability.

CVV Aircraft Carrier

With a displacement of about 60,000 tons and a 920 feet long flight deck, the medium size aircraft carrier could accommodate all CTOL aircraft types in the U.S. Navy inventory. Complement would be about 50 of these planes. The estimated cost of this carrier is about 2/3 that of a *Nimitz* class Supercarrier. A smaller hull in the 35,000 tons range could accommodate a small number of only a selected few types of aircraft in the U.S. Navy inventory which would cancel its effectiveness as a first-line carrier.

The 60,000 ton CVV does not appear to be a viable alternative to the *Nimitz* Supercarriers, mainly because of its small air wing, which would be about 1/2 that of the *Nimitz*. This increases the ship tonnage per plane from 917 to 1,200. The 60,000 ton CVV could, however, augment the single Supercarrier in each CVBG, as was done in World War II when the light cruiser hull *Independence* class light carriers served in the same task group with *Essex* class carriers. In fact, during peacetime the CVV could sail with the CVBG as a Supercarrier stand-in and, if a low level conflict got out of hand, the Supercarrier could join the CVBG, with a proper escort, of course.

VSS Aircraft Carrier

A very useful and popular type would be the VSS aircraft carrier operating V/STOL and STO/VL aircraft. V/STOL carriers are not new, having experienced the U.S. Navy LPD, LHA and LHD assault ships, as well as the Royal Navy carriers *Bulwark*, *Hermes* and *Invincible* class, plus the *Garibaldi*, *Principe De Asturias* and *Kiev*. Since the U.S. Congress rejected Admiral Elmo R. Zumwalt's

Sea Control Ship in 1974, the U.S. seems to have abandoned new sea control V/STOL-STO/VL aircraft carriers. The 15,000 to 25,000 ton VSS carrier can live with a Ski-Jump axial flight deck without catapults or arresting cables. The VSS flight deck can be any length; however, longer is better to enable V/STOL aircraft to make a deck run before takeoff. During an Operational Readiness Evaluation (ORE) on *USS Franklin D. Roosevelt* (CVB-42) in 1976 with AV-8A Harriers, the planes made STO (Short Take Offs) with runs of 300 to 600 feet, depending upon the takeoff weight. It must be remembered that the *Roosevelt* was not fitted with a Ski-Jump which would have shortened the takeoff runs. The very minimum carrier size that can operate a partial range of current U.S. Navy CTOL carrier aircraft is about 35,000 tons; therefore, it is imprudent to select a vessel of that size or larger as a VSS aircraft carrier. If a 600 feet long flight deck is selected, the displacement could be approximately 18,000 tons. From 25 to 30 V/STOL fixed-wing aircraft and helicopters could be flown from this VSS candidate.

The VSS cannot hope to replace the Supercarrier in the foreseeable future; however, it is ideal for very important missions: ASW operations using on-board Harriers and LAMPS III helicopters; dedicated SCS and convoy escort duty; close air support for amphibious operations using shipborne helicopter gunships and Harriers; and mine countermeasures using embarked MH-53E Sea Dragon helicopters with minesweeping sleds.

Vickers Versatile Aircraft Carrier

The prestigious British shipbuilder, Vickers, developed a 13,000 tons displacement V/STOL aircraft carrier design called the Vickers

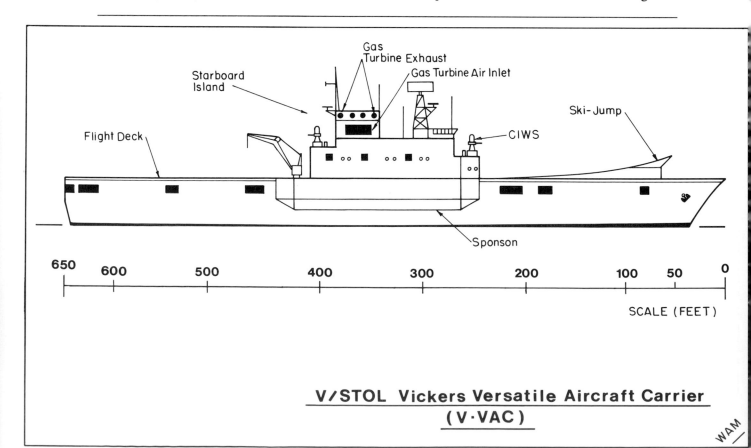

V/STOL Vickers Versatile Aircraft Carrier (V·VAC)

Versatile Aircraft Carrier (V-VAC). Compared to a Supercarrier, this seems small but its displacement is more than *USS Independence* class and *Garibaldi*, and a bit less than the *Invincible* class, defunct American SCS, and *Principe De Asturias* which puts it in good company. A flight deck of about 575 feet long could be fitted. Vickers drawings reveal a Ski-Jump flight deck. Air Group comprises a mixed bag of about a dozen Harriers and helicopters. Diesel engine power has been proposed. This design could engage in the same activities as the VSS; however, it is questionable if it could handle the large Sea Dragon mine countermeasures helicopter.

Litton/Ingalls Flight Deck DD-963

The reputable American Litton/Ingalls Shipyard is the builder of the gas turbine-powered DD-963 *Spruance* class destroyers and has developed a design for a 9,000 ton displacement STO/VL aircraft carrier based upon the 7,800 ton displacement *Spruance* class. Four General Electric LM2500 gas turbines are arranged COGAG in which two are connected to the twin-screw drive train for cruising while one or both of the remaining gas turbines can be clutched to the gears as additional power is needed. The 80,000 shaft horsepower can produce speeds in excess of 30 knots.

The original design divided the 560 foot flight deck into three sections: a 332 feet takeoff runway on the forward half; a 170 feet long full beam hangar just aft of midships; and a helicopter pad located aft of the hangar. Now that the Ski-Jump is here this could be added to the takeoff runway. About a half-dozen Harriers and helicopters could be carried.

Vosper Thornycroft Harrier Carrier

The innovative British Vosper Thornycroft shipbuilders conceived a frigate-size aircraft carrier in 1975, designed specifically to operate eight British Aerospace Sea Harriers. Alternatively, eight Westland Sea King antisubmarine helicopters could be flown from the new design.

Named the Harrier Carrier, this design was to displace just over 6,000 tons, had an overall length of 450 feet and could attain a top speed of 30 knots. A complement of 250 officers and crew were required to operate the ship. The full length Flight Deck was a conventional through type with an island offset to the starboard side which allowed about 40 feet between the island and the port side deck edge. Two aircraft elevators and a Flight Deck turntable were to be installed to ensure rapid and safe deployment of aircraft. In addition, it was planned to provide a pilot-released hold-back tie attached to the landing gear struts which was to enable the engine to reach full power before the Harrier began its short take off (STO).

The Harrier Carrier powerplant requires description because of its unusual and innovative selection and location within the hull. Gas turbine propulsion was selected in order to operate the ship as well as the aircraft with the same fuel; however, the unusual equipment selection was turbo-electric drive in which gas turbines were to drive electric generators and the generated electricity would then power electric motors that are connected to the propellers. It will be recalled that the U.S. Navy carriers *USS Lexington* and *USS Saratoga* of the 1920s were fitted with turbo-electric propulsion machinery; using steam turbines instead of gas turbines which had not yet been invented at that time.

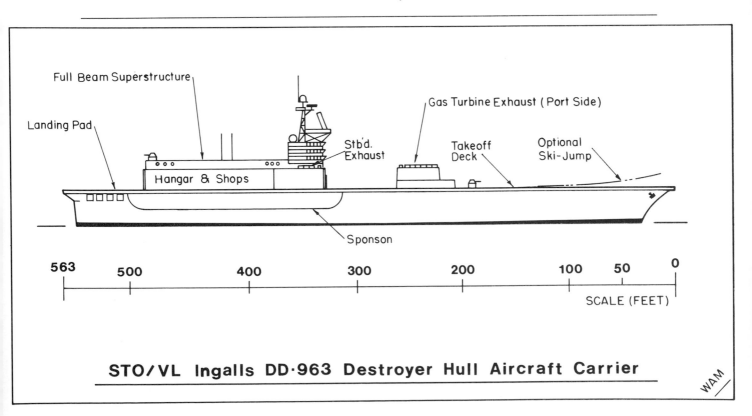

STO/VL Ingalls DD·963 Destroyer Hull Aircraft Carrier

The propulsion scheme was to use nine electric generators, each driven by a General Motors Detroit Allison 501K gas turbine producing 4,500 brake horsepower each. In view of the fact that the generators transmitted power to the two electric motors via flexible electrical cables rather than a conventional direct mechanical drive, it was not necessary to locate the turbo-generators in the same compartment or adjacent compartment to the electric motors. Vosper Thornycroft decided to locate the turbo-generator units high in the hull on the Hangar Deck. Five turbo-generator units were located beneath the Island while the remaining four turbo-generators were arranged at the aft end just forward of the transom. This arrangement has several advantages: the motor compartment becomes considerably smaller and, therefore, presents a smaller target to enemy fire and the distribution of turbo-generators into two compartments a safe distance apart from each other and from the motor room provides added safety from critical battle damage. In addition, the gas turbine air supply and exhaust ducts to the atmosphere are considerably shorter with the gas turbines on the Hangar Deck than if they were placed in the customary location – below, in the bowels of the ship.

It was planned to provide sufficient propulsion fuel for a 4,500 mile range at 16 knots plus 500 tons of fuel for aircraft operation. The basic premise and the advantages of creating the smallest and cheapest autonomous warship that was able to exploit the unique operational capabilities of the Sea Harrier was apparently lost in the minds of naval planners because, as with the Vickers Versatile Aircraft Carrier and the Litton/Ingalls Flight Deck DD-963, the advanced concepts of mini-carriers were either ignored or rejected and not even prototypes were constructed.

If constructed today, there is no doubt that the Harrier Carrier would be fitted with a Ski-Jump Flight Deck to enhance Harrier operation.

Air Cover For Small Combatants

Small V/STOL carriers will give every ship in the Navy air cover; especially those small ship formations that do not warrant the attention of a fleet carrier. Air Cover has become the all-important factor in naval and commercial ship safety during wartime or in hostile waters during peacetime.

Sea Control Ship Requirements

Many of the foregoing V/STOL carriers would qualify as a Sea Control Ship. Too many experts claim that long-range patrol planes, destroyer types and submarines can do the job. Sea Control's foremost challenge is the long-range missile launched from planes, ships or submarines and, in order to counter these, sea-based aircraft are

The Vosper Thornycroft Harrier Carrier is an excellent solution to achieve naval air striking power at modest cost when constructed on a frigate-size hull of about 6,000 tons displacement.

essential. Antennae must be as high as possible in order for radar to detect incoming missiles, ships and aircraft and this requires shipborne aircraft; not just one, but enough to cover all horizons. Sea Control Ships can be austere and inexpensive with no specific size necessary, but with acceptable displacement ranging from 9,000 to 15,000 tons. Numbers count in Sea Control with at least 25 to 30 ships at sea to not only protect the SLOC's, but to engage in power projection as well.

SCS Speed and Powerplant

Any SCS with a speed below 30 knots is underpowered. Speed should be the same as Supercarriers in order to be able to operate in CVBG's when necessary. Speed is also necessary if the SCS is called upon to deter a hostile force during Sea Control or Power Projection activities. The powerplant should be a combined type such as CODOG (COmbined Diesel Or Gas turbine) in which the gas turbines can be disengaged from the power drive for cruising in order to conserve fuel and extend the range. The SCS operates at cruising speed for most of its life on diesel or gas turbine power; however, it must have the capability of high speed when necessary by clutching the reserve gas turbines into the drive train. Gas turbo-electric drive can also be applied to the SCS.

Assault Ships Don't Qualify

Although the *Iwo Jima* class and *Tarawa* class ships have been repeatedly nominated as Sea Control Ships, it is felt that Sea Control demands a purpose-designed and built vessel. Using the assault ships for SCS would push them into a function for which they were not designed and, in the event of a war emergency, they would be forced to abandon the Sea Control role and return to their primary function. Assault ships are too slow and the newer designs are too big. To accomplish its mission the SCS must be leaner and faster.

Sea Control; Important Mission

The SCS can have an axial Ski-Jump flight deck without catapults or arresting cables. Sea Control has many interpretations, but the most descriptive is, ". . . to assure freedom of safe passage on the high seas for warships, merchantmen, and aircraft." This important task requires a large quantity of ships and aircraft because planes are the major weapons for successful control of the sea. SCS helicopters and V/STOL-STO/VL Jump-Jet aircraft have the capability to detect surface ships, missiles, submarines, and long-range reconnaissance planes, as well as destroy them.

Supercarriers For The Big Punch

The large, powerful Supercarrier and its overpowering air wing of sophisticated aircraft will always be necessary because it has the amazing ability to apply devastating force virtually anywhere on this planet. They cannot; however, be called upon to cover every one of the many trouble spots that erupt periodically, because Supercarriers are too few in number. Further, to apply Supercarriers to quench every brushfire in the Middle East, Latin America, Indian Ocean area and other flammable areas is exposing the Supercarrier to unreasonable risk and it would be like using a sledge hammer to kill a fly. A CVV or VSS could be sent to low-level problems or, in short notice situations, one or more SCS could be diverted to the troubled area; thereby, maintaining a national presence quickly and at moderate cost and risk.

ASW Operations
Instead of depending upon Supercarriers for ASW operations, smaller and more numerous VSS, SCS and even smaller Ski-Jump decked V/STOL carriers operating Jump-Jet Harriers can handle the task with greater efficiency because ASW operations demand a numerical superiority against a submerged submarine. The Jump-Jet Harrier is a force multiplier and is capable of filling the large performance gap between the shore-based, long-range patrol/reconnaissance plane and the short-range helicopter. The Jump-Jet provides quick response over a wide area and is capable of moderate-range coverage by using the new sensors available or those under development. ASW carriers must have a speed well in excess of 30 knots because submarines can reach that speed while submerged.

V/STOL's On CTOL Carriers
During the ORE on *USS Franklin D. Roosevelt* in 1976, previously mentioned, the Harriers took off quicker than the CTOL aircraft because of their self-starters and no need for catapult hook-up. On recovery only a small area was needed for Vertical Landing and there were no bolters or waveoffs because the Harriers could hover away from the CTOL landing path until it was clear to land. The amusing but valid Harrier doctrine is that: "It is better to stop and then land instead of landing and then trying to stop." During the ORE, Harriers transferred to *USS Guam* in the Mediterranean and then conducted operations in the Indian Ocean. *Guam* then returned to the Mediterranean where the Harriers flew back to *Roosevelt*. V/STOL aircraft can operate from CTOL carriers but CTOL aircraft cannot operate from V/STOL carriers; therefore, it is reasonable to include a squadron or more of V/STOL-STO/VL aircraft on every CTOL carrier to provide greater operational flexibility.

JUMP-JETS *AND* GIANTS
Until the awe-inspiring, supersonic, sophisticated, heavy punch, 70,000 pound carrier-based fighters can V/STOL or STO/VL, a well-balanced naval air service, comprising V/STOL and CTOL aircraft, plus Supercarriers and CVV's for CTOL and V/STOL aircraft, are necessary for high intensity conflicts. Also needed are VSS, SCS and smaller Ski-Jump carriers to employ helicopters and Harrier Jump-Jets for the many functions previously discussed.

The smaller carriers should complement and not replace the Supercarrier; however, many naval professionals argue for an all-giant carrier Navy while others debate for an all Jump-Jet aircraft and Ski-Jump carrier Navy. Actually, they all have their place and function so it is not a matter of Jump-Jet or Giant but an objective blend of JUMP-JETS *AND* GIANTS for a well-balanced navy.

BRITISH AEROSPACE-DOWTY GROUP SKY HOOK
It will be recalled that the Italian prophet of air power, Giulio Douhet, was quoted in the Prologue as saying: "To prepare for war demands exercise of imagination." The only nation on the winning side of World War II that has, ". . . exercised imagination" in shipborne aviation is Britain. Her austere economy has sharply curtailed military spending, otherwise Britain would no doubt have gone further than the Harrier and the many aircraft carrier innovations.

It is quite normal for a victorious nation to continue to produce and depend upon the same type weapons with which it won the previous war. The same is true regarding its strategy. Conversely, the loser researches new weapons and develops new strategies with the hope that these will be better than those it was using when the war was lost. Carl von Clausewitz experienced losing battles in the Napoleonic Wars and, therefore, went to work devising new philosophies on war.

Military Resist Change
In general the military resists rapid change. This was succinctly stated by military authority Basil Henry Liddell Hart: "The only thing harder than getting a new idea into the military mind is to get an old one out."

Small Carriers In Rough Seas
In the foregoing paragraphs V/STOL carriers as small as 6,000 tons were described. A ship of this size has one major disadvantage when operating as an aircraft carrier; it rolls and pitches more than a larger carrier during high sea states. The fantail portion of the flight deck on ships of this size can experience a vertical movement of about 35 feet in a sea state six (30 foot waves) which occurs an average of 130 hours per year in the North Atlantic. Obviously, this large vertical movement has a detrimental effect on the operation of fixed-wing VTOL or V/STOL aircraft.

Harriers Versus Helicopters
Although both are VTOL aircraft, helicopters and Harriers have diametrically opposite hovering characteristics. Helicopters are designed to hover for long periods with complete control. They have a relatively low wing loading and, although they are easily disturbed by turbulence, they have excellent vertical maneuverability. Helicopters are also fitted with RAST and Harpoon systems. Harriers and other fixed-wing VTOL aircraft have a higher wing loading and are insignificantly affected by wind gusts. Harriers are designed to land and takeoff vertically but not to hover for long periods and have very little vertical maneuverability. When the Harrier is in a vertical landing or takeoff mode, once committed, it must continue in that course of action from which it is difficult, but not impossible, to deviate. This makes landing on a wet, sharply rolling and pitching deck fraught with danger. In order to remedy this problem, British Aerospace and the Dowty Group conceived the Sky Hook in 1986 which clearly illustrates the "exercise of imagination."

Sky Hook Crane
Sky Hook consists of a space-stabilized, single-knuckle robot crane that is hinged to the deck of the mother ship. The digitally controlled crane compensates for the ship's roll, pitch and heave and yaw by isolating the crane head from all ship motion. This is accomplished very accurately by using an electronic control system which detects excursions of the ship relative to its mean path and articulates the crane to counteract the deviations in such a manner

that the crane head does not abandon its fixed position, irrespective of ship movement. The crane capture head is fitted with a female probe jack and four docking pads to secure the Harrier. Port and starboard cranes are fitted.

Sky Hook Harrier

The planes embarked on a Sky Hook ship can either keep the landing gear retracted or have the landing gear removed. The Sky Hook Harrier has a male fitting installed atop the fuselage at the balance point to match the female probe jack on the crane head.

Sky Hook Launching

Launching begins when the crane swings over the side of the ship with the Harrier secured to the crane capture head; pulled up firmly against the four docking pads. The engine is self-started and power is increased for effective power reaction control. The lock-on jack is then extended to place the aircraft in the center of the "capture window." When all is ready the pilot increases power until hover condition is achieved. Sensing this removal of weight, the lock-on jack female fitting automatically releases the aircraft and quickly retracts upwards. The jack is programmed so it cannot prematurely release the plane until the jack experiences zero weight. The aircraft is then free to hover and transition into forward flight.

Sky Hook Recovery

Recovery is accomplished automatically. The pilot hovers his plane within the "capture window" which is a 10-foot cube located 15 feet below the crane head. Sensors on the crane head determine the position of the aircraft and the capture control system guides the female lock-on jack to engage and lock on to the aircraft male pick-up point. This is proven technology, having been employed on numerous industrial robots. After lock-on has been accomplished power is reduced slightly as in a free hover. The lock-on jack senses the weight of the plane and pulls the Harrier up against the four docking pads. After an internal lock is engaged the aircraft engine may be shut down. Sky Hook then swings inboard at which time the space-stabilization inputs are progressively reduced until the crane moves in harmony with the ship, but also constraining the plane against the motion of the ship until the aircraft can be safely secured.

With the landing gear still retracted or removed the Harrier can be deposited in a special cradle from which it can be serviced, rearmed and refueled. The cradle can be mounted on tracks to facilitate stowage in a hangar as necessary.

A hypothetical Sky Hook operation would start with a Harrier (No.1) launching from the Ski-Jump rail runway (No.2) while another Harrier (No.3) is hoisted by space stabilized robot crane (No.4) This digitally controlled crane will place the Harrier on the launching rail (No.2). Meanwhile, another Harrier (No.5) returns from a mission to be caught by the Sky Hook Capture Head (No.6) and lowered to the cradle (No.7) for refueling and rearming in preparation for the next mission. (British Aerospace/Modified by author/Courtesy Brendan Morrissey)

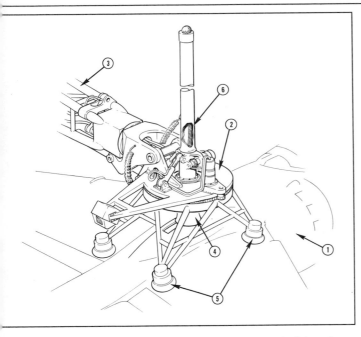

The Harrier (No.1) is held fast to the Capture Head (No.2) of the robot crane (No.3) by the Female Probe (No.4) The Jack (No.6) pulls the Harrier against the four Docking Pads (No.5) to secure the plane to the crane. (British Aerospace/Modified by author/Courtesy Brendan Morrissey)

Ski-Jump Deck
The mini-carrier can also be fitted with a Ski-Jump deck for STO (Short Take Off) operations conducted simultaneously with Sky Hook recoveries and helicopter flights.

Tested Ashore
The Sky Hook concept has been successfully tested ashore with wind gusts up to 25 miles per hour.

Unlimited Possibilities
The numerous possibilities of Sky Hook installations on small ships are exciting to the innovative mind. In addition to convoy, ASW, SCS, and amphibious assault air support, the Sky Hook-fitted small combatants can assist in CAP duties as AAW picket or screen ships patrolling the outer fringes of the CVBG. The VTOL fighter can remain on the Sky Hook or Ski-Jump ramp; armed, fueled and perhaps even manned and ready for instantaneous launching. This would result in continuous cover with fewer aircraft, less fuel consumed, less engine airframe life reduction, and reduced pilot fatigue.

AIR-CAPABLE AUXILIARIES
The Supercarrier will remain the keystone of naval aviation; however, the ability to operate aircraft from many smaller ships is an undeniable asset to any naval force. The Sky Hook-fitted frigate-size carrier has the stealth, unpredictability, and flexibility of operation that the Supercarrier lacks. Now, even merchantmen can be fitted with the Sky Hook during peacetime for defense in the event of an emergency such as the Mayaguez Incident, previously cov-

ered in Chapter VII, or in the event of war. For many years merchant ships have been successfully adapted to handle aircraft, and new ideas such as the Ski-Jump deck and Sky Hook will produce better aviation auxiliaries. Installing Sky Hook on freighters and tankers in peacetime can be accomplished without interfering with the normal operation of the ship.

World War I, World War II and the Falklands War proved the feasibility and advantages of employing commercial merchantmen and passenger ships as auxiliary aircraft carriers. This applies more today than ever with the advent of V/STOL and STO/VL aircraft, Ski-Jump decks and Sky Hook.

Fast Merchantmen Imperative
With submarines exceeding 30 knots while submerged, the fastest merchantman can barely reach that speed. If merchantmen are to run in convoys or be used as auxiliary carriers their speed must be increased to at least 35 knots. This will demand more power and slender hull lines, neither of which will please the ship owners because the former will increase the initial engine cost as well as the fuel cost, while the fine lines would reduce the ship's cargo capacity. This reduction in income should not be borne by the ship owner. The Navy must, therefore, compensate the ship owners/operators for this added expense and loss of revenue to assure an ample supply of commercial ships that will be useful in wartime. Higher speed will, of course, enable the ship owner to move his cargo faster.

Falklands War STUFT
It will be recalled that commercial ships were converted into seaplane carriers in World War I; cargo ships were converted into escort aircraft carriers in World War II; and during the Falklands War, the Royal Navy converted merchant ships into transports, auxiliary aircraft carriers, assault ships, ammunition and stores ships, minesweepers, hospital ships, and so many others that the modified commercial ships actually outnumbered the combatants. The British call these STUFT (Ships Taken Up From Trade). The Royal Navy has inducted many commercial ships into the service so it can arm them with missile launchers, infra-red decoy launchers, chaff launch-

RFA (Royal Fleet Auxiliary) Reliant is a commercial containership that served as an operational platform for ASW helicopters and related utility missions in the Falklands War. After the war RFA Reliant was fitted with U.S. Navy Arapaho containerized aviation support facilities. (Royal Navy Photograph [MoD])

ers and so forth. STUFT were a big factor in the British victory in the Falklands War.

VTOL FRS Mk.I Sea Harriers and GR.3 Harriers plus helicopters operated from the decks of containerships RFA (Royal Fleet Auxiliary), *Reliant, Atlantic Conveyor* and *Contender Bezant* in the Falklands action. This proved that fixed-wing, as well as rotary wing operations from commercial ships are feasible, safe and economical, and that the ship's rapid mobilization could mean the difference between victory and defeat.

Arapaho Helicopter Support System

RFA Reliant served as an operational platform for ASW helicopters and related utility missions. The ship had been fitted with leased U.S. Navy Arapaho equipment and demonstrated the successful use of this system under operational conditions in the Mediterranean and in the South Atlantic.

The Arapaho System

Arapaho is the first system that provided a modularized and self-sustaining seaborne facility for helicopters that was capable of performing aviation maintenance aboard a commercial containership while at anchor or at sea. It was also a seagoing ASW helicopter platform. The modular system consists of 8 x 8 x 40 feet standard transportation containers modified for workshops, electric generating units, air conditioning machinery, JP-5 fuel, potable water, sewage holding tank, and living quarters. The Arapaho system consists of 395 modules which are interconnected by means of integral vestibules and inclined ladders. About 130 modules must be installed above the main deck due to safety and functional requirements. A 57 x 180 feet hangar kit is designed for quick and easy assembly or disassembly as is the 73 x 165 feet Flight Deck. The entire system can be transported by train, trailer truck and by ship. It can be loaded aboard a commercial containership and made operable within 24 hours. Arapaho can also be installed on shore as necessary.

Operational Concepts

The U.S. Navy developed Arapaho in the late 1970s and early 1980s to provide convoy protection using a commercial containership as an ASW helicopter platform. In late 1982 Arapaho was demonstrated during sea trials on board the containership *Export Leader*. The ship was fitted with a Flight Deck supported above the Main Deck so the ship's crew could work on the Main Deck beneath the Flight Deck. Hundreds of helicopter takeoffs and landings were made during the demonstration.

U.S. Army interest in a floating aircraft maintenance facility had begun during the Vietnam War when USNS *Corpus Christie Bay* was extensively modified for this mission. Experience with the converted ship proved that Army depot maintenance on helicopters in a remote wartime theater for prolonged periods is successful. *Corpus Christie Bay* did not apply the modular concept.

The U.S. Army Arapaho system is arranged around a U.S. Army AVIM (AViation Intermediate Maintenance) company that could be erected on board a containership or ashore.

Useful to both Army and Navy needs, Arapaho's primary advantage is the rapid installation on ship or shore; however, the vari-

Commercial containerships and tankers are ideal candidates to operate STO/VL aircraft from permanent or temporary Ski-Jump decks. In this artist's conception a heavily loaded Rolls-Royce-powered Harrier is airborne from a temporary Ski-Jump deck on a containership. Permanent Ski-Jump decks can be installed on tankers and containerships without interfering with the commercial operation of the ship. (Rolls-Royce Ltd., Courtesy Edna Carrozza)

ous components of these massive kits must be previously constructed and ready for assembly.

Arapaho is an American Indian Algonquin tribe whose name in Crow language means "enemy with many skins." It is possible that the Arapaho name was selected because the Arapaho system converts a peacetime containership into a multi-purpose instrument of war, (many skins).

Permanent Air-Capable Installations

Tankers, bulk carriers and containerships are the ideal candidates for conversion to aviation auxiliaries because flight decks can be installed about 20 feet above the main deck without interfering with the commercial operation of the ship. On tankers, the flight deck will be well above the maze of piping, tank hatches, loading manifolds and walkways, while on containerships the flight deck can be fitted with removable rectangular sections as hatches to permit loading and unloading of containers. A 12 to 15 degree Ski-Jump should be built into the flight decks.

Containership flight decks will weigh about 1,000 tons while large tanker flight decks might weigh twice as much.

As was proposed for the SCS, MILVAN containers for aircraft refueling, rearming and basic maintenance would be located on the main deck, clear of the ship's basic operations. The flight deck designs can be standardized for tankers and containerships with sections constructed shoreside and erected on board. This is better than the MAC of World War II. (See Chapt.III photo and Chapt.IV story of the MAC.)

Tanker candidates must be crude oil carriers or heavy fuel oil carriers, but not those that transport refined petroleum products, in the interest of safety.

Using Ski-Jump decks, the Harriers can operate in the STO/VL mode to carry heavier loads and extend their range.

No Time To Convert

Under ordinary circumstances the flight decks would be installed in the event of war but in today's world of rapid-fire incidents the next conflagration will be a "come as you are" event. In order to satisfy this possibility it appears wise to construct or retrofit the fastest available tankers and containerships with permanent flight decks. This would make the auxiliary carriers ready for action as soon as the aircraft and air crew are aboard. Another reason for permanent flight decks is the growing feeling among U.S. naval officers that the first wave of attackers will not only target combatants but merchantmen as well in order to cut our SLOC's with Europe and Asia. A flight deck-fitted tanker or containership will have a better chance of survival with a few Harriers on board.

Sky Hook Installations

The Sky Hook can be installed on selected merchantmen instead of Ski-Jump flight decks. Air-Capable merchantmen can mean the difference between victory or defeat.

VCASS SUPER COCKPIT

The employment of video displays and a multitude of electronics in the fighter pilots' cockpit appeared to be the answer to display and control problems in a Buck Rogers world; however, under some conditions, the electronic cockpits are able to display more data and symbols than the pilot is able to absorb. Much of the data is in code which the pilot must decipher instantly from instrument panel-mounted displays. HUD and panel displays provide two-dimensional viewing ports into a three-dimensional world which could become confusing to the pilot in a high-stress situation.

Technology Outpacing Pilots' Capability

Fighter plane control columns bristle with as many as nine switches, and throttle knobs have as many as seven. The pilot must remember the purpose of each and select the proper switch by touch alone. Cockpits with contemporary high-tech displays make the pilot work very hard just to understand what the plane is trying to tell him and, once he gets the message, his somewhat unwieldy controls hinder his efforts to relay his decision to the plane. This is not a criticism of modern aircraft design but, rather, an example of how modern aircraft technology has outpaced the pilot's ability to fly the sophisticated planes with the traditional panel-mounted instruments and conventional controls. This is especially true of shipboard aircraft because of their need for complex navigational and sensing electronics. Cockpit clutter had to go.

Imaginary Virtual World

This problem has been studied by the engineers and scientists in the Visual Display Systems Branch of the U.S. Air Force Armstrong Aerospace Medical Research Laboratory. They have developed a solution for the two-dimensional versus three-dimensional worlds problem that confuse the supersonic aircraft pilots. The solution is called "cognitive port" that will permit the pilot to place himself in an imaginary "virtual world" which actually exists only as a mathematical model in the memory of a computer. The "virtual world" has the effect but not the actual form of what is specified, yet it would be understood by the pilot who is shut off from the real world.

Outside World Composed of Symbols

By 1982 Thomas A. Furness III, Dean Kocian and their fellow researchers had produced a large helmet called VCASS (Visually Coupled Airborne Systems Simulator). This "Darth Vader" helmet resembled something out of Star Wars and was wired to a cockpit mockup and computer. The VCASS projected computer-generated symbols of a "virtual world" of synthetic reality directly into the pilot's field of vision inside the helmet. The pilot wearing the VCASS helmet could not see the outside world because it had been replaced by exact duplicates composed of symbols generated by the computer and projected into the pilot's vision inside the helmet. The projected images were concentrated on the pilot's foreal vision, which is the area of clearest vision, so he could analyze and process the projected information more efficiently.

Weapons; Voice-Selected, Eyeball-Aimed

As research progressed, a voice command selector was added to the helmet that could choose a particular weapon and fire it to the target at which the pilot is looking. This is accomplished by means of a sensor that tracks the pilot's own eyeball movement to determine where he is looking. This eyeball movement actuates a selector that aims the weapon at the proper target.

Future Improvements

Work is scheduled through 1996 when the Super Cockpit, as the VCASS is called, will include a color display, head-aimed weapons, voice-control of system functions, display of flight situation and navigation data, weapons delivery and sensor control, reduction of helmet size and incorporating all video and audio equipment in the helmet into a fully enclosed shell.

Transphasors Lighten Helmet

By using photonics-based transphasors instead of electronics-based computer transistors (using light energy instead of electric current) the designers reduced the weight considerably so that the Super Cockpit helmet added only 3 1/4 pounds including the umbilical cable.

Conversation With An Artificial Intelligence

The final stage in Super Cockpit development is for it to perform the duties of a second crew member with expert artificial intelligence that will monitor the airplane as well as the pilot's physical and mental state. In the future, the "second pilot" or "associate" will converse with the pilot in a clear female voice. The "associate" will perform mundane tasks such as preflight cockpit check and engine start.

The Phantom Co-pilot

Once the umbilical is plugged in, the takeoff is conventional; however, once the Super Cockpit visor is closed, the outside world is obscured and the pilot is in the "virtual world" of the computerized helmet. As was done in German night-fighter aircraft of World War

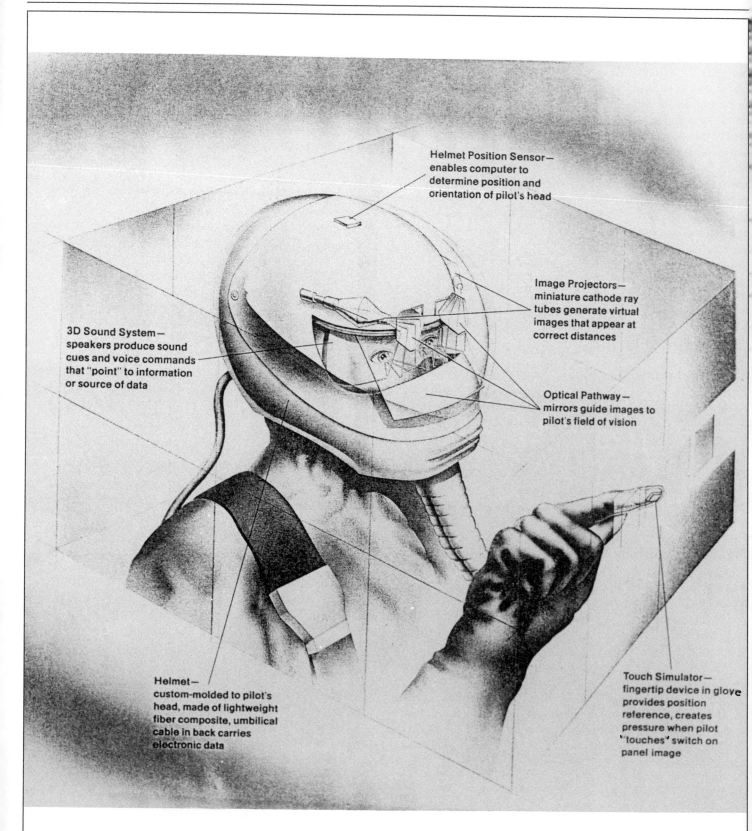

Helmet Position Sensor—
enables computer to
determine position and
orientation of pilot's head

Image Projectors—
miniature cathode ray
tubes generate virtual
images that appear at
correct distances

3D Sound System—
speakers produce sound
cues and voice commands
that "point" to information
or source of data

Optical Pathway—
mirrors guide images to
pilot's field of vision

Helmet—
custom-molded to pilot's
head, made of lightweight
fiber composite, umbilical
cable in back carries
electronic data

Touch Simulator—
fingertip device in glove
provides position
reference, creates
pressure when pilot
"touches" switch on
panel image

VCASS Super Helmet

II, when an enemy plane approaches a faint whine is heard in the helmet; the closer the enemy, the louder the whine. With the new helmet the pilot can choose his weapon, using a voice command to produce a large virtual weapons display in the helmet. He selects his weapon by raising his hand and "pushing" on a phantom button in mid-air on the virtual display he "sees." A tiny sensor on the fingertip of his glove gives off signals to indicate the weapon chosen by the location of the finger in the cockpit. The pilot senses a slight pressure on his fingertip and hears a click to confirm his selection. The hard-to-believe aspect of the flight is that should the pilot enter into a violent maneuver causing him to lose conciousness because of excessive "G" forces the "associate" will not only continue the turn but complete the encounter as well until the pilot regains conciousness.

Man Is Still Supreme

The pilots flying the latest agile, supersonic, shipborne aircraft need all the help they can get and the Super Cockpit helmet will project them into Star Wars and beyond! The revolutionary Super Cockpit is an aide but not a replacement for the pilot. As Admiral James S. Russell, Vice Chief of Naval Operations in the early 1960s, correctly forecast, ". . . the pilot is not obsolete, the missile has not replaced him and the space age has certainly not made him obsolete. Man is the maker, maintainer and operator of machines of war – the best, most versatile and by far the most reliable combination of sensing, deciding, acting device we can hope to see for a long time."

OPPOSITE: Artwork by Dale Glasgow. (Courtesy of Dale Glasgow)

Epilogue

The astounding advancements made by shipboard aviation during the past four-score years, literally one's lifetime, has no equal in its influence on ship and aircraft design; development of weapons and electronic devices; or impact on the implementation of strategic theories and tactical applications. In effect, it has revised the naval combat philosophies of the past several hundred years.

Beginning with the heroic flights of Eugene Ely from *USS Birmingham* and *USS Pennsylvania*, through the intensive planning and test flights of Murray Sueter, Washington Irving Chambers, Oliver Swann, Charles Samson, Arthur Longmore, Reginald Gregory, Glenn Curtiss, John Towers, Theodore Ellyson and many others, the vision of shipborne aircraft began to solidify out of the nebulous concept. Then, Flight Commander Edmonds made the first kill with an aerial torpedo which revealed the destructive power of the airplane as a war machine. *Ben-My-Chree*, *Campania* and other ramp-fitted converted merchantmen put the carrier theories into practice, followed by the through-deck carriers *HMS Eagle* and *HMS Argus* which were developed from experience with *HMS Furious*. *HMS Eagle*'s configuration then set the design pattern for future carriers.

The American gun turret takeoff platforms soon gave way to catapults on battleships and cruisers; then a collier was converted into the first U.S. aircraft carrier, *USS Langley*.

The Anglo-Americans took advantage of Japan at the Washington Naval and Disarmament Conference of 1921-1922. The Conference agreement treated carriers very lightly but concentrated heavily on the reduction of battleships and battlecruisers. Loathe to destroy their precious capital ships, Britain, Japan and the U.S. converted the powerful ships *HMS Glorious*, *HMS Courageous*, *Akagi*, *Amagi*, *USS Lexington* and *USS Saratoga* into aircraft carriers; not yet realizing the aircraft carrier's full potential.

Aircraft carrier construction boomed during the 1920s and 1930s while aircraft were being specially designed for operation from carriers; however, the British Fleet Air Arm was handicapped because of unification with the Royal Air Force. The Japanese launched the first purpose-built carrier, *Hosho*, in 1921, followed by the Royal Navy purpose-built carrier, *Hermes*, in 1923. The first U.S. Navy purpose-built carrier, *Ranger*, was launched 10 years later. After this time, virtually all fleet carriers were purpose-built, including classics such as *HMS Ark Royal*, *USS Yorktown*, *Enterprise* and *Hornet*, plus the Japanese *Hiryu*, *Soryu* and *Ryujo*.

Many classic Warbirds were developed during this period, including the American Curtiss Hawks, Boeing F4B series and Grumman F2F and F3F series; Fleet Air Arm Fairey Swordfish and Hawker Nimrod; and Japanese Navy Nakajima A2N1 and Aichi D1A2; however, these aircraft were eclipsed when the monoplane began replacing the biplane. The U.S. Navy Douglas Devastator and Dauntless, Brewster Buffalo, Grumman Wildcat and Vought Vindicator; Japanese Mitsubishi Zero-Sen, Aichi Val and Nakajima Kate; and Fleet Air Arm Blackburn Skua were some 1930s monoplanes that saw action in World War II.

Much had to be learned about aircraft carrier operation in hostile waters. This became obvious when *HMS Glorious* was sunk off Norway by German surface ship gunfire because it had been left unescorted and had no CAP in operation.

The Taranto and Pearl Harbor raids proved the advantage of a carrier force; however, only the Imperial Japanese Navy was aware of the potential devastation from a mass carrier attack.

History was made in the Battle of the Coral Sea because it was the first sea battle in which the opposing ships were never within sight of each other. Its aircraft had become the carrier's eyes and weapons. *USS Lexington* and the IJNS *Shoho* were sunk in this action. The sinking of *Lexington* was especially surprising because she was the largest and most formidable carrier in existence along with *Saratoga*. It was a greater shock than the sinking of *HMS Courageous*, *Ark Royal*, *Audacity* and *Hermes* because the big carrier was assumed to be impregnable.

The U.S. victory at Midway proved to be the turning point of the Pacific War in which Admiral Fletcher's *Yorktown* was sunk and put Admiral Spruance in command. The Japanese lost *Akagi*, *Kaga*, *Soryu* and *Hiryu* at Midway. Had the Japanese won the battle, the war would have lasted much longer.

The Battle of the Atlantic was saved through the use of escort carriers, most of which had been converted from commercial freighters. Armed with both Wildcats and Avengers they defeated the dual menace of submarines and Focke-Wulf 200 Kondors. Purpose-built escort carriers performed yeoman's service in the Pacific, covering beachheads, escorting transports and replenishing fleet carriers with aircraft. The *Essex* class and *Independence* class carriers were virtually mass-produced at this time.

After Midway the U.S. Navy went on the offensive with Fifth Fleet carriers leading the way to the Philippines via the Gilbert, Marshall and Mariana Island chains. This offensive culminated in the Battle of the Philippine Sea in which Admiral Spruance's fighter pilots scored heavily in the Marianas Turkey Shoot. The Japanese carriers IJNS *Shokaku*, *Hitaka* and *Taiho* were sunk during this fighting with no U.S. losses.

The Battle of Leyte Gulf followed; with "Doug Mac Arthur's Navy" (Seventh Fleet) covering the immediate beachhead with escort carriers which fought off Japanese capital ships. Meanwhile, Admiral Halsey's Third Fleet was speeding north to engage the Japanese decoy carriers of which *Zuikaku*, *Zuiho*, *Chiyoda* and *Chitose* were sunk. *USS Princeton* (CVL-23) was also sunk during the Battle of Leyte Gulf.

U.S. carriers then pounded Iwo Jima and Okinawa; finally hitting naval installations in the Japanese homeland. The last Japanese carriers to be sunk were the *Unru* and *Shinano* in late 1944.

The final tally of aircraft carriers sunk during World War II was: seven British; 11 American; and 22 Japanese.

In the Pacific fighting U.S. carrier planes sank 161 Japanese surface warships and 13 submarines. A total of 447 cargo ships and tankers were also sunk. U.S. naval aircraft also assisted in the sinking of an additional 26 surface warships and seven submarines plus 39 cargo ships and tankers.

During the Battle of the Atlantic U.S. carrier planes sank 63 German submarines and assisted in the destruction of 20 more U-boats.

About 250,000 sorties were flown against shore targets while about 36,000 sorties were flown against ships which illustrates that the brunt of aircraft carrier power was directed against land targets, usually in support of amphibious landings. Once the carrier versus carrier battles were over, carriers were directed against land installations. It was then discovered that the effective striking range of the carrier is governed by the range of the defending aircraft rather than that of the attacking carrier planes. Otherwise, it will be placed in danger of being attacked and sunk; therefore, the range of the carrier aircraft must exceed that of the defenders. This lesson appears to have been forgotten because a current U.S. Maritime strategy recommends using Supercarriers to support a land war on the European continent ignoring the enemy's potent land-based, long-range missile-equipped aircraft.

The war had renewed belief in the basic principles of maritime strategy. The troop landings on the far-flung Pacific islands demanded mastery of the sea which could not be achieved without the air supremacy attained by aircraft carriers. Britain was forced to shift from a continental strategy to a more fitting maritime strategy due to her reverses in France. Reverting to a maritime strategy Britain returned to the principles which had served her so well for almost four centuries. Now, as a member of NATO, Britain has again embraced the unnatural principle of continental strategy.

After interservice rivalry, Forrestal's death, the Admirals' Revolt and lessons learned from the Korean War, the U.S. Navy finally got its first Supercarrier *USS Forrestal* completed in 1955. The British-developed angled flight deck, steam catapult, and mirror landing device were incorporated in Forrestal.

Jet powered planes, swept wings and guided missiles were developed with amazing acceleration until it was foolishly suggested that the guided missile will make the manned combat aircraft obsolete. It was the massed bombing conducted by B-17 Flying Fortresses and B-29 Superfortresses that was made obsolete by virtue of the intense fire power of carrier-based jet powered strike/fighters. The atomic bomb had been reduced in size from 12,000 pounds in 1945 to 2,000 pounds by 1955 and could be delivered by much smaller planes than that for which *USS Forrestal* was designed. Nevertheless, the Supercarrier size was correct because carrier-based fighters eventually grew to the size of the atomic bombers.

Despite the many British technical achievements during the postwar years, the Royal Navy has no fleet carriers. The V/STOL Harrier and Ski-Jump deck are outstanding innovations that Britain incorporated in the *Invincible* class carriers. These set the pace for moderately priced, multi-purpose carriers which have become very popular for non-superpower navies.

The carrier proved indispensable in the Korean and Vietnam Wars despite the fact that it could not blockade the enemy's sources of supply.

The complex floating war machine called Supercarrier is very expensive to replace. The cost for *USS Forrestal* (CV-59) of under one billion dollars had risen to over three billion dollars each for *USS Abraham Lincoln* (CVN-72) and *USS George Washington* (CVN-73). In view of the fact that Supercarrier construction is lim-ited to only one American shipyard, Newport News Shipbuilding and Drydock Co., SLEP was conceived to reduce cost and to be certain that Newport News would be available for new carrier construction. Service Life Extension Program extends the Supercarrier's active life for 10 to 15 years at a cost of 700 to 800 million dollars over a period of just over two years and most shipyards can accomplish the work. SLEP consists of overhauling or replacing catapults, defensive armament upgrading, boiler overhauling, updating electronics, rehabilitating living quarters, motor rewinding and replacement of or overhauling other items as necessary.

The rapid developments in helicopter design and their many uses in naval operations caused a minor revolution in carrier design and increased the numbers of air capable ships. Purpose-built helicopter carriers, such as the *Moskva* class, were developed when helicopters expanded their SAR and ASW dunking sonar roles into more aggressive ASUW and ASW operations using depth bombs, homing torpedoes and antiship missiles. Amphibious assault ships and through deck cruisers would not exist without a complement of helicopters and Harriers. Troop carrying, LAMPS, mine countermeasures, AEW, and many more tasks are assigned to helicopters. The world's smaller navies deploy helicopters from destroyers, frigates and other small craft.

The foregoing chapters have included combat theorists, naval aircraft and carrier pioneers, plus air and naval combat heroes because without the human intelligence, determination, energy and courage, these marvelous machines would not exist nor perform. Unfortunately many of these intrepid souls have been forgotten and remain unsung; however, the U.S. Navy has honored many Americans by naming ships in their honor. Already mentioned is that the lead ship of the DD-963 class destroyers is named in honor of Admiral Spruance. The Spruance class also includes destroyers named in honor of other U.S. Navy heroes mentioned on previous pages. *Kinkaid* (DD-965); *Arthur W. Radford* (DD-968); *Oldendorf* (DD-972); and *Fletcher* (DD-992). The *Leahy* class destroyers includes *Richmond K. Turner* (DLG-20) and *Halsey* (DLG-23) while the *Forrest Sherman* class honors *Blandy* (DD-943); *Mullinnix* (DD-944); and *Turner Joy* (DD-951). The *Gearing* class includes the following name ships: *Chevalier* (DD-805); *Bordelon* (DD-881); and *O'Hare* (DD-889). The *Charles F. Adams* class honors *Towers* (DDG-9) while the *Edsall* class included *Chambers* (DER-391). The destroyer *Mitscher* (DD-927) honors that famous admiral and the *Coontz* class destroyer *Mahan* (DDG-11) honors the revered naval strategist. U.S. destroyers normally honor famous naval personalities; however, Admiral Chester Nimitz was exceptional by having the Supercarrier CVN-68 *USS Nimitz* named in his honor. Too many others who struggled to bring their dream of mating the airplane with the ship to life remain forgotten; men who spent years at the drawing board, conceived the unbelievable, and risked their lives to prove it could be done remain in virtual obscurity.

The argument of battleship versus aircraft carrier has been won but now the carrier finds itself in a confrontation with small attack craft. Since a Soviet-built Egyptian 83 foot *Komar* class missile patrol boat fired four Styx missiles at the Israeli destroyer *Elath* at a 15 mile range and sank it in 1967 an argument has raged against the Supercarrier because it is too "vulnerable" to attacks by small high-speed craft. As is customary in disputes of this sort, neither side will concede any point to its adversary despite the fact that both naval weapons are necessary. Ed Heinemann, who designed outstanding World War II carrier planes and numerous postwar carrier aircraft, has designed a very high speed attack patrol craft. The author, who spent more than a half century working on designs of carrier aircraft and aircraft carriers, is also working on the design of a revolutionary high speed attack patrol craft. This does not mean that the aircraft carrier has been abandoned. It means that the well balanced navy must have Supercarriers, fast attack craft (FAC) and smaller Ski-Jump carriers plus, of course, the ever-present destroyers, frigates, cruisers and submarines.

A myriad of ships and planes are needed for a comprehensive defense force; however, it is the aircraft carrier and its Warbirds that will always fill us with amazement and give us a sense of security as the Warbirds takeoff at the rate of three each minute.

Appendixes

APPENDIX A

NAVAL AIRCRAFT & AIRCRAFT CARRIER WEAPONRY

Introduction • Air Launched Air-to-Air Missiles (AAM) • Air Launched Antiship Missiles (ASM)
• Carrier Launched Surface-to-Air Missiles (SAM) • Carrier Mounted Antiaircraft Guns (CIWS)

INTRODUCTION

The remarkable development of aircraft carrier and shipboard aircraft design since 1945 was accompanied by simultaneous progress in air-launched weapons and aircraft carrier CIWS and SAM weapons. Many of the weapons are adaptable to both air and surface launch while others are equally potent against ships and aircraft.

The combat indicator for the effectiveness of smart naval weapons was the Falklands fighting in 1982 in which AAM's and ASM's played a major role.

It is not possible to include the hundreds of guns and missiles produced since 1945 because that would require a volume in itself; however, an attempt has been made to describe some weapons, mentioned in the foregoing pages, that are employed by aircraft carriers and shipboard aircraft.

AIR LAUNCHED AIR-TO-AIR MISSILES (AAM)

The Air-to-Air Missile appears to stimulate the most interest because it conjures the image of plane versus plane dogfight and the romantic fantasy of hand-to-hand combat in the sky. In reality, this is not always true because victories can be scored without visual sighting when launching AAM's with radar guidance and/or infra-red homing or other guidance systems.

Intercept AAM's are extremely important because of their capability to stop intruders before the enemy approaches to within missile range of the CVBG; therefore, the carrier's safety depends upon the reliability and accuracy of the fighter's AAM.

Ford/Raytheon Sidewinder

The Sidewinder AIM-9D is a short/medium range AAM of which over 1,000 have been constructed by Ford Aerospace and Raytheon Company.

Ordnancemen aboard USS Kitty Hawk (CVA-63) slide a Ford/Raytheon AIM-9D Sidewinder AAM onto the launching rail of a Grumman Tomcat fighter. (Official U.S. Navy Photograph Department of Defense by PHAN M. Langway)

An F/A-18 Hornet fires a Sidewinder from its wingtip launching rail. During the Falklands War air action 24 of the 27 Sidewinders that were launched hit their targets. (McDonnell Douglas, Courtesy Timothy J. Beecher)

The several variants of this missile equip the vast majority of U.S. and NATO fighters, usually mounted at the wing-tip or on the wing underside near the wing-tip.

Sidewinders had their baptism of fire in the Falklands War in which 24 of the 27 Sidewinders launched struck their targets! A high explosive warhead is fitted.

The 186 pound Sidewinder is 9 feet-6 inches long with a diameter of 5 inches. Fin span is 24 inches. A Rocketdyne solid fuel rocket motor propels the missile to a speed twice that of sound. Range at sea level is about 3,600 feet and ceiling is 50,000 feet.

The AIM-9D variant employs infra-red guidance which makes the Sidewinder home in on heat emissions from the target; especially from the jet tailpipe. The design is simple and the cost is inexpensive which makes this maneuverable and accurate missile very popular.

Over 20,000 of several variants have been produced by Ford Aerospace & Communications Corporation and Raytheon Company Missile Systems Division while an additional 9,000 have been produced for NATO by the German Bodenseewerk Geratetechnik GmbH. Guidance and control units for some variants are made by British Aerospace Dynamics.

Hughes/Raytheon Phoenix

One of the largest air-to-air missiles in production is the Phoenix which is the primary weapon of the Tomcat.

Designated AIM-54C, the Phoenix incorporates an auto-pilot which is set by the fire control system as the missile is fired. Enemy electronic countermeasures are frustrated because the Phoenix electronics illuminates the target only when it is closing in on the hostile aircraft. The semi-active homing system of the Phoenix also incorporates a short range active radar which enables the Phoenix to home itself as it approaches nearer the target. In order for this system to function properly the Tomcat must remain pointed in the direction of the targets to keep them all within its radar field of vision.

Overall length is 13 feet with a 15 inch diameter. Wingspan is 36 inches. Weight is 989 pounds. A North American Rockwell Mark 47 solid fuel rocket gives the Phoenix a range of over 104 miles and a speed of 3,040 miles per hour.

The warhead is a 135 pound proximity fused high explosive type. Phoenix is produced by Hughes Aircraft and Raytheon Company Missile Systems Division.

This Grumman F-14 Tomcat is loaded with four Hughes Raytheon Phoenix missiles under the fuselage (No.1), two Sparrow missiles (No.2), and two Sidewinder missiles (No.3). The Phoenix is unique to the Tomcat. (Grumman Corporation, Courtesy Lois Lovisolo)

A Grumman Tomcat launches a Phoenix. This missile is the major weapon to combat the long range Backfire menace and is one of the largest AAMS in production. (Grumman Corporation, Courtesy Lois Lovisolo)

Raytheon Sparrow

The venerable Sparrow AAM has been proven to be one of the most successful air-to-air missiles in the NATO inventory. The AIM-7M is one of the latest versions with exceptional invulnerability to ECM, improved target-tracking capability and a new low-altitude active fuse. The Sparrow is scheduled for replacement by AMRAM on a gradual basis.

Guidance comprises a control system using digital computers and a powered director-illuminator.

Sparrow overall length is 12 feet with an 8 inch diameter. Wingspan is 40 inches. Weight is 510 pounds and the warhead is a WAU-17 fragmentation type. The Hercules Mk 58 solid fuel rocket propellant gives the Sparrow a speed in excess of 2,660 miles per hour and a range of more than 30 miles. Six countries plus NATO use the Sparrow AAM.

The manufacturer of the AIM/RIM-7M Sparrow is Raytheon Company Missile Systems Division.

Ordnancemen aboard USS Nimitz (CVN-68) prepare Raytheon Sparrows for installation on the Tomcat. Observe that the missiles have no fins. The ordnancemen are about to install the fins from the fin cart to the right of the missiles. (Official U.S. Navy Photograph Department of Defense by PH3 Randy Morrell)

Assembled Sparrow AIM-7M missiles are shown installed on fuselage launchers (black arrow). This is one of the most successful missiles in the NATO inventory. A Ford/Raytheon Sidewinder is wing-mounted (white arrow). (Raytheon Company Courtesy Jonna D. Manes)

Hughes/Raytheon AMRAAM

The AMRAAM (Advanced Medium Range Air-to-Air Missile) Sparrow replacement weapon was developed after a lengthy investigation into the probable hostile air threats for the next quarter century. Produced by Hughes Aircraft and Raytheon Company Missile Systems Division, the AMRAAM is deployed on Tomcats and Hornets plus some NATO aircraft. A high explosive blast warhead is fitted.

The AMRAAM AIM-120 is a "launch and leave" missile with a beyond visual range combat capability of about 40 miles. The missile system is equipped with inertial navigation for mid-course direction and with active radar for terminal guidance to the target.

Overall length of the 300 pound missile is 11 feet-9 inches with a 7 inch diameter. The rocket motor is a directed type which does the steering; therefore, wingspan is only 21 inches. Speed is in excess of 760 miles per hour. The system enables the pilot to aim and fire at several targets simultaneously.

AIR LAUNCHED ANTISHIP MISSILES (ASM)

Air launched antiship missiles are the primary offensive weapon of aircraft carriers. As the heirs to the battleship, the carrier's fighters and attack planes have become the carriers' counterpart to the battleship guns with

In addition to the large selection of air-to-air missiles, many U.S. fighters and strike aircraft also depend upon rapid-fire cannon for offensive armament. During the post-World War II years guns were replaced by AAM's; however, combat experience in Asia revealed that rapid-fire guns were needed for close-in aerial combat and some ground attack missions. The standard rapid-fire gun installation on U.S. military aircraft has, for many years, been the rotating six-barrel 20 millimeter Gatling-type M-61 Vulcan cannon. Overheating is the most common restriction to a gun's rate of fire; therefore, by employing six barrels, each barrel fires only one of six shots and has time to cool while the remaining five shots are fired. This permits an increased rate of fire because the barrels remain cooler. The Vulcan cannon shown here is installed in the fuselage of a U.S. Navy Vought A-7E Corsair II attack plane. (Ling-Temco-Vought, Courtesy Arthur L. Schoeni)

the ASM's and bombs replacing the giant shells. The Warbirds' antiship and antisurface missiles and bombs are used against ship and shore targets.

Aerospatiale Exocet

Probably the most publicized and spectacular antiship missile used in action since 1982 is the French Exocet which system is manufactured by Aerospatiale. The Exocet is made for either surface or air launching and is in use by more than 20 navies. The air-launched version is responsible for the sinking of *HMS Sheffield* and the containership *Atlantic Conveyor* as well as crippling *USS Stark*.

Exocet weight is about 1,500 pounds. It is 17 feet long with a diameter of 14 inches. Wingspan is 40 inches. The tandem two-stage solid pro-

The Hughes/Raytheon AMRAAM Air-to-Air Missile is a "launch and leave" weapon with inertial navigation guidance to the target. Photo at left shows the AMRAAM mounted under the fuselage of a Grumman Tomcat while photo at right shows eight AMRAAM's mounted under the wings and two more mounted under the engine nacelles of a McDonnell Douglas Hornet. (Hughes Missile Systems Company)

The French Aerospatiale Exocet ASM is one of the best known antiship missiles. A Dassault Super Etendard is shown taking off a French carrier with an Exocet under its wing. (Marcel Dassault/Breguet, Courtesy Shirley Manfredi)

pellant rocket motor gives Exocet a high subsonic speed and a range of about 22 miles.

The missile guidance system is programmed with computed future target position data prior to launching and the missile follows this course until it is within six miles of the target. Then the active radar homing system leads Exocet to the target. During its flight the missile maintains a height of about eight feet above the water which makes it very difficult to detect. The proper altitude is controlled by a radio altimeter system.

McDonnell Douglas Harpoon

One of the most versatile American antiship cruise missiles is the McDonnell Douglas Astronautics Harpoon. This long range all-weather missile can be air-launched, submarine-launched or surface-launched. A new infra-red air-launched Harpoon SLAM (Standoff Land Attack Missile) has also been developed. Over 13 navies use the Harpoon which is fitted with a 500 pound high explosive, blast penetrator warhead.

A turbojet engine propels the 1,160 pound missile to 646 miles per hour to a range of 120 miles. Length is 12 feet-7 inches long while diameter is 14 inches. Wingspan is 36 inches. Target data is inserted just before launch. The missile then proceeds at wavetop level under altimeter control. When it approaches the objective the active radar homing system takes control to find and lock onto the target. In its final phase the Harpoon executes a sharp climb and then dives on the target.

The air-launched Harpoon was used successfully in the 1986 U.S. air attack in the Gulf of Sidra.

Sistel Sea Killer

Italy's Sea Killer Mark 2 antiship missile, manufactured by Sistel, can be surface-launched or air-launched. Originally called Vulcano this medium-range missile is a development of the Sea Killer Mark 1 formerly called Nettuno.

Italy's Sistel Sea Killer Mark 2 antiship missile is launched from an Agusta SH-3D helicopter and will be guided to the target by the Marte antiship system. (Regia Aeronautica)

OPPOSITE: Two 1,160 pound McDonnell Douglas Harpoon antiship missiles are mounted on this McDonnell Douglas F/A-18 Hornet. Over 13 navies use the Harpoon missile. Observe that the Hornet can perform aerobatics with the missiles installed. (McDonnell Douglas, Courtesy Thomas J. Downey)

The Mark 2 missile is used in the Marte helicopter and antiship system in which the APQ-706 radar is fitted to SH-3D Sea King helicopters. A Marte system with two modified Mark 2 missiles weighs less than 3520 pounds. Missile control is via beam riding in azimuth while a radio commanded altimeter controls the wave skimming altitude. If interference prevents beam riding, optical tracking and radio command can be substituted.

The missile has a light alloy body with a diameter of 8 1/2 inches. Overall length is 12 feet and wingspan is 40 inches. Solid fuel gives the Sea Killer Mark 2 a range of 15 miles at a subsonic speed. The Italian and Iranian Navies use this missile.

British Aerospace Sea Skua

The aluminum alloy, light weight Sea Skua is the Royal Navy's principal helicopter-borne ASM; having been proven ideal against high speed, ASM armed Fast Attack Craft (FAC). Designed and manufactured by British Aerospace Dynamics, the Sea Skua was used extensively in the Falklands War in which all Sea Skua missiles fired hit their targets.

The Royal Navy's British Aerospace Dynamics Sea Skua antiship missile was used extensively in the Falklands War in which all Sea Skua missiles fired hit their targets. A Westland Lynx is shown fitted with four British Aerospace Dynamics Sea Skua missiles. (Westland Helicopter Courtesy P.D. Batten)

A capsuled Sea Skua operating scenario is as follows: when the helicopter crew has detected and identified the target, the helicopter closes in at low level to a suitable attack position. It then climbs to the missile launching altitude when the aircrew select a Sea Skua and feed it information and instructions such as its terminal sea skimming height. The crew illuminates the target ship causing the missile homing head to lock onto the reflections from the target. Upon release the Sea Skua drops for a short distance under autopilot control until the rocket motors ignite. The missile then descends to an intermediate altitude under radio altimeter control and later drops to the preselected terminal sea skimming altitude as it homes to the target ship.

The Sea Skua is equipped with booster and sustainer solid fuel rocket motors, giving the missile a high subsonic speed. Length is 8 feet-2 1/2 inches with a 10 inch diameter. The 320 pound Sea Skua has a range of about nine miles. Wingspan is 28 inches.

British Aerospace Dynamics designed and produce the Sea Skua ASM.

Konigsberg Vaapenfabrikk Penguin

The Norwegian medium range Penguin antiship missile is made by A/S Konigsberg Vaapenfabrikk in air and surface-launched versions.

The inertially guided missile is fitted with an infrared search and homing system for the terminal phase as it closes in on the target. Penguin requires a backup data acquisition and fire control system.

A U.S. Navy Sikorsky SH-60B LAMPS has just launched a Konigsberg
Vaapenfabrikk Penguin antiship missile. Components are made in the U.S.,
England, Scotland, Sweden, Norway and France. (Official U.S. Navy Photo-
graph)

The Texas Instruments HARM AGM-88A antiradiation, defense suppression
missile renders hostile radar impotent thereby, protecting the waves of friendly
strike aircraft. (Official U.S. Navy Photograph)

With an overall length of 10 feet, the Penguin weighs 847 pounds and
has a diameter of 11 inches. The solid fuel rocket gives the missile a range
of 19 miles at a subsonic speed. Wingspan is 57 inches.

The Penguin warhead is semi-armor piercing. It is deployed on NATO
helicopters and the U.S. Navy LAMPS Mk. III.

The missile is also in service with the navies of Norway, Greece and
Sweden. Components are made in the U.S., France, Norway, England,
Sweden, and Scotland.

Texas Instruments HARM
HARM AGM-88A (High speed Anti Radar Missile) is a highly sophisticated air-to-surface antiradiation, defense suppression missile. It has a wide
frequency band to render hostile radar impotent by following the radiation
to its source to destroy the radar station. Its warhead contains a laser terminal and guidance aids. HARM replaced the previous Shrike and Arm
antiradiation missiles.

The HARM contractor is Texas Instruments. This 807 pound missile
is powered by a two-stage solid rocket motor which gives the missile a
speed of 760 miles per hour and a range of 22 miles. Overall length is 13
feet-8 inches while diameter is 8 inches. Wingspan is 44 inches.

The missile is deployed on Grumman A-6E and EA-6B, McDonnell
Douglas F/A-18, and Vought A-7E. HARM was used most effectively
against Libyan radar installations in the Gulf of Sidra fighting of 1986 and
the Persian Gulf War of 1991.

British Aerospace Sea Eagle
Sea Eagle is a second generation antiship missile designed to counter the
modern warship's improved defenses and resistance to attack.

It is a radar controlled, fire and forget missile with a powerful, active
radar target seeker which is capable of selecting a particular ship out of a
task force; such as the carrier. After launching, the Sea Eagle assumes a sea
skimming trajectory, homing in on the target by means of its onboard computers. The radar seeker remains silent until the missile is within radar
range of the target.

The 1,333 pound Sea Eagle is 13 feet long and has a diameter of 16
inches. Wingspan is 4 feet. Sea Eagle is powered by a Microturbo type
TRI-60 turbojet engine which is fitted with an air inlet duct cover to keep
the engine clean and reduce drag during carriage. The cover is jettisoned
upon launching.

The warhead is a high explosive blast type designed to penetrate a
ship's hull before exploding. The effect of the explosion is augmented by
the ignition of residual fuel in the missile. Sea Eagle has been designed to
cripple or sink even the largest ships.

Sea Eagle can also be surface launched in which event it is fitted with
two side mounted solid fuel booster rockets.

Designed and produced by British Aerospace Dynamics, the Sea Eagle
can be launched by helicopters as well as fixed wing aircraft.

Hughes Aircraft Maverick
The Maverick air-to-surface missile is produced in a Laser-guided short
range weapon for close air support and for the destruction of targets beyond the amphibious landing objective zone. Another version is an Imaging Infra-Red (IIR) air to surface direct-attack weapon for day or night
action.

Mavericks are carried by both U.S. Navy and U.S. Marine aircraft.
The U.S. Air Force is also equipped with the Maverick.

The British Aerospace Dynamics Sea Eagle antiship missile is a radar-controlled fire-and-forget weapon which augments the explosion with residual fuel. This Sea
Harrier is equipped with two Sea Eagles. (British Aerospace, Courtesy Brendan Morrissey)

Above: The innovative Stingray torpedo contains a propulsion battery that uses sea water as the electrolyte; thereby, starting the torpedo motor. (Marconi Space & Defence Systems) Left: The Royal Navy's Marconi Stingray antisubmarine homing torpedo is dropped by parachute which detaches in the water as the propulsion electric motor starts. (Ministry of Defence [Navy])

The 635 pound ASM is fitted with a warhead that carries 299 pounds of high explosive. Length is 8 feet-1 inch with a diameter of 11 3/4 inches. Wingspan is 28 inches. A two-stage solid fuel rocket motor gives the Maverick a range of 12 miles.

Almost 2,000 Mavericks have been produced by Hughes Aircraft.

Marconi Stingray Torpedo

The Stingray antisubmarine homing torpedo was designed by and is produced by Marconi Space and Defence Systems for Royal Navy service. It is intended to replace the U.S. Mk. 44 and Mk. 46 torpedoes.

The Stingray is a lightweight torpedo fitted with a digital computer which enables the independent acquisition, classification and tracking of the target. The computer has the capability of selecting the optimum com-

This McDonnell Douglas Hornet is equipped with four Mark 83 bombs under each wing. Bombs are still used to attack surface targets despite the amazing antiship missiles. (McDonnell Douglas, Courtesy Timothy J. Beecher)

An electronically laden Harrier is shown fitted with a Martel (Missile Anti Radar and TELevision) antiship missile under each wing. This missile was developed jointly by French SA Engins Matra and British Hawker Siddeley Dynamics. (British Aerospace Dynamics, Courtesy David Dodds)

This Harrier is equipped with a French Matra F.1 rocket pod under each wing; each containing 36 surface attack rockets. (British Aerospace, Courtesy Brendan Morrissey)

Above: Aviation ordnancemen load a Mark 83 1,000 pound bomb onto a Grumman Intruder A-6E aboard USS Nimitz (CVN-68). (Official U.S. Navy Photograph Department of Defense by PH3 Randy Morrell)

Right: Two McDonnell Douglas A-4 Skyhawks drop Mark 83 bombs on moving targets. Bombs are still very important antisurface and antiship weapons. (Official U.S. Navy Photo)

bination of sonar modes to suit the prevailing acoustic conditions including the presence of any underwater countermeasures.

The Stingray is propelled by a silent running electric motor which is powered by a sea water electrolyte battery. The torpedo is capable of operating in both shallow and deep water. When dropped from aircraft the torpedo's entry into the water is slowed by a small parachute which detaches in the water as the electric motor starts.

CARRIER LAUNCHED SURFACE TO AIR MISSILES (SAM)

Although aircraft carriers are equipped with superb fighter planes that form Combat Air Patrols, there always remains the possibility of at least one heavily armed enemy aircraft slipping through the patrol, as was related in the World War II narrative of Chapter V. It is; therefore, important for carriers to have their own air defenses, and missiles are the most effective medium and long range defense against air attack when a CAP is not available or otherwise distracted.

The Raytheon NATO Sea Sparrow SAM is fired from an 8-cell box-like launcher and is operational on surface ships from frigates to carriers. (Raytheon Company Courtesy Jonna D. Manes)

Raytheon/Mitsubishi NATO Sea Sparrow

The NATO Sea Sparrow SAM is operational aboard ships of the U.S. Navy, Norway, Denmark, Belgium, Germany and Japan. Although Raytheon Company Missile Systems Division is the prime manufacturer, Mitsubishi of Japan has acquired the rights to build the missile in Japan. Sea Sparrow is fired from an eight-cell box-like launcher employing a fire control system using digital computers plus a powered director-illuminator with continuous wave semi-active radar homing. The RIM-7H Sea Sparrow variant has folding wings and a monopulse seeker head. Installations aboard U.S. Navy high-value ships, such as aircraft carriers, were improved with the installation of the Hughes Mk. 23 pulse-Doppler Target Acquisition System which automatically detects and tracks targets as they come over the horizon. Specifications are basically the same as the AAM Sparrow except that the maximum altitude is 16,400 feet while minimum altitude is about 16 feet; and range is 18 miles. Sea Sparrow can also double as an SSM. The NATO Sea Sparrow program began in 1968 as a consortium comprised of the U.S., Germany, Belgium, Denmark, Italy, Britain, and Netherlands.

British Aerospace Sea Dart

Deployed on *HMS Invincible* class and many other Royal Navy combatants, the Sea Dart SAM is the result of an extensive development program by the manufacturer, British Aerospace Dynamics. Sea Dart performed well in the Falklands by scoring eight victories. The standard Royal Navy variant is the GWS 30 which has an overall length of 14 feet-6 inches and a diameter of 17 inches. Wingspan is 36 inches. Launch weight is 1,210 pounds with a fragmentation (HE) warhead. Power is a solid fuel booster rocket with a Rolls-Royce Odin ramjet sustainer which gives the Sea Dart a maximum range of 48 miles and a maximum altitude of 82,000 feet. Guidance consists of target tracking and illumination by Marconi Radar Systems Type 909 using semi-active radar homing in conjunction with a proportional navigation system that can be altered in flight. The Sea Dart missile is fired from a two-rail launcher that is reloaded automatically. The Sea Dart system had been developed to stop high altitude Soviet aircraft.

The U.S. Navy's BPDMS (Basic Point Defense Missile System) SAM was assembled from existing systems with a minimum of new development and new parts. (Raytheon Company, Courtesy Jonna D. Manes)

Raytheon Basic Point-Defense Missile System (BPDMS)

The American Basic Point-Defense Missile System (BPDMS) SAM or ASM was assembled from existing systems with a minimum of new development and new parts. An AIM-7E Sparrow III or similar missile is launched from a modified eight-cell ASROC launcher which is mounted on a three inch gun mounting.

This Raytheon-built system guidance comprises semi-active radar homing. Target data from the ship's Combat Information Center (CIC) is fed into a manually-operated fire-control system. When the target is located and identified it is illuminated for homing guidance by a manually controlled director/illuminator radar. BPDMS can also be used against surface targets because it is capable of low angle engagements. The BPDMS is produced by Raytheon Company Missile Systems Division.

Selenia Albatros /Aspide

The Italian Albatros SAM weapons system was originally designed to employ the Sea Sparrow but can also use the Italian Aspide missile as is done on the carrier *Garibaldi*. The Aspide is a high performance multipurpose SAM or ASM with an overall length of 12 feet-4 inches and a diameter of eight inches. Wingspan is 32 inches and finspan is 25 1/2 inches. Launch weight is 484 pounds. A single stage solid fuel rocket motor provides propulsion for the 77 pound warhead. Guidance consists of a semi-

With a maximum altitude of 82,000 feet, the Royal Navy's British Aerospace Dynamics Sea Dart SAM is ideal for stopping high altitude long-range aircraft and missiles. (British Aerospace Dynamics Courtesy David Dodds)

The Italian Albatros SAM weapons system can fire the Sea Sparrow or the Italian Aspide missile. The Aspide is a multipurpose SAM or ASM with a semi-active radar homing system. (Regia Aeronautica)

active radar homing system. Albatros and Aspide are manufactured by Selenia-Industrie Elettroniche Associate. Seven of the world's navies are using the Albatros system.

CARRIER MOUNTED ANTIAIRCRAFT GUNS (CIWS)

The vast majority of naval antiaircraft guns are short-range CIWS (Close In Weapons Systems) for close targets, while the more distant aerial targets are left to guided missiles and larger guns. Shipboard CIWS must be on target instantly because there is very little time between the sighting and the explosion of a hit. This demands very close cooperation between the radar tracking and the automatic mechanical servo operation of the gun in both vertical and horizontal movement. Some CIWS are programmed to automatically fire when they are on target.

The principal U.S. Navy CIWS (Close In Weapons System) on World War II carriers was the 40 millimeter rapid-fire gun. Observe the gunners loading the four-round clips and the expended shells on the deck at right plus the fact that it required eight men to operate the two twin units on USS Hornet (CV-12) in 1945. (U.S. National Archives)

General Dynamics/General Electric Phalanx CIWS

The Phalanx CIWS (Close In Weapons System) is the U.S. Navy's final defense against missiles, aircraft or even shells that have penetrated the CVBG multi-layered defense system. Contractors are General Dynamics Pomona Division and General Electric Pittsfield Division. The central component of the Phalanx is the six-barrel Gatling type gun which has been installed in the U.S. Navy fighter planes for more than a decade. The rotating barrel assembly has a rate of fire of 3,000 rounds per minute. The 20 millimeter projectiles are 2 1/2 times heavier than conventional rounds because the core of each projectile is made from high density depleted uranium known as Stabaloy. This ensures a high projectile velocity and exceptional penetration upon impact. Barrel elevation range is from negative 35 degrees to positive 90 degrees. The automatic integrated weapons system conducts the search, detection, threat evaluation, tracking and firing which incorporates closed-loop spotting. This involves tracking both the incoming target and the outgoing projectiles, correcting the gun's aim as is necessary to bring the two together. Phalanx is reputed to be able to shoot down an incoming five-inch shell. The Gatling type gun is the M61Al Vulcan with a magazine capacity of 989 rounds. System computers are located in a room below decks. Phalanx is deployed on U.S. Navy ships from patrol craft to aircraft carriers.

Empressa Meroka CIWS

Spain's Meroka 20 millimeter CIWS air defense system has a rate of fire of 2,700 to 3,600 rounds per minute. Similar in appearance to the Phalanx, the Meroka 96 inch long multiple barrels do not revolve as in the Gatling design. The 12 Oerlikon GA1-B01 gun barrels are mounted in two concentric circles of six barrels in each circle. Meroka is manufactured by Empressa Nacional Bazan. Initial aiming of the one mile range gun is through an optical gyro gunsight with a Lockheed Electronics Doppler radar system handling the target tracking phase. The Spanish Armada has deployed Meroka on combatants from frigates to aircraft carriers among which are the carriers *Dedalo* and *Principe De Asturias*.

Spain's Meroka 20 millimeter CIWS has a rate of fire of 2,700 to 3,600 rounds per minute. The (12) 96 inch gun barrels do not revolve as the Phalanx. (Empressa Nacional Bazan)

Resembling an android, the amazing General Dynamics/General Electric Phalanx CIWS is a far cry from the World War II 40 millimeter rapid-fire guns. This view shows the 20 millimeter rotating six-barrel gun that automatically aims and fires 3,000 rounds per minute. (General Electric)

This rear view of the Phalanx shows the magazine cylinder in the open space which holds 989 rounds of ammunition while the white dome houses a radar antenna. The shells weigh 2 1/2 times more than conventional rounds, which increases the velocity and penetration. System computers for the Phalanx are located below deck. (General Dynamics)

Breda/Bofors Dardo Point Defense System

The Italian Breda/Bofors Twin-mounted 40 millimeter 70 caliber antiaircraft/antimissile gun is well suited for point defense. The turreted guns are fully automatic using the Dardo point defense system which employs a high performance remote control servo installation.

This is coupled with a low inertia gun mounting design that results in rapid mechanical response to electronic commands. Angular movement velocities are 90 degrees per second in both vertical and horizontal directions. The barrel elevation range is from negative 13 degrees to positive 85 degrees. Muzzle velocity is about 3,300 feet per second and the rate of fire is 300 rounds per barrel per minute. The gun is manufactured by Breda Meccanica Bresciana and three sets are installed on the carrier *Garibaldi*.

The Italian Breda/Bofors Dardo Point Defense Systems twin-mounted 40 millimeter antiaircraft/antimissile twin-mounted turreted guns can move 90 degrees per second in both horizontal and vertical directions. (Breda Mechanica Bresciana)

APPENDIX B
U.S. NAVAL MUSEUMS

The following list of Naval Museums located in the continental United States is presented for the convenience of the readers who care to pursue the absorbing subject of Naval History.

USS Yorktown (CV-10)
Charleston Harbor, Charleston, South Carolina

U.S. Naval Academy Museum
Annapolis, Maryland, 21402

U.S. Naval Aviation Museum
Pensacola, Florida, 32508

U.S. Navy Memorial Museum
Washington, D.C., 20374

U.S. Naval Air and Test Evaluation Museum
Patuxent River, Maryland, 20670

U.S. Naval War College Museum
Newport, Rhode Island, 02840

U.S. Navy/Marine Corps Museum
Treasure Island, California, 94130

Intrepid Sea-Air Space Museum
Hudson River Pier at West 46th Street
New York, N.Y., (USS Intrepid CV-11)

Glossary & Acronyms

AAA	Anti Aircraft Artillery
AAM	Air-to-Air Missile
AAW	Anti Aircraft Warfare
ACV	Auxiliary Aircraft Carrier (U.S. Navy)
AEW	Airborne Early Warning
AEWC	Airborne Early Warning and Control
AFCS	Automatic Flight Control System (U.S. Navy)
AIM	Air Intercept Missile
Air Boss	Officer in charge of all operations on hangar deck and flight deck including aircraft launching and recovery.
Airdale	A flight deck crewman such as plane handlers.
Air Wing	Total aircraft complement on an aircraft carrier.
AMRAAM	Advanced Medium-Range Air-to-Air Missile
Angle of Attack	The angle of the wing relative to the flight path of an aircraft measured in plus or minus degrees. Used as a guide to determine the plane's glidepath during recovery.
AOE	Multi-Purpose Stores Ship
ASDIC	Anti Submarine Detecting Equipment
ASCAC	Anti Submarine Classification Analysis Center
ASM	Anti Ship Missile
ASO	Accoustic Sensor Operator (U.S. Navy)
ASPJ	Airborne Self Protection Jammer
ASR	Air-Sea Rescue
ASW	Anti Submarine Warfare
ASUW	Anti SUrface Warfare
ATA	Advanced Tactical Aircraft
ATACO	Air TActical Control Officer (U.S. Navy)
ATARS	Advanced Tactical Air Reconnaissance System
ATO	Airborne Tactical Officer
AV	Seaplane tender (U.S. Navy)
AVG	Aircraft escort vessel (U.S. Navy)
AVT	Auxiliary aircraft transport (U.S. Navy)
AWACS	Airborne Warning And Control System
BMEWS	Ballistic Missile Early Warning System
Bolter	An aborted landing in which the aircraft tail hook fails to engage the arresting cable and the plane climbs away to try again.
BPDMS	Basic Point-Defense Missile System
CAM	Catapult Aircraft Merchant (ship)
CAP	Combat Air Patrol
CAS	Close Air Support
CATCC	Carrier Air Traffic Control Center (U.S. Navy)
CATG	Commander Amphibious Task Group
CCA	Carrier Controlled Approach
Chaff	Metallic foil strips fired into the air to confuse radar signals
CINC	Commander IN Chief
CIC	Combat Information Center
CIWS	Close-In Weapon System
COD	Carrier Onboard Delivery
CTOL	Conventional Take Off and Landing
CV	Aircraft Carrier (U.S. Navy designation)
CVA	Attack Aircraft Carrier (U.S. Navy designation)
CVAN	Nuclear powered Attack Aircraft Carrier (U.S. Navy designation)
CVB	Battle Aircraft Carrier (U.S. Navy designation)
CVBG	Aircraft Carrier Battle Group (U.S. Navy designation)
CVE	Escort Aircraft Carrier (U.S. Navy designation)
CVHE	Helicopter Escort Aircraft Carrier (U.S. Navy)
CVL	Light Aircraft Carrier (U.S. Navy)
CVN	Nuclear powered Aircraft Carrier (U.S. Navy)
CVS	Support Aircraft Carrier, anti-submarine (U.S. Navy)
CVU	Utility Aircraft Carrier (U.S.)
Dropline	A vertical strip of amber lights on the center of the transom of an aircraft carrier to assist pilots in alignment during landing approaches.

DDG	Guided Missile Destroyer
DIANE	Digital Integrated Attack and Navigation Equipment
DLCO	Deck Landing Control Officer (Royal Navy)
DP	Dual Purpose (antiaircraft and antiship gun)
ECM	Electronic Counter Measures
EMCON	EMissions CONtrol conditions (electronics)
ESM	Electronics Surveillance Measures
ESMO	Electronic Support Measures Operator
EWO	Electronic Warfare Operator (U.S. Navy)
FAA	Fleet Air Arm (Royal Navy)
FAADS	Forward Area Air Defense System
FAC	Forward Air Controller
FFG	Guided Missile Frigate
FLAK	Anti-Aircraft Fire (FLieger Abwehr Kanonen) German acronym used by British, German and American Armed Forces.
FOD	Foreign Object Damage
Fouled Deck	When flight deck is not ready to receive incoming aircraft; such as severe congestion or accident.
FLIR	Forward Looking Infra Red (radar)
Fly by wire	Electronic controlled electro-mechanical operation of aircraft control surfaces which limits maneuvers to the extent the plane and pilot can endure.
Focsle	FOreCaStLE; the raised portion of a ship's bow.
FRAM	Fleet Rehabilitation And Modernization program (U.S. Navy)
Glidepath	The path of descent to a landing measured as an angle in degrees. (Also angle of descent)
GCI	Ground Control Intercept
HARM	High speed Anti Radiation Missile
Harpoon	System for guiding helicopters to the deck of a small ship in violent weather, similar to U.S. Navy RAST. (Royal Navy)
HOTAS	Hands On Throttle And Stick
HUD	Heads Up Display; aircraft instruments projected on a transparent screen inside the windshield so the pilot need not look down to read them.
IADS	Integrated Air Defense System
ICBM	Inter Continental Ballistic Missile
IFF	Identification Friend or Foe
IR	Infra Red
Island	The superstructure of an aircraft carrier above the flight deck containing the navigating bridge, Pri-Fly, radio room, smokestack if fitted, and other operational spaces. Islands are usually located at the extreme starboard side of the flight deck.
ITAWDS	Integrated Tactical Amphibious Warfare Data System
JCS	Joint Chiefs of Staff
Jet blast deflector	A water-cooled steel barrier located at the aft end of the catapult which is raised out of the flight deck to deflect the hot blast from the jet planes taking off.
JTIDS	Joint Tactical Information Distribution System (U.S. Navy)
Knot	Nautical term for ship's speed (nautical mile/hour equivalent to 1.15 statute miles/hour) Expressed as "Knots" and not as "Knots/Hour"
LAMPS	Light Airborne Multi-Purpose System helicopters (U.S. Navy)
LANTIRN	Low Altitude Navigation & Targeting Infra Red system for Night
LFC	Landing Force Commander
LHA	(Landing Helicopter Assault) Multi-purpose amphibious assault ship (U.S. Navy)
LIC	Low Intensity Conflict
LHD	(Landing Helicopter Dock) Multi-purpose amphibious assault ship (U.S. Navy)

579

LPD	(Landing Personnel Helicopter) Amphibious assault ship (U.S.Navy)
LSO	Landing Signal Officer
MAC	Merchant Aircraft Carriers (Royal Navy)
MAD	Magnetic Anomaly Detector
MAGTF	Marine Air-Ground Task Force (U.S.Navy)
MAG	Marine Aircraft Wing
MAS	Maritime Air Superiority
MiG	Mikoyan-Gurevich (Soviet Aircraft)
NASA	National Aeronautics and Space Administration (U.S.)
NATC	Naval Air Test Center (U.S.)
Navair	Naval Air Systems Command (U.S.)
NFO	Naval Flight Officer
OTH	Over The Horizon
Port Side	The left side of a ship or aircraft when looking from the stern to the bow.
Pri-Fly	Primary Flight Control (Glass enclosed space on inboard side of the Island from where all air operations are controlled.
R&D	Research and Development
RAST	Recovery Assist Secure & Traverse (a system for guiding a helicopter to the deck of a small ship, using a small winch and cable attached to the helicopter).
REMRO	REMote Radar Operator
RNAS	Royal Naval Air Service or Station
RIO	Radar Intercept Officer
SAC (A)	Supporting Arms Coordinator (Airborne)
SAG	Surface Action Group
SAM	Surface to Air Missile
SAR	Search And Rescue
SCS	Sea Control Ship
SEAD	Suppression of Enemy Air Defense
SENSO	SENSor Operator
SLEP	Service Life Extension Program (U.S.Navy)
SLOC	Sea Lines Of Communications
SNA	Soviet Naval Aviation
SSM	Surface to Surface Missile
Starboard side (Stbd.)	The right side of ship or aircraft when looking from the stern to the bow.
Stem	The extreme forward end of a ship.
STO	Short Take Off
STOL	Short Take Off and Landing
STO/VL	Short Take Off/Vertical Landing
TAC (A)	Tactical Air Coordinator (Airborne)
TACAN	TACtical Airborne Navigation
TACCO	TACtical COordinator
TAC-TAS	TACtical Towed Array Sonar system
TARPS	Tactical Air Reconnaissance Pod System
TASM	Tactical Air to Surface Missile
TINS	Thermal Imaging Navigation Set
TRAM	Target Recognition Attack Multisensor
VB	Bomber squadron (U.S.Navy)
VDS	Variable Depth Sonar
VF	Fighter squadron (U.S.Navy)
VFR	Visual Flight Rules
VIFF	Vectoring In Forward Flight (with reference to Harrier aircraft)
VOD	Vertical On board Delivery
V/STOL	Vertical/Short Take Off and Landing
VT	Torpedo bomber squadron (U.S.Navy)
VTOL	Vertical Take Off and Landing
Waveoff	An order from the LSO telling the pilot to abort the landing; either due to a dangerous approach or due to a fouled deck.
WOD	Wind Over Deck

Bibliography

The author has applied his half-century of naval design experience to the preparation of this volume. In addition to this he has, during the past several decades, sought out and read every available book, article and document to research the fascinating and complex subjects of aircraft carriers, carrier-based aircraft, international politics, history and sea battles plus strategists, tacticians, pilots, naval commanders, designers and early visionaries in order to establish a comprehensive background for the preparation of this book. Many friends and fellow researchers have generously helped in his quest with books, official records and documents from their own libraries and files. A partial list of the pertinent volumes is presented here to assist those who care to delve deeper into specific aspects of this absorbing subject.

Adamson, Hans Christian, and George Francis Kosco, *Halsey's Typhoons*, New York, 1967.

Agawa, Hiroyuki, *The Reluctant Admiral: Yamamoto and the Imperial Navy*, New York, 1979.

Baldwin, Hanson Weightman, *Battles Lost and Won: Great Campaigns of World War II*, New York, 1966.

Beard, Charles A., *American Foreign Policy in the Making, 1932-1940*, New Haven, Conn., 1948.

Beitzel, R., *The Uneasy Alliance: America, Britain and Russia, 1941-1943*, New York, 1972.

Bell, Roger John, *Unequal Allies: Australian-American Relations and the Pacific War*, Carlton, Victoria, 1977.

Belote, James H. and William M. Belote, *Titans of the Seas: The Development and Operations of Japanese Carrier Task Forces During World War II*, New York, 1975.

Borg, Dorothy and Shumpei Okamoto, *Pearl Harbor as History: Japanese-American Relations, 1931-1941*, New York, 1973.

British Ministry of Information (Official), *HMS Ark Royal*.

British Ministry of Information (Official), *Fleet Air Arm*.

Brown, David, *Carrier Operations in World War II. Vol.I The Royal Navy*, Annapolis, 1974.

Buell, Thomas B., *The Quiet Warrior: A Biography of Admiral Raymond A. Spruance*, Boston, 1974.

Caiden, Martin, *A Torch to the Enemy: The Fire Raid on Tokyo*, New York, 1960.

Churchill, Winston S., *The Second World War*, Vols. I-VI. Boston, 1948-1953, New York, 1973.

Coale, Griffith Baily, *Victory at Midway*, Farrar and Rinehart, Inc., New York.

Costello, John, *The Pacific War: 1941-1945*, New York, 1981.

Dallek, Robert, *Franklin D. Roosevelt and American Foreign Policy, 1932-1945*, New York, 1979.

Dull, Paul S., *A Battle History of the Japanese Navy, 1941-1945*, Annapolis, 1978.

Ellis, Paul, *Aircraft of the Royal Navy*, Jane's, London, 1982.

Field, James A. Jr., *The Japanese at Leyte Gulf*, Princeton University Press, Princeton.

Gallagher, Barrett, *Flattop*, Doubleday & Company, New York.

Green, William, *Famous Fighters of the Second World War*, New York, Vol.I 1958, Vol.II 1965.

Greenfield, Kent Roberts, *American Strategy in World War II*, Baltimore, 1963.

Halsey, William F. and Joseph Bryan Halsey, *Admiral Halsey's Story*, New York, 1947.

Herzog, James H., *Closing the Open Door: American-Japanese Diplomatic Negotiations, 1936-1941*, Annapolis, 1962.

Hough, Richard, *The Death of the Battleship*, New York, 1963.

Hoyt, Edwin Palmer, *The Battle of Leyte Gulf: The Death Knell of the Japanese Fleet*, New York, 1972.

Hughes, Terry and John Costello, *The Battle of the Atlantic*, London, 1977.

Ienaga, Saburo, *The Pacific War: World War II and the Japanese, 1931-1945*, New York, 1978.

Inoguchi, Rikihei and Roger Pineau, *The Divine Wind: Japan's Kamikaze Force in World War II*, Westport, Conn., 1978.

Inoguchi, Rikihei, Tadashi Nakajima and Roger Pineau, *The Divine Wind*, Annapolis, 1958.

Jackson, Robert, *Air War Over Korea*, New York, 1973.

Jensen, Oliver, *Carrier War*, Simon & Schuster, New York, 1945.

Johnston, Stanley, *Queen of the Flattops: USS Lexington at Coral Sea Battle*, E.P. Dutton & Company, Inc., New York.

Jones, Francis Gifford, *Japan's New Order in East Asia: Its Rise and Fall, 1937-1945*, London, 1954.

Karig, Walter and Wellbourn Kelley, *Pearl Harbor to Coral Sea*, New York, 1944.

Kato, Masuo, *The Lost War*, New York, 1946.

Kemp, P.K., *Fleet Air Arm*, Herbert Jenkins Ltd., London.

Kennan, George F., *American Diplomacy, 1900-1950*, Chicago, 1951.

Kennedy, Paul M., *The Rise and Fall of British Naval Mastery*, New York, 1976.

Kirby, Stanley Woodburn, *The War Against Japan*, London, Vol.II 1958, Vol.III 1961, Vol.IV 1965, Vol.V 1969.

Langer, William L., *The Undeclared War, 1940-1941*, New York, 1953.

Lenton, H.T., *British Battleships and Aircraft Carriers*, Garden City, 1972.

Lockwood, A. and Hans C. Adamson, *Battles of the Philippine Sea*, Thomas Y. Crowell Ltd., New York.

Lowe, P., *Great Britain and the Origins of the Pacific War*, Oxford, 1977.

Macintyre, Donald, *Aircraft Carrier: The Majestic Weapon*, New York, 1968.

Mahan, Alfred Thayer, *The Interests of America in Sea Power, Present and Future*, Boston, 1898.

Mason, Francis K., *The British Fighter Since 1912*, Annapolis, 1993.

Matloff, Maurice, *Strategic Planning for Coalition Warfare: 1943-1944*, Washington, D.C., 1959.

Middlebrook, Martin, *Battleship: The Loss of the Prince of Wales and the Repulse*, London, 1977.

Millis, W., ed., *The Forrestal Diaries*, London, 1952.

Morison, Samuel Eliot, *History of United States Naval Operations in World War II*, Vol.IV-XV. Boston, 1949-1962.

Morison, Samuel Eliot, *The Two-Ocean Navy*, New York, 1963.

Newton, Don and A. Cecil Hampshire, *Taranto*, William Kimber and Company, Ltd., London.

Odgers, George, *Air War Against Japan: 1943-1945*, Canberra, 1957.

Okumiya, Masatake and Jiro Horikoshi with Martin Caiden, *Zero*, New York, 1956.

Okumiya, Masatake and Mitsuo Fuchida, *Midway, the Battle that Doomed Japan*, Huchinsons, Ltd., London.

Perry, Hamilton Darby, *The Panay Incident: Prelude to Pearl Harbor*, New York, 1969.

Potter, E.B. and Chester W. Nimitz, *Triumph in the Pacific*, Trenton, 1963.

Potter, E.B., *Bull Halsey*, Annapolis, 1985.

Preston, Antony, *Navies of World War II*, London, 1976.

Reynolds, Clark G., *The Fast Carriers: The Forging of an Air Navy*, New York, 1968.

Roskill, S.W., *The War at Sea*, London, Vols. 1-3, 1954-1961.

Ross, Al, *The Escort Carrier Gambier Bay*, Annapolis, 1993.

Rutter, Owen, *The British Navy's Air Arm*, New York, 1944.

Seth, Ronald., *Two Fleets Surprised: Story of the Battle of C. Matapan*, Arthur Barker Ltd., London.

Sherrod, Robert L., *On to Westward: War in the Central Pacific*, New York, 1945.

Skiera, J.A., *Aircraft Carriers in Peace and War*, Franklin Watts Inc., New York.

Stern, Robert C., *The Lexington-Class Carriers*, Annapolis, 1993.

Swanborough, Gordon and Peter M. Bowers, *U.S. Navy Aircraft since 1911*, New York, 1968.

Tanaka, Raizo, *Japan's Losing Struggle for Guadalcanal*, Annapolis, 1956.

Tansill, Charles C., *Back Door to War: The Roosevelt Foreign Policy 1933-1941*, Chicago, 1952.

Terzibaschitsch, Stefan, *Escort Carriers and Aviation Support Ships of the U.S. Navy*, Annapolis, 1981.

Thetford, O.G., *Aircraft of the 1914-1918 War*, Letchworth, Herts., 1954.

Thorne, Christopher, *Allies of a Kind: The United States, Britain and the War Against Japan, 1941-1945*, Oxford, 1978.

Togo, Shigenori, *The Cause of Japan*, New York, 1956.

U.S. Navy Aviation History Unit OP-519B, DCNO (Air), *The Navy's Air War*, A.R. Buchanan, Ed. Harper & Brothers, New York, 1946.

U.S. Navy, *U.S. Naval Aviation 1910-1970*, Naval Air Systems Command, 1970.

Van der Vat, Dan, *The Atlantic Campaign*, New York, 1988.

Wallin, Homer Norman, *Pearl Harbor: Why, How, Fleet Salvage and Final Appraisal*, Washington, D.C., 1968.

Ward, Sharkey, *Sea Harrier Over the Falklands*, Annapolis, 1993.

Winton, John, *The Forgotten Fleet: The British Navy in the Pacific 1944-1945*, New York, 1969.

Indexes

AIRCRAFT

AIRCRAFT CARRIERS

CARRIER ACTIONS

PERSONALITIES